management

A PRACTICAL INTRODUCTION

third edition

The San Francisco–Oakland Bay Bridge—San Francisco's "other bridge." Well known for its famous Golden Gate Bridge, San Francisco also boasts another famous bridge, whose 8.25-mile span links it to Oakland and Berkely on the east side of San Francisco Bay in northern California. Completed in 1936, it carries approximately 280,000 vehicles every day across two major spans. Some great achievements of history were accomplished by individuals working quietly by themselves, such as scientific discoveries or works of art. But so much more has been achieved by people who were able to leverage their talents and abilities—and those of others—by being managers. None of the great architectural wonders, such as this one, was built single-handedly by one person. Rather, all represent triumphs of management.

management
A PRACTICAL INTRODUCTION

third edition

Angelo Kinicki
Arizona State University

Brian K. Williams

McGraw-Hill
Irwin

Boston   Burr Ridge, IL   Dubuque, IA   Madison, WI   New York   San Francisco   St. Louis
Bangkok   Bogotá   Caracas   Kuala Lumpur   Lisbon   London   Madrid   Mexico City
Milan   Montreal   New Delhi   Santiago   Seoul   Singapore   Sydney   Taipei   Toronto

**McGraw-Hill
Irwin**

MANAGEMENT: A PRACTICAL INTRODUCTION

Published by McGraw-Hill/Irwin, a business unit of The McGraw-Hill Companies, Inc., 1221 Avenue of the Americas, New York, NY, 10020. Copyright © 2008, 2006, 2003 by The McGraw-Hill Companies, Inc. All rights reserved. No part of this publication may be reproduced or distributed in any form or by any means, or stored in a database or retrieval system, without the prior written consent of The McGraw-Hill Companies, Inc., including, but not limited to, in any network or other electronic storage or transmission, or broadcast for distance learning.

Some ancillaries, including electronic and print components, may not be available to customers outside the United States.

This book is printed on acid-free paper.

3 4 5 6 7 8 9 0 QPD/QPD 0 9 8 7

ISBN: 978-0-07-353019-2
MHID: 0-07-353019-0

Editorial director: *John E. Biernat*
Executive editor: *John Weimeister*
Developmental editor: *Kirsten Guidero*
Senior marketing manager: *Anke Braun*
Producer, Media technology: *Greg Bates*
Senior project manager: *Harvey Yep*
Senior production supervisor: *Debra Sylvester*
Lead designer: *Kami Carter*
Photo research coordinator: *Kathy Shive*
Photo researcher: *PoYee Oster*
Media project manager: *Brian Nacik*
Cover photograph: *© Corbis*
Typeface: *10.5/12 Times Roman*
Compositor: *Techbooks*
Printer: *Quebecor World Dubuque Inc.*
Cover Designer: *Jenny El-Shamy*

Library of Congress Cataloging-in-Publication Data

Kinicki, Angelo.
  Management : a practical introduction / Angelo Kinicki, Brian K. Williams. — 3rd ed.
    p. cm.
  Includes index.
  ISBN-13: 978-0-07-353019-2 (alk. paper)
  ISBN-10: 0-07-353019-0 (alk. paper)
  1. Management. I. Williams, Brian K., 1938- II. Title.
HD31.K474 2008
658--dc22
                                        2006037793

www.mhhe.com

brief CONTENTS

ABOUT THE
authors

Angelo Kinicki Angelo is a Professor of Management at the W. P. Carey School of Business at Arizona State University. He also was awarded the Weatherup/Overby Chair in Leadership in 2005. He has held his current position since 1982 when he received his doctorate in Organizational Behavior from Kent State University.

Angelo is recognized for both his teaching and research. As a teacher, Angelo has been the recipient of several awards, including the John W. Teets Outstanding Graduate Teacher Award (2004–2005), Graduate Teaching Excellence Award (1998–1999), Continuing Education Teaching Excellence Award (1991–1992), and Undergraduate Teaching Excellence Award (1987–1988). He also was selected into Who's Who of American Colleges and Universities and Beta Gamma Sigma. Angelo is an active researcher. He has published over 80 articles in a variety of leading academic and professional journals and has coauthored six college textbooks (15 counting revisions). His textbooks have been used by hundreds of universities around the world. Angelo's experience as a researcher also resulted in his selection to serve on the editorial review boards for the *Academy of Management Journal, the Journal of Vocational Behavior,* and the *Journal of Management.* He received the "All-Time Best Reviewer Award" from the *Academy of Management Journal* for the period of 1996–1999.

Angelo also is an active international consultant who works with top management teams to create organizational change aimed at increasing organizational effectiveness and profitability. He has worked with many Fortune 500 firms as well as numerous entrepreneurial organizations in diverse industries. His expertise includes facilitating strategic/operational planning sessions, diagnosing the causes of organizational and work-unit problems, implementing performance management systems, designing and implementing performance appraisal systems, developing and administering surveys to assess employee attitudes, and leading management/executive education programs. He developed a 360° leadership feedback instrument called the Performance Management Leadership Survey (PMLS) that is used by companies throughout the United States and Europe.

One of Angelo's strengths is his ability to teach students at all levels within a university. He uses an interactive environment to enhance undergraduates' understanding about management and organizational behavior. He focuses MBAs on applying management concepts to solve complex problems; PhD students learn the art and science of conducting scholarly research.

Angelo and his wife, Joyce, have enjoyed living in the beautiful Arizona desert for 25 years but are natives of Cleveland, Ohio. They enjoy traveling, golfing, and hiking.

Brian Williams has been Managing Editor for college textbook publisher Harper & Row/Canfield Press in San Francisco; Editor-in-Chief for nonfiction trade-book publisher J. P. Tarcher in Los Angeles; Publications & Communications Manager for the University of California, Systemwide Administration, in Berkeley; and an independent writer and book producer based in the San Francisco and Lake Tahoe areas. He has a B.A. in English and an M.A. in Communication from Stanford University. He has co-authored 20 books (49, counting revisions), which include such best-selling college texts as *Using Information Technology* with his wife, Stacey C. Sawyer, now in its seventh edition with McGraw-Hill. He has also written a number of other information technology books, college success books, and health and social science texts. In his spare time, he and Stacey enjoy travel, music, cooking, hiking, and exploring the wilds of the American West.

dedication

To Lynne and Jim Penhollow, two of my best friends.
I admire and respect what you have accomplished.
You are entrepreneurial role models, starting,
growing, managing, and selling a successful business,
while staying happily married for over 40 years.
Luck made us neighbors, and love makes us friends.

— Love, A.K.

To Stacey, for her 21 years of steadfast, patient support
and for her collaboration and shared adventures; to
Sylvia, for her many years of being the apple of her
father's eye; to Kirk, for being the son who continues to
delight me; and to Nicolas, newest member of the family.

— Much love, B.K.W.

a promise: to make learning management easy, efficient, and effective

The Third Edition of *Management: A Practical Introduction*—a concepts book for the introductory course in management—uses a wealth of instructor feedback to identify which features from prior editions worked best and which should be improved and expanded. By blending our two strengths—Angelo's scholarship, teaching, and management-consulting experience with Brian's writing and publishing background—we have again tried to create a research-based yet highly readable, innovative, and practical text.

Our primary goal is simple to state but hard to execute: to make learning principles of management as easy, efficient, and effective as possible. Accordingly, the book integrates writing, illustration, design, and magazine-like layout in **a program of learning that appeals to the visual sensibilities and respects the time constraints and different learning styles of today's students**. In an approach initially tested in our First Edition and fine-tuned in the Second Edition, **we break topics down into easily grasped portions** and incorporate **frequent use of various kinds of reinforcement techniques**. Our hope, of course, is to make a difference in the lives of our readers: to produce a text that students will enjoy reading and that will provide them with practical benefits.

The text covers the principles that most management instructors have come to expect in an introductory text—planning, organizing, leading, and controlling—plus the issues that today's students need to be aware of in order to succeed: customer focus, globalism, diversity, ethics, information technology, entrepreneurship, work teams, the service economy, and small business. Also, **new to this edition**, we include an emphasis on the importance of using **evidence-based management**—basing decisions on the real world rather than on hunches or management fads.

Beyond these, our book has **four features that make it unique**:

 I. A student-centered approach to learning

 2. Imaginative writing for readability and reinforcement

 3. Emphasis on practicality

 4. Resources that work

> "This text does a superb job with the primary topics that ought to be covered in an introductory management course. Information is thorough, easy to read, and extraordinarily accessible and is presented in a visually appealing manner that encourages student engagement. Kinicki and Williams have knocked the ball out of the park with this text."
>
> —*Neil Burton, Clemson University*

feature #1: A Student-Centered Approach to Learning

CHAPTER OPENERS:
Designed to help students read with purpose

Each chapter begins with 4–8 provocative, motivational Major Questions, written to appeal to students' concern about "what's in it for me?" and help them read with purpose.

Instead of opening with the conventional case, as most texts do, we open with the Manager's Toolbox, a motivational device offering practical nuts-and-bolts advice pertaining to the chapter content students are about to read—and allowing for class discussion.

CHAPTER SECTIONS:
Structured into constituent parts for easier learning

Chapters are organized to cover each major question in turn, giving students bite-sized chunks of information. Each section begins with a recap of the Major Question and includes "The Big Picture," which presents students with an overview of how the section they are about to read answers the Major Question. See page 181 for the rest of the section shown at right.

"This is an excellent introductory management text designed for maximum student comprehension. The material is presented in a manner that permits students to see the concepts as tools, not merely as things to memorize."

—*David Bess, University of Hawaii*

Chapter tools help students learn how to learn

In focus groups, symposiums, and reviews, instructors told us that many students do not have the skills needed to succeed in college. To support students in acquiring these skills, we offer the following:

A One-Minute Guide to Success in This Class

Got one minute to read this section? It could mean the difference between getting an A instead of a B. Or a B instead of a C.

Four Rules for Success

There are four rules that will help you be successful in this (or any other) course.

- **Rule 1:** Attend every class. No cutting allowed.
- **Rule 2:** Don't postpone studying, then cram the night before a test.
- **Rule 3:** Read or review lectures and readings more than once.

Why Learn about International Management?

International management is management that oversees the conduct of operations in or with organizations in foreign countries, whether it's through a multinational corporation or a multinational organization.

- **A *multinational corporation*, or multinational enterprise, is a business firm with operations in several countries.** Our publisher, McGraw-Hill, is one such "multinational" (see the 17 foreign cities listed on our book's title page). In terms of revenue, the real behemoths in multinational corporations include the American firms Wal-Mart, ExxonMobil, General Motors, Ford Motor Co., General Electric, and Citigroup. The largest foreign companies are BP (Britain), Royal Dutch/Shell (Netherlands/Britain), DaimlerChrysler (Germany/USA), and Toyota (Japan).
- **A *multinational organization* is a nonprofit organization with operations in several countries.** Examples are the World Health Organization, the International Red Cross, the Church of Latter Day Saints.

Practical Action

Being a World Citizen: Learning to Be a Success Abroad

Whether you go abroad on your own or on a work assignment for your company, there are several ways to make your travel enhance your career success.

Learn How Not to Be an "Ugly American" Americans "are seen throughout the world as an arrogant people, totally self-absorbed and loud," says Keith Reinhard, former head of advertising conglomerate DDB Worldwide, who is leading an effort to reverse that through a nonprofit group called Business for Diplomatic Action (BDA), from which many suggestions here are drawn.[29] A survey conducted by DDB in more than 100 countries found that respondents repeatedly mentioned "arrogant," "loud," and "uninterested in the world" when asked their perceptions of Americans.[30] Some sample advice for Americans traveling abroad appears below. (See Table 4.1.)

Learn What's Appropriate Behavior Before you go, "Spend at least 10% of preparation time on interpersonal skills," suggests executive coach Arlene B. Isaacs.[31] In Japan it is considered rude to look directly into the eye for more than a few seconds. In Greece the hand-waving gesture commonly used in America is considered an insult. In Afghanistan, a man does not ask another man about his wife.[32]

Learn rituals of respect, including exchange of business cards. Understand that shaking hands is always permissible, but social kissing may not be. Dress professionally. For women, this means no heavy makeup, no flashy jewelry, no short skirts or sleeveless blouses (particularly in Islamic countries). In some countries, casual dressing is a sign of disrespect. Don't use first names and nicknames with fellow employees

---

The **"One-Minute Guide to Success in This Class,"** found on pg. l, lays down four rules for student success in class and suggestions for how to use this book most effectively.

"Getting Control of Your Time: Dealing with the Information Deluge in College and in Your Career," at the end of Chapter l on pages 27-30, gives students a crash course in time management skills, solid study habits, memory aids, learning from lectures, and becoming effective test takers.

Key terms are highlighted and terms and definitions are in boldface, to help students build their management vocabulary.

Other devices to help students develop understanding:

- Important **scholar names in boldface** so students remember key contributors to the field of management.
- Frequent use of **advance organizers, bulleted lists, and headings** to help students grasp the main ideas
- **Illustrations positioned close to relevant text discussion** so students can refer to them more easily and avoid flipping pages

---

"The Kinicki text is organized very, very well. It makes the relationships between the concepts of management very easy to identify and to understand for students. The visual elements of the Kinicki text are superb...the graphics are exceptional and will be of great help to students trying to get a clear visual picture of how the concepts relate. The coverage of the topics is excellent."
—Linda Koffel, Houston Community College

feature #2: Imaginative Writing for Readability

Research shows that textbooks written in **an imaginative, people-oriented style significantly improve students' ability to retain information**. We employ a number of journalistic devices to make the material as engaging as possible for students.

We use **colorful facts, attention-grabbing quotes, biographical sketches, and lively tag lines** to get students' attention as they read. See page 418 for the rest of these stories.

The year 2006 was not a good one for American men's sports teams on the world stage. The U.S. soccer team failed to muster one victory at the World Cup. The U.S. baseball team was defeated by Mexico, Korea, and Canada at the World Baseball Classic and did not even make it to the semifinals. And at the World Basketball Championship, the U.S. men's team—in a sport invented by Americans—failed for the third straight year to bring home the gold.[3] What went wrong?

Take the basketball team, which despite having such NBA stars as Dwyane Wade and LeBron James nevertheless lost to Greece 101–95 in the semifinals. Team USA players had been together for more than a year, but, says one account, "the lack of experience—and familiarity with each other—was glaringly obvious against a Greek squad that has been together three years."[4] But perhaps there was more to it than that. "Our best male athletes have regressed as team players—as *teammates,*" writes Michael Sokolove. "A couple of decades of free agency and lavish salaries freed the players from the grips of owners but also unbound them from one another. . . . If our greatest young athletes don't care enough about one another to commit to effort and team play, that can't be a good thing."[5]

More Teamwork: The Change Today's Employees Need to Make

"You lead today by building teams and placing others first," says General Electric CEO Jeffrey Immelt. "It's not about you."[6] According to management philosopher Peter Drucker, tomorrow's organizations will not only be flatter and information-based but also organized around teamwork.[7] "We have this mythology in America about the lone genius," says Tom Kelley, general manager of Ideo, an industrial design company in Palo Alto, California, that helped create the Apple mouse and the Palm V handheld computer. "We love to personify things. But Michelangelo didn't paint the Sistine Chapel alone, and Edison didn't invent the light bulb alone."[8]

Our emphasis on practicality and applications extends to the **Example boxes**, "mini-cases" that use snapshots of real-world situations to explain text concepts. **New to this edition: "Your Call" invites student critical thinking and class discussion at the end of each example**. Suggestions for how to use the example boxes are found in the Instructor's Manual. See page 420 for the remainder of this box on worker chit-chat as informal training.

Example

Informal Groups Can Help with Informal Learning: Worker Chitchat "Is Not Goofing Off, It's Training"

As a manager, what would you think when you saw employees making brief exchanges near the coffeepot? "The assumption was made," said Barry Blyston, director of training at a plant in Wendell, North Carolina, where managers wondered how to stop workers from gathering so often in the cafeteria, "that this was chitchat, talking about their golf game. But there was a whole lot of work activity."[14]

Or so a 2-year $1.6 million study by the Center for Workplace Development discovered.[15] At Siemens Power Transmission and Distribution, as well as companies such as Motorola and Boeing, the study found that 70% of workplace learning is informal, despite the $60 billion

organizations spend on formal training programs every year.[16]

Your Call
Following the study, Siemens managers placed overhead projectors and empty pads of paper in the lunchroom to facilitate informal meetings. They also alerted supervisors about the informal gatherings. What other things would you do to encourage employees to informally learn from each other?

Talking it out. Ever worked in a job in which you got a lot of informal training through conversations over coffee?

"This text does a wonderful job of being approachable from a student's perspective. It's conversational, lively, and engaging."

—Scott Droege, Western Kentucky University

feature #3: An Emphasis on Practicality

We want this book to be a "keeper" for students, a resource for future courses and for their careers—so we give students a great deal of practical advice in addition to covering the fundamental concepts of management. Application points are found not only throughout the text discussion, but also in the following specialized features:

Practical Action

Transition Problems on Your Way Up: How to Avoid the Pitfalls

Before you can become a good leader you need to become a good manager. Making the leap from individual contributor to a manager of several employees "is one of the most difficult in peoples' careers," suggests *Wall Street Journal* columnist Hal Lancaster.

Although corporations and managements may make noises about training and mentoring support, newly promoted managers may not see any of this and may simply be expected to know what to do. And, as managers move up the ladder, they may encounter other problems that they have not anticipated. How can you avoid some pitfalls as you make

since they have resources you need to get your job done. Don't make the mistake of thinking your own department is the center of the universe.

• **Think about what kind of manager or leader you want to be.** Make a list of all your previous bosses and their good and bad attributes. This may produce a list of dos and don'ts that can serve you well.

• **Get guidance from other managers.** You may not get advice on how to manage from your own manager, who may have promoted you to help reduce his or her workload, not add to it, by expecting

Practical Action boxes, appearing one or more times in each chapter, offer students practical and interesting advice on issues they will face in the workplace. See page 459 for the rest of this box on avoiding pitfalls in advancing your career.

End-of-Chapter Resources that reinforce applications

Each chapter continues our strategy of repetition for learning reinforcement. We include various unique pedagogical features to help students take away the most significant portions of the chapter's content:

Management in Action cases depict how companies students are familiar with respond to situations or issues featured in the text. Discussion questions are included for ease of use in class, as reflection assignments, or over online discussion boards. See pages 484–485 for an example on how Citigroup's new CEO is leading his company through changes.

Self-Assessment Exercises enable students to personally apply chapter content. These exercises include objectives for ease in assigning, instructions for use, guidelines for interpreting results, and questions for further reflection. They can also be found on the text Web site. See pages 141–143 for an example on learning how to manage globally.

Group Exercises offer a teamwork venue for further applying chapter topics. Instructions, objectives, and discussion questions are included. See pages 322–323 for a group exercise on human resource management.

Ethical Dilemmas present cases—often based on real events—that require students to think through how they would handle the situation, helping prepare them for decision-making in their careers. See page 354 for an example on the ethics of free prescription drug samples.

feature #4: Resources That Work

Video cases offer a visual way to focus in on chapter topics. Sixteen videos, 8 of them new for this edition, accompany this text on DVD, with corresponding cases within each chapter. Cases include newsreel footage, company interviews, and Manager's Hot Seat episodes to keep students thinking about how topics play out in the real world. See pages 105-106 for the rest of this video case.

Cases by chapter are:
1. A Look at eBay's Meg Whitman
2. Organizational Culture at New Belgium Brewery
3. The Rules of Engagement (NBC InDepth)
4. The Peace Corps: The Toughest Job You'll Ever Love
5. The Dale Grey Story
6. Strategy at Panera Bread
7. Partnership: The Unbalancing Act at The Living Room Café (MHS)
8. JetBlue's Culture
9. Human Resources at Patagonia
10. Managing Change at Hillerich and Bradsby
11. Project Management: Steering the Committee at TechBox (MHS)
12. Working for the Best: The Container Store
13. Pike Place Fish Market
14. Winning Advice from Jack Welch
15. Listening Skills at Midnight Visions
16. Starbucks: Building Relationships with Coffee Growers

Each video includes a case authored by Joe Santora of Essex County College as well as suggested uses and answers to questions in the IM.

NEW TO THIS EDITION

McGraw-Hill/Irwin is pleased to present the first **expanded cartridge** for the Kinicki/Williams text. Now you can benefit from a one-stop course cartridge that includes all digital supplements from the OLC, instructor resources, and the capability to record and store grades. Students can access all OLC elements plus additional interactive learning materials such as the now fully digital, fully functional study guide. Help keep your students accountable for course concepts by tracking their participation and grading their efforts! Talk to your publisher's representative today to find out more.

You asked for ways to tie resources to specific chapters, so we did it! **New to this edition, target icons** in the text margins denote **specific places where chapter content is augmented by a review activity, exercise, or self-assessment in the course cartridge system, Group and Video Resource Manual, and Hot Seat programs**, allowing you to help guide your students in remediation and making connections between concepts.

The **Group and Video Resource Manual**, authored by Amanda Johnson and Angelo Kinicki, was compiled to help you create a more lively and stimulating classroom environment. It contains interactive in-class group and individual exercises as well as notes on how to use the Build Your Management Skills modules and the Manager's Hot Seat scenarios. PowerPoint slides walk you through each exercise, and discussion questions help facilitate learning. Visit **www.mhhe.com/kw3e** to find out more.

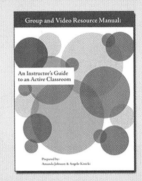

Manager's Hot Seat Online! Now you can put your students in the hot seat with access to our interactive program. Students are given an introduction to the situation, view a dossier of related management materials, and then watch 15 real managers apply their years of experience when confronting unscripted issues. As the scenario unfolds, questions about how the manager is handling the situation pop up, forcing the student to make decisions along with the manager. At the end of the scenario, students watch a post-interview with the manager, view how their responses matched up to the manager's decisions, and then submit a report critiquing the manager's choices while defending their own. Access to the online program is an optional package with this text.

NEW TO THIS EDITION

The **Online Learning Center** for this edition, **www.mhhe.com/kw3e**, is re-engineered to better meet your and your students' needs. Students can take self-assessments tied directly to chapters, use flashcards to test their vocabulary memory, take chapter quizzes to review concepts, access a career corner, and practice building their management skills through additional exercises also tagged to specific chapters. Instructors can view the IM and PowerPoint sets online, as well as access all student content to assign various exercises.

The Instructor's Resource CD includes multiple resources to make your teaching life easier.

- The **Instructor's Manual**, authored by Brian Williams and Stacey Sawyer, thoroughly covers each chapter by giving an overview of key points; lecture outlines incorporating use of PowerPoints, text pedagogy—including end-of-chapter resources, and videos; key terms discussion; critical thinking exercises; and lecture enhancers.

- Also included are two sets of **PowerPoint Presentations**, authored by Russell Casey of Clayton State University—a foundational, outline-based set and an expanded set with notes for use in the classroom.

- Finally, the **Test Bank**, authored by Amit Shah of Frostburg State University, includes 80-100 questions in a variety of formats, and is revised for this edition to include not just answers and rationales, but also tags to how each question fits in Bloom's Taxonomy levels and fulfills AACSB requirements.

McGraw-Hill offers **content for complete online** courses using delivery systems such as WebCT, Blackboard, and PageOut, which enable instructors to exert complete control over course content and how it is presented to students. Your publisher's representative can equip you with a cartridge for use with your online course system.

 McGraw-Hill/Irwin's PageOut enables you to **create a Web site for your management course** that incorporates your course materials and syllabus to build a custom Web site to your specifications—no HTML coding or graphic design knowledge needed! Simply fill in a series of boxes, click on one of our available designs, and in no time, your course is online. For more information, visit **www.pageout.net**.

acknowledgments

We could not have completed this product without the help of a great many others. The first edition was signed by Karen Mellon, to whom we are very grateful. Sincere thanks and gratitude go to our executive editor, John Weimeister, and his first-rate team at McGraw-Hill/Irwin. Key contributors included Kirsten Guidero, developmental editor; Anke Braun, senior marketing manager; Harvey Yep, project manager; Kami Carter, senior designer; and Greg Bates, media producer. We would also like to thank Russell Casey for his wonderful work on the PowerPoint presentations, Amit Shah for authoring the Test Bank and developing content for the Online Learning Center, Joe Santora for creating the Video Cases, Stacey C. Sawyer, for her work on The Study Guide and Instructor's Manual; and Paige Wolf for writing the teaching notes for the Manager's Hot Seat DVD segments.

Warmest thanks and appreciation go to the individuals who provided valuable input during the developmental stages of this edition, as follows:

Scott Anchors, *Maine Business School*

David Bess, *University of Hawaii*

Marit Brunsell, *Madison Area Technical College*

Neil Burton, *Clemson University*

Scott Droege, *Western Kentucky University*

Linda Durkin, *Delaware County Community College*

Samuel Hazen, *Tarleton State University*

Bobbie Knoblauch, *Wichita State University*

David Levy, *United States Air Force Academy*

Val Miskin, *Washington State University*

Jack Partlow, *Northern Virginia Community College*

Randi Sims, *Nova Southeastern University*

Isaiah Ugboro, *North Carolina Agricultural & Technical State University*

We would also like to thank the following colleagues who served as manuscript reviewers during the development of the first and second editions

G. Stoney Alder, *Western Illinois University*

Phyllis C. Alderdice, *Jefferson Community College*

John Anstey, *University of Nebraska at Omaha*

Maria Aria, *Camden County College*

James Bell, *Texas State University-San Marcos*

Victor Berardi, *Kent State University*

Stephen Betts, *William Paterson University*

Danielle Beu, *Louisiana Tech University*

Larry Bohleber, *University of Southern Indiana*

Melanie Bookout, *Greenville Technical College*

Robert S. Boothe, *University of Southern Mississippi*

Roger Brown, *Western Illinois University*

Jon Bryan, *Bridgewater State College*

Pamela Carstens, *Coe College*

Glen Chapuis, *St. Charles Community College*

Rod Christian, *Mesa Community College*

Mike Cicero, *Highline Community College*

Jack Cichy, *Davenport University*

Anthony Cioffi, *Lorain County Community College*

Deborah Clark, *Santa Fe Community College*

Sharon Clinebell, *University of Northern Colorado*

Ron Cooley, *South Suburban College*

Gary Corona, *Florida Community College*

Ajay Das, *Baruch College*

Kathleen DeNisco, *Erie Community College*

David Dore, *San Francisco City College*

Lon Doty, *San Jose State University*

Steven Dunphy, *University of Akron*

Subhash Durlabhji, *Northwestern State University*

Jack Dustman, *Northern Arizona University*

Ray Eldridge, *Freed-Hardeman University*

Judy Fitch, *Augusta State University*

David Foote, *Middle Tennessee State University*

Tony Frontera, *Broome Community College*

Michael Garcia, *Liberty University*

Evgeniy Gentchev, *Northwood University*

James Glasgow, *Villanova University*

Kris Gossett, *Ivy Tech State College*

Joyce Guillory, *Austin Community College*

Charles T. Harrington, *Pasadena City College*

Santhi Harvey, *Central State University*

Jack Heinsius, *Modesto Junior College*

Kim Hester, *Arkansas State University*

Mary Hogue, *Kent State University*

Edward Johnson, *University of North Florida*

Rusty Juban, *Southeastern Louisiana University*

Dmitriy Kalyagin, *Chabot College*

Heesam Kang, *Bacone College*

Marcella Kelly, *Santa Monica College*

Rebecca Legleiter, *Tulsa Community College*

David Leonard, *Chabot College*

Beverly Little, *Western Carolina University*

Mary Lou Lockerby, *College of DuPage*

Paul Londrigan, *Charles Stewart Mott Community College*

Tom Loughman, *Columbus State University*

Brenda McAleer, *University of Maine at Augusta*

David McArthur, *University of Nevada Las Vegas*

Tom McFarland, *Mount San Antonio College*

Joe McKenna, *Howard Community College*

Jeanne McNett, *Assumption College*

Spencer Mehl, *Coastal Carolina Community College*

Mary Meredith, *University of Louisiana*

Douglas Micklich, *Illinois State University*

Christine Miller, *Tennessee Tech University*

Gregory Moore, *Middle Tennessee State University*

Rob Moorman, *Creighton University*

Robert Myers, *University of Louisville*

Francine Newth, *Providence College*

Jack Partlow, *Northern Virginia Community College*

Don A. Paxton, *Pasadena City College*

John Paxton, *Wayne State College*

Sheila Petcavage, *Cuyahoga Community College*

Barbara Petzall, *Maryville University*

Leah Ritchie, *Salem State College*

Barbara Rosenthall, *Miami Dade Community College/Wolfson Campus I*

Gary Ross, *Barat College of DePaul University*

Cindy Ruszkowski, *Illinois State University*

William Salyer, *Morris College*

Diane R. Scott, *Wichita State University*

Marianne Sebok, *Community College of Southern Nevada*

Gerald F. Smith, *University of Northern Iowa*

Mark Smith, *University of Southwest Louisiana*

Jeff Stauffer, *Ventura College*

Raymond Stoudt, *DeSales University*

Virginia Anne Taylor, *William Patterson University*

Jerry Thomas, *Arapahoe Community College*

Robert Trumble, *Virginia Commonwealth University*

Anthony Uremovic, *Joliet Junior College*

Barry Van Hook, *Arizona State University*

Susan Verhulst, *Des Moines Area Community College*

Annie Viets, *University of Vermont*

Tom Voigt, Jr., *Aurora University*

Bruce C. Walker, *University of Louisiana at Monroe*

Charles Warren, *Salem State College*

Allen Weimer, *University of Tampa*

James Whelan, *Manhattan College*

John Whitelock, *Community College of Baltimore/Catonsville Campus*

Wendy Wysocki, *Monroe County Community College*

The following professors also participated in an early focus group that helped drive the development of this text. We appreciate their suggestions and participation immensely:

Rusty Brooks, *Houston Baptist University*

Kerry Carson, *University of Southwestern Louisiana*

Sam Dumbar, *Delgado Community College*

Subhash Durlabhji, *Northwestern State University*

Robert Mullins, *Delgado Community College*

Carl Phillips, *Southeastern Louisiana University*

Allayne Pizzolatto, *Nicholls State University*

Ellen White, *University of New Orleans*

We would also like to thank the following students for participating in a very important focus group to gather feedback from the student reader's point of view:

Marcy Baasch, *Triton College*

Diana Broeckel, *Triton College*

Lurene Cornejo, *Moraine Valley Community College*

Dave Fell, *Elgin Community College*

Lydia Hendrix, *Moraine Valley Community College*

Kristine Kurpiewski, *Oakton Community College*

Michelle Monaco, *Moraine Valley Community College*

Shannon Ramey, *Elgin Community College*

Arpita Sikand, *Oakton Community College*

Finally, we would like to thank our wives, Joyce and Stacey, for being understanding, patient, and encouraging throughout the process of writing this edition. Your love and support helped us endure the trials of completing this text.

We hope you enjoy reading and applying the book. Best wishes for success in your career.

Angelo Kinicki   **Brian K. Williams**

contents

Part 2
The Environment of Management

Chapter Three

Chapter Four

Part 3
Planning

Chapter Five

Chapter Six

Part 4
Organizing

Part 5
Leading

Chapter Thirteen

Chapter Fourteen

Chapter Fifteen

Part 6
Control

Chapter Sixteen

A One-Minute Guide to Success in This Class

Got one minute to read this section? It could mean the difference between getting an A instead of a B. Or a B instead of a C.

Four Rules for Success

There are four rules that will help you be successful in this (or any other) course.

- **Rule 1:** Attend every class. No cutting allowed.
- **Rule 2:** Don't postpone studying, then cram the night before a test.
- **Rule 3:** Read or review lectures and readings more than once.
- **Rule 4:** Learn how to use this book.

How to Use This Book Most Effectively

When reading this book, follow the steps below:

- Get an overview of the chapter by reading over the first page, which contains the section headings and Major Questions.
- Read "Forecast: What's Ahead in This Chapter."
- Look at the Major Question at the beginning of each section before you read it.
- Read the "The Big Picture," which summarizes the section.
- Read the section itself (which is usually only 2–6 pages), *trying silently to answer the Major Question.* This is important!
- After reading all sections, use the Key Terms and Summary at the end of the chapter to see how well you understand the major concepts. Reread any material you're unsure about.

If you follow these steps consistently, you'll probably absorb the material well enough that you won't have to cram before an exam; you'll need only to lightly review it before the test.

chapter I

The Exceptional Manager
What You Do, How You Do It

Major Questions You Should Be Able to Answer

I.I Management: What It Is, What Its Benefits Are
Major Question: What are the rewards of being an exceptional manager–of being a star in my workplace?

I.2 Six Challenges to Being a Star Manager
Major Question: Challenges can make one feel alive. What are six challenges I could look forward to as a manager?

I.3 What Managers Do: The Four Principal Functions
Major Question: What would I actually *do*—that is, what would be my four principal functions—as a manager?

I.4 Pyramid Power: Levels & Areas of Management
Major Question: What are the levels and areas of management I need to know to move up, down, and sideways?

I.5 Roles Managers Must Play Successfully
Major Question: To be an exceptional manager, what roles must I play successfully?

I.6 The Entrepreneurial Spirit
Major Question: Do I have what it takes to be an entrepreneur?

I.7 The Skills Star Managers Need
Major Question: To be a terrific manager, what skills should I cultivate?

Becoming a Star Manager: Rules for Advancing Your Career

Someday maybe you can afford to have a *personal career coach*—the kind long used by sports and entertainment figures and now adopted in the upper ranks of business. These individuals "combine executive coaching and career consulting with marketing and negotiations," says one account. "They plot career strategy, help build networks of business contacts, . . . and shape their clients' images."[1]

Because planning a career is increasingly bewildering in today's work world, in the following pages we are going to try to act much like your personal career coach. In that spirit, it is our desire *to make this book as practical as possible for you.* For instance, the **Manager's Toolbox,** like this one, which appears at the beginning of every chapter, offers practical advice appropriate to the subject matter you are about to explore.

Five Rules for Staying Ahead in Your Career The purpose of this book is to help you become a successful manager—indeed, a *star manager*—an *exceptional manager,* as this chapter's title has it, whose performance is far superior to that of other managers. The first thing star managers learn is how to stay ahead in their careers.

The following strategies for staying ahead in the workplace of tomorrow are adapted from rules offered by professional career counselor Richard L. Knowdell, president of Career Research and Testing in San Jose, California.[2]

- **Take charge of your career and avoid misconceptions:** Because you, not others, are in charge of your career, and it's an ongoing process, you should develop a career plan and base your choices on that plan. When considering a new job or industry, find out how that world *really* works, not what it's reputed to be. When considering a company you might want to work for, find out its corporate "style" or culture by talking to its employees.

- **Develop new capacities:** "Being good at several things will be more advantageous in the long run than being excellent at one narrow specialty," says Knowdell. "A complex world will not only demand *specialized knowledge* but also *general and flexible skills.*"

- **Anticipate and adapt to, even embrace, changes:** Learn to analyze, anticipate, and adapt to new circumstances in the world and in your own life. For instance, as technology changes the rules, *embrace* the new rules.

- **Keep learning:** "You can take a one- or two-day course in a new subject," says Knowdell, "just to get an idea of whether you want to use those specific skills and to see if you would be good at it. Then, if there is a match, you could seek out an extended course."

- **Develop your people and communications skills:** No matter how much communication technology takes over the workplace, there will always be a strong need for effectiveness in interpersonal relationships. In particular, learn to listen well.

For Discussion Which of these five rules do you think is the most important—and why?

forecast
What's Ahead in This Chapter

We describe the rewards, benefits, and privileges managers might expect. We also describe the six challenges to managers in today's world—not only staying ahead of rivals but also managing for diversity, globalization, information technology, ethical standards, and personal happiness and life goals. You'll be introduced to the four principal functions of management—planning, organizing, leading, and controlling—and levels and areas of management. Then we consider the contributions of entrepreneurship. Finally, we describe the three types of roles (interpersonal, informational, and decisional) and three skills (technical, conceptual, and human) required of a manager.

1.1 MANAGEMENT: WHAT IT IS, WHAT ITS BENEFITS ARE

✳ major question What are the rewards of being an exceptional manager—of being a star in my workplace?

THE BIG PICTURE

Management is defined as the pursuit of organizational goals efficiently and effectively. Organizations, or people who work together to achieve a specific purpose, value managers because of the multiplier effect: Good managers have an influence on the organization far beyond the results that can be achieved by one person acting alone. Managers are well paid, with the CEOs and presidents of even small and midsize businesses earning good salaries and many benefits.

Judy McGrath, from a blue-collar Irish neighborhood in Scranton, Pennsylvania, was 26 when she arrived in New York in 1978 with an English degree. After a period of writing articles for women's magazines, she was hired to create promotional materials for MTV. Today at age 53 she is chief executive officer (CEO) of MTV Networks, which was launched in 1981 as a music video channel but now comprises TV channels, Web sites, and wireless services reaching 440 million households in 169 countries. What brought about her rise to the top of this $7 billion company?

One quality she brought to her job is a strong sense of community. If she has been "smart or lucky at one thing," she says, "it has been [picking] good people." Another quality is perseverance. "It's a really undervalued asset," she points out, "but if you really want something, you've got to hang in there." A third quality: encouraging an anything-is-possible spirit by creating an atmosphere in which people feel safe and are not afraid to fail. "Falling flat is a great motivator," she says. "So is accident."[3]

In an era of broadband, iPods, and an "Always On" online generation, MTV faces a slew of threats. The company will now have to deliver services across new broadband channels, over cell phones, and via video games. Two important rules in the McGrath playbook, therefore, are "Make change part of your DNA" and "Companies don't innovate, people do."

Being prepared for surprises and change is important to any manager's survival, and continuing change—in the world and in the workplace—is a major theme of this book.

MTV in New York City. The sprawl of the MTV empire includes multiple online communities for various geographical locations, shops such as this one in the Big Apple, and, of course, TV channels. As CEO, Judy McGrath must understand the unique needs of customers from Stockholm to Toronto to Chicago, as well as how to reach them with MTV's offerings. If you were in her shoes, what would you consider to be the key component of managerial success? A strong sense of community? Perseverance? Making people not afraid to fail?

The Art of Management Defined

Is being an exceptional manager—a star manager—a gift, like a musician having perfect pitch? Not exactly. But in good part it may be an art. Fortunately, it is one that is teachable.

Management, said one pioneer of management ideas, is "the art of getting things done through people."[4]

Getting things done. Through people. Thus, managers are task oriented, achievement oriented, and people oriented. And they operate within an ***organization—a group of people who work together to achieve some specific purpose.***

More formally, ***management* is defined as (1) the pursuit of organizational goals efficiently and effectively by (2) integrating the work of people through (3) planning, organizing, leading, and controlling the organization's resources.**

Note the words *efficiently* and *effectively,* which basically mean "doing things right."

- *Efficiency—the means.* Efficiency is the means of attaining the organization's goals. **To be *efficient* means to use resources—people, money, raw materials, and the like—wisely and cost-effectively.**

- *Effectiveness—the ends.* Effectiveness is the organization's ends, the goals. **To be *effective* means to achieve results, to make the right decisions and to successfully carry them out so that they achieve the organization's goals.**

Good managers are concerned with trying to achieve both qualities. Often, however, organizations will erroneously strive for efficiency without being effective.

Why Organizations Value Managers: The Multiplier Effect

Some great achievements of history, such as scientific discoveries or works of art, were accomplished by individuals working quietly by themselves. But so much more has been achieved by people who were able to leverage their talents and abilities by being managers. For instance, of the top 10 great architectural wonders of the world named by the American Institute of Architects, none was built single-handedly by one person. All were triumphs of management, although some reflected the vision of an individual.

Example

Efficiency versus Effectiveness: Won't Someone Answer the Phone—*Please?*

We're all now accustomed to having our calls to companies answered not by people but by a recorded "telephone menu" of options. Certainly this arrangement is *efficient* for the companies, since they no longer need as many telephone receptionists. But it's not *effective* if it leaves us, the customers, fuming and not inclined to continue doing business.

The cost for self-service via an automated phone system averages $1.85, whereas the cost of using a live customer-service representative is $4.50, according to the Gartner Group, an information technology analyst.[5] Nevertheless, automated technologies often don't allow completion of transactions, because of customer confusion and technological glitches, so this leads to "ping-ponging"—customers calling back trying to find a live representative or other means of contacting the company.

Thus, Scott Broetzmann, president of CustomerCare Measurement Consulting, a firm that does surveys on customer service, says that 90% of consumers say they want nothing to do with an automated telephone system. "They just don't like it," he says. The most

Effective? How often do you encounter organizations using their telephone systems more efficiently than effectively?

telling finding is that 50% of those surveyed had become so aggravated that they were willing to pay an additional charge for customer service that avoids going through an automated phone system.[6]

Richard Shapiro, head of a firm that evaluates the experiences of customers calling in to toll-free call centers, says that companies "create more value through a dialogue with a live agent. A call is an opportunity to build a relationship, to encourage a customer to stay with the brand. There can be a real return on this investment."[7]

Your Call

Paul English, chief technology officer for a travel search engine business, was so fed up with automated voice services and other awful customer service that he started Get Human to "change the face of customer service." The Web site, **www.gethuman. com,** publishes the unpublicized codes for reaching a company's human operators, a list of the best and worst companies, and cut-through-automation tips.[8] What recent unpleasant customer experience would you want to post on this Web site?

(The wonders are the Great Wall of China, the Great Pyramid, Machu Picchu, the Acropolis, the Coliseum, the Taj Mahal, the Eiffel Tower, the Brooklyn Bridge, the Empire State Building, and Frank Lloyd Wright's Falling Water house in Pennsylvania.)

Good managers create value. The reason is that in being a manager you have a *multiplier effect:* your influence on the organization is multiplied far beyond the results that can be achieved by just one person acting alone. Thus, while a solo operator such as a salesperson might accomplish many things and incidentally make a very good living, his or her boss could accomplish a great deal more—and could well earn two to seven times the income. And the manager will undoubtedly have a lot more influence.

Star managers are in high demand. "The scarcest, most valuable resource in business is no longer financial capital," says a recent *Fortune* article. "It's talent. If you doubt that, just watch how hard companies are battling for the best people. . . . Talent of every type is in short supply, but the greatest shortage of all is skilled, effective managers.[9]

Financial Rewards of Being a Star Manager

How well compensated are managers? According to the U.S. Bureau of Labor Statistics, the median weekly wage in 2004 for American workers of all sorts was $638, or $33,176 a year. Education pays: The average 2003 income for full-time workers with a bachelor's degree was $43,000 and with a master's degree was $53,000. (For high-school graduates, it was $26,000.)

The business press frequently reports on the astronomical earnings of top chief executive officers such as Lee R. Raymond, chairman and chief executive of the oil giant ExxonMobil, who was compensated more than $686 million from 1993 to 2005, which works out to $144,573 a day.[10] However, this kind of compensation isn't common. In 2005, the median pay of CEOs running the nation's 100 largest companies was $17.9 million.[11] Another 2005 survey found that the median CEO salary and bonus of 350 big public companies was $2.4 million.[12] More usual is the take-home pay for the head of a small business: in 2000 (the latest year for which data are available), the chief executive of a $3 million firm had an average base salary of $159,543 plus about $30,000 in cash incentives, and the chief executive of a $10 million company had a total compensation of $268,092.[13] (As for nonprofits, the Council on Foundations reported that the median annual salary for CEOs and chief giving officers of nonprofits in 2004 was $110,000.)[14]

Managers farther down in the organization usually don't make this much, of course; nevertheless, they do fairly well compared to most workers. At the lower rungs, managers may make between $25,000 and $50,000 a year; in the middle levels, between $35,000 and $110,000.

There are also all kinds of fringe benefits and status rewards that go with being a manager, ranging from health insurance to stock options to large offices. And the higher you ascend in the management hierarchy, the more privileges may come your way: personal parking space, better furniture, lunch in the executive dining room, on up to—for those on the top rung of big companies—company car and driver, corporate jet, and even executive sabbaticals (months of paid time off to pursue alternative projects).

What Are the Rewards of Studying & Practicing Management?

Are you studying management but have no plans to be a manager? Or are you trying to learn techniques and concepts that will help you be an exceptional management practitioner? Either way there are considerable rewards.

The Rewards of Studying Management
Students sign up for the introductory management course for all kinds of reasons. Many, of course, are planning business careers, but others are taking it to fulfill a requirement or an elective or just to fill a hole in their course schedule. Some students are in technical fields, such as accounting, finance, computer science, and engineering, and never expect to have to supervise other people.

Lee Raymond. The former ExxonMobil CEO earned about $144,573 a day in the years before retirement—equivalent to the yearly salary of a well-paid middle manager. The company's shares rose an average of 13% a year on Raymond's watch. What do you think your chances are of making $400 million, as Raymond did in his final year?

Here are just a few of the payoffs of studying management as a discipline:

- **You will understand how to deal with organizations from the outside.** Since we all are in constant interaction with all kinds of organizations, it helps to understand how they work and how the people in them make decisions. Such knowledge may give you some defensive skills that you can use in dealing with organizations from the outside, as a customer or investor, for example.

- **You will understand how to relate to your supervisors.** Since most of us work in organizations and most of us have bosses, studying management will enable you to understand the pressures managers deal with and how they will best respond to you.

- **You will understand how to interact with co-workers.** The kinds of management policies in place can affect how your co-workers behave. Studying management can give you the understanding of teams and teamwork, cultural differences, conflict and stress, and negotiation and communication skills that will help you get along with fellow employees.

- **You will understand how to manage yourself in the workplace.** Management courses in general, and this book in particular, give you the opportunity to realize insights about yourself—your personality, emotions, values, perceptions, needs, and goals. We help you build your skills in areas such as self-management, listening, handling change, managing stress, avoiding groupthink, and coping with organizational politics.

The Rewards of Practicing Management It's possible you are planning to be a manager. Or it's possible you will start your career practicing a narrow specialty but find yourself tapped for some sort of supervisory or leadership position. However you become a management practitioner, there are many rewards—apart from those of money and status—to being a manager:

- **You and your employees can experience a sense of accomplishment.** Every successful goal accomplished provides you not only with personal satisfaction but also with the satisfaction of all those employees you directed who helped you accomplish it.

- **You can stretch your abilities and magnify your range.** Every promotion up the hierarchy of an organization stretches your abilities, challenges your talents and skills, and magnifies the range of your accomplishments.

- **You can build a catalog of successful products or services.** Every product or service you provide—the personal Eiffel Tower or Empire State Building you build, as it were—becomes a monument to your accomplishments. Indeed, studying management may well help you in running your own business.

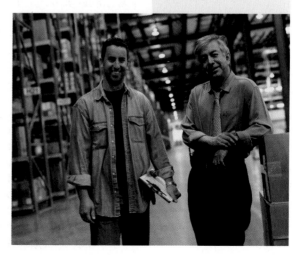

Mentoring. Being a manager is an opportunity "to counsel, motivate, advise, guide, empower, and influence" other people. Does this sense of accomplishment appeal to you?

Finally, points out Odette Pollar, who owns Time Management Systems, a productivity-improvement firm in Oakland, California, "Managers are able to view the business in a broader context, to plan and grow personally. Managers can play more of a leadership role than ever before. This is an opportunity to counsel, motivate, advise, guide, empower, and influence large groups of people. These important skills can be used in business as well as in personal and volunteer activities. If you truly like people and enjoy mentoring and helping others to grow and thrive, management is a great job."[15] ●

1.2 SIX CHALLENGES TO BEING A STAR MANAGER

❋ **major question** Challenges can make one feel alive. What are six challenges I could look forward to as a manager?

THE BIG PICTURE

Six challenges face any manager: You need to manage for competitive advantage—to stay ahead of rivals. You need to manage for diversity in race, ethnicity, gender, and so on, because the future won't resemble the past. You need to manage for the effects of globalization and of information technology. You always need to manage to maintain ethical standards. Finally, you need to manage for the achievement for your own happiness and life goals.

The ideal state that many people seek is an emotional zone somewhere between boredom and anxiety, in the view of psychologist Mihaly Csikzentmihalyi.[16] Boredom, he says, may arise because skills and challenges are mismatched: You are exercising your high level of skill in a job with a low level of challenge, such as licking envelopes. Anxiety arises when one has low levels of skill but a high level of challenge.

As a manager, could you achieve a balance between these two states? Certainly managers have enough challenges to keep their lives more than mildly interesting. Let's see what they are.

Challenge #1: Managing for Competitive Advantage— Staying Ahead of Rivals

Competitive advantage **is the ability of an organization to produce goods or services more effectively than competitors do, thereby outperforming them.** This means an organization must stay ahead in four areas: (1) being responsive to customers, (2) innovation, (3) quality, and (4) efficiency.

1. Being Responsive to Customers   The first law of business is: *take care of the customer.* Without customers—buyers, clients, consumers, shoppers, users, patrons, guests, investors, or whatever they're called—sooner or later there will be no organization. Nonprofit organizations are well advised to be responsive to their "customers," too, whether they're called citizens, members, students, patients, voters, rate-payers, or whatever, since they are the justification for the organizations' existence.

2. Innovation   **Finding ways to deliver new or better goods or services is called** *innovation.* No organization, for-profit or nonprofit, can allow itself to become complacent—especially when rivals are coming up with creative ideas. "Innovate or die" is an important adage for any manager.

We discuss innovation in Chapter 3.

3. Quality   If your organization is the only one of its kind, customers may put up with products or services that are less than stellar (as they have with some airlines whose hub systems give them a near-monopoly on flights out of certain cities), but only because they have no choice. But if another organization comes along and offers a better-quality travel experience, TV program, cut of meat, computer software, or whatever, you may find your company falling behind. Making improvements in quality has become an important management idea in recent times, as we shall discuss.

Losing Competitive Advantage: Network Television Battles "On-Demand" Technologies

The four major television networks—ABC, CBS, NBC, and Fox—have felt extreme pressure on revenues as the mass audience they used to take for granted has fragmented, causing the networks to lose their competitive advantage. Indeed, during the past dozen years, their share of the viewing audience has fallen from 72% to 46%. This has been caused by three developments, says television critic David Friend.[17]

First has been the rise of cable television, supported by its two revenue streams, advertisers and subscribers, and its offerings, which, says Friend, "made even the best network shows look strangely antique." Examples have been the HBO hits "The Sopranos" and "Deadwood," Comedy Central's "South Park," and FX's "The Shield." The major networks responded by premiering shows not just in the fall but throughout the year, by putting on serial dramas and reality shows, and by running shows in short series of only 10 or 12 episodes. However, these tactics adversely affected the ability of the networks to sell hit shows into syndication (reruns), causing them to lose further revenues.

Second has been further audience fragmentation occasioned by the change from a "linear" viewing model to an "on-demand" model. In the linear model, according to Friend, people watch a show at the time the network airs it, such as "Desperate Housewives" at 9 P.M. on ABC. In the on-demand model, viewers tune in whenever they want to, using ad-skipping digital video-recorders (TiVo systems), iPods, personal computers, and cell phones. This has two results: on-demand viewers frequently become distracted by other offerings (including "grassroots" content, such as skateboard wipeouts created by sk8hed), and they frequently skip or delete commercials. By the end of 2007, 20–40% of viewers could be in a position to zap ads.[18] This phenomenon has forced the networks to resort to more "product (or brand) integration," in which products are placed in scenes visible to viewers and advertisers are given roles in plots of shows, such as "a desperate housewife showing off a Buick at a shopping mall," in one description.[19]

Third has been the networks' obsession with beating other hit shows, moving successful shows around to different time slots in order to try to outdraw rivals. "By obsessing about whether 'Chicago Hope' will beat 'ER,'" says Friend, "the execs are making a classic *Time* vs. *Newsweek* . . . mistake: grappling with their longtime rival, oblivious of their surroundings, they all fall over the cliff together."

Your Call

As the networks go, will cable follow? What do you think the effect will be of iPods, DVRs, HDTV, video-on-demand, and the like on the cable industry?[20]

---

4. Efficiency Whereas a generation ago organizations rewarded employees for their length of service, today the emphasis is on efficiency: Companies strive to produce goods or services as quickly as possible using as few employees (and raw materials) as possible. While a strategy that downgrades the value of employees will probably backfire—resulting in the loss of essential experience and skills and even customers—an organization that is overstaffed may not be able to compete with leaner, meaner rivals. This is the reason why, for instance, today many managers—aided by their desktop computers—do much of their own correspondence and filing. Secretarial staffs have been reduced, but of course the secretarial work remains.

Challenge #2: Managing for Diversity—The Future Won't Resemble the Past

During the next half-century, the mix of American racial or ethnic groups will change considerably, with the U.S. becoming half minority. Nonhispanic whites are projected to decrease from 69% of the population at the turn of the 21st century to 50% in 2050.

African Americans will increase from 13% to 15%, Asians and Pacific Islanders from 4% to 8%, and Hispanics (who may be of any race) from 13% to 24%.[21] In addition, in the coming years there will be a different mix of women, immigrants, and older people in the general population, as well as in the workforce.

Clearly, the challenge to the manager of the near future is to maximize the contributions of employees diverse in gender, age, race, and ethnicity. We discuss this matter in more detail in Chapter 3.

Challenge #3: Managing for Globalization—The Expanding Management Universe

"In Japan it is considered rude to look directly in the eye for more than a few seconds," says a report about teaching Americans how to behave abroad, "and in Greece the hand-waving gesture commonly used in America for goodbye is considered an insult."[22]

The point: gestures and symbols don't have the same meaning to everyone throughout the world. Not understanding such differences can affect how well organizations manage globally.

American firms have been going out into the world in a major way. At the same time, the world has been coming to us. Indeed, despite political outcries about white-collar jobs disappearing overseas to places such as India, foreigners actually send far more office work to the U.S. than American companies send abroad.[23] Managing for globalization will be a complex, ongoing challenge, as we discuss at length in Chapter 4.

Challenge #4: Managing for Information Technology

The challenge of managing for information technology, not to mention other technologies affecting your business, will require your unflagging attention. Perhaps most important is the ***Internet*, the global network of independently operating but interconnected computers, linking hundreds of thousands of smaller networks around the world.**

By 2008, according to International Data Corp., Internet trade between businesses will surpass $650 billion in the United States and $1 trillion worldwide, representing a compound annual growth of 52%.[24] This kind of ***e-commerce*, or electronic commerce—the buying and selling of goods or services over computer networks**—is reshaping entire industries and revamping the very notion of what a company is. More important than e-commerce, the information technology has facilitated ***e-business*, using the Internet to facilitate *every* aspect of running a business.** As one article puts it, "at bottom, the Internet is a tool that dramatically lowers the cost of communication. That means it can radically alter any industry or activity that depends heavily on the flow of information."[25]

Some of the implications of e-business that we will discuss throughout the book are as follows:

- **Far-ranging e-management and e-communication.** Using wired and wireless telephones, fax machines, electronic mail, or ***e-mail*—text messages and documents transmitted over a computer network**—as well as ***project management software*—programs for planning and scheduling the people, costs, and resources to complete a project on time**—21st-century managers will find themselves responsible for creating, motivating, and leading teams of specialists all over the world. This will require them to be masters of organizational communication, able to create concise, powerful e-mail and voice-mail messages.

- **Accelerated decision making, conflict, and stress.** The Internet not only speeds everything up, it also, with its huge, interconnected ***databases*— computerized collections of interrelated files**—can overwhelm us with information, much of it useful, much of it not. The result affects the pace and quality of managerial decision making: one survey of 479 managers found that 77% reported making more decisions, and 43% said they had less time in

The famous golden arches. This McDonald's store in Beijing is an example of globalization.

which to make decisions.[26] Among the unavoidable by-products are increased conflict and stress, although, as we will show, these can be managed.

- **Changes in organizational structure, jobs, goal setting, and knowledge management.** With computers and telecommunications technology, organizations and teams become "virtual"; they are no longer as bound by time zones and locations. Employees, for instance, may *telecommute,* **or work from home or remote locations using a variety of information technologies.** Meetings may be conducted via *videoconferencing,* **using video and audio links along with computers to let people in different locations see, hear, and talk with one another.** In addition, *collaborative computing,* **using state-of-the-art computer software and hardware, will help people work better together.** Goal setting and feedback will be conducted via Web-based software programs such as eWorkbench, which enables managers to create and track employee goals. All such forms of interaction will require managers and employees to be more flexible, and there will be an increased emphasis on *knowledge management*—**the implementing of systems and practices to increase the sharing of knowledge and information throughout an organization.**

Challenge #5: Managing for Ethical Standards

With the pressure to meet sales, production, and other targets, managers can find themselves confronting ethical dilemmas. What do you do when you learn an employee dropped a gyroscope but put it in the helicopter anyway in order to hold the product's delivery date? How much should you allow your sales reps to knock the competition? (Rivals could sue for confusing or deceptive statements, according to one attorney.)[27] How much leeway do you have in giving gifts to prospective clients in a foreign country to try to land a contract? (American companies need to walk a fine line between observing the realities of the local business culture and complying with the Foreign Corrupt Practices Act, which prohibits bribery.)

Ethical behavior is not just a nicety, it is a very important part of doing business. This was made clear during the period 2003–2004 as executives from Enron, Tyco, WorldCom, Adelphia, and other companies were paraded in handcuffs before television cameras. Not since sociologist Edwin Sutherland invented the term "white-collar crime" in the 1930s were so many top-level executives being hauled into court. We consider ethics in Chapter 3 and elsewhere in the book.

Challenge #6: Managing for Your Own Happiness & Life Goals

Ann Garcia had the view that good managers push decision making down, spread the compliments, and take the blame, but after being given a team to manage at her technology company, she gave it up. "I'm just not a big enough person all the time to want to do that," she said. "Many of us realize that we don't want the career path that corporate America has to offer."[28]

Regardless of how well paid you are, you have to consider whether in meeting the organization's challenges you are also meeting the challenge of realizing your own happiness. Many people simply don't find being a manager fulfilling. They may complain that they have to go to too many meetings, that they can't do enough for their employees, that they are caught in the middle between bosses and subordinates. They may feel, at a time when Dilbert cartoons have created such an unflattering portrayal of managers, that they lack respect.[29] They may decide that, despite the greater income, money cannot buy happiness, as the adage goes.

In the end, however, recall what Odette Pollar said: "If you truly like people and enjoy mentoring and helping others to grow and thrive, management is a great job." And it helps to know, as she points out, that "one's experience in management is greatly affected by the company's culture."[30] Culture, or style, is indeed an important matter, because it affects your happiness within an organization, and we discuss it in detail in Chapter 8. ●

Cuffed. Former Merrill Lynch & Co. executive Daniel Bayly leaves the FBI offices in Houston to go to the federal courthouse in September 2003. Bayly was charged with helping Enron Corp. appear to have met earnings targets with a loan wrongly booked as a sale. If you're tempted to stretch your ethics in order to pass a college course, do you think you'd do the same in business, where the pressures can be even worse?

1.3 WHAT MANAGERS DO: THE FOUR PRINCIPAL FUNCTIONS

major question What would I actually *do*—that is, what would be my four principal functions—as a manager?

THE BIG PICTURE

Management has four functions: *planning, organizing, leading,* and *controlling.*

What do you as a manager do to "get things done"—that is, achieve the stated goals of the organization you work for? You perform what is known as the **management process,** also called the *four management functions:* **planning, organizing, leading, and controlling.** (The abbreviation "POLC" may help you to remember them.)

As the diagram below illustrates, all these functions affect one another, are ongoing, and are performed simultaneously. *(See Figure 1.1.)*

figure 1.1

THE MANAGEMENT PROCESS

What you as a manager do to "get things done"—to achieve the stated goals of your organization.

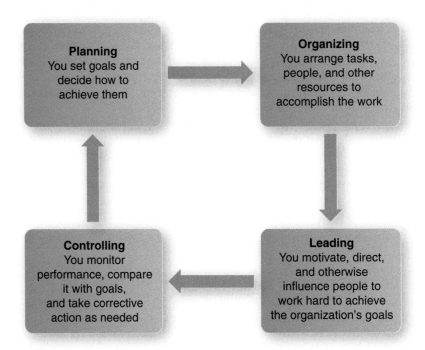

Although the process of management can be quite complex, these four functions represent its essential principles. Indeed, as a glance at our text's table of contents shows, they form four of the part divisions of the book. Let's consider what the four functions are, using the management (or "administration," as it is called in nonprofit organizations) of your college to illustrate them.

Planning: Discussed in Part 3 of This Book

Planning **is defined as setting goals and deciding how to achieve them.** Your college was established for the purpose of educating students, and its present managers, or administrators, now must decide the best way to accomplish this. Which of several possible degree programs should be offered? Should the college be a residential or a commuter campus? What sort of students should be recruited and admitted? What kind of faculty should be hired? What kind of buildings and equipment are needed?

Organizing: Discussed in Part 4 of This Book

Organizing **is defined as arranging tasks, people and other resources to accomplish the work.** College administrators must determine the tasks to be done, by whom, and what the reporting hierarchy is to be. Should the institution be organized into schools with departments, with department chairpersons reporting to deans who in return report to vice presidents? Should the college hire more full-time instructors than part-time instructors? Should English professors teach just English literature or also composition, developmental English, and "first-year experience" courses?

Leading: Discussed in Part 5 of This Book

Leading **is defined as motivating, directing, and otherwise influencing people to work hard to achieve the organization's goals.** At your college, leadership begins, of course, with the president (who would be the chief executive officer, or CEO, in a for-profit organization). He or she is the one who must inspire faculty, staff, students, alumni, wealthy donors, and residents of the surrounding community to help realize the college's goals. As you might imagine, these groups often have different needs and wants, so an essential part of leadership is resolving conflicts.

Controlling: Discussed in Part 6 of This Book

Controlling **is defined as monitoring performance, comparing it with goals, and taking corrective action as needed.** Is the college discovering that fewer students are majoring in nursing than they did five years previously? Is the fault with a change in the job market? with the quality of instruction? with the kinds of courses offered? Are the Nursing Department's student recruitment efforts not going well? Should the department's budget be reduced? Under the management function of controlling, college administrators must deal with these kinds of matters. ●

I.4 PYRAMID POWER: LEVELS & AREAS OF MANAGEMENT

> **major question** What are the levels and areas of management I need to know to move up, down, and sideways?

THE BIG PICTURE

Within an organization, there are managers at three levels: *top, middle,* and *first-line.* Managers may also be *general managers,* or they may be *functional managers,* responsible for just one organizational activity, such as Research & Development, Marketing, Finance, Production, or Human Resources. Managers may work for for-profit, non-profit, or mutual-benefit organizations.

The workplace of the future may resemble a symphony orchestra, famed management theorist Peter Drucker said.[31] Employees, especially so-called knowledge workers—those who have a great deal of technical skills—can be compared to concert musicians. Their managers can be seen as conductors.

In Drucker's analogy, musicians are used for some pieces of music—that is, work projects—and not others, and they are divided into different sections (teams) based on their instruments. The conductor's role is not to play each instrument better than the musicians but to lead them all through the most effective performance of a particular work.

This model is in sharp contrast to the traditional pyramid-like organizational model, where one leader sits at the top, with layers of managers beneath. We therefore need to take a look at the traditional arrangement first.

The Traditional Management Pyramid: Levels & Areas

A new Silicon Valley technology startup company staffed by young people in sandals and shorts may be so small and so loosely organized that only one or two members may be said to be a manager. General Motors or the U.S. Army, in contrast, has thousands of managers doing thousands of different things. Is there a picture we can draw that applies to all the different kinds of organizations that describes them in ways that make sense? Yes: by levels and by areas, as the pyramid opposite shows. *(See Figure 1.2 on the next page.)*

Three Levels of Management

Not everyone who works in an organization is a manager, of course, but those who are may be classified into three levels—top, middle, and first-line.

Top Managers   Their offices may be equipped with expensive leather chairs and have lofty views. Or, as with one Internet service provider (ISP), they may have plastic lawn chairs in the CEO's office and beat-up furniture in the lobby. Whatever their decor, an organization's top managers tend to have titles such as "chief executive officer (CEO)," "chief operating officer (COO)," "president," and "senior vice president."

Some may be the stars in their fields, the men and women whose pictures appear on the covers of business magazines, people such as Carly Fiorina of Hewlett-Packard, who appeared on the cover of *Forbes* in mid-2003, and Steve Jobs of Apple Computer and Pixar Animation, who appeared on the cover of *BusinessWeek* in early 2006.[32] The salaries and bonuses can average $290,000 a year for CEOs and presidents of small and midsize companies to far over $1 million for top executives in large companies.

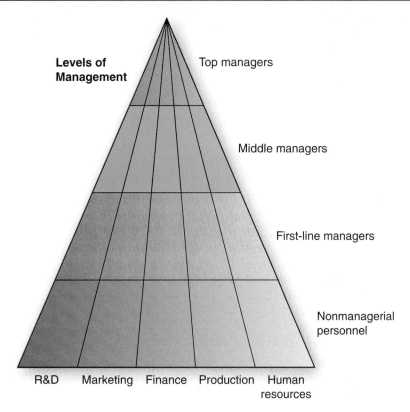

figure I.2

THE LEVELS AND AREAS OF MANAGEMENT

Top managers make long-term decisions, middle managers implement those decisions, and first-line managers make short-term decisions.

Levels of Management

Top managers

Middle managers

First-line managers

Nonmanagerial personnel

Functional Areas

R&D Marketing Finance Production Human resources

One kind of top manager. Welsh-born American Howard Stringer, CEO of Sony, and Japanese engineer Ryoji Chubachi, Sony's president, preside over a $63 billion company that is moving from being a traditional electronics manufacturer to a digital provider of software, services, and content as well as devices. Why do you think a Japanese company would go outside to recruit a top manager, as it did Stringer?

Top managers **make long-term decisions about the overall direction of the organization and establish the objectives, policies, and strategies for it.** They need to pay a lot of attention to the environment outside the organization, being alert for long-run opportunities and problems and devising strategies for dealing with them. Thus, executives at this level must be future oriented, dealing with uncertain, highly competitive conditions.

These people stand at the summit of the management pyramid. But the nature of a pyramid, as business consultant Jack Falvey observes, is that the farther you climb, the less space remains at the top. Thus, most pyramid climbers never get to the apex.[33] However, that doesn't mean that you shouldn't try. Indeed, you might end up atop a much smaller pyramid of some other organization than the one you started out in—and happier with the result.

Middle Managers *Middle managers* **implement the policies and plans of the top managers above them and supervise and coordinate the activities of the first-line managers below them.** In the nonprofit world, middle managers may have titles such as "clinic director," "dean of student services," and the like. In the for-profit world, the titles may be "division head," "plant manager," and "branch sales manager." Their salaries may range from $35,000 to $110,000 a year.

Sometimes the titles have become more creative, in accordance with the changing face of management. For

Top managers of another sort.
Entrepreneurs Larry Page (left) and Sergey Brin, former graduate students who founded the highly popular search engine Google six years earlier in a Menlo Park, Calif., garage, became instant billionaires before age 30 when they took their company public in 2004. Do you think a top manager is always adventurous?

instance, at Intuit, a California software company, Barb Karlin had the title of Director of Great People, which reflected the nature of her challenge—to recruit and retain programmers and other high-technology stars for her company. "I spent 19 years in marketing, bringing in new customers and keeping them," she said. "Now I do it with employees instead of customers. The stakes are equally high: If you lose great people, you lose success. It's that simple."[34]

First-Line Managers   The job titles at the bottom of the managerial pyramid tend to be on the order of "department head," "foreman" or "forewoman," "team leader," or "supervisor"—clerical supervisor, production supervisor, research supervisor, and so on. Indeed, *supervisor* is the name often given to first-line managers as a whole. Their salaries may run from $25,000 to $50,000 a year.

Following the plans of middle and top managers, *first-line managers* **make short-term operating decisions, directing the daily tasks of nonmanagerial personnel,** who are, of course, all those people who work directly at their jobs but don't oversee the work of others.

No doubt the job of first-line manager will be the place where you would start your managerial career. This can be a valuable experience because it will be the training and testing ground for your management ideas.

Areas of Management: Functional Managers versus General Managers

We can represent the levels of management by slicing the organizational pyramid horizontally. We can also slice the pyramid vertically to represent the organization's departments or functional areas, as we did in Figure 1.2.

In a for-profit technology company, these might be *Research & Development, Marketing, Finance, Production,* and *Human Resources.* In a nonprofit college, these might be *Faculty, Student Support Staff, Finance, Maintenance,* and *Administration.* Whatever the names of the departments, the organization is run by two types of managers—functional and general. (These are line managers, with authority to direct employees. Staff managers mainly assist line managers, as we discuss later.)

Functional Managers   If your title is Vice President of Production, Director of Finance, or Administrator for Human Resources, you are a functional manager. **A *functional manager* is responsible for just one organizational activity.** Danamichele Brennan, now chief technology officer for McGettigan Partners, was previously with Rosenbluth Travel, where her title—indicative of the trend in some companies toward use of more flexible job titles—was Chief Travel Scientist. Her job was heading a research team that developed services to turn reservation agents into travel consultants. The goal: not just cheaper travel but better travel.[35] Leading this specialized sort of research-and-development activity makes her a functional manager.

General Managers   If you are working in a small organization of, say, 100 people and your title is Executive Vice President, you are probably a general manager over several departments, such as Production and Finance and Human Resources. **A *general manager* is responsible for several organizational activities.** At the top of the pyramid, general managers are those who seem to be the subject of news stories in magazines such as *BusinessWeek, Fortune, Forbes, Inc.,* and *Fast Company.* Examples are big-company CEOs Kenneth I. Chenault of American Express, Jeffrey R. Immelt of General Electric, and Anne Mulcahy of Xerox Corp. It also includes small-company CEOs such as Gayle Martz, who heads Sherpa's Pet Trading Co., a $4 million New York company with 10 employees that sells travel carriers for dogs and cats. But not all general managers are in for-profit organizations.

Dr. Rick Aubrey is executive director of Rubicon Programs, a San Francisco–area nonprofit formed after California state psychiatric hospitals were closed in 1973. The organization funds training, housing, and employment programs that have helped thousands of former patients and disabled, impoverished, and homeless people reenter society. Aubrey says Rubicon funds more than 60% of its $13.6 million annual budget from its rental properties, enterprises, and services, such as the Rubicon Bakery and Rubicon Landscape Services, which also provide job training. Aubrey makes a point of running Rubicon like a business, reflecting the strategic vision of a top-level general manager.[36]

Managers for Three Types of Organizations: For-Profit, Nonprofit, Mutual-Benefit

There are three types of organizations classified according to the three purposes for which they are formed—*for-profit, nonprofit, and mutual-benefit.*[37]

Nonprofit manager. A general manager is responsible for several organizational activities. Rick Aubrey oversees a nonprofit organization with a $13.6 million budget. Do you think managerial skills are different for nonprofit and for-profit organizations?

1. For-Profit Organizations: For Making Money For-profit, or business, organizations are formed to make money, or profits, by offering products or services. When most people think of "management," they think of business organizations, ranging from Allstate to Zenith, from Amway to Zagat.

2. Nonprofit Organizations: For Offering Services Managers in nonprofit organizations are often known as "administrators." Nonprofit organizations may be either in the public sector, such as the University of California, or in the private sector, such as Stanford University. Either way, their purpose is to offer services to some clients, not to make a profit. Examples of such organizations are hospitals, colleges, and social-welfare agencies (the Salvation Army, the Red Cross).

One particular type of nonprofit organization is called the *commonweal organization.* Unlike nonprofit service organizations, which offer services to *some* clients, commonweal organizations offer services to *all* clients within their jurisdictions. Examples are the military services, the U.S. Postal Service, and your local fire and police departments.

3. Mutual-Benefit Organizations: For Aiding Members Mutual-benefit organizations are voluntary collections of members—political parties, farm cooperatives, labor unions, trade associations, and clubs—whose purpose is to advance members' interests.

Do Managers Manage Differently for Different Types of Organizations? If you become a manager, would you be doing the same types of things regardless of the type of organization? Generally you would be; that is, you would be performing the four management functions—planning, organizing, leading, and controlling—that we described in Section 1.3.

The single biggest difference, however, is that in a for-profit organization, the measure of its success is how much profit (or loss) it generates. In the other two types of organization, although income and expenditures are very important concerns, the measure of success is usually the effectiveness of the services delivered—how many students were graduated, if you're a college administrator, or how many crimes were prevented or solved, if you're a police chief. ●

I.5 ROLES MANAGERS MUST PLAY SUCCESSFULLY

➕ **major question** To be an exceptional manager, what roles must I play successfully?

THE BIG PICTURE

Managers tend to work long hours at an intense pace; their work is characterized by fragmentation, brevity, and variety; and they rely more on verbal than on written communication. According to management scholar Henry Mintzberg, managers play three roles—*interpersonal, informational,* and *decisional.* Interpersonal roles include figurehead, leader, and liaison activities. Informational roles are monitor, disseminator, and spokesperson. Decisional roles are entrepreneur, disturbance handler, resource allocator, and negotiator.

Clearly, as MTV Networks CEO Judy McGrath's experience suggests, being a successful manager requires playing several different roles and exercising several different skills. What are they?

The Manager's Roles: Mintzberg's Useful Findings

Maybe, you think, it might be interesting to shadow some managers to see what it is, in fact, they actually do. That's exactly what management scholar **Henry Mintzberg** did when, in the late 1960s, he followed five chief executives around for a week and recorded their working lives.[38] And what he found is valuable to know, since it applies not only to top managers but also to managers on all levels.

Consider this portrait of a manager's workweek: "There was no break in the pace of activity during office hours," reported Mintzberg about his subjects. "The mail (average of 36 pieces per day), telephone calls (average of five per day), and meetings (average of eight) accounted for almost every minute from the moment these executives entered their offices in the morning until they departed in the evening."[39]

Multitasking. Multiple activities are characteristic of a manager—which is why so many managers carry a personal digital assistant or smart phone to keep track of their schedules. Many students already use these. Do you?

Only five phone calls per day? And, of course, this was back in an era before e-mail, which nowadays can shower some executives with 100, even 300, messages a day. Indeed, says Ed Reilly, who heads the America Management Association, all the e-mail, cell phone calls, text messaging, and so on can lead people to end up "concentrating on the urgent rather than the important."[40]

Obviously, the top manager's life is extraordinarily busy. Here are three of Mintzberg's findings, important for any prospective manager:

I. A Manager Relies More on Verbal Than on Written Communication

Writing letters, memos, and reports takes time. Most managers in Mintzberg's research tended to get and transmit information through telephone conversations and meetings. No doubt this is still true, although the technology of e-mail now makes it possible to communicate almost as rapidly in writing as with the spoken word.

2. A Manager Works Long Hours at an Intense Pace "A true break seldom occurred," wrote Mintzberg about his subjects. "Coffee was taken during meetings, and lunchtime was almost always devoted to formal or informal meetings."

Long hours at work are standard, he found, with 50 hours being typical and up to 90 hours not unheard of. A 1999 survey by John P. Kotter of the Harvard Business School found that the general managers he studied worked just under 60 hours per week.[41]

Are such hours really necessary? Three decades following the Mintzberg research, Linda Stroh, Director of Workplace Studies at Loyola University Chicago, did a study that found that people who work more also earn more. "Those managers who worked 61 hours or more per week had earned, on average, about two promotions over the past five years," she reported.[42] However, researchers at Purdue and McGill universities have found that more companies are allowing managers to reduce their working hours and spend more time with their families yet still advance their high-powered careers.[43]

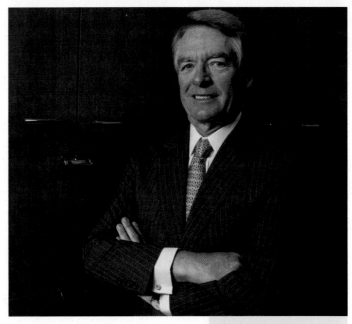

A Mintzberg manager. Charles Schwab, founder of the financial services firm, relies more on verbal than on written communication, works long hours, and experiences an "interrupt-driven day." Interestingly, Schwab is successful despite having had lifelong dyslexia, the common language-related learning disability. What kind of personal obstacles do you need to overcome?

3. A Manager's Work Is Characterized by Fragmentation, Brevity, & Variety Only about a tenth of the managerial activities observed by Mintzberg took more than an hour; about half were completed in under 9 minutes. Phone calls averaged 6 minutes, informal meetings 10 minutes, and desk-work sessions 15 minutes. "When free time appeared," wrote Mintzberg, "ever-present subordinates quickly usurped it."

No wonder the executive's work time has been characterized as "the interrupt-driven day" and that many managers—such as the late Mary Kay Ash, head of the Mary Kay Cosmetics company—get up as early as 5 A.M. so that they will have a quiet period in which to work undisturbed.[44] No wonder that finding balance between work and family lives is an ongoing concern and that many managers—such as Dawn Lepore, executive V.P. of discount broker Charles Schwab & Co.—have become "much less tolerant of activities that aren't a good use of my time" and so have become better delegators.[45]

It is clear from Mintzberg's work that *time and task management* are major challenges for every manager. The Practical Action box on the next page, "Managing Information Overload," offers some suggestions along this line, as does the box at the end of this chapter (page 27), "Getting Control of Your Time: Dealing with the Information Deluge in College & in Your Career."

Three Types of Managerial Roles

Three Types of Managerial Roles: Interpersonal, Informational, & Decisional From his observations and other research, Mintzberg concluded that managers play three broad types of roles or "organized sets of behavior": *interpersonal, informational,* and *decisional.*

Managing Information Overload: Keep Your Eye on the Big Picture

Chris Peters is a vice president of Microsoft, a company famous for its killer workdays, but he's known for keeping reasonable hours. How does he do it? Like other high achievers, he's able to get more work done in shorter time because he stays focused on things he *has* to do instead of unimportant things he might be doing.[46]

Stars like Peters keep their eye on the big picture. They "have this grasp of what the bottom line is, what 'the critical path' is, and they stay there rather than getting pulled off it all the time," says Carnegie Mellon professor Robert E. Kelley.[47] Stars keep their priorities straight by seeing projects through the eyes of the customers or the coworkers who depend on them. Says star manager Brian Graham, who sits out routine meetings and relies on coworkers to keep him informed, "The key for me is to know what not to do, and to always be looking for the path of quickest resolution."[48] Finally, stars avoid multitasking. "Successful CEOs do not multitask," says time-management guru Stephanie Winston, who advises people to turn off their instant messaging. "They concentrate intensely on one thing at a time."[49]

As a manager, how are you going to deal with information overload? College students already wrestle with this problem. Clearly, if you can come to grips with this beast now, you'll have developed some skills that can save your life in your career. Some strategies are given in the box ("Taking Something Practical Away from This Chapter") at the end of this chapter.

1. Interpersonal Roles—Figurehead, Leader, and Liaison In their *interpersonal roles,* **managers interact with people inside and outside their work units.** The three interpersonal roles include *figurehead, leader,* and *liaison* **activities.** *(See Table 1.1, opposite.)*

2. Informational Roles—Monitor, Disseminator, and Spokesperson The most important part of a manager's job, Mintzberg believed, is information handling, because accurate information is vital for making intelligent decisions. In their three *informational roles—as monitor, disseminator,* **and** *spokesperson—***managers receive and**

Doer. Frederick Smith (left), chairman and CEO of FedEx, is an example of a doer. When given a low grade on a graduate-school paper outlining his ideas for an overnight delivery service, he used his family's money to found the company.

table 1.1

THREE TYPES OF MANAGERIAL ROLES: INTERPERSONAL, INFORMATIONAL, AND DECISIONAL

Interpersonal Managerial Roles	**Figurehead role**	In your *figurehead role,* you show visitors around your company, attend employee birthday parties, and present ethical guidelines to your subordinates. In other words, you perform symbolic tasks that represent your organization.
	Leadership role	In your role of *leader,* you are responsible for the actions of your subordinates, since their successes and failures reflect on you. Your leadership is expressed in your decisions about training, motivating, and disciplining people.
	Liaison role	In your *liaison* role, you must act like a politician, working with other people outside your work unit and organization to develop alliances that will help you achieve your organization's goals.
Informational Managerial Roles	**Monitor role**	As a *monitor,* you should be constantly alert for useful information, whether gathered from newspaper stories about the competition or gathered from snippets of conversation with subordinates you meet in the hallway.
	Disseminator role	Workers complain they never know what's going on? That probably means their supervisor failed in the role of *disseminator.* Managers need to constantly disseminate important information to employees, as via e-mail and meetings.
	Spokesperson role	You are expected, of course, to be a diplomat, to put the best face on the activities of your work unit or organization to people outside it. This is the informational role of *spokesperson.*
Decisional Managerial Roles	**Entrepreneur role**	A good manager is expected to be an *entrepreneur,* to initiate and encourage change and innovation.
	Disturbance handler role	Unforeseen problems—from product defects to international currency crises—require you be a *disturbance handler,* fixing problems.
	Resource allocator role	Because you'll never have enough time, money, and so on, you'll need to be a resource *allocator,* setting priorities about use of resources.
	Negotiator role	To be a manager is to be a continual *negotiator,* working with others inside and outside the organization to accomplish your goals.

communicate information with other people inside and outside the organization. *(See Table 1.1.)*

3. Decisional Roles—Entrepreneur, Disturbance Handler, Resource Allocator, and Negotiator In their ***decisional roles,*** **managers use information to make decisions to solve problems or take advantage of opportunities. The four decision-making roles are** *entrepreneur, disturbance handler, resource allocator,* **and** ***negotiator.*** *(See Table 1.1.)*

Did anyone say a manager's job is easy? Certainly it's not for people who want to sit on the sidelines of life. Above all else, managers are *doers.* ●

❌ major question **Do I have what it takes to be an entrepreneur?**

THE BIG PICTURE

Entrepreneurship, a necessary attribute of business, means taking risks to create a new enterprise. It is expressed through two kinds of innovators, the entrepreneur and the intrapreneur.

Like many colleges, Harvard offers every freshman a copy of the class directory, known as the "facebook," that shows photographs of all members of the class along with their names, birth dates, hometowns, and high schools. Harvard administrators had planned to put the facebook online, but in early 2004 a psychology student and programming hobbyist named Mark Zuckerberg beat them to it.

Zuckerberg had already tried some other projects, including Coursematch, which allowed Harvard students to find out who was enrolled in a particular class, and Facemash, which enabled students to rate student pictures for attractiveness. A version of the latter site was online a bare 4 hours when Zuckerberg's Internet access was revoked by administration officials and he was charged with breaching security—an offense for which he escaped with a warning. Later, at the invitation of some fellow students, he was invited to help write the code for a "social networking" site, modeled after Friendster and Tribe.net, to be called Harvard Connection. Meanwhile he continued to work on his own projects.

Entrepreneur. Mark Zuckerberg (left) has become one of today's most watched techno entrepreneurs. Shown here in his Palo Alto home, Zuckerberg has opted for some time off school to engage in further business pursuits.

During a weeklong semester break, Zuckerberg stayed in his dorm room creating a Web site, and on February 4, 2004, Thefacebook.com went up. Within 24 hours it had between 1,200 and 1,500 registrants. Facebook allowed anyone with a Harvard e-mail address to join and to create a profile, consisting of a photograph and personal information. A search box helped users call up other profiles. Unlike Friendster and MySpace, social sites that are open to anyone, Facebook's members had a physical location, professors, and classes in common. That is, the site was not so much an online community as a directory that reinforces a physical community.

"By luck or design," says one account, "Zuckerberg had tapped into a powerful yearning: the desire of hundreds of ambitious and impressionable young people to establish themselves and make friends in an unfamiliar environment. . . . The site quickly became a platform for self-promotion, a place to boast and preen and vie for others' attention as much as for their companionship."[50] By the end of June 2004, the site had expanded to 40 schools and had 150,000 registered users. Zuckerberg and two friends who had pioneered Facebook then moved to Palo Alto, California, where later they began to meet with venture capitalists to expand the site. Today Facebook has about 7.5 million registered members.

Entrepreneurship Defined: Taking Risks in Pursuit of Opportunity

Facebook is one of the many small outfits in the United States that is one of the primary drivers of the nation's economy. Indeed, according to the Small Business Administration, small outfits create some 75% of all new jobs, represent 99.7% of all employers, and employ 50% of the private workforce.[51] Most small businesses originate with people like Zuckerberg. He and his partners are the entrepreneurs, the people with the idea, the risk takers.

So is Chip Conley, who has achieved success in the offbeat but expanding business of "boutique" hotels, each of which, unlike Hiltons and Hyatts, has its own one-of-a-kind charm. Conley likes magazines because they provide inspired themes for the hotels he buys and renovates. For instance, he says the Nob Hill Lambourne in San Francisco, which is oriented toward health-conscious travelers, resembles the magazine *Men's Health;* the hotel offers algae shakes, vitamins instead of chocolates on the pillows, and an on-call psychologist. The Hotel Rex, modeled on *The New Yorker,* features a book-lined cocktail lounge, old leather furniture, and poetry readings.[52]

The most successful entrepreneurs become wealthy and make the covers of business magazines: Fred Smith of Federal Express, Debbie Fields of Mrs. Fields' Cookies, Anita Roddick of The Body Shop, Michael Dell of Dell Computers. Failed entrepreneurs may benefit from the experience to live to fight another day—as did Henry Ford, twice bankrupt before achieving success with Ford Motor Co.

What Entrepreneurship Is   *Entrepreneurship* **is the process of taking risks to try to create a new enterprise.** There are two types of entrepreneurship:

- **The entrepreneur. An *entrepreneur* is someone who sees a new opportunity for a product or service and launches a business to try to realize it.** Most entrepreneurs run small businesses with fewer than 100 employees.

- **The intrapreneur. An *intrapreneur* is someone who works inside an existing organization who sees an opportunity for a product or service and mobilizes the organization's resources to try to realize it.** This person might be a researcher or a scientist but could also be a manager who sees an opportunity to create a new venture that could be profitable.

How Do Entrepreneurs & Managers Differ?   While the entrepreneur is not necessarily an inventor, he or she "always searches for change, responds to it, and exploits it as an opportunity," Peter Drucker pointed out.[53] How does this differ from being a manager?

Being an entrepreneur is what it takes to *start* a business; being a manager is what it takes to *grow or maintain* a business. As an entrepreneur/intrapreneur, you initiate new goods or services; as a manager you coordinate the resources to produce the goods or services.

Example

Example of an Intrapreneur: Art Fry & 3M's Post-it Notes

One of the most famous instances of intrapreneurship occurred at 3M Corp., a company famous for pumping out new products, when 3M employee Art Fry conceived of Post-it Notes, those bright-colored "sticky notes" that people use to post messages on walls and mark books. The company had invented an experimental adhesive for which it could find no use. Meanwhile, when attending church, Fry found that the bits of paper he used to mark hymns in his hymnbook kept slipping out. It dawned on him that 3M's experimental glue could provide adhesive-backed paper that would stick for a long time but could be easily removed without damaging the book.

Coming up with the product was only the first step. Market surveys were negative. Office-supply distributors thought the notion useless. Fry thereupon started giving samples to executives and secretaries at 3M, who began using the sticky paper and soon were hooked. Later Fry used the same approach with other executives and secretaries throughout the United States. After 12 years, the orders began to flow, and Post-its became a winning product for 3M.[54]

Your Call

What companies are you aware of that do their own in-house research and development of products?

Up and away. Gary Ream, president and partner of Woodward Camp, transformed this aging gymnastics camp in central Pennsylvania into an extreme-sports summer retreat. First he offered BMX lessons, then coached in-line skaters and skateboarders, then began hosting competitions, which attracted the attention of sports TV channel ESPN and generated further publicity. What is your passion that you might turn into a business?

The examples of success we mentioned above—Chip Conley, Fred Smith, Debbie Fields, Anita Roddick, Michael Dell—are actually *both* entrepreneurs and effective managers. Some people, however, find they like the start-up part but hate the management part. For example, Stephen Wozniak, entrepreneurial co-founder with Steve Jobs of Apple Computer, abandoned the computer industry completely and went back to college. Jobs, by contrast, went on to launch another business, Pixar, which among other things became the animation factory that made the movies *Toy Story* and *Finding Nemo.*

Entrepreneurial companies have been called "gazelles" for the two attributes that make them successful: *speed and agility.* "Gazelles have mastered the art of the quick," says Alan Webber, founding editor of *Fast Company* magazine. "They have internal approaches and fast decision-making approaches that let them move with maximum agility in a fast-changing business environment."[55]

Is this the kind of smart, innovative world you'd like to be a part of? Most people prefer the security of a job and a paycheck. Indeed, even young people—those ages 25–34—who might be expected to be attracted to the entrepreneurial life are about 40% less likely to be self-employed than their parents, according to the Bureau of Labor Statistics.[56]

Entrepreneurs do seem to have psychological characteristics that are different from managers, as follows:[57]

- **Characteristic of both—high need for achievement.** Both entrepreneurs and managers have a high need for achievement. However, entrepreneurs certainly seem to be motivated to pursue moderately difficult goals through their own efforts in order to realize their ideas and, they hope, financial rewards. Managers, by contrast, are more motivated by promotions and organizational rewards of power and perks.

- **Also characteristic of both—belief in personal control of destiny.** If you believe "I am the captain of my fate, the master of my soul," you have what is known as ***internal locus of control,* the belief that you control your own destiny,** that external forces will have little influence. (External locus of control means the reverse—you believe you don't control your destiny, that external forces do.) Both entrepreneurs and managers like to think they have personal control over their lives.

- **Characteristic of both, but especially of entrepreneurs—high energy level and action orientation.** Rising to the top in an organization probably requires that a manager put in long hours. For entrepreneurs, however, creating a new enterprise may require an extraordinary investment of time and energy. In addition, while some managers may feel a sense of urgency, entrepreneurs are especially apt to be impatient and to want to get things done as quickly as possible, making them particularly action oriented.

- **Characteristic of both, but especially of entrepreneurs—high tolerance for ambiguity.** Every manager needs to be able to make decisions based on ambiguous—that is, unclear or incomplete—information. However, entrepreneurs must have more tolerance for ambiguity because they are trying to do things they haven't done before.

- **More characteristic of entrepreneurs than managers—self-confidence and tolerance for risk.** Managers must believe in themselves and be willing to make decisions; however, this statement applies even more to entrepreneurs. Precisely because they are willing to take risks in the pursuit of new opportunities—indeed, even risk personal financial failure—entrepreneurs need the confidence to act decisively.

Test Your Knowledge Exercise: Characteristics of Successful Entrepreneurs

Ebay's Meg Whitman. Pierre Omidyar was the entrepreneurial founder of the online auction company, but Whitman is the professional manager who, in one fan's words, "has taken a brilliant idea, and with execution, monitoring, and constant improvement, made it infinitely better." Which are you, entrepreneur or manager?

Of course, not all entrepreneurs have this kind of faith in themselves. So-called *necessity* entrepreneurs are people such as laid-off corporate workers, discharged military people, immigrants, and divorced homemakers who suddenly must earn a living and are simply trying to replace lost income and are hoping a job comes along. These make up about 11% of entrepreneurs. However, so-called *opportunity* entrepreneurs—the other 89%—are those who start their own business out of a burning desire rather than because they lost a job. Unlike necessity types, they tend to be more ambitious and to start firms that can lead to high-growth businesses.[58]

Which do you think you would be happier doing—being an entrepreneur or being a manager? ●

1.7 THE SKILLS STAR MANAGERS NEED

> **✴ major question** To be a terrific manager, what skills should I cultivate?

THE BIG PICTURE

Good managers need to work on developing three principal skills. The first is *technical,* the ability to perform a specific job. The second is *conceptual,* the ability to think analytically. The third is *human,* the ability to interact well with people.

CEO Judy McGrath once broke her wrist during a food fight at an MTV staff party. Is this the kind of beyond-the-call-of-duty activity that's required to have the right management stuff? Let's see what the "right stuff" might be.

In the mid-1970s, researcher **Robert Katz** found that through education and experience managers acquire three principal skills—*technical, conceptual,* and *human.*[59]

1. Technical Skills—The Ability to Perform a Specific Job

McGrath clearly has acquired the job-specific knowledge needed to function in the world of television and digital entertainment (as opposed to another industry—say, tax law, engineering, or restaurant work). Indeed, she has a college degree in English literature from Cedar Crest College and previously worked as a copy chief at *Glamour* magazine and as a senior writer at *Mademoiselle.*

Technical skills consist of the job-specific knowledge needed to perform well in a specialized field. Having the requisite technical skills seems to be most important at the lower levels of management—that is, among first-line managers.

2. Conceptual Skills—The Ability to Think Analytically

McGrath also has the "big picture" knowledge to keep up with her job. Although she tries to get home every night at a sane hour to see her 11-year-old daughter and stay-at-home husband, she lugs a bagful of scripts and tapes and exchanges Blackberry messages with executives well past midnight. She networks constantly with film, TV, and music industry executives and stars but also reads widely, everything from *US Weekly* to novels such as Samuel Beckett's *Malone Dies.* "Judy was the only person I ever worked with who knew as much about great literature as what was going on between East Coast and West Coast rappers," says a former MTV executive. "I always thought her intuitive appreciation of storytelling and characters was an enormous secret weapon."[60]

Conceptual skills consist of the ability to think analytically, to visualize an organization as a whole and understand how the parts work together. Conceptual skills are particularly important for top managers, who must deal with problems that are ambiguous but that could have far-reaching consequences.

3. Human Skills—The Ability to Interact Well with People

This may well be the most difficult set of skills to master. **Human skills consist of the ability to work well in cooperation with other people to get things done.** These skills—the ability to motivate, to inspire trust, to communicate with others—are necessary for managers of all levels. But because of the range of people, tasks, and problems in an organization, developing your human-interacting skills may turn out to be an ongoing, lifelong effort.

McGrath "is known for her skillful management of talent and the chaos that comes with a creative enterprise," reports a *BusinessWeek* article. "Judy's ability to concentrate on people" is intense, says an MTV executive. She tries to listen to everyone, from interns to senior vice-presidents, then offer advice. As a result, she gets a lot of credit for fostering a company culture of inclusiveness, making it a better place for creativity and risk taking. "There is less testosterone," says her former boss. "It's not the system of the old Hollywood moguls where they are throwing chairs at each other. It's about listening and accepting ideas wherever and whoever they come from."[61]

Star manager. CEO Judy McGrath of MTV seems to have the three skills—technical, conceptual, and human—necessary to be a terrific manager. Which one do you think you need to work on the most? (Human skills are the most difficult to master.)

The Most Valued Traits in Managers

McGrath embodies the qualities sought in star managers, especially top managers. "The style for running a company is different from what it used to be," says a top executive recruiter of CEOs. "Companies don't want dictators, kings, or emperors."[62] Instead of someone who gives orders, they want executives who ask probing questions and force the people beneath them to think and find the right answers.

Among the chief skills companies seek in top managers are the following:

- The ability to motivate and engage others.
- The ability to communicate.
- Work experience outside the United States.
- High energy levels to meet the demands of global travel and a 24/7 world.[63]

Let's see how you can begin to acquire these and other qualities for success. ●

Taking Something Practical Away from This Chapter

Getting Control of Your Time: Dealing with the Information Deluge in College & in Your Career

One great problem most college students face—and that all managers face—is how to manage their time. This first box describes skills that will benefit you in college and later in your career.

"I've managed to ratchet my schedule down so I can have an outside life," says Doug Shoemaker, a San Francisco architect who tries to be home by 6:00 every night. "I'm a highly organized guy, I really focus on tasks, and I get them done."[64]

Professionals and managers all have to deal with this central problem: how not to surrender their lives to their jobs. The place to start, however, is in college. If you can learn to manage time while you're still a student, you'll find it will pay off not only in higher grades and more free time but also in more efficient information-handling skills that will serve you well as a manager later on.

Developing Study Habits: Finding Your "Prime Study Time"

Each of us has a different energy cycle. The trick is to use it effectively. That way your hours of best performance will coincide with your heaviest academic demands. For example, if your energy level is high during the evenings, you should plan to do your studying then.

Make a Study Schedule

First make a master schedule that shows all your regular obligations—especially classes and work—for the entire school term. Then insert the times during which you plan to study. Next write in major academic events, such as term paper due dates and when exams will take place. At the beginning of every week, schedule your study sessions. Write in the specific tasks you plan to accomplish during each session.

Find Some Good Places to Study

Studying means first of all avoiding distractions. Avoid studying in places that are associated with other activities, particularly comfortable ones, such as lying in bed or sitting at a kitchen table.

Avoid Time Wasters, but Reward Your Studying

While clearly you need to learn to avoid distractions so that you can study, you must also give yourself frequent rewards so that you will indeed be *motivated* to study. You should study with the notion that, after you finish, you will give yourself a reward. The reward need not be elaborate. It could be a walk, a snack, or some similar treat.

Improving Your Memory Ability

Memorizing is, of course, one of the principal requirements of staying in college. And it's a great help for success in life afterward.

Beyond getting rid of distractions, there are certain techniques you can adopt to enhance your memory.

Space Your Studying, Rather Than Cramming

Cramming—making a frantic, last-minute attempt to memorize massive amounts of material—is probably the least effective means of absorbing information. Indeed, it may actually tire you out and make you even more anxious before the test. Research shows that it is best to space out your studying of a subject on successive days. This is preferable to trying to do it all during the same number of hours on one day.[65] It is repetition that helps move information into your long-term memory bank.

Review Information Repeatedly—Even "Overlearn" It

By repeatedly reviewing information—"rehearsing"— you can improve both your retention and your understanding of it.[66] Overlearning can improve your recall substantially. Overlearning is continuing to repeatedly review material even after you appear to have absorbed it.

Use Memorizing Tricks

There are several ways to organize information so that you can retain it better. The exhibit opposite shows how to establish associations between items you want to remember. *(See Exhibit I.I.)*

How to Improve Your Reading Ability: The SQ3R Method

SQ3R Stands for *Survey, Question, Read, Recite, and Review*[67]

The strategy here is to break a reading assignment into small segments and master each before moving on. The five steps of the SQ3R method are as follows:

Survey the Chapter before You Read It

Get an overview of the chapter or other reading assignment before you begin reading it. If you have a sense what the material is about before you begin reading it, you can predict where it is going. Many textbooks offer some "preview"-type material—a list of objectives or an outline of topic headings at the beginning of the chapter. Other books offer a summary at the end of the chapter. This book offers "The Big Picture" at the beginning of each section. It also offers a Summary at the end of each chapter. The strategy for reading this book is presented on page I.

Question the Segment in the Chapter before You Read It

This step is easy to do, and the point, again, is to get involved in the material. After surveying the entire chapter, go to the first segment—section, subsection, or even paragraph, depending on the level of difficulty and density

- **Mental and physical imagery:** Use your visual and other senses to construct a personal image of what you want to remember. Indeed, it helps to make the image humorous, action-filled, sexual, bizarre, or outrageous in order to establish a personal connection. Example: To remember the name of the 21st president of the United States, Chester Arthur, you might visualize an author writing the number "21" on a wooden chest. This mental image helps you associate <u>chest</u> (Chester), <u>author</u> (Arthur), and <u>21</u> (21st president).

- **Acronyms and acrostics:** An acronym is a word created from the first letters of items in a list. For instance, Roy G. Biv helps you remember the colors of the rainbow in order: <u>r</u>ed, <u>o</u>range, <u>y</u>ellow, <u>g</u>reen, <u>b</u>lue, <u>i</u>ndigo, <u>v</u>iolet. An acrostic is a phrase or sentence created from the first letters of items in a list. For example, *Every Good Boy Does Fine* helps you remember that the order of musical notes on the stave is E-G-B-D-F.

- **Location:** Location memory occurs when you associate a concept with a place or imaginary place. For example, you could learn the parts of a computer system by imagining a walk across campus. Each building you pass could be associated with a part of the computer system.

- **Word games:** Jingles and rhymes are devices frequently used by advertisers to get people to remember their products. You may recall the spelling rule "*I* before *E* except after *C* or when sounded like *A* as in *neighbor* or *weigh*." You can also use narrative methods, such as making up a story.

Exhibit I.I SOME MEMORIZING TRICKS

of information. Look at the topic heading of that segment. In your mind, restate the heading as a question.

After you have formulated the question, go to steps 3 and 4 (read and recite). Then proceed to the next segment and restate the heading here as a question. For instance, consider the section heading in this chapter that reads "What Managers Do: The Four Principal Functions." You could ask yourself, "What *are* the four functions of a manager?" For the heading in Chapter 2 "Two Overarching Perspectives about Management & Four Practical Reasons for Studying Them," ask "What *are* the types of management perspectives, and what are reasons for studying them?"

Read the Segment about Which You Asked the Question

Now read the segment you asked the question about. Read with purpose, to answer the question you formulated. Underline or color-mark sentences you think are important, if they help you answer the question. Read this portion of the text more than once, if necessary, until you can answer the question. In addition, determine whether the segment covers any other significant questions, and formulate answers to these, too. After you have read the segment, proceed to step 4. (Perhaps you can see where this is all leading. If you read in terms of questions and answers, you will be better prepared when you see exam questions about the material later.)

Recite the Main Points of the Segment

Recite means "say aloud." Thus, you should speak out loud (or softly) the answer to the principal question about the segment and any other main points. Make notes on the principal ideas, so you can look them over later. Now that you have actively studied the first segment, move on to the second segment and do steps 2–4 for it. Continue doing this through the rest of the segments until you have finished the chapter.

Review the Entire Chapter by Repeating Questions

After you have read the chapter, go back through it and review the main points. Then, without looking at the book, test your memory by repeating the questions.

Clearly the SQ3R method takes longer than simply reading with a rapidly moving color marker or underlining pencil. However, the technique is far more effective because it requires your *involvement and understanding.* This is the key to all effective learning.

Learning from Lectures

Does attending lectures really make a difference? Research shows that students with grades of B or above were more apt to have better class attendance than students with grades of C— or below.[68]

Regardless of the strengths of the lecturer, here are some tips for getting more out of lectures.

Take Effective Notes by Listening Actively

Research shows that good test performance is related to good note taking.[69] And good note taking requires that you *listen actively*—that is, participate in the lecture process. Here are some ways to take good lecture notes:

- **Read ahead and anticipate the lecturer:** Try to anticipate what the instructor is going to say, based on your previous reading. Having background knowledge makes learning more efficient.

- **Listen for signal words:** Instructors use key phrases such as "The most important point is . . .," "There are four reasons for . . .," "The chief reason . . .," "Of special importance . . .," "Consequently . . . ." When you hear such signal phrases, mark your notes with an asterisk (*), or write *Imp* (for "Important").

- **Take notes in your own words:** Instead of just being a stenographer, try to restate the lecturer's thoughts in your own words. This makes you pay attention to the lecture and organize it in a way that is meaningful to you. In addition, don't try to write everything down. Just get the key points.

- **Ask questions:** By asking questions during the lecture, you participate in it and increase your understanding. Although many students are shy about asking questions, most professors welcome them.

Becoming an Effective Test Taker

Besides having knowledge of the subject matter, you can acquire certain skills that will help during the test-taking process. Some suggestions:[70]

Review Your Notes Regularly

Most students, according to one study, do take good notes, but they don't use them effectively. That is, they wait to review their notes until just before final exams, when the notes have lost much of their meaning.[71] Make it a point to review your notes regularly, such as the afternoon after the lecture or once or twice a week. We cannot emphasize enough how important this kind of reviewing is.

Reviewing: Study Information That Is Emphasized & Enumerated

Because you won't always know whether an exam will be an objective test or an essay test, you need to prepare for both. Here are some general tips.

- **Review material that is emphasized:** In the lectures, this consists of any topics your instructor pointed out as being significant or important. It also includes anything he or she spent a good deal of time discussing or specifically advised you to study. In the textbook, pay attention to key terms (often emphasized in *italic* or **boldface** type), their definitions, and their examples. In addition, of course, material that has a good many pages given over to it should be considered important.

- **Review material that is enumerated:** Pay attention to any numbered lists, both in your lectures and in your notes. Enumerations often provide the basis for essay and multiple-choice questions.

- **Review other tests:** Look over past quizzes, as well as the discussion questions or review questions provided at the end of chapters in many textbooks.

Prepare by Doing Final Reviews & Budgeting Your Test Time

Learn how to make your energy and time work for you. Whether you have studied methodically or must cram for an exam, here are some tips:

- **Review your notes:** Spend the night before the test reviewing your notes. Then go to bed without interfering with the material you have absorbed (as by watching television). Get up early the next morning, and review your notes again.

- **Find a good test-taking spot:** Make sure you arrive at the exam with any pencils or other materials you need. Get to the classroom early, or at least on time, and find a quiet spot. If you don't have a watch, sit where you can see a clock. Again review your notes. Avoid talking with others, so as not to interfere with the information you have learned or to increase your anxiety.

- **Read the test directions:** Many students don't do this and end up losing points because they didn't understand precisely what was required of them. Also, listen to any verbal directions or hints your instructor gives you before the test.

- **Budget your time:** Here is an important test strategy: Before you start, read through the entire test and figure out how much time you can spend on each section. There is a reason for budgeting your time: you would hate to find you have only a few minutes left and a long essay still to be written. Write the number of minutes allowed for each section on the test booklet or scratch sheet and stick to the schedule. The way you budget your time should correspond to how confident you feel about answering the questions.

Objective Tests: Answer Easy Questions & Eliminate Options

Some suggestions for taking objective tests, such as multiple-choice, true/false, or fill-in, are as follows:

- **Answer the easy questions first:** Don't waste time stewing over difficult questions. Do the easy ones first, and come back to the hard ones later. (Put a check mark opposite those you're not sure about.) Your unconscious mind may have solved them in the meantime, or later items may provide you with the extra information you need.

- **Answer all questions:** Unless the instructor says you will be penalized for wrong answers, try to answer all questions. If you have time, review all the questions and make sure you have written the responses correctly.

- **Eliminate the options:** Cross out answers you know are incorrect. Be sure to read all the possible answers, especially when the first answer is correct. (After all, other answers could also be correct, so that "All of the above" may be the right choice.) Be alert that subsequent questions may provide information pertinent to earlier questions. Pay attention to options that are long and detailed, since answers that are more detailed and specific are likely to be correct. If two answers have the opposite meaning, one of the two is probably correct.

Essay Tests: First Anticipate Answers & Prepare an Outline

Because time is limited, your instructor is likely to ask only a few essay questions during the exam. The key to success is to try to anticipate beforehand what the questions might be and memorize an outline for an answer. Here are the specific suggestions:

- **Anticipate 10 probable essay questions:** Use the principles we discussed above of reviewing lecture and textbook material that is *emphasized* and *enumerated.* You will then be in a position to identify 10 essay questions your instructor may ask. Write out these questions.

- **Prepare and memorize informal essay answers:** For each question, list the main points that need to be discussed. Put supporting information in parentheses. Circle the key words in each main point and below the question put the first letter of the key word. Make up catch phrases, using acronyms, acrostics, or word games, so that you can memorize these key words. Test yourself until you can recall the key words the letters stand for and the main points the key words represent.

collaborative computing 11
competitive advantage 8
conceptual skills 26
controlling 13
databases 10
decisional roles 21
e-business 10
e-commerce 10
e-mail 10
effective 5
efficient 5
entrepreneur 23
entrepreneurship 23

first-line manager 16
four management functions 12
functional manager 16
general manager 16
human skills 26
informational roles 20
innovation 8
internal locus of
  control 25
Internet 10
interpersonal roles 20
intrapreneur 23
knowledge management 11

leading 13
management 4
management process 12
middle manager 15
organization 4
organizing 13
planning 12
project management
  software 10
technical skills 26
telecommute 11
top manager 15
videoconferencing 11

summary

 1.1 Management: What It Is, What Its Benefits Are

- Management is defined as the pursuit of organizational goals, efficiently and effectively. Efficiently means to use resources wisely and cost-effectively. Effectively means to achieve results, to make the right decisions and successfully carry them out to achieve the organization's goals.

 1.2 Six Challenges to Being a Star Manager

- Challenge #1, managing for competitive advantage, means an organization must stay ahead in four areas: being responsive to customers; innovating new products or services; offering better quality; being more efficient.

- Challenge #2 is managing for diversity among different genders, ages, races, and ethnicities.

- Challenge #3 is managing for globalization, the expanding universe.

- Challenge #4 is managing for computers and telecommunications—information technology.

- Challenge #5 is managing for right and wrong, or ethical standards.

- Challenge #6 is managing for your own happiness and life goals.

 1.3 What Managers Do: The Four Principal Functions

- The four management functions are represented by the abbreviation POLC: *planning, organizing, leading, controlling.*

- The first function is defined as setting goals and deciding how to achieve them.

- The second function is defined as arranging tasks, people, and other resources to accomplish the work.

- The third function is defined as motivating, directing, and otherwise influencing people to work hard to achieve the organization's goals.

- The fourth function is defined as monitoring performance, comparing it with goals, and taking corrective action as needed.

 1.4 Pyramid Power: Levels & Areas of Management

- Within an organization, there are managers at three levels: top, middle, and first-line.

- Top managers make long-term decisions about the overall direction of the organization and establish the objectives, policies, and strategies for it.

- Middle managers implement the policies and plans of their superiors and supervise and coordinate the activities of the managers below them.

- First-line managers make short-term operating decisions, directing the daily tasks of nonmanagement personnel.

- There are three types of organizations classified according to the three different purposes for which they are formed. (1) For-profit organizations are formed to make money by offering products or services. (2) Nonprofit organizations offer services to some, but not to make a profit. (3) Mutual-benefit organizations are voluntary collections of members created to advance members' interests.

I.5 Roles Managers Must Play Successfully

- The Mintzberg study shows that, first, a manager relies more on verbal than on written communication; second, managers work long hours at an intense pace; and, third, a manager's work is characterized by fragmentation, brevity, and variety.

- From this, Mintzberg concluded that managers play three broad types of roles: interpersonal, informational, and decisional.

- In the first role, the manager acts as figurehead, leader, and liaison.

- In the second role, the manager acts as monitor, disseminator, and spokesperson.

- In the third role, the manager acts as entrepreneur, disturbance handler, resource allocator, and negotiator.

I.6 The Entrepreneurial Spirit

Entrepreneurship, a necessary attribute of business, is the process of taking risks to try to create a new enterprise. There are two types of entrepreneurship: (1) An entrepreneur is someone who sees a new opportunity for a product or service and launches a business to try to realize it. (2) An intrapreneur is someone who works inside an existing organization who sees an opportunity for a product or service and mobilizes the organization's resources to try to realize it.

Entrepreneurs, who are needed to start a business, and managers, who are needed to grow or maintain a business, differ somewhat. Both have a high need for achievement and a belief in personal control of their own destiny (internal locus of control). Both have a high energy level and action orientation as well as high tolerance for ambiguity, but these characteristics are especially true of entrepreneurs. Entrepreneurs are more self-confident than managers are and they have a higher tolerance for risk.

I.7 The Skills Star Managers Need

- The three skills that star managers cultivate are technical, conceptual, and human.

- The first set of skills consists of job-specific knowledge needed to perform well in a specialized field.

- The second set of skills consists of the ability to think analytically, to visualize an organization as a whole, and to understand how the parts work together.

- The third set of skills consists of the ability to work well in cooperation with other people to get things done.

management in action

A Road Map for Managers Who Find Themselves Taking on a Bigger Company Role

Thomas Swidarski was a senior vice president at Diebold, the Canton, Ohio, maker of automated teller machines [in the fall of 2005]. Hardly anything was going smoothly. New ATMs had fancy features but also costly bugs. A supply chain quagmire in overseas plants slowed the flow of products. Earnings plummeted. Every C-level executive left: the chief financial officer jumped ship and late last year, the COO and CEO both were ousted.

That's when directors named Mr. Swidarski, 47 years old, president and CEO. Before accepting the top job, he reminded Diebold's lead director that he didn't have any manufacturing expertise. What the 10-year veteran did have was experience overseeing marketing, global business development and acquisitions. And he hasn't lacked the ability to identify problems quickly and mobilize employees to work toward solutions.

His moves since taking charge offer a road map to other executives who suddenly find themselves attempting a turnaround or taking on a bigger company role than they ever anticipated.

Mr. Swidarski began his first day as CEO . . . by asking himself what he'd want from a new top boss. His answer: candid communication. He sent an email to Diebold's 14,500 employees inviting comments and outlining his priorities, including building customer loyalty by speeding the flow of products through the supply chain, and "providing quality products and outstanding service." He told them that leading Diebold "does not rest with one person—it rests with each and every one of us."

He received more than 1,000 responses. Some employees simply said "thanks for writing," but others wrote about a problem they wanted to solve. "People cared and were passionate, which is what you always want and need" to make changes, says Mr. Swidarski.

He then assembled a new senior team, relying mostly on insiders whose skills he knew and who complemented one another. "These are people I've witnessed in good and also bad times when they've been under fire," says Mr. Swidarski, a sports fan who likes reading football coaches' advice for management tips.

A few key jobs were redesigned to focus on the greatest needs. Diebold gets 50% of its revenue from service contracts, requiring it to keep thousands of ATMs up and running world-wide 24/7. In the past, the executive in charge of service didn't have a say in product development. Mr. Swidarski combined jobs, naming a new senior vice president of global development and service. It was a small change, but has the potential to save millions of dollars. And instead of relying on service technicians only to fix problems in the field, they and customers now give feedback for future product designs.

To tackle Diebold's supply-chain problems, Mr. Swidarski put one executive in charge of parts procurement and manufacturing. Until he took charge, the company's overseas plants received parts mostly from U.S. suppliers, running up shipping costs. Procurement managers, who reported to different bosses from the plant managers, focused too much on the cost of parts, rather than on how much inventory was needed, when and where.

That's changing as Diebold seeks overseas suppliers close to overseas plants and links procurement directly to supply-chain logistics.

Straightforward and unpretentious, Mr. Swidarski drops by employees' desks to ask about their work or invites them to lunch. He reminds executives to "make sure associates know the work they do is important, whatever their title," says Cassie Metzger, who oversees Diebold's global customer-satisfaction program.

He's demanding, however, quick to tell a manager he or she hasn't prepared for a meeting—not an easy thing to do with former peers. "I indicated that, make no mistake, this is a business not a fraternity, and I will be making tough business and personnel decisions in coming months," he says.

He told Wall Street analysts . . . he wanted to cut $100 million in costs over three years. Diebold recently announced plans to close its plant in France and move its European operation to Hungary. But Mr. Swidarski says most saving will come from more-efficient manufacturing and service processes, not job cuts. "Our head count will go up, not down," he says. "We need to make sure we have the right skills for us to compete."

He no longer makes quarterly projections to Wall Street. Companies don't reach goals by checking results every quarter, he says, "You get there by saying, 'Here is where we are going over the next two- to three-year period.'"

For Discussion

1. Which of the six managerial challenges discussed in this chapter did Thomas Swidarski face when he accepted the position of CEO of Diebold? Discuss.
2. Using Figure 1.1 as a guide, describe which functions of management were displayed by Swidarski.
3. Based on the information in the case, what type of managerial behaviors does Swidarski expect from his top managers? Explain.
4. Which of the three types of managerial roles did Swidarski display?
5. How would you evaluate Swidarski's technical, conceptual, and human skills? Explain your rationale.

Source: Excerpted from Carol Hymowitz, "Diebold's New Chief Shows How to Lead After a Sudden Rise," *The Wall Street Journal,* May 8, 2006, p. B1. Reprinted by permission of Dow Jones & Company, Inc. via The Copyright Clearance Center.

Can You Pass the CEO Test?

Objectives
1. To assess whether or not you have "it" at this time to be a CEO.
2. To assess whether or not you want to be a CEO.
3. To see what seems to be expected of a CEO.

Introduction
The Chief Executive Officer of a company is the person in charge, the top star. This person has tremendous power and, consequently, experiences incredible pressures. Not everyone is cut out to be a CEO or aspires to be one. Many people would not want the stress and expectations for greatness that come with the job.

Instructions
Take the following quiz at **www.mbajungle.com/ monthlysurvey/ceotest.cfm** to "test" whether you have "it." Leading a successful company requires a combination of talents and skills that few people seem to have—some people have it, some don't. Here's your chance to find out where you stand.

Accompanying the quiz is an article by John Scaizi for the MBA Jungle Online magazine. Read it; then take the test and see if you are a potential rising star. Once you have completed the test and have submitted your responses, ask yourself the following questions and be prepared to discuss them.

Questions for Discussion
1. Do you want to be a CEO? Explain.
2. Do you want to climb the corporate ladder to become a star?
3. At what level in the organization do you think you would be comfortable?
4. What are the ethics behind #7, #8, #11, # 15, and #16?
5. How would you describe what it takes to be a CEO?

group exercise

How Well Do Managers Manage Their Time?

Objectives
- To see how time is allocated in a top management position.
- To start to think about how you might spend your time in a top management position.
- To see what you think about this kind of job and what functions are performed.

Introduction
Managers must allocate their time appropriately. If as a manager you continuously misallocate your time in terms of work coordination, your company will not reach its goals or, at the very least, you will not achieve your own goals and may become a liability to the organization. So, you must understand how to allocate your time wisely.

Instructions
The following is from Charles Handy's *Understanding Organizations:*

A senior manager's diary: One senior division manager sat down to review what he regarded as the major responsibilities of his job. He listed six key areas for himself:

1. Relations with head office: communicating with the top managers.
2. Long-term and strategic planning: the plans that position the company over time.
3. Operational responsibilities for particular ongoing activities: the day-to-day activities of the company.
4. Co-coordinating function: working with other parts of the company to complete a task or tasks.
5. Standard setting, performance, morale priorities: setting up quality standards and other types of standards, operationalizing performance appraisals, and developing a climate where employees want to work.

6. External relations: working with customers, watching what competitors are doing, dealing with pressure groups, working with suppliers.

As a group, estimate in percentages how you think this senior manager allocated his time to these six key areas. (The senior manager's percentages are included at the end of this exercise.)

1.   %   4.   %
2.   %   5.   %
3.   %   6.   %

What areas would you add to his list? Why?

Questions for Discussion

1. How do your percentages compare to the senior division manager's time allocation?
2. Why do you think that 1, 3, and 4 take so much of his time?

3. In this changing world do you think that more time should be spent on 2, 5, and 6?
4. How do managers "know" how to allocate their time? In his position, would you allocate your time differently? Why or why not?

Answers

After outlining the six key areas of responsibility in his job, the division manager then analyzed his diary for the previous 3 months and came up with the following approximate percentages of time spent on each of the key areas:

1. 20%   4. 25%
2. 10%   5. 5%
3. 35%   6. 5%

Adapted and modified by Anne Cowden, PhD, from Charles Handy's *Understanding Organizations* (New York: Penguin, 1993), p. 338.

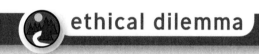 ethical dilemma

To Delay or Not to Delay?

You have been hired by a vice president of a national company to create an employee attitude survey, to administer it to all employees, and to interpret the results. You have known this vice president for over 10 years and have worked for her on several occasions. She trusts and likes you, and you trust and like her. You have completed your work and now are ready to present the findings and your interpretations to the vice president's management team. The vice president has told you that she wants your honest interpretation of the results, because she is planning to make changes based on the results. Based on this discussion, your report clearly identifies several strengths and weaknesses that need to be addressed. For example, employees feel that they are working too hard and that management does not care about providing good customer service. At the meeting you will be presenting the results and your interpretations to a group of 15 managers. You also have known most of these managers for at least 5 years.

You show up for the presentation armed with slides, handouts, and specific recommendations. Your slides are loaded on the computer, and most of the participants have arrived. They are drinking coffee and

telling you how excited they are about hearing your presentation. You also are excited to share your insights. Ten minutes before the presentation is set to begin, the vice president takes you out of the meeting room and says she wants to talk with you about your presentation. The two of you go to another office, and she closes the door. She then tells you that her boss's boss decided to come to the presentation unannounced. She feels that he is coming to the presentation solely looking for negative information in your report. He does not like the vice president and wants to replace her with one of his friends. If you present your results as planned, it will provide this individual with the information he needs to create serious problems for the vice president. Knowing this, the vice president asks you to find some way to postpone your presentation. You have 10 minutes to decide what to do.

Solving the Dilemma

What would you do?

1. Deliver the presentation as planned.
2. Give the presentation but skip over the negative results.

3. Go back to the meeting room and announce that your spouse has had an accident at home and you must leave immediately. You tell the group that you just received this message and that you will contact the vice president to schedule a new meeting.

4. Invent other options. Discuss.

 video case

A Look at eBay CEO Meg Whitman

Meg Whitman is Chief Executive Officer (CEO) at eBay, the giant online auction house that auctions more than three million items on its Web site (**www.eBay. com**) daily. Not only does Whitman boast a solid educational pedigree with undergraduate and graduate degrees from two Ivy League universities—Princeton (Economics) and Harvard (MBA)—but she also possesses the practical experience that enables her to run a mega-company such as eBay. During her career as a professional manager, Whitman has held middle level managerial positions at Bain & Company, Walt Disney, and Hasbro Inc., as well as CEO positions at both Stride Rite Corporation and FTD (Florists Transworld Delivery).

In addition, Whitman is a risktaker. True, she has worked as a CEO at several companies, but her corporate expertise was not connected to the Internet—in fact, she took the job at eBay without any real knowledge of the Internet. She credits her mother as the person from whom she learned to be risk tolerant.

To succeed in her role at eBay, Whitman has also taken the time to understand her employees. Most employees are younger and more technical than she. Such an understanding and connection with her employees has aided Whitman in developing a flexible corporate culture at eBay: employees (and she) dress down and are allowed to wear jeans to work. Like them, she too works from a cubicle. She has not reserved the coveted corner suite for herself.

Since Whitman became CEO at eBay in March 1998, the company's stock has experienced a 2,400 percent gain (its stock was selling slightly more than $24.00 in early August 2006), and its workforce, which attends to some eight million customers, has increased more than 60 percent to 800 from 500. In addition to these dramatic company gains, Whitman herself has been well compensated for her managerial leadership at the company. In 2005, she enjoyed a base salary, exclusive of stock options and other perks, of $995,016. Her personal worth tops $1 billion, and in 2005, *Fortune* magazine ranked her first among the 50 most powerful women in business. Without a doubt, Meg Whitman is an exceptional manager.

Questions

1. Would you consider Meg Whitman an entrepreneur as well as a risk taker in her current position as CEO at eBay? Why or why not?

2. Describe Whitman's managerial skills as CEO at eBay. How has she used these skills to compensate for her lack of technical skills?

3. Which managerial traits do you see in Whitman?

4. Which managerial roles does Whitman primarily play in her job as CEO? Which roles might she need to develop in order to ensure continued success?

5. What managerial challenges do you think Whitman, a star manager, faces at eBay?

Source: Joseph C. Santora, EdD, Essex County College.

chapter 2

Management Theory
Essential Background for the Successful Manager

Major Questions You Should Be Able to Answer

2.1 Evolving Viewpoints: How We Got to Today's Management Outlook
Major Question: What's the payoff in studying different management perspectives, both yesterday's and today's?

2.2 Classical Viewpoint: Scientific & Administrative Management
Major Question: If the name of the game is to manage work more efficiently, what can the classical viewpoint teach me?

2.3 Behavioral Viewpoint: Behaviorism, Human Relations, & Behavioral Science
Major Question: To understand how people are motivated to achieve, what can I learn from the behavioral viewpoint?

2.4 Quantitative Viewpoints: Management Science & Operations Research
Major Question: If the manager's job is to solve problems, how might the two quantitative approaches help?

2.5 Systems Viewpoint
Major Question: How can the exceptional manager be helped by the systems viewpoint?

2.6 Contingency Viewpoint
Major Question: In the end, is there one best way to manage in all situations?

2.7 Quality-Management Viewpoint
Major Question: Can the quality-management viewpoint offer guidelines for true managerial success?

2.8 The Learning Organization in an Era of Accelerated Change
Major Question: Organizations must learn or perish. How do I build a learning organization?

Mindfulness over Mindlessness: Being a Learner in a Learning Organization

Learn or die. Isn't that the challenge for us as individuals? It's the same with organizations. Thus has arisen the concept of the "learning organization," in which employees continually expand their ability to achieve results by obtaining the right knowledge and changing their behavior.

Throughout your career, you will have to constantly be a learner, evaluating all kinds of beliefs and theories—including those described in this chapter. However, one barrier to learning that all of us need to be aware of is *mindlessness.* Instead we need to adopt the frame of mind that Harvard psychology professor Ellen Langer has called *mindfulness,* a form of active engagement.

We've all experienced mindlessness. We misplace our keys. We write checks in January with the previous year's date. Mindlessness is characterized by the three following attributes:

- **Entrapment in old categories:** An avid tennis player, Langer says that at a tennis camp she, like all other students, was taught *exactly* how to hold her racquet and toss the ball when making a serve. But later, when watching a top tennis championship, she observed that none of the top players served the way she was taught and that all served slightly differently.[1]

  The significance: There is no one right way of doing things. In a conditional, or mindful, way of teaching, an instructor doesn't say "This is THE answer" but rather "This is ONE answer." Thus, all information—even in the hard sciences and mathematics, where it may seem as though there is just one correct answer—should be regarded with open-mindedness, since there may be exceptions. That is, you should act as though the information is true only for certain uses or under certain circumstances.

- **Automatic behavior:** Langer tells of the time she used a new credit card in a department store. Noticing that Langer hadn't signed the card yet, the cashier returned it to her to sign the back. After passing the credit card through the imprinting machine, the clerk handed her the credit card receipt to sign, which Langer did. Then, says Langer, the cashier "held the form next to the newly signed card to see if the signatures matched."[2]

  In automatic behavior, we take in and use limited signals from the world around us without letting other signals penetrate as well. By contrast, mindfulness is being open to new information—including that not specifically assigned to you. Mindfulness requires you engage more fully in whatever it is you're doing.

- **Acting from a single perspective:** Most people, says Langer, typically assume that other people's motives and intentions are the same as theirs. For example, she says, "If I am out running and see someone walking briskly, I assume she is trying to exercise and would run if only she could," when actually she may be intending to get her exercise only from walking.

For most situations, many interpretations are possible. "Every idea, person, or object is potentially simultaneously many things depending on the perspective from which it is viewed," says Langer.[3] Trying out different perspectives gives you *more choices in how to respond;* a single perspective that produces an automatic reaction reduces your options.

For Discussion Developing mindfulness means consciously adapting: Being open to novelty. Being alert to distinctions. Being sensitive to different contexts. Being aware of multiple perspectives. Being oriented in the present. What situations have you been in which by allowing yourself to be open-minded (mindfulness) you allowed in new information that completely changed your mind?

forecast
What's Ahead in This Chapter

This chapter gives you a short overview of the three principal *historical* perspectives or viewpoints on management—*classical, behavioral,* and *quantitative.* It then describes the three principal *contemporary* viewpoints—*systems, contingency,* and *quality-management.* Finally, we consider the concept of *learning organizations.*

2.1 EVOLVING VIEWPOINTS: HOW WE GOT TO TODAY'S MANAGEMENT OUTLOOK

> **✳ major question** What's the payoff in studying different management perspectives, both yesterday's and today's?

THE BIG PICTURE

Management began as an art but is evolving into a science. Two principal perspectives are the *historical* and the *contemporary.* Studying management theory provides a guide to action, a source of new ideas, clues to the meaning of your managers' decisions, and clues to the meaning of outside events.

"These days, there aren't any hot, new trends, just a lot of repackaged ones from the past," writes *Wall Street Journal* columnist Carol Hymowitz.[4] "Executives have been treated to an overdose of management guides that mostly haven't delivered what they promised. Many bosses have adopted them all, regardless of their company's business model, balance sheet, competition, employee bench strength, or any other unique qualities. They have become copycat managers, trying to find a one-stop, fix-it-all answer to their various problems."

How will you know whether the next "fit-it-all" book to hit the business bestseller list is simply a recycling of old ideas? The answer is: you have to have studied history—hence the reason for this chapter.

Is Management an Art or a Science?

There's no question that the practice of management can be an art. Judy McGrath, CEO of MTV Networks, has a background in English and journalism, not business. Bill Gates, the founder of Microsoft Corp. and today the richest man in the world, had no training in management—in fact, he was a college dropout (from Harvard) with a background in computer science. Great managers, like great painters or actors, are those who have the right mix of intuition, judgment, and experience.

But management is also a science. That is, rather than being performed in a seat-of-the-pants, trial-and-error, make-it-up-as-you-go-along kind of way—which can lead to some truly horrendous mistakes—management can be approached deliberately, rationally, systematically. That's what the scientific method is, after all—a logical process, embodying four steps:

1. You observe events and gather facts.
2. You pose a possible solution or explanation based on those facts.
3. You make a prediction of future events.
4. You test the prediction under systematic conditions.

This process is now known as *evidence-based management.* Throughout the book, we describe various scientific tools that managers use to solve problems.

Two Overarching Perspectives about Management & Five Practical Reasons for Studying Them

In this chapter, we describe two overarching perspectives about management:

- **Historical. The *historical perspective* includes three viewpoints—*classical, behavioral,* and *quantitative.***

- **Contemporary.** The *contemporary perspective* also includes three viewpoints—*systems, contingency,* and *quality-management.*

This is supposed to be a practical book. But what could be more practical than studying different approaches to management to see which seem to work best? After all, as philosopher George Santayana said, "Those who cannot remember the past are condemned to repeat it."

Indeed, there are five good reasons for studying theoretical perspectives:

1. **Understanding of the present.** When you view current management practices, an understanding of history will help you understand why they are still in favor, whether for the right reasons or the wrong ones.

2. **Guide to action.** Knowing management perspectives helps you develop a set of principles, a blueprint, that will guide your actions.

3. **Source of new ideas.** Being aware of various perspectives can also provide new ideas when you encounter new situations.

4. **Clues to meaning of your managers' decisions.** It can help you understand the focus of your organization, where the top managers are "coming from."

5. **Clues to meaning of outside events.** Finally, it may allow you to understand events outside the organization that could affect it or you. ●

Example

How Understanding Theory Can Help You: Is the Pyramid Hierarchy Useful or Useless?

Is there a reason for having the kind of management hierarchy that we described in Chapter 1? The idea that the company is shaped like a pyramid, with the CEO at the top and everybody else in layers below, is a legacy with strong roots in the military bureaucracy. German sociologist Max Weber thought bureaucracy was actually a rational approach to organizations, and in his day it probably was an improvement over the organizational arrangements then in place, as we'll discuss. The traditional pyramid hierarchy and bureaucracy have had a past history of great success in large corporations such as the Coca-Cola Company.

Knowing what you know about the pyramid hierarchy, can you think of any problems posed by the traditional organization chart? Could a hierarchy of boxes with lines showing who works in what department and who reports to whom actually become a corporate straitjacket?

That's what Lars Kolind, CEO of Danish digital hearing-aid producer Oticon, thought. In the early 1990s, he took Oticon's organization chart and simply threw it away. "He unilaterally abolished the old pyramid," says one account. In the new "spaghetti organization," as it came to be called, there was "no formal organization, no departments, no functions, no paper, no permanent desks."[5] All employees worked at mobile workstations, all desks were on wheels, and everybody worked on projects that were always subject to reorganization. Why such deliberate disorganization? Because if you want to have a company that is fast, agile, and innovative, as CEO Kolind did, you might want to have a flexible organizational structure that allows for fast reaction time. And it worked. By 1993, Oticon achieved the greatest profits since it was founded in 1904.

Your Call

Kolind says that the spaghetti organization structure has four characteristics: a much broader job definition, less formal structure, more open and informal physical layouts to facilitate communications, and management based on values (in Oticon's case, to help people achieve a better quality of life with the hearing they have) rather than on command-and-control mechanisms.[6] Do you think a spaghetti organization could be applied to a factory with hundreds or thousands of employees, such as a Coca-Cola bottling plant or a Ford assembly plant?

2.2 CLASSICAL VIEWPOINT: SCIENTIFIC & ADMINISTRATIVE MANAGEMENT

❋ major question — If the name of the game is to manage work more efficiently, what can the classical viewpoint teach me?

THE BIG PICTURE

The *three historical management viewpoints* we will describe include (1) the classical, described in this section; (2) the behavioral; and (3) the quantitative. The classical viewpoint, which emphasized ways to manage work more efficiently, had two approaches: (a) scientific management and (b) administrative management. *Scientific management,* pioneered by Frederick W. Taylor and Frank and Lillian Gilbreth, emphasized the scientific study of work methods to improve the productivity of individual workers. *Administrative management,* pioneered by Henry Fayol and Max Weber, was concerned with managing the total organization.

Bet you've never heard of a "therblig," although it may describe some physical motions you perform from time to time—perhaps when you have to wash dishes. A made-up word you won't find in most dictionaries, *therblig* was coined by Frank Gilbreth and is, in fact, "Gilbreth" spelled backward, with the "t" and the "h" reversed. It refers to 1 of 17 basic motions. By identifying the therbligs in a job, as in the tasks of a bricklayer (which he had once been), Frank and his wife, Lillian, were able to eliminate motions while simultaneously reducing fatigue.

The Gilbreths were a husband-and-wife team of industrial engineers who were pioneers in one of the classical approaches to management, part of the historical perspective. As we mentioned, there are *three historical management viewpoints* or approaches. *(See Figure 2.1, opposite page.)* They are

- Classical
- Behavioral
- Quantitative

In this section, we describe the classical perspective of management, which originated during the early 1900s. **The *classical viewpoint,* which emphasized finding ways to manage work more efficiently, had two branches—*scientific* and *administrative*—each of which is identified with particular pioneering theorists.** In general, classical management assumes that *people are rational.* Let's compare the two approaches.

Scientific Management: Pioneered by Taylor & the Gilbreths

The problem for which scientific management emerged as a solution was this: In the expansive days of the early 20th century, labor was in such short supply that managers were hard pressed to raise the productivity of workers. **Scientific management emphasized the scientific study of work methods to improve the productivity of individual workers.** Two of its chief proponents were **Frederick W. Taylor** and the team of **Frank and Lillian Gilbreth.**

Frederick Taylor & the Four Principles of Scientific Management   No doubt there are some days when you haven't studied, or worked, as efficiently as you could. This could be called "underachieving," or "loafing," or what Taylor called

① **Classical Viewpoint** Emphasis on ways to manage work more efficiently	② **Behavioral Viewpoint** Emphasis on importance of understanding human behavior and motivating and encouraging employees toward achievement	③ **Quantitative Viewpoint** Applies quantitative techniques to management
Scientific management Emphasized scientific study of work methods to improve productivity of individual workers *Proponents*: Frederick W. Taylor Frank and Lillian Gilbreth	**Early behaviorists** *Proponents*: Hugo Munsterberg Mary Parker Follet Elton Mayo	**Management science** Focuses on using mathematics to aid in problem solving and decision making
Administrative management Concerned with managing the total organization *Proponents*: Henri Fayol Max Weber	**Human relations movement** Proposed better human relations could increase worker productivity *Proponents*: Abraham Maslow Douglas McGregor	**Operations management** Focuses on managing the production and delivery of an organization's products or services more effectively
	Behavioral science approach Relies on scientific research for developing theory to provide practical management tools	

figure 2.1

THE HISTORICAL PERSPECTIVE

Three viewpoints are shown.

Frederick W. Taylor. Called the father of scientific management, Taylor published *The Principles of Scientific Management* in 1911.

it—*soldiering,* deliberately working at less than full capacity. Known as "the father of scientific management," Taylor was an American engineer from Philadelphia who believed that managers could eliminate soldiering by applying four principles of science:

1. Evaluate a task by scientifically studying each part of the task (not use old rule-of-thumb methods).
2. Carefully select workers with the right abilities for the task.
3. Give workers the training and incentives to do the task with the proper work methods.
4. Use scientific principles to plan the work methods and ease the way for workers to do their jobs.

Taylor based his system on *motion studies,* in which he broke down each worker's job at a steel company, say, into basic physical motions and then trained workers to use the methods of their best-performing co-workers. In addition, he suggested employers institute a *differential rate system,* in which more efficient workers earned higher wages.

Lillian and Frank Gilbreth. These industrial engineers pioneered time and motion studies. If you're an athlete, you would appreciate how small changes could make you efficient.

Although "Taylorism" met considerable resistance from employees fearing that working harder would lead to lost jobs except for the highly productive few, Taylor believed that by raising production both labor and management could increase profits to the point where they no longer would have to quarrel over them. If used correctly, the principles of scientific management can enhance productivity, and such innovations as motion studies and differential pay are still used today.

Frank & Lillian Gilbreth & Industrial Engineering   As mentioned, Frank and Lillian Gilbreth were a husband-and-wife team of industrial engineers who lectured at Purdue University in the early 1900s. Their experiences in raising 12 children—to whom they applied some of their ideas about improving efficiency (such as printing the Morse Code on the back of the bathroom door so that family members could learn it while doing other things)—later were popularized in a book, two movies, and a TV sitcom, *Cheaper by the Dozen.* The Gilbreths expanded on Taylor's motion studies—for instance, by using movie cameras to film workers at work in order to isolate the parts of a job.

Lillian Gilbreth, who received a PhD in psychology, was the first woman to be a major contributor to management science.

Administrative Management: Pioneered by Fayol & Weber

Scientific management is concerned with the jobs of individuals. ***Administrative management*** **is concerned with managing the total organization.** Among the pioneering theorists were **Henri Fayol** and **Max Weber.**

Test Your Knowledge Exercise:
"Managerial Functions"

Henri Fayol & the Functions of Management   Fayol was not the first to investigate management behavior, but he was the first to systematize it. A French engineer and industrialist, he became known to American business when his most important work, *General and Industrial Management,* was translated into English in 1930.

Fayol was the first to identify the major functions of management (p. 12)—planning, organizing, leading, and controlling, as well as coordinating—the first four of which you'll recognize as the functions providing the framework for this and most other management books.

Max Weber & the Rationality of Bureaucracy In our time, the word "bureaucracy" has come to have negative associations: impersonality, inflexibility, red tape, a molasseslike response to problems. But to German sociologist Max Weber, a *bureaucracy* was a rational, efficient, ideal organization based on principles of logic. After all, in Weber's Germany in the late 19th century, many people were in positions of authority (particularly in the government) not because of their abilities but because of their social status. The result, Weber wrote, was that they didn't perform effectively.

A better-performing organization, he felt, should have five positive bureaucratic features:

1. A well-defined hierarchy of authority.
2. Formal rules and procedures.
3. A clear division of labor.
4. Impersonality.
5. Careers based on merit.

Weber's work was not translated into English until 1947, but, as we mentioned in the box on page 41, it came to have an important influence on the structure of large corporations, such as the Coca-Cola Company.

The Problem with the Classical Viewpoint: Too Mechanistic

The essence of the classical viewpoint was that work activity was amenable to a rational approach, that through the application of scientific methods, time and motion studies, and job specialization it was possible to boost productivity. Indeed, these concepts are still in use today, the results visible to you every time you visit McDonald's or Pizza Hut.

The flaw in the classical viewpoint, however, is that it is mechanistic: it tends to view humans as cogs within a machine, not taking into account the importance of human needs. Behavioral theory addressed this problem, as we explain next. ●

Scientific management. Car makers have broken down automobile manufacturing into its constituent tasks. This reflects the contributions of the school of scientific management. Is there anything wrong with this approach? How could it be improved?

2.3 BEHAVIORAL VIEWPOINT: BEHAVIORISM, HUMAN RELATIONS, & BEHAVIORAL SCIENCE

> ❖ **major question** To understand how people are motivated to achieve, what can I learn from the behavioral viewpoint?

THE BIG PICTURE

The second of the three historical management perspectives was the *behavioral* viewpoint, which emphasized the importance of understanding human behavior and of motivating employees toward achievement. The behavioral viewpoint developed over three phases: (1) *Early behaviorism* was pioneered by Hugo Munsterberg, Mary Parker Follett, and Elton Mayo. (2) The *human relations movement* was pioneered by Abraham Maslow (who proposed a hierarchy of needs) and Douglas McGregor (who proposed a Theory X and Theory Y view to explain managers' attitudes toward workers). (3) The *behavioral science approach* relied on scientific research for developing theories about behavior useful to managers.

The *behavioral viewpoint* **emphasized the importance of understanding human behavior and of motivating employees toward achievement.** The behavioral viewpoint developed over three phases: (1) early behaviorism, (2) the human relations movement, and (3) behavioral science.

Early Behaviorism: Pioneered by Munsterberg, Follett, & Mayo

The three people who pioneered behavioral theory were **Hugo Munsterberg, Mary Parker Follett,** and **Elton Mayo.**

Mary Parker Follett. She proposed that managers and employees should work together cooperatively.

Hugo Munsterberg & the First Application of Psychology to Industry

Called "the father of industrial psychology," German-born Hugo Munsterberg had a PhD in psychology and a medical degree and joined the faculty at Harvard University in 1892. Munsterberg suggested that psychologists could contribute to industry in three ways. They could:

1. Study jobs and determine which people are best suited to specific jobs.
2. Identify the psychological conditions under which employees do their best work.
3. Devise management strategies to influence employees to follow management's interests.

His ideas led to the field of *industrial psychology,* the study of human behavior in workplaces, which is still taught in colleges today.

Mary Parker Follett & Power Sharing among Employees & Managers

A Massachusetts social worker and social philosopher, Mary Parker Follett was lauded on her death in 1933 as "one of the most important women America has yet produced in the fields of civics and sociology." Instead of following the usual hierarchical arrangement of managers as order givers and employees as order takers,

Follett thought organizations should become more democratic, with managers and employees working cooperatively.

The following ideas were among her most important:

1. Organizations should be operated as "communities," with managers and subordinates working together in harmony.
2. Conflicts should be resolved by having managers and workers talk over differences and find solutions that would satisfy both parties—a process she called *integration*.
3. The work process should be under the control of workers with the relevant knowledge, rather than of managers, who should act as facilitators.

With these and other ideas, Follett anticipated some of today's concepts of "self-managed teams," "worker empowerment," and "interdepartmental teams"—that is, members of different departments working together on joint projects.

Elton Mayo & the Supposed "Hawthorne Effect" Do you think workers would be more productive if they thought they were receiving special attention? This was the conclusion drawn by a Harvard research group in the late 1920s.

Conducted by Elton Mayo and his associates at Western Electric's Hawthorne (Chicago) plant, what came to be called the *Hawthorne studies* began with an investigation into whether workplace lighting level affected worker productivity. (This was the type of study that Taylor or the Gilbreths might have done.) In later experiments, other variables were altered, such as wage levels, rest periods, and length of workday. Worker performance varied but tended to increase over time, leading Mayo and his colleagues to hypothesize what came to be known as the *Hawthorne effect*—namely, that employees worked harder if they received added attention, if they thought that managers cared about their welfare and that supervisors paid special attention to them.

Hawthorne. Western Electric's Hawthorne plant, where Elton Mayo and his team conducted their studies in the 1920s. Do you think you'd perform better in a robotlike job if you thought your supervisor cared about you and paid more attention to you?

Ultimately, the Hawthorne studies were faulted for being poorly designed and not having enough empirical data to support the conclusions. Nevertheless, they succeeded in drawing attention to the importance of "social man" (social beings) and how managers using good human relations could improve worker productivity. This in turn led to the so-called human relations movement in the 1950s and 1960s.

The Human Relations Movement: Pioneered by Maslow & McGregor

The two theorists who contributed most to the *human relations movement*—**which proposed that better human relations could increase worker productivity**—were Abraham Maslow and Douglas McGregor.

Abraham Maslow & the Hierarchy of Needs   What motivates you to perform: Food? Security? Love? Recognition? Self-fulfillment? Probably all of these, Abraham Maslow would say, although some needs must be satisfied before others. The chairman of the psychology department at Brandeis University and one of the earliest researchers to study motivation, in 1943 Maslow proposed his famous *hierarchy of human needs:* physiological, safety, social, esteem, and self-actualization[7] (as we discuss in detail in Chapter 12).

Douglas McGregor & Theory X versus Theory Y   Having been for a time a college president (at Antioch College in Ohio), Douglas McGregor came to realize that it was not enough for managers to try to be liked; they also needed to be aware of their attitudes toward employees.[8] Basically, McGregor suggested in a 1960 book, these attitudes could be either "X" or "Y."

Theory X represents a pessimistic, negative view of workers. In this view, workers are considered to be irresponsible, to be resistant to change, to lack ambition, to hate work, and to want to be led rather than to lead.

Theory Y? Debra Stark (third from left) built her Concord, Massachusetts–based Debra's Natural Gourmet store into a $2.5 million business by assigning each of her 26 employees, whom she calls "co-workers," a management role, such as monitoring product turnover. Each quarter, Stark distributes 20% of her after-tax profits among everyone, divided according to not only hours worked and salary level but also "how I see they're interacting with customers, each other, and me."

Theory Y represents the outlook of human relations proponents—an optimistic, positive view of workers. In this view, workers are considered to be capable of accepting responsibility, self-direction, and self-control and of being imaginative and creative.

The principal contribution offered by the Theory X/Theory Y perspective is that it can help managers avoid falling into the trap of the *self-fulfilling prophecy*. This is the idea that if a manager expects a subordinate to act in a certain way, the worker may, in fact, very well act that way, thereby confirming the manager's expectations: The prophecy that the manager made is fulfilled.

The Behavioral Science Approach

The human relations movement was a necessary correction to the sterile approach used within scientific management, but its optimism came to be considered too simplistic for practical use. More recently, the human relations view has been superseded by the behavioral science approach to management. **Behavioral science relies on scientific research for developing theories about human behavior that can be used to provide practical tools for managers.** The disciplines of behavioral science include psychology, sociology, anthropology, and economics. ●

Example

Application of Behavioral Science Approach: Which Is Better—Competition or Cooperation?

A widely held assumption among American managers is that "competition brings out the best in people." From an economic standpoint, business survival depends on staying ahead of the competition. But from an interpersonal standpoint, critics contend competition has been overemphasized, primarily at the expense of cooperation.[9]

One strong advocate of greater emphasis on cooperation, Alfie Kahn, reviewed the evidence and found two reasons for what he sees as competition's failure.

First, he said, "success often depends on sharing resources efficiently, and this is nearly impossible when people have to work against one another." Competition makes people suspicious and hostile toward each other. Cooperation, by contrast, "takes advantage of all the skills represented in a group as well as the mysterious process by which that group becomes more than the sum of its parts."

Second, Kahn says, competition does not promote excellence, "because trying to do well and trying to beat others simply are two different things." Kahn points out the example of children in class who wave their arms to get the teacher's attention, but when they are finally recognized they then seem befuddled and ask the teacher to repeat the question—because they were more focused on beating their classmates than on the subject matter.[10]

What does the behavioral science research suggest about the question of cooperation versus competition? One team of researchers reviewed 122 studies encompassing a wide variety of subjects and settings and came up with three conclusions: (1) Cooperation is superior to competition in promoting achievement and productivity. (2) Cooperation is superior to individualistic efforts in promoting achievement and productivity. (3) Cooperation without intergroup competition promotes higher achievement and productivity than cooperation with intergroup competition.[11]

Your Call

What kind of office layout do you think would encourage more cooperation—a system of private offices or an open-office configuration with desks scattered about in a small area with no partitions?

2.4 QUANTITATIVE VIEWPOINTS: MANAGEMENT SCIENCE & OPERATIONS RESEARCH

> ✦ **major question** If it's the manager's job to solve problems, how might the two quantitative approaches help?

THE BIG PICTURE

The third and last category under historical perspectives consists of *quantitative viewpoints,* which emphasize the application to management of quantitative techniques, such as statistics and computer simulations. Two approaches of quantitative management are *management science* and *operations management.*

During the air war known as the Battle of Britain in World War II, a relative few Royal Air Force fighter pilots and planes were able to successfully resist the overwhelming might of the German military machine. How did they do it? Military planners drew on mathematics and statistics to determine how to most effectively allocate use of their limited aircraft.

When the Americans entered the war in 1941, they used the British model to form *operations research (OR)* teams to determine how to deploy troops, submarines, and other military personnel and equipment most effectively. For example, OR techniques were used to establish the optimum pattern that search planes should fly to try to locate enemy ships.

After the war, businesses also began using these techniques. One group of former officers, who came to be called the Whiz Kids, used statistical techniques at Ford Motor Co. to make better management decisions. Later Whiz Kid Robert McNamara, who had become Ford's president, was appointed Secretary of Defense and introduced similar statistical techniques and cost-benefit analyses throughout the Department of Defense. Since then, OR techniques have evolved into **quantitative management, the application to management of quantitative techniques, such as statistics and computer simulations. Two branches of quantitative management are** *management science* **and** *operations management.*

FedEx. What management tools do you use to schedule employees and aircraft to deal with wide variations in package volume—such as December 23 versus December 26?

Management Science: Using Mathematics to Solve Management Problems

How would you go about deciding how to assign utility repair crews during a blackout? Or how many package sorters you needed and at which times for an overnight delivery service such as FedEx or UPS? You would probably use the tools of management science.

Management science is not the same as Taylor's scientific management. ***Management science* focuses on using mathematics to aid in problem solving and decision making.** Sometimes management science is called *operations research.*

Management Science: Renting Hotel Rooms at Half the Price

"Anyone who spends more than a few nights in hotels each year should join a half-price hotel program," says travel writer Ed Perkinson.[12] "Like airlines, hotels use a yield-management system to set prices," says another travel writer, Robert Belsky. "The goal is to maximize occupancy when business is weak and hike rates when business is strong. Filling rooms in lean times means off-season deals at resorts, half-price weekends at downtown hotels that cater to business travelers, and cheap rooms in the summer at hotels booked with conventions the rest of the year."[13]

All it takes for the hotels to work out a half-price program is to do some management science–style math. Research shows that 80% occupancy is the standard for profitability. If the hotel is booked beyond that, half-price members don't get their discount; lower than 80%, they do. (There may be blackout periods for some days.)

Your Call

What other industries do you think might use this kind of discount system, and how might it work?

Operations Management: Helping Organizations Deliver Products or Services More Effectively

How does Costco decide when to reorder supplies? How does JetBlue decide which planes are to fly where and when? Managers use the techniques of operations management. A less sophisticated version of management science, **operations management focuses on managing the production and delivery of an organization's products or services more effectively.** It is concerned with work scheduling, production planning, facilities location and design, and decisions about the optimum levels of inventory a company should maintain. ●

Operations Management: Can a Car Maker's "Lean Management" Production Techniques Be Applied to a Hospital?

Over the years, Toyota Motor Corp. has developed a variety of production techniques that draw in part on operations research.[14]

First, it emphasizes the smoothest possible *flow of work*. To accomplish this, managers perform *value stream mapping,* identifying the many steps in a production process and eliminating unnecessary ones. They also perform *mistake proofing* or *root-cause analysis,* using teamwork to examine problems and fix them as soon as they appear. In addition, the car maker helped pioneer the *just-in-time* approach to obtaining supplies from vendors only as they are needed in the factory. All such techniques now come under the term "lean management."

However, doctors and nurses don't think of themselves as assembly-line workers. Can lean management be used to improve hospital patient flow? Actually, it can.

At Allegheny General in Pittsburgh, for example, its two intensive-care units had been averaging 5.5 infections per 1,000 patient days, and in a 12-month period 37 patients had 49 infections and 51% died. The medical staff in the two units applied the Toyota "root-cause analysis" system to investigating every new infection as soon as it occurred. They concluded that an intravenous line inserted into an artery near the groin had a particularly high rate of infections. Now the hospital makes a continuous effort to replace these lines with lower-risk ones in the arm or near the collarbone.[15]

Your Call

If "lean management" can be applied at automakers and hospitals, could it be applied in higher education to educate students better? How?

2.5 SYSTEMS VIEWPOINT

How can the exceptional manager be helped by the systems viewpoint?

THE BIG PICTURE

Three contemporary management perspectives are (1) the *systems,* (2) the *contingency,* and (3) the *quality-management* viewpoints. The *systems viewpoint* sees organizations as a system, either open or closed, with inputs, outputs, transformation processes, and feedback. The *contingency viewpoint* emphasizes that a manager's approach should vary according to the individual and environmental situation. The *quality-management viewpoint* has two traditional approaches: *quality control,* the strategy for minimizing errors by managing each stage of production, and *quality assurance,* which focuses on the performance of workers, urging employees to strive for zero defects. A third quality approach is the movement of *total quality management (TQM),* a comprehensive approach dedicated to continuous quality improvement, training, and customer satisfaction.

Being of a presumably practical turn of mind, could you run an organization or a department according to the theories you've just learned? Probably not. The reason: people are complicated. To be an exceptional manager, you need to learn to deal with individual differences in a variety of settings.

Thus, to the historical perspective on management (classical, behavioral, and quantitative viewpoints), let us now add the *contemporary perspective,* which consists of three viewpoints. *(See Figure 2.2 below.)* These consist of:

- Systems
- Contingency
- Quality-management

In this section, we discuss the systems viewpoint.

The Systems Viewpoint Regards the organization as systems of interrelated parts that operate together to achieve a common purpose	**The Contingency Viewpoint** Emphasizes that a manager's approach should vary according to—i.e., be contingent on—the individual and environmental situation	**The Quality-Management Viewpoint** Three approaches
Quality control Strategy for minimizing errors by managing each stage of production *Proponent*: Walter Shewart	**Quality assurance** Focuses on the performance of workers, urging employees to strive for "zero defects"	**Total quality management** Comprehensive approach dedicated to continuous quality improvement, training, and customer satisfaction *Proponents*: W. Edwards Deming Joseph M. Juran

figure 2.2

THE CONTEMPORARY PERSPECTIVE

Three viewpoints

The Systems Viewpoint

The 52 bones in the foot. The monarchy of Great Britain. A weather storm front. Each of these is a system. **A *system* is a set of interrelated parts that operate together to achieve a common purpose.** Even though a system may not work very well—as in the inefficient way the Russian government collects taxes, for example—it is nevertheless still a system.

The *systems viewpoint* **regards the organization as a system of interrelated parts.** By adopting this point of view, you can look at your organization both as (1) a collection of *subsystems*—**parts making up the whole system**—and (2) a part of the larger environment. A college, for example, is made up of a collection of academic departments, support staffs, students, and the like. But it also exists as a system within the environment of education, having to be responsive to parents, alumni, legislators, nearby townspeople, and so on.

The Four Parts of a System

The vocabulary of the systems perspective is useful because it gives you a way of understanding many different kinds of organizations. There are four parts:

1. ***Inputs*** **are the people, money, information, equipment, and materials required to produce an organization's goods or services.** Whatever goes into a system is an input.

2. ***Outputs*** **are the products, services, profits, losses, employee satisfaction or discontent, and the like that are produced by the organization.** Whatever comes out of the system is an output.

3. ***Transformation processes*** **are the organization's capabilities in management and technology that are applied to converting inputs into outputs.** The main activity of the organization is to transform inputs into outputs.

4. ***Feedback*** **is information about the reaction of the environment to the outputs that affects the inputs.** Are the customers buying or not buying the product? That information is feedback.

The four parts of a system are illustrated below. *(See Figure 2.3.)*

figure 2.3
THE FOUR PARTS OF A SYSTEM

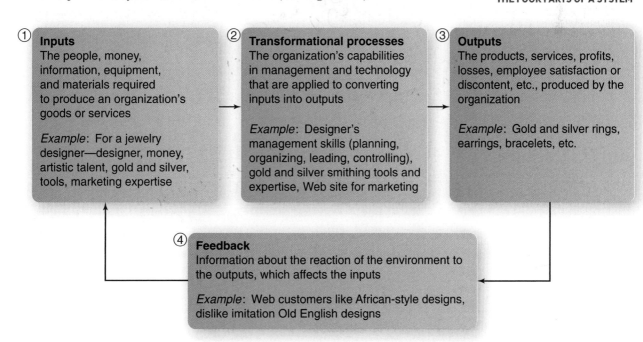

① **Inputs**
The people, money, information, equipment, and materials required to produce an organization's goods or services

Example: For a jewelry designer—designer, money, artistic talent, gold and silver, tools, marketing expertise

② **Transformational processes**
The organization's capabilities in management and technology that are applied to converting inputs into outputs

Example: Designer's management skills (planning, organizing, leading, controlling), gold and silver smithing tools and expertise, Web site for marketing

③ **Outputs**
The products, services, profits, losses, employee satisfaction or discontent, etc., produced by the organization

Example: Gold and silver rings, earrings, bracelets, etc.

④ **Feedback**
Information about the reaction of the environment to the outputs, which affects the inputs

Example: Web customers like African-style designs, dislike imitation Old English designs

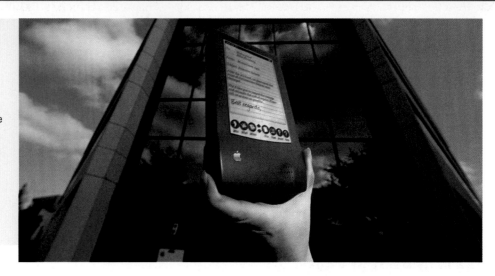

Closed system. The Apple Newton Messagepad, a personal digital assistant released in 1993 and killed in 1998, probably failed because it was developed as a closed system, with inadequate feedback from consumers before launch. It was panned for being too expensive, too large, and having faulty handwriting recognition. (It still survives because of the efforts of Newton enthusiasts, not Apple.)

Open & Closed Systems Nearly all organizations are, at least to some degree, open systems rather than closed systems. An ***open system* continually interacts with its environment.** A ***closed system* has little interaction with its environment;** that is, it receives very little feedback from the outside. The classical management viewpoint often considered an organization a closed system. So does the management science perspective, which simplifies organizations for purposes of analysis. However, any organization that ignores feedback from the environment opens itself up to possibly spectacular failures.

Open system. Levi's, whose flagship San Francisco store is shown here, confronted sinking sales arising from its closed system of market research. It now is actively trying to be an open-system company. Do you think a company that loses touch with its market can regain it?

The history of management is full of accounts of organizations whose services or products failed because they weren't open enough systems and didn't have sufficient feedback. One of the most famous gaffes was the introduction of the 1959 Edsel by the Ford Motor Co. despite mixed reactions about the car's eccentric styling by customers given a preview look at the vehicle. ●

Example

Open & Closed Systems: The Struggles of Levi's

Are generations really different? However fuzzy the notion of what a "generation" is, we have been accustomed to hearing them labeled: the Baby Boomers (born between 1945 and 1962), then Generation X (born 1963 to 1978), and now Generation Y (born 1979 to 1994). Generation Y—also tagged the Echo Boomers and the Millennium Generation—consists of 60 million people. While this is not as huge as the 72 million Baby Boomers, it is a great deal larger than the 17 million in Gen X, and no marketer can afford to ignore a demographic bulge of this size. But how to discover what's cool and what's not to this generation?

Having grown up with the Internet, Gen Yers are accustomed to high-speed information, research shows, which has made fashions faster changing, with young consumers inclined to switch brand loyalties in a millisecond. So far, however, Tommy Hilfiger has stayed ahead of the style curve. "When Hilfiger's distinctive logo-laden shirts and jackets started showing up on urban rappers in the early '90s," says a *BusinessWeek* account, "the company started sending researchers into music clubs to see how this influential group wore the styles. It bolstered its traditional mass-media ads with unusual promotions. . . . Knowing its customers' passion for computer games, it sponsored a Nintendo competition and installed Nintendo terminals in its stores." By having constant feedback—an open system—with young consumers, Hilfiger was rewarded: Its jeans became the No. 1 brand in this age group.[16] Indeed, designers like Hilfiger, Nike, and DKNY have even refused to crack down on the pirating of their logos for T-shirts and baseball hats in the inner cities in order to maintain the "got to be cool" presence of their brands.[17]

By contrast, Levi Strauss and Co., a veritable icon of Baby Boomer youth, was jolted awake in 1997 when its market share slid, and the company's researchers found the brand was losing popularity among teens. "We all got older, and as a consequence, we lost touch with teenagers," said David Spangler, director of market research. Levi's thereupon opened up its relatively closed system by instituting ongoing teen panels to keep tabs on emerging trends. Generation Y "is a generation that must be reckoned with," said Spangler. "They are going to take over the country."

As Levi's has struggled to regain its luster, it has recently been hit by another threat: private-label jeans, in which retailers like Wal-Mart, Macy's, Target, and JC Penney create brands of their own, cutting out the middleman. Wal-Mart, for instance, introduced an in-house brand, called Metro 7, that competes against Levi's low-priced Signature jeans.

Your Call

Whereas in 1975 private labels and private brands were 25% of the apparel market, by 2010 they are expected to be over 60%. Still, consumers who prefer national brands, such as Levi's, outspend other shoppers by nearly 3 to 1 in department stores.[18] What would you recommend Levi's do to broaden its feedback system and respond to changing business conditions?

2.6 CONTINGENCY VIEWPOINT

> ❌ **major question** In the end, is there one best way to manage in all situations?

THE BIG PICTURE

The second viewpoint in the contemporary perspective, the contingency viewpoint, emphasizes that a manager's approach should vary according to the individual and environmental situation.

The classical viewpoints advanced by Taylor and Fayol assumed that their approaches had universal applications—that they were "the one best way" to manage organizations. The contingency viewpoint began to develop when managers discovered that under some circumstances better results could be achieved by breaking the one-best-way rule.

Example

The Contingency Viewpoint: When Does Using Data-Mining Software to Build Business Make Sense?

Most managers believe that technology increases productivity, a notion that Taylor and the Gilbreths might subscribe to. But does it always? Consider the use of data-mining software to increase business.

Gary Loveman, a former Harvard Business School professor, is now CEO of gambling giant Harrah's Entertainment, which owns or manages 25 casinos. Over the past 6 years, he has helped to build Harrah's into what will soon probably be the world's largest gaming company. He has done this not by courting high rollers, as other gambling casinos do, but by, as one article describes it, "looking for frequent shoppers—the teachers, doctors, and accountants who walk through the doors to play the odds, again and again and again."[19]

The means of building business from this customer base, Loveman explained in a famous paper (and later book), "Diamonds in the Data Mine," was through the use of data-mining software, a computer-assisted process of sifting through and analyzing vast amounts of data in order to extract meaning and discover new knowledge.[20] Loveman identified its best customers through its Total Rewards incentive program and taught them to respond to the casino's marketing efforts in a way that added to their individual value.

But does data mining always boost productivity? New software enables companies to make faster sales by identifying and mining electronic networks of personal contacts. They allow people to get introductions to people they don't know, based on mathematical formulas that analyze tidbits of data in electronic calendars, phone logs, sales records, company databases, and the like.

Such software might seem a beneficial business-networking tool. However, the potential downside, one writer points out, is that a world "in which salespeople are using higher-powered electronic networking tools would inevitably be a world in which more pushy people engage in more intrusive behavior."[21] Such aggressive relationship mining might well backfire by angering and humiliating the very people you are trying to reach. Indeed, this has already happened in pharmaceutical sales, where drug sales representatives have computerized dossiers showing which physicians are prescribing what drugs and used that knowledge to pressure a doctor to write more prescriptions for a brand-name drug or fewer orders for a competitor's drug. Now many doctors are in revolt against this intrusive data gathering and the resulting overzealous sales practices.[22]

Your Call

Should you or should you not adopt data-mining tools in a future business? What would be the answer, according to the contingency viewpoint?

The *contingency viewpoint* emphasizes that a manager's approach should vary according to—that is, be contingent on—the individual and the environmental situation.

A manager subscribing to the Gilbreth approach might try to get workers to build a better mousetrap, say, by simplifying the steps. A manager of the Theory X/Theory Y persuasion might try to use motivational techniques to boost worker productivity. But the manager following the contingency viewpoint would simply ask, "What method is the best to use under these particular circumstances?" ●

Practical Action

Toward a More Open Workplace: Treating Employees Right

Some companies are "toxic organizations," Stanford University business professor Jeffrey Pfeffer's name for firms with high turnover and low productivity. Others take a contingency kind of approach, keeping employees through methods such as "open-book management," *Inc.* magazine editor John Case's term for a company's being completely open with employees about its financial status, projections, costs, expenses, and even salaries.[23]

"Companies that manage people right will outperform companies that don't by 30% to 40%," says Pfeffer. "If you don't believe me, look at the numbers."[24] The author of *The Human Equation: Building Profits by Putting People First,* Pfeffer says that employees' loyalty to employers isn't dead but that toxic companies drive people away.[25] Companies such as Hewlett-Packard, Starbucks, and The Men's Warehouse have had lower turnover—and hence lower replacement and training costs—than their competitors for a reason: They have bent over backward to create workplaces that make people want to stay.

One way of challenging traditional military-style management and empowering employees and increasing earnings is through open-book management. This approach "means training employees in how the company is run," says one account. "It means asking for employee input and acting on it. It means rewarding employees with bonuses when the goals they create are met."[26] By learning the key numbers, employees are able to use their heads instead of just do-

Starbucks. Offering better pay, health insurance, and even stock options, Starbucks' approach to employees results in a turnover rate of only 60%— compared with 140% average for hourly workers in the fast-food business.

ing their jobs and going home. "Whether or not you have equity ownership, open-book management helps employees to feel, think, and act like owners," says Gary T. Brown, director of human resources for Springfield ReManufacturing Corp., a rebuilder of truck engines in Springfield, Missouri.[27] "True open-book management means asking employees what the goals should be."

CompuWorks, a Pittsfield, Massachusetts, computer systems-integration company, cultivates employee loyalty by piling on personal and team recognition, as in giving the Wizard of the Week award to the employee who goes beyond the call of duty. It also operates the Time Bank, into which every month 10 hours of free time is "deposited" for each employee to use as he or she wishes. Employees are trained how to read financial statements and how to chart billable hours and watch cash-flow levels. Regular bonuses are given based on company profits.[28]

Sometimes, despite the mantra that "the customer is always right," companies will even side with employees against clients. For example, The Benjamin Group, a California public relations agency, has fired clients who have been arrogant and hard to work with. This reflects management theories that troublesome customers are often less profitable and less loyal and so aren't worth the extra effort.[29]

All these approaches reflect the application of knowledge derived from management theory and research.[30]

2.7 QUALITY-MANAGEMENT VIEWPOINT

major question Can the quality-management viewpoint offer guidelines for true managerial success?

THE BIG PICTURE

The quality-management viewpoint, the third category under contemporary perspectives, consists of *quality control, quality assurance,* and especially the movement of *total quality management (TQM),* dedicated to continuous quality improvement, training, and customer satisfaction.

During the 1960s and 1970s, word got around among buyers of American cars that one shouldn't buy a "Monday car" or a "Friday car"—cars built on the days when absenteeism and hangovers were highest among dissatisfied autoworkers. The reason, supposedly, was that, despite the efforts of quantitative management, the cars produced on those days were the most shoddily made of what were coming to look like generally shoddy products.

The energy crisis of 1973 showed different possibilities, as Americans began to buy more fuel-efficient cars made in Japan. Consumers found they could not only drive farther on a gallon of gas but that the cars were better made and needed repair less often. Eventually American car manufacturers began to adopt Japanese methods, leading to such slogans as "At Ford, Quality Is Job One." Today the average American car lasts 8 or 9 years compared to 5 or 6 just 20 years ago.[31]

Although not a "theory" as such, the **quality-management viewpoint, which includes quality control, quality assurance, and total quality management,** deserves to be considered because of the impact of this kind of thinking on contemporary management perspectives.

Quality Control & Quality Assurance

Quality **refers to the total ability of a product or service to meet customer needs.** Quality is seen as one of the most important ways of adding value to products and services, thereby distinguishing them from those of competitors. Two traditional strategies for ensuring quality are quality control and quality assurance.

Quality Control *Quality control* **is defined as the strategy for minimizing errors by managing each stage of production.** Quality control techniques were developed in the 1930s at Bell Telephone Labs by **Walter Shewart,** who used statistical sampling to locate errors by testing just some (rather than all) of the items in a particular production run.

Quality Assurance Developed in the 1960s, *quality assurance* **focuses on the performance of workers, urging employees to strive for "zero defects."** Quality assurance has been less successful because often employees have no control over the design of the work process.

Total Quality Management: Creating an Organization Dedicated to Continuous Improvement

In the years after World War II, the imprint "Made in Japan" on a product almost guaranteed that it was cheap and flimsy. That began to change with the arrival in Japan of two Americans, **W. Edwards Deming** and **Joseph M. Juran.**

TQM pioneer. W. Edwards Deming (right), shown with Kenzo Sasaoka, president of Yokogawa Hewlett-Packard, in Japan, 1982.

W. Edwards Deming   Desperate to rebuild its war-devastated economy, Japan eagerly received mathematician W. Edwards Deming's lectures on "good management." Deming believed that quality stemmed from "constancy of purpose"—steady focus on an organization's mission—along with statistical measurement and reduction of variations in production processes. However, he also emphasized the human side, saying that managers should stress teamwork, try to be helpful rather than simply give orders, and make employees feel comfortable about asking questions.

In addition, Deming proposed his so-called 85–15 rule—namely, when things go wrong, there is an 85% chance that the system is at fault, only a 15% chance that the individual worker is at fault. (The "system" would include not only machinery and equipment but also management and rules.) Most of the time, Deming thought, managers erroneously blamed individuals when the failure was really in the system.

Joseph M. Juran   Another pioneer with Deming in Japan's quality revolution was Joseph M. Juran, who defined quality as "fitness for use." By this he meant that a product or service should satisfy a customer's real needs. Thus, the best way to focus a company's efforts, Juran suggested, was to concentrate on the real needs of customers.

TQM: What It Is   From the work of Deming and Juran has come the strategic commitment to quality known as total quality management. ***Total quality management (TQM) is a comprehensive approach—led by top management and supported throughout the organization—dedicated to continuous quality improvement, training, and customer satisfaction.***

The four components of TQM are as follows:

1. **Make continuous improvement a priority.** TQM companies are never satisfied. They make small, incremental improvements an everyday priority in all areas of the organization. By improving everything a little bit of the time all the time, the company can achieve long-term quality, efficiency, and customer satisfaction.

2. **Get every employee involved.** To build teamwork and trust, TQM companies see that every employee is involved in the continuous improvement process. This requires that workers must be trained and empowered to find and solve problems. The goal is to build teamwork, trust, and mutual respect.

3. **Listen to and learn from customers and employees.** TQM companies pay attention to their customers, the people who use their products or services. In addition, employees within the companies listen and learn from other employees, those outside their own work areas.

4. **Use accurate standards to identify and eliminate problems.** TQM organizations are always alert to how competitors do things better, then try to improve on them—a process known as benchmarking. Using these standards, they apply statistical measurements to their own processes to identify problems. ●

2.8 THE LEARNING ORGANIZATION IN AN ERA OF ACCELERATED CHANGE

> ✴ major question — Organizations must learn or perish. How do I build a learning organization?

THE BIG PICTURE

Learning organizations actively create, acquire, and transfer knowledge within themselves and are able to modify their behavior to reflect new knowledge. There are three ways you as a manager can help build a learning organization.

Ultimately, the lesson we need to take from the theories, perspectives, and viewpoints we have described is this: We need to keep on learning. Organizations are the same way: Like people, they must continually learn new things or face obsolescence. A key challenge for managers, therefore, is to establish a culture that will enhance their employees' ability to learn—to build so-called learning organizations.

Learning organizations, says Massachusetts Institute of Technology professor **Peter Senge,** who coined the term, are places "where people continually expand their capacity to create the results they truly desire, where new and expansive patterns of thinking are nurtured, where collective aspiration is set free, and where people are continually learning how to learn together."[32]

The Learning Organization: Handling Knowledge & Modifying Behavior

More formally, a *learning organization* is an organization that actively creates, acquires, and transfers knowledge within itself and is able to modify its behavior to reflect new knowledge.[33] Note the three parts:

1. **Creating and acquiring knowledge.** In learning organizations, managers try to actively infuse their organizations with new ideas and information, which are the prerequisites for learning. They acquire such knowledge by constantly scanning their external environments, by not being afraid to hire new talent and expertise when needed, and by devoting significant resources to training and developing their employees.

2. **Transferring knowledge.** Managers actively work at transferring knowledge throughout the organization, reducing barriers to sharing information and ideas among employees. Electronic Data Systems (EDS), for instance, practically invented the information-technology services industry, but by 1996 it was slipping behind competitors—missing the onset of the Internet wave, for example. When a new CEO, Dick Brown, took the reins in 1999, he changed the culture from "fix the problem yourself" to sharing information internally.[34]

3. **Modifying behavior.** Learning organizations are nothing if not results oriented. Thus, managers encourage employees to use the new knowledge obtained to change their behavior to help further the organization's goals.[35]

Why Organizations Need to Be Learning Organizations: Living with Accelerated Change

Just as you as an individual will have to confront the challenges we mentioned in Chapter 1—globalization, information technology, diversity, and so on—so will organizations. The challenges posed by competition from a globalized marketplace and from the Internet and e-business revolution have led to unprecedented accelerated change, forcing organizations to be faster and more efficient.

Among some of the consequences of this fast-paced world:

1. **The rise of virtual organizations.** "Strip away the highfalutin' talk," says one industry observer, "and at bottom the Internet is a tool that dramatically lowers the cost of communication. That means it can radically alter any industry or activity that depends heavily on the flow of information."[36] One consequence of this is the ***virtual organization, an organization whose members are geographically apart, usually working with e-mail, collaborative computing, and other computer connections,*** while often appearing to customers and others to be a single, unified organization with a real physical location.[37]

2. **The rise of boundaryless organizations.** Computer connections and virtual organization have given rise to the concept of boundaryless organization. The opposite of a bureaucracy, with its numerous barriers and divisions, a ***boundaryless organization* is a fluid, highly adaptive organization whose members, linked by information technology, come together to collaborate on common tasks; the collaborators may include competitors, suppliers, and customers.** This means that the form of the business is ever-changing, and business relationships are informal.[38]

3. **The imperative for speed and innovation.** "Speed is emerging as the ultimate competitive weapon," says a *BusinessWeek* article. "Some of the world's most successful companies are proving to be expert at spotting new opportunities, marshaling their forces, and bringing to market new products or services in a flash. That goes for launching whole new ventures, too."[39] Speed is being driven by a new innovation imperative. "Competition is more intense than ever," the article continues, "because of the rise of the Asian powerhouses and the spread of disruptive new Internet technologies and business models."

4. **The increasing importance of knowledge workers. A *knowledge worker* is someone whose occupation is principally concerned with generating or interpreting information, as opposed to manual labor.** Knowledge workers add value to the organization by using their brains rather than the sweat of their brows, and as such they are the most common type of worker in 21st-century organizations. Because of globalization and information technology, the United States no longer has an advantage in knowledge workers. Indeed, because of the advancement of China, India, Russia, and Brazil; the offshoring of sophisticated jobs; the decrease in math and science skills among today's younger Americans; and other factors, the U.S. may be in danger of slipping behind.

5. **An appreciation for the importance of human capital. *Human capital* is the economic or productive potential of employee knowledge, experience, and actions.**[40] Thinking about people as human capital has an obvious basis: "Attracting, retaining, and developing great people is sometimes the only way our organizations can keep up with the competition across the street or around the globe," says Susan Meisinger, president and CEO of the Society for Human Resource Management. "Research has shown that highly educated, knowledgeable workers—*the most in demand*—are the hardest to find and easiest to lose."[41]

6. **An appreciation for the importance of social capital. *Social capital* is the economic or productive potential of strong, trusting, and cooperative relationships.**[42] Among aspects of social capital are goodwill, mutual respect, cooperation, trust, and teamwork. Relationships within a company are important: In one survey, 77% of the women and 63% of the men rated "good relationship with boss" extremely important, outranking such matters as good equipment, easy commute, and flexible hours.[43]

7. **New emphasis on evidence-based management.** Is it such a radical idea to base decisions on the latest and best knowledge of what actually works? Wouldn't you think this would be the way medicine operates? In fact, say Stanford business scholars Jeffrey Pfeffer and Robert Sutton, most doctors rely on "obsolete knowledge gained in school, long-standing but never proven traditions, patterns gleaned from experience, the methods they believe in and are most skilled in applying, and information from hordes of vendors with products and services."[44] Business decision makers operate much the same way. Challenging this is a push for the use of evidence-based management in business. ***Evidence-based management,* say Pfeffer and Sutton, is based on the belief that "facing the hard facts about what works and what doesn't, understanding the dangerous half-truths that constitute so much conventional wisdom about management, and rejecting the total nonsense that too often passes for sound advice will help organizations perform better."[45]** We continue the discussion about evidence-based management in Chapter 6.

How to Build a Learning Organization: Three Roles Managers Play

To create a learning organization, managers must perform three key functions or roles: (1) *build a commitment to learning,* (2) *work to generate ideas with impact,* and (3) *work to generalize ideas with impact.*[46]

1. **You can build a commitment to learning.** To instill in your employees an intellectual and emotional commitment to the idea of learning, you as a manager need to lead the way by investing in it, publicly promoting it, creating rewards and symbols of it, and performing other similar activities. For example, Mark Pigott, chairman of Piccar, Inc., which makes Kenworth and Peterbilt trucks, accomplished this by looking at other kinds of businesses and learning from their success. By focusing intently on how to improve quality, Paccar can charge up to ten percent more then competitors for its trucks.[47]

2. **You can work to generate ideas with impact.** As a manager, you need to try to generate ideas with impact—that is, ideas that add value for customers, employees, and shareholders—by increasing employee competence through training, experimenting with new ideas, and engaging in other leadership activities.

   Soon after Dick Brown became new CEO of EDS, he saw that the company had to be reinvented as a cool brand to make people feel good about working there. His marketing director decided to launch a new campaign at the biggest media event of all: the Super Bowl. EDS ran an ad showing rugged cowboys riding herd on 10,000 cats. The message: "We ride herd on complexity."

3. **You can work to generalize ideas with impact.** Besides generating ideas with impact, you can also generalize them—that is, reduce the barriers to learning among employees and within your organization. You can create a climate that reduces conflict, increases communication, promotes teamwork, rewards risk taking, reduces the fear of failure, and increases cooperation. In other words, you can create a psychologically safe and comforting environment that increases the sharing of successes, failures, and best practices.

We consider the learning organization again in Chapter 8. ●

key terms used in this chapter

administrative management 44
behavioral science 49
behavioral viewpoint 46
boundaryless organization 6l
classical viewpoint 42
closed system 54
contemporary perspective 4l
contingency viewpoint 57
evidence-based management 62
feedback 53
historical perspective 40
human capital 6l

human relations
  movement 48
inputs 53
knowledge worker 6l
learning organization 60
management science 50
open system 54
operations management 5l
outputs 53
quality 58
quality assurance 58
quality control 58

quality-management
  viewpoint 58
quantitative management 50
scientific management 42
social capital 6l
subsystems 53
system 53
systems viewpoint 53
total quality management
  (TQM) 59
transformation process 53
virtual organization 6l

 summary

2.I Evolving Viewpoints: How We Got to Today's Management Outlook

- Management is an art, but it is also a science. In this chapter we describe two overarching theoretical perspectives on management: (I) The historical perspective includes three viewpoints—classical, behaioral, and quantitative. (2) The contemporary perspective also includes three viewpoints—systems, contingency, and quality-management.

- There are five good reasons for studying theoretical perspectives. They provide (I) an understanding of the present, (2) a guide to action, (3) a source of new ideas, (4) clues to the meaning of your managers' decisions, and (5) clues to the meaning of outside ideas.

2.2 Classical Viewpoint: Scientific & Administrative Management

- The first of the historical perspectives includes the classical viewpoints, which emphasized finding ways to manage work more efficiently. It had two branches, scientific and administrative.

- Scientific management emphasized the scientific study of work methods to improve

productivity of individual workers. It was pioneered by Frederick W. Taylor, who offered four principles of science that could be applied to management, and by Frank and Lillian Gilbreth, who refined motion studies that broke job tasks into physical motions.

- Administrative management was concerned with managing the total organization. Among its pioneers were Henri Fayol, who identified the major functions of management (planning, organizing, leading, and controlling), and Max Weber, who identified five positive bureaucratic features in a well-performing organization.

- The problem with the classical viewpoint is that it is too mechanistic, viewing humans as cogs in a machine.

2.3 Behavioral Viewpoint: Behaviorism, Human Relations, & Behavioral Science

- The second of the historical perspectives, the behavioral viewpoint emphasized the importance of understanding human behavior and of motivating employees toward achievement. It developed over three phases.

Management Theory * CHAPTER 2

- The first phase, early behaviorism, had three pioneers. Hugo Munsterberg suggested that psychologists could contribute to industry by studying jobs, identifying the psychological conditions for employees to do their best work, and devising strategies to influence employees to follow management's interests.

- Mary Parker Follett thought organizations should be democratic, with employees and managers working together.

- Elton Mayo hypothesized a so-called Hawthorne effect, suggesting that employees worked harder if they received added attention from managers.

- The second phase was the human relations movement, which suggested that better human relations could increase worker productivity. It was pioneered by Abraham Maslow, who proposed a hierarchy of human needs (physiological, safety, social, esteem, and self-actualization). Another pioneer was Douglas McGregor, who proposed a Theory X (managers have pessimistic, negative view of workers) versus Theory Y (managers have optimistic, positive view of workers) and suggested that managers could avoid the self-fulfilling prophecy of expecting workers to behave a certain way and then being unsurprised when they acted that way.

- The third phase was the behavioral science approach, which relies on scientific research for developing theories about human behavior that can be used to provide practical tools for managers.

 ### 2.4 Quantitative Viewpoints: Management Science & Operations Research

- The third of the historical perspectives consists of quantitative viewpoints, which emphasized the application to management of quantitative techniques. Two approaches of quantitative management are management science and operations management.

- Management science focuses on using mathematics to aid in problem solving and decision making.

- Operations management focuses on managing the production and delivery of an organization's products or services more effectively.

 ### 2.5 Systems Viewpoint

- We turn from study of the historical management perspectives to the contemporary management perspectives, which include three viewpoints: (1) systems, (2) contingency, and (3) quality-management.

- The systems viewpoint regards the organization as a system of interrelated parts or collection of subsystems that operate together to achieve a common purpose. A system has four parts: inputs, outputs, transformation processes, and feedback. A system can be open, continually interacting with its environment, or closed, having little such interaction.

 ### 2.6 Contingency Viewpoint

- The second viewpoint in the contemporary perspective is the contingency viewpoint, which emphasizes that a manager's approach should vary according to the individual and the environmental situation.

 ### 2.7 Quality-Management Viewpoint

- The third category in the contemporary perspective is the quality-management viewpoint, which includes (1) quality control, (2) quality assurance, and (3) total quality management.

- Quality refers to the total ability of a product or service to meet customer needs. Two traditional strategies for ensuring quality are quality control and quality assurance. Quality control is defined as the strategy for minimizing errors by managing each stage of production. Quality assurance focuses on the performance of workers, urging employees to strive for "zero defects."

- Total quality management (TQM) is a comprehensive approach—led by top management and supported throughout the organization—dedicated to continuous quality improvement, training, and customer satisfaction. The four components of TQM are (1) make continuous improvement a priority, (2) get every employee involved, (3) listen to and learn from customers and employees, and (4) use accurate standards to identify and eliminate problems.

 ### 2.8 The Learning Organization in an Era of Accelerated Change

- A learning organization is an organization that actively creates, acquires, and transfers

- knowledge within itself and is able to modify its behavior to reflect new knowledge.
- Seven reasons why organizations need to become learning organizations are: (1) the rise of virtual organizations, with members connected by electronic networks; (2) the rise of fluid, adaptive boundaryless organizations; (3) the imperative for speed and innovation; (4) the increasing importance of knowledge workers, those principally concerned with generating or interpreting information; (5) an appreciation for the importance of human capital, the economic or productive potential of employees; (6) an appreciation for the importance of social capital, the economic or productive potential of strong and cooperative relationships; and (7) new emphasis on evidence-based management, in which managers face hard facts about what works and what doesn't.
- Three roles that managers must perform to build a learning organization are (1) build a commitment to learning, (2) work to generate ideas with impact, and (3) work to generalize ideas with impact.

 management in action

What Do NASCAR Pit Crews & Intel Employees Have in Common?

What does NASCAR racing have to do with computer chips?

Plenty, it turns out.

Intel Corp. employees in Chandler, Ariz., have been going to pit-stop school to learn how other pros get expensive equipment back on track accurately and in record time.

College graduates used to working in sterile jumpsuits and clean rooms got their hands dirty changing tires and tightening lug nuts under the tutelage of pit-stop experts from North Carolina. . . . The Intel crews might not know yet who NASCAR star Rusty Wallace is, and their racing coaches remain fuzzy about what a semiconductor is, but the lessons learned in the pits are being applied inside Intel's high-tech manufacturing plants.

"We're in a very capital-intensive business," said Steve Megli, co-plant manager of Intel's recently upgraded Fab 12 in Chandler. "So to be competitive, we really have to get the most out of our investment and our tools. And the key to doing that is excellence in maintenance."

Training for more than 1,000 Intel employees started with a quick history of pit stops and how they've improved over the years. Then it was outside to an Intel parking lot converted into pit row, complete with crew suits and kneepads, stacks of tires, lug-nut guns and three mock racecars plastered with Intel logos.

After brief coaching on their assigned tasks, teams of fab workers raced the clock, and, unofficially, each other.

The "jack man" came first, then tire carriers and tire changers, while the "gasman" fueled the car. The clock didn't stop until the last crewmember jumped back over the yellow line. If a tire rolled onto the track or the jack pulled out before a tire was on, a 10-second penalty was added. Video cameras rolled, and each coach took his sweaty crew aside to review the tape and show them where to stand, how to move and how to smooth out the process.

"The smoother you go, the faster you go," Matt Struve of PIT Instruction & Training LLC told his team of rookies. The Intel workers heard variations on that mantra all day, such as "Take your time to speed up" and "Go slow to go fast."

As the crews lined up for the second of their four tries, PIT instructors threw in a virtual monkey wrench: Switch jobs with another crewmember. The tactic is designed to make people realize that even though they have specific jobs, they need to pay attention to what the rest of the team does.

Real pit crews take roughly 13 seconds to get their cars up and running. The fastest Intel crew got it down to 33.4 seconds.

Intel workers then headed inside for a debriefing and to think of ways to apply the experience to their jobs.

It was all part of benchmarking, the practice of finding out how the best performers in other industries do things. Intel is focusing on maintenance because machine breakdowns cost the company time and money in lost production.

The root of quality problems is almost always maintenance, Megli said. Good maintenance also helps the company better predict its output and cycle times, he said.

"People think it's all about speed, but it's not. It's about the process," said Breon Klopp, senior director of development at PIT. "Being fast comes with having lean processes. If you just focus on speed, you wind up with mistakes."

A pit crew knows how long it takes to do each step, and if one step takes longer than it should, the whole process takes longer, he said. Missing one lug nut and going back to tighten it will turn a 13-second pit stop into a 14.3-second one, he said.

And even though pit and chip workers are recruited for very specific skills and positions, it pays to have them know what is going on upstream and downstream, he said.

"There are ways to help the other person with their job so the overall task takes less time," he said.

The Intel crews, for their part, were impressed by how pit crews plan and walk through everything they do, then review their performance after every stop.

Pit crews know each task that needs to be done, how long it takes and how important it is to have the right tools at the ready.

Process engineer Ray Bernal said the experience ought to help Intel.

"It's not working fast, it's working smart," he said. "If you have procedures, things should flow easily."

Intel came out of the week with "pages of 'We need to do this on our next preventative maintenance'," Megli said. Suggestions ran the gamut from better arranging tools and staffing to slowing down to do things right the first time.

For Discussion

1. Is the training program being used at Intel more reflective of managerial art or managerial science? Explain your rationale.
2. To what extent do pit crews use the principles suggested by Frederick Taylor and Frank and Lillian Gilbreth? Discuss.
3. How is Intel using management science and operations management techniques to improve its maintenance function? Explain.
4. Are the recommended changes being made at Intel consistent with suggestions from a quality-management viewpoint and evidence-based management? Explain.
5. Can pit crews really teach technical employees how to improve quality and productivity? Discuss.

Source: Excerpted from Jane Larson, "How Changing a Tire Helps Fix a Computer," *The Arizona Republic*, January 19, 2006, pp. D1, D3. Used by permission.

self-assessment

What Is Your Level of Self-Esteem?

Objectives
1. To get to know yourself a bit better.
2. To help you assess your self-esteem.

Introduction
Self-esteem, confidence, self-worth, and self-belief are all important aspects of being a manager in any organizational structure. However, the need for strong self-esteem is especially vital today because organizations demand that a manager manage people not as appendages of machines (as in Scientific Management) but as individuals who possess skills, knowledge, and self-will. Managers used to operate from a very strong position of centralized power and authority. However, in our modern organizational settings power is shared, and knowledge is to some extent "where you find it." To manage effectively in this situation, managers need strong self-esteem.

Instructions
To assess your self-esteem, answer the following questions. For each item, indicate the extent to which you agree or disagree by using the following scale. Remember, there are no right or wrong answers.

1 = strongly disagree
2 = disagree
3 = neither agree nor disagree
4 = agree
5 = strongly agree

Questions

1. I generally feel as competent as my peers.	1 2 3 4 5
2. I usually feel I can achieve whatever I want.	1 2 3 4 5
3. Whatever happens to me is mostly in my control.	1 2 3 4 5
4. I rarely worry about how things will work out.	1 2 3 4 5
5. I am confident that I can deal with most situations.	1 2 3 4 5
6. I rarely doubt my ability to solve problems.	1 2 3 4 5
7. I rarely feel guilty for asking others to do things.	1 2 3 4 5
8. I am rarely upset by criticism.	1 2 3 4 5
9. Even when I fail, I still do not doubt my basic ability.	1 2 3 4 5
10. I am very optimistic about my future.	1 2 3 4 5
11. I feel that I have quite a lot to offer an employer.	1 2 3 4 5
12. I rarely dwell for very long on personal setbacks.	1 2 3 4 5
13. I am always comfortable in disagreeing with my boss.	1 2 3 4 5
14. I rarely feel that I would like to be somebody else.	1 2 3 4 5

TOTAL SCORE_____

Arbitrary Norms

High Self-esteem = 56–70

Moderate Self-esteem = 29–55

Low Self-esteem = 14–28

Questions for Discussion

1. Do you agree with the assessment? Why or why not?
2. How might you go about improving your self-esteem?
3. Can you survive today without having relatively good confidence in yourself?

 group exercise

Which Are the Best Companies to Work for in the United States & Why?

Objectives

1. To assess your group's awareness of the best companies to work for in the United States in 2006.

2. To discover the different perceptions of these companies and their management practices.

Introduction

For decades *Fortune* has evaluated the 100 best companies to work for in the United States. The 100 best companies are chosen on the basis of aggregating information from three criteria. The first is a subjective assessment of each company's policies and organizational culture. The second is an evaluation of the company based on a 57-item survey given to a random sample of at least 400 employees from each company. The survey assesses topics such as job satisfaction, camaraderie, and attitudes toward management. The third criterion is an evaluation of each company's demographic makeup and pay and benefits. Overall, each company is scored in four areas: "credibility (communication to employees), respect (opportunities and benefits), fairness (compensation, diversity), and pride/camaraderie (philanthropy, celebrations)."[48] In this exercise, you will consider the extent to which the top 10 companies to work for in 2006 possess these characteristics.

Instructions

Four key organizational characteristics are used to rank all companies being considered as the best place to work—about 1,500 companies participated in the ranking process in 2006:

- Credibility
- Respect
- Fairness
- Pride/Camaraderie

Below is a list, in random order, of the top 10 companies to work for in 2006. After forming groups, your first task is to have each individual guess these companies' rankings based on the attributes listed above. (Number 1 is the highest ranking and number 10 the lowest.) If you do not know anything about some of these companies, we suggest that you search the Internet prior to conducting your evaluations. Next, share your rankings and come to a consensus ranking.

Here are the companies, in random order.

1. Vision Service Plan (not-for-profit eye-care insurance company)
2. S. C. Johnson (family-owned consumer products company)
3. Genentech (biotechnology)
4. W. L. Gore & Associates (maker of consumer products like Gore-Tex fabrics, Glide dental floss, Elixir guitar strings)
5. Valero Energy (largest oil refinery in the U.S.)
6. J. M. Smucker (jam and food company)
7. Griffin Hospital (nonprofit acute-care hospital)
8. Container Store (storage retailer)
9. Recreational Equipment (REI) (outdoor products manufacturer and retailer)
10. Wegmans Food Markets (privately held grocery store)

Questions for Discussion

1. How different was the group ranking from the individual rankings? Why do you think this occurred?
2. Why did the group order its ranking in the way that it did?
3. How close was the group ranking to *Fortune's*? See the results listed in the end notes—note 49.
4. Which of these companies would each of you like to work for? Explain your rationale.

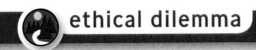
ethical dilemma

Should Medical Devices Be Used as an Aid in Marketing Products?

[Magnetic resonance imaging (MRI)] technology has been used since the 1980s to detect injury or disease in patients suffering from symptoms such as seizures, paralysis, or severe headaches. But in just the past few years, manufacturers have developed stronger MRI magnets and more sophisticated software that can sort through a flood of subtle signals the scans collect.

. . . Imaging technology has leaped far beyond its roots of looking for lumps and shadows. Psychiatrists are now studying the mental activities of patients suffering from depression and other emotional ills. Basic researchers are rolling thousands of healthy subjects . . . into MRI machines in order to explore the very essence of the mind, asking them to think, decide, feel, and learn inside the scanners. Pharma companies hope the new "functional" MRI (fMRI) technology will enhance drug development. Law enforcement experts hope it could become a more accurate lie detector. Even our most private tastes and impulses are under scrutiny as so-called neuromarketing takes off.

. . . Unlike other brain-scanning technologies such as positron emission tomography (PET), which exposes patients to radiation, fMRI simply tracks the response in the brain tissue to magnetic fields. It's noninvasive and believed to be harmless. That means even very young children can be scanned—and scanned repeatedly as they grow older.

. . . One intriguing, yet controversial use of fMRI is probing consumer preferences—a technique sometimes called *neuromarketing*. At California Institute of Technology, researcher Stephen R. Quartz is using fMRI to explore how the brain perceives a cool product vs. an uncool one. Among portable MP3 players, "the [Apple] iPod is by far the market leader. What about that gives us a different signal in the brain?" he asks. Quartz also has formed a company that will offer services to Hollywood studios, imaging the brains of test audiences as they view movie trailers to see which generate the most brain buzz.

Solving the Dilemma

You are part of a committee on medical ethics organized to vote on whether fMRI should be used in capacities other than medicine—i.e., law enforcement and consumer marketing. How would you vote?

1. Absolutely not. It is wrong to use medical technology in any capacity other than healing.
2. Absolutely not. I don't think anyone should be able to peek into my own private thoughts and preferences.
3. Yes, but only if the brain scan data are made public. Such data could be of scientific interest and could be used to combat social issues such as racism and terrorism. This kind of data would also be extremely useful for law enforcement, because it would help determine what really went on in the mind of a criminal.
4. Invent other options. Discuss.

Source: Excerpted from Joan C. O'Hamilton, "Journey to the Center of the Mind: 'Functional' MRI Is Yielding a Clearer Picture of What Thoughts Look Like," *BusinessWeek*, April 19, 2004, pp. 78–80.

video case

Organizational Culture at New Belgium Brewery

In 1991, Jeff Lebesch and his wife, Kim Jordan, began making beer in their home after Lebesch returned to Colorado from a trip to Belgium. Lebesch was impressed with the Belgian brew masters' methods of making beer and wanted to give it a try on his own. Friends, family and local people began praising the beer, and Lebesch and Jordan realized that they needed to grow their fledgling company. They hired a brewer and "the rest is history," as the saying goes. However, as the company expanded, co-owners Lebesch and Jordan felt strongly about the need to engage employees more fully and decided to create an organizational culture based on several fundamental operating principles. First, because Lebesch and Jordan recognized the importance of employees whose work ethic either helped or hurt the bottom line of the company, they decided to make employees co-owners. After one year of service, employees can become owners of the company. Second, they decided to practice "open book management," by allowing employees access to company financial information. Jordan calls it having "financial literacy." By acquiring financial knowledge about the company, employees recognize they have the power to improve company operations and financial earnings, which in turn benefit them directly. Third, New Belgium Brewery has created a departmental organizational structure that is flatter with less bureaucracy, and where employees are considered area leaders. This decentralized structure empowers employees to participate in the decision-making process, to work as a team, and to be held accountable for their successes and failures.

The management approach Lebesch and Jordan decided to take is part of the management-labor changes seen in some companies today. Insightful managers know that employees change jobs frequently today, and that managers do not have all the answers. In fact, employees often have keener insights at the operational level of the company. Finally, by giving employees a greater voice in decision-making and problem-solving processes, they can be held more accountable for their performance. In essence, besides creating a great product, Lebesch and Jordan have developed a real relationship with people through open communication at their Fort Collins, Colorado, brewery.

Questions

1. Discuss how Lebesch and Jordan have integrated total quality management (TQM) into the operations of their company.
2. What are the major management challenges facing Lebesch and Jordan? Discuss them.
3. Why is the organization culture that Lebesch and Jordan created so important in a company like New Belgium Brewery?
4. Do you think that New Belgium Brewery is a learning organization? Why or why not?

Source: Joseph C. Santora, EdD, Essex County College.

chapter 3

The Manager's Changing Work Environment & Ethical Responsibilities

Doing the Right Thing

Major Questions You Should Be Able to Answer

3.1 The Community of Stakeholders Inside the Organization
Major Question: Stockholders are only one group of stakeholders. Who are the stakeholders important to me inside the organization?

3.2 The Community of Stakeholders Outside the Organization
Major Question: Who are stakeholders important to me outside the organization?

3.3 The Ethical Responsibilities Required of You as a Manager
Major Question: What does the successful manager need to know about ethics and values?

3.4 The Social Responsibilities Required of You as a Manager
Major Question: Is being socially responsible really necessary?

3.5 The New Diversified Workforce
Major Question: What trends in workplace diversity should managers be aware of?

In Demand: Problem-Solving, Conscientious Managers Who Can Deal with Change

The world is changing, and changing fast. Thus, the greatest challenge to organizations is finding managers who can manage change. Yet despite great efforts, organizations can't seem to find enough managers and professionals with the qualities they want.

Consider the conclusions of a nationwide study by Caliper, a human-resources consulting firm based in Princeton, New Jersey, as reported by *Fortune* columnist Anne Fisher. It seems, says Fisher, that "people who do the serious hiring in companies these days are desperate—and no, that's not too strong a word—for candidates with two traits: (1) A talent for problem solving. By which they mean: If I give you a Serious Situation to fix, can you figure it out? . . . And (2) conscientiousness. That is, do you know what a deadline is, and will you meet it? . . . Will you try to do a good job even when you're having a bad day?"[1]

Why are these attributes in such demand? Because organizations today are being buffeted by tremendous changes of the sort we describe in this chapter—economic, technological, sociocultural, demographic, political-legal, and international.

How do you achieve and manage success in a workplace being rapidly transformed by change? Here is a new set of ABCs—for accountability, balance, and control:[2]

- **A is for Accountability.** "The job you are doing now might not have even existed six months ago and may be gone again next year," says time management consultant Odette Pollar. Even so, you need to take responsibility and

be accountable for you and your team's performance. The days when you could say "It's not my job" are long gone.

- **B is for Balance.** In many industries, there are managers who work 60 or even 80 hours a week. Pressures to do more, learn more, create more may make you feel you should take your work home with you every evening and weekend instead of using the time to recharge your batteries. But now, more than ever, it's important to maintain balance in your life.

- **C is for Control.** If the work environment keeps changing, you may feel you can't keep up. But there are some things you can control. The way to do so is to distinguish between urgent tasks and important tasks. "Things with deadlines—the ringing phone, a person at your desk with a question—are all urgent," says Pollar. But they may not be important. Important tasks add value and are closely tied to long-term organizational success. It's important to know when to say "No" to distracting activities so that you can say "Yes" to the important work. Otherwise you're not managing change. It's managing you.

For Discussion   How good are you at problem solving and meeting deadlines, as indicated by your schoolwork? Do you think these are indicative of the kind of manager you'll be?

forecast
What's Ahead in This Chapter

This chapter sets the stage for understanding the new world in which managers must operate and the responsibilities they will have. We begin by describing the community of stakeholders that managers have to deal with—first the internal stakeholders (of employees, owners, and directors), then the external stakeholders in two kinds of environments (task and general). We then consider the ethical and social responsibilities required in being a manager, as well as the new diversified workforce and the barriers and approaches to managing diversity.

3.I THE COMMUNITY OF STAKEHOLDERS INSIDE THE ORGANIZATION

✳ major question Stockholders are only one group of stakeholders. Who are stakeholders important to me inside the organization?

THE BIG PICTURE

Managers operate in two organizational environments—internal and external—both made up of stakeholders, the people whose interests are affected by the organization. The first, or internal, environment consists of employees, owners, and the board of directors.

Costco. In the war of big-box stores, is Costco or Wal-Mart better for everyone involved?

Which company is better—Wal-Mart Stores (2 million employees) or rival warehouse club Costco Wholesale (118,000)? Why?

The difference in the way the two companies treat their employees is dramatic. Costco's average pay of $17 an hour is 42% higher than that of Wal-Mart's Sam's Club. At Costco, 96% of eligible workers are covered by company health insurance; at Wal-Mart, it is 44%. Wal-Mart employees in California have been found to be 40% more likely to use public assistance and welfare programs than comparable employees of other big-box stores. Wal-Mart's low-wage policy has forced rivals, such as Safeway, to reduce benefits for their workers. Costco's wages have enabled its employees to buy homes and take vacation trips. Finally, Wal-Mart has reportedly locked out workers overnight, hired illegal immigrants to mop its floors, and was slapped with a big discrimination suit.[3]

Yet *Fortune* named Wal-Mart the number one Most Admired company for 2003 and 2004. Is this because its low prices probably save consumers $20 billion a year? Because it generates 3.5 cents for each dollar on sales compared with Costco's 1.7 cents?

"Where you stand on Wal-Mart," says one account, "seems to depend on where you sit. If you're a consumer, Wal-Mart is good for you. If you're a wage earner, there's a good chance it's bad. If you're a Wal-Mart shareholder, you want the company to grow. If you're a citizen, you probably don't want it growing in your backyard."[4]

How you feel about Costco may also vary with where you sit. "From the perspective of investors," says one stock analyst, "Costco's benefits are overly generous. Public companies need to care for shareholders first." Responds Costco president and chief executive Jim Sinegal, "I happen to believe that in order to reward the shareholder in the long term, you have to please your customers and workers."[5]

The differences may be seen in annual employee turnover—50% for Wal-Mart, 24% for Costco. It's been calculated that a 10% reduction in employee turnover can yield a 20% savings on labor costs. Thus, whereas Wal-Mart's labor costs amount to 12% of its annual sales, Costco's are only 7%. On a per-store basis, Wal-Mart's Sam's Club generates only half the sales of the average Costco store (in part because Costco attracts higher-income shoppers and because it charges a yearly membership fee, spending no money on advertising). Still, the more favorable employee benefits lead to a less favorable stock price for Costco compared with Wal-Mart.

Which should a company favor, its employees or its owners (stockholders)? Henry Ford, founder of Ford Motor Co., thought he could serve both. In 1914, he announced workers in his factories would receive $5 a day—a major boost over then-prevailing wages. The reason: He recognized that his promise to build a car affordable to the masses would be hypocritical if he didn't pay his own workers enough to buy it themselves.[6]

Internal & External Stakeholders

Should a company be principally responsible to just its stockholders? Perhaps we need a broader term to indicate all those with a stake in an organization. That term, appropriately, is *stakeholders*—**the people whose interests are affected by an organization's activities.**

Managers operate in two organizational environments, both made up of various stakeholders. *(See Figure 3.1.)* As we describe in the rest of this section, the two environments are these:

- Internal stakeholders
- External stakeholders

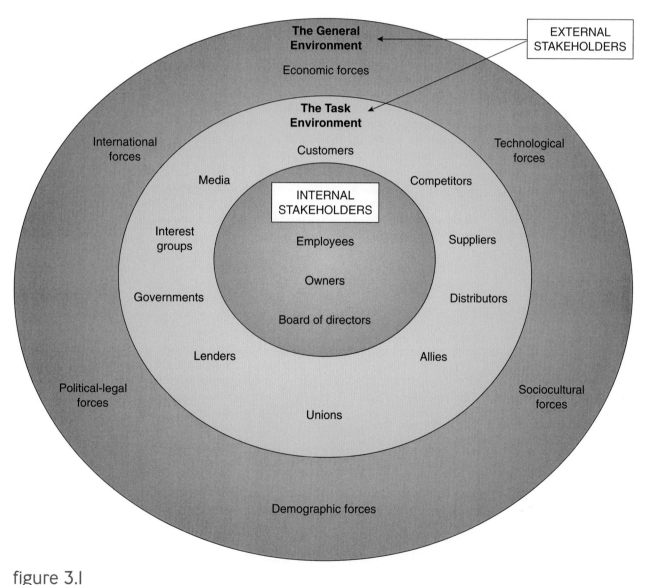

figure 3.1

THE ORGANIZATION'S ENVIRONMENT

The two main groups are internal and external stakeholders

Internal Stakeholders

Whether small or large, the organization to which you belong has people in it that have an important stake in how it performs. These *internal stakeholders* **consist of employees, owners, and the board of directors, if any.** Let us consider each in turn.

Employees   As a manager, could you run your part of the organization if you and your employees were constantly in conflict? Labor history, of course, is full of accounts of just that. But such conflict may lower the performance of the organization, thereby hurting everyone's stake. In many of today's forward-looking organizations, employees are considered "the talent"—the most important resource.

For instance, at Trilogy Software in Austin, Texas, workers aren't really considered "employees." "They're all shareholders," says former U.S. Labor Secretary Robert Reich in an article about cutting-edge kinds of companies. "They're all managers. They're all partners. That's how [Joe] Liemandt, Trilogy's CEO, has chosen to run his company—and that's what makes it successful."[7]

Owners   The *owners* of an organization consist of all those who can claim it as their legal property, such as Wal-Mart's stockholders. In the for-profit world, if you're running a one-person graphic design firm, the owner is just you—you're what is known as a sole proprietorship. If you're in an Internet startup with your brother-in-law, you're both owners—you're a partnership. If you're a member of a family running a car dealership, you're all owners—you're investors in a privately owned company. If you work for a company that is more than half owned by its employees (such as Food Giant, United Airlines, or W. L. Gore Associates, maker of Gore-Tex fabric), you are one of the joint owners—you're part of an Employee Stock Ownership Plan (ESOP).[8] And if you've bought a few shares of stock in a company whose shares are listed for sale on the New York Stock Exchange, such as General Motors, you're one of thousands of owners—you're a stockholder. In all these examples, of course, the goal of the owners is to make a profit.

Employee ownership. Zachary's Chicago Pizza, based in Oakland, California, uses a device known as an Employee Stock Ownership Plan, in which employees buy company stock in order to become owners. Although the idea was conceived over 50 years ago, there are only about 11,500 ESOPs today out of hundreds of thousands of businesses. Why do you suppose more companies aren't owned by their employees?

Board of Directors   Who hires the chief executive of a for-profit or nonprofit organization? In a corporation, it is the *board of directors,* whose members are elected by the stockholders to see that the company is being run according to their interests. In nonprofit organizations, such as universities or hospitals, the board may be called the *board of trustees* or *board of regents.* Board members are very important in setting the organization's overall strategic goals and in approving the major decisions and salaries of top management.

Not all firms have a board of directors. A lawyer, for instance, may operate as a sole proprietor, making all her own decisions. A large corporation might have eight or so members on its board of directors. Some of these directors (inside directors) may be top executives of the firm. The rest (outside directors) are elected from outside the firm. ●

"It's a Career, Not a Job": The Different Career Paths

As a manager, it's not enough that you be aware of all the changing trends and responsibilities in the workplace. You also need to have a sense of where you're going.

No doubt what you're looking for is something about which you can say "It's not just a job, it's a career," as the slogan goes. Your *career path* is the sequence of jobs and occupations you follow during your career.

Michael J. Driver has suggested there are different possible career paths, among them the *linear career,* the *steady-state career,* and the *spiral career.*[9]

The Linear Career: Climbing the Stairs

The *linear career* resembles the traditional view of climbing the stairs in an organization's hierarchy. That is, you move up the organization in a series of jobs—generally in just one functional area, such as finance—each of which entails more responsibility and requires more skills.

The legendary Roberto C. Goizueta of Coca-Cola Co., who started out as a chemist with a Havana-based Coke subsidiary, spent his entire career with the company, rising through the technical side before he became chairman and CEO. Some top executives may change companies during their ascent, as Lee Iaccoca did from Ford to Chrysler, but their careers are still always upwardly mobile—that is, linear.

Of course, it's possible that a linear career will *plateau.* That is, you'll rise to a certain level and then remain there; there will be no further promotions. Career plateaus actually happen a lot and need not signify disgrace, since they happen even to very successful managers. After all, the higher you get in the hierarchy, the fewer the managerial positions above you and the more intense the competition for them.

Another possibility, of course, is the *declining career,* in which a person reaches a certain level and then after a time begins descending back to the lower levels. This could come about, for instance, because technology changes the industry you're in and you're not willing or able to learn the necessary new skills. It can also happen because people

have addiction problems, for example, causing them to take their eye off the career ball. Or they are victims of age, gender, or racial discrimination.

The Steady-State Career: Staying Put

The *steady-state career* is almost the opposite of a linear career: you discover early in life that you're comfortable with a certain occupation and you stay with it. Or you accept a promotion for a while, decide you don't like the responsibility, and take a step down.

This kind of career is actually fairly commonplace: sales representatives, computer programmers, graphic artists, accountants, insurance agents, or physicians, for example, may decide they are perfectly happy being "hands-on" professionals rather than managers.

The Spiral Career: Holding Different Jobs That Build on One Another

The *spiral career* is, like the linear career, upwardly mobile. However, on this career path, you would have a number of jobs that are fundamentally different yet still build on one another, giving you more general experience and the skills to advance in rank and status. Nowadays this route may actually give you a better chance of reaching the top than the linear career because it provides such a broad base of experience.

For example, an engineer might start out in a company's research and development department, then become a product manager in the marketing department, then move into sales, all the while gradually moving up the organization chart.

Of course, it's possible that you might (like some salespeople, actors, chefs, or construction workers) favor a variant called the *transitory career.* That is, you're the kind of person who doesn't want the responsibility that comes with promotion. You're a free spirit who likes the variety of experience that comes with continually shifting sideways from job to job or place to place (or you're afraid of making the commitment to doing any one thing).

3.2 THE COMMUNITY OF STAKEHOLDERS OUTSIDE THE ORGANIZATION

> **✳ major question** Who are stakeholders important to me outside the organization?

THE BIG PICTURE

The external environment of stakeholders consists of the task environment and the general environment. The task environment consists of customers, competitors, suppliers, distributors, strategic allies, employee associations, local communities, financial institutions, government regulators, special-interest groups, and the mass media. The general environment consists of economic, technological, sociocultural, demographic, political-legal, and international forces.

In the first section we described the environment inside the organization. Here let's consider the environment outside it, which consists of *external stakeholders*—**people or groups in the organization's external environment that are affected by it.** This environment consists of:

- The task environment.
- The general environment.

The Task Environment

The *task environment* **consists of 11 groups that present you with daily tasks to handle: customers, competitors, suppliers, distributors, strategic allies, employee organizations, local communities, financial institutions, government regulators, special-interest groups, and mass media.**

Example

Taking Care of Customers: L.L. Bean's No Questions Asked

Only a handful of companies stand by their products for a lifetime—Parker Pens, Williams-Sonoma cookware, Zippo cigarette lighters, for example. For more than 90 years, L.L. Bean, the Freeport, Maine, mail-order seller of clothing and outdoor gear, has had an unconditional guarantee that it will give a replacement, refund, or charge credit and even pay shipping on a Bean product if a customer is dissatisfied with it—no matter when it was bought. No proof of purchase is required. No product defect need be cited. Even 30-year-old worn-out hiking boots can be exchanged.

Why don't more companies have such lifetime warranties or total-satisfaction guarantees? "Companies are worried about customers cheating them," says one writer. "That's nonsense. People cheat bad companies, because they think the companies have cheated them. Nobody cheats top companies."[10]

Your Call

Do you agree with this opinion— that people cheat only bad companies? What would you do to try to generate lifetime goodwill among customers?

1. Customers The first law of business, we've said, is *take care of the customer.* **Customers are those who pay to use an organization's goods or services.** Customers may be the focus not only of for-profit organizations but also non-profit ones. A 1998 survey found that, with crime rates falling, police forces scored the biggest 4-year gain in customer (citizen) satisfaction of all industries and services.[11]

2. Competitors Is there any line of work you could enter in which there would *not* be *competitors*—**people or organizations that compete for customers or resources,** such as talented employees or raw materials? Every organization has to be actively aware of its competitors. Florist shops and delicatessens must be aware that customers can buy the same products at Safeway or Kroger.

Take care of the customer. Apple manufactures and sells its personal computers not only over the Internet but also through its own stores. Does doing so give the company a competitive advantage over Internet sellers of PCs, such as Dell?

3. Suppliers A *supplier* is a person or an organization that provides supplies—that is, raw materials, services, equipment, labor, or energy—to other organizations. Suppliers in turn have their own suppliers: the publisher of this book buys the paper on which it is printed from a paper merchant, who in turn is supplied by several paper mills, who in turn are supplied wood for wood pulp by logging companies with forests in the United States or Canada.

4. Distributors A *distributor* is a person or an organization that helps another organization sell its goods and services to customers. Publishers of magazines, for instance, don't sell directly to newsstands; rather, they go through a distributor, or wholesaler. Tickets to Green Day, Evanescence, or other artists' performances might be sold to you directly by the concert hall, but they are also sold through such distributors as TicketMaster, Tower Records, and Blockbuster Video.

Distributors can be quite important because in some industries (such as movie theaters and magazines) there is not a lot of competition, and the distributor has a lot of power over the ultimate price of the product. However, the rise in popularity of the Internet has allowed manufacturers of personal computers, for example, to cut out the "middleman"—the distributor—and to sell to customers directly.

5. Strategic Allies Companies, and even nonprofit organizations, frequently link up with other organizations (even competing ones) in order to realize strategic advantages. The term *strategic allies* **describes the relationship of two organizations who join forces to achieve advantages neither can perform as well alone.**

In 2006, several major banks, normally fierce competitors, joined together to try to prevent federal regulators from granting Wal-Mart a charter to expand its empire into the consumer banking business.[12] In another example of strategic alliances, Wal-Mart itself in 2006 announced an effort to support its small business rivals—including the hardware stores, dress shops, and bakeries with which it competes—with training, financial grants, and free advertising in urban neighborhoods into which the giant discounter was planning to expand.[13]

6. Employee Organizations: Unions & Associations As a rule of thumb, labor unions (such as the United Auto Workers or the Teamsters Union) tend to represent hourly workers; professional associations (such as the National Education

Association or the Newspaper Guild) tend to represent salaried workers. Nevertheless, during a labor dispute, the salary-earning reporters in the Newspaper Guild might well picket in sympathy with the wage-earning circulation-truck drivers in the Teamsters Union.

In recent years, the percentage of the labor force represented by unions has steadily declined (from 35% in the 1950s to 12.5% in 2005).[14] Moreover, union agendas have changed. Strikes and violence are pretty much out. Benefits, stock ownership, and campaigns for "living-wage" ordinances are in.[15]

7. Local Communities

Local communities are obviously important stakeholders, as becomes evident not only when a big organization arrives but also when it leaves, sending government officials scrambling to find new industry to replace it. Schools and municipal governments rely on the organization for their tax base. Families and merchants depend on its employee payroll for their livelihoods. In addition, everyone from the United Way to the Little League may rely on it for some financial support.[16]

Anderson, Indiana, once had so many General Motors (GM) manufacturing plants that it had to stagger work schedules so that the streets would not be jammed with cars when the workday ended. Today there is not a single GM plant left, only two parts plants that the automaker once owned still survive, and Anderson's population has dropped from 70,000 to 58,000 people. Even so, the town is still dependent on GM. About 10,000 GM retirees plus surviving spouses and other family members receive health and pension checks, which in turn support local restaurants, shopping centers, doctors' offices, and hospitals.

For Anderson's mayor, Kevin Smith, the dependence on retiree income is a major concern. "We realize those retiree pensions will not be here in the coming years," he said. "That's why it's important that we are involved in new job creation that will employ the younger people now, too, and keep them in our community."[17]

While industrial states like Indiana and Michigan continue to lose manufacturing jobs as U.S. automakers struggle to survive, other towns, particularly in the South, are benefiting from Asian and European auto companies looking for skilled workers. For example, Osceola, Arkansas, a town of 9,000 on the west bank of the Mississippi, induced Denso Corp., an affiliate of Toyota Motor Corp., to locate a new plant in town for producing air-conditioning and heating systems. Denso was particularly persuaded by Osceola's efforts to improve local education by creating a charter school. "We got the strong feeling that in Osceola education was being integrated with industry," says Denso plant manager Jerry McGuire.[18]

8. Financial Institutions

Want to launch a small start-up company? As Visa, MasterCard, and Discover continue to flood mailboxes with credit-card offers, some entrepreneurs have found it convenient to use multiple cards to fund new enterprises. Joe Liemandt of Trilogy Software charged up 22 cards to finance his startup.

Established companies also often need loans to tide them over when revenues are down or to finance expansion, but they rely for assistance on lenders such as commercial banks, investment banks, and insurance companies.

Government as stakeholder. Santa Fe, New Mexico, which depends largely on state government and tourism, is an expensive place to live. To help lower-paid workers, the city council voted to raise the minimum wage to $9.50 an hour, but some small business owners believe that's too high. In what ways does your local government affect business in your area?

9. Government Regulators The preceding groups are external stakeholders in your organization since they are clearly affected by its activities. But why would *government regulators—***regulatory agencies that establish ground rules under which organizations may operate***—be considered stakeholders?

We are talking here about an alphabet soup of agencies, boards, and commissions that have the legal authority to prescribe or proscribe the conditions under which you may conduct business. To these may be added local and state regulators on the one hand and foreign governments and international agencies (such as the World Trade Organization, which oversees international trade and standardization efforts) on the other.

Such government regulators can be said to be stakeholders because not only do they affect the activities of your organization, they are in turn affected by it. The Federal Aviation Agency (FAA), for example, specifies how far planes must stay apart to prevent midair collisions. But when the airlines want to add more flights on certain routes, the FAA may have to add more flight controllers and radar equipment, since those are the agency's responsibility.

10. Special-Interest Groups "The Gap, a San Francisco-based national clothing chain, was slammed with high-profile demonstrations on Saturday by activists protesting its labor policies in the Mariana Islands . . . ," read the newspaper account.[19] Any organization can become the target of a special-interest group, as The Gap was by an outfit called Global Exchange, which denounced the chain's use of below-minimum-wage labor (so-called sweatshop labor) in its factory on Saipan, which is U.S. territory.

Special-interest groups **are groups whose members try to influence specific issues,** some of which may affect your organization. Examples are Mothers Against Drunk Driving, the National Organization for Women, and the National Rifle Association. Special-interest groups may try to exert political influence, as in contributing funds to lawmakers' election campaigns or in launching letter-writing efforts to officials. Or they may organize picketing and *boycotts*—holding back their patronage—of certain companies, as some African American groups did in recent years to protest reports of racism at Texaco and at Denny's restaurants.[20]

11. Mass Media On March 24, 1989, when the tanker *Exxon Valdez* ran aground in Prince William Sound, it dumped 11 million gallons of North Slope crude oil into the water, blackening 1,500 miles of magnificent Gulf of Alaska coastline. This was not only one of the nation's worst environmental disasters, but for the Exxon Corporation it was also the start of a gigantic public-relations nightmare that never seemed to end. Even 17 years later, the news media were running prominent stories on the effects of the incident, once again bringing it to public attention.[21]

Exxon's troubles were not the fault of the press. But no manager can afford to ignore the power of the mass media—print, radio, TV, and the Internet—to rapidly and widely disseminate news both bad and good. Thus, most companies, universities, hospitals, and even government agencies have a public-relations person or department to communicate effectively with the press. In addition, top-level executives often receive special instruction on how to best deal with the media.

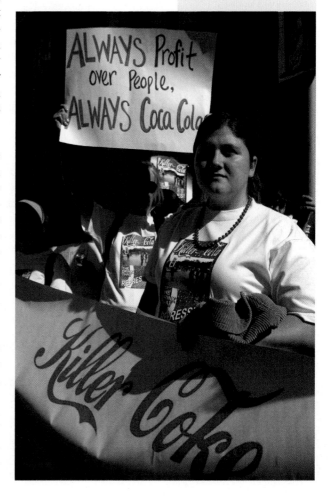

Special interests. Michigan State University students protest Coca-Cola Company's alleged practices of anti-union violence at plants in Colombia and damage to the environment in India. Protestors and special-interest groups are among the external stakeholders affecting businesses that managers must consider as they make decisions.

The General Environment

Beyond the task environment is the ***general environment,*** or ***macroenvironment,*** which includes six forces: economic, technological, sociocultural, demographic, political-legal, and international.

You may be able to control some forces in the task environment, but you can't control those in the general environment. Nevertheless, they can profoundly affect your organization's task environment without your knowing it, springing nasty surprises on you. Clearly, then, as a manager you need to keep your eye on the far horizon because these forces of the general environment can affect long-term plans and decisions.

I. Economic Forces *Economic forces* **consist of the general economic conditions and trends—unemployment, inflation, interest rates, economic growth—that may affect an organization's performance.** These are forces in your nation and region and even the world over which you and your organization probably have no control.

Are banks' interest rates going up in the United States? Then it will cost you more to borrow money to open new stores or build new plants. Is your region's unemployment rate rising? Then maybe you'll have more job applicants to hire from, yet you'll also have fewer customers with money to spend. Are natural resources getting scarce in an important area of supply? Then your company will need to pay more for them or switch to alternative sources.

One indicator that managers often pay attention to is productivity growth. Rising productivity leads to rising profits, lower inflation, and higher stock prices. In recent times, companies have been using information technology to cut costs, resulting in productivity growing at an annual rate of 3–3.5%, rather than the expected 2–2.5%.[22]

2. Technological Forces *Technological forces* **are new developments in methods for transforming resources into goods or services.** For example, think what the U.S. would have been like if the elevator, air-conditioning, the combustion engine, and the airplane had not been invented. No doubt changes in computer and communications technology—especially the influence of the Internet—will continue to be powerful technological forces during your managerial career. But other technological currents may affect you as well.

Socio-carbo forces. The meat industry was looking at a product glut in mid-2006 following the decline in popularity of the Atkins and other low-carb diets, which had driven up beef prices while they were still in vogue. What other food industries can you think of that are currently affected by sociocultural forces?

For example, biotechnology may well turn health and medicine upside down in the coming decades. Researchers can already clone animals, and some reports say they are close to doing the same with humans.

3. Sociocultural Forces "I have one client who has tattoos of all kinds of stuff on her body," says Doug, owner of Doug's Tattoos in Oakland, California. "There's no theme to it. She has favorite cartoon names, her children's and grandchildren's names— just anything she likes at the time."[23]

Some day, of course, our descendants will view these customs as old-fogyish and quaint. That's how it is with sociocultural changes. *Sociocultural forces* **are influences and trends originating in a country's, a society's, or a culture's human relationships and values that may affect an organization.**

Entire industries have been rocked when the culture underwent a lifestyle change that affected their product or service. The interest in health and fitness, for instance, led to a decline in sales of cigarettes, whiskey, red meat, and eggs. And it led to a boost in sales of athletic shoes, spandex clothing, and Nautilus and other exercise machines. Low-carbohydrate, high-protein diets like the Atkins and the South Beach diets triggered a rise in chicken, pork, and beef sales, but then led to an oversupply and consequent dip in prices as consumers turned to a more balanced eating approach.[24]

4. Demographic Forces *Demographics* derives from the ancient Greek word for "people"—*demos*—and deals with statistics relating to human populations. Age, gender, race, sexual orientation, occupation, income, family size, and the like are known as demographic characteristics when they are used to express measurements of certain groups. ***Demographic forces* are influences on an organization arising from changes in the characteristics of a population, such as age, gender, or ethnic origin.** In the United States, for instance, more women and minorities continue to join the workforce, making it more diverse.

A dozen years ago, for instance, the part of South-Central Los Angeles that experienced urban riots (following the acquittal of four white cops in the beating of black motorist Rodney King) was dominated by African Americans. Today nearly two thirds of South-Central is Hispanic, with many recent immigrants from Mexico and Central America. The area also is the first rung on the ladder of success for immigrants from Russia, Korea, China, Thailand, Israel, Iran, Italy, and Jamaica.[25]

5. Political-Legal Forces ***Political-legal forces* are changes in the way politics shape laws and laws shape the opportunities for and threats to an organization.** In the United States, whatever political view tends to be dominant at the moment may be reflected in how the government handles antitrust issues, in which one company tends to monopolize a particular industry. Should Microsoft, for instance, be allowed to dominate the market for personal-computer operating systems?

As for legal forces, some countries have more fully developed legal systems than others. And some countries have more lawyers per capita. (The United States has an estimated 25% of the world's lawyers, according to University of Wisconsin law professor Marc Galanter—not the 70% figure repeated for years by some conservative political figures.)[26] American companies may be more willing to use the legal system to advance their interests, as in suing competitors to gain competitive advantage. But they must also watch that others don't do the same to them.

6. International Forces ***International forces* are changes in the economic, political, legal, and technological global system that may affect an organization.**

This category represents a huge grab bag of influences. How does the economic integration of the European Union create threats and opportunities for American companies? U.S. companies that do significant business in Europe are subject to regulation by the European Union (EU). In 2004, for instance, the EU ruled that Microsoft Corp. had abusively wielded its Windows software monopoly and ordered it to produce a version of Windows without Microsoft's own digital media player included. Microsoft supporters complained that the ruling stepped on U.S. turf and interfered with a successful American industry.[27] We consider global concerns in Chapter 4.

How well Americans can handle international forces depends a lot on their training. The American Council on Education says there is a "dangerous" shortage of experts in non-European cultures and languages. The council urges that schools teach a wider variety of languages and that instruction begin as early as kindergarten, since waiting until students are in college to begin instruction in more obscure languages hinders their ability to become fluent speakers.[28] ●

3.3 THE ETHICAL RESPONSIBILITIES REQUIRED OF YOU AS A MANAGER

> ❖ **major question** What does the successful manager need to know about ethics and values?

THE BIG PICTURE
Managers need to be aware of what constitutes ethics, values, the four approaches to ethical dilemmas, and how organizations can promote ethics.

"It's a tough issue, choosing between being a law-abiding person and losing your job," says lawyer Gloria Allred, who represented a woman fired for complaining about running her boss's office football pool.[29] Imagine having to choose between *economic performance* and *social performance,* which in business is what most ethical conflicts are about.[30] This is known as an ***ethical dilemma,*** **a situation in which you have to decide whether to pursue a course of action that may benefit you or your organization but that is unethical or even illegal.**

Defining Ethics & Values

Most of us assume we know what "ethics" and "values" mean, but do we? Let's consider them.

Ethics *Ethics* **are the standards of right and wrong that influence behavior. These standards may vary among countries and among cultures.** ***Ethical behavior*** **is behavior that is accepted as "right" as opposed to "wrong" according to those standards.**

What are the differences among a tip, a gratuity, a gift, a donation, a commission, a consulting fee, a kickback, a bribe? Regardless of the amount of money involved, each one may be intended to reward the recipient for providing you with better service, either anticipated or performed. What should be the expectations of a medical society that accepts $700,000 from three pharmaceutical companies to be used for dinner lectures to brief doctors on the latest news about high blood pressure? What if the main point of these briefings is to expand the concept of high blood pressure, increasing the pool of people taking blood-pressure medications?[31]

Higher self. If you worked for a drug company, would you think it's acceptable to give a medical society several thousand dollars to use on dinner lectures to inform doctors about high blood pressure and how your company's products can treat the condition? Would your perspective change if you were a patient with high blood pressure?

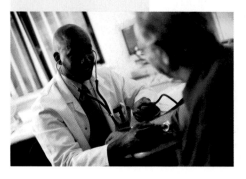

Values Ethical dilemmas often take place because of an organization's ***value system,*** **the pattern of values within an organization.** ***Values*** **are the relatively permanent and deeply held underlying beliefs and attitudes that help determine a person's behavior,** such as the belief that "Fairness means hiring according to ability, not family background." Values and value systems are the underpinnings for ethics and ethical behavior.

Organizations may have two important value systems that can conflict: (1) the value system stressing financial performance versus (2) the value system stressing cohesion and solidarity in employee relationships.[32]

Four Approaches to Deciding Ethical Dilemmas

How do alternative values guide people's decisions about ethical behavior? Here are four approaches, which may be taken as guidelines:

1. The Utilitarian Approach: For the Greatest Good   Ethical behavior in the *utilitarian approach* **is guided by what will result in the greatest good for the greatest number of people.** Managers often take the utilitarian approach, using financial performance—such as efficiency and profit—as the best definition of what constitutes "the greatest good for the greatest number."[33]

Thus, a utilitarian "cost-benefit" analysis might show that in the short run the firing of thousands of employees may improve a company's bottom line and provide immediate benefits for the stockholders. The drawback of this approach, however, is that it may result in damage to workforce morale and the loss of employees with experience and skills—actions not so readily measurable in dollars.

2. The Individual Approach: For Your Greatest Self-Interest Long Term, Which Will Help Others   Ethical behavior in the *individual approach* **is guided by what will result in the individual's best *long-term* interests, which ultimately are in everyone's self-interest.** The assumption here is that you will act ethically in the short run to avoid others harming you in the long run.

The flaw here, however, is that one person's short-term self-gain may *not,* in fact, be good for everyone in the long term. After all, the manager of an agribusiness that puts chemical fertilizers on the crops every year will always benefit, but the fishing industries downstream could ultimately suffer if chemical runoff reduces the number of fish. Indeed, this is one reason why Puget Sound Chinook, or king salmon, are now threatened with extinction in the Pacific Northwest.[34]

3. The Moral-Rights Approach: Respecting Fundamental Rights Shared by Everyone   Ethical behavior in the *moral-rights approach* **is guided by respect for the fundamental rights of human beings,** such as those expressed in the U.S. Constitution's Bill of Rights. We would all tend to agree that denying people the right to life, liberty, privacy, health and safety, and due process is unethical. Thus, most of us would have no difficulty condemning the situation of immigrants illegally brought into the United States and then effectively enslaved—as when made to work 7 days a week as maids.

The difficulty, however, is when rights are in conflict, such as employer and employee rights. Should employees on the job have a guarantee of privacy? Actually, it is legal for employers to listen to business phone calls and monitor all nonspoken personal communications.[35]

4. The Justice Approach: Respecting Impartial Standards of Fairness   Ethical behavior in the *justice approach* **is guided by respect for impartial standards of fairness and equity.** One consideration here is whether an organization's policies—such as those governing promotions or sexual harassment cases—are administered impartially and fairly regardless of gender, age, sexual orientation, and the like.

Fairness can often be a hot issue. For instance, many employees are loudly resentful when a corporation's CEO is paid a salary and bonuses worth hundreds of times more than what they receive—even when the company performs poorly—and when fired is then given a "golden parachute," or extravagant package of separation pay and benefits.

Enron, SarbOx, & Ethical Training

Their names have been repeatedly carved in headlines from 2001 on. Here's Dennis Kozlowski, former CEO of manufacturing conglomerate Tyco International, now serving time for grand larceny, conspiracy, securities fraud, and falsifying business records associated with looting $600 million to finance a lavish lifestyle. There's Bernard Ebbers, former head of WorldCom, currently free while his nine-count guilty verdict of conspiracy, securities fraud, and filing false reports with regulators is on appeal. Eighty-year-old John Rigas, former chair and CEO of Adelphia, is also free pending appeal after being found guilty of 18 counts of conspiracy and securities and bank fraud. Bringing up the rear is Jeffrey Skilling, former CEO for Enron, the Houston-based energy giant, found guilty for many similar kinds of crimes, facing a sentence of two to three more lifetimes in prison.[36]

Was this frenzy of white-collar crime an anomaly over which we can now breathe a sigh of relief? Unfortunately, probably not. Still, there is now a great deal more public and corporate awareness.

Public Outrage & the Sarbanes–Oxley Reform Act   The various forms of deceit practiced by top-level managers generated a great deal of public outrage, not only among the employees and shareholders who suffered great harm (most Enron workers and investors, for example, lost everything) but also among federal regulators and politicians. As a result, Congress passed the ***Sarbanes–Oxley Act of 2002,* often shortened to *SarbOx* or *SOX,* which establishes requirements for proper financial record keeping for public companies and penalties for noncompliance.**

Administered by the Securities and Exchange Commission, SarbOx requires a company's chief executive officer and chief financial officer to personally certify the organization's financial reports, prohibits them from taking personal loans or lines of credit, and makes them reimburse the organization for bonuses and stock options when required by restatement of corporate profits. It also requires the company to have established procedures and guidelines for audit committees. Penalties can be as much as 25 years in prison.[37]

How Do People Learn Ethics? Kohlberg's Theories   American business history is permeated with occasional corporate scandals, from railroad tycoons trying to corner the gold market (the 1872 Credit Mobilier scandal) to style mavens found to be lying to the government (Martha Stewart in 2004). Legislation such as SarbOx can't head off all such behavior. No wonder that now many colleges and universities have required more education in ethics.

"Schools bear some responsibility for the behavior of executives," says Fred J. Evans, dean of the College of Business and Economics at California State University at Northridge. "If you're making systematic errors in the [business] world, you have to go back to the schools and ask, 'What are you teaching?'"[38] There may be a ways to go, however: A 2006 survey of 50,000 undergraduates found that 26% of business majors admitted to serious cheating on exams, and 54% admitted to cheating on written assignments.[39]

Of course, most students' levels of moral development are established by personalities and upbringing long before they get to college, with some being more advanced than others. One psychologist, **Laurence Kohlberg,** has proposed three levels of personal moral development—preconventional, conventional, and postconventional.[40]

- **Level 1, preconventional—follows rules.** People who have achieved this level tend to follow rules and to obey authority to avoid unpleasant consequences. Managers of the Level 1 sort tend to be autocratic or coercive, expecting employees to be obedient for obedience's sake.

- **Level 2, conventional—follows expectations of others.** People whose moral development has reached this level are conformist but not slavish, generally adhering to the expectations of others in their lives. Level 2 managers lead by encouragement and cooperation and are more group and team oriented. Most managers are at this level.

- **Level 3, postconventional—guided by internal values.** The farthest along in moral development, Level 3 managers are independent souls who follow their own values and standards, focusing on the needs of their employees and trying to lead by empowering those working for them. Only about a fifth of American managers reach this level.

What level of development do you think you've reached?

How Organizations Can Promote Ethics

There are three ways an organization may foster high ethical standards:

I. Support by Top Managers of a Strong Ethical Climate The "tone at the top is critical—and it's always monkey see, monkey do," says Martha Clark Goss, VP and chief financial officer for consulting firm Booze Allen & Hamilton. At her firm, she says, "we have the sunshine rule, which asks employees to consider how they would feel if they had to stand in front of partners [that is, top managers] and explain a particular business expense. It's a good rule, but only a guideline. People almost always follow the example of the senior partners."[41]

If top executives "wink at the problem" or "look the other way" in ethical matters, so will employees farther down the organization.

2. Ethics Codes & Training Programs A *code of ethics* **consists of a formal written set of ethical standards guiding an organization's actions.** Most codes offer guidance on how to treat customers, suppliers, competitors, and other stakeholders. The purpose is to clearly state top management's expectations for all employees. As you might expect, most codes prohibit bribes, kickbacks, misappropriation of corporate assets, conflicts of interest, and "cooking the books"—making false accounting statements and other records. Other areas frequently covered in ethics codes are political contributions, workforce diversity, and confidentiality of corporate information.[42]

In addition, about 45% of the 1,000 largest U.S. corporations now provide ethics training.[43] The approaches vary, but one way is to use a case approach to present employees with ethical dilemmas. By clarifying expectations, this kind of training may reduce unethical behavior.[44]

3. Rewarding Ethical Behavior: Protecting Whistleblowers It's not enough to simply punish bad behavior; managers must also reward good ethical behavior, as in encouraging (or at least not discouraging) whistleblowers.

A *whistleblower* **is an employee who reports organizational misconduct to the public,** such as health and safety matters, waste, corruption, or overcharging of customers. For instance, the law that created the Occupational Safety and Health Administration allows workers to report unsafe conditions, such as "exposure to toxic chemicals; the use of dangerous machines, which can crush fingers; the use of contaminated needles, which expose workers to the AIDS virus; and the strain of repetitive hand motion, whether at a computer keyboard or in a meatpacking plant."[45]

The law prohibits employers from firing employees who report workplace hazards, although one study found that about two-thirds of those who complained lost their jobs anyway.[46] Clearly, top managers have to stress that the organization's ethics policy is more than just window dressing.

Public employees don't get the same break as everyone else. In 2006, the U.S. Supreme Court restricted the free-speech rights of the nation's 21 million government workers, ruling that the First Amendment to the Constitution does not protect them from being punished for reporting official misconduct.[47] ●

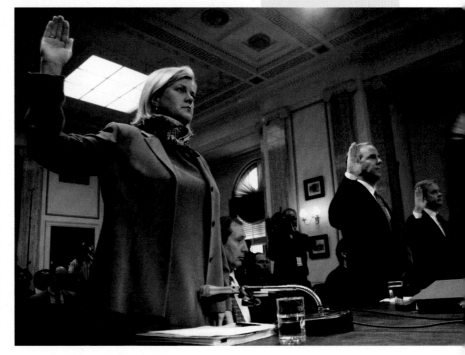

Whistleblower. Sherron Watkins, a former vice president of Enron, is sworn in alongside Jeffrey Skilling, former CEO, before testifying at a U.S. Congressional hearing. Watkins testified about her attempts to warn top managers of her fears that the company would "implode" because of irregular accounting practices. Close to half of all whistleblowers are fired; given this fact, what would it take for you to become a whistleblower?

3.4 THE SOCIAL RESPONSIBILITIES REQUIRED OF YOU AS A MANAGER

> ⊛ **major question** Is being socially responsible really necessary?

THE BIG PICTURE

Managers need to be aware of the viewpoints supporting and opposing social responsibility, four managerial approaches to social responsibility, and whether being and doing good pays off financially for the organization.

If ethical responsibility is about being a good individual citizen, social responsibility is about being a good organizational citizen. More formally *social responsibility* **is a manager's duty to take actions that will benefit the interests of society as well as of the organization.**

Social responsibility rests at the top of a pyramid of a corporation's obligations, right up there with economic, legal, and ethical responsibilities. That is, while some

Example

Social Responsibility: U.S. Companies Lend a Helping Hand to Victims of Tsunami

Originating in the sea floor off the coast of northwest Sumatra, the second-biggest earthquake in recorded history, the tsunami of December 26, 2004, traveled thousands of miles across the Indian Ocean, killing nearly a quarter-million people and leaving 1.8 million homeless in countries as far apart as Indonesia, the Maldives, Sri Lanka, and Somalia.[48]

Yet hours after the news of the devastation was heard round the world, many American companies had sprung into action, donating and delivering food, clothing, medicine, and other urgently needed goods and services, as well as funds.[49]

FedEx, for example, instantly revamped its delivery schedules to redeploy planes and pilots to ferry 230 tons of medical supplies to Sri Lanka and Indonesia. FedEx even chartered a plane at its own expense to deliver 344,000 pounds of Pedialyte, an oral rehydration solution for infants and children made by a division of Abbott. Pfizer pledged $35 million in money and medicine. Others stepping up to meet their social responsibilities were Coca-Cola (which donated $10 million), Dow Chemical ($5 million), ExxonMobil ($5 million), Merck ($3 million), Citigroup ($3 million), Wal-Mart ($2 million), and Microsoft ($2 million). Besides cash, Microsoft also donated servers and manpower to help relief organizations. Cisco supplied low-cost technology to connect Internet telephones to the Internet via satellite. DHL offered warehouses in Jakarta. Coke and Pepsi offered bottling facilities and distribution networks.

Many companies remained quite low-key about their contributions. "Fearing donations might be seen as public relations gimmicks," says one account, "some firms didn't announce—or even comment on—contributions."[50]

Your Call

Social responsibility may have benefits beyond the acts of selflessness themselves. In one survey of 2,000 people, 76% said they'd switch from their current brand to one associated with a good cause if price and quality were equal.[51] Can you think of any highly profitable and legal businesses that do not practice any kind of social responsibility?

people might consider that a company's first duty is to make a profit, most would hold that it is equally important that it obey the law, be ethical, and be a good corporate citizen.[52]

Is Social Responsibility Worthwhile? Opposing & Supporting Viewpoints

In the old days of cutthroat capitalism, social responsibility was hardly thought of. A company's most important goal was to make money pretty much any way it could, and the consequences be damned. Today for-profit enterprises generally make a point of "putting something back" into society as well as taking something out.

Not everyone, however, agrees with these new priorities. Let's consider the two viewpoints.

Against Social Responsibility "Few trends could so thoroughly undermine the very foundations of our free society," argues free-market economist Milton Friedman, "as the acceptance by corporate officials of social responsibility other than to make as much money for their stockholders as possible."[53]

Friedman represents the view that, as he says, "The social responsibility of business is to make profits." That is, unless a company focuses on maximizing profits, it will become distracted and fail to provide goods and services, benefit the stockholders, create jobs, and expand economic growth—the real social justification for the firm's existence.

This view would presumably support the efforts of companies to set up headquarters in name only in offshore Caribbean tax havens (while keeping their actual headquarters in the U.S.) in order to minimize their tax burden.

For Social Responsibility "A large corporation these days not only may engage in social responsibility," says famed economist Paul Samuelson, "it had damned well better to try to do so."[54] That is, a company must be concerned for society's welfare as well as for corporate profits.

Beyond the fact of ethical obligation, the rationale for this view is that since businesses create problems (environmental pollution, for example), they should help solve them. Moreover, they often have the resources to solve problems in ways that the non-profit sector does not. Finally, being socially responsible gives businesses a favorable public image that can help head off government regulation.

Four Managerial Approaches to Social Responsibility

The two extremes in managers' approaches to social responsibility range from "Do nothing" to "Do a lot."[55] Or, stated another way, from "obstructionist" to "proactive," as follows.[56]

1. The Obstructionist Manager Managers in an obstructionist organization not only resist being socially responsible, but they also behave unethically—maybe even illegally—whenever they think they can get away with it, or deny wrongdoing if found out. In the *obstructionist approach,* **managers put economic gain**

Sorry Sears. Sometimes even major companies are obstructionist. In the most serious ethical breach in its history, Sears, Roebuck and Co. was discovered in 1999 to have secretly violated federal law for a decade. It even, suggested U.S. Justice Department lawyers, may have put its illegal practice in its procedures manual. Sears allegedly used unenforceable agreements to collect debts that legally no longer existed with some bankrupt credit-card holders. "The company's 111 years old," said the relatively new CEO at the time, Arthur Martinez, "and I'm the guy in the chair when we plead guilty to a criminal offense. Wonderful."

Four Approaches to Social Responsibility

Obstructionist: "Just make money, forget any social responsibility."

Defensive: "Just do what the law requires, no more."

Accommodative: "Do the minimum that's ethically required."

Proactive: "Be a leader in social responsibility."

first and resist social responsibility as being outside the organization's self-interest.

Illegal drug dealers certainly represent the obstructionist approach. But so do some entirely legal companies. In 1999, according to a grand jury indictment, Waste Management, the largest trash hauler in the United States, hired Joseph Lauricella, who tried to undermine another company by swiping confidential data, sabotaging potential deals, and spreading rumors that tied the other company to illegal dumping and drug trafficking.[57]

2. The Defensive Manager In the *defensive approach,* **managers make the minimum commitment to social responsibility—obeying the law but doing nothing more.** The defensive approach probably represents Milton Friedman's position: Companies are in business to make money, and they shouldn't distract themselves by doing anything else.

3. The Accommodative Manager In the *accommodative approach,* **managers do more than the law requires, if asked, and demonstrate moderate social responsibility.** For months in 1998, Intel battled privacy groups that claimed its new Pentium III chip's hardwired identification number would give Web sites the power to monitor a user's every move online, until the company finally yielded and released the chip with the ID number turned off.[58]

4. The Proactive Manager In the *proactive approach,* **managers actively lead the way in being socially responsible for all stakeholders, using the organization's resources to identify and respond to social problems.** For example, Merck & Co., the pharmaceutical concern, spent millions developing a drug (Mectizan) to fight river blindness, then distributed it free in the West African countries in which the disease is mainly found.[59]

The Idea of Blended Value: Measuring Both Economic & Social Benefits

Jeb Emerson, a former social worker who became a lecturer at the Stanford Graduate School of Business, has gained some attention by asking, What if we did not judge business organizations on profits alone? According to Emerson, "We tend to categorize value as economic or social. You either work for a nonprofit that creates social value or you work for a for-profit that creates economic value."[60] In actuality, however, for-profits create social value: They create jobs (which lead to stable family units), they create products that improve people's lives, and they pay taxes that help build local communities. Conversely, nonprofits contribute economic value, because they also create jobs and they consume goods and services. (Nonprofits represent 7% of the gross domestic product.)

Social conscience. Bonnie Nixon-Gardner was only a middle-level manager at Hewlett-Packard, but in 2005 she was successful in spurring the company to enforce anti-sweatshop policies in low-wage countries to which they outsource products. Coercing a Chinese supplier to foot the bill for earplugs so that workers could be protected from excessive machine noise took six trips and much personal effort—would you be willing to do the same?

The notion of *blended value,* **then, is that all investments are understood to operate simultaneously in both economic and social realms.** "There is no 'trade off' between the two, but rather a concurrent pursuit of value—both social and financial," Emerson says. "The two operate together, in concert, at all times. They cannot be separated and considered as two distinct propositions, but are one and the same."[61]

Economic and social value (which includes environmental value) may well be all part of a piece, as Emerson proposes. The problem, of course, is that financial performance can be measured by numbers ("econometrics"), whereas measuring social performance is more difficult. However, just as society has been grappling with measuring environmental impacts for only the last 5–10 years, so it may take another 5–50 years to learn how to adequately track and report social value, Emerson believes. "There is increasing pressure on companies to understand, quantify, and measure their social impact," he says. "It's inevitable. Successful companies will be savvy about how understanding the full value proposition can create wider opportunity."

Two Types of Social Responsibility: Sustainability & Philanthropy

In 2006, some major stories hit the news media that probably raised the consciousness of a number of Americans about two significant issues linked to business and social responsibility—sustainability and philanthropy.

Sustainability: The Business of Green   Several companies—General Electric, Wal-Mart, Toyota, and others—launched "green marketing" campaigns promoting environmentally friendly causes, products, or stores.[62] In addition, an apparently changing climate, bringing increased damage from hurricanes, floods, and fires throughout the United States and the world, also brought the issue of "being green" to increased prominence. In mid-2006, former U.S. Vice President Al Gore's documentary film *An Inconvenient Truth,* along with his book by the same name, further popularized the concepts of global warming and the idea of sustainability as a business model.[63]

Our economic system has brought prosperity, but it has also led to unsustainable business practices because it has assumed that natural resources are limitless, which they are not. *Sustainability* **is defined as economic development that meets the needs of the present without compromising the ability of future generations to meet their own needs.**[64] G.E., which once polluted the Hudson River with PCBs from the transformers it manufactured, has been especially proactively green, promising to invest $1.5 billion a year in research in cleaner technologies. In part this is simply good business, because it enhances the efficiency of the products it sells.[65] But companies that have adopted an active pro-green stance have been able to avoid unfavorable publicity. ExxonMobil, for example, came under fire from shareholders and environmentalists in 2005 because it challenged the theory of global warming and wanted to drill in the Arctic National Wildlife Refuge. By contrast, BP (formerly British Petroleum), which has promoted a carbon-balanced world, did not.[66]

Philanthropy: "Not Dying Rich"   "He who dies rich dies thus disgraced," 19th-century steel magnate Andrew Carnegie is supposed to have said, after he turned his interests from making money to *philanthropy,* **making charitable donations to benefit humankind.** Carnegie became well known as a supporter of free libraries.

More recently, Bill Gates of Microsoft, the richest person in the world, made headlines when he announced that in 2008 he would step down from day-to-day oversight of the company he co-founded in order to focus on his $29 billion philanthropy, the Bill and Melinda Gates Foundation, which has pledged to spend billions on health, education, and overcoming poverty.[67] This news was closely followed by the announcement of the second-richest man in the world, investor Warren Buffet, chairman of Berkshire Hathaway, that he would channel $31 billion to the Gates Foundation to help in finding cures for the globe's most fatal diseases.[68]

Companies practice philanthropy, too. For example, Billiton, an international mining company, has joined forces with the government of Mozambique to reduce the threat of malaria in southern Africa, using new medicines, better bed nets, and old-fashioned pesticides.[69] But even ordinary individuals can become philanthropists of a sort. Mona Purdy, an Illinois hairdresser, noticed while vacationing in Guatemala in 1999 that many children coated their feet with tar in order to be able to run in a local race. So she went home and established the nonprofit Share Your Shoes, which collects shoes and sends them around the world. "I always thought I was too busy to help others," she says. "Then I started this and found myself wondering where I'd been all my life."[70]

How Does Being Good Pay Off?

From a hard-headed manager's point of view, does ethical behavior and high social responsibility pay off financially? Here's what some of the research shows.

Effect on Customers   According to one survey, 88% of the respondents said they were more apt to buy from companies that are socially responsible than from companies that are not.[71] Another survey of 2,037 adults found that 72% would prefer to purchase products and services from a company with ethical business practices and higher prices compared with 18% who would prefer to purchase from a company with questionable business practices and lower prices.[72]

Effect on Job Applicants & Employee Retention   Ethics can affect the quality of people who apply to work in an organization. One online survey of 1,020 people indicated that 83% rated a company's record of business ethics as "very important" when deciding whether to accept a job offer; only 2% rated it as "unimportant."[73] A National Business Ethics Survey found that 79% of employees said their firms' concern for ethics was a key reason they remained.[74]

Effect on Sales Growth   The announcement of a company's conviction for illegal activity has been shown to diminish sales growth for several years.[75] A 2003 survey found that 80% of people said they decide to buy a firm's goods or services partly on their perception of its ethics.[76]

Effect on Company Efficiency   One survey found that 71% of employees who saw honesty applied rarely or never in their organization had seen misconduct in the past year, compared with 52% who saw honesty applied only occasionally and 25% who saw it frequently.[77]

Effect on Company Revenue   Unethical behavior in the form of employee fraud costs U.S. organizations around $652 billion a year, according to the Association of Certified Fraud Examiners.[78] Employee fraud, which is twice as common as consumer fraud (such as credit card fraud and identity theft), costs employers about 20% of every dollar earned.[79]

Effect on Stock Price   A 2003 survey found that 74% of people polled said their perception of a firm's honesty directly affected their decision about whether to buy its stock.[80] Earlier research found that investments in unethical firms earn abnormally negative returns for long periods of time.[81]

Effect on Profits   Studies suggest that profitability is enhanced by a reputation for honesty and corporate citizenship.[82]

Ethical behavior and social responsibility are more than just admirable ways of operating. They give an organization a clear competitive advantage. ●

3.5 THE NEW DIVERSIFIED WORKFORCE

| What trends in workplace diversity should managers be aware of? | major + question |

THE BIG PICTURE

One of today's most important management challenges is working with stakeholders of all sorts who vary widely in diversity—in age, gender, race, religion, ethnicity, sexual orientation, capabilities, and socioeconomic background. Managers should also be aware of the differences between internal and external dimensions of diversity and barriers to diversity.

"Coors Cares," says one of the beer company's slogans.

Didn't it always? Actually, in the 1980s the Coors family's funding of right-wing causes—they helped start the conservative Heritage Foundation—gave the brewer such a bad reputation with minorities and unions that it was devastated financially. Today Coors still gives steady support to the political right. Ironically, however, the company goes far beyond government requirements in embracing sensitivity, diversity, and other politically left policies.

Inside Coors, workers get training in sexual harassment and attend diversity workshops. "Employees can choose among eight 'resource councils'—groups representing gays, women, and Native Americans, among others," says a *Time* article. It also claims to offer "the first corporate mammography program in the country." In addition, it sets aside a specific share of purchases for minority-owned firms. Outside, it provides sponsorship of such programs as the Mi Casa resource center for women, a black-heritage festival, and a marathon gay dance party. It is one of the three out of four Fortune 500 companies to have diversity programs to help attract and keep minorities.[83]

Coors and other companies have discovered they can benefit from a singular fact: minority markets buy more goods and services than any country that trades with the United States.[84] In this section, we describe one of the most important management challenges—dealing with diversity.

How to Think about Diversity: Which Differences Are Important?

Diversity **represents all the ways people are unlike and alike—the differences and similarities in age, gender, race, religion, ethnicity, sexual orientation, capabilities, and socioeconomic background.** Note here that diversity is not synonymous with differences. Rather, it encompasses both differences and similarities. This means that as a manager you need to manage both simultaneously.

To help distinguish the important ways in which people differ, diversity experts Lee Gardenswartz and Anita Rowe have identified a "diversity wheel" consisting of four layers of diversity: (1) personality, (2) internal dimensions, (3) external dimensions, and (4) organizational dimensions. *(See Figure 3.2, next page.)*

Let's consider these four layers:

Personality   At the center of the diversity wheel is personality. It is at the center because *personality* **is defined as the stable physical and mental characteristics responsible for a person's identity.** We cover the dimension of personality in Chapter 11.

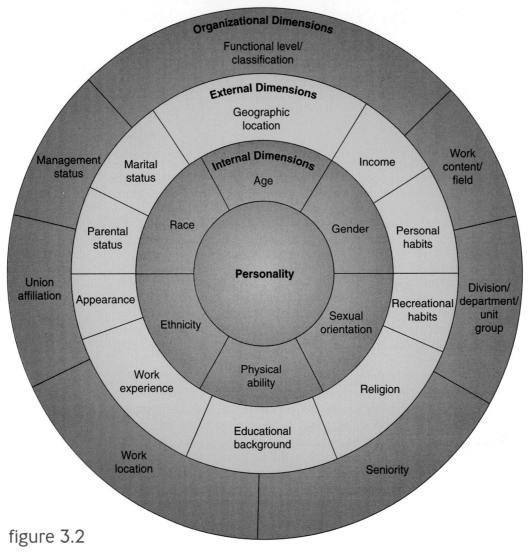

figure 3.2

THE DIVERSITY WHEEL

Four layers of diversity

Source: L. Gardenswartz and A. Rowe, *Diverse Teams at Work: Capitalizing on the Power of Diversity* (New York: McGraw-Hill, 1994), p. 33, © 1994. Reproduced with permission of The McGraw-Hill Companies and by permission of The Society for Human Resource Management via The Copyright Clearance Center. Internal dimensions and external dimensions are adapted from M. Loden and J. B. Rosener, *Workforce America! Managing Employee Diversity as a Vital Resource,* (Homewood, IL: Business One Irwin, 1991).

Internal Dimensions   *Internal dimensions of diversity* are those human differences that exert a powerful, sustained effect throughout every stage of our lives: gender, age, ethnicity, race, sexual orientation, physical abilities.[85] These are referred to as the *primary* dimensions of diversity because they are not within our control for the most part. Yet they strongly influence our attitudes and expectations and assumptions about other people, which in turn influence our own behavior.

What characterizes internal dimensions of diversity is that they are visible and salient in people. And precisely because these characteristics are so visible, they may be associated with certain stereotypes—for example, that black people work in menial jobs. For instance, an African American female middle manager reports that, while on vacation and sitting by the pool at a resort, she was approached by a 50ish white male who "demanded that I get him extra towels. I said, 'Excuse me?' He then said, 'Oh, you don't work here,' with no shred of embarrassment or apology in his voice."[86]

External Dimensions *External dimensions of diversity* **include an element of choice; they consist of the personal characteristics that people acquire, discard, or modify throughout their lives:** educational background, marital status, parental status, religion, income, geographic location, work experience, recreational habits, appearance, personal habits. They are referred to as the *secondary* dimensions of diversity because we have a greater ability to influence or control them than we do internal dimensions.

These external dimensions also exert a significant influence on our perceptions, behavior, and attitudes. If you are not a believer in the Muslim religion, for example, you may not perceive the importance of some of its practices—as with some managers at Atlanta-based Argenbright Security Inc., who sent seven Muslim female employees home for wearing Islamic head scarves at their security jobs at Dulles International Airport. Because wearing head scarves in no way affected their job performance, the company had to reimburse the women for back pay and other relief in a settlement negotiated with the Equal Employment Opportunity Commission.[87]

Organizational Dimensions Organizational dimensions include management status, union affiliation, work location, seniority, work content, and division or department.

Trends in Workforce Diversity

How is the U.S. workforce apt to become more diverse in the 21st century? Let's examine five categories on the internal dimension—*age, gender, race/ethnicity, sexual orientation, and physical/mental abilities*—and one category on the external dimension, *educational level.*

Age: More Older People in the Workforce
The most significant demographic event, management philosopher Peter Drucker suggested, "is that in the developed countries the number and proportion of younger people is rapidly shrinking. . . . Those shrinking numbers of younger people will have to both drive their economies and help support much larger numbers of older people."[88] In Europe and Japan, births are not keeping pace with deaths. Italy, for example, could drop from 60 million to 20 million by the end of the 21st century. Even China is faced with a nationwide aging gap, which means the country may face a shortage of cheap labor.[89]

The United States, suggested Drucker, is the only developed economy to have enough young people, and that is only because immigrants to the United States still have large families. Even so, the median age of the American worker was 36.2 in 2005, up from 34.3 in 1980.[90]

Diversity enriches. A diverse population in a company can provide ideas, experience, and points of view that strengthen the business culture.

Gender: More Women Working
Since the 1960s, women have been flooding into the workplace in great numbers, with about 75% of women ages 25–54 in the workforce, up from about 40% in the late 1950s.[91] (For men in the same age range, participation is about 90%.) Although women's participation in the labor force has declined a bit (in part because of delayed motherhood), today females hold half of all management and professional jobs. In addition, more and more businesses are owned by women—about 30% of all U.S. nonfarm companies.[92]

Traditionally, however, women have earned roughly the same pay as men only in jobs paying $25,000–$30,000 a year. The further up the pay scale and the higher the education level, the wider the earnings gap. Thus, for every dollar a man earns,

African-American success.
Police chief Annetta Nunn, the first woman African-American police chief of Birmingham, Alabama, prepares for a press conference. Nunn broke through a glass ceiling of a different sort, taking over the police operations in 2003 for a city known for its racial discrimination only a few decades earlier.

a woman cashier earns 93 cents, an administrative assistant 93 cents, and a registered nurse 88 cents. But for a woman physician or surgeon, it is 59 cents, a woman lawyer or judge 69 cents, a woman college professor 75 cents, and a woman psychologist 83 cents.[93] The obstacles to women's progress are known as the *glass ceiling*—**the metaphor for an invisible barrier preventing women and minorities from being promoted to top executive jobs.** For instance, women account for only about 8% of executive vice presidents and above at Fortune 500 companies.[94] Females also hold only 14.7% of seats on the boards of directors for these 500 largest companies.[95] (Black, Latina, and Asian women held only 3.4% of such seats.)

What factors are holding women back? Three that are mentioned are negative stereotypes, lack of mentors, and limited experience in line or general management.[96]

Interestingly, however, several studies have suggested that female managers outshine their male counterparts on almost every measure, from motivating others to fostering communication to producing high-quality work to goal-setting to mentoring employees.[97] Indeed, one study, by Catalyst, an advocacy group for women in business, found that companies with more women executives have better financial performance.[98] We discuss this further in a later chapter.

Race & Ethnicity: More People of Color in the Workforce By 2020, people of color are expected to make up 37% of the U.S. adult workforce (Hispanic/Latino 17%, African Americans 13%, Asian Americans 6%, and Native Americans 0.8%).[99] Unfortunately, three trends show that American businesses need to do a lot better by this population.

First, people of color, too, have hit the glass ceiling. For example, African Americans held only 11.3% and Hispanics only 10.9% of all managerial and professional jobs in 2001.[100]

Second, minorities tend to earn less than whites. Median household income in 2004 was $30,442 for African Americans and $33,884 for Hispanics. It was $49,061 for whites. (Asians had the highest median income, at $57,196.)[101]

Third, their chances of success have been hurt by perceived discrimination, as shown, for example, by a study of 200 black managers and 139 Hispanic employees.[102] African Americans also have been found to receive lower performance ratings than whites have.[103] Another study found 44 black managers experienced slower rates of promotion compared with 890 white managers.[104] No wonder the turnover rate is 40% higher for black than for white executives.[105]

Recently employers have had to become aware of another wrinkle in ethnic and race relations—namely, whether the labor they are hiring is legal. Illegal immigrants make up 1 in 20 workers, according to a 2006 Pew Hispanic Center study.[106] They account for nearly 1 in 4 farm workers, 1 in 6 maids and housekeepers, 1 in 7 in construction, and 1 in 8 in food preparation. Companies such as Georgia carpet maker Mohawk Industries depend substantially on immigrants from Mexico and other Latin American countries, many of whom are illegal.[107]

Sexual Orientation: Gays & Lesbians Become More Visible   Gays and lesbians make up, by some estimates, 6% of the U.S. population. Between a quarter and two-thirds report being discriminated against at work (with negative attitudes directed toward them held more by men than by women).[108] One 2003 study found that 41% of gay employees said they had been harassed, pressured to quit, or denied a promotion because of their sexual orientation.[109] Homosexual workers report higher levels of stress compared with heterosexual workers, and one source of this may be the fact that in 36 states homosexuality is still a legitimate legal basis for firing an employee. Finally, gay and bisexual male workers were found to earn 11–27% less than equally qualified heterosexual counterparts.[110]

How important is the issue of sexual preference? Once again, if managers are concerned about hiring and keeping workplace talent, they shouldn't ignore the motivation and productivity of 6% of the workforce. Many employers are recognizing this: 430 of the top 500 U.S. companies now offer policies prohibiting discrimination based on sexual preference, and more than half offer domestic partner benefits for same-sex couples.[111]

People with Differing Physical & Mental Abilities   One out of six Americans has a physical or mental disability, according to the U.S. Department of Labor. Since 1992 we have had the ***Americans with Disabilities Act*, which prohibits discrimination against the disabled** and requires organizations to reasonably accommodate an individual's disabilities. Despite what we've all heard about organizations having to spend hundreds of thousands of dollars building wheelchair ramps and the like, the costs actually aren't that great: half the disability accommodations cost less than $50 and 69% cost less than $500.[112]

Even so, disabled people have difficulty finding work. Although two-thirds of people with disabilities want to work, roughly two-thirds are unemployed. (Among blind adults, for example, about 70% are out of work.)[113] Those who are working tend to be in part-time, low-status jobs with little chance for advancement. Moreover, they earn up to 35% less than their more fully abled counterparts.[114] Here, too, is a talent pool that managers will no doubt find themselves tapping into in the coming years.

Educational Levels: Mismatches between Education & Workforce Needs   Two important mismatches between education and workplace are these:

- **College graduates may be in jobs for which they are overqualified.** About 27% of people working have a college degree. But some are ***underemployed*— *working at jobs that require less education than they have*—** such as tending bar, managing video stores, or other jobs that someone with less education could do.

  During the period 2000–2004, one national survey of 2,350 college graduates found that 18% were underemployed.[115] It is estimated that for the workforce in general, whether college educated or not, about a quarter is underemployed, a condition associated with higher absenteeism, arrest rates, and unmarried parenthood and with lower motivation, job involvement, and psychological well-being.[116]

- **High-school dropouts and others may not have the literacy skills needed for many jobs.** Among 16- to 24-year-olds in the United States, about 10% were high school dropouts in 2004.[117] In addition, an estimated 90 million adult Americans are functionally illiterate, that is, unable to use "printed and written information to function in society, to achieve one's goals, and to develop one's knowledge and potential."[118] In addition, more than two-thirds of the American workforce reads below ninth-grade level—a problem because about 70% of the on-the-job reading materials are written at or above that level.[119]

Disability. Everyone recognizes the wheelchair as signifying that a person is disabled, but other disabilities are not easily identified—and may not invite understanding. Do you think that mental disabilities, for example, should be accommodated in employment? If you were subject to mood swings, would you think that would prevent you from doing your job effectively?

Barriers to Diversity

Some barriers are erected by diverse people themselves. In the main, however, most barriers are put in their paths by organizations.[120] When we speak of "the organization's barriers," we are, of course, referring to the *people* in the organization—especially those who may have been there for a while—who are resistant to making it more diverse.

Resistance to change in general is an attitude that all managers come up against from time to time, and resistance to diversity is simply one variation. It may be expressed in the following six ways.

1. Stereotypes & Prejudices

Ethnocentrism **is the belief that one's native country, culture, language, abilities, or behavior is superior to those of another culture.** (An example is embodied in the title of the Wesley Snipes/Woody Harrelson movie about urban basketball hustlers: *White Men Can't Jump.*) When differences are viewed as being weaknesses—which is what many stereotypes and prejudices ultimately come down to—this may be expressed as a concern that diversity hiring will lead to a sacrifice in competence and quality.

2. Fear of Reverse Discrimination

Some employees are afraid that attempts to achieve greater diversity in their organization will result in reverse discrimination—that more black or Asian employees will be promoted to fire captain or police lieutenant, for example, over the heads of supposedly more qualified whites.

3. Resistance to Diversity Program Priorities

Some companies such as 3M offer special classes teaching tolerance for diversity, seminars in how to get along.[121] Some employees may see diversity programs as distracting them from the organization's "real work." In addition, they may be resentful of diversity-promoting policies that are reinforced through special criteria in the organization's performance appraisals and reward systems.

4. Unsupportive Social Atmosphere

Diverse employees may be excluded from office camaraderie and social events.

5. Lack of Support for Family Demands

In most families (63%, according to the Bureau of Labor Statistics), both parents work; in 29.5% only the father works, and in 4.5% only the mother works. But more and more women are moving back and forth between being at-home mothers and in the workforce, as

OUR GLOBAL DIVERSITY VISION

Johnson & Johnson's Credo sets forth our responsibilities to our employees. It recognizes their dignity and merit, their individuality, and the requirement for equal opportunity in employment, development and advancement for those qualified. From these principles, modified over the years, Johnson & Johnson has fostered and encouraged the development of a diverse workforce - a workforce for the future. ▼ While we can point with pride to a commitment to diversity deeply rooted in our value system, we recognize that our employees, customers and communities, then, were far different from those of today. However, our commitment to these core stakeholders as they have evolved and as Johnson & Johnson has evolved is as strong as ever. ▼ Today's customers and employees come from all over the world and represent different ages, cultures, genders, races and physical capabilities. Through their life experiences, they provide a diversity of thought and perspective that must be reflected in our corporate culture.

Our global diversity vision is to become
THE EMPLOYER OF CHOICE IN A DYNAMIC GLOBAL ENVIRONMENT.

To achieve this vision, we must build a workforce that is increasingly skilled, diverse, motivated and committed to dynamic leadership. This workforce should reflect our diverse customer base and be knowledgeable of the markets we serve. ▼ Being the Employer of Choice in a Dynamic Global Environment means embracing the differences and similarities of all our employees and prospective employees. It also means the execution of innovative diversity and marketing initiatives to ensure our ability to recruit, develop, retain and promote exceptional talent from an array of backgrounds and geographies, while continuing our pursuit of excellence. ▼ Our goal is to ensure our ability to meet the demands of a changing world with a vision worthy of our values and our commitment to be the leader in health care across the globe. When we achieve our vision, diversity becomes one of our most important competitive advantages.

Johnson & Johnson

economic circumstances dictate.[122] Yet in a great many households, it is still women who primarily take care of children, as well as other domestic chores. When organizations aren't supportive in offering flexibility in hours and job responsibilities, these women may find it difficult to work evenings and weekends or to take overnight business trips.

6. Lack of Support for Career-Building Steps   Organizations may not provide diverse employees with the types of work assignments that will help qualify them for positions in senior management. In addition, organizations may fail to provide the kind of informal training or mentoring that will help them learn the political savvy to do networking and other activities required to get ahead. ●

key terms used in this chapter

accommodative approach 90
Americans with Disabilities Act 97
blended value 90
code of ethics 87
competitors 79
customers 79
defensive approach 90
demographic forces 83
distributor 79
diversity 93
economic forces 82
ethnocentrism 98
ethical behavior 84
ethical dilemma 84
ethics 84
external dimensions of diversity 95

external stakeholders 78
general environment 82
glass ceiling 96
government regulators 81
individual approach 85
internal dimensions of diversity 94
internal stakeholders 76
international forces 83
justice approach 85
macroenvironment 82
moral-rights approach 85
obstructionist approach 89
owners 76
personality 93
philanthropy 91
political-legal forces 83

proactive approach 90
Sarbanes–Oxley Act of 2002 86
sociocultural forces 82
social responsibility 88
special-interest groups 81
stakeholders 75
strategic allies 79
supplier 79
sustainability 91
task environment 78
technological forces 82
underemployed 97
utilitarian approach 85
value system 84
values 84
whistleblower 87

summary

 3.1 The Community of Stakeholders Inside the Organization

- Managers operate in two organizational environments—internal and external—both made up of shareholders, the people whose interests are affected by the organization's activities. The first, or internal, environment, also includes employees, owners, and the board of directors.

 3.2 The Community of Stakeholders Outside the Organization

- The external environment of stakeholders consists of the task environment and the general environment.

- The task environment consists of 11 groups that present the manager with daily tasks to deal with. (1) Customers are those who pay to use an organization's goods and services. (2) Competitors are people or organizations that compete for customers or resources. (3) Suppliers are people or organizations that provide supplies—raw materials, services, equipment, labor, or energy—to other organizations. (4) Distributors are people or organizations that help another organization sell its goods and services to customers. (5) Strategic allies describe the relationship of two organizations who join forces to achieve advantages neither can perform as well alone. (6) Employee organizations consist of labor unions and employee associations. (7) Local communities consist of residents, companies, governments, and nonprofit entities that depend on the organization's taxes, payroll, and charitable contributions. (8) Financial institutions are commercial banks, investment banks, and insurance companies that deal with the organization. (9) Government regulators are regulatory agencies that establish the ground rules under which the organization operates. (10) Special-interest groups are groups whose members try to influence specific issues that may affect the organization. (11) The mass media are print, radio, TV, and Internet sources that affect the organization's public relations.

- The general environment includes six forces. (1) Economic forces consist of general economic conditions and trends—unemployment, inflation, interest rates, economic growth—that may affect an organization's performance. (2) Technological forces are new developments in methods for transforming resources into goods and services. (3) Sociocultural forces are influences and trends originating in a country, society, or culture's human relationships and values that may affect an organization. (4) Demographic forces are influences on an organization arising from changes in the characteristics of a population, such as age, gender, and ethnic origin. (5) Political-legal forces are changes in the way politics shapes laws and laws shape the opportunities for and threats to an organization. (6) International forces are changes in the economic, political, legal, and technological global system that may affect an organization.

3.3 The Ethical Responsibilities Required of You as a Manager

- Managers need to be aware of what constitutes ethics, values, the four approaches to ethical dilemmas, and how organizations can promote ethics.

- Ethics are the standards of right and wrong that influence behavior. Ethical behavior is behavior that is accepted as "right" as opposed to "wrong" according to those standards.

- Ethical dilemmas often take place because of an organization's value system. Values are the relatively permanent and deeply held underlying beliefs and attitudes that help determine a person's behavior.

- There are four approaches to deciding ethical dilemmas. (1) In the utilitarian approach, ethical behavior is guided by what will result in the greatest good for the greatest number of people. (2) In the individual approach, ethical behavior is guided by what will result in the individual's best long-term interests, which ultimately is in everyone's self-interest. (3) In the moral-rights approach, ethical behavior is guided by respect for the fundamental rights of human beings, such as those expressed in the U.S. Constitution's Bill of Rights. (4) In the justice approach, ethical behavior is guided by respect for the impartial standards of fairness and equity.

- Recent white-collar crime, such as that committed by the executives of Tyco and Enron, has led to further consideration of ethics. Public outrage led to the creation of the Sarbanes–Oxley Act of 2002 (SarbOx), which establishes requirements for proper financial record keeping for public companies and penalties for noncompliance.

- Concerns about business ethics have led colleges and universities to teach about moral development. Laurence Kohlberg proposed three levels of personal moral development: (1) People at the preconventional level of moral development are those who tend to follow rules and to obey authority; (2) people at the conventional level are conformist, generally adhering to the expectations of others; and (3) people at the highest, or postconventional, level are guided by internal values.

- There are three ways an organization may foster high ethical standards. (1) The top managers must support a strong ethical climate. (2) The organization may have a code of ethics, which consists of a formal written set of ethical standards guiding an organization's actions. (3) An organization must reward ethical behavior, as in not discouraging whistleblowers, employees who report organizational misconduct to the public.

3.4 The Social Responsibilities Required of You as a Manager

- Managers need to be aware of the viewpoints supporting and opposing social responsibility, four managerial approaches to responsibility, and whether being and doing good pays off financially for the organization.

- Social responsibility is a manager's duty to take actions that will benefit the interests of society as well as of the organization. An example of social responsibility is philanthropy, donating money to worthwhile recipients.

- For-profit companies generally make a point of "putting something back" into society as well as taking something out, but the idea of social responsibility has opposing and supporting viewpoints. The opposing viewpoint is that the social responsibility of business is to make profits. The supporting viewpoint is that since business creates some problems (such as pollution) it should help solve them.

- There are four approaches to social responsibility. (1) In the obstructionist approach, managers put economic gain first and resist social responsibility as being outside the organization's self-interest. (2) In the defensive approach, managers make the minimum commitment to social responsibility—obeying the law but doing nothing more. (3) In the accommodative approach, managers will do more than the law requires, if asked, and will demonstrate moderate social responsibility. (4) In the proactive approach, managers actively lead the way in being socially responsible for all stakeholders, using the organization's resources to identify and respond to social problems.

- It has been proposed that business organizations not be judged on profits alone— that there is blended value, in which all investments are understood to operate simultaneously in both economic and social realms.

- Two types of social responsibility are (1) sustainability, defined as economic development that meets the needs of the present without compromising the ability of future generations to meet their own needs, and (2) philanthropy, making charitable donations to benefit humankind.

- Positive ethical behavior and social responsibility can pay off in the form of customer goodwill, better quality of job applicants and retained employees, enhanced sales growth, less employee misconduct and fraud, better stock price, and enhanced profits.

3.5 The New Diversified Workforce

- One of today's most important management challenges is working with stakeholders of all sorts who vary widely in diversity. Diversity represents all the ways people are alike and unlike—the differences and similarities in age, gender, race, religion, ethnicity, sexual orientation, capabilities, and socioeconomic background.

- There are two dimensions of diversity— internal and external. Internal dimensions of diversity are those human differences that exert a powerful, sustained effect throughout every stage of our lives: gender, ethnicity, race, physical abilities, age, and sexual orientation. External dimensions of diversity have an element of choice; they consist of the personal characteristics that people acquire, discard, or modify throughout their lives: personal habits, educational background, religion, income, marital status, and the like.

- There are five categories in the internal dimension and one category in the external dimension in which the U.S. workforce is becoming more diverse: (1) age, (2) gender, (3) race and ethnicity, (4) sexual orientation, (5) disabilities, and (6) educational level.

- There are six ways in which employees and managers may express resistance to diversity: (1) Some express stereotypes and prejudices based on ethnocentrism, the belief that one's native country, culture, language, abilities, or behavior is superior to those of another country. (2) Some employees are afraid of reverse discrimination. (3) Some employees see diversity programs as distracting them from the organization's supposed "real work." (4) Diverse employees may experience an unsupportive social atmosphere. (5) Organizations may not be supportive of flexible hours and other matters that can help employees cope with family demands. (6) Organizations may show lack of support for career-building steps for diverse employees.

Hewlett-Packard Extends Its Social Responsibility across the Globe

Bonnie Nixon-Gardiner certainly knows how to throw her weight around. She's only a middle-level manager at Hewlett-Packard Co. and stands at just 5 foot 3. But the top brass snapped to attention last year when she showed up in Long Hua, China, to inspect working conditions at a massive electronics manufacturing complex owned by a key HP supplier. Executives from Foxconn Electronics, a unit of Hon Hai Precision Industry Co., tried to whisk her into a conference room for a PowerPoint presentation. But Nixon-Gardiner, 46, said bluntly that she wasn't interested.

Instead, remembers Grover Thurman, Foxconn's senior director of social and environmental responsibility, she demanded full freedom to walk around the 200,000-employee complex, the waste-treatment center, and the dorm rooms where workers live. When her hosts resisted, she sat them down for a talking-to. "Look, this isn't going to work unless you're totally transparent with me," she told the officials. Within minutes, she was off, a line of nervous, suit-clad executives in tow. "[We] were pretty uptight when she took a left turn when [we] wanted her to go straight," recalls Thurman.

Foxconn had reason to balk. A non-Chinese speaker was wandering around among 250-ton metalcutting machines that churn out parts for computers and cell phones. Perhaps of greater concern was Nixon-Gardiner's potential impact on the bottom line, despite her unimpressive title of program manager for HP's Supply Chain Social & Environmental Responsibility.

A big chunk of Foxconn's $25 billion in sales comes from HP, which buys $67 billion worth of electronics every year. So, a lot was riding on whether she gave the thumbs-up. On a bigger stage, Nixon-Gardiner has been a key behind-the-scenes catalyst for an ambitious new effort by the high-tech industry to improve working conditions at suppliers like Foxconn around the globe. "HP has taken the lead on this, and Bonnie did a lot of it on sheer passion," says Kevin O'Mara, vice-president at consultants AMR Research.

Back in 1999, as HP and other tech companies began outsourcing production of printers, motherboards, and laptops to the same low-wage countries that make Nike shoes and T-shirts sold at Wal-Mart, she began setting down strong anti-sweatshop policies for HP suppliers. By 2004, Nixon-Gardiner and her counterparts at Dell, IBM, Intel, and other companies had agreed to create the Electronic Industry Code of Conduct. The EICC sets out basic labor and environmental standards for the industry's contractors.

Modeled broadly on other industrywide groups such as the Fair Labor Assn. (FLA) founded a decade ago by Nike and other footwear and apparel companies, the EICC is a first for the tech industry, which is rarely associated with sweatshop issues. Still, it only goes so far. Unlike the FLA, for instance, the EICC isn't an independent body and to date doesn't conduct random inspections of member companies' overseas factories. The EICC simply spells out abuses—from child or forced labor to excessive overtime—that the companies agree are unacceptable on the part of their contractors. It leaves the inspection and enforcement of these standards to each member company.

Nixon-Gardiner isn't waiting for the perfect solution. A New Jersey native raised by a single mom, she grew up with a strong social conscience. At HP, she has set up a 70-auditor system that has inspected 200 factories owned by 150 key HP suppliers—more than any other EICC member. HP says allegations of labor problems contributed to its decision to break with three suppliers that didn't make the grade, including South Korea–based Trigem Computer Inc. Trigem says it wasn't aware of this issue. She is also trying to educate local suppliers. On June 1, HP announced a new training program to help Chinese manufacturers prevent labor and environmental abuses; Brazil, Malaysia, and India could be next. "My 10-year vision is for [consumers to know that] when you touch a technology product, you are guaranteed it was made in a socially and environmentally responsible way," she says.

Clearly, HP's activist has moved social responsibility up the high-tech priority list, even if the changes are taking place one plant at a time. During that first Foxconn audit, Nixon-Gardiner decided that the machinery was too loud. So Foxconn bought employees some flimsy orange earplugs. Not good enough. Six visits from Nixon-Gardiner later, the company had spent tens of thousands of dollars to put enclosures around the gear, change the blades, and give workers top-of-the-line ear protectors. Now, says Thurman, employees are complaining about how hot their ears get. Dealing with Nixon-Gardiner, he says, "is like being kissed and slapped at the same time. It can make you psychotic—but it needs to be done." That message is sinking in with the rest of high tech, too.

For Discussion

1. Which internal and external stakeholders are positively and negatively affected by HP's approach toward anti-sweatshop policies?
2. Which of the six general environmental forces are influencing HP's approach toward its suppliers? Discuss.
3. Use the four approaches to deciding ethical dilemmas to evaluate whether it is ethical for technical companies to create and impose the Electronic Industry Code of Conduct standards on organizations around the world.
4. Is HP being socially responsible or is the company going too far? Explain your rationale.
5. How would you evaluate Bonnie Nixon-Gardiner in terms of Kohlberg's three levels of moral development? Explain.

Source: Excerpted from Peter Burrows, "How HP's Bonnie Nixon-Gardiner Spurred the Industry to Police Worker Conditions," *BusinessWeek*, June 19, 2006, pp. 60–63.

self-assessment

What Is Your Guiding Ethical Principle?

Objectives

1. To understand your ethical approach.
2. To understand that there are different ways to perceive ethics in the workplace.

Introduction

Over the centuries human beings have grappled with defining ethics and behaving ethically. Many different principles have evolved to deal with ethics from different perspectives. None is better or worse than the other—they are simply perspectives. You may choose one to be your guiding principle while your friend follows another. This is also true of companies and their employees. For example, Johnson & Johnson has a valued reputation for being very ethical and socially responsible, whereas actions by companies like Ford and Arthur Andersen have placed a large question mark on their ethical conduct and social responsibility.

Instructions

Rank each of the following principles in order from 1 (my most important guiding principle) to 3 (least relevant to my ethical principles).

1. *Utilitarianism:* The greatest good for the greatest number, or any view that holds that actions and policies should be evaluated on the basis of benefits and costs they will impose on society.

   Violation? The Ford Motor Company knew of the problems with its tires 6 years before they became known in the United States, but this was information from Europe, and U.S. law did not require that the company report it if it did not happen here.

2. *Rights Theory:* A right is an individual's entitlement or claim to something. A person has a right when he or she is entitled to act in a certain way or is entitled to have others act in a certain way toward him or her. It can be a legal right, a moral right, or a human right.

   Violation? Many stockholders at Microsoft want the company to adopt the "U.S. Business Principles for Human Rights of Workers in China," a statement supported by other companies such as Levi Strauss and Reebok. Microsoft management did not agree, arguing that its own principles and code of ethics covered the important points and that the statement principles were too broad and vague. Other companies also thought that American companies should not promote human rights in China because they would be abandoning a position of political neutrality.

3. *Justice as Fairness:* A principle that aims to protect those least able to protect themselves.

   Examples: Companies should establish strong affirmative action plans to redress the wrongs of discrimination; or, if a company introduces pay cuts, the workers paid the least should receive the smallest pay cut and those who are paid the most should get the largest pay cut.

Questions for Discussion

1. What are the pros and cons of your primary ethical principle in terms of advancing up the corporate ladder? Discuss.

2. Why do you think ethical principles are important in the workplace? Explain.
3. Which of the previous three principles would you want the company that you work for to adopt? Why?

4. In such a competitive world, how ethical can any company really be?

Developed by Anne C. Cowden, PhD. Laura P. Hartman and Joseph R. DesJardins, *Business Ethics: Decision-Making for Personal Integrity and Social Responsibility* (Burr Ridge, IL: McGraw-Hill, 2008). See Chapter three for a detailed discussion for each approach.

group exercise

Ethical Application

Objectives

1. To assess how you apply your primary ethical principle (from the previous exercise) to a case.
2. To see how group members using different ethical principles approach a case.

Introduction

Because "perception is reality" people see situations differently and thus make different decisions. The subjectivity of perception makes it difficult for organizational members to reach a consensus on what the ethical conduct of the company should be—but consensus must be reached if the company is to be able to make coherent, consistent decisions concerning ethical issues.

Instructions

Divide your class into three groups: those who ranked Utilitarianism as their first choice (in the previous exercise); those who selected Rights Theory as their first choice; and those who ranked Justice as Fairness as their first choice. Each group is to read the following scenario and then discuss how they would manage it, according to their chosen principle. Next each group must in turn try to convince the other two groups that their approach is the best one. Finally, all three groups should try to agree on one approach.

Scenario

You are a U.S. pharmaceutical firm that has discovered a drug that will stop a terrible disease epidemic on the African continent. You have spent a great deal of time (5 years) and an immense amount of money ($100 million) on the drug's development. It has tied up the time of 25 specialists and a lot of lab space. To recoup costs, you are going to have to charge a high price for each pill. You have another, similar product in process, which your scientists are very excited about. Given the competitive nature of the drug market, your stockholders are asking for justification for the time and money spent on these and other such products.

Your marketing and salespeople are now looking for buyers and find that no one wants to meet your price of $10 per pill. The African people need it badly but cannot afford it. The disease causes early blindness in millions of children, and your drug would greatly improve the quality of living for these children as well as increase their society's human resources. What would you do and why? Explain in detail.

Questions for Discussion

1. Did your group easily agree on a solution? Explain why or why not.
2. Did the three groups propose similar or different solutions to the case? Why did this happen? Discuss.
3. What did you learn about the relationship between ethical principles and decision making from this exercise? Discuss.
4. How can people who possess competing ethical principles reach consensus when making decisions?

Developed by Anne C. Cowden, PhD.

ethical dilemma

Should Job Applicants Reveal Their Chronic Illnesses to Potential Employers?

You've just graduated from college and are excited to begin job hunting. You have many exciting prospects, but there is one thing holding you back—you were recently diagnosed with scleroderma. This chronic connective tissue disease is progressive and typically kills patients within 10 years. Your doctor is positive about your prognosis; however, you have already experienced some of the effects, such as swelling and stiffening in your fingers. Federal disability laws bar employers from asking about an applicant's health. However, the U.S. Supreme Court ruled that a company can refuse to hire an applicant whose medical condition might adversely affect the performance of a specific job function.

Solving the Dilemma

Knowing a company might be reluctant to hire you based on your condition, what would you do?

1. Don't immediately mention your disease during the interview. Instead, play up your abilities, experience, and enthusiasm for the job. If you get hired, you can explain your ill-

ness and make up for missed work owing to medical appointments and flare-ups by working on weekends.

2. Bring up your disease right away. You don't have to provide vivid details about your symptoms, but it is important for your employer to know you have a chronic disease and how it will affect you.

3. Don't mention your disease at all. If you get the job and have a flare-up and need to take sick days, it is your business.

4. Invent other options. Discuss.

Source: Based on Joann S. Lublin, "Should Job Hunters Reveal Chronic Illness? The Pros and Cons," *The Wall Street Journal*, January 13, 2004, p. B1.

video case

The Rules of Engagement

Harry Stonecipher, the 68-year-old Boeing CEO, hired to repair some of the public relations damage caused by the former CEO, was dismissed after only 15 months at the helm of the company. Stonecipher was caught having a consensual extra-marital affair with a Boeing female executive. Ironically, Stonecipher was fired using the very code of conduct policy he implemented at the company after its Chief Financial Officer offered a job to an air force official with whom the company was negotiating a $23 billion Air Force contract.

Corporate office romances are apparently nothing new. In a 2005 survey, careerbuilder.com found that some 50 percent of co-workers date, and some 25 percent of workers date their bosses. In the past, a one-time office affair was not grounds for firing a corporate executive, but today it may be part of the new morality many corporate boards of directors have embraced to deal with the infamous ethics scandals that have rocked corporate America and sent some CEOs to jail for their crimes.

CEOs now live in a fishbowl. Boards of directors and governmental agencies have become increasingly vigilant about their behavior, and the passage of the Sarbanes-Oxley Act of 2002 has created stricter auditing practices for companies to reduce inaccurate financial disclosures. In some instances, boards of directors have become personally liable for their actions as board members and can no longer be indemnified by the company. Moreover, they are under intense pressure from the public to safeguard their investments and from the government to protect all stakeholders including the company, its employees,

and its shareholders from any types of corporate mismanagement. Everyone connected to the company is being held to a higher standard so there is not even the slightest notion of impropriety. And while Bill Clinton may have gotten away unscathed from his indiscretion when he was the president of the United States, the rules of engagement in corporate America have changed the way business is conducted today. Plain and simple, unacceptable behavior will no longer be tolerated.

Today's boards of directors are sending a strong message to CEO and employees alike—a new day has arrived and heads will roll if their business affairs are anything less than above board.

Questions

1. Select one approach to deciding about an ethical dilemma and discuss it in relationship to this case.

2. Do you think the board of directors acted in an ethically responsible manner by firing Stonecipher?

3. List the internal and external stakeholders in this case. What would be the impact on each of them, if Stonecipher was allowed to "get away" with his office romance?

4. What could a company such as Boeing do to prevent office romances in the future?

Source: Joseph C. Santora, EdD, Essex County College.

Chapter 4

Global Management
Managing across Borders

Major Questions You Should Be Able to Answer

4.1 Globalization: The Collapse of Time & Distance
Major Question: What three important developments of globalization will probably affect me?

4.2 You & International Management
Major Question: Why learn about international management, and what characterizes the successful international manager?

4.3 Why & How Companies Expand Internationally
Major Question: Why do companies expand internationally, and how do they do it?

4.4 Economic & Political-Legal Differences
Major Question: How may foreign countries differ in their economic, political, and legal characteristics?

4.5 The World of Free Trade: Regional Economic Cooperation
Major Question: What are barriers to free trade, and what major organizations and trading blocs promote trade?

4.6 The Importance of Understanding Cultural Differences
Major Question: What are the principal areas of cultural differences?

Being a Star Road Warrior

Since business travelers who fly 100,000-plus miles a year are no longer a rare breed, should you prepare for the possibility of joining them?

As we discuss in this chapter, globalization has collapsed time and distance. Managers must be prepared to work for organizations that operate not only countrywide but also worldwide. To stay connected with colleagues, employees, clients, and suppliers, you may have to travel a lot.

Business travel can have its rewards. Many people enjoy going to different cities, meeting new people, encountering new cultures. In one survey, people who took business trips of five nights or more said that being on the road provided certain escapes: from their everyday workplace (35% of those polled); from putting out work "fires" (20%); from frequent meetings (12%); from co-worker distractions (11%).[1]

Here are two lessons that business travelers have learned:

- **Frequent travel may be needed because personal encounters are essential for teamwork.** "Flying is a waste of time, but it's a necessary evil," says management consultant Jeff Bowden, who flies about 500,000 miles a year. "I've done well financially, so I've been very lucky. I laugh at people who think they can be successful without flying."[2]

  Scott Collins lives in Michigan, where his $100,000 salary goes far. But he works at Netscape Communications in Mountain View, California, in the heart of Silicon Valley, and travels the 2,000 miles between home and workplace a couple of times a month. The reason: Phones, e-mail, and videoconferencing aren't entirely feasible. Teamwork requires personal encounters.

  "Paradoxically, location matters more than ever in high-tech," says futurist Paul Saffo. "To be a player in Silicon Valley, you have to be in people's faces."[3]

  The same is true in most other industries.

- **Frequent travel requires frequent adjustments.** How do you cope if you travel all the time? Management consultant Bowden keeps sets of clothes in Tampa, Los Angeles, and Vancouver, British Columbia. He is away so much that he has a problem getting rid of his household trash. If he puts his garbage cans out Tuesday morning, he may not be home to wheel them in. So he has learned to dispose of the trash in a trash can en route to the airport.

  Niki Leondakis, chief operating officer of a San Francisco–based hotel group, keeps a bag packed in her closet at all times that includes a second set of everything she might forget, such as power cords and chargers for cell phones and iPods. Tina Guzlec, vice president of a Chicago real estate development company, chooses travel clothes that enable her to get quickly through airport security, avoiding belts and coats that won't fit into a carry-on and wearing shoes that readily slip on and off.[4]

  Vicki Schubert-Martin, who works in the software industry, travels about 250,000 miles a year, which keeps her away from her Denver home about 5 days a week. To keep up her health, she maintains a high-fiber diet while on the road. She keeps a close relationship with her husband by phoning him daily and spending weekends hiking, biking, and seeing movies with him. "It's a matter of keeping a healthy attitude about it," she says.[5]

For Discussion Have you done much traveling? What tricks have you discovered to make it more efficient?

forecast

What's Ahead in This Chapter

This chapter covers the importance of globalization—the rise of the global village, of one big market, of both worldwide megafirms and minifirms. We also describe the characteristics of the successful international manager, why and how companies expand internationally, and some of the economic and political-legal differences between countries. We describe the barriers to free trade and the major organizations promoting trade. Finally, we describe some of the cultural differences you may encounter if you become an international manager.

4.1 GLOBALIZATION: THE COLLAPSE OF TIME & DISTANCE

✴ **major question** What three important developments of globalization will probably affect me?

THE BIG PICTURE

Globalization, the trend of the world economy toward becoming a more interdependent system, is reflected in three developments: the rise of the "global village" and e-commerce, the trend of the world's becoming one big market, and the rise of both megafirms and Internet-enabled minifirms worldwide.

Barry Salzman, president of DoubleClick International, a worldwide Internet advertising firm headquartered in New York, spends about 75% of his time traveling. "He takes a laptop and four battery packs so that he can wade through the 200 e-mail messages he averages daily," says one description. "He carries two mobile phones because he is on call, day or night, to handle problems anywhere in the world."[6]

Here is a manager who heads an Internet company—which can reach all corners of the globe in milliseconds. Yet he spends most of his time traveling because it's the only way he can see to manage his 13 offices worldwide.

Can you visualize yourself operating like this? Like Salzman, you are living in a world being rapidly changed by *globalization*—**the trend of the world economy toward becoming a more interdependent system.** Time and distance, which have been under assault for 150 years, have now virtually collapsed, as reflected in three important developments we shall discuss.[7]

1. The rise of the "global village" and electronic commerce.
2. The world's becoming one market instead of many national ones.
3. The rise of both megafirms and Internet-enabled minifirms worldwide.

The Rise of the "Global Village" & Electronic Commerce

The hallmark of great civilizations has been their great systems of communications. In the beginning, communications was based on transportation: the Roman Empire had its network of roads, as did other ancient civilizations, such as the Incas. Later the great European powers had their farflung navies. In the 19th century, the United States and Canada unified North America by building transcontinental railroads. Later the airplane reduced travel time between continents.

From Transportation to Communication   Transportation began to yield to the electronic exchange of information. Beginning in 1844, the telegraph ended the short existence of the Pony Express and, beginning in 1876, found itself in competition with the telephone. The amplifying vacuum tube, invented in 1906, led to commercial radio. Television came into being in England in 1925. During the 1950s and 1960s, as television exploded throughout the world, communications philosopher Marshall McLuhan posed the notion of a "global village," where we all share our hopes, dreams, and fears in a "worldpool" of information. **The *global village* refers to the "shrinking" of time and space as air travel and the electronic media have made it easier for the people of the globe to communicate with one another.**

 Then the world became even faster and smaller. Fifteen years ago, cell phones, pagers, fax, and voice-mail links barely existed. When AT&T launched the first cellular communications system in 1983, it predicted fewer than a million users by 2000. By the end of 1993, however, there were more than 16 million cellular phone subscribers in the United States.[8] And as of the end of 2005, there were nearly 195 million, and that number was predicted to grow to 270 million by 2009.[9]

The Net, the Web, & the World   Then came the Internet, the worldwide computer-linked "network of networks," where 1,018,057,389 people logged on in 2005, according to the *World Factbook* put out by the Central Intelligence Agency.[10] The Net might have remained the province of academicians had it not been for the contributions of Tim Berners-Lee, who came up with the coding system, linkages, and addressing scheme that debuted in 1991 as the World Wide Web. "He took a powerful communications system [the Internet] that only the elite could use," says one writer, "and turned it into a mass medium."[11]

The arrival of the Web quickly led to *e-commerce,* **or electronic commerce, the buying and selling of products and services through computer networks.** Total U.S. e-commerce sales were expected to top $100 billion in 2006, and some forecasters were predicting e-sales would make up 25–30% of all sales in the U.S. by 2012.[12]

One Big World Market: The Global Economy

"We are seeing the results of things started in 1988 and 1989," said Rosabeth Moss Kantor of the Harvard Business School a decade later.[14] It was in the late 1980s when the Berlin Wall came down, signaling the beginning of the end of communism in Eastern Europe. It was also when countries of the Pacific Rim began to open their economies to foreign investors. Finally, the trend toward governments deregulating their economies began sweeping the globe. These three events set up conditions by which goods, people, and money could move more freely throughout the world—a global economy.

Example

Worldwide E-Commerce: Amazon.com

amazon.com.

In 1994, Jeffrey Bezos left a successful career on Wall Street with a plan to exploit the potential for electronic retailing on the World Wide Web by launching an online bookstore called Amazon.com.

Bezos realized that no bookstore with four walls could possibly stock the more than 2.5 million books that are now active and in print. Moreover, he saw that an online bookstore wouldn't have to make the same investment in retail clerks, store real estate, or warehouse space (in the beginning, Amazon.com ordered books from the publisher *after* Amazon took an order), so it could pass savings along to customers in the form of discounts. In addition, he appreciated that there would be opportunities to obtain demographic information about customers in order to offer personalized services, such as books of interest to them. Finally, Bezos saw that

there could be a good deal of online interaction: customers could post reviews of books they read and could reach authors by e-mail to provide feedback.

Amazon.com sold its first book in July 1995 and by the end of 1998 had served 6.2 million customers in more than 100 countries. Later the firm began expanding into nonbook areas, such as online retailing of music CDs, toys, electronics, drugs, cosmetics, pet supplies, and technologies for planned digital media services. In early 2006, it reported sales rose 20%, to $2.3 billion, from a year earlier.[13]

Your Call

Can you think of any highly specialized worldwide medium-sized or small business that the invention of the Internet made possible? Could you see yourself launching a similar business?

The global economy. This purveyor of souvenirs and antiques is located in Beijing. It welcomes American Express cards. In China and other parts of the world, you can use your U.S. credit card or debit card in local cash machines to obtain the currency of your host country. You will see the amount deducted, in dollars, from your credit card or bank account when you get home.

The *global economy* refers to the increasing tendency of the economies of the world to interact with one another as one market instead of many national markets.

The economies of the world have never been more entangled. As Kevin Maney writes in *USA Today,* "They're tied together by instantaneous information arriving via everything from currency trading databases to Web sites to CNN broadcasts. Capital—the money used to build businesses—moves globally and moves in a matter of keystrokes."[15]

Positive Effects   Is a global economy really good for the United States? U.S. exports, international trade, and U.S. workers are connected, points out Nancy Birdsall, executive vice president of the Inter-American Development Bank in Washington, DC. "As consumers in other regions of the world see their income go up, they are going to be more interested in U.S. products," she said in 1995. "The bottom line is that growth of jobs and income in other countries will mean growth of jobs and income in [the United States]. It's a win-win situation."[16]

Negative Effects   However, global economic interdependency can also turn into a lose-lose situation. Its double-edged nature was shown when, following the devaluation of Thailand's currency in July 1997, the previously fast-growing "Asian Tiger" economies—Thailand, Indonesia, South Korea, Japan—became the "Asian crisis." (*Devaluation* means that a nation's currency is lowered relative to other countries' currencies.) The economic catastrophes of the Pacific Rim began affecting the economies of emerging nations from Latin America to Eastern Europe, eventually hurting Australia, Canada, and certain sectors of the United States.[17] National governments were powerless to stop the flight of capital from weakened economies to stronger ones. U.S. stock markets reacted, for a time losing one-fifth of their value.

Another negative effect is the movement, or outsourcing (discussed in Section 4.3), of formerly well-paying jobs overseas as companies seek cheaper labor costs. Two decades ago, the loss was in American manufacturing jobs; more recently, many service jobs have moved offshore. Part of the reason for this, as Microsoft's Bill Gates has observed, is that "American high schools are obsolete . . . Until we design them to meet the needs of the 21st century, we will keep limiting—even ruining—the lives of millions of Americans every year."[18] In the competition with low-wage countries (India, China, and Asia), Americans are falling behind in the skills required to excel.

But the global economy isn't going to go away just because we don't like some of its destabilizing aspects. "The process is irreversible, if only because of the information technology and communications revolutions," says Claude Smadja, managing director of the World Economic Forum in Switzerland. "The problem also is that, contrary to some illusions, one cannot pick and choose in the package. . . . The new globality means a tremendous emphasis on speed, flexibility, versatility, and permanent change—in some respects, insecurity."[19]

Cross-Border Business: The Rise of Both Megamergers & Minifirms Worldwide

The global market driven by electronic information "forces things to get bigger and smaller at the same time," suggests technology philosopher Nicholas Negroponte. "And that's so ironic, when things want to do both but not stay in the middle. There will be an increasing absence of things that aren't either very local or very global."[20]

If Negroponte is correct, this means we will see more and more of two opposite kinds of businesses: mergers of huge companies into even larger companies, and small, fast-moving start-up companies.

Megamergers Operating Worldwide AOL + Time Warner. Glaxo Wellcome + SmithKline Beecham. Verizon + MCI. SBC + AT&T. Home Depot + Hughes. Walt Disney + Pixar. Nokia + Siemens.

The last 10 years have been megamerger time, "corporations on steroids," in one writer's phrase.[21] Oil, telecommunications, automobiles, financial services, and pharmaceuticals, for instance, aren't suited to being midsize, let alone small and local, so companies in these industries are trying to become bigger and cross-border. The means for doing so is to merge with other big companies. In telecommunications, for instance, cell phone maker Nokia of Finland teamed up with network equipment maker Siemens of Germany because of growing competition from emerging rivals in Asia, which are increasingly finding ways to produce new technology while lowering costs.[22]

Minifirms Operating Worldwide The Internet and the World Wide Web allow almost anyone to be global, which Kevin Maney points out has two important results:

1. Small Companies Can Get Started More Easily Because anyone can put goods or services on a Web site and sell worldwide, this wipes out the former competitive advantages of distribution and scope that large companies used to have.

2. Small Companies Can Maneuver Faster Little companies can change direction faster, which gives them an advantage in terms of time and distance over large companies.

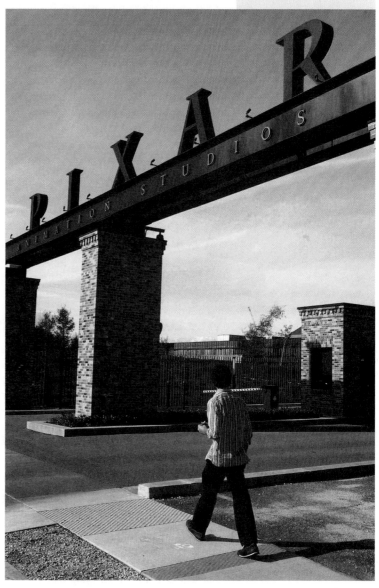

Pixar Animation Studios. Based in Richmond, California, and formed by Apple's Steve Jobs, Pixar started out selling animation software, with Disney as its biggest customer. In 1991, Disney backed Pixar's "Toy Story," which was followed by other hits such as "Finding Nemo" and "The Incredibles." In early 2006, Disney acquired Pixar in a $7.4 billion deal.

The most famous example of these two phenomena is Amazon.com, which has scared major retail store chains. But many small firms, such as online auction companies, have also come from nowhere to collapse time and distance. For instance, so-called Bay-traders make a living selling things on eBay, the online auction company. Bay traders find they get higher prices at Internet auctions than at swap meets or collectibles shows because bidding generates excitement and because the Internet's worldwide reach makes multiple bids more likely. Judi Henderson-Townsand's Oakland, California, company, Mannequin Madness, began when, while working in marketing for a failing dot-com firm, she saw an online ad from a former window dresser offering 50 mannequins. After purchasing the entire inventory, she started renting mannequins and later, after buying more from department stores, started selling them to special-event planners, retail stores, and artists. Henderson claims that the Internet, including eBay, has been by far her greatest marketing resource because it allows the firm to reach customers who could never be reached otherwise.[23] ●

4.2 YOU & INTERNATIONAL MANAGEMENT

> ✱ **major question** Why learn about international management, and what characterizes the successful international manager?

THE BIG PICTURE

Studying international management prepares you to work with foreign customers or suppliers, for a foreign firm in the United States or for a U.S. firm overseas. Successful international managers aren't ethnocentric or polycentric but geocentric.

Part of the action. If "all of the action in business is international," as one expert says, what role do you think you might play in it? Do you think cultural bias against women in some foreign countries contributes to the low percentage of U.S. female executives working abroad?

Working overseas "is an advantage to your career," says Lyric Merrie Hughes, head of a Chicago international marketing firm. "All of the action in business is international."[24] Hughes goes to Europe and Asia every 2 weeks, relying on a nanny and "a good support system" to care for her three children. "Just do it," she says, in urging women to accept overseas assignments. "It's going to enrich you and your family and enhance your career. Get on the plane!"

Julie Androshick spent 2 years teaching in Samoa, then worked as a journalist and as an analyst for consulting company McKinsey & Company. Now based in New York, she says working abroad expanded her worldview, gave her the courage to pursue long-shot jobs, and made her a more loyal employee.[25] After graduating from Northwestern University, Nate Linkon found a job in marketing with InfoSys Technologies, the Indian software giant, in Bangalore.[26] Scott Stapleton, formerly of Oakland, California, also took a marketing job with InfoSys in India. "The job blends practical work experience with life in a developing country," says Stapleton, adding that it's "a rare opportunity to actually witness globalization."[27]

Can overseas experience enhance your career? Foreign experience demonstrates independence, resourcefulness, and entrepreneurship, according to management recruiters. "You are interested in that person who can move quickly and is nimble and has an inquiring mind," says one. People who have worked and supported themselves overseas, she says, tend to be adaptive and inquisitive—valuable skills in today's workplace.[28]

Why Learn about International Management?

International management is management that oversees the conduct of operations in or with organizations in foreign countries, whether it's through a multinational corporation or a multinational organization.

- A *multinational corporation,* or multinational enterprise, **is a business firm with operations in several countries.** Our publisher, McGraw-Hill, is one such "multinational" (see the 17 foreign cities listed on our book's title page). In terms of revenue, the real behemoths in multinational corporations include the American firms Wal-Mart, ExxonMobil, General Motors, Ford Motor Co., General Electric, and Citigroup. The largest foreign companies are BP (Britain), Royal Dutch/Shell (Netherlands/Britain), DaimlerChrysler (Germany/USA), and Toyota (Japan).

- A *multinational organization* **is a nonprofit organization with operations in several countries.** Examples are the World Health Organization, the International Red Cross, the Church of Latter Day Saints.

Practical Action

Being a World Citizen: Learning to Be a Success Abroad

Whether you go abroad on your own or on a work assignment for your company, there are several ways to make your travel enhance your career success.

Learn How Not to Be an "Ugly American"
Americans "are seen throughout the world as an arrogant people, totally self-absorbed and loud," says Keith Reinhard, former head of advertising conglomerate DDB Worldwide, who is leading an effort to reverse that through a nonprofit group called Business for Diplomatic Action (BDA), from which many suggestions here are drawn.[29] A survey conducted by DDB in more than 100 countries found that respondents repeatedly mentioned "arrogant," "loud," and "uninterested in the world" when asked their perceptions of Americans.[30] Some sample advice for Americans traveling abroad appears below. *(See Table 4.1.)*

table 4.1

PROUD TO BE AMERICAN: SOME TIPS

- **Be patient.** Americans "talk fast. Eat fast. Move fast. Live fast. Many cultures do not."
- **Be quiet.** "A loud voice is often perceived as a bragging voice. Casual profanity is almost always considered unacceptable."
- **Listen at least as much as you talk.** Ask the people you're visiting about themselves and their way of life.
- **Don't use slang.** Slang means little or nothing in other cultures and can make you seem insensitive.
- **Talk small.** Talking about wealth, power, or status—corporate or personal—can create resentment.

Source: *World Citizens Guide,* Business for Diplomatic Action, May 2006, http://www.worldcitizensguide.org/index2.html (accessed July 4, 2006).

Study Up on Your Host Country

Study up on the host country's cultural landmarks, cultural shrines, painters, writers, and other outstanding personalities to show you respect their cultural heritage.

Learn What's Appropriate Behavior

Before you go, "Spend at least 10% of preparation time on interpersonal skills," suggests executive coach Arlene B. Isaacs.[31] In Japan it is considered rude to look directly into the eye for more than a few seconds. In Greece the hand-waving gesture commonly used in America is considered an insult. In Afghanistan, a man does not ask another man about his wife.[32]

Learn rituals of respect, including exchange of business cards. Understand that shaking hands is always permissible, but social kissing may not be. Dress professionally. For women, this means no heavy makeup, no flashy jewelry, no short skirts or sleeveless blouses (particularly in Islamic countries). In some countries, casual dressing is a sign of disrespect. Don't use first names and nicknames with fellow employees overseas, especially in countries with strict social strata.[33]

Know Your Field

If you know your field and behave with courtesy and assurance, Asian colleagues will respect your authority, whatever your gender but particularly if you're a woman. "They assume you've proven to other people that you deserve respect," says the female representative for an American health care organization in Singapore, "and so they give it to you."[34]

Become at Least Minimally Skilled in the Language

Whatever foreign country you're in, at the very least you should learn a few key phrases, such as "hello," "please," and "thank you," in your host country's language.

However, successful international managers have learned there is no adequate substitute for knowing the local language. Indeed, half of the top executives in one survey say that among the skills most needed "to maintain a competitive edge" that they find lacking in employees is knowledge of a foreign language.[35]

Even if in the coming years you never travel to the wider world outside North America—an unlikely proposition, we think—the world will assuredly come to you. That, in a nutshell, is why you need to learn about international management.

More specifically, consider yourself in the following situations:

You May Deal with Foreign Customers or Partners

While working for a U.S. company you may have to deal with foreign customers. Or you may have to work with a foreign company in some sort of joint venture. The people you're dealing with may be outside the United States or visitors to it. Either way you would hate to blow a deal—and maybe all future deals—because you were ignorant of some cultural aspects you could have known about.

A typical scenario is that described by *Fortune* columnist Anne Fisher: "You, a hotshot of either sex, show up alone in Tokyo to meet with the head honchos of a prospective joint-venture partner. You don't know how to say 'hello' or 'thank you' in Japanese, you don't have a proper business card, and you plop yourself down in any old seat at the conference table. Pretty soon your counterparts won't look you in the eye, and before you know it, you're on the plane home and the deal is off."[36] All because you didn't know some details of the culture.

You May Deal with Foreign Suppliers

While working for an American company you may have to purchase important components, raw materials, or services from a foreign supplier. And you never know where foreign practices may diverge from what you're accustomed to.

It is estimated, for example, that about 5% of U.S. information technology jobs, such as writing software, have been taken over by suppliers in India, New Zealand, and eastern Europe, and that by 2007 this figure will rise to 23%. Many U.S. software companies—Microsoft, IBM, Oracle, Motorola, Novell, Hewlett-Packard, and Texas Instruments—have opened offices in India to take advantage of high-quality labor.[37]

You May Work for a Foreign Firm in the United States

You may sometime take a job with a foreign firm doing business in the United States, such as an electronics, pharmaceutical, or car company. And you'll have to deal with managers above and below you whose outlook is different from yours. For instance, Japanese companies, with their emphasis on correctness and face saving, operate in significantly different ways from American companies.

Sometimes it is even hard to know that an ostensibly U.S. company actually has foreign ownership. For example, many American book publishers (though not McGraw-Hill) are British, German, or Canadian owned.

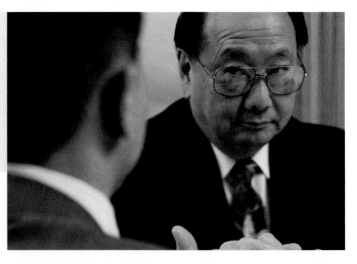

The challenge of interacting successfully with foreign customers. Beyond speaking the language of your host country, what *cultural* skills and awareness might help you gain an advantage over your international competitors?

You May Work for an American Firm Outside the United States—or for a Foreign One You might easily find yourself working abroad in the foreign operation of a U.S. company. Most big American corporations have overseas subsidiaries or divisions. For example, General Motors has plants in Mexico. Yahoo! has operations in the United Kingdom and many Asian countries. On the other hand, as we showed at the beginning of this section, you might also well work for a foreign firm in a foreign country, such as a big Indian company in Bangalore or Bombay.

The Successful International Manager: Geocentric, Not Ethnocentric or Polycentric

Maybe you don't really care that you don't have much understanding of the foreign culture you're dealing with. "What's the point?" you may think. "The main thing is to get the job done." Certainly there are international firms with managers who have this perspective. They are called *ethnocentric,* one of three primary attitudes among international managers, the other two being *polycentric* and *geocentric.*[38]

Ethnocentric Managers—"We Know Best" *Ethnocentric managers* **believe that their native country, culture, language, and behavior are superior to all others.** Ethnocentric managers tend to believe that they can export the managers and practices of their home countries to anywhere in the world and that they will be more capable and reliable. Often the ethnocentric viewpoint is less attributable to prejudice than it is to ignorance, since such managers obviously know more about their home environment than the foreign environment. Ethnocentrism might also be called *parochialism*—**that is, a narrow view in which people see things solely through their own perspective.**

Is ethnocentrism bad for business? It seems so. A survey of 918 companies with home offices in the United States, Japan, and Europe found that ethnocentric policies were linked to such problems as recruiting difficulties, high turnover rates, and lawsuits over personnel policies.[39]

Polycentric Managers—"They Know Best" *Polycentric managers* **take the view that native managers in the foreign offices best understand native personnel and practices, and so the home office should leave them alone.** Thus, the attitude of polycentric managers is nearly the opposite of that of ethnocentric managers.

Geocentric Managers—"What's Best Is What's Effective, Regardless of Origin" *Geocentric managers* **accept that there are differences and similarities between home and foreign personnel and practices and that they should use whatever techniques are most effective.** Clearly, being an ethno- or polycentric manager takes less work. But the payoff for being a geocentric manager can be far greater.

The lessons seem clear. If you become an *expatriate manager*—**a manager living or working in a foreign country**—it's imperative that you try to learn everything you can about the local culture so that you can deal effectively with it and avoid being beaten by your competitors. ●

4.3 WHY & HOW COMPANIES EXPAND INTERNATIONALLY

> ◆ **major question** Why do companies expand internationally, and how do they do it?

THE BIG PICTURE
Multinationals expand to take advantage of availability of supplies, new markets, lower labor costs, access to finance capital, or avoidance of tariffs and import quotas. Five ways they do so are by global outsourcing; importing, exporting, and countertrading; licensing and franchising; joint ventures; and wholly-owned subsidiaries.

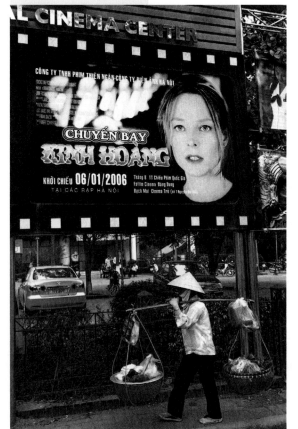

U.S. export. Popular entertainment is one of the major U.S. exports across the globe, as evidenced by this movie billboard. Now Jodie Foster fans in Chuyen Bay, Vietnam, can see her film *Flight Plan* at a cinema nearby. Can you think of any downsides to the globalization of entertainment, especially when it most often originates in the United States and is taken elsewhere?

In Austria, Indonesia, and South Korea, you can find Big Macs in the McDonald's franchises just like in the United States. However, there are also variations for the locals. In Vienna, "McCafés" offer coffee blended for local tastes. In Jakarta, you can get rice as well as French fries. And in Seoul, you can get roast pork on a bun with a garlicky soy sauce.

There's an important lesson here. Says a *New York Times* writer, "That combination of a globally recognized brand with a flexible menu that caters to local palates has helped McDonald's navigate the global economic turbulence that has knocked most of the other big corporations operating around the world way off course."[40]

Clearly, we could all benefit from learning why the McDonald's international division accounts for nearly 60% of the burger chain's profits. Let us consider why and how companies expand overseas.

Why Companies Expand Internationally

Many a company has made the deliberate decision to restrict selling its product or service to just its own country. Is anything wrong with that?

The answer is: It depends. It would probably have been a serious mistake for NEC, Sony, or Hitachi to have limited their markets solely to Japan during the 1990s, a time when the country was in an economic slump and Japanese consumers weren't consuming. During that same period, however, some American banks might have been better off not making loans abroad, when the U.S. economy was booming but foreign economies were not. Going international or not going international—it can be risky either way.

Why, then, do companies expand internationally? There are at least five reasons, all of which have to do with making or saving money.

1. Availability of Supplies   Antique and art dealers, mining companies, banana growers, sellers of hard woods—all have to go where their basic supplies or raw materials are located. For years oil companies, for example, have expanded their activities outside the United States in seeking cheaper or more plentiful sources of oil.

2. New Markets Elsewhere in this book (Chapter 6) we discuss the *product life cycle,* the natural rise and fall in the sales life of a product. Sometimes a company will find, as cigarette makers have, that the demand for their product has declined domestically but that they can still make money overseas. Or sometimes a company will steal a march on its competitors by aggressively expanding into foreign markets, as did Coca-Cola over PepsiCo under the leadership of legendary CEO Robert Goizueta.

3. Lower Labor Costs The decline in manufacturing jobs in the United States is directly attributable to the fact that American companies have found it cheaper to do their manufacturing outside the States. For example, the rationale for using *maquiladoras*—**manufacturing plants allowed to operate in Mexico with special privileges in return for employing Mexican citizens**—is that they provide less expensive labor for assembling everything from appliances to cars. However, even professional or service kinds of jobs may be shipped overseas. As mentioned, some makers of software applications programs are taking care of their programming needs by sending their jobs to India.

4. Access to Finance Capital Companies may be enticed into going abroad by the prospects of capital being put up by foreign companies. Or sometimes a foreign government will offer a subsidy in hopes of attracting a company that will create jobs, as Ireland did in the 1970s for Lotus sports-car maker John DeLorean.

5. Avoidance of Tariffs & Import Quotas Countries place tariffs (fees) on imported goods or impose import quotas—limitations on the numbers of products allowed in—for the purpose of protecting their own domestic industries. For example, Japan imposes tariffs on agricultural products, such as rice, imported from the United States. To avoid these penalties, a company might create a subsidiary to produce the product in the foreign country. General Electric and Whirlpool, for example, have foreign subsidiaries to produce appliances overseas.

How Companies Expand Internationally

Most companies don't start out to be multinationals. Generally, they edge their way into international business, making minimal investments and taking minimal risks, as shown in the drawing below. *(See Figure 4.1.)*
 Let's consider these five ways.

I. Global Outsourcing A common practice of many companies, *outsourcing* is **defined as using suppliers outside the company to provide goods and services.** For example, airlines are increasingly farming out aircraft maintenance to other

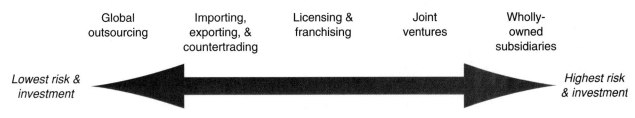

figure 4.1

FIVE WAYS OF EXPANDING INTERNATIONALLY

These range from lowest risk and investment *(left)* to highest risk and investment *(right).*

companies.[41] Management philosopher Peter Drucker believes that in the near future organizations may be outsourcing all work that is "support"—such as information systems—rather than revenue producing.

Global outsourcing (or simply *global sourcing* or *offshoring*) extends this technique outside the U.S. **Global outsourcing is defined as using suppliers outside the United States to provide labor, goods, or services.** The reason may be that the foreign supplier has resources not available in the United States, such as Italian marble. Or the supplier may have special expertise, as do Pakistani weavers. Or—more likely these days—the supplier's labor is cheaper than American labor. As a manager, your first business trip outside the U.S. might be to inspect the production lines of one of your outsourcing suppliers.

2. Importing, Exporting, & Countertrading When *importing,* **a company buys goods outside the country and resells them domestically.** Nothing might seem to be more American than Jeep Wranglers, but they are made not only in the United States but also in Canada, from which they are imported and made available for sale in the United States. Many of the products we use are imported, ranging from Heineken beer (Netherlands) to Texaco gasoline (Saudi Arabia) to Honda snowblowers (Japan).

Practical Action

Global Outsourcing: Which Jobs Are Likely to Fall Victim to Offshoring?

Will there be any good jobs left for new college graduates?

Americans are rightly concerned about the changing jobs picture, brought about in part by offshoring of work to low-wage countries such as China, India, the Philippines, and Ireland. Few of the 2.8 million factory jobs that were lost between 2001 and 2004, for instance, have been replaced, forcing many workers to accept lower-paying alternatives, such as jobs in retail and health care, which pay on average 21% less than manufacturing jobs.[42] Now the same trend—global outsourcing—is happening with white-collar jobs.[43]

Offshoring Is Not the Only Job Killer
Offshoring is not the only culprit in doing away with many U.S. jobs. Much more important are productivity gains—increased output per existing worker through use of labor-saving technology, procurement efficiencies, and extended work hours. Every one percentage point of annual productivity growth, it's estimated, eliminates about 1.3 million jobs. Another factor is employers' hiring of temporary instead of permanent workers to save on health care and retirement benefit costs.[44]

Does Global Outsourcing Actually Benefit the U.S.?
Supporters of free trade argue that jobs shipped offshore—even infotech and biotech jobs—generate returns to the U.S. "The money paid to foreign producers," says University of California at Berkeley business professor Hal Varian, "whether businesses or workers, typically comes back home to buy domestic goods and services, thereby generating domestic employment."[45] The difficulty is the political problem: "when the dollars flow offshore," he says, "it is easy to identify those who are hurt. But when the dollars flow back, it is much more difficult to discern the beneficiaries."

Observed management philosopher Peter Drucker: "Nobody seems to realize that we import twice or three times as many jobs as we export. I'm talking about the jobs created by foreign companies coming into the U.S. The most obvious [importers] are foreign auto companies. . . . We are exporting low-skill, low-paying jobs but are importing high-skill, high-paying jobs."[46]

How Can You Prepare for an Offshored World?
What career fields are apt to be most susceptible to offshoring?

"I believe you should outsource everything for which there is no career track that could lead into senior management," said Drucker. An example, he said, is the job of total-quality-control specialist, a job that can be done overseas. Among the jobs predicted by Forrester Research to move offshore: office support, computer, business operations, architecture, legal, sales, and art and design.[47]

"As soon as a job becomes routine enough to describe in a spec sheet, it becomes vulnerable to outsourcing," says another writer. "Jobs like data entry, which are routine by nature, were the first among obvious candidates for outsourcing." But even "design and financial-analysis skills can, with time, become well-enough understood to be spelled out in a contract and signed away."[48]

Says Fred Levy, a Massachusetts Institute of Technology economist, "If you can describe a job precisely, or write rules for doing it, it's unlikely to survive. Either we'll program a computer to do it, or we'll teach a foreigner to do it."[49] If you're a programmer or in a similar at-risk job, Bill Mitchell, CEO of a software company, suggests that you should "specialize to the point that you offer greater productivity, or change careers." Another option is to innovate; Mitchell mentions a friend who developed new programming methods, "which allowed him to write certain specialized applications about eight times faster than his typical Bangalore competitor."[50] However, this advantage might not last for long.

Which Jobs Will Remain in the U.S.?

It is difficult to predict which jobs will remain at home, since even the Bureau of Labor Statistics often can't get it right. However, jobs that endure may share certain traits, listed below, regardless of the industry they serve:

- **Face to face.** Some involve *face-to-face contact,* such as being a salesperson with a specific territory or an emergency room doctor.

- **Physical contact.** Other jobs involve *physical contact,* such as those of dentists, nurses, massage therapists, gardeners, and nursing-home aides.

- **Recognizing complex patterns.** Others involve the human ability to *recognize complex patterns,* which are hard to computerize, such as a physician's ability to diagnose an unusual disease (even if the X-rays are read by a radiologist in India). This also describes such high-end jobs as teaching first grade or selling a mansion to a millionaire or jobs that demand an intimate knowledge of the U.S., such as marketing to American teenagers or lobbying Congress.[51]

Finally, the Association for Computing Machinery has found after a year of study that the effects of offshoring on technical jobs have been overstated; that is, although 2–3% of information technology jobs are being offshored each year, this is offset by an annual 3% increase in technical jobs in the U.S.[52]

Survival Rules

For you, as a prospective manager, there are perhaps three ideas to take away from all this:

- **Teamwork and creativity.** "Jobs that persist are dynamic and creative and require the ability to team with others," says Jim Spohrer of the IBM Almaden Research Center in San Jose, California, which studies the business operations of IBM's corporate clients. "At its heart, a company is simply a group of teams that come together to create" products and services.[53]

- **Flexibility.** "Jobs used to change very little or not at all over the course of several generations," says Spohrer. "Now, they might change three or four times in a single lifetime." Flexibility—as in being willing to undergo retraining—thus becomes important. Fortunately, as Drucker pointed out, the United States is "the only country that has a very significant continuing education system. This doesn't exist anywhere else." The U.S. is also the only country, he said, in which it is easy for younger people to move from one area at work to another.[54]

- **Education.** The more education one has, the more one is apt to prevail during times of economic change. Men and women with 4 years of college, for instance, earn nearly 45% more on average than those with only a high school diploma.[55]

When *exporting,* **a company produces goods domestically and sells them outside the country.** One of the greatest U.S. exports is American pop culture, in the form of movies, CDs, and fashion. The United States is also a leader in exporting computers and other information technology.

Sometimes other countries may wish to import American goods but lack the currency to pay for them. In that case, the exporting U.S. company may resort to *countertrading—that is, bartering goods for goods.* When the Russian ruble plunged in value in 1998, some goods became a better medium of exchange than currency.

3. Licensing & Franchising   Licensing and franchising are two aspects of the same thing, although licensing is used by manufacturing companies and franchising is used more frequently by service companies.

In *licensing,* **a company allows a foreign company to pay it a fee to make or distribute the first company's product or service.** For example, the Du Pont chemical company might license a company in Brazil to make Teflon, the nonstick substance that is found on some frying pans. Thus, Du Pont, the licensor, can make money without having to invest large sums to conduct business directly in a foreign company. Moreover, the Brazilian firm, the licensee, knows the local market better than Du Pont probably would.

Franchising **is a form of licensing in which a company allows a foreign company to pay it a fee and a share of the profit in return for using the first company's brand name and a package of materials and services.** For example, Burger King, Hertz, and Hilton Hotels, which are all well-known brands, might provide the use of their names plus their operating know-how (facility design, equipment, recipes, management systems) to companies in Greece in return for an upfront fee plus a percentage of the profits.

By now Americans traveling throughout the world have become accustomed to seeing so-called U.S. franchises everywhere: Popeye's Chicken & Biscuits in China, DKNY and The GAP stores in Turkey, Coca-Cola in Mexico, Intercontinental hotels in Hungary.

4. Joint Ventures   *Strategic allies* (described in Chapter 3) are two organizations that have joined forces to realize strategic advantages that neither would have if operating alone. A U.S. firm may form a *joint venture,* **also known as a *strategic alliance,* with a foreign company to share the risks and rewards of starting a new enterprise together in a foreign country.** For instance, General Motors operates a joint venture in Canada with Suzuki Motor Corp. and an assembly plant called NUMMI in California with Toyota.

Sometimes a joint venture is the only way an American company can have a presence in a certain country, whose laws may forbid foreigners from ownership.

General Motors found that the best way to do business in the new nation of Namibia (after it became independent of South African control) was to ship GM vehicles to a plant in that country. The Namibians, who wanted to be producers, not just consumers, then converted them from U.S.-style left-hand drive to right-hand drive, as required in parts of Africa.

5. Wholly-Owned Subsidiaries   A *wholly-owned subsidiary* **is a foreign subsidiary that is totally owned and controlled by an organization.** The foreign subsidiary may be an existing company that is purchased outright. **A *greenfield venture* is a foreign subsidiary that the owning organization has built from scratch.**

General Motors owns Adam Opel AG in Germany, Vauxhall Motor Cars Ltd. in the United Kingdom, Holden's in Australia, and half of Saab Automobile AB in Sweden. ●

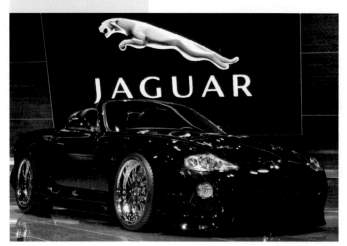

Jaguar. A number of formerly British-owned carmakers have gone over to foreign ownership. Jaguar is a subsidiary of Ford Motor Co., as is Land Rover. Ford also has provided the financial assistance to keep Aston-Martin going. Vauxhall is owned by General Motors. The rights to make Rolls-Royce cars (but not aircraft engines) are now held by German automaker Volkswagen, but Volkswagen's German rival BMW holds the rights to the name and the "RR" marque. Volkswagen owns the Rolls-Royce sister Bentley brand. Do you think the American companies General Motors and Ford could ever wind up under foreign ownership?

4.4 ECONOMIC & POLITICAL-LEGAL DIFFERENCES

How may foreign countries differ in their economic, political, and legal characteristics?

major question

THE BIG PICTURE
Countries' economies vary among free-market, command, and mixed economies, as well as in infrastructure and resources and currency exchange rates. Political systems may vary between democratic and totalitarian, in political risk, and in laws and regulations.

As an international manager, you might well have to operate amid many complexities. What should you be on the lookout for? First let us consider (1) *economic differences,* then (2) *political-legal differences.*

Economic Differences: Adjusting to Other Countries' Economies

How will you, as an international manager, adjust to economic changes? Let's discuss the following important topics: *economic systems, economic development, infrastructure and resources,* and *currency exchange rates.*

Principal Economic Systems: Free Market, Command, & Mixed Economies
How is doing business in Taiwan different from doing business in China? One is a *free-market economy,* the other traditionally a *command economy* (but changing). These are two of the three principal types of economic system around the globe, the third being a *mixed economy.*

1. Free-Market Economy   This is the kind of economy found, for example, in the United States and in Great Britain. **In a *free-market economy,* the production of goods and services is controlled by private enterprise and the interaction of the forces of supply and demand, rather than by the government.** As a manager you may prefer dealing with countries with this kind of system because there will be fewer hassles with government regulators. Moreover, in general the citizens of such countries may have higher incomes, which means there may be more markets for your product or service.

2. Command Economy   This is the kind of economy found in the old communist countries in and around the former Soviet Union. It is still found in Cuba and North Korea and, to a certain extent, in China and Vietnam. **In a *command economy,* or *central-planning economy,* the government owns most businesses and regulates the amounts, types, and prices of goods and services.** The failure of communism in Europe is largely because such economies proved to be unworkable. Other communist countries (Cuba, North Korea) have experienced great economic difficulties, and still others (China, Vietnam) have begun moving away from command economies.

3. Mixed Economy   This type of economy is found in many countries of Europe. **In a *mixed economy,* most of the important industries are owned by the government, but others are controlled by private enterprise.** This used to be the case in

Britain, where the government once owned the railroads, airlines, steel, telecommunications, and health industries. However, most of these industries underwent *privatization—that is, state-owned businesses were sold off to private enterprise.* Russia, too, has been moving away from state ownership of big utilities and other sectors of the economy.

Whatever the type of economy, some countries have *indigenization laws,* which require that citizens within the host country own a majority of whatever company is operating within that country.

Developed versus Less-Developed Countries

It used to be that the United States, Canada, western Europe, Australia, New Zealand, and Japan were known as "first-world" countries. The communist nations were called "second-world" countries. Pretty much all the rest, especially those in the Southern Hemisphere, were known as "third-world" or developing countries. With the end of the cold war, the world now seems to be divided between *developed countries* and *less-developed countries.*

Developed Countries   These are the first-world countries: the United States, Canada, most European countries, Australia, New Zealand, and Japan. ***Developed countries are those with a high level of economic development and generally high average level of income among their citizens.***

Most international organizations, whether International Paper Co. or the International Red Cross, Royal Dutch/Shell or the World Health Organization, are headquartered in developed countries. Also, about three-quarters of foreign investment has been directed toward developed countries.[56]

Less-Developed Countries   These are the third-world countries, such as Brazil, China, Haiti, Mexico, and Zambia, to name just a handful of the scores of nations in this category.

***Less-developed countries,* also known as *developing countries,* consist of nations with low economic development and low average incomes.** They also are usually characterized by high birth rates.

Today the five largest countries in population size are China, India, the United States, Indonesia, and Brazil. By the middle of the 21st century, because of population growth (most of it owing to birth rates, not immigration), the five largest will be India, China, the United States, Nigeria (today's No. 9), and Indonesia.[57]

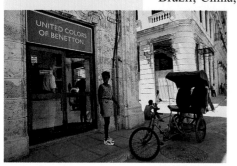

Infrastructure & Resources   In the United States, Canada, and much of Europe, we pretty much take the phone system for granted. In less-developed countries, getting a phone installed may take weeks, even months, and then it may still be inefficient. The significance of the cell phone is that countries with underdeveloped wired telephone systems can use cellular phones as a fast way of installing better communications, giving Pakistan, China, Nigeria, and others a chance of joining the world economy.

Telephone networks are an essential part of a country's infrastructure, especially since they are important to the development of information technology. **A country's *infrastructure* consists of the physical facilities that form the basis for its level of economic development.** Examples are schools, roads, airports, railroads, harbors, utilities, hospitals, and telecommunications systems. Before you as a manager begin

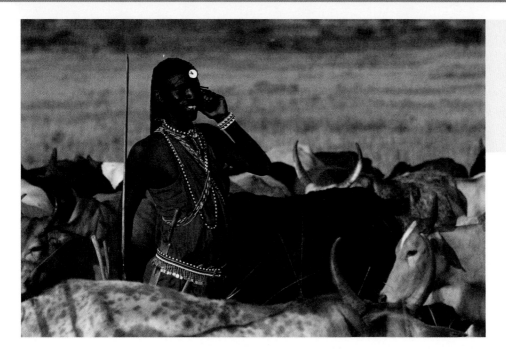

"Oh, same old thing." The cell phone represents a boon to less-developed countries because this kind of telephone infrastructure does not entail the costly process of installing miles of telephone poles and land lines.

getting involved in major projects in a particular foreign country, you need to be aware of any drawbacks in its infrastructure.

In addition, you'll need to be concerned about resources. If you've set up an apparel plant in Mexico, for example, you need to think about where the fabric and the sewing equipment are going to come from—whether you'll be able to get them from suppliers in that country or you'll have to import them.

Currency Exchange Rates   The *exchange rate* **is the rate at which one country's currency can be exchanged for another country's currency.** International managers have to keep a close eye on currency exchange rates because a change of just a few percentage points can have major implications. For example, if one year the American dollar is worth 1.10 Canadian dollars and the next year it is worth 1.34 Canadian dollars, this means that U.S. goods have become more expensive for Canadians, so they are apt to buy less. If the American dollar drops to the equivalent of 1.00 Canadian dollars, they will probably buy more.

Political-Legal Differences: Adjusting to Other Countries' Governments & Laws

When in the early 1990s McDonald's opened an outlet in Belgrade in the former Yugoslavia, should it have tried to anticipate the possibility that the restaurant might someday be wrecked by angry crowds of Serbs (as happened following air strikes by American and other NATO bombers on Serbia in 1999)? Perhaps someone was foresighted enough to take out political risk insurance, which is available for corporations investing in unstable areas.[58]

Such is one of the considerations of a company hoping to develop new markets overseas. A star international manager needs to always be aware of political-legal differences, including different government systems, political risks, and unfamiliar laws and regulations, as we discuss.

Governmental Systems: Democratic versus Totalitarian

No doubt you will have to deal with unfamiliar political systems. There are two extremes:

- **Democratic.** *Democratic governments* **rely on free elections and representative assemblies.** The government is supposed to represent the society as a whole, or at least the majority of its citizens.

  From the standpoint of ease in doing business, democratic systems of government, such as those in western Europe, generally seem more familiar to an American international manager. Nevertheless, different national attitudes toward bureaucracy, monopolies, and the acceptance of "gratuities" can make it difficult to do business.

- **Totalitarian.** *Totalitarian governments* **are ruled by a dictator, a single political party, or a special-membership group,** such as a handful of ruling families or a military junta (such as Cuba under Fidel Castro or Indonesia under Sukarno). The risk for you as an international manager is that the political tides may change, and through no fault of your own you may find yourself somehow on the wrong side.

  Some governments fall in between democratic and totalitarian. Mexico, for example, regularly features free elections, but for decades it was ruled by a single political party.

Political Risk

It's possible that a democratic country in which your company has started up an overseas operation could overnight become a totalitarian country, accompanied by a sudden change in all the rules. Thus, every firm contemplating establishing itself abroad must calculate its *political risk*—**the risk that political changes will cause loss of a company's assets or impair its foreign operations.** Two political risks an organization planning to do business abroad might anticipate are these:

- **Instability.** Even in a developed country a company may be victimized by political instability, such as riots or civil disorders, as happened during the 1989 Rodney King riots in Los Angeles. Overseas an international company may also have to try to anticipate revolutions or changes in government. Italy, for example, has had more than 60 governments since World War II.

- **Expropriation.** *Expropriation* **is defined as a government's seizure of a foreign company's assets.** After Fidel Castro overthrew the Batista government in Cuba in 1959, he expropriated millions of dollars' worth of assets of American companies. Early in the 20th century, Mexico expropriated American-owned oil fields and production facilities.

Laws & Regulations

"Ignorance of the law is no excuse," one hears. That assumes you're supposed to keep up with the important laws in your own country, which can be complicated enough. Now try keeping up with the laws in another country.

International companies have to work with numerous laws and regulations on subjects ranging from labor to libel to labeling. The United States, for instance, has legislation under the *Foreign Corrupt Practices Act* **of 1977, which makes it illegal for employees of U.S. companies to bribe political decision makers in foreign nations,** an acceptable practice in many countries.

Many of the laws and regulations have to do with tariffs, import quotas, and the like, as we discuss in the next section. ●

4.5 THE WORLD OF FREE TRADE: REGIONAL ECONOMIC COOPERATION

> **What are barriers to free trade, and what major organizations and trading blocs promote trade?**
>
> major + question

THE BIG PICTURE

Barriers to free trade are tariffs, import quotas, and embargoes. Organizations promoting international trade are the World Trade Organization, the World Bank, and the International Monetary Fund. Major trading blocs are NAFTA, the EU, APEC, and Mercosur.

If you live in the United States, you see foreign products on a daily basis—cars, appliances, clothes, foods, beers, wines, and so on. Based on what you see every day, which countries would you think are our most important trading partners? Japan? Germany? England? South Korea? France?

These five countries do indeed appear among the top 10 leading U.S. trading partners (measured in terms of imports and exports added together). Interestingly, however, our No. 1 and No. 2 trading partners are our immediate neighbors—Canada and Mexico, whose products may not be quite so visible. (Others at the top: 3. China; 4. Japan; 5. Germany; 6. United Kingdom; 7. South Korea; 8. Taiwan; 9. France; 10. Malaysia.)

Let's begin to consider *free trade,* **the movement of goods and services among nations without political or economic obstruction.**

Barriers to International Trade

Countries often use *trade protectionism—***the use of government regulations to limit the import of goods and services**—to protect their domestic industries against foreign competition. The justification they often use is that this saves jobs. Actually, protectionism is not considered beneficial, mainly because of what it does to the overall trading atmosphere.

The three devices by which countries try to exert protectionism consist of *tariffs, import quotas,* and *embargoes.*

I. Tariffs A *tariff* **is a trade barrier in the form of a customs duty, or tax, levied mainly on imports.** At one time, for instance, to protect the American shoe industry, the United States imposed a tariff on Italian shoes.

Actually, there are two types of tariffs: One is designed simply to raise money for the government (revenue tariff). The other, which concerns us more, is to raise the price of imported goods to make the prices of domestic

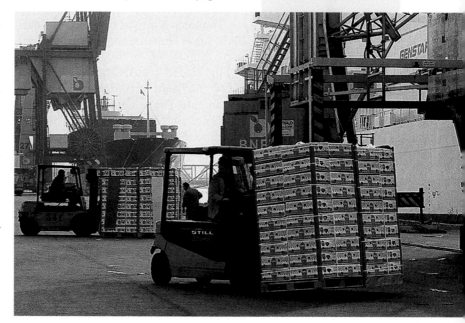

Going bananas. Stevedores unload Chiquita bananas from a ship in Antwerp harbor. The Netherlands is a member of the European Union, which had imposed a duty on bananas, including those grown by Cincinnati-based Chiquita Brands Inc. The reason for the duty was that Chiquita's bananas undercut those of the EU's longstanding suppliers. For retaliation, Chiquita successfully lobbied the U.S. government to place duties on European goods (such as paper products) imported into the United States. Such activities among governments are known as a "trade war."

products more competitive (protective tariff). For example, in 2001 President George W. Bush called for tariffs on imported steel, following influxes in imported foreign steel in the previous two years. Although the tariffs gave the U.S. domestic steel industry a chance to regroup and better compete with foreign steelmakers, the tariffs were lifted after the World Trade Organization (discussed below) ruled in 2003 that they were illegal.[59]

2. Import Quotas An *import quota* **is a trade barrier in the form of a limit on the numbers of a product that can be imported.** Its intent is to protect domestic industry by restricting the availability of foreign products.

Effective January 2005, China agreed (as a condition of being allowed into the World Trade Organization) to cancel car import quotas, which it had used to protect its domestic car manufacturing industry against imported vehicles from the United States, Japan, and Germany.[60]

Quotas are designed to prevent *dumping,* **the practice of a foreign company's exporting products abroad at a lower price than the price in the home market— or even below the costs of production—in order to drive down the price of the domestic product.**

3. Embargoes Ever had a Cuban cigar? They're difficult for Americans to get, since they're embargoed. **An** *embargo* **is a complete ban on the import or export of certain products.** It has been years since anyone was allowed to import Cuban cigars and sugar into the United States or for an American firm to do business in Cuba. The U.S. government also tries to embargo the export of certain supercomputers and other high-tech equipment with possible military uses to countries such as China.

Organizations Promoting International Trade

In the 1920s, the institution of tariff barriers did not so much protect jobs as depress the demand for goods and services, thereby leading to the loss of jobs anyway—and the massive unemployment of the Great Depression of the 1930s.[61] As a result of this lesson, after World War II the advanced nations of the world began to realize that if all countries could freely exchange the products that each could produce most efficiently, this would lead to lower prices all around. Thus began the removal of barriers to free trade.

The three principal organizations designed to facilitate international trade are the *World Trade Organization,* the *World Bank,* and the *International Monetary Fund.*

1. The World Trade Organization (WTO) Consisting of 146 member countries, the *World Trade Organization (WTO)* **is designed to monitor and enforce trade agreements.** The agreements are based on the *General Agreement on Tariffs and Trade (GATT),* an international accord first signed by 23 nations in 1947, which helped to reduce worldwide tariffs and other barriers. Out of GATT came a series of "rounds," or negotiations, that resulted in the lowering of barriers; for instance, the Uruguay Round, implemented in 1996, cut tariffs by one-third.

Founded in 1995 and headquartered in Geneva, Switzerland, WTO succeeded GATT as the world forum for trade negotiations and has the formal legal structure for deciding trade disputes. WTO also encompasses areas not previously covered by GATT, such as services and intellectual property rights. A particularly interesting area of responsibility covers telecommunications—cell phones, pagers, data transmission, satellite communications, and the like—with half of the WTO members agreeing in 1998 to open their markets to foreign telecommunications companies.[62]

2. The World Bank The World Bank was founded after World War II to help European countries rebuild. Today the purpose of the *World Bank* **is to provide low-interest loans to developing nations for improving transportation, education, health, and telecommunications.** The bank has 184 member nations, with most contributions coming from the United States, Europe, and Japan.

Most recently, the bank has concentrated on bringing the Internet to less-developed and developing countries, such as those in Africa, in hopes that it will attract more companies to those areas and lead to more rapid economic development.[63]

In recent years, the World Bank has been the target of demonstrations in Seattle, Washington, DC, Ottawa, and elsewhere. Some protestors believe it finances projects that could damage the ecosystem, such as the Three Gorges Dam on China's Yangtze River. Others complain it supports countries that permit low-paying sweatshops or that suppress religious freedom. Still others think it has dragged its feet on getting affordable AIDS drugs to less-developed countries in Africa. Many of the same protests were leveled against the International Monetary Fund, discussed next. The World Bank has responded by trying to support projects that are not harmful to the environment and that are aimed at helping lift people out of poverty.

3. The International Monetary Fund Founded in 1945 and now affiliated with the United Nations, the International Monetary Fund is the second pillar supporting the international financial community. Consisting of 182 member nations, **the** *International Monetary Fund (IMF)* **is designed to assist in smoothing the flow of money between nations.** The IMF operates as a last-resort lender that makes short-term loans to countries suffering from unfavorable balance of payments (roughly the difference between money coming into a country and money leaving the country, because of imports, exports, and other matters).

For example, during the late 1990s' "Asian crisis," the value of Thailand's currency dropped until at the end of 1997 it was worth half what it was at the start of the year. Because Thailand owed other countries, they, too, were affected: Indonesia's currency dropped 70% and South Korea's 45%. In response to pleas for help, the IMF loaned Asian countries billions of dollars—$57 billion to South Korea alone in 1997.

Major Trading Blocs: NAFTA, EU, APEC, & Mercosur

A *trading bloc,* **also known as an** *economic community,* **is a group of nations within a geographical region that have agreed to remove trade barriers with one another.** The four major trading blocs are the *NAFTA nations,* the *European Union,* the *APEC countries,* and the *Mercosur.*

I. NAFTA—the Three Countries of the North American Free Trade Agreement Formed in 1994, **the** *North American Free Trade Agreement (NAFTA)* **is a trading bloc consisting of the United States, Canada, and Mexico,** encompassing 435 million people. The agreement is supposed to eliminate 99% of the tariffs and quotas among these countries, allowing for freer flow of goods, services, and capital in North America. Since 1994, trade with Canada and Mexico now accounts for one-third of the U.S. total, up from one-quarter in 1989. Exports to Mexico and Canada rose from $12 billion in 1993 to $26 billion in 2002.[64]

Is NAFTA a job killer, as some have complained? In Mexico, it has failed to generate substantial job growth and has hurt hundreds of thousands of subsistence farmers, so that illegal immigration to the U.S. continues to grow. As for the United States, nearly 525,000 workers, mostly in manufacturing, have been certified by the U.S.

government as having lost their jobs or had their hours or wages reduced because of NAFTA's shifting of jobs south of the border. It's also spurred a $418 billion trade deficit.[65] However, supporters insist NAFTA ultimately will result in more jobs and a higher standard of living among all trading partners.

2. The EU—the 25 Countries of the European Union

Formed in 1957, **the *European Union (EU)* consists of 25 trading partners in Europe,** covering 455 million consumers.

Nearly all internal trade barriers have been eliminated (including movement of labor between countries), making the EU a union of borderless neighbors and the world's largest free market.

By 2002, such national symbols as the franc, the mark, the lira, the peseta, and the guilder had been replaced with the EU currency, the euro.[66] There has even been speculation that someday the euro could replace the dollar as the dominant world currency.[67] On May 1, 2004, the EU swelled to 25 countries with the addition of eight former Communist states from eastern Europe and two Mediterranean islands; Bulgaria and Romania hope to join by 2007.

3. APEC—21 Countries of the Pacific Rim

The *Asia-Pacific Economic Cooperation (APEC)* is a group of 21 Pacific Rim countries whose purpose is to improve economic and political ties. Most countries with a coastline on the Pacific Ocean are members of the organization, although there are a number of exceptions. Among the 21 members are the United States, Canada, and China. Since the founding in 1989, APEC members have worked to reduce tariffs and other trade barriers across the Asia-Pacific region. APEC member countries are highlighted below.

4. Mercosur—Six Countries of Latin America

The *Mercosur* is the largest trade bloc in Latin America and has four core members—Argentina, Brazil, Paraguay, and Uruguay—and two associate members, Chile and Bolivia. Besides reducing tariffs by 75%, Mercosur nations are striving for full economic integration, and the alliance is also negotiating trade agreements with NAFTA, the EU, and Japan.

Most Favored Nation Trading Status

Besides joining together in trade blocs, countries will also extend special, "most favored nation" trading privileges to one another. *Most favored nation* **trading status describes a condition in which a country grants other countries favorable trading treatment such as the reduction of import duties.** The purpose is to promote stronger and more stable ties between companies in the two countries. ●

4.6 THE IMPORTANCE OF UNDERSTANDING CULTURAL DIFFERENCES

What are the principal areas of cultural differences?

major ❌ question

THE BIG PICTURE

Managers trying to understand other cultures need to understand four basic cultural perceptions embodied in language, nonverbal communication, time orientation, and religion.

Americans living near San Jose, California, didn't like it when an Australian company acquired the local Valley Fair shopping center and renamed it Shoppingtown.[68]

"The first time I saw the word Shoppingtown, I nearly choked," complained one letter writer to the local paper. "The more I see it, the more it annoys me."

"We aren't the penny-pinchers this name indicates we are," said another. "What happened to that survey about Valley Fair customers having the area's most upscale lifestyle and money to back it up?"

Said a third: "These are the same people—Australians—who did not get [the U.S. television comedy] *Seinfeld*; the show failed miserably there. 'Shoppingtown' is a brand name in Australia. They are trying too hard to accomplish the same thing here in the U.S. Do you really care that your mall is a 'brand'. . . ? They have not done their homework, and do not understand Americans just yet." (Actually, Westfield's strategy may have been sound; in 2006, with 128 shopping centers in several areas of the English-speaking world, the son of the founder bragged, "We did what others didn't think you can do, which is to brand malls.")[69]

Don't Australians and Americans speak the same language? Could a shopping center risk failing simply because of a name change? And if there can be such misperceptions in English, what might it be like in trying to communicate in a different language? *Training* magazine offers some blunt advice: "The lesson for those [managers] plying foreign markets or hosting business visitors is: Slow down. Shut up. Listen."[70]

The Importance of National Culture

Some of the problems resulting from the experiences of companies such as that described above are the result of cultural differences. A nation's *culture* **is the shared set of beliefs, values, knowledge, and patterns of behavior common to a group of people.**

We begin learning our culture starting at an early age through everyday interaction with people around us. This is why, from the outside looking in, a nation's culture can seem so intangible and perplexing. As cultural anthropologist Edward T. Hall puts it, "Since much of culture operates outside our awareness, frequently we don't even know what we know. . . . We unconsciously learn what to notice and what not to notice, how to divide time and space, how to walk and talk and use our bodies, how to behave as men or women, how to relate to other people, how to handle responsibility. . . ."[71] Indeed, says Hall, what we think of as "mind" is really internalized culture.

And because a culture is made up of so many nuances, this is why visitors to another culture may experience culture shock—the feelings of discomfort and disorientation associated with being in an unfamiliar

Would you shop at "Shoppingtown"? That was the name new Australian owners gave to a California shopping center known as Valley Fair.

culture. According to anthropologists, culture shock involves anxiety and doubt caused by an overload of unfamiliar expectations and social cues.[72]

Cultural Dimensions: The Hofstede & GLOBE Project Models

Misunderstandings and miscommunications often arise in international business relationships because people don't understand the expectations of the other side. A person from North America, Great Britain, Scandinavia, Germany, or Switzerland, for example, comes from a *low-context culture* **in which shared meanings are primarily derived from written and spoken words.** Someone from China, Korea, Japan, Vietnam, Mexico, or many Arab cultures, on the other hand, comes from a *high-context culture* **in which people rely heavily on situational cues for meaning when communicating with others,** relying on nonverbal cues as to another person's official position, status, or family connections.

One way to avoid cultural collisions is to have an understanding of various cultural dimensions, as expressed in the Hofstede model and the GLOBE project.

Hofstede's Model of Four Cultural Dimensions   Thirty years ago Dutch researcher and IBM psychologist **Geert Hofstede** collected data from 116,000 IBM employees in 53 countries and proposed his *Hofstede model of four cultural dimensions,* **which identified four dimensions along which national cultures can be placed: (1) individualism/collectivism, (2) power distance, (3) uncertainty avoidance, and (4) masculinity/femininity.**[73]

- **Individualism/collectivism—how loosely or tightly are people socially bonded?** The United States, Australia, Sweden, France, Canada, and Great Britain have high individualistic values. *Individualism* indicates a preference for a loosely knit social framework in which people are expected to take care of themselves. Costa Rica, Thailand, Mexico, China, Guatemala, and Ecuador have high collectivist values. *Collectivism* indicates a preference for a tightly knit social framework in which people and organizations are expected to look after each other.

- **Power distance—how much do people accept inequality in power?** *Power distance* refers to the degree to which people accept inequality in social situations. *High power distance,* such as occurs in Mexico, India, Thailand, Panama, and the Philippines, means that people accept inequality in power among people, institutions, and organizations. *Low power distance,* such as occurs in Sweden, Germany, Israel, and Australia, means that people expect equality in power.

- **Uncertainty avoidance—how strongly do people desire certainty?** This dimension is about being comfortable with risk and uncertainty. Countries such as Japan, France, Greece, Portugal, and Costa Rica are very high in *uncertainty avoidance,* which expresses people's intolerance for uncertainty and risk. *High uncertainty avoidance* means people feel uncomfortable with uncertainty and support beliefs that promise certainty and conformity. Countries such as Sweden, India, the United States, Singapore, and Jamaica are very low on this dimension. *Low uncertainty avoidance* means that people have high tolerance for the uncertain and ambiguous.

- **Masculinity/femininity—how much do people embrace stereotypical male or female traits?** *Masculinity* expresses how much people value performance-oriented masculine traits, such as achievement, assertiveness, and material success. Countries with strong masculine preferences are Japan, Mexico, Austria, and Germany. *Femininity* expresses how much people embrace relationship-oriented feminine traits, such as cooperation and group decision making. Sweden, Norway, Thailand, Denmark, Costa Rica, and France are high on this cultural dimension.

In general, the United States ranked very high on individualism, relatively low on power distance, low on uncertainty avoidance, and moderately high on masculinity.

The GLOBE Project's Nine Cultural Dimensions Started in 1993 by University of Pennsylvania professor **Robert J. House, the *GLOBE project* is a massive and ongoing cross-cultural investigation of nine cultural dimensions involved in leadership and organizational processes.**[74] (GLOBE stands for Global Leadership and Organizational Behavior Effectiveness.) GLOBE has evolved into a network of more than 150 scholars from 62 societies, and most of the researchers are native to the particular cultures they study. The nine cultural dimensions are as follows:

- **Institutional collectivism—how much should leaders encourage and reward loyalty to the social unit?** *Institutional collectivism,* or *individualism/ collectivism,* expresses the extent to which individuals should be encouraged and rewarded for loyalty to the social group as opposed to the pursuit of individual goals. Countries ranking high in individualism: Argentina, Germany, Greece, Hungary, Italy. Countries ranking low: Denmark, Japan, Singapore, South Korea, Sweden. (The United States is rated moderate in individualism, a change from 30 years ago, when it ranked high.)

- **In-group collectivism—how much pride and loyalty should people have for their family or organization?** In contrast to individualism, *in-group collectivism* expresses the extent to which people should take pride in being members of their family, circle of close friends, and their work organization. High: China, Egypt, India, Iran, Morocco. Low: Denmark, Finland, Netherlands, New Zealand, Sweden.

- **Power distance—how much unequal distribution of power should there be in organizations and society?** *Power distance* expresses the degree to which a society's members expect power to be unequally shared. High: Argentina, Morocco, Russia, Spain, Thailand. Low: Costa Rica, Denmark, Israel, Netherlands, South Africa.

- **Uncertainty avoidance—how much should people rely on social norms and rules to avoid uncertainty?** *Uncertainty avoidance* expresses the extent to which a society relies on social norms and procedures to alleviate the unpredictability of future events. Countries high in uncertainty avoidance: Austria, Denmark, Germany, Sweden, Switzerland. Countries low in this dimension: Bolivia, Greece, Hungary, Russia, Venezuela. (The United States is rated moderate.)

- **Gender differentiation—how much should society maximize gender role differences?** *Gender differentiation* expresses the extent to which a society should minimize gender discrimination and role inequalities. High in gender egalitarianism: Denmark, Hungary, Poland, Slovenia, Sweden. Low: China, Egypt, India, Morocco, South Korea.

- **Assertiveness—how confrontational and dominant should individuals be in social relationships?** *Assertiveness* represents the extent to which a society expects people to be confrontational and competitive as opposed to tender and modest. High: Austria, Germany, Greece, Spain, United States. Low: Japan, Kuwait, New Zealand, Sweden, Switzerland.

- **Future orientation—how much should people delay gratification by planning and saving for the future?** *Future orientation* expresses the extent to which a society encourages investment in the future, as by planning and saving. High: Canada, Denmark, Netherlands, Singapore, Switzerland. Low: Argentina, Italy, Kuwait, Poland, Russia.

- **Performance orientation—how much should individuals be rewarded for improvement and excellence?** *Performance orientation* expresses the extent to which society encourages and rewards its members for performance improvement and excellence. High: Hong Kong, New Zealand, Taiwan, Singapore, United States. Low: Argentina, Greece, Italy, Russia, Venezuela.

- **Humane orientation—how much should society encourage and reward people for being kind, fair, friendly, and generous?** *Humane orientation* represents the degree to which individuals are encouraged to be altruistic, caring, kind, generous, and fair. High: Egypt, Indonesia, Ireland, Malaysia, Philippines. Low: Brazil, France, Germany, Singapore, Spain.

The United States, you may notice, scored high on assertiveness and performance orientation, which is why Americans are perceived as being pushy and hardworking.

Clearly, there is an important lesson in the Hofstede and GLOBE cultural dimensions—namely, knowing the cultural tendencies of foreign business partners and competitors can give you a strategic competitive advantage.

Other Cultural Variations: Language, Interpersonal Space, Time Orientation, & Religion

How do you go about bridging cross-cultural gaps? It begins with understanding. Let's consider variations in four basic culture areas: (1) *language,* (2) *interpersonal space,* (3) *time orientation,* and (4) *religion.*

Note, however, that such cultural differences are to be viewed as *tendencies* rather than absolutes. We all need to be aware that the *individuals* we are dealing with may be exceptions to the cultural rules. After all, there *are* talkative and aggressive Japanese, just as there are quiet and deferential Americans, stereotypes notwithstanding.[75]

I. Language More than 3,000 different languages are spoken throughout the world. However, even if you are operating in the English language, there are nuances between cultures that can lead to misperceptions. For instance, in Asia, a "yes" answer to a question "simply means the question is understood," says one well-traveled writer. "It's the beginning of negotiations."[76]

In communicating across cultures you have three options: (a) You can speak your own language. (The average American believes that about half the world can speak English, when actually it's about 20%.)[77] (b) You can use a translator. (If you do, try to get one that will be loyal to you rather than to your overseas host.) (c) You can learn the local language—by far the best option (as reflected in the *USA Today* headline: "U.S. Firms Becoming Tongue-Tied. Global Trade Requires Foreign Language Skills").[78]

2. Interpersonal Space People of different cultures have different ideas about what is acceptable interpersonal space—that is, how close or far away one should be when communicating with another person. For instance, the people of North America and northern Europe tend to conduct business conversations at a range of 3–4 feet. For people in Latin American and Asian cultures, the range is about 1 foot. For Arabs, it is even closer.

This can lead to cross-cultural misunderstandings. "Arabs tend to get very close and breathe on you," says anthropologist Hall. "The American on the receiving end can't identify all the sources of his discomfort but feels that the Arab is pushy. The Arab comes close, the American backs up. The Arab follows, because he can only interact at certain distances."[79] However, once the American understands that Arabs handle interpersonal space differently and that "breathing on people is a form of communication," says Hall, the situation can sometimes be redefined so that the American feels more comfortable.

3. Time Orientation Time orientation is different in many cultures. Anthropologist Hall makes a useful distinction between monochronic time and polychronic time:

- **Monochronic time.** This kind of time is standard American business practice. That is, **monochronic time is a preference for doing one thing at a time. In** this perception, time is viewed as being limited, precisely segmented, and schedule driven. This perception of time prevails, for example, when you schedule a meeting with someone and then give the visitor your undivided attention during the allotted time.[80]

Indeed, you probably practice monochronic time when you're in a job interview. You work hard at listening to what the interviewer says. You may well take careful notes. You certainly don't answer your cell phone or gaze repeatedly out the window.

- **Polychronic time.** This outlook on time is the kind that prevails in Mediterranean, Latin American, and especially Arab cultures. *Polychronic time* **is a preference for doing more than one thing at a time.** Here time is viewed as being flexible and multidimensional.

  This perception of time prevails when you visit a Latin American client, find yourself sitting in the waiting room for 45 minutes, and then find in the meeting that the client is dealing with three other people at the same time. (The American variant these days is referred to as "multitasking," as when you talk on the phone while simultaneously watching television and doing a crossword puzzle.)

As a manager, you will probably have to reset your mental clock when doing business across cultures.

4. Religion Are you a Protestant doing business in a predominantly Catholic country? Or a Muslim in a Buddhist country? How, then, does religion influence the work-related values of the people you're dealing with?

A study of 484 international students at a Midwestern university uncovered wide variations in the work-related values for different religious affiliations.[84] For example,

Example

Cultural Differences in Time: A Garment Factory in Mexico

Harry Mehserjian and his brothers own a garment factory near Los Angeles, and they still do the high-fashion work there. However, the T-shirts and other low-budget knitware are sent deep into Mexico, to a factory in a suburb of Guadalajara, where wages are one-seventh those in Los Angeles.[81]

"I never wanted to go to Mexico," Harry says. But since NAFTA removed quotas limiting how much clothing could be brought in from Mexico, that country has shot from sixth place to first place (passing China) in exporting garments to the U.S. The changes caused by NAFTA, along with a rise in minimum wage in California, aggressive unionization, and more regulations, made it difficult for the Mehserjians to continue doing all their business in the United States.

One of the challenges to the Mehserjians is to change their workers' attitudes about time. "If they come on Monday, they're out on Tuesday. If they come on Tuesday, they're out on Wednesday," says a plant manager. To try to overcome absenteeism, the Mehserjians offer a 10% bonus to those who come to work faithfully for the entire week. Even so, their factory is still plagued by absenteeism and turnover. The workplace culture in the interior of Mexico is looser than in the United States—or even in northern Mexico, such as Juarez.

Says one UCLA expert, "These workers don't necessarily see their lives revolving around a job. There's a great deal of informality that they have come to expect from factory employment. You work hard during certain periods of time, and relax during others."[82]

Your Call

A 2006 Associated Press poll found the United States to be an impatient nation, with Americans getting antsy after 5 minutes on hold on the phone and 15 minutes maximum in a Department of Motor Vehicles line.[83] If you were supervising this factory in Mexico, what would you do to adjust?

among Catholics, the primary work-related value was found to be consideration. For Protestants, it was employer effectiveness; for Buddhists, social responsibility; for Muslims, continuity. There was, in fact, virtually *no agreement* among religions as to what is the most important work-related value. This led the researchers to conclude: "Employers might be wise to consider the impact that religious differences (and more broadly, cultural factors) appear to have on the values of employee groups."

Current Followers of the Major World Religions	
Christianity	2.1 billion
Islam	1.3 billion
Hinduism	900 million
Buddhism	376 million
Judaism	15 million
Chinese traditional religions	394 million

After what some World War II veterans have been through, one can sympathize with their outrage over drivers who fly American flags from cars made by their former enemies—Toyotas, Mitsubishis, BMWs, Porsches, and other Japanese and German cars. "I drive all-American," boasts one vet.

But just what *is* an American car nowadays? "Is it a Honda Accord built by Americans in the Midwest," asks a newspaper reader, "or is it a Chrysler built in Mexico with parts from Canada by a company owned by Daimler-Benz?"[85] Perhaps the lesson is this: In a global economy, cultural arrogance is a luxury we can no longer afford. ●

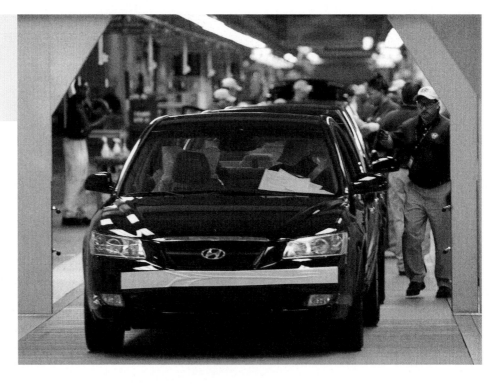

Who made this car? The assembly line producing these Hyundai Sonatas is located in Kentucky, but these days an automobile plant may be located nearly anywhere.

key terms used in this chapter

 summary

 4.1 Globalization: The Collapse of Time & Distance

- Globalization is the trend of the world economy toward becoming a more inter-dependent system. Globalization is reflected in three developments: (1) the rise of the global village and e-commerce; (2) the trend of the world's becoming one big market; and (3) the rise of both megafirms and Internet-enabled minifirms worldwide.

- The rise of the "global village" refers to the "shrinking" of time and space as air travel and the electronic media have made global communication easier. The Internet and the World Wide Web have led to e-commerce, the buying and selling of products and services through computer networks.

- The global economy is the increasing tendency of the economies of the nations of the world to interact with one another as one market instead of many national markets.

- The rise of cross-border business has led to the rise of megamergers, as giant firms have joined forces, and of minifirms, small companies in which managers can use the Internet and other technologies to get enterprises started more easily and to maneuver faster.

 4.2 You & International Management

- Studying international management prepares you to work with foreign customers or partners, with foreign suppliers, for a foreign firm in the U.S., or for a U.S. firm overseas. International management is management that oversees the conduct of operations in or with organizations in foreign countries.

- The successful international manager is not ethnocentric or polycentric but geocentric. Ethnocentric managers believe that their native country, culture, language, and behavior are superior to all others. Polycentric managers take the view that native managers in the foreign offices best understand native personnel and practices. Geocentric managers accept that there are differences and similarities between home and foreign personnel and practices, and they should use whatever techniques are most effective.

4.3 Why & How Companies Expand Internationally

- Companies expand internationally for at least five reasons, all of which have to do with making or saving money. They seek (1) cheaper or more plentiful supplies, (2) new markets, (3) lower labor costs, (4) access to finance capital, and (5) avoidance of tariffs on imported goods or import quotas.

- There are five ways in which companies expand internationally. (1) They engage in global outsourcing, using suppliers outside the company and the U.S. to provide goods and services. (2) They engage in importing, exporting, and countertrading (bartering for goods). (3) They engage in licensing (allow a foreign company to pay a fee to make or distribute the company's product or service) and franchising (allow a foreign company to pay a fee and a share of the profit in return for using the first company's brand name and a package of materials and services). (4) They engage in joint ventures, a strategic alliance with a foreign company to share the risks and rewards of starting a new enterprise together in a foreign country. (5) They become wholly-owned subsidiaries, or foreign subsidiaries that are totally owned and controlled by an organization.

4.4 Economic & Political-Legal Differences

- Among the differences with which international managers must cope are (1) economic differences and (2) political-legal differences.

- Four economic differences that managers must deal with include (1) different economic systems, (2) economic development, (3) infrastructure and resources, and (4) currency exchange rates.

- The principal economic systems are free market, command, and mixed economies. (1) In a free-market economy, the production of goods and services is controlled by private enterprise and the interaction of the forces of supply and demand, rather than by the government. (2) In a command economy, or central-planning economy, the government owns most businesses and regulates the amounts, types, and prices of goods and services. (3) In a mixed economy, most of the important industries are owned by the government, but others are controlled by private enterprise.

- Countries may be divided between developed countries (those with a high level of economic development and generally high average income) and less-developed countries (nations with low economic development and low average incomes).

- International companies are concerned about a foreign country's infrastructure (the physical facilities that form the basis for its level of economic development, such as roads and schools) and resources (labor and equipment).

- Companies operating internationally also have to be concerned about currency exchange rates. The exchange rate is the rate at which one country's currency can be exchanged for another country's currency.

- Managers operating internationally also need to be concerned about three kinds of political-legal differences: (1) democratic versus totalitarian political systems, (2) political risk, and (3) laws and regulations.

- Governmental systems may be democratic or totalitarian. Democratic governments rely on free elections and representative assemblies. Totalitarian governments are ruled by a dictator, a single political party, or a special-membership group.

- Political risk is defined as the risk that political changes will cause loss of a company's assets or impair its foreign operations. Two political risks a company doing business abroad might anticipate are instability, such as riots or civil disorders, and expropriation, defined as a government's seizure of a foreign company's assets.

- International companies have to work with numerous laws and regulations. The United States has legislation under the Foreign

Corrupt Practices Act of 1977 that makes it illegal for employees of U.S. companies to bribe decision makers in foreign nations.

4.5 The World of Free Trade: Regional Economic Cooperation

- Free trade is the movement of goods and services among nations without political or economic obstructions.

- Countries often use trade protectionism—the use of government regulations to limit the import of goods and services—to protect their domestic industries against foreign competition. Three barriers to free trade, or devices by which countries try to exert protectionism, are tariffs, import quotas, and embargoes. (1) A tariff is a trade barrier in the form of a customs duty, or tax, levied mainly on imports. (2) An import quota is a trade barrier in the form of a limit on the numbers of a product that can be imported. (3) An embargo is a complete ban on the import or export of certain products.

- Three principal organizations exist that are designed to facilitate international trade. (1) The World Trade Organization is designed to monitor and enforce trade agreements. (2) The World Bank is designed to provide low-interest loans to developing nations for improving transportation, education, health, and telecommunications. (3) The International Monetary Fund is designed to assist in smoothing the flow of money between nations.

- A trading bloc is a group of nations within a geographical region that have agreed to remove trade barriers. There are four major trading blocs: (1) North American Free Trade Agreement (NAFTA; U.S., Canada, and Mexico); (2) European Union (EU; 25 trading partners in Europe); (3) Asia-Pacific Economic Cooperation (APEC; 21 Pacific Rim countries); (4) Mercosur (Argentina, Brazil, Paraguay, Uruguay, Chile, and Bolivia).

- Besides joining together in trade blocs, countries also extend special, "most favored nation" trading privileges—that is, grant other countries favorable trading treatment such as the reduction of import duties.

4.6 The Importance of Understanding Cultural Differences

- Misunderstandings and miscommunications often arise because one person doesn't understand the expectations of a person from another culture. In low-context cultures, shared meanings are primarily derived from written and spoken words. In high-context cultures, people rely heavily on situational cues for meaning when communicating with others.

- Geert Hofstede proposed the Hofstede model of four cultural dimensions, which identified four dimensions along which national cultures can be placed: (1) individualism/collectivism, (2) power distance, (3) uncertainty avoidance, and (4) masculinity/femininity.

- Robert House and others created the GLOBE (for Global Leadership and Organizational Behavior Effectiveness) Project, a massive and ongoing cross-cultural investigation of nine cultural dimensions involved in leadership and organizational processes: (1) institutional collectivism, (2) in-group collectivism, (3) power distance, (4) uncertainty avoidance, (5) gender differentiation, (6) assertiveness, (7) future orientation, (8) performance orientation, and (9) humane orientation.

- A nation's culture is the shared set of beliefs, values, knowledge, and patterns of behavior common to a group of people. Visitors to another culture may experience culture shock—feelings of discomfort and disorientation. Managers trying to understand other cultures need to understand four basic cultural perceptions embodied in (1) language, (2) interpersonal space, (3) time orientation, and (4) religion.

- Regarding language, when you are trying to communicate across cultures you have three options: speak your own language (if others can understand you), use a translator, or learn the local language.

- Interpersonal space involves how close or far away one should be when communicating with another person, with Americans being comfortable at 3–4 feet but people in other countries often wanting to be closer.

- Time orientation of a culture may be either monochronic (preference for doing one thing at a time) or polychronic (preference for doing more than one thing at a time).

- Managers need to consider the effect of religious differences. In order of size (population), the major world religions are Christianity, Islam, Hinduism, Buddhism, Chinese traditional religion, and Judaism.

Effective Employee Training in Afghanistan Requires Cross-Cultural Awareness & Personal Fortitude

The following is an account from Steve Coyle, a U.S. citizen living in Malaysia and working for Malaysia-based ServiceWinners International. Coyle and his training team provided supervisory and sales development training to employees of a mobile phone operator in Kabul in 2005.

Training in Afghanistan may not be for everyone, but for our training team, it was an exhilarating experience. The team from our company consisted of myself, Dalwi Lee Wei Keat, a Malaysian of Chinese descent, and Jude Louis, a Malaysian of Indian descent. The chance to train in Afghanistan presented itself right after two of our trainers survived the December 26, 2004, Asian tsunami on Penang Island, Malaysia. After that experience, training employees at Telecom Development Company Afghanistan in Kabul sounded doable.

The learning environment in Kabul was more diverse than usual. As trainers, we were aware of multiple dynamics within the classroom. For example, some women felt uncomfortable sitting next to men. Also, taking a group photo is *de rigueur* in our home base of Malaysia, but in Afghanistan, it was a totally different story.

Afghanistan is comprised of multiple ethnic groups. We had Pashtuns, Hazaras, Uzbeks, and Tajiks in our classroom. These ethnic lines are further sub-divided by religious sects. Our client had Sunni and Shia Muslim employees. Then, the learners were further sub-divided by clans. Besides the local ethnic and religious groups, each of our workshops contained a few ex-pats who came from Algeria, France, Canada, and India.

There were other differences within the classroom—some learners had prejudices against those who fled the country to escape the wars. They were considered undeserving of good positions in the company, whereas those who fled considered themselves better educated and in possession of more valuable work experience than those who stayed behind.

There were age divisions. Our client's workforce consisted primarily of those in their late teens to early 20s since most of the middle-age population has been decimated by wars. Some older staff in a traditional society like Afghanistan had difficulty working for a supervisor in his or her late teens who was educated in Pakistan and spoke fluent English.

There was also a gender imbalance in the classroom; 80% of the learners were male. During the Taliban era, women were forbidden to work. As a result, women lack English-language and business skills.

Although the learners come from diverse backgrounds, it was refreshing to see that they considered themselves Afghans first. They were proud of their nation and genuinely wanted to better themselves both for their own good and the good of their nation. . . .

Conducting a training needs analysis (TNA) is important in any training assignment; however, it's critical when training in developing countries. We had been in contact with the client months before the actual training took place. In addition, we flew to Kabul for a week to determine the client's training needs. The on-site TNA showed us what e-mail could not. It was invaluable to truly understand their skill level and fears.

Our TNA took us out of town to discover the client's sales style and processes. We also interviewed the client's dealer channels. Our findings led us to completely revamp our supervisory and sales curricula. We could then create company-specific case studies, projects, and role-plays.

Our supervisory curriculum consisted of three stages: basic (five days), intermediate (three days), and advanced (three days). The client found that a typical supervisory program conducted by a training franchise using thick English-language manuals supported by Western videos would have failed for this audience's unique requirements. Instead, the client decided on our regional training house. We kept the content simple and instead focused more heavily on project work and class activities.

Per-capita income in Afghanistan is low, and life is tough. These conditions foster a scarcity mentality within the society that enters the classroom. For example, when we offered small tokens as prizes for best project work (a practice common in Southeast Asia), the learners were extremely keen to win. They perceived the value of the tokens far higher than other Asian learners we have trained. Competition sometimes got a bit out of control in the group work activities with some groups criticizing each other's group to win a token. They thrived on recognition from the trainers and wanted us to say which group was better.

The learning environment is fairly traditional. Afghans expect to be called on by the "teachers." As trainers, we are taught that adults are responsible for their own learning, but in Afghanistan the learners complained if we didn't call on or volunteer those who weren't participating. They wanted the whole group to be involved. We also found that generally the wallflowers, although stressed when called upon, liked the opportunity to be forced to participate. . . .

There are, of course, safety and health concerns when teaching in a politically unstable environment. Security is a topic that each individual must weigh. Our team never felt threatened at any time. There were a lot of uniformed people carrying machine guns in Kabul, but we never heard any gunfire. . . .

Additionally, health should be a primary concern. Kabul was experiencing a cholera and typhoid fever epidemic last summer. We took the necessary injections beforehand to protect ourselves.

Modern hospital facilities are difficult to find in Kabul. I recommend only those who are physically fit and willing to push their bodies to extremes travel to Afghanistan. Even physically fit bodies will likely eventually experience diarrhea or altitude sickness (Kabul has an altitude of 5,900 feet) at one time or another.

Training in Afghanistan is not for everyone. It was the most difficult international project my team has been involved in, yet it was also the most rewarding. Afghanistan has huge training needs for those who are mentally and physically ready to answer.

For Discussion

1. Which of the recommendations presented in this chapter's Practical Action box titled "Being a World Citizen: Learning to Be a Success Abroad" did Steve Coyle and his team of trainers follow? Explain.
2. Why was it important for the trainers to avoid ethnocentric and polycentric tendencies? Discuss.
3. To what extent was the training needs analysis consistent with a geocentric approach to management? Explain.
4. Based on information in the case, how would you rank Afghanistan in terms of Hofstede's model of cultural differences and the nine cultural dimensions identified in the GLOBE project? Discuss your rationale.
5. Would you like to conduct training in Afghanistan? Why or why not?

Source: Excerpted from Steve Coyle, "Training Day in Afghanistan," *Training*, April 2006, pp. 50–52.

self-assessment

How Well Are You Suited to Becoming a Global Manager?

Objectives
1. To see if you are ready to be a global manager.
2. To help you assess your comfort level with other cultures.

Introduction
As our business world becomes increasingly globalized, U.S. companies need more managers to work in other countries. This usually means vast adjustments for the manager and her or his family during this job assignment. Flexibility is critical as is the ability to adjust to new ways, new people, new foods, different nonverbal communication, a new language, and a host of other new things.

Before agreeing to such an assignment, you need to know more about yourself and how you function in such situations.

Instructions
Are you prepared to be a global manager? Rate the extent to which you agree with each of the following 14 items by circling your response on the rating scale shown below. If you do not have direct experience with a particular situation (for example, working with people from other cultures), respond by circling how you *think* you would feel.

1 = Very strongly disagree
2 = Strongly disagree
3 = Disagree
4 = Neither agree nor disagree
5 = Agree
6 = Strongly agree
7 = Very strongly agree

I. When working with people from other cultures, I work hard to understand their perspectives.	I	2	3	4	5	6	7
2. I have a solid understanding of my organization's products and services.	I	2	3	4	5	6	7
3. I am willing to take a stand on issues.	I	2	3	4	5	6	7
4. I have a special talent for dealing with people.	I	2	3	4	5	6	7
5. I can be depended on to tell the truth regardless of circumstances.	I	2	3	4	5	6	7
6. I am good at identifying the most important part of a complex problem or issue.	I	2	3	4	5	6	7
7. I clearly demonstrate commitment to seeing the organization succeed.	I	2	3	4	5	6	7
8. I take personal as well as business risks.	I	2	3	4	5	6	7
9. I have changed as a result of feedback from others.	I	2	3	4	5	6	7
I0. I enjoy the challenge of working in countries other than my own.	I	2	3	4	5	6	7
II. I take advantage of opportunities to do new things.	I	2	3	4	5	6	7
I2. I find criticism hard to take.	I	2	3	4	5	6	7
I3. I seek feedback even when others are reluctant to give it.	I	2	3	4	5	6	7
I4. I don't get so invested in things that I cannot change when something doesn't work.	I	2	3	4	5	6	7

Interpretation

This exercise assesses factors associated with being a successful global manager. These factors include general intelligence, business knowledge, interpersonal skills, commitment, courage, cross-cultural competencies, and the ability to learn from experience.

Total your scores, which will fall between 14 and 98. The higher your score, the greater your potential for success as an international manager.

Arbitrary Norms

High Potential for Success	70–98
Moderate Potential for Success	40–69
Low Potential for Success	39 and below

Questions for Discussion

1. What do the results suggest about your preparedness to be a global manager? Do you agree with these results?
2. How comfortable would you be going to another country at this time in your life?
3. How have your experiences as a citizen of a very diverse nation helped you to understand the other cultures of the world?
4. How might you improve your preparedness to one day assume an international position? Explain.

Modified and adapted from G. M. Spreitzer, M.W. McCall Jr., and J. D. Mahoney, "Early Identification of International Executive Potential," *Journal of Applied Psychology*, February 1997, pp. 6–29.

When in Rome, Do as the Romans Do!

Objectives

1. To raise your awareness regarding appropriate behavior in different nations.
2. To emphasize that different nations have truly different customs.

Introduction

Globalization means that people in business must know the customs of other nations. A mistake can alienate a potential business partner; rudeness, even if unconscious or unknowing, can create a lasting bad impression of Americans; and lack of knowledge about the country you're in shows disrespect for its people. For example, many people in the United States signal "OK" by making a round sign with the thumb and the first finger; however, in Brazil the same gesture is a very crude one, comparable to raising the middle index figure in the U.S.

Instructions

Divide the class into teams of five students. Everyone in each team should individually try to match each of the following countries to the custom/gesture described in the list below. Then score choices according to the answer key at the end of this exercise. After each team member has individually completed his or her answers and scored them, compare them and then share your results with other teams in the class. Which items were incorrectly matched the most times? What do you think are the reasons for this?

Country	Custom/Gesture associated with each country
1. Chile	_____
2. France	_____
3. Italy	_____
4. South Korea	_____
5. Denmark	_____
6. Thailand	_____
7. Poland	_____
8. Egypt	_____
9. Pakistan	_____
10. Germany	_____

Gesture/Custom

a. Never show the bottom of your foot; it is considered offensive.

b. While imported liquor is appropriate, a gift of locally available wine can be interpreted as saying that your host's wine cellar is inadequate.

c. Beckoning is done with the palm down rather than up, moving the fingers toward the body.

d. The "thumbs up" sign means zero.

e. The gesture North Americans use to indicate that someone is crazy—index finger circling while pointed at one's temple—is used here to insult other drivers while on the road.

f. At a meal, keep your hands above the table at all times.

g. Men greet each other with a slight bow and sometimes an accompanying handshake while maintaining eye contact.

h. Press your hands together as though in prayer, keeping arms and elbows close to your body, bow your head to touched fingers, and say Wai (pronounced "why").

i. You may see a disgruntled man quickly stroke his fingertips under his chin and thrust them forward. This is a sign of defiance and/or derision.

j. In social situations, when a man flicks his finger against his neck, he is inviting you to join him for a drink.

Interpretation & Scoring

If you matched the correct country with the correct gesture/custom 8–10 times, you are very cosmopolitan, or international; if you matched the correct country with the correct gesture/custom 4–7 times, you are moving toward becoming cosmopolitan; if you matched 0 to 3 accurately, you probably need to read more about other nations and travel outside the United States.

Questions for Discussion

1. What does it mean to you to be cosmopolitan or international? Explain.
2. Do you believe that it is important to know about diverse cultures? Why or why not?
3. Do you value knowledge about other cultures? Why or why not?
4. Does the knowledge provided in this exercise encourage you to learn more about other cultures? Why or why not?

 ethical dilemma

Who Should You Recommend for a Plant Maintenance Contract?

You are a maintenance supervisor at a clothing factory located in China. The plant's senior manager, Bin Wu, has just come to you and asked for a recommendation for a maintenance contractor. The current contractor has problems with service and delays and is experiencing high turnover. During your review of potential contractors, someone tells you that the owner of the current contractor is the son-in-law of the plant's maintenance manager, Zhaoli Song, to whom you report.

Solving the Dilemma

What would you do given the current situation?

1. Ask co-workers if the current contractor is in fact Zhaoli Song's son-in-law. If true, recommend the current contractor.
2. Tell Bin Wu about the potential conflict of interest.
3. Ignore the potential conflict of interest and recommend whomever you want.
4. Invent other options.

Source: Based on material contained in Erin White, "What Would You Do? Ethics Courses Get Context," *The Wall Street Journal*, June 12, 2006, p. B3.

 video case

The Peace Corps: The Hardest Job You'll Ever Love

In his presidential inaugural address in January 1961, John F. Kennedy gave the now famous directive, "Ask not what your country can do for you, ask what you can do for your country." Two months later in March 1961, with the passage of the Peace Corps Act, the Peace Corps was created to assist less developed countries by lending them skilled workers or Peace Corps volunteers who totally integrate themselves into the country by living among the people, eating local food, and learning the language and cultural nuances of the country. Peace Corps volunteers act as agents in creating cross-cultural understanding between the United States and the host country.

Today, many Peace Corps volunteers teach entrepreneurship and computer skills to indigenous people to enable them to become self-sufficient. In order to become a Peace Corps volunteer, a candidate must make a two-year commitment, cannot determine where she will be sent, must work very hard, and is often underpaid in comparison to other work positions. And despite all the potential hardships connected to working for the Peace Corps, volunteerism is at a 30 year high.

Peace Corps volunteers spend much time learning about the culture of their host country and building relationships with locals in order to be more effective. In particular, their education includes nine components: 1) aesthetics, 2) attitudes and beliefs, 3) religion, 4) material culture, 5) education, 6) language, 7) societal organization, 8) legal characteristics, and 9) political structures. Attitudes and beliefs, material culture, and language are especially relevant for learning about cultural differences and are closely connected with business. We know that in order to conduct any new endeavor, such as transacting business, we must learn the prevailing attitudes toward change in a specific country. In some eastern or African countries, that attitude toward change may be rather evolutionary—slow over time, vis-à-vis a quick-paced revolutionary change in the West.

Material culture deals with technology and marketing. Advanced technology increases productivity and thus enables producers to bring products to market more quickly and thereby increase a less developed country's economic growth and expansion, so it is essential for Peace Corps volunteers to understand their host country's material culture. Language, too, is viewed as important to a volunteer's success; therefore, Peace Corps volunteers live with local families of the host country and receive full-immersion language classes over a 3 to 4 month period to further their abilities to become integrated and be accepted by local people. Finally, the ethnic and racial diversity of Peace Corps volunteers paints a different portrait of America which is often unknown to residents of other countries. Through its role in assisting lesser-developed countries throughout the world over the past 45 years, the more than 170,000 Peace Corps volunteers who served in 135 countries worldwide have helped promote socio-cultural understanding between the United States and other nations.

Questions

1. If you were the human resource manager of a company, would you hire a former Peace Corps volunteer? Why or why not?
2. What qualities and skills do former Peace Corps volunteers bring to a corporate job?
3. Discuss some ways managers of international firms can use former Peace Corps volunteers effectively as new employees.
4. What lessons can managers of international companies learn from the Peace Corps about training employees for global assignments?

Source: Joseph C. Santora, EdD, Essex County College.

chapter 5

Planning
The Foundation of Successful Management

Major Questions You Should Be Able to Answer

5.1 Planning & Uncertainty
Major Question: How do I tend to deal with uncertainty, and how can planning help?

5.2 Fundamentals of Planning
Major Question: What are mission and vision statements, three types of planning and goals, and SMART goals?

5.3 The Planning/Control Cycle
Major Question: How does the planning/ control cycle help keep a manager's plans headed in the right direction?

5.4 Promoting Goal Setting: Management by Objectives
Major Question: What is MBO, and how can it be implemented successfully to achieve results?

5.5 Project Planning
Major Question: What is project planning, why is it important, and what is the project life cycle?

How Do Exceptional Managers Make Their Own Luck?

Risk and luck are two aspects of life that can't be ignored. But planning can improve your odds.

Many people think what happens to them is the result of fickle fate. However, with knowledge and planning, you can better learn what's risky and what's not.

What determines the way people perceive risk? The context in which the risk occurs is often important.[1] For example, you may tend to view something as more risky if you're not in control (as when traveling on an airplane). Another factor is trust: When a company or agency has a shady record, people conclude it can't be trusted and view what it's doing as more risky.

As a manager, you need to be aware of such outside factors when making plans about new endeavors involving some risk. You also need to be aware of how you yourself think about your luck.

Bad luck is when a flaming meteor hits you on the head. But failed business deals, lost promotions, and the like can't be blamed on just bad luck. "We're responsible for a good deal more of what happens to us than we realize," says research psychologist William F. Vitulli.[2]

People who are prone to bad luck are often impulsive. "They routinely speak before they think, make investments and purchases based on passing whims, and put themselves in dangerous spots by failing to plan ahead," says one writer.[3] Other people have bad luck in just one area (such as relationships) in which they are incapable of seeing life realistically. Still others have self-expectations that they will fail, and so

they generally do. Or they exaggerate their setbacks to gain sympathy.

How do you improve your luck? Some steps:[4]

- **Make a list and consider your motives.** If you think you could be the victim of self-induced misfortune, make a written list of specific examples in which you contributed to your own bad luck. Then fight it by putting Post-it® reminders (such as the word "Impulse?") on your phone, computer monitor, dashboard, and so on.

- **Cultivate optimism and confidence.** Can you actually *will* yourself to be in control of your life? The chances are that if you act like the person you want to become, you will become that person. Indeed, you are more apt to ACT your way into a new way of thinking than to THINK your way into it.[5] Thus, try to cultivate optimism. Don't automatically expect the worst in any situation.

- **Ask for help.** Many of us can't see ourselves objectively. If you have trouble figuring out a pattern of bad luck, the best solution is to talk to a counselor.

For Discussion In what kinds of transactions, especially business transactions, have you had bad luck? Why do you think that is?

forecast
What's Ahead in This Chapter

In this chapter, we describe planning, the first of the four management functions. We consider the benefits of planning and how it helps you deal with uncertainty. We deal with the fundamentals of planning, including the mission and vision statements and the three types of planning—strategic, tactical, and operational. We consider goals and action plans, SMART goals, the planning/control cycle, and management by objectives (MBO). We then consider project planning.

5.I PLANNING & UNCERTAINTY

✸ major question How do I tend to deal with uncertainty, and how can planning help?

THE BIG PICTURE

Planning, the first of four functions in the management process, involves setting goals and deciding how to achieve them. Planning helps you check your progress, coordinate activities, think ahead, and cope with uncertainty. Uncertainty is of three types—state, effect, and response. Organizations respond to uncertainty in various ways.

What is known as the *management process,* you'll recall (from Chapter 1, p. 12), involves the four management functions of *planning, organizing, leading,* and *controlling,* which form four of the part divisions of this book. In this and the next two chapters we discuss **planning, which we previously defined as setting goals and deciding how to achieve them. Another definition:** *Planning* **is coping with uncertainty by formulating future courses of action to achieve specified results.**[6] When you make a plan, you make a blueprint for action that describes what you need to do to realize your goals.

Planning & Strategic Management

Planning, which we discuss in this chapter, is used in conjunction with strategic management, as we describe in Chapter 6. As we will see, strategic management is a process that involves managers from all parts of the organization—top managers, middle managers, and first-line managers—in the formulation, implementation, and execution of strategies and strategic goals to advance the purposes of the organization. Thus, planning covers not only strategic planning (done by top managers) but also tactical planning (done by middle managers) and operational planning (done by first-line managers). Planning and strategic management derive from an organization's mission and vision about itself, as we describe in the next few pages. *(See Figure 5.1.)*

1. Establish the organization's mission and vision → 2. Formulate the grand strategy → 3. Formulate the strategic plans, then the tactical and operational plans → 4. Implement the strategic plans → 5. Control the strategy

figure 5.I

PLANNING AND STRATEGIC MANAGEMENT

The details of planning and strategic management are explained in Chapters 5 and 6.

Why Not Plan?

On the face of it, planning would seem to be a good idea—otherwise we would not be devoting three chapters to the subject. But there are two cautions to be aware of:

I. Planning Requires You to Set Aside the Time to Do It Time-starved managers may be quite resentful when superiors order them to prepare a 5-year plan for their work unit.

"What?" they may grouse. "They expect me to do that and *still* find time to meet this year's goals?" Somehow, though, that time for planning must be found. Otherwise, managers are mainly just reacting to events.

Planning means that you must involve the subordinates you manage to determine resources, opportunities, and goals. During the process, you may need to go outside the work unit for information about products, competitors, markets, and the like.

2. You May Have to Make Some Decisions without a Lot of Time to Plan In our time of Internet connections and speedy-access computer databases, can't nearly anyone lay hands on facts quickly to make an intelligent decision? Not always. A competitor may quickly enter your market with a highly desirable product. A change in buying habits may occur. A consumer boycott may suddenly surface. An important supplier may let you down. The caliber of employees you need may not be immediately available at the salary level you're willing to pay. And in any one of these you won't have the time to plan a decision based on all the facts.

Nevertheless, a plan need not be perfect to be executable. While you shouldn't shoot from the hip in making decisions, often you may have to "go with what you've got" and make a decision based on a plan that is perhaps only three-quarters complete.

How Planning Helps You: Four Benefits

You can always hope you'll luck out or muddle through the next time a hurricane, earthquake, tornado, or other natural disaster strikes your area. Or you can plan for it by stocking up on flashlight batteries and canned food. Which is better? The same consideration applies when you're a manager. Some day, after you've dealt with some crisis, you will be very happy that you had a plan for handling it. The benefits of planning are fourfold:

I. Planning Helps You Check on Your Progress The preprinted score card that golfers use when playing 18 holes of golf isn't blank. For each hole, the card lists the standard number of strokes ("par"), such as three or five, that a good player should take to hit the ball from the tee to the cup. The score card is the plan for the game, with objectives for each hole. After you play the hole, you write your own score in a blank space. At the end of the 18 holes, you add all your scores to see how you performed compared to the standard for the course.

How well is your work going in an organization? You won't know unless you have some way of checking your progress. That's why, like a golfer, you need to have some expectations of what you're supposed to do—in other words, a plan.

2. Planning Helps You Coordinate Activities "The right hand doesn't know what the left hand is doing!"

We may hear that expression used, for example, when a crisis occurs and an organization's public relations department, legal department, and CEO's office all give the press separate, contradictory statements. Obviously, such an embarrassment can be avoided if the organization has a plan for dealing with the media during emergencies. A plan defines the responsibilities of various departments and coordinates their activities for the achievement of common goals—such as, at minimum, making an organization not look confused and disorganized.

Looking ahead. In 2006, Andrea Wong, CEO of Avon, shown here at an Avon Foundation meeting, announced a new initiative to encourage sales representatives to move beyond traditional sales techniques to do more business on the Internet. What else do you think "Avon ladies," long known for door-to-door cosmetics selling, should be doing to stay ahead of their competitors?

3. Planning Helps You Think Ahead Founder and former CEO Michael Dell, of Dell Computer, which makes personal computers, says, "In my business, the life cycle of a product is six months, and so there are two types of people: the quick and the dead."[7] Dell is always trying to look into the future to try to plan for what might be the next big change in microcomputer products.

Similarly, as we describe under product life cycle (Chapter 6), the service or product with which you're engaged will probably at some point reach maturity, and sales will begin to falter. Thus, you need to look ahead, beyond your present phase of work, to try to be sure you'll be one of the quick rather than one of the dead.

4. Above All, Planning Helps You Cope with Uncertainty You don't care for unpleasant surprises? Most people don't. (Pleasant surprises, of course, are invariably welcome.) That's why trying to plan for unpleasant contingencies is necessary (as we'll describe in Chapter 6). Planning helps you deal with uncertainty, as we discuss next.

Three Types of Uncertainty: State, Effect, & Response

Experts tend to classify uncertainty as being of three types—*state, effect,* and *response*:[8]

State Uncertainty—"What Possible Harmful Event Could Occur?" On a summer day, you're setting out for a hike in the mountains. You scan the skies. Could it rain? Are you at a high enough elevation, and is it cold enough that it could even snow? This is an example of *state uncertainty,* **when the environment is considered unpredictable.**

Effect Uncertainty—"What Possible Harmful Effect Might an Environmental Change Have?" An unexpected rainstorm in the mountains could be just a slight inconvenience, forcing you to take cover until it passes. However, a snowstorm could cause you to lose the trail and perhaps risk freezing and hypothermia. This is an example of *effect uncertainty,* **when the effects of environmental changes are unpredictable.**

Response Uncertainty—"What Possible Harmful Consequence Might a Decision Have?" Which would be better to have in a mountain snowstorm, warm clothes or a cell phone? The clothes would help you survive the weather. The cell phone could help summon emergency aid—if anyone could receive your call from a wilderness area. This is an example of *response uncertainty,* **when the consequences of a decision are uncertain.**

How Organizations Respond to Uncertainty

How do you personally respond to uncertainty? Do you react slowly? conservatively? proactively? Do you watch to see what others do? Organizations act in similar ways.

Four Basic Strategy Types Scholars **Raymond E. Miles** and **Charles C. Snow** suggest that organizations adopt one of four approaches when responding to uncertainty in their environment. They become *Defenders, Prospectors, Analyzers,* or *Reactors.*[9]

Defenders—"Let's Stick with What We Do Best, Avoid Other Involvements"
Whenever you hear an organization's leader say that "We're sticking with the basics" or "We're getting back to our core business," that's the hallmark of a Defender

Planning for Uncertainty: How Did Nokia Jump Ahead on Cell Phones?

How do managers make decisions about uncertainty in cell phones and telecommunications, one of the most volatile industries on Earth?

In the early 1990s, Finland was principally engaged in selling wood, rubber, and similar ho-hum products to the former Soviet Union, then undergoing a great transformation following the collapse of old-style communism. Nokia was a Finnish company that for over 100 years had been engaged in heavy-manufacturing businesses, but it had a small radio-manufacturing unit that was just starting to make early cell phones. In that era of uncertainty (what kind?), Jorma Ollila, who had become CEO in 1992, and Nokia's board of directors confronted some crucial decisions about which direction to take the company.

"I started discussing with the board that the way to go was to put all our eggs in one basket, and divest the rest," Ollila said later. The board said, "Isn't this a bit extreme?" The discussion went on for 6 months. "It was very interesting and quite dramatic," Ollila says. "We were talking about selling businesses the company was born around."[10] The final decision was based on two facts: Projections for cell phone growth pointed up, and projections for the newly independent states of the Soviet Union as industrial customers pointed down.

By 2001, Nokia accounted for 25% of Finland's exports and 40% of the total worth of Finnish public companies. "These days," says technology writer Kevin Maney, "Finland's global image, its wealth, and its sense of self are entirely tied up in Nokia and wireless technology."[11]

Despite the success, Nokia has had to constantly struggle with un-

certainty. Should the company make one perfect phone, packed with every possible feature? Or should it make five different phones, each with different capabilities? "If you make too many phones you go bankrupt," said Erik Anderson, Nokia's head of production. "If you make lots of products but none are the best in their class, you will go bankrupt. If you make one good product, you might do really well with it, but there won't be enough profit, so you'll go bankrupt. In the end, it all really comes back to balance."[12]

All during its period of growth, Nokia has been in a see-saw race with Motorola, as well as Asian competitors such as Samsung, LG, and NEC. Twice it has had to overcome great difficulties: once in 1995, when logistics and supplier troubles couldn't keep up with growth; once in 2004, when it made too many feature-rich phones before the market was ready for them and when cell phone service providers (such as Verizon and AT&T) decided to play up their own brand names on handsets.[13] In 2006, as telecommunications went through a series of mergers that created billion-dollar giants (Alcatel/Lucent, Ericsson/Marconi), Nokia decided to join forces with German company Siemens to create Nokia Siemens Networks. With this, Nokia obtains the networking and wireline products that enable it to provide so-called quadruple-play services that include voice, video, data, and wireless.[14]

Your Call

Perhaps even greater challenges lie ahead. Wireless Internet—and Internet phone—technology could push wireless networking into all aspects of life, from cars and homes to offices and factories.[15] How should Nokia Siemens plan for this uncertainty?

---

organization. ***Defenders* are expert at producing and selling narrowly defined products or services.** Often they are old-line successful enterprises—such as Harley-Davidson motorcycles or Brooks Brothers clothiers—with a narrow focus. They do not tend to seek opportunities outside their present markets. They devote most of their attention to making refinements in their existing operations.

Edgy alternative. Using big black cans adorned with neon-colored claw marks, the high-caffeine, high-sugar Monster Energy drinks from Hansen Natural Corporation are positioned to compete as alternatives to Red Bull in the fast-growing energy drink market. What strategy type is being followed here?

Prospectors—"Let's Create Our Own Opportunities, Not Wait for Them to Happen" A company described as "aggressive" is often a Prospector organization. *Prospectors* **focus on developing new products or services and in seeking out new markets, rather than waiting for things to happen.** Like 19th-century gold miners, these companies are "prospecting" for new ways of doing things. The continual product and market innovation has a price: Such companies may suffer a loss of efficiency. Nevertheless, their focus on change can put fear in the hearts of competitors.

Analyzers—"Let Others Take the Risks of Innovating, & We'll Imitate What Works Best" Analyzers take a "me too" response to the world. By and large, you won't find them called "trendsetters." Rather, *Analyzers* **let other organizations take the risks of product development and marketing and then imitate (or perhaps slightly improve on) what seems to work best.**

Reactors—"Let's Wait Until There's a Crisis, Then We'll React" Whereas the Prospector is aggressive and proactive, the Reactor is the opposite—passive and reactive. *Reactors* **make adjustments only when finally forced to by environmental pressures.** In the worst cases, they are so incapable of responding fast enough that they suffer massive sales losses and are even driven out of business. Schwinn bicycles, for instance, failed to respond quickly enough to the sudden popularity of mountain bikes and lost its stature as the leading manufacturer of bicycles.

The Adaptive Cycle Miles and Snow also introduced the idea of the *adaptive cycle,* which portrays businesses as continuously cycling through decisions about three kinds of business problems: (1) *entrepreneurial* (selecting and making adjustments of products and markets), (2) *engineering* (producing and delivering the products), and (3) *administrative* (establishing roles, relationships, and organizational processes).

Thus, a business that makes decisions in the entrepreneurial area that take it in the direction of being a Prospector will in a short time also begin making Prospector-oriented decisions in the engineering area, then the administrative area, and then even more so in the entrepreneurial area, and so on. Thus, as one scholar points out, "With enough cycles and insight, a given business becomes a very good, comprehensively aligned Prospector, Analyzer, or Defender. If a business lacks insight, or if it fails to take advantage of alignment opportunities afforded by the adaptive cycle, it will be an incongruent, poorly performing Reactor."[16] ●

5.2 FUNDAMENTALS OF PLANNING

What are mission and vision statements, three types of planning and goals, and SMART goals?

major ✳ question

THE BIG PICTURE

Planning consists of translating an organization's mission into objectives. The organization's purpose is expressed as a mission statement, and what it becomes is expressed as a vision statement. From these are derived strategic planning, then tactical planning, then operational planning. Each kind specifies goals and action plans for accomplishing the goals, which should be S-M-A-R-T.

"Everyone wants a clear reason to get up in the morning," writes journalist Dick Leider. "As humans we hunger for meaning and purpose in our lives."[17]

And what is that purpose? "Life never lacks purpose," says Leider. "Purpose is innate—but it is up to each of us individually to discover or rediscover it."

An organization has a purpose, too—a mission. And managers must have an idea of where they want the organization to go—a vision. The approach to planning can be summarized in the following diagram, which shows how an organization's mission becomes translated into objectives. *(See Figure 5.2.)*

Test Your Knowledge: Elements of the Planning Process

figure 5.2

MAKING PLANS

An organization's reason for being is expressed in a *mission statement*. What the organization wishes to become is expressed in a *vision statement*. From these are derived *strategic planning,* then *tactical planning,* and finally *operational planning.* The purpose of each kind of planning is to specify *goals* and *action plans* for accomplishing those goals.

Mission & Vision Statements

The planning process begins with two attributes: a mission statement (which answers the question "What is our reason for being?") and a vision statement (which answers the question "What do we want to become?").

The Mission Statement—"What Is Our Reason for Being?" An organization's *mission* is its purpose or reason for being. Determining the mission is the responsibility of top management and the board of directors. It is up to them to formulate a *mission statement*, which expresses the purpose of the organization.

"Only a clear definition of the mission and purpose of the organization makes possible clear and realistic . . . objectives," said Peter Drucker.[18] Whether the organization is for-profit or nonprofit, the mission statement identifies the goods or services the organization provides and will provide, and the reasons for providing them (to make a profit or to achieve humanitarian goals, for example).

Example

Mission Statements: Why Are We Here?

amazon.com.

In less than 4 years—from July 1995 to June 1999—Internet retailer ("e-tailer") Amazon.com went from 0 to 10 million customers. "If anyone had predicted in 1995 that we'd have 10 million Amazonians by now, they'd have been locked up as dangerous," said a jubilant Jeff Bezos, Amazon's founder and CEO.[19]

That, of course, was a victory statement rather than a mission statement. The mission, as expressed on the company's Web site, is to "use the Internet to offer products that educate, inform, and inspire. We decided to build an online store that would be customer friendly and easy to navigate and would offer the broadest possible selection."[20] More prosaically, since Amazon is a for-profit organization, the mission is to make money: "We believe that a fundamental measure of our success will be the shareholder value we create over the *long term*," states one of the company's annual reports. "This

value will be a direct result of our ability to extend and solidify our current market leadership position. . . . Market leadership can translate directly to higher revenue, higher profitability. . . ."[21]

Your Call

Here is the mission statement for Nest Fresh Eggs, a Colorado-based family business that produces eggs from free-range hens: "Nest Fresh Eggs' mission is to remain profitable by producing or purchasing premium cage-free and natural eggs to supply supermarkets and restaurants in its markets, providing those customers with excellent service and product, and by being an environmentally responsible corporate citizen by using recyclable packaging and donating to targeted charities."[22] Do you think this statement could be adapted to a different company making different products? Give an example.

The Vision Statement—"What Do We Want to Become?" A *vision* is a long-term goal describing "what" an organization wants to become. It is a clear sense of the future and the actions needed to get there. "[A] vision should describe what's happening to the world you compete in and what you want to do about it," says one *Fortune* article. "It should guide decisions."[23]

Before Roger Enrico moved up to CEO of PepsiCo, the company thrived on "big-idea, renegade thinking," according to one report.[24] The problem was that the culture of autonomous business units led to decentralized control and managers who "were ricocheting off each other in search of their next promotion, or chasing new restaurant chains or joint ventures in far-flung parts of the world." Because Enrico had a clear sense of the future and the actions needed to get there—that is, a vision—he recentralized control and offered managers compensation schemes to encourage them to get their present jobs done rather than look for the next one.

After formulating a mission statement, top managers need to develop a *vision statement*, which expresses what the organization should become, where it wants to go strategically.[25]

Vision Statements: Where Do We Want to Go?

amazon.COM.

Jeff Bezos started out selling books as Amazon's first online product for the reason that, as one article reports, "there are far more of them in and out of print than any physical bookstore could ever line up on its shelves and that, unlike his second choice, music, the industry is not dominated by a cartel of half a dozen mega-distributors."[26]

However, his vision goes beyond books. "Our vision is to build a place to find and discover anything our customers might want to buy . . . [including] car parts and spark plugs," says Bezos.[27] The company expanded into several endeavors, including a music CD store, a video store, and an online auction business, and was offering a free electronic greeting card service, an Internet movie database, and (in April 2004) a jewelry and watches business. Yes, it also offers car parts and spark plugs.

As an extension of the vision, Bezos has said that Amazon intends "to build the world's most customer-centric company. . . . I constantly remind our employees to be afraid, to wake up every morning terrified. Not of our competition, but of our customers. . . . We're proud of the differentiation we've built through constant innovation and relentless focus on customer experience. . . ."[28]

Your Call

Here is Nest Fresh Eggs' vision statement: "Nest Fresh Eggs' vision is to influence the way the public views egg production in the U.S., to make it more economically feasible to reduce the number of hens in battery-caged facilities and/or to decrease cage density, and to create opportunities for small farmers to continue farming."[29] Do you think this meets *Fortune*'s criterion of describing "what's happening in the world you compete in and what you want to do about it. It should guide decisions"?

Three Types of Planning for Three Levels of Management: Strategic, Tactical, & Operational

Inspiring, clearly stated mission statements and vision statements provide the focal point of the entire planning process. Then three things happen:

- *Strategic planning by top management.* Using their mission and vision statements, top managers do *strategic planning*—**they determine what the organization's long-term goals should be for the next 1–5 years with the resources they expect to have available.** "Strategic planning requires visionary and directional thinking," says one authority.[30] It should communicate not only general goals about growth and profits but also ways to achieve them.

- *Tactical planning by middle management.* The strategic priorities and policies are then passed down to middle managers, who must do *tactical planning*—**that is, they determine what contributions their departments or similar work units can make with their given resources during the next 6–24 months.**

- *Operational planning by first-line management.* Middle managers then pass these plans along to first-line managers to do *operational planning*—**that is, they determine how to accomplish specific tasks with available resources within the next 1–52 weeks.**

The kinds of managers are described further in the figure on the next page. *(See Figure 5.3.)*

It is one thing to formulate a vision statement, however, and another to find concrete methods to manage and measure the performance that makes the vision a reality. One survey found that 73% of organizations said they had a clearly articulated strategic direction, but only 44% of them said they were able to communicate it well to the employees who must implement it.[31]

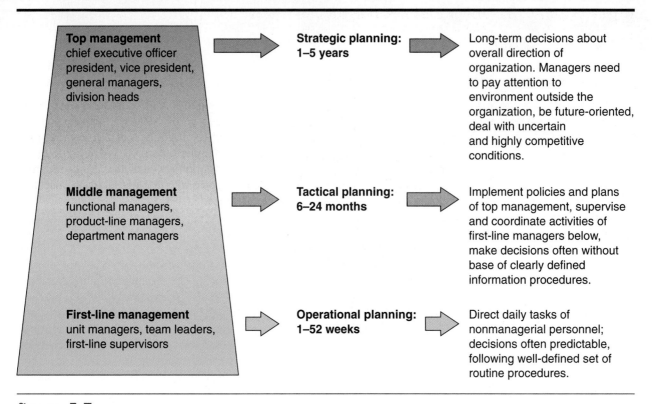

figure 5.3

THREE LEVELS OF MANAGEMENT, THREE TYPES OF PLANNING

Each type of planning has different time horizons, although the times overlap since the plans are somewhat elastic.

Goals, Action Plans, & Operating Plans

Whatever its type—strategic, tactical, or operational—the purpose of planning is to set a *goal* and then to formulate an *action plan.*

Goals   A *goal,* also known as an *objective,* is a specific commitment to achieve a measurable result within a stated period of time.

As with planning, goals are of the same three types—strategic, tactical, and operational. Also, like planning, goals are arranged in a hierarchy known as a **means-end chain** because in the chain of management (operational, tactical, strategic) the accomplishment of low-level goals is the means leading to the accomplishment of high-level goals or ends.

- *Strategic goals* are set by and for top management and focus on objectives for the organization as a whole.

- *Tactical goals* are set by and for middle managers and focus on the actions needed to achieve strategic goals.

- *Operational goals* are set by and for first-line managers and are concerned with short-term matters associated with realizing tactical goals.

The Action Plan & the Operating Plan   The goal should be followed by an *action plan,* which defines the course of action needed to achieve the stated goal, such as a marketing plan or sales plan. **The *operating plan,* which is typically designed for a 1-year period, defines how you will conduct your business based on the action plan; it identifies clear targets such as revenues, cash flow, and market share.**

Types of Plans: Standing Plans & Single-Use Plans

Plans are of two types—*standing plans* and *single-use plans. (See Table 5.1.)*

Plan	Description
Standing plan	For activities that occur repeatedly over a period of time
• Policy	Outlines general response to a designated problem or situation
• Procedure	Outlines response to particular problems or circumstances
• Rule	Designates specific required action
Single-use plan	For activities not likely to be repeated in the future
• Program	Encompasses a range of projects or activities
• Project	Has less scope and complexity than a program

table 5.1

STANDING PLANS AND SINGLE-USE PLANS

There are three types of standing plans and two types of single-use plans.

Standing Plans: Policies, Procedures, & Rules *Standing plans* **are plans developed for activities that occur repeatedly over a period of time.** Standing plans consist of policies, procedures, and rules.

- **A** *policy* **is a standing plan that outlines the general response to a designated problem or situation.** Example: "This workplace does not condone swearing." This policy is a broad statement that gives managers a general idea about what is allowable for employees who use bad language, but gives no specifics.

- **A** *procedure* **(or** *standard operating procedure***) is a standing plan that outlines the response to particular problems or circumstances.** Example: McDonald's specifies exactly how a hamburger should be dressed, including the order in which the mustard, ketchup, and pickles are applied.

- **A** *rule* **is a standing plan that designates specific required action.** Example: "No smoking is allowed anywhere in the building." This allows no room for interpretation.

Single-Use Plans: Programs & Projects *Single-use plans* **are plans developed for activities that are not likely to be repeated in the future.** Such plans can be programs or projects.

- **A** *program* **is a single-use plan encompassing a range of projects or activities.** Example: The U.S. government space *program* has several projects, including the *Challenger* project and the Hubble Telescope project.

- **A** *project* **is a single-use plan of less scope and complexity than a program.** Example: The space shuttle *Discovery* is one project in the government's space program.

Setting SMART Goals

Anyone can define goals. But the five characteristics of a good goal are represented by the acronym SMART. **A** *SMART goal* **is one that is** *S***pecific,** *M***easurable,** *A***ttainable,** *R***esults-oriented, and has** *T***arget dates.**

Example

Strategic, Tactical, & Operational Goals: Southwest Airlines

Strategic Goals

The goal of top managers of Dallas-based Southwest Airlines is to ensure that the airline is highly profitable, following the general strategy of (a) keeping costs and fares down and (b) offering a superior on-time arrival record. One of the most important strategic decisions Southwest made was to fly just one type of airplane—Boeing 737s. (The fleet has 462 jets.) Thus, it is able to hold down training, maintenance, and operating expenses.[32] As of this writing, the airline is achieving its strategic goals: By the end of 2005, it had made money for 33 consecutive years. It has continually lowered its costs, and it leads the industry in on-time performance.[33] In 2002, Southwest launched nonstop, coast-to-coast flights twice a day between Baltimore/Washington International and Los Angeles, thereby taking on the routes long dominated by higher-fare airlines. In doing so, however, it planned to stick with 737s, but the newer generation that would travel longer distances.[34]

Tactical Goals

Cutting costs and keeping fares low is a key tactical goal for Southwest's middle managers. For example, the organization cut costs in its maintenance program by doing more work on a plane when it's in for a check instead of bringing it in three different times. In addition, it gets more use out of its planes every day by limiting the turnaround time between flights to 20 minutes, compared to up to an hour for other airlines. Southwest also usually flies to less-congested airports, thus saving time and money by avoiding traffic. There is just one class of seating, doing away with the distinction between coach and first class. Even the boarding passes are reusable, being made of plastic. Finally, the airline saves by not feeding passengers: it serves mostly peanuts, no in-flight meals.

How do you make arrival times more reliable? To achieve this second tactical goal, middle managers did away with guaranteed seat reservations before ticketing, so that no-shows won't complicate (and therefore delay) the boarding process. In addition, as mentioned, the airline is religious about turning planes around in exactly 20 minutes, so that on-time departures are more apt to produce on-time arrivals. Although the airline is unionized, turnaround is helped by looser work rules, so that workers can pitch in to do tasks outside their normal jobs. "If you saw something that needed to be done," said one former employee, "and you thought you could do it, you did."[35]

Operational Goals

Consider how Southwest's first-line managers can enhance productivity in the unloading, refueling, and cleaning of arriving planes. "One example [of productivity] customers mention all the time," says chairman Herb Kelleher, "is if you look out the window when the airplane is taxiing toward the jetway, you see our ground crews charging before the airplane has even come to rest. Customers tell me that with other airlines nobody moves until the airplane has turned off its engines."[36]

First-line managers also make sure that seat assignments (boarding passes) are not given out until an hour before the plane is due to leave to make sure that the maximum number of passengers will be on hand to fill the seats available.

Your Call

The Southwest business model has inspired a host of low-fare imitators, such as JetBlue, Spirit, and AirTran. Competition has become so stiff that even old-line traditional carriers, such as United, American, and Delta, may beat Southwest's prices on certain routes.[37] If low-cost carriers' fares are no longer the cheapest, how should Southwest redefine its strategic, tactical, and operational goals in order to successfully compete?

Group Exercise:
Using SMART Goals to Plan a Student Organization

Specific Goals should be stated in *specific* rather than vague terms. The goal that "As many planes as possible should arrive on time" is too general. The goal that "Ninety percent of planes should arrive within 15 minutes of the scheduled arrival time" is specific.

Measurable Whenever possible, goals should be *measurable,* or quantifiable (as in "90% of planes should arrive within 15 minutes . . ."). That is, there should be some way to measure the degree to which a goal has been reached.

Of course, some goals—such as those concerned with improving quality—are not precisely quantifiable. In that case, something on the order of "Improve the quality of customer relations by instituting 10 follow-up telephone calls every week" will do. You can certainly quantify how many follow-up phone calls were made.

Attainable Goals should be challenging, of course, but above all they should be realistic and *attainable.* It may be best to set goals that are quite ambitious so as to challenge people to meet high standards. Always, however, the goals should be achievable within the scope of the time, equipment, and financial support available. *(See Figure 5.4.)*

figure 5.4

RELATIONSHIP BETWEEN GOAL DIFFICULTY AND PERFORMANCE

Source: Adapted from E. A. Locke and G. P. Latham, *A Theory of Goal Setting and Task Performance* (Englewood Cliffs, NJ: Prentice Hall, 1990).

If too easy (as in "half the flights should arrive on time"), goals won't impel people to make much effort. If impossible ("all flights must arrive on time, regardless of weather"), employees won't even bother trying. Or they will try and continually fail, which will end up hurting morale.

Results-Oriented Only a few goals should be chosen—say, five for any work unit. And they should be *results-oriented*—they should support the organization's vision.

In writing out the goals, start with the word "To" and follow it with action-oriented verbs—"complete," "acquire," "increase" ("to decrease by 10% the time to get passengers settled in their seats before departure").

Some verbs should not be used in your goal statement because they imply activities—the tactics used to accomplish goals (such as having baggage handlers waiting). For example, you should not use "to develop," "to conduct," "to implement."

Target Dates Goals should specify the *target dates* or deadline dates when they are to be attained. For example, it's unrealistic to expect an airline to improve its on-time arrivals by 10% overnight. However, you could set a target date—3 to 6 months away, say—by which this goal is to be achieved. That allows enough time for lower-level managers and employees to revamp their systems and work habits and gives them a clear time frame in which they know what they are expected to do. ●

5.3 THE PLANNING/CONTROL CYCLE

> ❖ major question   **How does the planning/control cycle help keep a manager's plans headed in the right direction?**

THE BIG PICTURE
The four-step planning/control cycle helps you keep in control, to make sure you're headed in the right direction.

Once you've made plans, how do you stay in control to make sure you're headed in the right direction? Actually, there is a continuous feedback loop known as the planning/control cycle. (The "organizing" and "leading" steps within the Planning-Organizing-Leading-Controlling sequence are implied here.) **The *planning/control cycle* has two planning steps (1 and 2) and two control steps (3 and 4), as follows: (1) Make the plan. (2) Carry out the plan. (3) Control the direction by comparing results with the plan. (4) Control the direction by taking corrective action in two ways— namely, (a) by correcting deviations in the plan being carried out, or (b) by improving future plans.** *(See Figure 5.5.)*

figure 5.5

THE PLANNING/CONTROL CYCLE

This describes a constant feedback loop designed to ensure plans stay headed in the right direction.

Source: Adapted from R. Kreitner, *Management,* 8th ed. (Boston: Houghton Mifflin, 2001), p. 177, Fig. 6.4. Used with permission.

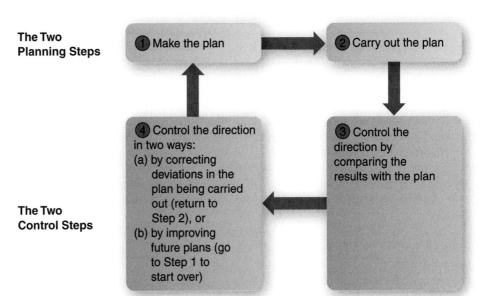

The Two Planning Steps

1. Make the plan
2. Carry out the plan

The Two Control Steps

4. Control the direction in two ways:
   (a) by correcting deviations in the plan being carried out (return to Step 2), or
   (b) by improving future plans (go to Step 1 to start over)

3. Control the direction by comparing the results with the plan

The planning/control cycle loop exists for each level of planning—strategic, tactical, and operational. The corrective action in Step 4 of the cycle (a) can get a project back on track before it's too late or (b) if it's too late, can provide data for improving future plans. ●

The Planning/Control Cycle: Apple Keeps Its Products Secret to Generate Buzz[38]

Most electronics and computer makers talk about their products well in advance of releasing them in order to give big customers and users a chance to prepare for them. Not Apple Computer Inc., maker of Macs and iPods. Secrecy is a big part of the company's marketing strategy. And the planning/control cycle figures closely in how well it is accomplished.

Step 1: The Plan

About 60% of all personal computers are bought by corporate customers and other big technology purchasers. Because of the hefty investment involved, these customers favor suppliers that let them see major product plans a year in advance. However, Apple co-founder and CEO Steve Jobs has determined that he favors selling technology directly to consumers rather than to corporate buyers and chief technology officers. By keeping a new product secret, Apple stimulates a great deal of public curiosity. "There's a great deal of mystery and speculation about what it will be," says one seasoned marketing executive. "That's created a marketing aura for them." Such was the plan in 2004, for example, when Apple and Hewlett-Packard made a deal to repackage Apple's iPod digital music player and sell it under the H-P label.

Step 2: Carrying Out the Plan

Following its plan to keep new products secret to generate marketing buzz, Apple often didn't tell H-P about new iPod models until the day before they were introduced to the public. It also insisted that H-P work on iPods under tight security, even though Apple's versions were already displayed on store shelves. The same has been true with other Apple products, with employees being sworn to secrecy for years. When, for example, the company decided to open its own chain of retail stores, an exact replica of a 6,000-square-foot store was built entirely inside a sealed-off warehouse away from Apple's main Cupertino, California, headquarters. When Apple decided to switch to Intel microprocessors, engineers worked on the project for five years under hush-hush conditions to adapt the Macintosh operating system to Intel chips.

Step 3: Comparing Results

The use of mystery "helps Apple attract crowds at its retail stores and generally garner much more visibility than its relatively modest advertising budget would suggest," says a *Wall Street Journal* story. "While new wares from Dell Inc. or H-P rarely get front-page treatment, Mr. Jobs has repeatedly appeared on the covers of *Time, Newsweek,* and *Fortune* showing off a new iPod or Macintosh computer." Secrecy, the article points out, has been a particular boon to Apple's fastest-growing product line, the iPod, which accounted for nearly 40% of the company's sales at the end of 2005. Consumers have shown their willingness to abandon their old iPods in favor of newer ones that Apple unveils with great publicity and fanfare. On the negative side, Hewlett-Packard decided to terminate its iPod partnership with Apple, in part because of the secrecy issue.

Step 4: Taking Corrective Action

Leaks have occurred, and Apple has learned that secrecy requires strong measures. Thus, Apple has fired and later sued employees who leaked news about unannounced products. It has even sued Web sites that have published gossip about Apple products. The company also assigns different departments dissimilar code names for the same product, so it can more easily track where leaks come from. Employees are outfitted with special electronic badges that grant them access only to specific areas within the fortress-like Apple corporate headquarters.

Your Call

Can you think of a more effective way to generate consumer interest in a forthcoming product than just keeping it secret? What kind of planning/control cycle issues would it raise?

5.4 PROMOTING GOAL SETTING: MANAGEMENT BY OBJECTIVES

> ⟐ major question | What is MBO, and how can it be implemented successfully to achieve results?

THE BIG PICTURE

A technique for setting goals, management by objectives (MBO) is a four-step process for motivating employees.

table 5.2

THREE TYPES OF OBJECTIVES USED IN MBO

Improvement objectives

Purpose Express performance to be accomplished in a specific way for a specific area
Examples "Increase sport-utility sales by 10%." "Reduce food spoilage by 15%."

Personal development objectives

Purpose Express personal goals to be realized
Examples "Attend five days of leadership training." "Learn basics of Microsoft Office software by June 1."

Maintenance objectives

Purpose Express the intention to maintain performance at previously established levels
Examples "Continue to meet the increased sales goals specified last quarter." "Produce another 60,000 cases of wine this month."

Do you perform better when you set goals or when you don't? What about when you set difficult goals rather than easy ones?

Research shows that if goals are made more difficult ("increase study time 30%"), people may achieve them less often than they would easy goals ("increase study time 5%"), but they nevertheless perform at a higher level. People also do better when the objectives are specific ("increase study time 10 hours a week") rather than general ("do more studying this semester").[39]

These are the kinds of matters addressed in the activity known as *management by objectives.* First suggested by **Peter Drucker** in 1954, MBO has spread largely because of the appeal of its emphasis on converting general objectives into specific ones for all members of an organization.[40]

What Is MBO? The Four-Step Process for Motivating Employees

Management by objectives (MBO) **is a four-step process in which (1) managers and employees jointly set objectives for the employee, (2) managers develop action plans, (3) managers and employees periodically review the employee's performance, and (4) the manager makes a performance appraisal and rewards the employee according to results.** The purpose of MBO is to *motivate* rather than control subordinates. Let's consider the four steps.

1. Jointly Set Objectives You sit down with your manager and the two of you jointly set objectives for you to attain. Later you do the same with each of your own subordinates. Joint manager/subordinate participation is important to the program. It's probably best if the objectives aren't simply imposed from above ("Here are the objectives I want you to meet"). Managers also should not simply approve the employee's objectives ("Whatever you aim for is okay with me"). It's necessary to have back-and-forth negotiation to make the objectives practicable. One result of joint participation, research shows, is that it impels people to set more difficult goals—to raise the level of their aspirations—which may have a positive effect on their performance.[41] The objectives should be expressed in writing and should be SMART. There are three types of objectives, shown at left. *(See Table 5.2 at left.)*

2. Develop Action Plan Once objectives are set, managers at each level should prepare an action plan for attaining them. Action plans may be prepared for both individuals and for work units, such as departments.

3. Periodically Review Performance You and your manager should meet reasonably often—either informally as needed or formally every 3 months—to review progress, as should you and your subordinates. Indeed, frequent communication is necessary so that everyone will know how well he or she is doing in meeting the objectives.

During each meeting, managers should give employees feedback, and objectives should be updated or revised as necessary to reflect new realities. If you were managing a painting or landscaping business, for example, changes in the weather, loss of key employees, or a financial downturn affecting customer spending could force you to reconsider your objectives.

4. Give Performance Appraisal & Rewards, If Any   At the end of 6 or 12 months, you and your subordinate should meet to discuss results, comparing performance with initial objectives. *Deal with results,* not personalities, emotional issues, or excuses.

Because the purpose of MBO is to *motivate* employees, performance that meets the objectives should be rewarded—with compliments, raises, bonuses, promotions, or other suitable benefits. Failure can be addressed by redefining the objectives for the next 6- or 12-month period, or even by taking stronger measures, such as demotion. Basically, however, MBO is viewed as being a learning process. After Step 4, the MBO cycle begins anew.

Cascading Objectives: MBO from the Top Down

For MBO to be successful, three things have to happen:

I. Top Management Must Be Committed   "When top-management commitment [to MBO] was high," said one review, "the average gain in productivity was 56%. When commitment was low, the average gain in productivity was only 6%."[42]

2. It Must Be Applied Organizationwide   The program has to be put in place throughout the entire organization. That is, it cannot be applied in just some divisions and departments; it has to be done in all of them.

3. Objectives Must "Cascade"   MBO works by *cascading* objectives down **through the organization; that is, objectives are structured in a *unified hierarchy,* becoming more specific at lower levels of the organization.** Top managers set general *organizational* objectives, which are translated into *divisional* objectives, which are translated into *departmental* objectives. The hierarchy ends in *individual* objectives set by each employee. ●

Example

Setting Objectives: Microsoft's "The List"

Although Microsoft Corp. has been the most profitable company in the technology industry, it now finds that its old businesses (such as its Windows operating system software and Office applications software) are growing only at the rate of the overall software industry, so it is having to focus much more on innovation. To achieve this innovation, chairman Bill Gates put together what is called "The List."

The List is a priority ranking of 50 or so initiatives that, in one description, "cut across product lines and are critical to making the next generation of products successful—everything from security software and the user interface to Web search and telephony." The List is so important that each of the items is assigned to one top executive, who is responsible for following through on it throughout the company. "We're using a lot of IQ to go after these things," Gates said.[43]

Your Call

In 2006, Microsoft announced its strategic vision for the future, to be rolled out over the next 2–3 years.[44] The company plans to create the means by which all kinds of programs and data would be stored not on individual PCs and network computers but rather "in the cloud"—all over the Internet—and be accessible via a variety of devices, from cell phones to full-powered computers. How do you think a unified hierarchy of objectives could be set for such an all-encompassing vision?

5.5 PROJECT PLANNING

major question What is project planning, why is it important, and what is the project life cyle?

THE BIG PICTURE

Project planning, designed to prepare single-use plans called projects, consists of a four-stage project life cycle: definition, planning, execution, and closing.

Project planning **is the preparation of single-use plans, or projects.** Planning is followed by *project management,* **achieving a set of goals through planning, scheduling, and maintaining progress of the activities that comprise the project.**[45] The purpose of project planning and project management is to lower the risk of uncertainty in the execution of a project. As we will see, the heart of project planning is the four-stage project life cycle.

Why care about project planning? Because more and more, this is becoming the fastest way of getting things done. Technology has sped everything up, including the process of getting a new product or service to market.[46] The age of terrorism has also changed the way strategic planners must look at their companies' futures.[47] To complete specific projects quickly, companies will now draw together people with different skills to work together on a temporary basis, then disband once the job is done. Since project management works outside an organization's usual chain of command, project managers need to be adept at people skills, able to communicate, motivate, and negotiate (as we discuss in later chapters).

Project management has long been a standard way of operating for movie production companies, which will pull together a talented team of people to make a film, then disband when the picture is "wrapped." It's also a familiar approach for professional sports teams, construction companies, and even some types of legal teams. However, it is just beginning to be employed by other for-profit organizations, such as manufacturers and insurance companies, as well as nonprofit organizations, such as those in health care and education.

An example of project planning is the *skunkworks,* **the term given to a project team whose members are separated from the normal operation of an organization and asked to produce a new, innovative product.**

The Project Life Cycle: The Predictable Evolution of a Project

Being a project manager is a challenging job if for no other reason than that you have to be attentive both to the big picture *and* to the details. Let us therefore look at the big picture—the four-stage project life cycle that any project goes through, whether it's developing an online magazine or staging an AIDS in Africa music benefit.

The *project life cycle* **has four stages from start to finish: definition, planning, execution, and closing.** *(See Figure 5.6, opposite.)* As we will see, the graph of the rise and fall of the *project* life cycle resembles that for the *product* life cycle, which we discuss in Chapter 6.

Stage I: Definition In the *definition* stage, you look at the big picture. You state the problem, look at the assumptions and risks, identify the project's goals and objectives, and determine the budget and schedule. You may also write a project proposal.

Project Planning: Skunkworks Operate Outside the Rules

In the old *Li'l Abner* comic strip about hillbillies, the Skonk Works was the site of the bootleg brewing operation for moonshine (called Kickapoo Joy Juice). In a skunkworks, says futurist Alvin Toffler, "a team is handed a loosely specified problem or goal, given resources, and allowed to operate outside the normal company rules. The skunkworks group thus ignores both the cubbyholes and the official channels—that is, the specialization and hierarchy of the existing corporate bureaucracy."[48]

In the 1960s through 1980s, Clarence "Kelly" Johnson managed Lockheed Aircraft's super-secret Advanced Development Projects Division facility—known as the Skunk Works—in Burbank, California, where under strict security some of the nation's most sophisticated aircraft, including the superfast Mach 3 SR-71 Blackbird, were developed. Among Johnson's basic operating rules were "The Skunk Works manager must be delegated practically complete control of his program in all respects" and "There must be a minimum number of reports required, but important work must be recorded thoroughly."

The computer industry has been particularly creative in employing the concept of the skunkworks. Racing to catch up with Apple Computer, which had been launched in 1976, International Business Machines launched its own version of the microcomputer, the IBM Personal Computer in 1981.[49] To get its PC to market quickly (it took only 12 months), it decided to abandon its traditional slow, methodical development process and instead gave the development of the PC to a nearly autonomous group in Boca Raton, Florida, whose members were reviewed quarterly by corporate headquarters but otherwise permitted to operate as they wished.

Google, the Mountain View, California, search-engine company, has extended the notion of skunkworks from protected place to protected idea. Google's managers keep a "Top 100" priorities list (which actually now numbers 240 items). An "S" next to the project stands for "skunkworks" and protects it from premature reviews and criticism. Engineers are rarely told what projects to work on. Instead they are allowed to gravitate to those that interest them, forming fluid work groups that can last weeks or months. They also spend a day a week working on their own personal research projects. "We're encouraging creativity and tolerating chaos," says Google's vice-president for engineering. "We turn that dial all the way over to loud."[50]

Your Call

With all this activity, you would expect Google to be churning out a flurry of products—and indeed it has. Strangely, however, despite the company's reputation as an Internet juggernaut, few of its nonsearch products (such as its instant-messaging service) have been very successful.[51] Does this mean there's something wrong with the skunkworks approach?

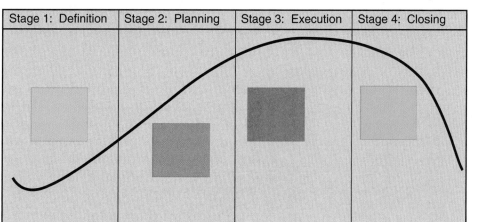

Giggling at Google. Bending the rules at Google entails greater freedom and less formality in the office so employees stay creative, as this meeting around a Ping-Pong table demonstrates.

Stage 1: Definition	Stage 2: Planning	Stage 3: Execution	Stage 4: Closing

figure 5.6

THE PROJECT LIFE CYCLE

Source: Adapted from J. W. Weiss and R. K. Wysocki, *5-Phase Project Management* (Reading, MA: Addison-Wesley, 1992) and J. K. Pinto and O. P. Kharbanda, *Successful Project Manager: Leading Your Team to Success* (New York: Van Nostrand Reinhold, 1995), pp. 17–21.

Stage 2: Planning In the *planning* stage, you consider the details needed to make the big picture happen. You identify the facilities and equipment, the people and their duties, and the schedule and co-ordination efforts needed.

Stage 3: Execution The *execution* stage is the actual work stage. You define the management style and establish the control tools. You will need to monitor progress, review the project schedule, issue change orders, and prepare status reports to the "client" (boss or customer) for whom the work is being done. Larry Bossidy, former CEO of AlliedSignal, believes many managers don't give execution the attention required to make a company's strategy really deliver results. We discuss his ideas at length in Chapter 6.

Your main focus is to complete the project on time and under budget while trying to meet the client's expectations.

Stage 4: Closing The *closing* stage occurs when the project is accepted by the client. This stage can be abrupt but could be gradual, as when you're required to install deliverables (such as a complete computer system) and carry out training.

You may also be required to write a report about the project in which you document everything that happened.

Example

Project Life Cycle: Writing a Research Paper

An example of a project is the approach recommended by one college-success book for producing a research paper.[52]

Stage 1: Definition

In the definition stage, you concentrate on picking a topic. That is, you set a deadline for when you will have decided on the topic, by which time you will have picked three alternative topics that are important to the instructor and interesting to you. You next refine the three proposed topics into three questions that your paper will be designed to answer. You then check the topic ideas with your instructor to see if he or she considers them satisfactory in importance and in scope.

Stage 2: Planning

When writing a term paper, in your planning stage you do initial research online and in the library to see if there is enough material available to you so that you can adequately research your paper. You then develop a rough outline so that you know the direction your paper will take.

Stage 3: Execution

When you're developing a research paper, the execution stage is the longest and most labor-intensive stage. This is when you do extensive research, sort your research notes, revise the outline to reflect changes suggested by your research, write a first draft, and then write and proofread your final draft.

Stage 4: Closing

The closing stage for your research paper occurs when you hand in your paper to your "client"—your instructor.

Your Call

Perhaps you've hurriedly written a paper in which you simply skipped stages 1 and 2. How successful was it? Would you try doing this for an employer who wanted you to investigate new markets for a product? Why or why not?

D
P
E
C

The Importance of Project Deadlines

There's no question that college is a pressure cooker for many students. The reason, of course, is the seemingly never-ending deadlines. But consider: Would you do all the course work you're doing—and realize the education you're getting—if you *didn't* have deadlines?

As we saw under the "T" in SMART ("has Target date"), deadlines are as essential to project planning as they are to your college career. Because the whole purpose of a planned project is to deliver to a client specified results within a specified period of time, deadlines become a great motivator, both for you and for the people working for you.

It's possible, of course, to let deadlines mislead you into focusing too much on immediate results and thereby ignore project planning—just as students will focus too much on preparing for a test in one course while neglecting others. In general, however, deadlines can help you keep your eye on the "big picture" while simultaneously paying attention to the details that will help you realize the big picture. Deadlines can help concentrate the mind, so that you make quick decisions rather than put them off.

Deadlines help you ignore extraneous matters (such as cleaning up a messy desk) in favor of focusing on what's important—achieving the project on time and on budget. Deadlines provide a mechanism for giving ourselves feedback. ●

Practical Action

Detail Thinkers versus Strategic Thinkers: Are You One or the Other?

When it comes to planning, are you a "big picture" person or a believer that "the importance is in the details"?

"Those with a natural inclination for either detail orientation or strategic thinking often choose jobs that allow them to rely on their preferred skills," says Intel Corp. senior manager Cheryl Shavers.

"It's no coincidence," she continues, "that manufacturing engineers have an ability to pay acute attention to detail—process flow, documentation, data—whereas technology licensing experts are likely to be strategic thinkers, focusing on long-term benefits and ramifications."[52]

So what happens when a person who is good at seeing the forest but not the trees meets up with a person who can see the trees but not the forest?

Someone told Shavers that he had been asked to work with a colleague to fix their flawed departmental approval process. However, the co-worker was "so process driven" that he was not very open to considering anything but an improved version of the old system, whereas the other wanted to explore a more innovative approach.

While most people with the necessary skills can, with practice, learn to move from detail orientation to strategic thinking (or the reverse), there are those who are inflexible because of fears of "not getting things right" or an inability to deal with ambiguity. Or they may get so wrapped up in a new idea they often fall short on implementation.

When detail and strategic thinkers meet, suggests Shavers, it may help to strike a balance by doing the following:

- **Use a visual to focus the discussion.** Developing a flowchart or other visual can help focus the discussion on how old processes may be stretched before new approaches are introduced.

- **Consider implementation.** The practicalities of implementation should be considered before new solutions are adopted.

- **Have mutual respect.** Both parties should respect the fact that neither approach is right or wrong, only different.

summary

 ### 5.1 Planning & Uncertainty

- Planning is defined as setting goals and deciding how to achieve them. It is also defined as coping with uncertainty by formulating future courses of action to achieve specified results.

- Planning has four benefits. (1) It helps you check your progress. (2) It helps you coordinate activities. (3) It helps you think ahead. (4) Above all, it helps you cope with uncertainty.

- Uncertainty is of three types. (1) State uncertainty is when the environment is considered unpredictable. (2) Effect uncertainty is when the effects of environmental changes are unpredictable. (3) Response uncertainty is when the consequences of a decision are uncertain.

- Organizations respond to uncertainty in one of four ways. (1) Defenders are expert at producing and selling narrowly defined products or services. (2) Prospectors focus on developing new products or services and in seeking out new markets, rather than waiting for things to happen. (3) Analyzers let other organizations take the risks of product development and marketing and then imitate (or perhaps slightly improve on) what seems to work best. (4) Reactors make adjustments only when finally forced to by environmental pressures.

 ### 5.2 Fundamentals of Planning

- An organization's reason for being is expressed in a mission statement. What the organization wishes to become and where it wants to go strategically—that is, its clear sense of the future and the actions needed to get there—are expressed in a vision statement.

- From these are derived strategic planning, then tactical planning, then operational planning. In strategic planning, managers determine what the organization's long-term goals should be for the next 1–10 years. In tactical planning, managers determine what contributions their departments or similar work units can make during the next 6–24 months. In operational planning, they determine how to accomplish specific tasks with available resources within the next 1–52 weeks.

- Whatever its type—strategic, tactical, or operational—the purpose of planning is to achieve a goal. A goal, also known as an objective, is a specific commitment to achieve a measurable result within a stated period of time. The goal should be followed by an action plan, which defines the course of action needed to achieve the stated goal. As with planning, goals are of the same three types—strategic, tactical, and operational.

- Strategic goals are set by and for top management and focus on objectives for the organization as a whole. Tactical goals are set by and for middle managers and focus on the actions needed to achieve strategic goals. Operational goals are set by and for first-line managers and are concerned with short-term matters associated with realizing tactical goals.

- The goal should be followed by an action plan, which defines the course of action needed to achieve the stated goal, such as a marketing plan or sales plan. The operating plan, which is typically designed for a 1-year period, defines how you will conduct your business based on the action plan; it identifies clear targets such as revenues, cash flow, and market share.

- Plans may be either standing plans, developed for activities that occur repeatedly over a period of time, or single-use plans, developed for activities that are not likely to be repeated in the future. There are three types of standing plans: (1) A policy is a standing plan that outlines the general response to a designated problem or situation. (2) A procedure outlines the response to particular problems or circumstances. (3) A rule designates specific required action. There are two types of single-use plans: (1) A program encompasses a range of projects or activities. (2) A project is a single-use plan of less scope and complexity than a program.

- The five characteristics of a good goal are represented by the acronym SMART. A SMART goal is one that is Specific, Measurable, Attainable, Results oriented, and has Target dates.

5.3 The Planning/Control Cycle

- Once plans are made, managers must stay in control using the planning/control cycle, which has two planning steps (1 and 2) and two control steps (3 and 4), as follows: (1) Make the plan. (2) Carry out the plan. (3) Control the direction by comparing results with the plan. (4) Control the

direction by taking corrective action in two ways—namely, (a) by correcting deviations in the plan being carried out, or (b) by improving future plans.

5.4 Promoting Goal Setting: Management by Objectives

- Management by objectives (MBO) is a four-step process in which (1) managers and employees jointly set objectives for the employee, (2) managers develop action plans, (3) managers and employees periodically review the employee's performance, and (4) the manager makes a performance appraisal and rewards the employee according to results. The purpose of MBO is to *motivate* rather than control subordinates.

- For MBO to be successful three things have to happen. (1) The commitment of top management is essential. (2) The program must be applied organizationwide. (3) Objectives must cascade—becoming more specific at lower levels of the organization.

5.5 Project Planning

- Project planning is becoming the fastest way of getting things done. Project management works outside an organization's usual chain of command. An example of project planning is the skunkworks.

- A project evolves through a project life cycle involving four stages: (1) In the definition stage, a project manager looks at the big picture, stating the problem, identifying the project's goals and objectives, and determining the budget and schedule. (2) In the planning stage, managers consider the details needed to make the big picture happen, such as identifying equipment, people, and coordination efforts needed. (3) In the execution stage, the actual work stage, managers define the management style and establish the control tools, then ensure the work is being done on time and under budget. (4) In the closing stage, the project is accepted by the client.

- Deadlines are essential to project planning because they become great motivators both for the manager and for subordinates.

In Spite of Much Uncertainty, Effective Planning & Execution Helped Toyota to Design & Produce Its Hybrid, the Prius

In late 1995, six months after Toyota decided to move forward with its revolutionary hybrid, the Prius, and two years before the car was supposed to go into production in Japan, the engineers working on the project had a problem. A big problem.

The first prototypes wouldn't start. "On the computer, the hybrid power system worked very well," says Satoshi Ogiso, the team's chief powertrain engineer. "But simulation is different from seeing if the actual part can work." It took Ogiso and his team more than a month to fix the software and electrical problems that kept the Prius stationary. Then, when they finally got it started, the car motored only a few hundred yards down the test track before coming to a stop.

It's hard to imagine Toyota, with its aura of invincibility, running into such trouble. But the story of how it brought the Prius to market—a tale of technological potholes, impossible demands, and multiple miscalculations—reveals how a great company can overcome huge obstacles to make the improbable seem inevitable. The gas-electric auto represents only a tiny fraction of the nine million cars and trucks the Japanese company will produce this year. But it is the first vehicle to provide a serious alternative to the internal combustion engine since the Stanley Steamer ran out of steam in 1924. It has become an automotive landmark: a car for the future, designed for a world of scarce oil and surplus greenhouse gases. . . .

Toyota's push into hybrids is only going to accelerate. Although the Prius first came to life under Hiroshi Okuda and Fujio Cho, Toyota's two previous presidents, new boss Katsuaki Watanabe wants hybrids to become the automotive mainstream. Watanabe, 64, who became the company's top executive [in June 2005], has the deferential air of a longtime family retainer. But he is intent on continuing Toyota's explosive growth of the past five years, in which worldwide production rose by nearly half. In an interview [in early 2006] at company headquarters in Toyota City, he stressed that a key part of his strategy is making hybrids more affordable for consumers. "We need to improve the production engineering and develop better technology in batteries, motors, and inverters," he said. "My quest is to produce a third-generation Prius quickly and cheaply." By early in the next decade he expects Toyota to be selling one million hybrids a year. . . .

The car that became the Prius began life in 1993, when Eiji Toyoda, Toyota's chairman and the patriarch of its ruling family, expressed concern about the future of the automobile. Yoshiro Kimbara, then executive vice president in charge of R&D, heard the rumblings and embarked on a project known as G21 (for global 21st century) to develop a new small car that could be sold worldwide. He set two goals: to develop new production methods and to wring better fuel economy from the traditional internal combustion engine. His target was 47.5 miles per gallon, a little more than 50% better than what the Corolla, Toyota's popular small car, was getting at the time.

By the end of 1993 the development team had determined that higher oil prices and a growing middle class around the world would require the new car to be both roomy and fuel-efficient. Other than that, they were given no guidance. "I was trying to come up with the future direction of the company," says Watanabe, who headed corporate planning at the time. "I didn't have a very specific idea about the vehicle."

Direct responsibility for the project lay with executive vice president Akihiro Wada. To lead the team, Wada went looking for an engineer with the right blend of experience and open-mindedness. He found it in Takeshi Uchiyamada. As Wada, now an advisor to Aisin Seiki, a Toyota brake supplier, explains, "Uchiyamada was originally an expert in noise and vibration control. But he was serious and hardworking, and we thought it would develop his capability to make him chief engineer of a product that could go rapidly into production."

At first Uchiyamada assumed he could increase the G21's fuel economy by making refinements to existing technology. In a plan he submitted to Wada in 1994, he wrote that the introduction of an improved engine and transmission system could boost fuel efficiency by 50%. But that wasn't audacious enough for Wada, who didn't want to be remembered for producing yet another Japanese econobox. "It was not enough to be a simple extension of existing technology," Wada says. One possible solution intrigued him: a hybrid power system.

The concept wasn't new. Toyota had been dabbling for 20 years with the idea of placing a traditional gasoline motor alongside an electric one powered by batteries that are recharged whenever the car coasts or brakes. (Honda was working on a version too.) Masatami Takimoto, now an executive vice president, says he was developing a hybrid minivan at the time but that the project had run into trouble. "There was a split between the engineers and sales executives," he says. "Engineers had the firm belief that the hybrid was the answer to all those questions—oil depletion, emissions, and the long-term future of the automobile society—but the businesspeople weren't in agreement." They thought the premium price for the hybrid would make it impossible to sell.

Wada sided with the engineers and ordered the team to develop a concept car with a hybrid powertrain for the 1995 Tokyo Motor Show, just 12 months away. To reinforce his directive, he demanded that they raise the fuel-economy target even higher to compensate for higher hybrid costs. "Don't settle for anything less than a 100% improvement," he says he told Uchiyamada. "Otherwise competitors would catch up quickly." As Uchiyamada, now an executive vice president and a member of Toyota's board, concedes, "At that moment I felt he demanded too much."

To find the right hybrid system for the G21, by now called the Prius, Uchiyamada's team went through 80 alternatives before narrowing the list to four, based largely on fuel efficiency. . . .

Watching developments from across the Pacific were the product planners at the company's U.S. division, Toyota Motor Sales, in Torrance, Calif. The TMS planners had first heard about hybrids at a meeting in Japan in 1995. "It was all new and unconventional," recalls marketing executive Mark Amstock. "There was skepticism within the company about whether the hybrids were really cars." Early consumer research in the U.S. supported the skeptics. "It wasn't clear that better fuel economy alone could drive premium pricing," says Andrew Coetzee, now vice president of product planning for TMS. But another factor was at play at TMS: the ever more stringent emission targets set by the California Air Resources Board. Gradually support began to build around hybrid's ecological potential.

Thirty miles to the south, at Toyota's design studio in Newport Beach, stylists were competing with colleagues in Japan to develop body concepts for the Prius. Like everything else, it was a rush job. "Ordinarily we get two to three months to make sketches and prepare models," recalls designer Erwin Lui. "For Prius we got two to three weeks." . . .

Meanwhile the engineers in Japan kept running into problems. According to a 1999 account written by Hideshi Itazaki and published in Japan, the batteries continued to be a nightmare. The Prius needed a large battery pack to power the car at low speeds and to store energy, but it would shut down when it became too hot or too cold. During road tests with Toyota executives, a team member had to sit in the passenger seat with a laptop and monitor the temperature of the battery so that it wouldn't burst into flames.

Okuda kept up the pressure. He told Wada in December 1996 that he wanted to announce by the following March that Toyota had developed a hybrid technology. . . .

Toyota unveiled the Prius in Japan in October 1997, two months ahead of schedule, and it went on sale that December. The total cost of development was an estimated $1 billion—after all the anguish, about average for a new car. But the Prius's initial reception took some executives, including Watanabe, by surprise. "I did not envisage such a major success at that time," he says. "Some thought it would grow rapidly, and others thought it would grow gradually. I was in the second camp." Production was quickly doubled to 2,000 cars a month.

Over in California, TMS executives were still worried about sales prospects in the U.S. Introducing cars with novel powertrains wasn't something they were used to. . . .

The two biggest decisions TMS had to make were how many cars to order and how much to charge, the latter causing friction between California and Japan. Under the Toyota system, the U.S. sales group buys cars from the parent company at a negotiated price, then resells them to dealers. Japan wanted the Prius to sell for more than $20,000, putting it in Camry territory. But the Americans saw a car about the size of the smaller Corolla and produced research showing that buyers would balk at paying that much. A compromise was reached when TMS cut the dealer margin on the car from 14% to 10% so that it could pay Japan more and still make a decent profit. Since the Prius was expected to account for less than 1% of their total sales, dealers didn't complain. The car went on sale with a base price of $19,995. Japan lost money on the first batch—not unusual for a small car. . . .

The Prius made its U.S. debut in July 2000. It wasn't a delight to drive, requiring 13 seconds to get to 60 miles per hour (the Corolla needed just ten). A Car and Driver writer reported, "The Prius alternatively lurches and bucks down the road, its engine noise swelling and subsiding for no apparent reason."

But the Prius caught on anyway and, as in Japan, sales were much higher than the company dared hope. Buyers didn't care about the jerky ride or premium price—they focused on the improved fuel economy, lower emissions (as much as 80% lower), and advanced technology. Resale value protected them on the downside: The Prius retained 57% of its value after three years. Pride of ownership was so high that only 2% of buyers opted to lease.

For Discussion

1. What is your evaluation of the planning process used by Toyota? Discuss.
2. What types of uncertainty were faced by the development team and members of TMS in California?

3. Which of the four basic strategy types were used by Toyota? Explain your rationale.
4. What is your feeling about the vision Katsuaki Watanabe has for hybrids? Do you think his vision can be achieved? Explain.
5. What did you learn about planning based on this case? Explain.
6. Would you purchase a hybrid? Why or why not?

Source: Excerpted from Alex Taylor III, "The Birth of the Prius," *Fortune,* March 6, 2006, pp. 111–124.

self-assessment

Holland Personality Types & You: Matching Your Personality to the Right Work Environment & Occupation

Objectives

1. To understand the need to plan for your career.
2. To try to match your personality with an occupation.

Introduction

What do you want to be when you grow up? Some people seem to know early in life. Others come to a realization in college. Still others may be forced to such awareness by a crisis in later life, such as being dismissed from a job. Of course, most of us make some sort of plans for our careers. But in doing so we may not always be knowledgeable about how to match our personalities with the choices available.

Instructions

There are four parts to this exercise.

First, select a number from the list of six personality types.

Second, match that choice with the personality you think that type would have.

Third, select the work environment you think would be best for that personality type and personality.

Fourth, based on the preceding three choices, select which occupation would fit best. (For example, if you selected #1, C, and f, the best fit for an occupation would be artist, musical conductor, and other related occupations.)

Try to connect each of the four parts and then check the key to see if your pairings are correct. After that, go through the list again, identifying what you think your personality type is, what your personality is, the work environment you like or think you would like best, and then the occupation that you would or do like best. See if there is an alignment by using the scoring guidelines

and interpretation shown below; if there is such an alignment, this suggests you may be on your way to a successful career.

Personality Type

1. Artistic
2. Conventional
3. Realistic
4. Enterprising
5. Social
6. Investigative

Personality

A. Prefers to work with things; is present-oriented, athletic, and mechanical.

B. Is analytical, a problem solver, scientific, and original.

C. Relies on feelings and imagination, is expressive, is intuitive, and values esthetics.

D. Sensitive to needs of others, enjoys interpersonal gatherings, and values educational and social issues.

E. Adventurous, has leadership qualities, persuasive, and values political and economic matters.

F. Structured, accurate, detail-oriented, and loyal follower.

Work Environments

a. Technical/mechanical and industrial.

b. Traditional and rewards conformity and dependability.

c. Cooperative and rewards personal growth.

d. Managerial role in organizations and rewards monetary gains and achievements.

e. Rewards high academic achievement and uses technical abilities to complete tasks.

f. Unstructured and allows nonconformity and rewards creativity.

Occupations

7. Chemist/biological scientist, computer analyst, and emergency medical technician.
8. Lawyer, flight attendant, sales representative, reporter.
9. Accountant, bank teller, medical record technician.
10. Cook, drywall installer, auto mechanic.
11. Artist/commercial artist, musical director, architect, writer/editor.
12. Teacher, clergy, nurse, counselor, librarian.

Scoring Guidelines & Interpretation
Scoring is as follows:

1-C-f-11

2-F-b-9

3-A-a-10

4-E-d-8

5-D-c-12

6-B-e-7

The purpose of this type of exercise is to see how personality type, personality, work environment, and occupation can best fit together. When the elements mesh, you will usually feel more competent and more satisfied with your work conditions and occupation. When these elements or factors are mismatched, one can be very frustrated, feel incompetent, or not be good at one's job.

If you wish to know more about career planning, you can avail yourself of a much more in-depth planning process at **www.soice.state.nc.us/sociss/planning/jh-types.htm.**

Questions for Discussion
1. Does your assessment suggest that your career choice is best for your personality type? How do you feel about this assessment?
2. What do you think the management challenges are for those who are mismatched in their work? Explain.
3. Can you see and describe yourself more clearly in terms of personality type, personality, work environment, and occupation given the results of your scoring? Explain.

Developed by Anne C. Cowden, PhD, based on the information provided by the Web site **www.soice.state.nc.us/sociss/planning/jh-types.htm.**

group exercise

Trying to Solve an "Electric" Problem in Managerial Planning

Objectives

1. To assess a specific problem where planning is required.
2. To arrive at a mutual and effective solution as a group, taking into consideration different perspectives and different goals.

Introduction

Increasingly problems are being solved by groups of people, each with a different stake in the outcome. However, for a company to achieve its goals successfully, these problems must be solved without alienating members of the group.

Scenario

The company, a large processing center operating in a highly bureaucratic fashion, was experiencing challenging problems in a major division of its operations. Fifteen months earlier, when an electrical storm caused loss of power in one company building, five of the seven members of the night-shift service staff reported strange sensations emanating from their computer terminals causing tingling in their hands. In the following days, other staff members reported similar sensations, as well as numbness, headaches, and nausea. Two weeks later there were almost 100 reports of such "electrical shocks." Union representatives requested immediate action on the problems. The issues of workplace health and safety at the company became a hot topic in the local media. Various health and government agencies began to investigate.

Reports of the shocks continued sporadically for the next nine months, then began to rise significantly. During a 10-week period, there were more than 150 reports, many from people working in other parts of the company. The ensuing uproar produced a walkout lasting three days, costing the company an estimated $1 million in lost revenue. The problem didn't seem to be solvable simply by top managers' exercising their authority and dictating a solution. What could be done to get the company back on the right track?

Instructions

The class should divide into groups of seven people each. Within each group, each person should assume one of the roles described below. Take turns discussing the case from each of the seven perspectives, with each person staying within his or her role, until your group has solved the problem by consensus. The goal of the group is to arrive at a solution that will get the company moving efficiently and effectively again.

Roles: The Perspectives of the Positions Involved

1. **Senior management.** "We don't need this problem. We have to restore normal levels of control and efficiency, based on measured results."

2. **The ergonomists.** "There are some routine ergonomic problems that can be improved through the physical redesign of equipment. But there is no evidence of major health and safety problems."

3. **Labor leaders.** "This mess has got to be cleaned up. The health and safety features are critical. Management has to take action, but we don't trust them. We are strong and can apply a lot of pressure if necessary."

4. **The politicians.** "We don't want more media coverage on this one and more charges of mismanagement that consume our time. We

don't want the unions asking us to solve their problems."

5. **The service staff.** "We're working with a poor system. We don't want the strain and stress. Management has to sort the situation out. More stress breaks. Safer equipment. Find the 'techies' that are 'zapping us.'"

6. **The human resources people.** "The problem rests with the stressful nature of the work itself. We need to redesign the work process. We also need to deal with the collective stress phenomenon that's emerged."

7. **Line managers.** "The situation has changed on us. We're held accountable, but we don't have the power to deliver. We need to get better informed and to learn new skills for managing in a turbulent world."

Questions for Discussion

1. How did your group resolve the situation? Explain.
2. How did you feel, as you had to stay "in role" and respond from that position's perspective?
3. How difficult do you think it is it for people to see each other's perspectives and manage a situation? Explain.
4. How would you manage people who are in conflict about a situation such as the one presented above? Describe.

Written by Anne C. Cowden, PhD; adapted from a case in Gareth Morgan, *Imagination: The Art of Creative Management* (Newbury Park, CA.: Sage, 1993), Chapter 5.

 ethical dilemma

Should PricewaterhouseCoopers Pass on Rebates to Its Customers?

Assume you are the CEO from PricewaterhouseCoopers, and Neal Roberts brings the following information to your attention.

In early 2000, Neal A. Roberts discovered that his employer, PricewaterhouseCoopers LLP, was pocketing millions of dollars a year from what he considered to be a dubious billing gimmick: the accounting giant obtained large rebates on airline tickets used for client business but didn't pass along the savings to its clients. Travel expenses had become an undisclosed source

of profits at PricewaterhouseCoopers, and unknowing clients paid the tab.

Solving the Dilemma

As the CEO of PricewaterhouseCoopers, what would you do?

1. Keep the rebates. Inform all employees of the practice and explain that you support this policy because the rebates offset other administrative costs, such as the cost to run your travel department. Further, if you don't do

this, then the company will have to charge clients higher hourly rates.

2. Because it would be impractical and difficult to retroactively refund all your clients, keep the rebates the company has already received but initiate a new policy passing future rebates on to clients.

3. Disclosure is important. Inform your clients of the practice, and explain that the rebates offset other costs (for example, running your travel department) and this practice allows you to bill them at a lower hourly rate.

4. Invent other options. Discuss.

Source: Excerpted from Jonathan Weil, "Disputed Discounts: Court Files Offer Inside Look at Pricewaterhouse Billing Clash," *The Wall Street Journal*, January 5, 2004, p. A1.

 video case

The Dale Grey Story

The Dale Grey story starts in Denver, Colorado. In 1983 Dale started Grey & Associates with two weeks' vacation pay (but no associates). Today, the company has evolved into Communication Services and employs over 100 people in six offices and is one of the top 20 companies in telecommunications infrastructure development.

For 17 years now, Grey has enjoyed being an entrepreneur. A turning point came when, as a young man, Grey's boss asked him to slow down his work production because he was outshining the other employees. Grey soon recognized a personal desire and a passion that he didn't see in other people, and he decided that he needed to build his own company. Almost two decades later, he's still excited to work in an environment that's fun, challenging, and profitable.

Grey's initial goal was to build a million-dollar company. After successfully attaining this goal, he and his employees held an off-site planning retreat to determine the company's future goals and direction. Grey and his team considered a number of factors, including what the company was doing right, necessary changes, and the future of the industry. The group articulated and recorded a company vision and decided they wanted to be a 10-million-dollar company by the year 2005 (which they accomplished early).

Like most entrepreneurs, Grey initially shouldered all the workload himself. However, his proudest accomplishment is being just another member of the team. As the name of the company evolved from "Grey & Associates" to "Grey Communications" and finally to "Communication Services," clients relied less and less on Grey and more on the capable talents of company employees. Thus, Grey became "just part of the team," which suits him just fine.

According to Grey, self-confidence is the most important quality of a successful entrepreneur. Even though there are hundreds of opportunities to fail, an entrepreneur must see only the certainty of success.

The most difficult aspect of being an entrepreneur is learning the business skills that do not initially interest one or that one does not feel strong in. For example, in the beginning, the company didn't have a business plan (and wasn't required to create one, since the business grew using internally generated profits). However, as the firm grew larger, it became necessary to create the business plan simply to understand how the organization ran and to meet financial expectations and staffing requirements.

Staffing was a critical element in building a successful company. According to Grey, the key is to find people who have the same passion and energy for the organization as he does. Next, training should be viewed as an investment in both the Communication Services team members and the industry as a whole. Finally, Grey respects the need for a balance between work and home life. Although he expects his employees to work hard in the workplace, he knows that they need time with family and friends to rejuvenate and recharge. After all, Grey and his team are prepared for a marathon, not a short race.

Discussion Questions

1. Experts classify uncertainty as three different types: state, effect, and response. Define each of these types. At the planning retreat held by Grey and his colleagues, the group attempted to predict the direction of the telecommunications industry. Which type of uncertainty does this represent?

2. At the off-site planning retreat, were Grey and his team developing strategic, tactical, or operational goals?

3. According to Dale Grey, what is the most critical quality for a successful entrepreneur? What is the most difficult aspect of being an entrepreneur?

chapter 6

Strategic Management
How Star Managers Realize a Grand Design

Major Questions You Should Be Able to Answer

6.1 The Dynamics of Strategic Planning
Major Question: Am I really managing if I don't have a strategy?

6.4 Formulating Strategy
Major Question: How can two techniques—Porter's competitive strategies and the product life cycle—help me formulate strategy?

6.2 The Strategic-Management Process
Major Question: What's the five-step recipe for the strategic-management process?

6.5 Implementing & Controlling Strategy: Execution
Major Question: How does effective execution help managers during the strategic-management process?

6.3 Establishing the Grand Strategy
Major Question: How can SWOT and forecasting help me establish my strategy?

What Does the Successful Top Manager Do to Stay Successful?

Management tools and techniques, says Darrell K. Rigby, a director of global business consulting firm Bain & Co., "are to some extent fashion items," becoming popular or unpopular as intellectual and economic currents change.[1]

One year the big buzz words may be *reengineering* or *activity-based costing*, according to Rigby, who prepares Bain's annual Management Tools & Trends survey of the use of and satisfaction with the most popular management tools. Another year may favor *customer relationship management* or *contingency planning*. But "management tools are not silver bullets," says Rigby. "They are more like chain saws—potentially powerful when applied to the right problems but extraordinarily dangerous in the wrong hands."

There seem to be two lessons here:

- **Lesson #1—In an era of management fads, strategic planning is still tops.** Over the years, some tools still retain their popularity. The Bain & Company 2005 Management Tools survey found that the most widely used management tool in 2004 was the same as that used 4 years and even 6 years earlier— namely, *strategic planning*, which is concerned with developing a comprehensive program for long-term success. Strategic planning, which we discuss in this chapter, scored 4.14 on a one-to-five "satisfaction scale" among respondents in Bain's global database of 7,000 executives who were asked how satisfied they were with this particular tool.[2]

- **Lesson #2—A manager's most valuable character trait: be willing to make large, painful decisions to suddenly alter strategy.** But there's another lesson. In a world of rapid and discontinuous change, managers must always be prepared to make large, painful decisions and radically alter their business design—the very basis of how the company makes money. Today, say two consultants with Boston's Mercer Management Consulting, "a static business model is death."[3]

Intel, for example, used to make memory chips. When that began to look like a hypercompetitive commodity business (a commodity is a mass-produced, unspecialized product), Intel switched to making processor chips. When processors were threatened with becoming commodities, it began marketing them as branded consumer products ("Intel Inside!").[4] Later it focused on making chips for communications and consumer electronics—the chips that power everything. And recently it has become one of the prime backers of high-speed wireless technologies, including Wi-Fi (which can cover a few hundred feet) and WiMax (which has a range up to 30 miles).[5] Because of fast-spreading world conditions such as the threat of products becoming commodities, rapidly increasing productivity, and global overcapacity, managers must be able to make difficult decisions: "exiting businesses, firing people, admitting you were wrong (or at least not omniscient)," as writer Geoffrey Colvin puts it. "So the future will demand ever more people with the golden trait, the fortitude to accept and even seek psychic pain."[6]

Many managers think they can make painful decisions about things that obviously need doing. But, Colvin points out, "those with the far greater courage to make unpleasant decisions based on what they see that *no one else sees*—these people will dominate." These decisions are at the very heart of strategic management.

For Discussion Earlier we described the importance of practicing so-called *evidence-based management*, with managers "seeing the truth as a moving target," always facing the hard facts, avoiding falling prey to half-truths, and being willing to admit when they're wrong and change their ways.[7] Do you think you have this mind-set when thinking about the overall direction of your organization or work unit?

forecast

What's Ahead in This Chapter

We describe strategic management and strategic planning and why they're important. We go through the five steps in the strategic-management process. Then we show how grand strategy is developed, using two strategic-planning tools—SWOT analysis and forecasting. Next we show how strategy is formulated, using such techniques as Porter's four competitive strategies, product life cycles, single-product versus diversification strategies, and competitive intelligence. Finally, we show how strategy is carried out and controlled.

6.1 THE DYNAMICS OF STRATEGIC PLANNING

major question Am I really managing if I don't have a strategy?

THE BIG PICTURE

This section distinguishes among strategy, strategic management, and strategic planning. We describe three reasons why strategic management and strategic planning are important and how they may work for both large and small firms.

Is thinking strategically really necessary?

After all, in the 1970s and 1980s, Japanese companies rarely developed strategic positions. Instead, they pioneered in what is known as *operational effectiveness,* which means they learned to perform *similar* activities *better* than rivals performed them. Through such practices as total quality management and continuous improvement, Japanese manufacturers gained substantial cost and quality advantages, and for many years they appeared unstoppable.

But most Japanese companies try to imitate one another, so that competitors match one another's plant designs, employ the same distribution channels, and offer most of the same product features and varieties. In the 1990s, as the gap narrowed in operational effectiveness, these companies found themselves engaged in mutually destructive battles. Now they have had to learn strategic positioning—that is, to perform activities that are *different* from those of their rivals or similar activities that are performed in *different* ways.

In this section, we do the following:

- Define strategy and strategic management.
- Explain why strategic planning is important.

Operational effectiveness, not strategic effectiveness. Japanese makers of television sets have been more apt to imitate one another than do strategic planning. When you buy a TV set made in Japan, do you see any difference among those made by Sony, Toshiba, and Panasonic?

- Describe the three key principles that underlie strategic positioning.
- Discuss strategic management in large versus small firms.

Strategy, Strategic Management, & Strategic Planning: What They Are, Why They're Important

Every organization needs to have a "big picture" about where it's going and how to get there. These are matters of strategy, strategic management, and strategic planning.

Strategy   A *strategy* **is a large-scale action plan that sets the direction for an organization.** It represents an "educated guess" about what must be done in the long term for the survival or the prosperity of the organization or its principal parts.

We hear the word expressed in terms like "Budweiser's ultimate strategy . . ." or "Visa's overseas strategy . . ." or *financial strategy, marketing strategy,* and *human resource strategy.*

An example of a strategy is "Find out what customers want, then provide it to them as cheaply and quickly as possible" (the strategy of Wal-Mart). As we stated in this chapter's introduction, however, strategy is not something that can be decided on just once. Because of fast-changing conditions, it needs to be revisited from time to time, whether every year or every 5 years.

Strategic Management   In the late 1940s, most large U.S. companies were organized around a single idea or product line. By the 1970s, Fortune 500 companies were operating in more than one industry and had expanded overseas. It became apparent that to stay focused and efficient, companies had to begin taking a strategic-management approach.

Strategic management **is a process that involves managers from all parts of the organization in the formulation and the implementation of strategies and strategic goals.** This definition doesn't mean that managers at the top dictate ideas to be followed by people lower down. Indeed, precisely because middle managers are the ones who will be asked to understand and implement the strategies, they should also help to formulate them. The steps in this process are covered in Section 6.2.

Strategic Planning   *Strategic planning,* as we stated in Chapter 5, determines not only the organization's long-term goals for the next 1–5 years regarding growth and profits but also the ways the organization should achieve them.

As Bryan W. Barry, author of *Strategic Planning Workbook for Nonprofit Organizations,* states: "Strategic planning is the process of determining what your organization intends to accomplish, and how you will direct the organization and its resources toward accomplishing these goals in the coming months and years."[8]

Why Strategic Management & Strategic Planning Are Important

There are three reasons why an organization should adopt strategic management and strategic planning: They can (1) provide *direction and momentum,* (2) *encourage new ideas,* and above all (3) *develop a sustainable competitive advantage.*[9] Let's consider these three matters.

I. Providing Direction & Momentum

"Leaders of some groups become so preoccupied with day-to-day pressures," says Bryan Barry, "that their organizations lose momentum." Strategic planning can help people focus on the most critical problems, choices, and opportunities. If everyone is involved in the process, that can also help create teamwork, promote learning, and build commitment across the organization.

Unless a strategic plan is in place, managers may well focus on just whatever is in front of them, the usual run-of-the-mill problems—until they get an unpleasant jolt when a competitor moves out in front because it has been able to take a long-range view of things and act more quickly. Recently this surprise has been happening over and over as companies have had an attack of Internet anxiety because some upstart online company or trend suddenly emerged as a threat—as Schwab.com did to Merrill Lynch, as Amazon.com did to Barnes & Noble, and as Napster and Kazaa did to the Big Five record companies.[10]

But there are many other instances in which a big company didn't take a competitor seriously (as Sears didn't Wal-Mart, IBM didn't Microsoft, and GM didn't Toyota). "We were five years late in recognizing that [microbreweries] were going to take as much market as they did," says August Busch III, CEO of massive brewer Anheuser-Busch, "and five years late in recognizing we should have joined them."[11]

Of course, a poor plan can send an organization in the wrong direction. Bad planning usually results from faulty assumptions about the future, poor assessment of an organization's capabilities, ineffective group dynamics, and information overload.[12]

2. Encouraging New Ideas

Some people object that planning can foster rigidity, that it creates blinders that block out peripheral vision and reduces creative thinking and action. "Setting oneself on a predetermined course in unknown waters," says one critic, "is the perfect way to sail straight into an iceberg."[13]

Actually, far from being a straitjacket for new ideas, strategic planning can help encourage them by stressing the importance of innovation in achieving long-range success. Gary Hamel, head of Strategos, an international consulting firm specializing in strategy, says that companies such as Nike have been successful because they have been able to unleash the spirit of "strategy innovation." Strategy innovation, he says, is "the ability to reinvent the basis of competition within existing industries and to invent entirely new industries."

Some successful innovators are companies creating new wealth in the grocery business, where Starbucks Coffee, Trader Joe's, Petco, ConAgra, and Wal-Mart, for

New concept, new store. Electronics retailer Best Buy is trying to lure younger, savvier customers by opening experimental stores, such as Escape (shown here at its flagship location in a trendy Chicago neighborhood). Escape carries cutting-edge products not carried by other Best Buys, as well as videogame-testing rooms and a snack bar. As of mid-2006, there was only one Escape store—what Best Buy calls a "learn-and-earn" model. Do you think such stores could have mass appeal?

Developing Competitive Advantage: Staples Simplifies Its Shopping Experience

Staples practically invented the office-retail store to supply small and medium-sized businesses, when it launched its first one in 1986. By the early 2000s, however, the field had become crowded with competitors and Staples sales were falling off. Market research found that shoppers expected stores to carry everything but wanted helpful sales people to help them with hassle-free shopping. From this was born the tag line "Staples: That was easy."

But then Staples did something more than just create a new marketing message: it took a year to give its stores a major makeover, removing 800 superfluous items from inventory (such as Britney Spears backpacks), adding larger signs, removing office chairs from the rafters to the floor so customers could try them out, and retraining sales people ("sales associates") to walk shoppers to the correct aisle. Then they launched the new tag line, along with the iconic object, the "Easy Button."

Many marketers believe that if they just pronounce an advertising message long and loud enough, customers will come to believe it. In Staples' case, however, it is more likely that changing the customer experience within the stores did more. After 5 years of the rebranding effort, Staples became the runaway leader in office retail. In 2005, its profit was up 18%, while its major competitors Office Depot and OfficeMax posted losses.[14]

Your Call

What other competitive retail industries can you think of where the Staples model could be extended for competitive advantage?

example, have developed entirely new product categories and retailing concepts. For instance, says Hamel, Starbucks "took a sleepy supermarket commodity—coffee—and began selling it in infinite varieties in trendy stores, thereby establishing a whole new market."[15]

3. Developing a Sustainable Competitive Advantage Strategic management provides a sustainable *competitive advantage,* which, you'll recall (from Chapter 1), is the ability of an organization to produce goods or services more effectively than its competitors do, thereby outperforming them. Sustainable competitive advantage occurs when an organization is able to get and stay ahead in four areas: (1) in being responsive to customers, (2) in innovating, (3) in quality, and (4) in effectiveness.

What Is an Effective Strategy? Three Principles

Harvard Business School professor **Michael Porter** "is the single most important strategist working today, and maybe of all time," raves Kevin Coyne of consulting firm McKinsey & Co.[16]

Is this high praise deserved? Certainly Porter's status as a leading authority on competitive strategy is unchallenged. The Strategic Management Society, for instance, voted him the most influential living strategist. We will refer to him repeatedly in this chapter.

According to Porter, ***strategic positioning* attempts to achieve sustainable competitive advantage by preserving what is distinctive about a company.** "It means," he says, "performing *different* activities from rivals, or performing *similar* activities in different ways."[17]

Three key principles underlie strategic positioning:[18]

1. Strategy Is the Creation of a Unique & Valuable Position

Strategic position emerges from three sources:

- **Few needs, many customers.** Strategic position can be derived from serving the few needs of many customers. Example: Jiffy Lube provides only lubricants, but it provides them to all kinds of people with all kinds of motor vehicles.
- **Broad needs, few customers.** A strategic position may be based on serving the broad needs of just a few customers. Example: Bessemer Trust targets only very high wealth clients.
- **Broad needs, many customers.** Strategy may be oriented toward serving the broad needs of many customers. Example: Carmike Cinemas operates only in cities with populations of fewer than 200,000 people.

2. Strategy Requires Trade-offs in Competing

As a glance at the choices above shows, some strategies are incompatible. Thus, a company has to choose not only what strategy to follow but what strategy *not* to follow. Example: Neutrogena soap, points out Porter, is positioned more as a medicinal product than as a cleansing agent. In achieving this narrow positioning, the company gives up sales based on deodorizing, gives up large volume, and accordingly gives up some manufacturing efficiencies.

3. Strategy Involves Creating a "Fit" among Activities

"Fit" has to do with the ways a company's activities interact and reinforce one another. Example: A mutual fund such as Vanguard Group follows a low-cost strategy and aligns all its activities accordingly, distributing funds directly to consumers and minimizing portfolio turnover. However, when Continental Lite tried to match some but not all of Southwest Airlines' activities, it was not successful because it didn't apply Southwest's whole interlocking system.

Does Strategic Management Work for Small as Well as Large Firms?

You would expect that a large organization, with its thousands of employees and even larger realm of "stakeholders," would benefit from strategic management and planning. After all, how can a huge company such as Ford Motor Co. run without some sort of grand design?

But what about smaller companies, which account for more than half of total employment and the bulk of employment growth in recent years? One analysis of several studies found that strategic planning was appropriate not just for large firms—companies with fewer than 100 employees could benefit as well, although the improvement in financial performance was small. Nevertheless, the researchers concluded, "it may be that the small improvement in performance is not worth the effort involved in strategic planning unless a firm is in a very competitive industry where small differences in performance may affect the firm's survival potential."[19] ●

6.2 THE STRATEGIC-MANAGEMENT PROCESS

What's the five-step recipe for the strategic-management process?

major question

THE BIG PICTURE

The strategic-management process has five steps: Establish the mission and the vision, establish the grand strategy, formulate the strategic plans, carry out those plans, and maintain strategic control. In addition, all the steps may be affected by feedback that enables the taking of constructive action.

When is a good time to begin the strategic-management process? Often it's touched off by some crisis.

Coca-Cola was compelled to do serious soul searching when in 1985 buyers turned away in droves from its New Coke, one of the worst marketing disasters in history. For Clorox Co., the crisis came in 1988, when it introduced a line of powdered detergents, which was rejected by consumers who not only favored liquid detergents but also identified Clorox with bleach. For ValuJet, it was the crash of one of its DC-9 jets in the Florida Everglades, which gave the no-frills airline so much bad publicity that ultimately it had to merge with AirTran Airways and adopt the AirTran name.[20] And the backers of the DVD were confronted by the DivX disk.

The Five Steps of the Strategic-Management Process

The strategic-management process has five steps, plus a feedback loop, as shown below. *(See Figure 6.1.)* Let's consider these five steps.

Feedback: Revise actions, if necessary, based on feedback

figure 6.1

THE STRATEGIC-MANAGEMENT PROCESS

The process has five steps.

Step 1: Establish the Mission & the Vision We discussed mission and vision in Chapter 5. If you were called on to write a mission statement and a vision statement, how would you go about it?

Characteristics of a Good Mission Statement The *mission,* you'll recall, is the organization's purpose or reason for being, and it is expressed in a *mission statement.*

Crisis Leading to the Strategic-Management Process: The Video-Disk War—DVD versus DivX

Every new technology must overcome resistance. And the DVD, short for digital video disk, had some major hurdles.[21]

First, the VCR was perhaps the most popular consumer-electronics product in a generation. The DVD, intended to replace it, not only cost more, it offered few new features. Second, just as the DVD was beginning to sell, in 1997 a rival disk appeared, the DivX, backed by the huge electronics chain of Circuit City Stores (along with a Hollywood law firm). The key idea behind DivX was that it would be a movie-on-a-disk that could offer an alternative to renting VCR tapes. Consumers could buy a disk with a movie on it for the price of a video rental, then have 48 hours in which to view it. After that, they could choose between simply throwing the disk away or paying an extra $15—billed by DivX directly to their credit card. This credit card fee authorized the company's central computer, through a modem connection to the customer's home computer—to grant outright ownership for unlimited viewing, thereby obviating further rental fees at video stores.

The crisis forced DVD backers, led by Warner Home Video, to re-examine their business design. They were able to take advantage of three external factors. First, only 750 of some 10,000 electronics stores nationwide agreed to carry DivX, most not wishing to boost the revenues of rival Circuit City. Second, only three manufacturers agreed to make DivX players, mainly because they didn't wish to offend the mammoth retailer. Third, video stores realized

the DivX would cut their rentals in half, so they started offering DVD rentals.

The DVD strategy for success was based on forming an alliance among Hollywood movie studios, hardware makers, and retailers. Hollywood wanted not only better image and audio quality but also longer playing time and a parental "lockout" feature. As the film studios began making more and more movies available on DVD, Toshiba, Sony, and other DVD hardware manufacturers began slicing prices and pouring millions into promotion, including giving away five DVDs with every player sold.

In June 1999, after losing $375 million, Circuit City announced it was discontinuing DivX.

Your Call

Now DVD is nearing the end of its product life, and there's a new disk war, this time between two high-definition disk formats: Toshiba's HD-DVD and Sony's Blu-ray. HD-DVD is backed by Microsoft, Sanyo, NEC, and movie studios like New Line and Universal. Blu-ray has in its camp Apple, Panasonic, Philips, Samsung, Sharp, Pioneer, Dell, and movie studios like Sony, 20th Century Fox, and Disney.[22] Probably only one format will ultimately prevail (as VHS did over Betamax 30 years ago), and losers will be left with obsolete players. If you were a video-rental outfit like Netflix, this either-or choice might be seen as a crisis that would force you to consider your long-range strategy. What would influence your decision?

For example, the mission statement of McGraw-Hill, publisher of this book, is as follows:

> *To serve the worldwide need for knowledge at a fair profit by gathering, evaluating, producing, and distributing valuable information in a way that benefits our customers, employees, authors, investors, and our society.*

Characteristics of a Good Vision Statement An organization's vision, you'll recall, is its long-term goal describing what it wants to become. It is expressed in a *vision* *statement,* which describes its long-term direction and strategic intent. For example, Walt Disney's original vision for Disneyland went in part like this:

> *Disneyland will be something of a fair, an exhibition, a playground, a community center, a museum of living facts, and a showplace of beauty and magic. It will be filled with the accomplishments, the joys and hopes of the world we live in. And it will remind us and show us how to make those wonders part of our own lives.*[23]

Sometimes a vision statement can be short. When Ciba Vision's sales of conventional contacts were threatened by a new, disposable contact lens from Johnson & Johnson in 1987, Ciba president Glenn Bradley reorganized the company into six formal development projects to produce eye-ware product breakthroughs. While each unit was free to shape its own organization, processes, and culture, Bradley knew they had to share expertise and resources. Accordingly, he and his team enunciated a new vision statement: "Healthy Eyes for Life." The statement was not only meaningful to all parts of the business but also underscored the connections between the breakthrough initiatives and the conventional operation. The slogan, Bradley noted, also gave people a social value as well as an economic reason for working together.[24]

Guidelines for constructing powerful mission statements and vision statements are shown below. *(See Table 6.1.)* "Visions that have these properties challenge and inspire people in the organization and help align their energies in a common direction," says Burt Nanus of the University of Southern California's School of Business Administration. "They prevent people from being overwhelmed by immediate problems because they help distinguish what is truly important from what is merely interesting."[25]

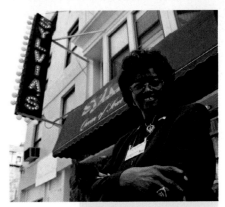

Family business. Do small, family-owned businesses need a vision statement? If yes, what should be the one for Sylvia's soul food restaurant, the landmark Harlem eatery? If no, why not?

table 6.1

MISSION STATEMENTS AND VISION STATEMENTS

Mission statements: Does your company's mission statement answer these questions?

1. Who are our customers?
2. What are our major products or services?
3. In what geographical areas do we compete?
4. What is our basic technology?
5. What is our commitment to economic objectives?
6. What are our basic beliefs, values, aspirations, and philosophical priorities?
7. What are our major strengths and competitive advantages?
8. What are our public responsibilities, and what image do we wish to project?
9. What is our attitude toward our employees?

Vision statements: Does your company's vision statement answer "yes" to these questions?

1. Is it appropriate for the organization and for the times?
2. Does it set standards of excellence and reflect high ideals?
3. Does it clarify purpose and direction?
4. Does it inspire enthusiasm and encourage commitment?
5. Is it well articulated and easily understood?
6. Does it reflect the uniqueness of the organization, its distinctive competence, what it stands for, what it's able to achieve?
7. Is it ambitious?

Sources: F. R. David, "How Companies Define Their Mission," *Long Range Planning,* February 1989, pp. 90–97; and B. Nanus, *Visionary Leadership: Creating a Compelling Sense of Direction for Your Organization* (San Francisco: Jossey-Bass, 1992), pp. 28–29.

Step 2: Establish the Grand Strategy The next step is to translate the broad mission and vision statements into a ***grand strategy,*** which, after an assessment of current organizational performance, then explains how the organization's mission is to be accomplished.[26] Three common grand strategies are growth, stability, and defensive.

The first part of the process of developing a grand strategy, then, is to make a rigorous analysis of the organization's present situation to determine *where it is presently headed.* The second part is to determine where it *should be headed in the future.*

Let's consider the three common grand strategies.

1. The Growth Strategy A *growth strategy* is a grand strategy that involves expansion—as in sales revenues, market share, number of employees, or number of customers or (for nonprofits) clients served.

2. The Stability Strategy A *stability strategy* is a grand strategy that involves little or no significant change.

3. The Defensive Strategy A *defensive strategy* or a *retrenchment strategy,* is a grand strategy that involves reduction in the organization's efforts.

Examples of the three strategies are shown in the table below. *(See Table 6.2.)*

table 6.2

HOW COMPANIES CAN IMPLEMENT GRAND STRATEGIES

Growth strategy

- It can improve an existing product or service to attract more buyers.
- It can increase its promotion and marketing efforts to try to expand its market share.
- It can expand its operations, as in taking over distribution or manufacturing previously handled by someone else.
- It can expand into new products or services.
- It can acquire similar or complementary businesses.
- It can merge with another company to form a larger company.

Stability strategy

- It can go for a no-change strategy (if, for example, it has found that too-fast growth leads to foul-ups with orders and customer complaints).
- It can go for a little-change strategy (if, for example, the company has been growing at breakneck speed and feels it needs a period of consolidation).

Defensive strategy

- It can reduce costs, as by freezing hiring or tightening expenses.
- It can sell off (liquidate) assets—land, buildings, inventories, and the like.
- It can gradually phase out product lines or services.
- It can divest part of its business, as in selling off entire divisions or subsidiaries.
- It can declare bankruptcy.
- It can attempt a turnaround—do some retrenching, with a view toward restoring profitability.

How do you establish a grand strategy? Among the strategic-planning tools and techniques used are (1) *SWOT analysis* and (2) *forecasting,* as we describe in Section 6.3.

Step 3: Formulate Strategic Plans
The grand strategy must then be translated into more specific *strategic plans,* which determine what the organization's long-term goals should be for the next 1–5 years. These should communicate not only the organization's general goals about growth and profits but also information about how these goals will be achieved. Moreover, like all goals, they should be SMART—Specific, Measurable, Attainable, Results-oriented, and specifying Target dates (Chapter 5).

Growth Strategy. One growth strategy Starbucks has employed is to set up small kiosks in large supermarket chain locations—drawing in more customers who may find that they need a tall, skim-milk, double-shot latte in order to finish their grocery shopping.

Strategy formulation is the process of choosing among different strategies and altering them to best fit the organization's needs. Because the process is so important, formulating strategic plans is a time-consuming process. Among the techniques used to formulate strategy are *Porter's competitive forces and strategies* and *product life cycles,* which we describe in Section 6.4.

Step 4: Carry Out the Strategic Plans
Putting strategic plans into effect is *strategy implementation.* Strategic planning isn't effective, of course, unless it can be translated into lower-level plans. This means that top managers need to check on possible roadblocks within the organization's structure and culture and see if the right people and control systems are available to execute the plans.[27]

Often implementation means overcoming resistance by people who feel the plans threaten their influence or livelihood. This is particularly the case when the plans must be implemented rapidly, since delay is the easiest kind of resistance there is (all kinds of excuses are usually available to justify delays). Thus, top managers can't just announce the plans; they have to actively sell them to middle and supervisory managers.

Step 5: Maintain Strategic Control: The Feedback Loop
Strategic control **consists of monitoring the execution of strategy and making adjustments, if necessary.** To keep strategic plans on track, managers need control systems to monitor progress and take corrective action—early and rapidly—when things start to go awry. Corrective action constitutes a feedback loop in which a problem requires that managers return to an earlier step to rethink policies, redo budgets, or revise personnel arrangements. To keep a strategic plan on track, suggests Bryan Barry, you need to do the following:[28]

- **Engage people.** You need to actively engage people in clarifying what your group hopes to accomplish and how you will accomplish it.

- **Keep it simple.** Keep your planning simple, unless there's a good reason to make it more complex.

- **Stay focused.** Stay focused on the important things.

- **Keep moving.** Keep moving toward your vision of the future, adjusting your plans as you learn what works.

To see how good you think you'd be, see the Self-Assessment, "Core Skills Required in Strategic Planning," at the end of this chapter.

Now, in Section 6.3, let us consider some of the tools used for Step 2, establishing a grand strategy—SWOT and forecasting. ●

How to Streamline Meetings

"Beware of designing a planning process that requires 40 hours of meetings if your staff or board cannot realistically make the time commitment," advises Bryan W. Barry. "Frustration and failure can result. Effective strategic planning can be done in 10 to 15 hours of meeting time, with good preparation between meetings."[29]

Meetings are a fact of management life—one study of 299 managers found they spent half their time in meetings.[30] If you're not in a position to call meetings but have to attend them regularly, it is frustrating to have to be a victim of a poorly run meeting.

In one survey, 50% of workers at big companies said they had attended a meeting where at least one participant fell asleep.[31] (At smaller companies, where it is harder to hide, the figure was 26%.) Problem meetings can result from a lack of focus, nobody watching the clock, and no leader to keep the meeting on track.[32] Patrick Lencioni, author of *Death by Meeting,* believes one reason meetings are so ineffective is that top executives discourage conflict.[33] But that tactic backfires, he says, because it makes meetings boring and ignores crucial issues.[34]

As a participant, you can always pull an off-track conversation back by saying, for example, "We were discussing the 2007 budget, but now we seem to be discussing the shortfalls of last year." Or you can try making a summary of a series of comments to prevent others from covering the same ground again. If you're constantly exposed to ineffective meetings, you can also offer your assistance to the meeting leader in creating an agenda, with time frames attached for each item, suggests productivity specialist Odette Pollar. She adds: "Your approach, timing, and tone of voice are important. You must avoid appearing to tell the person what to do."[35]

If you're leading meetings, here are three good ways to streamline them:[36]

Eliminate Unnecessary Meetings & Meeting Attendance

Don't call a meeting if the same result can be accomplished in some other way: phone call, e-mail, memo, one-on-one visit, and so on. Invite only people who need to attend, and let them know they need stay for only those parts of the meeting that concern them. Hold the meeting in a place where distractions will be minimal. Consider using telephone conferencing or videoconferencing.

Distribute an Action Agenda in Advance

Do your homework about the issues. Prepare a list of meeting objectives, topics to be covered and the number of minutes allowed for discussion, and information participants should bring. Organize the topics with the most important ones first. Distribute this agenda a day or more in advance, if possible. For informal meetings, phone conversations, and one-on-one appointments, make a list of items to cover.

Stay in Control of the Meeting

Start on time and stay within the time frame of the agenda items. (Coffee breaks, lunchtime, or quitting time provide built-in limits.) Announce politely at the start of the meeting that you value everyone's time and so you will intervene if discussion becomes off-point, rambling, or unintelligible. Reserve judgments and conclusions until after discussion so that everyone will feel free to give their input. Don't allow a few members to monopolize the discussion. Encourage silent members to participate. Try to reach a decision or make an assignment for every item. Use two notepads or pieces of paper, one for general notes, the other for tasks and assignments. Summarize the highlights at the end of the meeting. Map out a timetable for actions to be taken.

Do Follow-Up

After the meeting, type up tasks and assignments for distribution. Set a date for a follow-up meeting to assess progress.

For more about running meetings, go to Effective-Meetings.com (*www.effectivemeetings.com*).

6.3 ESTABLISHING THE GRAND STRATEGY

How can SWOT and forecasting help me establish my strategy?

major question ◈

THE BIG PICTURE
To develop a grand strategy, you need to gather data and make projections, using the tools of SWOT analysis and forecasting.

The first part in developing a grand strategy, Step 2 of the five-step strategic management process, is intelligence gathering—internally and externally. The next part is to make some projections.

Two kinds of strategic-planning tools and techniques are (1) *SWOT analysis* and (2) *forecasting*—trend analysis and contingency planning.

SWOT Analysis

The starting point in establishing a grand strategy is often a **SWOT analysis—also known as *a situational analysis*—which is a search for the Strengths, Weaknesses, Opportunities, and Threats affecting the organization.** A SWOT analysis should provide you with a realistic understanding of your organization in relation to its internal and external environments so you can better formulate strategy in pursuit of its mission. *(See Figure 6.2.)*

INSIDE MATTERS—analysis of internal Strengths & Weaknesses

S—Strengths: inside matters
Strengths could be work processes, organization, culture, staff, product quality, production capacity, image, financial resources & requirements, service levels, other internal matters

W—Weaknesses: inside matters
Weaknesses could be in the same categories as stated for Strengths: work processes, organization, culture, etc.

O—Opportunities: outside matters
Opportunities could be market segment analysis, industry & competition analysis, impact of technology on organization, product analysis, governmental impacts, other external matters

T—Threats: outside matters
Threats could be in the same categories as stated for Opportunities: market segment analysis, etc.

OUTSIDE MATTERS—analysis of external Opportunities & Threats

figure 6.2

SWOT ANALYSIS
SWOT stands for Strengths, Weaknesses, Opportunities, Threats.

The SWOT analysis is divided into two parts: inside matters and outside matters—that is, an analysis of *internal strengths and weaknesses* and an analysis of *external opportunities and threats.*

Inside Matters: Analysis of Internal Strengths & Weaknesses   Does your organization have a skilled workforce? a superior reputation? strong financing? These are examples of ***organizational strengths—the skills and capabilities that give the organization special competencies and competitive advantages in executing strategies in pursuit of its mission.***

Or does your organization have obsolete technology? outdated facilities? a shaky marketing operation? These are examples of ***organizational weaknesses— the drawbacks that hinder an organization in executing strategies in pursuit of its mission.***

Outside Matters: Analysis of External Opportunities & Threats   Is your organization fortunate to have weak rivals? emerging markets? a booming economy? These are instances of ***organizational opportunities—environmental factors that the organization may exploit for competitive advantage.***

Alternatively, is your organization having to deal with new regulations? a shortage of resources? substitute products? These are some possible ***organizational threats—environmental factors that hinder an organization's achieving a competitive advantage.***

Forecasting: Predicting the Future

Once they've analyzed their organization's Strengths, Weaknesses, Opportunities, and Threats, planners need to do forecasting for making long-term strategy. **A *forecast* is a vision or projection of the future.**

Lots of people make predictions, of course—and often they are wrong. In the 1950s, the head of IBM, Thomas J. Watson, estimated that the demand for computers would never exceed more than five for the entire world. In the late 1990s, many computer experts predicted power outages, water problems, transportation disruptions, bank shutdowns, and far worse because of computer glitches (the "Y2K bug") associated with the change from year 1999 to 2000.

Of course, the farther into the future one makes a prediction, the more difficult it is to be accurate, especially in matters of technology. Yet forecasting is a necessary part of planning.

Two types of forecasting are *trend analysis* and *contingency planning.*

Trend Analysis   A ***trend analysis* is a hypothetical extension of a past series of events into the future.**[37] The basic assumption is that the picture of the present can be projected into the future. This is not a bad assumption, if you have enough historical data, but it is always subject to surprises. And if your data are unreliable, they will produce erroneous trend projections.

An example of trend analysis is a time-series forecast, which predicts future data based on patterns of historical data. Time-series forecasts are used to predict long-term trends, cyclic patterns (as in the up-and-down nature of the business cycle), and seasonal variations (as in Christmas sales versus summer sales).

Contingency Planning: Predicting Alternative Futures   ***Contingency planning—also known as scenario planning* and *scenario analysis—is the creation of alternative hypothetical but equally likely future conditions.*** The scenarios present alternative combinations of different factors—different economic pictures, different strategies by competitors, different budgets, and so on.

Example

SWOT Analysis: How Would You Analyze Starbucks Coffee?

If you were presently a manager for Starbucks Corp., what would be the kinds of things you would identify in a SWOT analysis?[38]

First, the internal *Strengths:* No small part of the company's success is based on the loyalty of the staff—most of whom are young (average age: 26) and 85% of whom have some education beyond high school—which Starbucks calls "partners." Because the company offers above-average pay for food service, health insurance for all, stock options, and channels such as e-mail for employee feedback, partners feel quite involved with the company, and turnover is half the industry average. Employees receive painstaking training in the art of making a high-quality cup of coffee, handling coffee beans and equipment, and dealing with customers. Following a McDonald's-like strategy, Starbucks has been breaking into new markets, opening retail stores throughout the country and the world, expanding into different retail channels such as supermarkets, bookstores, and airports. The payoff: Starbucks's revenues continue to climb, and in May 2006 its stock was up about 5,775% since it went public in 1992.[39]

Second, the internal *Weaknesses:* To be able to charge $1.75 for a cup instead of 50 cents, Starbucks's focus has been to turn coffee—traditionally an inexpensive commodity-type product—into a premium-placed brand, imitating Coca-Cola's strategy of getting people to think "Coke" versus plain old "cola." But if customers are to continue to pay top dollar for specialty coffee, Starbucks can't slip on quality and service. Thus, complaints about "tepid coffee, gruff employees, long waits" in New York can't be ignored. Nor can press accounts expressing disappointment in the company's new food ventures. In addition, the company can't allow itself to be distracted from its core business. In early 1999, for example, CEO Howard Schultz became infatuated with the Internet and began aggressively pursuing a Web e-commerce strategy; as a

result of taking his eye off the ball, the company suffered an earnings shortfall, which caused the price of the stock to drop.

Third, the external *Opportunities:* Other chains—Boston Chicken, Rainforest Café, Planet Hollywood—have found the restaurant business tough sledding. But the fact that Starbucks has extremely loyal customers (another Strength) gives the company an Opportunity. Many of the aforementioned theme restaurants were done in because they couldn't get customers to return after the novelty wore off. Moreover, it's been pointed out that coffee is not a fad but rather "the last socially acceptable addiction." Starbucks is also fortunate to have numerous overseas opportunities such as Asia. Indeed, it is even invading Europe, despite Europe's age-old coffee culture.

Fourth, the external *Threats:* Specialty-coffee companies like Starbucks account for only 12% of the coffee roasted in the United States. Most coffee is bought in supermarkets and is dominated by Folgers, Maxwell House, Taster's Choice, and Hills Bros. In years past, they could have turned coffee into either a special beverage, as Starbucks has done, or a drink with mass appeal, like Coke and Pepsi, but they did neither. Instead, they got into price wars with one another, and to cut costs they gradually reduced the quality of coffee. And in fighting one another, they ignored the biggest threat to their industry: soda pop. The result: the coffee industry lost a generation of consumers, who were wooed away by the aggressive marketing of soft drinks. Starbucks is also a victim of its own success, so that in some areas when it moves into a new neighborhood and displaces existing coffee shops it is viewed as a Darth Vader–like corporate giant. A possible recent threat is the Fair Trade coffee movement.

Your Call

Which part of the SWOT analysis should Starbucks managers pay the closest attention to, in your opinion? Why?

Fuel proof. Locking in the price of jet fuel with long-term contracts with suppliers, a form of contingency planning, has put low-cost airlines such as Southwest in a competitive position with rivals in controlling costs.

Example

Contingency Planning: Southwest Airlines Uses Hedging to Hold Down Price of Aviation Fuel

In mid-2004, when the price of crude oil hit 20-year highs ($41 a barrel), the cost of jet fuel threatened to take a big bite out of airline profits, which were only beginning to return after a prolonged financial downturn. Jet fuel makes up 10–25% of an airline's operating costs, the second-biggest expense after labor.[40]

Some airlines tried to pass the extra cost along to passengers by raising fares on some routes. Low-cost carriers such as Southwest, JetBlue, and America West, however, were better able to weather the fuel price increase without raising seat prices. Southwest Airlines, for example, was in better shape than many larger competitors because it had done effective contingency planning—by hedging the rise of fuel prices in the futures market. Airlines hedge fuel price increases by locking in contracts that allow them to buy fuel at a fixed price. Southwest and JetBlue were in a better position to buy favorable futures contracts because of their financial strengths: they avoid expensive labor contracts, operate only one or two types of aircraft, and fly high-traffic routes.[41]

Thus, Southwest's hedging reduced its energy costs by $455 million in 2004. "You have to have foresight, wisdom, and some courage to hedge," says Tammy Romo, Southwest's treasurer.[42]

Your Call

In 2005, Southwest was able to hedge 85% of its fuel at $26 a barrel (far less than half the market price, which averaged $72 a barrel). In 2006, it had 70% of its fuel hedged at $36 a barrel (when fuel prices were expected to be $70 a barrel). However, no investment banks will be willing to cover $36 barrels of oil, no matter how much cash an airline puts up front, when oil prices continue to soar. What do you think Southwest will have to do in, say, 2009 in order to continue being profitable?[43]

Because the scenarios try to peer far into the future—perhaps 5 or more years—they are necessarily written in rather general terms. Nevertheless, the great value of contingency planning is that it not only equips an organization to prepare for emergencies and uncertainty, it also gets managers thinking strategically. ●

6.4 FORMULATING STRATEGY

How can three techniques—Porter's competitive forces, competitive strategies, and the product life cycle—help me formulate strategy?

major question

THE BIG PICTURE

Strategy formulation makes use of several concepts. Here we discuss Porter's five competitive forces, four competitive strategies, the four-stage product life cycle, diversification and synergy, and competitive intelligence.

After the grand strategy has been determined (Step 2 in the strategic-management process), it's time to turn to strategy formulation (Step 3). Examples of techniques that can be used to formulate strategy are *Porter's five competitive forces, Porter's four competitive strategies, the product life cycle, diversification and synergy,* and *competitive intelligence.*

Porter's Five Competitive Forces

What determines competitiveness within a particular industry? After studying several kinds of businesses, strategic management expert Michael Porter suggested in his **Porter's model for industry analysis** that business-level strategies originate in five primary competitive force in the firm's environment: **(1) threats of new entrants, (2) bargaining power of suppliers, (3) bargaining power of buyers, (4) threats of substitute products or services, and (5) rivalry among competitors.**[44]

Test Your Knowledge:
Porter's Five Forces

I. Threats of New Entrants   New competitors can affect an industry almost overnight, taking away customers from existing organizations. Example: Kraft Macaroni & Cheese is a venerable, well-known brand but is threatened from the low end by store brands, such as Wal-Mart's brand, and from the high end by Annie's Creamy Macaroni and Cheese with Real Aged Wisconsin Cheddar.[45]

2. Bargaining Power of Suppliers   Some companies are readily able to switch suppliers in order to get components or services, but others are not. Example: Clark Foam of Laguna Niguel, California, supplied nearly 90% of the foam cores used domestically to make custom surfboards. When it suddenly closed shop in late 2005, blaming government agencies for trying to shut it down, many independent board shapers and small retailers found they couldn't afford to get foam from outside the country. On the other hand, Surftech in Santa Cruz, California, was one of the few board manufacturers to use resin instead of foam, and so it saw a spike in sales.[46]

3. Bargaining Power of Buyers   Customers who buy a lot of products or services from an organization have more bargaining power than those who don't. Customers who use the Internet to shop around are also better able to negotiate a better price. Example: Buying a car used to be pretty much a local activity, but now potential car buyers can use the Net to scout a range of offerings within a 100-mile or larger radius, giving them the power to force down the asking price of any one particular seller.

4. Threats of Substitute Products or Services   Again, particularly because of the Internet, an organization is in a better position to switch to other products or services when circumstances threaten their usual channels. Example: Oil companies might worry that Brazil is close to becoming energy self-sufficient because it is able to meet its growing demand for vehicle fuel by substituting ethanol derived from sugar cane for petroleum.[47]

5. Rivalry among Competitors   The preceding four forces influence the fifth force, rivalry among competitors. Think of the wild competition among makers and sellers of portable electronics, ranging from cell phones to PDAs to MP3 audio players to videogame systems. Once again, the Internet has intensified rivalries among all kinds of organizations.

An organization should do a good SWOT analysis that examines these five competitive forces, Porter felt. Then it was in a position to formulate effective strategy, using what he identified as four competitive strategies, as we discuss next.

Porter's Four Competitive Strategies

Porter's four competitive strategies (also called *four generic strategies*) are (1) cost-leadership, (2) differentiation, (3) cost-focus, and (4) focused-differentiation.[48] The first two strategies focus on *wide* markets, the last two on *narrow* markets. *(See Figure 6.3.)* Time Warner, which produces lots of media and publications, serves wide markets around the world. Your neighborhood video store serves a narrow market of just local customers.

figure 6.3

PORTER'S FOUR COMPETITIVE STRATEGIES

	Type of market targeted	
Strategy	Wide	Narrow
1. Cost-leadership	√	
2. Differentiation	√	
3. Cost-focus		√
4. Focused-differentiation		√

Let's look at these four strategies.

I. Cost-Leadership Strategy: Keeping Costs & Prices Low for a Wide Market   The *cost-leadership strategy* is to keep the costs, and hence prices, of a product or service below those of competitors and to target a wide market.

This puts the pressure on R&D managers to develop products or services that can be created cheaply, production managers to reduce production costs, and marketing managers to reach a wide variety of customers as inexpensively as possible.

Firms implementing the cost-leadership strategy include computer maker Dell, watch maker Timex, hardware retailer Home Depot, and pen maker Bic.

2. Differentiation Strategy: Offering Unique & Superior Value for a Wide Market   The *differentiation strategy* is to offer products or services that are of unique and superior value compared to those of competitors but to target a wide market.

Because products are expensive, managers may have to spend more on R&D, marketing, and customer service. This is the strategy followed by Ritz-Carlton hotels and the makers of Lexus automobiles.

The strategy is also pursued by companies trying to create *brands* to differentiate themselves from competitors. Although Pepsi may cost only cents more than a supermarket's own house brand of cola, PepsiCo. spends millions on ads.

3. Cost-Focus Strategy: Keeping Costs & Prices Low for a Narrow Market
The *cost-focus strategy* is to keep the costs, and hence prices, of a product or service below those of competitors and to target a narrow market.

This is a strategy you often see executed with low-end products sold in discount stores, such as low-cost beer or cigarettes, or with regional gas stations, such as the Terrible Herbst or Rotten Robbie chains in parts of the West.

Needless to say, the pressure on managers to keep costs down is even more intense than it is with those in cost-leadership companies.

4. Focused-Differentiation Strategy: Offering Unique & Superior Value for a Narrow Market
The *focused-differentiation strategy* is to offer products or services that are of unique and superior value compared to those of competitors and to target a narrow market.

Some luxury cars are so expensive—Rolls-Royce, Ferrari, Lamborghini—that only a few car buyers can afford them. Other companies following the strategy are jeweler Cartier and shirtmaker Turnbull & Asser. Yet focused-differentiation products need not be expensive. The publisher Chelsea Green has found success with niche books, such as *The Straw Bale House*.

The Product Life Cycle: Different Stages Require Different Strategies

In Chapter 5, we described a *project* life cycle. A *product* life cycle has a similar curve (although the end is usually not quite so abrupt). **A *product life cycle* is a model that graphs the four stages that a product or a service goes through during the "life" of its marketability: (1) introduction, (2) growth, (3) maturity, and (4) decline.** *(See Figure 6.4.)*

Focused differentiation. The world's largest cruise ship, the 1,112-foot-long, 15-deck *Freedom of the Seas,* features such amenities as a skating rink, rock-climbing facilities, basketball, a surfing pool, a miniature golf course, a three-story-high dining room, and lavish lodging quarters. Clearly, there's something here for everyone—if you can afford it.

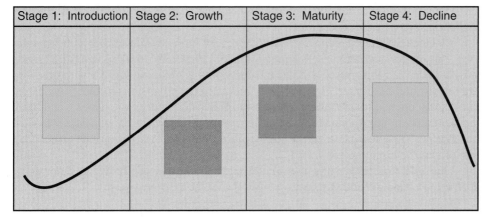

Stage 1: Introduction	Stage 2: Growth	Stage 3: Maturity	Stage 4: Decline

figure 6.4

THE PRODUCT LIFE CYCLE

Managers can use this cycle to create strategies appropriate to each stage.

Some products, such as faddish toys or collectibles (for example, Beanie Babies), may have a life cycle of only months or a year or so. Others, such as a shopping center, may have a life cycle equivalent to a human generation (about 30 years) before they begin to decline and need to be redesigned for fresh appeal and modern sensibilities.

For you as a manager it's useful to know about the concept of product life cycle because different strategies—such as those advanced by Michael Porter—can be used to support different products or services in different stages of the cycle. Let's look at these stages.

Stage I: Introduction—Getting the Product to Market   The *introduction stage* is the stage in the product life cycle in which a new product is introduced into the marketplace.

This is the stage that is heavy on start-up costs for production, marketing, and distribution. Managers have to concentrate on building inventory and staff without loss of quality. With sales usually low during this period, the product is probably losing the company money.

There is also the huge risk that the product may be rejected. Following the smashing reception of the original Apple II (and II-Plus) personal computer, for example, Apple Computer introduced the Lisa—which was a good deal less than a resounding success. Fortunately for Apple, the Lisa evolved into the company's best-selling Macintosh.

During the introduction stage, one should, to use a military analogy, follow a strategy of infiltration. A differentiation or a focus (cost-focus or focused-differentiation) strategy may be appropriate.

Stage 2: Growth—Demand Increases   The *growth stage,* which is the most profitable stage, is the period in which customer demand increases, the product's sales grow, and (later) competitors may enter the market.

At the start, the product may have the marketplace to itself and demand for it may be high. Managers need to worry about getting sufficient product into the distribution pipeline, maintaining quality, and expanding the sales and distribution effort.

This phase may go on for years. But all the while, competitors will be scrambling to enter the market. "For 40 years, all we had to do was open restaurants," said McDonald's CEO Jack Greenberg in 1999. "That's not enough anymore."[49] The reason: the competition has become fierce, with other fast-food giants spending millions on promotions.

During the growth stage, managers would advance their attack, probably continuing Stage 1 differentiation or focus strategies.

Stage 3: Maturity—Growth Slows   The *maturity stage* is the period in which the product starts to fall out of favor and sales and profits begin to fall off.

In this phase, sales start to decline as competition makes inroads. At this point, managers need to concentrate on reducing costs and instituting efficiencies to maintain the product's profitability. Sometimes they can extend the life of the product by tinkering with its various features.

McDonald's CEO Greenberg, for instance, put a lid on domestic growth, opening only 92 new restaurants in 1998 compared to 1,130 in 1995, and he laid off 525 employees. He also introduced a $350 million cooking system that allows food to be served fresher and hotter. He increased international expansion, so that 90% of the new stores opened in 1999 were outside the U.S.[50] His successor, James Cantalupo, concentrated on improving the menu (offering entrée salads and McGriddle breakfast sandwiches) and service, trying to draw more diners to existing outlets rather than building more restaurants.[51]

During the maturity stage, managers would become more defensive, perhaps using a cost-leadership or focus strategy.

Stage 4: Decline—Withdrawing from the Market   The *decline stage* is the period in which the product falls out of favor and the organization withdraws from the marketplace.

In this stage, the product falls out of favor, and managers sound the bugle for retreat, scaling down relevant inventory, supplies, and personnel.

While this phase may mean withdrawal of support for the old product, it doesn't necessarily mean a complete shutdown for the organization. Much of the same expertise will be required to support new products.

Hismanal was a once-promising prescription antihistamine drug for Johnson & Johnson, but the company announced its discontinuation in 1999. "This was a voluntary decision in response to a marketplace crowded with alternatives," said a company spokesman.

Hismanal was one of the first prescription antihistamines that did not cause drowsiness, but later it was found to produce heart problems when taken with other drugs.[52]

Single-Product Strategy versus Diversification Strategy

You might begin to see why, with the birth-to-death stages of the product life cycle, a company needs to think about whether to have a *single-product strategy* or a *diversification strategy*. After all, if you have only one product to sell, what do you do if that product fails?

What stage in the life cycle? This shopping center clearly has seen better days. Do you think a shopping center could be built that would last 100 years?

The Single-Product Strategy: Focused but Vulnerable   In a *single-product strategy,* **a company makes and sells only one product within its market.** This is the kind of strategy you see all the time as you drive past the small retail businesses in a small town: there may be one shop that sells only flowers, one that sells only security systems, and so on. It's also a strategy used by some bigger companies. For instance, Indian Motorcycle Company, which was once a worthy rival to Harley-Davidson, sold only motorcycles.

The single-product strategy has both positives and negatives:

- **The benefit—focus.** Making just one product allows you to focus your manufacturing and marketing efforts just on that product. This means that your company can become savvy about repairing defects, upgrading production lines, scouting the competition, and doing highly focused advertising and sales. See's Candies, for instance, is a San Francisco–based chain of 200 stores throughout the West that specializes in making boxed chocolates—something it does so well that when it was acquired by Berkshire Hathaway, its corporate owner chose not to tamper with success and runs it with a "hands-off" policy.

- **The risk—vulnerability.** The risk, of course, is that if you do *not* focus on all aspects of the business, if a rival gets the jump on you, or if an act of God intervenes (for a florist, roses suffer a blight right before Mother's Day), your entire business may go under. For instance, in 2003, Gilroy, California–based Indian Motorcycle went bankrupt a second time (it went under in 1953, too) because it was unable to focus on meeting its projected production targets.[53]

The Diversification Strategy: Operating Different Businesses to Spread the Risk   The obvious answer to the risks of a single-product strategy is **diversification, operating several businesses in order to spread the risk.** You see this at the small retailer level when you drive past a store that sells gas *and* food *and* souvenirs *and* rents videotape and DVD movies. Big companies do it, too: all the major entertainment/media companies, such as Disney, Time Warner, and Sony, run different divisions specializing in television, music, publishing, and the like (a divisional structure we explain further in Chapter 8).

There are two kinds of diversification—*unrelated* and *related.*

Unrelated Diversification: Independent Business Lines   If you operate a small shop that sells flowers on one side and computers on the other, you are exercising a strategy of **unrelated diversification** —**operating several businesses under one ownership that are not related to one another.** This has been a common big-company strategy in the recent past. General Electric, for instance, which began by making lighting products, diversified into such unrelated areas as plastics, broadcasting, and financial services (a so-called conglomerate structure that we discuss in Chapter 8).

Related Diversification: Related Business Lines   In some parts of the world you have to do all your grocery shopping in separate stores—the butcher, the baker, the green grocer, and so on. In most U.S. grocery stores, all these businesses appear under the same roof, an example of the strategy of ***related diversification,*** **in which an organization under one ownership operates separate businesses that are related to one another.** The famous British raincoat maker Burberry, for instance, started by making and marketing outerwear clothing but since then has expanded into related business lines, including accessories such as umbrellas, children's clothing, and even fragrances, which it sells in its own stores.

Related diversification has three advantages:

- **Reduced risk—because more than one product.** Unlike Indian Motorcycles, Burberry is able to reduce its risks. During seasons when rainwear sales are slow, for instance, Burberry's economic risk is reduced by sales of other product lines.

- **Management efficiencies—administration spread over several businesses.** Whatever the business, it usually has certain obligatory administrative costs—accounting, legal, taxes, and so on. Burberry need not have separate versions of these for each business line. Rather, it can actually save money by using the same administrative services for all its businesses.

- **Synergy—the sum is greater than the parts.** When a company has special strengths in one business, it can apply those to its other related businesses—as PepsiCo, for instance, can do in marketing not only Pepsi Cola but also 7-Up and Mountain Dew. This is an example of ***synergy*** **—the economic value of separate, related businesses under one ownership and management is greater together than the businesses are worth separately.**

Competitive Intelligence

Regardless of the kind of diversification (or lack of) a company may have, if it is to survive it must keep track of what its competitors are doing—what is known as competitive intelligence. Practicing ***competitive intelligence*** **means gaining information about one's competitors' activities so that you can anticipate their moves and react appropriately.** If you are a manager, one of your worst nightmares is that a competitor will come out with a service or product—whether it's boutique beer to a major brewer or mountain bikes to a major bicycle maker—that will revolutionize the market and force you to try to play catch-up, if indeed that's even possible.

Gaining competitive intelligence isn't always easy, but there are several avenues—and, surprisingly, most of them are public sources—including the following:

- **The public prints and advertising.** A product may be worked on in secret for several years, but at some point it becomes subject to announcement—through a press release, advertising piece, news leak, or the like. Much of this is available free through the Internet or by subscription to certain specialized databases, such as Nexus, which contains hundreds of thousands of news stories.

- **Investor information.** Information about new products and services may also be available through the reports filed with the Securities and Exchange Commission and through corporate annual reports.

- **Informal sources.** People in the computer industry every year look forward to major trade shows, as Comdex in Las Vegas has been, when companies roll out their new products. At such times, people also engage in industry-gossip conversation to find out about future directions. Finally, salespeople and marketers, who are out calling on corporate clients, may return with tidbits of information about what competitors are doing. ●

6.5 IMPLEMENTING & CONTROLLING STRATEGY: EXECUTION

How does effective execution help managers during the strategic management process?

major + question

THE BIG PICTURE

Strategic implementation is closely aligned with strategic control. Execution is a process that helps align these two phases of the strategic-management process.

Stage 1 of the strategic-management process was establishing the mission and the vision. Stage 2 was establishing the grand strategy. Stage 3 was formulating the strategic plans. Now we come to the last two stages—4, strategic implementation, and 5, strategic control.

Execution: Getting Things Done

Larry Bossidy, former CEO of AlliedSignal (later Honeywell), and **Ram Charan,** a business advisor to senior executives, are authors of *Execution: The Discipline of Getting Things Done.*[54] ***Execution,*** **they say, is not simply tactics, it is a central part of any company's strategy; it consists of using questioning, analysis, and follow-through in order to mesh strategy with reality, align people with goals, and achieve results promised.** As we will discuss, execution consists of linking the three core processes of any business—the people process, the strategy, and the operating plan—together to get things done on time.

Many executives appear to have an aversion to execution, which they associate with tactics—with the tedium of doing, as opposed to visioning, and which they hand off to subordinates. But, Bossidy and Charan point out, this notion can be a fatal flaw. "There's an enormous difference between leading an organization and presiding over it," they write. "The leader who boasts of her hands-off style or puts her faith in empowerment is not dealing with the issues of the day. . . . Leading for execution is not about micromanaging. . . . Leaders who excel at execution immerse themselves in the substance of execution and even some of the key details. They use their knowledge of the business to constantly probe and question. They bring weaknesses to light and rally their people to correct them."[55]

The Building Blocks of Execution

Three building blocks underlie the process of effective execution:

- Leadership must be based on seven essential behaviors.
- A framework for cultural change must be created.
- There must be effective selection and evaluation of people.

The First Building Block: Develop Seven Essential Behaviors To be a leader who executes, you need to possess seven behaviors:

- **Know your people and your business.** In companies that don't execute, leaders are usually out of touch with the day-to-day realities. Bossidy and Charan insist leaders must engage intensely and personally with their organization's people and its businesses; they cannot rely on second-hand knowledge through other people's observations, assessments, and recommendations.

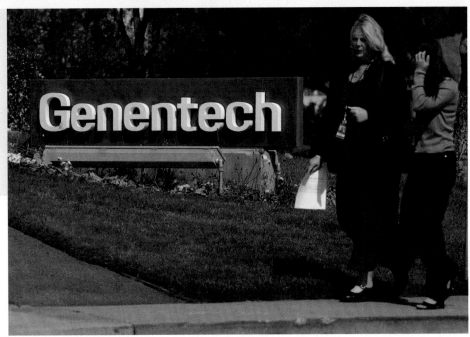

Execution. A biotechnology company located in South San Francisco, California, Genentech was rated the No. 1 company on *Fortune*'s 2006 list of "Best Companies to Work For." In early 2006, it was adding an average of 151 new employees a month. It plows 50% of its revenues back into research. What other measures would you evaluate to see if Genentech is truly successful?

- **Insist on realism.** Many people want to avoid or shade reality, hiding mistakes or avoiding confrontations. Making realism a priority begins with the leaders being realistic themselves, and making sure realism is the goal of all dialogues in the organization.

- **Set clear goals and priorities.** Leaders who execute focus on a very few clear priorities that everyone can grasp.

- **Follow through.** Failing to follow through is a major cause of poor execution. "How many meetings have you attended where people left without firm conclusions about who would do what and when?" Bossidy and Charan ask. Accountability and follow-up are important.

- **Reward the doers.** If people are to produce specific results, they must be rewarded accordingly, making sure that top performers are rewarded far better than ordinary performers.

- **Expand people's capabilities.** Coaching is an important part of the executive's job, providing useful and specific feedback that can improve performance.

- **Know yourself.** Leaders must develop "emotional fortitude" based on honest self-assessments. Four core qualities are authenticity, self-awareness, self-mastery, and humility.

The Second Building Block: Create a Framework for Cultural Change
Culture (which we discuss thoroughly in Chapter 8) is the sum of an organization's values, beliefs, and norms of behavior. The culture consists of dozens of social operating mechanisms, which the leader must understand so that he or she can change the beliefs and behavior of people in ways that are directly linked to bottom-line results. Cultural change becomes real when it is linked to execution. "First you tell people clearly what results you're looking for," Bossidy and Charan write. "Then you discuss how to get those results.... Then you reward people for producing the results."[56] Doing these things creates a culture of getting things done.

The Third Building Block: Selecting & Evaluating People
Many executives delegate most of their human resource responsibilities, but they shouldn't. By personally choosing the right people—especially those who are good at getting things done—the

effective leader creates the circumstances that lead to sustainable competitive advantage.

The Three Core Processes of Business

The three building blocks just described are the foundation for the three core processes of execution:

- People
- Strategy
- Operations

The First Core Process: People "If you don't get the people process right," say Bossidy and Charan, "you will never fulfill the potential of your business." But today most organizations focus on evaluating the jobs people are doing at present, rather than considering which individuals can handle the jobs of the future. An effective leader tries to evaluate talent by linking people to particular strategic milestones, developing future leaders, dealing with nonperformers, and transforming the mission and operations of the human resource department.

The Second Core Process: Strategy In most organizations, the strategies developed fail to consider the "how" of execution. According to the authors, a good strategic plan addresses nine questions. *(See Table 6.3.)* In considering whether the organization can execute the strategy, a leader must take a realistic and critical view of its capabilities and competencies. If it does not have the talent in finance, sales, and manufacturing to accomplish the vision, the chances of success are drastically reduced.

table 6.3

QUESTIONS A STRONG STRATEGIC PLAN MUST ADDRESS

1. What is the assessment of the external environment?

2. How well do you understand the existing customers and markets?

3. What is the best way to grow the business profitably, and what are the obstacles to growth?

4. Who is the competition?

5. Can the business execute the strategy?

6. Are the short term and long term balanced?

7. What are the important milestones for executing the plan?

8. What are the critical issues facing the business?

9. How will the business make money on a sustainable basis?

Source: From L. Bossidy and R. Charan, *Execution: The Discipline of Getting Things Done* (New York: Crown Business, 2002), pp. 188–189. Copyright © 2002 by Larry Bossidy and Ram Charan. Used by permission of Crown Business, a division of Random House.

The Third Core Process: Operations The strategy process defines where an organization wants to go, and the people process defines who's going to get it done. The third core process, operations, or the operating plan, provides the path for people to follow. The operating plan, as we described in Chapter 5, should address all the major activities in which the company will engage—marketing, production, sales, revenue, and so on—and then define short-term objectives for these activities, to provide targets for people to aim at.

Success in Linking the Three Processes = Success in Execution   How well leaders master the three individual processes of strategy, people, and operations and link them together will determine the success of the execution—"the differentiation between you and your competitors," as Bossidy and Charan put it. ●

key terms used in this chapter

competitive intelligence 196
contingency planning 188
cost-focus strategy 193
cost-leadership strategy 192
decline stage 194
defensive strategy 184
differentiation strategy 192
diversification 195
execution 197
focused-differentiation
  strategy 193
forecast 188
grand strategy 184

growth stage 194
growth strategy 184
introduction stage 194
maturity stage 194
organizational opportunities 188
organizational strengths 188
organizational threats 188
organizational weaknesses 188
Porter's four competitive
  strategies 192
Porter's model for industry
  analysis 191
product life cycle 193

related diversification 196
single-product strategy 195
stability strategy 184
strategic control 185
strategic management 177
strategic positioning 179
strategy 177
strategy formulation 185
strategy implementation 185
SWOT analysis 187
synergy 196
trend analysis 188
unrelated diversification 195

 summary

 6.1 The Dynamics of Strategic Planning

- Every organization needs to have a "big picture" about where it's going and how to get there. These are matters of strategy, strategic management, and strategic planning. A strategy is a large-scale action plan that sets the direction for an organization. Strategic management involves managers from all parts of the organization in the formulation and implementation of strategies and strategic goals. Strategic planning determines the organization's long-term goals and ways to achieve them.

- Strategic positioning attempts to achieve sustainable competitive advantage by preserving what is distinctive about a company. Three key principles underlie strategic positioning: (1) Strategy is the creation of a unique and valuable position, such as serving the few needs of many customers, the broad needs of just a few customers, or the broad needs of many customers. (2) Strategy requires trade-offs in competing, because some of the strategies just mentioned are incompatible. (3) Strategy involves creating a "fit" among a company's activities.

- There are three reasons why an organization should adopt strategic management and strategic planning. They can (1) provide direction and momentum, (2) encourage new ideas, and above all (3) develop a sustainable competitive advantage. Sustainable competitive advantage occurs when an organization is able to get and stay ahead in four areas: (1) in being responsive to customers, (2) in innovating, (3) in quality, and (4) in effectiveness.

6.2 The Strategic Management Process

- The strategic management process has five steps plus a feedback loop.

- Step 1 is to establish the mission statement and the vision statement. The mission statement expresses the organization's purpose or reason for being. The vision statement describes the organization's long-term direction and strategic intent.

- Step 2 is to translate the broad mission and vision statements into a grand strategy that explains how the organization's mission is to be accomplished. Three common grand strategies are growth, stability, and defensive. (1) A growth strategy involves expansion—as in sales revenues. (2) A stability strategy involves little or no significant change. (3) A defensive strategy involves reduction in the organization's efforts. Among the strategic planning tools and techniques used are (1) SWOT analysis and (2) forecasting, as described in Section 6.3.

- Step 3 is strategy formulation, the translation of the grand strategy into more specific strategic plans, choosing among different strategies and altering them to best fit the organization's needs. Among the techniques used to formulate strategy are Porter's competitive strategies and product life cycles, as described in Section 6.4.

- Step 4 is strategy implementation—putting strategic plans into effect. Step 5 is strategic control, monitoring the execution of strategy and making adjustments.

- Corrective action constitutes a feedback loop in which a problem requires that managers return to an earlier step to rethink policies, budgets, or personnel arrangements.

6.3 Establishing the Grand Strategy

- To develop a grand strategy (Step 2 above), you need to gather data and make projections, using the tools of SWOT analysis and forecasting.

- SWOT analysis is a search for the Strengths, Weaknesses, Opportunities, and Threats affecting the organization. The SWOT analysis is divided into two parts: an analysis of internal strengths and weaknesses and an analysis of external opportunities and threats. Organizational strengths are the skills and capabilities that give the

organization special competencies and competitive advantages. Organizational weaknesses are the drawbacks that hinder an organization in executing strategies. Organizational opportunities are environmental factors that the organization may exploit for competitive advantage. Organizational threats are environmental factors that hinder an organization's achieving a competitive advantage.

- Another tool for developing a grand strategy is forecasting—creating a vision or projection of the future. Two types of forecasting are (1) trend analysis, a hypothetical extension of a past series of events into the future; and (2) contingency planning, the creation of alternative hypothetical but equally likely future conditions.

6.4 Formulating Strategy

- Strategy formulation (Step 3 in the strategic-management process) makes use of several concepts, including (1) Porter's five competitive forces, (2) Porter's four competitive strategies, and (3) product life cycles.

- Porter's model for industry analysis suggests that business-level strategies originate in five primary competitive forces in the firm's environment: (1) threats of new entrants, (2) bargaining power of suppliers, (3) bargaining power of buyers, (4) threats of substitute products or services, and (5) rivalry among competitors.

- Porter's four competitive strategies are as follows: (1) The cost-leadership strategy is to keep the costs, and hence the prices, of a product or service below those of competitors and to target a wide market. (2) The differentiation strategy is to offer products or services that are of unique and superior value compared to those of competitors but to target a wide market. (3) The cost-focus strategy is to keep the costs and hence prices of a product or service below those of competitors and to target a narrow market. (4) The focused-differentiation strategy is to offer products or services that are of unique and superior value compared to those of competitors and to target a narrow market.

- A product life cycle is a model of the four stages a product or service goes through: (1) In the introduction stage, a new product is introduced into the marketplace and is heavy on start-up costs for production, marketing, and distribution. (2) In the growth stage, customer demand increases, the product's sales grow, and later competitors may enter the market. (3) In the maturity stage, the product starts to fall out of favor and sales and profits fall off. (4) In the decline stage, the product falls out of favor, and the organization withdraws from the marketplace.

6.5 Implementing & Controlling Strategy: Execution

- The last two stages of the strategic-management process are 4, strategic implementation, and 5, strategic control.

- Execution, say Larry Bossidy and Ram Charan, is not simply tactics, it is a central part of any company's strategy; it consists of using questioning, analysis, and follow-through in order to mesh strategy with reality, align people with goals, and achieve results promised.

- Three building blocks underlie the process of effective execution. The first building block is that leadership must be based on seven essential behaviors: (1) know your people and your business; (2) insist on realism; (3) set clear goals and priorities; (4) follow through; (5) reward the doers; (6) expand people's capabilities; and (7) know yourself. The second building block is that a framework for cultural change must be created. The third building block is that there must be effective selection and evaluation of people.

- The three building blocks are the foundation for the three core processes of execution—people, strategy, and operations. (1) You have to evaluate talent by linking people to particular strategic milestones, developing future leaders, dealing with nonperformers, and transforming the mission and operations of the human resource department. (2) In considering whether the organization can execute the strategy, a leader must take a realistic and critical view of its capabilities and competencies. If it does not have the talent in finance, sales, and manufacturing to accomplish the vision, the chances of success are drastically reduced. (3) The third core process, operations, or the operating plan, provides the path for people to follow. The operating plan should address all the major activities in which the company will engage—marketing, production, sales, revenue, and so on—and then define short-term objectives for these activities, to provide targets for people to aim at.

management in action

Should Home Depot Expand into China?

When will Home Depot Inc. make its move in China? The home improvement market on the mainland is the most promising in the world: $50 billion in sales in 2005 and growing at 12% a year. Homeownership has skyrocketed, from near zero two decades ago, when there was virtually no private property, to 70% of all housing today. Home Depot CEO Robert L. Nardelli has labeled China a top priority: A successful strategy there would offset the challenge of sustaining strong sales growth back home and could even boost the stock. Chuck Elias, Home Depot's China head, is studying the terrain. He has visited 25 Chinese cities

in the past 14 months, scouring competitors' outlets and prowling the traditional markets. "China is an incredibly exciting opportunity," says Elias.

Sure looks like something is up. Rumors about a pending Home Depot deal have been building steadily. The latest is that the Atlanta-based company will buy a 49% stake in Orient Home, a well-managed local chain and a strong presence in northern and northeastern China with $350 million in sales. Home Depot would not confirm that it's in talks with Orient Home. "We're going to make the prudent decision," says Elias. "We're going to make sure we have the right business model."

Is Home Depot blowing it? Or is it biding its time for the right reasons? The China home improvement market is a lot trickier to navigate than those hot growth numbers would indicate. For starters, it barely resembles the do-it-yourself market back in America, where Home Depot workers dispense advice, then send customers back home to lay their own tiles and install some track lighting.

In China, purchasers of newly constructed homes don't have bathrooms to tile. They don't have bedrooms or kitchens. Or even interior walls. Chinese contractors just build concrete shells: They do no finishing work. "Imagine in the U.S. if you bought a home with just interior framing studs and cement floors." says Elias. "You have no doorways, or even wiring or pipes."

So Chinese homeowners fix up these shells themselves. They have to hire handymen to install everything. The home improvement stores already operating in China provide those workers. When first-time home buyer Angeline Xu took possession of her new Shanghai apartment last July, she found herself staring at a shell without plumbing, flooring, doors, or windows. Travel agent Xu headed over to B&Q, a British home improvement chain. B&Q staffers helped her design a floor plan and choose materials, and then performed all the installation work. The retailer offers a complete package, with installation included, which is aimed at entry-level property buyers and priced at around $6,000 for a two-bedroom, 900-square-foot apartment. "I bought everything here," says Xu.

If Home Depot decides to take the plunge, it would have to train thousands of its staffers to do such floor-to-ceiling installation, something it doesn't do in the U.S. Meanwhile, it faces stiffening competition from the likes of B&Q and homegrown players, including Homemart, Homeway, and Orient Home. Homeway, which had a brief dalliance with Home Depot in the mid-1990s, has adopted much of the Home Depot model, right down to the orange work aprons. These chains have spent years cultivating relationships with local suppliers and have already grabbed prime retail locations in the big cities.

In B&Q especially, Home Depot faces a rival that has already learned many lessons about operating in China. The chain, a subsidiary of Europe's do-it-yourself giant Kingfisher, inaugurated its first Chinese store in Shanghai in 1999 but soon realized that a cookie-cutter version of its British stores would not pass muster. . . .

Since those wobbly first steps, B&Q has hit its stride in China. Its 49 stores on the mainland rang up $542 million in sales in 2005, a 48% increase over the previous year. B&Q China President David Wei says

his company plans to double its store count in the country by 2010.

B&Q's Chinese outlets bear little resemblance to the cavernous warehouses filled with piles of drywall, paint, and potted plants typical of a Home Depot in the U.S. It's more like the macho big-box store meets Queer Eye for the Straight Guy. Designer chopsticks compete for space with professional-grade power tools. For feng shui followers, there's an extensive selection of aquariums (Chinese believe fish bring good luck), with some costing as much as $3,000. Not your standard Home Depot fare.

As they try to gauge the risks and rewards in China. Home Depot executives don't want to get off on the wrong foot. While the retailer has found success in Canada and Mexico, forays into more distant markets have ended badly. After a half-hearted expansion into Chile and Argentina, Home Depot sold off its stores there in 2001 and has not ventured into any other countries since.

It's likely that Home Depot will try some mix of building its own stores and buying share in China through an acquisition. Yet the longer it waits, the tougher it will be to break in. Securing the best locations requires good government connections. Getting to know the market and forging relationships with local suppliers can take years. Says Tian Guanyong, CEO of CGen Media, a company that installs flat-panel screens that play ads in retail outlets: "Home Depot had better make up its mind about China before it's too late."

For Discussion

1. Based on Michael Porter's discussion of the characteristics of an effective strategy, does Home Depot have a good strategy when it comes to China? Discuss.

2. To what extent is Home Depot following the five steps of the strategic-management process?

3. Conduct a SWOT analysis of Home Depot's potential expansion into China and recommend whether the company should enter the home improvement market in China.

4. To what extent will Porter's five competitive forces help or hurt Home Depot's potential entry into China? Explain.

5. Which of the three core processes of any business are going to create the biggest problems for a Home Depot expansion in China? Discuss your rationale.

Source: Excerpted from Frederik Balfour, with Brian Grow, "Home Depot: One Foot in China," *BusinessWeek* May 1, 2006, pp. 44–45.

self-assessment

Core Skills Required in Strategic Planning

Objectives
1. To assess if you have the skills to be in strategic planning.
2. To see what you think are the important core skill areas in strategic planning.

Introduction
Strategic planning became important as a method of managing the increasing velocity of change. The business environment no longer evolves at a manageable pace but increasingly through a process Charles Handy calls "discontinuous change"—change that radically alters how we think, work, and often behave. The com-puter, for instance, has completely changed how we communicate, research, write, and work. To meet this challenge, companies have strategic planners and others knowledgeable about their organizations, culture, and environment to shape strategy. Individuals must develop knowledge about their own abilities so that they formulate their own kind of strategic planning.

Instructions
To see whether or not you have the required skills needed to be a strategic planner, truthfully and thoughtfully assess your ability level for the following list of 12 skills. Rate each skill by using a five-point scale in which 1 = exceptional, 2 = very high, 3 = high, 4 = low, and 5 = very low.

	1	2	3	4	5
1. Ability to synthesize	1	2	3	4	5
2. Analytical skills	1	2	3	4	5
3. Computer skills	1	2	3	4	5
4. Decisiveness	1	2	3	4	5
5. Interpersonal skills	1	2	3	4	5
6. Listening skills	1	2	3	4	5
7. Persuasiveness	1	2	3	4	5
8. Problem-solving skills	1	2	3	4	5
9. Research skills	1	2	3	4	5
10. Team skills	1	2	3	4	5
11. Verbal skills	1	2	3	4	5
12. Written skills	1	2	3	4	5

Scoring & Interpretation
According to research conducted at the Ohio State University College of Business, the core required skills for the 12 skills above rate as follows:

Ability to synthesize:	2
Analytical skills:	1
Computer skills:	3
Decisiveness:	3
Interpersonal skills:	1
Listening skills:	2
Persuasiveness:	2

Problem-solving skills:	3
Research skills:	3
Team skills:	2
Verbal skills:	2
Written skills:	3

If you scored mostly 4s and 5s, strategic planning is probably not for you.

If you scored near the "perfect" score, it may be a possible career path.

If you scored all 1s and 2s, you might do extremely well at this type of work and might want to look into it more.

Questions for Discussion

1. Based on your results, do you think you would like to make a career out of strategic planning? Why or why not?
2. What appeals or does not appeal to you about this career? Explain.
3. How might you enhance your strategic skills? Discuss.

Developed by Anne C. Cowden, PhD.

 group exercise

Strategizing for Real

Objectives

1. To help you understand the complexity of the strategic-planning process.
2. To more completely familiarize yourself with strategic planning.

Introduction

Social psychologist Kurt Lewin argued that there is nothing as useful as a good theory. The important word here is *good* since bad theories can cause a great deal of trouble. An example of a bad theory was the introduction of the New Coke in 1985 by Coca-Cola, one of the world's most successful companies. Management's "theory" was that customers wanted a New Coke. But its introduction was an enormous fiasco, and furious customers demanded that traditional Coke be brought back. Companies that effectively use strategic planning can try to avoid these blunders.

To have a sense of what function a strategic plan can have, you must (1) look at the theory and (2) apply it to an actual situation that you know. In this way, you can see if you like doing strategic planning, what it entails in terms of complexity and insight, and whether or not you think it is a career area you might like to pursue. Because of transitions in the world economy, the demand for strategists will likely increase. The purpose of this exercise is to provide you the opportunity to create a strategic plan for your college or university.

Instructions

Students should be divided into groups of five each. One person should go to the Web site for the New Mexico State University Planning Process at **www.nmsu.edu/Strategic/process/fig1.html,** download the chart there, and make copies for everyone. The task of the group is to use this chart as a guide to develop a strategic plan for your college or university. Your first step is to discover if such a document already exists, acquire a copy, and then compare it to your chart, filling in the specifics and trying to improve the process as you go along. This exercise should help make you a better strategic planner of your own education and career.

Questions for Discussion

1. Why is it important for an organization—whether private, public, or not-for-profit—to have a strategic plan? Explain your rationale.
2. Do you think that a strategic plan can ever be totally accurate? Why or why not?
3. Who do you think should be involved in developing and maintaining a strategic plan?
4. How would you grade (A through F) the strategic plan at your college? Explain your rationale.

Developed by Anne C. Cowden, PhD.

ethical dilemma

Should Companies Stockpile the Avian-Influenza Drug Tamiflu?

In 2005, Procter & Gamble asked its company doctors whether P&G should try to secure a private stash of the avian-influenza drug Tamiflu for its staff of 25,000 in Asia. A year later they were still debating the question.

"How ethical would it be if we were holding supplies that the general public didn't have access to but badly needed?" asked Shivanand Priolkar, the company's medical leader for southern Asia. He even worried that "people could come to know you have a life-saving medicine and you could make yourself a target."

Here the tensions are between a company's obligations to its employees and shareholders and its responsibility to the community. "We always believe we support the communities in which we operate," said P&G's Dr. Shivanand. Stockpiling Tamiflu "would take supplies out of the system."

Solving the Dilemma

Suppose you were on a committee at P&G that was considering the issue of stockpiling Tamiflu. What would you recommend?

1. Even though the Avian flu has not killed many people to date, your most important responsibilities are to your employees and shareholders. Stockpile the drug for your employees.
2. Don't worry about the situation because the avian flu has not mutated to a form that is transmissible to humans. A pandemic is very unlikely.
3. Develop stockpiles of the drug in remote areas where you have operations, like Vietnam. Employees in these areas are more likely to get the flu and they are less likely to have access to top-notch health care.
4. Invent other options. Discuss.

Source: Excerpted from Cris Prystay, Murray Hiebert, and Kate Linebaugh, "Companies Face Ethical Issues Over Tamiflu," *The Wall Street Journal,* January 16, 2006, pp. B1, B3

video case

Panera Bread Company: A Recipe for Growth

Panera Bread Company (PBC), with corporate headquarters in Richmond Heights, Missouri, began in 1981 as Au Bon Pain Company ("where the good bread is at"). The company's mission was to change the way America eats by focusing on healthier eating and more balanced living for its customers. Panera has a long history of strategic changes that have allowed the company to get to the successful place it currently enjoys today. In 1993, Au Bon Pain acquired Saint Louis Bread Company with 19 St. Louis bakery-cafes, and over the next five years, the company grew tremendously, making several additional acquisitions. In 1999, all Au Bon Pain business units, except Panera Bread, were divested when the company encountered financial difficulties, and Panera Bread was renamed Panera Bread Company (PBC) with a bakery-café model. This model is essentially a fast-food eat-in restaurant where healthy eating is stressed. Customers can purchase "real artisan bread" sans chemicals or preservatives; food choices contain minimally processed ingredients.

Today, Panera Bread Company consists of more than 900 bakery-cafes (approximately one third of the bakery-cafes are company owned and two-thirds of the bakery-cafes are franchises) in 37 states. Panera stores serve breakfast, lunch, and "lunch in the evening" in a "gathering place" atmosphere. Unlike fast food chains, each Panera store has its unique character and design. Salespeople do not rush customers out of the store, but rather encourage them to spend time there. In fact, some Panera stores have Wi-Fi network capabilities to entice customers to remain in the store. Independent surveys show Panera's high approval ratings from customers. It has been ranked as #1 of 110 new business concepts and has won the prestigious JD Power Award. In one survey,

6,000 customers ranked Panera highest in the food quality category. Not only does the company offer a unique product line, it created a good corporate image through its philosophy of distributing baked goods to soup kitchens and food banks. Last year, the company as a whole gave away some $12 million worth of baked goods to soup kitchens as part of its policy for baked goods to never exceed a one-day shelf life.

Challenges that continue to face Panera include growing too fast, something the company has already responded to with its earlier divestments. Additionally, the Panera Bread Company may encounter high employee turnover rates that seem to plague the food industry in general. Also, the current lo-carb rage in American eating diets may present another problem for PBC as does the continuing issue of differentiating itself from its competitors. Panera has had to deal with the Atkins Diet and South Beach Diet craze. It responded to these competitors by offering different menu items and introducing new whole grain breads. It offers what CEO Shaich calls "good-carbs" that allow customers to stay healthy.

CEO Shaich believes that Panera Bread Company has remained close to its 1994 vision. As part of its 2006 corporate goal, Panera plans opening between 150–160 new bakery-cafes, almost evenly split between company ownership and franchisees. Today, Panera generates some $2 billion in business annually and is well-positioned for continued success in the fast-food market.

Questions

1. Describe how Panera Bread Company has carried out the 5 steps of strategic management. Which area do you think they have made the most changes in? Which areas do you think need more development, and what would your recommendations be?
2. Which category of Porter's Five Forces do you think represents the most significant challenge for Panera today? Why? If you were in Shaich's shoes, how would you try to meet this challenge?
3. Develop a brief SWOT analysis for the Panera Bread Company.
4. How does the culture at Panera reinforce and contribute to their strategic goals?

Source: Joseph C. Santora, EdD, Essex County College.

chapter 7

Individual & Group Decision Making
How Managers Make Things Happen

Major Questions You Should Be Able to Answer

7.1 The Nature of Decision Making
Major Question: How do I decide to decide?

7.2 Two Kinds of Decision Making: Rational & Nonrational
Major Question: How do people know when they're being logical or illogical?

7.3 Evidence-Based Decision Making & Analytics
Major Question: How can I improve my decision making using evidence-based management and business analytics?

7.4 Making Ethical Decisions
Major Question: What guidelines can I follow to be sure that decisions I make are not just lawful but ethical?

7.5 Group Decision Making: How to Work with Others
Major Question: How do I work with others to make things happen?

7.6 How to Overcome Barriers to Decision Making
Major Question: Trying to be rational isn't always easy. What are the barriers?

How Exceptional Managers Make Decisions

"Failure is a great teacher."

That is one of the life lessons of David Dorman, who at age 45 is the CEO of a $10 billion joint venture between AT&T and British Telecommunications.[1] During his meteoric career, Dorman has had to make many decisions—the subject of this chapter—for which failure is always a possible outcome. But he has learned that that possibility can't stop one from making decisions And one can probably always learn from the result.

- **When should you make a decision and when should you delay?** Often you want to stay open-minded before making a decision. But sometimes that can just be a cover for procrastination. (After all, *not* making a decision is in itself a kind of decision.) How do you know when you're keeping an open mind or are procrastinating? Ralph L. Keeney, coauthor of *Smart Choices: A Practical Guide to Making Better Decisions,* offers some questions to consider:[2]

  Understanding: Do you have a reasonable grasp of the problem?

  Comfort level about outcome: Would you be satisfied if you chose one of the existing alternatives?

  Future possible alternatives: Would it be unlikely that you could come up with a better alternative if you had more time?

  Seizing the opportunity: Could the best alternatives disappear if you wait?

  If you can answer "yes" to those questions, you almost certainly should decide now, not wait.

- **Making tough choices.** To reach the top, as Dorman has, a manager needs to be able to make tough choices. "On a daily and weekly basis we can be faced with making hundreds of decisions," says management consultant

Odette Pollar. "Most of them are small, but the larger ones where more is at stake can be truly painful." Here are some ways she suggests making decision making easier, some of which resemble Keeney's:[3]

Decide in a timely fashion: "Rarely does waiting significantly improve the quality of the decision," says Pollar. In fact, delay can result in greater unpleasantness in loss of money, time, and peace of mind.

Don't agonize over minor decisions: Postponing decisions about small problems can mean that they simply turn into large ones later.

Separate outcome from process: Does a bad outcome mean you made a bad decision? Not necessarily. The main thing is to go through a well-reasoned process of choosing among alternatives, which increases the chances of success. But even then you can't be sure there will always be a positive outcome.

Learn when to stop gathering facts: "Gather enough information to make a sound decision," suggests Pollar, "but not all the possible information." Taking extra time may mean you'll miss a window of opportunity.

When overwhelmed, narrow your choices: Sometimes there are many good alternatives, and you need to simplify decision making by eliminating some options.

For Discussion "Facing the hard facts about what works and what doesn't" is how evidence-based management was characterized in Chapter 2. How able do you think you are to make the tough choices that effective managers have to make? For instance, could you reverse a wrong decision—your decision—that led to an expensive mistake?

forecast

What's Ahead in This Chapter

We describe decision making and types of decisions, and we describe the range of decision-making conditions. Next we distinguish between rational and nonrational decision making, and we describe five nonrational models. We then consider evidence-based decision making and the use of analytics. We discuss four steps in practical decision making. We follow with a discussion of group decision making, including participative management and group problem-solving techniques. We conclude by considering how individuals respond to decision situations and four common decision-making biases.

7.1 THE NATURE OF DECISION MAKING

 major question **How do I decide to decide?**

THE BIG PICTURE

Decision making, the process of identifying and choosing alternative courses of action, may be programmed or nonprogrammed. Decision-making conditions range from certainty to risky to uncertainty to confusion.

Success. Basketball coach Pat Riley, surrounded by some of his Miami Heat players, celebrates winning the 2006 NBA Championship. One of pro basketball's most successful coaches, Riley previously led the Los Angeles Lakers and the New York Knicks. As a manager, a coach must make many decisions about what is the right way to success. Riley maintains a standard of excellence both on and off the court. If you were a coach, what would you do differently?

Ben Swett—former Vassar English major, University of Chicago MBA, TV comedy writer, and Quaker Oats executive—started windowbox.com in 1997 after failing in the seemingly simple task of growing a plant on his balcony in Los Angeles. His mission: to run an online organization that satisfied the needs of urban gardeners, as well as to contribute to the social good.

Selling plants to patio and balcony gardeners, it turns out, is an extremely seasonal business. About half of Swett's annual sales occur at three times: Valentine's Day, Mother's Day, and the 2 weeks before Christmas. What kinds of decisions do Swett and his managers have to make to scale up and down for such a volatile business?[4]

Decision Making Defined

A *decision* **is a choice made from among available alternatives.** For example, should your college offer (if it currently does not) computer-based distance learning to better serve students who work odd hours or are homebound and can't easily get to lectures on campus? That question is a decision that the college administrators must make.

Decision making **is the process of identifying and choosing alternative courses of action.** For example, the college could offer distance learning by televising the lectures of a single professor into several classrooms or to community centers off campus. Or it could offer distance learning interactively over the Internet. It could offer distance learning only for certain subjects (business and education, say) or for selected courses in all majors. It could offer distance learning only during the summer or only during the evenings. It could charge extra for such courses. It could offer them for credit to high school students or to students attending other colleges. Identifying and sorting out these alternatives is the process of decision making.

Types of Decisions: Programmed versus Nonprogrammed

In most day-to-day matters, you automatically know what kind of decision needs to be made and when, who will decide it, who will need to be consulted about it, who should be informed about it. That is, the decisions are *programmed.* However, when you have to stop and think about these matters, then the decisions are *nonprogrammed.*[5]

Let's distinguish further between programmed and nonprogrammed decisions.

Distance learning. This student is logged on to the distance-learning Web site at Camden County (New Jersey) College. Today students frequently have the option to take many courses online that previously were not available to them. Do you think that the addition of distance-learning courses gives you greater freedom of choice and new opportunities—or simply more headaches?

Programmed Decisions   *Programmed decisions* **are repetitive and routine,** such as those involving customer complaints or customer payments. Because they are fairly structured and occur fairly frequently, such decisions tend to follow established rules and so are virtually automatic. This does not mean, however, that the issues are necessarily simple. Even a complicated issue, if its components can be analyzed, may be decided by a programmed decision.

Example: The three-times-a-year peak load times for windowbox.com are predictable. During these periods, plant shipments jump from 2,000 to 32,000, nursery workers go from 8 to 60, and back-office workers triple to 18. Owner Ben Swett taps pools of friends and family, many of whom are used to doing temp work. Even so, says Swett, "I freak out four weeks before the holiday and ask everyone questions like, 'What if the power goes off?' " As a result, a generator is on standby. Thus, says one account, Swett "devises a backup for every problem he can imagine and then is free to focus on those he didn't anticipate."[6]

Nonprogrammed Decisions   *Nonprogrammed decisions* **are those that occur under nonroutine, unfamiliar circumstances.** Because they occur in response to unusual, unpredictable opportunities and threats—the conditions of uncertainty we mentioned in Chapter 5—nonprogrammed decisions are relatively unstructured. Often, too, they tend to involve complex, important situations. The farther you move up the organizational hierarchy, the more important your ability to make nonprogrammed decisions becomes.

Example: Although Ben Swett badgers customers to give their best forecasts, surprises happen anyway. Thus, shortly after moving into an older building with space for plants on the roof, Swett realized that the small elevator would not be able to move all the plants in time for the Mother's Day crunch. Accordingly, he got a nearby tailor to fashion a chute out of canvas, which was used to slide boxed plants down four stories to waiting Federal Express trucks. The lesson, says a *Wall Street Journal* story: "plan for knowable contingencies, be ready to wing the rest."[7]

General Decision-Making Styles: Directive, Analytical, Conceptual, Behavioral

Do men and women differ in the way they make decisions? Do they, for example, differ in risk propensity? *Risk propensity* **is the willingness to gamble or to undertake risk for the possibility of gaining an increased payoff.**

Perhaps another name for this is competitiveness. And research does seem to show that, as one scholar summarized it, "Even in tasks where they do well, women seem to shy away from competition, whereas men seem to enjoy it too much."[8] In an experiment involving winning small amounts of money in number-memorizing tournaments, men were avid competitors and were eager to continue, partly from overconfidence regardless of their success in earlier rounds, and they rated their abilities more highly than the women rated theirs. Most women declined to compete, even when they had done the best in earlier rounds.[9]

This brings us to the subject of decision-making style. **A *decision-making style* reflects the combination of how an individual perceives and responds to information.** A team of researchers developed a model of decision-making styles based on the idea that styles vary along two different dimensions: value orientation and tolerance for ambiguity.[10]

Self-Assessment Exercise:
Your Preferred Decision-Making Style

Value orientation reflects the extent to which a person focuses on either task and technical concerns or people and social concerns when making decisions. Some people, for instance, are very task focused at work and do not pay much attention to people issues, whereas others are just the opposite.

The second dimension pertains to a person's *tolerance for ambiguity.* This individual difference indicates the extent to which a person has a high need for structure or control in his or her life. Some people desire a lot of structure in their lives (a low tolerance for ambiguity) and find ambiguous situations stressful and psychologically uncomfortable. In contrast, others do not have a high need for structure and can thrive in uncertain situations (a high tolerance for ambiguity). Ambiguous situations can energize people with a high tolerance for ambiguity.

When the dimensions of value orientation and tolerance for ambiguity are combined, they form four styles of decision making: *directive, analytical, conceptual,* and *behavioral. (See Figure 7.1.)*

figure 7.1

DECISION-MAKING STYLES

I. Directive People with a directive style have a low tolerance for ambiguity and are oriented toward task and technical concerns in making decisions. They are efficient, logical, practical, and systematic in their approach to solving problems.

People with this style are action oriented and decisive and like to focus on facts. In their pursuit of speed and results, however, these individuals tend to be autocratic, to exercise power and control, and to focus on the short run.

2. Analytical This style has a much higher tolerance for ambiguity and is characterized by the tendency to overanalyze a situation. People with this style like to consider more information and alternatives than managers following the directive style.

Analytic individuals are careful decision makers who take longer to make decisions but who also respond well to new or uncertain situations.

3. Conceptual People with a conceptual style have a high tolerance for ambiguity and tend to focus on the people or social aspects of a work situation. They take a broad perspective to problem solving and like to consider many options and future possibilities.

Conceptual types adopt a long-term perspective and rely on intuition and discussions with others to acquire information. They also are willing to take risks and are good at finding creative solutions to problems. However, a conceptual style can foster an indecisive approach to decision making.

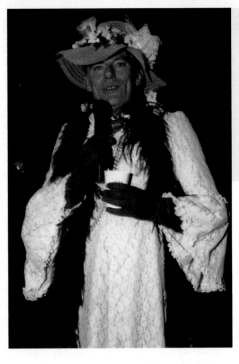

Who is this, er, man? Herb Kelleher, former CEO of highly successful Southwest Airlines, was much beloved by his employees for his humor, informal management style, and extraordinary people orientation. What kind of decision-making styles do you think his successors should try to follow?

4. Behavioral This style is the most people oriented of the four styles. People with this style work well with others and enjoy social interactions in which opinions are openly exchanged. Behavioral types are supportive, receptive to suggestions, show warmth, and prefer verbal to written information.

Although they like to hold meetings, people with this style have a tendency to avoid conflict and to be concerned about others. This can lead behavioral types to adopt a wishy-washy approach to decision making and to have a hard time saying no.

Which Style Do You Have? Research shows that very few people have only one dominant decision-making style. Rather, most managers have characteristics that fall into two or three styles. Studies also show that decision-making styles vary across occupations, job level, and countries.[11] There is not a best decision-making style that applies to all situations.

You can use knowledge of decision-making styles in three ways:

- Knowledge of styles helps you to understand yourself. Awareness of your style assists you in identifying your strengths and weaknesses as a decision maker and facilitates the potential for self-improvement.
- You can increase your ability to influence others by being aware of styles. For example, if you are dealing with an analytical person, you should provide as much information as possible to support your ideas.
- Knowledge of styles gives you an awareness of how people can take the same information and yet arrive at different decisions by using a variety of decision-making strategies. Different decision-making styles represent one likely source of interpersonal conflict at work.

To get a sense of your own decision-making style, see the Self-Assessment at the end of this chapter. ●

7.2 TWO KINDS OF DECISION MAKING: RATIONAL & NONRATIONAL

> ✳ major question
>
> How do people know when they're being logical or illogical?

THE BIG PICTURE

Decision making may be rational, but often it is nonrational. Four steps in making a rational decision are (1) identify the problem or opportunity, (2) think up alternative solutions, (3) evaluate alternatives and select a solution, and (4) implement and evaluate the solution chosen. Two examples of nonrational models are satisficing and incremental.

Group Exercise:
Stranded in the Desert: An Exercise in Decision Making

Iridium LLC's network of 66 low-orbit satellites was supposed to revolutionize telecommunications by allowing people to make phone calls at any time from anywhere in the world. But 9 months after its splashy 1998 launch, the Motorola-led consortium had filed for bankruptcy protection.

What happened? Critics say that Iridium and Motorola became so focused on making the technology work they failed to pay attention to marketing problems. In an era of pocket-size cell phones, the clunky Iridium "space phone" weighed 1 pound, was the size of a brick, and featured an array of ungainly accessories and adapters. Moreover, because of technology limitations, phone users had to position themselves so nothing blocked the line of sight between the phone's antenna and the satellites overhead. This meant the handset couldn't be used inside buildings, moving cars, or many other locations where the high-powered managers Iridium was targeting tended to make calls. Finally, the phones retailed for $3,000 apiece, and calls ran $2–$8 a minute—at a time when competitors were even giving phones away to induce consumers to subscribe to their low-cost calling plans.[12]

Were Iridium's decisions rational? Let us look at the two approaches managers may take to making decisions: They may follow a *rational model* or various kinds of *nonrational models*.

Rational Decision Making: Managers Should Make Logical & Optimal Decisions

The *rational model of decision making*, also called the *classical model*, explains how managers *should* make decisions; it assumes managers will make logical decisions that will be the optimum in furthering the organization's best interests. The rational model is appropriate for making programmed decisions, such as how to respond to customer complaints.

Typically there are four stages associated with rational decision making. *(See Figure 7.2.)*

figure 7.2

THE FOUR STEPS IN RATIONAL DECISION MAKING

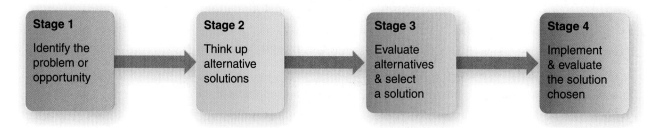

Stage 1	Stage 2	Stage 3	Stage 4
Identify the problem or opportunity	Think up alternative solutions	Evaluate alternatives & select a solution	Implement & evaluate the solution chosen

Stage I: Identify the Problem or Opportunity— Determining the Actual versus the Desirable

As a manager, you'll probably find no shortage of **problems, or difficulties that inhibit the achievement of goals.** Customer complaints. Supplier breakdowns. Staff turnover. Sales shortfalls. Competitor innovations.

However, you'll also often find **opportunities—situations that present possibilities for exceeding existing goals.** It's the farsighted manager, however, who can look past the steady stream of daily problems and seize the moment to actually do *better* than the goals he or she is expected to achieve. When a competitor's top salesperson unexpectedly quits, that creates an opportunity for your company to hire that person away to promote your product more vigorously in that sales territory.

Whether you're confronted with a problem or an opportunity, the decision you're called on to make is how to make *improvements*—how to change conditions from the present to the desirable. This is a matter of *diagnosis*—**analyzing the underlying causes.**

Example

NASCAR

Making a Correct Diagnosis: Pit Crew Chief Wins NASCAR Races

Ray Evernham, a former NASCAR driver and now owner of the Evernham Motorsports racing team, has also headed up Jeff Gordon's pit crew, keeping charge of a team of seven who changed tires and added fuel during pit stops. Using two-way radio communication with his drivers, Evernham made all decisions as each race progressed, such as when to make pit stops, how many tires to change, how much fuel to pump, and which repairs to make. Thus, if a driver complained that his car was oversteering or understeering, Evernham would determine how to adjust the weight-jacking bolts on each corner of the car before the pit stop even began. By carefully watching how other drivers made their pit stops, Evernham planned his, always trying to save a little time. This paid off big time at the 1994 Coca-Cola 600, when Evernham observed rival driver Rusty Wallace's crew spending 17 seconds changing all four tires. When Gordon arrived for his pit stop, Evernham ordered only two tires changed, saving 8 seconds that allowed Gordon to claim his first major win with a margin of 3.91 seconds. [13]

Your Call

What should you do if you make a mistaken diagnosis of a problem?

Stage 2: Think Up Alternative Solutions— Both the Obvious & the Creative

Employees burning with bright ideas are an employer's greatest competitive resource. "Creativity precedes innovation, which is its physical expression," says *Fortune* magazine writer Alan Farnham. "It's the source of all intellectual property."[14]

After you've identified the problem or opportunity and diagnosed its causes, you need to come up with alternative solutions. For a programmed decision (for which the rational model is most appropriate), the alternatives will probably be easy and obvious. For nonprogrammed decisions, the more creative and innovative the alternatives, the better.

Stage 3: Evaluate Alternatives & Select a Solution— Ethics, Feasibility, & Effectiveness

In this stage, you need to evaluate each alternative not only according to cost and quality but also according to the following questions: (1) Is it *ethical?* (If it isn't, don't give it a second look.) (2) Is it *feasible?* (If time is short, costs are high, technology unavailable, or customers resistant, for example, it is not.) (3) Is it ultimately *effective?* (If the decision is merely "good enough" but not optimal in the long run, you might reconsider.)

Stage 4: Implement & Evaluate the Solution Chosen

With programmed decisions, implementation is usually straightforward (though not necessarily easy—firing employees who steal may be an obvious decision but it can still be emotionally draining). With nonprogrammed decisions, implementation can be quite difficult; when one company acquires another, for instance, it may take months to consolidate the departments, accounting systems, inventories, and so on.

Successful Implementation   For implementation to be successful, you need to do two things:

- **Plan carefully.** Especially if reversing an action will be difficult, you need to make careful plans for implementation. Nonprogrammed decisions may require written plans.

- **Be sensitive to those affected.** You need to consider how the people affected may feel about the change—inconvenienced, insecure, even fearful, all of which can trigger resistance. This is why it helps to give employees and customers latitude during a changeover in business practices or working arrangements.

Evaluation   One "law" in economics is the Law of Unintended Consequences—things happen that weren't foreseen. For this reason, you need to follow up and evaluate the results of the decision.

What should you do if the action is not working? Some possibilities:

- **Give it more time.** You need to make sure employees, customers, and so on have had enough time to get used to the new action.

Example

Faulty Implementation: Customer Service Is Often "Just Talk"

"My claim to fame, the only thing I've ever been really good at, is returning people's phone calls every single day," says Mark Powers. No doubt it is that kind of customer service that is the reason why Excelsior Roofing of San Francisco, founded by Powers's grandfather 100 years ago, is still in business.[15]

"Executives talk about the importance of responding to customers' needs with top-notch customer service," writes *Wall Street Journal* columnist Carol Hymowitz. "But often it's just talk."[16]

The problem with faulty customer service, however, is that sometimes the company may be the last to hear about it, but a great many other potential customers may hear of it by word of mouth. One study found that only 6% of shoppers who experienced a problem with a retailer contacted the company. However, 31% went on to tell friends, family, and colleagues

what had happened. Indeed, if 100 people have a bad experience, a retailer stands to lose between 32 and 36 current or potential customers, according to the study.[17]

Consultants working for one large telecommunications company encourage customer service reps at one call center to share their problems and successes with each other and bring in customers to report their positive and negative experiences with the call center. To encourage customer reps to "step inside the shoes of customers," the consultants also presented a weekly award of a pair of baby shoes to the employee who solved the most customer problems.[18]

Your Call

What frustrations have you experienced with an organization's customer service policy? What recommendations could you make to correct the policy?

Evaluation: The Boeing 787 Dreamliner, a Bet-the-Company Decision

The airline industry is one of the most volatile around, and Boeing Co., the Chicago-headquartered aerospace giant, has been through some rough boom-and-bust cycles. In 1997, for instance, production problems shut down two assembly lines and cost the company $2.5 billion.

Then, at a time when Boeing was losing business to its European rival Airbus, the company was wracked by scandals involving Pentagon contracts, and rising fuel costs were dramatically impacting the commercial airline industry, Boeing management made a bold decision: It would build a new medium-sized commercial jet, the 787 Dreamliner, its first new aircraft in 10 years, that would fly faster than the competition and would consume 20% less fuel than similar-sized planes. To achieve this, the 787 would feature more fuel-efficient engines and the fuselage would be built from plastic composite materials instead of aluminum, cutting down on structural fatigue and corrosion, thereby reducing the number of inspections necessary and increasing the number of flights possible. "A light, strong plane is the big payoff for the huge technical risk Boeing is taking in crafting parts out of composites," says aerospace reporter Stanley Holmes.[19]

However, in mid-2006, as the scheduled 2008 delivery date neared, the company was encountering bad news. The fuselage section had failed in testing, and engineers had discovered worrisome bubbles in its skin. The carbon-fiber wing was too heavy, adding to the plane's overall weight. To hold costs down, Boeing had outsourced 80% of the 787's parts, making it dependent on 43 "top-tier" suppliers on three continents, but these subcontractors were struggling to meet the exacting technological demands and deadlines and their software programs were having trouble communicating with each other. "The Dreamliner's mounting challenges call into question whether such a radical business model can succeed, and whether the advantages of collaboration on such a scale are outweighed by the loss of logistical and design control," says Holmes. "For Boeing in particular, it raises the question of whether the company is entering a danger zone that could result in a serious blow to its credibility."

Your Call

By now you, the reader, may be in a position to know whether Boeing's bet on the Dreamliner paid off, or whether it blew its deadline and thus had to pay large financial penalties along with losing airline orders. How would you evaluate the company's decisions?

- **Change it slightly.** Maybe the action was correct, but it just needs "tweaking"—a small change of some sort.
- **Try another alternative.** If Plan A doesn't seem to be working, maybe you want to scrap it for another alternative.
- **Start over.** If no alternative seems workable, you need to go back to the drawing board—to Stage 1 of the decision-making process.

What's Wrong with the Rational Model?

The rational model is *prescriptive,* describing how managers ought to make decisions. It doesn't describe how managers *actually* make decisions. Indeed, the rational model makes some highly desirable assumptions—that managers have complete information, are able to make an unemotional analysis, and are able to make the best decision for the organization. *(See Table 7.1, next page.)*

table 7.1

ASSUMPTIONS OF
THE RATIONAL MODEL

- **Complete information, no uncertainty:** You should obtain complete, error-free information about all alternative courses of action and the consequences that would follow from each choice.

- **Logical, unemotional analysis:** Having no prejudices or emotional blind spots, you are able to logically evaluate the alternatives, ranking them from best to worst according to your personal preferences.

- **Best decision for the organization:** Confident of the best future course of action, you coolly choose the alternative that you believe will most benefit the organization.

Nonrational Decision Making: Managers Find It Difficult to Make Optimal Decisions

In contrast to models that show how decisions should be made are various models of how decisions actually *are* made. ***Nonrational models of decision making* explain how managers make decisions; they assume that decision making is nearly always uncertain and risky, making it difficult for managers to make optimal decisions.** The nonrational models are *descriptive* rather than prescriptive: They describe how managers *actually* make decisions rather than how they should. Two nonrational models are *satisficing* and *incremental*.

I. Bounded Rationality & the Satisficing Model: "Satisfactory Is Good Enough"
During the 1950s, economist **Herbert Simon**—who later received the Nobel Prize—began to study how managers actually make decisions. From his research he proposed that managers could not act truly logically because their rationality was bounded by so many restrictions.[20] Called ***bounded rationality,* the concept suggests that the ability of decision makers to be rational is limited by numerous constraints,** such as complexity, time and money, and their cognitive capacity, values, skills, habits, and unconscious reflexes. *(See Figure 7.3.)*

figure 7.3

SOME HINDRANCES TO
PERFECTLY RATIONAL
DECISION MAKING

- **Complexity:**
The problems that need solving are often exceedingly complex, beyond understanding.

- **Time and money constraints:**
There is not enough time and money to gather all relevant information.

- **Different cognitive capacity, values, skills, habits, and unconscious reflexes:**
Managers aren't all built the same way, of course, and all have personal limitations and biases that affect their judgment.

- **Imperfect information:**
Managers have imperfect, fragmentary information about the alternatives and their consequences.

- **Information overload:**
There is too much information for one person to process.

- **Different priorities:**
Some data are considered more important, so certain facts are ignored.

- **Conflicting goals:**
Other managers, including colleagues, have conflicting goals.

Because of such constraints, managers don't make an exhaustive search for the best alternative. Instead, they follow what Simon calls the ***satisficing model*—that is, managers seek alternatives until they find one that is satisfactory, not optimal.** Iridium's decision to proceed with a clunky 1-pound satellite phone instead of waiting to improve the technology is an example of satisficing.

While looking for a solution that is merely "satisficing" might seem to be a weakness, it may well outweigh any advantages gained from delaying making a decision until all information is in and all alternatives weighed. However, making snap decisions can also backfire.

2. The Incremental Model: "The Least That Will Solve the Problem" Another nonrational decision-making model is the *incremental model,* **in which managers take small, short-term steps to alleviate a problem,** rather than steps that will accomplish a long-term solution. Of course, over time a series of short-term steps may move toward a long-term solution. However, the temporary steps may also impede a beneficial long-term solution.

Making Better Decisions through Knowledge Management

No doubt you have made decisions that later you realized you would have made differently if you had had more complete information. The same happens with decision making in organizations. There, however, managers often find that they need information possessed by people working elsewhere in the system. Accordingly, there is now a growing interest in what is known as knowledge management. ***Knowledge management* is the development of an organizational culture—and the tools, processes, systems, and structures—that encourages continuous learning and sharing of knowledge and information among employees, for the purpose of making better decisions.**[21]

The Two Types of Knowledge: Explicit versus Tacit To begin to comprehend this subject, it helps to understand that there are two types of knowledge—*explicit* and *tacit.*[22]

Explicit Knowledge: "Textbook Knowledge" That Can Be Easily Expressed & Shared An expert in a certain field (tax lawyer, mortgage broker, whatever) may be said to have surface knowledge or "textbook knowledge." This is ***explicit knowledge*, information that can be easily put into words, graphics, and numbers and shared with others.** An example is information about the U.S. tax code that can be looked up.

Tacit Knowledge: "Tricks of the Trade" Learned from Experience & Difficult to Express An expert of many years' experience also has a lot of deep knowledge or "tricks of the trade." This is ***tacit knowledge,* which is individual-based, intuitive, acquired through considerable experience, and hard to express and to share.** Examples are how to swing a golf club, write a speech, or find one-of-a-kind exceptions in the tax code.

Sharing Knowledge to Help Decision Making Both explicit and tacit knowledge affect decision making. However, it's suggested that it is the sharing of tacit knowledge in particular that creates competitive advantage.[23] Two ways to share knowledge are high-tech solutions and low-tech solutions.[24]

High-Tech Solutions: To Share Explicit Knowledge As you might expect, information technology—e-mail, intranets, Web sites, databases—can be of considerable benefit in helping employees learn and share knowledge. This is particularly the case for explicit knowledge.

Sharing knowledge. Medical professionals acquire considerable tacit knowledge, or "tricks of the trade." If they are able to share this with others in their organization, they can build a considerable competitive advantage.

Low-Tech Solutions: To Share Tacit Knowledge But technology alone is not enough. As Anne Mulcahy, chair and CEO of Xerox, says, "Technology requires changes in the way humans work, yet companies continue to inject technology without making the necessary changes"— that is, increase learning.[25] Tacit knowledge is best shared directly, as through informal networking, periodic meetings, and interaction with mentors and coaches. Particularly crucial is an organizational culture that encourages the spread of tacit knowledge. ●

7.3 EVIDENCE-BASED DECISION MAKING & ANALYTICS

❖ major
question

How can I improve my decision making using evidence-based management and business analytics?

THE BIG PICTURE

Evidence-based decision making, which depends on an "attitude of wisdom," rests on three truths. This section describes seven principles for implementing evidence-based management. We also describe why it is hard to bring this approach to bear on one's decision making. Finally, we describe analytics and its three key attributes.

"Too many companies and too many leaders are more interested in just copying others, doing what they've always done, and making decisions based on beliefs in what ought to work rather than what actually works," say Stanford professors **Jeffrey Pfeffer** and **Robert Sutton.** "They fail to face the hard facts and use the best evidence to help navigate the competitive environment."[26] But companies that use evidence-based management, they suggest, routinely trump the competition.

Evidence-Based Decision Making

The trend toward evidence-based management, which means translating principles based on best evidence into organizational practice, is very much in the spirit of bringing rationality to the decision making process.[27] Evidence-based management derives from evidence-based medicine, embracing what Pfeffer and Sutton call *an attitude of wisdom.* This is a mind-set that, first, is willing to set aside belief and conventional wisdom and to act on the facts and, second, has an unrelenting commitment to gathering information necessary to make informed decisions and to keeping pace with new evidence to update practices.[28]

"The way a good doctor or a good manager works," Sutton says, "is to act with knowledge while doubting what you know. So if a patient goes to a doctor, you hope the doctor would do two things: first look at the literature and make the best decision given what's available. Then actually track the progress of the treatment and see what unexpected side effects you're having and what things are working."[29]

Three Truths Evidence-based management is based on three truths:

- **There are few really new ideas.** Most supposedly new ideas are old, wrong, or both.
- **True is better than new.** Effective organizations and managers are more interested in what is true than in what is new.
- **Doing well usually dominates.** Organizations that do simple, obvious, and even seemingly trivial things well will dominate competitors who search for "silver bullets and instant magic."

Seven Implementation Principles Pfeffer and Sutton identify seven implementation principles to help companies that are committed to doing what it takes to profit from evidence-based management, as follows:[30]

- **Treat your organization as an unfinished prototype.** Leaders practicing the "attitude of wisdom" think and act as if their organization is an unfinished prototype that won't be ruined by dangerous new ideas or impossible to change because of employee or management resistance. Example: The products home-shopping network QVC sells are selected through a process of constant experimentation, punctuated by evidence-based analysis as to why some sell and some don't.

- **No brag, just facts.** This slogan is an antidote for assertions made with complete disregard for whether they correspond to facts. Example: Hewlett-Packard CEO Carly Fiorina bragged to the press about HP's merger with Compaq but failed to consider facts about consumer dissatisfaction with Compaq products until after the merger. Other companies, such as DaVita, which operates dialysis centers, take pains to evaluate data before making decisions.

- **See yourself and your organization as outsiders do.** Most managers are afflicted with "rampant optimism," with inflated views of their own talents and prospects for success, which causes them to downplay risks and continue on a path despite evidence things are not working. "Having a blunt friend, mentor, or counselor," Pfeffer and Sutton suggest, "can help you see and act on better evidence."

- **Evidence-based management is not just for senior executives.** The best organizations are those in which everyone, not just the top managers, is guided by the responsibility to gather and act on quantitative and qualitative data and share results with others.

- **Like everything else, you still need to sell it.** "Unfortunately, new and exciting ideas grab attention even when they are vastly inferior to old ideas," the Stanford authors say. "Vivid, juicy stories and case studies sell better than detailed, rigorous, and admittedly dull data—no matter how wrong the stories or how right the data." To sell an evidence-based approach, you may have to identify a preferred practice based on solid if unexciting evidence, then use vivid stories to grab management attention.

- **If all else fails, slow the spread of bad practice.** Because many managers and employees face pressures to do things that are known to be ineffective, it may be necessary for you to practice "evidence-based misbehavior"—that is, ignore orders you know to be wrong or delay their implementation.

- **The best diagnostic question: what happens when people fail?** "Failure hurts, it is embarrassing, and we would rather live without it," the authors write. "Yet there is no learning without failure. . . . If you look at how the most effective systems in the world are managed, a hallmark is that when something goes wrong, people face the hard facts, learn what happened and why, and keep using those facts to make the system better." From the U.S. civil aviation system, which rigorously examines airplane accidents, near misses, and equipment problems, to Intel's Andy Grove's willingness to learn from mistakes, evidence-based management makes the point that failure is a great teacher. This means, however, that the organization must "forgive and remember" people who make mistakes, not be trapped by preconceived notions, and confront the best evidence and hard facts.

What Makes It Hard to Be Evidence Based Despite your best intentions, it's hard to bring the best evidence to bear on your decisions. Among the reasons:[31] (1) There's too much evidence. (2) There's not enough *good* evidence. (3) The evidence doesn't quite apply. (4) People are trying to mislead you. (5) *You* are trying to mislead you. (6) The side effects outweigh the cure. (Example: Despite the belief that social promotion in school is a bad idea—that is, that schools shouldn't advance children to the next grade when they haven't mastered the material—the side effect is skyrocketing costs because it crowds schools with older students, and angrier students, demanding more resources.) (7) Stories are more persuasive, anyway.

In Praise of Analytics

Perhaps the purest application of evidence-based management is the use of ***analytics,*** **or *business analytics,* the term used for sophisticated forms of business data analysis.** One example of analytics is portfolio analysis, in which an investment advisor evaluates the risks of various stocks. Another example is the time-series forecast, which predicts future data based on patterns of historical data.

Use of Analytics: The Oakland A's Play "Moneyball"

As one of the poorest teams in Major League Baseball, with the second-lowest payroll ($55 million in 2005/2006, compared with the New York Yankees' $205 million), how did the Oakland Athletics win so many games? That was the question writer Michael Lewis set out to investigate, and he provides answers in *Moneyball: The Art of Winning an Unfair Game.*[34]

Clearly, the A's couldn't afford superstar talent by competing on the open market for it. Thus, the organization had to find players who could contribute in ways that other clubs didn't value as much, and then minimize the risk in their investment by using players in unconventional ways to maximize their value. Avoiding the use of traditional baseball statistics, the California club found, for example, that better indicators of success lay in on-base percentage and slugging percentage, and that avoiding an out was more important than getting a hit.

Armed with an unprecedented seven first-round draft picks for the 2002 season, the A's crunched the numbers and concentrated primarily on college players (rather than veteran professionals), taking 25 college players with their first 28 picks. Despite the low budget for player salaries, the analytics paid off, and the A's have won as many as 102 games a season and emerged as a perennial playoff team.[35]

Your Call

Executives and personnel people in other lines of work are often like the old baseball traditionalists, relying on résumé, degree, years of experience, and even looks in evaluating job applicants. What other, more quantifiable measures might be used instead?

Some leaders and firms have become exceptional practitioners of analytics. Elsewhere (Chapter 2) we mentioned Harrah's Gary Loveman, whose famous paper and book *Diamonds in the Data Mine* explained how data-mining software was used to analyze vast amounts of casino customer data to target profitable patrons.[32] Others are Marriott International, which through its Total Hotel Optimization program has used quantitative data to establish the optimal price for hotel rooms, evaluate use of conference facilities and catering, and develop systems to optimize offerings to frequent customers.[33]

Thomas H. Davenport and others at Babson College's Working Knowledge Research Center studied 32 organizations that made a commitment to quantitative, fact-based analysis and found three key attributes among analytics competitors.[36]

I. Use of Modeling: Going beyond Simple Descriptive Statistics   Companies such as Capital One look well beyond basic statistics, using data mining and predictive modeling to identify potential and most profitable customers. ***Predictive modeling*** **is a data mining technique used to predict future behavior and anticipate the consequences of change.** Thus, Capital One conducts more than 30,000 experiments a year, with different interest rates, incentives, direct-mail packaging, and other variables to evaluate which customers are most apt to sign up for credit cards and will pay back their debt.

2. Having Multiple Applications, Not Just One   UPS (formerly United Parcel Service) applies analytics not only to tracking the movement of packages but also to examining usage patterns to try to identify potential customer defections so that salespeople can make contact and solve problems. Analytics competitors "don't gain advantage from one killer app [application], but rather from multiple applications supporting many parts of the business," says Davenport.

3. Support from the Top   "A companywide embrace of analytics impels changes in culture, processes, behavior, and skills for many employees," says Davenport. "And so, like any major transition, it requires leadership from executives at the very top who have a passion for the quantitative approach." ●

7.4 MAKING ETHICAL DECISIONS

What guidelines can I follow to be sure that decisions I make are not just lawful but ethical?

THE BIG PICTURE
A graph known as a decision tree can help one make ethical decisions. In addition, one should be aware of "the magnificent seven" general moral principles for managers.

"Have we saved capitalism from the capitalists?" writes Mortimer Zuckerman, editor-in-chief of *U.S. News & World Report* (and, incidentally, quite a capitalist himself, being a self-made billionaire, mainly through real estate). In the early 2000s, one business scandal followed another, from Enron to WorldCom. "The supposedly 'independent' auditors, directors, accountants, and stock market advisers and accountants were all tarnished," Zuckerman goes on, "the engine of the people's involvement, the mutual fund industry, was shown to be permeated by rip-off artists rigging the system for the benefit of insiders and the rich. To crown it all, the high temple of capitalism, the New York Stock Exchange, was polluted by cronyism and greed."[37]

The images of handcuffed executives has forced the subject of right-minded decision making to the top of the agenda in many organizations. Indeed, many companies now have an *ethics officer,* **someone trained about matters of ethics in the workplace, particularly about resolving ethical dilemmas.** More and more companies are also creating values statements to guide employees as to what constitutes desirable business behavior.[38] As a result of this raised consciousness, managers now must try to make sure their decisions are not just lawful but also ethical, a subject discussed in detail in Chapter 3.

Road Map to Ethical Decision Making: A Decision Tree

One of the greatest pressures—if not *the* greatest pressure—on top executives is to maximize shareholder value, to deliver the greatest return on investment to the owners of their company. But is a decision that is beneficial to shareholders yet harmful to employees—such as forcing them to contribute more to their health benefits, as IBM has done—unethical? Harvard Business School professor Constance Bagley suggests that what is needed is a decision tree to help with ethical decisions.[39] **A *decision tree* is a graph of decisions and their possible consequences; it is used to create a plan to reach a goal.** Decision trees are used to aid in making decisions. Bagley's

When confronted with any proposed action for which a decision is required, a manager should ask the following questions:

Self Assessment Exercise:
Assessing Your Ethical Decision-Making Skills

1. **Is the Proposed Action Legal?** This may seem an obvious question. But, Bagley observes, "recent [2002–2003] corporate shenanigans suggest that some managers need to be reminded: If the action isn't legal, don't do it."

2. **If "Yes," Does the Proposed Action Maximize Shareholder Value?** If the action is legal, one must next ask whether it will profit the shareholders. If the answer is "yes," should you do it? Not necessarily.

3. **If "Yes," Is the Proposed Action Ethical?** As Bagley, points out, though directors and top managers may believe they are bound by corporate law to always maximize shareholder value, the courts and many state legislatures

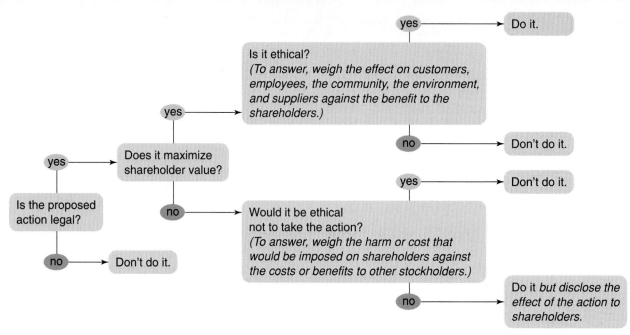

ethical decision tree is shown on the next page. *(See Figure 7.4.)*

figure 7.4

THE ETHICAL DECISION TREE: WHAT'S THE RIGHT THING TO DO?

Source: C. E. Bagley, "The Ethical Leader's Decision Tree," *Harvard Business Review,* February 2003, p. I9. Copyright © 2003 by the Harvard Business School Publishing Corporation. Reprinted with permission; all rights reserved.

have held they are not. Rather, their main obligation is to manage "for the best interests of the corporation," which includes the larger community.

Thus, says Bagley, building a profitable-but-polluting plant in a country overseas may benefit the shareholders but be bad for that country—and for the corporation's relations with that nation. Ethically, then, managers should add pollution-control equipment.

4. **If "No," Would It Be Ethical *Not* to Take the Proposed Action?** If the action would not directly benefit shareholders, might it still be ethical to go ahead with it?

Not building the overseas plant might be harmful to other stakeholders, such as employees or customers. Thus, the ethical conclusion might be to build the plant with pollution-control equipment but to disclose the effects of the decision to shareholders.

Applying the Ethical Decision Tree

Group Exercise:
Applying the Ethical Decision-
Making Tree

When IBM raised the amount of the contribution it required of its retirees to continue their health benefits, in order to save the company money, was that an ethical decision? Certainly it created a positive impact on shareholder value. However, at the same time it hurt employees, some of whom were not able to easily pay for health-related expenses. For instance, retiree Fran Asbeck, an IBM programmer for 32 years, had to get another job in order to pay for his health insurance. "I'm just going to have to work until I'm in the box and hear the dirt hit the lid," he says.[40] Retirees realize that IBM is covered legally, but they feel betrayed. "We feel that IBM has a social contract with the retirees . . . for which they are now reneging," says a former IBM employee in Vermont.[41]

As a basic guideline to making good ethical decisions on behalf of a corporation, Bagley suggests that directors, managers, and employees need to follow their own individual ideas about right and wrong. There is a lesson, she suggests, in the response of the pension fund manager who, when asked whether she would invest in a company doing business in a country that permits slavery, responded, "Do you mean me, personally, or as a fund manager?" When people feel entitled or compelled to compromise their own personal ethics to advance the interests of a business, "it is an invitation to mischief."[42]

General Moral Principles for Managers

Management consultant and writer Kent Hodgson suggests there are no absolute ethical answers for managerial decision makers. Rather, the goal for managers, he believes, should be to rely on moral principles so that their decisions are *principled, appropriate,* and *defensible.*[43] Accordingly, Hodgson has put forth what he calls "the magnificent seven" general moral principles for managers. *(See Table 7.2)* ●

table 7.2

THE MAGNIFICENT SEVEN: GENERAL MORAL PRINCIPLES FOR MANAGERS

1. **Dignity of human life: The lives of people are to be respected.** Human beings, by the fact of their existence, have value and dignity. We may not act in ways that directly intend to harm or kill an innocent person. Human beings have a right to live; we have an obligation to respect that right to life. Human life is to be preserved and treated as sacred.
2. **Autonomy: All persons are intrinsically valuable and have the right to self-determination.** We should act in ways that demonstrate each person's worth, dignity, and right to free choice. We have a right to act in ways that assert our own worth and legitimate needs. We should not use others as mere "things" or only as means to an end. Each person has an equal right to basic human liberty, compatible with a similar liberty for others.
3. **Honesty: The truth should be told to those who have a right to know it.** Honesty is also known as integrity, truth telling, and honor. One should speak and act so as to reflect the reality of the situation. Speaking and acting should mirror the way things really are. There are times when others have the right to hear the truth from us; there are times when they do not.
4. **Loyalty: Promises, contracts, and commitments should be honored.** Loyalty includes fidelity, promise keeping, keeping the public trust, good citizenship, excellence in quality of work, reliability, commitment, and honoring just laws and policies.
5. **Fairness: People should be treated justly.** One has the right to be treated fairly, impartially, and equitably. One has the obligation to treat others fairly and justly. All have the right to the necessities of life—especially those in deep need and the helpless. Justice includes equal, impartial, unbiased treatment. Fairness tolerates diversity and accepts differences in people and their ideas.
6. **Humaneness.** There are two parts: (1) **Our actions ought to accomplish good,** and (2) **we should avoid doing evil.** We should do good to others and to ourselves. We should have concern for the well-being of others; usually, we show this concern in the form of compassion, giving, kindness, serving, and caring.
7. **The common good: Actions should accomplish the "greatest good for the greatest number" of people.** One should act and speak in ways that benefit the welfare of the largest number of people, while trying to protect the rights of individuals.

Source: K. Hodgson, *A Rock and a Hard Place: How to Make Ethical Business Decisions When the Choices Are Tough* (New York: AMACOM, 1992), pp. 69–73. ©1992 Kent Hodgson. Published by AMACOM, a division of the American Management Association. Used with permission.

7.5 GROUP DECISION MAKING: HOW TO WORK WITH OTHERS

➕ major question **How do I work with others to make things happen?**

THE BIG PICTURE
Group decision making has five potential advantages and four potential disadvantages. There are a number of characteristics of groups that a manager should be aware of, as well as participative management and group problem-solving techniques.

The movies celebrate the lone heroes who, like Clint Eastwood, make their own moves, call their own shots. Most managers, however, work with groups and teams (as we discuss in Chapter 13). Although groups don't make as high-quality decisions as the best individual acting alone, research suggests that groups make better decisions than *most* individuals acting alone.[44] Thus, to be an effective manager, you need to learn about decision making in groups.

Advantages & Disadvantages of Group Decision Making

Because you may often have a choice as to whether to make a decision by yourself or to consult with others, you need to understand the advantages and disadvantages of group-aided decision making.

Advantages Using a group to make a decision offers five possible advantages.[45] For these benefits to happen, however, the group must be made up of diverse participants, not just people who all think the same way.

- **Greater pool of knowledge.** When several people are making the decision, there is a greater pool of information from which to draw. If one person doesn't have the pertinent knowledge and experience, someone else might.

- **Different perspectives.** Because different people have different perspectives—marketing, production, legal, and so on—they see the problem from different angles.

- **Intellectual stimulation.** A group of people can brainstorm or otherwise bring greater intellectual stimulation and creativity to the decision-making process than is usually possible with one person acting alone.

- **Better understanding of decision rationale.** If you participate in making a decision, you are more apt to understand the reasoning behind the decision, including the pros and cons leading up to the final step.

- **Deeper commitment to the decision.** If you've been part of the group that has bought into the final decision, you're more apt to be committed to seeing that the course of action is successfully implemented.

Disadvantages The disadvantages of group-aided decision making spring from problems in how members interact.[46]

- **A few people dominate or intimidate.** Sometimes a handful of people will talk the longest and the loudest, and the rest of the group will simply give in. Or one individual, such as a strong leader, will exert disproportional influence, sometimes by intimidation. This cuts down on the variety of ideas.

- **Groupthink.** *Groupthink* **occurs when group members strive to agree for the sake of unanimity and thus avoid accurately assessing the decision situation.** Here the positive team spirit of the group actually works against sound judgment.

- **Satisficing.** Because most people would just as soon cut short a meeting, the tendency is to seek a decision that is "good enough" rather than to push on in pursuit of other possible solutions. Satisficing can occur because groups have limited time, lack the right kind of information, or are unable to handle large amounts of information.[47]

- **Goal displacement.** Although the primary task of the meeting may be to solve a particular problem, other considerations may rise to the fore, such as rivals trying to win an argument. *Goal displacement* **occurs when the primary goal is subsumed by a secondary goal.**

What Managers Need to Know about Groups & Decision Making

If you're a manager deliberating whether to call a meeting for group input, there are four characteristics of groups to be aware of:

I. They Are Less Efficient Groups take longer to make decisions. Thus, if time is of the essence, you may want to make the decision by yourself. Faced with time pressures or the serious effect of a decision, groups use less information and fewer communication channels, which increases the probability of a bad decision.[48]

2. Their Size Affects Decision Quality The larger the group, the lower the quality of the decision.[49]

3. They May Be Too Confident Groups are more confident about their judgments and choices than individuals are. This, of course, can be a liability because it can lead to groupthink.

4. Knowledge Counts Decision-making accuracy is higher when group members know a good deal about the relevant issues. It is also higher when a group leader has the ability to weight members' opinions.[50] Depending on whether group members know or don't know one another, the kind of knowledge also counts. For example, people who are familiar with one another tend to make better decisions when members have a lot of unique information. However, people who aren't familiar with one another tend to make better decisions when the members have common knowledge.[51]

Remember that individual decisions are not *necessarily* better than group decisions. As we said at the outset, although groups don't make as high-quality decisions as the *best* individual acting alone, groups generally make better decisions than *most* individuals acting alone. Some guidelines to using groups are presented on the next page. *(See Figure 7.5.)*

Different perspectives or groupthink? A diversified team can offer differing points of view, as well as a greater pool of knowledge and intellectual stimulation. Or it can offer groupthink and satisficing. What has been your experience as to the value of decision making in the groups you've been in?

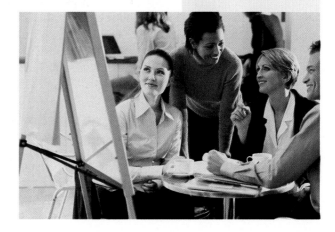

1 When it can increase quality: If additional information would increase the quality of the decision, managers should involve those people who can provide the needed information. Thus, if a type of decision occurs frequently, such as deciding on promotions or who qualifies for a loan, groups should be used because they tend to produce more consistent decisions than individuals do.

2 When it can increase acceptance: If acceptance within the organization is important, managers need to involve those individuals whose acceptance and commitment are important.

3 When it can increase development: If people can be developed through their participation, managers may want to involve those whose development is most important.

figure 7.5

WHEN A GROUP CAN HELP IN DECISION MAKING: THREE PRACTICAL GUIDELINES

The guidelines may help you as a manager decide whether to include people in a decision-making process and, if so, which people.

Source: Derived from George P. Huber, *Managerial Decision Making* (Glenview, IL: Scott Foresman, 1980), p. 149.

Participative Management: Involving Employees in Decision Making

"Only the most productive companies are going to win," says former General Electric CEO Jack Welch about competition in the world economy. "If you can't sell a top-quality product at the world's lowest price, you're going to be out of the game. In that environment, 6% annual improvement may not be good enough anymore; you may need 8% to 9%."[52]

What Is PM?   One technique that has been touted for meeting this productivity challenge is *participative management (PM),* **the process of involving employees in (a) setting goals, (b) making decisions, (c) solving problems, and (d) making changes in the organization.**[53] Employees themselves seem to want to participate more in management: in one nationwide survey of 2,408 workers, two-thirds expressed the desire for more influence or decision-making power in their jobs.[54] Thus, participative management is predicted to increase motivation, innovation, and performance because it helps employees fulfill three basic needs: autonomy, meaningfulness of work, and interpersonal contact.[55]

Is PM Really Effective?   Does participative management really work? Certainly it can increase employee job involvement, organizational commitment, and creativity, and it can lower role conflict and ambiguity.[56] Yet it has been shown that, although participation has a significant effect on job performance and job satisfaction, that effect is small—a finding that calls into question the practicality of using PM at all.[57]

So what's a manager to do? In our opinion, PM is not a quick-fix solution for low productivity and motivation. Yet it can probably be effective in certain situations, assuming that managers and employees interact constructively—that is, have the kind of relationship that fosters cooperation and respect rather than competition and defensiveness.[58]

Although participative management doesn't work in all situations, it can be effective if certain factors are present, such as supportive managers and employee trust. *(See Table 7.3, opposite page.)*

Group Problem-Solving Techniques: Reaching for Consensus

Using groups to make decisions generally requires that they reach a *consensus,* **which occurs when members are able to express their opinions and reach agreement to support the final decision.** More specifically, consensus is reached "when all

table 7.3

FACTORS THAT CAN HELP MAKE PARTICIPATIVE MANAGEMENT WORK

- **Top management is continually involved:** Implementing PM must be monitored and managed by top management.

- **Middle and supervisory managers are supportive:** These managers tend to resist PM because it reduces their authority. Thus, it's important to gain the support and commitment of managers in these ranks.

- **Employees trust managers:** PM is unlikely to succeed when employees don't trust management.

- **Employees are ready:** PM is more effective when employees are properly trained, prepared, and interested in participating.

- **Employees don't work in interdependent jobs:** Interdependent employees generally don't have a broad understanding of the entire production process, so their PM contribution may actually be counterproductive.

- **PM is implemented with TQM:** A study of Fortune 1000 firms during three different years found employee involvement was more effective when it was implemented as part of a broader total quality management (TQM) program.

Sources: P. E. Tesluk, J. L. Farr, J. E. Matheieu, and R. J. Vance, "Generalization of Employee Involvement Training to the Job Setting: Individual and Situational Effects," *Personnel Psychology,* Autumn 1995, pp. 607–632; R. Rodgers, J. E. Hunter, and D. L. Rogers, "Influence of Top Management Commitment on Management Program Success," *Journal of Applied Psychology,* February 1993, pp. 151–155; and S. A. Mohrman, E. E. Lawler III, and G. E. Ledford Jr., "Organizational Effectiveness and the Impact of Employee Involvement and TQM Programs: Do Employee Involvement and TQM Programs Work?" *Journal for Quality and Participation,* January/February 1996, pp. 6–10.

members can say they either agree with the decision or have had their 'day in court' and were unable to convince the others of their viewpoint," says one expert in decision making. "In the final analysis, everyone agrees to support the outcome."[59] This does not mean, however, that group members agree with the decision, only that they are willing to work toward its success.

One management expert offers the following dos and don'ts for achieving consensus.[60]

Toward consensus. Working to achieve cooperation in a group can tell you a lot about yourself. How well do you handle the negotiation process? What do you do when you're disappointed in a result achieved by consensus?

- **Dos:** Use active listening skills. Involve as many members as possible. Seek out the reasons behind arguments. Dig for the facts.

- **Don'ts:** Avoid log rolling and horse trading ("I'll support your pet project if you'll support mine"). Avoid making an agreement simply to keep relations amicable and not rock the boat. Finally, don't try to achieve consensus by putting questions to a vote; this will only split the group into winners and losers, perhaps creating bad feelings among the latter.

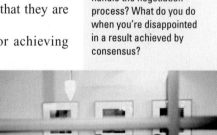

More Group Problem-Solving Techniques

Decision-making experts have developed three group problem-solving techniques to aid in problem solving: (1) *brainstorming,* (2) *nominal groups,* and (3) *Delphi groups.* These may be assisted with (4) *computer-aided decision making.*

1. Brainstorming: For Increasing Creativity *Brainstorming* is a technique used to help groups generate multiple ideas and alternatives for solving problems.[61] Developed by advertising executive A. F. Osborn, the technique consists in having members of a group meet and review a problem to be solved. Individual members are then asked to silently generate ideas or solutions, which are then collected (preferably without identifying their contributors) and written on a board or flip chart. A second session is then used to critique and evaluate the alternatives. A modern-day variation is *electronic brainstorming,* sometimes called *brainwriting,* in which members of a group come together over a computer network to generate ideas and alternatives.

2. The Nominal Group Technique: For Generating Ideas Members of a nominal group don't talk to one another—at least in the beginning. Rather, **the purpose of a *nominal group* is to generate ideas and evaluate solutions, which members do by writing down as many ideas as possible. The ideas are then listed on a blackboard, then discussed, then voted on in a secret ballot.**

During the discussion period, there may be a "30-second soapbox" format, in which every participant is allowed 30 seconds to argue for or against any idea listed. After discussion, group members may vote—anonymously—using a weighted voting procedure (for example, first choice = 3 points, second choice = 2 points, third choice = 1 point). The group leader tallies the points to determine the group's choice.[62]

3. The Delphi Group: For Consensus of Experts The Delphi group technique was originally designed for technological forecasting but now is used as a multipurpose planning tool.[63] **The *Delphi group* uses physically dispersed experts who fill out questionnaires to anonymously generate ideas; the judgments are combined and in effect averaged to achieve a consensus of expert opinion.**

The Delphi group technique is useful when face-to-face discussions are impractical. It's also practical when disagreement and conflicts are likely to impair communication, when certain individuals might try to dominate group discussions, and when there is a high risk of groupthink.[64]

4. Computer-Aided Decision Making As in nearly every other aspect of business life, computers have entered the area of decision making, where they are useful not only in collecting information more quickly but also in reducing roadblocks to group consensus.

The two types of computer-aided decision-making systems are *chauffeur driven* and *group driven,* as follows:[65]

- **Chauffeur-driven systems—for push-button consensus.** *Chauffeur-driven computer-aided decision-making systems* ask participants to answer predetermined questions on electronic keypads or dials. These have been used as polling devices, for instance, with audiences on live television shows such as *Who Wants to Be a Millionaire,* allowing responses to be computer-tabulated almost instantly.

- **Group-driven systems—for anonymous networking.** A *group-driven computer-aided decision system* involves a meeting within a room of participants who express their ideas anonymously on a computer network. Instead of talking with one another, participants type their comments, reactions, or evaluations on their individual computer keyboards. The input is projected on a large screen at the front of the room for all to see. Because participation is anonymous and no one person is able to dominate the meeting on the basis of status or personality, everyone feels free to participate, and the roadblocks to consensus are accordingly reduced.

Compared to the nominal-group technique or traditional brainstorming, group-driven systems have been shown to produce greater quality and quantity of ideas for large groups of people, although there is no advantage with groups of 4–6 people.[66] The technique also produces more ideas as group size increases from 5 to 10 members.

Problem-Solving Techniques, Pros & Cons Each of these problem-solving techniques has pros and cons.

- **Brainstorming:** Brainstorming is an effective technique for encouraging the expression of as many useful new ideas or alternatives as possible. However, it can waste time generating a lot of unproductive ideas, and it is not appropriate for evaluating alternatives or selecting solutions.

- **Nominal group technique:** The nominal group technique has been found to generate more ideas than a standard brainstorming sessions.[67] Because of the secret ballot, however, there is no way to tell why individual members voted as they did.

- **Delphi technique:** The Delphi technique is useful when face-to-face discussions are impractical, when disagreements and conflict are likely to impair communication, when certain individuals might severely dominate group discussion, and when groupthink is a probable outcome of the group process.[68] A disadvantage is that contributors can't ask questions of one another.

- **Computer-aided decision making:** Computer-aided decision making has been found to produce greater quality and quantity of ideas than either traditional brainstorming or the nominal group technique for both small and large groups of people.[69] However, other research reveals that the use of online chat groups led to decreased group effectiveness and member satisfaction and increased time to complete tasks compared with face-to-face groups.[70] ●

Traditional, face-to-face group work. This photo shows the kind of traditional arrangement we expect of groups—colleagues are seated close together in clusters to better focus on their particular projects. Do you think you'd rather work in this type of arrangement than in one that is more individually based? Why or why not?

> **✕ major question** Trying to be rational isn't always easy. What are the barriers?

THE BIG PICTURE

Responses to a decision situation may take the form of four ineffective reactions or three effective reactions. Managers should be aware of four common decision-making biases.

Do you make decisions based on how happy or unhappy you think you're going to feel about the outcome? Then here's some interesting news.

It seems that people expect certain life events to have a much greater emotional effect than in fact they do, according to Harvard University psychologist Daniel Gilbert, who has studied individual emotional barometers in decision making. College professors, for example, expect to be quite happy if they are given tenure and quite unhappy if they aren't. However, Gilbert found those who received tenure were happy but not as happy as they themselves had predicted, whereas those denied tenure did not become very unhappy.

The expectation about the level of euphoria or disappointment was also found to be true of big-jackpot lottery winners and of people being tested for HIV infection. That is, people are often right when they describe what outcome will make them feel good or bad, but they are often wrong when asked to predict how strongly they will feel that way and how long the feeling will last. "Even severe life events have a negative impact on people's sense of well-being and satisfaction for no more than three months," says one report, "after which their feelings at least go back to normal."[71]

Perhaps knowing that you have this "immune system" of the mind, which blunts bad feelings and smoothes out euphoric ones, can help make it easier for you to make difficult decisions.

How Do Individuals Respond to a Decision Situation? Ineffective & Effective Responses

What is your typical response when you're suddenly confronted with a challenge in the form of a problem or an opportunity? There are perhaps four ineffective reactions and three effective ones.[72]

Four Ineffective Reactions   There are four defective problem-recognition and problem-solving approaches that act as barriers when you must make an important decision in a situation of conflict:

1. Relaxed Avoidance—"There's no point in doing anything; nothing bad's going to happen" **In *relaxed avoidance,* a manager decides to take no action in the belief that there will be no great negative consequences.** This condition, then, is a form of complacency: You either don't see or you disregard the signs of danger (or of opportunity).

For example, you might decide to accept a job offer without checking the financial status of your new employer, even though the company is in an industry being whipsawed by technological change. After his first employer went out of business because of poor money management, programmer Bryan Galdrikian began asking prospective employers more about their finances.[73]

2. Relaxed Change—"Why not just take the easiest way out?" **In *relaxed change*, a manager realizes that complete inaction will have negative consequences but opts for the first available alternative that involves low risk.** This is, of course, a form of "satisficing"; the manager avoids exploring a variety of alternatives in order to make the best decision.

For example, if you go to the college career center, sign up for one job interview, and are offered and accept a job based on that single interview, you may have no basis for comparison to know that you made the right choice.

3. Defensive Avoidance—"There's no reason for me to explore other solution alternatives" **In *defensive avoidance*, a manager can't find a good solution and follows by (a) procrastinating, (b) passing the buck, or (c) denying the risk of any negative consequences.** This is a posture of resignation and a denial of responsibility for taking action. By procrastinating, you put off making a decision ("I'll get to this later"). In passing the buck, you let someone else take the consequences of making the decision ("Let George do it"). In denying the risk that there will be any negative consequences, you are engaging in rationalizing ("How bad could it be?").

According to one report, many college students graduating in 2004, following the 2-year recession and dismal job prospects, are doing anything but practicing defensive avoidance. Aware of the economy's inherent instability, many have taken steps that will help them find jobs with more security. Thus, when a Ford Motor Co. recruiter visited Ohio State University, he was amazed not to get the usual questions about salaries and vacations from graduating seniors. Armed with Wall Street analysts' reports, the job candidates peppered him with questions about layoff prospects and foreign competition. "They had independent research and were trying to put me on the spot," said the recruiter. "This is a level of inquiry that I didn't use to see from a bachelor of business administration."[74]

4. Panic—"This is so stressful, I've got to do something—anything—to get rid of the problem" **This reaction is especially apt to occur in crisis situations. In *panic*, a manager is so frantic to get rid of the problem that he or she can't deal with the situation realistically.** This is the kind of situation in which the manager has completely forgotten the idea of behaving with "grace under pressure," of staying cool and calm. Troubled by anxiety, irritability, sleeplessness, and even physical illness, if you're experiencing this reaction, your judgment may be so clouded that you won't be able to accept help in dealing with the problem or to realistically evaluate the alternatives.

Panic can even be life-threatening. When in 1999 a jetliner skidded off the runway at Little Rock National Airport, passenger Clark Brewster and a flight attendant tried repeatedly to open an exit door that would not budge. "About that time I hear someone say the word 'Fire!'" Brewster said. "The flight attendant bends down and says, 'Please pray with me.'" Fortunately, cooler, quicker-thinking individuals were able to find another way out.[75]

Three Effective Reactions: Deciding to Decide   In *deciding to decide,* a manager agrees that he or she must decide what to do about a problem or opportunity and take effective decision-making steps. Three ways to help you decide whether to decide are to evaluate the following:[76]

1. Importance—"How high priority is this situation?" You need to determine how much priority to give the decision situation. If it's a threat, how extensive might prospective losses or damage be? If it's an opportunity, how beneficial might the possible gains be?

2. *Credibility—"How believable is the information about the situation?"* You need to evaluate how much is known about the possible threat or opportunity. Is the source of the information trustworthy? Is there credible evidence?

3. *Urgency—"How quickly must I act on the information about the situation?"* Is the threat immediate? Will the window of opportunity stay open long? Can actions to address the situation be done gradually?

Example

Deciding to Decide: How Should PayPal React to a Possible Google Threat?

Want to buy some clothes from an online merchant you've never heard of but are afraid it might rip off your credit card or banking information? One solution is to give such details to PayPal, the San Jose, California, online-payment company, and let it make the payment, while shielding your financial privacy. To use the service, you set up an account online with PayPal with your credit card or bank account data, fill out the payment amount and the e-mail address of the merchant, and send the payment via the Internet to PayPal.

Founded in 1998 and presently controlling 24% of the U.S. online payments market, PayPal now boasts 96 million accounts with consumers. It also is expanding beyond its core business of handling transactions for its owner, eBay, the online auction service, by introducing new software and tools so both small and large vendors (such as Dell Inc. and Sharper Image) can process PayPal transactions on their own Web sites.

So after PayPal CEO Jeff Jordan learns in May 2006 that Google Inc. is building its own Internet-payment service, to be called GBuy, how does he decide to decide?

The first decision—*Should this be considered a high-priority matter?*—would seem to be obvious. After all, the threat comes from Google, the Mountain View, California, Web-search giant, which, as one writer points out, "has terrified Silicon Valley with its ability to create new consumer products and services."[77]

The second decision—*How believable is the information?*—also needs to be taken seriously. Jordan had directed PayPal employees to learn everything they could about Google's plans, not only monitoring news reports and blogs, but also gleaning details from customers who had been approached by Google. Although Google confirmed in press reports that it was building a payment service, it denied it would compete directly with PayPal. Nevertheless, Jordan decides to take the threat seriously, since in the past Google had denied it would launch such a service, only to take it back later. "We took [the Google comments] as 'Thou doth protest too much,'" says Jordan.

The answer to the final decision—*How quickly should this information be acted on?*—becomes apparent when Jordan finds out that for the last 9 months Google has been recruiting online retailers to test GBuy. He also learns that Google plans to feature an icon alongside its paid-search ads of merchants, hoping to tempt consumers to click on the ads and store their credit-card information on GBuy.

Your Call

After deciding that the Google threat is serious, real, and immediate, how would you try to reshape PayPal's business strategy, if you were the CEO?

Six Common Decision-Making Biases: Rules of Thumb, or "Heuristics"

If someone asked you to explain the basis on which you make decisions, could you even say? Perhaps, after some thought, you might come up with some "rules of thumb." Scholars call them *heuristics* (pronounced "hyur-*ris*-tiks")—strategies that simplify the process of making decisions.

Despite the fact that people use such rules of thumb all the time, that doesn't mean they're reliable. Indeed, some are real barriers to high-quality decision making. Among those that tend to bias how decision makers process information are (1) *availability,* (2) *confirmation,* (3) *representativeness,* (4) *sunk cost,* (5) *anchoring and adjustment,* and (6) *escalation of commitment.*[78]

1. The Availability Bias: Using Only the Information Available

If you had a perfect on-time work attendance record for 9 months but then were late for work 4 days during the last 2 months because of traffic, shouldn't your boss take into account your entire attendance history when considering you for a raise? Yet managers tend to give more weight to more recent behavior. This is because of the *availability bias*—**managers use information readily available from memory to make judgments.**

The bias, of course, is that readily available information may not present a complete picture of a situation. The availability bias may be stoked by the news media, which tends to favor news that is unusual or dramatic. Thus, for example, because of the efforts of interest groups or celebrities, more news coverage may be given to AIDS or to breast cancer than to heart disease, leading people to think the former are the bigger killers when in fact the latter is the biggest killer.

2. The Confirmation Bias: Seeking Information to Support One's Point of View

The *confirmation bias* **is when people seek information to support their point of view and discount data that do not.** Though this bias would seem obvious, people practice it all the time.

3. The Representativeness Bias: Faulty Generalizing from a Small Sample or a Single Event

As a form of financial planning, playing state lotteries leaves something to be desired. When, for instance, in a recent year the New York jackpot reached $70 million, a New Yorker's chance of winning was 1 in 12,913,588.[79] (A person would have a greater chance of being struck by lightning.) Nevertheless, millions of people buy lottery tickets because they read or hear about a handful of fellow citizens who have been the fortunate recipients of enormous winnings. This is an example of the *representativeness bias,* **the tendency to generalize from a small sample or a single event.**

The bias here is that just because something happens once, that doesn't mean it is representative—that it will happen again or will happen to you. For example, just because you hired an extraordinary sales representative from a particular university, that doesn't mean that same university will provide an equally qualified candidate next time. Yet managers make this kind of hiring decision all the time.

4. The Sunk Cost Bias: Money Already Spent Seems to Justify Continuing

The *sunk cost bias* or *sunk cost fallacy,* **is when managers add up all the money already spent on a project and conclude it is too costly to simply abandon it.**

Most people have an aversion to "wasting" money. Especially if large sums have already been spent, they may continue to push on with an iffy-looking project so as to justify the money already sunk into it. The sunk cost bias is sometimes called the "Concorde" effect, referring to the fact that the French and British governments continued to invest in the Concorde supersonic jetliner even when it was evident there was no economic justification for the aircraft.

5. The Anchoring & Adjustment Bias: Being Influenced by an Initial Figure

Managers will often give their employees a standard percentage raise in salary, basing the decision on whatever the workers made the preceding year. They may do this even though the raise may be completely out of alignment with what other companies are paying for the same skills. This is an instance of the *anchoring and adjustment bias,* **the tendency to make decisions based on an initial figure.**

The bias is that the initial figure may be irrelevant to market realities. This phenomenon is sometimes seen in real estate sales. A homeowner may at first list his or her house at an extremely high (but perhaps randomly chosen) selling price. The seller is then unwilling later to come down substantially to match the kind of buying offers that reflect what the marketplace thinks the house is really worth.

6. The Escalation of Commitment Bias: Feeling Overly Invested in a Decision

If you really hate to admit you're wrong, you need to be aware of the *escalation of commitment bias* **whereby decision makers increase their commitment to a project despite negative information about it.** History is full of examples of heads of state who escalated their commitment to an original decision in the face of overwhelming evidence that it was producing detrimental consequences. A noteworthy example was President Lyndon B. Johnson's pressing on of the Vietnam War despite mounting casualties abroad and political upheavals at home.

The bias is that what was originally made as perhaps a rational decision may continue to be supported for irrational reasons—pride, ego, the spending of enormous sums of money, and being "loss averse." Indeed, scholars have advanced what is known as the *prospect theory,* which suggests that decision makers find the notion of an actual loss more painful than giving up the possibility of a gain.[80] We saw a variant of this when we described the tendency of investors to hold on to their losers but cash in their winners. ●

Example

Avoiding Escalation of Commitment: L.L. Bean CEO Is Glad to Reverse Big Decision, Even at a Cost of $500,000

Most executives, like most people, tend to stick with their initial decisions because they hate to admit they were wrong, or simply because it is the path of least resistance, according to management experts. Indeed, they say, top executives are even less likely to reverse themselves because their position seems to require projecting self-assurance. This is the kind of mind-set that can lead to escalation of commitment.

Thus, Christopher McCormick, chief executive of outdoor-clothing retailer L.L. Bean, is unusual for being more concerned about making the best decision rather than being bothered about appearing wishy-washy. This makes him very much in the spirit of evidence-based decision making.

In the fall of 2004, L.L. Bean began building a call center near Waterville, Maine. A few months later, mobile-phone carrier T-Mobile USA said it would build its own call center next door, one that would house 700 or more employees. McCormick immediately ordered construction on the Bean center halted, even though $500,000 beyond the land cost had already been spent on it. A few weeks later, the company announced it would abandon the Waterville site entirely and would open a new call center about 55 miles away.

What circumstances led to this evaluation? McCormick worried that Waterville, population 16,000, didn't have enough workers to supply both companies or that employees would prefer year-round employment with T-Mobile to seasonal employment with Bean.

Your Call

Even though thousands of dollars had already been spent on the Waterville center, McCormick says he had no reservations about his decision. He said he also wanted to send a signal to other Bean executives. "I want my people to consider all the options," he said. "I don't want them to be a champion of one point of view."[81] Do you think you're capable of making such a momentous decision?

Being Aware of Your Possible Biases: How Can Your Judgment Be Distorted?

The six common decision-making biases described in the text may be expressed in more specific distortions of judgment. Here are five types of questions that you might ask yourself next time you're poised to make a decision:

"Am I Being Too Cocky?" The Overconfidence Bias

If you're making a decision in an area in which you have considerable experience or expertise, you're less likely to be overconfident. Interestingly, however, you're more apt to be overconfident when dealing with questions on subjects you're unfamiliar with or questions with moderate to extreme difficulty.[82]

In addition, many sorts of managers—especially top managers who worked their way up to the top—have a kind of overconfidence that makes them overestimate their ability to control events (the *illusion-of-control bias*).

Recommendation: When dealing with unfamiliar or difficult matters, think how your impending decision might go wrong. Afterward pay close attention to the consequences of your decision for feedback about your judgment.

"Am I Considering the Actual Evidence, or Am I Wedded to My Prior Beliefs?" The Prior-Hypothesis Bias

Do you tend to have strong beliefs? When confronted with a choice, decision makers with strong prior beliefs tend to make their decision based on their beliefs—even if evidence shows those beliefs are wrong. This is known as the *prior-hypothesis bias.* In addition, people tend to look for evidence to support their beliefs rather than contradict them.[83]

Recommendation: Although it's always more comforting to look for evidence to support your prior beliefs, you need to be tough-minded and weigh the evidence.

"Are Events Really Connected, or Are They Just Chance?" The Ignoring-Randomness Bias

Is a rise in sales in athletic shoes because of your company's advertising campaign or because it's the start of the school year? Many managers don't understand the laws of randomness and believe chance events—even multiple chance events—are connected to one another.

Recommendation: Don't attribute trends or connections to a single, random event.

"Is There Enough Data on Which to Make a Decision?" The Unrepresentative Sample Bias

If all the secretaries in your office say they prefer dairy creamer to real cream or milk in their coffee, is that enough data on which to launch an ad campaign trumpeting the superiority of dairy creamer? It might if you polled 3,000 secretaries, but not if you asked only 3 or even 30. This is too small a sample to reflect the sentiments of secretaries everywhere.

Recommendation: You need to be attuned to the importance of the size of your sample when making a decision.

"Looking Back, Did I (or Others) Really Know Enough Then to Have Made a Better Decision?" The 20-20 Hindsight Bias

Once managers know what the consequences of a decision are, they may begin to think they could have predicted it ahead of time. They can no longer recall how uncertain the circumstances were at the time they made the decision. Instead, they may remember the facts as being a lot clearer than they actually were.[84]

Recommendation: Try to keep in mind—especially when you're evaluating negative outcomes of decisions made by subordinates—that hindsight does not equal foresight.

summary

7.1 The Nature of Decision Making

- A decision is a choice made from among available alternatives. Decision making is the process of identifying and choosing alternative courses of action.

- Decisions are of two types: programmed and nonprogrammed. Programmed decisions are repetitive and routine. They tend to follow established rules and so are virtually automatic. Nonprogrammed decisions are those that occur under nonroutine, unfamiliar circumstances. Because they occur in response to unusual, unpredictable opportunities and threats, nonprogrammed decisions are relatively unstructured.

- A decision-making style reflects the combination of how an individual perceives and responds to information. Decision-making styles may tend to have a value orientation, which reflects the extent to which a person focuses on either task or technical concerns versus people and social concerns when making decisions. Decision-making styles may also reflect a person's tolerance for ambiguity, the extent to which a person has

a high or low need for structure or control in his or her life. When the dimensions of value orientation and tolerance for ambiguity are combined, they form four styles of decision making: directive, analytical, conceptual, and behavioral.

7.2 Two Kinds of Decision Making: Rational & Nonrational

- Two models managers follow in making decisions are rational and nonrational.

- In the rational model, there are four steps in making a decision: Stage 1 is identifying the problem or opportunity. A problem is a difficulty that inhibits the achievement of goals. An opportunity is a situation that presents possibilities for exceeding existing goals. This is a matter of diagnosis—analyzing the underlying causes. Stage 2 is thinking up alternative solutions. For programmed decisions, alternatives will be easy and obvious. For nonprogrammed decisions, the more creative and innovative the alternatives, the better. Stage 3 is evaluating the alternatives and selecting a solution. Alternatives should be evaluated according to cost, quality, ethics, feasibility, and effectiveness. Stage 4 is implementing and evaluating the solution chosen.

- The rational model of decision making assumes managers will make logical decisions that will be the optimum in furthering the organization's best interests. The rational model is prescriptive, describing how managers ought to make decisions. It assumes that managers have complete information and there is no uncertainty, that they can do unemotional analysis, and that they are coolly capable of making the best decision for the organization.

- Nonrational models of decision making assume that decision making is nearly always uncertain and risky, making it difficult for managers to make optimum decisions. Two nonrational models are satisficing and incremental. (1) Satisficing falls under the concept of bounded rationality—that is, that the ability of decision makers to be rational is limited by enormous constraints, such as time and money. These constraints force managers to make decisions according to the satisficing model—that is, managers seek alternatives until they find one that is satisfactory, not optimal. (2) In the incremental model, managers take small, short-term steps to alleviate a problem rather than steps that will accomplish a long-term solution.

7.3 Evidence-Based Decision Making & Analytics

- Evidence-based management means translating principles based on best evidence into organizational practice. It is intended to bring rationality to the decision-making process. Evidence-based management is based on three truths: (1) there are few really new ideas; (2) true is better than new; and (3) organizations that do simple, obvious, and even seemingly trivial things well will dominate competitors who search for silver bullets and instant magic.

- Scholars Jeffrey Pfeffer and Robert Sutton identify seven implementation principles to help companies that are committed to doing what it takes to profit from evidence-based management: (1) treat your organization as

an unfinished prototype; (2) "no brag, just facts"; (3) see yourself and your organization as outsiders do; (4) have everyone, not just top executives, be guided by the responsibility to gather and act on quantitative and qualitative data; (5) you may need to use vivid stories to sell unexciting evidence to others in the company; (6) at the very least, you should slow the spread of bad practices; and (7) you should learn from failure by using the facts to make things better.

- Applying the best evidence to your decisions is difficult, for seven reasons: (1) There's too much evidence. (2) There's not enough *good* evidence. (3) The evidence doesn't quite apply. (4) People are trying to mislead you. (5) *You* are trying to mislead you. (6) The side effects outweigh the cure. (7) Stories are more persuasive, anyway.

- Perhaps the purest application of evidence-based management is the use of analytics, or business analytics, the term used for sophisticated forms of business data analysis. Among organizations that have made a commitment to quantitative, fact-based analysis, scholars have found three key attributes: (1) They go beyond simple descriptive statistics and use data mining and predictive modeling to identify potential and most profitable customers. (2) Analytics competitors don't gain advantage from one principal application but rather from multiple applications supporting many parts of the business. (3) A companywide embrace of analytics impels changes in culture, processes, behavior, and skills for many employees, and so requires the support of top executives.

7.4 Making Ethical Decisions

- Corporate corruption has made ethics in decision making once again important. Many companies have an ethics officer to resolve ethical dilemmas, and more companies are creating values statements to guide employees as to desirable business behavior.

- To help make ethical decisions, a decision tree—a graph of decisions and their possible consequences—may be helpful. Managers should ask whether a proposed action is legal and, if it is intended to maximize shareholder value, whether it is ethical—and whether it would be ethical *not* to take the proposed action.

- A goal for managers should be to rely on moral principles so that their decisions are principled, appropriate, and defensible, in accordance with "the magnificent seven" general moral principles for managers.

7.5 Group Decision Making: How to Work with Others

- Groups make better decisions than most individuals acting alone, though not as good as the best individual acting alone.

- Using a group to make a decision offers five possible advantages: (1) a greater pool of knowledge; (2) different perspectives; (3) intellectual stimulation; (4) better understanding of the reasoning behind the decision; and (5) deeper commitment to the decision. It also has four disadvantages: (1) a few people may dominate or intimidate; (2) it will produce groupthink, when group members strive for agreement among themselves for the sake of unanimity and so avoid accurately assessing the decision situation; (3) satisficing; and (4) goal displacement, when the primary goal is subsumed to a secondary goal.

- Some characteristics of groups to be aware of are (1) groups are less efficient, (2) their size affects decision quality, (3) they may be too confident, and (4) knowledge counts—decision-making accuracy is higher when group members know a lot about the issues.

- Participative management (PM) is the process of involving employees in setting goals, making decisions, solving problems, and making changes in the organization. PM can increase employee job involvement, organizational commitment, and creativity and can lower role conflict and ambiguity.

- Using groups to make decisions generally requires that they reach a consensus, which occurs when members are able to express their opinions and reach agreement to support the final decision.

- Four problem-solving techniques aid in problem solving. (1) Brainstorming is a technique used to help groups generate multiple ideas and alternatives for solving problems. A variant is electronic brainstorming, in which group members use a computer network to generate ideas. (4) In nominal groups, members generate ideas and evaluate solutions by writing down as many ideas as possible; the ideas are then listed on a blackboard, then discussed, then voted on in a secret ballot. (3) In Delphi groups, physically dispersed experts fill out questionnaires to anonymously generate ideas; the judgments are combined and in effect averaged to achieve consensus of expert opinion. (4) In computer-aided decision making, chauffeur-driven systems may be used, which ask participants to answer predetermined questions on electronic keypads or dials, or group-driven systems may be used, in which participants in a room express their ideas anonymously on a computer network.

✖ 7.6 How to Overcome Barriers to Decision Making

- When confronted with a challenge in the form of a problem or an opportunity, individuals may respond in perhaps four ineffective ways and three effective ones.

- The ineffective reactions are as follows: (1) In relaxed avoidance, a manager decides to take no action in the belief that there will be no great negative consequences. (2) In relaxed change, a manager realizes that complete inaction will have negative consequences but opts for the first available alternative that involves low risk. (3) In defensive avoidance, a manager can't find a good solution and follows by procrastinating, passing the buck, or denying the risk of any negative consequences. (4) In panic, a manager is so frantic to get rid of the problem that he or she can't deal with the situation realistically.

- The effective reactions consist of deciding to decide—that is, a manager agrees that he or she must decide what to do about a problem or opportunity and take effective decision-making steps. Three ways to help a manager decide whether to decide are to evaluate (1) importance—how high priority the situation is; (2) credibility—how believable the information about the situation is; and (3) urgency—how quickly the manager must act on the information about the situation.

- Heuristics are rules of thumb or strategies that simplify the process of making decisions. Some heuristics or barriers that tend to bias how decision makers process information are availability, confirmation representativeness, sunk cost anchoring and adjustment, and escalation of commitment. (1) The availability bias means that managers use information readily available from memory to make judgments. (2) The confirmation bias means people seek information to support their own point of view and discount data that do not. (3) The representativeness bias is the tendency to generalize from a small sample or a single event. (4) The sunk cost bias is when managers add up all the money already spent on a project and conclude that it is too costly to simply abandon it. (5) The anchoring and adjustment bias is the tendency to make decisions based on an initial figure or number. (6) The escalation of commitment bias describes when decision makers increase their commitment to a project despite negative information about it. An example is the prospect theory, which suggests that decision makers find the notion of an actual loss more painful than giving up the possibility of a gain.

 management in action

Does the Use of Analytics Produce Better Decisions?

Business today is awash in data and data crunchers, but only certain companies have transformed this technology from a supporting tool into a strategic weapon. Their ability to collect, analyze and act on data is the essence of their competitive advantage and the source of their superior performance.

A prime example is Anheuser-Busch Companies Inc., brewer of many of the world's best-selling beers, based in St. Louis. It has made a science out of monitoring the metrics that allow it to understand when, where and why consumers buy beer—insights that have allowed the company to post double-digit profit gains for 20 straight quarters.

The core of the company's competitive capability is BudNet, a real-time network capable of gathering data on dozens of key performance indicators which the company's distributors report as they review shelves and product positioning in the field. Analysts at corporate HQ regularly analyze and mine the data for decision support.

What's more, Anheuser-Busch combines the figures it gleans from its distributors' information systems with other key data, such as U.S. Census figures on the ethnic and economic makeup of neighborhoods, allowing the company to design local promotions that match their markets to a tee.

Recently, Anheuser-Busch was the first to identify an important shift in customer purchasing preferences toward more healthy beverages, information the company harnessed to successfully capture the low-carb beer market.

Granted, organizations have been gathering massive amounts of data on customers' buying habits and the efficiency of their operational processes for decades. But

Anheuser-Busch is one of a new breed of data-driven companies that has taken analytics to a new level.

"Firms like Anheuser-Busch are outsmarting and outmaneuvering the competition because they have made information analysis and management a distinctive capability, one that is fundamental to their formula for doing business," observes Paul F. Nunes, an executive research fellow at the Accenture Institute for High Performance Business in Wellesley, Mass.

Accenture's continuing research into the components of high performance proves that information can indeed be power. The global management consultancy, technology services and outsourcing company recently surveyed 450 executives in 370 companies spread across 35 countries and 19 industries. The company identified a strong link between extensive and sophisticated use of analytics and sustained high performance.

Of the respondents, high-performance companies—businesses that Accenture research has identified on the basis of their ability to substantially and consistently outperform their competitors over the long term, over economic and industry cycles and through generations of leadership—were five times more likely than low performers to single out analytics as critical to their competitive edge.

"It's not about better number crunching, it's about reinventing a company's core value algorithm to embrace analytics and make it part of the company's distinctive capability," notes Jeanne Harris, a director of Accenture's Institute for High Performance Business who spearheaded the survey. "This focus consistently distinguishes the market leaders from the also-rans."

In addition, Accenture has identified three categories of companies that win on analytics.

"Some were born that way," Ms. Harris explains. Prime examples include Internet giants such as Google, the dominant search-engine company; Amazon, the leading online retailer; and Netflix, the pioneering online DVD rental company. Such companies were built from the ground up on new ways of capturing and analyzing data. "They correctly view their algorithms as a key weapon in their competitive arsenal."

Other companies, such as Procter & Gamble and General Electric, have a "long and proud history" of using analytics to drive high performance, Ms. Harris continues.

Finally, there are the companies that have come to embrace analytics, either as part of a turnaround strategy or a plan to dramatically change their market position. "These are the companies that have transformed themselves by harnessing technology to drive results and pull away from the competition," she says.

In line with this, Accenture has pinpointed the three approaches companies can choose from to join the ranks of analytics juggernauts.

Put simply, organizations can, first, leverage analytics to add value to their offer in the form of service improvements, such as better or more timely delivery of goods and services; second, they can develop and deliver more personalized services to their customers; or third, they can expand their participation in the value chain.

Cemex S.A., a global supplier of cement and building solutions headquartered in Monterrey, Mexico, grew from a regional player to a world leader by using analytics to deliver its products to its customers on time and on their terms.

A deep understanding of its customers—which the company gained by meticulously gathering data about its customers' needs—allowed it to identify a crucial and unmet demand: quick delivery.

Ready-mix concrete is perishable and begins to set when a truck is loaded. Cemex found that, on average, it took three hours from the receipt of a contractor's order to the delivery of the concrete. These delays were costly to contractors, whose crews were at a standstill until the concrete arrived.

To complicate matters, Mexico, like other developing countries, is plagued by traffic congestion in its major cities, making it hard for a company to accurately plan deliveries.

Cemex determined that it could charge a premium to time-pressed contractors—as well as reduce costs by decreasing the amount of concrete that hardened en route—if they could reduce delivery times.

To accomplish this, Cemex again turned to analytics, this time to collect data and study the techniques and technologies used by couriers, delivery firms, police and paramedics.

Based on this research, Cemex devised a strategy to cut response times by equipping its concrete-mixing trucks in Mexico with global-positioning satellite locators and Web-based vehicle dispatch technology. Using these systems to reconfigure its business processes allowed the company to deliver cement to its customers within a 20-minute window, boosting both productivity and customer loyalty.

For Discussion

1. Are analytics more useful for programmed or nonprogrammed decisions? Explain.
2. Which of the four steps associated with the rational model of decision making are most likely to be affected by the use of analytics? Discuss your rationale.
3. Which of the seven evidence-based decision-making implementation principles were used by Anheuser-Busch and Cemex? Provide examples to support your conclusions.
4. Would the use of analytics lead to more or less ethical decisions? Explain.
5. Why don't more companies rely on evidence-based management?

Source: Excerpted from Peggy Anne Salz, "Intelligent Use of Information Is a Powerful Corporate Tool," *The Wall Street Journal*, April 27, 2006, p. A10. Reprinted by permission of Dow Jones & Company, Inc. via The Copyright Clearance Center.

 ## self-assessment

What Is Your Decision-Making Style?

Objectives

1. To assess your decision-making style.
2. To consider the implications of your decision-making style.

Introduction

This chapter discussed a model of decision-making styles. Decision-making styles are thought to vary according to a person's tolerance for ambiguity and value orientation. In turn, the combination of these two dimensions results in four different decision-making styles (see Figure 7.1). This exercise gives you the opportunity to assess your decision-making style.

Instructions

Following are nine items that pertain to decision making. Read each statement and select the option that best represents your feelings about the issue. Remember, there are no right or wrong answers.

1. I enjoy jobs that
   a. are technical and well defined.
   b. have considerable variety.
   c. allow independent action.
   d. involve people.
2. In my job, I look for
   a. practical results.
   b. the best solutions.
   c. new approaches or ideas.
   d. a good working environment.
3. When faced with solving a problem, I
   a. rely on proven approaches.
   b. apply careful analysis.
   c. look for creative approaches.
   d. rely on my feelings.
4. When using information, I prefer
   a. specific facts.
   b. accurate and complete data.
   c. broad coverage of many options.
   d. limited data that are easily understood.
5. I am especially good at
   a. remembering dates and facts.
   b. solving difficult problems.
   c. seeing many possibilities.
   d. interacting with others.
6. When time is important, I
   a. decide and act quickly.
   b. follow plans and priorities.
   c. refuse to be pressured.
   d. seek guidance and support.
7. I work well with those who are
   a. energetic and ambitious.
   b. self-confident.

   c. open-minded.
   d. polite and trusting.
8. Others consider me
   a. aggressive.
   b. disciplined.
   c. imaginative.
   d. supportive.
9. My decisions typically are
   a. realistic and direct.
   b. systematic or abstract.
   c. broad and flexible.
   d. sensitive to the needs of others.

Scoring & Interpretation

Score the exercise by giving yourself one point for every time you selected an A, one point for every B, and so on. Add up your scores for each letter. Your highest score represents your dominant decision-making style. If your highest score was A, you have a directive style; B = analytical; C = conceptual; and D = behavioral. See the related material in this chapter for a thorough description of these four styles.

Questions

1. What are your highest- and lowest-rated styles?
2. Do the results accurately reflect your self-perceptions? Explain.
3. What are the advantages and disadvantages of your style? Discuss.
4. Which of the other decision-making styles is least consistent with your style? How might you work more effectively with someone who has this style? Discuss.

Adapted from A. J. Rowe, J. D. Boulgarides, and M. R. McGrath, *Managerial Decision Making* (Chicago: SRA, 1984).

 group exercise

Ethical Decision Making

Objectives

1. To look at the stages in practical decision making.
2. To gain practice in ethical decision making.

Introduction

In this chapter you learned there are four stages in making practical decisions. The third stage involves evaluating alternatives and selecting a solution. Part of this evaluation entails deciding whether the solution is ethical. The purpose of this exercise is to examine the stages in practical decision making and consider the issue of ethical decision making.

Instructions

Break into groups of five or six people and read the following case. As a group discuss the decision made by the company and answer the questions for discussion at the end of the case. Before answering questions 5–6, brainstorm alternative decisions the managers at TELECOMPROS could have made. Finally, the entire class can reconvene and discuss the alternative solutions that were generated.

The Case

For large cellular service providers, maintaining their own customer service call center can be very expensive. Many have found they can save money by outsourcing their customer service calls to outside companies.

TELECOMPROS is one such company. It specializes in cell phone customer service, saving large cellular companies money by eliminating overhead costs associated with building a call center, installing additional telephone lines, and so on. Once TELECOMPROS is hired by large cellular service providers, TELECOMPROS employees are trained on the cellular service providers' systems, policies, and procedures. TELECOMPROS derives its income from charging a per-hour fee for each employee.

Six months ago, TELECOMPROS acquired a contract with Cell2U, a large cellular service provider serving the western United States. At the beginning of the contract, Cell2U was very pleased. As a call center, TELECOMPROS has a computer system in place that monitors the number of calls the center receives and how quickly the calls are answered. When Cell2U received its first report, the system showed that TELECOMPROS was a very productive call center and handled the call volume very well. A month later, however, Cell2U launched a nationwide marketing campaign. Suddenly, the call volume increased and TELECOMPROS customer service reps were unable to keep up. The phone-monitoring system showed that some customers were on hold for 45 minutes or longer, and at any given time throughout the day there were as many as 50 customers on hold. It was clear to Cell2U that the original number of customer service reps they had contracted for was not enough. They renegotiated with upper management at TELECOMPROS and hired additional customer service reps. TELECOMPROS managers were pleased because they were now receiving more money from Cell2U for the extra employees, and Cell2U was happy because the call center volume was no longer overwhelming and its customers were happy with the attentive customer service.

Three months later, though, TELECOMPROS customer service supervisors noticed a decrease in the number of customer service calls. It seemed that the reps had done such a good job that Cell2U customers had fewer problems. There were too many people and not enough calls; with little to do, some reps were playing computer games or surfing the Internet while waiting for calls to come in.

Knowing that if Cell2U analyzed its customer service needs it would want to decrease the number of reps to save money, TELECOMPROS upper management made a decision. Rather than decrease its staff and lose the hourly pay from Cell2U, upper management told customer service supervisors to call the customer service line. Supervisors called in and spent enough time on the phone with reps to ensure that the computer registered the call and the time it took to "resolve" the call. They would then hang up and call the call center again. Thus, TELECOMPROS did not have to decrease its customer service reps, and Cell2U continued to pay for the allotted reps until the end of the contract.

Questions for Discussion

1. Was the decision made by TELECOMPROS an ethical one? Why or why not?
2. What stages in the Practical Decision-Making Process did TELECOMPROS managers skip? Describe and explain.
3. Which of the Nonrational Models of Decision Making did managers at TELECOMPROS follow? Explain.
4. Which of the hindrances to rational decision making listed in Figure 7.3 explain the decision made by TELECOMPROS managers? Explain.
5. What is your recommended solution? Explain why you selected this alternative.
6. How would you implement your preferred solution? Describe in detail.

 ethical dilemma

Should the Principal of Westwood High Allow an Exception to the Graduation Dress Code?

This dilemma involves a situation faced by Helen Riddle, the principal of Westwood High School in Mesa, Ariz. Westwood High has 225 Native American students, including 112 from the Salt River Pima-Maricopa Indian Community, most of which lies within the boundaries of the Mesa Unified School District. Districtwide there are 452 Native American high school students, 149 of whom are from the Salt River Reservation.

Here is the situation: Native American students asked the principal if they could be allowed to wear eagle feathers during their graduation ceremony. Although this may seem like a reasonable request given these students' customs and traditions, Westwood High had a rule stating that, according to a newspaper report, "students were only allowed to wear a traditional cap and gown for graduation, with no other adornments or clothing, including military uniforms. The rules were based on past practice and tradition at schools, not school board policy."

Advocates for the Native American students argued that students should be allowed to wear the eagle feathers because they represent a significant achievement in the lives of those individuals. In contrast, one school board member opposed the exception to the rule because "it would open the door for other students wanting to display symbols of their own culture or background."

Solving the Dilemma

What would you do if you were the principal of Westwood High?

1. Allow the Native American students to wear the eagle feathers now and in the future. This shows an appreciation for diversity.

2. Do not allow the Native American students to wear the eagle feathers because it violates an existing rule. Allowing an exception opens the door for additional requests about changing the dress code. How will you defend one exception over another?

3. Allow the students to wear the eagle feathers only in this year's ceremony, then form a committee to review the dress code requirements.

4. Invent other options. Discuss.

Souce: Excerpted from J. Kelley, "Westwood Students Get OK for Eagle Feathers," *The Mesa Republic*, May 25, 2006, p. 15.

 video case

Living Room Café

As the video case opens, partners Jonas Goldberg and Rande Gedaliah exchange greetings. In addition to being business partners, Rande and Jonas are long-time friends. Rande is under increasing stress and doesn't feel that Jonas is "holding up his end" of running the business. Jonas agrees. His spouse is extra busy at work, and he is taking on greater child-care responsibilities. But after all, they always agreed that their families would come first. However, Rande's family life is also affected.

Jonas has missed several meetings. He had "things to do" and felt confident that Rande could handle anything that arose. He twice missed payroll deadlines, delaying salary payments to employees. According to Jonas this is not a significant issue. Jonas feels he can accomplish his normal workload, it just might not be on the tight schedule that Rande is expecting. "It will all get done anyway." However, Rande feels the work is getting done because she is picking up the slack, causing her to be "totally stressed out." Rande senses a lack of concern for both their friendship and the business. She suggests a solution: find a partner to buy Jonas's share of the business. However, at this important juncture Jonas abruptly ends the meeting.

Privately Rande expresses frustration at the tone of the meeting, acknowledging that Jonas is likely frustrated as well. Jonas's goals have changed, and he is no longer taking an active interest in the business. She sees no hope of salvaging the partnership and would rather retain their friendship. Saving both no longer seems possible.

When Rande and Jonas reconvene, Jonas puts forth a proposal. He will "bow out gracefully" and sell his share of the business. For Jonas as well, maintaining their friendship is important. So far, the two partners are in agreement. However, a major point of contention arises. Jonas wants complete control over the choice of

buyer, with the intention to sell to the highest bidder. Rande strongly opposes this idea, because the buyer would be her day-to-day partner. She should have total control over that decision and legally has the right of first refusal. Rande has reviewed their contract and consulted with their attorneys, but Jonas is unaware of the legal ramifications. Jonas doesn't want to leave Rande with an undesirable partner but still feels he has the right to sell to whomever he pleases. The discussion becomes heated, and again Jonas must abruptly leave to attend to family business. However, at least the friends have agreed that their partnership can no longer continue.

Privately Rande reflects on Jonas's proposal. With certainty, she states, "we will not be partners." Rande also perceives that the situation has been influenced by their gender differences and that she has been forced into the mother-like role of disciplinarian. Perhaps a female partner would be a better choice, because they would likely have more similar communication and management styles.

Discussion Questions

1. Are Rande and Jonas experiencing functional or dysfunctional conflict? Support your response with evidence from the case.

2. Critique Rande and Jonas's decision-making process thus far. What might they do to improve this process?

3. Jonas is clearly attempting to maintain a comfortable balance between work and family life. Suggest how he might more successfully maintain this balance.

4. Did gender differences play a role in this situation? Support your answer with evidence from the case.

Chapter 8

Organizational Culture, Structure, & Design
Building Blocks of the Organization

Major Questions You Should Be Able to Answer

8.1 What Kind of Organizational Culture Will You Be Operating In?
Major Question: How do I find out about an organization's "social glue," its normal way of doing business?

8.2 Developing High-Performance Cultures
Major Question: What can be done to an organization's culture to increase its economic performance?

8.3 What Is an Organization?
Major Question: How are for-profit, nonprofit, and mutual-benefit organizations structured?

8.4 The Major Elements of an Organization
Major Question: When I join an organization, what seven elements should I look for?

8.5 Basic Types of Organizational Structures
Major Question: How would one describe the eight organizational structures?

8.6 Contingency Design: Factors in Creating the Best Structure
Major Question: What factors affect the design of an organization's structure?

8.7 Toward Building a Learning Organization
Major Question: Why do organizations resist learning, and what is a new way for employees in an organization to view themselves?

Mentoring: The New Rules

Who's going to help you learn the ropes in a new organization? Maybe you need a mentor.

If you can find an experienced employee to mentor you—to be your organizational sponsor and help you understand and navigate the organization's culture and structure—it can be a great asset to your career. Indeed, mentoring may be especially useful for female and minority managers, for whom there may be fewer role models within their particular organizations. One survey of 4,561 respondents from 42 countries found that 46% felt that coaching or mentoring had a great impact and 45% a moderate impact on their career success.[1]

What's the best advice about acquiring a mentor? Here are some of the new rules.[2]

- **Choose anyone you can learn from, not just someone higher up:** It used to be thought that a mentor should be a seasoned manager higher up in the organization. But a mentor can also be a peer—someone at your own level inside the organization.

- **Choose more than one mentor:** It might be nice to have a single mentor who can give you lots of one-on-one attention. But everyone's busy, so look around and see if there are two or three people who might be helpful to you. "Diversify your mentor portfolio," goes one piece of advice.

- **Pick your mentors, don't wait to be picked:** Don't wait for organizational veterans to select you to be their protégé. It's up to you to make the first move, to be assertive in a nice way.

- **Do a self-assessment:** Before you begin contacting people to be mentors, assess where you want to go and what skills and knowledge you need to get there, so that you'll know the kind of help you need.

- **Look for someone different from you:** It used to be thought the mentor and mentee should have a lot in common, as in personal chemistry or personal style. But someone who is different from you will challenge you and help you be more objective.

- **Investigate your prospects:** Before approaching prospective mentors, call their administrative assistants, explain your plans, and ask what their bosses are like to work with. Find out the best time to approach them.

- **Show your prospective mentor how you can be helpful:** "Mentoring is a two-way street," says Anne Hayden, senior vice president of Metropolitan Life insurance company. "The person being mentored gets help, advice, and coaching, and the person doing the mentoring generally gets extra effort—someone very committed to working on special projects or on assignments that maybe don't fall within the boxes on the organizational chart."[3]

- **Agree on how your mentoring relationship will work:** In your first meeting, set the ground rules for how frequently you will meet and the type of contact, such as whether it will be in the office, over lunch, or at the gym. A minimum of one meeting a month is recommended, and in between the two of you should keep in touch by phone and e-mail.

For Discussion Mentoring has taken a new twist. The CEO of California-based Freedom Communications, Scott Flanders, has told his managers that they can't afford to constantly offer advice and guidance to their staffs. "We can't tolerate mediocrity," he says, "but we have to presume the competence of employees—and then, when we're disappointed, spend time coaching and training," or weed out failures. On the other hand, Stanford business professor Jeffrey Pfeffer, advocate of evidence-based management, cautions that "it's penny wise and pound foolish" for companies not to want managers to train and mentor employees—that such firms are simply muddling along, hoping their staffs will somehow be self-reliant.[4] If you were a boss, how would you handle mentoring? If you were a new employee, how would you want to be helped?

forecast

What's Ahead in This Chapter

In this chapter, we consider organizational cultures and why they are important. We then consider the three types of organizations and seven basic characteristics of an organization. We next consider eight types of organizational structures. We look at five factors that should be considered when one is designing the structure of an organization. Finally, we describe the characteristics of a learning organization, why people resist learning, and what a manager can do to help build a learning organization.

8.1 WHAT KIND OF ORGANIZATIONAL CULTURE WILL YOU BE OPERATING IN?

✳ major question How do I find out about an organization's "social glue," its normal way of doing business?

THE BIG PICTURE

The study of organizing, the second of the four functions in the management process, begins with a study of organizational culture, which exists on two levels, invisible and visible. An organizational culture has four functions.

Want to get ahead in the workplace but hate the idea of "office politics"?

Probably you can't achieve the first without mastering the second. Although hard work and talent can take you a long way, "there is a point in everyone's career where politics becomes more important," says management professor Kathleen Kelley Reardon. You have to know the political climate of the company you work for, says Reardon, who is author of *The Secret Handshake* and *It's All Politics.*[5] "Don't be the last person to understand how people get promoted, how they get noticed, how certain projects come to attention. Don't be quick to trust. If you don't understand the political machinations, you're going to fail much more often."[6]

A great part of learning to negotiate the politics—that is, the different behavioral and psychological characteristics—of a particular office means learning to understand the organization's *culture.* The culture consists not only of the slightly quirky personalities you encounter but also all of an organization's normal way of doing business.

What Is an Organizational Culture?

According to scholar **Edgar Schein,** *organizational culture,* **sometimes called** *corporate culture,* **is a system of shared beliefs and values that develops within an organization and guides the behavior of its members.**[7] This is the "social glue" that binds members of the organization together. Just as a human being has a personality—fun-loving, warm, uptight, competitive, or whatever—so an organization has a "personality," too, and that is its culture. For instance, at Pfizer Pharmacy, the Connecticut pharmaceutical company, drug discovery is a high-risk,

Risky business. In the organizational culture of Pfizer Pharmacy, failure and disappointment are taken for granted.

costly endeavor in which hundreds of scientists screen thousands of chemicals against specific disease targets, but 96% of these compounds are ultimately found to be unworkable. The culture, then, is one of managing failure and disappointment, of helping drug researchers live for the small victories. Thus, says one account, "when a researcher publishes a paper, or when a lab gets some positive results on a new therapy, it's trumpeted throughout the organization."[8] The corporate culture at Houston energy trader Enron was said to have been a "very arrogant place, with a feeling of invincibility," according to whistleblower Sherron Watkins.[9] In some unhealthy corporate cultures, so-called passive-aggressive organizations, more effort is expended on thwarting things than starting them—but in the nicest way.[10]

Culture can vary considerably, with different organizations having differing emphases on risk taking, treatment of employees, teamwork, rules and regulations, conflict and criticism, and rewards. And the sources of these characteristics also vary. They may represent the strong views of the founders, of the reward systems that have been instituted, of the effects of competitors, and so on.[11]

The Two Levels of Culture: Invisible & Visible

Culture exists on two levels—invisible and visible.

The Invisible Level: The Core Culture
The invisible level is the *core culture,* which consists of values, beliefs, and assumptions. These underlying beliefs and values are so widely shared that they are rarely discussed. Considered "the right way to behave," the core culture is followed nearly automatically—indeed, people feel threatened when their assumptions are challenged, often saying, "That's the way it's always been done here."

The invisible culture often has two sources: (1) the vision, assumptions, and biases of the organization's founders and (2) the outlook that the initial employees learned from their own experiences of the formative years.[12] For example, the founders of technology company Hewlett-Packard stressed a collegial, egalitarian culture that gave as much authority and job security to employees as possible. When a new CEO, Carleton (Carly) Fiorina, joined the company, she arranged a merger with computer maker Compaq that resulted in massive layoffs—a direct challenge to the company's cherished "HP Way" culture of trying to keep employees on.[13] (In the end, because of a lack of focus and vision, the Fiorina strategy failed and she had to step down.)

HP founders. David Packard (left) and William Hewlett created a close-knit organizational culture that gave a lot of authority and job security to Hewlett-Packard employees.

The Visible Level: The Observable Culture   The *visible level* is the *observable culture,* which—besides such obvious manifestations as slogans, office layout, and manner of dress—is expressed in symbols, stories, heroes, and rites and rituals.[14]

- **Symbols. A *symbol* is an object, act, quality, or event that conveys meaning to others.** In an organization, symbols convey its most important values. For instance, 3M has a trophy known as the Gold Step award, which is presented every year to employees whose new products achieve significant revenue levels.

- **Stories. A *story* is a narrative based on true events, which is repeated—and sometimes embellished—to emphasize a particular value.** Stories are oral histories that are told and retold by members about the organization's history.

     An example is the one told at Home Depot about the irate customer who called the Tampa store a couple of days before Christmas to complain that they had delivered a carpet that was way too small. The store delivered the right size of carpet via air freight the next day—which happened to be December 24th—and the installation was completed by midday, just in time for Christmas Eve.[15]

- **Heroes. A *hero* is a person whose accomplishments embody the values of the organization.** The accomplishments of heroes, past and present, are put forth to motivate other employees to do the right thing.

     For instance, famed pro football coach Vince Lombardi took over the losing Green Bay Packers in 1959 and forged a juggernaut team that won five championships in the next 9 years. Although he was reputed to be tough, he was also patient, teaching quarterbacks fewer plays than his predecessor had but with more options within each play, which he explained so they would not feel confused or overwhelmed. Along with each play, he presented its logic. "They call it coaching, but it is teaching," he said. "You do not just tell them it is so, but you show them the reasons why it is so, and you repeat and repeat until they are convinced, until they know."[16]

- **Rites and rituals. *Rites and rituals* are the activities and ceremonies, planned and unplanned, that celebrate important occasions and accomplishments in the organization's life.**

     Of course, military units have long known the value of rites and rituals, which is why ceremonies awarding decorations and medals are so important. Sports teams, too, appreciate the importance of awards ceremonies recognizing winners and "most valuable player." But many companies, too, have rites and rituals.

     Mary Kay, Inc., for instance, annually hosts five back-to-back conventions attended by 50,000 independent Beauty Consultants to recognize and reward its top producers for outstanding achievements in sales and recruiting. The founder, the late Mary Kay Ash, would personally present the best salespeople with jewelry, trips, and pink Cadillacs—items still awarded today.[17]

The Importance of Culture

Culture can powerfully shape an organization's long-term success.

"If employees know what their company stands for, if they know what standards they are to uphold, then they are much more likely to make decisions that will support those standards," write management experts Terrence Deal and Alan Kennedy. "They are also more likely to feel as if they are an important part of the organization. They are motivated because life in the company has meaning for them."[18] Much the same thing could be said for employees in nonprofit organizations.

figure 8.1

FOUR FUNCTIONS OF ORGANIZATIONAL CULTURE

Source: Adapted from discussion in L. Smircich, "Concepts of Culture and Organizational Analysis," *Administrative Science Quarterly,* September 1983, pp. 339–58. Copyright © 1983 Johnson Graduate School of Management, Cornell University. Reprinted with permission.

An organization's culture has four functions.[19] *(See Figure 8.1, above.)*

I. It Gives Members an Organizational Identity At Southwest Airlines, for instance, top executives constantly reinforce the company's message that workers should be treated like customers, and they continually celebrate employees whose contributions go beyond the call of duty.[20]

2. It Facilitates Collective Commitment Consider 3M, one of whose corporate values is to be "a company that employees are proud to be part of." This collective commitment results in a turnover rate of less than 3% among salaried personnel. "I'm a 27-year 3Mer because, quite frankly, there's no reason to leave," says one manager. "I've had great opportunities to do different jobs and to grow a career. It's just a great company."[21]

3. It Promotes Social-System Stability The more effectively conflict and change are managed within an organization and the more that employees perceive the work environment to be positive and reinforcing, the more stable the social system within the organization. At 3M, social stability is encouraged by promoting from within, by hiring capable college graduates in a timely manner, and by providing displaced workers 6 months to find new jobs.

4. It Shapes Behavior by Helping Employees Make Sense of Their Surroundings The culture helps employees understand why the organization does what it does and how it intends to accomplish its long-term goals. 3M sets expectations for innovation, for example, by having an internship and co-op program, which provides 30% of the company's new college hires.

Sometimes culture can be strong enough to take the place of structure; that is, the expectations of the culture replace formal rules and regulations. In these cases, the sense of orderliness and predictability that employees look to for guidance are provided by the culture rather than by a rule book. ●

How to Stand Out in a New Job: Fitting into an Organization's Culture in the First 90 Days

"As an ambitious 22-year-old readying to enter the corporate world, how can I quickly distinguish myself as a winner?" asked Dain Zaitz of Corvallis, Oregon.

"Once you are in the real world—and it doesn't make any difference if you are 22 or 62, starting your first job or your fifth," answered *BusinessWeek* columnists Jack and Suzy Welch, "the way to look great and get ahead is to overdeliver."[22]

This means that, among other things, when you take a new job, it's important to go into it with a sense of urgency and make the first 90 days really count by overdelivering on the tasks asked of you (while at the same time curbing the expression of personal ambition so you won't alienate other people by seeming to be an unrestrained striver). Overdelivering means doing more than what is asked of you—not just doing the report your boss requests, for example, but doing the extra research to provide him or her with something truly impressive.

As the Welches put it, "Do the extra legwork and data-crunching to give her something that really expands her thinking—an analysis, for instance, of how the entire industry might play over the next three years. What new companies and products might emerge? What technologies could change the game?"

Here are a few things, among others, you should do in the first 3 months.[23]

Get to Know Some People & Listen to What They Have to Say

During the first 2 weeks, get to know a few people and try to have lunch with them. Find out how the organization works, how people interact with the boss, what the corporate culture encourages and discourages. Your role here is to listen, rather than to slather on the charm. Realize that you have a lot to learn.

Be Aware of the Power of First Impressions

Within 3 minutes of meeting someone new, people form an opinion about where the future of the relationship is headed, according to one study.[24] (Actually, first im-

pressions can be formed as quickly as 1/20th of a second, according to a study of human reactions to Web pages.)[25]

Roger Ailes, CEO of Fox News and former top Republican strategist, points out that 7 seconds are all people need to start making up their minds about you, so this is the period in which to make a good first impression. "When meeting someone for the first time, concentrate on one thing: your energy level," Ailes says. Amp it up. "If you don't demonstrate energetic attitude on your first day, you're already screwing up."[26] And don't wear a poker face, Ailes advises. Be warm and open, which is generally perceived as being stronger and less afraid. Finally, dress at or above the conservative median for the company.

Note: If you feel you've blown it in trying to make a positive first impression on someone, don't be too distressed. What's key, research shows, is making sure you have second, third, and fourth chances to meet that person so that you can show different sides of yourself.[27]

Make It Easy for Others to Give You Feedback

Ask your boss, co-workers, and subordinates to give you feedback about how you're doing. Be prepared to take unpleasant news gracefully. "Don't get defensive," advises Lois P. Frankel, author of *Overcoming Your Strengths.* "It's not other people's job to tell you how to correct your performance."[28]

At the end of 30 days, have a "How am I doing?" meeting with your boss. And review how your job differs from the initial job description and what opportunities you might pursue.

Overdeliver

Because performance reviews for new-hires generally take place at 60–90 days, you need to have accomplished enough—and preferably something big—to show your boss your potential. In other words, do as the Welches suggest: overdeliver.

Delighted to meet you. When meeting someone new, how much time do you take to start forming an impression about them? About 7 seconds? What cues do you look for?

8.2 DEVELOPING HIGH-PERFORMANCE CULTURES

What can be done to an organization's culture to increase its economic performance?

 major question

THE BIG PICTURE

Three perspectives have been suggested to explain why an organization's culture can enhance the firm's economic performance: strength, fit, and adaptive. There are many ways in which a particular culture can become embedded in an organization, 11 of which are described here.

What does a company do when the growth of its most successful product starts slowing down? This was the situation that confronted financial software maker Intuit Inc., as we shall see. How successfully an organization reacts depends on its culture.

Cultures for Enhancing Economic Performance: Three Perspectives

What types of organizational culture can increase an organization's economic performance in terms of increasing competitiveness and profitability? Three perspectives have been proposed: (1) strength, (2) fit, and (3) adaptive.

1. The Strength Perspective: Success Results When a Firm Has a Strong Culture
The *strength perspective* **assumes that the strength of a corporate culture is related to a firm's long-term financial performance.** A culture is said to be "strong" when employees adhere to the organization's values because they believe in its purpose. A culture is said to be "weak" when employees are forced to adhere to the organization's values through extensive procedures and bureaucracies. The strength perspective embraces the point of view that strong cultures create goal alignment, employee motivation, and the appropriate structure and controls needed to improve organizational performance.[29]

The downside of a strong culture, critics believe, is that such financial success can so reinforce cultural norms that managers and employees become arrogant, inwardly focused, and resistant to change, with top managers becoming blinded to the need for new strategic plans. Example: A case could be made that the strong cultures of American auto makers for many years made them resistant to the need to make radical adjustments.

2. The Fit Perspective: Success Results When Culture Fits with the Firm's Business Context
The *fit perspective* **assumes that an organization's culture must align, or fit, with its business or strategic context.** A "correct" fit is expected to foster higher financial performance.

Example: Prior to the arrival of Carleton Fiorina, Hewlett-Packard's "HP Way" culture from 1957 to the early 1990s pushed authority as far down as possible in the organization and created an environment that emphasized integrity, respect for individuals, teamwork, innovation, and an emphasis on customers and community improvement. This fit perspective was a key contributor to HP's success—until the high-technology industry began to change in the late 1990s.[30]

3. The Adaptive Perspective: Success Results When Culture Helps the Firm Adapt
The *adaptive perspective* **assumes that the most effective cultures help organizations anticipate and adapt to environmental changes.**

Which Perspective Is Accurate?
An investigation of 207 companies from 22 industries during the years 1977–1988 partly supported the strength and fit perspectives. However, findings were completely consistent with the adaptive perspective. Long-term financial performance was highest for organizations with an adaptive culture.[32]

Intuit Demonstrates an Adaptive Culture

Intuit Inc. of Mountain View, California is well known as the maker of finance software, such as TurboTax, QuickBooks, and Quicken. In 2003, however, the company's culture began to change, especially at Quicken, where sales had begun to stall as online banking reduced the need for software for managing personal finances. Peter Karpas, who was then in charge of Quicken Solutions Group, began spurring his staff to think of innovative ideas beyond just simply improving their core software program. He identified several people who had "that entrepreneurial spark," then challenged them to "Find something that excites you, go forward, and answer these questions."

One of them was engineering manager Dan Robinson, father to a son, Zane, who had been born in 2000 with a rare genetic disorder that required open heart surgery, an operation on his stomach, and other treatment. For 6 months, Robinson and his wife were so overwhelmed that they paid little attention to the medical bills arriving almost daily. "When Robinson finally sat down with the file box of papers he had accumulated," says a *Business-Week* account, "among them were a $100,000 bill for Zane's heart surgery that had not been sent to his insurance company, threatening letters about charges he had never received, and dozens of 'explanation of benefits' statements from his insurer that he couldn't match to any bills."[31]

To keep track of everything, Robinson thereupon sat down and wrote a software program. In doing so, he came to the realization that there were probably many other people with health problems who needed something like it. In the fall of 2003, he pitched his idea to Karpas. Robinson and a partner, Kate Welker, were given time and resources to visit dozens of people to see how they handled their health care bills and statements. They found that people would spend hours to get even a few dollars out of their insurers, and they wanted some way to assert control over their medical paperwork.

Eventually Medical Expense Manager was born, and it was quickly adopted by a select group of people dealing with serious medical matters. So far it is only a modest money maker by Intuit's standards, but the company is convinced that it could revolutionize health care.

Your Call

Do you think most organizations are capable of being adaptable under changing circumstances? What does it take to implant a culture of adaptability within an organization?

Eleven Ways Cultures Become Embedded in Organizations

Those who found a business, and the managers who follow them, essentially use a teaching process to embed the values, beliefs, expectations, behaviors, and business philosophy that constitute the organization's culture. Among the mechanisms used are the following.[33]

I. Formal Statements The first way to embed preferred culture is through the use of formal statements of organizational philosophy, mission, vision, values, as well as materials used for recruiting, selecting, and socializing employees. Example: Wal-Mart founder Sam Walton stated that three basic values represented the core of the retailer's culture: (1) respect for the individual, (2) service to customers, and (3) striving for excellence.[34]

2. Slogans & Sayings The desirable corporate culture can be expressed in language, slogans, sayings, and acronyms. Example: Bank One's slogan, "Whatever it takes," encourages employees to do whatever it takes to exceed customer expectations.

3. Stories, Legends, & Myths As with the stories and heroes we mentioned earlier as signs of the visible culture, stories, legends, or myths about key people and events can be used to implant desirable organizational values. Example: Jim Sinegal, founder and CEO of multibillion-dollar Costco, doesn't distance himself from his employees. He even wears a name tag that just says "Jim," and he could easily be mistaken for a stock clerk. His philosophy is simple: "We have said from the very beginning," he says, "'We're going to be a company that's on a first-name basis with everyone.'" He even answers his own phone. "If a customer's calling and they have a gripe," he says, "don't you think they kind of enjoy the fact that I picked up the phone and talked to them?"[35]

4. Leader Reactions to Crises   How top managers respond to critical incidents and organizational crises sends a clear cultural message. Example: Canadian Dov Charney got into the clothing business as a college student, when he would buy thousands of T-shirts at Kmart, then import them via a U-Haul truck into Canada. Then he dropped out of college, borrowed $10,000 from his father, and moved to South Carolina to manufacture clothes—just at a time when the rest of the garment industry found it was cheaper to make clothing overseas. Charney filed for bankruptcy but then moved his company to California, determined to make it work. "I knew I could do it differently, and I knew I could turn it around," he said. "Passion" is the key to success. "When you believe in what you're doing, that's the first thing. And you have to be resilient, because people are going to try to knock you down." Today his company, American Apparel, has 4,000 employees. And it does something other garment makers have abandoned: it makes all its clothing in the United States.[36]

5. Role Modeling, Training, & Coaching   Managers can use role modeling, training programs, teaching, and coaching to demonstrate the organizational culture they want to promote. Example: To role model the corporate value of "having fun," Southwest Airlines CEO Gary Kelly showed up at a Halloween party dressed as Gene Simmons, front man for the rock group Kiss.[37]

6. Physical Design   Another means of embedding culture is through the design of physical space, work environments, and buildings. Example: By building a one-floor facility, insurance company Acordia Inc. encouraged interactive workflow procedures and interactions among team members, as well as more positive morale.[38]

7. Rewards, Titles, Promotions, & Bonuses   Offering explicit rewards, status symbols, promotions, and bonuses are traditional ways used by managers to reinforce desirable organizational behavior. Example: Putnam Investments CEO Charles Haldeman wanted to encourage his mutual fund managers to aim for reliable returns rather than for occasional spectacular returns, as had been the goal in the go-go 1990s. Accordingly, bonuses were given to managers whose funds ranked in the top half of their categories each year—and they received not a penny more for edging their funds into the top 10%, as they once did.[39]

8. Organizational Goals & Performance Criteria   Many organizations establish organizational goals and criteria for recruiting, selecting, developing, promoting, dismissing, and retiring people, all of which reinforce the desired organizational culture. Example: PepsiCo sets challenging goals that reinforce a culture aimed at high performance.

9. Measurable & Controllable Activities   There are a number of activities, processes, or outcomes that an organization's leaders can pay attention to, measure, and control that can foster a certain culture. Example: ExxonMobil's credo is "efficiency in everything we do," so that managers make a concerted effort to measure, control, and reward cost efficiency. As a result, the company is famous for delivering consistent returns, regardless of whether the price of oil is up or down.[40]

10. Organizational Structure   The hierarchical structure found in most traditional organizations is more likely to reinforce a culture oriented toward control and authority compared to the flatter organization that eliminates management layers in favor of giving employees more power. Example: The hierarchical structure of a railroad provides a much different culture from that of the former "spaghetti" organization of Danish hearing-aid maker Oticon, described in Chapter 2.

11. Procedures for Self-Development   Companies may set up procedures to reinforce employee self-development to align with organizational goals. Example: Credit card company Capital One has a program in which employees can learn how to develop themselves, with individual objectives being aligned with corporate goals and with performance being reinforced by appropriate rewards, coaching, and evaluations.[41] ●

8.3 WHAT IS AN ORGANIZATION?

THE BIG PICTURE

The organizational structure of the three types of organizations—for-profit, nonprofit, and mutual-benefit—may be expressed vertically or horizontally on an organization chart.

The changing organization. For-profit Time Warner was once known as AOL Time Warner, but in 2003 it dropped AOL from its name. Like other media companies, it also changed its corporate vision, separating or casting off parts of itself that it had previously consolidated in the hopes that divisions such as its Internet empire could be fed by its other media divisions.

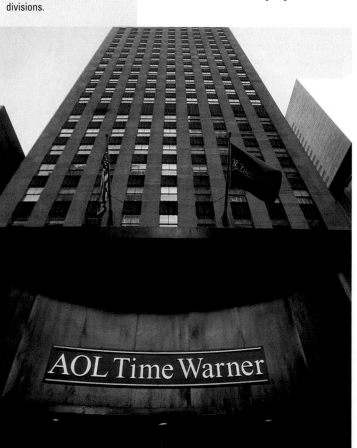

According to **Chester I. Barnard's** classic definition, **an *organization* is a system of consciously coordinated activities or forces of two or more people.**[42] By this definition, a crew of two coordinating their activities to operate a tuna fishing boat is just as much an organization as the entire StarKist Tuna Co.—assuming the two fishers are catching tuna for a living and not just for fun.

The Organization: Three Types

As we stated in Chapter 1, there are three types of organizations classified according to the three different purposes for which they are formed:[43]

- **For-profit organizations.** These are formed to make money, or profits, by offering products or services.
- **Nonprofit organizations.** These are formed to offer services to some clients, not to make a profit (examples: hospitals, colleges).
- **Mutual-benefit organizations.** These are voluntary collectives whose purpose is to advance members' interests (examples: unions, trade associations).

Clearly, you might have an occupation (such as auditor or police officer) that is equally employable in any one of these three sectors. As a manager, however, you would be principally required to focus on different goals—making profits, delivering public services, or satisfying member needs—depending on the type of organization.

The Organization Chart

Whatever the size or type of organization, it can be represented in an organization chart. **An *organization chart* is a box-and-lines illustration showing the formal lines of authority and the organization's official positions or work specializations.** This is the

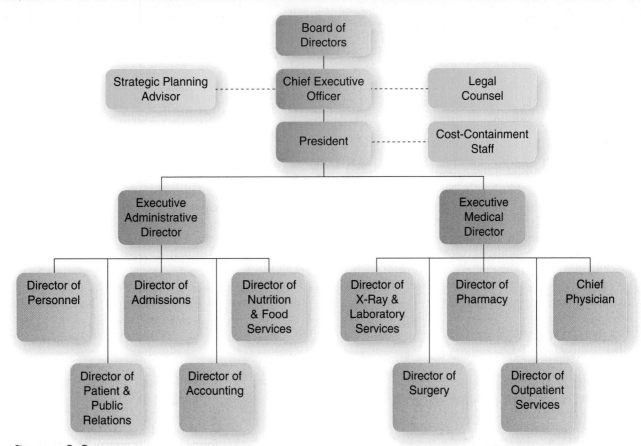

figure 8.2

ORGANIZATION CHART

Example for a hospital

family-tree-like pattern of boxes and lines posted on workplace walls and given to new hires. *(See Figure 8.2, above.)*

Two kinds of information that organization charts reveal about organizational structure are (1) the *vertical hierarchy of authority*—who reports to whom, and (2) the *horizontal specialization*—who specializes in what work.

The Vertical Hierarchy of Authority: Who Reports to Whom   A glance up and down an organization chart shows the *vertical hierarchy,* the chain of command. A formal vertical hierarchy also shows the official communication network— who talks to whom. In a simple two-person organization, the owner might communicate with just a secretary or an assistant. In a complex organization, the president talks principally to the vice presidents, who in turn talk to the assistant vice presidents, and so on.

The Horizontal Specialization: Who Specializes in What Work   A glance to the left and right on the line of an organization chart shows the *horizontal specialization,* the different jobs or work specialization. The husband-and-wife partners in a two-person desktop-publishing firm might agree that one is the "outside person," handling sales, client relations, and finances, and the other is the "inside person," handling production and research. A large firm might have vice presidents for each task—marketing, finance, and so on. ●

Practical Action

When Should You Delegate & When Not? Using Your Authority Wisely

Failure to delegate can happen even with high-powered executives, including those you might least suspect—such as the president of Harvard University. Dr. Neil L. Rudenstine, who became president of Harvard in 1991, initially became so exhausted from overwork that he had to stay home for 2 weeks to recover. The incident sent a message that his future survival would depend on his ability to set priorities and delegate responsibility.[44]

There are many reasons why managers fail to delegate.[45] An excessive need for perfection. A belief that only they should handle "special," "difficult," or "unusual" problems or clients. A wish to keep the parts of a job that are fun. A fear that others will think them lazy. A reluctance to let employees lower down in the hierarchy take risks. A worry that subordinates won't deliver. A concern that the subordinates will do a better job and show them up.

If you find yourself often behind, always taking work home, doing your subordinates' work for them, and constantly having employees seeking your approval before they can act, you're clearly not delegating well. "To do more in a day, you must do less—not do everything faster," says productivity expert Odette Pollar.

How do you decide when to delegate and when not to? Here are some guidelines:[46]

Delegation. For delegation to be effective, workers must be able to function independently. Managers often depend on assistants doing independent—and careful—supporting work to help them attain their more important goals.

Delegate Routine & Technical Matters

Always try to delegate routine tasks and routine paperwork. When there are technical matters, let the experts handle them.

Delegate Tasks That Help Your Subordinates Grow

Let your employees solve their own problems whenever possible. Let them try new things so they will grow in their jobs.

Don't Delegate Confidential & Personnel Matters

Any tasks that are confidential or that involve the evaluation, discipline, or counseling of subordinates should never be handed off to someone else.

Don't Delegate Emergencies

By definition, an emergency is a crisis for which there is little time for solution, and you may have to handle this yourself.

Don't Delegate Special Tasks That Your Boss Asked You to Do—Unless You Have His or Her Permission

If your supervisor entrusts you with a special assignment, such as attending a particular meeting, don't delegate it unless you have permission to do so.

Match the Tasks Delegated to Your Subordinates' Skills & Abilities

While recognizing that delegation involves some risk, make your assignments appropriate to the training, talent, skills, and motivation of your employees.

Finally, be prepared to live with a less-than-perfect result.

8.4 THE MAJOR ELEMENTS OF AN ORGANIZATION

When I join an organization, what seven elements should I look for?

major question

THE BIG PICTURE

Seven basic elements or features of an organization are described in this section.

Whether for-profit, nonprofit, or mutual-benefit, organizations have a number of elements in common. We discuss four proposed by an organizational psychologist, then describe three others that most authorities agree on.

Common Elements of Organizations: Four Proposed by Edgar Schein

Organizational psychologist **Edgar Schein** proposed the four common elements of (1) *common purpose,* (2) *coordinated effort,* (3) *division of labor,* and (4) *hierarchy of authority.*[47] Let's consider these.

I. Common Purpose: The Means for Unifying Members   An organization without purpose soon begins to drift and become disorganized. **The *common purpose* unifies employees or members and gives everyone an understanding of the organization's reason for being.**

2. Coordinated Effort: Working Together for Common Purpose   The common purpose is realized through *coordinated effort,* **the coordination of individual efforts into a group or organization-wide effort.** Although it's true that individuals can make a difference, they cannot do everything by themselves.

3. Division of Labor: Work Specialization for Greater Efficiency   *Division of labor,* **also known as *work specialization,* is the arrangement of having discrete parts of a task done by different people.** Even a two-person crew operating a fishing boat probably has some work specialization—one steers the boat, the other works the nets. With division of labor, an organization can parcel out the entire complex work effort to be performed by specialists, resulting in greater efficiency.

4. Hierarchy of Authority: The Chain of Command   The *hierarchy of authority,* or *chain of command,* **is a control mechanism for making sure the right people do the right things at the right time.** If coordinated effort is to be achieved, some people—namely, managers—need to have more authority, or the right to direct the work of others. Even in member-owned organizations, some people have more authority than others, although their peers may have granted it to them.

Test Your Knowledge:
Allocating Authority

In addition, authority is most effective when arranged in a hierarchy. Without tiers or ranks of authority, a lone manager would have to confer with everyone in his or her domain, making it difficult to get things done. Even in newer organizations that flatten the hierarchy, there still exists more than one level of management.

Finally, a principle stressed by early management scholars was that of ***unity of command,* in which an employee should report to no more than one manager** in order to avoid conflicting priorities and demands. Today, however, with advances in computer technology and networks, there are circumstances in which it makes sense for a person to communicate with more than one manager (as is true, for instance, with the organizational structure known as the matrix structure, as we'll describe).

Common Elements of Organizations: Three More That Most Authorities Agree On

To Schein's four common elements we may add three others that most authorities agree on: (5) *span of control,* (6) *authority, responsibility, and delegation,* and (7) *centralization versus decentralization of authority.*

5. Span of Control: Narrow (or Tall) versus Wide (or Flat)   The *span of control, or span of management,* **refers to the number of people reporting directly to a given manager.**[48] There are two kinds of spans of control, narrow (or tall) and wide (or flat).

Narrow Span of Control   This means a manager has a limited number of people reporting—three vice presidents reporting to a president, for example, instead of nine vice presidents. An organization is said to be *tall* when there are many levels with narrow spans of control.

Wide Span of Control   This means a manager has several people reporting—a first-line supervisor may have 40 or more subordinates, if little hands-on supervision is required, as is the case in some assembly-line workplaces. An organization is said to be *flat* when there are only a few levels with wide spans of control.

Historically, spans of five or seven subordinates were considered best, but there is no consensus as to what is ideal. In general, when managers must be closely involved with their subordinates, as when the management duties are complex, they are advised to have a narrow span of control. This is why presidents tend to have only a handful of vice presidents reporting to them. By contrast, first-line supervisors directing subordinates with similar work tasks may have a wide span of control.

The recent emphasis on lean management staffs and more efficiency has meant that spans of control need to be as wide as possible while still providing adequate supervision. Wider spans also fit in with the trend toward allowing workers greater autonomy in decision making.

6. Authority, Responsibility, & Delegation: Line versus Staff Positions   Male sea lions have to battle other males to attain authority over the herd. In human organizations, however, authority is related to the management authority in the organization; it has nothing to do with the manager's fighting ability or personal characteristics. With authority goes *accountability, responsibility,* and the ability to *delegate* one's authority.

Accountability   **Authority refers to the rights inherent in a managerial position to make decisions, give orders, and utilize resources.** (Authority is distinguished from *power,* which, as we discuss in Chapter 14, is the extent to which a person is able to influence others so they respond to orders.) In the military, of course, orders are given with the expectation that they will be obeyed, disobedience making one liable to a dishonorable discharge or imprisonment. In civilian organizations, disobeying orders may lead to less dire consequences (demotion or firing), but subordinates are still expected to accept that a higher-level manager has a legitimate right to issue orders.

Authority means *accountability*—**managers must report and justify work results to the managers above them.** Being accountable means you have the responsibility for performing assigned tasks.

Responsibility   With more authority comes more responsibility. **Responsibility is the obligation you have to perform the tasks assigned to you.** A car assembly-line worker has little authority but also little responsibility: just install those windshields over and over. A manager, however, has greater responsibilities.

It is a sign of faulty job design when managers are given too much authority and not enough responsibility, in which case they may become abusive to subordinates and capricious in exerting authority.[49] Conversely, managers may not be given enough authority, so the job becomes difficult.

Delegation   **Delegation is the process of assigning managerial authority and responsibility to managers and employees lower in the hierarchy.** To be more efficient, most managers are expected to delegate as much of their work as possible.

However, a business entrepreneur may fall into the common trap of perfection, believing, as one writer puts it, that "you are the only person who can handle a given situation, work with a special client, design a program."[50] But a surprising number of managers fail to realize that delegation is an important part of their job.

Regarding authority and responsibility, the organization chart distinguishes between two positions, *line* and *staff*. *(See Figure 8.3.)*

figure 8.3

LINE AND STAFF

Line have solid lines, staff have dotted lines.

Line Position **Line managers have authority to make decisions and usually have people reporting to them.** Examples: the president, the vice presidents, the director of personnel, and the head of accounting. Line positions are indicated on the organization chart by a *solid line* (usually a vertical line).

Staff Position **Staff personnel have authority functions; they provide advice, recommendations, and research to line managers** (examples: specialists such as legal counsels and special advisors for mergers and acquisitions or strategic planning). Staff positions are indicated on the organization chart by a *dotted line* (usually a horizontal line).

7. Centralization versus Decentralization of Authority Who makes the important decisions in an organization? That is what the question of centralization versus decentralization of authority is concerned with.

Centralized Authority **With *centralized authority*, important decisions are made by higher-level managers.** Very small companies tend to be the most centralized, although nearly all organizations have at least some authority concentrated at the top of the hierarchy. Kmart and McDonald's are examples of companies using this kind of authority.

An advantage in using centralized authority is that there is less duplication of work, because fewer employees perform the same task; rather, the task is often performed by a department of specialists. Another advantage of centralization is that procedures are uniform and thus easier to control; all purchasing, for example, may have to be put out to competitive bids.

Decentralized Authority **With *decentralized authority*, important decisions are made by middle-level and supervisory-level managers.** Here, obviously, power has been delegated throughout the organization. Among the companies using decentralized authority are General Motors and Harley-Davidson.

An advantage in having decentralized authority is that managers are encouraged to solve their own problems rather than to buck the decision to a higher level. In addition, decisions are made more quickly, which increases the organization's flexibility and efficiency. ●

8.5 BASIC TYPES OF ORGANIZATIONAL STRUCTURES

⊕ major question How would one describe the eight organizational structures?

THE BIG PICTURE

Eight types of organizational structures are simple, functional, divisional, conglomerate, hybrid, matrix, team-based, and network.

Small firm. What type of organizational structure is best suited to a local floral shop? Should the number of employees influence the decision?

figure 8.4

SIMPLE STRUCTURE: AN EXAMPLE

There is only one hierarchical level of management beneath the owner.

Culture and structure are often intertwined. When in 1997 the Federal Railroad Administration (FRA) sent inspectors to Union Pacific's headquarters in Omaha, Nebraska, to examine why the railroad had had a series of fatal accidents, they learned that the company had a top-down, military-style hierarchy and culture that seemed to discourage teamwork and communication. The antiquated style of management had its roots in the days when railroads' executive ranks were filled with combat-hardened former Civil War officers. "When something happened," said a railroad vice president explaining the attitude of leading by fear, "you pulled out your gun and shot the guy in charge of the territory." Said the head of the FRA of Union Pacific's dysfunctional working arrangements, "They were separated from each other in a way that almost guaranteed problems."[51]

We may categorize the arrangements of organizations into eight types of structures: (1) *simple,* (2) *functional,* (3) *divisional,* (4) *conglomerate,* (5) *hybrid,* (6) *matrix,* (7) *team-based,* and (8) *network.*

1. The Simple Structure: For the Small Firm

The first organizational form is the simple structure. This is the form often found in a firm's very early, entrepreneurial stages, when the organization is apt to reflect the desires and personality of the owner or founder. **An organization with a *simple structure* has authority centralized in a single person, a flat hierarchy, few rules, and low work specialization.** *(See Figure 8.4, at left.)*

There are hundreds of thousands of organizations that are arranged according to a simple structure—for instance, small mom 'n' pop firms running landscaping, construction, insurance sales, and similar businesses. Some of these firms, of course, grow into larger organizations with different kinds of structures. Both Hewlett-Packard and Apple Computer began as two-man garage startups that later became large.

2. The Functional Structure: Grouping by Similar Work Specialties

The second organizational form is the functional structure. **In a *functional structure,* people with similar occupational specialties are put together in formal groups.** This is a quite commonplace structure, seen in all kinds of organizations, for-profit and nonprofit. *(See Figure 8.5, opposite page.)*

A manufacturing firm, for example, will often group people with similar work skills in a Marketing Department, others in a Production Department, others in Finance, and so on. A nonprofit educational institution might group employees according to work specialty under Faculty, Admissions, Maintenance, and so forth.

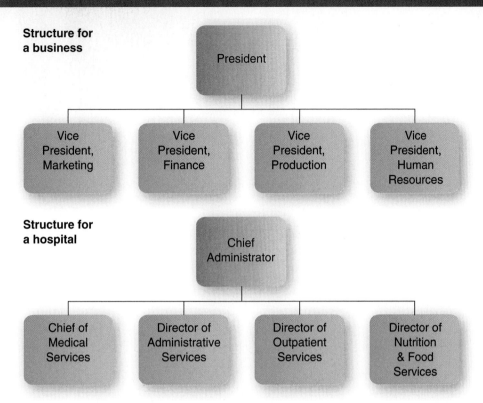

Structure for a business

President

- Vice President, Marketing
- Vice President, Finance
- Vice President, Production
- Vice President, Human Resources

Structure for a hospital

Chief Administrator

- Chief of Medical Services
- Director of Administrative Services
- Director of Outpatient Services
- Director of Nutrition & Food Services

figure 8.5

FUNCTIONAL STRUCTURE: TWO EXAMPLES

This shows the functional structure for a business and for a hospital.

3. The Divisional Structure: Grouping by Similarity of Purpose

The third organizational form is the divisional structure. **In a *divisional structure*, people with diverse occupational specialties are put together in formal groups by similar products or services, customers or clients, or geographic regions.** *(See Figure 8.6, next page.)*

Product Divisions: Grouping by Similar Products or Services ***Product divisions* group activities around similar products or services.** For instance, the media giant Time Warner has different divisions for magazines, movies, recordings, cable television, and so on. The Warner Bros. part of the empire alone has divisions spanning movies and television, a broadcast network, retail stores, theaters, amusement parks, and music.

Customer Divisions: Grouping by Common Customers or Clients ***Customer divisions* tend to group activities around common customers or clients.** For instance, Ford Motor Co. has separate divisions for passenger-car dealers, for large trucking customers, and for farm products customers. A savings and loan might be structured with divisions for making consumer loans, mortgage loans, business loans, and agricultural loans.

Geographic Divisions: Grouping by Regional Location ***Geographic divisions* group activities around defined regional locations.** This arrangement is frequently used by government agencies. The Federal Reserve Bank, for instance, has 12 separate districts around the United States. The Internal Revenue Service also has several districts.

figure 8.6

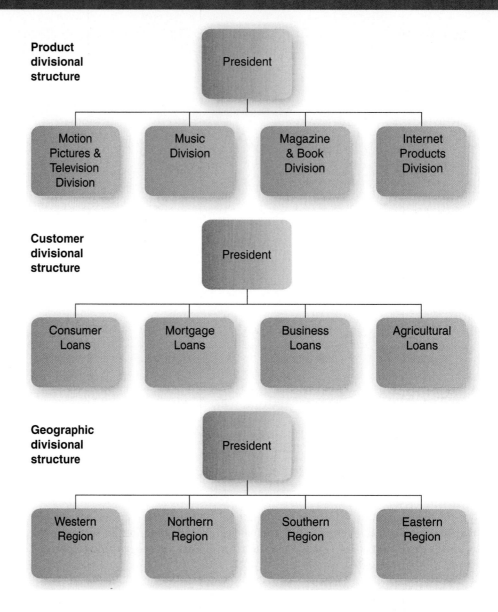

4. The Conglomerate Structure: Grouping by Industry

A large-scale variant on the divisional structure is the conglomerate structure. A *conglomerate* is a large company that is doing business in different, quite unrelated areas. For example, Tyco International has electronics, fire and security, health care, plastics and adhesives, and engineered products and services. **The *conglomerate structure* groups divisions or business units around similar businesses or industries.** *(See Figure 8.7.)*

figure 8.7

CONGLOMERATE STRUCTURE

This resembles the structure of Tyco International.

5. The Hybrid Structure: Functional & Divisional Used within the Same Organization

The fifth organizational form is the hybrid structure. **In a *hybrid structure*, an organization uses functional and divisional structures in different parts of the same organization.** *(See Figure 8.8.)*

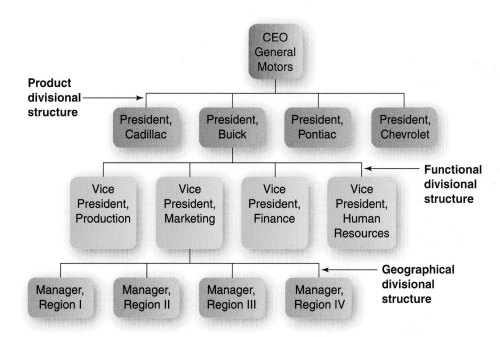

figure 8.8

HYBRID STRUCTURE

Hypothetical example of General Motors

Many different kinds of possible hybrid structures exist. One example is General Motors, which at the top rung of the hierarchy could be organized into product (or customer) divisions: Cadillac, Buick, Pontiac, Chevrolet. (Oldsmobile was recently discontinued.) Within each product division, there could be a functional division according to type of work. Thus, Buick would be organized into Production, Marketing, Finance, Human Resources. Each functional division in turn is organized into a geographical division. Thus, Marketing would be organized into Region I, Region II, Region III, and Region IV.

6. The Matrix Structure: A Grid of Functional & Divisional for Two Chains of Command

The sixth organizational form is the matrix structure. **In a *matrix structure,* an organization combines functional and divisional chains of commands in a grid so that there are two command structures—vertical and horizontal.** The functional structure usually doesn't change—it is the organization's normal departments or divisions, such as Finance, Marketing, Production, and Research & Development. The divisional structure may vary—as by product, brand, customer, or geographic region.*(See Figure 8.9.)*

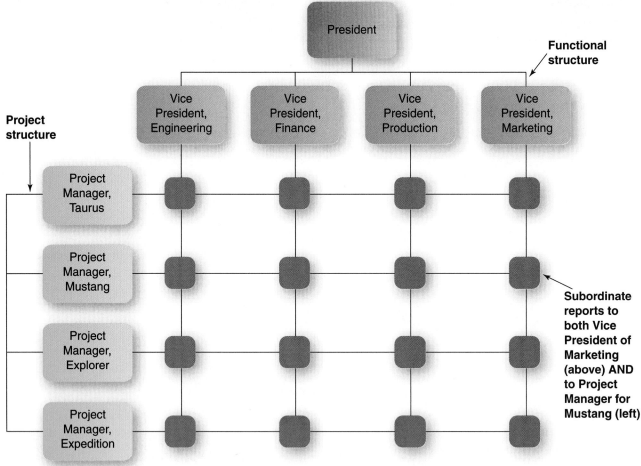

figure 8.9

MATRIX STRUCTURE

An example of an arrangement that Ford might use.

For example, the functional structure might be the departments of Engineering, Finance, Production, and Marketing, each headed by a vice president. Thus, the reporting arrangement is vertical. The divisional structure might be by product (the new models of Taurus, Mustang, Explorer, and Expedition, for example), each headed by a project manager. This reporting arrangement is horizontal. Thus, a marketing person, say, would report to *both* the Vice President of Marketing *and* to the Project Manager for the Ford Mustang. Indeed, Ford Motor Co. used the matrix approach to create the Taurus and a newer version of the Mustang.

7. The Team-Based Structure: Eliminating Functional Barriers to Solve Problems

The seventh organizational form is the team-based structure. **In a *team-based structure*, teams or workgroups, either temporary or permanent, are used to improve horizontal relations and solve problems throughout the organization.**[52] When managers from different functional divisions are brought together in teams—known as cross-functional teams—to solve particular problems, the barriers between the divisions break down. The focus on narrow divisional interests yields to a common interest in solving the problems that brought them together. Yet team members still have their full-time functional work responsibilities and still formally report to their own managers above them in the functional-division hierarchy. *(See Figure 8.10.)*

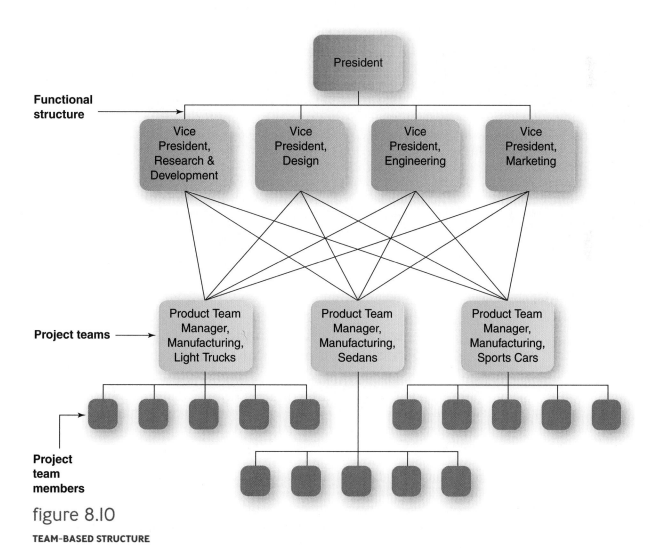

figure 8.10

TEAM-BASED STRUCTURE

This shows a mix of functional and team arrangements.

Use of a Team-Based Structure: Designing Motorola's RAZR Cell Phone

In early 2003, the mood was grim at Motorola, which had watched rival cell phone maker Nokia leap to No. I worldwide in market share on the basis of its "candy bar" phone designs. But engineers in Motorola's concept-phone unit had a vision for something different, having produced a mock-up of what was described as "an impossibly thin phone—at ten millimeters . . . half the girth of a typical flip-flop" cell phone.[53] Engineer Roger Jellicoe was told to pull a team together and produce the thinnest phone ever released—and to do it within a year in order to make a splash by handing it out as a high-end niche product to celebrities at the February 2004 Academy Awards.

Eventually the team grew to as many as 20 engineers, who met daily in a conference room in Motorola's Libertyville, Illinois, office, to deliberate over how to cram a checklist of components—antenna, speaker, keypad, camera, display, light source, and so on—into minimal space. Operating as a skunkworks that kept the project secret even from their colleagues, the team members used materials and techniques that Motorola had never tried before and threw out accepted models of what a cell phone was supposed to look and feel like. "In short," says a *Fortune* account, "the team that created the RAZR broke the mold, and in the process rejuvenated the company."

As engineers worked on the components, industrial designer Chris Arnholt worked on the look, rendering designs onto a page and then letting another designer translate them info three-dimensional computer graphics, which model makers could use to craft plastic mockups. Nearly every activity came down to a trade-off of functionality versus thinness, which eventually led to two compromises: the phone exceeded the original targeted size by about an eighth of an inch and the team missed the February 2004 deadline.

When the RAZR was finally unveiled in a splashy presentation in July, it became an instant hit. And the company realized that the product it had designed to be a high-priced, high-end jewel had mass market appeal.

Your Call

The team approach, known as *concurrent engineering* or *integrated product development,* has been found to speed up the design of new products because all the specialists meet at once, instead of separately doing their own thing, then handing off the result to the next group of specialists. Indeed, the team-based structure has even been applied successfully by Boeing to the design of its 777 jumbo jet. Can you think of circumstances in which the old-fashioned nonteam approach would probably work better?

8. The Network Structure: Connecting a Central Core to Outside Firms by Computer Connections

In the eighth organizational form, **network structure, the organization has a central core that is linked to outside independent firms by computer connections, which are used to operate as if all were a single organization.** Corporations using this structure are sometimes called *virtual corporations* or *virtual organizations,* as we mentioned in Chapter 2.[54] *(See Figure 8.11, opposite page.)*

"The notion of where a corporation starts and stops is going to be very different in the future," said a Hewlett-Packard chief information officer and vice president. "Your expertise might be harvesting timber or processing lumber, but you also need to move your product to the construction industry. Traditionally, we brought all those steps together in a soup-to-nuts operation. Now, given [network structures], someone else can run your truck fleet, but it will still operate like your own fleet."[55]

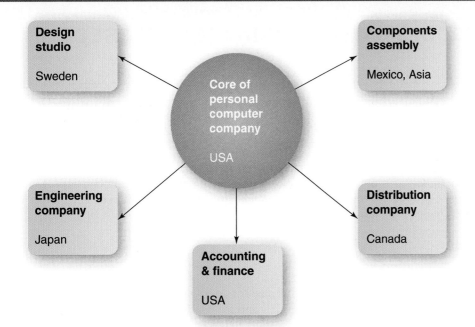

figure 8.11

NETWORK STRUCTURE

This is an example of a personal computer company.

Design studio

Sweden

Core of personal computer company

USA

Components assembly

Mexico, Asia

Engineering company

Japan

Distribution company

Canada

Accounting & finance

USA

With a network structure, an organization can become a *boundaryless organization,* as we described in Chapter 2, operating with extensive, even worldwide operations, yet its basic core can remain small, thus keeping payrolls and overhead down. The glue that holds everything together is information technology, along with strategic alliances and contractual arrangements with supplier companies. ●

Self Assessment Exercise:
Identify Your Preferred Organizational Structure

Example

Network Structure: MySQL Manages a Virtual Worldwide Workforce

MySQL (pronounced "my S-Q-L") is a $40 million software maker that employs 320 workers in 25 countries, 70% of whom work from home. Although Thomas Basil, MySQL's director of support, operates from his basement home office in Baltimore, he keeps his clocks set 7 hours ahead to Helsinki time, the time zone of many of his team members.

Employees stay in touch through Internet Relay Chat (IRC), which acts as a companywide chatroom, as well as Skype, which allows them to make free voice calls over the Internet—"and just as important," adds writer Josh Hyatt, "to keep themselves from perishing in what can quickly intensify into . . . e-mail storms."[56] As Basil says, "Voice is more personal than text and more helpful in building real understanding."

A virtual, boundaryless company like MySQL operates differently from a traditional company, with managers learning to evaluate people and give feed-back differently. "Productivity is measured strictly by output; mushy factors like charisma don't pertain in cyberspace," says Hyatt. "The company has developed software called Worklog, which requires employees to check off tasks as they finish them." As might be expected, the company hires strictly for skill, not "the ability to play nicely with others."

Your Call

Many people like the social interaction that comes with working in a physical office with other people. Others, however, are turned off by the "office politics" and time-wasting activities that seem to be a necessary concomitant and welcome the opportunity to do task-oriented work in a makeshift home office, occasionally having to cope with loneliness and restlessness. Which would you favor?

8.6 CONTINGENCY DESIGN: FACTORS IN CREATING THE BEST STRUCTURE

> ## ✖ major question
> ## What factors affect the design of an organization's structure?

THE BIG PICTURE

Five factors affecting an organization's structure are whether its environment is mechanistic or organic, whether its environment stresses differentiation or integration, and size, technology, and life cycle.

Frontier Airlines. Denver's hometown carrier, Frontier Airlines, is in a competitive struggle with Southwest Airlines, which entered its market in early 2006. One of the strategies Frontier uses to cut costs and keep fares down is to employ a mostly nonunion workforce to hustle planes through gates.

What is the optimal size for an organization? How big is too big?

"The real growth and innovation in this country," said famed management consultant Peter F. Drucker, "has been in medium-size companies that employ between 200 and 4,000 workers." Despite the informality, smaller than 200 is not necessarily better. "If you are in a small company, you are running all out," Drucker pointed out. "You have neither the time nor the energy to devote to anything but yesterday's crisis." A medium-size company, by contrast, "has the resources to devote to new products and markets, and it's still small enough to be flexible and to move fast. And these companies now have what they once lacked—they've learned how to manage."[57]

When managers are considering what organizational arrangements to choose from, size is one of several factors, or *contingencies,* to consider. Recall from Chapter 2 that the *contingency approach* to management emphasizes that a manager's approach should vary according to—that is, be contingent on—the individual and environmental situation. Thus, the manager following the contingency approach simply asks, "What method is the best to use under these particular circumstances?" **The process of fitting the organization to its environment is called *contingency design.***

Managers taking a contingency approach must consider the following factors in designing the best kind of structure for their particular organization at that particular time:

1. *Environment—mechanistic versus organic*
2. *Environment—differentiation versus integration*
3. *Size*
4. *Technology*
5. *Life cycle*

I. The Environment: Mechanistic versus Organic Organizations—the Burns & Stalker Model

"Here every job is broken down into the smallest of steps, and the whole process is automated," wrote *BusinessWeek* correspondent Kathleen Deveny, reporting about a day she spent working in a McDonald's restaurant. "Anyone could do this, I think."[58]

Actually, Deveny found that she fell behind in, say, bagging French fries, but it was certainly the intention of McDonald's guiding genius Ray Kroc that, in fact, nearly anyone *should* be able to do this—and that a Big Mac should taste the same anywhere. Thus, for example, procedure dictates that a hamburger is always dressed the same way: first the mustard, then the ketchup, then two pickles.

McDonald's is a hugely successful example of what British behavioral scientists **Tom Burns** and **G. M. Stalker** call a *mechanistic organization,* as opposed to an *organic organization.*[59] *(See Table 8.1.)*

Could anyone do this? McDonald's follows the model of a mechanistic organization.

table 8.1

MECHANISTIC VERSUS ORGANIC ORGANIZATIONS

Mechanistic Organizations	Organic Organizations
Centralized hierarchy of authority	Decentralized hierarchy of authority
Many rules and procedures	Few rules and procedures
Specialized tasks	Shared tasks
Formalized communication	Informal communication
Few teams or task forces	Many teams or task forces
Narrow span of control, taller structures	Wider span of control, flatter structures

Test Your Knowledge:
Mechanistic vs Organic Organizational Structure

Mechanistic Organizations: When Rigidity & Uniformity Work Best In a *mechanistic organization,* **authority is centralized, tasks and rules are clearly specified, and employees are closely supervised.** Mechanistic organizations, then, are bureaucratic, with rigid rules and top-down communication. This kind of structure is effective at McDonald's because the market demands uniform product quality, cleanliness, and fast service.

In general, mechanistic design works best when an organization is operating in a stable environment. Yet new companies that have gone through a rough-and-tumble start-up period may decide to change their structures so that they are more mechanistic, with clear lines of authority.

Organic Organizations: When Looseness & Flexibility Work Best In an *organic organization,* **authority is decentralized, there are fewer rules and procedures, and networks of employees are encouraged to cooperate and respond quickly to unexpected tasks.** Tom Peters and Robert Waterman called this kind of organization a "loose" structure.[60]

Organic organizations are sometimes termed "adhoc-racies" because they operate on an ad hoc basis, improvising as they go along. As you might expect, information-technology companies such as Motorola favor the organic arrangement because they constantly have to adjust to technological change—yet so also do companies that need to respond to fast-changing consumer tastes, such as clothing retailer The Worth Collection, which operates as a virtual company offering high-end women's clothing through direct selling in people's homes.[61]

2. The Environment: Differentiation versus Integration—the Lawrence & Lorsch Model

Burns and Stalker's ideas were extended in the United States by Harvard University researchers **Paul R. Lawrence** and **Jay W. Lorsch**.[62] Instead of a *mechanistic-organic dimension,* however, they proposed a *differentiation-integration* dimension—forces that impelled the parts of an organization to move apart or to come together. The stability of the environment confronting the parts of the organization, according to Lawrence and Lorsch, determines the degree of differentiation or integration that is appropriate.

Differentiation: When Forces Push the Organization Apart   *Differentiation* **is the tendency of the parts of an organization to disperse and fragment.** The more subunits into which an organization breaks down, the more highly differentiated it is.

This impulse toward dispersal arises because of technical specialization and division of labor. As a result, specialists behave in specific, delimited ways, without coordinating with other parts of the organization. For example, a company producing dental floss, deodorants, and other personal-care products might have different product divisions, each with its own production facility and sales staff—a quite differentiated organization.

Integration: When Forces Pull the Organization Together   *Integration* **is the tendency of the parts of an organization to draw together to achieve a common purpose.** In a highly integrated organization, the specialists work together to achieve a common goal. The means for achieving this are a formal chain of command, standardization of rules and procedures, and use of cross-functional teams and computer networks so that there is frequent communication and coordination of the parts.

3. Size: The Larger the Organization, the More Mechanistic

Organizational size **is usually measured by the number of full-time employees.** In general, research shows that larger organizations—those with 2,000 or more full-time employees (or the equivalent workload in a mix of full- and part-timers)—tend to have more rules, regulations, and procedures and more job specialization, as well as greater decentralization. That is, larger firms tend to be more mechanistic.[63] Small organizations tend to be more informal, to have fewer rules and regulations, and to have less work specialization. In other words, small firms tend to be more organic.

Economists have long extolled the virtues of economies of scale, suggesting that "bigger is better" because the per-unit cost of production decreases as the organization grows. Opponents, however, contend that "small is beautiful," because large organizations tend to breed apathy, alienation, absenteeism, and turnover. Indeed, bigger is not always better: The world's largest company, Japan's Mitsubishi, with revenues of $176 billion (bigger than those of AT&T, Du Pont, CitiCorp, and Procter & Gamble combined) in a recent year had a puny profit margin of just 0.12%, although the inefficiencies may be related to complexity rather than size.[64] Similarly, the electronics giant Sony has expanded into fields like financial services and beauty products, but some financial analysts believe the company should be

Cutting Sony back. The huge Japanese company is well known as an electronics giant that has expanded into music and movies, but it also has branched into products as diverse as flashlight batteries and online banking services, thus blurring its identity. This threatens one of the company's most profitable assets—the so-called Sony premium, its ability to charge higher prices for its electronics products. What do you think Sony should do about its size?

cut back to a rational size or the blurring of identity could affect its ability to command higher prices in electronics.[65]

According to Tom Peters and Robert Waterman, most top-performing organizations keep their division size between $50 million and $100 million, "with a maximum of 1,000 or so employees each. Moreover, they grant their divisions extraordinary independence—and give them the functions and resources to exploit."[66] For example, Parker Hannifin, maker of industrial valves, auto parts, and programmable motion controls, among many other products, has 100 autonomous divisions, with 263 plants in 46 countries. Each division operates only a few plants in order to keep the company nonunion and the managers close to their customers. "Whenever we get more than 200 people in a plant," says chairman Patrick Parker, "we like to move 50 miles down the road and start another."[67]

4. Technology: Small-Batch, Large-Batch, or Continuous-Process—the Woodward Model

Technology has an important influence on organizational design. *Technology* **consists of all the tools and ideas for transforming materials, data, or labor (inputs) into goods or services (outputs).** A hand-cranked ice-cream-making machine, for instance, is the technology that, with your muscle power, transforms cream, ice, sugar, and flavoring into ice cream. This book, the classroom, the blackboard, the instructor's lectures, and so on are the technologies that deliver an education about management.

In a study of 100 manufacturing firms in England, **Joan Woodward** classified firms according to three forms of technology in increasing levels of complexity: *small-batch, large-batch,* and *continuous process.*[68]

Small-Batch Technology: Custom-Made Products Made by Organic Organizations
In *small-batch technology,* **often the least complex technology, goods are custom-made to customer specifications in small quantities.** The one-of-a-kind portrait painting, the Saville Row bespoke suit, the *Columbia* space shuttle, the personal stationery you had designed and printed just for you are all examples.

Small-batch organizations, Woodward found, tend to be informal and flexible—that is, organic.

Large-Batch Technology: Mass-Produced Products Made by Mechanized Organizations
So-called *large-batch technology* **is mass-production, assembly-line technology.** Large volumes of finished products are made by combining easily available component parts. The clothes you buy at Macy's, Kenmore washers and dryers, Toyota automobiles, and most of the products we purchase on a daily basis fall into this category.

Large-batch organizations tend to have a higher level of specialization and to be more bureaucratic, according to Woodward.

Continuous-Process: Highly Routinized Products Made by Organic Organizations
Continuous-process technology **is highly routinized technology in which machines do all the work.** Examples of this kind of technology are found in petroleum refineries, vodka distilleries, nuclear power plants, and steel mills, in which human operators mainly read dials and repair machine breakdowns.

Successful continuous-process organizations, Woodward found, tend to be more organic than mechanistic—less rigid and formal.

5. Life Cycle: Four Stages in the Life of an Organization

Like the four stages of a *project* life cycle (described in Chapter 5) and of a *product* life cycle (Chapter 6), organizations, too, have a life cycle. **The four-stage *organizational life cycle* has a natural sequence of stages: birth, youth, midlife, and maturity.** In general, as an organization moves through these stages, it becomes not only larger but also more mechanistic, specialized, decentralized, and bureaucratic. Each stage offers different managerial challenges and different organizational design issues.[69]

Stage I. The Birth Stage—Nonbureaucratic

The *birth stage* is the nonbureaucratic stage, the stage in which the organization is created. Here there are no written rules and little if any supporting staff beyond perhaps a secretary.

The founder may be a lone entrepreneur, such as Michael Dell, who began Dell Computers by selling microcomputers out of his University of Texas college dorm room. Or the founders may be pals who got together, as did Apple Computer founders Steven Jobs and Stephen Wozniak, who built the first computer in Wozniak's parents' Palo Alto, California, garage, using the proceeds from the sale of an old Volkswagen.

Stage 2. The Youth Stage—Prebureaucratic

In the *youth stage,* the organization is in a prebureaucratic stage, a stage of growth and expansion.

Now the company has a product that is making headway in the marketplace, people are being added to the payroll (most clerical rather than professional), and some division of labor and setting of rules are being instituted.

For Apple Computer, this stage occurred during the years 1978–1981, with the establishment of the Apple II product line.

Stage 3. The Midlife Stage—Bureaucratic

In the *midlife stage,* the organization becomes bureaucratic, a period of growth evolving into stability.

Now the organization has a formalized bureaucratic structure, staffs of specialists, decentralization of functional divisions, and many rules.

In the 1980s, Apple Computer became a large company with many of these attributes. In 1983, Pepsi-Cola marketer John Scully was hired as a professional manager. Jobs became chairman; Wozniak left.

Stage 4. The Maturity Stage—Very Bureaucratic

In the *maturity stage,* the organization becomes very bureaucratic, large, and mechanistic. The danger at this point is lack of flexibility and innovation.

After Jobs was fired in a boardroom struggle in 1985, Apple entered a period in which it seemed to lose its way, having trouble developing successful products and getting them to market. Scully, who emphasized the wrong technology (a "personal data assistant" called Newton, which failed to establish a following) was followed by two more CEOs who were unable to arrest the company's declining market share.

In 1997, Jobs was brought back as a "temporary" chairman, and Apple's fortunes began to revive.

Group Exercise:
Designing an Organization

Employees who were present during birth and youth stages may long for the good old days of informality and fewer rules as the organization moves toward more formalized and bureaucratic structures. Whereas clearly some organizations jump the gun and institute such structures before they are appropriate, some expanding companies in effect never grow up, holding on to the prebureaucratic way of life for too long, hindering their ability to deliver goods or services efficiently in relation to their size. ●

8.7 TOWARD BUILDING A LEARNING ORGANIZATION

> **Why do organizations resist learning, and what is a new way for employees in an organization to view themselves?** **major question** ✳

THE BIG PICTURE

Learning organizations are able to modify their behavior to reflect new knowledge. There are three reasons why organizations resist learning. A way to encourage learning is for all employees to view themselves as collaborators, not competitors.

The film *Gorillas in the Mist,* which was being shot in the middle of a jungle in Rwanda and was to use more than 200 animals, had turned into a nightmare, says Peter Guber, who was the producer. In large part, he reports, this was because "the screenplay required the gorillas to do what we wrote—in other words, to 'act.' If they couldn't or wouldn't, we'd have to fall back on a formula that the studio had seen fail before: using dwarfs in gorilla suits on a sound stage."

During an emergency meeting, a young intern had asked, "What if you let the gorillas write the story? . . . . What if you sent a really good cinematographer into the jungle with a ton of film to shoot the gorillas? Then you could write a story around what the gorillas did on the film."

Everyone had laughed and wondered what the intern was doing in a meeting with experienced filmmakers. But ultimately they did exactly what she suggested, and the cinematographer "came back with phenomenal footage that practically wrote the story for us," Guber says. "We shot the film for $20 million—half of the original budget." The moral: the woman's inexperience enabled her to see opportunities where others saw problems.[70]

Guber adopted ideas appropriate to what is known as a *learning organization.* As we said in Chapter 2, a learning organization is an organization that actively creates, acquires, and transfers knowledge within itself and is able to modify its behavior to reflect new knowledge.[71] Learning organizations, says MIT professor **Peter Senge,** who coined the term, are places "where people continually expand their capacity to create the results they truly desire, where new and expansive patterns of thinking are nurtured, where collective aspiration is set free, and where people are continually learning how to learn together."[72]

To identify whether an organization you're currently working for, if any, is a learning organization, see the Self-Assessment at the end of this chapter. Being a learning organization is the basis for having a culture of intrapreneurship, as we discussed in Chapter 3.

Why Organizations Might Resist Learning

Like people, organizations must continually learn new things or face obsolescence. A key challenge for managers in today's competitive environment, therefore, is to establish a culture that will enhance their employees' ability to learn. Organizations, like the people in them, do not *consciously* resist learning. But resistance arises anyway, for three reasons.[73] *(See Table 8.2, next page.)*

1. People believe that competition is always better than collaboration.
2. Fragmentation leads to specialized fiefdoms that resist learning.
3. Unless encouraged, people won't take risks, the basis for learning.

table 8.2

REASONS THAT RESISTANCE TO LEARNING DEVELOPS IN ORGANIZATIONS

1. People Believe Competition Is Always Better Than Collaboration	2. Fragmentation Leads to Specialized Fiefdoms That Resist Learning	3. Unless Encouraged, People Won't Take Risks, the Basis for Learning
One of the most important beliefs (or paradigms—see text) in business is that competition is superior to collaboration. This belief can lead employees within an organization to battle one another when success depends on their cooperation.	Today most people are specialists, trained to work in specific areas. This fragmented, piecemeal approach solves some kinds of problems but not organization-wide problems, such as the effect of new technology.	Do you resist learning a new software program because you've gotten along just fine with the one you've used so far? Most of us tend to resist change, choosing to stay within our comfort zones, because change can be frustrating, even stressful.
Overemphasis on competition also makes people more concerned about "looking good rather than doing good," hampering learning because they are reluctant to admit ignorance or mistakes. It also makes everyone more concerned about short-term measurable results rather than long-term solutions to root causes of problems.	Fragmentation not only creates specialists working in functional areas, it also erects walls between them, with workers battling one another for power and resources. Left behind on the battlefield are important ideas such as sharing and collaboration and, as a consequence, learning.	Learning requires taking some risks, as in making mistakes or in revealing your ignorance for all to see. But if our natural tendency to want others' approval is coupled with an organizational climate that favors management by fear and intimidation, people will resist taking risks, and so little learning will take place.

The New Paradigm: "We're All Stakeholders"

Most of us live by certain *paradigms,* **generally accepted ways of viewing the world.** As stated in Table 8.2, one of the most important in business—and in American society in general—is the paradigm ("*pare*-uh-dime") that competition is superior to collaboration.

Many paradigms have outlived their usefulness, and you need to seriously challenge them if you want to create a learning organization. A principal challenge is to create a climate in which managers and employees stop thinking in terms of "us" versus "them" and start thinking of themselves as mutual stakeholders in the same enterprise.

"This is a company of owners, of partners, of businesspeople," reads one company's mission statement. "We are in business together. . . . No one in this company is just an employee. People have different jobs, make different salaries, have different levels of authority. But all workers will see the same basic information and will have a voice in matters affecting them. And it will be everyone's responsibility to understand how the business operates, to keep track of its results, and to make decisions that contribute to its success in the marketplace."[74]

Here the writer could well be making a case for the importance of *evidence-based management,* the world view we have stressed in earlier chapters. And there could be no better statement of the new managerial paradigm. ●

summary

 ### 8.1 What Kind of Organizational Culture Will You Be Operating In?

- Organizational culture is a system of shared beliefs and values that develops within an organization and guides the behavior of its members. Culture exists on two levels—invisible and visible. (1) The invisible level is the core culture, which consists of values, beliefs, and assumptions—beliefs and values so widely shared that they are rarely discussed. (2) The visible level is the observable culture, which is expressed in symbols, stories, heroes, and rites and rituals. A symbol is an object, act, quality, or event that conveys meaning to others. A story is a narrative based on true events, which is repeated—and sometimes embellished on—to emphasize a particular value. A hero is a person whose accomplishments embody the values of the organization. Rites and rituals are the activities and ceremonies, planned and unplanned, that celebrate important occasions and accomplishments in the organization's life.

- Culture, which can powerfully shape an organization's success over the long term, has four functions. (1) It gives members an organizational identity. (2) It facilitates collective commitment. (3) It promotes social-system stability. (4) It shapes behavior by helping employees make sense of their surroundings.

 ### 8.2 Developing High-Performance Cultures

- What types of organizational culture can increase an organization's competitiveness and profitability? Three perspectives have been proposed: (1) The strength perspective assumes that the strength of a corporate culture is related to a firm's long-term financial performance; (2) the fit perspective assumes that an organization's culture must align, or fit, with its business or strategic context; and (3) the adaptive perspective assumes that the most effective cultures help organizations anticipate and adapt to environmental changes.

- Among the mechanisms managers use to embed a culture in an organization are: (1) formal statements; (2) slogans and sayings; (3) stories, legends, and myths; (4) leader reactions to crises; (5) role modeling, training, and coaching; (6) physical design; (7) rewards, titles, promotions, and bonuses; (8) organizational goals and performance criteria; (9) measurable and controllable activities; (10) organizational structure; and (11) procedures for self-development.

 ## 8.3 What Is an Organization?

- An organization is a system of consciously coordinated activities or forces of two or more people. There are three types of organizations classified according to the three different purposes for which they are formed: for-profit, nonprofit, and mutual-benefit. It has been proposed that business organizations not be judged on profits alone—that there is blended value, in which all investments are understood to operate simultaneously in both economic and social realms.

- Whatever the size of organization, it can be represented in an organization chart, a boxes-and-lines illustration showing the formal lines of authority and the organization's official positions or division of labor. Two kinds of information that organizations reveal about organizational structure are (1) the vertical hierarchy of authority—who reports to whom, and (2) the horizontal specialization—who specializes in what work.

 ## 8.4 The Major Elements of an Organization

- Organizations have seven elements: (1) common purpose, which unifies employees or members and gives everyone an understanding of the organization's reason for being; (2) coordinated effort, the coordination of individual efforts into a group or organization-wide effort; (3) division of labor, having discrete parts of a task done by different people; (4) hierarchy of authority, a control mechanism for making sure the right people do the right things at the right time; (5) span of control, which refers to the number of people reporting directly to a given manager; (6) authority and accountability, responsibility, and delegation. Authority refers to the rights inherent in a managerial position to make decisions, give

orders, and utilize resources. Accountability means that managers must report and justify work results to the managers above them. Responsibility is the obligation you have to perform the tasks assigned to you. Delegation is the process of assigning managerial authority and responsibility to managers and employees lower in the hierarchy. Regarding authority and responsibility, the organization chart distinguishes between two positions, line and staff. Line managers have authority to make decisions and usually have people reporting to them. Staff personnel have advisory functions; they provide advice, recommendations, and research to line managers. (7) Centralization versus decentralization of authority. With centralized authority, important decisions are made by higher-level managers. With decentralized authority, important decisions are made by middle-level and supervisory-level managers.

 ## 8.5 Basic Types of Organizational Structures

- Organizations may be arranged into eight types of structures. (1) In a simple structure, authority is centralized in a single person; this structure has a flat hierarchy, few rules, and low work specialization. (2) In a functional structure, people with similar occupational specialties are put together in formal groups. (3) In a divisional structure, people with diverse occupational specialties are put together in formal groups by similar products or services, customers or clients, or geographic regions. (4) In a conglomerate structure, divisions are grouped around similar businesses or industries. (5) In a hybrid structure, an organization uses functional and divisional structures in different parts of the same organization. (6) In a matrix structure, an organization combines functional and divisional chains of commands in grids so that there are two command structures—vertical and horizontal. (7) In a team-based structure, teams or workgroups are used to improve horizontal relations and solve problems throughout the organization. (8) In a network structure, the organization has a central core that is linked to outside independent firms by computer connections, which are used to operate as if all were a single organization.

8.6 Contingency Design: Factors in Creating the Best Structure

- The process of fitting the organization to its environment is called contingency design. Managers taking a contingency approach must consider five factors in designing the best kind of structure for their organization at that particular time.

- (1) An organization may be either mechanistic or organic. In a mechanistic organization, authority is centralized, tasks and rules are clearly specified, and employees are closely supervised. In an organic organization, authority is decentralized, there are fewer rules and procedures, and networks of employees are encouraged to cooperate and respond quickly to unexpected tasks.

- (2) An organization may also be characterized by differentiation or integration. Differentiation is the tendency of the parts of an organization to disperse and fragment. Integration is the tendency of the parts of an organization to draw together to achieve a common purpose.

- (3) Organizational size is usually measured by the number of full-time employees. Larger organizations tend to have more rules, regulations, job specialization, and decentralization. Smaller organizations tend to be more informal, have fewer rules, and have less work specialization.

- (4) Technology consists of all the tools and ideas for transforming materials, data or labor (inputs) into goods or services (outputs). Firms may be classified according to three forms of technology in increasing levels of complexity. In small-batch technology, often the least complex technology, goods are custom-made to customer specifications in small quantities. Large-batch technology is mass-production, assembly-line technology. Continuous-process technology is highly routinized technology in which machines do all the work.

- (5) The four-stage organizational life cycle has a natural sequence of stages: birth, youth, midlife, and maturity. The birth stage is the nonbureaucratic stage, the stage in which the organization is created. The youth stage is the prebureaucratic stage, a stage of growth and expansion. In the midlife stage, the organization becomes bureaucratic, a period of growth evolving into stability. In the maturity stage, the organization becomes very bureaucratic, large, and mechanistic. The danger at this point is lack of flexibility and innovation.

8.7 Toward Building a Learning Organization

- Learning organizations are able to modify their behavior to reflect new knowledge. There are three reasons why organizations resist learning. (1) People believe that competition is always better than collaboration. (2) Fragmentation leads to specialized fiefdoms that resist learning. (3) Unless encouraged, people won't take risks, the basis for learning.

- A way to encourage learning is a new paradigm—namely, for all employees to view themselves as collaborators, not competitors.

management in action

Is It Good to Foster a Culture That Reinforces Failure?

Ever heard of Choglit? How about OK Soda or Surge? Long after "New Coke" became nearly synonymous with innovation failure, these products joined Coca-Cola Co.'s graveyard of beverage busts.

Choglit, in case you blinked and missed it, was a chocolate-flavored milk drink test-marketed with Nestlé in 2002. OK Soda, unveiled in 1994, tried to capture Generation X with edgy marketing. The "OK Manifesto," parts of which were printed on cans in an attempt at hipster irony, asked: "What's the point of OK Soda?" It turned out customers wondered the same thing. And while Surge did well initially, this me-too Mountain Dew later did anything but. Sales began drying up after five years.

Given that history, failure hardly seems like a subject Chairman and CEO E. Neville Isdell would want to trot out in front of investors. But Isdell did just that, deliberately airing the topic at Coke's annual meeting in April. "You will see some failures," he told the crowd. "As we take more risks, this is something we must accept as part of the regeneration process."

Warning Coke investors that the company might experience some flops is a little like warning Atlantans they might experience afternoon thunderstorms in July. But Isdell thinks it's vital. He wants Coke to take bigger risks, and to do that, he knows he needs to convince employees and shareholders that he will tolerate the failures that will inevitably result. That's the only way to change Coke's traditionally risk-averse culture. And given the importance of this goal, there's no podium too big for sending the signal. "Using [the annual meeting] occasion elevates the statement to another order of importance," Isdell said in an interview with *BusinessWeek.*

While few CEOs are as candid about the potential for failure as Isdell, many are wrestling with the same problem, trying to get their organizations to cozy up to the risk-taking that innovation requires. A warning: It's not going to be an easy shift. After years of cost-cutting initiatives and growing job insecurity, most employees don't exactly feel like putting themselves on the line. Add to that the heightened expectations by management on individual performance, and it's easy to see why so many opt to play it safe.

Indeed, for a generation of managers weaned on the rigors of Six Sigma error-elimination programs, embracing failure—gasp!—is close to blasphemy. [But, says] Stefan H. Thomke, a professor at Harvard Business School, . . . "[Failure] is so important to the experimental process."

That it is. Crucial, in fact. After all, that's why true, breakthrough innovation—an imperative in today's globally competitive world, in which product cycles are shorter than ever—is so extraordinarily hard. It requires well-honed organizations built for efficiency and speed to do what feels unnatural: Explore. Experiment. Foul up, sometimes. Then repeat.

Granted, not all failures are praiseworthy. Some flops are just that: bad ideas. The eVilla, Sony Corp.'s $500 "Internet appliance." The Pontiac Aztek, General Motors Corp.'s ugly duckling "cross-over" SUV. . . .

But intelligent failures—those that happen early and inexpensively and that contribute new insights about your customers—should be more than just tolerable. They should be encouraged. "Figuring out how to master this process of failing fast and failing cheap and fumbling toward success is probably the most important thing companies have to get good at," says Scott Anthony, the managing director at consulting firm Innosight.

"Getting good" at failure, however, doesn't mean creating anarchy out of organization. It means leaders—not just on a podium at the annual meeting, but in the trenches, every day—who create an environment safe for taking risks and who share stories of their own mistakes. It means bringing in outsiders unattached to a project's past. It means carving out time to reflect on failure, not just success.

Perhaps most important, it means designing ways to measure performance that balance accountability with the freedom to make mistakes. People may fear failure, but they fear the consequences of it even more. "The performance culture really is in deep conflict with the learning culture," says Paul J. H. Schoemaker, CEO of consulting firm Decision Strategies International Inc. "It's an unusual executive who can balance these."

Some organizations have tried to measure performance in a way that accounts for these opposing pressures. At IBM Research, engineers are evaluated on both one- and three-year time frames. The one-year term determines the bonus, while the three-year period decides rank and salary. The longer frame can help neutralize a year of setbacks. "A three-year evaluation cycle sends an important message to our researchers, demonstrating our commitment to investing in the early, risky stages of innovation," says Armando Garcia, vice-president for technical strategy and worldwide operations at IBM Research.

In addition to making sure performance evaluations take a long-term view, managers should also think about celebrating smart failures. (Those who repeat their mistakes, of course, should hardly be rewarded.) . . .

Intuit Inc., based in Mountain View, Calif., recently celebrated an adventurous marketing campaign that failed. The company had never targeted young tax filers before, and in early 2005 it tried to reach them through an ill-fated attempt to combine tax-filing drudgery with hip-hop style. . . . Through a postmortem process, the team that developed the campaign documented its insights, such as the fact that Gen Yers don't visit destination Web sites that feel too much like advertising. Then, on a stage at the Dolce Hayes Mansion in San Jose, Calif., last October in front of some 200 Intuit marketers, the team received an award from Intuit Chairman Scott Cook. "It's only a failure if we fail to get the learning," says Cook.

In addition to postmortems, Intuit has begun plucking insights from its flops through sessions that focus on failure. Jana Eggers, who heads up Intuit's Innovation Lab, held the first such "When Learning Hurts" session recently. There, she recounted the story of QuickBase, a software application that failed for its initial market, small business customers, but is now finding fans among large companies. Eggers hopes future conferences will feature even more presentations on failures. She also plans to distribute "narrative storytelling booklets" about failed projects so people can "feel the pain."

Unlike Intuit, most companies don't spend enough time and resources looking backward, says Chris Trimble, a professor at the Tuck School of Business at Dartmouth College and co-author of *10 Rules for Strategic Innovators*. That's a mistake. "How do you learn if you don't examine the past?" asks Trimble.

General Electric Co. is trying to do just that. The company, which is well-known for sharing best practices across its many units, has recently begun formally discussing failures, too. Last September the company set up a two-hour conference call for managers of eight "imagination breakthroughs" that didn't live up to expectations and were being shelved, or "retired," in GE's parlance. ("Imagination breakthroughs"—IBs—are new businesses or products that have potential sales of $100 million within three to five years.)

Such discussions can be nerve-racking, especially in companies where failure has traditionally been met with tough consequences. That was the case at GE, which is now three years into the effort spearheaded by Chairman and CEO Jeffrey R. Immelt to make

innovation the new mantra at the $150 billion behemoth. "I had some offline conversations with some of the IB leaders reassuring them that this was not a call where they were going to get their pink slips," says Patia McGrath, a GE marketing director who helped put together the call. "The notion of taking big swings, and that it's O.K. to miss the swing, is something that's quite new with Jeff."

For Discussion

1. Is it good to foster a culture that reinforces failure? What are the pros and cons?
2. How can storytelling be used to embed an innovative culture? Explain.
3. How can organizations use reward systems to embed the positive aspects of failure? Discuss.
4. How is Jeff Immelt trying to embed a culture that fosters innovation?
5. Which of the eight types of organizational structures are most likely to promote innovation? Explain your rationale.

Source: Excerpted from Jena McGregor, "How Failure Breeds Success," *BusinessWeek*, July 10, 2006, pp. 42, 44–46.

self-assessment

Is Your Organization a Learning Organization?

Objectives

1. To gain familiarity with the characteristics of learning organizations.
2. To identify whether your organization is a learning organization.

Introduction

As we learned in this chapter, a learning organization is one that actively creates, acquires, and transfers new knowledge. Learning organizations are places in which new ideas and patterns of thinking are nurtured and in which people are allowed to continually expand their abilities to achieve desired results. Most importantly, a learning organization is

a place in which the organization and individuals in it are continually learning in order to achieve its goals. The purpose of this exercise is to identify whether the organization in which you work is a learning organization.

Instructions

The following survey was created to assess the extent to which an organization follows the principles of a learning organization. If you are currently working, you should answer the questions in regard to this organization. If you are not currently working but have worked in the past, use a past job in completing the survey. If you have never had a job, you can use your school as a reference or use an organization you might be familiar with. For example, you might interview your parents to determine the extent to which the organization they work for follows the principles of a learning organization. Read each statement and use the following scale to indicate which answer most closely matches your response: 1 = strongly disagree; 2 = disagree; 3 = neither agree nor disagree; 4 = agree; 5 = strongly agree.

1. Management uses rewards, praise, and recognition to get what they want done.		1 2 3 4 5
2. The company promotes teamwork.		1 2 3 4 5
3. People are recognized and rewarded on the basis of what they do rather than *who* they know.		1 2 3 4 5
4. I see more examples of optimistic attitudes/behaviors rather than negative and cynical ones.		1 2 3 4 5
5. I have a clear picture of the organization's vision and my role in helping to accomplish it.		1 2 3 4 5
6. This organization relies more on team-based solutions than individual ones.		1 2 3 4 5
7. This organization tends to look at the big picture rather than analyzing problems from a narrow perspective.		1 2 3 4 5
8. People have an open mind when working with others.		1 2 3 4 5
9. This company looks for the root cause of a problem rather than a "quick fix."		1 2 3 4 5
10. I have the skills and knowledge to continuously improve the way I do my job.		1 2 3 4 5
	Total _____	

Scoring

To get your score, add up the numbers that correspond to your responses. The range will be from 10 to 50. Comparative norms for learning organizations are as follows:

Total score of 10–23 = low learning organization

Total score of 24–36 = moderate learning organization

Total score of 37–50 = high learning organization

 group exercise

Designing Your Own Organization

Objectives

- To learn more about organizational structures.
- To consider the relationship between organizational culture and structure.

Introduction

As we learned in this chapter, an organization's culture consists of a system of shared beliefs and values that develops within the organization and guides the behavior of its members. An organization's culture and its structure are closely intertwined.

The purpose of this exercise is to examine the relationship between an organization's culture and its structure. To accomplish this, you will design your own company.

Instructions

Break into groups of five or six people. Your first task is to start your own organization. Your organization can be anything from a baseball team to a car company to a bank. Once you have determined what type of organization your group wants to create, the group needs to establish the organizational values that will underlie your organization's culture. Once the values are established, we want you to propose two different organizational structures. Begin by examining the eight types of organizational structures covered in the text. Your first organizational chart should represent your proposed structure at the beginning of your organization's inception. The second organization chart should represent the structure of your organization once it has 300 or more employees.

Questions for Discussion

1. What are your organization's values? Explain why they were chosen.
2. How do the values and culture of your organization correspond to its structure? Explain.
3. How did your organization chart change once your company reached 300 employees? What type of structure does this chart represent? Explain.
4. Do you believe your organization is more mechanistic or organic? Explain.

 # ethical dilemma

When Your Brother-in-Law Is Bending the Rules

Assume you are the purchasing manager for a small, family-run homebuilding firm. Your brother-in-law works in the framing department and your sister is the company's chief financial officer (CFO). The firm has a policy that employees can do small homebuilding jobs (projects valued at less than $2,000) on the side and can purchase their building supplies for these projects through the company. This policy allows employees to make some extra cash while purchasing materials at much discounted rates.

Because of your role, you are aware of all side projects taking place and the dollar amount of materials purchased through the company for these projects. You recently noticed that your brother-in-law has been purchasing raw materials that you suspect will exceed the $2,000 threshold—he purchased $3,000 worth of materials for one project and $1,500 for another.

You approved both of the purchases even though you suspect that he is doing projects that are valued at around $5,000-$8,000. These types of projects are not permitted as side jobs because the company itself does work in this price range. You sense that your brother-in-law's behavior is OK because your sister also knows about these purchases, given her role as CFO.

Solving the Dilemma

Your brother-in-law just submitted a purchase request for materials valued at $10,000 for side jobs. What should you do?

1. Approve the purchase. It's not your job to police your brother-in-law, and your sister is aware of what he's doing.
2. Call your sister and express your concern about what your brother-in-law is doing. Let her deal with any potential ethical breaches.
3. Contact your brother-in-law and ask him if he is abiding by the company policy of not doing side jobs valued at over $2,000. If he says yes, approve the purchases.
4. Go to the CEO and let him know about the details of your brother-in-law's purchases. The CEO can then do whatever he thinks is best.
5. Invent other options.

JetBlue Airways: Is "High-Touch Service" the Key Driver for Future Success?

On February 11, 2000, JetBlue Airways, the highest-funded startup U.S. airline in history, began flight service between JFK International Airport (New York) and Fort Lauderdale International Airport (Florida). With $130 million in the bank, David Neeleman, chief executive officer (CEO), took the position that his startup airline would "bring humanity back to air travel."

Since its maiden flight a few short years ago, JetBlue has been quite successful in competing with larger airline companies. It attributes its success to "high touch services" and low fares for customers. The company's mission statement consists of five core values: 1) safety, 2) caring, 3) integrity, 4) fun, and 5) passion, and CEO Neeleman wants all employees to act according to those values. Neeleman wants to delight customers, which in turn, he believes, will make clients think "JetBlue" when they make travel plans. To that end, all employees go the extra mile for customers, who receive pre-boarding and on-board courtesies called the "JetBlue Experience." Neeleman himself has been known to distribute snacks to passengers when he flies aboard a JetBlue aircraft.

The "JetBlue Experience" is a strategy of differentiation, providing customer delivery service with the goal to demonstrate how JetBlue goes beyond its competitors. For example, once on board the aircraft, passengers enjoy leather seats, direct TV, and additional leg room, despite the fact that the company has lost some additional revenue by giving up extra seating capacity for comfort. But Neeleman remains constant about making customer service a priority and he stands by his decision, since it directly reflects company strategies.

As an integral part of meeting its mission, JetBlue takes pains to develop employees through communication and continuous training. Employees are constantly mindful that they work in a customer-driven business. In addition to learning about any airline regulatory changes, they are also taught to become the best employees possible. They are taught the importance of teamwork, and rather than just filling their job description, all employees approach work in a holistic manner, helping out whenever necessary as part of a work culture where the operative slogan is "I can make a difference." By fostering this kind of culture, JetBlue believes customers will return, in greater and greater numbers. Neeleman says JetBlue's core beliefs will continue to lead the way for the company's success.

Questions

1. Describe the organizational culture at JetBlue.
2. How important is culture to the success of an organization such as JetBlue?
3. JetBlue does not seem to follow a traditional hierarchical organization structure. Does its nontraditional approach to organizations give it any advantage over its competitors? If so, discuss some of these advantages.
4. Discuss JetBlue's philosophy in light of the new paradigm: "We're All Stakeholders."

Source: Joseph C. Santora, EdD, Essex County College.

chapter 9

Human Resource Management

Getting the Right People for Managerial Success

Major Questions You Should Be Able to Answer

9.1 Strategic Human Resource Management
Major Question: How do star managers view the role of people in their organization's success?

9.2 The Legal Requirements of Human Resource Management
Major Question: To avoid exposure to legal liabilities, what areas of the law do I need to be aware of?

9.3 Recruitment & Selection: Putting the Right People into the Right Jobs
Major Question: How can I reduce mistakes in hiring and find great people who might work for me?

9.4 Orientation, Training, & Development
Major Question: Once people are hired, what's the best way to see that they do what they're supposed to do?

9.5 Performance Appraisal
Major Question: How can I assess employees' performance more accurately and give more effective feedback?

9.6 Managing an Effective Workforce: Compensation & Benefits
Major Question: What are the various forms of compensation?

9.7 Managing Promotions, Transfers, Disciplining, & Dismissals
Major Question: What are some guidelines for handling promotions, transfers, disciplining, and dismissals?

Keeping Employees Invested in Their Jobs

"Get a life!" everyone says. But what, exactly, is a "life," anyway?

As more and more people have begun asking this question, it has spilled over into organizational life. The result has been a new category of work rewards called *work-life benefits.*

As one definition has it, work-life benefits are programs "used by employers to increase productivity and commitment by removing certain barriers that make it hard for people to strike a balance between their work and personal lives."[1] Examples are nonsalary incentives such as flexible work arrangements, tuition assistance, and paid time off for community service.

Managing human resources, the subject of this chapter, focuses on managing people. You need to be thinking about employees not as "human capital" or "capital assets" but as people who are *investors:* They are investing their time, energy, and intelligence—their lives—in your organization, for which they deserve a return that makes sense to them.[2]

To keep your employees invested in their jobs and performing well, it helps to know what the Gallup Organization discovered in surveying 80,000 managers and 1 million workers over 25 years.[3] Gallup found that in the best workplaces employees gave strong "Yes" answers to the following 12 questions:

1. Do I know what's expected of me?
2. Do I have the right materials and equipment I need to do my work right?
3. Do I have the opportunity to do what I do best every day?
4. In the last 7 days, have I received recognition or praise for good work?
5. Does my supervisor, or someone at work, seem to care about me as a person?
6. Is there someone at work who encourages my development?
7. Does my opinion seem to count?
8. Does the mission of my company make me feel like my work is important?
9. Are my co-workers committed to doing quality work?
10. Do I have a best friend at work?
11. In the last 6 months, have I talked with someone about my progress?
12. Have I had opportunities to learn and grow?

The best managers, Gallup says, meet with workers individually at least every 3 months, not just once or twice a year. In doing so, they not only discuss performance but also try to find out what employees want to accomplish and how the manager can help. In addition, good managers focus on strengths, rather than weaknesses, allowing employees to devote time to what they do best.

Since *Fortune* magazine began publishing its annual list of "The 100 Best Companies to Work For," managers have been concerned about trying to take better care of their employees. The best organizations, according to a project leader who helps with the *Fortune* list, keep their employees an average of 6 years, as opposed to the nationwide average of 3.6 years. They accomplish this by pushing for employees at all levels to feel involved in the company's success.[4]

For Discussion Which 3 of the 12 questions listed above are most important to you? Which do you think are most important to most employees?

forecast

What's Ahead in This Chapter

This chapter considers human resource (HR) management—planning for, attracting, developing, and retaining an effective workforce. We consider how this subject fits in with the overall company strategy, how to evaluate current and future employee needs, and how to recruit and select qualified people. We discuss orientation, training, and development; how to assess employee performance and give feedback; and what HR laws managers should be aware of. Finally, we consider how to manage compensation and benefits, promotions and discipline, and workplace performance problems.

9.1 STRATEGIC HUMAN RESOURCE MANAGEMENT

> ❋ major question | How do star managers view the role of people in their organization's success?

THE BIG PICTURE

Human resource management consists of the activities managers perform to plan for, attract, develop, and retain an effective workforce. Planning the human resources needed consists of understanding current employee needs and predicting future employee needs.

One company that has appeared on *Fortune*'s "The 100 Best Companies to Work For" list (#1 in 2005, #2 in 2006) is Wegmans Food Markets, Inc., a 71-store regional supermarket chain with stores in New York, Pennsylvania, New Jersey, Virginia, and Maryland. The company, which is headquartered in Rochester, is in its third generation of family management. In an industry facing severe challenges from nontraditional grocery outlets like club stores and discounters, Wegmans' sales per square foot are 50% higher than the industry average, owing to a prepared-foods department that features dishes "that rival those of any top restaurant," according to *Fortune* writer Matthew Boyle.[5] The vast selection, ranging from Cocoa Puffs to organic gourmet fare, both at competitive prices, explains the zeal that customers have for the stores.

But what really contributes to the grocer's success as a retailer is its success with its employees. Hourly wages and annual salaries are at the high end of the market. Employees earning less than $55,000 a year get 100% coverage of health insurance premiums. The company has shelled out more than $54 million for college scholarships to more than 17,500 full- and part-time employees over the past 20 years. Employees are sent on company-sponsored trips to California wineries and European cheese makers to raise the level of product knowledge and education. Thus, labor costs are high, estimated at 15–17% of sales, compared with 12% for most supermarkets. But annual turnover for full-time employees is just 6%, compared with 19% for grocery chains with a similar number of stores. (Indeed, the supermarket industry's annual turnover costs can exceed its entire profits by more than 40%.) Moreover, employees feel there's a cachet to working at Wegmans. "You're a culinary whiz, an ambassador of fine cuisine—even if you only stock shelves at night," says Boyle.

How does Wegmans do so well? One reason is that it is a privately held company, as are about a third of the Fortune 100 Best Companies to Work For. As Boyle remarks, "It's no doubt easier to pamper employees . . . when you don't have Wall Street breathing down your neck" to deliver quick profits, as is the case with publicly held companies.

Human Resource Management: Managing an Organization's Most Important Resource

Human resource (HR) management **consists of the activities managers perform to plan for, attract, develop, and retain an effective workforce.** Whether it's McKenzie looking for entry-level business consultants, the U.S. Navy trying to fill its ranks, or churches trying to reverse the declining number of priests and ministers, all organizations must deal with staffing.

The fact that the old Personnel Department is now called the Human Resources Department is not just a cosmetic change. It is intended to suggest the importance of staffing to a company's success. Although talking about people as "resources" might seem to downgrade them to the same level as financial resources and material resources, in fact people are an organization's most important resource. Indeed, companies such as South San Francisco biotechnology firm Genentech (#1 on the 2006 *Fortune* magazine Best Companies list), jam maker J. M. Smucker (#1 in 2004), stockbroker Edward Jones (#1 in 2003 and 2002), and box retailer The Container Store (#1 in 2001 and 2000) have discovered that putting employees first has been the foundation for their success. "If you're not thinking all the time about making every person valuable, you don't have a chance," says former General Electric head Jack Welch. "What's the alternative? Wasted minds? Uninvolved people? A labor force that's angry or bored? That doesn't make sense!"[6]

Human Resources as Part of Strategic Planning   At many companies, human resources has become part of the strategic-planning process. Thus, HR departments deal not only with employee paperwork and legal accountability—a very important area, as we describe in Section 9.2—but also with helping to support the organization's overall strategy.

For example, is it important, as Wegmans owners think, to have loyal, innovative, smart, passionate employees who will give their best to promote customer satisfaction (the grocery chain's mission)? Who, then, should be recruited? How should they be trained? What's the best way to evaluate and reward their performance? The answers to these questions should be consistent with the firm's strategic mission. The purpose of the strategic human resource process, then—shown in the yellow-orange shaded boxes at right—is to get the optimal work performance that will help the company's mission and goals.[7] *(See Figure 9.1.)*

Two concepts important in this view of human resource management, which we mentioned in Chapter 2, are *human capital* and *social capital.*

Human Capital: Potential of Employee Knowledge & Actions   *Human capital,* you'll recall, is the economic or productive potential of employee knowledge and actions.[8] A present or future employee with the right combination of knowledge, skills, and motivation to excel represents human capital with the potential to give the organization a competitive advantage. Why is human capital important? "We are living in a time," says one team of human resource management authors, "when a new economic paradigm—characterized by speed, innovation, short cycle times, quality, and customer satisfaction—is highlighting the importance of intangible assets, such as brand recognition, knowledge, innovation, and particularly human capital."[9]

Social Capital: Potential of Strong & Cooperative Relationships   *Social capital,* we said, is the economic or productive potential of strong, trusting, and cooperative relationships.[10] Relationships do matter. For instance, the brothers running family-owned J. M. Smucker follow a simple code of conduct set forth by their father: "Listen with your full attention, look for the good in others, have a sense of humor, and say thank you for a job well done."[11] (The company's voluntary employee turnover rate is a mere 3%.)

Planning the Human Resources Needed

When a building contractor, looking to hire someone for a few hours to dig ditches, drives by a group of idle day laborers standing on a street corner, is that a form of HR planning? Certainly it shows the contractor's awareness that a pool of laborers usually

figure 9.1

THE STRATEGIC HUMAN RESOURCE MANAGEMENT PROCESS

Establish the mission & the vision

Establish the grand strategy

Formulate the strategic plans

Plan human resources needed

Recruit & select people

Orient, train, & develop

Perform appraisals of people

Purpose: Get optimal work performance to help realize company's mission & vision

Big Brown. A UPS driver's problems of driving in a big city—traffic, double parking, addressees not at home—are different from those of driving in rural areas, where there may be long stretches of boredom. Specialists in job analysis can interview drivers about their problems in order to write job descriptions that allow for varying circumstances.

can be found in that spot. But what if the builder needs a lot of people with specialized training—to give him or her the competitive advantage that the strategic planning process demands?

Here we are concerned with something more than simply hiring people on an "as needed" basis. *Strategic human resource planning* **consists of developing a systematic, comprehensive strategy for (a) understanding current employee needs and (b) predicting future employee needs.** Let's consider these two parts.

Understanding Current Employee Needs   To plan for the future, you must understand the present—what today's staffing picture looks like. This requires that you (or a trained specialist) do, first, a *job analysis* and from that write a *job description* and a *job specification.*[12]

- **Job analysis.** The purpose of *job analysis* **is to determine, by observation and analysis, the basic elements of a job.** Specialists who do this interview job occupants about what they do, observe the flow of work, and learn how results are accomplished. For example, United Parcel Service has specialists who ride with the couriers and time how long it takes to deliver a load of packages and note what problems are encountered (traffic jams, vicious dogs, recipients not home, and so on).

- **Job description and job specification.** Once the fundamentals of a job are understood, then you can write a *job description,* **which summarizes what the holder of the job does and how and why he or she does it.** Next you can write a *job specification,* **which describes the minimum qualifications a person must have to perform the job successfully.**

This process can produce some surprises. Jobs that might seem to require a college degree, for example, might not after all. Thus, the process of writing job analyses, descriptions, and specifications can help you avoid hiring people who are overqualified (and presumably more expensive) or underqualified (and thus not as productive) for a particular job.

In addition, by entering a job description and specification with their attendant characteristics into a database, an organization can do computer-searching for candidates by matching keywords (nouns) on their résumés with the keywords describing the job. A position in desktop publishing, for instance, might be described by the kinds of software programs with which applicants should be familiar: *Adobe Illustrator, Adobe PageMaker, Adobe Photoshop, Quark, Adobe Acrobat.*

Predicting Future Employee Needs Job descriptions change, of course: auto mechanics, for instance, now have to know how computer chips work in cars. (A C-class Mercedes may have 153 processors on board.) And new jobs are created: who could have visualized the position of "e-commerce accountant" 10 years ago, for example?

As you might expect, predicting future employee needs means you have to become knowledgeable about the *staffing the organization might need* and the *likely sources for that staffing*:

- **The staffing the organization might need.** You could assume your organization won't change much. In that case, you can fairly easily predict that jobs will periodically become unoccupied (because of retirement, resignations, and so on) and that you'll need to pay the same salaries and meet the same criteria about minority hiring to fill them.

  Better, however, to assume the organization will change. Thus, you need to understand the organization's vision and strategic plan so that the proper people can be hired to meet the future strategies and work.

- **The likely sources for staffing.** You can recruit employees from either inside or outside the organization. In looking at those inside, you need to consider which employees are motivated, trainable, and promotable and what kind of training your organization might have to do. A device for organizing this kind of information is a ***human resource inventory,* a report listing your organization's employees by name, education, training, languages, and other important information.**

  In looking outside, you need to consider the availability of talent in your industry's and geographical area's labor pool, the training of people graduating from various schools, and such factors as what kind of people are moving into your area. The U.S. Bureau of Labor Statistics and the U. S. Census Bureau issue reports on such matters. ●

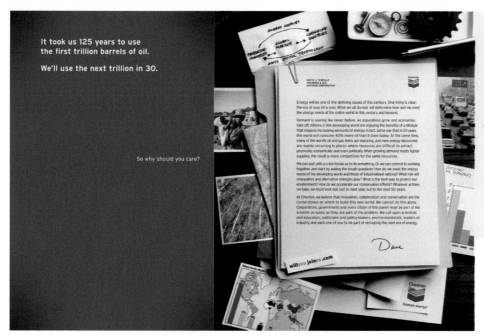

It took us 125 years to use the first trillion barrels of oil.

We'll use the next trillion in 30.

So why should you care?

One way to attract potential employees. Chevron's slick new ads serve two purposes: encouraging people to get involved in the energy crisis discussion and appealing to socially responsible engineers, scientists, and strategists looking to work for a company with an active conscience. The Web site noted in the ad includes additional close-ups of each component of the ad collage and a link to Chevron's careers portal.

9.2 THE LEGAL REQUIREMENTS OF HUMAN RESOURCE MANAGEMENT

> ❋ **major question** To avoid exposure to legal liabilities, what areas of the law do I need to be aware of?

THE BIG PICTURE

Four areas of human resource law any manager needs to be aware of are labor relations, compensation and benefits, health and safety, and equal employment opportunity.

Whatever your organization's human resource strategy, in the United States (and in U.S. divisions overseas) it has to operate within the environment of American law. Four areas you need to be aware of are as follows. Some important laws are summarized in the table opposite. *(See Table 9.1.)*

1. Labor Relations

The earliest laws affecting employee welfare had to do with unions, and they can still have important effects. Legislation passed in 1935 (the Wagner Act) resulted in the *National Labor Relations Board,* **which enforces procedures whereby employees may vote to have a union and for collective bargaining.** *Collective bargaining* **consists of negotiations between management and employees about disputes over compensation, benefits, working conditions, and job security.**

A 1947 law (the Taft-Hartley Act) allows the President of the United States to prevent or end a strike that threatens national security.

2. Compensation & Benefits

The Social Security Act in 1935 established the U.S. retirement system. The passage of the *Fair Labor Standards Act* **of 1938 established minimum living standards for workers engaged in interstate commerce, including provision of a federal minimum wage** (currently $5.25 an hour) and a maximum workweek (now 40 hours, after which overtime must be paid), along with banning products from child labor. Salaried executive, administrative, and professional employees are exempt from overtime rules. (We discuss compensation further in Section 9.6.)

3. Health & Safety

From miners risking tunnel cave-ins to cotton mill workers breathing lint, industry has always had dirty, dangerous jobs. Beginning with the Occupational Safety and Health Act (OSHA) of 1970, there has grown a body of law requiring organizations to provide employees with nonhazardous working conditions. Later laws extended health coverage for employees.

4. Equal Employment Opportunity

The effort to reduce discrimination in employment based on racial, ethnic, and religious bigotry and gender stereotypes began with Title VII of the Civil Rights Act of 1964. This established the *Equal Employment Opportunity (EEO) Commission,* **whose job it is to enforce antidiscrimination and other employment-related laws.** Title VII

table 9.1

SOME IMPORTANT RECENT U.S. FEDERAL LAWS AND REGULATIONS PROTECTING EMPLOYEES

Year	Law or regulation	Provisions
Labor relations		
1974	Privacy Act	Gives employees legal right to examine letters of reference concerning them
1986	Immigration Reform & Control Act	Requires employers to verify the eligibility for employment of all their new hires (including U.S. citizens)
1988	Polygraph Protection Act	Limits employer's ability to use lie detectors
1988	Worker Adjustment & Retraining Notification Act	Requires organizations with 100 or more employees to give 60 days' notice for mass layoffs or plant closings
2003	Sarbanes-Oxley Act	Prohibits employers from demoting or firing employees who raise accusations of fraud to a federal agency
Compensation and benefits		
1974	Employee Retirement Income Security Act (ERISA)	Sets rules for managing pension plans; provides federal insurance to cover bankrupt plans
1993	Family & Medical Leave Act	Requires employers to provide 12 weeks of unpaid leave for medical and family reasons, including for childbirth, adoption, or family emergency
1996	Health Insurance Portability & Accountability Act (HIPPA)	Allows employees to switch health insurance plans when changing jobs and receive new coverage regardless of preexisting health conditions; prohibits group plans from dropping ill employees
Health and safety		
1970	Occupational Safety & Health Act (OSHA)	Establishes minimum health and safety standards in organizations
1985	Consolidated Omnibus Budget Reconciliation Act (COBRA)	Requires an extension of health insurance benefits after termination
Equal employment opportunity		
1963	Equal Pay Act	Requires men and women be paid equally for performing equal work
1964, amended 1972	Civil Rights Act, Title VII	Prohibits discrimination on basis of race, color, religion, national origin, or sex
1967, amended 1978 and 1986	Age Discrimination in Employment Act (ADEA)	Prohibits discrimination in employees over 40 years old; restricts mandatory retirement
1978	Pregnancy Discrimination Act	Broadens discrimination to cover pregnancy, childbirth, and related medical conditions; protects job security during maternity leave
1990	Americans with Disabilities Act (ADA)	Prohibits discrimination against essentially qualified employees with physical or mental disabilities or chronic illness; requires "reasonable accommodation" be provided so they can perform duties
1991	Civil Rights Act	Amends and clarifies Title VII, ADA, and other laws; permits suits against employers for punitive damages in cases of intentional discrimination

applies to all organizations or their agents engaged in an industry affecting interstate commerce that employs 15 or more employees. Contractors who wish to do business with the U.S. government (such as most colleges and universities, which receive federal funds) must be in compliance with various executive orders issued by the President covering antidiscrimination. Later laws prevented discrimination against older workers and people with physical and mental disabilities.

Three important concepts covered by EEO laws are *discrimination, affirmative action,* and *sexual harassment.*

Discrimination   *Discrimination* **occurs when people are hired or promoted—or denied hiring or promotion—for reasons not relevant to the job,** such as skin color or eye shape, gender, religion, natural origin, and the like. When the organization is found to have been practicing discrimination, the people discriminated against may sue for back pay and punitive damages.

table 9.2

GUIDELINES FOR PREVENTING SEXUAL HARASSMENT

- Don't do uninvited touching, hugging, or patting of someone's body.

- Don't request or suggest sexual favors for rewards related to work or promotion.

- Don't make suggestive jokes of a sexual nature, demeaning remarks, slurs, or obscene gestures or sounds.

- Don't create sexual pictures or displays or written notes of a sexual nature.

- Don't laugh at others' sexually harassing words or behaviors.

Source: Adapted from U.S. Equal Employment Opportunity Commission, "Sexual Harassment," March 29, 2006, www.eeoc.gov/types/sexual_harassment.html (accessed August 12, 2006); and CCH Inc., "Business Owners' Tool Kit," © 2006 CCH Inc., www.toolkit.cch.com/tools/sxhrst_m.asp (accessed August 12, 2006).

Affirmative Action   *Affirmative action* **focuses on achieving equality of opportunity within an organization.** It tries to make up for past discrimination in employment by actively finding, hiring, and developing the talents of people from groups traditionally discriminated against. Steps include active recruitment, elimination of prejudicial questions in interviews, and establishment of minority hiring goals. It's important to note that EEO laws *do not* allow use of hiring quotas.[13]

Affirmative action has created tremendous opportunities for women and minorities, but it has been resisted more by some white males who see it as working against their interests. Affirmative action plans are more successful when employees view them as being fair and equitable and when whites are not prejudiced against people of color.[14] In addition, research shows that women and minorities hired on the basis of affirmative action felt stigmatized as unqualified and incompetent and experienced lower job satisfaction and more stress than employees supposedly selected on the basis of merit.[15]

Sexual Harassment   *Sexual harassment* **consists of unwanted sexual attention that creates an adverse work environment.** This means obscene gestures, sex-stereotyped jokes, sexually oriented posters and graffiti, suggestive remarks, unwanted dating pressure, physical nonsexual contact, unwanted touching, sexual propositions, threatening punishment unless sexual favors are given, obscene phone calls, and similar verbal or physical actions of a sexual nature.[16] The harassment may be by a member of the opposite sex or a member of the same sex, by a manager, by a co-worker, or by an outsider. If the harasser is a manager or an agent of the organization, the organization itself can be sued, even if it had no knowledge of the situation.[17]

There are two types of sexual harassment, according to the U.S. Supreme Court and the EEO:

- *Quid pro quo—tangible economic injury.* In the *quid pro quo* type, the person to whom the unwanted sexual attention is directed is put in the position of jeopardizing being hired for a job or obtaining job benefits or opportunities unless he or she implicitly or explicitly acquiesces.

- *Hostile environment—offensive work environment.* In the *hostile environment* type, the person being sexually harassed doesn't risk economic harm but experiences an offensive or intimidating work environment, as might be the case when one has to put up with lewd jokes or sexually oriented graffiti or remarks belittling the target's competence.

Sexual harassment does not refer to occasional compliments of a socially acceptable nature. Rather, it refers to offensive, unwelcome behavior that negatively affects morale and therefore job performance. The table at left shows some guidelines for preventing sexual harassment. *(See Table 9.2.)* ●

9.3 RECRUITMENT & SELECTION: PUTTING THE RIGHT PEOPLE INTO THE RIGHT JOBS

> **How can I reduce mistakes in hiring and find great people who might work for me?**
>
> major
> question

THE BIG PICTURE

Qualified applicants for jobs may be recruited from inside or outside the organization. The task of choosing the best person is enhanced by such tools as reviewing candidates' application forms, résumés, and references; doing interviews, either structured or unstructured; and screening with ability, personality, performance, and other kinds of employment tests.

"Digital résumés, digital employment advertising, digital résumé searches—it's a rebuilding of the [employment] infrastructure," says former Intel chairman Andy Grove.[18]

Companies have been using the public Internet with their own internal intranets to revolutionize their human resource departments, going online for everything from listing job openings to conducting new employee orientations. Recruitment efforts have migrated from simple online classified-ad–like job postings to Web sites that attract candidates with video and audio feeds. Yet as tempting as it is to think that most job-hunting activity has migrated to the Internet, only a minority of job-seekers used the Net in their last job search.[19]

Recruitment: How to Attract Qualified Applicants

At some time nearly every organization has to think about how to find the right kind of people. *Recruiting* **is the process of locating and attracting qualified applicants for jobs open in the organization.** The word "qualified" is important: You want to find people whose skills, abilities, and characteristics are best suited to your organization. Recruiting is of two types: *internal* and *external*.

Test Your Knowledge:
Recruitment Sources

1. Internal Recruiting: Hiring from the Inside   *Internal recruiting* **means making people already employed by the organization aware of job openings.** Indeed, most vacant positions in organizations are filled through internal recruitment, mainly through *job posting,* **placing information about job vacancies and qualifications on bulletin boards, in newsletters, and on the organization's intranet.**

2. External Recruiting: Hiring from the Outside   *External recruiting* **means attracting job applicants from outside the organization.** Notices of job vacancies are placed through newspapers, employment agencies, executive recruiting firms, union hiring halls, college job-placement offices, technical training schools, and word of mouth through professional associations. Many organizations—and not just high-technology companies—are advertising job openings on the Internet.

Both methods have advantages and disadvantages. *(See Table 9.3, next page.)*

Which External Recruiting Methods Work Best?   In general, the most effective sources are employee referrals, say human resource professionals, because, to protect their own reputations, employees are fairly careful about whom they

table 9.3

INTERNAL AND EXTERNAL RECRUITING: ADVANTAGES AND DISADVANTAGES

Internal recruiting

Advantages

1. Employees tend to be inspired to greater effort and loyalty. Morale is enhanced because they realize that working hard and staying put can result in more opportunities.

2. The whole process of advertising, interviewing, and so on is cheaper.

3. There are fewer risks. Internal candidates are already known and are familiar with the organization.

Disadvantages

1. Internal recruitment restricts the competition for positions and limits the pool of fresh talent and fresh viewpoints.

2. It may encourage employees to assume that longevity and seniority will automatically result in promotion.

3. Whenever a job is filled, it creates a vacancy elsewhere in the organization.

External recruiting

Advantages

1. Applicants may have specialized knowledge and experience.

2. Applicants may have fresh viewpoints.

Disadvantages

1. The recruitment process is more expensive and takes longer.

2. The risks are higher because the persons hired are less well known.

recommend, and they know the qualifications of both the job and the prospective employee.[20] Other above-average sources are college recruiters and executive search firms, and average sources are professional associations and newspaper ads.

At one time, the Internet seemed to offer the promise of an effective online hiring hall. Although a few companies do a majority of hiring via online systems, many job-seekers find their applications simply disappear into a black hole.[21] John Challenger, head of a Chicago outplacement firm, says there's a lot of good information on the Internet, but the popular job sites are simply time wasters.[22]

Realistic Job Previews   Often an organization will put on its best face to try to attract the best outside candidates—and then wonder why the new hires leave when the job doesn't turn out to be as rosy as promised.

A better approach is to present what's known as a **_realistic job preview,_ which gives a candidate a picture of both positive and negative features of the job and the organization before he or she is hired.**[28] People with realistic expectations tend to quit less frequently and be more satisfied than those with unrealistic expectations.

Selection: How to Choose the Best Person for the Job

Whether the recruitment process turns up a handful of job applicants or thousands, now you turn to the **_selection process,_ the screening of job applicants to hire the best candidate.** Essentially this becomes an exercise in _prediction:_ how well will the candidate perform the job and how long will he or she stay?

Screening Résumés & References

Because it seems to be getting harder to distinguish honest job applicants from the great number of dishonest ones, companies now routinely check résumés or hire companies that do so, such as Illinois-based Credentials LLC, which signs contracts with most major universities to tap into their databases to glean information about their students.

As far as recommendations from previous employers, however, many such employers don't give honest assessments of former employees, for two reasons: (1) They fear that if they say anything negative, they can be sued by the former employee. (2) They fear that if they say anything positive, and the job candidate doesn't pan out, they can be sued by the new employer.

In addition, some companies now resort to computer prescreening, which job seekers must pass before obtaining an in-person interview. Macy's, for instance, requires applicants to undergo an 8- or 10-minute screening, using a phone's keypad to answer multiple-choice questions (such as "If a customer complained to you about the selection of merchandise in a store, what would you do?").[23] Information services firm EDS has an entire Web site for screening candidates.[24]

Because honest references are so hard to get (see text), candidates are now being scrutinized more carefully for character and candor, with 96% of employers conducting background checks, according to a study by the Society for Human Resource Management.[25] And here's something to think about if you are a MySpace, Facebook, YouTube enthusiast or a blogger or vlogger (video logger): employers now frequently use search engines such as Google as a way to do continuous and stealthy background checks on prospective employees, effectively making an end run around discrimination laws.[26] And the background checks may continue throughout the period of your employment.[27]

Three types of selection tools are *background information, interviewing,* and *employment tests.*

I. Background Information: Application Forms, Résumés, & Reference Checks

Application forms and résumés provide basic background information about job applicants, such as citizenship, education, work history, and certifications.

Unfortunately, a lot of résumé information consists of mild puffery and even outrageous fairy tales. InfoLink Screening Services, which does background checks, reported that 14% of the tens of thousands of applicants it had screened had lied about their education.[29] Vermont-based ResumeDoctor.com, a résumé-writing service, surveyed 1,133 résumés that had been uploaded to its site and found that nearly 42.7% had at least one inaccuracy and 12.6% had two or more factual errors.[30] A 2003 survey by the Society of Human Resource Management found that 44% of 2.6 million respondents said they had misstated their work experience on their résumés.[31] And Background Information Services, a pre-employment screening company in Cleveland, found 56% of résumés contained falsehoods of some kind.[32]

Lying about education is the most prevalent distortion (such as pretending to hold a degree or an advanced degree). RadioShack CEO David Edmondson achieved some notoriety in 2006 and had to resign after a newspaper discovered he had falsely claimed on his résumé to hold degrees in psychology and theology (the college did not even offer degrees in psychology).[33] Automatic Data Processing of Roseland, New Jersey, which has studied employee background verification, reported that 41% of education records showed a difference between the information provided by an applicant and that provided by the educational institution.[34]

Another common fabrication includes creative attempts to cover gaps in employment history (although there are straightforward ways of dealing with this, such as highlighting length of service instead of employment dates).[35] People also lie about their ages for fear of seeming to be too experienced (hence expensive) or too old.[36] As you might expect, people also embellish their salary histories, job titles, and achievements on projects.[37]

2. Interviewing: Unstructured, Situational, & Behavioral-Description

Group Exercise:
Practicing Your Interview
Skills

Interviewing, the most commonly used employee-selection technique, may take place face to face, by videoconferencing, or—as is increasingly the case—via the Internet.[38] (However, face-to-face interviews have been found to be perceived as more fair and to lead to higher job acceptance intentions than were videoconferencing and telephone interviews.[39]) To help eliminate bias, interviews can be designed, conducted, and evaluated by a committee of three or more people. The most commonly used employee-selection technique, interviewing, takes three forms.

- **Unstructured interview.** Like an ordinary conversation, an ***unstructured interview* involves asking probing questions to find out what the applicant is like.** There is no fixed set of questions asked of all applicants and no systematic scoring procedure. As a result, the unstructured interview has been criticized as being overly subjective and apt to be influenced by the biases of the interviewer. Equally important, nowadays it is susceptible to legal attack, because some questions may infringe on non-job-related matters such as privacy, diversity, or disability.[40] However, compared with the structured interview method, the unstructured interview has been found to provide a more accurate assessment of an applicant's job-related personality traits.[41]

- **Structured interview type 1—the situational interview.** The ***structured interview* involves asking each applicant the same questions and comparing their responses to a standardized set of answers.**

   In one type of structured interview, the ***situational interview,* the interviewer focuses on hypothetical situations.** Example: "What would you do if you saw two of your people arguing loudly in the work area?" The idea here is to find out if the applicant can handle difficult situations that may arise on the job.

- **Structured interview type 2—the behavioral-description interview.** In the second type of structured interview, the ***behavioral-description interview,* the interviewer explores what applicants have actually done in the past.** Example: "What was the best idea you ever sold to a supervisor, teacher, peer, or subordinate?" This question (asked by the U.S. Army of college students applying for its officer training program) is designed to assess the applicant's ability to influence others.

3. Employment Tests: Ability, Personality, Performance, & Others

It used to be that employment selection tests consisted of paper-and-pencil, performance, and physical-ability tests. Now, however, ***employment tests* are legally considered to consist of any procedure used in the employment selection decision process.** Thus, even application forms, interviews, and educational and experience requirements are now considered tests.[45]

Probably the three most common employment tests are the following.

- **Ability tests.** *Ability tests* measure physical abilities, strength and stamina, mechanical ability, mental abilities, and clerical abilities. Telephone operators, for instance, need to be tested for hearing. Assembly-line workers are tested for manual dexterity.

- **Performance tests.** *Performance tests* measure performance on actual job tasks, as when secretarial applicants take a typing test or middle managers work on a small project. Some companies have an ***assessment center,* in which management candidates participate in activities for a few days while being assessed by evaluators.**

Practical Action

The Right Way to Conduct an Interview

Because hiring people who later have to be let go is such an expensive proposition, companies are now putting a great deal of emphasis on effective interviewing. Although this is a subject worth exploring further, here are some minimal suggestions:[42]

Before the Interview: Define Your Needs & Review Applicant's Résumé

Write out what skills, traits, and qualities the job requires. "Looking to hire somebody is like going to the supermarket," says one HR manager. "You need to have a list and know what you need."[43]

Look at the applicant's résumé or application form to determine relevant experience, gaps, and discrepancies.

Write Out Interview Questions

You should ask each candidate the same set of questions, so that you can compare their answers. (This helps keep you out of legal trouble, too.) In general, the questions should be designed to elicit the following types of information.

- **Does the applicant have the knowledge to do the job?** Examples: "Give an example where you came up with a creative solution." "How do you do research on the Internet?"

- **Can the applicant handle difficult situations?** Examples: "Tell me about a time when you dealt with an irate customer. How did you handle the situation and what was the outcome?"

- **Is the applicant willing to cope with the job's demands?** Examples: "How do you feel about making unpopular decisions?" "Are you willing to travel 30% of the time?"

- **Will the applicant fit in with the organization's culture?** Examples: "How would your last supervisor describe you?" "How much leeway did they give you in your previous job in charging travel expenses?"

Follow a Three-Scene Interview Scenario

The interview itself may follow a three-scene script.

- **Scene 1: The first 3 minutes—small talk and "compatibility" test.** The first scene is really a "compatibility test." It takes about 3 minutes and consists of exchanging small talk, giving you a chance to establish rapport and judge how well the candidate makes a first impression.

  Note: As many as four out of five hiring decisions are made within the first 10 minutes of an interview, according to some research. Thus, be aware that if you are immediately impressed with a candidate, you may spend more time talking than listening—perhaps trying to sell the candidate on the job rather than screen his or her qualifications.[44]

- **Scene 2: The next 15–60 minutes—asking questions and listening to the applicant's "story."** In the next scene, you ask the questions you wrote out (and answer those the candidate directs to you). Allow the interviewee to do 70%–80% of the talking.

  Take notes to remember important points. Don't ignore your "gut feelings." Intuition plays a role in hiring decisions. (But be careful you don't react to people as stereotypes.)

- **Scene 3: The final 1–2 minutes—closing the interview and setting up the next steps.** In the final minute, you listen to see whether the candidate expresses interest in taking the job.

After the Interview

Write a short report making some sort of quantitative score of the candidate's qualifications. Indicate your reasons for your decision.

Check the applicant's references before inviting him or her to a second interview.

- **Personality tests.** *Personality tests* measure such personality traits as adjustment, energy, sociability, independence, and need for achievement. One of the most famous such tests, in existence for 60-plus years, is the 93-question Myers-Briggs Type Indicator, with about 2.5 million tests given each year throughout the world. Myers-Briggs endures, observers say, "because it does a good job of pointing up differences between people, offers individuals a

Personality Tests: A Sporting-Goods Chain Uses a Web-Based Test to Screen Job Applicants

About 30% of American companies, from tiny independents to giant General Motors, use personality tests, according to one 2003 survey.[48] At Finish Line, a nationwide chain of sporting-goods stores, store managers use the results of Web-based personality tests developed by Unicru, of Beaverton, Oregon, to screen applicants for jobs as retail sales clerks. Candidates may apply through Unicru's kiosks or computer phones, which are installed in the stores. One Finish Line store in Chicago screens as many as 70 applicants a week during the store's pre-holiday season.

Unicru's computer scores test takers according to how strongly they agree or disagree (on a four-point scale) with statements such as "You do not fake being polite" and "You love to listen to people talk about themselves." High scores on attributes such as sociability and initiative reward applicants with a "green" rating that allows them to move on to an interview with a human manager. Scores in the middle earn a "yellow," and a lesser chance of landing a job; low-scoring "reds" are out of luck.

"The kinds of people who do well," says Unicru psychologist David Scarborough, ". . . obviously have to have good self-control. They have to be patient. They have to enjoy helping people. All those characteristics are quite measurable."[49] Finish Line says that Unicru's system has reduced turnover by 24%.

Your Call

There are, by some estimates, around 2,500 cognitive and personality employment tests on the market, and it's important that employers match the right test for the right purpose.[50] Moreover, tests aren't supposed to have a disparate impact on a protected class of people, such as certain racial or ethnic groups.[51] What questions would you want to ask about a personality test before you submitted yourself to it?

Lie detectors. Defense contractors and other security-minded companies are apt to require polygraph testing.

Test Your Knowledge: *Reliability and Validity*

revealing glimpse of themselves, and is a valuable asset in team-building, improving communication, and resolving personality-based conflict."[46]

Myers-Briggs and other personality tests should be used with caution because of the difficulty of measuring personality characteristics and of making a legal defense if the results are challenged.[47]

Other Tests The list of employment testing techniques has grown to include—in appropriate cases—drug testing, polygraph (lie detectors), genetic screening, and even (a questionable technique) handwriting analysis. (Human resource professionals need to be aware, incidentally, that there are a variety of products available on the Internet to help employees beat a company's drug tests.[52])

With any kind of test, an important legal consideration is the test's *reliability*—**the degree to which a test measures the same thing consistently**—so that an individual's score remains about the same over time, assuming the characteristics being measured also remain the same.

Another legal consideration is the test's *validity*—**the test measures what it purports to measure and is free of bias.** If a test is supposed to predict performance, then the individual's actual performance should reflect his or her score on the test. Using an invalid test to hire people can lead to poor selection decisions. It can also create legal problems if the test is ever challenged in a court of law. ●

9.4 ORIENTATION, TRAINING, & DEVELOPMENT

Once people are hired, what's the best way to see that they do what they're supposed to do?

major question

THE BIG PICTURE

Three ways newcomers are helped to perform their jobs are through *orientation,* to fit them into the job and organization; *training,* to upgrade the skills of technical and operational employees; and *development,* to upgrade the skills of professionals and managers.

In muckraker Upton Sinclair's 1906 novel *The Jungle,* "employers barely paused when a worker swooned from overwork or fell into a rendering tank," writes columnist Sue Shellenbarger. "They just got another warm body to replace him."[53]

That's hardly the case anymore. Now, as we said, the emphasis is on "human capital." Only a third to half of most companies' stock-market value is accounted for by hard assets such as property, plant, and equipment, according to a Brookings Institution report. Most of a firm's value is in such attributes as patents, processes, and—important to this discussion—employee or customer satisfaction.[54] The means for helping employees perform their jobs are *orientation, training,* and *development.*

Orientation: Helping Newcomers Learn the Ropes

The finalist candidate is offered the job, has accepted it, and has started work. Now he or she must begin, in that old sailor's phrase, to "learn the ropes." This is the start of *orientation,* **helping the newcomer fit smoothly into the job and the organization.**

Helping New Employees Get Comfortable: The First 6 Months

"How well will I get along with other employees?" "What if I screw up on a project?" Coming into a new job can produce a lot of uncertainty and anxiety. In part this is because, depending on the job, a new hire can accomplish only 60% as much in the first 3 months as an experienced worker, according to MCI Communications.[55]

The first 6 months on a job can be critical to how one performs over the long haul, because that's when the psychological patterns are established. Thus, employers have discovered that it's far better to give newcomers a helping hand than to let them learn possibly inappropriate behavior that will be hard to undo later.[56]

The Desirable Characteristics of Orientation

Like Orientation Week for new college students, the initial socialization period is designed to give new employees the information they need to be effective. In a large organization, orientation may be a formal, established process. In a small organization, it may be so informal that employees find themselves having to make most of the effort themselves.

Following orientation, the employee should emerge with information about three matters (much of which he or she may have acquired during the job-application process):

- **The job routine.** At minimum, the new employee needs to have learned what is required in the job for which he or she was hired, how the work will be evaluated, and who the immediate co-workers and managers are. This is basic.

Group training. In large companies, orientation and on-going training are often conducted in group sessions led by a presenter while the employees follow along. Do you see any problems with this approach?

- **The organization's mission and operations.** Certainly all managers need to know what the organization is about—its purpose, products or services, operations, and history. And it's now understood that low-level employees perform better if they, too, have this knowledge.

- **The organization's work rules and employee benefits.** A public utility's HR department may have a brochure explaining formalized work rules, overtime requirements, grievance procedures, and elaborate employee benefits. A technology startup may be so fluid that many of these matters will have not been established yet. Even so, there are matters of law (such as those pertaining to sexual harassment) affecting work operations that every employee should be made aware of.

Training & Development: Helping People Perform Better

Test Your Knowledge:
Training Methods

Which business strategy offers the highest returns: (1) downsizing; (2) total quality management, which focuses on work methods and process control; or (3) employee involvement, which focuses on upgrading workers' skills and knowledge? According to a study of 216 big firms, the winner is employee involvement, which had an average return on investment of 19.1% (versus 15.4% for downsizing and 15% for TQM).[57]

In hiring, you always try to get people whose qualifications match the requirements of the job. Quite often, however, there are gaps in what new employees need to know. These gaps are filled by training. The training process involves five steps, as shown below. *(See Figure 9.2.)*

figure 9.2

FIVE STEPS IN THE TRAINING PROCESS

HR professionals distinguish between *training* and *development.*

- **Training—upgrading skills of technical and operational employees.** Electronics technicians, word processors, computer network administrators, and X-ray technicians, among many others, need to be schooled in new knowledge as the requirements of their fields change. *Training,* **then, refers to educating technical and operational employees in how to better do their current jobs.**

- **Development—upgrading skills of professionals and managers.** Accountants, nurses, lawyers, and managers of all levels need to be continually educated in how to do their jobs better not just today but also tomorrow. *Development* **refers to educating professionals and managers in the skills they need to do their jobs in the future.**

Typical areas for which employee training and development are given are customer service, safety, leadership, computer skills, quality initiatives, communications, human relations, ethics, diversity, and sexual harassment.[58]

The Different Types of Training or Development   There are all kinds of training and development methods, and their effectiveness depends on whether what is being taught are facts or skills. If people are to learn *facts*—such as work rules or legal matters—lectures, videotapes, and workbooks are effective. If people are to learn *skills*—such as improving interpersonal relations or using new tools—then techniques such as discussion, role playing, and practice work better.

Another way to categorize training methods is to distinguish on-the-job from off-the-job methods. *On-the-job training* takes place in the work setting while employees are performing job-related tasks. Four major training methods are coaching, training positions, job rotation, and planned work activities. *Off-the-job training* consists of classroom programs, videotapes, workbooks, and the like. Lots of off-the-job training consists of **computer-assisted instruction (CAI), in which computers are used to provide additional help or to reduce instructional time.**

Example

Off-the-Job Training: Getting Ahead through E-Learning

College students, of course, have already discovered e-learning (electronic learning), and by 2008 an estimated 1 out of 10 college students will be enrolled in an online degree program.[59] Besides college students, several score million other people are taking short-term, practical courses related to their careers, mostly at business schools and continuing-education institutions around the country. Even top managers are brushing up. For instance, John Klotsche, 56, chairman of Baker & McKenzie, a global law firm, decided he and his 550 partners didn't know enough about managing a business in today's fast-changing marketplace, so all attorneys in his firm took a 2-week executive-education course at Northwestern University.[60]

But while most students are taking classes on campuses, the fastest-growing method of continuing education is via e-learning from videotapes, satellite lectures, or courses offered on the World Wide Web. The benefits of a virtual education are that no transportation is needed and you can follow a flexible schedule and often work at your own pace. However, there are

Off-the-job training. How does receiving feedback from an instructor affect your retention of knowledge?

some drawbacks. "The one thing e-learning boosters don't want to talk about is the simple fact that very few people ever actually finish an e-learning course when it involves a technically complex or lengthy subject such as software training or programming," says corporate trainer Roland Van Liew. "People perform the complex process of assimilating information best in socially interactive environments."[61]

The result is that there has been somewhat of a backlash against self-paced e-learning in favor of more instructor-led training. Because of the lack of classroom interaction between students and teachers in online education, both must assume more responsibility. "If students do not receive adequate teacher feedback and reinforcement," points out one writer, "they will not always know whether they possess an accurate knowledge of the subject matter."[62]

Your Call

Have you found e-learning (also known as online learning or distance learning) difficult? What problems can you identify with this as a training method?

What If No One Shows Up?   Many employers offer employee training, whether internal or external, or funding to attend seminars. But research has shown that a surprisingly high percentage of employees simply don't know about it. For instance, while 92% of employers in one survey offered funding to attend seminars and trade shows, only 28% of employees were aware the funding existed.[63] Clearly, then, employers need to find out whether the training offered fits with the majority of employee development goals. ●

9.5 PERFORMANCE APPRAISAL

➕ **major question** How can I assess employees' performance more accurately and give more effective feedback?

THE BIG PICTURE

Performance appraisal, assessing employee performance and providing them feedback, may be objective or subjective. Appraisals may be by peers, subordinates, customers, oneself. Feedback may be formal or informal.

"Ask most managers the most difficult part of their job, and they'll likely answer having to fire someone," writes Carol Hymowitz in *The Wall Street Journal*. "Ask what they endlessly put off doing, and they'll say advising weak employees that they must improve or risk losing their jobs."[64]

Clearly, it's unfair to underperforming employees to assume that time alone will enable them to shape up. And it's unfair to the organization to allow those employees to continue to stumble along without direction. It's part of your job as a manager to give the people who work for you honest appraisals.

Test Your Knowledge:
Appraisal Methods

Defining Performance Appraisal

Performance appraisal **consists of (1) assessing an employee's performance and (2) providing him or her with feedback.** Thus, this management task has two purposes: First, performance appraisal helps employees understand how they are doing in relation to objectives and standards; here you must *judge* the employee. Second, it helps in their training and personal development; here you must *counsel* the employee.[65]

Appraisals are of two general types—objective and subjective:

I. Objective Appraisals *Objective appraisals,* **also called *results appraisals,* are based on facts and are often numerical.** In these kinds of appraisals, you would keep track of such matters as the numbers of products the employee sold in a month, customer complaints filed against an employee, miles of freight hauled, and the like.

There are two good reasons for having objective appraisals:

How'm I doing? One of the most important tasks of being a manager is giving employees accurate information about their work performance. Which would you be more comfortable giving—objective appraisals or subjective appraisals?

- **They measure results.** It doesn't matter if two appliance salespeople have completely different personal traits (one is formal, reserved, and patient; the other informal, gregarious, and impatient) if each sells the same number of washers and dryers. Human resource professionals point out that, just as in business we measure sales, profits, shareholder value, and other so-called metrics, so it's important to measure employee performance, benefit costs, and the like as an aid to strategy.[66]

- **They are harder to challenge legally.** Not being as subject to personal bias, objective appraisals are harder for employees to challenge on legal grounds, such as for age, gender, or racial discrimination.

We discussed an objective approach in Chapter 5 under *management by objectives,* which can encourage employees to feel empowered to adopt behavior that will produce specific results. MBO, you'll recall, is a four-step process in which (1) managers and employees jointly set objectives for the employee, (2) managers develop action plans, (3) managers and employees periodically review the employee's performance, and (4) the manager makes a performance appraisal and rewards the employee according to results. For example, an objective for a copier service technician might be to increase the number of service calls 15% during the next 3 months.

2. Subjective Appraisals Few employees can be adequately measured just by objective appraisals—hence the need for *subjective appraisals,* **which are based on a manager's perceptions of an employee's (1) traits or (2) behaviors.**

Test Your Knowledge: *Potential Errors in the Rating Process*

- **Trait appraisals.** *Trait appraisals* are ratings of such subjective attributes as "attitude," "initiative," and "leadership." Trait evaluations may be easy to create and use, but their validity is questionable because the evaluator's personal bias can affect the ratings.

- **Behavioral appraisals.** Behavioral appraisals measure specific, observable aspects of performance—being on time for work, for instance—although making the evaluation is still somewhat subjective. An example is the *behaviorally anchored rating scale (BARS),* **which rates employee gradations in performance according to scales of specific behaviors.** For example, a five-point BARS rating scale about attendance might go from "Always early for work and has equipment ready to fully assume duties" to "Frequently late and often does not have equipment ready for going to work," with gradations in between.

Who Should Make Performance Appraisals?

As you might expect, most performance appraisals are done by managers. However, to add different perspectives, sometimes appraisal information is provided by other people knowledgeable about particular employees.

Peers, Subordinates, Customers, & Self Among additional sources of information are co-workers and subordinates, customers and clients, and the employees themselves.

- **Peers and subordinates.** Co-workers, colleagues, and subordinates may well see different aspects of your performance. Such information can be useful for development, although it probably shouldn't be used for evaluation. (Many managers will resist soliciting such information about themselves, of course, fearing negative appraisals.)

- **Customers and clients.** Some organizations, such as restaurants and hotels, ask customers and clients for their appraisals of employees. Publishers ask authors to judge how well they are doing in handling the editing, production, and marketing of their books. Automobile dealerships may send follow-up questionnaires to car buyers.

- **Self-appraisals.** How would you rate your own performance in a job, knowing that it would go into your personnel file? Probably the bias would be toward the favorable. Nevertheless, *self-appraisals* help employees become involved in the whole evaluation process and may make them more receptive to feedback about areas needing improvement.

360-Degree Assessment: Appraisal by Everybody We said that performance appraisals may be done by peers, subordinates, customers, and oneself. Sometimes all these may be used, in a technique called 360-degree assessment.

In a "theater in the round," the actors in a dramatic play are watched by an audience on all sides of them—360 degrees. Similarly, as a worker, you have many people watching you from all sides. Thus has arisen the idea of the *360-degree assessment,* **or** *360-degree feedback appraisal,* **in which employees are appraised not only by their managerial superiors but also by peers, subordinates, and sometimes clients,** thus providing several perspectives.

Typically, an employee chooses between six and 12 other people to make evaluations, who then fill out anonymous forms, the results of which are tabulated by computer. The employee then goes over the results with his or her manager and together they put into place a long-term plan for performance goals.

There are advantages and disadvantages to incorporating 360-degree feedback into the performance appraisal process. Recent research found that "improvement is most likely to occur when feedback indicates that change is necessary, recipients have a positive feedback orientation, perceive a need to change their behavior, react positively to feedback, believe change is feasible, set appropriate goals to regulate their behavior, and take actions that lead to skill and performance improvement."[67] At the heart of the process is the matter of *trust*. "Trust determines how much an individual is willing to contribute for an employer," says one expert. "Using 360 confidentially, for developmental purposes, builds trust; using it to trigger pay and personnel decisions puts trust at risk."[68]

Example

The 360-Degree Assessment: How Can It Be Compromised?

The 360-degree assessment can be very effective for performance improvement, career development, and even training. Texas computer maker Dell Inc., for instance, has realized that it needs to nurture its talent in order to achieve better performance. Accordingly, it designed an in-house training program taught primarily by Dell's own top executives, chairman Michael Dell and CEO Kevin Rollins, who submitted to 360-degree assessments in the hope of inspiring the executives beneath them to do the same. "Pay," says one report, "is now determined in part by how well a manager does at nurturing people."[69]

There are many ways, however, in which 360-degree assessments can become disasters. Curtiss Peck describes a health care organization in which the vice president of human resources was rated by his staff as being a strong, positive, effective leader, but his boss, the corporate senior vice president, did not rate him as being very effective. At a meeting to review the 360-degree assessment, the HR manager asked to discuss the differences in perceptions, but his boss said, "Obviously, everyone else is right and I am wrong. So, we'll just go along with what others have said"—thereby destroying the opportunity to give constructive feedback or coaching to the HR VP.

In another case, a manager confronted specific employees about their 360 assessments, effectively compromising the integrity of the process. In a third case, a sales organization executed an effective assessment and feedback, but, Peck says, "there was no accountability for development plans, there was no follow-up after the initial feedback meetings, and no training was offered or provided for clearly identified weaknesses in a majority of the sales people."[70]

Your Call

If you were the recipient of a 360-degree assessment, what kind of steps would you like to see taken to ensure that you could trust the process?

Forced Ranking: Grading on a Curve   To increase performance, as many as a quarter of Fortune 500 companies (such as General Electric, Ford, Cisco, and Intel) have instituted performance review systems known as forced ranking (or "rank and yank") systems.[71] **In *forced ranking performance review systems,* all employees within a business unit are ranked against one another and grades are distributed along some sort of bell curve**—just like students being graded in a college course. Top performers (such as the top 20%) are rewarded with bonuses and promotions, the worst performers (such as the bottom 20%) are rehabilitated or dismissed. For instance, every year 10% of GE's managers are assigned the bottom grade, and if they don't improve, they are asked to leave the company.

Proponents of forced ranking say it encourages managers to identify and remove poor performers and also structures a predetermined compensation curve, which enables them to reward top performers. If, however, the system is imposed on an organization overnight without preparation, by pitting employees against one another it can produce shocks to morale, productivity, and loyalty. There may also be legal ramifications, as when employees filed class-action lawsuits alleging that the forced-ranking methods had a disparate effect on particular groups of employees.[72]

Effective Performance Feedback

The whole point of performance appraisal, of course, is to stimulate better job performance. To gather information to feed back to the employee, a manager can use two kinds of appraisals—formal and informal.

I. Formal Appraisals *Formal appraisals* **are conducted at specific times throughout the year and are based on performance measures that have been established in advance.** An emergency medical technician might be evaluated twice a year by his or her manager, using objective performance measures such as work attendance time sheets and more subjective measures such as a BARS to indicate the employee's willingness to follow emergency procedures and doctors' and nurses' orders.

As part of the appraisal, the manager should give the employee feedback, describing how he or she is performing well and not so well and giving examples. Managers are sometimes advised to keep diaries about specific incidents so they won't have to rely on their memories (and so that their evaluations will be more lawsuit-resistant). Facts should always be used rather than impressions.

2. Informal Appraisals Formal appraisals are the equivalent of a student receiving a grade on a midterm test and a grade on a final test—weeks may go by in which you are unaware of how well you're doing in the course. Informal appraisals are the equivalent of occasional unscheduled pop quizzes and short papers or drop-in visits to the professor's office to talk about your work—you have more frequent feedback about your performance. *Informal appraisals* **are conducted on an unscheduled basis and consist of less rigorous indications of employee performance.**

You may not feel comfortable about critiquing your employees' performance, especially when you have to convey criticism rather than praise. Nevertheless, giving performance feedback is one of the most important parts of the manager's job.

Some suggestions for improvement appear below. *(See Table 9.4.)* ●

table 9.4

HOW TO GIVE PERFORMANCE FEEDBACK TO EMPLOYEES

Think of yourself as a coach, as though you were managing a team of athletes.

- *Take a problem-solving approach, avoid criticism, and treat employees with respect.* Recall the worst boss you ever worked for. How did you react to his or her method of giving feedback? Avoid criticism that might be taken personally.

  Example: Don't say "You're picking up that bag of cement wrong" (which criticizes by using the word "wrong"). Say "Instead of bending at the waist, a good way to pick up something heavy is to bend your knees. That'll help save your back."

- *Be specific in describing the employee's present performance and in the improvement you desire.* Describe your subordinate's current performance in specific terms and concentrate on outcomes that are within his or her ability to improve.

  Example: Don't say "You're always late turning in your sales reports." Say "Instead of making calls on Thursday afternoon, why don't you take some of the time to do your sales reports so they'll be ready on Friday along with those of the other sales reps."

- *Get the employee's input.* In determining causes for a problem, listen to the employee and get his or her help in crafting a solution.

  Example: Don't say "You've got to learn to get here at 9:00 every day." Say "What changes do you think could be made so that your station is covered when people start calling at 9:00?"

9.6 MANAGING AN EFFECTIVE WORKFORCE: COMPENSATION & BENEFITS

> ❌ **major question** What are the various forms of compensation?

THE BIG PICTURE
Managers must manage for compensation—which includes wages or salaries, incentives, and benefits.

Do we work only for a paycheck? Many people do, of course. But money is only one form of compensation.

Compensation **has three parts: (1) wages or salaries, (2) incentives, and (3) benefits.** In different organizations one part may take on more importance than another. For instance, in some nonprofit organizations (education, government), salaries may not be large, but health and retirement benefits may outweigh that fact. In a high-technology startup, the salary and benefits may actually be somewhat humble, but the promise of a large payoff in incentives, such as stock options or bonuses, may be quite attractive. Let's consider these three parts briefly. (We expand on them in Chapter 12 when we discuss ways to motivate employees.)

Wages or Salaries

Base pay **consists of the basic wage or salary paid employees in exchange for doing their jobs.** The basic compensation is determined by all kinds of economic factors: the prevailing pay levels in a particular industry and location, what competitors are paying, whether the jobs are unionized, if the jobs are hazardous, what the individual's level is in the organization, and how much experience he or she has.

Incentives

To induce employees to be more productive or to attract and retain top performers, many organizations offer incentives, such as commissions, bonuses, profit-sharing plans, and stock options. We discuss these in detail in Chapter 12.

Stock options. Companies like to offer favored employees stock options rather than higher salaries as benefits. Not only do employees place a high value on options, but companies can issue as many as they want without hurting corporate profits because, under present accounting rules, they don't have to count the options' value as an expense.

How to Make Incentive Pay Plans Meet Company Goals: Communicate Them to Employees[74]

There are many incentive compensation plans, ranging from cash awards and gifts to profit sharing and stock ownership, as we discuss in detail in Chapter 12.

Here let's ask the question: Do they work?

A 1998 survey of 139 companies, more than a third of them in the Fortune 500, found that 72% had variable pay plans. But only 22% said their plans had helped them achieve all their business objectives, and 28% said their plans had achieved none of them.

What explains the difference? Good plan design is important but so is good communication and oversight.

According to Ken Abosch, a consultant at Chicago-based Hewett Associates, which conducted the survey, often plans fail to deliver on their intended goals because employees aren't told enough about them and aren't kept up to date on the progress of the plans. Eighty-nine percent of companies that regularly communicated with their employees said their incentive plans met their goals, compared with only 57% of companies that did not discuss them with their employees.

Five keys to a successful incentive-pay plan are the following, according to Abosch:

- **Simplicity.** Does the plan pass the simplicity test? As Abosch puts it, "Can you explain it on an elevator ride?"

- **Clear goals.** Are the goals clear? Are the goals fully supported by management?

- **Realistic goals.** Are the goals realistic—that is, neither too difficult nor too easy to achieve?

- **Consistency with present goals.** Is the plan in line with the organization's present goals? Company goals change. "There are very few organizations that have the same business objective for five to seven years," points out Abosch.

- **Regular communication.** Do managers regularly communicate with employees about the plan? "People want a scorecard," Abosch says.

Benefits

Benefits, or *fringe benefits,* **are additional nonmonetary forms of compensation** designed to enrich the lives of all employees in the organization, which are paid all or in part by the organization. Examples are many: health insurance, dental insurance, life insurance, disability protection, retirement plans, holidays off, accumulated sick days and vacation days, recreation options, country club or health club memberships, family leave, discounts on company merchandise, counseling, credit unions, legal advice, and education reimbursement. For top executives, there may be "golden parachutes," generous severance pay for those who might be let go in the event the company is taken over by another company.

Benefits are no small part of an organization's costs. According to the U.S. Chamber of Commerce, employee benefit costs were 40.2% of payroll costs in 2005, with medical benefit costs constituting the largest part.[73] ●

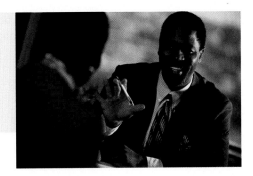

Communication is everything. The questions human resource managers need to keep in mind are: What good does it do a company to have attractive incentive plans if employees don't understand them? Will an employee exert the extra effort in pursuit of rewards if he or she doesn't know what the rewards are?

> ✴ **major question** What are some guidelines for handling promotions, transfers, disciplining, and dismissals?

THE BIG PICTURE

As a manager, you'll have to manage employee replacement actions, as by promoting, transferring, demoting, laying off, or firing.

American society, points out George Washington University sociologist Amitai Etzioni, can be depicted by the term "pluralism within unity." Unlike Europeans, who have great difficulty accepting the idea of diversity—of Turkish-Germans, Algerian-Frenchmen, or Romanian-Austrians, for example—in the United States we pretty much take it for granted that hyphenated Americans can be good workers and citizens.[75]

Indeed, our sense of inclusiveness seems to be gradually growing to embrace not only ethnic and racial diversity but also both genders and different ages, religions, sexual orientation, and physical and mental abilities. And there's more, as roles continue to change. Now more men seek paternity leaves, working parents want flexible hours, employees want to telecommute from home, and questions of "work-life balance" are receiving greater priority. What this shows is that as a manager you may have quite a complex workforce.

Among the major—and most difficult—decisions you will make as a manager are those about employee movement within an organization: whom should you promote? transfer? discipline? fire? All these matters go under the heading of *employee replacement*. And, incidentally, any time you need to deal with replacing an employee in a job, that's a time to reconsider the job description to see how it might be made more effective for the next person to occupy it.

You'll have to deal with replacement whenever an employee quits, retires, becomes seriously ill, or dies. Or you may initiate the replacement action by promoting, transferring, demoting, laying off, or firing.

Promotion

Promotion—moving an employee to a higher-level position—is the most obvious way to recognize that person's superior performance (apart from giving raises and bonuses). Three concerns are these:

Fairness It's important that promotion be *fair*. The step upward must be deserved. It shouldn't be for reasons of nepotism, cronyism, or other kind of favoritism.

Nondiscrimination The promotion cannot discriminate on the basis of race, ethnicity, gender, age, or physical ability.

Others' Resentments If someone is promoted, someone else may be resentful about being passed over. As a manager, you may need to counsel the people left behind about their performance and their opportunities in the future.

Transfer

Transfer is movement of an employee to a different job with *similar responsibility*. It may or may not mean a change in geographical location (which might be part of a promotion as well).

There are four principal reasons why employees might be transferred: to solve organizational problems by using their skills at another location; to broaden their experience in being assigned to a different position; to retain their interest and motivation by being presented with a new challenge; or to solve some employee problems, such as personal differences with their bosses.

Disciplining & Demotion

Poorly performing employees may be given a warning or a reprimand and then disciplined. That is, they may be temporarily removed from their jobs, as when a police officer is placed on suspension or administrative leave—removed from his or her regular job in the field and perhaps given a paperwork job or told to stay away from work.

Alternatively, an employee may be demoted—that is, have his or her current responsibilities, pay, and perquisites taken away, as when a middle manager is demoted to a first-line manager. (Sometimes this may occur when a company is downsized, resulting in fewer higher-level management positions.)

Dismissal

Dismissals are of three sorts:

Layoffs The phrase being *laid off* tends to suggest that a person has been dismissed *temporarily*—as when a car maker doesn't have enough orders to justify keeping its production employees—and may be recalled later when economic conditions improve.

Downsizings A *downsizing* is a *permanent* dismissal; there is no rehiring later. An auto maker discontinuing a line of cars or on the path to bankruptcy might permanently let go of its production employees.

Firings The phrase being *fired,* with all its euphemisms and synonyms—being "terminated," "separated," "let go," "canned"—tends to mean that a person was dismissed *permanently "for cause"*: absenteeism, sloppy work habits, failure to perform satisfactorily, breaking the law, and the like.

It used to be that managers could use their discretion about dismissals. Today, however, because of the changing legal climate, steps must be taken to avoid employees suing for "wrongful termination." That is, an employer has to carefully *document* the reasons for dismissals.

The Practical Action box on the next page offers some suggestions for handling dismissals. ●

Practical Action

The Right Way to Handle a Dismissal

"Employment at will" is the governing principle of employment in the great majority of states, which means that anyone can be dismissed at any time for any reason at all—or for no reason. Exceptions are whistleblowers and people with employment contracts. Civil-rights laws also prohibit organizations' dismissing people for their gender, skin color, or physical or mental disability.[76]

Four suggestions for handling a dismissal follow.

Give the Employee a Chance First

If you're dealing with someone who has a problem with absenteeism, alcohol/drug dependency, or the like, articulate to that employee what's wrong with his or her performance, then set up a plan for improvement (which might include counseling). Or if you're dealing with an employee who has a bad cultural or personality fit with the company—a buttoned-down, by-the-book style, say, that's at odds with your flexible, fast-moving organization—have a conversation and give the employee time to find a job elsewhere.[77]

Don't Delay the Dismissal, & Make Sure It's Completely Defensible

If improvements aren't forthcoming, don't carry the employee along because you feel sorry for him or her. Your first duty is to the performance of the organization. Make sure, however, that you've *documented* all the steps taken in advance of the dismissal. Also be sure that they follow the law and all important organizational policies.

Be Aware How Devastating a Dismissal Can Be—Both to the Individual & to Those Remaining

To the person being let go, the event can be as much of a blow as a divorce or a death in the family. Dismissals can also adversely affect those remaining with the company. This is what psychiatrist Manfred Kets de Vries calls *layoff survivor sickness,* which is characterized by anger, depression, fear, guilt, risk aversion, distrust, vulnerability, powerlessness, and loss of motivation. Indeed, a 5-year study by Cigna and the American Management Association found an enormous increase in medical claims, particularly for stress-related illnesses, not only among those dismissed but among continuing employees as well.[78]

Offer Assistance in Finding Another Job

Dismissing a long-standing employee with only a few weeks of severance pay not only hurts the person let go but will also hurt the organization itself, as word gets back to the employees who remain, as well as to outsiders who might be prospective employees. Knowledgeable employers offer assistance in finding another job.

"The best demonstration that a company's values are real," says management scholar Rosabeth Moss Kanter, "is to act on them today even for people who will not be around tomorrow. A company, like a society, can be judged by how it treats its most vulnerable. . . . Bad treatment of departing employees can destroy the commitment of those who stay."[79]

key terms used in this chapter

summary

 ### 9.1 Strategic Human Resource Management

- Human resource management consists of the activities managers perform to plan for, attract, develop, and retain an effective workforce. The purpose of the strategic human resource management process is to get the optimal work performance that will help realize the company's mission and vision.

- Two concepts important to human resource management are human capital and social capital. (1) Human capital is the economic or productive potential of employee knowledge. (2) Social capital is the economic or productive potential of strong, trusting, and cooperative relationships.

- Strategic human resource planning consists of developing a systematic, comprehensive strategy for (a) understanding current employee needs and (b) predicting future employee needs.

- Understanding current employee needs requires first doing a job analysis and then writing a job description and job specification. The purpose of job analysis is to determine, by observation and analysis, the basic elements of a job. Once the fundamentals of a job are understood, a job description can be written, which summarizes what the holder of the job does and how and why he or she does it. Next comes the job specification, which describes the minimum qualifications a person must have to perform the job successfully.

- Predicting employee needs means a manager needs to become knowledgeable about the staffing an organization might need and the likely sources of staffing, perhaps using a human resource inventory to organize this information.

 ### 9.2 The Legal Requirements of Human Resource Management

- Four areas of human resource law that any manager needs to be aware of are as follows: (1) Labor relations are dictated in part by the National Labor Relations Board, which enforces procedures whereby employees may vote to have a union and for collective bargaining. Collective bargaining consists of negotiations between management and employees about disputes over compensation, benefits, working conditions, and job security. (2) Compensation and benefits are covered by the Social Security Act of 1935 and the Fair Labor Standards Act, which established minimum wage and overtime pay regulations. (3) Health and safety are covered by the Occupational Safety and Health Act of 1970, among other laws. (4) Equal employment opportunity is covered by the Equal Employment Opportunity (EEO) Commission, whose job it is to enforce antidiscrimination and other employment-related laws. Three important concepts covered by EEO are (a) discrimination, which occurs when people are hired or promoted—or denied hiring or promotion—for reasons not relevant to the job, such as skin color or national origin; (b) affirmative action, which focuses on achieving equality of opportunity within an organization; and (c) sexual harassment, which consists of unwanted sexual attention that creates an adverse work environment and which may be of two types—the quid pro quo type, which may cause direct economic injury, and the hostile environment type, in which the person being harassed experiences an offensive work environment.

9.3 Recruitment & Selection: Putting the Right People into the Right Jobs

- Recruiting is the process of locating and attracting qualified applicants for jobs open in the organization. Recruiting is of two types: internal and external. (1) Internal recruiting means making people already employed by the organization aware of job openings. (2) External recruiting means attracting job applicants from outside the organization. A useful approach with external recruitment is the realistic job preview, which gives a candidate a picture of both positive and negative features of the job and organization before he or she is hired.

- The selection process is the screening of job applicants to hire the best candidates. Three types of selection tools are background information, interviewing, and employment tests. (1) Background information is ascertained through application forms, résumés, and reference checks. (2) Interviewing takes three forms. (a) The unstructured interview involves asking probing questions to find out what the applicant is like. (b) The structured interview involves asking each applicant the same questions and comparing their responses to a standardized set of answers. The first type of structured interview is the situational interview, in which the interview focuses on hypothetical situations. (c) The second type of structured interview is the behavioral-description interview, in which the interviewer explores what applicants have actually done in the past. (3) Employment tests are legally considered to consist of any procedure used in the employment selection decision process, but the three most common tests are ability tests, personality tests, and performance tests. Some companies have assessment centers, in which management candidates participate in activities for a few days while being assessed in performance tests by evaluators. Other tests include drug testing, polygraphs, and genetic screening. With any kind of test, an important legal consideration is the test's reliability, the degree to which a test measures the same thing consistently, and validity, whether the test measures what it purports to measure and is free of bias.

 9.4 Orientation, Training, & Development

- Three ways in which newcomers are helped to perform their jobs are through orientation, training, and development.

- Orientation consists of helping the newcomer fit smoothly into the job and organization. Following orientation, the employee should emerge with information about the job routine, the organization's mission and operations, and the organization's work rules and employee benefits.

- Training must be distinguished from development. Training refers to educating technical and operational employees in how to better do their current jobs.

- Development is the term describing educating professionals and managers in the skills they need to do their jobs in the future.

- Both training and development may be effected through on-the-job training methods and off-the-job training methods.

 9.5 Performance Appraisal

- Performance appraisal consists of assessing an employee's performance and providing him or her with feedback. Appraisals are of two general types—objective and subjective. Two good reasons for having objective appraisals are that they measure results and they are harder to challenge legally. (1) Objective appraisals are based on facts and are often numerical. An example is management by objectives. (2) Subjective appraisals are based on a manager's perceptions of an employee's traits or behaviors. Trait appraisals are ratings of subjective attributes such as attitude and leadership. Behavioral appraisals measure specific, observable aspects of performance. An example is the behaviorally anchored rating scale (BARS), which rates employee gradations in performance according to scales of specific behaviors.

- Most performance appraisals are made by managers, but they may also be made by co-workers and subordinates, customers and clients, and employees themselves (self-appraisals). Sometimes all of these may be used, in a technique called the 360-degree assessment, in which employees are appraised not only by their managerial superiors but also by their peers, subordinates, and sometimes clients. In another evaluation technique, forced ranking performance review systems, all employees within a business unit are ranked against one another, and grades are distributed along some sort of bell curve.

- Effective performance feedback can be effected in two ways: formal and informal. Formal appraisals are conducted at specific times throughout the year and are based on performance measures that have been established in advance. Informal appraisals are conducted on an unscheduled basis and consist of less rigorous indications of employee performance.

 9.6 Managing an Effective Workforce: Compensation & Benefits

- Compensation has three parts: wages or salaries, incentives, and benefits. (I) In the category of wages or salaries, the concept of base pay consists of the basic wage or salary paid employees in exchange for doing their jobs. (2) Incentives include commis-

sions, bonuses, profit-sharing plans, and stock options. (3) Benefits are additional nonmonetary forms of compensation, such as health insurance, retirement plans, and family leave.

 9.7 Managing Promotions, Transfers, Disciplining, & Dismissals

- Managers must manage promotions, transfers, disciplining, and dismissals. (I) In considering promotions, managers must be concerned about fairness, nondiscrimination, and other employees' resentment. (2) Transfers, or moving employees to a different job with similar responsibility, may take place in order to solve organizational problems, broaden managers' experience, retain managers' interest and motivation, and solve some employee problems. (3) Poor-performing employees may need to be disciplined or demoted. (4) Dismissals may consist of layoffs, downsizings, or firings.

---

management in action

How Should Managers Fire Good Workers Who Don't Fit?

Valerie Frederickson, a human-resources consultant in Silicon Valley, had a delicate problem: Her office administrator was smart and well-spoken, but after two months on the job, she didn't seem to like the work. "We needed to have her do things like data entry and clean the refrigerator, and she wanted to plan events for us," Ms. Frederickson says.

So Ms. Frederickson decided to let the administrator go—gently. She gave the woman a small amount of severance pay, helped her get a new job and assured her that the firing wasn't personal. "I told her, 'I like you a lot, and I think of you like a little sister, but I don't want you working here any more,'" Ms. Frederickson recalls.

That humane approach to firing may seem like common sense. But human-resources professionals say that figuring out how to handle employees who aren't fitting into the workplace is one of the trickiest tasks a manager can face.

Employers are well-schooled in how to eliminate jobs or fire poor performers. Yet they often don't know what to do with people who are doing their work passably, or even better, but aren't suited for the job, for reasons ranging from personal chemistry to mismatched skills.

In that gray area, employers often fumble, either keeping people on because they don't know what else to do, or seeking evidence of poor performance—even when that isn't the real issue. Badly handled firings can damage workplace morale, traumatize the employee, and end up in court, says Maureen Clark, a human-resources consultant in Menlo Park, Calif., who is asked often to investigate when things go wrong.

Employers need a graceful way to say, "It's not working; it's not your fault; let's figure out how to get you somewhere else," Ms. Clark says.

U.S. employers generally can fire employees not protected by a labor contract without a reason. In practice, however, courts often act to protect employees, faulting companies for firing longtime workers or those who have had good performance reviews. Judges also scrutinize disputed firings to ensure there was no race, gender, or other discrimination, employment attorneys say.

At the same time, increasing job mobility and changing skill requirements are producing more personnel problems that "don't fit in the box," says Rhoma Young, a human-resources consultant in Oakland, Calif.

In one case Ms. Young is investigating for a high-technology concern, the company shifted an engineer out of a programming position where he was doing well and into a job with more responsibility that required communication skills he lacked. The stress, combined with pressure from management, led the engineer to take several months of disability leave, and eventually the situation cost him his job. Now, he is threatening to sue.

Employment attorneys and human-resources consultants say companies can stay out of trouble by following some guidelines when thinking of firing a worker who doesn't fit in.

Managers should make sure they understand the problem—and be certain that the employee does, too. Sometimes bosses haven't properly explained what they want, or what the job requires, Ms. Young says.

Marlene Muraco, an attorney at labor-law specialist Littler Mendelson in San Jose, Calif., suggests considering options other than termination, such as training, a different post or another boss.

At Banco Popular North America, a unit of Puerto Rico's Popular Inc., human-resources chief Jeannette Frett says managers are instructed to tell employees who aren't fitting in exactly where they aren't meeting expectations and to offer training to fix the problem before considering dismissal. That has been important, because jobs at the bank have changed a lot in the past few years, as Banco Popular has snapped up other lenders—along with their staff—and has pushed its bankers to market the bank's services more aggressively.

If an employee must be fired, be honest and nice, experts say. Ms. Frett says Banco Popular gives employees it is letting go as much notice as possible, and sometimes it offers outplacement counseling or severance pay. "They walk out with their dignity and respect," Ms. Frett says.

Ms. Clark, the human-resources consultant, advises clients to specify in employee handbooks that the company will offer support to workers who are fired because they don't fit in.

One of those clients, the chief executive of public relations firm McGrath/Power in Silicon Valley, used the clause a few years ago when he fired a new account executive. Jonathan Bloom says the executive wasn't as experienced as he had hoped, and he felt that she was disturbing other employees by gossiping a lot. The company gave her a small severance payment and agreed with her about how to describe the dismissal.

"The more honest you are, the smoother the process tends to go," Mr. Bloom says.

Managers should remember that employees who aren't fitting in well are often unhappy themselves and may agree that they would be better off elsewhere, says Ms. Frederickson, the recruiter who fired her office administrator. "You want them to admit it is a bad fit and get out of there," she says.

Ms. Frederickson should know: She was fired years ago from a human-resources firm, largely because she didn't get along with her boss. She started her own firm later and competes with her former employer.

For Discussion

1. How might companies inadvertently discriminate when firing good employees who don't fit? Explain.
2. How can an employer use its recruitment and selection process to minimize the problem of hiring people who don't fit? Provide specific recommendations.
3. How can companies revise their performance appraisal procedures and processes to reduce the problem of employing people who don't fit? Discuss your recommendations.
4. Why is it hard for managers to fire employees who don't fit in? What can be done to overcome these causes? Explain.

Source: Excerpted from Phred Dvorak, "Firing Good Workers Who Are a Bad Fit," *The Wall Street Journal,* May 1, 2006. p. B5. Reprinted by permission of Dow Jones & Company, Inc. via The Copyright Clearance Center.

self-assessment

HR 101: An Overview

Objectives

1. To learn that there is more to HR than recruitment and hiring.
2. To assess your skills and determine if a career in HR is right for you.

Introduction

Your chosen career should optimally be based on your interests. The HR field, for example, offers many different career paths that require many different skills. The purpose of this exercise is to help you become familiar with the different career paths available to an HR professional and to see which path best fits your interests. This experience may help you decide if an HR career is right for you.

Among the professionals in the HR field are the following:

The HR generalist: HR generalists take on many different roles, whether negotiating a company's employee benefits package or interviewing a candidate for a director-level position. An HR generalist is supposed to be flexible and able to change gears at a moment's notice.

Compensation professional: Compensation professionals, who are very much in demand, design reward systems that attract, retain, and motivate employees. The job requires not only good technical skills but good people skills as well, a rare combination. It also requires a great deal of number crunching, creativity, and ingenuity, because a compensation package that might work for one employee might not work for another.

HRIS professional: HRIS stands for Human Resource Information Systems. With technology now such a key part of human resources, HRIS products help companies manage their personnel. Because the information systems are now so sophisticated, there is great demand for experienced HRIS professionals, who must be very detail oriented and, of course, enjoy working with computers. Such professionals are involved in product selection, systems customization, implementation, and ongoing administration.

Benefits professional: This individual is responsible for designing and implementing benefits plans. The job requires strong technical and communication skills.

Training and development professional: This individual is responsible for building environments that foster learning and management and leadership development. People in this field may be involved in distance learning programs as well as on-site, computer-based training programs.

Organizational development professional: Organizational development professionals work with top management to make sure that the organizational design sticks to the company's mission, vision, and goals. Besides doing some training and development, an OD professional must be able to embrace change and work long hours.

Instructions

Ask yourself the following questions and circle whether the statement applies to you. Once you have answered all of the questions, use the interpretation guidelines to analyze your responses and determine if a career in HR is right for you.

1. Do I enjoy changing gears on a moment's notice?	Yes	No
2. Am I open to learning about areas in which I currently have no expertise?	Yes	No
3. Am I comfortable leaving a project unfinished to handle emergency situations?	Yes	No
4. Do I consider myself fairly flexible?	Yes	No
5. Am I good at creatively solving problems when resources and instructions are scarce?	Yes	No
6. Do I have an aptitude for numbers?	Yes	No
7. Am I comfortable seeing other people's salaries?	Yes	No
8. Do I have strong communication skills?	Yes	No
9. Do I have strong computer skills?	Yes	No
10. Am I comfortable working at a computer all day?	Yes	No
11. Am I well organized?	Yes	No
12. Am I detail oriented?	Yes	No
13. Am I comfortable constantly reworking projects I thought were already done?	Yes	No

14. Am I willing to pay for and donate my free time to professional certifications?	Yes	No
15. Am I good at taking complex ideas and making them understandable to the average person?	Yes	No
16. Am I good at expressing my ideas and getting people to go along with them?	Yes	No
17. Am I a creative person with strong computer skills?	Yes	No
18. Am I comfortable in front of an audience?	Yes	No
19. Am I comfortable working one very long project instead of lots of small projects?	Yes	No
20. Am I passionate about learning and about teaching others?	Yes	No
21. Can I handle change? Can I handle it well?	Yes	No
22. Do I enjoy pulling together pieces of a puzzle?	Yes	No
23. Do I perform well in times of stress?	Yes	No
24. Am I a big-picture person?	Yes	No

Interpretation

If you answered "yes" to three or more of questions 1–4 (which apply to the HR generalist), three or more of questions 5–8 (compensation professional), three or more of questions 9–12 (HRIS professional), three or more of questions 13–16 (benefits professional), three or more of questions 17–20 (training and development professional), and three or more of questions 21–24 (organizational development professional), then you are well suited for the field of HR.

If you answered "no" to most of the previous 24 questions, the field of HR may not be right for you. (However, since this is only a small sampling of the many aspects of this field, there may still be a place for you in HR.)

Questions for Discussion

1. To what extent did the results fit your interests? Explain.
2. Look at the top two areas of HR for which you tested as being best suited. Look over the descriptions of these fields. What skills do you need to have to be successful? Describe.
3. Even if you do not pursue a career in HR, which skills do you feel you should continue to develop? Explain.

Adapted from R.C. Matuson, "HR 101: An Overview, Parts I and II," *Monster HR*, **www.monster.com,** June 2002.

 group exercise

Choosing the Best Person for the Job

Objectives

- To gain further knowledge of the selection process.
- To practice looking for the skills that help HR professionals find the best person for a job.

Introduction

As you learned from this chapter, the recruitment process may turn up a handful of applicants or it may turn up thousands. During the selection process, how do hiring managers make their decisions? What can an applicant do to stand out in the crowd? It is important for applicants to be able to highlight the skills that make them unique. Skills can be looked at in three ways: (1) those gained from past experience, (2) those that can carry through to any job (portable skills), and (3) personal skills. The purpose of this exercise is to enable you to practice looking for skills that help HR professionals find the best person for the job.

Instructions

Break into groups of five to six people. Read the following case about Gina, who has applied for a job at a high-technology company. The company has its own ideas about the ideal applicant, but it hasn't given out much information about them. You are going to try to help Gina get the job. (Remember, she's not the only applicant, so she needs to stand out.) After reading the case:

1. Take a piece of paper and divide it into three columns—the first headed "Past experience," the second "Portable skills" (skills that will carry to any job), and the third "Personality skills." Your group is to identify what skills you think Gina should have based on "Past experience," "Portable skills," and "Personality skills."
2. Using these skills as a guide, brainstorm which of these skills you think Gina has. Make sure you put them in the correct column.
3. Then examine Gina's case again and come up with as many different skills as you can that go *beyond* what the company is looking for. Think about what past skills Gina has besides marketing experience that would make her the perfect candidate.

The Case

After 5 years, Gina was laid off as a marketing manager for a high-tech company. "Gina hates not having a job," her roommate says. "She always has to have something to do. If not, she'll jump up and start cleaning just to be productive. She's also very organized. For instance, she files all her CDs in alphabetical order."

At her old job, Gina was in charge of marketing the company over the World Wide Web and so she spent a lot of time at the computer. Since being laid off, she has been using the computer to look for another job, as well as searching the Web for art projects to do in her spare time. Her friends describe her as being not only fiercely independent but also very creative. In college, they say, she was always writing. "She used to write short stories," her roommate recalls, "and also worked part time on the college newspaper."

Her friends also say Gina's sense of humor keeps her from feeling unbearably depressed about the layoff, and they believe she will find a new job quickly. Her mother agrees. "Gina is the oldest child," she says, "and she has always been a very good team leader. She's very organized and ever since she was a little girl she's been good at coordinating things." Her father says his daughter has a great head for numbers, and he hoped she would follow in his tracks and become an accountant.

Gina's supervisor at her old job says they hated to see her go. "She was so good at dealing with our customers," he says. "She was also one of the few marketing managers who had a close business relationship with our vendors. In addition, she was very goal oriented: We would tell her what we wanted to achieve and she would dive in head first." Her direct reports state that Gina had a good attitude, a great sense of humor, excellent follow-through, and a superior ability to solve problems. Her colleagues and supervisor all comment on Gina's creativity and her ability to learn things quickly. One co-worker noted that Gina was "very flexible" and "always showed good judgment."

Questions for Discussion

1. If you were the HR professional at this high-tech company, would you hire Gina? Do you feel she has the appropriate skills? Why or why not?
2. Are there any skills Gina does not exhibit that you feel she should develop in order to be a more appealing candidate? Discuss.
3. What are some things Gina can do to improve her skills for her future job in marketing? Explain.

Adapted from "Assessing Your Skills: What Makes You Different from All the Others?" **http://interview.monster.com/** accessed June 2002.

ethical dilemma

More Companies Want the FBI to Screen Employees for Terrorist Connections

A wide range of industry groups, from trucking associations to sporting-event organizers, are trying to gain access to the FBI's closely guarded data on suspected terrorists and criminals in an effort to screen their own employees.

The American Trucking Association, for one, is lobbying Congress to give it authority to go directly to the Federal Bureau of Investigation with names and fingerprints of drivers, loading-dock workers, and job applicants of its member companies. . . .

Fueling this push is the supposition that, next time around, terrorists may attack something besides an airplane. But allowing companies to tap into FBI intelligence banks opens a can of worms both for the government and civil liberties advocates. Unions protest that employers could use the system to find old skeletons in people's closets and use them as a pretext for dismissal. . . .

Giving an industry access to the FBI lists typically requires an act of Congress or a new federal regulation. Some industries, such as banking, airlines, and nuclear power plants, already have such access. . . .

Of particular interest to this latest round of companies are the FBI's watch lists of suspected terrorists, including people who may have infiltrated the American workplace years ago as "sleeper" agents. One of these lists, from the State Department, contains 64,000 names from around the world. The FBI keeps its own list and won't say how many people are on it. . . .

Although terrorists typically are trained to avoid detection, at least a few of the Sept. 11 hijackers were on watchlists because their names had popped up in connection with prior attacks: Mohamed Atta had been flagged by the Customs Service, and Khalid al-Midhar was on a CIA list.

FBI background checks should turn up anybody with, among other things, an arrest record, criminal conviction, or protective order filed against them.

Not all this information is readily accessible to those outside the agency, and companies are concerned about missing such information in a check on their own. . . .

But truckers and others who want FBI background checks say the pros outweigh the cons. Tony Chrestman, president of the trucking unit of Ruan Transportation Management Systems, says: "Previously, I would never have thought about anyone taking one of our loads of propane and running it into a building. There's got to be improvements to background checks."

Solving the Dilemma

What would you do if you were evaluating the trucking industry's desire for FBI background checks?

1. Allow the trucking industry to obtain FBI background checks.
2. Not allow the trucking industry access to FBI records because such information might adversely affect employment conditions for potential and existing employees.
3. Allow the trucking industry to obtain limited information (that is, only information pertaining to terrorism) about people.
4. Invent other options. Explain.

Source: Excerpted from Ana Davis, "Companies Want the FBI to Screen Employees for Suspected Terrorists," *The Wall Street Journal*, February 6, 2002, pp. B1, B4. Reprinted by permisssion of Dow Jones & Company, Inc. via The Copyright Clearance Center.

 video case

Patagonia: Nurturing the Environment & Employees

Patagonia is certainly not your father's company. Patagonia, a pioneer in designing outdoor apparel, receives some 900 résumés for every vacancy. It seeks dedicated and passionate employees, not restricting the applicant pool to sports enthusiasts, athletes, or environmental activists. Believe it or not, the company has a mere 4% turnover rate. Its culture is based on its environmental, moral, ethical, and philosophical culture, and therefore, it hires like-minded people for careers based on psychological, not financial, success.

Worker satisfaction is important at Patagonia. Four keystone projects help employees derive satisfaction at work. First, the "Let my people surf" motto adapts a "do it while you can" philosophy. Employees enjoy a flexible schedule and can leave their workplace at any-time to pursue their passion. If the spirit moves her, an employee can leave work to go fishing or surfing—the work will get done. Second, Patagonia's internship program allows employees a 60-day "sabbatical" to work for a grassroots organization of their choice. Upon their return from the sabbatical, employees must make a slideshow presentation and submit a written report about their sabbatical activities. On occasion, some employees have completed their internship and left the company to take up their cause as full-time activists. Patagonia's emphasis on growing employees into good people, not just into cogs in the wheel of their company, means that they consider this just as much a successful outcome as if the employee in question had returned for another five years. The third major employee benefit, the on-site child care program, offers employees the opportunity to bring their children to work in a nurturing and safe environment. Employees can visit their children during the workday, and the childcare facility is integrated into the life of the offices surrounding it. This program has increased job satisfaction and helped to strengthen work-family relationships. Finally, the company has imposed an "earth tax" on itself through its "1% for the planet" program. In essence, the company gives 1% of sales and 10% of pre-tax profits to environmental grassroots organizations worldwide. Last year, this percentage amounted to nearly $2.5 million.

The company also sponsors a foundation essentially run by employees. Every 18 months, the foundation holds a conference for advocacy groups who lack sophistication in writing and executing business plans. By the end of the conference, after being trained by employees, these groups leave with a business plan and are ready to implement it. In addition to these unique company benefits, Patagonia offers employees surf lessons, free civil disobedience classes, and bail money (yes, like in jail) for participating in nonviolent actions that are consistent with company values.

Given these unique employee benefits, it's no surprise that *Fortune* has named Patagonia one of the best companies to work for, nor that the company needs to undertake little recruiting for employees. With this kind of work environment, Patagonia ensures that it will continue to enjoy its extremely high reputation as an employer.

Questions

1. People are an organization's most important asset. How does Patagonia let employees know how important they are?
2. Discuss Patagonia's hiring and selection process. Does it follow the typical process? What makes it different than other similar organizations?
3. Discuss some of the nontraditional benefits Patagonia offers employees. Do you believe they enhance worker satisfaction? Why? Why not?

Source: Joseph C. Santora, EdD, Essex County College.

chapter 10

Organizational Change & Innovation

Lifelong Challenges for the Exceptional Manager

Major Questions You Should Be Able to Answer

10.1 The Nature of Change in Organizations
Major Question: Since change is always with us, what should I understand about it?

10.2 Organization Development: What It Is, What It Can Do
Major Question: What are the uses of OD, and how effective is it?

10.3 Promoting Innovation within the Organization
Major Question: What do I need to know to encourage innovation?

10.4 The Threat of Change: Managing Employee Fear & Resistance
Major Question: How are employees threatened by change, and how can I help them adjust?

Managing for Innovation & Change Takes a Careful Hand

"What I try to do is go out and grab lightning every day."

That's the way Terry Fadem, head of business development at DuPont Co., describes the company's never-ending search for tomorrow's breakthroughs.[1]

Managing for innovation and change takes a careful hand. "Even when their jobs depend on adopting and inventing new maneuvers," says columnist Carol Hymowitz, "most workers hold fast to old ones. The majority either are overwhelmed when asked to do things differently or become entrenched, clinging harder to the past. . . ."[2]

Because the revolution in technology is inflicting what Tom Peters calls Discontinuous Times, or "a brawl with no rules," dealing with change is an ongoing challenge for every manager.[3] "The one constant factor in business today is we live in a perpetual hurricane season," says Mellon Bank Corp. Vice Chairman Martin McGuinn. "A leader's job is less about getting through the current storm and more about enabling people to navigate the ongoing series of storms."[4]

Some ways to deal with change and innovation:[5]

- **Allow room for failure.** "If somebody has an idea, don't stomp on it," says a psychologist and developer of ideas at Intuit, the software company famous for TurboTax and QuickBooks. "It's more important to get the stupidest idea out there and build on it than not to have it in the first place."[6] At Intuit, failure is very much an option as long as one learns from it.

- **Give one consistent explanation for the change.** When a company is undergoing change, myriad rumors will fly and employees will be uneasy; you and the managers who report to you need to give one consistent explanation. In McGuinn's case, the explanation for overhauling Mellon Bank's retail division was "We want to be the best retailer in financial services."

- **Look for opportunities in unconventional ways.** Most "new" products and services are really knockoffs or marginal variations of the things already on the market and hence are doomed to failure, says Robert Cooper, professor of marketing at Ontario's McMaster University. This doesn't mean, of course, that there isn't room for leveraging existing products with utterly unoriginal ideas. But most people are blinded by the limits of conventional wisdom and their own experience and fail to see huge potential markets in unconventional concepts. Try this advice from a Yale entrepreneurship instructor: Write down every hassle you encounter during the day. "At the end of the month, you will have 20 business ideas," he says, "and some of them will work."[7]

- **Have the courage to follow your ideas.** This may be the hardest job of all—trying to convince others that your ideas for change are feasible, especially if the ideas are radical. This may mean working to gain allies within the organization, standing up to intimidating competitors inside and out, and perhaps being prepared to follow a lonely course for a long time.

- **Allow grieving, then move on.** Managers overseeing change need to give long-term employees a chance to grieve over the loss of the old ways, says McGuinn, who found that staffers were more willing to change after they had a chance to vent their fears.

For Discussion If you were going to instill a climate of innovation in a company you worked for, what kinds of things would you do?

forecast

What's Ahead in This Chapter

In this chapter, we consider the nature of change in organizations, including the two types of change—reactive and proactive—and the forces for change originating outside and inside the organization. We describe the four areas in which change is often needed: people, technology, structure, and strategy. We then discuss organizational development, a set of techniques for implementing planned change. We next discuss how to promote innovation within an organization. Finally, we explore the threat of change and how you can manage employee fear and resistance.

10.1 THE NATURE OF CHANGE IN ORGANIZATIONS

✻ major question Since change is always with us, what should I understand about it?

THE BIG PICTURE
Two types of change are reactive and proactive. Forces for change may consist of forces outside the organization—demographic characteristics, market changes, technological advancements, and social and political pressures. Or they may be forces inside the organization—employee problems and managers' behavior. Four areas in which change is often needed are people, technology, structure, and strategy.

People are generally uncomfortable about change, even change in apparently minor matters. Philosopher Eric Hoffer told how as a younger man he spent a good part of one year as an agricultural worker picking peas, starting in southern California in January and working his way northward. He picked the last of the peas in June, then moved to another area where, for the first time, he was required to pick string beans. "I still remember," he wrote, "how hesitant I was that first morning as I was about to address myself to the string bean vines. Would I be able to pick string beans? Even the change from peas to string beans had in it elements of fear."[8]

If small changes can cause uneasiness, large changes can cause considerable stress. And as a manager, you will no doubt have to deal with both.

Fundamental Change: What Will You Be Called On to Deal With?

"It is hard to predict, especially the future," physicist Niels Bohr is supposed to have quipped.

But it is possible to identify and prepare for *the future that has already happened*, in the words of management theorist Peter Drucker, by looking at some of the fundamental changes that are happening now.[9] Declining population in developed countries. More diversity in the workforce. The ascent of knowledge work. Increased globalization. The rise of business-to-business (B2B) technology. Digital long-distance networks. The increase in data storage. The capturing of customer-specific information. The customization of mass goods. Sales in the form of auctions instead of fixed prices.[10]

Beyond these overarching trends there are also some supertrends shaping the future of business:[11]

1. The Marketplace Is Becoming More Segmented & Moving Toward More Niche Products
In the recent past, managers could think in terms of mass markets—mass communication, mass behavior, and mass values. Now we have "demassification," with customer groups becoming segmented into smaller and more specialized groups responding to more narrowly targeted commercial messages. "Our culture and economy are increasingly shifting away from a focus on a relatively small number of hits (mainstream products and markets) . . . and moving toward a huge number of niches," says Chris Anderson in *The Long Tail*. "In an era without the constraints of physical shelf space and other bottlenecks of distribution, narrowly targeted goods and services can be as economically attractive as mainstream fare."[12] Or, as the book's subtitle states, "the future of business is selling less of more."

Example: In the Internet Age, retailers like Amazon.com and Apple Computer are not constrained by physical shelf space and can offer consumers a much wider variety of products, yet small sales, one or two rather than millions of items at a time, can produce big profits.

2. There Are More Competitors Offering Targeted Products, Requiring Faster Speed-to-Market Companies offering a broad range of products or services are now experiencing intense pressure from competitors offering specialized solutions—and beating them to the punch by devising novel speed-to-market strategies. Indeed, "Speed is emerging as the ultimate competitive weapon," says one report. "Some of the world's most successful companies are proving to be expert at spotting new opportunities, marshaling their forces, and bringing to market new products or services in a flash."[13]

Example: Virgin Group Ltd., headed by Sir Richard Branson, is known mainly for its music and airline businesses, but it has entered several new businesses one after the other—mobile phones, credit cards, hotels, games, trains, even space travel—and very quickly. Virgin Comics, aimed at India's multibillion-dollar comics market, went from idea to public announcement in less than 11 months.

3. Some Traditional Companies May Not Survive Radically Innovative Change In *The Innovator's Dilemma: When New Technologies Cause Great Firms to Fail,* Clayton Carlson, a Harvard Business School professor, argues that when successful companies are confronted with a giant technological leap that transforms their markets, all choices are bad ones. Indeed, he thinks, it's very difficult for an existing successful company to take full advantage of a technological breakthrough such as digitalization— what he calls "disruptive innovation." Instead, he argues that such a company should set up an entirely separate organization that can operate much like a startup.[14]

Example: Eastman Kodak found its sales hit $14 billion in 1999 and dropped to $13.3 billion in 2003 as digital cameras began to take their toll on the chemical-based film business. The company quit making big investments in film and shifted its resources to digital cameras and accessories, digital health-imaging technologies, and inkjet printing and liquid displays. Time will tell whether the new strategy will succeed.

Rising to the challenge.
An indication that Kodak is inventing innovative solutions to the problem of the digital revolution, this billboard advertises a digital camera that can transmit photos wirelessly.

4. China, India, & Other Offshore Suppliers Are Changing the Way We Work As we said in Chapter 2, globalization and outsourcing are transforming whole industries and changing the way we work. China, India, Mexico, the Philippines, and other countries offer workers and even professionals willing to work twice as hard for half the pay, giving American businesses substantial labor savings. These developing nations also, says *BusinessWeek,* offer "enormous gains in efficiency, productivity, quality, and revenues that can be achieved by fully leveraging offshore talent."[15] While unquestionably some American jobs are lost, others become more productive, with some engineers and salespeople, for example, being liberated from routine tasks so that they can spend more time innovating and dealing with customers.

Example: In 3 years, California-based IndyMac Bancorp has risen from the 22nd-largest U.S. mortgage issuer to the ninth, using not only innovations in technology to process loan applications but also by following an offshoring strategy, using mostly Indian staff to do customer calls and bill collection and to write more efficient software. "Yet rather than losing any American jobs," points out *BusinessWeek,* "IndyMac has doubled its U.S. workforce to nearly 6,000 in four years—and is still hiring."[16]

5. Knowledge, Not Information, Is Becoming the New Competitive Advantage "Information is rapidly becoming a profitless commodity, and knowledge is becoming the new competitive advantage," says San Diego management consultant Karl Albrecht.[17] That is, as information technology does more of the work formerly done by humans, even in high-tech areas (such as sorting data for relevance), many low-level employees previously thought of as knowledge workers are now being recognized as "data workers," who contribute very little added value to the processing of information. Unlike routine information handling, knowledge work is analytic and involves problem solving and abstract reasoning—exactly the kind of thing required of skillful managers, professionals, salespeople, and financial analysts. As futurists Alvin and Heidi Toffler suggest, knowledge work drives the future and creates wealth.[18]

Example: Many so-called *back-office* systems and functions, those the customer does not see, such as inventory management and accounts payable, are rapidly being outsourced, although even some tasks of software engineers and other technical experts are also being sent overseas.

Clearly, we are all in for an interesting ride.

Two Types of Change: Reactive versus Proactive

As a manager, you will typically have to deal with two types of change: *reactive* and *proactive.*

I. Reactive Change: Responding to Unanticipated Problems & Opportunities When managers talk about "putting out fires," they are talking about **reactive change, making changes in response to problems or opportunities as they arise.** When you have to respond to surprises, there is usually less time to get all the information and resources you need to adequately manage the change, and serious mistakes

---

Example

Reactive Change: Bausch & Lomb Responds to a Serious Eye Infection among Contact Lens Wearers

Many companies do not handle crises well. Among the instances: Exxon's handling of the 1989 *Exxon Valdez* oil spill in the Gulf of Alaska, Jack In The Box's management of the 1993 botulism crisis in Washington, TWA's actions on the 1996 crash of Flight 800 off Long Island, and Coca-Cola's reactions to the 1999 illness in Europe attributed to bottlers in Belgium and France. Could some of these have been anticipated and managed better?

More recently, in 2006, Bausch & Lomb, the Rochester, New York, maker of eye-care products, was presented with "about the worst thing that can happen to a consumer-products company," according to *BusinessWeek,* "a suggestion that your product is harming customers."[19] The Centers for Disease Control & Prevention reported an upsurge in a particular fungal eye infection that can cause blindness, and a large number of the more than 100 reported cases involved contact lens wearers who used Bausch & Lomb's contact lens cleaner MoistureLoc. After some retailers began removing the product from their shelves, B&L asked all retailers to stop selling the lens cleaner while public health officials examined the company's South Carolina plant to see if there was a link to the infections.

MoistureLoc is part of B&L's ReNu line, which has helped make lens care the company's most profitable sector. But as the crisis played out, the company made a crucial decision. When the CDC made its first announce-

ment about an outbreak on April 10, B&L said it was halting shipments of MoistureLoc in the United States as a precaution, a move short of a product recall. But this left retailers with potential liability for continued sales. It also made the company appear to be more concerned about its commercial future than the health risks to its customers. Three days later B&L announced a full United States recall, then a global withdrawal.[20] Four months later, Bausch & Lomb had lost market share, was facing legal costs related to the recall, and had slashed its 2006 earnings forecast by 80%.[21]

Bausch & Lomb had had plenty of opportunity to learn from a famous crisis faced down by Johnson & Johnson years before. In 1982, someone in the Chicago area added cyanide to J&J's best-selling Extra-Strength Tylenol packages on store shelves, and seven people died. The company took immediate and unprecedented action, recalling all unsold Tylenol at a cost of $100 million, offering refunds, creating a consumer hotline, introducing tamper-resistant packaging, and making managers (including the CEO) available to the media. The result: three months after the crisis, a poll showed that 93% of the public felt the company had done a good job.[22]

Your Call

Do you think Bausch & Lomb reacted appropriately by waiting 5 days before issuing a complete recall?

---

may be made. Nevertheless, some of the best stories in business concern the intelligent management of unanticipated calamities.

2. Proactive Change: Managing Anticipated Problems & Opportunities   In contrast to reactive change, *proactive change* or planned change involves **making carefully thought-out changes in anticipation of possible or expected problems or opportunities.**[23]

Example

Proactive Change: Being Ahead of the Curve with Natural Beef

The high-desert cattle ranch, 180 miles southeast of Denver in Colorado's San Luis Valley, is the home of Coleman Natural Foods, founded by Mel Coleman Sr. in 1979 on the ranch of his ancestors, who had moved there in 1875. Coleman sold "natural" beef back when most shoppers were unaware of the term. On a sales trip in the 1980s, Coleman would pitch grocers that his cows were not given antibiotics and growth hormones like those of the big producers, but were fed a vegetarian diet.

It took Coleman years to win converts, says a *New York Times* story, "not only among retailers but also among consumers and government regulators. Now, paradoxically, natural and organic meats have become so popular that even the big conventional meat producers are getting into the business, and Coleman is left in the unexpected position of scrambling for shelf space."[24]

The word "natural" can signify many things—that the animals were not given hormones or antibiotics, not fed rendered animal by-products, or were raised entirely out of doors—or it can mean nothing at all. "Organic," however, means the meat adheres to more stringent standards—no use of antibiotics, growth hormones, or parasite-killing chemicals and animals were given feed grown without pesticides or chemical fertilizers.[25] Regardless, shoppers have learned to pay a premium, as much as 50% more, particularly for organic beef. Indeed, organic meat is now the fastest-growing segment of the organic food business. The Coleman ranch is now run by Mel Coleman Jr., but his father's legacy lives on. "Mel Sr. was one of the pioneers to develop a truly natural meat company," says an admirer.

Your Call

Most instances of proactive change involve technology, such as Wal-Mart's ordering suppliers to replace the conventional bar code on their products with RFID tags, radio-wave tracking technology that can contain much more information.[26] Can you think of other examples of proactive change?

The Forces for Change: Outside & Inside the Organization

How do managers know when their organizations need to change? The answers aren't clear-cut, but you can get clues by monitoring the forces for change—both outside and inside the organization. *(See Figure 10.1, next page.)*

Test Your Knowledge:
Macroenvironmental Forces

Forces Originating Outside the Organization   External forces consist of four types, as follows.

1. Demographic Characteristics   Earlier we discussed the demographic changes occurring in the U.S. workforce. We've pointed out that the workforce is now more diverse, and organizations need to effectively manage this diversity.

2. Market Changes   As discussed in Chapter 4, the global economy is forcing companies to change the way they do business, with U.S. companies forging new partnerships and alliances with employees, suppliers, and competitors.

Outside Forces

Demographic characteristics
- Age
- Education
- Skill level
- Gender
- Immigration

Market changes
- Mergers & acquisitions
- Domestic & international competition
- Recession

Technological advancements
- Manufacturing automation
- Office automation

Social & political pressures
- Leadership
- Values

Inside Forces

Employee problems
- Unmet needs
- Job dissatisfaction
- Absenteeism & turnover
- Productivity
- Participation/suggestions

Managers' behavior
- Conflict
- Leadership
- Reward systems
- Structural reorganization

THE NEED FOR CHANGE

figure IO.I

FORCES FOR CHANGE OUTSIDE AND INSIDE THE ORGANIZATION

3. Technological Advancements   Information technology may be one of the greatest forces for productivity in our lifetime. But it can also create headaches.

4. Social & Political Pressures   Social events can create great pressures. Changing drinking habits, for example, have led to a rise in wine sales and a decline in whiskey sales.

Forces Originating Inside the Organization   Internal forces affecting organizations may be subtle, such as low job satisfaction, or more dramatic, such as constant labor-management conflict. Internal forces may be of the two following types.

1. Employee Problems   Is there a gap between the employees' needs and desires and the organization's needs and desires? Job dissatisfaction—as expressed through high absenteeism and turnover—can be a major signal of the need for change. Organizations may respond by addressing job design, reducing employees' role conflicts, and dealing with work overload, to mention a few matters.

For instance, when Martin McGuinn was reorganizing the retail division of Mellon Bank, many of the employees who were upset over expanded banking hours were appeased when they were given more freedom to arrange their own schedules.

2. Managers' Behavior   Excessive conflict between managers and employees may be another indicator that change is needed. Perhaps there is a personality conflict, so that an employee transfer may be needed. Or perhaps some interpersonal training is required.

Phil Dusenberry, chairman of ad agency BBDO, says that he used to have a gentle way of letting people down because he didn't want to hurt their feelings. Often, however, this would simply confuse people. "They'd go off thinking that I liked their work even if I didn't," he says. "Over time I realized that dealing in terms of black and white wasn't a bad thing. I became much more direct."[27]

Areas in Which Change Is Often Needed: People, Technology, Structure, & Strategy

Change can involve any part of the organization. However, the four areas in which change is most apt to be needed are *people, technology, structure,* and *strategy.*

1. Changing People
Even in a two-person organization, people changes may be required. The changes may take the following forms:

- **Perceptions.** Employees might feel they are underpaid for what they do. Managers might be able to show that pay and benefits are comparable or superior to those offered by competitors.

- **Attitudes.** In old-line manufacturing industries, employees may feel that it is the nature of things that they should be in an adversarial relationship with their managers. It may be up to management to try to change the culture and

Example

Changing Technology: Web 2.0 Could Radically Alter How Business Is Done

Futurist Paul Saffo, director of the think tank Institute for the Future in Menlo Park, California, says that new technologies lead to new products. The invention of television, for example, led to TV dinners and TV trays. The invention of the iPod led to the selling of music singles—something that hadn't happened since the 45 rpm record. "Each time it gets cheaper to do something," says Saffo, "you get more players. It's irreversibly more complex."[28]

Thus, the original World Wide Web has led to what is known as Web 2.0, a second generation of Internet-based services that lets people collaborate and share information online in a new way.[29] Among the results are social networking sites (MySpace, Facebook, TagWorld), photo-sharing sites (Flickr), and wikis (group-editable Web pages, such as the reference source Wikipedia), which all demand active participation and social interaction. Now Web 2.0 services are coming into the business world. For example, wikis are being used by Walt Disney Co., investment bank Dresdner Kleinwort Wasserstein, and other companies to enhance collaboration. Other corporations are using social networking services such as LinkedIn Corp. and

Visible Path Corp. to gain sales leads and hiring prospects. Mash-ups, in which existing Web services are combined and put to new uses, have been used by the U.S. Chamber of Commerce Center for Corporate Citizenship to help people displaced by Hurricane Katrina to look for jobs. "In essence," says a *BusinessWeek* article, "these services are coalescing into one giant computer that anyone with access to an Internet-connected PC can use, from anywhere in the world."[30]

A significant structural result of Web 2.0 will be a further assault on conventional reporting arrangements, already being transformed by globalization and outsourcing. That is, the new freeform technologies will help to further flatten clear lines of authority between managers and employees and to reduce organizational boundaries between the company and its partners and customers.

Your Call

What possibilities do you see for applying the social networking services, photo-sharing sites, blogs, and wikis you are familiar with as a college student to business uses?

Cell phone power. Camera phones with e-mail access have become commonplace, but the cell phone is still evolving—and rapidly. In South Korea, where cell phones operate at broadband speeds, young commuters on the subway are forsaking print matter and occupying themselves with cell phone news services, videos, and music downloads, as well as e-mail and phone calls. Cell phones there can double as credit cards: a consumer can point his or her phone at an infrared terminal on a store counter, which sends credit card information straight to the card company. In the future, cell phones might also take the place of ID cards such as driver's licenses. When cell phones and accompanying text-messaging features are joined to advanced search engines and huge databases the technology will no doubt stand several industries on their heads. Which ones do you think these might be?

the attitudes by using educational techniques to show why the old labor wars should become a thing of the past.

- **Performance.** Should an organization pay the people who contract to wash its windows by the hour? by the window? or by the total job? Will one method cause them to work fast and sloppily but cost less? Will one cause them to do pristine windows but cost too much? It's often a major challenge to find incentives to improve people's performance.

- **Skills.** Altering or improving skill levels is often an ongoing challenge, particularly these days, when new forms of technology can change an organization's way of doing business, as we describe next.

2. Changing Technology   Technology is a major area of change for many organizations. *Technology* **is not just computer technology; it is any machine or process that enables an organization to gain a competitive advantage in changing materials used to produce a finished product.** Breweries, for example, used to make beer by letting malted cereal grain flavored with hops brew slowly by fermentation; nowadays, the process is often sped up by the direct injection of carbonation (from carbon dioxide) into the process.

3. Changing Structure   When one organization acquires another, the structure often changes—perhaps from a divisional structure, say, to a matrix structure. The recent trend is toward "flattening the hierarchy," eliminating several middle layers of management, and to using work teams linked by electronic networks.

4. Changing Strategy   Shifts in the marketplace often may lead organizations to have to change their strategy. As a result of the sudden rise in popularity of the Netscape Navigator Web browser, Microsoft Corp. found itself having to shift from a PC-based strategy to an Internet strategy. ●

10.2 ORGANIZATION DEVELOPMENT: WHAT IT IS, WHAT IT CAN DO

What are the uses of OD, and how effective is it?

major question

THE BIG PICTURE
Organization development (OD) is a set of techniques for implementing change, such as managing conflict, revitalizing organizations, and adapting to mergers. OD has three steps: diagnosis, intervention, and evaluation. Four factors have been found to make OD programs effective.

Organization development (OD) **is a set of techniques for implementing planned change to make people and organizations more effective.** Note the inclusion of people in this definition. OD focuses specifically on people in the change process. Often OD is put into practice by a person known as a *change agent,* **a consultant with a background in behavioral sciences who can be a catalyst in helping organizations deal with old problems in new ways.**

What Can OD Be Used For?

OD can be used to address the following three matters:

I. Managing Conflict   Conflict is inherent in most organizations. Sometimes an OD expert in the guise of an executive coach will be brought in to help advise an executive on how to improve relationships with others in the organization.

For instance, David Hitz and Michael Malcolm, two cofounders of Network Appliance, a data-storage firm in Sunnyvale, California, were feuding with each other. The problem: Malcolm couldn't stick to his decisions, which drove Hitz crazy. An organization behavior specialist began working with the warring executives in separate sessions to solve the problem.

2. Revitalizing Organizations   Information technology is wreaking such change that nearly all organizations these days are placed in the position of having to adopt new behaviors in order to resist decline. OD can help by opening communication, fostering innovation, and dealing with stress.

3. Adapting to Mergers   Mergers and acquisitions are associated with increased anxiety, stress, absenteeism, and turnover and decreased productivity.[31] What is the organizational fit between two disparate organizations, such as Chrysler and DaimlerBenz? OD experts can help integrate two firms with varying cultures, products, and procedures.

How OD Works

Like physicians, OD managers and consultants follow a medical-like model. (Or, to use our more current formulation, they follow the rules of evidence-based management.) They approach the organization as if it were a sick patient, using *diagnosis, intervention,* and *evaluation*—"diagnosing" its ills, "prescribing" treatment or intervention, and "monitoring" or evaluating progress. If the evaluation

figure 10.2

THE OD PROCESS

Sources: Adapted from W. L. French and C. H. Bell Jr., *Organization Development: Behavioral Interventions for Organizational Improvement* (Englewood Cliffs, NJ: Prentice-Hall, 1978); and E. G. Huse and T. G. Cummings, *Organizational Development and Change,* 3rd ed. (St. Paul: West, 1985).

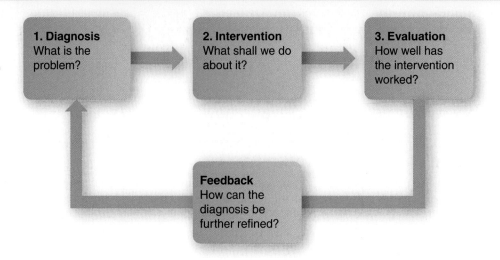

shows that the procedure is not working effectively, the conclusions drawn are then applied (see feedback loop) to refining the diagnosis, and the process starts again. *(See Figure 10.2 above.)*

I. Diagnosis: What Is the Problem?   To carry out the diagnosis, OD consultants or managers use some combination of questionnaires, surveys, interviews, meetings, records, and direct observation to ascertain people's attitudes and to identify problem areas.

2. Intervention: What Shall We Do about It?   "Treatment" or ***intervention is the attempt to correct the diagnosed problems.*** Often this is done using the services of an OD consultant who works in conjunction with management teams. Some OD activities for implementing planned change are communicating survey results to employees to engage them in constructive problem solving, observing employee communication patterns and teaching them skills to improve them, helping group members learn to function as a team, stimulating better cohesiveness among several work groups, and improving work technology or organizational design.

3. Evaluation: How Well Has the Intervention Worked?   An OD program needs objective evaluation to see if it has done any good. Answers may lie in hard data about absenteeism, turnover, grievances, and profitability, which should be compared with earlier statistics. The change agent can use questionnaires, surveys, interviews, and the like to assess changes in employee attitudes.

The Effectiveness of OD

Among organizations that have practiced organization development are American Airlines, B.F. Goodrich, General Electric, Honeywell, ITT, Polaroid, Procter & Gamble, Prudential, Texas Instruments, and Westinghouse Canada—companies covering a variety of industries.

Research has found that OD is most apt to be successful under the following circumstances.

I. Multiple Interventions   OD success stories tend to use multiple interventions. Goal setting, feedback, recognition and rewards, training, participation, and challenging job design have had good results in improving performance and satisfaction.[32] Combined interventions have been found to work better than single interventions.[33]

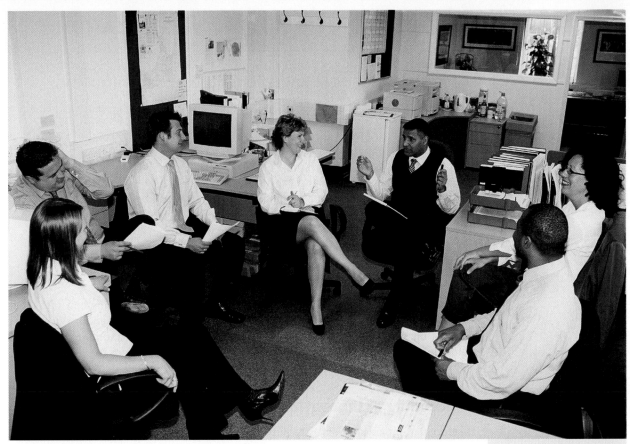

Team building. One technique for implementing change is team building. Teams are often diverse in gender, age, ethnicity, and educational background and experience. Would you prefer to work with a highly diverse team of people?

2. Management Support   OD is more likely to succeed when top managers give the OD program their support and are truly committed to the change process and the desired goals of the change program.[34] Also, the expectations for change were not unrealistic.[35]

3. Goals Geared to Both Short- & Long-Term Results   Change programs are more successful when they are oriented toward achieving both short-term and long-term results. Managers should not engage in organizational change for the sake of change. Change efforts should produce positive results.[36]

4. OD Is Affected by Culture   OD effectiveness is affected by cross-cultural considerations. Thus, an OD intervention that worked in one country should not be blindly applied to a similar situation in another country.[37] ●

> ◆ **major question** What do I need to know to encourage innovation?

THE BIG PICTURE

Innovation may be a product innovation or a process innovation, an incremental innovation or a radical innovation. Four characteristics of innovation are that it is uncertain, people closest to it know the most about it, it may be controversial, and it may be complex. Three ways to encourage innovation are by providing the organizational culture, the resources, and the reward system. To make innovation happen, you need to recognize problems and opportunities, gain allies, and overcome employee resistance.

Innovation, as we've said earlier in the book, is the activity of creating new ideas and converting them into useful applications—specifically new goods and services. The spirit of innovation is essential to keeping an organization vital and in maintaining a competitive advantage. Otherwise, the innovation will come from your competitors, forcing you to scramble to catch up—if you can.

Succeeding at Innovation

American companies constantly put forth ads touting the spirit of innovation, but how well are they actually doing? Ironically, a survey of 4,559 corporate managers in 36 industries found that U.S. executives thought their own companies gave innovation or creativity short shrift—only 4% felt their organizations could be respected for their leadership in this area.[38]

Why Are U.S. Firms Lagging? Scholars Larry Selden and Ian MacMillan argue that firms are focusing their innovation efforts in the wrong way: "Companies are pouring money into their insular R&D [research and development] labs, instead of working to understand what the customer wants and then using the understanding to drive innovation."[39]

Cynthia Barton Rabe, a former innovation strategist for Intel, suggests that too much knowledge and experience can actually kill innovation. "When we become expert," she says, "we often trade our 'what if' flights of fancy for the grounded reality of 'what is,'" thereby limiting our approaches to challenges.[40]

Curtis Carlson, head of research and development firm SRI International, and William Wilmot, director of the Collaboration Institute, say that if organizations are to innovate more effectively they must change their mindset by becoming more focused. That is, firms must, among other things, concentrate on important customer needs, create teams to make solutions happen, and find a champion to keep a team on track.[41]

Picking Many People's Brains: The Open-Source Idea Innovation can happen by design or by accident, and it need not come about because of a for-profit orientation. For instance, the computer operating system Linux was written by Finnish programmer Linus Torvalds, who then put his work in the public domain. It is now a free, "open-source" operating system created by hundreds of programmers around the world who contribute to its source code, its underlying instructions available to anyone.[42]

Some companies have extended the open source idea by taking a Linux-style approach that taps masses of people for inspiration. Tim O'Reilly, founder of computer publisher O'Reilly Media, believes, according to one report, that "creativity is no longer about which companies have the most visionary executives, but who has the most compelling 'architecture of participation.' That is, which companies make it easy, interesting, and rewarding for a wide range of contributors to offer ideas, solve problems, and improve products?"[43] Padmasree Warrior, Motorola's chief technology officer, in pursuit of a follow-up success story to the best-selling RAZR cell phone, oversees a Web-based system called Innovate, in which 25,000 Motorola engineers are encouraged to blog new ideas nonstop. "I'm a firm believer in the idea that the future belongs to the genius of the collaborative innovator," she says.[44]

Linus Torvalds, innovator. In 1991, computer programmer Torvalds, then a graduate student in Finland, posted his free Linux operating system on the Internet. Linux is a free version of Unix, and its continual improvements result from the efforts of tens of thousands of volunteer programmers. Can you think of any other innovations that occurred that did not come about because of a for-profit orientation?

The Culture of Innovation   As we will see, a big part of what makes innovation happen is a country and a corporation's culture. Unlike most Europeans, who abhor "precariousness," or the absence of security, Americans as a whole seem to be more comfortable with taking risks. As one writer puts it, "Risk, movement, and personal ambition are fundamental. . . . The United States is about the endless possibility of self-invention through hard work. It is inseparable from change." [45] It is not an accident that so many risk-averse countries that have tried to generate Silicon Valley–style entrepreneurial magic through government-sponsored technical havens—Malaysia with its Multimedia Supercorridor, Dubai with its Internet City, Singapore with its Singapore One—have been unsuccessful.[46] In the United States, by contrast, innovation is propelled not just by big-company research labs or by high-tech 24/7 "geek houses" (such as Meetro in Palo Alto and Box.net in Berkeley) manned by young college graduates.[47] It is also pushed by an "entrepreneurial melting pot" of enterprises owned by Asians, Latinos, and African Americans, whose business initiatives have far outstripped the national rate of U.S. business growth.[48]

Types of Innovation: Product or Process, Incremental or Radical

Innovations may be of the following two types.

Product versus Process Innovations   As a manager, you may need to improve your organization's product or service itself; this is generally a technological innovation. Or you may need to improve the process by which the product or service is created, manufactured, or distributed; this is generally a managerial innovation.

More formally, a **_product innovation_ is a change in the appearance or the performance of a product or a service or the creation of a new one. A _process innovation_ is a change in the way a product or service is conceived, manufactured, or disseminated.**

Today, says an article about the world's most innovative companies, "innovation is about much more than new products. It is about reinventing business processes and building entirely new markets that meet untapped customer needs."[54]

Practical Action

What Makes a Startup?

Lots of books are written about creativity and innovation in organizational life. In general, the message is the same: "Fire up your companywide brainpower to hatch ideas," as one *BusinessWeek* writer put it, "and make sure the ideas reach the people who can implement them." But it's difficult to come up with a formula for turning companies into prodigious idea factories.[49] As Gina O'Connor, a marketing professor at Rensselaer Polytechnic Institute, points out: "American companies are doing a great job of developing better products. But there's been very little improvement in radical, or 'discontinuous,' innovation."[50]

Interestingly, though, many startups don't begin with radical ideas. According to Amar V. Bhidé, author of *The Origin and Evolution of New Businesses,* successful entrepreneurs start out by making "a small modification in what somebody else is doing."[51] One has only to think of how the notion of disposability has been extended to so many products—phone cards, DVDs, even cell phones.[52]

Most entrepreneurs, he explains, see a small niche opportunity—one in which the company he or she is working for is already involved, or a supplier or customer is involved. "And the person jumps in with very little preparation and analysis," he says, "but with direct firsthand knowledge of the profitability of that opportunity—and pretty much does what somebody else is already doing, but does it better and faster."

And "better and faster" seems to be the main difference. Such entrepreneurs don't have anything in the way of technology or concept that differentiates them from other businesses. "They just work harder, hustle for customers, and know that the opportunity may not last for more than six or eight months," says Bhidé. "But they expect to make a reasonable return on those six to eight months. And along the way they'll figure out something else that will keep the business going."

Another quality of entrepreneurs is "a tolerance for ambiguity," Bhidé says. They are willing to jump into things when it's hard to even imagine what the possible outcomes will be, going ahead in the absence of information, very much capital—or even a very novel idea.

An example of a startup fitting these criteria is Netflix, which rents DVD movies by mail to customers ordering online. This concept does not seem very innovative. The wrinkle, however, which struck founder Reed Hastings when he was charged $40 for returning a movie late to a video rental outfit, is that for a $19.95 monthly subscription, customers can keep three films out at a time. "If you rent five or six a month," says one California retired engineer, "you're ahead compared to what you pay at Blockbuster." (In one month, he watched more than 40 movies.) Another differentiating feature: when you rate the movie you rented, Netflix will recommend other movies you might enjoy that you might not have heard of.

No entrepreneur can afford to rest easily, however. Both Blockbuster and Wal-Mart have also entered the online DVD rental business. And new technology is a big uncertainty, with pay-per-view, TiVo set-top boxes, and digital movie downloads being possible challengers.[53]

Incremental versus Radical Innovations   An innovation may be small or large. The difference is in modifying versus replacing existing products or services. That is, you might have *incremental innovations*—**the creation of products, services, or technologies that modify existing ones.** Or you might have *radical innovations*—**the creation of products, services, or technologies that replace existing ones.**

Four Characteristics of Innovation

According to Harvard management scholar Rosabeth Moss Kanter, innovation has four characteristics:[55]

I. Innovating Is an Uncertain Business Being an innovator means being like the first driver in a line of cars in a snowstorm: You're dealing with the unknown while the less adventurous souls behind you may be carping about your performance. When you're innovating, progress is difficult to predict, and the ultimate success of your endeavor is always somewhat in doubt.

2. People Closest to the Innovation Know the Most about It, at Least Initially Innovation is knowledge-intensive. The people closest to the development of the idea know the most about it, at least in the early stages. Consequently, it is often difficult for outsiders—such as co-workers or managers who are removed from the process—to understand and appreciate it. This leads to characteristic #3.

Self-Assessment Exercise: Assessing Your Creativity Quotient

3. Innovation May Be Controversial Whoever is doing the innovating is using the organization's people and funds for that purpose. Since there is always competition for resources, others in the organization may take issue with the way they are being used here—especially since the innovation has not yet shown positive results.

4. Innovation Can Be Complex Because It May Cross Organizational Boundaries An innovation may involve more than one department or business unit. This, of course, increases the complexity of the process. Thus, you as a manager need to understand not only how the process of innovation works in general but also how it requires special handling to make it successful within different parts of the organization. Shepherding an innovation, therefore, may require you to draw on your finest communication skills—especially because of characteristic #2 above.

Celebrating Failure: Cultural & Other Factors Encouraging Innovation

Innovation doesn't happen as a matter of course. Organizations have to develop ways to make it happen—over and over. Three ways to do so are by providing (1) the right organizational *culture*, (2) the appropriate *resources*, and (3) the correct *reward system*.

I. Culture: Is Innovation Viewed as a Benefit or a Boondoggle?

Although much of American culture seems oriented toward punishing failure, an organizational culture that doesn't just allow but *celebrates* failure is vital toward fostering innovation. Pharmaceutical company Eli Lilly, for example, is said to have "long had a culture that looks at failure as an inevitable part of discovery and encourages scientists to take risks."[56] Most new ideas will fail. Only a few will be successful. But if an organization doesn't encourage this kind of risk taking—if people tend to view experimentation as a boondoggle—that organization won't become a superstar in innovation.

An organizational culture, as we said in Chapter 8, is the "social glue," or system of shared beliefs and values, that binds members together. The top 10 companies with cultures that strongly encourage innovation, according to *BusinessWeek*, are Apple, Google, 3M, Toyota, Microsoft, General Electric, Procter & Gamble, Nokia, Starbucks, and IBM.[57]

2. Resources: Do Managers Put Money Where Their Mouths Are?

An organization's managers may say they encourage innovation, but if they balk at the expense, they aren't putting their money where their mouths are. Innovation doesn't come cheap. Its costs can be measured in all kinds of ways: dollars, time, energy, and focus. For instance, an organization's research and development (R&D) department may need to hire top scientists, whose salaries may be high.

Of course, because there is always competition within an organization for resources, innovation may simply be given short shrift because other concerns seem so urgent—even within a company with a culture encouraging experimentation. But the risk of downgrading innovation in favor of more immediate concerns is that a company may "miss the next wave"—the next big trend, whatever that is.

3. Rewards: Is Experimentation Reinforced in Ways That Matter?

Top-performing salespeople are often rewarded with all kinds of incentives, such as commissions, bonuses, and perks. Are R&D people rewarded the same way? Every year Monsanto Corp., for instance, presents a $50,000 award to the scientist or scientists who developed the largest commercial breakthrough.

The converse is also important: People should not be punished when their attempts to innovate don't work out, or else they won't attempt new things in the future. By the nature of experimentation, the end result can't be foreseen. Top managers at 3M, for instance, recognize that three-fifths of the new ideas suggested each year fail in the marketplace. Only when people attempting an innovation are acting half-heartedly, sloppily, or otherwise incompetently should sanctions be used such as the withholding of raises and promotions.

Example

Achieving Success by Celebrating Failure: 3M's Culture of Innovation

In Chapter 3 we mentioned 3M's Art Fry, inventor of Post-it Notes, as an example of an intrapreneur. But 3M is also famous for having a culture of innovation that celebrates taking chances—which means achieving success by celebrating failure.

A story told around 3M is about an outside inventor, Francis Okie, who in the 1920s wrote 3M for samples of various sandpaper grit. Okie had an idea for a waterproof sandpaper, which he thought might have use in shaving and would reduce the cuts inflicted by razor blades. That idea turned out to be a failure. However, 3M was still interested in the sandpaper, later named Wetordry, and Okie sold them his idea after the company agreed to help bring the product to market. The result was a hugely successful product that became widely used in the automotive market, where previously dry sanding had created clouds of dust and lead-based paint that made people sick. Okie joined 3M in 1921 and became the company's first real inventor.

Only with 20-20 hindsight can people see that a policy of celebrating failure can lead to success. No one can know, when setting out on a new course, whether the effort will yield positive results, and usually, in fact, most such experiments *are* failures. But the *attempts* must be encouraged, or innovation will never happen.

3M builds innovation and intrapreneurship into its culture. Mistakes are allowed, destructive criticism is forbidden, experimentation is encouraged, and divisions and individuals are allowed to operate with a good deal of autonomy. 3M sets goals decreeing that 25%–30% of annual sales must come from products that are only 5 years old or less. Investment in research and development is almost double the rate of that of the average American company. In addition, 3M employees are permitted to spend 15% of their time pursuing personal research interests that are not related to current company projects, knowing that if their ideas aren't successful, they will be encouraged to pursue other paths.[58]

Your Call

Stanford University organizational behavior scholar Jerker Denrell believes that there is too much study of successes and not enough of failure, although it's very likely that firms pursuing risky strategies tend to achieve either a very high or very low performance whereas firms pursuing conservative strategies always achieve an average performance.[59] But while risk taking can lead to either spectacular success or disastrous failure, looking only at successes will show a positive correlation between success and risk taking. Do you think this is true?

How You Can Foster Innovation: Three Steps

If you're going to not just survive but *prevail* as a manager, you need to know how to make innovation happen within an organization. Here we offer three steps for doing so. *(See Figure 10.3.)*

1. Recognize problems & opportunities & devise solutions → 2. Gain allies by communicating your vision → 3. Overcome employee resistance, & empower & reward them to achieve progress

figure 10.3

THREE STEPS FOR FOSTERING INNOVATION

Source: Adapted from eight steps in K. M. Bartol and D. C. Martin, *Management,* 3rd ed. (Burr Ridge, IL: Irwin/McGraw-Hill, 1998), pp. 360–363. Copyright © 1998 by the McGraw-Hill Companies, Inc. Used by permission.

I. Recognize Problems & Opportunities & Devise Solutions   Change may be needed because you recognize a *problem* or recognize an *opportunity.*

- **Recognizing a problem—find a "better way."** Problems, whether competitive threat or employee turnover, tend to seize our attention.

  Sometimes problems lead to new business ideas. When John Decker of Maui, Hawaii, took up classical guitar, he discovered Hawaii's tropical climate was hard on wooden instruments. This led to his forming a company to turn out high-quality classical guitars made of synthetic materials known for their stiffness and durability.[60]

- **Recognizing an opportunity.** Recognition of opportunities may come from long-term employees who regularly expose themselves to new ideas ("technological gate-keepers" in one phrase).[61] Ideas originating at the grassroots level of an organization may be a particularly fruitful source of innovation.[62]

2. Gain Allies by Communicating Your Vision   Once you've decided how you're going to handle the problem or opportunity, you need to start developing and communicating your vision. You need to create a picture of the future and paint in broad strokes how your innovation will be of benefit. That is, you need to start persuading others inside—and perhaps outside—the organization to support you. Having hard data helps. Others will be more persuaded, for example, if you can demonstrate that a similar idea has been successful in another industry. Or if you can take current trends (such as sales or demographics) and project them into the future.

But a great deal of innovation comes about precisely because the future has no resemblance to the past. Thus, you may have to use your imagination to paint the brightest picture you can of the possible payoffs of your innovation.

3. Overcome Employee Resistance, & Empower & Reward Them to Achieve Progress   Once you've persuaded and gotten the blessing of your managerial superiors, then you need to do the same with the people reporting to you. It's possible, of course, that the idea for innovation came from them and that you already have their support.

Alternatively, you may have to overcome their resistance. Then you'll need to remove obstacles that limit them in executing the vision, such as having to get management to sign off on all aspects of a project. Finally, you'll need to hand out periodic rewards—recognition, celebrations, bonuses—for tasks accomplished. And the rewards should not be withheld until the end of the project, which may be many months away, but given out for the successful accomplishment of short-term phases in order to provide constant encouragement. ●

10.4 THE THREAT OF CHANGE: MANAGING EMPLOYEE FEAR & RESISTANCE

major question How are employees threatened by change, and how can I help them adjust?

THE BIG PICTURE

This section discusses the degree to which employees fear change, from least threatening to most threatening. It also describes Lewin's three-stage change model: unfreezing, changing, and refreezing. Finally, it describes Kotter's eight steps for leading organizational change, which correspond to Lewin's three stages.

As a manager, particularly one working for an American organization, you may be pressured to provide short-term, quick-fix solutions. But when applied to organizational problems, this approach usually doesn't work: quick-fix solutions have little staying power.

What, then, are effective ways to manage organizational change and employees' fear and resistance to it? In this section, we discuss the following:

- The extent to which employees fear change and reasons why employees resist change.
- Lewin's change model.
- Kotter's eight stages for leading organizational change.

The Degree to Which Employees Fear Change: From Least Threatening to Most Threatening

Whether organizational change is administrative or technological, the degree to which employees feel threatened by it in general depends on whether the change is *adaptive, innovative,* or *radically innovative.*[63]

Hot Seat DVD Application:
Change: More Pain Than Gain

Least Threatening: Adaptive Change *Adaptive change* **is reintroduction of a familiar practice**—the implementation of a kind of change that has already been experienced within the same organization. This form of change is lowest in complexity, cost, and uncertainty. Because it is familiar, it is the least threatening to employees and thus will create the least resistance.

For example, during annual inventory week, a department store may ask its employees to work 12 hours a day instead of the usual 8. During tax-preparation time, the store's accounting department may imitate this same change in work hours. Although accounting employees are in a different department from stockroom and sales employees, it's expected they wouldn't be terribly upset by the temporary change in hours since they've seen it in effect elsewhere in the store.

Somewhat Threatening: Innovative Change *Innovative change* **is the introduction of a practice that is new to the organization.** This form of change involves moderate complexity, cost, and uncertainty. It is therefore apt to trigger some fear and resistance among employees.

For example, should a department store decide to adopt a new practice of competitors by staying open 24 hours a day, requiring employees to work flexible schedules, it may be felt as moderately threatening.

Very Threatening: Radically Innovative Change *Radically innovative change* **involves introducing a practice that is new to the industry.** Because it is the most complex, costly, and uncertain, it will be felt as extremely threatening to managers' confidence and employees' job security and may well tear at the fabric of the organization.[64]

For example, a department store converting some of its operations to e-commerce—selling its goods on the Internet—may encounter anxiety among its staff, especially those fearing being left behind.

Ten Reasons Employees Resist Change Whether changes are adaptive, innovative, or radically innovative, employees may resist them for all kinds of reasons. Ten of the leading ones are as follows.[65]

Group Exercise:
Overcoming Resistance
to Change

- **Individual's predisposition toward change.** How people react to change depends a lot on how they learned to handle change and ambiguity as children. One person's parents may have been patient, flexible, and understanding, and from the time the child was weaned she may have learned there were positive compensations for the loss of immediate gratification. Thus, she will associate making changes with love and approval. Another person's parents may have been unreasonable and unyielding, forcing him to do things (piano lessons, for example) that he didn't want to do. Thus, he will be distrustful of making changes because he will associate them with demands for compliance.[66]

- **Surprise and fear of the unknown.** When radically different changes are introduced without warning—for example, without any official announcements—the office rumor mill will go into high gear and affected employees will become fearful of the implications of the changes. Harvard business scholar Rosabeth Moss Kanter recommends that in such cases a transition manager should be appointed who is charged with keeping all relevant parties adequately informed.[67]

- **Climate of mistrust.** Trust involves reciprocal faith in others' intentions and behavior. Mistrust encourages secrecy, which causes deeper mistrust, putting even well-conceived changes at risk of failure. Managers who trust their employees make the change process an open, honest, and participative affair. Employees who trust their managers are more apt to expend extra effort and take chances with something different.

- **Fear of failure.** Intimidating changes on the job can cause employees to doubt their capabilities. Self-doubt erodes self-confidence and cripples personal growth and development.

- **Loss of status or job security.** Administrative and technological changes that threaten to alter power bases or eliminate jobs—as often happens during corporate restructurings that threaten middle-management jobs—generally trigger strong resistance.

- **Peer pressure.** Even people who are not themselves directly affected by impending changes may actively resist in order to protect the interests of their friends and co-workers.

- **Disruption of cultural traditions or group relationships.** Whenever individuals are transferred, promoted, or reassigned, it can disrupt existing cultural and group relationships. Traditionally, for example, Sony Corp. promoted insiders to new positions; when an outsider, Howard Stringer, was named as the next chairman and CEO and six corporate officers were asked to resign, creating a majority board of foreigners, the former CEO, Nobuyuki Idei, worried the moves might engender strong employee resistance.[68]

- **Personality conflicts.** Just as a friend can get away with telling us something we would resent hearing from an adversary, the personalities of change agents can breed resistance.

- **Lack of tact or poor timing.** Introducing changes in an insensitive manner or at an awkward time can create employee resistance. Employees are more apt to accept changes when managers effectively explain their value, as, for example, in demonstrating their strategic purpose to the organization.

- **Nonreinforcing reward systems.** Employees are likely to resist when they can't see any positive rewards from proposed changes, as, for example, when one is asked to work longer hours without additional compensation.

To gauge how adaptable you're apt to be to organizational change, complete the Self-Assessment at the end of this chapter.

Lewin's Change Model: Unfreezing, Changing, & Refreezing

Most theories of organizational change originated with the landmark work of social psychologist **Kurt Lewin.** Lewin developed a model with three stages—*unfreezing, changing,* and *refreezing*—to explain how to initiate, manage, and stabilize planned change.[69]

I. "Unfreezing": Creating the Motivation to Change

In the *unfreezing stage,* managers try to instill in employees the motivation to change, encouraging them to let go of attitudes and behaviors that are resistant to innovation. For this "unfreezing" to take place, employees need to become dissatisfied with the old way of doing things. Managers also need to reduce the barriers to change during this stage.

2. "Changing": Learning New Ways of Doing Things

In the *changing stage,* employees need to be given the tools for change: new information, new perspectives, new models of behavior. Managers can help here by providing benchmarking results, role models, mentors, experts, and training. It's advisable, experts say, to convey the idea that change is a continuous learning process, not just a one-time event.[70]

3. "Refreezing": Making the New Ways Normal

In the *refreezing stage,* employees need to be helped to integrate the changed attitudes and behavior into their normal ways of doing things. Managers can assist by encouraging employees to exhibit the new change and then, through additional coaching and modeling, by reinforcing the employees in the desired change.

One technique used in Stage 1, to help unfreeze organizations, is **benchmarking, a process by which a company compares its performance with that of high-performing organizations.**[71] Professional sports teams do this all the time, but so do other kinds of organizations, including nonprofit ones.

For example, one company discovered that their costs to develop a computer system were twice as high as those of the best companies in their industry. They also learned that the time it took to get a new product to market was four times longer than the benchmarked organizations. These data were ultimately used to unfreeze employees' attitudes and motivate people to change the organization's internal processes in order to remain competitive.[72]

Kotter's Eight Steps for Leading Organizational Change

An expert in leadership and change management, **John Kotter** believes that, to be successful, organizational change needs to follow eight steps to avoid the eight common errors senior management usually commits.[73] *(See Table 10.1, opposite page.)* These correspond with Lewin's unfreezing-changing-refreezing steps.

Steps 1–4 represent unfreezing: establish a sense of urgency, create the guiding coalition, develop a vision and strategy, and communicate the change vision.

Steps 5–7 represent the changing stage: empower broad-based action, generate short-term wins, and consolidate gains and produce more change.

table 10.1

**STEPS TO LEADING
ORGANIZATIONAL CHANGE**

Step	Description
1. Establish a sense of urgency.	Unfreeze the organization by creating a compelling reason for why change is needed.
2. Create the guiding coalition.	Create a cross-functional, cross-level group of people with enough power to lead the change.
3. Develop a vision and a strategy.	Create a vision and a strategic plan to guide the change process.
4. Communicate the change vision.	Create and implement a communication strategy that consistently communicates the new vision and strategic plan.
5. Empower broad-based action.	Eliminate barriers to change, and use target elements of change to transform the organization. Encourage risk taking and creative problem solving.
6. Generate short-term wins.	Plan for and create short-term "wins" or improvements. Recognize and reward people who contribute to the wins.
7. Consolidate gains and produce more change.	The guiding coalition uses credibility from short-term wins to create more change. Additional people are brought into the change process as change cascades throughout the organization. Attempts are made to reinvigorate the change process.
8. Anchor new approaches in the culture.	Reinforce the changes by highlighting connections between new behaviors and processes and organizational success. Develop methods to ensure leadership development and succession.

Source: These steps were developed by J. P. Kotter, *Leading Change* (Boston: Harvard Business School Press, 1996). Copyright © 1996 by the Harvard Business School Publishing Corporation. Reprinted by permission of Harvard Business School Press; all rights reserved.

Step 8, corresponding to refreezing, is to anchor new approaches in the organization's culture.

The value of Kotter's steps is that they provide specific recommendations about behaviors that managers need to exhibit to successfully lead organizational change. It is important to remember that Kotter's research reveals that it is ineffective to skip steps and that successful organizational change is 70%–90% leadership and only 10%–30% management. Senior managers are thus advised to focus on leading rather than on managing change.[74] ●

Lookalikes. One key to the success of Southwest Airlines is that all the planes in its fleet have been the same type, Boeing 737s, which saves on maintenance and training costs. As Southwest expands from being a short-haul, low-fare carrier to running long-haul flights as well, it has needed to add new-generation 737s, which can travel longer distances than the older planes did. Southwest still offers no-frills service—no seat assignments and snacks instead of meals—and competes principally on fare price. In evolving from short routes to long ones, should the company expect to have to undergo any of the steps in Lewin's change model—unfreezing, changing, and refreezing?

summary

 10.1 The Nature of Change in Organizations

- Among supertrends shaping the future of business: (1) The marketplace is becoming more segmented and moving toward more niche products. (2) There are more competitors offering targeted products, requiring faster speed-to-market. (3) Some traditional companies may not survive radically innovative change. (4) China, India, and other offshore suppliers are changing the way we work. (5) Knowledge, not information, is becoming the new competitive advantage.

- Two types of change are reactive and proactive. Reactive change is making changes in response to problems or opportunities as they arise. Proactive change involves making carefully thought-out changes in anticipation of possible or expected problems or opportunities.

- Forces for change may consist of forces outside the organization or inside it. (1) External forces consist of four types: demographic characteristics, market changes, technological advancements, and social and political pressures. (2) Internal forces may be of two types: employee problems and managers' behavior.

- Four areas in which change is most apt to be needed are people, technology, structure, and strategy. (1) People changes may require changes in perceptions, attitudes, performance, or skills. (2) Technology is any machine or process that enables an organization to gain a competitive advantage in changing materials used to produce a finished product. (3) Changing structure may happen when one organization acquires another. (4) Changing strategy may occur because of changes in the marketplace.

 10.2 Organization Development: What It Is, What It Can Do

- Organization development (OD) is a set of techniques for implementing planned change to make people and organizations more effective. Often OD is put into practice by a change agent, a consultant with a background in behavioral sciences who can be a catalyst in helping organizations deal with old problems in new ways. OD can be used to manage conflict, revitalize organizations, and adapt to mergers.

- The OD process follows a three-step process: (1) Diagnosis attempts to ascertain the problem. (2) Intervention is the attempt to correct the diagnosed problems. (3) Evaluation attempts to find out how well the intervention worked.

- Four factors that make OD work successfully are (1) multiple interventions are used; (2) top managers give the OD program their support; (3) goals are geared to both short- and long-term results; and (4) OD is affected by culture.

 10.3 Promoting Innovation within the Organization

- Innovations may be a product innovation or a process innovation. A product innovation is a change in the appearance or performance of a product or service or the creation of a new one. A process innovation is a change in the way a product or service is conceived, manufactured, or disseminated. Innovations may also be an incremental innovation or a radical innovation. An incremental innovation is the creation of a product, service, or technology that modifies an existing one. A radical innovation is the creation of a product, service, or technology that replaces an existing one.

- Four characteristics of innovation are that (1) it is an uncertain business; (2) people closest to the innovation know the most about it, at least initially; (3) it may be controversial; and (4) it can be complex because it may cross organizational boundaries.

- Innovation doesn't happen as a matter of course. Three ways to make it happen are to provide the right organizational culture, so that it is viewed as a benefit rather than as a boondoggle; to provide the resources; and to provide the rewards, so that experimentation is reinforced in ways that matter. Three steps for fostering innovation are as follows. (1) Recognize problems and opportunities and devise solutions. (2) Gain allies by communicating your vision. (3) Overcome employee resistance and empower and reward them to achieve progress.

 ### 10.4 The Threat of Change: Managing Employee Fear & Resistance

- The degree to which employees feel threatened by change depends on whether the change is adaptive, innovative, or radically innovative. Adaptive change, the least threatening, is reintroduction of a familiar practice. Innovative change is the introduction of a practice that is new to the organization. Radically innovative change, the most threatening, involves introducing a practice that is new to the industry.

- Ten reasons employees resist change are as follows: (1) individuals' predisposition toward change; (2) surprise and fear of the unknown; (3) climate of mistrust; (4) fear of failure; (5) loss of status or job security; (6) peer pressure; (7) disruption of cultural traditions or group relationships; (8) personality conflicts; (9) lack of tact or poor timing; and (10) nonreinforcing reward systems.

- Kurt Lewin's change model has three stages—unfreezing, changing, and refreezing—to explain how to initiate, manage, and stabilize planned change. (1) In the unfreezing stage, managers try to instill in employees the motivation to change. One technique used is benchmarking, a process by which a company compares its performance with that of high-performing organizations. (2) In the changing stage, employees need to be given the tools for change, such as new information. (3) In the refreezing stage, employees need to be helped to integrate the changed attitudes and behavior into their normal behavior.

- In a model corresponding with Lewin's, John Kotter's suggests an organization needs to follow eight steps to avoid the eight common errors senior management usually commits. The first four represent unfreezing: establish a sense of urgency, create the guiding coalition, develop a vision and strategy, and communicate the change vision. The next three steps represent the changing stage: empower broad-based action, generate short-term wins, and consolidate gains and produce more change. The last step, corresponding to refreezing, is to anchor new approaches in the organization's culture.

management in action

Speed Is the New Competitive Advantage

Speed is emerging as the ultimate competitive weapon. Some of the world's most successful companies are proving to be expert at spotting new opportunities, marshaling their forces, and bringing to market new products or services in a flash. That goes for launching whole new ventures, too. . . .

At Nissan Motor Co., the development of new cars used to take 21 months. Now, the company is shifting to a 10½-month process. In the cell phone business, Nokia, Motorola, and others used to take 12 to 18 months to develop basic models. Today: Six to nine months.

It's all being driven by a new innovation imperative. Competition is more intense than ever because of the rise of the Asian powerhouses and the spread of disruptive new Internet technologies and business models. Companies realize that all of their attention to efficiency in the past half-decade was fine—but it's not nearly enough. If they are to thrive in this hypercompetitive environment, they must innovate more and faster.

Of course, speed has been important in business ever since the California Gold Rush. What's changed in recent years is that a slew of new techniques make it possible to get things done much faster. Start with global outsourcing. A vast network of suppliers around the world stands ready to do everything from manufacturing products to drawing up legal contracts. This helps companies create supply chains that are faster, more flexible, and more efficient than ever before.

Take clothing retailer H&M. Every time it designs a new outfit, the Swedish company can choose on the fly among more than 700 manufacturers worldwide. It looks for the right skills, geographic proximity, and ability to finish the job quickly—and then gets the plant rolling in a matter of hours or days. Or consider Wipro Ltd., the Indian outsourcing firm. It does engineering and design for clients, and in some cases, part of its fee is based on the success of the product it delivers. Customers can keep costs low, until they know they've got a hit on their hands. "Our clients are under a lot of pressure to get new products faster into the market. Their core employment isn't adequate for it, so they're looking for partners who can do it for them," says Azim Premji, Wipro's chairman.

Then there's technology. The Internet has become ubiquitous, so companies can connect with talent anywhere in the blink of an eye, inside or outside the company. Open-source software can be plucked off the shelf to become the foundation of new software programs or Web sites. Algorithms can be used to slice and dice market information and spot new trends.

Perhaps most important, today's fleet companies are embracing a management approach that would have been heresy just a decade ago: If you don't fail occasionally, you're not pushing hard enough. Executives tend to try lots of things, expecting a number of them to flop. It doesn't matter as long as you produce a steady stream of hits. Even losers can burnish a company's reputation for innovation if they're seen as exciting experiments. "It's not just O.K. to fail; it's imperative to fail," says Seth Godin, a marketing expert and author of several books, including *Unleashing the Ideavirus*. . . .

While focus groups and market research are useful, they're not sufficient. So companies have come up with new techniques for sussing out great ideas. Electronics retailer Best Buy Co. has begun checking with venture capitalists to find out what their startups are working on. Procter & Gamble Co. uses online networks to get in touch with thousands of experts worldwide. That helped the company produce 100 new products in the past two years. One example: It found a professor in Bologna, Italy, who had invented an ink-jet method for printing edible images on cakes. P&G used it to create Pringles potato chips with jokes and pictures printed on them—boosting Pringles growth into double digits. "This was terrific. We found a ready-to-go solution we could put into the marketplace," says Larry Huston, P&G's vice-president for research

and development. The product came out in one year, rather than the usual three or four.

Everybody knows that bureaucracy means death to new ideas, yet most companies still insist on forcing innovative products and ventures through a gauntlet of presentations and reviews and refinements. Not at Raving Brands, an Atlanta-based fast-casual restaurant franchiser. Chief Executive Martin Sprock talks a mile a minute and launches concepts nearly as fast. In the past five years, Sprock has unveiled six, including Fresh Mex, Asian fusion, and gourmet salads, and has another on the way. Raving Brands typically goes from finished concept to store opening in about a year. For some franchisers, it takes two years or more.

Raving Brands isn't so much a company as a SWAT team in chinos and polo shirts. Sprock meets with four or five senior partners every Monday to handle problems and talk over new ideas. They don't have a corporate office, so they gather at one of the restaurants. Sprock might come in with a new concept. (The gourmet salad idea came after he saw fancy salads being custom-made for busy New York office workers.) They'll bat around ideas. Then they'll split up to handle their specialties—recipes, say, or real estate. If somebody needs a quick O.K., they get Sprock on his cell. . . .

Fast and lean has a nice ring to it, but it's not a claim many companies can make. While some organizations have speeded up their innovation and formation of new businesses, they're the exceptions. Most are still bogged down in bureaucracy and old modes of doing things. That's a recipe for trouble. "There are two kinds of businesses: the quick and the dead," warns analyst Bruce Richardson of tech industry consultancy AMR Research Inc. That's probably an overstatement. But in an era in which once-mighty dinosaurs are struggling to survive, the alternative to fast and lean may soon be . . . gone.

For Discussion

1. Is the need for speed creating reactive or proactive change in organizations? Explain.
2. What are the forces of change that are creating the need for organizations to increase the speed with which they respond to marketplace opportunities and produce their products? Discuss.
3. Will a focus on speed tend to create incremental or radical innovation? Explain.
4. How can organizations increase the speed by which they innovate? Discuss.
5. How does this case show the interrelationship among strategy, innovation, and organizational change? Explain.

Source: Excerpted from Steve Hamm, "Speed Demons," *BusinessWeek*, March 27, 2006, pp. 70–76.

How Adaptable Are You?

Objectives

1. To assess your adaptability.
2. To examine how being adaptable can help you cope with organizational change.

Introduction

Ultimately all organizational change passes through an organization's people. People who adapt more easily are better suited to cope with organizational changes and so they clearly are important assets to any organization. The purpose of this exercise is to determine your adaptability.

Instructions

Read the following statements. Using the scale provided, circle the number that indicates the extent to which you agree or disagree with each statement:

1 = strongly disagree
2 = disagree
3 = neither agree nor disagree
4 = agree
5 = strongly agree

I. In emergency situations, I react with clear, focused thinking and maintain emotional control in order to step up to the necessary actions.	1 2 3 4 5	
2. In stressful circumstances, I don't overreact to unexpected news. I keep calm, focused, and manage frustration well.	1 2 3 4 5	
3. I solve problems creatively by turning them inside out and upside down looking for new approaches to solving them that others may have missed.	1 2 3 4 5	
4. I easily change gears in response to uncertain or unexpected events, effectively adjusting my priorities, plans, goals, and actions.	1 2 3 4 5	
5. I enjoy learning new ways to do my work and I do what is necessary to keep my knowledge and skills current.	1 2 3 4 5	
6. I adjust easily to changes in my workplace by participating in assignments or training that prepares me for these changes.	1 2 3 4 5	
7. I am flexible and open-minded with others. I listen and consider others' viewpoints, adjusting my own when necessary.	1 2 3 4 5	
8. I am open to both negative and positive feedback. I work well in teams.	1 2 3 4 5	
9. I take action to learn and understand the values of other groups, organizations, or cultures. I adjust my own behavior to show respect for different customs.	1 2 3 4 5	

10. I adjust easily to differing environmental states such as extreme heat, humidity, cold, or dirtiness.	1	2	3	4	5
11. I frequently push myself to complete strenuous or demanding tasks.	1	2	3	4	5
Total					_____

Interpretation

When you are done, add up your responses to get your total score to see how adaptable you are. Arbitrary norms for adaptability:

11−24 = Low adaptability

25−39 = Moderate adaptability

40−55 = High adaptability

Questions for Discussion

1. Were you surprised by your results? Why or why not?

2. Look at the areas where your score was the lowest. What are some skills you can work on or gain to increase your adaptability? Describe and explain.

3. What are some ways being adaptable can improve the way you handle change? Discuss.

Adapted from S. Arad, M. A. Donovan, K. E. Plamondon, and E. D. Pulakos, "Adaptability in the Workplace: Development of Taxonomy of Adaptive Performance," *Journal of Applied Psychology*, August 2000, pp. 612–624.

group exercise

Understanding Resistance to Change

Objectives

- To examine reasons why employees resist change.
- To practice using ways to overcome resistance to change.

Introduction

Managers who need to implement planned change find that success depends on how much their employees accept the change. If errors are made in the ways changes are introduced, employee resistance is likely to increase. The purpose of this exercise is to examine ways managers can overcome employee resistance to change.

Instructions

Break into groups of five to six people. Read the following case of the Canadian Furniture Corp. (CFC).

Discuss the case with your group and brainstorm, using Lewin's Change Model, and Kotter's Eight Steps for Organizational Change, to find errors in the way managers at CFC implemented change. After your group has identified the errors, compare your notes with other groups. As a class, discuss some managerial strategies that would prevent errors such as the ones at CFC from occurring.

The Case

The Canadian Furniture Corp. is a manufacturer of household furniture located in southern Ontario. It has been in business since the early 1950s and has always experienced steady growth, even in periods of economic downturn. . . . At present, CFC has an assembly plant in 8 of the 10 Canadian provinces. Because of Canada's geography, the unique provincial differences in consumer preferences, and early transportation problems, CFC has traditionally given local assembly plants considerable freedom of action in all aspects of the business. This is especially true in purchasing.

The business was purchased by Centrex, a manufacturer of office furniture headquartered in Toronto that wanted to expand into household furniture. Shortly after the takeover, Mr. Benton, president of Centrex, decided that CFC's operations should be brought more in line with those of Centrex. These included introducing a new position at CFC—Vice President of Purchasing. To fill this position, Benton selected John Speedman, who had been with Centrex for seven years. Benton assured Speedman that he had authority to make whatever changes he wanted, to bring the CFC operations into line with Centrex. . . . In addition, Benton assigned Bob Hestent as Speedman's assistant. Hestent had been with CFC purchasing group since 1984 and was familiar with the assembly plant managers. The new Purchasing Department was to be located at CFC's Toronto home office.

Speedman decided there was no reason to delay efforts to restructure CFC. As far as he was concerned, this was what Benton and the board of directors at Centrex wanted and that's what they would get. His first move was to centralize the purchasing practices of CFC. All assembly plant purchases over $50,000 would be made through the Toronto office. Speedman thought the coordination of assembly plant purchases would ensure a standard quality of furniture and allow the company to obtain quantity discounts when purchasing high-demand items. He presented his plan to Benton and the Board, and they gave it their complete backing.

At the time Speedman enacted his changes, CFC experienced a major increase in demand for furniture. This was likely to have a major impact on future purchases. Nevertheless, Speedman prepared this letter to be sent to assembly plant managers in order to explain his position:

Dear _____:

The home office has recently authorized a change in the way CFC obtains its resources. Starting immediately, all purchases over $50,000 will be sent first to my office for approval. This should be done well before the material is actually needed so that quantity purchases can be made where possible. I am sure that you will agree that such a move will improve the quality of CFC's product and help CFC save money. By accomplishing both these objectives, CFC will be better able to compete in what appears to be a very aggressive industry.

Sincerely yours,

(signed) John Speedman

Before mailing the letters, Speedman asked Hestent (his assistant) for his opinion. Hestent thought the letter was good and clearly made its point. However, he suggested that Speedman first meet with some of the assembly plant managers. Speedman was quick to say no because he was too busy, and, as Hestent said, the letter was clear and to the point. There would be no wasteful field trips.

In the weeks that followed, Speedman's office received positive replies from all assembly plant managers. The following is one such response:

Dear Mr. Speedman:

In response to your letter of the 13th, I see no problems in meeting your request. We at South Shore will do our best to inform you of all purchases over $50,000 and will give you the required lead time.

Although the anticipated increase in sales did occur over the next four months and reports from the field indicated a high level of activity, Speedman's office did not receive purchase information from the assembly plant managers.

Questions for Discussion

1. Which steps in Lewin's Change Model did Speedman ignore? Describe and explain.
2. How could Speedman have used these steps to overcome the employees' resistance to change? Discuss in detail.
3. How could Speedman have used Kotter's eight steps to more successfully implement change? Explain.
4. Using Table 10.1 and Figure 10.2 as a guide, describe how Speedman could have used organizational development to implement change. Explain in detail.

ethical dilemma

Should Drug Salespeople Be Allowed to Give Doctors Free Drug Samples & Gifts?

For years, they've been the standard freebies that drug companies have offered in an attempt to get doctors to prescribe their medications: expensive dinners, golf outings, trips to ski resorts and drug samples. . . .

This week, 11 current and former sales executives from TAP Pharmaceutical Products—a leading drug company—go on trial, accused of conspiring to pay kickbacks to doctors, hospitals, and other customers. The charges focus on efforts to get doctors to prescribe Lupron, the company's prostate cancer drug, as well as Prevacid, its heartburn drug. . . .

Doctors approached by the 11 TAP employees were offered gifts including trips to swanky golf and ski resorts and "educational grants," used to pay for cocktail parties, office Christmas parties and travel, according to prosecutors. Defense lawyers say the sales executives were simply doing their jobs. "As far as I can tell, this is the first time there has ever been a prosecution under the health care statute in which salespeople are being charged with a crime [for things] that they thought were completely within their job descriptions," says Roal Martine, a Chicago attorney who represents Carey Smith, a former TAP executive.

Solving the Dilemma

What is your feeling about drug salespeople giving doctors free drug samples and trips and/or "educational grants" as a way to get doctors to prescribe their products?

1. There is nothing wrong with this practice. Giving drug samples and gifts is simply another form of advertising.
2. Although this practice amounts to bribery, the doctors should not take the gifts. But I think it is all right for doctors to take only free drug samples. Doctors who take trips and "educational grants" for cocktail parties should be punished.
3. The salespeople and TAP should be punished. This practice drives up the costs of drugs, which ultimately are passed along to consumers.
4. Because guidelines established by the American Medical Association are vague, the TAP employees should not be punished. We need clear guidelines that include real penalties for not following them.

Source: *Excerpted from D. Lavoie, "Drug Firm Sales Reps Go on Trial,"* San Francisco Chronicle, *April 13, 2004, pp. C1, C5.*

video case

Louisville Slugger

Hillerich & Bradsby (H&B) is best known for making the Louisville Slugger, the first name in wooden bats. The company now produces aluminum bats as well as golf, hockey, and other sporting good products. But the privately held family company founded in 1857 eventually had to address substantial issues requiring difficult organizational changes.

Coming up with creative and innovative ideas wasn't the problem. Product users, customers, and sales reps provide a wealth of ideas. H&B's role is to take those ideas and synthesize them into forms useful for customers. The company's internal systems, however, weren't running smoothly. Existing computer systems didn't provide up-to-date access to important company information. Departments weren't communicating with one another. Inventory updating was woefully inade-

quate. Delivery personnel would attempt to ship inventory that wasn't ready or prepare to ship hundreds of items when only dozens were needed. On-time and complete shipping occurred about 30% of the time. Simple communications between production, management, and sales personnel took weeks to complete.

After listening to numerous proposals, H&B decided on an enterprise resource planning (ERP) system and contracted with SAP, a German business solutions software firm. ERP systems are designed to simplify all of the processes of the firm by storing all information in a centralized database and automatically updating information in each stage of the production process. However, even with ample warning from H&B's information systems personnel, CEO John Hillerich underestimated the difficulty of the transition process by "at least ten- or a hundredfold." Several years into the implementation process, top management was still debating whether to continue. Even though the new ERP system was designed with flexibility in mind, there was an inevitable period of trial and error while the software was customized to the needs of H&B. Implementation can take years, and the transition period is difficult. Employees are forced to abandon the old ways and learn new methods. Productivity sinks as employees struggle to meet demand while operating a completely foreign system. Employee morale slumped during the transition period, as longtime workers struggled to change the way they operated. In fact, several employees chose to retire rather than learn the new system.

But according to H&B top managers, the cost of implementation is worth the savings down the road. Although it took 5 years before H&B saw quantifiable cost savings from their new ERP system, an estimated 80% of employees are now happy dealing with the new system. Importantly, the company now ships 85% of its orders on time and complete, and customer satisfaction is high. Labor costs were reduced, and employees are free to work more productively.

Discussion Questions

1. Managers have to deal with two types of change: reactive and proactive. Define each of these types. Which type of change occurred at H&B?

2. The forces for change that originate outside the organization include demographic characteristics, market changes, technological advancements, and social and political pressures. Which of these forces is operating at H&B?

3. The degree to which employees feel threatened by change depends on whether the change is adaptive, innovative, or radically innovative. Define each of these levels of change. Which type of change is evident at H&B? Use evidence from the video to support your answer.

chapter II

Managing Individual Differences & Behavior

Supervising People as People

Major Questions You Should Be Able to Answer

II.I Values, Attitudes, & Behavior
Major Question: How do the hidden aspects of individuals—their values and attitudes—affect employee behavior?

II.2 Work-Related Attitudes & Behavior Managers Need to Deal With
Major Question: Is it important for managers to pay attention to employee attitudes?

II.3 Personality & Individual Behavior
Major Question: In the hiring process, do employers care about one's personality and individual traits?

II.4 Perception & Individual Behavior
Major Question: What are the distortions in perception that can cloud one's judgment?

II.5 Understanding Stress & Individual Behavior
Major Question: What causes workplace stress, and how can it be reduced?

Leading Younger Workers in Attaining Job Satisfaction

Will there be a labor shortage in the United States in the near future? Predictions vary. By 2010, the Bureau of Labor Statistics has said, there will be a need for 8 million more jobs than there are workers to do them, although other forecasters disagree. If true, however, it means that companies will not only have to do a better job of retaining mature workers. They will also have to learn how to keep younger workers.[1]

"Younger employees want success now, and on their own terms, but paying dues is often a foreign concept. They are less trusting of organizations, institutions, and authority in general." So writes one management consultant about younger workers. Is it possible for them to find satisfaction in the workplace?

A survey by the Gallup Organization suggests that supposedly discontented twentysomethings may fit into the workplace better than employers previously thought. But managers need to know how to manage for individual and generational differences.[2]

Young people today are much more apt to have had both parents working, or to come from a single-parent family, and are more likely to have been latch-key kids compared to those in previous generations. As a result, they have been left alone to make their own decisions and have had to assume greater responsibility. They are also used to television as entertainment and to a faster pace of life. In the workplace, these translate into a skepticism about rules, policies, and procedures; a requirement for more autonomy; and a need for constant stimulation.[3]

If you're going to be a leader, what should you know about managing this group? Following are some suggestions, some of which may benefit employees of all ages.[4]

- **Make training an obsession.** Just waiting to move up the organizational ladder is no longer good enough. Employer-sponsored training and education is a major attraction for young workers. In the Gallup survey, 84% of those who received at least 6 days of training within the previous year said they were satisfied. (Only 70% of those who received no training said they were satisfied.) Fifty-eight percent of workers 32 years old and younger said training was useful in preparing them for higher-level jobs. (Among those older, only 42% had the same opinion.)

- **Allow them independent learning while creating bonds with mentors.** The best kind of training for younger workers is not classroom training but forms of independent learning such as internships, work-study programs, and independent study. At the same time, they should be given the chance to create long-term bonds with teaching managers and mentors.

- **Teach people by showing them their results.** Younger workers need to see the daily tangible results of their work. Managers can help by carving a job up into bite-size chunks—as in dividing a sales job into categories such as making cold calls, making second-round calls, meeting in person with hot leads, and so on. A daily checklist helps workers see their results.

- **Provide frequent feedback.** Six-month and 12-month reviews are not as effective with young workers. More important is frequent, timely, and specific feedback each time a task is completed, with concrete suggestions for improvement.

- **Provide frequent rewards for great performance.** Incentives need not always be financial. Such rewards as praise, flex time, telecommuting, and extra responsibility are also recommended.

For Discussion As a worker, you might hope to be led by someone who would follow the above suggestions. But suppose your boss is of the old "tough guy" school and doesn't manage this way. In a tough job market, would you stick it out? How would you try to let your supervisor know how you would prefer to be managed?

forecast
What's Ahead in This Chapter

This first of five chapters on leadership discusses how to manage for individual differences and behaviors. We describe values, attitudes, and behavior; personality dimensions and traits; and specific work-related attitudes and behaviors managers need to be aware of. We next discuss distortions in perception, which can affect managerial judgment. Finally, we consider what stress does to individuals.

11.1 VALUES, ATTITUDES, & BEHAVIOR

> ✱ **major question** How do the hidden aspects of individuals—their values and attitudes—affect employee behavior?

THE BIG PICTURE
Organizational behavior (OB) considers how to better understand and manage people at work. In this section, we discuss individual values and attitudes and how they affect people's actions and judgments.

In this and the next four chapters we discuss the third management function (after planning and organizing)—namely, leading. *Leading,* as we said in Chapter 1, is defined as *motivating, directing, and otherwise influencing people to work hard to achieve the organization's goals.*

If you look at a company's annual report or at a brochure from its corporate communications department, you are apt to be given a picture of its *formal aspects:* Goals. Policies. Hierarchy. Structure. Could you exert effective leadership if the formal aspects were all you knew about the company? What about the *informal aspects*? Values. Attitudes. Personalities. Perceptions. Conflicts. Culture. Clearly, you need to know about these hidden, "messy" characteristics as well. *(See Figure 11.1, at left.)*

figure 11.1

FORMAL AND INFORMAL ASPECTS OF AN ORGANIZATION

Organizational Behavior: Trying to Explain & Predict Workplace Behavior

The informal aspects are the focus of the interdisciplinary field known as **organizational behavior (OB), which is dedicated to better understanding and management of people at work.** In particular, OB tries to help managers not only *explain* workplace behavior but also to *predict* it, so that they can better lead and motivate their employees to perform productively. OB looks at two areas:

- **Individual behavior.** This is the subject of this chapter. We discuss such individual attributes as values, attitudes, personality, perception, and learning.

- **Group behavior.** This is the subject of later chapters, particularly Chapter 13, where we discuss norms, roles, and teams.

Let us begin by considering individual values, attitudes, and behavior.

Values: What Are Your Consistent Beliefs & Feelings about *All* Things?

Values are abstract ideals that guide one's thinking and behavior across all situations.[5] Lifelong behavior patterns are dictated by values that are fairly well set by the time people are in their early teens. After that, however, one's values can be reshaped by significant life-altering events, such as having a child, undergoing a business failure, or surviving the death of a loved one, a war, or a serious health threat.

From a manager's point of view, it's helpful to know that values are those concepts, principles, things, people, or activities for which a person is willing to work hard—even make sacrifices for. Compensation, recognition, and status are common values in the workplace.[6] Younger people, however, may hold the value that it's best to have balance between work and life. According to the Families and Work Institute, 60% of men and women under the age of 25 with children are willing to make significant sacrifices in money and career to spend more time with their families.[7] With these employees, it helps managers to know there are limits to the inducements they can offer.

Attitudes: What Are Your Consistent Beliefs & Feelings about *Specific* Things?

Values are abstract ideals—global beliefs and feelings—that are directed toward all objects, people, or events.[8] Values tend to be consistent both over time and over related situations. By contrast, attitudes are beliefs and feelings that are directed toward *specific* objects, people, or events. More formally, an **attitude is defined as a learned predisposition toward a given object.**[9]

Example: If you dislike your present job, will you be happier if you change to a different job? Not necessarily. It depends on your attitude. In one study, researchers found that the attitudes of 5,000 middle-aged male employees toward their jobs were very stable over a 5-year period. Men with positive attitudes tended to stay positive, those with negative attitudes tended to stay negative. More revealingly, even those who changed jobs or occupations generally expressed the same attitudes they had previously.[10]

The Three Components of Attitudes: Affective, Cognitive, & Behavioral Attitudes have three components.[11] *(See Table 11.1.)*

table 11.1

EXAMPLES OF THE THREE COMPONENTS OF ATTITUDES

Affective	"I hate people who talk on cell phones in restaurants." "I hate putting on a suit for work." "I really like working from home." "I like commuting by train because I have time to myself." "I don't like working in office cubicles because they don't have doors and so there's no privacy."
Cognitive	"I can't appoint Herschel because creative people don't make good administrators." "The tallest building in the world is in Chicago." (Actually, it's in Taiwan.)
Behavioral	"I intend to fill out my expense report tomorrow." "I'm going to turn over a new leaf at New Year's and stop eating junk food." "I'm going to try to avoid John because he's a Democrat." "I'm never going to talk to George because he's a Republican."

- **The affective component—"I feel."** The *affective component of an attitude* consists of the feelings or emotions one has about a situation.

- **The cognitive component—"I believe."** The *cognitive component of an attitude* consists of the beliefs and knowledge one has about a situation.

- **The behavioral component—"I intend."** The *behavioral component of an attitude,* also known as the *intentional component,* refers to how one intends or expects to behave toward a situation.

All three components are often manifested at any given time. For example, if you call a corporation and get one of those telephone-tree menus ("For customer service, press 1 . . .") that never seems to connect you to a human being, you might be so irritated that you would say:

"I hate being given the run-around." [*affective component—your feelings*]

"That company doesn't know how to take care of customers." [*cognitive component—your perceptions*]

"I'll never call them again." [*behavioral component—your intentions*]

When Attitudes & Reality Collide: Consistency & Cognitive Dissonance

One of the last things you want, probably, is to be accused of hypocrisy—to be criticized for saying one thing and doing another. Like most people, you no doubt want to maintain consistency between your attitudes and your behavior.

But what if a strongly held attitude bumps up against a harsh reality that contradicts it? Suppose you're extremely concerned about getting AIDS, which you believe you might get from contact with body fluids, including blood. Then you're in a life-threatening auto accident in a third-world country and require surgery and blood transfusions—including transfusions of blood from (possibly AIDS-infected) strangers in a blood bank. Do you reject the blood to remain consistent with your beliefs about getting AIDS?

In 1957, social psychologist **Leon Festinger** proposed the term *cognitive dissonance* **to describe the psychological discomfort a person experiences between his or her cognitive attitude and incompatible behavior.**[12] Because people are uncomfortable with inconsistency, Festinger theorized, they will seek to reduce the "dissonance" or tension of the inconsistency. How they deal with the discomfort, he suggested, depends on three factors:

- **Importance.** How important are the elements creating the dissonance? Most people can put up with some ambiguities in life. For example, many drivers don't think obeying speed limits is very important, even though they profess to be law-abiding citizens. People eat greasy foods even though they know that ultimately they may contribute to heart disease.

- **Control.** How much control does one have over the matters that create dissonance? A juror may not like the idea of voting the death penalty but believe that he or she has no choice but to follow the law in the case. A taxpayer may object to his taxes being spent on, say, special-interest corporate welfare for a particular company but not feel that he or she can withhold taxes.

- **Rewards.** What rewards are at stake in the dissonance? You're apt to cling to old ideas in the face of new evidence if you have a lot invested emotionally or financially in those ideas. If you're a police officer who worked 20 years to prove a particular suspect guilty of murder, you're not apt to be very accepting of contradictory evidence after all that time.

Among the main ways to reduce cognitive dissonance are the following. *(See Table 11.2, opposite page.)*

- **Change your attitude and/or behavior.** This would seem to be the most obvious, even rational, response to take when confronted with cognitive dissonance.

- **Belittle the importance of the inconsistent behavior.** This happens all the time.

- **Find consonant elements that outweigh the dissonant ones.** This kind of rationalizing goes on quite often, as when employees are confronted with ethical dilemmas but fear losing their jobs.

Behavior: How Values & Attitudes Affect People's Actions & Judgments

Values (global) and attitudes (specific) are generally in harmony, but not always. For example, a manager may put a positive *value* on helpful behavior (global) yet may have a negative *attitude* toward helping an unethical co-worker (specific). Together, however, values and attitudes influence people's workplace *behavior*—**their actions and judgments.** ●

Leon Festinger. In 1957, the psychologist and his associates penetrated a cult whose members predicted that most people on earth would perish in a cataclysmic event except for a handful that would be rescued by aliens in a flying saucer. Festinger found himself standing with cult members on a hilltop awaiting the event, which, of course, did not happen. Later he proposed the term *cognitive dissonance* to explain how they rationalized the failure of their prophecy. Have you observed people employing this mechanism when the sure-fire thing they predicted did not occur?

table 11.2

EXAMPLES OF WAYS TO REDUCE COGNITIVE DISSONANCE

Technique	Examples
Change attitude and/or behavior	Gregory Withow once belonged to the White Aryan Resistance and other racist groups. He preached hatred and bashed Japanese tourists in San Francisco. Then he met Sylvia, who rejected his white-supremacist ideas. As he grew to love her, he found himself caught between his ideas and her disapproval. To decrease this cognitive dissonance, he renounced his old racist beliefs and changed his behavior, even becoming a spokesperson for the antiracist Anti-Defamation League.
Belittle importance of the inconsistent behavior	All cigarette smokers are repeatedly exposed to information that smoking is hazardous to health. But many belittle the habit as not being as risky as the antismoking messages suggest. ("My grandmother smokes, and she's in her 80s.")
Find consonant elements that outweigh dissonant ones	Ethics professor Sissela Bok says students may justify cheating on an exam by saying "I don't usually do this, but here I really have to do it." As one MIT graduate student said, students see cheating take place and "feel they have to. People get used to it, even though they know it's not right."

Sources: R. Plotnik, *Introduction to Psychology,* 3rd ed. (Pacific Grove, CA: Brooks/Cole, 1993), p. 602; S. Bok, cited in E. Venant, "A Nation of Cheaters," *San Francisco Chronicle,* January 7, 1992, p. D3, reprinted from *Los Angeles Times;* A. Dobrzeniecki, quoted in D. Butler, "MIT Students Guilty of Cheating," *Boston Globe,* March 2, 1991, p. 25.

Example

How Values & Attitudes Affect Behavior: IBM Uses an "Innovation Jam" to Move Beyond Incremental Improvements to Catalytic Innovations

As a manager, would you think most employees would agree that innovation is beneficial—that the original Silicon Valley firms prospered because they were constantly creating new products and services? Employees may have the *value,* then, that innovation is good—that it leads to productivity and profitability.

However, for a particularly successful product within your company, your employees might have the *attitude* that radical innovation is unnecessary. If the product is so successful, they may feel, why mess with it? Why not just make incremental improvements?

IBM found that the company's current reputation for constant incremental innovation hadn't inspired investors, resulting in its stock price remaining flat for 3 years. Recent earnings had come through cost-cutting, not the leaps in growth propelled by new business. Accordingly, CEO Samuel J. Palmisano decided to create what he called an "Innovation Jam," pulling together thousands of people—clients, consultants, and employees' family members, as well as IBM workers—in the online equivalent of a town meeting. His hope, according to one account, is that "The opinions of some 100,000 minds will lead to catalytic innovations so powerful they will transform industries, alter human behavior, and lead to new businesses for IBM."[13] IBM wouldn't own any ideas emerging from the two 72-hour "open source" sessions; they could be used by anyone.

When the first jam went online in July 2006, it dealt with four topics: transportation, health, the environment, and finance and commerce. IBM reported that 53,000 participants from over 70 countries created 37,000 posts in the first 72 hours. The photo at left shows one jam site filled with participants.

Your Call

Beyond providing new ideas, the Innovation Jam could further IBM's image as a forward-thinking global competitor. Do you think this could be a transformative event that could change IBM employees' values and attitudes?

> ✳ **major question** Is it important for managers to pay attention to employee attitudes?

THE BIG PICTURE

Attitudes are important because they affect behavior. Managers need to be alert to work-related attitudes having to do with job satisfaction, job involvement, organizational commitment, and organizational citizenship behaviors. Among the types of employee behavior they should attend to are their on-the-job performance and productivity as well as their absenteeism and turnover.

"Keep the employees happy."

It's true that attitudes are important, the reason being that *attitudes affect behavior.* But is keeping employees happy all that managers need to know to get results? We discuss motivation for performance in the next chapter. Here let us consider what managers need to know about work-related attitudes and behaviors.

Work-Related Attitudes: Job Satisfaction, Job Involvement, Organizational Commitment, & Organizational Citizenship Behaviors

Employees will gripe about almost anything. About working in cubicles instead of offices. About not having enough help. About the mediocre cafeteria food. About managers "who don't know anything." They may also say some good things. About the great retirement plan. About flex time. About a product beating competing products. About how cool Manager X is.

Four types of attitudes managers are particularly interested in are (1) *job satisfaction,* (2) *job involvement,* (3) *organizational commitment,* and (4) *organizational citizenship behaviors.*

I. Job Satisfaction: How Much Do You Like or Dislike Your Job? *Job satisfaction* **is the extent to which you feel positively or negatively about various aspects of your work.** Most people don't like everything about their jobs. Their overall satisfaction depends on how they feel about several components, such as *work, pay, promotions, co-workers, and supervision.*[14] Among the key correlates of job satisfaction are stronger motivation, job involvement, organizational commitment, and life satisfaction and less absenteeism, tardiness, turnover, and perceived stress.[15]

Many middle managers are dissatisfied with their jobs, feeling overworked and underappreciated, especially during economic downturns, when companies cut staff and managers work longer hours for small pay increases and little recognition.[16] But what is the relationship between job satisfaction and job performance—does more satisfaction cause better performance or does better performance cause more satisfaction? This is a subject of much debate among management scholars.[17] One comprehensive study found that (1) job satisfaction and performance are moderately related, meaning that employee job satisfaction is a key work attitude managers should consider when trying to increase performance; but (2) the relationship between satisfaction and performance is complex and it seems that both variables influence each other through a host of individual differences and work-environment characteristics.[18]

2. Job Involvement: How Much Do You Identify with Your Work? *Job involvement* **is the extent to which you identify or are personally involved with your job.** Many people, of course, work simply to put bread on the table; they have no interest in excelling at their jobs. More fortunate are those who actively participate in their jobs and consider their work performance important to their self-worth.

Analysis of nearly 28,000 individuals from 87 different studies demonstrates that job involvement is moderately correlated with job satisfaction.[19] Thus, managers are encouraged to foster satisfying work environments to fuel employees' job involvement.[20]

3. Organizational Commitment *Organizational commitment* **reflects the extent to which an employee identifies with an organization and is committed to its goals.** For instance, some managers question whether mothers with children can be fully committed to their jobs, although one survey found that only 4% of more than 2,612 women said that their bosses think that they are not as committed to their jobs because they have children.[21] Research shows a strong relationship between organizational commitment and job satisfaction.[22] Thus, managers are advised to increase job satisfaction to elicit higher levels of commitment. In turn, higher commitment can facilitate higher performance.[23]

4. Organizational Citizenship Behaviors *Organizational citizenship behaviors* **are those employee behaviors that are not directly part of employees' job descriptions—that exceed their work-role requirements.** Examples, according to one description, include "such gestures as constructive statements about the department, expression of personal interest in the work of others, suggestions for improvement, training new people, respect for the spirit as well as the letter of housekeeping rules, care for organizational property, and punctuality and attendance well beyond standard or enforceable levels."[24] Several studies reveal a significant and moderately positive correlation between organizational citizenship behaviors and job satisfaction.[25]

Important Workplace Behaviors

Why, as a manager, do you need to learn how to manage individual differences? The answer, as you might expect, is so that you can influence employees to do their best work. Among the types of behavior are (1) performance and productivity and (2) absenteeism and turnover.

Evaluating Behavior When Employees Are Working: Performance & Productivity Every job has certain expectations, but in some jobs performance and productivity are easier to define than in others. How many contacts should a telemarketing sales rep make in a day? How many sales should he or she close? Often a job of this nature will have a history of accomplishments (from what previous job holders have attained) so that it is possible to quantify performance behavior.

However, an advertising agency account executive handling major clients such as a carmaker or a beverage manufacturer may go months before landing this kind of big account. Or a researcher in a pharmaceutical company may take years to develop a promising new prescription drug.

In short, the method of evaluating performance must match the job being done.

Evaluating Behavior When Employees Are Not Working: Absenteeism & Turnover Should you be suspicious of every instance of *absenteeism*—**when an employee doesn't show up for work?** Of course, some absences—illness, death in the family, or jury duty, for example—are legitimate. Such no-show behavior is to be expected from time to time. However, absenteeism is related to job dissatisfaction.[26]

Absenteeism may be a precursor to *turnover,* **when employees leave their jobs.** Every organization experiences some turnover, as employees leave for reasons of family, better job prospects, or retirement. However, except in low-skill industries, a continual revolving door of new employees is usually not a good sign, since replacement and training is expensive.[27] For instance, one study found the direct and indirect costs of recruiting and training a new midlevel manager—along with lost business to competitors, lost technical knowledge, decreased morale among remaining employees, and the like—came to $64,000.[28] Another study found it costs nearly $108,000 to replace a key worker or a manager.[29] ●

Performance monitors. These British Airways customer service reps are being monitored by software that keeps track not only of ticket sales and customer-complaint resolutions but also of the amount of time spent on breaks and personal phone calls. In tracking employee effectiveness, the technology can count incentive dollars tied to performance and immediately direct them into employee paychecks. Do you think these incentive calculators are justified or do you think they intrude too much on employee privacy?

II.3 PERSONALITY & INDIVIDUAL BEHAVIOR

 major question In the hiring process, do employers care about one's personality and individual traits?

THE BIG PICTURE
Personality consists of stable psychological and behavioral attributes that give you your identity. We describe five personality dimensions and five personality traits that managers need to be aware of to understand workplace behavior.

How would you describe yourself? Are you outgoing? aggressive? sociable? tense? passive? lazy? quiet? Whatever the combination of traits, which result from the interaction of your genes and your environment, they constitute your personality.

More formally, ***personality* consists of the stable psychological traits and behavioral attributes that give a person his or her identity.**[30] As a manager, you need to understand personality attributes because they affect how people perceive and act within the organization.

The Big Five Personality Dimensions

In recent years, the many personality dimensions have been distilled into a list of factors known as the Big Five.[31] **The *Big Five personality dimensions* are (1) extroversion, (2) agreeableness, (3) conscientiousness, (4) emotional stability, and (5) openness to experience.**

Self-Assessment Exercise:
Assessing Your Flexibility

- **Extroversion.** How outgoing, talkative, sociable, and assertive a person is.
- **Agreeableness.** How trusting, good-natured, cooperative, and soft-hearted one is.
- **Conscientiousness.** How dependable, responsible, achievement-oriented, and persistent one is.

Assertive and sociable.
Does it take a certain kind of personality to be a good salesperson? Have you ever known people who were quiet, unassuming, even shy but who were nevertheless very persistent and persuasive—that is, good salespeople?

- **Emotional stability.** How relaxed, secure, and unworried one is.
- **Openness to experience.** How intellectual, imaginative, curious, and broad-minded one is.

Standardized personality tests are used to score people on each dimension to draw a person's personality profile that is supposedly as unique as his or her fingerprints. For example, if you scored low on the first trait, extroversion, you would presumably be prone to shy and withdrawn behavior. If you scored low on emotional stability, you supposedly would be nervous, tense, angry, and worried.

Do Personality Tests Work for the Workplace?
As a manager, you would want to know if the Big Five model in particular and personality testing in

general can help predict behavior in the workplace. Is a personality test helpful in predicting a match between personality and job performance? Two findings:

- **Extroversion—the outgoing personality.** As might be expected, extroversion (an outgoing personality) has been associated with success for managers and salespeople. Also, extroversion is a stronger predictor of job performance than agreeableness, across all professions, according to researchers. "It appears that being courteous, trusting, straightforward, and soft-hearted [that is, agreeableness] has a smaller impact on job performance," conclude the researchers, "than being talkative, active, and assertive [that is, extroversion]."[32]

- **Conscientiousness—the dependable personality.** Conscientiousness (strong work ethic) has been found to have the strongest positive correlation with job performance and training performance. According to researchers, "those individuals who exhibit traits associated with a strong sense of purpose, obligation, and persistence generally perform better than those who do not."[33]

The table below presents tips to help managers avoid abuses and discrimination lawsuits when using personality and psychological testing for employment decisions.[34] *(See Table 11.3.)*

table 11.3

CAUTIONS ABOUT USING PERSONALITY TESTS IN THE WORKPLACE

• *Use professionals.* Rely on reputable, licensed psychologists for selecting and overseeing the administration, scoring, and interpretation of personality and psychological tests. This is particularly important, since not every psychologist is expert at these kinds of tests.	• *Don't hire on the basis of personality test results alone.* Supplement any personality test data with information from reference checks, personal interviews, ability tests, and job performance records. Also avoid hiring people on the basis of specified personality profiles. As a case in point, there is no distinct "managerial personality."	• *Be alert for gender, racial, and ethnic bias.* Regularly assess any possible adverse impact of personality tests on the hiring of women and minorities. This is truly a matter of great importance, since you don't want to find your company (or yourself) embroiled in a lawsuit at some point downstream.	• *Graphology tests don't work, but integrity tests do.* Personality traits and aptitudes cannot be inferred from samples of people's penmanship, as proponents of graphology tests claim. However, dishonest job applicants can often be screened by integrity tests, since dishonest people are reportedly unable to fake conscientiousness, even on a paper-and-pencil test.

The Proactive Personality   A person who scores well on the Big Five dimension of conscientiousness is probably a good worker. He or she may also be a *proactive personality,* **someone who is more apt to take initiative and persevere to influence the environment.**[35] People of this sort identify opportunities and act on them, which makes them associated not only with success—individual, team, and organizational—but also with entrepreneurship.

Five Traits Important in Organizations

Five of the most important personality traits that managers need to be aware of to understand workplace behavior are (1) *locus of control,* (2) *self-efficacy,* (3) *self-esteem,* (4) *self-monitoring,* and (5) *emotional intelligence.*

I. Locus of Control: "I Am/Am Not the Captain of My Fate"   As we discussed briefly in Chapter 3, **locus of control indicates how much people believe they control their fate through their own efforts.** If you have an *internal locus of control,* you believe you control your own destiny. If you have an *external locus of control,* you believe external forces control you.

Research shows internals and externals have important workplace differences. Internals exhibit less anxiety, greater work motivation, and stronger expectations that effort leads to performance. They also obtain higher salaries.[36]

These findings have two important implications for managers:

- **Different degrees of structure and compliance for each type.** Employees with internal locus of control will probably resist close managerial supervision. Hence, they should probably be placed in jobs requiring high initiative and lower compliance. By contrast, employees with external locus of control might do better in highly structured jobs requiring greater compliance.

- **Different reward systems for each type.** Since internals seem to have a greater belief that their actions have a direct effect on the consequences of that action, internals likely would prefer and respond more productively to incentives such as merit pay or sales commissions. (We discuss incentive compensation systems in Chapter 12.)

2. Self-Efficacy: "I Can/Can't Do This Task"   A related trait is **self-efficacy, belief in one's personal ability to do a task.** Unlike locus of control, this characteristic isn't about how much fate controls events (as in believing whether getting a high grade in a course is determined by you or by outside factors, such as the grade curve or trick questions). Rather, it's about your personal belief that you have what it takes to succeed. (Erik Weihenmayer, 35, is blind but also a self-described "unrealistic optimist," who was the first blind climber to scale Mt. Everest.)[37]

Have you noticed that those who are confident about their ability tend to succeed, whereas those preoccupied with failure tend not to? Indeed, high expectations of self-efficacy have been linked with all kinds of positives: not only success in varied physical and mental tasks but also reduced anxiety and increased tolerance for pain.[38] One study found that the sales performance of life-insurance agents was much better among those with high self-efficacy.[39] Low self-efficacy is associated with **learned helplessness, the debilitating lack of faith in one's ability to control one's environment.**[40]

Among the implications for managers:

- **Job assignments.** Complex, challenging, and autonomous jobs tend to enhance people's perceptions of their self-efficacy. Boring, tedious jobs generally do the opposite.

- **Developing self-efficacy.** Self-efficacy is a quality that can be nurtured. Employees with low self-efficacy need lots of constructive pointers and positive feedback.[41] Goal difficulty needs to match individuals' perceived self-efficacy, but goals can be made more challenging as performance improves.[42] Small successes need to be rewarded. Employees' expectations can be improved through guided experiences, mentoring, and role modeling.[43]

3. Self-Esteem: "I Like/Dislike Myself"

How worthwhile, capable, and acceptable do you think you are? The answer to this question is an indicator of your *self-esteem,* **the extent to which people like or dislike themselves, their overall self-evaluation.**[44] Research offers some interesting insights about how high or low self-esteem can affect people and organizations.

- **People with high self-esteem.** Compared to people with low self-esteem, people with high self-esteem are more apt to handle failure better, to emphasize the positive, to take more risks, and to choose more unconventional jobs.[45] However, when faced with pressure situations, high-self-esteem people have been found to become egotistical and boastful.[46] Some have even been associated with aggressive and violent behavior.

- **People with low self-esteem.** Conversely, low-self-esteem people confronted with failure have been found to have focused on their weaknesses and to have had primarily negative thoughts. Moreover, they are more dependent on others and are more apt to be influenced by them and to be less likely to take independent positions.

Can self-esteem be improved? According to one study, "low self-esteem can be raised more by having the person think of *desirable* characteristics *possessed* rather than of undesirable characteristics from which he or she is free."[47] Some ways in which managers can build employee self-esteem are shown below. *(See Table 11.4.)*

- Reinforce employees' positive attributes and skills.

- Provide positive feedback whenever possible.

- Break larger projects into smaller tasks and projects.

- Express confidence in employees' abilities to complete their tasks.

- Provide coaching whenever employees are seen to be struggling to complete tasks.

table 11.4

SOME WAYS THAT MANAGERS CAN BOOST EMPLOYEE SELF-ESTEEM

4. Self-Monitoring: "I'm Fairly Able/Unable to Adapt My Behavior to Others"

As you're rushing to an important meeting, you are stopped by a co-worker, who starts to discuss a personal problem. You need to break away, so you glance at your watch.

(a) Does your co-worker Get It? Seeing you look at your watch, he says, "Sorry, I see you're busy. Catch you later." Or (b) does he Not Get It? He keeps talking, until you say "I'm late for a big meeting" and start walking away.

The two scenarios show the difference between a high self-monitor and a low self-monitor. *Self-monitoring* **is the extent to which people are able to observe their own behavior and adapt it to external situations.** Of course, we would all like to think we are high in self-monitoring—able to regulate our "expressive self-presentation for the sake of desired public appearances," as some experts write, "and thus be highly responsive to social and interpersonal cues" of others.[48] But whereas some high self-monitors are criticized for being chameleons, always able to adapt their self-presentation to their surroundings, low self-monitors are often criticized for being on their own planet and insensitive to others. Instead, their behavior may reflect their own inner states, including their attitudes and feelings.

It might be expected that people in top management are more apt to be high self-monitors able to play different roles—even contradictory roles—to suit different situations. Research shows a positive relationship between high self-monitoring and career success. Among 139 MBA graduates who were tracked for 5 years, high self-monitors enjoyed more internal and external promotions than did their low self-monitoring classmates.[49] Other research has found that managerial success (in terms of speed of promotions) was tied to political savvy (knowing how to socialize, network, and engage in organizational politics).[50]

Self-Assessment Exercise:
Assessing Your Emotional
Intelligence

5. Emotional Intelligence: "I'm Pretty Good/Not Good at Empathizing with Others & Being Self-Motivated"

Daniel Goleman is co-chairman of the Consortium for Research on Emotional Intelligence in Organizations at Rutgers University and author of the popular 1995 book *Emotional Intelligence*. In 1998, he argued that the most important attribute in a leader is **emotional intelligence, the ability to cope, empathize with others, and be self-motivated.**[51] "When I compared star performers with average ones in senior leadership positions," Goleman wrote, "nearly 90% of the difference in their profiles was attributable to emotional intelligence factors rather than cognitive abilities."[52] The traits of emotional intelligence are (1) self-awareness, (2) self-management, (3) social awareness, and (4) relationship management. *(See Table 11.5.)*

table 11.5

THE TRAITS OF EMOTIONAL INTELLIGENCE

1. ***Self-awareness.*** The most essential trait. This is the ability to read your own emotions and gauge your moods accurately, so you know how you're affecting others.
2. ***Self-management.*** This is the ability to control your emotions and act with honesty and integrity in reliable and adaptable ways. You can leave occasional bad moods outside the office.
3. ***Social awareness.*** This includes empathy, allowing you to show others that you care, and organizational intuition, so you keenly understand how your emotions and actions affect others.
4. ***Relationship management.*** This is the ability to communicate clearly and convincingly, disarm conflicts, and build strong personal bonds.

Sources: Adapted from D. Goleman, R. Boyatzis, and A. McKee, "Primal Leadership: The Hidden Driver of Great Performance," *Harvard Business Review,* December 2001, p. 49; and *Primal Leadership: Realizing the Power of Emotional Intelligence* (Boston: Harvard Business School Press, 2002), p. 39. Copyright © 2001 and 2002 by the Harvard Business School Publishing Corporation. Reprinted with permission; all rights reserved.

The self-awareness and self-management components constitute *personal competence;* the social awareness and relationship management components feed into *social competence.* These emotional intelligence skills need to be well polished in today's pressure-packed workplace.

Are Goleman's ideas accurate? Preliminary evidence suggests that emotional intelligence can land you a job. A simulated interview process indicated that interviewers' assessments of an applicant's emotional intelligence were positively associated with their impression of the application.[53] However, given the difficulty of measuring emotional intelligence, further research is needed on this new leadership trait.[54]

The Self-Assessment at the end of this chapter enables you to evaluate your own emotional intelligence. ●

Self-Assessment Exercise:
Assessing Your Empathy Skills

II.4 PERCEPTION & INDIVIDUAL BEHAVIOR

> **What are the distortions in perception that can cloud one's judgment?**
>
> major **✦** question

THE BIG PICTURE

Perception, a four-step process, can be skewed by four types of distortion: selective perception, stereotyping, the halo effect, and causal attribution. We also consider the self-fulfilling prophecy, which can affect our judgment as well.

If you were a smoker, which warning on a cigarette pack would make you think more about quitting? "Smoking seriously harms you and others around you." A blunt "Smoking kills." Or a stark graphic image showing decaying teeth.

This is the kind of decision public health authorities in various countries are wrestling with. (And a Canadian Cancer Society study in 2000 found that 58% of smokers who saw graphic images thought twice about the health effects of smoking.)[55] These officials, in other words, are trying to decide how *perception* might influence behavior.

The Four Steps in the Perceptual Process

***Perception* is the process of interpreting and understanding one's environment.** The process of perception is complex, but it can be boiled down to four steps. *(See Figure 11.2.)*

figure II.2

THE FOUR STEPS IN THE PERCEPTUAL PROCESS

In this book, we are less concerned about the theoretical steps in perception than in how perception is distorted, since this has considerable bearing on the manager's judgment and job. In any one of the four stages of the perception process there is the possibility for misunderstandings or errors in judgment. Perceptual errors can lead to mistakes that can be damaging to yourself, other people, and your organization.

Four Distortions in Perception

Although there are other types of distortion in perception, we will describe the following: (1) *selective perception,* (2) *stereotyping,* (3) the *halo effect,* and (4) *causal attribution.*

I. Selective Perception: "I Don't Want to Hear about That" Are there topics that you find especially uncomfortable—your own death, say, or child molestation, or cheating in college—so that you tune out these subjects when people bring them up? For example, many people avoid making a will because they find it too awful to think about their future nonexistence. ***Selective perception* is the tendency to filter out information that is discomforting, that seems irrelevant, or that contradicts one's beliefs.**

One classic study found that when executives were asked to determine the key problem in a complex business case, they identified the problem as falling within their particular functional areas of work—they evidently filtered out information about other areas. That is, human resource managers said the principal problem was a people issue, marketing executives said it was a sales issue, and production people said it was a manufacturing issue.[56] This shows how managers can distort problem solving through selective perception.

Group Exercise:
Do Stereotypes Unconsciously Influence the Perception Process?

2. Stereotyping: "Those Sorts of People Are Pretty Much the Same" If you're a tall African American man, do people make remarks about basketball players? If you're of Irish descent, do people believe you drink a lot? If you're Jewish, do people think you're money-oriented? If you're a woman, do people think you're automatically nurturing? All these are stereotypes. ***Stereotyping* is the tendency to attribute to an individual the characteristics one believes are typical of the group to which that individual belongs.**[57]

Principal areas of stereotyping that should be of concern to you as a manager are (1) *sex-role stereotypes,* (2) *age stereotypes,* and (3) *race/ethnicity stereotypes.*

- **Sex-role stereotypes.** A *sex-role stereotype* is the belief that differing traits and abilities make males and females particularly well suited to different roles.

  A classic study found that women were viewed "as relatively less competent, less independent, less objective, and less logical than men; men are perceived as lacking interpersonal sensitivity, warmth, and expressiveness in comparison to women." Moreover, the study found, "stereotypically masculine traits are more often perceived to be desirable than are stereotypically feminine characteristics."[58]

  Although research shows that men and women do not differ in such a stereotypical manner, the stereotypes still persist.[59] And, unfortunately, promotional decisions may still be affected by sex-role stereotyping. A study of a multinational Fortune 500 company, for example, revealed that men received more favorable evaluations than women in spite of controlling for age, education, organizational tenure, salary grade, and type of job.[60]

- **Age stereotypes.** *Age stereotypes* tend to depict older workers as less involved in their work, less satisfied, less motivated, and less committed than younger workers. But in fact research shows that as employees' age increases, so does their job involvement and satisfaction, work motivation, and organizational commitment.[61]

  Stereotypes also depict older workers as being less productive; however, this is not borne out.[62] Finally, the stereotype that older workers have higher absenteeism is not supported by the research; if anything, managers should focus more attention on absenteeism among younger rather than older workers.[63]

  Because the median age of Americans is currently 35.3 years—the oldest in our history—it seems clear that managers will probably be dealing with an older workforce.[64] Moreover, by 2030, about one-fifth of the population will be over age 65, but many, whether by choice or by necessity, will continue working. World-famous heart surgeon Michael DeBakey, for instance, who was born in 1908, has continued to work into his late nineties.[65]

- **Race/ethnicity stereotypes.** *Race/ethnicity stereotypes* don't bear repeating here, but it is noteworthy that there are not a lot of African American, Hispanic, and Asian managers in the United States. For instance, the Labor Department estimates that women and minorities hold only 5% of senior-level positions—and the majority of those are held by women rather than minorities.[66]

3. The Halo Effect: "One Trait Tells Me All I Need to Know" Do you think physically attractive people have more desirable traits than unattractive people—that they are happier, kinder, more successful, more socially skilled, more sensitive, more interesting, independent, exciting, sexually warm, even smarter and nicer? All of these

Example

The Halo Effect: Are Attractive Men & Women Paid More Than Ordinary People?

Are attractive employees paid more than ordinary (or unattractive) people for the same work? Two economists, Markus Mobius of Harvard and Tanya Rosenblat of Wesleyan University, decided to look into that question.[71]

Students were recruited to play the roles of both applicants and employers for a job that involved solving mazes. To determine how attractive applicants were, a separate panel of students was shown their photographs and asked to rate them on a beauty scale. After applicants solved mazes, employers considered the prospective employees under different circumstances. They examined (1) only an applicant's résumé, which listed age, sex, university, graduation date, job experience, and activities and hobbies; (2) the résumé and a photograph; (3) the résumé and a telephone interview; (4) the résumé, a telephone interview, and a photograph; and (5) the résumé, a telephone interview, and a face-to-face interview. The employers used the interview information to form their own estimates of the number of mazes the subjects would solve during their 15-minute jobs, and the subjects then solved the mazes as best they could.

The economists found some interesting results: (1) Although beautiful people are no better than ordinary people at solving mazes, they are more self-

confident about their abilities. "Being good looking," says one article about the study, "seems to be strongly associated with self-confidence, a trait that is apparently attractive to employers."[72] (2) When employers looked only at résumés, physical appearance had no effect on their judgments, as you might expect. With all of the other treatments, employers showed higher estimates for beautiful people's productivity—especially when they had face-to-face interviews but even with telephone-only interviews, the result, apparently, of the effect of self-confidence that came across on the phone. (3) Good-looking people are good communicators, which also contributes to employers' positive perceptions. In sum, "Employers (wrongly) expect good-looking workers to perform better than their less-attractive counterparts under both visual and oral interaction," said the researchers, "even after controlling for individual worker characteristics and worker confidence."

Your Call

Are you yourself influenced in your judgment of people by how attractive they are? Do you think as a manager you could look beyond people's physical appearances to be a good judge of their competence?

Handsomely compensated. Attractive employees are generally paid better than unattractive ones are. Why do you think that is? Do you think it's inevitable?

traits have been attributed to attractive people.[67] This situation is an example of the *halo effect*, **in which we form an impression of an individual based on a single trait.** (The phenomenon is also called the *horn-and-halo effect*, because not only can a single positive trait be generalized into an array of positive traits but the reverse is also true.)

As if we needed additional proof that life is unfair, it has been shown that attractive people generally are treated better than unattractive people. Teachers have higher expectations of them in terms of academic achievement.[68] Potential employers are more apt to view them favorably.[69] Attractive employees are generally paid higher salaries than unattractive ones are.[70] Clearly, however, if a manager fails to look at *all* an individual's traits, he or she has no right to complain if that employee doesn't work out.

4. Causal Attributions   *Causal attribution* **is the activity of inferring causes for observed behavior.** Rightly or wrongly, we constantly formulate cause-and-effect explanations for our own and others' behavior. Attributional statements such as the following are common: "Joe drinks too much because he has no willpower; but I need a couple of drinks after work because I'm under a lot of pressure." Even though our causal attributions tend to be self-serving and are often invalid, it's important to understand how people formulate attributions because they profoundly affect organizational behavior. For example, a supervisor who attributes an employee's poor performance to a lack of effort might reprimand that person. However, training might be deemed necessary if the supervisor attributes the poor performance to a lack of ability.

As a manager, you need to be alert to two attributional tendencies that can distort one's interpretation of observed behavior—the *fundamental attribution bias* and the *self-serving bias.*

- **Fundamental attribution bias.** In the *fundamental attribution bias,* **people attribute another person's behavior to his or her personal characteristics rather than to situational factors.**

     Example: A study of manufacturing employees found that top managers attributed the cause of industrial back pain to individuals, whereas workers attributed it to the environment.[73]

- **Self-serving bias.** In the *self-serving bias,* **people tend to take more personal responsibility for success than for failure.**

     Example: The way students typically analyze their performance on exams shows self-serving bias, with "A" students likely to attribute their grade to high ability or hard work and "D" students blaming factors such as bad luck, unclear lectures, and unfair testing.[74] Another example: Disgraced Enron CEO Ken Lay asserted that his company failed not because of his doings but because it was the victim of "a real conspiracy"—by *The Wall Street Journal;*

by one-time chief financial officer Andrew Fastow, who testified for the government; and by short sellers, investors who bet that Enron's shares would fall.[75]

The Self-Fulfilling Prophecy, or Pygmalion Effect

The *self-fulfilling prophecy*, also known as the *Pygmalion* ("pig-*mail*-yun") *effect*, describes the phenomenon in which people's expectations of themselves or others lead them to behave in ways that make those expectations come true.

Expectations are important. An example is a waiter who expects some poorly dressed customers to be stingy tippers, who therefore gives them poor service and so gets the result he or she expected—a much lower tip than usual. Research has shown that by raising managers' expectations for individuals performing a wide variety of tasks, higher levels of achievement and productivity can be achieved.[76] The lesson for you as a manager is that when you expect employees to perform badly, they probably will, and when you expect them to perform well, they probably will. (In the G. B. Shaw play *Pygmalion,* a speech coach bets he can get a lower-class girl to change her accent and her demeanor so that she can pass herself off as a duchess. In 6 months, she successfully "passes" in high society, having become a woman of sensitivity and taste.) ●

Practical Action

How Can Managers Harness the Pygmalion Effect to Lead Employees?

Does the self-fulfilling prophecy really work? Research in a variety of industries and occupations shows that the effect can be quite strong. [77]

At Microsoft Corp., employees routinely put in 75-hour weeks, especially when trying to meet shipping deadlines for new products. Because Microsoft prides itself on trying to meet its deadlines, positive group-level expectations help create and reinforce an organizational culture of high expectancy for success. This process then excites people about working for the organization, thereby reducing turnover.[78]

This shows the Pygmalion effect at work—that is, managerial expectations powerfully influence employee behavior and performance. Managers can harness this effect by building a hierarchical framework that reinforces positive performance expectations throughout the organization. The foundation of this framework is employee self-expectations. In turn, positive self-expectations improve interpersonal expectations by encouraging people to work toward common goals. This cooperation enhances group-level productivity and promotes positive performance expectations within the work group.

How to Create a Pygmalion Effect

Because positive self-expectations are the foundation for creating an organization-wide Pygmalion effect, let us consider how managers can create positive performance expectations. This task may be accomplished using various combinations of the following:

1. Recognize that everyone has the potential to increase his or her performance.
2. Instill confidence in your staff.
3. Set high performance goals.
4. Positively reinforce employees for a job well done.
5. Provide constructive feedback when necessary.
6. Help employees advance through the organization.
7. Introduce new employees as if they have outstanding potential.
8. Become aware of your personal prejudices and non-verbal messages that may discourage others.
9. Encourage employees to visualize the successful execution of tasks.
10. Help employees master key skills and tasks.[79]

II.5 UNDERSTANDING STRESS & INDIVIDUAL BEHAVIOR

➕ major question | What causes workplace stress, and how can it be reduced?

THE BIG PICTURE

Stress is what people feel when enduring extraordinary demands or opportunities and are not sure how to handle them. There are six sources of stress: individual differences, individual task, individual role, group, organizational, and nonwork demands. We describe some consequences of stress and three ways to reduce it in the organization.

Although most workers are satisfied with their jobs, 24% say their work is "very stressful," and 43% say it is "moderately stressful."[80] A study by one health plan of 46,000 people working for six large employers found that the employers paid nearly 8% a year of total health care for treatment of what employees characterized as out-of-control stress. Such workers, who suffered from a variety of stress-related illnesses, such as migraines, back pain, and gastrointestinal disorders, had 46% higher health costs.[81]

Work stress can also, as you might guess, put managers at risk. Researchers who interviewed 800 hospital heart-attack patients over a 5-year period found that managers run twice the normal risk of heart attack the week after they have had to fire someone or face a high-pressure deadline.[82]

Workplace stress is negatively related to positive emotions, job satisfaction, organizational commitment, and job performance.[83] Indeed, historically researchers have generally believed that there is an *inverted U-shaped relationship* between stress and performance. That is, low levels of stress lead to low performance (because people are not "charged up" to perform), but high levels of stress also lead to an energy-sapping fight-or-flight response that produces low performance. Optimal performance, according to this hypothesis, results when people are subjected to moderate levels of stress.

What Is Stress?

Stress **is the tension people feel when they are facing or enduring extraordinary demands, constraints, or opportunities and are uncertain about their ability to handle them effectively.**[84] Stress is the feeling of tension and pressure; **the source of stress is called a** *stressor.*

Stress has both physical and emotional components. Physically, according to Canadian researcher Hans Selye, considered the father of the modern concept of stress, stress is "the nonspecific response of the body to any demand made upon it."[85] Emotionally, stress has been defined as the feeling of being overwhelmed, "the perception that events or circumstances have challenged, or exceeded, a person's ability to cope."[86]

Stressors can be *hassles,* or simple irritants, such as misplacing or losing things, concerns about one's physical appearance, and having too many things to do.[87] Or they can be *crises,* such as sudden occasions of overwhelming terror—a horrible auto accident, an incident of childhood abuse. Or they can be *strong stressors,* which can dramatically strain a person's ability to adapt—extreme physical discomfort, such as chronic severe back pain.

Stressors can be both *negative* and *positive.* That is, one can understand that being fired or being divorced can be a great source of stress but so can being promoted or getting married. As Selye writes, "It is immaterial whether the agent or the situation we face is pleasant or

Trading frenzy. Many jobs are stressful, but some are more stressful than others, such as those of traders on the floor of the New York Stock Exchange. What occupations do you think are the most stress-inducing?

unpleasant; all that counts is the intensity of the demand for adjustment and adaptation."[88] In addition, Selye distinguished between bad stress (what he called "distress"), in which the result of the stressor can be anxiety and illness, and good stress ("eustress"), which can stimulate a person to better coping and adaptation, such as performing well on a test. In this discussion, however, we are mainly concerned with how stress negatively affects people and their performance.

The Sources of Job-Related Stress

There are six sources of stress on the job: (1) *demands created by individual differences,* (2) *individual task demands,* (3) *individual role demands,* (4) *group demands,* (5) *organizational demands,* and (6) *nonwork demands.*

1. Demands Created by Individual Differences: The Stress Created by Personality Characteristics

Do you become extremely irritated if you have to wait in line? Do you walk, talk, or eat rapidly? Do you always feel you should be working or studying when you're supposed to be relaxing? If you answered yes, you belong to a hurried, deadline-ridden, and competitive group who have the personality characteristic known as ***Type A behavior pattern,* meaning they are involved in a chronic, determined struggle to accomplish more in less time.**[89] Type A behavior has been associated with increased performance in the work of professors, students, and life insurance brokers.[90] However, it also has been associated with greater cardiovascular activity and higher blood pressure, as well as to heart disease, especially for individuals who showed strong feelings of anger, hostility, and aggression.[91]

2. Individual Task Demands: The Stress Created by the Job Itself

Some occupations are more stressful than others. Directing a play is more stressful than selling tickets. Doing brain surgery is more stressful than processing medical claims. Managing employees is more stressful than being a receptionist (usually).

Nevertheless, low-level jobs can be more stressful than high-level jobs because employees often have less control over their lives and thus have less work satisfaction. Being a high-speed word processor or doing telemarketing sales, for instance, can be quite stressful.

There is also considerable stress caused by worries over the prospective loss of a job. Recent surveys indicate that employees frequently worry about being laid off.[92] Job security is an important stressor to manage because it can result in reduced job satisfaction, organizational commitment, and performance.[93]

3. Individual Role Demands: The Stress Created by Others' Expectations of You

***Roles* are sets of behaviors that people expect of occupants of a position.**[94] Stress may come about because of *role overload, role conflict,* and *role ambiguity.*

- **Role overload.** Role overload occurs when others' expectations exceed one's ability. Example: If you as a student are carrying a full course load plus working two-thirds time plus trying to have a social life, you know what role overload is—and what stress is. Similar things happen to managers and workers.

- **Role conflict.** Role conflict occurs when one feels torn by the different expectations of important people in one's life. Example: Your supervisor says the company needs you to stay late to meet an important deadline, but your family expects you to be present for your child's birthday party.

- **Role ambiguity.** Role ambiguity occurs when others' expectations are unknown. Example: You find your job description and the criteria for promotion vague, a complaint often voiced by newcomers to an organization.

4. Group Demands: The Stress Created by Co-workers & Managers
Even if you don't particularly care for the work you do but like the people you work with, that can be a great source of satisfaction and prevent stress. When people don't get along, that can be a great stressor.

In addition, managers can create stress for employees in a number of ways: Exhibiting inconsistent behaviors. Failing to provide support. Showing lack of concern. Providing inadequate direction. Creating a demanding, high-productivity environment. Focusing on negatives while ignoring good performance.[95] People who have bad managers are five times more likely to have stress-induced headaches, upset stomachs, and loss of sleep.[96]

5. Organizational Demands: The Stress Created by the Environment & Culture
The physical environments of some jobs are great sources of stress: poultry processing, asbestos removal, coal mining, fire fighting, police work, ambulance driving, and so on. Even white-collar work can take place in a stressful environment, with poor lighting, too much noise, improper placement of furniture, and no privacy.[97]

An organizational culture that promotes high-pressure work demands on employees will fuel the stress response.[98] The pace of information technology certainly adds to the stress. "For example," says Michael Patsalos-Fox, chairman of the Americas region for consulting firm McKinsey & Company, "you used to have media companies and you used to have telecom [telecommunications] companies, right? . . . The problem is that they are encroaching on each other. The onset of a lot of technologies is blurring the boundary between industries that were quite separate, creating opportunities for industries to attack each other."[99] Such rapidly changing technologies and financial pressures are what keep top executives up at night.

Research shows preliminary support for the idea that organizational stress can be reduced by participatory management.[100]

6. Nonwork Demands: The Stresses Created by Forces Outside the Organization
As anyone knows who has had to cope with money problems, divorce, support of elderly relatives, or other serious nonwork concerns, the stresses outside one's work life can have a significant effect on work. And people with lower incomes, education level, and work status are particularly apt to have higher stress.[101] But even people with ordinary lives can find the stress of coping with family life rugged going.

The Consequences of Stress

Positive stress is constructive and can energize you, increasing your effort, creativity, and performance. Negative stress is destructive, resulting in poorer-quality work, dissatisfaction, errors, absenteeism, and turnover.

Symptoms of Stress   Negative stress reveals itself in three kinds of symptoms:

- **Physiological signs.** Lesser physiological signs are sweaty palms, restlessness, backaches, headaches, upset stomach, and nausea. More serious signs are hypertension and heart attacks.

- **Psychological signs.** Psychological symptoms include boredom, irritability, nervousness, anger, anxiety, hostility, and depression.

- **Behavioral signs.** Symptoms include sleeplessness, changes in eating habits, and increased smoking/alcohol/drug abuse. Stress may be revealed through reduced performance and job satisfaction.

Burnout   "When you keep investing more energy and the return remains low, that's when you burn out," suggests Michael Staver, founder of an executive training company.[102]

***Burnout* is a state of emotional, mental, and even physical exhaustion,** expressed as listlessness, indifference, or frustration. Clearly, the greatest consequence of negative stress for the organization is reduced productivity. Overstressed employees are apt to call in sick, miss deadlines, take longer lunch breaks, and show indifference to performance. However, some may put in great numbers of hours at work without getting as much accomplished as previously.

Mental health experts estimate that 10% of the workforce suffers from depression or high levels of stress that may ultimately affect job performance. In addition, researchers estimate that in a recent year stress caused 11% of employee absenteeism.[103]

De-stressing. Experts say that exercise can be a tremendous stress reliever. Many companies maintain physical-fitness centers not only as an employee perk but also because they realize that exercise helps to improve stamina and endurance while reducing tension.

Alcohol & Other Drug Abuse   Have an employee who's often late? Who frequently calls in sick on Mondays? Who is somewhat sloppy? Maybe he or she is afflicted with *alcoholism,* a chronic, progressive, and potentially fatal disease characterized by a growing compulsion to drink. Alcoholics come from every social class, from students to college professors to priests to airline pilots. Alcoholism may not interfere with a person's job in an obvious way until it shows up in absenteeism, accidents, slipshod work, or significant use of a company's medical benefits.

Alcohol is the most common drug of abuse, but the misuse of others may also affect a person's productivity—legal drugs such as tranquilizers or illegal drugs such as marijuana, ecstasy, cocaine, or heroin. It is estimated that productivity losses caused by alcohol problems amount to $86 billion a year and by drug problems to $54 billion a year. Fortunately, workplace drug use seems to have steadily declined over the past 15 years.[104]

If you as a manager think you might be dealing with an employee with a substance-abuse problem, it's suggested you not try to make accusations but firmly point out that productivity is suffering and that it's up to the subordinate to do something about it. While not doing any counseling yourself, you can try steering the employee to the Human Resources Department, which may have an employee assistance program that may help employees overcome personal problems affecting their job performance.

Incidentally, although many people swear by 12-step programs, such as that offered by Alcoholics Anonymous, an examination of several studies found that such programs were no more and no less successful than any other interventions in reducing alcohol dependence and alcohol-related problems.[105]

Reducing Stressors in the Organization

There are all kinds of *buffers,* **or administrative changes, that managers can make to reduce the stressors that lead to employee burnout.** Examples: Extra staff or equipment at peak periods. Increased freedom to make decisions. Recognition for accomplishments. Time off for rest or personal development. Assignment to a new position.[106] Three- to 5-day employee retreats at offsite locations for relaxation and team-building activities. Sabbatical leave programs to replenish employees' energy and desire to work.[107]

Some general organizational strategies for reducing unhealthy stressors are the following:[108]

- **Create a supportive organizational climate.** Job stress often results because organizations have evolved into large, formal, and inflexible bureaucracies. Wherever possible, it's better to try to keep the organizational environment less formal, more personal, and more supportive of employees.

- **Make jobs interesting.** Stress also results when jobs are routinized and boring. Better to try to structure jobs so that they allow employees some freedom.

- **Make career counseling available.** Companies such as IBM make career planning available, which reduces the stress that comes when employees don't know what their career options are and where they're headed. ●

summary

 II.I Values, Attitudes, & Behavior

- Organizational behavior (OB) is dedicated to better understanding and managing people at work. OB looks at two areas: individual behavior (discussed in this chapter) and group behavior (discussed in later chapters).

- Values must be distinguished from attitudes and from behavior.
(I) Values are abstract ideals that guide one's thinking and behavior across all situations.
(2) Attitudes are defined as learned predispositions toward a given object. Attitudes have three components. The affective component consists of the feelings or emotions one has about a situation. The cognitive component consists of the beliefs and knowledge one has about a situation. The behavioral component refers to how one intends or expects to behave toward a situation. When attitudes and reality collide, the result may be cognitive dissonance, the psychological discomfort a person experiences between his or her cognitive attitude and incompatible behavior. Cognitive dissonance depends on three factors: importance, control, and rewards. The ways to reduce cognitive dissonance are to change your attitude and/or

your behavior, belittle the importance of the inconsistent behavior, or find consonant elements that outweigh the dissonant ones. (3) Together, values and attitudes influence people's workplace behavior—their actions and judgments.

 II.2 Work-Related Attitudes & Behaviors Managers Need to Deal With

- Managers need to be alert to work-related attitudes having to do with (I) job satisfaction, the extent to which you feel positively or negatively about various aspects of your work; (2) job involvement, the extent to which you identify or are personally involved with your job; (3) organizational commitment, reflecting the extent to which an employee identifies with an organization and is committed to its goals; and (4) organizational citizenship behaviors, those employee behaviors that are not directly part of employees' job descriptions—that exceed their work-role requirements.

- Among the types of behavior that managers need to influence are (I) performance and productivity and (2) absenteeism, when an employee doesn't show up for work, and turnover, when employees leave their jobs.

II.3 Personality & Individual Behavior

- Personality consists of the stable psychological traits and behavioral attributes that give a person his or her identity. There are five personality dimensions and five personality traits that managers need to be aware of to understand workplace behavior.

- The Big Five personality dimensions are extroversion, agreeableness, conscientiousness, emotional stability, and openness to experience. Extroversion, an outgoing personality, is associated with success for managers and salespeople. Conscientiousness, or a dependable personality, is correlated with successful job performance. A person who scores well on conscientiousness may be a proactive personality, someone who is more apt to take initiative and persevere to influence the environment.

- There are five personality traits that managers need to be aware of in order to understand workplace behavior. (1) Locus of control indicates how much people believe they control their fate through their own efforts. (2) Self-efficacy is the belief in one's personal ability to do a task. Low self-efficacy is associated with learned helplessness, the debilitating lack of faith in one's ability to control one's environment. (3) Self-esteem is the extent to which people like or dislike themselves. (4) Self-monitoring is the extent to which people are able to observe their own behavior and adapt it to external situations. (5) Emotional intelligence indicates the ability to cope, empathize with others, and be self-motivated.

II.4 Perception & Individual Behavior

- Perception is the process of interpreting and understanding one's environment. The process can be boiled down to four steps: selective attention, interpretation and evaluation, storing in memory, and retrieving from memory to make judgments and decisions. Perceptual errors can lead to mistakes that affect management.

- Four types of distortion in perception are (1) selective perception, the tendency to filter out information that is discomforting, that seems irrelevant, or that contradicts one's beliefs; (2) stereotyping, the tendency to attribute to an individual the characteristics one believes are typical of the group to which that individual belongs; (3) the halo effect, the forming of an impression of an individual based on a single trait; and (4) causal attribution, the activity of inferring causes for observed behavior. Two attributional tendencies that can distort one's interpretation of observed behavior are the fundamental attribution bias, in which people attribute another person's behavior to his or her personal characteristics rather than to situational factors, and the self-serving bias, in which people tend to take more personal responsibility for success than for failure.

- The self-fulfilling prophecy (Pygmalion effect) describes the phenomenon in which people's expectations of themselves or others leads them to behave in ways that make those expectations come true.

II.5 Understanding Stress & Individual Behavior

- Stress is the tension people feel when they are facing or enduring extraordinary demands, constraints, or opportunities and are uncertain about their ability to handle them effectively. Stress is the feeling of tension and pressure; the source of stress is called a stressor.

- There are six sources of stress on the job: demands created by individual differences, individual task demands, individual role demands, group demands, organizational demands, and nonwork demands. (1) Demands created by individual differences may arise from a Type A behavior pattern, meaning people have the personality characteristic that involves them in a chronic, determined struggle to accomplish more in less time. (2) Individual task demands are the stresses created by the job itself. (3) Individual role demands are the stresses created by other people's expectations of you. Roles are sets of behaviors that people expect of occupants of a position. Stress may come about because of role overload, role conflict, or role ambiguity. (4) Group demands are the stresses created by co-workers and managers. (5) Organizational demands are the stresses created by the environment and culture of the organization. (6) Nonwork demands are the stresses created by forces outside the organization, such as money problems or divorce.

- Positive stress can be constructive. Negative stress can result in poor-quality work; such stress is revealed through physiological, psychological, or behavioral signs. One sign is burnout, a state of emotional, mental, and even physical exhaustion. Stress can lead to alcohol and other drug abuse.

- There are buffers, or administrative changes, that managers can make to reduce the stressors that lead to employee burnout, such as adding extra staff or giving employees more power to make decisions. Some general organizational strategies for reducing unhealthy stressors are to create a supportive organizational climate, make jobs interesting, and make career counseling available.

 ## management in action

The Problem with Working for a Yes Man

Susan Loring remembers working for a yes man. "Oh God, I'm so glad I'm not there anymore," she moans.

It wasn't just the overabundance of work. Her boss reported to the company founder, who shared with him lots of new ideas that required major changes to projects well under way. Then, the moment of untruth always came for her yes man: He never pointed to the merits of the old plan or the flaws in the new one. The yes man caved. "What a wonderful idea!" Ms. Loring recalls him saying. "We'll have it for you on Monday."

Whenever she said "no" to her boss, she was told she didn't get either "it" or "the big picture." And there was always someone willing to bend to her yes man, making her look worse. "So you give up. You turn into the worst thing possible, which is a yes man's yes man," she says.

Her yes man became a founder favorite while Ms. Loring "had a stomachache every day getting ready for work."

Yes men, defined as stooges, flunkies, and pushovers, are so full of follow that they can't lead. They head up the corporate ladder because their agreeability is in direct proportion to their lust for power. Yes men create a make-work marathon, darting goals and work-life imbalance. They render their staffers as goose chasers, wasting time if not company money. Everyone gets tired working for the yes man, longing for a can't-do spirit.

The problem is you can't say "no" to a yes man. Having rarely uttered it, they don't value the currency of a "no." This is not about the get-lost "no," but even the most well reasoned, softly peddled, bad-for-the-bottom-line "no." No matter how deftly delivered, a "no" to a yes man is transformed into one of corporate America's most career-limiting charges: You're not a team player. . . .

This would be amusing if human yessers didn't seem even more satirical. One middle manager at an insurance company has a yes-man supervisor who tells his boss, "I was thinking the same thing myself." That was said when his boss's boss wanted a group that worked on compliance to do a task better done by accounting. "It made absolutely no sense," she says.

Similarly, Linda Shoemaker, a former sales manager, had a boss who would say, "'No' is not in my vocabulary!" And she routinely got sent on make-work missions, like reorganizing the office files. Near the end of three weeks, her boss told her it needed to be done differently, even though she had checked with her twice. It was deflating, to put it mildly.

Working for yes men, notes Robert Sutton, a professor of management science at Stanford University, "just s---s." Because a yes man can't filter out extraneous tasks the way good leaders can, he says, his staffers are "cognitively overloaded and condemned to do many things, almost all of them badly."

Innovation also takes a hit. "In an organization where innovation happens, very often people ignore orders and don't do what they're told," he says.

To avoid pointless tasks that a yes man has greenlighted, says Prof. Sutton, you can try to reason with facts. Or you can implement the best of bad alternatives, which may actually cost the company less than full compliance: "You say you're going to do it and you do it slowly and incompetently," he says.

That maneuver can make the boss's interest in the request fade fast, he says. . . .

Lee Folger, a former salesman, is a recovered yesser. He used to yes his clients constantly only to discover that on a few occasions, he couldn't deliver on promises. The failures torched his credibility.

So after he learned his lesson, instead of yes, he'd say, "I'm just not sure we can meet your expectations."

It's better managing but he misses seeing the satisfaction, even the romance, in the other person's eyes. "It's like a wonderful, romantic dinner—and someone stops the record."

For Discussion

1. Have you ever worked for a yes man? What was it like?
2. How would you describe Susan Loring's work attitudes while working in her previous job? Explain.

3. How does the perception process explain the behavior of yes men?

4. To what extent would a yes man likely possess the Big Five personality dimensions? Explain your rationale.

5. How can employees combat the stress of working for a yes man? Discuss.

Source: Excerpted from Jared Sandberg, "How Do You Say 'No' to a Yes Man? Often Unsuccessfully," *The Wall Street Journal*, July 25, 2006, p. B1. Reprinted by permission of Dow Jones & Company, Inc. via The Copyright Clearance Center.

self-assessment

What Is Your Emotional Intelligence Score?

Objectives
1. To help you assess your emotional intelligence.
2. To expand your knowledge of the new interpretations of intelligence.

Introduction
Employers have long been guided by one dimension of our personality, our intelligence quotient (IQ). However, a number of researchers and observers of human behavior have been examining components of intelligence that include emotions. Your Emotional Intelligence (EI) includes your abilities to motivate yourself and persist even when you are frustrated, to control your impulses and delay gratification, to regulate your mood and keep distress from overwhelming your thinking ability, to empathize with others, and to hope. The recognition of the emotional dimension to intelligence is vital today in a world of constant change and increased stress. Having a sense of your own EI is fundamental to being successful. The purpose of this exercise is to determine your own EI.

Instructions
Use this scale to indicate the extent to which you agree or disagree with each statement below.

1 = strongly disagree
2 = disagree
3 = neither agree nor disagree
4 = agree
5 = strongly agree

1. I am usually aware—from moment to moment—of my feelings as they change.	1 2 3 4 5
2. I think before I act.	1 2 3 4 5
3. I am impatient when I want something.	1 2 3 4 5
4. I bounce back quickly from life's setbacks.	1 2 3 4 5
5. I can pick up subtle social cues that indicate others' needs or wants.	1 2 3 4 5
6. I'm very good at handling myself in social situations.	1 2 3 4 5
7. I'm persistent in going after the things I want.	1 2 3 4 5
8. When people share their problems with me, I'm good at putting myself in their shoes.	1 2 3 4 5
9. When I'm in a bad mood, I make a strong effort to get out of it.	1 2 3 4 5
10. I can find common ground and build rapport with people from all walks of life.	1 2 3 4 5

Scoring & Interpretation

This questionnaire taps the five basic dimensions of EI: self-awareness (items 1 and 9), self-management (2, 4), self-motivation (3, 7), empathy (5, 8), and social skills (6, 10). Compute your total EI score by adding your responses to all 10 statements. Your total score will fall between 10 and 50. While no definite cutoff scores are available, scores of 40 or higher indicate a high EI. Scores of 20 or less suggest a relatively low EI.

Emotional intelligence is a collection of abilities and competencies that have an effect on a person's capacity to succeed in dealing with demands and pressures. People with high EI have the capacity to correctly perceive, evaluate, articulate, and manage emotions and feelings.

EI may be most predictive of performance in jobs such as sales or management, in which achievement is based as much on interpersonal skills as on technical ability. People with low EI are likely to have trouble managing others, making successful sales presentations, and functioning on teams.

Questions for Discussion

1. Did the results surprise you? Why or why not?
2. Look at the three items on which your score was lowest. What are some skills or attitudes you can work on to improve your EI? Explain.
3. Do you think your EI would help or hinder you when working in a team?

Based on D. Goleman, *Emotional Intelligence: Why It Can Matter More Than IQ* (New York: Bantam, 1995).

group exercise

Using Attribution Theory to Resolve Performance Problems: The Case of Mary Martin

Objectives

1. To gain experience determining the causes of performance.
2. To decide on corrective action for employee performance.

Introduction

Attributions are typically made to internal and external factors. Perceivers arrive at their assessments by using various informational cues or antecedents. To determine the types of antecedents people use, we have developed a case containing various informational cues about an individual's performance. You will be asked to read the case and make attributions about the causes of performance. To assess the impact of attributions on managerial behavior, you will also be asked to recommend corrective action.

Instructions

Presented is a case that depicts the performance of Mary Martin, a computer programmer. Please read the case and then identify the causes of her behavior by answering the questions following the case. Then determine whether you made an internal or external attribution. After completing this task, decide on the appropriateness of various forms of corrective action. A list of potential recommendations has been developed. The list is divided into four categories. Read each action, and evaluate its appropriateness by using the scale provided. Next, compute a total score for each of the four categories.

The Case

Mary Martin, 30, received her baccalaureate degree in computer science from a reputable state school in the Midwest. She also graduated with above-average grades. Mary is currently working in the computer support/analysis department as a programmer for a nationally based firm. During the past year, Mary has missed 10 days of work She seems unmotivated and rarely has her assignments completed on time. Mary is usually given the harder programs to work on.

Past records indicate Mary, on the average, completes programs classified as "routine" in about 45 hours. Her co-workers, on the other hand, complete "routine" programs in an average time of 32 hours. Further, Mary finishes programs considered "major problems," on the average, in about 115 hours. Her co-workers, however, finish these same "major problem" assignments, on the average, in about 100 hours. When Mary has worked in programming teams, her peer performance reviews are generally average to negative. Her male peers have noted she is not creative in attacking problems and she is difficult to work with.

The computer department recently sent a questionnaire to all users of its services to evaluate the usefulness and accuracy of data received. The results indicate many departments are not using computer output because they cannot understand the reports. It was also determined that the users of output generated from Mary's programs found the output chaotic and not useful for managerial decision making.

Causes of Performance

To what extent was each of the following a cause of Mary's performance? Use the following scale:

Very little				Very much
I———2———3———4———5				

a. High ability	I	2	3	4	5
b. Low ability	I	2	3	4	5
c. Low effort	I	2	3	4	5
d. Difficult job	I	2	3	4	5
e. Unproductive co-workers	I	2	3	4	5
f. Bad luck	I	2	3	4	5
Internal attribution (total score for causes a, b, and c) _____					
External attribution (total score for causes d, e, and f) _____					

Appropriateness of Corrective Action

Evaluate the following courses of action by using the scale below:

Very inappropriate				Very appropriate
I———2———3———4———5				

Coercive Actions					
a. Reprimand Mary for her performance	I	2	3	4	5
b. Threaten to fire Mary if her performance does not improve	I	2	3	4	5
Change Job					
c. Transfer Mary to another job	I	2	3	4	5
d. Demote Mary to a less demanding job	I	2	3	4	5
Nonpunitive Actions					
e. Work with Mary to help her do the job better	I	2	3	4	5
f. Offer Mary encouragement to help her improve	I	2	3	4	5
No Immediate Actions					
g. Do nothing	I	2	3	4	5
h. Promise Mary a pay raise if she improves	I	2	3	4	5

Compute a score for the four categories:
Coercive actions = a + b =
Change job = c + d =
Nonpunitive actions = e + f =
No immediate actions = g + h =

Questions for Discussion

1. How would you evaluate Mary's performance?
2. Is Mary's performance due to internal or external causes?
3. What did you identify as the top two causes of Mary's performance? Explain why.
4. Which of the four types of corrective action do you think is most appropriate? Explain.

Can you identify any negative consequences of this choice?

Developed by Robet Kreitner and Angelo Kinicki, *Organizational Behavior,* 7th edition. (Burr Ridge, IL: McGraw-Hill/Irwin, 2007), pp 231–232. Copyright © 2007 by the McGraw-Hill Companies, Inc. Used by permission.

 ethical dilemma

Enron Employees Create a Positive Impression for Wall Street Analysts

Some current and former employees of Enron's retail-energy unit say the company asked them to pose as busy electricity and natural-gas sales representatives one day in 1998 so the unit could impress Wall Street analysts visiting its Houston headquarters.

Enron rushed 75 employees of Enron Energy Services—including secretaries and actual sales representatives—to an empty trading floor and told them to act as if they were trying to sell energy contracts to businesses over the phone, the current and former employees say.

"When we went down to the sixth floor, I remember we had to take the stairs so the analysts wouldn't see us," said Kim Garcia, who at the time was an administrative assistant for Enron Energy Services and was laid off in December [of 2001].

"We brought some of our personal stuff, like pictures, to make it look like the area was lived in," Ms. Garcia said in an interview. "There were a bunch of trading desks on the sixth floor, but the desks were totally empty. Some of the computers didn't even work, so we worked off of our laptops. When the analysts arrived, we had to make believe we were on the phone buying and selling electricity and natural gas. The whole thing took like 10 minutes."

Penny Marksberry—who also worked as an Enron Energy Services administrative assistant in 1998 and was laid off in December—and two employees who still work at the unit also say they were told to act as if they were trying to sell contracts.

"They actually brought in computers and phones, and they told us to act like we were typing or talking on the phone when the analysts were walking through," Ms. Marksberry said. "They told us it was very important for us to make a good impression, and if the analysts saw that the operation was disorganized, they wouldn't give the company a good rating."

Solving the Dilemma

What would you do if you were asked to act busy in front of the analysts?

1. Follow the company's instructions by going to the sixth floor and pretending to be busy for the analysts.
2. Explain to your manager that this behavior is inconsistent with your personal values and that you will not participate.
3. Go to the sixth floor in support of the company's request but not act busy or bring personal artifacts to create a false impression.
4. Invent other options. Explain.

Source: Jason Leopold, "En-Ruse? Workers at Enron Say They Posed as Busy Traders to Impress Visitng Analysts," *The Wall Street Journal,* February 17, 2002, p. C1. Reprinted by permission by Dow Jones & Company, Inc. via The Copyright Clearance Center.

 video case

TechBox

TechBox produces a specialized computer chip for a large client base. Patrick Bennett is the supervising manager overseeing the production of the main component of the chip. Recently, he and his team began implementing a computerized tracking system to increase quality control and workflow. Historically, the quality control team expended significant time and resources reworking failed chips. This new system is expected to raise quality and productivity levels substantially. This is Patrick's first opportunity to lead a project of this magnitude. Although the new system is costly, it is relatively unproven. Still, expectations are high.

Patrick supervises 50 floor employees. In the two years he's worked at TechBox, he's built a reputation for numerous successes and improvements that have financially benefited the organization. Patrick possesses a unique combination of technical expertise and managerial skill. He is greatly admired by his team and generally well received by top management. At a recent progress meeting, however, Patrick was stunned by the attitudes of top executives. At the meeting were Sam Adelson, Lucinda Bergen, and Morgan Baines.

Sam Adelson is a longtime employee who worked his way up from the mailroom to vice president of operations. He is wary of change and skeptical of computerized system enhancements (which is unusual for someone employed in the high-tech industry). Others perceive him as stodgy, grumpy, and difficult. Lucinda Bergen is director of product management and the sole female executive at TechBox. She is generally perceived as compassionate, understanding, and easygoing. She seems comfortable with change and new ideas. However, she's quick to defend her position within the company and overassert herself when she feels confronted. Morgan Baines is vice president of distribution. He's perceived as the "jokester" of the company. He often speaks without thinking and seems to provide support, to attack, or to withdraw without rhyme or reason. Everyone has the impression that they have his support. Although unconventional, the approach seems to work. He's been at TechBox for years.

Mistakenly, Patrick assumes this to be a routine meeting. Once there, he feels ambushed. In Adelson's opinion, the entire project should be scrapped. He's concerned about the expense and fears that the system won't live up to expectations. Additionally, there are rumors that Patrick's team is intentionally slowing work production. Lucinda Bergen is generally supportive of the project but concerned about the slow rate of progress. Before Patrick can build on her supportive attitude, Adelson sidetracks the issue. Finally, Baines is completely disruptive. He's a total wildcard; Patrick has no clue where Baines stands on the issue. Patrick leaves the meeting frustrated and confused. He'll need to be better prepared for the follow-up meeting, which is scheduled in 1 week.

Although better informed for the next meeting, Patrick is still nervous. To benefit both the organization and his own career, he must somehow accommodate all three executives so that they will let him complete the project. Adelson's main concerns seem to be effectiveness and general cost. Bergen is focused on the project's conclusion date, and Baines is still the wildcard. Patrick will need to take charge of this meeting and diffuse these volatile personalities. In doing so, he'll have to appeal to the right person on the right issue.

Discussion Questions

1. Does Patrick Bennett have an internal or an external locus of control? Define these terms and provide evidence to support your answer.
2. What is the difference between stress and a stressor? What stressors is Patrick Bennett facing?
3. Managers need to learn about individual differences so that they can influence employees to do their best work. Measuring performance and productivity are ways to evaluate work behaviors. How can the executive team at TechBox evaluate Patrick's work performance?

chapter 12

Motivating Employees
Achieving Superior Performance in the Workplace

Major Questions You Should Be Able to Answer

12.1 Motivating for Performance
Major Question: What's the motivation for studying motivation?

12.2 Content Perspectives on Employee Motivation
Major Question: What kinds of needs motivate employees?

12.3 Process Perspectives on Employee Motivation
Major Question: Is a good reward good enough? How do other factors affect motivation?

12.4 Job Design Perspectives on Motivation
Major Question: What's the best way to design jobs—adapt people to work or work to people?

12.5 Reinforcement Perspectives on Motivation
Major Question: What are the types of incentives I might use to influence employee behavior?

12.6 Using Compensation & Other Rewards to Motivate
Major Question: How can I use compensation and other rewards to motivate people?

Managing for Motivation: The Flexible Workplace

Can a company slice and dice the 24 hours in a day, the 7 days a week, in ways that can better motivate employees?

With the parents of so many two-paycheck families, single parents, and other diverse kinds of employees in the workforce, employers have begun to develop the so-called *flexible workplace* as a way of recruiting, retaining, and motivating employees. Among the types of alternative work schedules available:

- **Part-time work—less than 40 hours:** Part-time work is any work done on a schedule less than the standard 40-hour workweek. Some part-time workers—so-called temporary workers or contingency workers—do want to work 40 hours or more but can't find full-time jobs. Others, however, work part time by choice. Today an organization can hire not only part-time clerical help, for instance, but also part-time programmers, market researchers, lawyers, even part-time top executives.

- **Flextime—flexible working hours:** Flextime, or flexible time, consists of flexible working hours or any schedule that gives one some choices in working hours. If, for example, an organization's normal working hours are 9 A.M. to 5 P.M., a flextime worker might be allowed to start and finish an hour earlier or an hour later—for instance, to work from 8 A.M. to 4 P.M. The main requirement is that the employee be at work during certain "core" hours, so as to be available for meetings, consultations, and so on. By offering flextime hours, organizations can attract and keep employees with special requirements such as the need to take care of children or elderly parents. It also benefits employees who wish to avoid commuting during rush hour.

- **Compressed workweek—40 hours in four days:** In a compressed workweek, employees perform a full-time job in less than 5 days of standard 8- (or 9-) hour shifts. The most common variation is a 40-hour week performed in 4 days of 10 hours each, which gives employees three (instead of two) consecutive days off. The benefits are that organizations can offer employees more leisure time and reduced wear and tear and expense from commuting. The disadvantages are possible scheduling problems, unavailability of an employee to co-workers and customers, and fatigue from long workdays.

- **Job sharing—two people split the same job:** In job sharing, two people divide one full-time job. Usually, each person works a half day, although there can be other arrangements (working alternate days or alternate weeks, for example). As with a compressed workweek, job sharing provides employees with more personal or leisure time. The disadvantage is that it can result in communication problems with co-workers or customers.

- **Telecommuting & other work-at-home schedules:** There have always been some employees who have had special full-time or part-time arrangements whereby they are allowed to work at home, keeping in touch with their employers and co-workers by mail and phone. The fax machine, the personal computer, the Internet, and overnight-delivery services have now made work-at-home arrangements much more feasible.

Working at home with telecommunications between office and home is called *telecommuting*. The advantage to employers is increased productivity because telecommuters experience less distraction at home and can work flexible hours.

For Discussion Which of these alternative work schedules most appeals to you? Why?

forecast

What's Ahead in This Chapter

This chapter discusses how to motivate people to perform well. We consider motivation from four perspectives: content (covering theories by Maslow, McClelland, and Herzberg); process (covering equity, expectancy, and goal-setting theories); job design; and reinforcement. Finally, we apply these perspectives to compensation and other rewards for motivating performance.

12.1 MOTIVATING FOR PERFORMANCE

 What's the motivation for studying motivation?

THE BIG PICTURE

Motivation is defined as the psychological processes that arouse and direct people's goal-directed behavior. The model of how it works is that people have certain needs that motivate them to perform specific behaviors for which they receive rewards, both extrinsic and intrinsic, that feed back and satisfy the original need. The three major perspectives on motivation are need-based, process, and reinforcement.

What would make you rise a half hour earlier than usual to ensure you got to work on time—and to perform your best once there?

A new leased car? Help with college tuition? Bringing your dog to work? Onsite laundry, gym, or childcare? Free lunch? Really nice bosses?

Believe it or not, these are among the perks available to some lucky employees—and not just high-level managers.[1] Especially when employment rates are high, companies are desperate to attract, retain, and motivate key people. But even in tough economic times, there are always industries and occupations in which employers feel they need to bend over backward to retain their "human capital."

Motivation: What It Is, Why It's Important

Why do people do the things they do? The answer is this: they are mainly motivated to fulfill their wants, their needs.

What Is Motivation & How Does It Work? *Motivation* **may be defined as the psychological processes that arouse and direct goal-directed behavior.**[2] Motivation is difficult to understand because you can't actually see it or know it in another person; it must be *inferred* from one's behavior. Nevertheless, it's imperative that you as a manager understand the process of motivation if you are to guide employees in accomplishing your organization's objectives.

The way motivation works actually is complex. However, in a simple model of motivation, people have certain *needs* that *motivate* them to perform specific *behaviors* for which they receive *rewards* that *feed back* and satisfy the original need. *(See Figure 12.1.)*

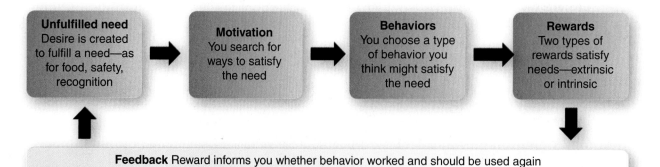

figure 12.1

A SIMPLE MODEL OF MOTIVATION

For example, you find you are hungry (need), which impels you to seek food (motive). You make a sandwich and eat it (behavior), which provides satisfaction (reward) and informs you (feedback loop) that sandwiches will reduce hunger and so should be used in the future. Or as an hourly worker you desire more money (need), which impels you (motivates you) to work more hours (behavior), which provides you with more money (reward) and informs you (feedback loop) that working more hours will fulfill your need for more money in the future.

Rewards (as well as motivation itself) are of two types—*extrinsic* and *intrinsic.*[3] Managers can use both to encourage better work performance.

- **Extrinsic rewards—satisfaction in the payoff from others. An *extrinsic reward* is the payoff, such as money, a person receives from others for performing a particular task.** An extrinsic reward is an external reward; the payoff comes from pleasing others.

  Example: In performing your job as a maker of custom sailboats, you get your principal satisfaction from receiving the great amount of money buyers pay you for a boat—an extrinsic reward.

- **Intrinsic rewards—satisfaction in performing the task itself. An *intrinsic reward* is the satisfaction, such as a feeling of accomplishment, a person receives from performing the particular task itself.** An intrinsic reward is an internal reward; the payoff comes from pleasing yourself.

  Example: In making custom sailboats, you derive satisfaction—warm feelings of accomplishment and heightened self-esteem—from the process of building a sailboat.

Group Exercise:
What Motivates You?

Why Is Motivation Important?   It seems obvious that organizations would want to motivate their employees to be more productive. Actually, though, there are five reasons why you as a manager will find knowledge of motivation important.[4] In order of importance, you want to motivate people to . . .

- *Join your organization.* You need to instill in talented prospective workers the desire to come to work for you.

- *Stay with your organization.* Whether you are in good economic times or bad, you always want to be able to retain good people.

- *Show up for work at your organization.* In many organizations, absenteeism and lateness are tremendous problems.[5]

- *Perform better for your organization.* Some employees do just enough to avoid being fired.[6] But what you really want is employees who will give you high productivity.

- *Do extra for your organization.* You hope your employees will perform extra tasks above and beyond the call of duty (be organizational "good citizens").

The Four Major Perspectives on Motivation: Overview

There is no theory accepted by everyone as to what motivates people. In this chapter, therefore, we present the four principal perspectives. From these, you may be able to select what ideas seem most workable to you. The four perspectives on motivation are (1) *content,* (2) *process,* (3) *job design,* and (4) *reinforcement,* as described in the following four main sections. ●

12.2 CONTENT PERSPECTIVES ON EMPLOYEE MOTIVATION

THE BIG PICTURE

Content perspectives are theories emphasizing the needs that motivate people. Needs are defined as physiological or psychological deficiencies that arouse behavior. The content perspective includes three theories: Maslow's hierarchy of needs, McClelland's acquired needs theory, and Herzberg's two-factor theory.

Content perspectives, **also known as** *need-based perspectives,* **are theories that emphasize the needs that motivate people.** Content theorists ask, "What kind of needs motivate employees in the workplace?" *Needs* **are defined as physiological or psychological deficiencies that arouse behavior.** They can be strong or weak, and, because they are influenced by environmental factors, they can vary over time and from place to place.

In addition to McGregor's Theory X/Theory Y (see Chapter 2), content perspectives include three theories:

- Maslow's hierarchy of needs theory
- McClelland's acquired needs theory
- Herzberg's two-factor theory

Maslow's Hierarchy of Needs Theory: Five Levels

In 1943, Brandeis University psychology professor **Abraham Maslow,** one of the first researchers to study motivation, put forth his *hierarchy of needs theory,* **which proposes that people are motivated by five levels of needs: (1) physiological, (2) safety, (3) belongingness, (4) esteem, and (5) self-actualization.**[7]

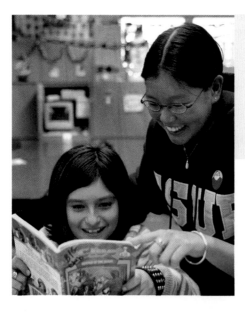

Self-actualization. No one has to engage in volunteerism, as this teacher is doing with a young girl at a Garden Grove, California, after-school reading program. But for some people, according to Maslow's theory, it represents the kind of realization of the best life has to offer—after other needs are satisfied. What activity or experience within your lifetime would represent self-fulfillment for you, the best that would realize your potential?

The Five Levels of Needs   In proposing this hierarchy of five needs, ranging from basic to highest level, Maslow suggested that needs are never completely satisfied. That is, our actions are aimed at fulfilling the "deprived" needs, the needs that remain unsatisfied at any point in time. Thus, for example, once you have achieved security, which is the second most basic need, you will then seek to fulfill the third most basic need—belongingness.

In order of ascendance, from bottom to top, the five levels of needs are as follows. (See Figure 12.2.)

figure 12.2

MASLOW'S HIERARCHY OF NEEDS

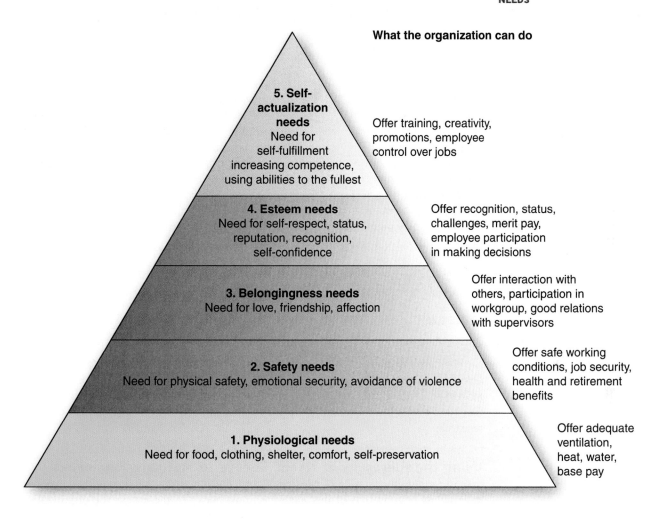

What the organization can do

5. Self-actualization needs
Need for self-fulfillment increasing competence, using abilities to the fullest

Offer training, creativity, promotions, employee control over jobs

4. Esteem needs
Need for self-respect, status, reputation, recognition, self-confidence

Offer recognition, status, challenges, merit pay, employee participation in making decisions

3. Belongingness needs
Need for love, friendship, affection

Offer interaction with others, participation in workgroup, good relations with supervisors

2. Safety needs
Need for physical safety, emotional security, avoidance of violence

Offer safe working conditions, job security, health and retirement benefits

1. Physiological needs
Need for food, clothing, shelter, comfort, self-preservation

Offer adequate ventilation, heat, water, base pay

1. Physiological Needs   These are the most basic human physical needs, in which one is concerned with having food, clothing, shelter, and comfort and with self-preservation.

2. Safety Needs   These needs are concerned with physical safety and emotional security, so that a person is concerned with avoiding violence and threats.

3. Belongingness Needs   Once basic needs and security are taken care of, people look for love, friendship, and affection.

4. Esteem Needs   After they meet their social needs, people focus on such matters as self-respect, status, reputation, recognition, and self-confidence.

5. Self-Actualization Needs The highest level of need, self-actualization is self-fulfillment—the need to develop one's fullest potential, to become the best one is capable of being.

Example

Higher-Level Needs: One Man Finds a Way to Measure Integrity

Software engineer Firinn Taisdeal of Walnut Creek, California, designed a social event database, now called LinkUp Central, that offers its 19,000 San Francisco Bay-area members 12,000 events per year, from rock climbing to theater, for $5 a month. But he discovered early on that events were being ruined and hosts disappointed by people who didn't show up. "Flakes," he calls them.

So he modified the database to chart patterns of flakiness—an accountability system. Thus, if a person RSVPs for events but doesn't show up 50% of the time, his or her "reliability threshold" goes down. With some events, such as restaurant dinners, guests can sign up only if they have a reliability index of 50% or more. "By changing their behavior over time," says one report, "people can improve their ratings."[9]

Driven to raise the level of integrity in the culture, Taisdeal is an example of a "cultural creative," a term coined by sociologists Paul Ray and Sherry Ruth Anderson to describe people who long to create deep and meaningful change in their lives and in the world.[10] Another name for people like Taisdeal is "tempered radical," the term that Stanford organizational behavior professor Debra Meyerson uses to describe people who work to strike a balance between what they believe in and what the system expects.[11] In this way, they fulfill their safety needs while also striving to fulfill their self-actualization needs.

Your Call

What kind of higher-level needs do you think you could fulfill through your work?

Research does not clearly support Maslow's theory, although it remains popular among managers. "There are still very few studies that can legitimately confirm (or refute) it," one scholar writes. "It may be that the dynamics implied by Maslow's theory of needs are too complex to be operationalized and confirmed by scientific research."[8]

Using the Hierarchy of Needs Theory to Motivate Employees For managers, the importance of Maslow's contribution is that he showed that workers have needs beyond that of just earning a paycheck. To the extent the organization permits, managers should first try to meet employees' level 1 and level 2 needs, of course, so that employees won't be preoccupied with them. Then, however, they need to give employees a chance to fulfill their higher-level needs in ways that also advance the goals of the organization.

McClelland's Acquired Needs Theory: Achievement, Affiliation, & Power

David McClelland, a well-known psychologist, investigated the needs for affiliation and power and as a consequence proposed the ***acquired needs theory,*** **which states that three needs—achievement, affiliation, and power—are major motives determining people's behavior in the workplace.**[12] McClelland believes that we are not born with our needs; rather we learn them from the culture—from our life experiences.

The Three Needs Managers are encouraged to recognize three needs in themselves and others and to attempt to create work environments that are responsive to them. The three needs, one of which tends to be dominant in each of us, are as follows. *(See Figure 12.3, at right.)*

- **Need for achievement—"I need to excel at tasks."** This is the desire to excel, to do something better or more efficiently, to solve problems, to achieve excellence in challenging tasks.

- **Need for affiliation—"I need close relationships."** This is the desire for friendly and warm relations with other people.

- **Need for power—"I need to control others."** This is the desire to be responsible for other people, to influence their behavior or to control them.[13]

McClelland identifies two forms of the need for power.

The negative kind is the need for *personal power,* as expressed in the desire to dominate others, and involves manipulating people for one's own gratification.

The positive kind, characteristic of top managers and leaders, is the desire for *institutional power,* as expressed in the need to solve problems that further organizational goals.

Using Acquired Needs Theory to Motivate Employees McClelland associates the three needs with different sets of work preferences, as follows:[14]

- **Need for achievement.** If you (or an employee) are happy with accomplishment of a task being its own reward, don't mind or even prefer working alone, and are willing to take moderate risks, then you probably have a *high need for achievement.* That being the case, you (or your employee) would probably

figure 12.3

McCLELLAND'S THREE NEEDS

A "well-balanced" individual: achievement, affiliation, and power are of equal size

A "control freak" individual: achievement is normal, but affiliation is small and power is large

Example

Acquired Needs Theory: The Need for Power of an Ad Agency CEO

In their book *The 100-Mile Walk: A Father and Son on a Quest to Find the Essence of Leadership,* Sander A. Flaum and his son, Jonathan, describe the generational values that divide them.[16] Sander, 69, became CEO of health care ad agency Robert A. Becker Euro RSCG in New York, a $1.7 billion business with 975 employees. Jonathan, 38, started his own public/corporate relations firm, WriteMind Communications, in Asheville, North Carolina, and hires people by the project. Sander learned to be diligent and loyal and to put work ahead of family, which led to his divorce. Jonathan grew up to be self-reliant, skeptical, and determined to balance work and family.

When the two decided to coauthor a book on leadership, they arranged to walk a combined total of 100 miles together in various places, from New York City to pre-Hurricane Katrina New Orleans, during which they talked about their views of the workplace. The book offers a comparison of their outlooks. Sander's

view: "Show company loyalty." Jonathan's view: "Move on if recognition and growth opportunities are absent." Sander: "Young people in India and China are not talking about work/life balance or . . . worrying about how to spend more time at home." Jonathan: "Work without adequate time for intimate connection and personal time has long-term degenerative effects." Sander: "I think you should be attuned to the knowledge that, at any time, every competitor of yours is out to recruit your best people, steal your ideas, take over your customers, and reinvent and improve your products." Jonathan: "Paranoia works . . . sometimes. But it robs us of fully enjoying those times when everything is just fine."

Your Call

In acquired needs theory, Sander would seem to embody the need for power. What needs do you think Jonathan embodies?

prefer doing the kind of work that offers feedback on performance, challenging but achievable goals, and individual responsibility for results. People high in need for achievement tend to advance in technical fields requiring creativity and individual skills.[15]

- **Need for power.** If you, like most effective managers, have a *high need for power,* that means you enjoy being in control of people and events and being recognized for this responsibility. Accordingly, your preference would probably be for work that allows you to control or have an effect on people and be publicly recognized for your accomplishments.

- **Need for affiliation.** If you tend to seek social approval and satisfying personal relationships, you may have a *high need for affiliation.* In that case, you may not be the most efficient manager because at times you will have to make decisions that will make people resent you. Instead, you will tend to prefer work, such as sales, that provides for personal relationships and social approval.

Herzberg's Two-Factor Theory: From Dissatisfying Factors to Satisfying Factors

Frederick Herzberg arrived at his needs-based theory as a result of a landmark study of 203 accountants and engineers, who were interviewed to determine the factors responsible for job satisfaction and dissatisfaction.[17] Job satisfaction was more frequently associated with achievement, recognition, characteristics of the work, responsibility, and advancement. Job dissatisfaction was more often associated with working conditions, pay and security, company policies, supervisors, and interpersonal relationships. The result was Herzberg's *two-factor theory,* **which proposed that work satisfaction and dissatisfaction arise from two different factors—work satisfaction from so-called *motivating factors* and work dissatisfaction from so-called *hygiene factors*.**

Hygiene Factors versus Motivating Factors In Herzberg's theory, the hygiene factors are the lower-level needs, the motivating factors are the higher-level needs. The two areas are separated by a zone in which employees are neither satisfied nor dissatisfied. *(See Figure 12.4, opposite page.)*

- **Hygiene factors—"Why are my people dissatisfied?"** The lower-level needs, *hygiene factors,* **are factors associated with job *dissatisfaction*—such as salary, working conditions, interpersonal relationships, and company policy—all of which affect the job *context* in which people work.**

  An example of a hygiene factor is the temperature in a factory that's not air-conditioned during the summer. Installing air-conditioning will remove a cause of job dissatisfaction. It will not, however, spur factory workers' motivation and make them greatly satisfied in their work. Because motivating factors are absent, workers become, in Herzberg's view, merely neutral in their attitudes toward work—neither dissatisfied nor satisfied.

- **Motivating factors—"What will make my people satisfied?"** The higher-level needs, *motivating factors,* or simply *motivators,* **are factors associated with job *satisfaction*—such as achievement, recognition, responsibility, and advancement—all of which affect the job content or the rewards of work performance.** Motivating factors—challenges, opportunities, recognition—must be instituted, Herzberg believed, to spur superior work performance.

  An example of a motivating factor would be to give factory workers more control over their work. For example, instead of repeating a single task over

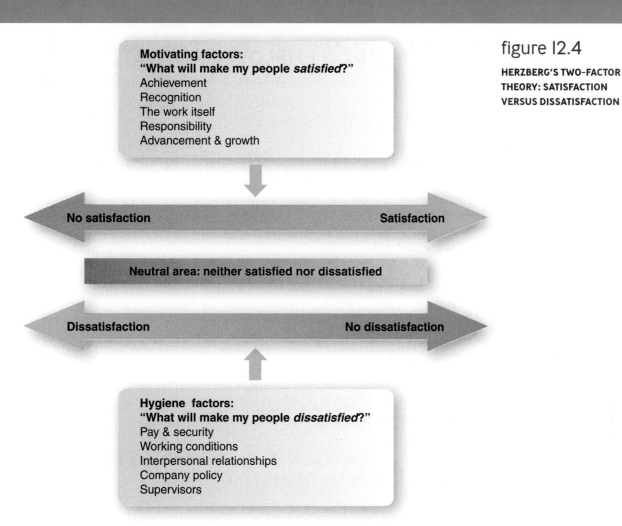

figure 12.4

HERZBERG'S TWO-FACTOR THEORY: SATISFACTION VERSUS DISSATISFACTION

and over, a worker might join with other workers in a team in which each one does several tasks. This is the approach that Swedish automaker Volvo has taken in building cars.

Using Two-Factor Theory to Motivate Employees The basic lesson of Herzberg's research is that managers should first eliminate dissatisfaction, making sure that working conditions, pay levels, and company policies are reasonable. They should then concentrate on spurring motivation by providing opportunities for achievement, recognition, responsibility, and personal growth.

The three needs theories are compared below. *(See Figure 12.5.)* ●

figure 12.5

A COMPARISON OF NEEDS THEORIES: MASLOW, McCLELLAND, AND HERZBERG.

McClelland has no classification for lower-level needs.

Is a good reward good enough? How do other factors affect motivation?

THE BIG PICTURE

Process perspectives, which are concerned with the thought processes by which people decide how to act, have three viewpoints: equity theory, expectancy theory, and goal-setting theory.

Process perspectives **are concerned with the thought processes by which people decide how to act**—how employees choose behavior to meet their needs. Whereas need-based perspectives simply try to understand employee needs, process perspectives go further and try to understand why employees have different needs, what behaviors they select to satisfy them, and how they decide if their choices were successful.

In this section we discuss three process perspectives on motivation:

- Equity theory
- Expectancy theory
- Goal-setting theory

Equity Theory: How Fairly Do You Think You're Being Treated in Relation to Others?

Fairness—or, perhaps equally important, the *perception* of fairness—can be a big issue in organizations. For example, if you received a 10% bonus from Circuit City for doubling your sales, would that be enough? What if other Circuit City salespeople received 15%?

Equity theory **focuses on employee perceptions as to how fairly they think they are being treated compared to others.** Developed by psychologist **J. Stacy Adams,** equity theory is based on the idea that employees are motivated to see fairness in the rewards they expect for task performance.[18] Clearly, this is an important matter. The U.S. Department of Commerce estimates that employee theft, for example, costs American business about $50 billion a year. This may represent employees' attempts to even the score when they feel that they haven't been treated fairly by their organizations.[19]

The Elements of Equity Theory: Comparing Your Inputs & Outputs with Those of Others The key elements in equity theory are *inputs, outputs (rewards),* and *comparisons. (See Figure 12.6, opposite page.)*

- **Inputs—"What do you think you're putting into the job?"** The inputs that people perceive they give to an organization are their time, effort, training, experience, intelligence, creativity, seniority, status, and so on.

- **Outputs or rewards—"What do you think you're getting out of the job?"** The outputs are the rewards that people receive from an organization: pay, benefits, praise, recognition, bonuses, promotions, status perquisites (corner office with a view, say, or private parking space), and so on.

- **Comparison—"How do you think your ratio of inputs and rewards compares with those of others?"** Equity theory suggests that people

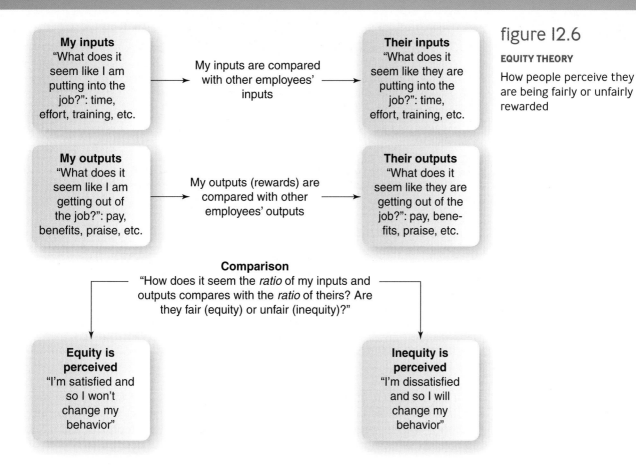

compare the *ratio* of their own outcomes to inputs against the *ratio* of someone else's outcomes to inputs. When employees compare the ratio of their inputs and outputs (rewards) with those of others—whether co-workers within the organization or even other people in similar jobs outside it—they then make a judgment about fairness. Either they perceive there is *equity*—they are satisfied with the ratio and so they don't change their behavior. Or they perceive there is *inequity*—they feel resentful and act to change the inequity.

To get a sense of your own reaction to equity differences, see the Self-Assessment at the end of this chapter.

Using Equity Theory to Motivate Employees Adams suggests that employees who feel they are being underrewarded will respond to the perceived inequity in one or more negative ways, as by reducing their inputs, trying to change the outputs or rewards they receive, distorting the inequity, changing the object of comparison, or leaving the situation. *(See Table 12.1, next page.)*

By contrast, employees who think they are treated fairly are more likely to support organizational change, more apt to cooperate in group settings, and less apt to turn to arbitration and the courts to remedy real or imagined wrongs.

Three practical lessons that can be drawn from equity theory are as follows.

1. Employee Perceptions Are What Count Probably the most important result of research on equity theory is this: no matter how fair managers think the organization's policies, procedures, and reward system are, each employee's *perception* of those factors is what counts.

table 12.1

SOME WAYS EMPLOYEES TRY TO REDUCE INEQUITY

- **They will reduce their inputs:** They will do less work, take long breaks, call in "sick" on Mondays, leave early on Fridays, and so on.

- **They will try to change the outputs or rewards they receive:** They will lobby the boss for a raise, or they will pilfer company equipment.

- **They will distort the inequity:** They will exaggerate how hard they work so they can complain they're not paid what they're worth.

- **They will change the object of comparison:** They may compare themselves to another person instead of the original one.

- **They will leave the situation:** They will quit, transfer, or shift to another reference group.

2. Employee Participation Helps Managers benefit by allowing employees to participate in important decisions. For example, employees are more satisfied with their performance appraisal when they have a "voice" during their appraisal review.[20]

3. Having an Appeal Process Helps When employees are able to appeal decisions affecting their welfare, it promotes the belief that management treats them fairly. Perceptions of fair treatment promote job satisfaction and commitment and reduce absenteeism and turnover.[21]

Expectancy Theory: How Much Do You Want & How Likely Are You to Get It?

Introduced by **Victor Vroom,** *expectancy theory* **suggests that people are motivated by two things: (1) how much they want something and (2) how likely they think they are to get it.**[22] In other words, assuming they have choices, people will make the choice that promises them the greatest reward if they think they can get it.

The Three Elements: Expectancy, Instrumentality, Valence What determines how willing you (or an employee) are to work hard at tasks important to the success of the organization? The answer, says Vroom, is: You will do what you *can* do when you *want* to.

Your motivation, according to expectancy theory, involves the relationship between your *effort,* your *performance,* and the desirability of the *outcomes* (such as pay or recognition) of your performance. These relationships, which are shown in the accompanying drawing, are affected by the three elements of *expectancy, instrumentality,* and *valence.* (See Figure 12.7, opposite page.)

1. Expectancy—"Will I be able to perform at the desired level on a task?" **Expectancy** is the belief that a particular level of effort will lead to a particular level of performance. *This is called the* effort-to-performance expectancy.

Example: If you believe that putting in more hours working at Circuit City selling videogame machines will

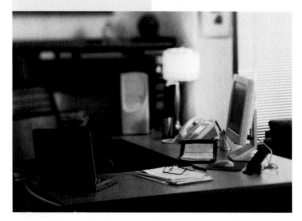

How much do you want? Would a well-appointed office represent the tangible realization of managerial success for you? How likely do you think you are to get it? The answers to these questions represent your important motivations, according to expectancy theory.

figure 12.7

EXPECTANCY THEORY: THE MAJOR ELEMENTS

result in higher sales, then you have high effort-to-performance expectancy. That is, you believe that your efforts will matter. You think you have the ability, the product knowledge, and so on so that putting in extra hours of selling can probably raise your sales of videogame machines.

2. Instrumentality—"What outcome will I receive if I perform at this level?" **Instrumentality is the expectation that successful performance of the task will lead to the outcome desired.** This is called the *performance-to-reward expectancy.*

Example: If you believe that making higher sales will cause Circuit City to give you a bonus, then you have high performance-to-reward expectancy. You believe *if* you can achieve your goals, the outcome will be worthwhile. This element is independent of the previous one—you might decide you don't have the ability to make the extra sales, but if you did, you'll be rewarded. (Lately, because of constant shareholder complaints about overpaid top executives, boards of directors have made stronger efforts to tie CEO pay more tightly to performance.)[23]

3. Valence—"How much do I want the outcome?" **Valence is value, the importance a worker assigns to the possible outcome or reward.**

Example: If you assign a lot of importance or a high value to Circuit City's prospective bonus or pay raise, then your valence is said to be high.

For your motivation to be high, you must be high on all three elements—expectancy, instrumentality, and valence. If any element is low, you will not be motivated. Your effort-to-performance expectancy might be low, for instance, because you doubt making an effort will make a difference (because retail selling has too much competition from Internet sellers). Or your performance-to-reward expectancy might be low because you don't think Circuit City is going to give you a bonus for being a star at selling. Or your valence might be low because you don't think the bonus or raise is going to be high enough to justify working evenings and weekends.

Using Expectancy Theory to Motivate Employees
The principal problem with the expectancy theory is that it is complex. Even so, the underlying logic is understandable, and research seems to show that managers are not following its principles.[24]

When attempting to motivate employees, managers should ask the following questions:

- **What rewards do your employees value?** As a manager, you need to get to know your employees and determine what rewards (outcomes) they value, such as pay raises or recognition.

Group Exercise:
What Rewards Motivate Student Achievement?

Champions. Members of Italy's football (soccer) team celebrate winning the 2006 World Cup. For sports teams, performance seems easily measured by a simple outcome—whether you win or not. Do you think performance can be as clearly measured in the business world?

- **What are the job objectives and the performance level you desire?** You need to clearly define the performance objectives and determine what performance level or behavior you want so that you can tell your employees what they need to do to attain the rewards.

- **Are the rewards linked to performance?** You want to reward high performance, of course. If high-performing employees aren't rewarded, they may

Example

Use of Expectancy Theory: Tying Teacher Pay to Student Achievement in the Denver Public Schools

The concept of instrumentality can be seen in practice by considering the debate over pay-for-performance compensation for teachers. Many educational and political leaders have been promoting the idea of providing financial rewards to teachers for improving the achievement of students, as a way to improve both student achievement and teacher quality in public schools.

A landmark 4-year study sponsored jointly by the Denver public schools and the Denver Classroom Teachers Association of a pay-for-performance program found that linking teacher compensation to student achievement can trigger fundamental improvements in school systems.[26] In the pilot program, which was implemented in 13% of the district schools, teachers developed two annual objectives for the achievement of their students that required the approval of the principal. Teachers received additional compensation if they met their objectives. The study found that students whose teachers had excellent objectives achieved higher scores, on average, than other students. The findings held

true at elementary, middle, and high school levels.

Since then, similar programs have been initiated in other states, including California, Florida, Kentucky, Louisiana, Minnesota, Texas, and Wisconsin.[27] Previous pay-for-performance programs have been unsuccessful because they were based on the belief that compensation is the primary incentive for teachers to perform at high levels or they were designed to punish teachers who were labeled as underperforming. The study referred to above notes that for the program to work, school districts need to align and improve the quality of the curriculum, instructional delivery, and supervision and training. In addition, districts need to be sure they have high-quality assessments that can measure student progress based on what teachers are being asked to teach.

Your Call

Do you think a pay-for-performance program can work if it is simply imposed on teachers without the teachers' collaboration? If you were a teacher, what would you recommend?

leave or slow down and affect the performance of other employees. Thus, employees must be aware that X level of performance within Y period of time will result in Z kinds of rewards.[25]

- **Do employees believe you will deliver the right rewards for the right performance?** Your credibility is on the line here. Your employees must believe that you have the power, the ability, and the will to give them the rewards you promise for the performance you are requesting.

Goal-Setting Theory: Objectives Should Be Specific & Challenging but Achievable

Goal-setting theory **suggests that employees can be motivated by goals that are specific and challenging but achievable.** According to psychologists **Edwin Locke** and **Gary Latham,** who developed the theory, it is natural for people to set and strive for goals; however, the goal-setting process is useful only if people *understand* and *accept* the goals. Thus, the best way to motivate performance is to set the right objectives in the right ways.[28]

Self-Assessment Exercise: Assessing How Personality Type Impacts Your Goal-Setting Skills

The benefits of setting goals is that a manager can tailor rewards to the needs of individual employees, clarify what is expected of them, provide regular reinforcement, and maintain equity.

Three Elements of Goal-Setting Theory A *goal* is defined as an objective that a person is trying to accomplish through his or her efforts. To result in high motivation and performance, according to goal-setting theory, goals must be *specific, challenging,* and *achievable.*

1. Goals Should Be Specific Goals such as "Sell as many cars as you can" or "Be nicer to customers" are too vague and therefore have no effect on motivation. Instead, goals need to be specific—usually meaning *quantitative.* As a manager, for example, you may be asked to boost the revenues of your unit by 25% and to cut absenteeism by 10%, all specific targets.

Small business. Do employees in small businesses, such as this worker in a bakery, need the same kind of motivational goals as employees in large corporations? Is setting goals in small businesses, where there's apt to be less specialization, more or less difficult than in large organizations?

2. Goals Should Be Challenging Goal theory suggests you not set goals that a lot of people can reach, since this is not very motivational. Rather you should set goals that are challenging, which will impel people to focus their attention in the right place and to apply more effort or inputs toward their jobs—in other words, motivate them toward higher performance.

3. Goals Should Be Achievable Goals can't be unattainable, of course. You might ask data-entry clerks to enter 25% more names and addresses an hour into a database, but if they don't have touch-typing skills, that goal won't be attainable. Thus, managers need to make sure employees have additional training, if necessary, to achieve difficult goals.

Using Goal-Setting Theory to Motivate Employees In addition, when developing employee goals, you need to follow the recommendation made in Chapter 5 that goals should be SMART— that is, Specific, Measurable, Attainable, Results-oriented, and have Target dates. It is also important to make sure that employees have the abilities and resources to accomplish their goals.

Finally, make sure that you give feedback so that employees know of their progress—and don't forget to reward people for doing what they set out to do. ●

12.4 JOB DESIGN PERSPECTIVES ON MOTIVATION

major question What's the best way to design jobs—adapt people to work or work to people?

THE BIG PICTURE

Job design, the division of an organization's work among employees, applies motivational theories to jobs to increase performance and satisfaction. The traditional approach to job design is to fit people to the jobs; the modern way is to fit the jobs to the people, using job enlargement and enrichment. The job characteristics model offers five job attributes for better work outcomes.

Job design is (1) the division of an organization's work among its employees and (2) the application of motivational theories to jobs to increase satisfaction and performance. There are two different approaches to job design, one traditional, one modern, that can be taken in deciding how to design jobs. The traditional way is *fitting people to jobs;* the modern way is *fitting jobs to people.*

Fitting people to jobs is based on the assumption that people will gradually adapt to any work situation. Even so, jobs must still be tailored so that nearly anyone can do them. This is the approach often taken with assembly-line jobs and jobs involving routine tasks. For managers the main challenge becomes *"How can we make the worker most compatible with the work?"*

One technique is *job simplification,* **the process of reducing the number of tasks a worker performs.** When a job is stripped down to its simplest elements, it enables a worker to focus on doing more of the same task, thus increasing employee efficiency and productivity. This may be especially useful, for instance, in designing jobs for mentally disadvantaged workers, such as those run by Goodwill Industries. However, research shows that simplified, repetitive jobs lead to job dissatisfaction, poor mental health, and a low sense of accomplishment and personal growth.[29]

Fitting Jobs to People

Fitting jobs to people is based on the assumption that people are underutilized at work and that they want more variety, challenges, and responsibility. This philosophy, an outgrowth of Herzberg's theory, is one of the reasons for the popularity of work teams in the United States. The main challenge for managers is *"How can we make the work most compatible with the worker so as to produce both high performance and high job satisfaction?"* Two techniques for this type of job design include (1) *job enlargement* and (2) *job enrichment.*

Job Enlargement: Putting More Variety into a Job The opposite of job simplification, *job enlargement* **consists of increasing the number of tasks in a job to increase variety and motivation.** For instance, the job of installing television picture tubes could be enlarged to include installation of the circuit boards.

Although proponents claim job enlargement can improve employee satisfaction, motivation, and quality of production, research suggests job enlargement by itself won't have a significant and lasting positive effect on job performance. After all, working at two boring tasks instead of one doesn't add up to a challenging job. Instead, job enlargement is just one tool of many that should be considered in job design.[30]

Job Enrichment: Putting More Responsibility & Other Motivating Factors into a Job Job enrichment is the practical application of Frederick Herzberg's two-factor motivator-hygiene theory of job satisfaction.[31] Specifically, *job enrichment*

consists of building into a job such motivating factors as responsibility, achievement, recognition, stimulating work, and advancement.

However, instead of the job-enlargement technique of simply giving employees additional tasks of similar difficulty (known as *horizontal loading*), with job enrichment employees are given more responsibility (known as *vertical loading*). Thus, employees take on chores that would normally be performed by their supervisors. For example, one department store authorized thousands of its sales clerks to handle functions normally reserved for store managers, such as handling merchandise-return problems and approving customers' checks.[32]

The Job Characteristics Model: Five Job Attributes for Better Work Outcomes

Developed by researchers **J. Richard Hackman** and **Greg Oldham,** the job characteristics model of design is an outgrowth of job enrichment.[33] **The *job characteristics model* consists of (a) five core job characteristics that affect (b) three critical psychological states of an employee that in turn affect (c) work outcomes—the employee's motivation, performance, and satisfaction.** The model is illustrated below. *(See Figure 12.8.)*

figure 12.8

THE JOB CHARACTERISTICS MODEL

Source: Adapted from J. R. Hackman and G. R. Oldham, *Work Redesign* (Reading, MA: Addison-Wesley, 1980), p. 90.

Five Job Characteristics   The five core job characteristics are as follows.

1. Skill Variety—"How Many Different Skills Does Your Job Require?"   *Skill variety* describes the extent to which a job requires a person to use a wide range of different skills and abilities.

Example: The skill variety required by a rocket scientist is higher than that for a short-order cook.

2. Task Identity—"How Many Different Tasks Are Required to Complete the Work?"   *Task identity* describes the extent to which a job requires a worker to perform all the tasks needed to complete the job from beginning to end.

Example: The task identity for a craftsperson who goes through all the steps to build a hand-made acoustic guitar is higher than it is for an assembly-line worker who just installs windshields on cars.

Skill variety. Being a jewelry designer—or airline pilot, building contractor, physician, or orchestra conductor—requires a greater number of skills than, say, driving a truck. Do highly skilled employees typically make good managers? What skills do jewelry designers have that would make them effective managers in other kinds of work?

3. Task Significance—"How Many Other People Are Affected by Your Job?" *Task significance* describes the extent to which a job affects the lives of other people, whether inside or outside the organization.

Example: A technician who is responsible for keeping a hospital's electronic equipment in working order has higher task significance than does a person wiping down cars in a carwash.

4. Autonomy—"How Much Discretion Does Your Job Give You?" *Autonomy* describes the extent to which a job allows an employee to make choices about scheduling different tasks and deciding how to perform them.

Example: College-textbook salespeople have lots of leeway in planning which campuses and professors to call on. Thus, they have higher autonomy than do toll-takers on a bridge, whose actions are determined by the flow of vehicles.

5. Feedback—"How Much Do You Find Out How Well You're Doing?" *Feedback* describes the extent to which workers receive clear, direct information about how well they are performing the job.

Example: Professional basketball players receive immediate feedback on how many of their shots are going into the basket. Engineers working on new weapons systems may go years before learning how effective their performance has been.

How the Model Works   According to the job characteristics model, these five core characteristics affect a worker's motivation because they affect three critical psychological states: *meaningfulness of work, responsibility for results,* and *knowledge of results.* (Refer to Figure 12.8 again.) That is, the more that workers (1) feel that they are doing meaningful work, (2) feel that they are responsible for outcomes of the work, and (3) have knowledge of the actual results of the work and how they affect others, then the more likely they are to have favorable work outcomes: *high motivation, high performance, high satisfaction,* and *low absenteeism and turnover.*

One other element—shown at the bottom of Figure 12.8—needs to be discussed: *contingency factors.* This refers to the degree to which a person wants personal and psychological development. Job enrichment will be more successful for employees with high growth-need strength. Not everyone will respond well to enriched jobs. To be motivated, a person must have three attributes: (1) necessary knowledge and skill, (2) desire for personal growth, and (3) context satisfactions—that is, the right physical working conditions, pay, and supervision.

Applying the Job Characteristics Model   There are three major steps to follow when applying the model.

- **Diagnose the work environment to see whether a problem exists.** Hackman and Oldham developed a self-report instrument for managers to use called the *job diagnostic survey.* This will indicate whether an individual's so-called motivating potential score (MPS)—the amount of internal work motivation associated with a specific job—is high or low.

- **Determine whether job redesign is appropriate.** If a person's MPS score is low, an attempt should be made to determine which of the core job characteristics is causing the problem. You should next decide whether job redesign is appropriate for a given group of employees. Job design is most likely to work in a participative environment in which employees have the necessary knowledge and skills.

- **Consider how to redesign the job.** Here you try to increase those core job characteristics that are lower than national norms.

   Example: At one time, the 470 workers at Alexander Doll Co. individually produced parts for dolls. Based on input from the workers, owners organized employees into seven- or eight-person teams, each responsible for completing about 300 doll or wardrobe assemblies a day. The result: orders can now be filled in 1 or 2 weeks instead of 8.[34] ●

12.5 REINFORCEMENT PERSPECTIVES ON MOTIVATION

What are the types of incentives I might use to influence employee behavior?

major + **question**

THE BIG PICTURE
Reinforcement theory suggests behavior will be repeated if it has positive consequences and won't be if it has negative consequences. There are four types of reinforcement: positive reinforcement, negative reinforcement, extinction, and punishment. This section also describes how to use some reinforcement techniques to modify employee behavior.

Reinforcement evades the issue of people's needs and thinking processes in relation to motivation, as we described under the need-based and process perspectives. Instead, the reinforcement perspective, which was pioneered by **Edward L. Thorndike** and **B. F. Skinner,** is concerned with how the consequences of a certain behavior affect that behavior in the future.[35]

Test Your Knowledge:
Reinforcing Performance

Skinner was the father of *operant conditioning,* the process of controlling behavior by manipulating its consequences. Operant conditioning rests on Thorndike's *law of effect,* which states that behavior that results in a pleasant outcome is likely to be repeated and behavior that results in unpleasant outcomes is not likely to be repeated.

From these underpinnings has come ***reinforcement theory,*** **which attempts to explain behavior change by suggesting that behavior with positive consequences tends to be repeated, whereas behavior with negative consequences tends not to be repeated.** The use of reinforcement theory to change human behavior is called *behavior modification.*

The Four Types of Reinforcement: Positive, Negative, Extinction, & Punishment

Reinforcement **is anything that causes a given behavior to be repeated or inhibited,** whether praising a child for cleaning his or her room or scolding a child for leaving a tricycle in the driveway. There are four types of reinforcement: (1) *positive reinforcement,* (2) *negative reinforcement,* (3) *extinction,* and (4) *punishment. (See Figure 12.9, next page.)*

Positive Reinforcement: Giving Rewards
Positive reinforcement **is the use of positive consequences to encourage desirable behavior.**

Example: A supervisor who's asked an insurance salesperson to sell more policies might reward successful performance by saying, "It's great that you exceeded your quota, and you'll get a bonus for it. Maybe next time you'll sell even more and will become a member of the Circle of 100 Top Sellers and win a trip to Paris as well." Note the rewards: praise, more money, recognition, awards. Presumably this will *strengthen* the behavior and the sales rep will work even harder in the coming months.

Negative Reinforcement: Avoiding Unpleasantness
Negative reinforcement **is the removal of unpleasant consequences following a desired behavior.**

Example: A supervisor who has been nagging a salesperson might say, "Well, so you exceeded your quota" and stop the nagging. Note the neutral statement; there is no

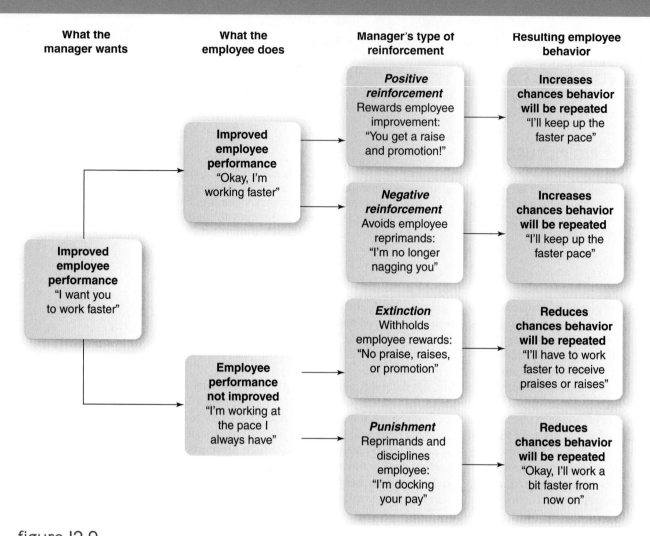

What the manager wants	What the employee does	Manager's type of reinforcement	Resulting employee behavior
Improved employee performance "I want you to work faster"	**Improved employee performance** "Okay, I'm working faster"	***Positive reinforcement*** Rewards employee improvement: "You get a raise and promotion!"	**Increases chances behavior will be repeated** "I'll keep up the faster pace"
		Negative reinforcement Avoids employee reprimands: "I'm no longer nagging you"	**Increases chances behavior will be repeated** "I'll keep up the faster pace"
	Employee performance not improved "I'm working at the pace I always have"	***Extinction*** Withholds employee rewards: "No praise, raises, or promotion"	**Reduces chances behavior will be repeated** "I'll have to work faster to receive praises or raises"
		Punishment Reprimands and disciplines employee: "I'm docking your pay"	**Reduces chances behavior will be repeated** "Okay, I'll work a bit faster from now on"

figure 12.9

FOUR TYPES OF REINFORCEMENT

These are different ways of changing employee behavior.

praise but also no longer any negative statements. This could cause the sales rep to *maintain* his or her existing behavior.

Extinction: Withholding Rewards *Extinction* **is the withholding or withdrawal of positive rewards for desirable behavior, so that the behavior is less likely to occur in the future.**

Example: A supervisor might tell a successful salesperson, "I know you exceeded your quota, but now that our company has been taken over by another firm, we're not giving out bonuses any more." Presumably this will *weaken* the salesperson's efforts to perform better in the future.

Punishment: Applying Negative Consequences *Punishment* **is the application of negative consequences to stop or change undesirable behavior.**

Example: A supervisor might tell an unsuccessful salesperson who's been lazy about making calls to clients and so didn't make quota, "Well, if this keeps up, you'll probably be let go." This could *inhibit* the salesperson from being so lackadaisical about making calls to clients.

Using Reinforcement to Motivate Employees

The following are some guidelines for using two types of reinforcement—positive reinforcement and punishment.

Positive Reinforcement   There are several aspects of positive reinforcement, which should definitely be part of your toolkit of managerial skills:

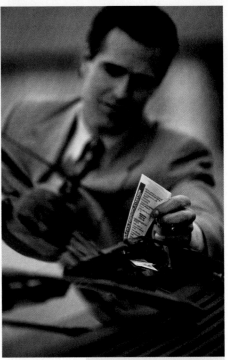

- **Reward only desirable behavior.** You should give rewards to your employees only when they show *desirable* behavior. Thus, for example, you should give praise to employees not for showing up for work on time (an expected part of any job) but for showing up early.

- **Give rewards as soon as possible.** You should give a reward as soon as possible after the desirable behavior appears. Thus, you should give praise to an early-arriving employee as soon as he or she arrives, not later in the week.

- **Be clear about what behavior is desired.** Clear communication is everything. You should tell employees exactly what kinds of work behaviors are desirable and you should tell everyone exactly what they must do to earn rewards.

- **Have different rewards and recognize individual differences.** Recognizing that different people respond to different kinds of rewards, you should have different rewards available. Thus, you might give a word of praise verbally to one person, shoot a line or two by e-mail to another person, or send a hand-scrawled note to another.

Punishment. Does getting a wallet-busting traffic violation ticket change your behavior? What if it happens several times? Yet consider also other, presumably stronger forms of governmental punishment that are supposed to act as deterrents to bad behavior. Does the possibility of the death punishment really deter homicides? Why or why not?

Punishment   Unquestionably there will be times when you'll need to threaten or administer an unpleasant consequence to stop an employee's undesirable behavior. Sometimes it's best to address a problem by combining punishment with positive reinforcement. Some suggestions for using punishment are as follows.

- **Punish only undesirable behavior.** You should give punishment only when employees show frequent *undesirable* behavior. Otherwise, employees may come to view you negatively as a tyrannical boss. Thus, for example, you should reprimand employees who show up, say, a half hour late for work but not 5 or 10 minutes late.

- **Give reprimands or disciplinary actions as soon as possible.** You should mete out punishment as soon as possible after the undesirable behavior occurs. Thus, you should give a reprimand to a late-arriving employee as soon as he or she arrives.

- **Be clear about what behavior is undesirable.** Tell employees exactly what kinds of work behaviors are undesirable and make any disciplinary action or reprimand match the behavior. A manager should not, for example, dock an hourly employee's pay if he or she is only 5 or 10 minutes late for work.

- **Administer punishment in private.** You would hate to have your boss chew you out in front of your subordinates, and the people who report to you also shouldn't be reprimanded in public, which would lead only to resentments that may have nothing to do with an employee's infractions.

- **Combine punishment and positive reinforcement.** If you're reprimanding an employee, be sure to also say what he or she is doing right and state what rewards the employee might be eligible for. For example, while reprimanding someone for being late, say that a perfect attendance record over the next few months will put that employee in line for a raise or promotion. ●

Test Your Knowledge:
Reinforcement Theory

12.6 USING COMPENSATION & OTHER REWARDS TO MOTIVATE

✖ major question How can I use compensation and other rewards to motivate people?

THE BIG PICTURE

Compensation, the main motivator of performance, includes pay for performance, bonuses, profit sharing, gain sharing, stock options, and pay for knowledge. Other nonmonetary incentives address needs that aren't being met, such as work-life balance, growth in skills, and commitment.

Perhaps the first thing that comes to mind when you think about motivating performance is compensation—how much money you or your employees can make. But consider how motivation worked for software engineer Firinn Taisdeal, mentioned previously. In 2003, he walked away from a job just before a historic public offering that probably would have made him rich. Why? Because the people he worked with repelled him. "They were not just greedy," he says. "They had no integrity."[36] Or consider Mary Morse, another software engineer, who turned down several offers from other Silicon Valley firms, at least one of which would have made her wealthy, in order to stay with the computer-aided design firm Autodesk. The reason? She liked her bosses.[37]

Morse in particular demonstrates the truth of a Gallup Organization poll that found that most workers rate having a caring boss higher than they value monetary benefits.[38] Clearly, then, motivating doesn't just involve dollars.

Motivation & Compensation

Most people are paid an hourly wage or a weekly or monthly salary. Both of these are easy for organizations to administer, of course. But by itself a wage or a salary gives an employee little incentive to work hard. Incentive compensation plans try to do so, although no single plan will boost the performance of all employees.

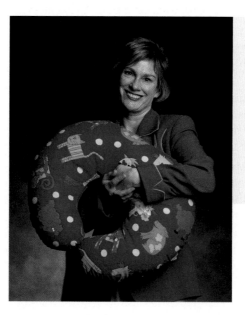

Motivation as a small business owner. Susan Brown of Golden, Colorado, had dreamed of opening her own business since she was a child. However, she invented the Boppy, a simple pillow stuffed with foam, almost accidentally, when her daughter's day care center asked parents to bring in pillows to prop up infants who couldn't sit up on their own. Today the Boppy Co. has annual sales of $15 million to $25 million. For some people, like Brown, the only way to merge motivation and compensation is to own and manage their own business. What factors or incentives motivate you to work hard?

Characteristics of the Best Incentive Compensation Plans In accordance with most of the theories of motivation we described earlier, for incentive plans to work, certain criteria are advisable, as follows. (1) Rewards must be linked to performance and be measurable. (2) The rewards must satisfy individual needs. (3) The rewards must be agreed on by manager and employees. (4) The rewards believable, and achievable by employees.

Popular Incentive Compensation Plans How would you like to be rewarded for your efforts? Some of the most well-known incentive compensation plans are *pay for performance, bonuses, profit sharing, gainsharing, stock options,* and *pay for knowledge.*

- **Pay for performance.** Also known as *merit pay,* **pay for performance bases pay on one's results.** Thus, different salaried employees might get different pay raises and other rewards (such as promotions) depending on their overall job performance.[39]

  Examples: One standard pay-for-performance plan, already mentioned, is payment according to a *piece rate,* **in which employees are paid according to how much output they produce,** as is often used with farmworkers picking fruit and vegetables. Another is the *sales commission,* **in which sales representatives are paid a percentage of the earnings the company made from their sales,** so that the more they sell, the more they are paid. We discussed teacher pay for performance under expectancy theory. A good deal of the criticism of excessive executive pay is that it has not been tied to company performance.[40]

- **Bonuses.** *Bonuses* **are cash awards given to employees who achieve specific performance objectives.**

  Example: Nieman Marcus, the department store, pays its salespeople a percentage of the earnings from the goods they sell.

- **Profit sharing.** *Profit sharing* **is the distribution to employees of a percentage of the company's profits.**

  Example: In one T-shirt and sweatshirt manufacturing company, 10% of pretax profits are distributed to employees every month, and more is given out at the end of the year. Distributions are apportioned according to such criteria as performance, attendance, and lateness for individual employees.

- **Gainsharing.** *Gainsharing* **is the distribution of savings or "gains" to groups of employees who reduced costs and increased measurable productivity.**

  Example: There are different types of gainsharing plans, but in one known as the *Scanlon plan,* developed in the 1920s by a steel-industry union leader named Joseph Scanlon, a portion of any cost savings, usually 75%, are distributed back to employees; the company keeps the other 25%.[41]

- **Stock options.** With *stock options,* **certain employees are given the right to buy stock at a future date for a discounted price.** The motivator here is that employees holding stock options will supposedly work hard to make the company's stock rise so that they can obtain it at a cheaper price. By giving stock options to all employees who work 20 or more hours a week, Starbucks Corp. has been able to hold its annual turnover rate to 60%—in an industry (fast food and restaurants) in which 300% is not unheard of.[42] (The use of stock options has been criticized recently because many companies allowed "backdating"— permitting their executives to buy company stock at low purchase prices from previous days or weeks. As one writer points out, this is sort of like being able to make a fortune by betting on a Kentucky Derby whose outcome you've known for some time.[43])

- **Pay for knowledge.** Also known as *skill-based pay,* **_pay for knowledge_ ties employee pay to the number of job-relevant skills or academic degrees they earn.**

  Example: The teaching profession is a time-honored instance of this incentive, in which elementary and secondary teachers are encouraged to increase their salaries by earning further college credit. However, firms such as FedEx also have pay-for-knowledge plans.

Nonmonetary Ways of Motivating Employees

Employees who can behave autonomously, solve problems, and take the initiative are apt to be the very ones who will leave if they find their own needs aren't being met—namely:[44]

- **The need for work-life balance.** A PricewaterhouseCoopers survey of 2,500 university students in 11 countries found that 57% named as their primary career goal "attaining a balance between personal life and career."[45] A 25-year study of values in the United States found that "employees have become less convinced that work should be an important part of one's life or that working hard makes one a better person."[46]

- **The need to expand skills.** Having watched their parents undergo downsizing, younger workers in particular are apt to view a job as a way of gaining skills that will enable them to earn a decent living in the future.

- **The need to matter.** Workers now want to be with an organization that allows them to feel they matter. They want to commit to their profession or fellow team members rather than have to profess a blind loyalty to the corporation.

There is a whole class of nonmonetary incentives to attract, retain, and motivate employees. The foremost example is the *flexible workplace*—including part-time work, flextime, compressed workweek, job sharing, and telecommuting. Other incentives can be expressed simply as *treat employees well,* some examples of which follow.

Thoughtfulness: The Value of Being Nice
A study by Walker Information, an Indianapolis-based research firm, found that employers spend too little time showing workers they matter, as manifested in lack of communication and lack of interest in new ideas and contributions.[47] A majority of employees feel underappreciated, according to a 1999 survey. Forty percent of employees who rated their boss's performance as poor said they were likely to look for a new job; only 11% of those who rated it excellent said they would.[48] "Being nice" to employees means, for example, reducing criticism, becoming more effusive in your praise, and writing thank-you notes to employees for exceptional performance.[49]

The No. 1 reason people quit their jobs, it's believed, is their dissatisfaction with their supervisors, not their paychecks. Thus, industrial psychologist B. Lynn Ware suggests that if you learn valued employees are disgruntled, you should discuss it with them.[50] "It's extraordinary how often it is the small and often banal gestures that are the most meaningful," says another expert. "People will often say things like, 'I'm not really happy, but not yet prepared to jump ship because my boss was really good to me when my mother was sick.'"[51] Employers can promote personal relationships, which most employees are concerned about on the job, by offering breaks or other opportunities in which people can mix and socialize.

Work-Life Benefits
Work-life benefits, according to Kathie Lingle, are programs "used by employers to increase productivity and commitment by removing certain barriers that make it hard for people to strike a balance between their work and personal lives."[52]

Lingle, who is national work-life director for KPMG, an accounting and consulting firm, emphasizes that work-life benefits "are not a reward, but a way of getting work done." After all, some employees are low performers simply because of a lack of life-work balance, with great demands at home. "If you only give these 'rewards' to existing high performers," says Lingle, "you're cutting people off who could, with some support, be high performers." Nevertheless, handing out extra time off can be used to reward performance and prevent burnout.[53]

Besides alternative scheduling, work-life benefits include helping employees with daycare costs or even establishing on-site centers; domestic-partner benefits; job-protected leave for new parents; and provision of technology such as mobile phones and laptops to enable parents to work at home.[54]

Surroundings   The cubicle, according to new research, is stifling the creativity and morale of many workers, and the bias of modern-day office designers for open spaces and neutral colors is leading to employee complaints that their workplaces are too noisy or too bland.

"There is no such thing as something that works for everybody," says Alan Hedge, a professor of environmental analysis at Cornell University.[55] An 8-foot-by-8-foot cubicle may not be a good visual trigger for human brains, and companies wanting to improve creativity and productivity may need to think about giving office employees better things to look at.

Skill-Building & Educational Opportunities   Learning opportunities can take two forms. Managers can see that workers are matched with co-workers from whom they can learn, allowing them, for instance, to "shadow" workers in other jobs or be in interdepartmental task forces. There can also be tuition reimbursement for part-time study at a college or university.[56]

Sabbaticals   Intel and Apple understand that in a climate of 80-hour weeks people need to recharge themselves. But even McDonald's offers sabbaticals to longtime employees, giving a month to a year of paid time off in which to travel, learn, and pursue personal projects. The aim, of course, is to enable employees to recharge themselves but also, it is hoped, to cement their loyalty to the organization.[57] ●

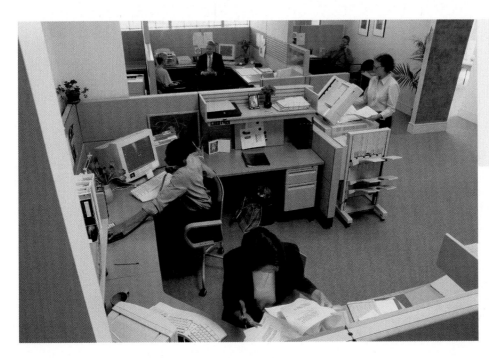

Cubicle culture. It might be too difficult to design a setup in which everyone has an office with a view. But would it be possible to design a layout in which everyone has a private office? Do you think it would better motivate employees?

summary

 12.1 Motivating for Performance

- Motivation is defined as the psychological processes that arouse and direct goal-directed behavior. In a simple model of motivation, people have certain needs that motivate them to perform specific behaviors for which they receive rewards that feed back and satisfy the original need. Rewards are of two types: extrinsic and intrinsic. An extrinsic reward is the payoff, such as money, a person receives from others for performing a particular task. An intrinsic reward is the satisfaction, such as a feeling of accomplishment, that a person receives from performing the particular task itself.

- As a manager, you want to motivate people to do things that will benefit your organization—join it, stay with it, show up for work at it, perform better for it, and do extra for it.

- Four major perspectives on motivation are (1) content, (2) process, (3) job design and (4) reinforcement.

 12.2 Content Perspectives on Employee Motivation

- Content perspectives or need-based perspectives emphasize the needs that motivate people. Needs are defined as physiological or psychological deficiencies that arouse behavior. Besides the McGregor Theory X/

Theory Y (Chapter 1), need-based perspectives include (1) the hierarchy of needs theory, (2) the two-factor theory, and (3) the acquired needs theory.

- The hierarchy of needs theory proposes that people are motivated by five levels of need: physiological, safety, belongingness, esteem, and self-actualization needs.

- The acquired needs theory states that three needs—achievement, affiliation, and power—are major motives determining people's behavior in the workplace.

- The two-factor theory proposes that work satisfaction and dissatisfaction arise from two different factors—work satisfaction from so-called motivating factors, and work dissatisfaction from so-called hygiene factors. Hygiene factors, the lower-level needs, are factors associated with job dissatisfaction—such as salary and working conditions—which affect the environment in which people work. Motivating factors, the higher-level needs, are factors associated with job satisfaction—such as achievement and advancement—which affect the rewards of work performance.

 12.3 Process Perspectives on Employee Motivation

- Process perspectives are concerned with the thought processes by which people decide how to act. Three process perspectives on motivation are (1) equity theory, (2) expectancy theory, and (3) goal-setting theory.

- Equity theory focuses on employee perceptions as to how fairly they think they are being treated compared to others. The key elements in equity theory are inputs, outputs (rewards), and comparisons. (1) With inputs, employees consider what they are putting into the job in time, effort, and so on. (2) With outputs or rewards, employees consider what they think they're getting out of the job in terms of pay, praise, and so on. (3) With comparison, employees compare the ratio of their own outcomes to inputs against the ratio of someone else's outcomes to inputs. Three practical lessons of equity theory are that employee perceptions are what count, employee participation helps, and having an appeal process helps.

- Expectancy theory suggests that people are motivated by how much they want something and how likely they think they are to get it. The three elements affecting motivation are expectancy, instrumentality, and valence. (1) Expectancy is the belief that a particular level of effort will lead to a particular level of performance. (2) Instrumentality is the expectation that successful performance of the task will lead to the outcome desired. (3) Valence is the value, the importance a worker assigns to the possible outcome or reward. When attempting to motivate employees, according to the logic of expectancy theory, managers should ascertain what rewards employees value, what job objectives and performance level they desire, whether there are rewards linked to performance, and whether employees believe managers will deliver the right rewards for the right performance.

- Goal-setting theory suggests that employees can be motivated by goals that are specific and challenging but achievable. Three elements of this theory are that goals must be specific, challenging, and achievable. In addition, the theory suggests that goals should be set jointly with the employee, be measurable, and have a target date for accomplishment and that employees should receive feedback and rewards.

12.4 Job Design Perspectives on Motivation

- Job design is, first, the division of an organization's work among its employees and, second, the application of motivational

theories to jobs to increase satisfaction and performance. Two approaches to job design are fitting people to jobs (the traditional approach) and fitting jobs to people.

- Fitting jobs to people assumes people are underutilized and want more variety. Two techniques for this type of job design include job enlargement, (1) increasing the number of tasks in a job to increase variety and motivation, and (2) job enrichment, building into a job such motivating factors as responsibility, achievement, recognition, stimulating work, and advancement.

- An outgrowth of job enrichment is the job characteristics model, which consists of (a) five core job characteristics that affect (b) three critical psychological states of an employee that in turn affect (c) work outcomes—the employee's motivation, performance, and satisfaction. The five core job characteristics are (1) skill variety—how many different skills does a job require; (2) task identity—how many different tasks are required to complete the work; (3) task significance—how many other people are affected by the job; (4) autonomy—how much discretion does the job allow the worker; and (5) feedback—how much do employees find out how well they're doing. These five characteristics affect three critical psychological states: meaningfulness of work, responsibility for results, and knowledge of results. Three major steps to follow when applying the job characteristics model are (1) diagnose the work environment to see if a problem exists, (2) determine whether job redesign is appropriate, and (3) consider how to redesign the job.

 12.5 Reinforcement Perspectives on Motivation

- Reinforcement theory attempts to explain behavior change by suggesting that behavior with positive consequences tends to be repeated whereas behavior with negative consequences tends not to be repeated. Reinforcement is anything that causes a given behavior to be repeated or inhibited.

- There are four types of reinforcement. (1) Positive reinforcement is the use of positive consequences to encourage desirable behavior. (2) Negative reinforcement is the removal of unpleasant consequences followed by a desired behavior. (3) Extinction is the withholding or withdrawal of positive rewards for desirable behavior, so that the behavior is less likely to occur in the future. (4) Punishment is the application of negative consequences to stop or change undesirable behavior.

- In using positive reinforcement to motivate employees, managers should reward only desirable behavior, give rewards as soon as possible, be clear about what behavior is desired, and have different rewards and recognize individual differences. In using punishment, managers should punish only undesirable behavior, give reprimands or disciplinary actions as soon as possible, be clear about what behavior is undesirable, administer punishment in private, and combine punishment and positive reinforcement.

12.6 Using Compensation & Other Rewards to Motivate

- Compensation is only one form of motivator. For incentive compensation plans for work, rewards must be linked to performance and be measurable; they must satisfy individual needs; they must be agreed on by manager and employee; and they must be perceived as being equitable, believable, and achievable by employees.

- Popular incentive compensation plans are the following. (1) Pay for performance bases pay on one's results. One kind is payment according to piece rate, in which employees are paid according to how much output they produce. Another is the sales commission, in which sales representatives are paid a percentage of the earnings the company made from their sales. (2) Bonuses are cash awards given to employees who achieve specific performance objectives. (3) Profit sharing is the distribution to employees of a percentage of the company's profits. (4) Gainsharing is the distribution of savings or "gains" to groups of employees who reduced costs and increased measurable productivity. (5) Stock options allow certain employees to buy stock at a future date for a discounted price. (6) Pay for knowledge ties employee pay to the number of job-relevant skills or academic degrees they earn.

- There are also nonmonetary ways of compensating employees. Some employees will leave because they feel the need for work-life balance, the need to expand their skills, and the need to matter. To retain such employees, nonmonetary incentives have been introduced, such as the flexible workplace. Other incentives that keep employees from leaving are thoughtfulness by employees' managers, work-life benefits such as daycare, attractive surroundings, skill-building and educational opportunities, and work sabbaticals.

 management in action

ARUP Laboratories, IBM, Versant Inc., and Great River Health Systems Rely on Positive Work Environments to Motivate Employees

U.S. industries lose nearly $300 billion a year—or $7,500 per worker—in employee absenteeism, diminished productivity, employee turnover and direct medical, legal, and insurance fees related to workplace stress, according to the American Institute of Stress.

Some organizations have responded to this and other business challenges, by creating workplaces that do more than just improve productivity; they aim to build a strong, vibrant organizational culture that supports the company itself. For instance, the Comporium Group, a South Carolina-based group of telecommunications companies, recently created a joint employee-management committee that evaluates ideas for new products and services in order to empower employees and reinforce their worth to the company. . . .

Large For-Profit: ARUP Laboratories. This Salt Lake City-based reference laboratory aims to create a balanced workplace by promoting the health and well-being of employees and their families. To do so, the lab offers a free, on-site health clinic that is open six days a week to provide services ranging from preventive to urgent care to employees and their families. The laboratory also aims to involve employees in a broad spectrum of company decisions through employee surveys, town hall meetings, and "brown bag" lunches where executives answer other employees' questions. The bottom line? ARUP staff have increased their productivity, with an average of 598 tests per person per month in 2005, up from 530 tests per person per month in 2001.

Large For-Profit: IBM–T.J. Watson Research Center. Health and safety at IBM's Yorktown Heights, New York, research facility are a high priority. IBM maintains an extensive menu of employee wellness resources that includes online tools, classes on a variety of health-related topics and access to a workout center and other sports and recreation facilities. Other opportunities available to IBM employees at the worksite include health screenings, wellness evaluations, immunizations, and lunch-and-learn presentations. The company's corporate commitment to the "whole employee" is also evident in the educational and training resources available through IBM's Global Campus Web site, which features thousands of online training options on topics ranging from nanoscience to business administration. The bottom line? Repeat measurements show a reduction in employee health risks and IBM's U.S. health insurance premiums from 1999–2005 were, on average, 4.7% lower than the national average and 6 to 15% lower than industry norms. . . .

Small For-Profit: Versant Inc. This marketing communications firm, based in Milwaukee, makes a commitment to enhancing employee growth and development to help each associate reach his or her potential. As such, Versant's culture allows all employees to make important decisions, contribute to the company's success and assume responsibility for results. Versant encourages employees' continuous learning and development through coaching and mentoring, roundtable discussions, funded membership in trade organizations, and on- and off-site education as a means of improving client solutions. The bottom line? Since 2001, Versant's productivity has increased 36% and fees billed per full-time worker have increased 31%.

Not-for-Profit: Great River Health Systems. This West Burlington, Iowa, health-care system's corporate culture is built upon a customer service philosophy dubbed EXCEL, or "being Enthusiastically friendly, X-ceeding expectations, showing Care and compassion, displaying Energetic teamwork, and through Leadership and professionalism." Building upon those values, Great River has developed programs that train employees to help new staff members transition into the organization and that support cross-training to improve services and workplace relationships. The company also provides a number of services to help employees manage other life demands, such as adoption assistance, sick-child day care services in the pediatrics department, and a lactation room for nursing mothers. The bottom line? Great River's turnover rate is 12.8%—compared with an average of 18% for hospitals in Iowa, and 17% for hospitals nationally.

For Discussion

1. Which of the four companies profiled in the case would you most like to work for? Explain your rationale.
2. How have ARUP Laboratories and Great River Health Systems used recommendations derived from content perspectives of motivation to motivate their employees? Discuss.
3. To what extent do the four companies discussed use hygiene factors and motivating factors to provide a positive work environment? Provide examples to support your conclusions.
4. To what extent are the motivation systems used at these companies consistent with expectancy theory? Explain.
5. What are the key lessons learned from the examples discussed in this case? Discuss.

 ## self-assessment

What Is Your Reaction to Equity Differences?

Objectives
1. Assess your reaction to equity differences.
2. Gain more insight into yourself.

Introduction
Have you ever noticed that certain people scream "No fair!" whenever they perceive something as unequal? Have you also noticed that other people don't seem bothered by inequity at all? According to researchers, when given the same amount of inequity, people respond differently depending on their individual equity sensitivity. There are varying degrees of equity sensitivity:

Benevolents are individuals who prefer their outcome/input ratios to be less than the others being compared. These are people who don't mind being underrewarded.

Equity Sensitives are individuals who prefer outcome/input ratios to be equal. These people are concerned with obtaining rewards that they perceive to be fair in relation to what others are receiving.

Entitleds are individuals who prefer that their outcome/input ratios go above those of the others being compared. These people aren't worried by inequities and actually prefer situations in which they see themselves as overrewarded.

The purpose of this exercise is to assess your equity sensitivity.

Instructions

The five statements below ask what you would like your relationship to be within any organization. For each question, *divide* 10 points between the two answers (A and B) *by giving the most points to the answer that is most like you and the fewest points to the answer least like you.* You can give an equal number of points to A and B. You can make use of zeros if you like. Just be sure to use all 10 points on each question. (For instance, if statement A is completely appropriate and B is not at all appropriate, give A 10 points and B zero points. If A is somewhat appropriate and B is not completely appropriate, give A 7 points and B 3 points.) Place your points next to each letter.

In any organization where I might work . . .

I. It would be more important for me to:
   A. Get from the organization   _____
   B. Give to the organization   _____

2. It would be more important for me to:
   A. Help others   _____
   B. Watch out for my own good   _____

3. I would be more concerned about:
   A. What I received from the organization   _____
   B. What I contributed to the organization   _____

4. The hard work I would do should:
   A. Benefit the organization   _____
   B. Benefit me   _____

5. My personal philosophy in dealing with the organization would be:
   A. If you don't look out for yourself, nobody else will   _____
   B. It's better to give than to receive   _____

Calculate your total score by adding the points you allocated to the following items: 1B, 2A, 3B, 4A, and 5B. Total score = _____

Analysis & Interpretation

Your total will be between 0 and 50. If you scored less than 29, you are an Entitled; if your score was between 29 and 32, you are Equity Sensitive; and if your score was above 32, you are a Benevolent.

Questions for Discussion

1. To what extent are the results consistent with your self-perception? Explain.
2. Using the survey items as a foundation, how should managers try to motivate Benevolents, Equity Sensitives, and Entitleds? Discuss in detail.

R. C. Huseman, J. D. Hatfield, and E. W. Miles, "Test for Individual Perceptions of Job Equity: Some Preliminary Findings," *Perceptual and Motor Skills* 62 (1985), pp. 1055–1064. Copyright © 1985, Perceptual and Motor Skills. Reproduced with permission of the authors and publisher.

 group exercise

Applying the Job Characteristics Model

Objectives

1. To assess the motivating potential score (MPS) of several jobs.
2. To determine which core job characteristics need to be changed for each job.
3. To explore how you might redesign one of the jobs.

Introduction

The first step in applying the job characteristics model is to diagnose the work environment to determine if a performance problem is due to demotivating job characteristics. This can be accomplished by having employees complete the job diagnostic survey (JDS).* The JDS is a self-report instrument that assesses the extent to which a specific job possesses the five core job characteristics. With this instrument, it also is possible to calculate a motivating potential score for a job. The motivating potential score (MPS) is a summary index that represents the extent to which the job characteristics foster internal work motivation. Low scores indicate that an individual will not experience high intrinsic motivation from the job. Such a job is a prime candidate for job redesign. High scores reveal that a job is capable of stimulating intrinsic motivation and suggest that a performance problem is not due to demotivating job characteristics. The MPS is computed as follows:

$$\text{MPS} = \frac{\left(\begin{array}{c}\text{Skill} \\ \text{variety}\end{array} + \begin{array}{c}\text{Task} \\ \text{identity}\end{array} + \begin{array}{c}\text{Task} \\ \text{significance}\end{array}\right)}{23}$$
$$\times \text{ Autonomy}$$
$$\times \text{ Feedback}$$

Judging from this equation, which core job characteristic do you think is relatively more important in determining the motivational potential of a job? Because autonomy and feedback are not divisible by another number, low amounts of autonomy and feedback have a greater chance of lowering MPS than the job characteristics of skill variety, task identity, and task significance.

Since the JDS is a long questionnaire, we would like you to complete a subset of the instrument. This will enable you to calculate the MPS and to identify deficient job characteristics.

Instructions

Your instructor will divide the class into groups of four to six. Each group member will first assess the MPS of his or her current or former job and then will identify which core job characteristics need to be changed. Once each group member completes these tasks, the group will identify the job with the lowest MPS and devise a plan for redesigning it. The following steps should be used.

You should first complete the 12 items from the JDS. For each item, indicate whether it is an accurate or inaccurate description of your current or most recent job by selecting one number from the scale provided. Write your response in the space provided next to each item. After completing the JDS, use the scoring key to compute a total score for each of the core job characteristics.

1 = very inaccurate 5 = slightly accurate
2 = mostly inaccurate 6 = mostly accurate
3 = slightly inaccurate 7 = very accurate
4 = uncertain

_____ 1. Supervisors often let me know how well they think I am performing the job.

_____ 2. The job requires me to use a number of complex or high-level skills.

_____ 3. The job is arranged so that I have the chance to do an entire piece of work from beginning to end.

_____ 4. Just doing the work required by the job provides many chances for me to figure out how well I am doing.

_____ 5. The job is not simple and repetitive.

_____ 6. This job is one where a lot of other people can be affected by how well the work gets done.

_____ 7. The job does not deny me the chance to use my personal initiative or judgment in carrying out the work.

_____ 8. The job provides me the chance to completely finish the pieces of work I begin.

_____ 9. The job itself provides plenty of clues about whether or not I am performing well.

_____ 10. The job gives me considerable opportunity for independence and freedom in how I do the work.

_____ 11. The job itself is very significant or important in the broader scheme of things.

_____ 12. The supervisors and co-workers on this job almost always give me "feedback" about how well I am doing in my work.

Scoring Key

Compute the *average* of the two items that measure each job characteristic.

Skill variety (2 and 5)	_____
Task identity (3 and 8)	_____
Task significance (6 and 11)	_____
Autonomy (7 and 10)	_____
Feedback from job itself (4 and 9)	_____
Feedback from others (I and 12)	_____

Now you are ready to calculate the MPS. First, you need to compute a total score for the feedback job characteristic. This is done by computing the average of the job characteristics entitled "feedback from job itself" and "feedback from others." Second, use the MPS formula presented earlier to compute the MPS. Finally, use the JDS norms provided to interpret the relative status of the MPS and each individual job characteristic.

Once all group members have finished these activities, convene as a group to complete the exercise. Each group member should present his or her results and interpretations of the strengths and deficiencies of the job characteristics. Next, pick the job within the group that has the lowest MPS. Prior to redesigning this job, however, each group member needs more background information. The individual who works in the lowest MPS job should thus provide a thorough description of the job, including its associated tasks, responsibilities, and reporting relationships. A brief overview of the general working environment is also useful. With this information in hand, the group should now devise a detailed plan for how it would redesign the job.

Norms

	TYPE OF JOB			
	Professional/ Technical	Clerical	Sales	Service
Skill variety	5.4	4.0	4.8	5.0
Task Identity	5.1	4.7	4.4	4.7
Task significance	5.6	5.3	5.5	5.7
Autonomy	5.4	4.5	4.8	5.0
Feedback from job itself	5.1	4.6	5.4	5.1
Feedback from others	4.2	4.0	3.6	3.8
MPS	135	90	106	114

Questions for Discussion

1. Using the norms, which job characteristics are high, average, or low for the job being redesigned?
2. Which job characteristics did you change? Why?
3. How would you specifically redesign the job under consideration?

4. What would be the difficulties in implementing the job characteristics model in a large organization?

Source: R. Kreitner and A. Kinicki, *Organizational Behavior,* 5th ed. (Burr Ridge, IL: McGraw-Hill, 2001), pp. 265–267. Copyright © 2001 by The McGraw-Hill Companies, Inc. Used by permission.

*The complete JDS can be found in J. R. Hackman and G. R. Oldham, *Work Redesign* (Reading, MA: Addison-Wesley, 1980). The JDS and its norms were adapted from Hackman and Oldham, *Work Redesign,* pp. 280, 281, 317.

 ethical dilemma

Should I Ignore the Cheating?

You are taking a college course. The tests and quizzes are online through the class Web site. The professor gives you a 3-day window and you take the tests in your personal time. The professor has strict guidelines about cheating. At the beginning of the semester, he told all of you that the tests and quizzes will be timed so you will not have enough time to look the answers up in the book. You are in the computing commons taking one of the quizzes and notice a group of your classmates huddled around a computer. They are taking the quiz as well. One student is looking up the answers in the book, one is taking the quiz, and the other is recording the answers.

Solving the Dilemma

As a student, what would you do?

1. Immediately contact your professor about what is going on. It is unfair to the rest of your classmates if these three get away with cheating.
2. Form a similar test group of your own. The professor never specifically said you couldn't take the tests in groups.
3. Ignore the group's behavior and continue taking the test. You are sure these three will be caught eventually and at least you will know you *earned* your grade.
4. Invent other options. Discuss.

The Container Store

The Container Store was voted "best company to work for in America" twice and was runner-up two additional times. So what's the secret to hiring highly motivated people who believe that their company is America's best? First, you need good products. Employees are motivated when they know that the products they sell are top quality and desired by customers. Second, you have to empower workers to do everything possible to exceed customer expectations (even if that means giving a customer a driving lesson in the parking lot).

One of the cornerstones at the Container Store is "Hire Great People." According to top management, one great person is worth three (or maybe four) good people. In support, they cite famed home-run hitter Babe Ruth, who hit 56 homers in one year; the second-best player hit only 13. The challenge is to find and keep great workers. The Container Store does this by hiring part-time people and then motivating the best of them to stay with the company.

Employees provide astonishing levels of customer service. For example, one worker in Houston loaned her car to a stranded customer! How exactly does the organization encourage this level of outstanding service? By successfully implementing numerous motivational principles. Wages are above the industry standard. Mistakes are tolerated and viewed as learning opportunities. Employees are continually encouraged to go the extra mile to please customers. Throughout the organization, emphasis is placed on a core set of values such as integrity, honesty, and open communication. Outstanding employees are recognized for their contributions, and the social atmosphere is one of "family." The importance of the job environment is recognized, including the quality of co-workers. People like to work with others who are equally motivated and committed.

Employees are cross-trained for a variety of jobs in an effort to prepare them to become managers when openings are available. Stores make use of daily coaching to help employees understand and implement managerial objectives. Through open communication channels, employees learn that good work will be amply rewarded. The communication system includes peer-to-peer communication so that everyone helps everybody else to do the best job possible.

The Container Store employs a humanistic approach coupled with employee empowerment, strong corporate values, cross-training, and open communication to motivate employees. As a result, employees are committed to one of the best companies to work for in America.

Discussion Questions

1. List Maslow's hierarchy of needs. Does the Container store help satisfy employees' needs in the workplace? Provide evidence to support your response.
2. What are the two factors in Herzberg's two-factor theory? Provide examples of each of these factors at the Container Store.
3. Equity theory focuses on employee perceptions of how fairly they think they are being treated compared to how others are treated. Identify the inputs and the outputs that employees use to determine equity perceptions at the Container Store.

chapter 13

Groups & Teams
Increasing Cooperation, Reducing Conflict

Major Questions You Should Be Able to Answer

13.1 Groups versus Teams
Major Question: How is one collection of workers different from any other?

13.2 Stages of Group & Team Development
Major Question: How does a group evolve into a team?

13.3 Building Effective Teams
Major Question: How can I as a manager build an effective team?

13.4 Managing Conflict
Major Question: Since conflict is a part of life, what should a manager know about it in order to deal successfully with it?

Dealing with Disagreements

Even if you're at the top of your game as a manager, working with groups and teams of people—the subject of this chapter—will now and then put you in the middle of disagreements, sometimes even destructive conflict. How can you deal with it?

There are five conflict-handling styles, or techniques, a manager can use for handling disagreements with individuals, as follows:[1]

- **Avoiding—"Maybe the problem will go away."** *Avoiding* involves ignoring or suppressing a conflict. Avoidance is appropriate for trivial issues, when emotions are high and a cooling-off period is needed, or when the cost of confrontation outweighs the benefits of resolving the conflict. It is not appropriate for difficult or worsening problems.

   The benefit of this approach is that it buys time in unfolding and ambiguous situations. The weakness is that it provides only a temporary fix and sidesteps the underlying problem.

- **Accommodating—"Let's do it your way."** An accommodating manager is also known as a "smoothing" or "obliging" manager. *Accommodating* is allowing the desires of the other party to prevail. As one writer describes it, "An obliging [accommodating] person neglects his or her own concern to satisfy the concern of the other party."[2] Accommodating may be an appropriate conflict-handling strategy when it's possible to eventually get something in return or when the issue isn't important to you. It's not appropriate for complex or worsening problems.

   The advantage of accommodating is that it encourages cooperation. The weakness is that once again it's only a temporary fix that fails to confront the underlying problem.

- **Forcing—"You have to do it my way."** Also known as "dominating," *forcing* is simply ordering an outcome, when a manager relies on his or her formal authority and power to resolve a conflict. Forcing is appropriate when an unpopular solution must be implemented and when it's not important that others be committed to your viewpoint.

   The advantage of forcing is speed: It can get results quickly. The disadvantage is that in the end it doesn't resolve personal conflict—if anything, it aggravates it by breeding hurt feelings and resentments.

- **Compromising—"Let's split the difference."** In *compromising,* both parties give up something in order to gain something. Compromise is appropriate when both sides have opposite goals or possess equal power. But compromise isn't workable when it is used so often that it doesn't achieve results—for example, continual failure to meet production deadlines.

   The benefit of compromise is that it is a democratic process that seems to have no losers. However, since so many people approach compromise situations with a win-lose attitude, they may be disappointed and feel cheated.

- **Collaborating—"Let's cooperate to reach a win-win solution that benefits both of us."** *Collaborating* strives to devise solutions that benefit both parties. Collaboration is appropriate for complex issues plagued by misunderstanding. It is inappropriate for resolving conflicts rooted in opposing value systems.

   The strength of collaborating is its longer lasting effect: it deals with the underlying problem, not just its symptoms. Its weakness is that it's very time-consuming. Nevertheless, collaboration is the best approach for dealing with groups and teams of people.

For Discussion Which kind of conflict-handling style are you most likely to use, based on your experience? Which kind do you feel comfortable trying?

forecast

What's Ahead in This Chapter

In this chapter, we consider groups versus teams and discuss different kinds of teams. We describe how groups evolve into teams and discuss how managers can build effective teams. We also consider the nature of conflict, both good and bad.

13.1 GROUPS VERSUS TEAMS

> ✳ **major question**
>
> **How is one collection of workers different from any other?**

THE BIG PICTURE

Teamwork promises to be a cornerstone of future management. A team is different from a group. A group typically is management-directed, a team self-directed. Groups may be formal, created to do productive work, or informal, created for friendship. Work teams, which engage in collective work requiring coordinated effort, may be organized according to four basic purposes: advice, production, project, and action. Two types of teams are quality circles and self-managed teams.

The year 2006 was not a good one for American men's sports teams on the world stage. The U.S. soccer team failed to muster one victory at the World Cup. The U.S. baseball team was defeated by Mexico, Korea, and Canada at the World Baseball Classic and did not even make it to the semifinals. And at the World Basketball Championship, the U.S. men's team—in a sport invented by Americans—failed for the third straight year to bring home the gold.[3] What went wrong?

Take the basketball team, which despite having such NBA stars as Dwyane Wade and LeBron James nevertheless lost to Greece 101–95 in the semifinals. Team USA players had been together for more than a year, but, says one account, "the lack of experience—and familiarity with each other—was glaringly obvious against a Greek squad that has been together three years."[4] But perhaps there was more to it than that. "Our best male athletes have regressed as team players—as *teammates,*" writes Michael Sokolove. "A couple of decades of free agency and lavish salaries freed the players from the grips of owners but also unbound them from one another. . . . If our greatest young athletes don't care enough about one another to commit to effort and team play, that can't be a good thing."[5]

More Teamwork: The Change Today's Employees Need to Make

"You lead today by building teams and placing others first," says General Electric CEO Jeffrey Immelt. "It's not about you."[6] According to management philosopher Peter Drucker, tomorrow's organizations will not only be flatter and information-based but also organized around teamwork.[7] "We have this mythology in America about the lone genius," says Tom Kelley, general manager of Ideo, an industrial design company in Palo Alto, California, that helped create the Apple mouse and the Palm V handheld computer. "We love to personify things. But Michelangelo didn't paint the Sistine Chapel alone, and Edison didn't invent the light bulb alone."[8]

There are many reasons why teamwork is now the cornerstone of progressive management, as the table opposite shows. *(See Table 13.1.)* Regardless, when you take a job in an organization, the chances are you won't be working as a lone genius or even as a lone wolf. You'll be working with others in situations demanding teamwork.

table 13.1

WHY TEAMWORK IS IMPORTANT

The improvements	Example
Increased productivity	At one GE factory, teamwork resulted in a workforce that was 20% more productive than comparable GE workforces elsewhere.
Increased speed	Guidant Corp., maker of life-saving medical devices, halved the time it took to get products to market.
Reduced costs	Boeing used teamwork to develop the 777 at costs far less than normal.
Improved quality	Westinghouse used teamwork to improve quality performance in its truck and trailer division and within its electronic components division.
Reduced destructive internal competition	Men's Wearhouse fired a salesman who wasn't sharing walk-in customer traffic, and total clothing sales volume among all salespeople increased significantly.
Improved workplace cohesiveness	Cisco Systems told executives they would gain or lose 30% of their bonuses based on how well they worked with peers and in 3 years had record profits.

Groups & Teams: How Do They Differ?

Aren't a group of people and a team of people the same thing? By and large, no. One is a collection of people, the other a powerful unit of collective performance. One is typically management-directed, the other self-directed.

Consider the differences.

What a Group Is: Collection of People Performing as Individuals
A **group** is defined as two or more freely interacting individuals who share collective norms, share collective goals, and have a common identity.[9] A group is different from a crowd, a transitory collection of people who don't interact with one another, such as a crowd gathering on a sidewalk to watch a fire. And it is different from an organization, such as a labor union, which is so large that members also don't interact.[10]

An example of a work group would be a collection of, say, 10 employees meeting to exchange information about various companies' policies on wages and hours.

What a Team Is: Collection of People with Common Commitment
McKinsey & Company management consultants Jon R. Katzenbach and Douglas K. Smith say it is a mistake to use the terms *group* and *team* interchangeably. Successful teams, they say, tend to take on a life of their own. Thus, a **team** is defined as a small group of people with complementary skills who are committed to a common purpose, performance goals, and approach for which they hold themselves mutually accountable.[11] "The essence of a team is common commitment," say Katzenbach and Smith. "Without it, groups perform as individuals; with it, they become a powerful unit of collective performance."[12]

An example of a team would be a collection of 2–10 employees who are studying industry pay scales with the goal of making recommendations for adjusting pay grades within their own company.

Formal versus Informal Groups

Groups may be either formal or informal.

- **Formal groups—created to do productive work. A *formal group* is a group established to do something productive for the organization and is headed by a leader.** A formal group may be a division, a department, a work group, or a committee. It may be permanent or temporary. In general, people are assigned to them according to their skills and the organization's requirements.

- **Informal groups—created for friendship. An *informal group* is a group formed by people seeking friendship and has no officially appointed leader, although a leader may emerge from the membership.** An informal group may be simply a collection of friends who hang out with one another, such as those who take coffee breaks together, or it may be as organized as a prayer breakfast, a bowling team, a service club, or other voluntary organization.

What's important for you as a manager to know is that informal groups can advance or undercut the plans of formal groups. The formal organization may make efforts, say, to speed up the plant assembly line or to institute workplace reforms. But these attempts may be sabotaged through the informal networks of workers who meet and gossip over lunch pails and after-work beers.[13]

However, interestingly, informal groups can also be highly productive—even more so than formal groups.

Example

Informal Groups Can Help with Informal Learning: Worker Chitchat "Is Not Goofing Off, It's Training"

As a manager, what would you think when you saw employees making brief exchanges near the coffeepot? "The assumption was made," said Barry Blyston, director of training at a plant in Wendell, North Carolina, where managers wondered how to stop workers from gathering so often in the cafeteria, "that this was chitchat, talking about their golf game. But there was a whole lot of work activity."[14]

Or so a 2-year $1.6 million study by the Center for Workplace Development discovered.[15] At Siemens Power Transmission and Distribution, as well as companies such as Motorola and Boeing, the study found that 70% of workplace learning is informal, despite the $60 billion

Talking it out. Ever worked in a job in which you got a lot of informal training through conversations over coffee?

organizations spend on formal training programs every year.[16]

Your Call

Following the study, Siemens managers placed overhead projectors and empty pads of paper in the lunchroom to facilitate informal meetings. They also alerted supervisors about the informal gatherings. What other things would you do to encourage employees to informally learn from each other?

Work Teams for Four Purposes: Advice, Production, Project, & Action

The names given to different kinds of teams can be bewildering. We have identified some important ones. *(See Table 13.2.)*

table 13.2

VARIOUS TYPES OF TEAMS

These teams are not mutually exclusive. Work teams, for instance, may also be self-managed, cross-functional, or virtual.

Cross-functional team	Members composed of people from different departments, such as sales and production, pursuing a common objective
Problem-solving team	Knowledgeable workers who meet as a temporary team to solve a specific problem and then disband
Quality circle	Volunteers of workers and supervisors who meet intermittently to discuss workplace and quality-related problems
Self-managed team	Workers are trained to do all or most of the jobs in a work unit, have no direct supervisor, and do their own day-to-day supervision
Top-management team	Members consist of the CEO, president, and top department heads and work to help the organization achieve its mission and goals
Virtual team	Members interact by computer network to collaborate on projects
Work team	Members engage in collective work requiring coordinated effort; purpose of team is advice, production, project, or action *(see text discussion)*

You will probably benefit most by understanding the various types of work teams distinguished according to their purpose. Work teams, which engage in collective work requiring coordinated effort, are of four types, which may be identified according to their basic purpose: *advice, production, project,* or *action.*[17]

1. Advice Teams *Advice teams* are created to broaden the information base for managerial decisions. Examples are committees, review panels, advisory councils, employee involvement groups, and quality circles (as we'll discuss).

2. Production Teams *Production teams* are responsible for performing day-to-day operations. Examples are mining teams, flight-attendant crews, maintenance crews, assembly teams, data processing groups, and manufacturing crews.

3. Project Teams *Project teams* work to do creative problem solving, often by applying the specialized knowledge of members of a **cross-functional team, which is staffed with specialists pursuing a common objective.** Examples are task forces, research groups, planning teams, architect teams, engineering teams, and development teams.

4. Action Teams *Action teams* work to accomplish tasks that require people with (1) specialized training and (2) a high degree of coordination, as on a baseball team, with specialized athletes acting in coordination. Examples are hospital surgery teams, airline cockpit crews, mountain-climbing expeditions, police SWAT teams, and labor contract negotiating teams.

Self-Managed Teams: Workers with Own Administrative Oversight

To give you an idea of how teams work, consider self-managed teams. These kinds of teams have emerged out of **quality circles,** **which consist of small groups of volunteers or workers and supervisors who meet intermittently to discuss workplace- and quality-related problems.** Typically a group of 10–12 people will meet for 60–90 minutes once or twice a month, with management listening to presentations and the important payoff for members usually being the chance for meaningful participation and skills training.[18]

In many places, such as the Texas Instruments electronics factory in Malaysia, the quality circles have evolved into a system made up almost entirely of self-managed teams, with routine activities formerly performed by supervisors now performed by team members. "Self-managed" does not, however, mean simply turning workers loose to do their own thing. **Self-managed teams are defined as groups of workers who are given administrative oversight for their task domains.** Administrative oversight involves delegated activities such as planning, scheduling, monitoring, and staffing. Nearly 70% of *Fortune* 1000 companies have created self-managed work teams.[19]

Self-managed teams are an outgrowth of a blend of behavioral science and management practice.[20] The goal has been to increase productivity and employee quality of work life. The traditional clear-cut distinction between manager and managed is being blurred as nonmanagerial employees are delegated greater authority and granted increased autonomy.

A Volvo team. This Volvo assembly plant in Torslanda, Sweden, makes cars by using team-based portable assembly platforms rather than a single constantly moving assembly line. Volvo puts the names of team members on every engine they build to instill pride in their work. Although teams have been used since the Egyptians built the pyramids, the idea didn't really gain currency in the workplace until it was promoted by management theorists such as Frederick Taylor and Douglas McGregor. In the 1930s, teams were adopted in factories to streamline manufacturing. In the 1960s, teams gained popularity as ways to improve worker satisfaction. Ironically, Volvo was acquired in 1999 by the company that was instrumental in using the assembly-line concept in manufacturing—Ford Motor Company.

In creating self-managed teams, both technical and organizational redesign are necessary. Self-managed teams may require special technology. Volvo's team-based auto assembly plant, for example, relies on portable assembly platforms rather than traditional assembly lines. Structural redesign of the organization must take place because self-managed teams are an integral part of the organization, not patched onto it, as is the case with quality circles. Personnel and reward systems need to be adapted to encourage teamwork. Staffing decisions may shift from management to team members who hire their own co-workers. Individual bonuses must give way to team bonuses. Supervisory development workshops are needed to teach managers to be facilitators rather than order givers.[21] Finally, extensive team training is required to help team members learn more about technical details, the business as a whole, and how to be team players.[22] ●

Practical Action

The Challenge of Managing Virtual Teams: Reaching across Time & Space

Once upon a time, managers subscribed to the so-called Fifty-Foot Rule—namely, "If people are more than 50 feet apart, they are not likely to collaborate." That is no longer true in today's era of virtual teams. Virtual teams are groups of people who use information technology—computers and telecommunications—to collaborate across space, time, and organizational boundaries.[23]

Teams are generally defined as consisting of 2–16 people. But virtual collaborations may be even larger. For instance, NCR Corp. created a virtual "team" (group) of more than 1,000 people working at 17 locations to develop a next-generation computer system. Using a high-bandwidth audio-video-data telecommunications network, members completed the project on budget and ahead of schedule.[24] And Hong Kong–based Cathay Pacific Airlines designed a network, called GalaCXy, appropriate for a company where employees are never in one place for very long but need to be able to communicate intelligently wherever they go. "GalaCXy users can set up meetings with each other without calling to check one another's schedules," says one account. "They can access one another's schedules to see when they're available and then suggest a time by e-mail."[25]

As technology has made it easier for workers to function from remote places, it has posed challenges for managers. Following are some suggestions for managing virtual workers, especially those working at home:[26]

- **Take baby steps.** When trying out virtual arrangements with new employees, take it slow. Let them show they can handle the challenge.

- **State expectations.** Nip problems in the bud by letting virtual workers know what you expect from them. With home-based workers, for example, go over the terms of your virtual arrangement—whether, for example, you want them to carry an office cell phone—and tell them if there are specific ways you want the job done.

- **Write it down.** Record directions, project changes, and updates in writing, by sending an e-mail or fax or using Web-based services that allow for sharing calendars and tracking projects.

- **Communicate.** Whether your virtual workers take an occasional day away or work from home full-time, make sure they're reachable during business hours. Phone call, e-mail, fax, and chat all work well—but they have to be able to reach you, too.

- **Manage by results.** Focus on what's accomplished, not whether your employee is working from her patio or at 10 P.M. Set interim deadlines on projects and stick to them.

- **Meet regularly.** Human contact still matters. When possible, schedule periodic and regular meetings at which all team members can discuss current projects, and telecommuters can catch up on office gossip. Fly out-of-towners in at least quarterly, so they can develop working friendships with your in-office staff.

13.2 STAGES OF GROUP & TEAM DEVELOPMENT

 major question How does a group evolve into a team?

THE BIG PICTURE
Groups may evolve into teams by going through five stages of development: forming, storming, norming, performing, and adjourning.

Elsewhere in this book we have described how products and organizations go through stages of development. Groups and teams go through the same thing. One theory proposes five stages of development: *forming, storming, norming, performing, adjourning.*[27] *(See Figure 13.1.)* Let us consider these stages in which groups may evolve into teams—bearing in mind that the stages aren't necessarily of the same duration or intensity.

figure 13.1

FIVE STAGES OF GROUP AND TEAM DEVELOPMENT

Hot Seat DVD Applications:
Working in Teams: Cross-Functional Dysfunction

Stage I: Forming—"Why Are We Here?"

The first stage, *forming,* **is the process of getting oriented and getting acquainted.** This stage is characterized by a high degree of uncertainty as members try to break the ice and figure out who is in charge and what the group's goals are. For example, if you were to become part of a team that is to work on a class project, the question for you as an individual would be "How do I fit in here?" For the group, the question is "Why are we here?"[28]

At this point, mutual trust is low, and there is a good deal of holding back to see who takes charge and how. If the formal leader (such as the class instructor or a supervisor) does not assert his or her authority, an emergent leader will eventually step in to fill the group's need for leadership and direction.

What the Leader Should Do Leaders typically mistake this honeymoon period as a mandate for permanent control, but later problems may force a leadership change. During this stage, leaders should allow time for people to become acquainted and socialize.

Stage 2: Storming—"Why Are We Fighting Over Who Does What & Who's in Charge?"

The second stage, *storming,* **is characterized by the emergence of individual personalities and roles and conflicts within the group.** For you as an individual, the question is "What's my role here?" For the group, the issue is "Why are we fighting over who does what and who's in charge?" This stage may be of short duration or painfully long, depending on the goal clarity and the commitment and maturity of the members.

This is a time of testing. Individuals test the leader's policies and assumptions as they try to determine how they fit into the power structure.[29] Subgroups take shape, and subtle forms of rebellion, such as procrastination, occur. Many groups stall in stage 2 because power politics may erupt into open rebellion.

What the Leader Should Do   In this stage, the leader should encourage members to suggest ideas, voice disagreements, and work through their conflicts about tasks and goals.

Stage 3: Norming—"Can We Agree on Roles & Work as a Team?"

In the third stage, *norming,* **conflicts are resolved, close relationships develop, and unity and harmony emerge.** For individuals, the main issue is "What do the others expect me to do?" For the group, the issue is "Can we agree on roles and work as a team?" Note, then, that the *group* may now evolve into a *team.*

Teams set guidelines related to what members will do together and how they will do it. The teams consider such matters as attendance at meetings, being late, and missing assignments as well as how members treat one another.

Groups that make it through stage 2 generally do so because a respected member other than the leader challenges the group to resolve its power struggles so something can be accomplished. Questions about authority are resolved through unemotional, matter-of-fact group discussion. A feeling of team spirit is experienced because members believe they have found their proper roles. **Group cohesiveness, a "we feeling" binding group members together,** is the principal by-product of stage 3. (We discuss cohesiveness next, in Section 13.3.)

What the Leader Should Do   This stage generally does not last long. Here the leader should emphasize unity and help identify team goals and values.

Stage 4: Performing—"Can We Do the Job Properly?"

In *performing,* **members concentrate on solving problems and completing the assigned task.** For individuals, the question here is "How can I best perform my role?" For the group/team, the issue is "Can we do the job properly?"

What the Leader Should Do   During this stage, the leader should allow members the empowerment they need to work on tasks.

Stage 5: Adjourning—"Can We Help Members Transition Out?"

In the final stage, *adjourning,* **members prepare for disbandment.** Having worked so hard to get along and get something done, many members feel a compelling sense of loss. For the individual, the question now is "What's next?" For the team, the issue is "Can we help members transition out?"

What the Leader Should Do   The leader can help ease the transition by rituals celebrating "the end" and "new beginnings." Parties, award ceremonies, graduations, or mock funerals can provide the needed punctuation at the end of a significant teamwork project. The leader can emphasize valuable lessons learned in group dynamics to prepare everyone for future group and team efforts. ●

13.3 BUILDING EFFECTIVE TEAMS

> ◈ **major question** How can I as a manager build an effective team?

THE BIG PICTURE

Two types of change are reactive and proactive. Forces for change may consist of forces outside the organization—demographic characteristics, market changes, technological advancements, and social and political pressures. Or they may be forces inside the organization—employee problems and managers' behavior.

Within an organization, you may hear managers loosely (and incorrectly) use the word *team* to describe any collection of people that have been pulled together. But because traditional managers are often reluctant to give up control, no thought is given to providing the "team" (really just a group) with training and support. That is, no attempt is made to sharpen communication skills, reward innovation, or encourage independence without group members running away and losing control.[30]

Thus, as a manager, the first thing you have to realize is that building a high-performance team is going to require some work. But the payoff will be a stronger, better-performing work unit.

The considerations in building a group into an effective team are (1) *performance goals and feedback,* (2) *motivation through mutual accountability,* (3) *size,* (4) *roles,* (5) *norms,* (6) *cohesiveness,* and (7) *groupthink.*

I. Performance Goals & Feedback

As an individual, you no doubt prefer to have measurable goals and to have feedback about your performance. The same is true with teams. Teams are not just collections of individuals. They are individuals organized for a collective purpose. That purpose needs to be defined in terms of specific, measurable performance goals with continual feedback to tell team members how well they are doing.

An obvious example are the teams you see on television at Indianapolis or Daytona Beach during automobile racing. When the driver guides the race car off the track to make a pit stop, a team of people swarm over the wall and quickly jack up the car to change tires, refuel the tank, and clean the windshield—all operating in a matter of seconds. The performance goals are to have the car back on the track as quickly as possible. The number of seconds of elapsed time—and the driver's place among competitors once back in the race—tells them how well they are doing.

2. Motivation through Mutual Accountability

Do you work harder when you're alone or when you're in a group? When clear performance goals exist, when the work is considered meaningful, when members believe their efforts matter, and when they don't feel they are being exploited by others, this kind of culture supports teamwork.[31] Being mutually accountable to other members of the team rather than to a supervisor makes members feel mutual trust and commitment—a key part in motivating members for team effort. To bring about this team culture, managers often allow teams to do the hiring of new members.

Learning teamwork from a NASCAR pit crew. Randy Darcy, chief technical officer for cereal maker General Mills, was given the challenge of cutting $1 billion out of the company's supply chain, Darcy's approach was to adapt lessons in efficiency and high performance learned elsewhere—watching Air Force mechanics fix Stealth bombers, participating in predawn raids with a U.S. Marshals Service SWAT team, and getting time- and money-saving ideas by observing a NASCAR pit crew. Learning how the pit crew was able to work with blinding speed through better team organization, the cereal company was able to cut the time workers changed a production line for a Betty Crocker product from 4.5 hours to just 12 minutes.

3. Size: Small Teams or Large Teams?

Size, which is often determined by the team's purpose, can be important in affecting members' commitment and performance. Whereas in some flat-organization structures groups may consist of 30 or more employees, teams seem to range in size from 2–16 people, with those of 5–12 generally being the most workable and 5–6 considered optimal.[32] A survey of 400 workplace team members in the United States found that the average team consisted of 10 members, with 8 being the most common size.[33]

Small and large teams have different characteristics, although the number of members is, to be sure, somewhat arbitrary.[34]

Small Teams: 2–9 Members for Better Interaction & Morale
Teams with 9 or fewer members have two advantages:

- **Better interaction.** Members are better able to interact, share information, ask questions of one another, and coordinate activities than are those in larger teams. In particular, teams with five or fewer offer more opportunity for personal discussion and participation.

- **Better morale.** They are better able to see the worth of their individual contributions and thus are more highly committed and satisfied. Members are less apt to feel inhibited in participating. Team leaders are subject to fewer demands and are able to be more informal.[35]

However, small teams also have some disadvantages:

- **Fewer resources.** With fewer hands, there will be fewer resources—less knowledge, experience, skills, and abilities to apply to the team's tasks.

- **Possibly less innovation.** A group that's too small may show less creativity and boldness because of the effect of peer pressure.

- **Unfair work distribution.** Because of fewer resources and less specialization, there may be an uneven distribution of the work among members.

Large Teams: 10–16 Members for More Resources & Division of Labor
Teams with 10–16 members have different advantages over small teams. (Again, the numbers are somewhat arbitrary.)

- **More resources.** Larger teams have more resources to draw on: more knowledge, experience, skills, abilities, and perhaps time. These will give them more leverage to help them realize the team's goals.

- **Division of labor.** In addition, a large team can take advantage of ***division of labor,*** **in which the work is divided into particular tasks that are assigned to particular workers.**

Yet bigness has its disadvantages:

- **Less interaction.** With more members, there is less interaction, sharing of information, and coordinating of activities. Leaders may be more formal and autocratic, since members in teams this size are apt to be more tolerant of autocratic leadership. The larger size may also lead to the formation of cliques.

- **Lower morale.** Because people are less able to see the worth of their individual contributions, they show less commitment and satisfaction and more turnover and absenteeism. They also express more disagreements and turf struggles and make more demands on leaders.

- **Social loafing.** The larger the size, the more likely performance is to drop, owing to the phenomenon known as ***social loafing,*** **the tendency of people to exert less effort when working in groups than when working alone.**[36]

Team Size: And the Magic Number Is . . .

The subject of team size has become a topic of fascination, according to two scholars, because "in the past decade, research on team effectiveness has burgeoned as teams have become increasingly common in organizations of all kinds."[37] What's the right number of people for a team? Various companies have various rules. At Amazon.com, there is a "two-pizza rule"—namely, if a team can't be fed by two pizzas, it's too large.[38] Other companies have their own ideal sizes: Titeflex, 6–10 people; EDS, 8–12; Johnsonville Foods, 12; Volvo, 20. Microsoft Corp. felt the optimal size for a software-development team was 8.[39]

J. Richard Hackman, Harvard professor of social and organizational psychology, thinks there should be no more than 6—the maximum he will allow for students forming project groups.[40] In 1970, Hackman and colleague Neil Vidmar set out to discover the perfect size, asking various teams large and small whether their number was too large or too small for the task. The optimal number: 4.6.[41]

Size is not the only consideration, however. For instance, says Wharton management professor Katherine J. Klein, the nature of the team's task is key because it defines the type of skills you are looking for and the type of coordination necessary.[42]

Your Call

What's been your experience, if any, with team size? At what point does adding members begin to hurt a team's performance as people become less motivated and group coordination becomes more difficult?

4. Roles: How Team Members Are Expected to Behave

Group Exercises:
Identifying Task and Maintenance Roles within Groups

A *role* is a socially determined expectation of how an individual should behave in a specific position. As a team member, your role is to play a part in helping the team reach its goals. Members develop their roles based on the expectations of the team, of the organization, and of themselves, and they may do different things. You, for instance, might be a team leader. Others might do some of the work tasks. Still others might communicate with other teams.

Two types of team roles are task and maintenance.[43]

Self-Assessment Exercise:
Team Roles Preference Scale

Task Roles: Getting the Work Done A *task role,* or *task-oriented role,* **consists of behavior that concentrates on getting the team's tasks done.** Task roles keep the team on track and get the work done. If you stand up in a team meeting and say, "What is the real issue here? We don't seem to be getting anywhere," you are performing a task role.

Examples: Coordinators, who pull together ideas and suggestions; orienters, who keep teams headed toward their stated goals; initiators, who suggest new goals or ideas; and energizers, who prod people to move along or accomplish more are all playing task roles.

Maintenance Roles: Keeping the Team Together A *maintenance role,* or *relationship-oriented role,* **consists of behavior that fosters constructive relationships among team members.** Maintenance roles focus on keeping team members. If someone at a team meeting says, "Let's hear from those who oppose this plan," he or she is playing a maintenance role.

Examples: Encouragers, who foster group solidarity by praising various viewpoints; standard setters, who evaluate the quality of group processes; harmonizers, who mediate conflict through reconciliation or humor; and compromisers, who help resolve conflict by meeting others "halfway."

5. Norms: Unwritten Rules for Team Members

Norms are more encompassing than roles. ***Norms* are general guidelines or rules of behavior that most group or team members follow.** Norms point up the boundaries between acceptable and unacceptable behavior.[44] Although norms are typically unwritten and seldom discussed openly, they have a powerful influence on group and organizational behavior.[45]

Example

Team Norms: A Steelmaker Treats Workers Like Owners

When the electrical grid at Nucor Corp.'s steelmaking plant in Hickman, Arkansas, failed, electricians drove or flew in from other Nucor plants as far away as Alabama and North Carolina. No supervisor asked them to do so, nor was there any direct financial incentive for them to blow their weekends to help out. The electricians were following team norms. They came because, as a *BusinessWeek* article states, "Nucor's flattened hierarchy and emphasis on pushing power to the front line lead its employees to adopt the mindset of owner-operators."[46]

Nucor's close-knit culture is the outgrowth of former CEO F. Kenneth Iverson's insight that employees would make extraordinary efforts if they were treated with respect, given real power, and rewarded richly. Instead of following the typical command-and-control model typical of most American businesses in recent decades, Nucor executives motivate their front-line people by "talking to them, listening to them, taking a risk on their ideas, and accepting the occasional failure," says *BusinessWeek*.

Good work is rewarded—production of defect-free steel can triple a worker's pay—but bad work is penalized, with employees losing bonuses they normally would have made. Executive pay is tied to team building, with bonuses tied not just to the performance of a particular plant but to the entire corporation's performance. There is not only healthy competition among facilities and shifts but also cooperation and idea-sharing. The result: Nucor is highly profitable, producing a 387% return to shareholders in the past 5 years.

Your Call

Can you think of any kind of businesses in which Nucor's model for strengthening team norms would not work very well? Could American manufacturing companies, automakers, and certain airlines make a comeback if their work and pay rules were made to copy Nucor's?

Why Norms Are Enforced: Four Reasons Norms tend to be enforced by group or team members for four reasons:[47]

- **To help the group survive—"Don't do anything that will hurt us."** Norms are enforced to help the group, team, or organization survive.

  Example: The manager of your team or group might compliment you because you've made sure it has the right emergency equipment.

- **To clarify role expectations—"You have to go along to get along."** Norms are also enforced to help clarify or simplify role expectations.

  Example: At one time, new members of Congress wanting to buck the system by which important committee appointments were given to those with the most seniority were advised to "go along to get along"—go along with the rules in order to get along in their congressional careers.

- **To help individuals avoid embarrassing situations—"Don't call attention to yourself."** Norms are enforced to help group or team members avoid embarrassing themselves.

Special norms. Enterprise Rent-A-Car, the largest and most prosperous car-rental company in the United States (more than Hertz and Avis), operates on the principle that "If you take care of your customers and employees, the bottom line will take care of itself." In a 2006 survey, 80% of customers said they were "completely satisfied" with their Enterprise rental—which *FORTUNE* magazine calls "an extraordinary score."

Examples: You might be ridiculed by fellow team members for dominating the discussion during a report to top management ("Be a team player, not a show-off"). Or you might be told not to discuss religion or politics with customers, whose views might differ from yours.

- **To emphasize the group's important values and identity— "We're known for being special."** Finally, norms are enforced to emphasize the group, team, or organization's central values or to enhance its unique identity.

Examples: Nordstrom's department store chain emphasizes the great lengths to which it goes in customer service. Every year a college gives an award to the instructor whom students vote best teacher.

6. Cohesiveness: The Importance of Togetherness

Another important characteristic of teams is *cohesiveness,* **the tendency of a group or team to stick together.** This is the familiar sense of togetherness or "we-ness" you feel, for example, when you're a member of a volleyball team, a fraternity or a sorority, or a company's sales force.

Managers can stimulate cohesiveness by allowing people on work teams to pick their own teammates, allowing off-the-job social events, and urging team members to recognize and appreciate each other's contributions to the team goal.[48] Cohesiveness is also achieved by keeping teams small, making sure performance standards are clear and accepted, and following the tips in the following table. *(See Table 13.3.)*

table 13.3

WHAT MANAGERS CAN DO TO ENHANCE TEAM COHESIVENESS

• Keep the team relatively small	• Regularly update and clarify the team's goals
• Strive for a favorable public image to increase the status and prestige of belonging	• Give every group member a vital "piece of the action"
• Encourage interaction and cooperation	• Channel each team member's special talents toward the common goals
• Emphasize members' common characteristics and interests	• Recognize and equitably reinforce each member's contributions
• Point out environmental threats— e.g., competitors' achievements—to rally the team	• Frequently remind group members they need each other to get the job done

7. Groupthink: When Peer Pressure Discourages "Thinking Outside the Box"

Cohesiveness isn't always good. An undesirable by-product that may occur, according to psychologist **Irvin Janis**, is *groupthink*—**a cohesive group's blind unwillingness to consider alternatives.** In this phenomenon, group or team members are friendly and tight-knit, but they are unable to think "outside the box." Their "strivings for unanimity override their motivation to realistically appraise alternative courses of action," says Janis.[49]

The word "groupthink" regained some prominence in mid-2004 when the Senate Intelligence Committee said the U.S. invasion of Iraq had occurred because too many people in the government tended to think alike and failed to challenge basic assumptions about Iraq's weapons capability.[50] It cannot be said, however, that group opinion is always risky. Indeed, financial writer James Surowiecki, author of *The Wisdom of Crowds,* argues that "Under the right circumstances, groups are remarkably intelligent, and are often smarter than the smartest people in them."[51] As evidence, he cites how groups have been used to predict the election of the President of the United States, find lost submarines, and correct the spread on a sporting event.

Symptoms of Groupthink   How do you know that you're in a group or team that is suffering from groupthink? Some symptoms:[52]

- **Invulnerability, inherent morality, and stereotyping of opposition.** Because of feelings of invulnerability, group members have the illusion that nothing can go wrong, breeding excessive optimism and risk taking. Members may also be so assured of the rightness of their actions that they ignore the ethical implications of their decisions. These beliefs are helped along by stereotyped views of the opposition, which leads the group to underestimate its opponents.

- **Rationalization and self-censorship.** Rationalizing protects the pet assumptions underlying the group's decisions from critical questions. Self-censorship also stifles critical debate. It is especially hard to argue with success, of course. But if enough key people, such as outside analysts, had challenged the energy giant Enron when it seemed to be flying high, it might not have led to the largest bankruptcy in corporate history.

- **Illusion of unanimity, peer pressure, and mindguards.** The illusion of unanimity is another way of saying that silence by a member is interpreted to mean consent. But if people do disagree, peer pressure leads other members to question the loyalty of the dissenters. In addition, in a groupthink situation there may exist people who might be called *mindguards*—self-appointed protectors against adverse information.

- **Groupthink versus "the wisdom of crowds."** Groupthink is characterized by a pressure to conform that often leads members with different ideas to censor themselves—the opposite of collective wisdom, says James Surowiecki, in which "each person in the group is offering his or her best independent forecast. It's not at all about compromise or consensus."[53]

The Results of Groupthink: Decision-Making Defects   Groups with a moderate amount of cohesiveness tend to produce better decisions than groups with low or high cohesiveness. Members of highly cohesive groups victimized by groupthink make the poorest decisions—even though they show they express great confidence in those decisions.[54]

Among the decision-making defects that can arise from groupthink are the following.

- **Reduction in alternative ideas.** The principal casualty of groupthink is a shrinking universe of ideas. Decisions are made based on few alternatives. Once preferred alternatives are decided on, they are not reexamined, and, of course, rejected alternatives are not reexamined.

- **Limiting of other information.** When a groupthink group has made its decision, others' opinions, even those of experts, are rejected. If new information is considered at all, it is biased toward ideas that fit the group's preconceptions. Thus, no contingency plans are made in case the decision turns out to be faulty.

Groupthink: Is Dell a "One-Trick Pony"?[55]

Dell Inc. became a success story through one core idea: becoming a lean, mean, direct sales machine. Using the slogan "Direct from Dell," it made personal computers cheaply by being super-efficient in acquiring and assembling their components (supply chain management) and selling them directly to consumers via the Internet.

In 2006, however, sales began to decline as competitors stepped up their efforts and markets shifted away from some of Dell's key advantages. Instead of adapting, however, Dell stuck to its old way of doing things, cutting costs to the point that, critics say, they compromised customer service and possibly product quality. Said a rival, "They're a one-trick pony. It was a great trick for over 10 years, but the rest of us have figured it out and Dell hasn't plowed any of its profits into creating a new trick." Even back in 2003, Dell revealed the limits of its business model. "There are some organizations where people think they're a hero if they invent a new thing," said CEO Kevin Rollins. "Being a hero at Dell means saving money."

The depth of groupthink at Dell was revealed in the extent to which new ideas were discouraged. Says one former manager, "You had to be very confident and thick-skinned to stay on an issue that wasn't popular. A lot of red flags got waved—but only once." Adds Geoffrey Moore, author of *Dealing with Darwin: How Great Companies Innovate at Every Phase of Their Evolution,* "Dell's culture is not inspirational or aspirational. This is when they need to be imaginative, but [Dell's] culture only wants to talk about execution."[56]

Your Call

The primacy of groups and teamwork "is so ingrained that we seldom stop to think about it anymore," says an *Inc. Magazine* writer. However, he adds, "In many cases, individuals do *much* better on their own. Our bias toward groups is counterproductive."[57] If you were chairman Michael Dell, who originally founded the company in his University of Texas dorm room, what would you do to break the groupthink culture at Dell?

Preventing Groupthink: Making Criticism & Other Perspectives Permissible

Janis believes it is easier to prevent groupthink than to cure it. As preventive measures, he suggests the following:

- **Allow criticism.** Each member of a team or group should be told to be a critical evaluator, able to actively voice objections and doubts. Subgroups within the group should be allowed to discuss and debate ideas. Once a consensus has been reached, everyone should be encouraged to rethink his or her position to check for flaws.

Fighting groupthink. For a long time, the Coca-Cola Co. had a culture of politeness and consensus that kept it from developing new products, at a time when consumers were flocking to a new breed of coffees, juices, and teas. Under Mary Minnick, who heads marketing, strategy, and innovation, the company is developing new beverages, such as the coffee-flavored Coca-Cola Blak. Do you think Coke can move beyond groupthink and "me-too" products to become cutting edge?

- **Allow other perspectives.** Outside experts should be used to introduce fresh perspectives. Different groups with different leaders should explore the same policy questions. Top-level executives should not use policy committees to rubber-stamp decisions that have already been made. When major alternatives are discussed, someone should be made devil's advocate to try to uncover all negative factors. ●

13.4 MANAGING CONFLICT

Since conflict is a part of life, what should a manager know about it in order to deal successfully with it?

major question

THE BIG PICTURE

Conflict, an enduring feature of the workplace, is a process in which one party perceives that its interests are being opposed or negatively affected by another party. Conflict can be negative (bad) or functional (good). Indeed, either too much or too little conflict can affect performance. This section identifies seven sources of conflict in organizations and also describes four ways to stimulate constructive conflict.

"I've fired many employees through the years," writes a manager to an advice columnist, "but right now I've got a guy who scares me. Maybe there's been one too many postal shootings, but I'm afraid this guy could turn violent."[58]

Firings, of course, generate strong emotions and can easily trigger outbursts, though dismissed workers seldom "go postal"—become violent and start shooting people. (About 20 American workers are murdered on the job every week, but few are by enraged co-workers; around 75% of workplace homicides occur during robberies.)[59] Nevertheless, employee dismissals—along with increased workloads, pressure-cooker deadlines, demands for higher productivity, and other kinds of stress—are among the sources of that enduring feature of the workplace: conflict.

Hot Seat DVD Applications:
Project Management:
Steering the Committee

Hot Seat DVD Application:
Partnership: The Unbalancing Act

The Nature of Conflict: Disagreement Is Normal

Mention the term *conflict* and many people envision shouting and fighting. But as a manager, during a typical workday you will encounter more subtle, nonviolent types of conflict: opposition, criticism, arguments. Thus, a definition of conflict seems fairly mild: ***Conflict* is a process in which one party perceives that its interests are being opposed or negatively affected by another party.**[60] Conflict is simply disagreement, a perfectly normal state of affairs. Conflicts may take many forms: between individuals, between an individual and a group, between groups, within a group, and between an organization and its environment. (To see what your own conflict-management style is, see the Self-Assessment at the end of this chapter.)

While all of us might wish to live lives free of conflict, it is now recognized that certain kinds of conflict can actually be beneficial.[61] Let us therefore distinguish between *negative conflict* (bad) and *constructive conflict* (good).

- **Negative conflict—bad for organizations.** From the standpoint of the organization, ***negative conflict* is conflict that hinders the organization's performance or threatens its interests.** As a manager, you need to do what you can to remove negative conflict, sometimes called *dysfunctional conflict.*

- **Constructive conflict—good for organizations.** The good kind of conflict is ***constructive conflict,* which benefits the main purposes of the organization and serves its interests.**[62] There are some situations in which this kind of conflict—also called *functional conflict* or *cooperative conflict*—is considered advantageous.

Negative & Positive Conflict: Do Nasty Bosses Get Better Performance?

In the 2006 film *The Devil Wears Prada,* Meryl Streep stars as a fear-inspiring fashion-magazine editor who keeps her new assistant quivering with dread. Is the portrait real? Says Liz Lange, a maternity-clothes designer, who was herself an editorial assistant, "If you happen to be working for the wrong editor, you could find yourself doing their kid's homework or being yelled at, or crying in the bathroom."[63] Real-life bosses renowned for their tempers include former Superior Oil head Fred Ackman and Walt Disney CEO Michael Eisner—and also Apple's Steve Jobs.

Does such negative conflict get results? Surprisingly, often it does. One study of 173 randomly chosen employees in a wide range of work found that, although some reacted to abusive bosses by doing little or nothing, others performed better—in part, it's speculated, to make themselves look good and others look worse.[64] Yet other research shows that abuse flows downhill, and when supervisors feel they have been unjustly treated, they may vent their resentment by abusing those who report to them. Subordinates generally cope either through avoidance or, less commonly, through confrontation, and are in any case less inclined to feel committed to their organizations, to speak unfavorably about their companies to outsiders, and to seek jobs elsewhere.[65]

When Stanford organizational psychologist Robert Sutton published a short essay in which he urged more civility in organizations by steady application of what he calls "the no-jerk rule" (although he used a far stronger word than "jerk"), he elicited more e-mails than he had received on any other subject, showing the topic had touched a nerve.[66] Jerks may be everywhere, he says, but "the key is to make explicit to everyone involved in hiring decisions that candidates who have strong skills but who show signs they will belittle and disrespect others cannot be hired under any circumstances." In addition, "Insults, put-downs, nasty teasing, and rude interruptions [should be] dealt with as soon as possible, preferably by the most respected and powerful members" of the company.[67]

Your Call

Have you ever worked for jerks (otherwise known, as Sutton puts it, as "tyrants, bullies, boors, destructive narcissists, and psychologically abusive people")? How did you respond to them?

Can Too Little or Too Much Conflict Affect Performance?

It's tempting to think that a conflict-free work group is a happy work group, as indeed it may be. But is it a productive group? In the 1970s, social scientists specializing in organizational behavior introduced the revolutionary idea that organizations could suffer from *too little* conflict.

- **Too little conflict—indolence.** Work groups, departments, or organizations that experience too little conflict tend to be plagued by apathy, lack of creativity, indecision, and missed deadlines. The result is that organizational performance suffers.

On strike. Home health care workers, members of a workforce that is chronically underpaid, are shown here on strike in New York City, demanding to be paid a living wage. What other issues do you think lead to too much conflict in the workplace?

- **Too much conflict—warfare.** Excessive conflict, on the other hand, can erode organizational performance because of political infighting, dissatisfaction, lack of teamwork, and turnover. Workplace aggression and violence are manifestations of excessive conflict.[68]

Thus, it seems that a moderate level of conflict can induce creativity and

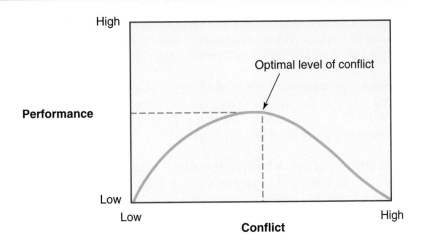

figure 13.2

THE RELATIONSHIP BETWEEN LEVEL OF CONFLICT AND LEVEL OF PERFORMANCE

Too little conflict or too much conflict causes performance to suffer.

initiative, thereby raising performance, as shown in the diagram above. *(See Figure 13.2.)* As might be expected, however, the idea as to what constitutes "moderate" will vary among managers.

Seven Causes of Conflict

There are a variety of sources of conflict—so-called conflict triggers. Seven of the principal ones are listed below. By understanding these, you'll be better able to take charge and manage the conflicts rather than letting the conflicts take you by surprise and manage you.

1. Competition for Scarce Resources: When Two Parties Need the Same Things   Within organizations there is often a scarcity of needed resources—for example, funds, office space, equipment, employees, and money for raises. When resources are scarce, being a manager becomes more difficult and conflict more likely.[69]

Example: There are lots of computer software glitches but not enough programmers to fix them.

2. Time Pressure: When People Believe There Aren't Enough Hours to Do the Work   Setting a deadline is a useful way of inducing people to perform. Or it can be a source of resentment, rage, and conflict if employees think their manager has unrealistic expectations.

Example: If you're in the business of marketing Christmas items to department stores and gift shops, it's imperative that you have your product ready for those important trade shows at which store buyers will appear. But the product-ready deadline for Marketing may be completely unworkable for your company's Production Department, leading to angry conflict.

3. Inconsistent Goals or Reward Systems: When People Pursue Different Objectives   It's natural for people in functional organizations to be pursuing different objectives and to be rewarded accordingly, but this means that conflict is practically built into the system.

Example: The sales manager for a college textbook publisher may be rewarded for achieving exceptional sales of newly introduced titles. But individual salespeople are rewarded for how many books they sell overall, which means they may promote the old tried and true books they know.

Test Your Knowledge:
Styles of Handling Conflict

Group Exercise:
Assessing the Effectiveness of Conflict-Handling Styles

Self-Assessment Exercise:
What Is Your Preferred Conflict-Handling Style?

4. Ambiguous Jurisdictions: When Job Boundaries Are Unclear   "That's not my job and those aren't my responsibilities." "Those resources belong to me because I need them as part of my job." When task responsibilities are unclear, that can often lead to conflict.

Examples: Is the bartender or the waiter supposed to put the lime in the gin and tonic and the celery in the Bloody Mary? Is management or the union in charge of certain work rules? Is Marketing or Research & Development supposed to be setting up focus groups to explore ideas for new products?

5. Status Differences: When There Are Inconsistencies in Power & Influence   It can happen that people who are lower in status according to the organization chart actually have disproportionate power over those theoretically above them, which can lead to conflicts.

Examples: If a restaurant patron complains his or her steak is not rare enough, the chef is the one who cooked it, but the waiter—who is usually lower in status—is the one who gave the chef the order. Airlines could not hold their schedules without flight crews and ground crews working a certain amount of overtime. But during labor disputes, pilots, flight attendants, and mechanics may simply refuse managers' requests to work overtime.

6. Personality Clashes: When Individual Differences Can't Be Resolved
Personality, values, attitudes, and experience can be so disparate that sometimes the only way to resolve individual differences—personality clashes—is to separate two people.

Example: Are you easygoing, but she's tense and driven? Does he always shade the facts, while you're a stickler for the truth? If you're basically Ms. Straight Arrow and he's Mr. Slippery, do you think you could adapt your personality to fit his? Maybe you should ask for a transfer.

7. Communication Failures: When People Misperceive & Misunderstand   The need for clear communication is a never-ending, ongoing process. Even under the best of circumstances, people misunderstand others, leading to conflict.

Example: Hewlett-Packard hired a consulting firm to explore acquisition of the computer maker Compaq, and at a crucial directors' meeting the consultant gave HP board members a document about the two companies to discuss. However, an important board member, Walter Hewlett, son of one of the founders, wasn't there. He was playing his cello somewhere—at an annual event he had appeared in for the past 3 years—and had assumed the board would accommodate him, as it had in the past. But the board plowed ahead, believing Hewlett wouldn't miss such an important session. This turned out to be a crucial misstep for HP management.[70] The miscommunication ultimately led to a major battle between Hewlett and top HP officers, including CEO Carleton Fiorina. Heirs of the company's founders, which owned 18% of the stock, were upset at the personal tone Fiorina took in painting Hewlett as a musician and academic who flip-flopped over board decisions.

How to Stimulate Constructive Conflict

As a manager you are being paid not just to manage conflict but even to create some, where it's constructive and appropriate, in order to stimulate performance. Constructive conflict, if carefully monitored, can be very productive under a number of circumstances: when your work group seems afflicted with inertia and apathy, resulting in low performance. When there's a lack of new ideas and resistance to change. When there seem to be a lot of yes-men and yes-women (expressing group-think) in the work unit. When there's high employee turnover. When managers seem unduly concerned with peace, cooperation, compromise, consensus, and their own popularity rather than in achieving work objectives.

The following four devices are used to stimulate constructive conflict:

I. Spur Competition among Employees
Competition is, of course, a form of conflict, but competition is often healthy in spurring people to produce higher results. Thus, a company will often put its salespeople in competition with each other by offering bonuses and awards for achievement—a trip to a Caribbean resort, say, for the top performer of the year.

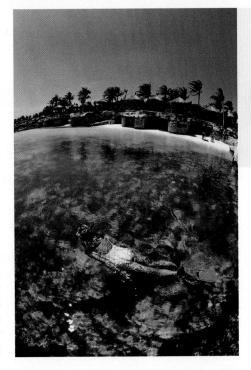

Top employee. Companies frequently stimulate constructive competition among employees to produce better performance. Top salespeople, for instance, may be rewarded with a trip to a Mexican resort. Do you think you would do well in a company that makes you compete with others to produce higher results?

2. Change the Organization's Culture & Procedures
Competition may also be established by making deliberate and highly publicized moves to change the corporate culture—by announcing to employees that the organization is now going to be more innovative and reward original thinking and unorthodox ideas. Procedures, such as paperwork sign-off processes, can also be revamped. Results can be reinforced in visible ways through announcements of bonuses, raises, and promotions.

3. Bring in Outsiders for New Perspectives
Without "new blood," organizations can become inbred and resistant to change. This is why managers often bring in outsiders—people from a different unit of the organization, new hires from competing companies, or consultants. With their different backgrounds, attitudes, or management styles, these outsiders can bring a new perspective and can shake things up.

4. Use Programmed Conflict: Devil's Advocacy & the Dialectic Method
Programmed conflict **is designed to elicit different opinions without inciting people's personal feelings.**[71]

Sometimes decision-making groups become so bogged down in details and procedures that nothing of substance gets done. The idea here is to get people, through role playing, to defend or criticize ideas based on relevant facts rather than on personal feelings and preferences.

The method for getting people to engage in this debate of ideas is to do disciplined role-playing, for which two proven methods are available: *devil's advocacy* and the *dialectic method.*

These two methods work as follows:

- **Devil's advocacy—role-playing criticism to test whether a proposal is workable.** *Devil's advocacy* **is the process of assigning someone to play the role of critic** to voice possible objections to a proposal and thereby generate critical thinking and reality testing.[72]

  Periodically role-playing devil's advocate has a beneficial side effect in that it is good training for developing analytical and communicative skills. However, it's a good idea to rotate the job so no one person develops a negative reputation.

- **The dialectic method—role-playing two sides of a proposal to test whether it is workable.** Requiring a bit more skill training than devil's advocacy does, the *dialectic method* is the process of having two people or groups play opposing roles in a debate in order to better understand a proposal. After the structured debate, managers are better able to make a decision.[73]

Example

Use of the Dialectic Method: How Anheuser-Busch Debates Important Moves

When the corporate policy committee of Anheuser-Busch is considering a major move—such as whether to make a big capital expenditure or get into or out of a business—it sometimes assigns two, even three, groups of people to make the case for each side of the question. Each team is knowledgeable about the subject, and each has the same information. Sometimes an opponent of the project is asked to argue for it—and vice versa.

The exercise may produce a final decision that represents a synthesis of the opposing views. "We end

up with decisions and alternatives we hadn't thought of," says Pat Stokes, who heads the company's beer empire. "You become a lot more anticipatory, better able to see what might happen, because you have thought through the process."[74]

Your Call

What kind of specific business move can you think of in which it would be helpful to apply the dialectic method?

Whatever kind of organization you work for, you'll always benefit from knowing how to manage conflict. ●

key terms used in this chapter

adjourning 425
cohesiveness 430
conflict 433
constructive conflict 433
cross-functional team 421
devil's advocacy 437
dialectic method 438
division of labor 427
formal group 420

forming 424
group 419
group cohesiveness 425
groupthink 430
informal group 420
maintenance role 428
negative conflict 433
norming 425
norms 429

performing 425
programmed conflict 437
quality circles 422
role 428
self-managed teams 422
social loafing 427
storming 424
task role 428
team 419

 summary

13.1 Groups versus Teams

- Groups and teams are different—a group is typically management-directed, a team self-directed. A group is defined as two or more freely interacting individuals who

share collective norms, share collective goals, and have a common identity. A team is defined as a small group of people with complementary skills who are committed to a common purpose, performance goals, and approach for which they hold themselves mutually accountable.

- Groups may be either formal, established to do something productive for the organization and headed by a leader, or informal, formed by people seeking friendship with no officially appointed leader.

- Teams are of various types, but one of the most important is the work team, which engages in collective work requiring coordinated effort. Work teams may be of four types, identified according to their basic purpose: advice, production, project, and action. A project team may also be a cross-functional team, staffed with specialists pursuing a common objective.

- Two types of teams worth knowing about are quality circles, consisting of small groups of volunteers or workers and supervisors who meet intermittently to discuss workplace and quality-related problems, and self-managed teams, defined as groups of workers given administrative oversight for their task domains.

 13.2 Stages of Group & Team Development

- A group may evolve into a team through five stages. (1) Forming is the process of getting oriented and getting acquainted. (2) Storming is characterized by the emergence of individual personalities and roles and conflicts within the group. (3) In norming, conflicts are resolved, close relationships develop, and unity and harmony emerge. (4) In performing, members concentrate on solving problems and completing the assigned task. (5) In adjourning, members prepare for disbandment.

 13.3 Building Effective Teams

- There are seven considerations managers must take into account in building a group into an effective team.
  (1) They must establish measurable goals and have feedback about members' performance.
  (2) They must motivate members by making them mutually accountable to one another.
  (3) They must consider what size is optimal. Teams with nine or fewer members have better interaction and morale, yet they also have fewer resources, are possibly less innovative, and may have work unevenly distributed among members. Teams of 10–16 members have more resources, and can

take advantage of division of labor, yet they may be characterized by less interaction, lower morale, and social loafing.
  (4) They must consider the role each team member must play. A role is defined as the socially determined expectation of how an individual should behave in a specific position. Two types of team roles are task and maintenance. A task role consists of behavior that concentrates on getting the team's tasks done. A maintenance role consists of behavior that fosters constructive relationships among team members.
  (5) They must consider team norms, the general guidelines or rules of behavior that most group or team members follow. Norms tend to be enforced by group or team members for four reasons: to help the group survive, to clarify role expectations, to help individuals avoid embarrassing situations, and to emphasize the group's important values and identity.
  (6) They must consider the team's cohesiveness, the tendency of a group or team to stick together.
  (7) They must be aware of groupthink, a cohesive group's blind unwillingness to consider alternatives. Symptoms of groupthink are feelings of invulnerability, certainty of the rightness of their actions, and stereotyped views of the opposition; rationalization and self-censorship; and illusion of unanimity, peer pressure, and the appearance of self-appointed protectors against adverse information. The results of groupthink can be reduction in alternative ideas and limiting of other information. Two ways to prevent groupthink are to allow criticism and to allow other perspectives.

 13.4 Managing Conflict

- Conflict is a process in which one party perceives that its interests are being opposed or negatively affected by another party. Conflict can be negative. However, constructive, or functional, conflict benefits the main purposes of the organization and serves its interests. Too little conflict can lead to indolence; too much conflict can lead to warfare.

- Seven causes of conflict are (1) competition for scarce resources, (2) time pressure, (3) inconsistent goals or reward systems, (4) ambiguous jurisdictions, (5) status differences, (6) personality clashes, and (7) communication failures.

- Four devices for stimulating constructive conflict are (1) spurring competition among employees, (2) changing the organization's culture and procedures, (3) bringing in outsiders for new perspectives, and (4) using programmed conflict to elicit different opinions without inciting people's personal feelings.

Two methods used in programmed conflict are (1) devil's advocacy, in which someone is assigned to play the role of critic to voice possible objections to a proposal, and (2) the dialectic method, in which two people or groups play opposing roles in a debate in order to better understand a proposal.

 management in action

Samsung Uses Product Development Teams to Increase Innovation & Sales of New Products

[In June 2006] a group of 11 Samsung Electronics Co. employees pledged to do the last thing most people desire just as spring bursts into summer: stay inside a drab room with small, curtained windows for the bulk of the next six weeks. The product planners, designers, programmers, and engineers had recently entered Samsung's so-called Value Innovation Program (VIP) Center, just south of Seoul. They were asked to outline the features and design of the company's mainstay flat-screen TV, code-named Bordeaux. And their bosses had vowed to keep them posted there until they had completed the assignment. . . .

It's all part of a new mantra at Samsung: "market-driven change." In the past decade Samsung has radically improved the quality and design of its products. Yun Jong Yong, Samsung's 62-year-old chief executive, now wants the company to rival the likes of Microsoft Corp. and IBM as a key shaper of information technology. By 2010 he aims to double sales, from $85 billion last year to $170 billion. . . .

How to make Samsung more innovative? One key initiative is the VIP Center. Yun set up the program in 1998 after concluding that as much as 80% of cost and quality is determined in the initial stages of product development. By bringing together everyone at the very beginning to thrash out differences, he believed, the company could streamline its operations and make better gadgets. In the past two years, though, the center's primary aim has shifted to "creating new value for customers," says Vice-President Lee Dong Jin, who heads the facility. Translation: Find that perfect balance of cost, innovation, and technology that makes a product great.

If it weren't such hard work, it might almost be fun. The center, at Suwon, Samsung's main manufacturing site, 20 miles from Seoul, is open 24 hours a day. Housed in a five-story former dormitory, it has 20 project rooms, 38 bedrooms for those who need to spend the night, a kitchen, a gym, traditional baths,

and Ping-Pong and pool tables. Last year some 2,000 employees cycled through, completing 90 projects with names such as Rainbow, Rapido, and Rocky. . . . While some teams wrap up their work within weeks, other projects drag on for months, and all division leaders sign a pledge that participants won't return to their regular jobs until they have finished the project.

The Bordeaux team shows how the VIP Center works. The goal was to create a flat-screen TV that would sell at least 1 million units. But the team members quickly discovered that they had strongly differing opinions about what consumers want in a TV. The designers proposed a sleek, heavily sculpted model. Engineers wanted to pack in plenty of functions and the best picture and sound quality. Product planners were concerned primarily with creating something that would beat the offerings of Sharp Corp., then the leader in LCD TVs.

Every step of the way, team members drew what Samsung calls "value curves." These are graphs that rank various attributes such as picture quality and design on a scale of 1 to 5, from outright bad to excellent. The graphs compared the proposed model with those of rival products and Samsung's existing TVs. The VIP Center specialists also guided the team in discussions exploring ideas and concepts from entirely different industries, picking up hints about the importance of the emotional appeal in the offerings of furniture makers and Hollywood. "We wanted a curve resembling a wine glass, and a glossy back to make the TV fit in with other furniture," says designer Lee Seung Ho, who worked on the Bordeaux project.

One challenge the team faced: Surveys showed that shoppers buy a flat-screen TV as much for its look as a piece of furniture as for its technological muscle. Some members went to furniture stores to figure out what made buyers tick, and discovered that the design of the set trumps most other considerations. So the group started shedding function in favor of form, cutting corners on high-tech features to spend more to make a TV that looks good even when it's turned off. . . .

The initial response is encouraging. In the last week of May [2006], Samsung inched ahead of Sony to become the No. 1 LCD TV brand in the U.S., garnering market share (in terms of value) of 26.4%, compared with Sony's 24.6% and Sharp's 8.2%, according to researcher NPD Group. In January, Samsung was No. 3, with just 12.1%. Yun now says he wants to become the top maker of digital TVs, including those using plasma and rear-projection technologies, in the U.S. this year.

Pretty grand ambitions. But Yun has a strong record of setting stretch goals and achieving them. Under his stewardship, Samsung has transformed itself from an industry also-ran into the richest electronics maker in Asia. Now it could also become the coolest if Yun can reinvent Samsung one more time and get his engineers, designers, and marketers to dream up products such as the Bordeaux and really fire consumers' imaginations.

For Discussion
1. What kind of work team is represented by the Bordeaux team? Explain.
2. How does Yun Jong Yong's goal to double sales to $170 billion help or hinder the performance of product development teams? Discuss.
3. What techniques are being used to help effective product development teams at Samsung? Provide examples.
4. How did the Bordeaux team manage conflict among team members? Discuss.

Source: Excerpted from Moon Ihlwan, "Camp Samsung," *BusinessWeek*, July 3, 2006, pp. 46–48.

self-assessment

What Is Your Conflict-Management Style?

Objectives
1. To assess your conflict-management style.
2. To gain insight on how you manage conflict.

Introduction
Have you ever had a professor whose viewpoints were in conflict with your own? Have you worked in a group with someone who seems to disagree just to cause conflict? How did you react in that situation? In this chapter, you learned that there are five different ways of handling conflict: (1) *avoiding*—this approach is seen in people who wish to suppress conflict or back down from it altogether; (2) *accommodating*—this approach is seen in people who place the other party's interests above their own; (3) *forcing*—this approach is seen when people rely on their authority to solve conflict; (4) *compromising*—this approach is seen in people who are willing to give up something in order to reach a solution; and (5) *collaboration*—this approach is seen in people who desire a win-win situation, striving to address concerns and desires of all the parties involved in the conflict. The purpose of this exercise is to determine your conflict handling style.

Instructions
Read each of the statements below and use the following scale to indicate how often you rely on each tactic.

1 = very rarely
2 = rarely
3 = sometimes
4 = fairly often
5 = very often

1. I work to come out victorious no matter what.	1 2 3 4 5
2. I try to put the needs of others above my own.	1 2 3 4 5
3. I look for a mutually satisfactory solution.	1 2 3 4 5
4. I try to get involved in conflicts.	1 2 3 4 5
5. I strive to investigate and understand the issues involved in the conflict.	1 2 3 4 5

(continued)

| 6. I never back away from a good argument. | | 2 | 3 | 4 | 5 |

6. I never back away from a good argument.   1 2 3 4 5

7. I strive to foster harmony.   1 2 3 4 5

8. I negotiate to get a portion of what I propose.   1 2 3 4 5

9. I avoid open discussion of controversial subjects.   1 2 3 4 5

10. When I am trying to resolve disagreements, I openly share information.   1 2 3 4 5

11. I would rather win than compromise.   1 2 3 4 5

12. I work through conflict by accepting suggestions of others.   1 2 3 4 5

13. I look for a middle ground to resolve disagreements.   1 2 3 4 5

14. I keep my true opinions to myself to avoid hard feelings.   1 2 3 4 5

15. I encourage the open sharing of concerns and issues.   1 2 3 4 5

16. I am reluctant to admit I am wrong.   1 2 3 4 5

17. I try to save others from embarrassment in a disagreement.   1 2 3 4 5

18. I stress the advantages of give and take.   1 2 3 4 5

19. I give in early on rather than argue about a point.   1 2 3 4 5

20. I state my position and stress that it is the only correct point of view.   1 2 3 4 5

Scoring & Interpretation

Enter your responses, item by item, in the five categories below. Add your responses to get your total for each of the five conflict handling styles. Your primary conflict-handling style will be the area where you scored the highest. Your back-up conflict-handling style will be your second highest score.

Avoiding		Accommodating		Forcing		Compromising		Collaborating	
Item	Score	Item	Score	Item	Score	Item	Score	Item	Score
4.	_____	2.	_____	1.	_____	3.	_____	5.	_____
9.	_____	7.	_____	6.	_____	8.	_____	10.	_____
14.	_____	12.	_____	11.	_____	13.	_____	15.	_____
19.	_____	17.	_____	16.	_____	18.	_____	20.	_____
Total = _____		Total = _____		Total = _____		Total = _____		Total = _____	

1. Were you surprised by the results? Why or why not? Explain.
2. Were the scores for your primary and back-up conflict-handling styles relatively similar, or was there a large gap? What does this imply? Discuss.
3. Is your conflict-handling style one that can be used in many different conflict scenarios? Explain.

4. What are some skills you can work on to become more effective at handling conflict? Describe and explain.

The survey was developed using conflict-handling styles defined by K. W. Thomas, "Conflict and Conflict Management," in M. Dunnette ed., *Handbook of Industrial and Organizational Psychology* (Chicago: Rand McNally, 1976), pp. 889–935.

 group exercise

Managing Conflict

Objectives

- To examine workplace conflict.
- To assess ways in which third parties manage conflict.

Introduction

As you learned in this chapter, conflict is not only a way of life but is sometimes necessary to generate new ideas. Conflict can be constructive or dysfunctional. Managers stimulate conflict by spurring competition among employees, changing the organization's culture and procedures, bringing in outsiders for a fresh perspective and sometimes playing devil's advocate, using programmed conflict. However, if there is too much conflict in an organization, it can be very destructive, leading to warfare. The purpose of this exercise is to examine a situation and consider alternative solutions for resolving the conflict.

Instructions

Break into groups of five to six people and read the following case study. Once you have read the case, discuss it with your group by brainstorming ways you could handle the situation if you were senior vice-president of operations at the furniture company. Use the questions for discussion at the end of the case to aid in your discussion.

The Case

Jack Smith is the senior vice-president of operations at a major producer of muscle-car performance accessories. His close personal friend Joe Black reports to him as vice-president and general manager of his largest engine-parts assembly plant. Joe has been with the company for nearly 40 years and will retire soon. Joe worked his way up from the assembly line to his current position and has successfully operated the division for 5 years. Joe is a hard worker and very professional; his staff, however, is rumored to be only marginally competent. Jack always felt that Joe purposely hired only moderately competent people. He agrees with another manager that Joe is threatened by talented assistants.

Last week, Jack went to lunch with another friend, Charles Williams, who happens to be Joe's second in command. Jack has been concerned about Joe's replacement for some time, and Charles seemed to be a good candidate. He is bright and well liked and a business-school graduate. Jack, who has known Charles for some time, also knows that Charles loves muscle cars and spends his free time restoring them. He shows a huge amount of enthusiasm for the company and its operations. At Jack's insistence, Joe hired him at the plant. Jack was relieved because there would finally be someone in the plant with talent and competence.

As Jack ate his lunch, however, he soon learned that Charles and Joe seemed to be engaged in some sort of feud. Jack was disappointed that Joe had not taken to Charles as he had hoped. It seems that Joe is in the process of developing a 5-year plan for his plant. The plan will lead to some major reinvestment and reorganization decisions that will be proposed to Jack and the rest of senior management. However, Joe has not included Charles at all in developing the plan. Because he did not feel like he was part of the team, Charles complained to Jack that he was no longer enthused about his job. Charles told Jack that his dissatisfaction was affecting his performance and that he was not putting forth any effort at managing the plant team. He told Jack he was considering a transfer to another plant or a transfer to a rising competitor's company.

Jack left the restaurant very worried and upset. He did not know the details of Joe's plan; he knew only what he had heard from Charles, but it worried him that Joe was making arbitrary decisions without including the rest of his staff. If Charles did stay at the company, Jack knew that once Joe retired, then Charles would have to live with Joe's plan. Jack was also frustrated because Joe's support is necessary if Charles is to develop as a leader. Jack also felt that Joe ran a good ship, and he did not want to undermine his authority or upset him. Despite some of his hiring choices, Joe had shown really good judgment, and the plant was one of the most successful in the company. Jack didn't know if Joe had a good reason for excluding Charles.

Questions for Discussion

1. Does this situation fit into one or more of the Seven Causes of Conflict discussed in section 13.4? Which ones? Discuss your rationale.
2. If you were Jack, what would you do to ease the rising conflict between Joe and Charles? Would you intervene? Explain.
3. Why would you take this action? Discuss.
4. If you were Charles, which conflict-handling style would work best to get Joe to include you in developing the plan? Discuss your rationale.

 ethical dilemma

When Employees Smoke Marijuana Socially: A Manager's Quandary

You are a supervisor at a telephone call center and have very positive relationships with members of your work team and your manager. A friend of yours, Christina, is also a supervisor, and her younger brother, Blake, is a member of her work team.

Christina invites you to her birthday party at her home, and you happily agree to attend. During the party, you walk out to the backyard to get some fresh air and notice that Blake and several other employees of your company are smoking marijuana. You have been told on several occasions by members of your own work team that these same individuals have used marijuana at other social events.

Blake and his friends are not part of your work team, and you never noticed any of them being impaired at work.

Solving the Dilemma

As a supervisor, what would you do?

1. Report the drug users and the incident to the company's human resources department.
2. Mind your own business. The employees are not on your team and don't appear to be impaired at work.
3. Talk to your boss and get her opinion about what should be done.
4. Invent other options. Discuss.

 video case

Pike Place Fish Market

When John Yokoyama of Pike Place Fish Market took over the business at age 25, he knew only one management style: tyrannical. He watched his employees every second, always vigilant for mistakes, and expected workers to do as they were told. Through his association with Jim Bergquist, owner of Big Features Consulting Company, his style evolved into the highest degree of employee empowerment and trust.

It took Bergquist's idea that a person can "create reality" many meetings to take hold. But one by one, owner and employees began to buy into the idea. According to Bergquist, the only known fact about the future is that it's unknown. This idea makes people feel uncomfortable. We prefer to view the future as

predictable because it gives us a sense of comfort and control. However, if we're willing to accept the unknown nature of the future, we then realize that anything's possible. We can create our own reality. It's up to management to create a context in which that can happen.

Several other key concepts guide management philosophies at Pike Place. One such concept is "you have the choice." According to Yokoyama, the power of personal responsibility is vital. We are responsible for all that enters our lives and how we react to it. But most people don't recognize this fact and as a result live as victims of circumstances. As a manager, Yokoyama recognizes that he has a choice when responding to a poorly performing employee. He can choose to pursue his initial negative reaction, or he can choose to recognize a quality employee who needs support in dealing with a problem.

Another founding principle at Pike Place is that employees be "committed to the purpose." When new employees enter the workplace they soon realize that they are not applying for a job opening but rather for the opportunity to try out for the team. Being committed to the purpose is one of the criteria for being on the team. With this committment, the team can "produce outrageous results." Management must allow employees to express their own creativity and empower them to create their own reality. According to Bergquist, the best way to manage that kind of team is to stay out of the way. After all, 15 heads are better than one.

Coaching is key to personal growth and development at Pike Place. Manager Justin Hall explains that everyone, from the newest hire to the owner, has permission to coach one another. Coaching works by recognizing when another person can benefit from your experience and is most powerful when the intention is to empower. If you see someone who needs to be coached, you must speak up, even if it's uncomfortable.

Yokoyama now recognizes that "people aren't numbers" and that managers should relate to employees as human beings and commit to making a difference in their lives. Yokoyama's current management style is best characterized as "management by inspiration." It's his hope that this attitude becomes a widespread movement in the business world.

Discussion Questions

1. Would you characterize the employees of Pike Place Fish Market as a group or a team? Support your answer.
2. Do the employees of Pike Place most closely embody the characteristics of a quality circle or a self-managed team? Support your answer.
3. Explain the phenomenon of groupthink. Do you see any evidence of groupthink at Pike Place? Why or why not?airline cockpit crews,

chapter 14

Power, Influence, & Leadership

From Becoming a Manager to Becoming a Leader

Major Questions You Should Be Able to Answer

14.1 The Nature of Leadership: Wielding Influence
Major Question: I don't want to be just a manager; I want to be a leader. What's the difference between the two?

14.2 Trait Approaches: Do Leaders Have Distinctive Personality Characteristics?
Major Question: What does it take to be a successful leader?

14.3 Behavioral Approaches: Do Leaders Show Distinctive Patterns of Behavior?
Major Question: Do effective leaders behave in similar ways?

14.4 Contingency Approaches: Does Leadership Vary with the Situation?
Major Question: How might effective leadership vary according to the situation at hand?

14.5 The Full-Range Model: Uses of Transactional & Transformational Leadership
Major Question: What does it take to truly inspire people to perform beyond their normal levels?

14.6 Six Additional Perspectives
Major Question: If there are many ways to be a leader, which one would describe me best?

How to Become a Star in the Workplace

People who are stars at work "are made, not born," says Carnegie Mellon professor Robert E. Kelley. "They have a fundamentally different conception of what work is."

Here are nine "star strategies" Kelly has identified, which average performers can adopt to become star performers—even leaders, the subject of this chapter.[1]

- **Initiative:** Initiative, says Kelley, is doing something outside your regular job that makes a difference to the company's core mission—doing something beyond your job description that helps other people. Initiative means you need to see the activity through to the end and you may need to take some risks.

- **Networking:** Star performers use networking to multiply their productivity, to do their current jobs better. "Average performers wait until they need some information, then cold-call someone to get it," Kelley says. "Stars know that you can't get work done today without a knowledge network and that you've got to put it in place beforehand."

- **Self-management:** Stars know how to get ahead of the game instead of waiting for the game to come to them. They look at the big picture and think about managing their whole life at work. They understand who they are and how they work best.

- **Perspective:** Average performers tend to see things just from their own points of view, says Kelley. Star performers try to think how things look through the eyes of their boss, co-workers, clients, and competitors. That depth of perspective can lead to better solutions.

- **Followership:** Stars know not only how to stand out but also how to help out—to be a follower as well as a leader. The idea is that if you help out others, they will later look out for you.

- **Leadership:** Star performers lead by understanding other people's interests and by using persuasion to bring out the best in people. People want leaders who are knowledgeable, who bring energy to a project and create energy in other people, and who pay close attention to the needs of everyone involved in the project.

- **Teamwork:** Stars join only workplace teams in which they think they will make a difference, and they become very good participants. They "make sure, once the team is put together, that it actually gets the job done," says Kelley.

- **Organizational savvy:** Average performers think of office politics as being dirty. Stars avoid getting needlessly involved in office melodramas, but they learn how to manage competing interests to achieve their work goals. They learn that not just one perspective is right, but that there are different perspectives.

- **Show and tell:** In both formal and informal meetings, stars learn how to craft their messages and to time them so that people pay attention. To excel at "show and tell," they learn to match the language of their communication to the language that people speak, then deliver the message in a way that works for them.

The good news is that these nine strategies can be learned. Like improving yourself in a sport, you identify the areas in which you need to improve and then practice those improvements every day. Take a look at yourself, then at the star performers you know. Then become a student of the stars—do what they do.

For Discussion   Which two of these qualities do you think you need to work on most in order to develop into a star performer?

forecast

What's Ahead in This Chapter

Are there differences between managers and leaders? This chapter considers this question. We discuss the sources of a leader's power and how leaders use persuasion to influence people. We then consider the following approaches to leadership: trait, behavioral, contingency, full-range, and six additional perspectives.

14.1 THE NATURE OF LEADERSHIP: WIELDING INFLUENCE

 major question

I don't want to be just a manager; I want to be a leader. What's the difference between the two?

THE BIG PICTURE

Being a manager and being a leader are not the same. A leader is able to influence employees to voluntarily pursue the organization's goals. Leadership is needed for organizational change. We describe five sources of power leaders may draw on. Leaders use the power of persuasion or influence to get others to follow them. Five approaches to leadership are described in the next five sections.

Leadership. What is it? Is it a skill anyone can develop?

Leadership **is the ability to influence employees to voluntarily pursue organizational goals.**[2] In an effective organization, leadership is present at all levels, say Tom Peters and Nancy Austin in *A Passion for Excellence,* and it represents the sum of many things. Leadership, they say, "means vision, cheerleading, enthusiasm, love, trust, verve, passion, obsession, consistency, the use of symbols, paying attention as illustrated by the content of one's calendar, out-and-out drama (and the management thereof), creating heroes at all levels, coaching, effectively wandering around, and numerous other things."[3]

Managers & Leaders: Not Always the Same

Group Exercise:
What Kind of Leader Do You Prefer?

Group Exercise:
What Is Your Motivation to Lead?

You see the words "manager" and "leader" used interchangeably all the time. However, as one leadership expert has said, "leaders manage and managers lead, but the two activities are not synonymous."[4]

Retired Harvard Business School professor **John Kotter** suggests that one is not better than the other, that in fact they are complementary systems of action. The difference is that . . .

- *Management* is about coping with *complexity,*
- *Leadership* is about coping with *change.*[5]

Let's consider these differences.

Being a Manager: Coping with Complexity   Management is necessary because complex organizations, especially the large ones that so much dominate the economic landscape, tend to become chaotic unless there is good management.

According to Kotter, companies manage complexity in three ways:

- **Determining what needs to be done—planning and budgeting.** Companies manage complexity first by *planning and budgeting*—setting targets or goals for the future, establishing steps for achieving them, and allocating resources to accomplish them.

- **Creating arrangements of people to accomplish an agenda—organizing and staffing.** Management achieves its plan by *organizing and staffing,* Kotter says—creating the organizational structure and hiring qualified individuals to fill the necessary jobs, then devising systems of implementation.

- **Ensuring people do their jobs—controlling and problem solving.** Management ensures the plan is accomplished by *controlling and problem solving,* says

Kotter. That is, managers monitor results versus the plan in some detail by means of reports, meetings, and other tools. They then plan and organize to solve problems as they arise.

Being a Leader: Coping with Change   As the business world has become more competitive and volatile, doing things the same way as last year (or doing it 5% better) is no longer a formula for success. More changes are required for survival—hence the need for leadership.

Leadership copes with change in three ways:

- **Determining what needs to be done—setting a direction.** Instead of dealing with complexity through planning and budgeting, leaders strive for constructive change by *setting a direction.* That is, they develop a vision for the future, along with strategies for realizing the changes.

- **Creating arrangements of people to accomplish an agenda—aligning people.** Instead of organizing and staffing, leaders are concerned with *aligning people,* Kotter says. That is, they communicate the new direction to people in the company who can understand the vision and build coalitions that will realize it.

- **Ensuring people do their jobs—motivating and inspiring.** Instead of controlling and problem solving, leaders try to achieve their vision by *motivating and inspiring.* That is, they appeal to "basic but often untapped human needs, values, and emotions," says Kotter, to keep people moving in the right direction, despite obstacles to change.

Do Kotter's ideas describe real leaders in the real business world? Certainly many participants in a seminar convened by *Harvard Business Review* appeared to agree. "The primary task of leadership is to communicate the vision and the values of an organization," Frederick Smith, chairman and CEO of FedEx, told the group. "Second, leaders must win support for the vision and values they articulate. And third, leaders have to reinforce the vision and the values."[6]

Managers have legitimate power (as we'll describe) that derives from the formal authority of the positions to which they have been appointed. This power allows managers to hire and fire, reward and punish. Managers plan, organize, and control, but they don't necessarily have the characteristics to be leaders.

Whereas management is a process that lots of people are able to learn, leadership is more visionary. As we've said, leaders inspire others, provide emotional support, and try to get employees to rally around a common goal. Leaders also play a role in creating a vision and strategic plan for an organization, which managers are then charged with implementing.[7]

Do you have what it takes to be a leader? To learn more about the skills required and to assess your own leadership ability, try the Self-Assessment at the end of this chapter.

Amazing Amazon. Jeffrey Bezos, founder and CEO of online retailer Amazon.com, has done nearly everything Kotter suggests. For instance, Bezos's "culture of divine discontent" permits employees to plunge ahead with new ideas even though they know that most will probably fail.

Five Sources of Power

To really understand leadership, we need to understand the concept of power and authority. *Authority* is the right to perform or command; it comes with the job. In contrast, *power* is the extent to which a person is able to influence others so they respond to orders.

People who pursue ***personalized power—power directed at helping oneself***—as a way of enhancing their own selfish ends may give the word power a bad name. However, there is another kind of power, ***socialized power—power directed at helping others.***[8] This is the kind of power you hear in expressions such as "My goal is to have a powerful impact on my community."

Within organizations there are typically five sources of power leaders may draw on: *legitimate, reward, coercive, expert,* and *referent.*

I. Legitimate Power: Influencing Behavior Because of One's Formal Position

Legitimate power, **which all managers have, is power that results from managers' formal positions within the organization.** All managers have legitimate power over their employees, deriving from their position, whether it's a construction supervisor, ad account supervisor, sales manager, or CEO. This power may be exerted both positively or negatively—as praise or as criticism, for example.

2. Reward Power: Influencing Behavior by Promising or Giving Rewards

Reward power, **which all managers have, is power that results from managers' authority to reward their subordinates.** Rewards can range from praise to pay raises, from recognition to promotions.

Example: Lloyd D. Ward, former CEO of Maytag and among the highest-ranking African Americans in corporate America, skillfully uses praise to reward positive behavior both on and off the job. For instance, while teaching karate moves during a workout with a reporter, he used such phrases as "You got it. Cool!" and "Outstanding! . . . Go! Go, David!"[9]

3. Coercive Power: Influencing Behavior by Threatening or Giving Punishment

Coercive power, **which all managers have, results from managers' authority to punish their subordinates.** Punishment can range from verbal or written reprimands to demotions to terminations. In some lines of work, fines and suspensions may be used. Coercive power has to be used judiciously, of course, since a manager who is seen as being constantly negative will produce a lot of resentments among employees. But there have been many leaders who have risen to the top of major corporations—such as Disney's Michael Eisner, Miramax's Harvey Weinstein, and Hewlett-Packard's Carly Fiorina—who have been abrasive and intimidating.[10]

4. Expert Power: Influencing Behavior Because of One's Expertise

Expert power **is power resulting from one's specialized information or expertise.** Expertise, or special knowledge, can be mundane, such as knowing the work schedules and assignments of the people who report to you. Or it can be sophisticated, such as having computer or medical knowledge. Secretaries may have expert power because, for example, they have been in a job a long time and know all the necessary contacts. CEOs may have expert power because they have strategic knowledge not shared by many others.

5. Referent Power: Influencing Behavior Because of One's Personal Attraction

Referent power **is power deriving from one's personal attraction.** As we will see later in this chapter (under the discussion of transformational leadership), this kind of power characterizes strong, visionary leaders who are able to persuade their followers by dint of their personality, attitudes, or background. Referent power may be associated with managers, but it is more likely to be characteristic of leaders.

Leadership & Influence: Using Persuasion to Get Your Way at Work

What would you do if you discovered your car stolen from the parking lot? Here's what Doug Dusenberg, a Houston, Texas, businessman, did on noticing his Jeep Cherokee missing. He telephoned the number of his car phone, and when one of the pair of young

A Strong Leader: Andy Grove, Former CEO of Intel Corp.

Symbolic of his ability to reinvent himself, Andy Grove has had three different names in his life. Born in 1936 as a Hungarian Jew, he was known as Andras Istvan Grof until 1944, when the Nazis invaded Hungary, at which point his mother changed his name to the Slavic Andras Malesevics. The following year, when the communists arrived, he changed back to Andras Grof. Nauseated by Communism, he escaped and arrived in the U.S. in 1957, where he enrolled at City College of New York and changed his name to Andrew Stephen Grove.

In 1968, with a PhD in chemical engineering, Grove joined two engineering colleagues in starting Intel Corporation in Mountain View, California, where at age 32 he found himself in the role of leader in a manufacturing startup. It was then that he began to teach himself about management. "Grove succeeded where others didn't," says historian Richard Tedlow, "in part, by approaching management as a discipline unto itself. There's a real urgency in his efforts to school himself: He never lost his Hungarian refugee's apprehension of the risk of imminent failure."[12]

By 1983, Intel was a $1.1 billion maker of memory chips and Grove had become its president. But something was about to happen that would reinforce in him a lesson he would later write about in his book *Only the Paranoid Survive*—namely, that in business you often don't see the cliff until you've already walked off it.[13] In the mid-1980s, Intel woke up to find that Japanese companies had mastered the industry it had invented and were turning memory chips into a commodity, so that in a single year Intel profits plunged from $198 million to $2 million.

A key to Grove's leadership was that he seemed to be one of the original practitioners of what we in this text have described as

"evidence-based management." His management style was "direct and confrontational," says *BusinessWeek*. "His shouts echoed down company halls."[14] Adds Tedlow, "At Intel he fostered a culture in which 'knowledge power' would trump 'position power.' Anyone could challenge anyone else's idea, so long as it was about the idea and not the person—and so long as you were ready for the demand 'Prove it.' That required data. Without data, an idea was only a story—a representation of reality and thus subject to distortion."[15]

It was at that point that Grove made the painful decision to abandon Intel-the-memory-chip-company, firing some 8,000 people, and to stake its future on the microprocessor. The personal computer was just coming into being, and once IBM chose to base its PCs on Intel's processor chip, the former memory company started a successful 11-year run. In 1986, it took a chance when launching the Intel 386 microprocessor to license it not just to IBM but to other computer makers as well. With the success of Microsoft's smash-hit Windows 3.0, designed to work on 386-chip machines, Intel began a compound annual growth rate of nearly 30%.

Andy Grove is celebrated as a leader because, as Tedlow says, he "was willing to let go of his instincts—since they could be wrong—and view himself as a student might: from outside, peering down with the wide-angle, disinterested perspective of the observer. . . . It is the singular ability to inhabit both roles at once—subject and object, actor and audience, master and student—that sets Grove apart."

Your Call

Which of the five sources of leadership power do you think Grove represents? Do you think you could follow Grove's example?

---

joyriders answered, he talked them into returning the car in exchange for keeping $20 that was in the glove compartment.[11]

Dusenberg probably would be considered to have leadership skills because of his powers of persuasion, or *influence*. Influence is the ability to get others to follow your wishes. There are nine general tactics for trying to influence others, but some work better than others. In one pair of studies, employees were asked in effect, "How do you get your boss, coworker, or subordinate to do something you want?" The nine answers—ranked from most used to least used tactics—were as follows.[16]

1. Rational Persuasion   Trying to convince someone by using reason, logic, or facts.
   Example: "You know, all the cutting-edge companies use this approach."

2. Inspirational Appeals   Trying to build enthusiasm or confidence by appealing to others' emotions, ideals, or values.
   Example: "If we do this as a goodwill gesture, customers will love us."

3. Consultation   Getting others to participate in a decision or change.
   Example: "Wonder if I could get your thoughts about this matter."

4. Ingratiating Tactics   Acting humble or friendly or making someone feel good or feel important before making a request.
   Example: "I hate to impose on your time, knowing how busy you are, but you're the only one who can help me."

5. Personal Appeals   Referring to friendship and loyalty when making a request.
   Example: "We've known each other a long time, and I'm sure I can count on you."

6. Exchange Tactics   Reminding someone of past favors or offering to trade favors.
   Example: "Since I backed you at last month's meeting, maybe you could help me this time around."

7. Coalition Tactics   Getting others to support your effort to persuade someone.
   Example: "Everyone in the department thinks this is a great idea."

8. Pressure Tactics   Using demands, threats, or intimidation to gain compliance.
   Example: "If this doesn't happen, you'd better think about cleaning out your desk."

9. Legitimating Tactics   Basing a request on one's authority or right, organizational rules or policies, or express or implied support from superiors.
   Example: "This has been green-lighted at the highest levels."

These influence tactics are considered *generic* because they are applied in all directions—up, down, and sideways within the organization. The first five influence tactics are considered "soft" tactics because they are considered friendlier than the last four "hard," or pressure, tactics. As it happens, research shows that of the three possible responses to an influence tactic—enthusiastic commitment, grudging compliance, and outright resistance—commitment is most apt to result when the tactics used are consultation, strong rational persuasion, and inspirational appeals.[17]

Knowing this, do you think you have what it takes to be a leader? To answer this, you need to understand what factors produce people of leadership character. We consider these in the rest of the chapter.

Five Approaches to Leadership

The next five sections describe five principal approaches or perspectives on leadership, which have been refined by research. They are (1) *trait,* (2) *behavioral,* (3) *contingency,* (4) *full-range,* and (5) *six additional. (See Table 14.1.)* ●

table 14.1

FIVE APPROACHES TO LEADERSHIP

1. **Trait approaches**
   - *Kouzes & Posner's five traits*—honest, competent, forward-looking, inspiring, intelligent
   - *Bossidy*—ability to execute, career runway, team orientation, multiple experiences
   - *Judge & colleagues*—two meta-analyses: importance of extroversion, conscientiousness, and openness; importance of personality over intelligence
   - *Gender studies*—motivating others, fostering communication, producing high-quality work, and so on
   - *Leadership lessons from the GLOBE project*—visionary and inspirational charismatic leaders who are good team builders are best worldwide

2. **Behavioral approaches**
   - *Michigan model*—two leadership styles: job-centered and employee-centered
   - *Ohio State model*—two dimensions: initiating-structure behavior and consideration behavior

3. **Contingency approaches**
   - *Fiedler's contingency model*—task-oriented style and relationship-oriented style—*and three dimensions of control:* leader-member, task structure, position power
   - *House's path*-goal revised leadership model—clarifying paths for subordinates' goals—and employee characteristics and environmental factors that affect leadership behaviors
   - *Hersey & Blanchard's situational leadership model*—adjusting leadership style to employee readiness

4. **Full-range approach**
   - *Transactional leadership*—clarify employee roles and tasks and provide rewards and punishments
   - *Transformational leadership*—transform employees to pursue organizational goals over self-interests, using inspirational motivation, idealized influence, individualized consideration, intellectual stimulation

5. **Six additional perspectives**
   - *Leader–member exchange (LMX) model*—leaders have different sorts of relationships with different subordinates
   - *Shared leadership*—mutual influence process in which people share responsibility for leading
   - *Greenleaf's servant leadership model*—providing service to others, not oneself
   - *Loyalty*—Reichheld's six principles: preach what one practices, pay win-win, be picky, keep it simple, reward right results, listen hard and talk straight
   - *Collins's Level 5 Leadership*—leader has humility plus fearless will to succeed, plus four other capabilities
   - *E-Leadership*—using information technology for one-to-one, one-to-many, and between group and collective interactions

14.2 TRAIT APPROACHES: DO LEADERS HAVE DISTINCTIVE PERSONALITY CHARACTERISTICS?

❋ major question | What does it take to be a successful leader?

THE BIG PICTURE
Trait approaches attempt to identify distinctive characteristics that account for the effectiveness of leaders. We describe (1) two trait perspectives expressed by Kouzes and Posner and by Bossidy; (2) Judge's research on traits; (3) some results of gender studies; and (4) leadership lessons from the GLOBE project.

Consider two high-powered leaders of the late 20th century. Each "personifies the word 'stubborn,'" says a *Fortune* magazine account. Both "are piercingly analytical thinkers who combine hands-on technical smarts with take-no-prisoners business savvy. Both absolutely hate to lose."[18]

Who are they? They are two of the most successful former CEOs in American business—Bill Gates of Microsoft and Andy Grove of Intel. Do they have distinctive personality traits that might teach us something about leadership? Perhaps they do. They would seem to embody the traits of (1) dominance, (2) intelligence, (3) self-confidence, (4) high energy, and (5) task-relevant knowledge.

These are the five traits that researcher **Ralph Stogdill** in 1948 concluded were typical of successful leaders.[19] Stogdill is one of many contributors to *trait approaches to leadership,* **which attempt to identify distinctive characteristics that account for the effectiveness of leaders.** Indeed, over the past 70 years, over 300 trait studies have been done.[20]

Trait theory is the successor to what used to be thought of as the "great man" approach to leadership, which held that leaders such as Napoleon Bonaparte and Abraham Lincoln were supposed to have some inborn ability to lead. Trait theorists believed that leadership skills were not innate, that they could be acquired through learning and experience. Today traits still often play a central role in how we perceive leaders, and organizations may find it beneficial to consider selected leadership traits when choosing among candidates for leadership positions. Gender, race, and ethnicity should not be used as any of these traits.

Two Trait Perspectives: Kouzes & Posner, & Bossidy

Two examples of trait approaches are those represented in the perspectives presented by Kouzes and Posner and by Larry Bossidy.

Kouzes & Posner's Research: Is Honesty the Top Leadership Trait?   During the 1980s, **James Kouzes** and **Barry Posner** surveyed more than 7,500 managers throughout the United States as to what personal traits they looked for and admired in their superiors.[21] The respondents suggested that a credible leader should have five traits. He or she should be (1) honest, (2) competent, (3) forward-looking, (4) inspiring, and (5) intelligent. The first trait, honesty, was considered particularly important, being selected by 87% of the respondents, suggesting that people want their leaders to be ethical.

Although this research does reveal the traits preferred by employees, it has not, however, been able to predict which people might be successful leaders.

Bossidy's Observations: A Working CEO Tells How to Find & Develop Great Leaders We mentioned **Larry Bossidy** earlier in Chapter 6 (Section 6.5) in conjunction with execution. Bossidy became CEO of AlliedSignal in 1991, when the company was suffering from low everything—morale, stock price, operating margins, and return on equity. Based on his experience of 34 years at General Electric, he realized that AlliedSignal's "inattention to leadership was a major problem."[22] He thereupon began a 2-year program of devoting up to 40% of his time to the task of hiring and developing leaders, a successful effort to which he attributes the company's turnaround.

Bossidy's approach represents the kinds of judgments that working top managers have to practice when they go about the empirical job of finding people who can be groomed into future leaders. The four qualities he looks for when interviewing and evaluating job candidates are (1) the ability to execute, (2) a career runway, (3) a team orientation, and (4) multiple experiences. *(See Table 14.2.)* Bossidy claims a 70% success rate in hiring leaders, and his approach contributed to a ninefold return for AlliedSignal shareholders from 1991 to 1999.

table 14.2

THE LEADERSHIP TRAITS BOSSIDY LOOKS FOR IN JOB CANDIDATES

1. ***Ability to execute.*** Look for a demonstrated history of real accomplishment and execution. Are you honest?	3. ***A team orientation.*** Someone able to work with other people has better potential than someone who's an individual contributor.
2. ***A career runway.*** Leaders have "plenty of runway" left in their careers, with the perspective to go beyond the present job.	4. ***Multiple experiences.*** People with significant responsibility in two or three different industries or companies have a range of good experience.

Judge's Research: Is Personality More Important Than Intelligence in Leadership?

Timothy Judge and his colleagues recently published the results of two meta-analyses that bear on the subject of traits and leaderships. **A *meta-analysis* is a statistical pooling technique that permits behavioral scientists to draw general conclusions about certain variables from many different studies.**

The Importance of Extroversion, Conscientiousness, & Openness The Big Five personality dimensions, you'll recall (from Chapter 11, Section 11.3), are extroversion, agreeableness, conscientiousness, emotional stability, and openness to experience. Judge and his group examined the Big Five personality traits and their relationship to leadership in 94 studies. Their conclusion: extroversion was most consistently and positively related to both leadership emergence and leadership effectiveness. Conscientiousness and openness to experience also were positively related to leadership effectiveness.[23]

The Importance of Personality over Intelligence In the second meta-analysis, which involved 151 samples, Judge and his colleagues found that intelligence was modestly related to leadership effectiveness. The study concluded that in the selection of leaders personality is more important than intelligence.[24] This conclusion is supported by research that found that managers who were leadership failures showed several personality flaws, including being overly controlling, irritable, exploitative, arrogant, abrasive, selfish, and lacking in emotional intelligence.[25]

Gender Studies: Do Women Have Traits That Make Them Better Leaders?

WOMEN ASPIRE TO BE CHIEF AS MUCH AS MEN DO, declared the headline in *The Wall Street Journal.* A study by a New York research firm found that 55% of women and 57% of men aspire to be CEO, challenging the notion that more women aren't at the top because they don't want to be there.[26] And, in fact, it's possible that women may have traits that make them better managers—indeed, better leaders—than men.

A number of management studies conducted in the United States for companies ranging from high-tech to manufacturing to consumer services were reviewed by *BusinessWeek*.[27] By and large, the magazine reports, the studies showed that "women executives, when rated by their peers, underlings, and bosses, score higher than their male counterparts on a wide variety of measures—from producing high-quality work to goal-setting to mentoring employees." Researchers accidentally stumbled on these findings about gender differences while compiling hundreds of routine performance evaluations and analyzing the results. In one study of 425 high-level executives, women won higher ratings on 42 of the 52 skills measured.[28]

What are the desirable traits in which women excel? Among those traits mentioned are teamwork and partnering, being more collaborative, seeking less personal glory, being motivated less by self-interest than in what they can do for the company, being more stable, and being less turf-conscious. Women were also found to be better at producing quality work, recognizing trends, and generating new ideas and acting on them. A gender comparison of skills is summarized below. *(See Table 14.3.)*

table 14.3

WHERE FEMALE EXECUTIVES DO BETTER: A SCORECARD

The check mark denotes which group scored higher on the respective studies. The asterisk indicates that in one study women's and men's scores in these categories were statistically even.

Skill	Men	Women
Motivating others		√√√√
Fostering communication		√√√√*
Producing high-quality work		√√√√
Strategic planning	√√	√√*
Listening to others		√√√√
Analyzing issues	√√	√√*

Source: Data from Hagberg Consulting Group, Management Research Group, Lawrence A. Pfaff, Personnel Decisions International Inc., and Advanced Teamware Inc., in table in R. Sharpe, "As Leaders, Women Rule," *BusinessWeek*, November 20, 2000, p. 75.

Why, then, aren't more women in positions of leadership? Males and females disagree about this issue. A team of researchers asked this question of 461 executive women holding titles of vice president or higher in Fortune 100 companies and all the male Fortune 100 CEOs. CEOs believed that women are not in senior leadership positions because (1) they lack significant general management experience and (2) women have not been in the executive talent pool long enough to get selected. Women, by contrast, believed that (1) male stereotyping and (2) exclusion from important informal networks are the biggest barriers to promotability.[29]

There are two additional possible explanations. First, as we suggested earlier in the book, there are many women who, though hard working, simply aren't willing to compete as hard as most men are or are not willing to make the required personal sacrifices.[30] (As Jamie Gorelick, former vice chair of Fannie Mae but also mother of two children ages 10 and 15, said when declining to be considered for CEO: "I just don't want that pace in my life.")[31] Second, women have a tendency to be overly modest and to give credit to others rather than taking it for themselves, which can undermine opportunities for promotions and raises.[32]

Leadership Lessons from the GLOBE Project

Project GLOBE (Global Leadership and Organizational Behavior Effectiveness), you'll recall from Chapter 4, is a massive and ongoing attempt to develop an empirically based theory to "describe, understand, and predict the impact of specific cultural variables on leadership and organizational processes and the effectiveness of these processes."[33] Surveying 17,000 middle managers working for 951 organizations across 62 countries, the researchers determined that certain attributes of leadership were universally liked or disliked. *(See Table 14.4.)* Visionary and inspirational *charismatic leaders* who are good team builders generally do the best. *Self-centered leaders* seen as loners or face-savers generally receive a poor reception worldwide. ●

table 14.4

LESSONS FROM GLOBE: LEADERSHIP ATTRIBUTES UNIVERSALLY LIKED AND DISLIKED ACROSS 62 NATIONS

Universally positive leader attributes	Universally negative leader attributes
Trustworthy	Loner
Just	Asocial
Honest	Noncooperative
Foresight	Irritable
Plans ahead	Nonexplicit
Encouraging	Egocentric
Positive	Ruthless
Dynamic	Dictatorial
Motive arouser	
Confidence builder	
Motivational	
Dependable	
Intelligent	
Decisive	
Effective bargainer	
Win-win problem solver	
Administrative skilled	
Communicative	
Informed	
Coordinator	
Team builder	
Excellence oriented	

Source: Excerpted and adapted from P. W. Dorfman, P. J. Hanges, and F. C. Brodbeck, "Leadership and Cultural Variation: The Identification of Culturally Endorsed Leadership Profiles," in R. J. House, P. J. Hanges, M. Javidan, P. W. Dorfman, and V. Gupta eds., *Culture, Leadership and Organizations: The GLOBE Study of 62 Societies* (Thousand Oaks, CA: Sage, 2004), Tables 21.2 and 21.3, pp. 677–678.

14.3 BEHAVIORAL APPROACHES: DO LEADERS SHOW DISTINCTIVE PATTERNS OF BEHAVIOR?

> ✸ major question Do effective leaders behave in similar ways?

THE BIG PICTURE
Behavioral leadership approaches try to determine the distinctive styles used by effective leaders. Two models we describe are the University of Michigan model and the Ohio State model.

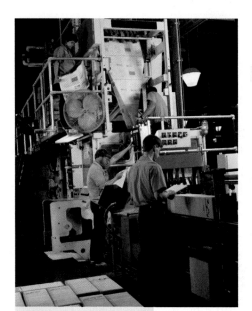

Printing press. What kind of leadership behavior is appropriate for directing these kinds of workers?

Maybe what's important to know about leaders is not their *personality traits* but rather their *patterns of behavior* or *leadership styles.* This is the line of thought pursued by those interested in **behavioral leadership approaches,** which attempt to determine the distinctive styles used by effective leaders. By *leadership styles,* we mean the combination of traits, skills, and behaviors that leaders use when interacting with others.

What all models of leadership behavior have in common is the consideration of *task orientation versus people orientation.* Two classic studies came out of the universities of Michigan and Ohio State.

The University of Michigan Leadership Model

In the late 1940s, researchers at the University of Michigan came up with what came to be known as the **University of Michigan Leadership Model.** A team led by **Rensis Likert** began studying the effects of leader behavior on job performance, interviewing numerous managers and subordinates.[34] The investigators identified two forms of leadership styles: *job-centered* and *employee-centered.*

- **Job-centered behavior—"I'm concerned more with the needs of the job."** In *job-centered behavior,* managers paid more attention to the job and work procedures. Thus, their principal concerns were with achieving production efficiency, keeping costs down, and meeting schedules.

- **Employee-centered behavior—"I'm concerned more with the needs of employees."** In *employee-centered behavior,* managers paid more attention to employee satisfaction and making work groups cohesive. By concentrating on subordinates' needs they hoped to build effective work groups with high-performance goals.

The Ohio State Leadership Model

A second approach to leadership research was begun in 1945 at Ohio State University under **Ralph Stogdill** (mentioned in the last section). Hundreds of dimensions of leadership behavior were studied, resulting in what came to be known as the **Ohio State**

Leadership Model.[35] From surveys of leadership behavior, two major dimensions of leader behavior were identified, as follows.

- **Initiating structure—"What do I do to get the job done?"** *Initiating structure* is leadership behavior that organizes and defines what group members should be doing. It consists of the efforts the leader makes to get things organized and get the job done. This is much the same as Likert's "job-centered behavior."

- **Consideration—"What do I do to show consideration for my employees?"** *Consideration* is leadership behavior that expresses concern for employees by establishing a warm, friendly, supportive climate. This behavior, which resembles Likert's "employee-centered behavior," is sensitive to subordinates' ideas and feelings and establishes mutual trust.

All in all, one management expert concluded from the Michigan and Ohio studies that effective leaders (1) tend to have supportive or employee-centered relationships with employees, (2) use group rather than individual methods of supervision, and (3) set high performance goals.[36] ●

Practical Action

Transition Problems on Your Way Up: How to Avoid the Pitfalls

Before you can become a good leader you need to become a good manager. Making the leap from individual contributor to a manager of several employees "is one of the most difficult in peoples' careers," suggests *Wall Street Journal* columnist Hal Lancaster.

Although corporations and managements may make noises about training and mentoring support, newly promoted managers may not see any of this and may simply be expected to know what to do. And, as managers move up the ladder, they may encounter other problems that they have not anticipated. How can you avoid some pitfalls as you make your ascent? Some suggestions:[37]

- **Have realistic expectations.** New managers often focus on the rights and privileges of their new jobs and underestimate the duties and obligations.

- **Don't forget to manage upward and sideways as well as downward.** You not only need to manage your subordinates but also the perceptions of your peers and your own managers above you.

- **Stay in touch with managers in other departments.** In addition, you need to have good relationships with managers in other departments—and be perceptive about their needs and priorities—

since they have resources you need to get your job done. Don't make the mistake of thinking your own department is the center of the universe.

- **Think about what kind of manager or leader you want to be.** Make a list of all your previous bosses and their good and bad attributes. This may produce a list of dos and don'ts that can serve you well.

- **Get guidance from other managers.** You may not get advice on how to manage from your own manager, who may have promoted you to help reduce his or her workload, not add to it by expecting some coaching. If this is the case, don't be shy about consulting other managers as well as people in professional organizations.

- **Resist isolation.** If you're promoted beyond supervisor of a small team and you have to manage hundreds rather than dozens, or thousands rather than hundreds, you may find the biggest surprise is isolation. The way to stay in touch is to talk daily with your senior managers, perhaps have "town meetings" with staffers several times a year, and employ "management by walking around"—bringing teams together to talk.

14.4 CONTINGENCY APPROACHES: DOES LEADERSHIP VARY WITH THE SITUATION?

> ⊛ major question — How might effective leadership vary according to the situation at hand?

THE BIG PICTURE

Effective leadership behavior depends on the situation at hand, say believers in the three contingency approaches: Fiedler's contingency leadership model, House's path-goal leadership model, and Hersey and Blanchard's situational leadership model.

Perhaps leadership is not characterized by universally important traits or behaviors. Perhaps there is no one best style that will work in all situations. This is the point of view of proponents of the *contingency approach* to leadership, **who believe that effective leadership behavior depends on the situation at hand.** That is, as situations change, different styles become appropriate.

Let's consider three contingency approaches: (1) the *contingency leadership model* by Fiedler, (2) the *path-goal leadership model* by House, and (3) the *situational leadership model* by Hersey and Blanchard.

I. The Contingency Leadership Model: Fiedler's Approach

The oldest model of the contingency approach to leadership was developed by **Fred Fiedler** and his associates in 1951.[38] **The *contingency leadership model* determines if a leader's style is (1) task-oriented or (2) relationship-oriented and if that style is effective for the situation at hand.** Fiedler's work was based on 80 studies conducted over 30 years.

Two Leadership Orientations: Tasks versus Relationships Are you task-oriented or relationship-oriented? That is, are you more concerned with task accomplishment or with people?

To find out, you or your employees would fill out a questionnaire (known as the least preferred co-worker, or LPC, scale), in which you think of the co-worker you least enjoyed working with and rate him or her according to an eight-point scale of 16 pairs of opposite characteristics (such as friendly/unfriendly, tense/relaxed, efficient/inefficient). The higher the score, the more the relationship-oriented the respondent; the lower the score, the more task-oriented.

Tile style. Do successful entrepreneurs or small-business managers need to be task-oriented, relationship-oriented, or both? What style of leadership model would best suit a small tile manufacturing business in which employees need to work with a great deal of independence?

The Three Dimensions of Situational Control Once the leadership orientation is known, then you determine *situational control*—how much control and influence a leader has in the immediate work environment.

There are three dimensions of situational control: *leader-member relations, task structure,* and *position power.*

- **Leader-member relations—"Do my subordinates accept me as a leader?"** This dimension, the most important component of situational control, reflects the extent to which a leader has or doesn't have the support, loyalty, and trust of the work group.

- **Task structure—"Do my subordinates perform unambiguous, easily understood tasks?"** This dimension refers to the extent to which tasks are routine, unambiguous, and easily understood. The more structured the jobs, the more influence a leader has.

- **Position power—"Do I have power to reward and punish?"** This dimension refers to how much power a leader has to make work assignments and reward and punish. More power equals more control and influence.

For each dimension, the amount of control can be *high*—the leader's decisions will produce predictable results because he or she has the ability to influence work outcomes. Or it can be *low*—he or she doesn't have that kind of predictability or influence. By combining the three different dimensions with different high/low ratings, we have eight different leadership situations.

Which Style Is Most Effective?   Neither leadership style is effective all the time, Fiedler's research concludes, although each is right in certain situations.

- **When task-oriented style is best.** The task-oriented style works best in either *high-control* or *low-control* situations.

  Example of *high-control* situation (leader decisions produce predictable results because he or she can influence work outcomes): Suppose you were supervising parking-control officers ticketing cars parked illegally in expired meter zones, bus zones, and the like. You have (1) high leader-member relations because your subordinates are highly supportive of you and (2) high task structure because their jobs are clearly defined. (3) You have high position control because you have complete authority to evaluate their performance and dole out punishment and rewards. Thus, a task-oriented style would be best.

  Example of *low-control* situation (leader decisions can't produce predictable results because he or she can't really influence outcomes): Suppose you were a high school principal trying to clean up graffiti on your private-school campus, helped only by students you can find after school. You might have (1) low leader-member relations because many people might not see the need for the goal. (2) The task structure might also be low because people might see many different ways to achieve the goal. And (3) your position power would be low because the committee is voluntary and people are free to leave. In this low-control situation, a task-oriented style would also be best.

- **When relationship-oriented style is best.** The relationship-oriented style works best in situations of *moderate control.*

  Example: Suppose you were working in a government job supervising a group of firefighters fighting wildfires. You might have (1) low leader-member relations if you were promoted over others in the group but (2) high task structure, because the job is fairly well defined. (3) You might have low position power, because the rigidity of the civil-service job prohibits you from doing much in the way of rewarding and punishing. Thus, in this moderate-control situation, relationship-oriented leadership would be most effective.

Test Your Knowledge:
Fiedler's Contingency Model of Leadership

What do you do if your leadership orientation does not match the situation? Then, says Fiedler, it's better to try to move leaders into suitable situations rather than try to alter their personalities to fit the situations.[39]

2. The Path–Goal Leadership Model: House's Approach

A second contingency approach, advanced by **Robert House** in the 1970s and revised by him in 1996, is the ***path–goal leadership model,* which holds that the effective leader makes available to followers desirable rewards in the workplace and increases their motivation by clarifying the *paths,* or behavior, that will help them achieve those *goals* and providing them with support.** A successful leader thus helps followers by tying meaningful rewards to goal accomplishment, reducing barriers, and providing support, so as to increase "the number and kinds of personal payoffs to subordinates for work-goal attainment."[40]

figure 14.1

GENERAL REPRESENTATION OF HOUSE'S REVISED PATH–GOAL THEORY

Numerous studies testing various predictions from House's original path–goal theory provided mixed results.[41] As a consequence, he proposed a new model, a graphical version, shown below. *(See Figure 14.1.)*

① Leader behaviors are . . .

. . . influenced by the two contingency factors of ② employee characteristics and ③ environmental factors . . .

. . . in determining ④ the most effective leadership.

② Employee characteristics
- Locus of control
- Task ability
- Need for achievement
- Experience
- Need for path–goal clarity

① Leader behaviors
- Path–goal clarifying
- Achievement-oriented
- Work facilitation
- Supportive
- Interaction facilitation
- Group-oriented decision making
- Representation & networking
- Value-based

③ Environmental factors
- Task structure
- Work group dynamics

④ Leadership effectiveness
- Employee motivation
- Employee satisfaction
- Employee performance
- Leader acceptance
- Interaction facilitation
- Work-unit performance

What Determines Leadership Effectiveness: Employee Characteristics & Environmental Factors Affect Leader Behavior   As the drawing indicates, two contingency factors, or variables—*employee characteristics* and *environmental factors*—cause some *leadership behaviors* to be more effective than others.

- **Employee characteristics.** Five employee characteristics are locus of control (described in Chapter 11), task ability, need for achievement, experience, and need for path–goal clarity.

- **Environmental factors.** Two environmental factors are task structure (independent versus interdependent tasks) and work group dynamics.

- **Leader behaviors.** Originally House proposed that there were four leader behaviors, or leadership styles—*directive* ("Here's what's expected of you and here's how to do it"), *supportive* ("I want things to be pleasant, since everyone's about equal here"), *participative* ("I want your suggestions in order to help me make decisions"), and *achievement-oriented* ("I'm confident you can accomplish the following great things"). The revised theory expands the number of leader behaviors from four to eight. *(See Table 14.5, opposite.)*

Thus, for example, employees with an internal locus of control are more likely to prefer achievement-oriented leadership or group-oriented decision making (formerly participative) leadership because they believe they have control over the work environment. The same is true for employees with high task ability and experience.

Employees with an external locus of control, however, tend to view the environment as uncontrollable, so they prefer the structure provided by supportive or path–goal clarifying (formerly directive) leadership. The same is probably true of inexperienced employees.

Besides expanding the styles of leader behavior from four to eight, House's revision of his theory also puts more emphasis on the need for leaders to foster intrinsic motivation

table 14.5

EIGHT LEADERSHIP STYLES OF THE REVISED PATH–GOAL THEORY

Style of leader behaviors	Description of behavior toward employees
1. Path–goal clarifying ("Here's what's expected of you and here's how to do it")	Clarify performance goals. Provide guidance on how employees can complete tasks. Clarify performance standards and expectations. Use positive and negative rewards contingent on performance.
2. Achievement-oriented ("I'm confident you can accomplish the following great things")	Set challenging goals. Emphasize excellence. Demonstrate confidence in employee abilities.
3. Work facilitation ("Here's the goal, and here's what I can do to help you achieve it")	Plan, schedule, organize, and coordinate work. Provide mentoring, coaching, counseling, and feedback to assist employees in developing their skills. Eliminate roadblocks. Provide resources. Empower employees to take actions and make decisions.
4. Supportive ("I want things to be pleasant, since everyone's about equal here")	Treat as equals. Show concern for well-being and needs. Be friendly and approachable.
5. Interaction facilitation ("Let's see how we can all work together to accomplish our goals")	Emphasize collaboration and teamwork. Encourage close employee relationships and sharing of minority opinions. Facilitate communication, resolve disputes.
6. Group-oriented decision making ("I want your suggestions in order to help me make decisions")	Pose problems rather than solutions to work group. Encourage members to participate in decision making. Provide necessary information to the group for analysis. Involve knowledgeable employees in decision making.
7. Representation & networking ("I've got a great bunch of people working for me whom you'll probably want to meet")	Present work group in positive light to others. Maintain positive relationships with influential others. Participate in organization-wide social functions and ceremonies. Do unconditional favors for others.
8. Value-based ("We're destined to accomplish great things")	Establish a vision, display passion for it, and support its accomplishment. Communicate high performance expectations and confidence in others' abilities to meet their goals. Give frequent positive feedback. Demonstrate self-confidence.

Source: Adapted from R. J. House, "Path–Goal Theory of Leadership: Lessons, Legacy, and a Reformulated Theory," *Leadership Quarterly*, Autumn 1996, pp. 323–352.

through empowerment. Finally, his revised theory stresses the concept of shared leadership, the idea that employees do not have to be supervisors or managers to engage in leader behavior but rather may share leadership among all employees of the organization.

Does the Revised Path–Goal Theory Work?   There have not been enough direct tests of House's revised path–goal theory using appropriate research methods and statistical procedures to draw overall conclusions. Research on charismatic leadership, however, which is discussed in Section 14.5, is supportive of the revised model.[42]

Although further research is needed on the new model, it offers two important implications for managers:

- *Use more than one leadership style.* Effective leaders possess and use more than one style of leadership. Thus, you are encouraged to study the eight styles

Test Your Knowledge:
Path–Goal Theory

Cranium's grand poo-bah and chief noodler. Richard Tait (left), responsible for business operations and marketing for the 14-person, Seattle-based game company Cranium, takes the unorthodox title of grand poo-bah. Whit Alexander, who focuses on product development, editorial content, and manufacturing, is called chief noodler. In devising the board game Cranium, the two entrepreneurs decided to adopt the acronym CHIFF— for "clever, high quality, innovative, friendly, and fun"— as the criterion by which all decisions would be guided. "Our survival and success will come from optimizing fun, focus, passion, and profits," says Tait. Which one of the eight path–goal leadership styles would you expect to find dominating this organization?

offered in path–goal theory so that you can try new leader behaviors when a situation calls for them.

- *Modify leadership style to fit employee and task characteristics.* A small set of employee characteristics (ability, experience, and need for independence) and environmental factors (task characteristics of autonomy, variety, and significance) are relevant contingency factors, and managers should modify their leadership style to fit them.[43]

3. The Situational Leadership Theory Model: Hersey & Blanchard's Approach

A third contingency approach has been proposed by management writers **Paul Hersey** and **Kenneth Blanchard.**[44] **In their *situational leadership theory,* leadership behavior reflects how leaders should adjust their leadership style according to the readiness of the followers.** The model suggests that managers should be flexible in choosing a leadership behavior style and be sensitive to the readiness level of their employees. ***Readiness* is defined as the extent to which a follower possesses the ability and willingness to complete a task.** Subordinates with high readiness (with high ability, skills, and willingness to work) require a different leadership style than do those with low readiness (low ability, training, and willingness).

The appropriate leadership style is found by cross-referencing follower readiness (low–high) with one of four leaderships styles. *(See Figure 14.2, opposite.)*

How the Situational Leadership Model Works   Let's see what the illustration means.

- **Leadership styles—relationship behavior plus task behavior.** The upper part of the drawing shows the leadership style, which is based on the combination of relationship behavior (vertical axis) and task behavior (horizontal axis).

    Relationship behavior is the extent to which leaders maintain personal relationships with their followers, as in providing support and keeping communication open.

    Task behavior is the extent to which leaders organize and explain the role of their followers, which is achieved by explaining what subordinates are to do and how tasks are to be accomplished.

- **Four leadership styles—telling, selling, participating, delegating.** The bell-shaped curve indicates when each of the four leadership styles—telling (S1), selling (S2), participating (S3), and delegating (S4)—should be used.

- **When a leadership style should be used—depends on the readiness of the followers.** How do you know which leadership style to employ? You need to have an understanding of the *readiness* of your followers, as represented by the scale at the bottom of the drawing, where R1 represents low readiness and R4 represents high readiness.

    Let's consider which leadership style to apply when.

    Telling represents the guiding and directing of performance. This leadership style works best for followers with a low level of readiness—that is, subordinates are neither willing nor able to take responsibility.

    Selling is explaining decisions and persuading others to follow a course of action. Because it offers both direction and support, this leadership style is most suitable for followers who are unable but willing to assume task responsibility.

    Participating involves encouraging followers to solve problems on their own. Because it shares decision making, this leadership style encourages subordinates in performing tasks. Thus, it is most appropriate for followers whose readiness is in the moderate to high range.

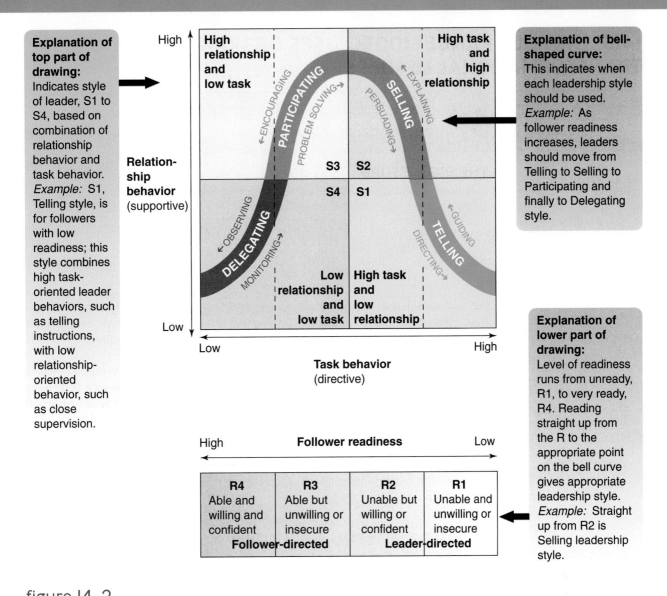

Explanation of top part of drawing: Indicates style of leader, S1 to S4, based on combination of relationship behavior and task behavior. *Example:* S1, Telling style, is for followers with low readiness; this style combines high task-oriented leader behaviors, such as telling instructions, with low relationship-oriented behavior, such as close supervision.

Explanation of bell-shaped curve: This indicates when each leadership style should be used. *Example:* As follower readiness increases, leaders should move from Telling to Selling to Participating and finally to Delegating style.

Explanation of lower part of drawing: Level of readiness runs from unready, R1, to very ready, R4. Reading straight up from the R to the appropriate point on the bell curve gives appropriate leadership style. *Example:* Straight up from R2 is Selling leadership style.

High relationship and low task — PARTICIPATING — High task and high relationship — SELLING

Relationship behavior (supportive)

S3 S2
S4 S1

DELEGATING — Low relationship and low task — High task and low relationship — TELLING

Low ————— Task behavior (directive) ————— High

High ————— Follower readiness ————— Low

R4	R3	R2	R1
Able and willing and confident	Able but unwilling or insecure	Unable but willing or confident	Unable and unwilling or insecure
Follower-directed		**Leader-directed**	

figure 14. 2

HERSEY AND BLANCHARD'S SITUATIONAL LEADERSHIP MODEL

Source: Adapted from P. Hersey, K. H. Blanchard, and D. E. Johnson, *Management of Organizational Behavior: Leading Human Resources,* 8th ed. (Upper Saddle River, NJ: Prentice Hall, 2000). Situational leadership® is a registered trademark of the Center for Leadership Studies, Inc. Copyright © 2002, Center for Leadership Studies, Inc. All rights reserved.

Delegating is providing subordinates with little support or direction. As such, the leader's role is to observe and monitor. This leadership style is best for followers who have a high level of readiness, both able and willing to perform tasks.

Does the Hersey-Blanchard Model Work? The situational leadership model is widely used as a training tool, but it is not strongly supported by scientific research. For instance, a study of 459 salespeople found that leadership effectiveness was not attributable to the predicted interaction between follower readiness and leadership style.[45] This is consistent with another study, in which 57 chief nurse executives were found not to delegate in accordance with situational leadership theory.[46] Researchers also have concluded that the self-assessment instrument used to measure leadership style and follower readiness is inaccurate.[47] In sum, managers should exercise discretion when using prescriptions from this model. ●

14.5 THE FULL-RANGE MODEL: USES OF TRANSACTIONAL & TRANSFORMATIONAL LEADERSHIP

major question What does it take to truly inspire people to perform beyond their normal levels?

THE BIG PICTURE

Full-range leadership describes leadership along a range of styles, with the most effective being transactional/transformational leaders. Four key behaviors of transformational leaders in affecting employees are they inspire motivation, inspire trust, encourage excellence, and stimulate them intellectually.

We have considered the major traditional approaches to understanding leadership—the trait, behavioral, and contingency approaches. But newer approaches seem to offer something more by trying to determine what factors inspire and motivate people to perform beyond their normal levels.

One recent approach proposed by **Bernard Bass and Bruce Avolio,** known as *full range leadership,* **suggests that leadership behavior varies along a full range of leadership styles, from take-no-responsibility (*laissez-faire*) "leadership" at one extreme, through transactional leadership, to transformational leadership at the other extreme.**[48] Not taking responsibility can hardly be considered leadership (although it often seems to be manifested by CEOs whose companies got in trouble, as when they say "I had no idea about the criminal behavior of my subordinates"). Transactional and transformational leadership behaviors, however, are both positive aspects of being a good leader.

Transactional versus Transformational Leaders

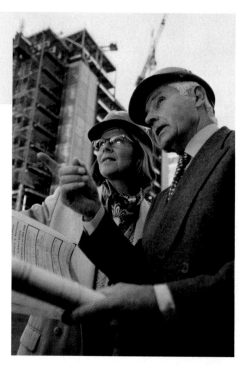

Plans, budgets, schedules. Would you expect management in the construction field to focus more on the nonpeople aspects of work?

Jim McNerney, chairman and CEO of 3M, is able to be both a transactional and a transformational leader. Let us consider the differences.

Transactional Leadership As a manager, your power stems from your ability to provide rewards (and threaten reprimands) in exchange for your subordinates' doing the work. When you do this, you are performing *transactional leadership,* **focusing on clarifying employees' roles and task requirements and providing rewards and punishments contingent on performance.** Transactional leadership also encompasses the fundamental managerial activities of setting goals and monitoring progress toward their achievement.[49]

"[3M's] McNerney's secret to success is elementary," says a *BusinessWeek* article. "He sets high goals that can be measured, such as business-unit sales or the rate of product introductions, and demands that his managers meet them. Granted, many CEOs do that today. But like a dedicated teacher or coach, McNerney also works with his team day in, day out, to help them make the grade."[50]

We shouldn't think of a transactional leader as being a mediocre leader—indeed, competent transactional leaders are badly needed. But transactional leaders are best in stable situations. What's needed in rapidly changing situations, as is often the case in many organizations today, is a transformational leader.

Transformational Leadership *Transformational leadership* **transforms employees to pursue organizational goals over self-interests.** Transformational leaders, in one description, "engender trust, seek to develop leadership in others, exhibit self-sacrifice, and serve as moral agents, focusing themselves and followers on objectives that transcend the more immediate needs of the work group."[51] Whereas transactional leaders try to get people to do *ordinary things,* transformational leaders encourage their people to do *exceptional* things—significantly higher levels of intrinsic motivation, trust, commitment, and loyalty—that can produce significant organizational change and results.

Transformational leaders are influenced by two factors:

- **Individual characteristics.** The personalities of such leaders tend to be more extroverted, agreeable, and proactive than nontransformational leaders. (Female leaders tend to use transformational leadership more than male leaders do.)[52]

- **Organizational culture.** Adaptive, flexible organizational cultures are more likely than are rigid, bureaucratic cultures to foster transformational leadership.

The Best Leaders Are Both Transactional & Transformational

It's important to note that transactional leadership is an essential *prerequisite* to effective leadership, and the best leaders learn to display both transactional and transformational styles of leadership to some degree. Indeed, research suggests that transformational leadership leads to superior performance when it "augments" or adds to transactional leadership.[53]

This is apparent in the case of 3M CEO McNerney. "Some people think you either have a demanding, command-and-control management style or you have a nurturing, encouraging style," he says. "I believe you can't have one without the other." *BusinessWeek* points out that McNerney is praised for being an inspirational leader who is comfortable speaking either one-on-one or to large groups. He also is quick to attribute the company's achievements to the entire organization and praises employees for their work ethic.[54]

Four Key Behaviors of Transformational Leaders

Whereas transactional leaders are dispassionate, transformational leaders excite passion, inspiring and empowering people to look beyond their own interests to the interests of the organization. They appeal to their followers' self-concepts—their values and personal identity—to create changes in their goals, values, needs, beliefs, and aspirations.

Transformational leaders have four key kinds of behavior that affect followers.[55]

1. Inspirational Motivation: "Let Me Share a Vision That Transcends Us All" Transformational leaders have *charisma* ("kar-*riz*-muh"), **a form of interpersonal attraction that inspires acceptance and support.** Such leaders inspire motivation

Sir Branson. One of today's most flamboyant businessmen, Britain's Richard Branson (middle), is shown here in May 2003 in Sydney Australia, with Paul Pester (right), CEO for the Virgin Money Group Ltd (UK) at the launch of the new Virgin credit card (shown behind them). Branson left school at 16 to start a 1960s counterculture magazine. By 2006, he was heading a $5 billion-plus empire—the Virgin Group—that includes airlines, entertainment companies, car dealerships, railroads, bridal gowns, soft drinks, financial services, a space tourism company, and his latest venture, Virgin Fuel. Knighted in 2000—which entitles him to be called "Sir"—Branson, who is dyslexic, says he is not for scrutinizing spreadsheets and plotting strategies based on estimates of market share. "In the end," he says, "it is your own gut and your own experience of running businesses." Do you think charismatic business leaders like Sir Branson are able to be more successful than more conventional and conservative managers?

by offering an agenda, a grand design, an ultimate goal—in short, a *vision,* "a realistic, credible, attractive future" for the organization, as leadership expert Burt Nanus calls it. The right vision unleashes human potential, says Nanus, because it serves as a beacon of hope and common purpose. It does so by attracting commitment, energizing workers, creating meaning in their lives, establishing a standard of excellence, promoting high ideals, and bridging the divide between the organization's problems and its goals and aspirations.[56]

Examples: Civil rights leader Martin Luther King Jr. had a vision—a "dream," as he put it—of racial equality. United Farm Workers leader Cesar Chavez had a vision of better working conditions and pay for agricultural workers. Candy Lightner, founder of Mothers Against Drunk Driving, had a vision of getting rid of alcohol-related car crashes. Apple Computer's Steve Jobs had a vision of developing an "insanely great" desktop computer.

2. Idealized Influence: "We Are Here to Do the Right Thing" Transformational leaders are able to inspire trust in their followers because they express their integrity by being consistent, single-minded, and persistent in pursuit of their goal. Not only do they display high ethical standards and act as models of desirable values, but they are also able to make sacrifices for the good of the group.[57]

Examples: In 1982, when seven people died consuming cyanide-laced Tylenol capsules, Johnson & Johnson CEO James Burke retained consumer confidence by his actions in taking the drug off the market. Anita Roddick of The Body Shop cosmetics company has been a model for her beliefs in fair trade, environmental awareness, animal protection, and respect for human rights.

3. Individualized Consideration: "You Have the Opportunity Here to Grow & Excel" Transformational leaders don't just express concern for subordinates' well-being. They actively encourage them to grow and to excel by giving them challenging work, more responsibility, empowerment, and one-on-one mentoring.

Example: Curt "Curre" Linström as head coach of the Finnish national ice hockey team was able to be the caring, fatherly figure to his athletes that enabled them to trust his leadership—and to go from gloomy failure to world championship victory in 1995.

4. Intellectual Stimulation: "Let Me Describe the Great Challenges We Can Conquer Together" These leaders are gifted at communicating the organization's strengths, weaknesses, opportunities, and threats so that subordinates develop a new sense of purpose. Employees become less apt to view problems as insurmountable or "that's not my department." Instead they learn to view them as personal challenges that they are responsible for overcoming, to question the status quo, and to seek creative solutions.

Example: Ben Cohen, co-founder of Ben & Jerry's, was able to communicate his vision that making ice cream shouldn't be just about profits but also about using some profits for good works.

Implications of Transformational Leadership for Managers

The research shows that transformational leadership yields several positive results. For example, it is positively associated with (1) measures of organizational effectiveness;[58] (2) measures of leadership effectiveness and employee job satisfaction;[59] (3) more employee identification with their leaders and with their immediate work groups;[60] and (4) higher levels of intrinsic motivation, group cohesion, work engagement, and setting of goals consistent with those of the leader.[61]

Besides the fact that, as we mentioned, the best leaders are *both* transactional and transformational, there are three important implications of transformational leadership for managers, as follows.

1. It Can Improve Results for Both Individuals & Groups   You can use the four types of transformational behavior just described to improve results for individuals—such as job satisfaction, organizational commitment, and performance. You can also use them to improve outcomes for groups—an important matter in today's organization, where people tend not to work in isolation but in collaboration with others.

2. It Can Be Used to Train Employees at Any Level   Not just top managers but employees at any level can be trained to be more transactional and transformational.[62] This kind of leadership training among employees should be based on a corporate philosophy, however. Johnson & Johnson, for instance, bases its training on seven principles of leadership development. *(See Table 14.6.)*

table 14.6

SEVEN PRINCIPLES OF LEADERSHIP DEVELOPMENT

These were developed by Johnson & Johnson.

1. Leadership development is a key business strategy.
2. Leadership excellence is a definable set of standards.
3. People are responsible for their own development.
4. Johnson & Johnson executives are accountable for developing leaders.
5. Leaders are developed primarily on the job.
6. People are an asset of the corporation; leadership development is a collaborative, corporation-wide process.
7. Human resources are vital to the success of leadership development.

Source: Excerpted from R. M. Fulmer, "Johnson & Johnson: Framework for Leadership," *Organizational Dynamics,* Winter 2001, p. 214.

3. It Can Be Used by Both Ethical & Unethical Leaders   Ethical transformational leaders help employees to enhance their self-concepts. Unethical leaders may select or produce obedient, dependent, and compliant followers. To better ensure positive results from transformational leadership, top managers should do the following:[63]

- **Employ a code of ethics.** The company should create and enforce a clearly stated code of ethics.
- **Choose the right people.** Recruit, select, and promote people who display ethical behavior.
- **Make performance expectations reflect employee treatment.** Develop performance expectations around the treatment of employees; these expectations can be assessed in the performance-appraisal process.
- **Emphasize value of diversity.** Train employees to value diversity.
- **Reward high moral conduct.** Identify, reward, and publicly praise employees who exemplify high moral conduct. ●

14.6 SIX ADDITIONAL PERSPECTIVES

❌ major question **If there are many ways to be a leader, which one would describe me best?**

THE BIG PICTURE

We consider six other kinds of leadership. The *leader–member exchange model* emphasizes that leaders have different sorts of relationships with different subordinates. In *shared leadership*, people share responsibility for leading with others. In *servant leadership*, leaders provide service to employees and the organization. *Loyalty leaders* inspire others by their integrity in words and deeds. *Level 5 leaders* possess the paradoxical qualities of humility and fearless will to succeed. *E-leadership* involves leader interactions with others via information technology.

Six additional kinds of leadership deserve discussion: (1) *leader–member exchange (LMX) model of leadership*, (2) *shared leadership*, (3) *servant leadership*, (4) *loyalty leadership*, (5) *Level 5 leadership*, and (6) *e-leadership*.

Self-Assessment Exercise:
Assessing Your
Leader–Member
Exchange

Leader–Member Exchange (LMX) Leadership

Proposed by **George Graen and Fred Dansereau, the *leader–member exchange (LMX) model of leadership* emphasizes that leaders have different sorts of relationships with different subordinates.**[64] Unlike other models we've described, which focus on the behaviors or traits of leaders or followers, the LMX model looks at the quality of relationships between managers and subordinates. Also, unlike other models, which presuppose stable relationships between leaders and followers, the LMX model assumes each manager-subordinate relationship is unique (what behavioral scientists call a "vertical dyad").

In-Group Exchange versus Out-Group Exchange

The unique relationship, which supposedly results from the leader's attempt to delegate and assign work roles, can produce two types of leader–member exchange interactions:[65]

- **In-group exchange.** In the *in-group exchange,* the relationship between leader and follower becomes a partnership characterized by mutual trust, respect and liking, and a sense of common fates. Subordinates may receive special assignments and may also receive special privileges.

- **Out-group exchange.** In the *out-group exchange,* leaders are characterized as overseers who fail to create a sense of mutual trust, respect, or common fate. Subordinates receive less of the manager's time and attention than those in in-group exchange relationships.

Is the LMX Model Useful?

It is not clear why a leader selects particular subordinates to be part of the in-group, but presumably the choice is made for reasons of compatibility and competence. Certainly, however, a positive (that is, in-group) leader–member exchange is positively associated with goal commitment, trust between managers and employees, work climate, satisfaction with leadership, and—important to any employer—job performance and job satisfaction.[66] The type of leader–member exchange also was found to predict not only turnover among nurses and computer analysts but also career outcomes, such as promotability, salary level, and receipt of bonuses, over a 7-year period.[67]

Shared Leadership

Which is better—leadership in a single chain of command or shared leadership responsibility among two or more individuals? Perhaps, it's suggested, shared leadership is more optimal.[68] **Shared leadership is a simultaneous, ongoing, mutual influence process in which people share responsibility for leading.** It is based on the idea that people need to share information and collaborate to get things done. This kind of leadership is most likely to be needed when people work in teams, are involved in complex projects, or are doing knowledge work—work requiring voluntary contributions of intellectual capital by skilled professionals.[69] Researchers are beginning to explore the process of shared leadership, and the results are promising. For example, shared leadership in teams has been found to be positively associated with group cohesion, group citizenship, and group effectiveness.[70]

Example

Shared Leadership: Tech Companies Spread the Power

All kinds of organizations are run with shared leadership. The famed Mayo Clinic, for example, which employs more than 42,000 employees in various hospitals and clinics, relies on shared leadership to provide high-quality health care and customer service.[71] For a while, Ford Motor Company was run by three individuals at the top.[72] At Dell, founder and chairman Michael Dell shares power with Chief Executive Officer and President Kevin Rollins.[73] At Google, cofounders Sergey Brin, President, Technology, and Larry Page, President, Products, are part of a triumvirate with Eric Schmidt, Chief Executive Officer.[74]

The fastest-growing Web site on the planet, with 100 million "friends," is MySpace.com. The founders, Tom Anderson and Chris DeWolfe, who live in Los Angeles, created the site, according to *Fortune,* "to promote local acts and connect fans and friends . . . who connected friends . . . who connected friends. . . . The two had a friendship based on business, then they—quite literally—founded a business based on friendship." When News Corp. CEO Rupert Murdoch offered $580 million for MySpace's parent company, they accepted the deal but remained on as the top executives, with DeWolfe as CEO and Anderson as President. DeWolfe is the business brain, the smart person with the compelling vision; Anderson is the "soul" of the enterprise, the one who understands the users.[75]

Your Call

If you were leading a business with a friend of yours, which role do you think would suit you best—the "business brain" or the "soul"?

Servant Leadership: Meeting the Goals of Followers & the Organization, Not of Oneself

The term *servant leadership,* coined in 1970 by **Robert Greenleaf,** reflects not only his one-time background as a management researcher for AT&T but also his views as a lifelong philosopher and devout Quaker.[76] **Servant leaders focus on providing increased service to others—meeting the goals of both followers and the organization—rather than to themselves.**

Former UCLA coach John Wooden, described as "a humble, giving person who wants nothing in return but to see other people succeed," is one such example. Wooden led the university's men's basketball teams to 10 national championships.[77] Wal-Mart's Sam Walton believed that leadership consisted of providing employees with the products, training, and support needed to serve customers and then standing back and letting them do their jobs.[78] Max De Pree, former chairman of furniture maker Herman Miller Inc., promoted a "covenant" with his employees. Leaders, he wrote, should give employees "space so that we can both give and receive such beautiful things as ideas, openness, dignity, joy, healing, and inclusion."[79] Starbucks CEO Howard Schultz is also cited as being one of the foremost practitioners of servant-style leadership. Schultz has made sure his employees have health insurance and work in a positive environment and as a result Starbucks has a strong brand following.[80]

Servant leadership is not a quick-fix approach to leadership. Rather, it is a long-term, transformational approach to life and work. Ten characteristics of the servant leader are shown below. *(See Table 14.7.)* One can hardly go wrong by trying to adopt these characteristics.

table 14.7

TEN CHARACTERISTICS OF THE SERVANT LEADER

1. Focus on listening.

2. Ability to empathize with others' feelings.

3. Focus on healing suffering.

4. Self-awareness of strengths and weaknesses.

5. Use of persuasion rather than positional authority to influence others.

6. Broad-based conceptual thinking.

7. Ability to foresee future outcomes.

8. Belief they are stewards of their employees and resources.

9. Commitment to the growth of people.

10. Drive to build community within and outside the organization.

Source: L. C. Spears, "Introduction: Servant-Leadership and the Greenleaf Legacy," in L. C. Spears, ed., *Reflections on Leadership: How Robert K. Greenleaf's Theory of Servant-Leadership Influenced Today's Top Management* (New York: John Wiley & Sons, 1995), pp. 1–14. Reprinted with permission of John Wiley & Sons, Inc.

Leading for Loyalty: Six Principles for Generating Faithful Employees, Customers, & Investors

Frederick F. Reichheld, former director of Bain & Company in Boston, is the author of books on loyalty, the latest being *The Loyalty Effect: The Hidden Force Behind Growth, Profits, and Lasting Value.*[81] After a dozen years of research, he has concluded that companies that are most successful in winning and retaining the allegiance of employees, customers, and investors are those that inspire loyalty. And outstanding loyalty, he suggests, "is the direct result of the words and deeds—the decisions and practices—of committed top executives who have personal integrity."[82]

Loyalty leader companies are quite diverse, ranging from Enterprise Rent-A-Car to Harley-Davidson to Northwestern Mutual. But what all have in common, says Reichheld, are six principles designed to engender and retain loyalty—principles that begin with executives at the top of the organization and affect all the relationships within it. *(See Table 14.8, opposite page.)* Let's consider them.

I. Preach What You Practice "Many business leaders are vaguely embarrassed by the idea of trumpeting their deepest values," says Reichheld. They feel that their actions should speak louder than their words.

1. Preach what you practice. Explain your principles, then live by them.

2. Play to win/win. Never profit at the expense of partners. It's a short-cut to a dead end.

3. Be picky. Membership must be a privilege.

4. Keep it simple. Complexity is the enemy of speed and responsiveness.

5. Reward the right results. Worthy partners deserve worthy goals.

6. Listen hard, talk straight. Insist on honest, two-way communication and learning.

Source: Adapted from F. F. Reichheld and T. Teal, *The Loyalty Effect: The Hidden Force Behind Growth, Profits, and Lasting Value* (Boston: Harvard Business School Press, 2001); F. F. Reichheld, *Loyalty Rules! How Today's Leaders Build Lasting Relationships* (Boston: Harvard Business School Press, 2001). Copyright © 2001 by the Harvard Business School Publishing Coporation. Reprinted by permission of Harvard Business School Press; all rights reserved.

Loyalty leaders realize that more is required—that they need to constantly preach the importance of loyalty in clear, powerful terms to fight beliefs that today loyalty is irrelevant to success. Scott Cook, CEO of personal-finance software maker Intuit, constantly delivers the message to employees that the company's mission is to treat customers right.

2. Play to Win-Win "In building loyalty, it's not enough that your competitors lose," says Reichheld. "Your partners must win." It is not a good strategy, he suggests, to browbeat employees, unions, and suppliers to make concession after concession or to tolerate dealers who abuse customers, as U.S. carmakers used to do. By treating employees right, loyalty leaders inspire them to deliver superior value to their customers.

Harley-Davidson, for example, has respectful dealings with its unions, and both labor and management have such good relations with customers that many even tattoo the company's logo on their bodies.

3. Be Picky "Arrogance is thinking your company can be all things to all customers," says Reichheld. "A truly humble company knows it can satisfy only certain customers, and it goes all out to keep them happy." Enterprise Rent-A-Car has become successful by satisfying its existing customer base, not chasing after frequent travelers in every air terminal.

Loyalty leaders are also picky about their employees. Not everyone can get a job with Southwest Airlines, which accepts only 4% of its applicants. As a result, Southwest is known for both service and customer loyalty.

4. Keep It Simple In a complex world, people need simple rules to guide their decision making, and they work better in small teams that simplify responsibility and accountability. Simplicity also helps companies deal with fast-changing business demands. And small teams help keep customers from getting lost in a faceless bureaucracy.

Northwestern Mutual CEO Jim Ericson piloted the insurance company through a "brutally complex business," Reichheld says, "by keeping his company on one simple rule: Do whatever is in the customer's best interest."

5. Reward the Right Results Many companies reward the wrong customer or employee, Reichheld points out. For example, they may reward employees who work for short-term profits rather than for long-term value and customer loyalty.

Enterprise Rent-A-Car CEO Andy Taylor devised a pay system that balanced profit inducements with incentives for building long-term employee and customer loyalty, as reflected in a survey measuring customer satisfaction and repeat business.

6. Listen Hard, Talk Straight "Long-term relationships require honest, two-way communication and learning," writes Reichheld. "True communication promotes trust, which in turn engenders loyalty. Communication also enables businesses to clarify their priorities and coordinate responses to problems and opportunities as they develop."

Dell Computer, for instance, posts all costs on a Web site, so customers are never confused about prices. It also grades its vendors on a publicly posted online supplier report card, so that suppliers can see how their performance measures against other vendors.

The High Road "Low-road" companies can survive for some time—maybe even generate impressive financial returns in the short run—by taking advantage of customers, employees, and vendors when they are vulnerable. Ultimately, however, such companies fail to anticipate market shifts or are blindsided by competitors.

Leaders of "high-road" companies realize that high standards of decency and consideration don't diminish profitability. Rather they enable it. Loyalty leaders, says Reichheld, show "they believe that business is not a zero-sum game, that an organization thrives when its partners and customers thrive."

Example

A Leader Who Bucked Conventional Wisdom: Scott McNealy of Sun Microsystems

Considered one of Silicon Valley's highest profile but also most colorful and controversial CEOs, Scott McNealy stepped down from that position at computer maker Sun Microsystems in Santa Clara, California, in April 2006, although continuing in his role as chairman of the board. McNealy, who had cofounded Sun in 1982, was famously combative, honing his competitive business strategy through a passion for ice hockey and golf.

A great innovator, in the 1980s McNealy bucked conventional wisdom by overruling his own executives and launching several Sun initiatives (selling machines based on a chip and an operating system of Sun's own design and putting Java software into Sun's servers when the Internet boom took off). Those strategies paid off hugely.[83] In the 1990s, he offered consumers alternatives to rivals IBM, Hewlett-Packard, and Dell, which offered computers based on industry standard chips and operating systems such as Windows and Linux. As a result, says one writer, McNealy "led Sun during a glorious run in the dot-com years, when every Internet startup seemed to rely on an army of Sun server computers."[84] But many

companies considered Sun's machines too expensive, and the company reported frequent losses over the past 5 years.[85]

Still, McNealy tried to restore growth and profit without slashing spending on research and development.[86] He also spoke of his sense of responsibility toward Sun's roughly 39,000 employees and had strongly resisted Wall Street's push to make steep job cuts.

"He was a powerful visionary and a determined business person," says marketing professor Peter Sealey at the Haas School of Business at the University of California, Berkeley. His failure, however, was that "he was not able to adjust to a profoundly changed marketplace."[87]

Tough call. Scott McNealy led Sun with a determination not to cut jobs even when times were difficult. Faced with similar circumstances, do you think you would choose similarly?

Your Call

After McNealy stepped down, a business columnist wrote: "I know that the company needs to do something to right the ship, but I think it's worth tipping the hat to a guy that's passionate about his company and has done everything possible to maintain jobs. It's a downright rarity in modern American business."[88] Despite his failures, do you think McNealy has been a strong loyalty leader?

Level 5 Leadership

Can a good company become a great company, and, if so, how? That was the question that **Jim Collins** asked, who then proceeded to perform a longitudinal research study to find the answer. The results were summarized in his 2001 bestseller *Good to Great.*[89]

Collins and his team identified a set of companies that shifted from "good" performance to "great" performance, defined as "fifteen-year cumulative stock returns at or below the general stock market, punctuated by a transition point, then cumulative returns at least three times the market over the next fifteen years."[90] From a sample of 1,435 Fortune 500 companies from 1965 to 1995, 11 good-to-great companies were identified: Abbot, Circuit City, Fannie Mae, Gillette, Kimberly-Clark, Kroger, Nucor, Philip Morris, Pitney Bowes, Walgreens, and Wells Fargo. These companies were then compared with a targeted set of direct-comparison companies to uncover the drivers of the good-to-great transformations. One of the key drivers was that the successful companies had what Collins called Level 5 leadership. Collins' research data revealed "all the good-to-great companies had Level 5 leadership at a time of transition. Furthermore, the absence of Level 5 leadership showed up as a consistent pattern in comparison companies."[91]

Level 5 Leadership: What Is It? *Level 5 leadership* means an organization is led by a person, a Level 5 executive, who possesses the paradoxical characteristics of humility and a fearless will to succeed, as well as the capabilities associated with levels 1-4. *(See Figure 14.3.)*

LEVEL 5 Executive
Builds enduring greatness through a paradoxical blend of personal humility & professional will

LEVEL 4 Effective Leader
Catalyzes commitment to and vigorous pursuit of a clear & compelling vision, stimulating higher performance standards

LEVEL 3 Competent Manager
Organizes people & resources toward the effective & efficient pursuit of predetermined objectives

LEVEL 2 Contributing Team Member
Contributes individual capabilities to the achievement of group objectives & works effectively with others in a group setting

LEVEL 1 Highly Capable Individual
Makes productive contributions through talent, knowledge, skills, and good work habits

figure 14.3

THE LEVEL 5 HIERARCHY

Source: Jim Collins, *Good to Great* (New York: Harper Business, 2001), p. 20. Copyright © 2001 by Jim Collins.

An example of a Level 5 executive was President Abraham Lincoln, who, though humble, soft spoken, and shy, possessed great will to keep the American Republic united during the Civil War of 1861–1865, despite a loss of 250,000 Confederate and 360,000 Union soldiers. Like other Level 5 leaders, however, Lincoln also possessed the capabilities of the other four levels of the hierarchy, ranging upward from being a highly capable individual, to a contributing team member, to a competent manager, to an effective leader. Although a Level 5 leader does not move up the hierarchy, he or she must possess the capabilities of levels 1–4 before being able to use the Level 5 characteristics to transform an organization.

Note the resemblances to Level 5 theory and other leadership theories we've discussed. For example, Level 1 is consistent with research on trait theory, which suggests that leaders are intelligent and possess the personality characteristics of extraversion, conscientiousness, and openness to experience. Levels 3 and 4 seem to contain behaviors associated with transactional and transformational leadership. But what is a novel contribution of Level 5 theory is that good-to-great leaders are not only transactional and transformational but, most importantly, are also humble and fiercely determined.

Three Observations about Level 5 Theory   There are three points to keep in mind about Level 5 leadership.

- **Additional drivers.** Collins notes that, besides having a Level 5 leader, additional drivers are required to take a company from good to great.[92] Level 5 leadership, however, enables the implementation of these additional drivers.

- **Further research needed.** To date there has been no additional testing of Collins's conclusions. Future research is clearly needed to confirm the Level 5 hierarchy.

- **Hindrances.** Collins believes that some people will never become Level 5 leaders because their narcissistic and boastful tendencies do not allow them to subdue their own ego and needs to the greater good of others.

E-Leadership: Managing for Global Networks

The Internet and other forms of advanced information technology have led to new possible ways for interacting within and between organizations (e-business) and with customers and suppliers (e-commerce). Leadership within the context of this electronic technology, called *e-leadership,* **can involve one-to-one, one-to-many, and within- and between-group and collective interactions via information technology.**[93]

An e-leader doesn't have to be a tech guru, but he or she does have to know enough about information technology to overhaul traditional corporate structures. E-leaders, says one writer, "have a global mind-set that recognizes that the Internet is opening new markets and recharging existing ones. They don't bother fighting mere battles with competitors because they're too busy creating businesses that will surround and destroy them."[94] Harvard Business School professor D. Quinn Mills, author of *E-Leadership,* suggests that individual companies will be replaced by much broader global networks that a single CEO will not be able to manage. Thus, while 20th-century management emphasized competition, he says, future organizations will run on knowledge sharing and open exchange.[95]

These observations suggest that e-leadership means having to deal with quite a number of responsibilities, some of which are suggested opposite. *(See Table 14.9.)* Some of these responsibilities are developing business opportunities through cooperative relationships, restructuring a company into global networks, decentralizing the company's organization, and energizing the staff.[96] ●

table 14.9

SIX SECRETS OF SUCCESSFUL E-LEADERS

These tips are offered by Don MacRae, president of the Lachlan Group, Toronto.

1. **Create the future rather than a better status quo.** No matter how successful your business is now, it can be wiped out overnight by the swiftness of the Internet economy. Pay attention to new possibilities rather than simply reacting to today's problems.

2. **Create a "teachable vision."** When Steve Jobs started Apple Computer, his teachable vision was to develop a computer that was as simple to use as a bicycle. Think about how your organization needs to act differently in order to stay at the top of your industry. Have the best and brightest stars in your company investigate how your traditional markets are shifting and what new opportunities might be up for grabs.

3. **Follow a strategy your customers set, not you.** Get over your love affair with your own products and services. What matters most is whether your customers love them. Talk to them about their needs and how you could serve them better. Let them set corporate direction.

4. **Foster a collaborative culture.** E-leaders don't give orders from the top. They let teams form organically in their organizations and encourage people to question the way things are done. Be open to unorthodox strategies.

5. **Think globally.** Technology allows you to build ties with customers, suppliers, and strategic partners all over the world. Don't neglect the opportunity. Be disciplined about finding the best places to do business and seeing opportunities where they exist.

6. **Thrive on information.** This means all kinds of information: overnight sales figures, customer-satisfaction scores, employee turnover, on-time delivery rates, canceled orders, and so on. Technology allows e-leaders to track their companies by every conceivable detail. Without taking a 360-degree view of what's going on in your business—and adjusting your strategy accordingly—you can forget about leading for much longer.

Source: Adapted from D. MacRae, *BusinessWeek online*, September 6, 2001, www.businessweek.com/technology/content/sep2001/tc2001096_619.htm, accessed August 15, 2004.

key terms used in this chapter

behavioral leadership approaches 458
charisma 467
contingency approach 460
contingency leadership model 460
coercive power 450
e-leadership 476
expert power 450
full-range leadership 466
leader–member exchange (LMX) model 470

leadership 448
legitimate power 450
Level 5 leadership 475
meta-analysis 455
path–goal leadership model 461
personalized power 449
readiness 464
referent power 450
reward power 450
servant leaders 471

shared leadership 471
situational leadership theory 464
socialized power 449
trait approaches to leadership 454
transactional leadership 466
transformational leadership 467

summary

14.1 The Nature of Leadership: Wielding Influence

- Leadership is the ability to influence employees to voluntarily pursue organizational goals. Being a manager and being a leader are not the same. Management is about coping with complexity, whereas leadership is about coping with change. Companies manage complexity by planning and budgeting, organizing and staffing, and controlling and problem solving. Leadership copes with change by setting a direction, aligning people to accomplish an agenda, and motivating and inspiring people.

- To understand leadership, we must understand authority and power. Authority is the right to perform or command; it comes with the manager's job. Power is the extent to which a person is able to influence others so they respond to orders. People may pursue personalized power, power directed at helping oneself, or, better, they may pursue socialized power, power directed at helping others.

- Within an organization there are typically five sources of power leaders may draw on; all managers have the first three. (1) Legitimate power is power that results from managers' formal positions within the organization. (2) Reward power is power that results from managers' authority to reward their subordinates. (3) Coercive power results from managers' authority to punish their subordinates. (4) Expert power is power resulting from one's specialized information or expertise. (5) Referent power is power deriving from one's personal attraction.

- There are nine influence tactics for trying to get others to do something you want, ranging from most used to least used tactics as follows: rational persuasion, inspirational appeals, consultation, ingratiating tactics, personal appeals, exchange tactics, coalition tactics, pressure tactics, and legitimating tactics.

- Four principal approaches or perspectives on leadership, as discussed in the rest of the chapter, are (1) trait, (2) behavioral, (3) contingency, and (4) emerging.

14.2 Trait Approaches: Do Leaders Have Distinctive Personality Characteristics?

- Trait approaches to leadership attempt to identify distinctive characteristics that account for the effectiveness of leaders. Representatives of this approach are Kouzes and Posner, Bossidy, Judge, gender studies, and leadership lessons from the GLOBE project.
  (1) Kouzes and Posner identified five traits of leaders. A leader should be honest, competent, forward-looking, inspiring, and intelligent.
  (2) Bossidy, a working CEO, identifies four qualities he looks for when assessing prospective leaders: ability to execute, a career runway (ability to go beyond present job), a team orientation, and multiple experiences.
  (3) Meta-analyses by Judge and colleagues suggest that the Big Five personality traits of extroversion, as well as conscientiousness and openness, are important to leadership effectiveness and that part 5 Leading personality is more important than intelligence for leadership.
  (4) Women may rate higher than men do on producing high-quality work, goal setting, mentoring employees, and other measures. Women excel in such traits as teamwork and partnering, being more collaborative, seeking less personal glory, being motivated less by self-interest than company interest, being more stable, and being less turf-conscious.
  (5) Project GLOBE surveyed 17,000 middle managers in 62 countries and determined that visionary and inspirational charismatic leaders who are good team builders do best.

14.3 Behavioral Approaches: Do Leaders Show Distinctive Patterns of Behavior?

- Behavioral leadership approaches try to determine the distinctive styles used by effective leaders. Leadership style means the combination of traits, skills, and behaviors that leaders use when interacting with others. We described some important models of leadership behavior.

- In the University of Michigan Leadership Model, researchers identified two forms of leadership styles. In job-centered behavior, managers paid more attention to the job and work procedures. In employee-centered behavior, managers paid more attention to employee satisfaction and making work groups cohesive.

- In the Ohio State Leadership Model, researchers identified two major dimensions of leader behavior: Initiating structure organizes and defines what group members should be doing. Consideration is leadership behavior that expresses concern for employees by establishing a supportive climate.

- One expert concludes from the Michigan and Ohio studies that effective leaders tend to have supportive relationships with employees, use group rather than individual methods of supervision, and set high performance goals.

14.4 Contingency Approaches: Does Leadership Vary with the Situation?

- Proponents of the contingency approach to leadership believe that effective leadership behavior depends on the situation at hand—that as situations change, different styles become effective. Three contingency approaches are described.

- The Fiedler contingency leadership model determines if a leader's style is task-oriented or relationship-oriented and if that style is effective for the situation at hand. Once it is determined whether a leader is more oriented toward tasks or toward people, then it's necessary to determine how much control and influence a leader has in the immediate work environment. The three dimensions of situational control are leader-member relations, which reflects the extent to which a leader has the support of the work group; the task structure, which reflects the extent to which tasks are routine and easily understood; and position power, which reflects how much power a leader has to reward and punish and make work assignments. For each dimension, the leader's control may be high or low. A task-oriented style has been found to work best in either high-control or low-control situations; the relationship-oriented style best in situations of moderate control.

- The House path–goal leadership model, in its revised form, holds that the effective leader clarifies paths through which subordinates can achieve goals and provides them with support. Two variables, employee characteristics and environmental factors, cause one or more leadership behaviors—which House expanded to eight from his original four—to be more effective than others.

- Hersey and Blanchard's situational leadership theory suggests that leadership behavior reflects how leaders should adjust their leadership style according to the readiness of the followers. Readiness is defined as the extent to which a follower possesses the ability and willingness to complete a task. The appropriate leadership style is found by cross-referencing follower readiness (low to high) with one of four leadership styles: telling, selling, participating, delegating.

14.5 The Full-Range Model: Uses of Transactional & Transformational Leadership

- Full-range leadership describes leadership along a range of styles, with the most effective being transactional/transformational leaders. Transactional leadership focuses on clarifying employees' roles and task requirements and providing rewards and punishments contingent on performance. Transformational leadership transforms employees to pursue goals over self-interests. Transformational leaders are influenced by two factors: (1) Their personalities tend to be more extroverted, agreeable, and proactive. (2) Organizational cultures are more apt to be adaptive and flexible.

- The best leaders are both transactional and transformational. Four key behaviors of transformational leaders in affecting employees are they inspire motivation, inspire trust, encourage excellence, and stimulate them intellectually.

- Transformational leadership has three implications. (1) It can improve results for both individuals and groups. (2) It can be used to train employees at any level. (3) It can be used by both ethical or unethical leaders.

14.6 Six Additional Perspectives

- Six additional kinds of leadership are (1) leader–membership exchange model, (2) shared leadership, (3) servant leadership,

- (4) loyalty leadership, (5) Level 5 leadership, and (6) e-leadership.
- The leader–member exchange (LMX) model of leadership emphasizes that leaders have different sorts of relationships with different subordinates.
- Shared leadership is a simultaneous, ongoing, mutual influence process in which people share responsibility for leading. It is based on the idea that people need to share information and collaborate to get things done.
- Servant leaders focus on providing increased service to others—meeting the goals of both followers and the organization—rather than to themselves.
- Loyalty leadership is embodied in six principles suggested by Reichheld for generating faithful employees, customers, and investors: preach what you practice, play to win-win, be picky, keep it simple, reward the right results, and listen hard and talk straight.
- Level 5 leadership means an organization is led by a person, a Level 5 executive, who possesses the paradoxical characteristics of humility and a fearless will to succeed, as well as the capabilities associated with levels I–4: being an effective leader, a competent manager, a contributing team member, and a highly capable individual.
- E-leadership involves leader interactions with others via the Internet and other forms of advanced information technology, which have made possible new ways for interacting within and between organizations (e-business) and with customers and suppliers (e-commerce). E-leadership can involve one-to-one, one-to-many, and within- and between-group and collective interactions via information technology.

 ## management in action

Charles Prince Makes Big Changes at Citigroup

Assuming the role of chief executive of the world's largest financial institution in October 2003 didn't come easily to Charles O. Prince III. His natural inclination from day one was to hole up in his office and attend to the company's many pressing matters, just as he had done for almost two decades at Citigroup and its predecessor companies. As general counsel to former CEO Sanford I. "Sandy" Weill, Prince's preference was to blend into the paneled woodwork of his spacious Park Avenue office.

Today, he is a different man. Prince is stepping out of the long shadow of his legendary former boss and pursuing his own strategy. . . .

Prince, now 56, came to recognize that a sprawling company like Citigroup needed more than competence and accountability in the corner office; it needed a charismatic leader. He had no choice but to try filling the bill. "I'm not used to operating in the limelight," he concedes, "but the difficulty of the moment demanded it. I had to get out front and say, 'we're going in this direction, follow me.'" . . .

He took over just as regulatory and public-relations troubles brought on by the collapse of Enron and WorldCom were doing maximum damage to the bank.

One year on the job and billions in legal fines later, Prince had met investors' low expectations, focusing mostly on regulatory matters and failing to become the commander in chief the bank sorely needed. His main objective at the time: "to keep Citigroup out of the headlines." He was failing there as well. Two big scandals erupted during his tenure: the Japanese private banking fiasco and charges of illegal European bond trading. And last summer the Federal Reserve, in a severe and unprecedented rebuke, banned Citi from making any future acquisitions until it got its house in order. It was a smack-down not only of the company's business practices, but also Weill's strategy of growth by acquisitions.

Looking back, Prince says he felt like he was flying with no navigation. He heard himself emphasizing to employees that he was in charge and that a plan was on its way. "I may not have known what it was going to be," he concedes, "but I knew it was coming."

Prince is making great efforts to change his management style. He has deliberately distanced himself from the qualities that landed him the job in the first place. His initial approach to leadership was to dictate rules and regulations; now he's fashioning himself a big thinker. He's working on his image, calling on CEOs like Michael S. Dell and Johnson & Johnson's William C. Weldon for advice. He has cut ties with key Citi veterans, cultivating what he calls a "new generation" of leaders. And he is turning away from the Weill strategy of being all things to all customers. . . .

In the face of such adversity, Prince is getting out from behind his desk. On Dec. 16, 2004, at the annual Citigroup Investor Day, he dispensed with the long-held tradition of department heads making individual presentations. Instead, he emceed the two-hour event himself. "Bad behavior is aberrational," he told the audience, and although "never is a big word . . . the chances of [the company] getting into trouble again are virtually nil." Then he enthusiastically punched the air and declared: "I know where Citigroup is going!" Coming from someone else, a line like that might have been met with snickering. But from the understated Prince, it was reassuring, even inspiring.

"Chuck is trying to introduce a change of culture rather than reinforce a long-held one, and that's . . . difficult," says his friend Weldon. "It's one thing to talk, it's another to go out there and make sure it's reinforced and people understand you're serious. That's what [he] has to do." . . .

Prince may not have had a plan, but he wasn't afraid to act. In his first month, he summoned Thomas W. Jones, chairman and CEO of Global Investment Management & Citigroup Asset Management; Deryck Maughan, vice-chairman and CEO of Citigroup International; and Peter K. Scaturro, CEO of Citigroup Private Bank. He wanted to know why the scandals in Japan had happened and why they hadn't yet met regulators' demands for a clean-up. No one would take responsibility. So Prince fired all three on the spot, a move that would have seemed unimaginable even a few months earlier. . . .

Then, on March 1, 2005, operation charisma began. Prince launched his "five-point plan," which included new standards for training, development, compensation, and annual reviews, all designed to inspire and monitor good behavior. Citi created a slick DVD sent to employees and journalists around the globe. Within two months, Prince personally addressed some 45,000 employees in 11 town hall meetings in 10 countries. . . .

Prince says inertia is his biggest obstacle. "I have to be able to inspire people, to motivate people," he says. "That's my job. It cuts against traditional patterns of doing business, it's new, and it feels awkward at first." . . .

Prince says the key requirement of a strong leader is to accept change.

For Discussion

1. How many of the five sources of power is Charles Prince using? Explain.
2. Which of the eight influence tactics is Mr. Prince using?
3. Which different leadership traits and styles does Charles Prince display? Cite examples and discuss.
4. To what extent is Charles Prince using the full-range model of leadership? Explain.
5. Evaluate the extent to which Prince displays the components of Level 5 leadership.

Source: Excerpted from M. D. Hovanesian, "Rewiring Chuck Prince," *BusinessWeek*, February 20, 2006, pp 75–78.

 self-assessment

Do You Have What It Takes to Be a Leader?

Objectives

1. To learn more about the skills required for being a leader.
2. To assess your own leadership ability.

Introduction

Managers cope with complexity: They look at what needs to be done (planning and budgeting), pull together the people needed to get the job done together (organizing and staffing), and ensure that people do their jobs (controlling and problem solving). Leaders, however, cope with change: They look at what needs to be done by setting a direction rather than planning and budgeting, pull people together to do the job through alignment rather than organizing and staffing, and ensure people do their jobs through motivation and inspiration instead of controlling and problem solving. The purpose of this exercise is to assess your skills and determine if you have what it takes to be a leader.

Instructions

Read each of the following statements, and circle the number that best represents your self-perceptions, where 1 = strongly disagree, 2 = disagree, 3 = neither agree nor disagree, 4 = agree, 5 = strongly agree. There is no right or wrong answer.

1. I can separate my personal life from work/school.	1	2	3	4	5
2. I'm honest with myself.	1	2	3	4	5
3. I communicate my ideas clearly.	1	2	3	4	5
4. I regularly prioritize what I need to get done.	1	2	3	4	5
5. I am on time for meetings/classes.	1	2	3	4	5
6. I am positive and upbeat.	1	2	3	4	5
7. I am solution oriented rather than problem oriented.	1	2	3	4	5
8. I take responsibility for my actions.	1	2	3	4	5
9. I do not blame others for my mistakes.	1	2	3	4	5
10. When working in a group, I work with members to solve and prevent problems.	1	2	3	4	5
11. I don't have to redo things because my work is thorough and complete.	1	2	3	4	5
12. I do not procrastinate on projects/tasks.	1	2	3	4	5
13. I do not get distracted when working on projects/tasks.	1	2	3	4	5
14. I work well in a group.	1	2	3	4	5
15. I am people oriented, not just results oriented.	1	2	3	4	5
16. I listen to others beyond just the words being spoken.	1	2	3	4	5
17. When working in a group, I am more concerned with the group's success than my own.	1	2	3	4	5
18. I adjust well to different communication styles.	1	2	3	4	5
19. I praise others when they are doing a good job.	1	2	3	4	5
20. I work at getting ahead, but within appropriate boundaries.	1	2	3	4	5
Total					_____

Scoring & Interpretation

Compute your score by adding the responses for all 20 items. The questions in this survey were designed to give you feedback on your skills in the following areas: (1) personal stability, (2) productivity, (3) self-management, (4) communication, (5) boundary setting, (6) work quality, (7) teamwork. All of these skills are found in good managers, and they represent necessary skills for leaders.

Arbitrary norms for leadership skills:

Excellent leadership skills (95–100)

Good leadership skills (85–90)

Moderate leadership skills (75–80)

Low leadership skills (65–70)

Poor leadership skills (60 and below)

Questions for Discussion

1. Were you surprised by your results? Why or why not?
2. Look at the five questions where you scored the lowest. What can you do to improve or develop your skills represented by these items? Explain.

3. Does the content in the five lowest areas relate to Table 14.2? If it does, can you identify additional ways you can improve these skills? Describe and explain.

Questions for this survey were adapted from Interlink Training and Coaching, "The Leadership Assessment Tool," *www.interlinktc.com/assessment.html.* Interlink Training and Coaching, 3655 W. Anthem Way, Box 315, Anthem, AZ 85086.

 group exercise

How Do They Do It? Examining the Skills of Famous Leaders

Objectives

- To examine the leadership skills of famous leaders.
- To further explore different approaches to leadership.

Introduction

In this chapter you learned four different approaches to explaining leadership. We know that leaders possess traits and skills that make them successful. They are effective communicators. They are guided by a vision that is shared by others. They are skillful planners. They are champions for their cause. They are successful at motivating people to voluntarily pursue goals. Leaders can be villains or heroes, trailblazers and visionaries, revolutionaries or college students. The purpose of this exercise is to examine the skills displayed by famous leaders and to determine how you might use this knowledge to improve your leadership skills.

Instructions

Break into groups of five to six people. First, brainstorm a list of famous leaders—CEOs, presidents, politicians, monarchs, or whoever, as long as the group knows something about their skills as leaders. Next, the group needs to pick two leaders to compare and contrast. Try to pick leaders that seem vastly different from one another—for example, Joan of Arc and Mother Teresa. Once you have decided on the two leaders, use the following survey to profile them in terms of their skills and traits. Use the panels and additional material in this chapter to help guide your discussion. Answer the questions for discussion after completing the survey.

Profile Survey	Leader A Name		Leader B Name:	
In terms of power: This person uses/used which sources of power?	Personalized power	_____	Personalized power	_____
	Socialized power	_____	Socialized power	_____
	Legitimate power	_____	Legitimate power	_____
	Reward power	_____	Reward power	_____
	Coercive power	_____	Coercive power	_____
	Expert power	_____	Expert power	_____
	Referent power	_____	Referent power	_____
In terms of influence: What influence tactics does/did this person use?	Consultation	_____	Consultation	_____
	Rational persuasion	_____	Rational persuasion	_____
	Inspirational appeals	_____	Inspirational appeals	_____

(continued)

	Leader 1		Leader 2	
	Ingratiating tactics	_____	Ingratiating tactics	_____
	Coalition tactics	_____	Coalition tactics	_____
	Pressure tactics	_____	Pressure tactics	_____
	Upward appeals	_____	Upward appeals	_____
	Exchange tactics	_____	Exchange tactics	_____
In terms of the trait approach to leadership: Which traits does/did this person exhibit?	Honest	_____	Honest	_____
	Competent	_____	Competent	_____
	Forward-looking	_____	Forward-looking	_____
	Inspiring	_____	Inspiring	_____
	Intelligent	_____	Intelligent	_____
	Self-awareness	_____	Self-awareness	_____
	Self-management	_____	Self-management	_____
	Social awareness	_____	Social awareness	_____
	Relationship management	_____	Relationship management	_____
In terms of behavioral approaches to leadership: Which leadership behaviors did/does this person exhibit?	**U of Michigan Model**	_____	**U of Michigan Model**	_____
	Job-centered behavior	_____	Job-centered behavior	_____
	Employee-centered behavior	_____	Employee-centered behavior	_____
	Ohio State Model	_____	**Ohio State Model**	_____
	Initiating structure	_____	Initiating structure	_____
	Consideration	_____	Consideration	_____
In terms of transactional and charismatic leadership: What general type of leader is/was this person?	Transactional leader	_____	Transactional leader	_____
	Charismatic leader	_____	Charismatic leader	_____
	Servant leader	_____	Servant leader	_____

Questions for Discussion

1. What criteria did your group use to determine which two leaders you would profile? Describe.
2. In what ways are the leadership styles of these leaders similar? In what ways are they different? Explain.
3. After completing this survey, were you surprised at the similarity or dissimilarity between these leaders? Discuss.
4. Which one of these leaders would you want to work for? Explain your rationale.

 ethical dilemma

Covering for a Laid-Off Friend

You manage a group of software developers for a large organization and several days ago had the difficult task of notifying a friend who works for the company that he is being laid off. Even though he has performed wonderfully in the past and you hate to see him go, your company lost a contract with a major client and thus his position has become obsolete.

The employee wants to build a house, and you're aware that he is 10 days away from closing on a loan

for it. He has sold his previous home and now is living with his in-laws. He asks you for a favor: could you extend his employment just 10 more days so that he can qualify for his new home loan? Unfortunately, you don't have the authority to do so, and you tell him you can't help him.

He then tells you that the mortgage company will be calling sometime soon to get a verbal confirmation of his employment. The confirmation is an essential prerequisite if your friend is to obtain the loan for his new home. Would you, he asks, tell the mortgage company that he is still employed?

Solving the Dilemma

As a manager, what would you do?

1. Tell the mortgage company your friend is still employed by the company. Your friend needs a break, and you're confident that he'll find a job in the near future.

2. Refuse to lie. It is unethical to falsify information regarding employment.

3. Simply avoid the mortgage company's phone call.

4. Invent other options. Discuss.

 video case

Winning Advice: Jack Welch

Jack Welch, the former Chief Executive Officer (CEO) at General Electric (GE), has been described as the greatest manager in modern times. Under his direction, GE dominated every sector of its industry. In addition, many top managers who lead American companies today worked at one time under Welch at GE. Welch defines successful leaders as those who "grow others," and he believes this was one of his greatest legacies as a CEO and leader.

In one of his latest books, *Winning*, Welch, who co-authored the book with his wife Suzy, reveals secrets about winning as a manager and leader. For Welch, winning isn't just something—it's everything. He believes that winners have more fun, are financially better off, and are excited about their jobs. He cautions leaders about the real purpose of their job—the leader should focus on the employees, not themselves.

For Welch, the role of a leader is to "let people know where they stand." He believes that for employees to be successful, they should have a deep burning passion for their work, and he views employees through a three-tier model he constructed at GE to gauge effectiveness within a company: 1) the top 20% (those whom the leader praises); 2) the middle 70% (those who can improve); and 3) the bottom 10% (those who should leave the company on their own and seek employment elsewhere). When told how they stand by an honest manager, employees know where they are successful and where they need to improve.

Unfortunately, Welch feels that most bosses aren't totally honest with their employees, which leads to lack of productivity and does employees no service.

When discussing the best and the worst aspects about being the boss, Welch states that the best part is "growing people" and watching their lives change for the better as a result of their growth. On the other hand, Welch believes the biggest hurdle for a boss is losing an employee. Welch also maintains that while it may be difficult for managers to separate the work-life phenomenon, they should view it instead as an opportunity to involve their families in many work-related activities. Certainly, Welch has statistics to back up his leadership practices: during his 20-year tenure at GE, the company's market value increased nearly 40% from $13 billion to $500 billion.

Questions

1. Do you think Jack Welch is a transformational leader? Why or why not?

2. Can a leader like Jack Welch share leadership? If so, how?

3. What makes leaders like Jack Welch successful?

4. Jack Welch's leadership seems to fit House's path–goal leadership model. Discuss how Welch fits this leadership model.

Source: Joseph C. Santora, EdD, Essex County College.

chapter 15

Interpersonal & Organizational Communication

Mastering the Exchange of Information

Major Questions You Should Be Able to Answer

15.1 The Communication Process: What It Is, How It Works
Major Question: What do I need to know about the communication process to be an effective communicator?

15.2 Barriers to Communication
Major Question: What are the important barriers I need to be aware of, so I can improve my communication skills?

15.3 How Managers Fit into the Communication Process
Major Question: How can I use the different channels and patterns of communication to my advantage?

15.4 Communication in the Information Age
Major Question: How do contemporary managers use information technology to communicate more effectively?

15.5 Improving Communication Effectiveness
Major Question: How can I be a better listener, reader, writer, and speaker?

Becoming a Better Communicator: Being Telephone Savvy

Some communication doesn't matter much (such as small talk with the latte server). Some matters a lot, as when you're using the phone to try to get a job interview. Indeed, despite e-mail, the phone is still the most used business tool, so you need to become skilled at it.

Ever feel that someone you called (whether a prospective date or prospective employer) is ignoring you because they never call back? Maybe the reason is inadequate telephone skills. Following are some suggestions for becoming phone-savvy, which will give you a practical introduction to the subject of communication.[1]

- **Consider the impression you make on the phone:** Watch out for self-defeating telephone behavior. Talking too fast, for instance, makes what you say seem unimportant. Talking too slowly makes you sound tired or uninterested. Talking too softly makes you hard to understand. Talking too loudly grates on others' ears. Talking too much—giving more details than your listener wants—makes people impatient.

- **When you call someone:** When you make a call to someone you don't know, do you speak briefly and above all *clearly*? When leaving a message, do you *slowly* give your name, organization, and phone number (*twice*)? Do you give the date and time you called? If you want a call back, do you specify a *time when you'll be available*? (Don't say: "Uh, I'll be around maybe later.")

- **When someone calls you:** Do you give a favorable first impression, showing the caller that you're helpful and confident? Do you identify yourself? Do you repeat (and *jot down*) the caller's name? (Don't say: "Um, what'd you say your name was again?")

- **Being courteous:** Do you keep your voice interested, attentive, and friendly? Do you say "please" and "thank you"? Do you ask callers if it's okay to put them on hold or if you should call back in a few minutes? Do you say "Thank you for waiting" when you come back on? Do you let the caller hang up first? (Of course, as a time-starved manager you'll sometimes have to politely terminate the conversation first.)

- **Making difficult calls:** When you have to make a difficult telephone call, such as when you're angling for a job interview, are you prepared? Do you have a script that you wrote out beforehand and practiced? Do you get to the point right away? (Attention spans are shorter on the phone.) Do you repeat the other person's name once in a while to make the conversation more personal?

- **Dealing with phone tag:** You phone. Your caller isn't in. That person calls you back. You're not in. That's "phone tag." To deal with it, you need to be aware of the following tricks. (1) Persistence is important. Four or five calls are fine. More than that and the other person may consider you a pest. (2) Don't just use the other person's answering machine or voice mail. If he or she has a secretary or administrative assistant, leave messages with that person as well. (And get to know that person by name and become allies.) (3) Describe your schedule and your availability. (4) If the other person calls back, note the time, which may be when he or she is always at a desk making calls. (5) When you leave a message, make it clear and complete but not overly long.

For Discussion From this list, can you tell there are some things you do that need improvement? Which ones?

forecast

What's Ahead in This Chapter

This chapter describes the process of transferring information and understanding from one person to another. It also describes three communications barriers—physical, semantic, and personal. It shows how you can use different channels and patterns of communication, both formal and informal, to your advantage. It discusses how star managers use information technology to communicate more effectively. Finally, we talk about how to be a better listener, talker, writer, and reader.

> ✳ **major question** What do I need to know about the communication process to be an effective communicator?

THE BIG PICTURE

Communication is the transfer of information and understanding from one person to another. The process involves sender, message, and receiver; encoding and decoding; the medium; feedback; and dealing with "noise," or interference. Managers need to tailor their communication to the appropriate medium (rich or lean) for the appropriate situation.

"Good writing is one of two key abilities I focus on when hiring," says Richard Todd at the Federal Reserve Bank of Minneapolis; "the other is the ability to read critically. I can train people to do almost anything else, but I don't have time to teach this."[2] In another survey of 300 executives, 71% said they believed written communication skills were a critical competency that needed enhancement via training; 68% said they believed the same about interpersonal communications skills.[3]

Because many students have not had sufficient training of this sort and because today's work environment is so fast-paced, faulty communication has become a real problem in the workplace. According to one survey, executives say 14% of each 40-hour workweek is wasted because of poor communication between staff and managers.[4] That's the equivalent of 7 workweeks of lost productivity a year. Thus, there's a hard-headed argument for better communication: It can save money.

Communication Defined: The Transfer of Information & Understanding

Communication—**the transfer of information and understanding from one person to another**—is an activity that you as a manager will have to do a lot of. Indeed, one study found that 81% of a manager's time in a typical workday is spent communicating.[5]

I hear you. Today some people can work almost anywhere, even more so as the cell phone becomes a more versatile instrument permitting Internet and e-mail access, text messaging, and access to huge databases. Do you think our ability to work outside traditional offices because of today's technology will negatively affect the communication process and employee camaraderie?

The fact that managers do a lot of communicating doesn't mean they're necessarily good at it—that is, that they are efficient or effective. You are an *efficient communicator* when you can transmit your message accurately in the least time. You are an *effective communicator* when your intended message is accurately understood by the other person. Thus, you may well be efficient in sending a group of people a reprimand by e-mail. But it may not be effective if it makes them angry so that they can't absorb its meaning.

From this, you can see why it's important to have an understanding of the communication process.

How the Communication Process Works

Communication has been said to be a process consisting of "a sender transmitting a message through media to a receiver who responds."[6] Let's look at these and other parts of the process.

Sender, Message, & Receiver   The *sender* **is the person wanting to share information—called a** *message*—**and the** *receiver* **is the person for whom the message is intended,** as follows.

Sender → Message → Receiver

Encoding & Decoding   Of course, the process isn't as simple as just sender/message/receiver. If you were sending the message over a telegraph line, you would first have to encode the message, and the receiver would have to decode it. But the same is true if you are sending the message by voice to another person in the same room, when you have to decide what language to speak in and what terms to use.

Encoding **is translating a message into understandable symbols or language.** *Decoding* **is interpreting and trying to make sense of the message.** Thus, the communication process is now

Sender **[Encoding]** → Message → **[Decoding]** Receiver

The Medium   The means by which you as a communicator send a message is important, whether it is by typing an e-mail traveling over the Internet, by voice over a telephone line, or by hand-scrawled note. This is the *medium,* **the pathway by which a message travels:**

Sender [Encoding] → Message **[Medium]** Message → [Decoding] Receiver

Feedback   "Flight 123, do you copy?" In the movies, that's what you hear the flight controller say when radioing the pilot of a troubled aircraft to see if he or she received ("copied") the previous message. And the pilot may radio back, "Roger, Houston, I copy." This is an example of *feedback* —**the receiver expresses his or her reaction to the sender's message.**

Sender [Encoding] → Message [Medium] Message → [Decoding] Receiver

[Feedback]   Message

Noise   Unfortunately, the entire communication process can be disrupted at several different points by what is called *noise* —**any disturbance that interferes with the transmission of a message.** The noise can occur in the medium, of course, as when you have static in a radio transmission or fade-out on a cell phone or when there's loud music when you're trying to talk in a noisy restaurant. Or it can occur in the encoding or decoding, as when a pharmacist can't read a prescription because of a doctor's poor handwriting.[7]

Noise also occurs in *nonverbal communication* (discussed later in this chapter), as when our physical movements send a message that is different from the one we are speaking, or in *cross-cultural communication* (discussed in Chapter 4), as when we make assumptions about other people's messages based on our own culture instead of theirs. We discuss noise further in the next section.

The communication process is shown below. *(See Figure 15.1.)*

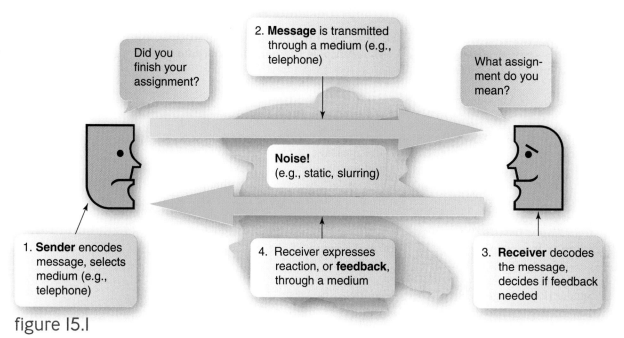

figure 15.1

THE COMMUNICATION PROCESS

"Noise" is not just noise or loud background sounds but any disturbance that interferes with transmission—static, fadeout, distracting facial expressions, uncomfortable meeting site, competing voices, and so on.

Selecting the Right Medium for Effective Communication

There are all kinds of communications tools available to managers, ranging from one-to-one face-to-face conversation all the way to use of the mass media. However, managers need to know how to use the right tool for the right condition—when to use e-mail, when to meet face to face, for example. Should you praise an employee by voicing a compliment, sending an e-mail, posting an announcement near the office coffee machine—or all three? How about when carrying out a reprimand?

Is a Medium Rich or Lean in Information?   As a manager, you will have many media to choose from: conversations, meetings, speeches, the telephone, e-mail, memos, letters, bulletin boards, PowerPoint presentations, videoconferencing, printed publications, videos, and so on. Beyond these are the sophisticated communications possibilities of the mass media: public relations; advertising; news reports via print, radio, TV, the Internet.

Media richness **indicates how well a particular medium conveys information and promotes learning.** That is, the "richer" a medium is, the better it is at conveying information. The term *media richness* was proposed by respected organizational theorists Richard Daft and Robert Lengel as part of their contingency model for media selection.[8]

Ranging from high media richness to low media richness, types of media may be positioned along a continuum as follows:

High media richness
(Best for nonroutine,
ambiguous situations)

Low media richness
(Best for routine,
clear situations)

Face-to-face
presence

Video-
conferencing

Telephone

Personal written
media (e-mail,
memos, letters)

Impersonal written
media (newsletters,
fliers, general reports)

Face-to-face communication, also the most personal form of communication, is the richest. It allows the receiver of the message to observe multiple cues, such as body language and tone of voice. It allows the sender to get immediate feedback, to see how well the receiver comprehended the message. At the other end of the media richness scale, impersonal written media is just the reverse—only one cue and no feedback—making it low in richness.

Matching the Appropriate Medium to the Appropriate Situation In general, follow these guidelines:

- **Rich medium—best for nonroutine situations and to avoid oversimplification.** A *rich* medium is more effective with nonroutine situations.

  Examples: In what way would you like to learn the facts from your boss of a nonroutine situation such as a major company reorganization, which might affect your job? Via a memo tacked on the bulletin board (a lean medium)? Or via face-to-face meeting or phone call (rich medium)?

  The danger of using a rich medium for routine matters (such as monthly sales reports) is that it results in information *overloading*—more information than necessary.

- **Lean medium—best for routine situations and to avoid overloading.** A *lean* medium is more effective with routine situations.

  Examples: In what manner would you as a sales manager like to get routine monthly sales reports from your 50 sales reps? Via time-consuming phone calls (somewhat rich medium)? Or via written memos or e-mails (somewhat lean medium)? The danger of using a lean medium for nonroutine manners (such as a company reorganization) is that it results in information *oversimplification*—it doesn't provide enough of the information the receiver needs and wants. ●

15.2 BARRIERS TO COMMUNICATION

 major question What are the important barriers I need to be aware of, so I can improve my communication skills?

THE BIG PICTURE

We describe three barriers to communication. Physical barriers include sound, time, and space. Semantic barriers include unclear use of words and jargon. Personal barriers include variations in communication skills, trustworthiness and credibility, stereotypes and prejudices, and faulty listening skills.

Test Your Knowledge:
Barriers to Effective Communication

Stand up and give a speech to a group of co-workers? Connecticut businessman Robert Suhoza would prefer to be trampled by elephants, says a news story. "Make small talk at a cocktail party?" it goes on. "Just go ahead and shoot him. Introduce himself to a room full of strangers? Maybe he'll just come back some other time. . . . Even answering the phone seemed at times an insurmountable task: He knew he should pick up the receiver, but he was paralyzed by not knowing who was on the other end, or what the caller wanted."[9]

Suhoza is 53 years old, but all his life he has suffered from social phobia or social anxiety disorder. In this he has plenty of company: One in every eight Americans apparently meets the diagnostic criteria for social anxiety disorder at some point in their lives, making it the third most common psychiatric condition. More women suffer from it than men, although men are more likely to seek treatment.[10]

Social anxiety disorder is an example (though an extreme one) of a communication *barrier*—a barrier being anything interfering with accurate communication between two people. Some barriers may be thought of as happening within the communication

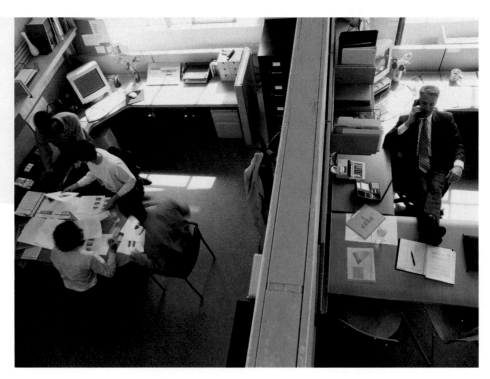

Without walls. Supposedly businesses that have open floor plans with cubicles instead of private offices function better because people can more easily talk across the shoulder-high partitions. But do you think the absence of floor-to-ceiling physical barriers might, in fact, lead to other kinds of barriers—such as others talking making it hard to hear while on the phone?

table 15.1

SOME BARRIERS THAT HAPPEN WITHIN THE COMMUNICATION PROCESS

All it takes is one blocked step in the communication process described in the text for communication to fail. Consider the following.

- **Sender barrier—no message gets sent.** Have you ever had an idea but were afraid to voice it because (like Robert Suhoza) you feared criticism? Then obviously no message got sent.

  But the barrier need not be for psychological reasons. Suppose as a new manager you simply didn't realize (because you weren't told) that supervising your subordinates' expense accounts was part of your responsibility. In that case, it may be understandable why you never call them to task about fudging their expense reports—why, in other words, no message got sent.

- **Encoding barrier—the message is not expressed correctly.** No doubt you've sometimes had difficulty trying to think of the correct word to express how you feel about something. If English is not your first language, perhaps, then you may have difficulty expressing to a supervisor, co-worker, or subordinate what it is you mean to say.

- **Medium barrier—the communication channel is blocked.** You never get through to someone because his or her phone always has a busy signal. The computer network is down and the e-mail message you sent doesn't go through. These are instances of the communication medium being blocked.

- **Decoding barrier—the recipient doesn't understand the message.** Your boss tells you to "lighten up" or "buckle down," but because English is not your first language, you don't understand what the messages mean. Or perhaps you're afraid to show your ignorance when someone is throwing computer terms at you and says that your computer connection has "a bandwidth problem."

- **Receiver barrier—no message gets received.** Because you were talking to a co-worker, you weren't listening when your supervisor announced today's work assignments, and so you have to ask him or her to repeat the announcement.

- **Feedback barrier—the recipient doesn't respond enough.** No doubt you've had the experience of giving someone street directions, but since they only nod their heads and don't repeat the directions back to you, you don't really know whether you were understood. The same thing can happen in many workplace circumstances.

process itself, as the table above shows. *(See Table 15.1.)* It's more practical, however, to think of barriers as being of three types: (1) *physical barriers,* (2) *semantic barriers,* and (3) *personal barriers.*

I. Physical Barriers: Sound, Time, Space, & So On

Try shouting at someone on the far side of a construction site—at a distance of several yards over the roar of earth-moving machinery—and you know what physical barriers are. Other such barriers are time-zone differences, telephone-line static, and crashed computers. Office walls can be physical barriers, too, which is one reason for the trend toward open floor plans with cubicles instead of offices in many workplace settings.

2. Semantic Barriers: When Words Matter

When a supervisor tells you, "We need to get this done right away," what does it mean? Does "We" mean just you? You and your co-workers? Or you, your co-workers, and the boss? Does "right away" mean today, tomorrow, or next week? These are examples of semantic barriers. **Semantics is the study of the meaning of words.**

In addition, we may encounter semantic difficulties when dealing with other cultures (as we discussed in Chapter 4). When talking on the phone with Indians

Practical Action

Minding Your Manners: Workplace Etiquette Can Be Crucial to Your Career

Even when you're not talking, you're often communicating—nonverbally (as we discuss elsewhere in this chapter). Manners are a big part of this.

Consider: While at lunch with your business clients, do you eat your soup by swiping the spoon from 12 o'clock to 6 o'clock in the bowl? (It should be the reverse.) Do you order a glass of wine with your meal? (Best not to drink alcohol on someone else's clock.) Do you squeeze lemon into your ice tea with a client across the table? (Best not—you might squirt him or her in the eye.) Do you scratch your back with your fork?

We are talking about a form of communication known as *etiquette* or *manners.* Despite the informality (including not just dress-down Fridays but dress-down every-days) of many offices, managers need to learn business etiquette—manners, politeness, appropriate behavior—if they are to achieve career success. Etiquette is more than table manners; it is the expression of being considerate. If you have to take clients out to dinner a couple times a week, you'll be glad if you know which fork to use. MBA candidates at Daniels College of Business at the University of Denver are required to attend an etiquette dinner, and the Massachusetts Institute of Technology also runs a not-for-credit charm school. These and similar courses provide lessons in dining etiquette, pager protocol, cell phone politeness, and the like. "In climbing the slippery ladder of success," says the founder of an etiquette training firm, "people have to recognize that they will never get promoted if their bosses and customers don't see them as looking and acting the part."

Some matters to be aware of:[11]

- **Handshakes.** The proper manner is to clasp firmly at an angle, then give two or three pumps.

- **Introductions.** When your boss is meeting your client, you should start with the person you want to honor—the client. ("Mr. Smith, I'd like you to meet my boss, Janet Jones. Jan, this is Horatio Smith, vice-president of Associated Success Inc.") Also, you should give some information about each person in order to get a conversation started. ("Jan is head of our Far West Division, and she just got back from a rock-climbing vacation.")

- **Thank-you notes.** When someone prepares an all-day or all-week program in which you've participated, send him or her a thank-you note. When the boss entertains you on her boat, send her a thank-you note. When a client gives you a plant tour, send him a note. And ALWAYS send a thank-you note after a job interview.

- **Dining tips and table manners.** Don't order the most expensive item. Don't start eating before your host. Avoid ordering food you think you might have difficulty handling properly because of splattering (such as soup or pasta). Know what to do with your bread. (Take the bread or roll, hold it over your plate—it's the plate on the left—break off a piece of it, and then put butter on it. If you drop a roll on the floor, don't pick it up; point it out to the waiter.) Don't kick your shoes off under the table. Turn off your cell phone so it won't beep. When you leave the table and plan to return, leave your napkin on your chair; when you're leaving for good, leave it on the table. In the U.S., you should keep your elbows off the table, and it's okay to keep your hands beneath it. In European countries, however, the reverse is considered polite.

working in call centers in India, for example, we may find their pronunciation unusual. Perhaps that is because, according to one Indian speech-voice consultant, whereas "Americans think in English, we think in our mother tongue and translate it while speaking."[12] As our society becomes more technically oriented, semantic meaning becomes a problem because jargon develops. ***Jargon* is terminology specific to a particular profession or group.** (Example: "The HR VP wants the RFP to go out ASAP." Translation: "The Vice President of Human Resources wants the Request For Proposal to go out as soon as possible.") As a manager in a specialized field, you need to remember that what are ordinary terms for you may be mysteries to outsiders.[13]

3. Personal Barriers: Individual Attributes That Hinder Communication

Self-Assessment Exercise:
What Is Your Communication
Style under Stress?

"Is it them or is it me?"

How often have you wondered, when someone has shown a surprising response to something you said, how the miscommunication happened? Let's examine nine personal barriers that contribute to miscommunication.[14]

Variable Skills in Communicating Effectively   As we all know, some people are simply better communicators than others. They have the speaking skills, the vocabulary, the facial expressions, the eye contact, the dramatic ability, the "gift of gab" to express themselves in a superior way. Conversely, other people don't have this quality. But better communication skills can be learned.

Variations in How Information Is Processed & Interpreted   Are you from a working-class or privileged background? Are you from a particular ethnic group? Are you better at math or at language? Are you from a chaotic household filled with alcoholism and fighting, which distracts you at work?

Because people use different frames of reference and experiences to interpret the world around them, they are selective about what things have meaning to them and what don't. All told, these differences affect what we say and what we think we hear.

Variations in Trustworthiness & Credibility   Without trust between you and the other person, communication is apt to be flawed. Instead of communicating, both of you will be concentrating on defensive tactics, not the meaning of the message being exchanged.[15] How will subordinates react to you as a manager if your predecessors in your job lied to them? They may give you the benefit of a doubt, but they may be waiting for the first opportunity to be confirmed in the belief that you will break their trust.

Oversized Egos   Our egos—our pride, our self-esteem, even arrogance—are a fifth barrier. Egos can cause political battles, turf wars, and the passionate pursuit of power, credit, and resources. Egos influence how we treat each other as well as how receptive we are to being influenced by others. Ever had someone take credit for an idea that was yours? Then you know how powerful ego feelings can be.

Faulty Listening Skills   When you go to a party, do people ever ask questions of you and about who you are and what you're doing? Or are they too ready to talk about themselves? And do they seem to be waiting for you to finish talking so that they can then resume saying what they want to say? (But here's a test: Do you actually *listen* when they're talking?)

Tendency to Judge Others' Messages   Suppose another student in this class sees you reading this text and says, "I like the book we're reading." You might say, "I agree." Or you might say, "I disagree—it's boring." The point is that we all have a natural tendency, according to psychologist Carl Rogers, to judge others' statements from our own point of view (especially if we have strong feelings about the issue).[16]

Inability to Listen with Understanding   To really listen with understanding, you have to imagine yourself in the other person's shoes. Or, as Rogers and his coauthor put it, you have to "see the expressed idea and attitude from the other person's point of view, to sense how it feels to him, to achieve his frame of reference in regard to the thing he is talking about."[17] When you listen with understanding, it makes you feel less defensive (even if the message is criticism) and improves your accuracy in perceiving the message.

Stereotypes & Prejudices   A *stereotype* **consists of oversimplified beliefs about a certain group of people.** There are, for instance, common stereotypes about old people, young people, males, and females. Wouldn't you hate to be categorized according to just a couple of exaggerated attributes—by your age and gender, for example? ("Young men are reckless." "Old women are scolds." Yes, *some* young men and *some* old women are this way, but it's unrealistic and unfair to tar every individual in these groups with the same brush.)

We consider matters of gender communication later in this chapter.

Nonverbal Communication   Do your gestures and facial expressions contradict your words? This is the sort of nonverbal communication that you may not even be aware of. We discuss this subject in more detail next.

Group Exercise:
Noverbal Communication:
A Twist on Charades

Nonverbal Communication

Nonverbal communication **consists of messages sent outside of the written or spoken word.** Says one writer, it includes such factors as "use of time and space, distance between persons when conversing, use of color dress, walking behavior, standing, positioning, seating arrangement, office locations, and furnishings."[18] Nonverbal communication is responsible for perhaps as much as 60% of a message being communicated, according to some researchers.[19] Others estimate it as high as 90%.[20] Given the prevalence of nonverbal communication and its impact on organizational behavior (such as hiring decisions, perceptions of others, and getting one's ideas accepted by others), it is important that you become familiar with the various sources of nonverbal communication.[21] Indeed, this is particularly so when you are dealing with people of other cultures around the world.[22]

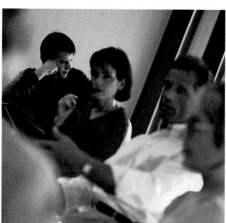

Body language. Who's paying attention and who isn't? If you were a manager speaking at this meeting and you noticed the man at the end of the row looking out the window as you talked, would you continue to speak to those who seem attentive? Or would you try to adjust your remarks—and your own body language—to try to reach the man who is tuning you out?

Seven ways in which nonverbal communication is expressed are through (1) *interpersonal space,* (2) *eye contact,* (3) *facial expressions,* (4) *body movements and gestures,* (5) *touch,* (6) *setting,* and (7) *time.*

I. Interpersonal Space   People of different cultures have different ideas about what is acceptable interpersonal space—that is, how close or far away one should be when communicating with another person. For instance, the people of North America and northern Europe tend to conduct business conversations at a range of 3–4 feet. For people in Latin American and Asian cultures, the range is about 1 foot. For Arabs, it is even closer.

This can lead to cross-cultural misunderstandings. "Arabs tend to get very close and breathe on you," says anthropologist Edward Hall. "The American on the receiving end can't identify all the sources of his discomfort but feels that the Arab is pushy. The Arab comes close, the American backs up. The Arab follows, because he can only interact at certain distances."[23] However, once the American understands that Arabs handle interpersonal space differently and that "breathing on people is a form of communication," says Hall, the situation may be redefined so that the American feels more comfortable.

2. Eye Contact   Eye contact serves four functions in communication: (1) It signals the beginning and end of a conversation; there is a tendency to look *away* from others when beginning to speak and to look *at* them when done. (2) It expresses emotion; for instance, most people tend to avoid eye contact when conveying bad news or negative feedback. (3) Gazing monitors feedback because it reflects interest and attention. (4) Depending on the culture, gazing also expresses the type of relationship between the people communicating. For instance, Westerners are taught at an early age to look at their parents when spoken to. However, Asians are taught to avoid eye contact with a parent or superior in order to show obedience and subservience.[24]

3. Facial Expressions   Probably you're accustomed to thinking that smiling represents warmth, happiness, or friendship whereas frowning represents dissatisfaction or anger. But these interpretations of facial expressions don't apply across all cultures.[25] A smile, for example, doesn't convey the same emotions in different countries.

4. Body Movements & Gestures An example of a body movement is leaning forward; an example of a gesture is pointing. Open body positions, such as leaning backward, express openness, warmth, closeness, and availability for communication. Closed body positions, such as folding one's arms or crossing one's legs, represent defensiveness.

Some body movements and gestures are associated more with one sex than the other, according to communication researcher Judith Hall. For instance, women nod their heads and move their hands more than men do. Men exhibit large body shifts and foot and leg movements more than women do.[26]

We need to point out, however, that interpretations of body language are subjective, hence easily misinterpreted, and highly dependent on the context and cross-cultural differences.[27] You'll need to be careful when trying to interpret body movements, especially when you're operating in a different culture.

5. Touch Norms for touching vary significantly around the world. In the Middle East, for example, it is normal for two males who are friends to walk together holding hands—not commonplace behavior in the U.S.

People tend to touch those they like, and women tend to do more touching during conversations than men do.[28] It needs to be noted, however, that men and women interpret touching differently, and in the United States, at least, sexual harassment claims might be reduced by keeping this perceptual difference in mind.

Still, women clearly have the advantage here, at least in the U.S. One study found that, whereas men are "largely boxed into the formality of a handshake," women are freer to emphasize a point with a brief (nonsexual) touch to the forearm of a man or a woman, give a playful mock push to a man's shoulder, and even place a firm hand on a man's shoulder to signal, if necessary, who is in charge. The risk of touching for a woman, however, is that she may appear flirtatious.[29]

6. Setting How do you feel when you visit someone who sits behind a big desk and is backlit by a window so her face is obscured? What does it say when someone comes out from behind his desk and invites you to sit with him on his office couch? The location of an office (such as corner office with window versus interior office with no window), its size, and the choice of furniture often expresses the accessibility of the person in it.

7. Time When your boss keeps you waiting 45 minutes for an appointment with him, how do you feel? When she simply grunts or makes one-syllable responses to your comments, what does this say about her interest in your concerns? As a manager yourself, you should always give the people who work for you adequate time. You should also talk with them frequently during your meetings with them so they will understand your interest.

The table below gives some suggestions for better nonverbal communication skills. *(See Table 15.2.)*

Do	Don't
Maintain eye contact	Look away from the speaker
Lean toward the speaker	Turn away from the speaker
Speak at a moderate rate	Speak too quickly or slowly
Speak in a quiet, reassuring tone	Speak in an unpleasant tone
Smile and show animation	Yawn excessively
Occasionally nod head in agreement	Close your eyes

Source: Adapted from W. D. St. John, "You Are What You Communicate," *Personnel Journal*, October 1985, p. 43.

table 15.2

TOWARD BETTER NONVERBAL COMMUNICATION SKILLS

You can practice these skills by watching TV with the sound off and interpreting people's emotions and interactions.

Gender-Related Communication Differences

Men are eight times as likely as women to bargain over starting pay. Indeed, says one account, "Women often are less adroit at winning better salaries, assignments, and jobs—either because they don't ask or because they cave in when they do."[30] In other words, women need to hone their negotiation skills, or else they will fall behind.

Some possible general differences in communication between genders are summarized below. *(See Table 15.3.)* Note, however, that these don't apply in all cases, which would constitute stereotyping.

table 15.3

COMMUNICATION DIFFERENCES

How do men and women differ?

Linguistic characteristic	Men	Women
Taking credit	Greater use of "I" statements (e.g., "I did this" and "I did that"); more likely to boast about their achievements	Greater use of "We" statements (e.g., "We did this" and "We did that"); less likely to boast about their achievements
Displaying confidence	Less likely to indicate that they are uncertain about an issue	More likely to indicate a lack of certainty about an issue
Asking questions	Less likely to ask questions (e.g., asking for directions)	More likely to ask questions
Conversation rituals	Avoid making apologies because it puts them in a one-down position	More frequently say "I'm sorry"
Giving feedback	More direct and blunt	More tactful; tend to temper criticism with praise
Giving compliments	Stingy with praise	Pay more compliments than men
Indirectness	Indirect when it comes to admitting fault or when they don't know something	Indirect when telling others what to do

Source: Derived from D. Tannen, "The Power of Talk: Who Gets Heard and Why," *Harvard Business Review,* September–October 1995; and D. Tannen, *You Just Don't Understand: Women and Men in Conversation* (New York: Ballantine Books, 1990).

How useful do you think these specific styles are in a managerial context? (Recall the discussion of men and women with reference to leadership in Chapter 14.)

Author Judith Tingley suggests that women and men should learn to "genderflex"—temporarily use communication behaviors typical of the other gender to increase the potential for influence.[31] For example, a female manager might use sports analogies to motivate a group of males.

Deborah Tannen, by contrast, recommends that everyone become aware of how differing linguistic styles affect our perceptions and judgments. For example, in a meeting, regardless of gender, "those who are comfortable speaking up in groups, who need little or no silence before raising their hands, or who speak out easily without waiting to be recognized are more apt to be heard," she says. "Those who refrain from talking until it's clear that the previous speaker is finished, who wait to be recognized, and who are inclined to link their comments to those of others will do fine at a meeting

Do Female Executives Have an Edge in Business? Women & Communication

Women in business have the edge in two ways, says Chris Clarke, head of an executive search firm with offices in more than 40 countries. "There is increasing evidence," he says, "that women are superior at multitasking, which is needed to handle business complexities, and that they are better at relationships, which is important developing effective teams."[33]

There is another way that women also have an edge, suggests a *BusinessWeek* article: instead of tightly controlling information, they are more willing to share it.[34] A representative of this viewpoint is Anu Shukla, who sold her Internet marketing company for $390 million and made 65 of her 85 employees millionaires. "It's better to overcommunicate," she says. As an example, she made it her policy to share information with all her employees rather than to impart it to selected employees on a need-to-know basis. In addition, she created what she called the "CEO lunch," in which she invited six to eight employees at a time to discuss the business with her.

Your Call

Anne Cummings, professor of business administration at the University of Minnesota at Duluth, suggests there are "masculine" and "feminine" styles in business, in which men tend to be more task-oriented and assertive and to take greater intellectual risks whereas women tend to be more relationship oriented and "democratic" and to be more efficient at solving problems.[35] (Of course, all this behavior operates on a continuum, and most people have a multitude of styles.) Do you think a woman can be successful by taking on the "masculine" style? Can a man be successful taking on the "feminine" style?

where everyone else is following the same rules but will have a hard time getting heard in a meeting with people whose styles are more like the first pattern."[32]

By now most male students and managers know they should avoid the use of masculine wording for jobs or roles that are occupied by both genders, using *police officer* instead of *policeman; supervisor* rather than *foreman.* (Conversely, secretaries, nurses, and babysitters should no longer be referred to as "she.") If you stay alert, it's fairly easy to avoid sentence constructions that are demeaning to women. (Instead of saying "he is," say "he or she is" or "they are.")

But, of course, there's more to effective managerial communication than that. Indeed, there are executive-training programs designed to teach men the value of emotion in relationships—the use of "soft skills" to communicate, build teams, and develop flexibility. "The nature of modern business requires what's more typical to the female mold of building consensus as opposed to the top-down male military model," says Millington F. McCoy, managing director of a New York executive search firm. One program given by London-based James R. Traeger helps participants break down the stereotype of the aggressive, controlling man who always wants to take charge and solve problems and to learn to listen and work in harmony.

Interestingly, although men hold 94% of the top corporate jobs, when they want the advice of an executive coach—a trained listener to help them with their goals and personal problems—they usually turn to a woman. And, in fact, females always want another female as a coach. As a result, 7 out of 10 graduates of Coach U, the largest training school for executive coaches, are women. Because good coaches, says Coach U's CEO Sandy Vilas (who is male), are intuitive communicators and have done a lot of personal development work, "that profile tends to fit women better." Says Susan Bloch, who heads an executive coaching practice, "When a man is asked to coach another, they have a tendency to compete. Man to man, they have to show each other how great they are."[36] ●

15.3 HOW MANAGERS FIT INTO THE COMMUNICATION PROCESS

> ◆ major question | **How can I use the different channels and patterns of communication to my advantage?**

THE BIG PICTURE

Formal communication channels follow the chain of command, which is of three types—vertical, horizontal, and external. Informal communication channels develop outside the organization's formal structure. One type is gossip and rumor. Another is management by wandering around, in which a manager talks to people across all lines of authority.

If you've ever had a low-level job in nearly any kind of organization, you know that there is generally a hierarchy of management between you and the organization's president, director, or CEO. If you had a suggestion that you wanted him or her to hear, you doubtless had to go up through management channels. That's formal communication. However, you may have run into that top manager in the elevator. Or in the restroom. Or in a line at the bank. You could have voiced your suggestion casually then. That's informal communication.

Formal Communication Channels: Up, Down, Sideways, & Outward

Formal communication channels **follow the chain of command and are recognized as official.** The organizational chart we described in Chapter 8 (page 257) indicates how official communications—memos, letters, reports, announcements—are supposed to be routed.

Formal communication is of three types: (1) *vertical*—meaning upward and downward, (2) *horizontal*—meaning laterally (sideways), and (3) *external*—meaning outside the organization.

I. Vertical Communication: Up & Down the Chain of Command   Vertical communication is the flow of messages up and down the hierarchy within the organization: bosses communicating with subordinates, subordinates communicating with

Upward bound. How do you communicate with a manager two or three levels above you in the organization's hierarchy? You can send a memo through channels. Or you can watch for when that manager goes to the water cooler or the coffee pot.

bosses. As you might expect, the more management levels through which a message passes, the more it is prone to distortion.

- **Downward communication—from top to bottom.** *Downward communication flows from a higher level to a lower level (or levels).* In small organizations, top-down communication may be delivered face to face. In larger organizations, it's delivered via meetings, e-mail, official memos, and company publications.

- **Upward communication—from bottom to top.** *Upward communication flows from a lower level to a higher level(s).* Often this type of communication is from a subordinate to his or her immediate manager, who in turn will relay it up to the next level, if necessary. Effective upward communication depends on an atmosphere of trust. No subordinate is going to want to be the bearer of bad news to a manager who is always negative and bad-tempered.

Types of downward and upward communication are shown below. *(See Table 15.4.)*

table 15.4

TYPES OF DOWNWARD AND UPWARD COMMUNICATION

Downward communication

Most downward communication involves one of the following kinds of information:

- Instructions related to particular job tasks. Example (supervisor to subordinate): "The store will close Monday for inventory. All employees are expected to participate."
- Explanations about the relationship between two or more tasks. Example: "While taking inventory, employees need to see what things are missing. Most of that might be attributable to shoplifting."
- Explanations of the organization's procedures and practices. Example: "Start counting things on the high shelves and work your way down."
- A manager's feedback about a subordinate's performance. Example: "It's best not to try to count too fast."
- Attempts to encourage a sense of mission and dedication to the organization's goals. Example: "By keeping tabs on our inventory, we can keep our prices down and maintain our reputation of giving good value."

Upward communication

Most upward communication involves the following kinds of information:

- Reports of progress on current projects. Example: "We shut down the store yesterday to take inventory."
- Reports of unsolved problems requiring help from people higher up. Example: "We can't make our merchandise count jibe with the stock reports."
- New developments affecting the work unit. Example: "Getting help from the other stores really speeded things up this year."
- Suggestions for improvements. Example: "The stores should loan each other staff every time they take inventory."
- Reports on employee attitudes and efficiency. Example: "The staff likes it when they go to another store and sometimes they pick up some new ways of doing things."

Sources: D. Katz and R. Kahn, *The Social Psychology of Organizations* (New York: Wiley, 1966); and E. Planty and W. Machaver, "Upward Communications: A Project in Executive Development," *Personnel* 28 (1952), pp. 304–318.

2. Horizontal Communication: Within & Between Work Units *Horizontal communication flows within and between work units; its main purpose is coordination.* As a manager, you will spend perhaps as much as a third of your time in this form of communication—consulting with colleagues and co-workers at the same level as you within the organization. In this kind of sideways communication, you will be sharing information, coordinating tasks, solving problems, resolving conflicts, and getting the support of your peers. Horizontal communication is encouraged through the use of committees, task forces, and matrix structures.

Horizontal communication can be impeded in three ways: (1) by specialization that makes people focus just on their jobs alone; (2) by rivalry between workers or work units, which prevents sharing of information; and (3) by lack of encouragement from management.[37]

3. External Communication: Outside the Organization *External communication* **flows between people inside and outside the organization.** These are other stakeholders: customers, suppliers, shareholders or other owners, and so on. Companies have given this kind of communication heightened importance, especially with customers or clients, who are the lifeblood of any company.

Informal Communication Channels

Informal communication channels **develop outside the formal structure and do not follow the chain of command**—they skip management levels and cut across lines of authority.

Two types of informal channels are (1) the *grapevine* and (2) *management by wandering around.*

The *grapevine* **is the unofficial communication system of the informal organization,** a network of gossip and rumor of what is called "employee language." Research shows that the grapevine is faster than formal channels, is about 75% accurate, and is used by employees to acquire the majority of their on-the-job information.[38]

Management by wandering around (MBWA) **is the term used to describe a manager's literally wandering around his or her organization and talking with people across all lines of authority.**[39] Management by wandering around helps to reduce the problems of distortion that inevitably occur with formal communication flowing up a hierarchy. MBWA allows managers to listen to employees and learn about their problems as well as to express to employees what values and goals are important. ●

MBWA. Management by wandering around is sort of the reverse of employees exchanging informal views with top managers at the water cooler. That is, by wandering around the organization, top managers can stop and talk to nearly anyone—and thus perhaps learn things that might be screened out by the formal up-the-organization reporting process. If top managers can do MBWA, do you think mid-level managers can as well?

15.4 COMMUNICATION IN THE INFORMATION AGE

How do contemporary managers use information technology to communicate more effectively?

major question

THE BIG PICTURE
We discuss seven communications tools of information technology: (1) the Internet and its associated intranets and extranets, (2) e-mail, (3) videoconferencing, (4) group support systems, (5) telecommuting, (6) handheld devices, and (7) blogs. We also discuss impediments to productivity: (1) misuse of technology, (2) fussing with computers, and (3) information overload.

"I'm dangerous," jokes Gregory Summe between runs at a Utah ski resort, as he pulls out his tiny cell phone and his electronic organizer with its 12,000-name contact list. With this kind of portable information technology, Summe, CEO of EG&G Inc., is able to work anywhere and contact anyone. "There's an expectation for CEOs to be much more in touch with customers, employees, and investors than in the past," he says. "A big part of the reason may be [portable information] technology."[40]

Communications Tools of Information Technology: Offspring of the Internet

Here we explore some of the more important aspects of information technology: (1) the Internet along with intranets and extranets, (2) e-mail, (3) videoconferencing, (4) group support systems, (5) telecommuting, (6) handheld devices, and (7) blogs.

I. The Internet, Intranets, & Extranets The Internet, or more simply "the Net," is more than a computer network. As we said in Chapter 1, it is a network of computer networks. The Internet is a global network of independently operating but interconnected computers, linking hundreds of thousands of smaller networks around the world. The Internet connects everything from personal computers to supercomputers in organizations of all kinds.[41]

Two private uses of the Internet are as intranets and extranets.

- **Intranets. An *intranet* is nothing more than an organization's private Internet.** Intranets also have *firewalls* that block outside Internet users from accessing internal information. This is done to protect the privacy and confidentiality of company documents. The top four uses for intranets are information sharing, information publishing, e-mail, and document management.[42]

- **Extranets. An *extranet* is an extended intranet in that it connects internal employees with selected customers, suppliers, and other strategic partners.** Ford Motor Co., for instance, has an extranet that connects its dealers worldwide. Ford's extranet was set up to help support the sales and servicing of cars and to enhance customer satisfaction.

No rigorous studies have demonstrated productivity increases from using the Internet, intranets, or extranets. However, research reveals some other organizational benefits. For example, Cisco Systems used the Internet to recruit potential employees, hiring 66% of its people and receiving 81% of its résumés from the Net.[43] General Mills used to send researchers across country to conduct focus groups or poll consumers on prospective products, but now it conducts 60% of its consumer research online, reducing its costs by half.[44]

2. E-mail E-mail, short for *electronic mail,* uses the Internet to send computer-generated text and documents between people. E-mail has become a major communications medium because of four key benefits: (1) reduced cost of distributing information, (2) increased teamwork, (3) reduced paper costs, and (4) increased flexibility. On the other hand, it has three drawbacks: It can lead to (1) wasted time, as in having to deal with **spam, or unsolicited jokes and junk mail;** (2) information overload; and (3) neglect of other media. *(See Table 15.5.)*

table 15.5

E-MAIL: BENEFITS, DRAWBACKS, AND TIPS FOR DOING BETTER

Benefits

- *Reduced cost of distributing information.* One software developer found that its telephone bill dropped by more than half after its employees and dealers were told to use e-mail instead of the phone.
- *Increased teamwork.* Users can send messages to colleagues anywhere, whether in the office or around the world.
- *Reduced paper costs.* E-mail reduces the costs and time associated with print duplication and paper distribution.
- *Increased flexibility.* Employees with portable computers, PDAs, and cell phones can access their e-mail from anywhere.

Drawbacks

- *Wasted time.* E-mail can distract employees from critical job duties. Employees now average nearly an hour a day managing their e-mail.
- *Information overload.* E-mail users tend to get too much information—in some cases, only 10 of 120 daily inbox messages may be worthwhile.
- *Neglect of other media.* Increased use of e-mail can be found to be associated with decreased face-to-face interactions and decreased overall organizational communication, with lessened cohesion.

Tips for better e-mail handling

- *Treat all e-mail as confidential.* Pretend every message is a postcard that can be read by anyone. (Supervisors may legally read employee e-mail.)
- *Be careful with jokes and informality.* Nonverbal language and other subtleties are lost, so jokes may be taken as insults or criticism.
- *Avoid sloppiness, but avoid criticizing others' sloppiness.* Avoid spelling and grammatical errors, but don't criticize errors in others' messages.
- *When replying, quote only the relevant portion.* Edit long e-mail messages you've received down to the relevant paragraph and put your response immediately following.
- *Not every topic belongs on e-mail.* Complicated topics may be better discussed on the phone or in person to avoid misunderstandings.

Sources: R. F. Federico and J. M. Bowley, "The Great E-Mail Debate," *HR Magazine,* January 1996, pp. 67–72; M. S. Thompson and M. S. Feldman, "Electronic Mail and Organizational Communication: Does Saying 'Hi' Really Matter?" *Organizational Science,* November–December 1998, pp. 685–698; J. Yaukey, "E-Mail Out of Control for Many," *Reno Gazette-Journal,* May 7, 2001, p. IE; D. Halpern, "Dr. Manners on E-Mail Dos and Don'ts," *Monitor of Psychology,* April 2004, p. 5; and B. K. Williams and S. C. Sawyer, *Using Information Technology,* 7th ed. (New York: McGraw-Hill/Irwin, 2007), p. 91.

3. Videoconferencing Also known as *teleconferencing, videoconferencing* uses video and audio links along with computers to enable people located at different locations to see, hear, and talk with one another. This enables people from many locations to conduct a meeting without having to travel. Video-conferencing can thus significantly reduce an organization's travel expenses.

Many organizations set up special videoconferencing rooms or booths with specially equipped television cameras. More recent equipment enables people to attach small cameras and microphones to their desks or computer monitors. This enables employees to conduct long-distance meetings and training classes without leaving their office or cubicle.[45]

Videoconferencing. In this arrangement, three people in different locations can computer-conference—view and interact with one another—while studying a layout on-screen. Videoconferencing offers considerable savings in time and money over the cost of travel. Do you think you would feel inhibited working with people in this way?

4. Group Support Systems *Group support systems* (GSSs) entail using state-of-the-art computer software and hardware to help people work better together. They enable people to share information without the constraints of time and space. This is accomplished using computer networks to link people across a room or across the globe. Collaborative applications include messaging and e-mail systems, calendar management, videoconferencing, and electronic whiteboards. GSS applications have demonstrated increased productivity and cost savings. In addition, groups using GSSs during brainstorming experienced greater participation and influence quality, a greater quantity of ideas generated, and less domination by individual members than did groups meeting face to face.[46]

Organizations that use full-fledged GSSs have the ability to create virtual teams (described in Chapter 13), who tend to use Internet or intranet systems, collaborative software, and videoconferencing to communicate with team members anytime.

It is important to keep in mind that modern-day information technology enables people to interact virtually, but it doesn't guarantee effective communications. Indeed, there is a host of unique communication problems associated with using information technology to operate virtually.[47]

5. Telecommuting *Telecommuting* involves doing work that is generally performed in the office away from the office, using a variety of information technologies. Employees typically receive and send work from home via phone and fax or by using a modem to link a home computer to an office computer. Among the benefits are (1) reduction of capital costs, because employees work at home; (2) increased flexibility and autonomy for workers; (3) competitive edge in recruiting hard-to-get employees; (4) increased job satisfaction and lower turnover; (5) increased productivity; and (6) ability to tap nontraditional labor pools (such as prison inmates and homebound disabled people).[48]

Telecommuting is more common for jobs that involve computer work, writing, and phone or brain work that requires concentration and limited interruptions. A 2006 Deloitte report states that by 2008 41 million corporate employees globally may spend at least 1 day a week teleworking and that 200 million will work from home at least 1 day a month.[49] A report by the Reason Foundation, a California-based think tank, found that telecommuters presently outnumbered actual mass-transit commuters in 27 of the largest U.S. metropolitan areas, and that two-thirds of Fortune 1000 companies now have telecommuting programs.[50]

Although telecommuting represents an attempt to accommodate employee needs and desires, it requires adjustments and is not for everybody. People who enjoy the social camaraderie of the office setting, for instance, probably won't like it. Others lack the self-motivation needed to work at home.

6. Handheld Devices   Handheld devices such as personal digital assistants (PDAs) and smartphones offer users the portability to do work from any location. PDAs, for example, are used to track appointments, work spreadsheets, manage e-mail, organize photos, play games, and watch videos. Multimedia smartphones, which combine some of the capabilities of a personal computer with a handset, offer a wealth of gadgetry: text messaging, cameras, music players, videogames, e-mail access, digital-TV viewing, search tools, personal information management, GPS locators, Internet phone service, and even phones doubling as credit cards (which, among other things, can be used to pay for parking time on a new generation of wireless parking meters).[51] As one newspaper headline put it, "It's Not Just a Phone, It's an Adventure."[52]

7. Blogs   **A *blog* is an online journal in which people write whatever they want about any topic.** According to a study from the Pew Internet and American Life Project, in 2006 there were an estimated 12 million adult bloggers in the United States, a threefold increase in 2 years.[53] Four million teens are also blogging.[54]

The benefits of blogs include the opportunity for people to discuss issues in a casual format, serving much like a chat group and thus providing managers with insights from a variety of employees and customers. Thus, managers such as Paul Otellini, CEO of Intel, who was one of the first executive bloggers, use blogs to discuss matters of importance.[55] Blogs also give people the opportunity to air their opinions, grievances, and creative ideas. In addition, blogs can be used to obtain feedback.

But blogs also have some drawbacks. One is the lack of legal and organizational guidelines about what can be posted online, resulting in some people being fired after posting information online (such as suggestive pictures or information about company finances).[56] Another problem is that employees can use blogs to say unflattering things or leak confidential information about their employers. There is also the problem of believability; can you trust what you read on blogs when, for example, bloggers are being paid to push products without disclosure?[57]

Workplace Problems: Impediments to Productivity

First the mainframe computer, then the desktop stand-alone personal computer, and then the networked computer were all brought into the workplace for one reason only: to improve productivity. But there are several ways in which information technology actively interferes with productivity. We consider (1) *misuse of technology,* (2) *fussing with computers,* and (3) *information overload.*

I. Misuse of Technology   Employees may look busy, as they stare into their computer screens with brows crinkled, but sometimes they are just hard at work playing video games. Or browsing online malls, or looking at their investments or pornography sites. Indeed, one study found that recreational Web surfing accounts for nearly one-third of office workers' time online.[58] In 2006, one survey found the average U.S. worker fritters away 1.86 hours per 8-hour workday and that the biggest time killer was personal use of the Internet (52% said they wasted more time online than any other way).[59]

2. Fussing with Computers   Most computer users at some point have to get involved with making online connections work or experience the frustrations of untangling complications caused by spam, viruses, and other Internet deviltry.

A Stanford study found that junk e-mail and computer maintenance take up a significant amount of time spent online each day. Indeed, people surveyed said they spent 14 minutes daily dealing with computer problems, which would add up to a total of 10 days a year. [60]

3. Information Overload *Information overload* **occurs when the amount of information received exceeds a person's ability to handle or process it.** Clearly, information technology is a two-edged sword. The average businessperson sends and receives 84 email messages a day, according to some research, and that average will increase to 110 messages a day by the end of 2008.[61] Cell phones, pagers, and laptops may untether employees from the office, but these employees tend to work longer hours under more severe deadline pressure than do their tethered counterparts who stay at the office, according to one study.[62] Moreover, the devices that once promised to do away with irksome business travel by ushering in a new era of communications have done the opposite. They have created the office-in-a-bag that allows businesspeople to continue to work from airplane seats, hotel desks, and their own kitchen tables. The diminishing difference between work and leisure is what Motorola calls the "blurring of life segments."[63]

Makers of handheld devices claim that the combination of portability and multitasking features makes people more productive, but David Greenfield, director of the Center for Internet Studies, thinks this idea "is a scam and illusion," because multitasking can easily become "multislacking" and in fact may make us take more time to accomplish basic tasks.[64] Probably a better information-management strategy is to reduce your information load and increase your information-processing capacity. *(See Table 15.6.)* ●

table 15.6

INFORMATION MANAGEMENT STRATEGY

Reducing information load and increasing information-processing capacity

Reducing your information load

- *Preview and ignore messages.* When going through your e-mail, quickly glance at the subject line and immediately delete anything that looks like spam or (if you can) messages from people you don't know. Do the same with voice mail or phone slips.

- *Filter messages.* Many e-mail programs have message filtering, so that an urgent message from the boss, for example, will go to the top of your e-mail queue. Spam-killer software is available to help eliminate junk mail. Some executives put all "cc" e-mails in a special file and rarely read them.

- *Organize your e-mail inbox.* Set up a folder for e-mails you want to keep. Don't use your e-mail inbox for general storage.

Increasing your information-processing capacity

- *Use discipline.* Check e-mail only three times a day. Handle every message only once. When an e-mail message arrives, deal with it immediately—read it and then either respond to it, delete it, or file it away in a folder.

- *Get a unified messaging site.* It's possible to get one unified messaging site to which all your e-mails, faxes, and voice mails are delivered. Voice mails arrive as audio files that you can listen to, while e-mails are read to you over the phone by a virtual (robot) assistant.

- *Use your company address for work-related e-mails only.* Have personal messages go to a separate account.

Sources: C. Hymowitz, "Taking Time to Focus on the Big Picture Despite the Flood of Data," *The Wall Street Journal,* February 27, 2001, p. B1; R. Strauss, "You've Got Maelstrom," *The New York Times,* July 5, 2001, pp. D1, D9; C. Canabou, "A Message about Managing E-mail," *Fast Company,* August 2001, p. 38; C. Cavanagh, *Managing Your Email: Thinking Outside the Inbox* (New York: John Wiley & Sons, 2003); and J. Zaslow, "Hoarders vs. Deleters: How You Handle Your Email Inbox Says a Lot About You," *The Wall Street Journal,* August 10, 2006, p. D1.

> **major question** How can I be a better listener, reader, writer, and speaker?

THE BIG PICTURE

We describe how you can be a more effective listener, as in learning to concentrate on the content of a message. We also describe how to be an effective reader. We offer four tips for becoming a more effective writer. Finally, we discuss how to be an effective speaker, through three steps.

Self-Assessment Exercise:
Active Listening Skills Inventory

The principal activities the typical manager does have to do with communication—listening, 40%; talking, 35%; reading, 16%; and writing, 9%.[65] Listening and speaking often take place in meetings (see the Practical Action box "How to Streamline Meetings" in Chapter 5), although they are not the only occasions. Regardless of the environment, let's see how you can be more effective at these four essential communication skills.

Understand me. What's the recipe for effective listening—for really finding out what someone has to say? Probably it is *listen, watch, write, think, question.* What do you do to fight flagging concentration if you're tired or bored? You suppress negative thoughts, ignore distractions about the speaker's style of delivery or body language, and encourage the speaker with eye contact, an interested expression, and an attentive posture. This will make you more involved and interested in the subject matter.

Being an Effective Listener

Is listening something you're good at? Then you're the exception. Generally, people comprehend only about 35% of a typical verbal message, experts say.[66] Two-thirds of all employees feel management isn't listening to them.[67] Interestingly, the average speaker communicates 125 words per minute, while we can process 500 words per minute. Poor listeners use this information-processing gap to daydream. They think about other things, thus missing the important parts of what's being communicated.[68] Good listeners know how to use these gaps effectively, mentally summarizing the speaker's remarks, weighing the evidence, and listening between the lines.

How do you become the kind of manager who others say is a good listener? Following are some suggestions (you can practice them in your college lectures and seminars).[69]

Concentrate on the Content of the Message Don't think about what you're going to say until the other person has finished talking.

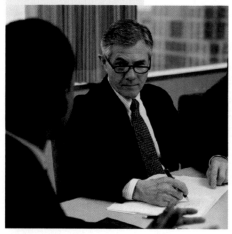

- **Judge content, not delivery.** Don't tune out someone because of his or her accent, clothing, mannerisms, personality, or speaking style.

- **Ask questions, summarize remarks.** Good listening is hard work. Ask questions to make sure you understand. Recap what the speaker said.

- **Listen for ideas.** Don't get diverted by the details; try to concentrate on the main ideas.

- **Resist distractions, show interest.** Don't get distracted by things other people are doing, paperwork on your desk, things happening outside the window, television or radio, and the like. Show the speaker you're listening, periodically restating in your own words what you've heard.

Communication by Listening

Often the reason that people act subversively against their employers is that they can't or are afraid to communicate with their managers.

Resistance may take the form of "malicious compliance" (following supervisors' instructions to the letter while ignoring the real goal), withholding crucial data, or sabotaging projects that reflect directly on the manager.

One bookstore employee sabotaged his non-listening, always-angry boss by going through the store and discreetly pocketing any pens, pencils, even crayons, then hiding them in a backroom cabinet. "My already preternaturally enraged boss," he reported later, "reached glorious heights of apoplexy."[70]

As we discuss in the text, effective communication begins with listening. There is a technique for doing this. "To begin with, listen to people as if you don't know the answer," suggests Meg Price, a Reno, Nevada, human resource professional. "This means that you will ask more questions to try to understand the situation from the other person's perspective. When you think you've got it, make a statement to the speaker summarizing what you believe they have told you. Only when they agree that indeed you do 'get it' should you begin to offer potential solutions or answers."[71]

Of course, sometimes there are true disagreements, and no amount of listening on your part is going to change that fact. Here, according to David Stiebel, author of *When Talking Makes Things Worse! Resolving Problems When Communication Fails,* is how to identify the nature of a dispute:

- If you only listened to the other person, would she feel satisfied and stop opposing you?
- If you succeed in explaining yourself, would you really change the other person's mind?
- If the other person explained himself more, would you change your mind?

When true disagreements occur, one person ultimately must be willing to change so that negotiations can begin.[72]

- **Give a fair hearing.** Don't shut out unfavorable information just because you hear a term—"Republican," "Democrat," "union," "big business," "affirmative action," "corporate welfare"—that suggests ideas you're not comfortable with. Try to correct for your biases.

Hot Seat DVD Application:
Listening Skills: Yeah, Whatever

Being an Effective Reader

Reading shares many of the same skills as listening. You need to concentrate on the content of the message, judge the content and not the delivery, and concentrate on the main ideas. But because managers usually have to do so much reading, you also need to learn to apply some other strategies.

Realize That Speed Reading Doesn't Work   Perhaps you've thought that somewhere along the line you could take a course on speed reading. By and large, however, speed reading isn't effective. Psychologists have found that speed reading or skimming may work well with easy or familiar reading material, but it can lead to problems with dense or unfamiliar material. For instance, in one study, when questioned about their reading of difficult material, average readers got half the questions right, while speed readers got only one in three.[73]

Learn to Streamline Reading   Management consultant and UCLA professor Kathryn Alesandrini offers a number of suggestions for streamlining your reading.[74]

- **Be savvy about periodicals and books.** Review your magazine and newspaper subscriptions and eliminate as many as possible. You can subscribe to just

Speed-read this? Maybe you could—if it's easy or familiar material. But lots of things managers are required to read take patient study. How are you going to manage such reading day after day?

a few industry publications, scan and mark interesting material, later read what's marked, and pitch the rest. Read summaries and reviews that condense business books and articles.

- **Transfer your reading load.** With some material you can ask some of your employees to screen or scan it first, then post an action note on each item that needs additional reading by you. You can also ask your staff to read important books and summarize them in four or five pages.

- **Make internal memos and e-mail more efficient.** Ask others to tell you up front in their e-mails, memos, and reports what they want you to do. Instruct them to include a one-page executive summary of a long report. When you communicate with them, give them specific questions you want answered.

Do Top-Down Reading—SQ3R "The key to better reading is to be a productive rather than a passive reader," writes Alesandrini. "You'll get more out of what you read if you literally produce meaningful connections between what you already know and what you're reading."[75] This leads to what she calls a "top-down" strategy for reading, a variant on the SQ3R (Survey, Question, Read, Recite, Review) method we discussed in the box at the end of Chapter 1.

The top-down system has five steps:

- **Rate reasons to read.** Rate your reasons for reading ("Why should I read this? Will reading it contribute to my goals?").

- **Question and predict answers.** Formulate specific questions you want the reading to answer. This will give you reasons for reading—to get answers to your questions.

- **Survey the big picture.** Survey the material to be read so you can get a sense of the whole. Take a few minutes to get an overview so that you'll be better able to read with purpose.

- **Skim for main ideas.** Skimming the material is similar to surveying, except it's on a smaller scale. You look for the essence of each subsection or paragraph.

- **Summarize.** Summarize as you skim. Verbally restate or write notes of the main points, using your own words. Visualize or sketch the main points. Answer your initial questions as you skim the material.

Being an Effective Writer

Writing is an essential management skill, all the more so because e-mail has replaced the telephone in so much of business communication. In addition, downsizing has eliminated the administrative assistants who used to edit and correct business correspondence, so even upper-level executives often write their own letters and e-mail now.[76] A lot of students, however, don't get enough practice in writing, which puts them at a career disadvantage. Taking a business writing class can be a real advantage. (Indeed, as a manager, you may have to identify employees who need writing training.)

Following are some tips for writing more effectively. These apply particularly to memos and reports but are also applicable to e-mail messages.

Don't Show Your Ignorance E-mail correspondence has made people more relaxed about spelling and grammar rules. While this is fine among friends, as a manager you'll need to create a more favorable impression in your writing. Besides using the spelling checkers and grammar checkers built in to most word processing programs, you should reread, indeed proofread, your writing before sending it on.

Understand Your Strategy before You Write　Following are three strategies for laying out your ideas in writing.

- **Most important to least important.** This is a good strategy when the action you want your reader to take is logical and not highly political.
- **Least controversial to most controversial.** This builds support gradually and is best used when the decision is controversial or your reader is attached to a particular solution other than the one you're proposing.
- **Negative to positive.** This strategy establishes a common ground with your reader and puts the positive argument last, which makes it stronger.[77]

Start with Your Purpose　Often people organize their messages backward, putting their real purpose last, points out Alesandrini. You should *start* your writing by telling your purpose and what you expect of the reader.

Write Simply, Concisely, & Directly　Keep your words simple and use short words, sentences, and phrases. Be direct instead of vague, and use the active voice rather than the passive. (Directness, active voice: "Please call a meeting for Wednesday." Vagueness, passive voice: "It is suggested that a meeting be called for Wednesday.")

Telegraph Your Writing with a Powerful Layout　Make your writing as easy to read as possible, using the tools of highlighting and white space.

- **Highlighting.** Highlighting consists of using **boldface** and *italics* to emphasize key concepts and introduce new concepts, and bullets—small circles or squares like the ones in the list you're reading—to emphasize list items. (Don't overuse any of these devices, or they'll lose their effect. And particularly don't use ALL CAPITAL LETTERS for emphasis, except rarely.)
- **White space.** White space, which consists of wide margins and a break between paragraphs, produces a page that is clean and attractive.[78]

Being an Effective Speaker

Speaking or talking covers a range of activities, from one-on-one conversations, to participating in meetings, to giving formal presentations. In terms of personal oral communication, most of the best advice comes under the heading of listening, since effective listening will dictate the appropriate talking you need to do.

However, the ability to talk to a room full of people—to make an oral presentation—is one of the greatest skills you can have. A study conducted by AT&T and Stanford University found that the top predictor of success and professional upward mobility is how much you enjoy public speaking and how effective you are at it.[79]

The biggest problem most people have with public speaking is controlling their nerves. Author and lecturer Gael Lindenfield suggests that you can prepare your nerves by practicing your speech until it's near perfect, visualizing yourself performing with brilliance, getting reassurance from a friend, and getting to the speaking site early and releasing physical tension by doing deep breathing. (And staying away from alcohol and caffeine pick-me-ups before your speech.)[80] As for the content of the speech, some brief and valuable advice is offered by speechwriter Phil Theibert, who says a speech comprises just three simple rules: (1) Tell them what you're going to say. (2) Say it. (3) Tell them what you said.[81]

1. Tell Them What You're Going to Say   The introduction should take 5%–15% of your speaking time, and it should prepare the audience for the rest of the speech. Avoid jokes and such phrases as "I'm honored to be with you here today . . ." Because everything in your speech should be relevant, try to go right to the point. For example:

"Good afternoon. The subject of identity theft may seem far removed from the concerns of most employees. But I intend to describe how our supposedly private credit, health, employment, and other records are vulnerable to theft by so-called identity thieves and how you can protect yourself."

2. Say It   The main body of the speech takes up 75%–90% of your time. The most important thing to realize is that your audience won't remember more than a few points anyway. Thus, you need to decide which three or four points must be remembered.[82] Then cover them as succinctly as possible.

Be particularly attentive to transitions during the main body of the speech. Listening differs from reading in that the listener has only one chance to get your meaning. Thus, be sure you constantly provide your listeners with guidelines and transitional phrases so they can see where you're going. Example:

"There are five ways the security of your supposedly private files can be compromised. The first way is . . ."

3. Tell Them What You Said   The end might take 5%–10% of your time. Many professional speakers consider the conclusion to be as important as the introduction, so don't drop the ball here. You need a solid, strong, persuasive wrap-up.

Use some sort of signal phrase that cues your listeners that you are heading into your wind-up. Examples:

"Let's review the main points . . ."

"In conclusion, what CAN you do to protect against unauthorized invasion of your private files? I point out five main steps. One . . ."

Give some thought to the last thing you will say. It should be strongly upbeat, a call to action, a thought for the day, a little story, a quotation. Examples:

"I want to leave you with one last thought . . ."

"Finally, let me close by sharing something that happened to me . . ."

"As Albert Einstein said, 'Imagination is more important than knowledge.'"

Then say "Thank you" and stop talking. ●

blog 506
communication 488
decoding 489
downward communication 50I
encoding 489
external communication 502
extranet 503
feedback 489
formal communication
 channels 500
grapevine 502

group support system 505
horizontal communication 50I
informal communication
 channels 502
information overload 507
intranet 503
jargon 494
management by wandering around
 (MBWA) 502
media richness 49I
medium 489

message 489
noise 490
nonverbal communication 496
receiver 489
semantics 493
sender 489
spam 504
stereotype 495
upward communication 50I

summary

 I5.I The Communication Process: What It Is, How It Works

- Communication is the transfer of information and understanding from one person to another. The process involves sender, message, and receiver; encoding and decoding; the medium; feedback; and dealing with "noise." The sender is the person wanting to share information. The information is called a message. The receiver is the person for whom the message is intended. Encoding is translating a message into understandable symbols or language. Decoding is interpreting and trying to make sense of the message. The medium is the pathway by which a message travels. Feedback is the process in which a receiver expresses his or her reaction to the sender's message. The entire communication process can be disrupted at any point by noise, defined as any disturbance that interferes with the transmission of a message.

- For effective communication, a manager must select the right medium. Media richness indicates how well a particular medium conveys information and promotes learning. The richer a medium is, the better it is at conveying information. Face-to-face presence is the richest; an advertising flyer would be one of the lowest. A rich medium is best for nonroutine situations and to avoid oversimplification. A lean medium is best for routine situations and to avoid overloading.

 I5.2 Barriers to Communication

- Barriers to communication are of three types:

  (I) Physical barriers are exemplified by walls, background noise, and time-zone differences.

  (2) Semantics is the study of the meaning of words. Jargon, terminology specific to a particular profession or group, can be a semantic barrier.

  (3) Personal barriers are individual attributes that hinder communication. Nine such barriers are (a) variable skills in communicating effectively, (b) variations in frames of reference and experiences that affect how information is interpreted, (c) variations in trustworthiness and credibility, (d) oversized egos, (e) faulty listening skills, (f) tendency to judge others' messages, (g) inability to listen with understanding, (h) stereotypes (oversimplified beliefs about a certain group of people) and prejudices, and (i) nonverbal communication (messages sent outside of the written or spoken word, including body language).

- Seven ways in which nonverbal communication is expressed are through (I) interpersonal space, (2) eye contact, (3) facial expressions, (4) body movements and gestures, (5) touch, (6) setting, and (7) time.

15.3 How Managers Fit into the Communication Process

- Communication channels may be formal or informal.

- Formal communication channels follow the chain of command and are recognized as official. Formal communication is of three types:

  (1) Vertical communication is the flow of messages up and down the organizational hierarchy.

  (2) Horizontal communication flows within and between work units; its main purpose is coordination.

  (3) External communication flows between people inside and outside the organization.

- Informal communication channels develop outside the formal structure and do not follow the chain of command. Two aspects of informal channels are the grapevine and management by wandering around.

  (1) The grapevine is the unofficial communication system of the informal organization. The grapevine is faster than formal channels, is about 75% accurate, and is used by employees to acquire most on-the-job information.

  (2) In management by wandering around (MBWA), a manager literally wanders around his or her organization and talks with people across all lines of authority; this reduces distortion caused by formal communication.

15.4 Communication in the Information Age

- This section considers seven communications tools of information technology:

  (1) The Internet is a global network of independently operating but interconnected computers, linking smaller networks. Two private uses of the Internet are for intranets, organizations' private Internets, and for extranets, extended intranets that connect a company's internal employees with selected customers, suppliers, and other strategic partners.

  (2) E-mail, for electronic mail, uses the Internet to send computer-generated text and documents between people. E-mail has become a major communication medium because it reduces the cost of distributing information, increases teamwork, reduces paper costs, and increases flexibility. However, e-mail has three drawbacks: wasted

time; information overload, in part because of spam, or unsolicited jokes and junk mail; and it leads people to neglect other media.

  (3) Videoconferencing uses video and audio links along with computers to enable people located at different locations to see, hear, and talk with one another.

  (4) Group support systems entail using state-of-the-art computer software and hardware to help people work better together.

  (5) Telecommuting involves doing work that is generally performed in the office away from the office, using a variety of information technologies.

  (6) Handheld devices such as personal digital assistants and smartphones offer users the portability to work from any location.

  (7) Blogs are online journals in which people write whatever they want about any topic.

- Three impediments to productivity of information technology are (1) the technology is misused, as for video games; (2) it requires a lot of fussing with, as in untangling complications caused by spam and viruses; and (3) it can produce information overload—the amount of information received exceeds a person's ability to handle or process it.

15.5 Improving Communication Effectiveness

- This section describes how to be more effective at listening, reading, writing, and speaking.

- To become a good listener, you should concentrate on the content of the message. You should judge content, not delivery; ask questions and summarize the speaker's remarks; listen for ideas; resist distractions and show interest; and give the speaker a fair hearing.

- To become a good reader, you need to first realize that speed reading usually doesn't work. You should also be savvy about how you handle periodicals and books, transfer your reading load to some of your employees, and ask others to use e-mails and reports to tell you what they want you to do. A top-down reading system that's a variant on the SQ3R system (survey, question, read, recite, review) is also helpful.

- To become an effective writer, you can follow several suggestions. Use spelling and grammar checkers in word processing software. Use three strategies for laying out your ideas in writing: go from most important topic to least important; go from least controversial topic to most controversial; and go from negative to positive. When organizing your message, start with your purpose. Write simply, concisely, and directly. Telegraph your writing through use of highlighting and white space.

- To become an effective speaker, follow three simple rules. Tell people what you're going to say. Say it. Tell them what you said.

 ## management in action

Boeing Co. Uses Blogging to Improve Communication Both Inside & Outside the Organization

Defense contractors and aerospace companies aren't known for their openness. After all, this is an industry built on security clearances and classified government projects. But today Boeing Co. is embracing a kind of management *glasnost* that would have been unthinkable a few years ago.

The evidence? Boeing's use of blogs. The Chicago aerospace giant—no stranger to recent and well-publicized ethical and political scandals—is among a small but growing group of large non-tech companies such as Walt Disney, General Motors, and McDonald's that are embracing the power of blogging. That means Boeing has learned to cede some control and expose itself to stinging criticism in exchange for a potentially more constructive dialogue with the public, customers, and employees. "Companies are nervous about creating external blogs because they fear the negative comments," says Charlene Li, an analyst at Forrester Research Inc. "But negative comments do exist. A company is better off knowing about them."

Boeing's early results suggest that the rewards outweigh the risks. The company's two public blogs give Boeing a direct link to the public, something the 91-year-old company has never had before. And executives are starting to use internal blogs to get conversations going and allow employees to raise issues anonymously. "I've always been a big believer in open and honest dialogue that gets the issues on the table," says James F. Albaugh, the chief executive of Boeing Integrated Defense Systems (IDS). He championed using blogs at the defense unit's meeting of 1,000 executives in February. "I was a little concerned and I had no idea how it would turn out, but I'm sold on it."

Boeing's entry into the blogosphere got off to a rocky start. Eighteen months ago, Randy Baseler, vice-president for marketing at Boeing Commercial Airplanes, started a Web log to talk about the company's view of the commercial airplane world. Almost immediately, he was blasted by the blogerati for not allowing comments, considered to be a key component of blogging. And he was dinged for the perception that his posts gave more of a marketing spin than an inside perspective. In one e-mail, an outside reader wrote: "Take down your blog. You embarrass us, everyone who reads it, and you make the world a dumber place."

Instead of backing down, Baseler responded. As the blog evolved, he found his voice. He began to offer insights into the industry that would be hard to find elsewhere, such as a post about emerging airplane markets in Latin America, called "Latin Rhythm." His explanation of the differences between Boeing's and Airbus' strategy, particularly an ongoing controversy about how they handle seat width, has been light on emotion and heavy on facts. The site drew 30,000 visitors in April, a new high for a blog that started with low expectations. . . .

Boeing's latest experiments have focused inward. In February, Boeing's senior IDS leaders set up blog kiosks at the annual strategy meeting in Los Angeles for the company's top 1,000 defense executives. During a series of briefings, managers went over new company policies and the division's top strategic and business priorities for the year. While Albaugh and his team discussed hot topics such as ethical compliance rules and a new management compensation plan, executives responded at the kiosks located outside the conference room. "As each exec talked, they would talk about comments from the blog," says DL Byron, a blogging consultant to Boeing.

In the end, the blog helped air questions about the unit's strategy and made sure everyone understood the human resources and diversity policies. It also let Albaugh understand what his top people knew or didn't know. For instance, he asked how many executives were actively using the division's Vision Support Plan software that helps managers track how their units are doing. About 30% said they weren't. Thanks to the blog, Albaugh can now try to create converts.

1. To what extent are blogs helping Boeing to provide better customer service? Explain.
2. How would you rate blogs in terms of their media richness? Given this conclusion, was Boeing's senior IDS leader's use of blogs consistent with the recommendations for matching the appropriate medium to the appropriate situation? Discuss your rationale.
3. What are the pros and cons of Boeing's use of blogs? Provide your rationale.
4. Which of the three key barriers to communication are most likely to influence the effectiveness of blogs? Discuss.

Source: Excerpted from Stanley Holmes, "Into the Wild Blog Yonder," BusinessWeek, May 22, 2006, pp. 84, 86.

self-assessment

What Is Your Most Comfortable Learning Style?

Objectives

1. To learn about your visual, auditory, and kinesthetic learning/communication style.
2. To consider how knowledge about learning/communication styles can be used to enhance your communication effectiveness.

Introduction

The purpose of this exercise is to find out what your most prominent learning style is—that is, what forms of communication can you best learn from. You should find the information of value for understanding not only your own style but those of others. Knowing your own style should also allow you to be a much more effective learner.

Instructions

Read the following 36 statements and indicate the extent to which each statement is consistent with your behavior by using the following rating scale: 1 = almost never applies; 2 = applies once in a while; 3 = sometimes applies; 4 = often applies; 5 = almost always applies.

1. I take lots of notes.	1 2 3 4 5
2. When talking to others, I have the hardest time handling those who do not maintain good eye contact with me.	1 2 3 4 5
3. I make lists and notes because I remember things better when I write them down.	1 2 3 4 5
4. When reading a novel, I pay a lot of attention to passages picturing the clothing, scenery, setting, etc.	1 2 3 4 5
5. I need to write down directions so that I can remember them.	1 2 3 4 5
6. I need to see the person I am talking to in order to keep my attention focused on the subject.	1 2 3 4 5
7. When meeting a person for the first time, I initially notice the style of dress, visual characteristics, and neatness.	1 2 3 4 5

(continued)

8. When I am at a party, one of the things
I love to do is stand back and "people watch."   1 2 3 4 5

9. When recalling information, I can see it in
my mind and remember where I saw it.   1 2 3 4 5

10. If I had to explain a new procedure or technique,
I would prefer to write it out.   1 2 3 4 5

11. With free time I am most likely to watch
television or read.   1 2 3 4 5

12. If my boss has a message for me, I am most
comfortable when he or she sends a memo.   1 2 3 4 5

Total A (the minimum is 12 and the maximum is 60)   _____

1. When I read, I read out loud or move my lips to
hear the words in my head.   1 2 3 4 5

2. When talking to someone else, I have the hardest
time handling those who do not talk back with me.   1 2 3 4 5

3. I do not take a lot of notes, but I still remember
what was said. Taking notes distracts me
from the speaker.   1 2 3 4 5

4. When reading a novel, I pay a lot of attention
to passages involving conversations.   1 2 3 4 5

5. I like to talk to myself when solving a problem
or writing.   1 2 3 4 5

6. I can understand what a speaker says, even if
I am not focused on the speaker.   1 2 3 4 5

7. I remember things easier by repeating them
again and again.   1 2 3 4 5

8. When I am at a party, one of the things
I love to do is have in-depth conversations
about a subject that is important to me.   1 2 3 4 5

9. I would rather receive information from
the radio than a newspaper.   1 2 3 4 5

10. If I had to explain a new procedure or technique,
I would prefer telling about it.   1 2 3 4 5

11. With free time I am most likely to listen to music.   1 2 3 4 5

12. If my boss has a message for me, I am most
comfortable when he or she calls on the phone.   1 2 3 4 5

Total B (the minimum is 12 and the maximum is 60)   _____

(continued)

1. I am not good at reading or listening to directions.	1	2	3	4	5
2. When talking to someone else, I have the hardest time handling those who do not show any kind of emotional support.	1	2	3	4	5
3. I take notes and doodle, but I rarely go back and look at them.	1	2	3	4	5
4. When reading a novel, I pay a lot of attention to passages revealing feelings, moods, action, drama, etc.	1	2	3	4	5
5. When I am reading, I move my lips.	1	2	3	4	5
6. I will exchange words and places and use my hands a lot when I can't remember the right thing to say.	1	2	3	4	5
7. My desk appears disorganized.	1	2	3	4	5
8. When I am at a party, one of the things I love to do is enjoy activities, such as dancing, games, and totally losing myself.	1	2	3	4	5
9. I like to move around. I feel trapped when seated at a meeting or desk.	1	2	3	4	5
10. If I had to explain a new procedure or technique, I would prefer actually demonstrating it.	1	2	3	4	5
11. With free time, I am most likely to exercise.	1	2	3	4	5
12. If my boss has a message for me, I am most comfortable when he or she talks to me in person.	1	2	3	4	5
Total C (the minimum is 12 and the maximum is 60)					_____

Scoring & Interpretation

Total A is your Visual Score _____; Total B is your Auditory Score _____; and Total C is your Kinesthetic Score _____. The area in which you have your highest score represents your "dominant" learning style. You can learn from all three, but typically you learn best using one style. Communication effectiveness is increased when your dominant style is consistent with the communication style used by others. For example, if you are primarily kinesthetic and your boss gives you directions orally, you may have trouble communicating because you do not learn or process communication well by just being told something. You must consider not only how you communicate but also how the people you work with communicate.

Questions for Discussion

1. Do you agree with the assessment? Why or why not? Explain.
2. How valuable is it to know your learning style? Does it help explain why you did well in some learning situations and poorly in others? Describe and explain.
3. How important is it to know the learning style of those you work with? Explain.

Source: www.nwlink.com/~donclark/hrd/vak.html. Used by permission.

How Well Does Your Group Swim in a Fishbowl?

Objectives

- To see how you communicate in a fishbowl setting.
- To assess how you communicate when under pressure.

Introduction

You can learn a great deal about your communication style by receiving feedback from others. Although we communicate all day long, we do not always stop to check whether we are actually communicating the intended message. By practicing our communication skills and receiving feedback, this exercise helps you become a more effective communicator. The purpose of this exercise is twofold: to see how you communicate in a group and to see how others communicate—and to learn how to develop your skills from both experiences.

Instructions

The fishbowl technique has been used for many years as a vehicle for providing feedback to individuals or groups. The class should first divide into groups of five or six people. Next these subgroups are formed into teams comprised of two groups of five or six people. Once the groups/teams are formed, one group is selected to be the discussion group, the other group will form the observing group. The seats should be arranged so that members of one group sit in the middle and members in the second group arrange their desks to form a circle around this group. The center group is the discussion group. This group will discuss a topic from the list below for approximately 10 minutes. The group surrounding the center group will observe and take notes on the center group's discussion and interaction with one another.

After time is up, the groups switch—the outer group moves to the center and begins discussion on a topic while the center group moves to the outer circle and begins observing and taking notes.

Once all of the groups have had a chance to observe and discuss, all of the two groups/teams should share their observations with one another. The feedback you receive from the group can be used or discarded by you. It is often hard to hear that we are different from how we think we are in terms of how others see and hear us, but this is an opportunity to learn both.

Topics for Discussion

1. Paris Hilton and Bono should be UN Ambassadors for the United States.
2. The Internet should be regulated.
3. Gnutella and other Web sites that allow you to download free music should not be regulated, and it is okay to burn CDs with music downloaded from these sites.
4. Chief executive officers who make over $10 million a year are overpaid.
5. The minimum wage should be $10 an hour.
6. All U.S. citizens should be allowed to attend college at the taxpayers' expense.

Observation Guidelines

Use the form shown below to take notes on how the center group communicates. Use the following guidelines.

What personal barriers to communication do you see in this group? That is, do any of the members have a tendency to judge others' messages? Do any of the members exhibit faulty listening skills? What types of communication styles do you see? Do some members appear to be better communicators? Do any members seem to have "the gift of gab"?

How well does this group communicate nonverbally? Do any group members look away from the speaker? Do any of the members speak too quickly or too slowly? Is there a group member that smiles and is animated? Do any of the members yawn excessively?

Questions for Discussion

1. Were you surprised at some of your behavior that your classmates noted? Explain.
2. Based on the feedback from your classmates, what are some things you can do to work on your communication style?
3. During your observation role, did you notice any gender-related communication differences? Explain.
4. Do you think the fishbowl technique is a valuable tool for obtaining feedback on interpersonal skills? Why or why not?

Group One:	Communication Styles Noted:

Student Name:

Student Name:

Student Name:

Student Name:

Student Name:

Student Name:

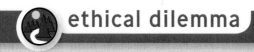

ethical dilemma

Are Camera Cell Phones Creating Ethical Problems?

Although camera phones have been broadly available for only a few months in the United States, more than 25 million of the devices are out on the streets of Japan. . . .

Now that the use of cell phones with little digital cameras has spread throughout Asia, so have new brands of misbehavior. Some people are secretly taking photos up women's skirts and down into bathroom stalls. Others are avoiding buying books by snapping free shots of desired pages.

"The problem with a new technology is that society has yet to come up with a common understanding about appropriate behavior," said Mizuko Ito, an expert on mobile phone culture at Keio University Tokyo.

Samsung Electronics is banning their use in semiconductor and research facilities, hoping to stave off industrial espionage. Samsung, a leading maker of cell phones, is taking a low-tech approach, requiring employees and visitors to stick tape over the handset's camera lens.

Solving the Dilemma

You are the manager of a large bookstore. You have seen customers use their camera phones to take pictures of one another in the store. Yesterday, for the first time, you observed a customer taking photos of 10 pages of material in a cookbook (and not buying the book). Although you did not say anything to this customer, you wonder what to do in the future. Which of the following options would you select?

1. Place a sign on the door asking customers to mind their "cell phone manners." This way you don't have to prevent people from using their phones; you can rely on common decency.
2. Ask customers to leave their camera cell phones with an employee at the front of the store. The employee will give the customer a claim check, and they can retrieve their phones once they finish shopping.
3. Station an employee at the front of the store who places tape over the lens of camera phones as customers come in.
4. Don't do anything. There is nothing wrong with people taking pictures of materials out of a book.
5. Invent other options. Discuss.

Source: *Excerpted from Yuri Kageyama, "Cellphones with Cameras Creating Trouble: Concerns Include Voyeurism,"* The Arizona Republic, *July 10, 2003, p. A18.*

Wolinsky & Williams

Wolinsky & Williams, Inc. (W&W) is an international architectural firm employing over 400 individuals in nine countries. They primarily specialize in office parks and corporate high rises. The company has grown quickly over the past 8 years—so quickly, in fact, that changes have occurred inefficiently and without proper planning. For instance, new offices were opened without any sense of continuity of process or corporate culture. Each of the offices is using different levels of computerization and different technologies for different tasks. The lack of consistency increases the complexity of all processes, from collaboration and revisions to cost and time management.

Recently, however, business has hit a plateau, and senior management now sees the opportunity to assess practices and make across-the-board improvements.

A committee has been appointed to formulate a proposal for streamlining the antiquated blueprint-generation process. Currently, the committee consists of four account managers. Joe Tanney has been employed at W&W for 6 years, working his way up from assistant to account manager and has held his current position for 1 year. Joe is a diligent and motivated worker, eager to move up the corporate ladder. Simon Mahoney has been with the company for over 15 years. Although his job performance is more than adequate, it's clear that he's running on "auto pilot" most of the time. His passion for his job is no longer there. In fact, he seems jaded, tired, and reluctant to step outside his comfortable routine. Cheng Jing has 2 years' experience as an account manager, but his true passion is designing. He will finish his graduate degree within the next few months and expects to be transferred to a position in the design department. Needless to say, his heart is not in account management. Rosa Denson transferred to her current location from the Dallas office about 3 years ago. She is known for her enthusiastic attitude and quality work. However, she has a reputation for letting difficulties in her personal life distract her from the work at hand.

For several weeks the team has been trying but unable to agree on a meeting date. In the meantime, all members agreed to individually generate ideas and identify necessary tasks. When the first meeting is finally convened, only Joe Tanney has completed this assignment. In fact, he has created a thorough analysis of the project. All others have come to the first meeting completely unprepared. During this meeting, it is clear that the committee needs to plan a course of action, assign tasks, and set deadlines. Because Simon Mahoney is the most senior manager, everyone, including senior management, assumes that he will assume the role of team leader.

At the second meeting, however, again nobody except Tanney has met a single deadline or shared a single memo. It's clear that Mahoney is not leading the committee; in fact, he's barely even participating. Cheng Jing would like to be more helpful, but committee tasks are still low on his priority list. Rosa Denson realizes the committee will have difficulty meeting deadlines, yet she is willing to work nights and weekends even in the face of continued hardship in her family life.

Discussion Questions

1. It's important to select the right medium for effective communication. Evaluate the richness of the communication media used by the committee. Are these media appropriate for the situation? Why or why not?
2. Identify the three types of barriers to effective communication. Which type is evident in the interactions among committee members?
3. Formal communication comes in three types: vertical, horizontal, and external. Explain each of these types. Which is/are being used by the committee at W&W?

chapter 16

Control
Techniques for Enhancing Organizational Effectiveness

Major Questions You Should Be Able to Answer

16.1 Managing for Productivity
Major Question: How do managers influence productivity?

16.2 Control: When Managers Monitor Performance
Major Question: Why is control such an important managerial function?

16.3 The Balanced Scorecard, Strategy Maps, & Measurement Management
How can three techniques—balanced scorecard, strategy maps, and measurement management—help me establish standards and measure performance?

16.4 Levels & Areas of Control
Major Question: How do successful companies implement controls?

16.5 Some Financial Tools for Control
Major Question: Financial performance is important to most organizations. What are the financial tools I need to know about?

16.6 Total Quality Management
Major Question: How do top companies improve the quality of their products or services?

16.7 Managing Control Effectively
Major Question: What are the keys to successful control, and what are the barriers to control success?

Improving Productivity: Going Beyond Control Techniques to Get the Best Results

How, as a manager, can you increase productivity—get better results with what you have to work with?

In this chapter we discuss control techniques for achieving better results. What are other ways for improving productivity? Following are some suggestions:[1]

- **Establish base points, set goals, and measure results.** To be able to tell whether your work unit is becoming more productive, you need to establish systems of measurement. You can start by establishing the base point, such as the number of customers served per day, quantity of products produced per hour, and the like. You can then set goals to establish new levels that you wish to attain, and institute systems of measurement with which to ascertain progress. Finally, you can measure the results and modify the goals or work processes as necessary.

- **Use new technology.** Clearly, this is a favorite way to enhance productivity. With a word processor, you can produce more typed pages than you can with a typewriter. With a computerized database, you can store and manipulate information better than you can using a box of file cards. Still, computerization is not a panacea; as we have seen, information technology also offers plenty of opportunities for simply wasting time.

- **Improve match between employees and jobs.** You can take steps to ensure the best fit between employees and their jobs, including improving employee selection, paying attention to training, redesigning jobs, and providing financial incentives that are tied to performance.

- **Encourage employee involvement and innovation.** Companies improve productivity by funding research and development (R&D) departments. As a manager, you can encourage your employees, who are closest to the work process, to come up with suggestions for improving their own operations. And, of course, you can give workers a bigger say in doing their jobs, allow employee flextime, and reward people for learning new skills and taking on additional responsibility.

- **Encourage employee diversity.** By hiring people who are diverse in gender, age, race, and ethnicity, you're more likely to have a workforce with different experience, outlooks, values, and skills. By melding their differences, a team can achieve results that exceed the previous standards.

- **Redesign the work process.** Some managers think productivity can be enhanced through cost cutting, but this is not always the case. It may be that the work process can be redesigned to eliminate inessential steps.

For Discussion Some observers think the pressure on managers to perform will be even more intense than before, because the world is undergoing a transformation on the scale of the industrial revolution 200 years ago as we move toward an information-based economy.[2] In what ways do you think you'll have to become a champion of adaptation?

forecast

What's Ahead in This Chapter

This final chapter explores the final management function—control. Controlling is monitoring performance, comparing it with goals, and taking corrective action as needed. In the first section, we discuss managing for *productivity*, defining what it is and explaining why it's important. We then discuss *controlling*, identify six reasons it's needed, explain the steps in the control process, and describe three types of control managers use. Next we discuss levels and areas of control. In the fifth section, we discuss financial tools for control—budgets, financial statements, ratio analysis, and audits. We then discuss total quality management (TQM), identifying its core principles and showing some TQM techniques. We conclude the chapter by describing the four keys to successful control and five barriers to successful control.

16.1 MANAGING FOR PRODUCTIVITY

 major question   **How do managers influence productivity?**

THE BIG PICTURE

The purpose of a manager is to make decisions about the four management functions—planning, organizing, leading, and controlling—to get people to achieve productivity and realize results. Productivity is defined by the formula of outputs divided by inputs for a specified period of time. Productivity is important because it determines whether the organization will make a profit or even survive.

In Chapter 1, we pointed out that as a manager in the 21st century you will operate in a complex environment in which you will need to deal with six challenges—managing for (1) competitive advantage, (2) diversity, (3) globalization, (4) information technology, (5) ethical standards, and (6) your own happiness and life goals.

Within this dynamic world, you will draw on the practical and theoretical knowledge described in this book to make decisions about the four management functions of planning, organizing, leading, and controlling.

The purpose is to get the people reporting to you *to achieve productivity and realize results.*

This process is diagrammed below. *(See Figure 16.1.)*

figure 16.1

MANAGING FOR PRODUCTIVITY AND RESULTS

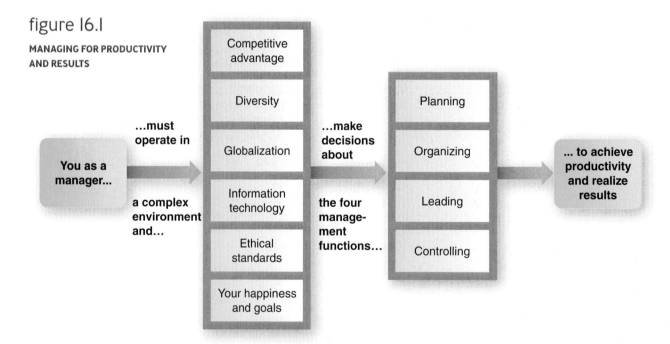

What Is Productivity?

Productivity can be applied at any level, whether for you as an individual, for the work unit you're managing, or for the organization you work for. Productivity is defined by the formula of *outputs divided by inputs* for a specified period of time. Outputs are all the goods and services produced. Inputs are not only labor but also capital, materials, and energy.[3] That is,

$$\text{productivity} = \frac{\text{outputs}}{\text{inputs}} \quad \text{or} \quad \frac{\text{goods} + \text{services}}{\text{labor} + \text{capital} + \text{materials} + \text{energy}}$$

What does this mean to you as a manager? It means that you can increase overall productivity by making substitutions or increasing the efficiency of any one element: labor, capital, materials, energy. For instance, you can increase the efficiency of labor by substituting capital in the form of equipment or machinery, as in employing a bulldozer instead of laborers with shovels to dig a hole.[4] Or you can increase the efficiency of materials inputs by expanding their uses, as when lumber mills discovered they could sell not only boards but also sawdust and wood chips for use in gardens. Or you can increase the efficiency of energy by putting solar panels on a factory roof so the organization won't have to buy so much electrical power from utility companies.

Why Increasing Productivity Is Important

"For a company and for a nation," said former General Electric CEO Jack Welch, "productivity is a matter of survival."[5]

Productivity is important to companies because ultimately it determines whether the organization will make a profit or even survive. But the productivity of the nation is important to us individually and collectively. The more goods and services that are produced and made easily available to us and for export, the higher our standard of living.

During the 1960s, productivity in the United States averaged a spectacular 2.9% a year, then sank to a disappointing 1.5% right up until 1995. Because the decline in productivity no longer allowed the improvement in wages and living standards that had benefited so many Americans in the 1960s, millions of people took second jobs or worked longer hours to keep from falling behind. From 1995 to 2000, however, during the longest economic boom in American history, the productivity rate jumped to 2.5% annually, as the total output of goods and services rose faster than the total hours needed to produce them. The 10-year productivity growth rate ending with the second quarter of 2006 was 2.8%.[6]

Most economists seem to think the recent productivity growth is the result of organizations' huge investment in information technology—computers, the Internet, other telecommunications advances, and computer-guided production line improvements.[7] For example, it used to be thought that service industries are so labor-intensive that productivity improvements are hard to come by. But from 1995 to 2001, labor productivity in services grew at a 2.6% rate, outpacing the 2.3% for goods-producing sectors. The consensus among economists is that information technology played a major role.[8]

Productivity, argues William Lewis, founding director of the McKinsey Global Institute, is produced by product market competition. Although Japan's auto industry, for example, is the most productive in the world—because it is sharpened by bruising global competition—its food-processing industry, which is still dominated by mom-and-pop stores, is only 39% as productive as the U.S. industry (in which Wal-Mart and other retailers have bargained down prices, making wholesalers improve their own operations). As a result, Japanese consumers pay unnecessarily high prices for food.[9]

Maintaining productivity depends on *control*. Let's look at this. ●

Competing internationally for productivity. This oil tanker represents the continual competition among companies and among nations to achieve productivity—"a matter of survival," as GE's Jack Welch put it. Is the United States doing everything it could to be more productive? What about taking measures to reduce dependence on foreign oil?

16.2 CONTROL: WHEN MANAGERS MONITOR PERFORMANCE

 major question | Why is control such an important managerial function?

THE BIG PICTURE

Controlling is monitoring performance, comparing it with goals, and taking corrective action. This section describes six reasons why control is needed and four steps in the control process.

figure 16.2

CONTROLLING FOR PRODUCTIVITY

What you as a manager do to get things done, with controlling shown in relation to the three other management functions. (These are not lockstep; all four functions happen concurrently.)

Control is making something happen the way it was planned to happen. **Controlling is defined as monitoring performance, comparing it with goals, and taking corrective action as needed.** Controlling is the fourth management function, along with planning, organizing, and leading, and its purpose is plain: to make sure that performance meets objectives.

- **Planning** is setting goals and deciding how to achieve them.
- **Organizing** is arranging tasks, people, and other resources to accomplish the work.
- **Leading** is motivating people to work hard to achieve the organization's goals.
- **Controlling** is concerned with seeing that the right things happen at the right time in the right way.

All these functions affect one another and in turn affect an organization's productivity. *(See Figure 16.2.)*

Why Is Control Needed?

There are six reasons why control is needed.

1. To Adapt to Change & Uncertainty   Markets shift. Consumer tastes change. New competitors appear. Technologies are reborn. New materials are invented. Government regulations are altered. All organizations must deal with these kinds of environmental changes and uncertainties. Control systems can help managers anticipate, monitor, and react to these changes.[10]

Example: Until the 1980s, urban department stores had restaurants within the stores (suburban ones did not) but closed them to use the space for merchandise. Now Macy's is reinventing department store dining in an effort to add convenience and induce customers to linger. The new notion: eat while you shop. The offerings, in one description, "can be gobbled while shopping, usually with one hand, leaving the other free to browse." And instead of being restaurants, the new food shops "operate as pit stops amid the merchandise." Of course, this means having to allow for possible food spills and smears on the merchandise. How does management deal with that?[11]

2. To Discover Irregularities & Errors

Small problems can mushroom into big ones. Cost overruns, manufacturing defects, employee turnover, bookkeeping errors, and customer dissatisfaction are all matters that may be tolerable in the short run. But in the long run, they can bring about even the downfall of an organization.

Example: You might not even miss a dollar a month looted from your credit card account. But an Internet hacker who does this with thousands of customers can undermine the confidence of consumers using their credit cards to charge online purchases at Amazon.com, Priceline.com, and other Web retailers. Thus, a computer program that monitors Internet charge accounts for small, unexplained deductions can be a valuable control strategy.

3. To Reduce Costs, Increase Productivity, or Add Value

Control systems can reduce labor costs, eliminate waste, increase output, and increase product delivery cycles. In addition, controls can help add value to a product so that customers will be more inclined to choose them over rival products. For example, as we have discussed early in the book (and will again in this chapter), the use of quality controls among Japanese car manufacturers resulted in cars being produced that were perceived as being better built than American cars.

4. To Detect Opportunities

Hot-selling products. Competitive prices on materials. Changing population trends. New overseas markets. Controls can help alert managers to opportunities that might have otherwise gone unnoticed.

Example: A markdown on certain grocery-store items may result in a rush of customer demand for those products, signaling store management that similar items might also sell faster if they were reduced in price.

5. To Deal with Complexity

Does the right hand know what the left hand is doing? When a company becomes larger or when it merges with another company, it may find it has several product lines, materials-purchasing policies, customer bases, even workers from different cultures. Controls help managers coordinate these various elements.

Example: Following the merger between media conglomerate Time Warner and online giant America Online, the two companies had to learn to deal with two very different cultures—an old-media, lavish-spending culture meshing with a fast-paced, highly reactive, tightwad new-media culture. (Five years after the January 10, 2000, merger, the company was worth about $83 billion—a staggering loss from the premerger combined value of about $240 billion.)[12]

6. To Decentralize Decision Making & Facilitate Teamwork

Controls allow top management to decentralize decision making at lower levels within the organization and to encourage employees to work together in teams.

Example: At General Motors, former chairman Alfred Sloan set the level of return on investment he expected his divisions to achieve, enabling him to push decision-making authority down to lower levels while still maintaining authority over the sprawling GM organization.[13] Later GM used controls to facilitate the team approach in its joint venture with Toyota at its California plant.

The six reasons are summarized on the next page. *(See Figure 16.3.)*

figure 16.3

SIX REASONS WHY CONTROL IS NEEDED

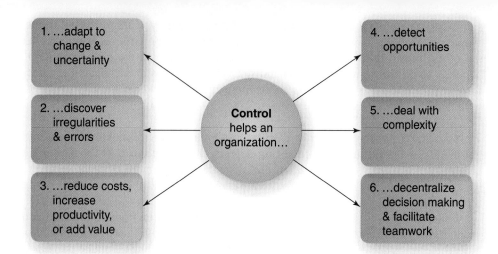

1. ...adapt to change & uncertainty

2. ...discover irregularities & errors

3. ...reduce costs, increase productivity, or add value

Control helps an organization...

4. ...detect opportunities

5. ...deal with complexity

6. ...decentralize decision making & facilitate teamwork

Steps in the Control Process

Control systems may be altered to fit specific situations, but generally they follow the same steps. The four *control process steps* **are (1) establish standards; (2) measure performance; (3) compare performance to standards; and (4) take corrective action, if necessary.** *(See Figure 16.4.)*

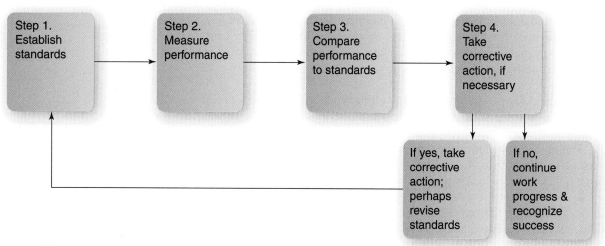

Step 1. Establish standards

Step 2. Measure performance

Step 3. Compare performance to standards

Step 4. Take corrective action, if necessary

If yes, take corrective action; perhaps revise standards

If no, continue work progress & recognize success

figure 16.4

STEPS IN THE CONTROL PROCESS

Let's consider these four steps.

1. Establish Standards: "What Is the Desired Outcome We Want?" A *control standard,* or *performance standard* or simply *standard,* **is the desired performance level for a given goal.** Standards may be narrow or broad, and they can be set for almost anything, although they are best measured when they can be made quantifiable. Nonprofit institutions might have standards for level of charitable contributions, number of students retained, or degree of legal compliance. For-profit organizations might have standards of financial performance, employee hiring, manufacturing defects, percentage increase in market share, percentage reduction in costs, number of customer complaints, and return on investment. More subjective standards, such as level of employee morale, can also be set, although they may have to be expressed more quantifiably as reduced absenteeism and sick days and increased job applications.

Example: United Parcel Service (UPS) establishes certain standards for its drivers that set projections for the number of miles driven, deliveries, and pickups. Because conditions vary depending on whether routes are urban, suburban, or rural, the standards are different for different routes.[14]

One technique for establishing standards is to use *the balanced scorecard,* as we explain later in this chapter.

2. Measure Performance: "What Is the Actual Outcome We Got?" The second step in the control process is to measure performance, such as by number of products sold, units produced, or cost per item sold. Less quantifiable activities, such as new products or patents created by a research scientist or scholarly writings produced by a college professor, may be measured by opinions expressed in peer reports.

Performance measures are usually obtained from three sources: (1) written reports, including computerized printouts; (2) oral reports, as in a salesperson's weekly recitation of accomplishments to the sales manager; and (3) personal observation, as when a manager takes a stroll of the factory floor to see what employees are doing.

Example: Every day, UPS managers look at a computer printout showing the miles, deliveries, and pickups a driver attained during his or her shift the previous day.

As we've hinted, measurement techniques can vary for different industries, as for manufacturing industries versus service industries. We discuss this further later in the chapter.

3. Compare Performance to Standards: "How Do the Desired & Actual Outcomes Differ?" The third step in the control process is to compare measured performance against the standards established. Most managers are delighted with performance that exceeds standards, which becomes an occasion for handing out bonuses, promotions, and perhaps offices with a view. For performance that is below standards, they need to ask: Is the deviation from performance significant? The greater the difference between desired and actual performance, the greater the need for action.

How much deviation is acceptable? That depends on *the range of variation* built in to the standards in step 1. In voting for political candidates, for instance, there is supposed to be no range of variation; as the expression goes, "every vote counts" (although the 2000 U.S. Presidential election was an eye-opener for many people in this regard). In political polling, however, a range of 3%–4% error is considered an acceptable range of variation. In machining parts for the space shuttle, the range of variation may be a good deal less tolerant than when machining parts for a power lawnmower.

The range of variation is often incorporated in computer systems into a principle called management by exception. ***Management by exception* is a control principle that states that managers should be informed of a situation only if data show a significant deviation from standards.**

Example: UPS managers compare the printout of a driver's performance (miles driven and number of pickups and deliveries) with the standards that were set for his or her particular route. A range of variation may be allowed to take into account such matters as winter or summer driving or traffic conditions that slow productivity.

4. Take Corrective Action, If Necessary: "What Changes Should We Make to Obtain Desirable Outcomes?" There are three possibilities here: (1) Make no changes. (2) Recognize and reinforce positive performance. (3) Take action to correct negative performance.

When performance meets or exceeds the standards set, managers should give rewards, ranging from giving a verbal "Job well done" to more substantial payoffs such as raises, bonuses, and promotions to reinforce good behavior.

When performance falls significantly short of the standard, managers should carefully examine the reasons why and take the appropriate action. Sometimes it may turn out the standards themselves were unrealistic, owing to changing conditions, in which case the standards need to be altered. Sometimes it may become apparent that employees haven't been given the resources for achieving the standards. And sometimes the employees may need more attention from management as a way of signaling that they have been insufficient in fulfilling their part of the job bargain.

Example: When a UPS driver fails to perform according to the standards set for him or her, a supervisor then rides along and gives suggestions for improvement. If drivers are unable to improve, they are warned, then suspended, and then dismissed. ●

Small business. How important is it for small businesses to implement all four steps of the control process? Do you think that employees in small companies—such as a restaurant—typically have more or less independence from managerial control than those in large companies do?

> **◆ major question** — How can three techniques—balanced scorecard, strategy maps, and measurement management—help me establish standards and measure performance?

THE BIG PICTURE

To establish standards, managers often use the balanced scorecard, which provides four indicators for progress. A visual representation of the balanced scorecard is the strategy map. Measurement management techniques help managers measure performance.

Wouldn't you, as a top manager, like to have displayed in easy-to-read graphics all the information on sales, orders, and the like assembled from data pulled in real-time from corporate software? The technology exists and it has a name: a *dashboard,* like the instrument panel in a car. "The dashboard puts me and more and more of our executives in real-time touch with the business," says Ivan Seidenberg, CEO at Verizon Communications. "The more eyes that see the results we're obtaining every day, the higher the quality of the decisions we can make."[15]

Throughout this book we have stressed the importance of *evidence-based management*—the use of real-world data rather than fads and hunches in making management decisions. When properly done, the dashboard is an example of the important tools that make this kind of management possible. Others are *the balanced scorecard, strategy maps,* and *measurement management,* techniques that even new managers will find useful.

The Balanced Scorecard

Robert Kaplan is a professor of accounting at the Harvard Business School. David Norton is founder and president of Renaissance Strategy Group, a Massachusetts consulting firm. Kaplan and Norton developed what they call the **balanced scorecard, which gives top managers a fast but comprehensive view of the organization via four indicators: (1) customer satisfaction, (2) internal processes, (3) innovation and improvement activities, and (4) financial measures.**

"Think of the balanced scorecard as the dials and indicators in an airplane cockpit," write Kaplan and Norton. For a pilot, "Reliance on one instrument can be fatal. Similarly, the complexity of managing an organization today requires that managers be able to view performance in several areas simultaneously."[16] It is not enough, say Kaplan and Norton, to simply measure financial performance, such as sales figures and return on investment. Operational matters, such as customer satisfaction, are equally important.

The Balanced Scorecard: Four "Perspectives" The balanced scorecard establishes (a) *goals* and (b) *performance measures* according to four "perspectives" or areas—*financial, innovation and learning, customer,* and *internal business. (See Figure 16.5, opposite page.)*

1. Financial Perspective: "How Do We Look to Shareholders?" Typical financial goals have to do with profitability, growth, and shareholder values. Financial

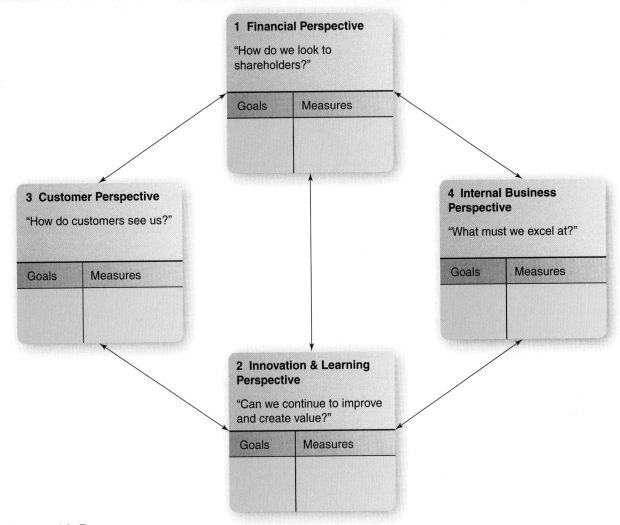

figure 16.5

THE BALANCED SCORECARD: FOUR PERSPECTIVES

measures such as quarterly sales have been criticized as being short-sighted and not reflecting contemporary value-creating activities. Moreover, critics say that traditional financial measures don't improve customer satisfaction, quality, or employee motivation.

However, making improvements in just the other three operational "perspectives" we will discuss won't *necessarily* translate into financial success. Kaplan and Norton mention the case of an electronics company that made considerable improvements in manufacturing capabilities that did not result in increased profitability.

The hard truth is that "if improved [operational] performance fails to be reflected in the bottom line, executives should reexamine the basic assumptions of their strategy and mission," say Kaplan and Norton. "Not all long-term strategies are profitable strategies. . . . A failure to convert improved operational performance, as measured in the scorecard, into improved financial performance should send executives back to their drawing boards to rethink the company's strategy or its implementation plans."[17]

2. Innovation & Learning Perspective: "Can We Continue to Improve & Create Value?"   Learning and growth of employees is the foundation for innovation and creativity. Thus, the organization must create a culture that encourages rank-and-file employees to make suggestions and question the status quo and it must provide employees with the environment and resources needed to do their jobs. The company can use employee surveys and analysis of training data to measure the degree of learning and growth.

3. Customer Perspective: "How Do Customers See Us?"   Many organizations make taking care of the customer a high priority. The balanced scorecard translates the mission of customer service into specific measures of concerns that really matter to customers—time between placing an order and taking delivery, quality in terms of defect level, performance and service, and cost.

Examples of customer measures are mean-time response to a service call, customer report cards of price and quality compared to the competition, and third-party surveys (such as the J.D. Powers quality survey of automobiles).

4. Internal Business Perspective: "What Must We Excel At?"   This part translates what the company must do internally to meet its customers' expectations. These are business processes such as quality, employee skills, and productivity.

Top management's judgment about key internal processes must be linked to measures of employee actions at the lower levels, such as time to process customer orders, get materials from suppliers, produce products, and deliver them to customers. Computer information systems can help, for example, in identifying late deliveries, tracing the problem to a particular plant.

The Visual Balanced Scorecard: Strategy Maps

Since they devised the balanced scorecard, Kaplan and Norton have come up with an improvement called the strategy map.[18] **A *strategy map* is a visual representation of the four perspectives of the balanced scorecard that enables managers to communicate their goals so that everyone in the company can understand how their jobs are linked to the overall objectives of the organization.** As Kaplan and Norton state, "Strategy maps show the cause-and-effect links by which specific improvements create desired outcomes," such as objectives for revenue growth, targeted customer markets, the role of excellence and innovation in products, and so on. An example of a strategic map for a company such as Target is shown opposite, with the goal of creating long-term value for the firm by increasing productivity growth and revenue growth. *(See Figure 16.6.)* Measures and standards can be developed in each of the four operational areas—financial goals, customer goals, internal goals, and learning and growth goals—for the strategy.

Measurement Management

"You simply can't manage anything you can't measure," says Richard Quinn, vice president of quality at the Sears Merchandising Group.[19]

Is this really true? Concepts such as the balanced scorecard seem like good ideas, but how well do they actually work? John Lingle and William Schiemann, principals in a New Jersey consulting firm specializing in strategic assessment, decided to find out.[20]

In a survey of 203 executives in companies of varying size they identified the organizations as being of two types: *measurement-managed* and *non–measurement-managed*. The measurement-managed companies were those in which senior management reportedly agreed on measurable criteria for determining strategic

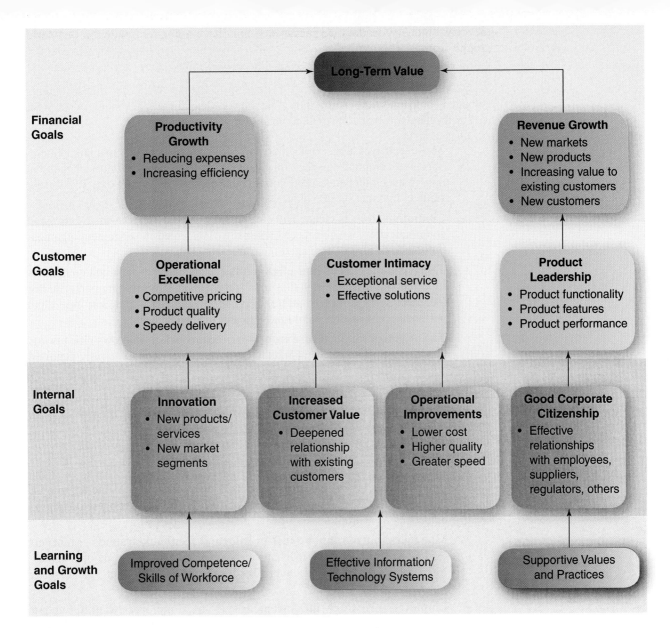

figure 16.6

THE STRATEGY MAP

This example might be used for a retail chain such as Target or Wal-Mart.

Source: T. S. Bateman and S. A. Snell, *Management: Leading & Collaborating in a Competitive World,* 7th ed. (Burr Ridge. IL: McGraw-Hill/Irwin, 2007), Fig. 4.3, p. 124. Adapted from R. Kaplan and D. Norton, "Plotting Success with Strategy Maps," *Optimize,* February 2004, http://www.optimizemag.com/article/showArticle.jhtml?articleId=18200733 (accessed September 18, 2006); and R. S. Kaplan and D. P. Norton, "Having Trouble with Your Strategy? Then Map It," *Harvard Business Review,* September–October 2000, pp. 167–176.

success, and management updated and reviewed semiannual performance measures in three or more of six primary performance areas. The six areas were financial performance, operating efficiency, customer satisfaction, employee performance, innovation/change, and community/environment. The results, concluded Lingle and Schiemann: "A higher percentage of measurement-managed companies were identified as industry leaders, as being financially in the top third of their industry, and as successfully managing their change effort." (The last indicator suggests that measurement-managed companies tend to anticipate the future and are likely to remain in a leadership position in a rapidly changing environment.) "Forget magic," they say. "Industry leaders we surveyed simply have a greater handle on the world around them."

Why Measurement-Managed Firms Succeed

Why do measurement-managed companies outperform those that are less disciplined? The study's data point to four mechanisms that contribute to these companies' success:

- **Top executives agree on strategy.** Most top executives in management-managed companies agreed on business strategy, whereas most of those in non–management-measured companies reported disagreement. Translating strategy into measurable objectives helps make them specific.
- **Communication is clear.** The clear message in turn is translated into good communication, which was characteristic of managed-measurement organizations and not of non–managed-measurement ones.
- **There is better focus and alignments.** Measurement-managed companies reported more frequently that unit (division or department) performance measures were linked to strategic company measures and that individual performance measures were linked to unit measures.
- **The organizational culture emphasizes teamwork and allows risk taking.** Managers in measurement-managed companies more frequently reported strong teamwork and cooperation among the management team and more willingness to take risks.

The Barriers to Effective Measurement

The four most frequent barriers to effective measurement, according to Lingle and Schiemann, are:

- **Objectives are fuzzy.** Company objectives are often precise in the financial and operational areas but not in areas of customer satisfaction, employee performance, and rate of change. Managers need to work at making "soft" objectives measurable.
- **Managers put too much trust in informal feedback systems.** Managers tend to overrate feedback mechanisms such as customer complaints or sales-force criticisms about products. But these mechanisms aren't necessarily accurate.
- **Employees resist new measurement systems.** Employees want to see how well measures work before they are willing to tie their financial futures to them. Measurement-managed companies tend to involve the workforce in developing measures.
- **Companies focus too much on measuring activities instead of results.** Too much concern with measurement that is not tied to fine-tuning the organization or spurring it on to achieve results is wasted effort.

Are There Areas That Can't Be Measured?

It's clear that some areas are easier to measure than others—manufacturing, for example, as opposed to services. We can understand how it is easier to measure the output of, say, a worker in a steel mill than that of a bellhop in a hotel or a professor in a classroom. Nevertheless, human resource professionals are trying to have a greater focus on employee productivity "metrics."[21] In establishing quantifiable goals for "hard to measure" jobs, managers should seek input from the employees involved, who are usually more familiar with the details of the jobs. ●

16.4 LEVELS & AREAS OF CONTROL

How do successful companies implement controls?

THE BIG PICTURE
This section describes three levels of control—strategic, tactical, and operational—and six areas of control: physical, human, informational, financial, structural (bureaucratic and decentralized), and cultural.

How are you going to apply the steps and types of control to your own management area? Let's look at this in three ways: First, you need to consider the *level* of management at which you operate—top, middle, or first level. Second, you need to consider the *areas* that you draw on for resources—physical, human, information, and/or financial. Finally, you need to consider the *style* or control philosophy—bureaucratic, market, or clan, as we will explain.

Levels of Control: Strategic, Tactical, & Operational

There are three levels of control, which correspond to the three principal managerial levels: *strategic* planning by top managers, *tactical* planning by middle managers, and *operational* planning by first-line (supervisory) managers.

1. Strategic Control by Top Managers *Strategic control* **is monitoring performance to ensure that strategic plans are being implemented and taking corrective action as needed.** Strategic control is mainly performed by top managers, those at the CEO and VP levels, who have an organization-wide perspective. Monitoring is accomplished by reports issued every 3, 6, 12, or more months, although more frequent reports may be requested if the organization is operating in an uncertain environment.

2. Tactical Control by Middle Managers *Tactical control* **is monitoring performance to ensure that tactical plans—those at the divisional or departmental level—are being implemented and taking corrective action as needed.** Tactical control is done mainly by middle managers, those with such titles as "division head," "plant manager," and "branch sales manager." Reporting is done on a weekly or monthly basis.

3. Operational Control by First-Level Managers *Operational control* **is monitoring performance to ensure that operational plans—day-to-day goals—are being implemented and taking corrective action as needed.** Operational control is done mainly by first-level managers, those with titles such as "department head," "team leader," or "supervisor." Reporting is done on a daily basis.

Considerable interaction occurs among the three levels, with lower-level managers providing information upward and upper-level managers checking on some of the more critical aspects of plan implementation below them.

Six Areas of Control

The six areas of organizational control are *physical, human, informational, financial, structural,* and *cultural.*

1. Physical Area The physical area includes buildings, equipment, and tangible products. Examples: There are equipment controls to monitor the use of computers, cars, and other machinery. There are inventory-management controls to keep track of how many products are in stock, how many will be needed, and what their delivery dates are from suppliers. There are quality controls to make sure that products are being built according to certain acceptable standards.

2. Human Resources Area The controls used to monitor employees include personality tests and drug testing for hiring, performance tests during training, performance evaluations to measure work productivity, and employee surveys to assess job satisfaction and leadership.

3. Informational Area Production schedules. Sales forecasts. Environmental impact statements. Analyses of competition. Public relations briefings. All these are controls on an organization's various information resources.

4. Financial Area Are bills being paid on time? How much money is owed by customers? How much money is owed to suppliers? Is there enough cash on hand to meet payroll obligations? What are the debt-repayment schedules? What is the advertising budget? Clearly, the organization's financial controls are important because they can affect the preceding three areas.

5. Structural Area How is the organization arranged from a hierarchical or structural standpoint?[22] Two examples are *bureaucratic control* and *decentralized control.*

- *Bureaucratic control* **is an approach to organizational control that is characterized by use of rules, regulations, and formal authority to guide performance.** This form of control attempts to elicit employee compliance, using strict rules, a rigid hierarchy, well-defined job descriptions, and administrative mechanisms such as budgets, performance appraisals, and compensation schemes (external rewards to get results). The foremost example of use of bureaucratic control is perhaps the traditional military organization.

  Bureaucratic control works well in organizations in which the tasks are explicit and certain. While rigid, it can be an effective means of ensuring that performance standards are being met. However, it may not be effective if people are looking for ways to stay out of trouble by simply following the rules, or if they try to beat the system by manipulating performance reports, or if they try to actively resist bureaucratic constraints.

- *Decentralized control* **is an approach to organizational control that is characterized by informal and organic structural arrangements,** the opposite of bureaucratic control. This form of control aims to get increased employee commitment, using the corporate culture, group norms, and workers taking responsibility for their performance. Decentralized control is found in companies with a relatively flat organization.

6. Cultural Area The cultural area is an informal method of control. It influences the work process and levels of performance through the set of norms that develop as a result of the values and beliefs that constitute an organization's culture. If an organization's culture values innovation and collaboration, then employees are likely to be evaluated on the basis of how much they engage in collaborative activities and enhance or create new products. The biotechnology company Genentech, ranked by *Fortune* in 2006 as the best U.S. company to work for, is a good example of an organization that promotes, measures, and rewards employee motivation. For instance, all scientists and engineers are encouraged to spend 20% of their workweek on pet projects. Genentech's tremendous revenue growth over the last decade is clearly driven by a set of cultural values, norms, and internal processes that reinforce creativity.[23] ●

Bureaucratic control. In businesses such as large railroads, tasks are explicit and certain, and employees are expected to perform them the same way each time. However, a small railroad, such as one line serving tourists, need not be bureaucratic.

16.5 SOME FINANCIAL TOOLS FOR CONTROL

Financial performance is important to most organizations. What are the financial tools I need to know about?

major + question

THE BIG PICTURE
Financial controls are especially important. These include budgets, financial statements, ratio analysis, and audits.

As you might expect, one of the most important areas for control is in regard to money—financial performance. Just as you need to monitor your personal finances to ensure your survival and avoid catastrophe, so managers need to do likewise with an organization's finances. Whether your organization is for-profit or nonprofit, you need to be sure that revenues are covering costs.

There are a great many kinds of financial controls, but here let us look at the following: *budgets, financial statements, ratio analysis,* and *audits.* (Necessarily this is merely an overview of this topic; financial controls are covered in detail in other business courses.)

Budgets: Formal Financial Projections

A *budget* **is a formal financial projection.** It states an organization's planned activities for a given period of time in quantitative terms, such as dollars, hours, or number of products. Budgets are prepared not only for the organization as a whole but also for the divisions and departments within it. The point of a budget is to provide a yardstick against which managers can measure performance and make comparisons (as with other departments or previous years).

Two Budget Approaches: Incremental & Zero-Based   Managers can take essentially two budget-planning approaches—*incremental budgeting* and *zero-based budgeting.*

- **Incremental budgeting—using the last budget period as reference point.** Incremental budgets are the traditional form of budget. *Incremental budgeting* **allocates increased or decreased funds to a department by using the last budget period as a reference point; only incremental changes in the budget request are reviewed.**

  One difficulty is that incremental budgets tend to lock departments into stable spending arrangements; they are not flexible in meeting environmental demands. Another difficulty is that a department may engage in many activities—some more important than others—but it's not easy to sort out how well managers performed at the various activities. Thus, the department activities and the yearly budget increases take on lives of their own.

- **Zero-based budgeting—starting over at each budget period.** Developed by the U.S. Department of Agriculture and later adopted by Texas Instruments, *zero-based budgeting* **(ZBB) forces each department to start from zero in projecting its funding needs for the coming budget period.** Thus, ZBB forces managers to reexamine their departments' activities and justify their need for funds for the coming budget period based on strategic plans for that period.

  One difficulty with ZBB is that it requires managers to spend more time rationalizing the need for more funds.

Coca-Cola's fleet. The truck fleet represents a huge part of a beverage distributor's capital expenditures budget. What types of data would be needed to justify expansion of this delivery system?

Another difficulty is that it tends to work better in small work units or departments that are declining in resources.[24]

table 16.1

EXAMPLES OF TYPES OF BUDGETS

Fixed versus Variable Budgets There are numerous kinds of budgets, and some examples are listed below. *(See Table 16.1.)* In general, however, budgets may be categorized as two types: *fixed* and *variable.*

Type of budget	Description
Cash or cashflow budget	Forecasts all sources of cash income and cash expenditures for daily, weekly, or monthly period
Capital expenditures budget	Anticipates investments in major assets such as land, buildings, and major equipment
Sales or revenue budget	Projects future sales, often by month, sales area, or product
Expense budget	Projects expenses (costs) for given activity for given period
Financial budget	Projects organization's source of cash and how it plans to spend it in the forthcoming period
Operating budget	Projects what an organization will create in goods or services, what financial resources are needed, and what income is expected
Nonmonetary budget	Deals with units other than dollars, such as hours of labor or office square footage

- **Fixed budgets—where resources are allocated on a single estimate of costs.** Also known as a *static budget,* a **fixed budget** allocates resources on the basis of a single estimate of costs. That is, there is only one set of expenses; the budget does not allow for adjustment over time. For example, you might have a budget of $50,000 for buying equipment in a given year—no matter how much you may need equipment exceeding that amount.

- **Variable budgets—where resources are varied in proportion with various levels of activity.** Also known as a *flexible budget,* a **variable budget** allows the allocation of resources to vary in proportion with various levels of activity. That is, the budget can be adjusted over time to accommodate pertinent changes in the environment. For example, you might have a budget that allows you to hire temporary workers or lease temporary equipment if production exceeds certain levels.

Financial Statements: Summarizing the Organization's Financial Status

A *financial statement* **is a summary of some aspect of an organization's financial status.** The information contained in such a statement is essential in helping managers maintain financial control over the organization.

There are two basic types of financial statements: the *balance sheet* and the *income statement.*

The Balance Sheet: Picture of Organization's Financial Worth for a Specific Point in Time A *balance sheet* **summarizes an organization's overall financial worth—that is, assets and liabilities—at a specific point in time.**

Assets are the resources that an organization controls; they consist of current assets and fixed assets. *Current assets* are cash and other assets that are readily convertible to cash within 1 year's time. Examples are inventory, sales for which payment has not been received (accounts receivable), and U.S. Treasury bills or money market mutual funds. *Fixed assets* are property, buildings, equipment, and the like that have a useful life that exceeds 1 year but that are usually harder to convert to cash. *Liabilities* are claims, or debts, by suppliers, lenders, and other nonowners of the organization against a company's assets.

The Income Statement: Picture of Organization's Financial Results for a Specified Period of Time   The balance sheet depicts the organization's overall financial worth at a specific point in time. By contrast, the ***income statement* summarizes an organization's financial results—revenues and expenses—over a specified period of time,** such as a quarter or a year.

Revenues are assets resulting from the sale of goods and services. *Expenses* are the costs required to produce those goods and services. The difference between revenues and expenses, called the *bottom line,* represents the profits or losses incurred over the specified period of time.

Ratio Analysis: Indicators of an Organization's Financial Health

The bottom line may be the most important indicator of an organization's financial health, but it isn't the only one. Managers often use ***ratio analysis*—the practice of evaluating financial ratios**—to determine an organization's financial health.

Among the types of financial ratios are those used to calculate liquidity, debt management, asset management, and return. *Liquidity ratios* indicate how easily an organization's assets can be converted into cash (made liquid). *Debt management* ratios indicate the degree to which an organization can meet its long-term financial obligations. *Asset management* ratios indicate how effectively an organization is managing its assets, such as whether it has obsolete or excess inventory on hand. *Return ratios*— often called return on investment (ROI) or return on assets (ROA)—indicate how effective management is generating a return, or profits, on its assets.

Audits: External versus Internal

When you think of auditors, do you think of grim-faced accountants looking through a company's books to catch embezzlers and other cheats? That's one function of auditing, but besides verifying the accuracy and fairness of financial statements it also is intended to be a tool for management decision making. ***Audits* are formal verifications of an organization's financial and operational systems.**

Audits are of two types—*external* and *internal.*

External Audits—Financial Appraisals by Outside Financial Experts   An ***external audit* is a formal verification of an organization's financial accounts and statements by outside experts.** The auditors are certified public accountants (CPAs) who work for an accounting firm (such as PricewaterhouseCoopers) that is independent of the organization being audited. Their task is to verify that the organization, in preparing its financial statements and in determining its assets and liabilities, followed generally accepted accounting principles.

Internal Audits—Financial Appraisals by Inside Financial Experts   An ***internal audit* is a verification of an organization's financial accounts and statements by the organization's own professional staff.** Their jobs are the same as those of outside experts— to verify the accuracy of the organization's records and operating activities. Internal audits also help uncover inefficiencies and thus help managers evaluate the performance of their control systems. ●

Accountants at the Academy Awards? No, these are the Oscar-winning Philip Seymour Hoffman, who in 2006 was voted Best Actor (for his role in *Capote*), and Reese Witherspoon, voted Best Actress (for her role in *Walk the Line*). But every year since 1929 the secret ballots for Oscar nominees voted on by members of the Academy of Motion Picture Arts and Sciences have been tabulated by accountants from the firm now known as PricewaterhouseCoopers. The accounting firm takes this event very seriously; secrecy is tight, and there is no loose gossip around the office water cooler. Two accountants tally the votes, stuff the winners' names in the envelopes—the ones that will be handed to award presenters during the Academy Awards—and then memorize the winners' names, just in case the envelopes don't make it to the show. Accounting is an important business because investors depend on independent auditors to verify that a company's finances are what they are purported to be.

16.6 TOTAL QUALITY MANAGEMENT

❌ **major question** How do top companies improve the quality of their products or services?

THE BIG PICTURE

Total quality management (TQM) is dedicated to continuous quality improvement, training, and customer satisfaction. Two core principles are people orientation and improvement orientation. Some techniques for improving quality are employee involvement, benchmarking, outsourcing, reduced cycle time, and statistical process control.

The Ritz-Carlton Hotel Co., LLC, a luxury chain of 61 hotels worldwide that is an independently operated division of Marriott International, puts a premium on doing things right. First-year managers and employees receive 250–310 hours of training. The president meets each employee at a new hotel to ensure he or she understands the Ritz-Carlton standards for service. The chain has also developed a database that records the preferences of more than 1 million customers, so that each hotel can anticipate guests' needs.[25]

Because of this diligence, the Ritz-Carlton has twice been the recipient (in 1992 and in 1999) of the Malcolm Baldrige National Quality Award. (The 2005 award for service went to DynMcDermott Petroleum Operations in New Orleans.) As we mentioned in Chapter 2, the Baldrige awards were created by Congress in 1987 to be the most prestigious recognition of quality in the United States, which is given annually to U.S. organizations in manufacturing, service, education, health care, and small business.

The Baldrige award is an outgrowth of the realization among U.S. managers in the early 1980s that three-fourths of Americans were telling survey takers that the label "Made in America" no longer represented excellence—that they considered products made overseas, especially Japan, equal or superior in quality to U.S.-made products. As we saw in Chapter 2, much of the impetus for quality improvements in Japanese products came from American consultants W. Edwards Deming and Joseph M. Juran, whose work led to the strategic commitment to quality known as total quality management.

Core TQM Principles: Deliver Customer Value & Strive for Continuous Improvement

Total quality management (TQM) **is defined as a comprehensive approach—led by top management and supported throughout the organization—dedicated to continuous quality improvement, training, and customer satisfaction.**

In Chapter 2 we said there are four components to TQM:

1. Make continuous improvement a priority.
2. Get every employee involved.
3. Listen to and learn from customers and employees.
4. Use accurate standards to identify and eliminate problems.

These may be summarized as *two core principles of TQM*—namely, **(1)** *people orientation*—**everyone involved with the organization should focus on delivering value to customers—and (2)** *improvement orientation*—**everyone should work on continuously improving the work processes.**[26] Let's look at these further.

I. People Orientation—Focusing Everyone on Delivering Customer Value Organizations adopting TQM value people as their most important resource—both those who create a product or service and those who receive it. Thus, not only are employees given more decision-making power, so are suppliers and customers.

This people orientation operates under the following assumptions.

- **Delivering customer value is most important.** The purpose of TQM is to focus people, resources, and work processes to deliver products or services that create value for customers.

- **People will focus on quality if given empowerment.** TQM assumes that employees and suppliers will concentrate on making quality improvements if given the decision-making power to do so. Customers can also be a valuable part of the process if they are allowed to express choices.

- **TQM requires training, teamwork, and cross-functional efforts.** Employees and suppliers need to be well trained, and they must work in teams. Teamwork is considered important because many quality problems are spread across functional areas. For example, if car or cell phone design specialists conferred with marketing specialists (as well as customers and suppliers), they would find the real challenge of using a cell phone in a car is not talking on it but pushing 11 tiny buttons to call a phone number while driving 65 miles an hour.

2. Improvement Orientation—Focusing Everyone on Continuously Improving Work Processes Americans seem to like big schemes, grand designs, and crash programs. While these approaches certainly have their place, the lesson of the quality movement from overseas is that the way to success is through continuous small improvements. *Continuous improvement* **is defined as ongoing small, incremental improvements in all parts of an organization**—all products, services, functional areas, and work processes.[27]

This improvement orientation has the following assumptions.

- **It's less expensive to do it right the first time.** TQM assumes that it's better to do things right the first time than to do costly reworking. To be sure, there are many costs involved in creating quality products and services—

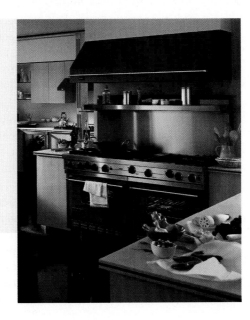

Continuous improvement. In the 1980s, building contractor Fred Carl found restaurant-style commercial stoves impractical for his own home kitchen, so he designed his own, then opened a manufacturing plant in Greenwood, Mississippi, under the name Viking Range Corporation. From Toyota Viking borrowed Japanese manufacturing techniqes grouped under the word "kaizen," which translates into "continuous improvement." Production is set up so that if there is a problem everyone on the line is instantly aware of it, and the problem is solved right on the plant floor—so that customers are continuously supplied with elegant yet dependable stoves like the one shown here.

training, equipment, and tools, for example. But they are less than the costs of dealing with poor quality—those stemming from lost customers, junked materials, time spent reworking, and frequent inspection, for example.[28]

- **It's better to do small improvements all the time.** This is the assumption that continuous improvement must be an everyday matter, that no improvement is too small, that there must be an ongoing effort to make things better a little bit at a time all the time.

- **Accurate standards must be followed to eliminate small variations.** TQM emphasizes the collection of accurate data throughout every stage of the work process. It also stresses the use of accurate standards (such as benchmarking, as we discuss) to evaluate progress and eliminate small variations, which are the source of many quality defects.

- **There must be strong commitment from top management.** Employees and suppliers won't focus on making small incremental improvements unless managers go beyond lip service to support high-quality work.

Some TQM Techniques

Several techniques are available for improving quality. Here we describe *employee involvement, benchmarking, outsourcing, reduced cycle time,* and *statistical process control.*

Employee Involvement: Quality Circles, Self-Managed Teams, & Special-Purpose Teams
As part of the TQM people orientation, employees (and often suppliers and customers) are given more decision-making power than is typical in non-TQM organizations. The reasoning here is that the people actually involved with the product or service are in the best position to detect opportunities for quality improvements.

Three means for implementing employee involvement are as follows.

- **Quality circles.** *Quality circles,* mentioned briefly in Chapter 13, consist of small groups of workers and supervisors who meet intermittently to discuss workplace and quality-related problems. A quality circle may consist of a group of 10–12 people meeting an hour or so once or twice a month, with management listening to presentations. Members of the quality circle attempt to identify and solve problems in production and quality in the work performed in their part of the company.

- **Self-managed teams.** *Self-managed teams,* also described in Chapter 13, are groups of workers who are given administrative oversight of activities such as planning, scheduling, monitoring, and staffing for their task domains. A common feature of self-managed teams is cross-functionalism—that is, a team is made up of technical specialists from different areas.

- **Special-purpose teams.** Quality circles and self-managed teams usually meet on a regular basis. Sometimes, however, an organization needs a *special-purpose team to meet to solve a special or one-time problem.* The team then disbands after the problem is solved. These teams are often cross-functional, drawing on members from different departments.

Benchmarking: Learning from the Best Performers
We discussed benchmarking briefly in Chapter 10. As we stated there, *benchmarking* is a process by which a company compares its performance with that of high-performing organizations. For example, at Xerox Corp., generally thought to be the first American company to use benchmarking, it is defined as, in one description, "the continuous process of measuring products, services, and practices against the toughest competitors or those companies recognized as industry leaders."[29]

Searching for "Best Practices": What Kind of Newspaper Ads Work Best?

Benchmarking is a search for "best practices" that can be applied to one's own business. Southwest Airlines, for instance, studied auto-racing pit crews to learn how to reduce the turnaround time of its aircraft at each scheduled stop. Toyota managers got the idea for just-in-time inventory deliveries by looking at how U.S. supermarkets replenish their shelves.

Sometimes companies go far afield in their search for best practices that might benefit them. QualPro Inc. of Knoxville, Tennessee, was able to use multivariable testing (MVT), a statistical technique that originated during World War II when the British were seeking ways to shoot down German bombers more effectively, to help AutoNation, a conglomeration of car dealers, test what combination of up to 30 factors made for more effective newspaper ads. Typically scientific experiments try to test one variable at a time while keeping all other factors constant. But one-at-a-time experiments can take a long time and miss instances involving multiple factors. QualPro tested numerous variables at the same time—for example, half-page versus full-page ads, or color ads versus black-and-white—to see the effect on dealer sales. "Some surprises popped out," says an account of the experiment. "A full-page ad was no more effective than a half-page one. The addition of color—a considerable expense—did not generate any extra sales."[30]

Your Call

Jeffrey Pfeffer and Robert Sutton, authors of a book on evidence-based management, worry that managers use benchmarking too casually ("GE does it? We should too!").[31] Are you aware of any instances in which a company simply picked up or copied a practice that turned out not to be useful?

Outsourcing: Let Outsiders Handle It *Outsourcing* (discussed in detail in Chapter 4) is the subcontracting of services and operations to an outside vendor. Usually this is done because the subcontractor vendor can do the job better or cheaper. Or, stated another way, when the services and operations are done in-house, they are not done as efficiently or are keeping personnel from doing more important things. For example, when Eastman Kodak farmed out its computer operations to IBM, it found it got higher-quality computing operations at less cost.[32] And when IBM and other companies outsource components inexpensively for new integrated software systems, says one researcher, offshore programmers make information technology affordable to small and medium-size businesses and others who haven't yet joined the productivity boom.[33]

Outsourcing is also being done by many state and local governments, which, under the banner known as privatization, have subcontracted traditional government services such as fire protection, correctional services, and medical services.

The ISO 9000 Series: Meeting Standards of Independent Auditors If you're a sales representative for Du Pont, the American chemical company, how will your overseas clients know that your products have the quality they are expecting? If you're a purchasing agent for an Ohio-based tire company, how can you tell if the synthetic rubber you're buying overseas is adequate?

At one time, buyers and sellers simply had to rely on a company's past reputation or personal assurances. In 1979, the International Organization for Standardization (ISO), based in Geneva, Switzerland, created a set of quality standards known as the 9000 series—"a kind of Good Housekeeping seal of approval for global business," in one description.[34] **The *ISO 9000 series* consists of quality-control procedures companies must install—from purchasing to manufacturing to inventory to shipping—that can be audited by independent quality-control experts, or "registars."** The goal is to

Outsourcing Public Services: Does Privatization Always Work?

Do public services work better when they're privatized? Privatization has been a popular idea in the last several years. As the term is used in the United States, this means farming out, or outsourcing, to private-sector companies traditional public-sector services such as prison supervision, fire protection, and road maintenance.

The driving force behind privatization is the idea that the for-profit sector is more *motivated* than the nonprofit sector to deliver services in a more customer-friendly, cost-efficient way. However, private companies can also make expensive, bad decisions. One has only to look at the example of Texas-based energy giant Enron, once the seventh-largest company in the U.S., whose off-books investments led it into bankruptcy. Or consider such money-losing private-sector projects as New Coke or the movie *Gigli* or Intel's Itanium processor. As one writer points out, "Is there much difference, after all, between the Defense Department paying $600 for an ordinary toilet seat and a private-sector corporation paying $600 a share for an Internet start-up with no assets, no profits, and no plan for producing either?"[35]

In Elliott Sclar's book *You Don't Always Get What You Pay For: The Economics of Privatization,* the Columbia University economist and urban planning professor points out that privatization alone is not a substitute for good public management.[36] For example, in the 1980s, the Metro-Dade Transit Agency in Florida hired a private company to run 10 of its bus routes, keeping 10 comparable routes in public operation for comparison. The result after 18 months, when the experiment was abandoned: Complaints had more than doubled on the private-sector routes, and ridership had plummeted. Moreover, the 40 new buses that the agency gave the contractor were so poorly maintained that only 10 could be kept in service.

Another example that Sclar gives is that of a mutual-aid pact among several small-town fire departments, in which one town had hired a private corporation to provide fire protection. Responding to its profit motive, the corporation kept smaller crews on each shift than the surrounding nonprofit fire companies did. The effect was to increase the reliance of that department on its public-sector neighbors for reinforcements. And on a day when the reinforcements could not show up, the for-profit department was unable to quell the fire in a $1 million home, which burned to the ground.

The lesson: Municipalities letting out contracts to the private sector have to make sure that the contracts are carefully drawn, that the contractor's performance is adequately monitored, and that the costs are measured against accurate internal costs to protect the public's interest against the company's overzealous pursuit of profit.

In other words, there must be effective *controls.*

---

reduce flaws in manufacturing and improve productivity. Companies must document the procedures and train their employees to use them. For instance, DocBase Direct is a Web-delivered document and forms-management system that helps companies comply with key ISO management standards, such as traceable changes and easy reporting.

The ISO 9000 designation is now recognized in 100 countries around the world, and a quarter of the corporations around the globe insist that suppliers have ISO 9000 certification. "You close some expensive doors if you're not certified," says Bill Ekeler, general manager of Overland Products, a Nebraska tool-and-die-stamping firm.[37] In addition, because the ISO process forced him to analyze his company from the top down, he found ways to streamline manufacturing processes that improved his bottom line.

Reduced Cycle Time: Increasing the Speed of Work Processes   Another TQM technique is the emphasis on increasing the speed with which an organization's operations and processes can be performed. This is known as ***reduced cycle time,* or reduction in steps in a work process,** such as fewer authorization steps required to let a contract to a supplier. The point is to improve the organization's performance by eliminating wasteful motions, barriers between departments, unnecessary procedural steps, and the like.

Statistical Process Control: Taking Periodic Random Samples As the pages of this book were being printed, every now and then a press person would pull a few pages out of the press run and inspect them (under a bright light) to see that the consistency of the color and quality of the ink were holding up. This is an ongoing human visual check for quality control.

All kinds of products require periodic inspection during their manufacture: hamburger meat, breakfast cereal, flashlight batteries, wine, and so on. The tool often used for this is *statistical process control,* **a statistical technique that uses periodic random samples from production runs to see if quality is being maintained within a standard range of acceptability.** If quality is not acceptable, production is stopped to allow corrective measures.

Statistical process control is the technique that McDonald's uses, for example, to make sure that the quality of its burgers is always the same, no matter where in the world they are served. Companies such as Intel and Motorola use statistical process control to ensure the reliability and quality of their products.

Six Sigma & Lean Six Sigma: Data-Driven Ways to Eliminate Defects
"The biggest problem with the management technique known as Six Sigma is this: It sounds too good to be true," says a *Fortune* writer. "How would your company like a 20% increase in profit margins within one year, followed by profitability over the long-term that is *ten times* what you're seeing now? How about a 4% (or greater) annual gain in market share?"[38]

What is this name, Six Sigma, which is probably Greek to you, and is it a path to management heaven? The name comes from *sigma,* the Greek letter that statisticians use to define a standard deviation. The higher the sigma, the fewer the deviations from the norm—that is, the fewer the defects. Developed by Motorola in 1985 and since embraced by General Electric, Allied Signal, American Express, and other companies, *Six Sigma* **is a rigorous statistical analysis process that reduces defects in manufacturing and service-related processes.** By testing thousands of variables and eliminating guesswork, a company using the technique attempts to improve quality and reduce waste to the point where errors nearly vanish. In everything from product design to manufacturing to billing, the attainment of Six Sigma means there are no more than 3.4 defects per million products or procedures.

"Six Sigma gets people away from thinking that 96% is good, to thinking that 40,000 failures per million is bad," says a vice president of consulting firm A. T. Kearney.[39] Six Sigma means being 99.9997% perfect. By contrast, Three Sigma or Four Sigma means settling for 99% perfect—the equivalent of no electricity for 7 hours each month, two short or long landings per day at each major airport, or 5,000 incorrect surgical operations per week.[40]

Six Sigma may also be thought of as a philosophy—to reduce variation in your company's business and make customer-focused, data-driven decisions. The method preaches the use of Define, Measure, Analyze, Improve, and Control (DMAIC). Team leaders may be awarded a Six Sigma "black belt" for applying DMAIC.

More recently, companies are using an approach known as *lean Six Sigma,* **which focuses on problem solving and performance improvement—speed with excellence—of a well-defined project.**[41] Xerox Corp., for example, has focused on getting new products to customers faster, which has meant taking steps out of the design process without loss of quality. A high-end, $200,000 machine that can print 100 pages a minute traditionally has taken three to five cycles of design; removing just one of those cycles can shave up to a year off time to market.[42] The grocery chain Albertsons Inc. announced in 2004 that it was going to launch Six Sigma training to reduce customer dissatisfaction and waste to the lowest level possible.[43]

Six Sigma may not be a perfect process, since it cannot compensate for human error or control events outside a company. Still, it lets managers approach problems with the assumption that there's a data-oriented, tangible way to approach problem solving.[44] ●

16.7 MANAGING CONTROL EFFECTIVELY

⁕ **major question** What are the keys to successful control, and what are the barriers to control success?

THE BIG PICTURE
This section describes four keys to successful control and five barriers to successful control.

How do you as a manager make a control system successful, and how do you identify and deal with barriers to control? We consider these topics next.[45]

The Keys to Successful Control

Successful control systems have a number of common characteristics: (1) They are strategic and results oriented. (2) They are timely, accurate, and objective. (3) They are realistic, positive, and understandable and they encourage self-control. (4) They are flexible.[46]

I. They Are Strategic & Results Oriented   Control systems support strategic plans and are concentrated on significant activities that will make a real difference to the organization. Thus, when managers are developing strategic plans for achieving strategic goals, that is the point at which they should pay attention to developing control standards that will measure how well the plans are being achieved.

Example: "In the 1970s and 1980s, environmental groups did a great job of making people aware that the environment was in trouble," said Marcelo Carvalho de Andrade. "In the [new] millennium, we must direct our efforts toward solutions that don't depend on charity." Solutions, Andrade realized, need money, "and corporations have it." In 1986, the 40-year-old Brazilian mountain climber, former fashion model,

One of 10 million trees. Established in 1986, Pro-Natura is a nongovernmental organization that specializes in sustainable development. The mission of the organization is to conserve biodiversity through integrated sustainable development projects adapted as models that can be replicated at regional levels.

and orthopedic surgeon had persuaded enough corporations—including Coca-Cola, Shell, Goodyear, and Christian Dior—to create Pro-Natura. One of its strategic goals is to arrest global warming. One results-oriented project intended to reduce carbon in the rain forest is to plant 10 million trees.[47]

2. They Are Timely, Accurate, & Objective Good control systems—like good information of any kind—should . . .

- **Be timely—meaning when needed.** The information should not necessarily be delivered quickly, but it should be delivered at an appropriate or specific time, such as every week or every month. And it certainly should be often enough to allow employees and managers to take corrective action for any deviations.

- **Be accurate—meaning correct.** Accuracy is paramount, if decision mistakes are to be avoided. Inaccurate sales figures may lead managers to mistakenly cut or increase sales promotion budgets. Inaccurate production costs may lead to faulty pricing of a product.

- **Be objective—meaning impartial.** Objectivity means control systems are impartial and fair. Although information can be inaccurate for all kinds of reasons (faulty communication, unknown data, and so on), information that is not objective is inaccurate for a special reason: It is biased or prejudiced. Control systems need to be considered unbiased for everyone involved so that they will be respected for their fundamental purpose—enhancing performance.

3. They Are Realistic, Positive, & Understandable & Encourage Self-Control Control systems have to focus on working for the people who will have to live with them. Thus, they operate best when they are made acceptable to the organization's members who are guided by them. Thus, they should . . .

- **Be realistic.** They should incorporate realistic expectations. If employees feel performance results are too difficult, they are apt to ignore or sabotage the performance system.

- **Be positive.** They should emphasize development and improvement. They should avoid emphasizing punishment and reprimand.

- **Be understandable.** They should fit the people involved, be kept as simple as possible, and present data in understandable terms. They should avoid complicated computer printouts and statistics.

- **Encourage self-control.** They should encourage good communication and mutual participation. They should not be the basis for creating distrust between employees and managers.

4. They Are Flexible Control systems must leave room for individual judgment, so that they can be modified when necessary to meet new requirements.

Barriers to Control Success

Among the several barriers to a successful control system are the following:[48]

1. Too Much Control Some organizations, particularly bureaucratic ones, try to exert too much control. They may try to regulate employee behavior in everything from dress code to timing of coffee breaks. Allowing employees too little discretion for analysis and interpretation may lead to employee frustration—particularly among professionals, such as college professors and medical doctors. Their frustration may lead them to ignore or try to sabotage the control process.

2. Too Little Employee Participation
As we've noted elsewhere in the book (Chapter 12), employee participation can enhance productivity. Involving employees in both the planning and execution of control systems can bring legitimacy to the process and heighten employee morale.

3. Overemphasis on Means Instead of Ends
We said that control activities should be strategic and results oriented. They are not ends in themselves but the means to eliminating problems. Too much emphasis on accountability for weekly production quotas, for example, can lead production supervisors to push their workers and equipment too hard, resulting in absenteeism and machine breakdowns. Or it can lead to game playing—"beating the system"—as managers and employees manipulate data to seem to fulfill short-run goals instead of the organization's strategic plan.

4. Overemphasis on Paperwork
A specific kind of misdirection of effort is management emphasis on getting reports done, to the exclusion of other performance activity. Reports are not the be-all and end-all. Undue emphasis on reports can lead to too much focus on quantification of results and even to falsification of data.

Example: A research laboratory decided to use the number of patents the lab obtained as a measure of its effectiveness. The result was an increase in patents filed but a decrease in the number of successful research projects.[49]

5. Overemphasis on One Instead of Multiple Approaches
One control may not be enough. By having multiple control activities and information systems, an organization can have multiple performance indicators, thereby increasing accuracy and objectivity.

Example: An obvious strategic goal for gambling casinos is to prevent employee theft of the cash flowing through their hands. Thus, casinos control card dealers by three means. First, they require they have a dealer's license before they are hired. Second, they put them under constant scrutiny, using direct supervision by on-site pit bosses as well as observation by closed-circuit TV cameras and through overhead one-way mirrors. Third, they require detailed reports at the end of each shift so that transfer of cash and cash equivalents (such as gambling chips) can be audited.[50] ●

Temptation. Because legal gambling is a heavy cash business, casinos need to institute special controls against employee theft. One of them is the "eye in the sky" over card and craps tables.

FINALE: SOME LIFE LESSONS

What are four keys to personal managerial success?

major question

THE BIG PICTURE
As we end the book, this section describes some life lessons to take away.

We have come to the end of the book, our last chance to offer some suggestions to take with you that we hope will benefit you in the coming years. Following are some life lessons pulled from various sources that can make you a "keeper" in an organization and help you be successful.[51]

- **Initiative is always in short supply.** Many people still hold back in showing initiative because they have the unreasonable fear of getting reprimanded. That may still be possible with short-sighted supervisors, and of course it never hurts to put your boss in the best possible light. But here's a life lesson: "If you set the bar high, even if you don't reach it, you end up in a pretty good place—that is, achieving a pretty high mark."

- **If you have an active desire to learn new things, you'll be ready for the next step.** You should always be learning—whether through classes, on-the-job training, getting tips from a co-worker, or reading a book. Learning makes you more valuable to your current employer and gives you more options in the wider work world. Here's a life lesson: "Be brutally honest with yourself about what you know or don't know, and ask what skills you need to take the next step."

- **Think ahead, understand what your obstacles are, and develop a strategy to win.** Ask for the most difficult job, study how to master it, and be willing to be accountable for outcomes. A life lesson: "Remove 'It's not my job' from your vocabulary." And another: "Don't sacrifice understanding for speed."

- **Be flexible, keep your cool, and take yourself lightly.** Things aren't always going to work out your way, so flexibility is important. In addition, the more unflappable you appear in difficult circumstances, the more you'll be admired by your bosses and co-workers. Having a sense of humor helps, since there are enough people spreading gloom and doom in the workplace. Life lesson: "When you're less emotional, you're better able to assess a crisis and develop a workable solution."

We wish you the very best of luck. And we mean it!

Angelo Kinicki
Brian K. Williams

key terms used in this chapter

summary

16.1 Managing for Productivity

- A manager has to deal with six challenges—managing for competitive advantage, diversity, globalization, information technology, ethical standards, and his or her own happiness and life goals. The manager must make decisions about the four management functions—planning, organizing, leading, and controlling—to get people to achieve productivity and realize results. Productivity is defined by the formula of outputs divided by inputs for a specified period of time. Productivity is important because it determines whether the organization will make a profit or even survive. Productivity depends on control.

16.2 Control: When Managers Monitor Performance

- Controlling is defined as monitoring performance, comparing it with goals, and taking corrective action as needed. There are six reasons why control is needed: (1) to adapt to change and uncertainty; (2) to discover irregularities and errors; (3) to reduce costs, increase productivity, or add value; (4) to detect opportunities; (5) to deal with complexity; and (6) to decentralize decision making and facilitate teamwork.

- There are four control process steps. (1) The first step is to set standards. A control standard is the desired performance level for a given goal. (2) The second step is to measure performance, based on written reports, oral reports, and personal observation. (3) The third step is to compare measured performance against the standards established. (4) The fourth step is to take corrective action, if necessary, if there is negative performance.

16.3 The Balanced Scorecard, Strategy Maps, & Measurement Management

- To establish standards, managers often use the balanced scorecard, which provides a fast but comprehensive view of the organization via four indicators: (1) customer satisfaction, (2) internal processes, (3) innovation and improvement activities, and (4) financial measures.

- The strategy map, a visual representation of the four perspectives of the balanced scorecard—financial, innovation and learning, customer, and internal business—enables managers to communicate their goals so that everyone in the company can understand how their jobs are linked to the overall objectives of the organization.

- Measurement-managed companies use measurable criteria for determining strategic success, and management updates and reviews three or more of six primary performance areas: financial performance, operating efficiency, customer satisfaction, employee performance, innovation/change, and community/environment. Four mechanisms that contribute to the success of such companies are top executives agree on strategy, communication is clear, there is better focus and alignments, and the organizational culture emphasizes teamwork and allows risk taking. Four barriers to effective measurement are objectives are fuzzy, managers put too much trust in informal feedback systems, employees resist new management systems, and companies focus too much on measuring activities instead of results.

- Some areas are difficult to measure, such as those in service industries.

16.4 Levels & Areas of Control

- In applying the steps and types of control, managers need to consider (1) the level of management at which they operate, (2) the areas they can draw on for resources, and (3) the style of control philosophy.

- There are three levels of control, corresponding to the three principal managerial levels. (1) Strategic control, done by top managers, is monitoring performance to ensure that strategic plans are being implemented. (2) Tactical control, done by middle managers, is monitoring performance to ensure that tactical plans are being implemented. (3) Operational control, done by first-level or supervisory managers, is monitoring performance to ensure that day-to-day goals are being implemented.

- Most organizations have six areas that they can draw on for resources. (1) The physical area includes buildings, equipment, and tangible products; these use equipment control, inventory-management control, and quality controls. (2) The human resources area uses personality tests, drug tests, performance tests, employee surveys, and the like as controls to monitor people. (3) The informational area uses production schedules, sales forecasts, environmental impact statements, and the like to monitor the organization's various resources. (4) The financial area uses various kinds of financial controls, as we discuss in Section 16.5. (5) The structural area uses hierarchical or other arrangements such as bureaucratic control, which is characterized by use of rules, regulations, and formal authority to guide performance, or decentralized control, which is characterized by informal and organic structural arrangements. (6) The cultural area influences the work process and levels of performance through the set of norms that develop as a result of the values and beliefs that constitute an organization's culture.

16.5 Some Financial Tools for Control

- Financial controls include (1) budgets, (2) financial statements, (3) ratio analysis, and (4) audits.

- A budget is a formal financial projection. There are two budget-planning approaches, incremental and zero-based. (1) Incremental budgeting allocates increased or decreased funds to a department by using the last budget period as a reference point; only incremental changes in the budget request are reviewed. (2) Zero-based budgeting (ZBB) forces each department to start from zero in projecting the funding needs for the coming budget period. Whether incremental or zero-based, budgets are either fixed, which allocate resources on the basis of a single estimate of costs, or variable, which allow resource allocation to vary in proportion with various levels of activity.

- A financial statement is a summary of some aspect of an organization's financial status. One type, the balance sheet, summarizes an organization's overall financial worth—assets and liabilities—at a specific point in time. The other type, the income statement, summarizes an organization's financial results—revenues and expenses—over a specified period of time.

- Ratio analysis is the practice of evaluating financial ratios. Managers may use this tool to determine an organization's financial health, such as liquidity ratios, debt management ratios, or return ratios.

- Audits are formal verifications of an organization's financial and operational systems. Audits are of two types. An external audit is formal verification of an organization's financial accounts and statements by outside experts. An internal audit is a verification of an organization's financial accounts and statements by the organization's own professional staff.

16.6 Total Quality Management

- Total quality management (TQM) is defined as a comprehensive approach—led by top management and supported throughout the organization—dedicated to continuous quality improvement, training, and customer satisfaction. The two core principles of TQM are people orientation and improvement orientation.

- In the people orientation, everyone involved with the organization is asked to focus on delivering value to customers, focusing on quality. TQM requires training, teamwork, and cross-functional efforts.

- In the improvement orientation, everyone involved with the organization is supposed to make ongoing small, incremental improvements in all parts of the organization. This orientation assumes that it's less expensive to do things right the first time, to do small improvements all the time, and to follow accurate standards to eliminate small variations.

- Several techniques are available for improving quality. (I) Employee involvement can be implemented through quality circles, self-managed teams, and special-purpose teams—teams that meet to solve a special or one-time problem. (2) Benchmarking is a process by which a company compares its performance with that of high-performing organizations. (3) Outsourcing is the subcontracting of services and operations to an outside vendor. (4) Reduced cycle time consists of reducing the number of steps in a work process. (5) Statistical process control is a statistical technique that uses periodic random samples from production runs to see if quality is being maintained within a standard range of acceptability.

16.7 Managing Control Effectively

- Successful control systems have four common characteristics: (I) They are strategic and results oriented. (2) They are timely, accurate, and objective. (3) They are realistic, positive, and understandable and they encourage self-control. (4) They are flexible.

- Among the barriers to a successful control system are the following: (I) Organizations may exert too much control. (2) There may be too little employee participation. (3) The organization may overemphasize means instead of ends. (4) There may be an overemphasis on paperwork. (5) There may be an overemphasis on one approach instead of multiple approaches.

---

 management in action

Dashboards Are Becoming a Key Control Technique for Enhancing Organizational Effectiveness

Since the advent of the mainframe in the 1950s, companies have dreamed of using computers to manage their businesses. But early efforts came up short, with technology that was too costly or too clunky. Now, thanks to the Net and dashboards, those dreams are starting to come true. Forrester Research Inc. analyst Keith Gile estimates that 40% of the 2,000 largest companies use the technology. Some of the most prominent chief executives in the world are believers, from Steven A. Ballmer at Microsoft and Ivan G. Seidenberg at Verizon Communications to Robert L. Nardelli at Home Depot. . . .

The dashboard is the CEO's killer app, making the gritty details of a business that are often buried deep within a large organization accessible at a glance to senior executives. So powerful are the programs that

they're beginning to change the nature of management, from an intuitive art into more of a science. Managers can see key changes in their businesses almost instantaneously—when salespeople falter or quality slides—and take quick, corrective action. At Verizon, Seidenberg and other executives can choose from among 300 metrics to put on their dashboards, from broadband sales to wireless subscriber defections. At General Electric Co., James P. Campbell, chief of the Consumer & Industrial division, which makes appliances and lighting products, tracks the number of orders coming in from each customer every day and compares that with targets. "I look at the digital dashboard the first thing in the morning so I have a quick global view of sales and service levels across the organization," says Campbell. "It's a key operational tool in our business." . . .

Still, dashboards have drawn some flak. Critics say CEOs can miss the big picture if they're glued to their computer screens. GE agrees with that point. While business unit chiefs such as Campbell are active dashboard users, CEO Jeffrey Immelt is not, since he focuses on issues such as broad strategy and dealmaking that the technology can't yet capture.

Other critics fear dashboards are an alluring but destructive force, the latest incarnation of Big Brother. The concern is that companies will use the technology to invade the privacy of workers and wield it as a whip to keep them in line. Even managers who use dashboards admit the tools can raise pressure on employees, create divisions in the office, and lead workers to hoard information.

One common concern is that dashboards can hurt morale. Consider the case of Little Earth Productions Inc., a Pittsburgh clothing manufacturer. The company uses NetSuite's tools to monitor the amount of business each salesperson has brought in and then displays it publicly. "You do feel bummed out sometimes if you are low on the list," says Ronisue Koller, a Little Earth salesperson. . . .

Still, most management experts think the rewards are well worth the risks. They caution that executives should roll out the systems slowly and avoid highlighting individual performance, at least at first. They also underscore the need for business leaders to spend time up-front figuring out which metrics are the most useful to track. But that's a question of how to use the technology, not whether to implement it. . . .

One big fan of dashboards is Microsoft Corp., which of course makes plenty of business software itself. Jeff Raikes, president of the Microsoft division that makes its Microsoft Office software, says that more than half of its employees use dashboards, including Ballmer and chief software architect William H. Gates III. "Every time I go to see Ballmer, it's an expectation that I bring my dashboard with me," says Raikes. Ballmer, he says, reviews the dashboards of his seven business heads during one-on-one meetings, zeroing in on such metrics as sales, customer satisfaction, and the status of key products under development.

As for Gates, Raikes says the Microsoft founder uses a dashboard during his "think week," when he leaves the office and reads more than 100 papers about the tech industry prepared by employees. "He uses the dashboard to track what he has read and the feedback and actions that should be taken," says Raikes.

Dashboards are a natural for monitoring operations. In manufacturing, GE execs use them to follow the production of everything from lightbulbs to dishwashers, making sure production lines are running smoothly. In the software business, Raikes uses his dashboard to track the progress of the upcoming version of Office. Shaygan Kheradpir, the chief information officer at Verizon, has on his dashboard what co-workers call the Wall of Shaygan, a replica of every single node on the telecom giant's network. All green is good. Yellow or red merits a click. Red means an outage somewhere. "It makes you move where you need to move," he says.

Dashboard technology can help keep customers happy, too. Before NetSuite, American Reporting's Porter says customer-service reps just answered the phone and had no place to store client requests. Now the company's entire customer-service team uses the software. As a result, customer-service managers can see who is responding to calls. And service reps have access to every repair ticket, making it easier to handle customer problems. "It allows us to compete against some of the bigger boys," says Porter.

American Reporting isn't the only small fry that's benefiting. Jerry Driggs, chief operating office of Little Earth, took four months last winter to move his business onto the NetSuite system. Little Earth sells funky eco-fashion products, such as a handbag made with recycled license plates. Today half of the company's 50 employees use the system to manage their production, sales, and financial operations. "Once you see it is so intuitive, you wonder how we ran the business before," says Driggs.

In fact, Driggs ran the business by the seat of his pants, and it showed. Because the company had no system to measure its production requirements or level of raw materials, much of which came from China, it took about six weeks to make and ship a handbag. And Little Earth constantly struggled with cash problems because Driggs would often buy more trim pieces and twist-knob closures than he needed. "You used to see dollars sitting on the shelves," he says. Now, using NetSuite, Driggs can monitor his purchase orders and inventory levels, and the system even alerts him when he is running low on closures and other parts. The result: Little Earth has slashed its shipping time to three days. "All of those things that used to drive us crazy are literally at our fingertips," says Driggs.

For Discussion

1. What are the pros and cons of using dashboards as a control technique? Explain.
2. How can the use of the balanced scorecard and strategy mapping be integrated within the dashboard technology? Discuss.
3. Which of the three levels of control can be provided through the use of dashboards? Provide examples to support your conclusions.
4. How can dashboards be used to improve quality and customer service? Explain.

Source: Excerpted from Spencer E. Ante with Jena McGregor, "Giving the Boss the Big Picture," *BusinessWeek,* February 13, 2006, pp. 48–51.

self-assessment

Do You Have Good Time-Management Skills?

Objectives

1. To determine how productive you are.
2. To discuss what time-management skills need developing.

Introduction

As we learned in this chapter, productivity is important to companies because it determines their profitability. For managers, productivity depends on effective time management, a skill involving planning and self-discipline that should be perfected in college. The purpose of this exercise is to evaluate your time-management skills.

Instructions

Read each question, and answer each one "Yes" or "No." Answer not as you feel you *should* but rather as you feel you *would* if you were being completely truthful.

1. I have a hard time saying "no."
2. I sometimes postpone a task so long that I'm embarrassed to do it.
3. I feel like I'm always in a hurry.
4. I feel guilty when I play or goof off instead of studying.
5. I tend to make excuses when I don't finish my work.
6. I often feel like I have too much to do.
7. I work better under pressure.
8. I feel resentful when someone reminds me I haven't finished my work.
9. I have difficulty deciding how to use my time.
10. I generally put off semester projects until the week before they're due.

Interpretation

Count the number of "No" responses. Your time-management skills may be characterized as follows:

9 – 10: Excellent

8 – 9: Good, but they could be improved in minor ways

6 – 8: Somewhat inadequate; you could benefit from training

4 – 6: Poor; you definitely need training.

4 or less: Emergency! You know little about time management and need to pay immediate attention here

Questions for Discussion

1. Were you surprised by the results? Why or why not?
2. Many statements in the assessment represent procrastination, with good intentions being eclipsed by excuses and bad time management. Do you frequently procrastinate?
3. What are some ways you could improve your time-management skills? Discuss.

Source: Adapted from www.ecu.edu/artsci/cas/advising/TimeManagement.com, © Thomas Harriot College of Arts & Sciences 2001, Advising Center, East Carolina University, Greenville, NC; last updated August 26, 2005.

group exercise

Keeping an Eye on Employee Performance

Objectives

- To look at ways in which companies monitor employee productivity.

- To look at how monitoring productivity can be used as a control mechanism.

Introduction

In this chapter you learned that monitoring can be an effective tool for managers to identify ways to improve productivity. This control device can help them establish standards, measure performance, compare performance to goals, and assess whether corrective action is needed. The purpose of this exercise is to gain familiarity about ways managers can monitor employee productivity.

Instructions

Break into groups of five or six people. Read the following scenario, which your group is then to role-play. Discuss with your group the concerns listed in the scenario. The group should then decide whether your organization should use ProMax software to monitor employee productivity. Once all of the groups in the class have reached their decisions, the various groups should have a class discussion comparing their decisions and their reasoning to those of other groups.

Scenario

Your group is a team of managers for a large organization. Each of you represents a different department. Recently your CEO, who has not been happy with the organization's performance, learned from a golfing friend that the latter's company had spent $1,000 installing a software program—ProMax, made by Replicon Inc.—to monitor employee productivity. Your CEO likes the idea, but he has learned that because your company is bigger, with 2,000 employees, it would cost $20,000 to install the software. Unsure about spending this amount, he has charged all the managers with deciding whether the software would work for your company.

He is open to all feedback because he wants to improve the company's productivity, though not at the employees' expense. He wants all of you to do some research and decide whether the software would be an effective monitoring tool. He understands that each manager has a different department and that the software might not meet the needs of some of them. Among the concerns he wants you to consider: Will the software really increase productivity? In a company of 2,000 employees, will increased productivity justify the software's cost of $20,000? What are some of the ethical issues involved with using this software? What other concerns should he be made aware of?

Your group does some research and finds the following article: E. Goodridge, "Replicon Keeps a Close Watch on Employee Performance: ProMax Software Provides Managers with a Reliable Barometer of Worker's Productivity," *Information Week.com,*

November 2001. **www.informationweek.com/story/ WK20011101S0023,** June 2002.

Measuring the amount of time an employee spends on a job is easy. Measuring employee productivity is another matter, one that poses a challenge for project managers trying to determine accurate time expenditures when billing clients or projects. Workforce-management software supplier Replicon Inc. says it can help with an Internet-based application that tracks employee productivity in real time.

ProMax lets managers set productivity goals for employees, contract workers, projects teams, and departments. When employees enter their billable hours for the day into the software, they can immediately see how their time on the job measures up against expectations set for each individual or project team. Managers receive real-time notifications of employee productivity from the software and can immediately see if a project is running on time and spot potential problems.

While managers may appreciate the hands-on knowledge, the software's ability to measure productivity could raise concerns about employee privacy issues. Replicon CEO John Eddy insists the software will be well received by both managers and employees. "It's a barometer to let an employee know 'where do I stand this month?' and 'where do I need to focus?'" he says. "We've found employees have a natural curiosity to compare their work performance against peers."

ProMax is an application suite from Replicon that tracks and manages time and expense data. FundTech Ltd., a Jersey City, New Jersey, developer of cash-management infrastructure software, implemented Replicon's Web-TimeSheet 4.0, an application that tracks billable employee and project hours across international time zones and foreign currencies.

FundTech needed the software to manage its international professional services group, which develops software for clients such as Citigroup and Merrill Lynch, says Cenk Ipeker, FundTech's director of information systems and financial analysis.

Installing ProMax "is the natural progression for the company next quarter," Ipeker says. "My job is a hybrid of installing and maintaining systems while tracking project reporting. Having a tool that acts like a scorecard, offering immediate insight to worker productivity, would be helpful."

ProMax will be bundled with TimeSheet software, which is used by major companies such as AT&T, Charles Schwab, Compaq, Kraft, and Sony Music Entertainment. Pricing will range from $1,000 for up to 50 users to $20,000 for up to 2,000 users.

1. Refer to Figure 16.4. Which steps in the control process would use this software? Do you feel this software could make any of these steps easier? How? Discuss and explain.

2. What level of control would this software be most effective in: strategic, tactical, or operational? Explain.

3. Do you feel the ethical concerns with this software outweigh the positive aspects of improving productivity? Why or why not?

ethical dilemma

Was Kenneth Lay Acting Ethically When He Bought & Sold Enron Stock?

In 2001, Enron Corp. was quietly lurching from crisis to crisis. Whatever he did or didn't know about Enron's woes at the time, Kenneth L. Lay rarely missed an opportunity to talk up the oil-and-gas trading concern with analysts and Enron employees. The exchairman and CEO even urged workers to follow his lead and buy stock. From August through October, 2001, Lay bought $4 million worth of Enron shares—which he cites as proof that he had faith in the company.

But there's a hitch. Privately, Lay was dumping far more stock than he publicly acquired, according to criminal and civil charges filed against him on July 8 [2004]. In the same three months, he sold $26 million of Enron shares. Altogether in 2001 he unloaded Enron stock for $90 million. But because those shares were sold back to Enron, Lay did not have to disclose the sales until 2002, thanks to a loophole—since closed—in Securities & Exchange Commission rules.

The difference between Lay's public statements and private actions is the foundation of the SEC's civil charges—one of the more aggressive interpretations of insider-trading law in decades.

Solving the Dilemma

What is your opinion about Kenneth Lay's behavior in 2001?

1. He's a crook and should be held liable in the civil suit against him.
2. Although he may have shown bad judgment, give the guy a break. After all, because he was not required to disclose the sale of his stock in 2001, he did not break the law.
3. Regardless of the technicalities about disclosing his stock sales, his behavior is unethical.
4. He is being used as a scapegoat by the SEC.

Source: Excerpted from Paula Dwyer, "The SEC to Top Execs: Read the Fine Print," *BusinessWeek*, July 26, 2004, pp. 33–34.

video case

Starbucks

Starbucks has nearly 6,000 outlets in more than 30 countries and annual revenues in excess of $3.3 billion. All this success rides on the back of a very small product: the coffee bean. Three-quarters of the world's coffee supply comes from small farms in the third world, and coffee producers are in the midst of a crisis. Current selling prices are less than the cost of production, and farmers constantly struggle to survive. So how does Starbucks ensure that it will continue to have access to needed products in a market that has the potential to put its suppliers out of business? To start with, Starbucks purchases only specialty coffee at prices that are almost always higher than the prevailing price for commodity-grade coffee. After

all, quality comes at a price. Starbucks also negotiates prices with individual growers and co-ops for their products, which can run significantly above market prices. However, the higher prices provide stability for both the growers and the organization. Stability is also enhanced through the use of long-term contracts. Dealing directly with growers delivers more of the purchase price to the farmers. Recently, Starbucks has partnered with Ecologic Enterprise Ventures and Conservation International to provide affordable credit to producers, helping farmers break the cycle of debt plaguing their industry.

Fair Trade coffee is a recent development in the worldwide production of coffee. Coffee producers must belong to democratically run cooperatives and must implement crop management and environmental protection plans. In exchange, they are guaranteed a fair price, long-term relationships with importers, and preharvest financing. Most small farms, however, have difficulty meeting all the requirements for Fair Trade certification. For these farmers, Starbucks still honors long-standing relationships, to the benefit of all involved. Even for those producers who cannot meet the Fair Trade standards, Starbucks is becoming more involved in addressing environmental issues. After all, maintaining a sustainable coffee supply means preserving the environment in which it is grown. At one time, all coffee was grown among shade trees. The trees continually provide mulch and nitrogen to the soil, reducing the likelihood of erosion and the need for fertilizers and herbicides. Recently, however, many farmers have switched to high-yielding plants grown under direct sun. Not only does this practice destroy the forests, but sun-grown coffee requires chemical fertilizers that contaminate water supplies. In contrast, a healthy farm of shade-grown coffee can rival a tropical forest in biodiversity.

Investing in its suppliers has created a number of unexpected results. The financial effect of selling to Starbucks is immense. Farmers and their families who sell to Starbucks have access to better clothing, medicine, and education. Entire communities benefit from a strengthened infrastructure. The growers who work with Starbucks are as committed to the organization as Starbucks is to them. At Starbucks, leaders recognize that being socially aware is good for business.

Discussion Questions

1. There are three levels of control: strategic, tactical, and operational. Define each of these types. Which is most evident in the case?
2. Do you see any evidence of total quality management (TQM) principles at Starbucks? Explain.

appendix

The Project Planner's Toolkit
Flowcharts, Gantt Charts, & Break-Even Analysis

How can you use planning tools to enhance your performance and achieve utmost success?

major question

THE BIG PICTURE

Three tools used in project planning, which was covered in Chapter 5, are flowcharts, Gantt charts, and break-even analysis.

Project planning may begin (in the definition stage) as a back-of-the-envelope kind of process, but the client will expect a good deal more for the time and money being invested. Fortunately, there are various planning and monitoring tools that give the planning and execution of projects more precision. Three tools in the planner's tool-kit are (1) flowcharts, (2) Gantt charts, and break-even analysis.

Tool #1: Flowcharts—for Showing Event Sequences & Alternate Decision Scenarios

A *flowchart* is a useful graphical tool for representing the sequence of events required to complete a project and for laying out "what-if" scenarios. Flowcharts have been used for decades by computer programmers and systems analysts to make a graphical "road map," as it were, of the flow of tasks required. These professionals use their own special symbols (indicating "input/output," "magnetic disk," and the like), but there is no need for you to make the process complicated. Generally, only three symbols are needed: (1) an oval for the "beginning" and "end," (2) a box for a major activity, and (3) a diamond for a "yes or no" decision. *(See Figure A.1, next page.)*

Computer programs such as Micrographix's ABC Flow Charter are available for constructing flowcharts. You can also use the drawing program in word processing programs such as Microsoft Word.

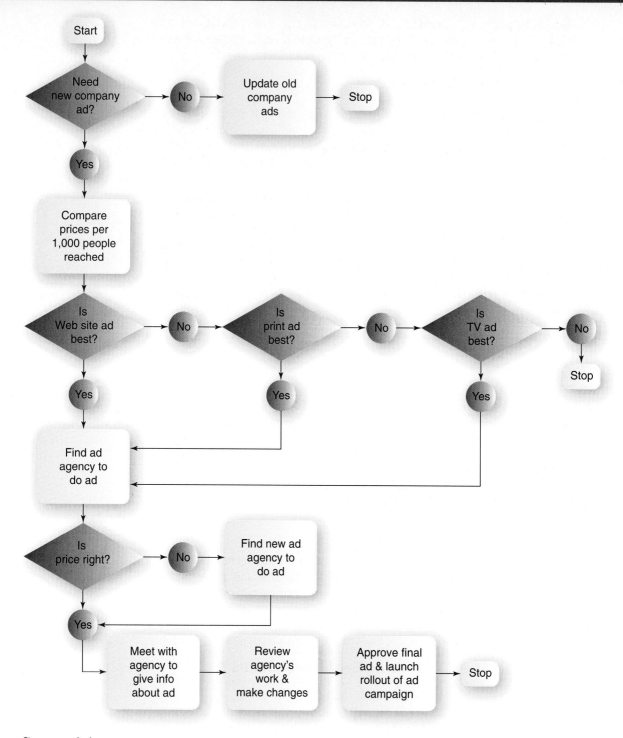

figure A.I

FLOWCHART: WEB SITE, PRINT, OR TELEVISION?

Example of a flowchart for improving a company's advertising

Benefits   Flowcharts have two benefits:

- **Planning straightforward activities.** A flowchart can be quite helpful for planning ordinary activities—figuring out the best way to buy textbooks or a car, for example. It is also a straightforward way of indicating the sequence of events in, say, thinking out a new enterprise that you would then turn into a business plan.

- **Depicting alternate scenarios.** A flowchart is also useful for laying out "what-if" scenarios—as in if you answer "yes" to a decision question you should follow Plan A, if you answer "no" you should follow Plan B.

Limitations   Flowcharts have two limitations:

- **No time indication.** They don't show the amounts of time required to accomplish the various activities in a project. In building a house, the foundation might take only a couple of days, but the rough carpentry might take weeks. These time differences can't be represented graphically on a flowchart (although you could make a notation).

- **Not good for complex projects.** They aren't useful for showing projects consisting of several activities that must all be worked on at the same time. An example would be getting ready for football season's opening game, by which time the players have to be trained, the field readied, the programs printed, the band rehearsed, the ticket sellers recruited, and so on. These separate activities might each be represented on their own flowcharts, of course. But to try to express them all together all at once would produce a flowchart that would be unwieldy, even unworkable.

Tool #2: Gantt Charts—Visual Time Schedules for Work Tasks

We have mentioned how important deadlines are to making a project happen. Unlike a flowchart, a Gantt chart can graphically indicate deadlines.

The Gantt chart was developed by **Henry L. Gantt,** a member of the school of scientific management (discussed in Chapter 2). **A _Gantt chart_ is a kind of time schedule—a specialized bar chart that shows the relationship between the kind of work tasks planned and their scheduled completion dates.** *(See Figure A.2, next page.)*

A number of software packages can help you create and modify Gantt charts on your computer. Examples are CA-SuperProject, Microsoft Project Manager, SureTrak Project Manager, and TurboProject Professional.

Benefits   There are three benefits to using a Gantt chart:

- **Express time lines visually.** Unlike flowcharts, Gantt charts allow you to indicate visually the time to be spent on each activity.

- **Compare proposed and actual progress.** A Gantt chart may be used to compare planned time to complete a task with actual time taken to complete it, so that you can see how far ahead or behind schedule you are for the entire project. This enables you to make adjustments so as to hold to the final target dates.

- **Simplicity.** There is nothing difficult about creating a Gantt chart. You express the time across the top and the tasks down along the left side. As Figure A.2 shows, you can make use of this device while still in college to help schedule and monitor the work you need to do to meet course requirements and deadlines (for papers, projects, tests).

Limitations   Gantt charts have two limitations:

- **Not useful for large, complex projects.** Although a Gantt chart can express the interrelations among the activities of relatively small projects, it becomes cumbersome and unwieldy when used for large, complex projects. More sophisticated management planning tools may be needed, such as PERT networks.

- **Time assumptions are subjective.** The time assumptions expressed may be purely subjective; there is no range between "optimistic" and "pessimistic" of the time needed to accomplish a given task.

Accomplished: ||||||||||
Planned: \\\\\\\\

Stage of development	Week 1	Week 2	Week 3	Week 4	Week 5
1. Examine competitors' Web sites	|||||||||||||||||| |||||||||||	|||||||||||			
2. Get information for your Web site	|||||||||||||||||| |||||||||||	||||||||||||||||||| |||||||||||			
3. Learn Web authoring software		|||||||||||||||||| |||||||||||	|||||||||||||||| |||||||||||		
4. Create (design) your Web site			\\\\\\\\\\	\\\\\\\\\\\\\\\\\\ \\	\\\\\\
5. "Publish" (put) Web site online					\\\\\\\\\\\\\\

figure A.2

GANTT CHART FOR DESIGNING A WEB SITE.

This shows the tasks accomplished and the time planned for remaining tasks to build a company Web site.

Tool #3: Break-Even Analysis—How Many Items Must You Sell to Turn a Profit?

Break-even analysis **is a way of identifying how much revenue is needed to cover the total costs of developing and selling a product.** Let's walk through the computation of a break-even analysis, referring to the illustration. *(See Figure A.3.)* We

figure A.3

BREAK-EVEN ANALYSIS

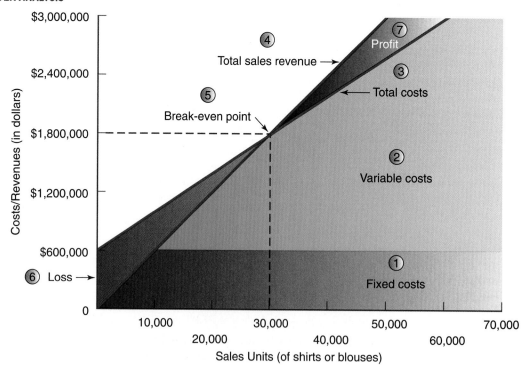

① **Fixed costs (green area):** Once you start up a business, whether you sell anything or not, you'll have expenses that won't vary much, such as rent, insurance, taxes, and perhaps salaries. These are called **fixed costs, expenses that don't change regardless of your sales or output.** Fixed costs are a function of time—they are expenses you have to pay out on a regular basis, such as weekly, monthly, or yearly. Here the chart shows the fixed costs (green area) are $600,000 per year no matter how many sales units (of shirts or blouses) you sell.

② **Variable costs (blue area):** Now suppose you start producing and selling a product, such as blouses or shirts. At this point you'll be paying for materials, supplies, labor, sales commissions, and delivery expenses. These are called **variable costs, expenses that vary directly depending on the numbers of the product that you produce and sell.** (After all, making more shirts will cost you more in cloth, for example.) Variable costs, then, are a function of volume—they go up and down depending on the number of products you make or sell. Here the variable costs (blue area) are relatively small if you sell only a few thousand shirts but they go up tremendously if you sell, say, 70,000 shirts.

③ **Total costs (first right upward-sloping line—green plus blue area added together):** The sum of the fixed costs and the variable costs equals the total costs (the green and blue areas together). This is indicated by the line that slopes upward to the right from $600,000 to $3,000,000.

④ **Total sales revenue (second right upward-sloping line):** This is the total dollars received from the sale of however many units you sell. The sales revenue varies depending on the number of units you sell. Thus, for example, if you sell 30,000 shirts, you'll receive $1,800,000 in revenue. If you sell 40,000 shirts, you'll receive somewhat more than $2,400,000 in revenue.

⑤ **Break-even point (intersection of dashed lines):** Finding this point is the purpose of this whole exercise. **The break-even point is the amount of sales revenue at which there is no profit but also no loss to your company.** On the graph, this occurs where the "Total sales revenues" line crosses the "Total costs" line, as we've indicated here where the dashed lines meet. This means that you must sell 30,000 shirts and receive $1,800,000 in revenue in order to recoup your total costs (fixed plus variable). Important note: Here is where pricing the shirts becomes important. If you raise the price per shirt, you may be able to make the same amount of money (hit your break-even point) by selling fewer of them—but that may be harder to do because customers may resist buying at the higher price.

⑥ **Loss (red area):** If you fail to sell enough shirts at the right price (the break-even point), you will suffer a loss. **Loss means your total costs exceed your total sales revenue.** As the chart shows, here you are literally "in the red"—you've lost money.

⑦ **Profit (black area):** Here you are literally "in the black"—you've made money. All the shirts you sell beyond the break-even point constitute a profit. **Profit is the amount by which total revenue exceeds total costs.** The more shirts you sell, of course, the greater the profit.

    The kind of break-even analysis demonstrated here is known as the **graphic method.** The same thing can also be done algebraically.

assume you are an apparel manufacturer making shirts or blouses. Start in the lower-right corner of the diagram on the previous page and follow the circled numbers as you read the descriptions above.

Benefits   Break-even analysis has two benefits:

- **For doing future "what-if" alternate scenarios of costs, prices, and sales.** This tool allows you to vary the different possible costs, prices, and

Break-Even Analysis: Why Do Airfares Vary So Much?

Why do some airlines charge four times more than others for a flight of the same distance?

There are several reasons, but break-even analysis enters into it.

United Airlines' average cost for flying a passenger 1 mile in 2003 was 11.7 cents, whereas Southwest's was 7.7 cents. Those are the break-even costs. What they charged beyond that was their profit.

Why the difference? One reason, according to a study by the U.S. Department of Transportation, is that Southwest's expenses are lower. United flies more long routes than short ones, so its costs are stretched out over more miles, making its costs for flying shorter routes higher than Southwest's.

Another factor affecting airfares is the type of passengers flying a particular route—whether they are high-fare-paying business travelers or more price-conscious leisure travelers. Business travelers often don't mind paying a lot (they are reimbursed by their companies), and those routes (such as Chicago to Cincinnati) tend to have more first-class seats, which drives up the average price. Flights to vacation spots (such as Las Vegas) usually have more low-price seats because people aren't willing to pay a lot for pleasure travel. Also, nonstop flight fares often cost more than flights with connections.

sales quantities to do rough "what-if" scenarios to determine possible pricing and sales goals. Since the numbers are interrelated, if you change one, the others will change also.

- **For analyzing the profitability of past projects.** While break-even analysis is usually used as a tool for future projects, it can also be used retroactively to find out whether the goal of profitability was really achieved, since costs may well have changed during the course of the project. In addition, you can use it to determine the impact of cutting costs once profits flow.

Limitations   Break-even analysis is not a cure-all.

- **It oversimplifies.** In the real world, things don't happen as neatly as this model implies. For instance, fixed and variable costs are not always so readily distinguishable. Or fixed costs may change as the number of sales units goes up. And not all customers may pay the same price (some may get discounts).

- **The assumptions may be faulty.** On paper, the formula may work perfectly for identifying a product's profitability. But what if customers find the prices too high? Or what if sales figures are outrageously optimistic? In the marketplace, your price and sales forecasts may really be only good guesses. ●

chapter notes

CHAPTER I

1. H. Lancaster, "If Your Career Needs More Attention, Maybe You Should Get an Agent," *The Wall Street Journal,* October 20, 1998, p. BI. See also L. K. Hardie, "Joelle K. Jay: Leadership Coach Inspires Businesspeople to Succeed," *Reno Gazette-Journal,* January 15, 2006, pp. IE, I3E; R. Berman, "Coached Toward Brighter Management," *San Francisco Chronicle,* March 5, 2006, pp. GI, G6; Nadine Brozan, "Top Brokers Hire Coaches to Climb Higher," *The New York Times,* May 7, 2006, sec. 4, p. 9.

2. R. L. Knowdell, "The 10 New Rules for Strategizing Your Career," *The Futurist,* June–July 1998, pp. 19–24.

3. Judy McGrath, quoted in T. Lowry, "Can MTV Stay Cool?" *BusinessWeek,* February 20, 2006, pp. 50–60.

4. M. P. Follett, quoted in J. F. Stoner and R. E. Freeman, *Management,* 5th ed. (Englewood Cliffs, NJ: Prentice Hall, 1992), p. 6.

5. The Gartner Group, cited in Don Oldenburg, Associated Press, "Tired of Automated Phone Menus? Press 1," *Reno Gazette-Journal,* March 15, 2004, p. 3E.

6. Scott Broetzmann, quoted in Oldenburg, 2004.

7. Richard Shapiro, quoted in W. C. Taylor, "Your Call Should Be Important to Us, but It's Not," *The New York Times,* February 26, 2006, sec. 3, p. 3; G. J. Carter, "How to Get a Human to Answer the Phone," *USA Weekend,* April 14–16, 2006, p. 4 See also the gethuman Web site at www.gethuman.com.

8. Taylor, 2006.

9. G. Colvin, "Catch a Rising Star," *Fortune,* February 6, 2006, pp. 46–50.

10. J. Mouawad, "For Leading Exxon to Its Riches, $144,573 a Day," *The New York Times,* April 15, 2006, pp. AI, B4.

11. G. Strauss and B. Hansen, "Median Pay for CEOs of 100 Largest Companies Rose 25%," *USA Today,* April 10, 2006, pp. IB, 2B.

12. The Wall Street Journal/Mercer Human Resource Consulting, *2005 CEO Human Resource Consulting and Trends,* May 15, 2006, p. 3, http://mercerhr.com/knowledgecenter/reportsummary.jhtml/dynamic/idContent/I089750:jsessionid=EOYOPZBJO3APECTGOUGCHPQKMZOQUI2C (accessed May 16, 2006). See also J. S. Lublin, "Adding It All Up," *The Wall Street Journal,* April 10, 2006, pp. RI, R3.

13. Naween Mangi, "What's Pushing Small-Biz Salaries Sky-High," *BusinessWeek,* August 8, 2000; www.businessweek.com/smallbiz/0008/sb000808.htm (accessed March 18, 2004).

14. Council on Foundations, cited in R. Berman, "Profiting from Your Passion," *San Francisco Chronicle,* July 3, 2005, pp. GI, G6.

15. O. Pollar, "Are You Sure You Want to Be a Manager?" *San Francisco Examiner,* October 4, 1998, p. J-3.

16. M. Csikszentmihalyi, *Flow: The Psychology of Optimal Experience* (New York: HarperCollins, 1990), and *Beyond Boredom and Anxiety* (San Francisco: Jossey-Bass, 1975). *Creativity: Flow and the Psychology of Discovery and Invention* (New York: Harper Perennial, 1996); (1998). *Finding Flow: The Psychology of Engagement with Everyday Life* (New York: Basic Books, 1998); and *Good Business. Leadership, Flow, and the Making of Meaning* (New York: Penguin Books, 2003).

17. T. Friend, "Don't Touch That Dial," *The New Yorker,* May 22, 2006, pp. 81–82.

18. R. Gover, "The Sound of Many Hands Zapping," *BusinessWeek,* May 22, 2006, p. 38.

19. S. Elliott and J. Bosman, "That New Show Starring . . . a Tube of Toothpaste," *The New York Times,* May 18, 2006, p. CIO. See also N. A. Hira, "The Evolving Art of Outwitting TiVo," *Fortune,* May 15, 2006, p. 36.

20. J. Heilemann, "Cable's Niche Player," *Business 2.0,* May 2006, pp. 36–39.

21. U.S. Census Bureau, "U.S. Interim Projections by Age, Sex, Race, and Hispanic Origin," Table Ia, 2004; www.census.gov/ipc/www/usinterimproj (accessed May 16, 2006).

22. S. McCartney, "Teaching Americans How to Behave Abroad," *The Wall Street Journal,* April 11, 2006, pp. DI, D4. See also J. Clark, "That 'Ugly American' Image Is Getting a Makeover Guide," *USA Today,* April 28, 2006, p. 9D.

23. Michael M. Phillips, "More Work Is Outsourced to U.S. Than Away from It, Data Show," *The Wall Street Journal,* March 15, 2004, p. A2.

24. International Data Corp. estimates, cited in L. Harris, "B2B E-Commerce Sites Increase Profitability Through Intelligent Search," *B2B Marketing Trends,* January 17, 2006; http://www.b2bmarketingtrends.com/abstract.asp?id=198&groupid=10 (accessed May 17, 2006).

25. M. J. Mandel and R. D. Hof, "Rethinking the Internet," *BusinessWeek,* March 26, 2001, p. 118. See also B. Powell, "The New World Order," *Fortune,* May 14, 2001, pp. 134, 136.

26. Data from "Hurry Up and Decide!" *BusinessWeek,* May 14, 2001.

27. S. Cabot, reported in D. Jones, "Sales Reps Must Watch Step When Rapping Rivals," *USA Today,* June 17, 1997, p. 3B.

28. J. Sandberg, "Down Over Moving Up: Some Bosses Find They Hate Their Jobs," *The Wall Street Journal,* July 27, 2005, p. BI. See also D. Jones, "Besides Being Lonely at the Top, It Can Be 'Disengaging' as Well," *USA Today,* June 21, 2005, pp. IB, 2B.

29. S. Armour, "Management Loses Its Allure," *USA Today,* October 15, 1997, pp. IB, 2B. See also J. Kornik, "With Leaders Like These . . . ," *Training,* December 2005, p. 10.

30. Pollar, 1998.

31. P. Drucker, reported in R. L. Knowdell, "A Model for Managers in the Future Workplace: Symphony Conductor," *The Futurist,* June–July 1998, p. 22.

32. P. Burrows, "Steve Jobs' Magic Kingdom," cover story, *BusinessWeek,* February 6, 2006, pp. 62–69.

33. J. Falvey, *After College: The Business of Getting a Job* (Charlotte, VT: Williamson, 1986).

34. B. Karlin, quoted in S. Spring, "Job Titles of the Future: Director of Great People," *Fast Company,* February–March, 1999, p. 46.

35. S. Spring, "Job Titles of the Future: Chief Travel Scientist," *Fast Company,* February–March, 1999, p. 68.

36. A. Thompson, "The Hardest Management Job, "*The Costco Connection,* August 2005, pp. 30–33.

37. P. M. Blau and W. R. Scott, *Formal Organizations* (San Francisco: Chandler, 1962).

38. H. Mintzberg, *The Nature of Managerial Work* (New York: Harper & Row, 1973).

39. Mintzberg, 1973.

40. Ed Reilly, quoted in W. J. Holstein, "Attention-Juggling in the High-Tech Office," *The New York Times,* June 4, 2006, sec. 3, p. 9.

41. J. P. Kotter, "What Effective General Managers Really Do," *Harvard Business Review,* March–April 1999, pp. 145–159.

42. L. Stroh, quoted in A. Muoio, "Balancing Acts," *Fast Company,* February–March 1999, pp. 83–90.

43. S. MacDermid, Purdue University, and M. D. Lee, McGill University, two-year study cited in R. W. Huppke, Associated Press, "Take This Job, and Love It," *San Francisco Chronicle,* January 28, 1999, p. B2.

44. A. Deutschman, "The CEO's Secret of Managing Time," *Fortune,* June 1, 1992, pp. 135–146.

45. D. G. Lepore, quoted in Muoio, 1999.

46. H. Lancaster, "Managing Your Time in Real-World Chaos Takes Real Planning," *The Wall Street Journal,* August 19, 1997, p. B1.

47. R. E. Kelley, quoted in S. Shellenbarger, "You Don't Have to Be Chained to Your Desk to Be a Star Performer," *The Wall Street Journal,* August 12, 1998, p. B1.

48. B. Graham, quoted in Shellenbarger, 1998.

49. S. Winston, quoted in A. Fisher, "Get Organized at Work—Painlessly," *Fortune,* January 10, 2005, p. 30.

50. J. Cassidy, "Me Media," *The New Yorker,* May 15, 2006, pp. 50–59. See also A. Saracevic, "Facebook Will Protect You—Sort of," *San Francisco Chronicle,* May 9, 2006, p. C3; "Mark Zuckerberg," Wikipedia, http://en.wikipedia.org/wiki/Mark_Zuckerberg (accessed June 8, 2006); "Exclusive Interview with Mark Zuckerberg," Current Magazine—MSNBC.com, November 30, 2004, www.msnbc.com/id/6596533/site/newsweek (accessed June 8, 2006).

51. S. Perman, "The Entrepreneurial Melting Pot," BusinessWeek Online, June 6, 2005; www.businessweek.com/smallbiz/content/jun2006/sb20060606_980_521.htm?chan=smallbiz_smallbiz+index+page_getting+started (accessed June 8, 2006). See also J. Mehring, "The Real Job Engines," *BusinessWeek SmallBiz,* Spring 2006, p. 42; and A. Weintraub, "Hot Growth," *BusinessWeek,* June 5, 2006, pp. 48–52.

52. N. Templin, "Boutique-Hotel Group Thrives on Quirks," *The Wall Street Journal,* March 1999, pp. B1, B9.

53. P. F. Drucker, *Innovation and Entrepreneurship* (New York: Harper & Row, 1986), pp. 27–28.

54. J. M. Higgins, "Innovate or Evaporate: Seven Secrets of Innovative Corporations," *The Futurist,* September–October 1995, pp. 42–43; K. Yakal, "Now You Can Use Your Post-It Notes Electronically," *Computer Shopper,* June 1997, p. 547; and "A Notable Idea," *Selling Power,* May 1998, p. 81.

55. A. M. Webber, "Danger: Toxic Company," *Fast Company,* November 1998, pp. 152–161.

56. Bureau of Labor Statistics, 1998.

57. D. C. McClelland, *The Achieving Society* (New York: Van Nostrand, 1961); D. C. McClelland, *Human Motivation* (Glenview, IL: Scott, Foresman, 1985); D. L. Sexton and N. Bowman, "The Entrepreneur: A Capable Executive and More," *Journal of Business Venturing* 1 (1985), pp. 129–140; D. Hisrich, "Entrepreneurship/Intrapreneurship," *American Psychologist,* February 1990, p. 218; T. Begley and D. P. Boyd, "Psychological Characteristics Associated with Performance in Entre-preneurial Firms and Smaller Businesses," *Journal of Business Venturing* 2 (1987), pp. 79–93; and C. R. Kuehl and P. A. Lambing, *Small Business: Planning and Management* (Fort Worth, TX: Dryden Press, 1990).

58. Global Entrepreneurship Monitor, 2002 study by London Business School and Babson College, reported in J. Bailey, "Desire—More Than Need—Builds a Business,"*The Wall Street Journal,* May 21, 2002, p. B4.

59. R. L. Katz, "Skills of an Effective Administrator," *Harvard Business Review,* September–October, 1974, p. 94.

60. Sara Levinson, quoted in Lowry, 2006, p. 60.

61. Lowry, 2006, p. 55.

62. CEO recruiter, quoted in Colvin, 2006.

63. Colvin, 2006.

64. D. Shoemaker, quoted in I. DeBare, "The Incredible Growing Workweek," *San Francisco Chronicle,* February 12, 1999, pp. B1, B2.

65. E. B. Zechmeister and S. E. Nyberg, *Human Memory: An Introduction to Research and Theory* (Pacific Grove, CA: Brooks/Cole, 1982).

66. B. K. Bromage and R. E. Meyer, "Quantitative and Qualitative Effects of Repetition on Learning from Technical Text," *Journal of Educational Psychology,* 1982, vol. 78, pp. 271–278.

67. F. P. Robinson, *Effective Study,* 4th ed. (New York: Harper & Row, 1970).

68. H. C. Lindgren, The *Psychology of College Success: A Dynamic Approach* (New York: Wiley, 1969).

69. R. J. Palkovitz and R. K. Lore, "Note Taking and Note Review: Why Students Fail Questions Based on Lecture Material," *Teaching of Psychology,* 1980, vol. 7, pp. 159–161.

70. J. Langan and J. Nadell, *Doing Well in College: A Concise Guide to Reading, Writing, and Study Skills* (New York: McGraw-Hill, 1980), pp. 93–110.

71. Palkovitz and Lore, 1980, pp. 159–161.

CHAPTER 2

1. E. J. Langer, *The Power of Mindful Learning* (Reading, MA: Addison-Wesley, 1997), p. 4.

2. E. J. Langer, *Mindfulness* (Reading, MA: Addison-Wesley, 1989), pp. 12–13.

3. Langer, 1989, p. 69.

4. C. Hymowitz, "Executives Must Stop Jumping Fad to Fad and Learn to Manage," *The Wall Street Journal,* May 15, 2006, p. B1.

5. A. Webber, "The Best Organization Is No Organization," *USA Today,* March 6, 1997, p. 13A.

6. "The Leader as Naval Architect: Beyond the Spaghetti Organization," interview with Lars Kolind, *Wharton @ Work: e-Buzz,* July 2005; http://execed-web.wharton.upenn.edu/ebuzz/0507/fellows.html (accessed May 23, 2006). See also N. J. Foss, "Selective Intervention and Internal Hybrids: Interpreting and Learning from the Rise and Decline of the Oticon Spaghetti Organization," *Organization Science* 14(2003), pp. 331–349.

7. A. Maslow, "A Theory of Human Motivation," *Psychological Review,* July 1943, pp. 370–396.

8. D. McGregor, *The Human Side of Enterprise* (New York: McGraw-Hill, 1960).

9. See J. T. Delaney, "Workplace Cooperation: Current Problems, New Approaches," *Journal of Labor Research,* Winter 1996, pp. 45–61; H. Mintzberg, D. Dougherty, J. Jorgensen, and F. Westley, "Some Surprising Things About Collaboration—Knowing How People Connect Makes It Work Better," *Organizational Dynamics,* Spring 1996, pp. 60–71; R. Crow, "Institutionalized Competition and Its Effects on Teamwork,"

Journal for Quality and Participation, June 1995, pp. 46–54; K. G. Smith, S. J. Carroll, and S. J. Ashford, "Intra- and Interorganizational Cooperation: Toward a Research Agenda," *Academy of Management Journal,* February 1995, pp. 7–23; M. E. Haskins, J. Liedtka, and J. Rosenblum, "Beyond Teams: Toward an Ethic of Collaboration," *Organizational Dynamics,* Spring 1998, pp. 34–50; and C. C. Chen, X. P. Chen, and J. R. Meindl, "How Can Cooperation Be Fostered? The Cultural Effects of Individualism-Collectivism," *Academy of Management Review,* April 1998, pp. 285–304.

10. A. Kohn, "How to Succeed without Even Vying," *Psychology Today,* September 1986, pp. 27–28. Sports psychologists discuss "cooperative competition" in S. Sleek, "Competition: Who's the Real Opponent?" *APA Monitor,* July 1996, p. 8.

11. D. W. Johnson, G. Maruyama, R. Johnson, D. Nelson, and L. Skon, "Effects of Cooperative, Competitive, and Individualistic Goal Structures on Achievement: A Meta-Analysis," *Psychological Bulletin,* January 1981, pp. 56–57. An alternative interpretation of the foregoing study that emphasizes the influence of situational factors can be found in J. L. Cotton and M. S. Cook, "Meta-Analysis and the Effects of Various Reward Systems: Some Different Conclusions from Johnson et al.," *Psychological Bulletin,* July 1982, pp. 176–183. Also see A. E. Ortiz, D. W. Johnson, and R. T. Johnson, "The Effect of Positive Goal and Resource Interdependence on Individual Performance," *The Journal of Social Psychology,* April 1996, pp. 243–249; and S. L. Gaertner, J. F. Dovidio, M. C. Rust, J. A. Nier, B. S. Banker, C. M. Ward, G. R. Mottola, and M. Houlette, "Reducing Intergroup Bias: Elements of Intergroup Cooperation," *Journal of Personality and Social Psychology,* March 1999, pp. 388–402.

12. E. Perkins, "How to Book Hotel Rooms at Half the Price," *San Francisco Examiner,* December 13, 1998, p. T-2.

13. R. W. Belsky, "Being Hotel Savvy," *The Dollar Stretcher;* www.stretcher.com/stories/00/000515c.cfm (accessed March 25, 2004).

14. S. F. Brown, "Wresting New Wealth from the Supply Chain," *Fortune,* November 9, 1998, pp. 204[C]–204[Z]. See also M. Maynard, "Toyota Shows Big Three How It's Done," *The New York Times,* January 13, 2006, pp. C1, C4.

15. B. Wysocki Jr., "To Fix Health Care, Hospitals Take Tips from Factory Floor," *The Wall Street Journal,* April 9, 2004, pp. A1, A6.

16. J. Strasburg, "Shaking the Blues," *San Francisco Chronicle,* February 3, 2002, pp. G1, G3; N. Munk, "How Levi's Trashed a Great American Brand," *Fortune,* April 12, 1999, pp. 83–90; and E. Neuborne, K. Kerwin, and bureau reports, "Generation Y," *BusinessWeek,* February 15, 1999, pp. 80–88.

17. N. Klein, *No Logo: Taking Aim at the Brand Bullies* (New York: St. Martin's Press, 1999).

18. NPD Group retail analyst Marshal Cohen, cited in P. Sarkar, "Stores Boost Sales with Own Labels," *San Francisco Chronicle,* May 5, 2006, pp. D1, D6.

19. J. Schlosser, "Teacher's Bet," *Fortune,* March 8, 2004, pp. 158–164.

20. G. Loveman, "Diamonds in the Data Mine," *Harvard Business Review,* May 2003, pp. 109–113.

21. L. Walker, "Data-Mining Software Digs for Business Leads," *San Francisco Chronicle,* March 8, 2004, p. E6; reprinted from *Washington Post.*

22. S. Saul, "Doctors Object as Drug Makers Learn Who's Prescribing What," *The New York Times,* May 4, 2006, pp. A1, C4.

23. J. Case, *Open-Book Management: The Coming Business Revolution* (New York: HarperBusiness, 1996).

24. J. Pfeffer, in A. M. Webber, "Danger: Toxic Company," *Fast Company,* November 1998, pp. 152–161.

25. J. Pfeffer, *The Human Equation: Building Profits by Putting People First* (Cambridge, MA: Harvard Business School Press, 1996).

26. C. Kleiman, "Companies Embracing 'Open-Book' Management," *San Jose Mercury News,* May 18, 1997, pp. PC1, PC2.

27. G. T. Brown, quoted in Kleiman, 1997.

28. K. Carney, "How to Keep Staff in a Boom Economy," *Inc.,* November 1998, p. 110.

29. I. Mochari, "How Motley Fools Talk Back," *Inc.,* June 1999, p. 108.

30. G. Bylinsky, "How to Bring Out Better Products Faster," *Fortune,* November 23, 1998, pp. 238[B]–238[T].

31. P. Senge, *The Fifth Discipline* (New York: Doubleday, 1990), p. 1.

32. R. Hodgetts, F. Luthans, and S. Lee, "New Paradigm Organizations: From Total Quality to Learning to World-Class," *Organizational Dynamics,* Winter 1994, pp. 5–19D; and A. Garvin, "Building a Learning Organization," *Harvard Business Review,* July/August 1993, pp. 78–91.

33. A. S. Miner and S. J. Mezias, "Ugly Duckling No More: Pasts and Futures of Organizational Learning Research," *Organization Science,* January–February 1996, pp. 88–99; and R. P. Mai, *Learning Partnerships: How Leading American Companies Implement Organizational Learning* (Chicago: Irwin, 1996).

34. R. Schultz, quoted in J. Martin, "Are You as Good as You Think You Are?" *Fortune,* September 30, 1996, p. 146.

35. D. M. Noer, *Breaking Free: A Prescription for Personal and Organizational Change* (San Francisco: Jossey-Bass, 1996); S. F. Slater, "Learning to Change," *Business Horizons,* November–December 1995, pp. 13–20; and D. Ulrich, T. Jick, and M. Von Glinow, "High-Impact Learning: Building and Diffusing Learning Capability," *Organizational Dynamics,* Autumn 1993, pp. 52–66.

36. M. J. Mandel and R. D. Hof, "Rethinking the Internet," *BusinessWeek,* March 26, 2001, p. 118.

37. Adapted from "Virtual Organization," Whatis.com; http://whatis.techtarget.com/definition/0,,sid9_gci213301,00.html (accessed June 12, 2006).

38. Adapted from "Boundaryless," *Encyclopedia of Small Business,* ed. K. Hillstrom and L. C. Hillstrom (Farmington Hills, MI: Thomson Gale, 2002, and Seattle, WA: eNotes.com, 2006) http://business.enotes.com/small-business-encyclopedia/boundaryless (accessed June 12, 2006). Regarding the impact of Web services on organizational boundaries, see R. D. Hof, "Web 2.0: The New Guy at Work," *BusinessWeek,* June 19, 2006, pp. 58–59.

39. S. Hamm, "Speed Demons," *BusinessWeek,* March 27, 2006, pp. 68–75. See also J. McGregor, "The World's Most Innovative Companies," *BusinessWeek,* April 24, 2006, pp. 63–74.

40. G. Bollander, S. Snell, and A. Sherman, *Managing Human Resources,* 12th ed. (Cincinnati, OH: South-Western Publishing, 2001), pp. 13–15; and B. E. Becker, M. A. Huselid, and D. Ulrich, *The HR Scorecard: Linking People, Strategy, and Performance* (Boston: Harvard Business School Press, 2001), p. 4.

41. S. Meisinger, "Taking the Measure of Human Capital," *HR Magazine,* January 2003, p. 10. See also R. J. Grossman, "Blind Investment," *HR Magazine,* January 2005, pp. 40–47.

42. Inspired by P. S. Adler and S. Kwon, "Social Capital: Prospects for New Concept," *Academy of Management Review,* January 2002, pp. 17–40. See also R. A. Baaron and G. D. Markman, "Beyond Social Capital: How Social Skills Can Enhance Entrepreneurs' Success," *Academy of Management Executive,* February 2000, pp. 106–116.

43. Data from "What Makes a Job Okay," *USA Today,* May 15, 2000, p. 1B.

44. J. Pfeffer and R. I. Sutton, "Evidence-Based Management," *Harvard Business Review,* January 2006, pp. 63–74. See also D. M. Rousseau, "Is There Such a Thing as 'Evidence-Based Management'?" *Academy of Management Review,* April 2006, pp. 256–269.

45. J. Pfeffer and R. I. Sutton, "Profiting from Evidence-Based Management," *Strategy & Leadership* 34(2) (2006), pp. 35–42.

46. Excerpted from J. L. Lunsford, "Lean Times: With Airbus on Its Tail, Boeing Is Rethinking How It Builds Planes," *The Wall Street Journal,* October 5, 2001, pp. A1, A16.

47. M. Arndt, "Built for the Long Haul," *BusinessWeek,* January 30, 2006, p. 66.

48. A description of the rating process can be found in "*Fortune* 100 Best Companies to Work For 2006," http://money.cnn.com/element/ssi/sections/mag/fortune/bestcompanies/how.popup.html (accessed July 21, 2006).

49. (1) Genentech; (2) Wegmans Food Markets; (3) Valero Energy; (4) Griffin Hospital; (5) W. L. Gore & Associates; (6) Container Store; (7) Vision Service Plan; (8) J. M. Smucker; (9) Recreational Equipment (REI); and (10) S. C. Johnson.

CHAPTER 3

1. Survey by Caliper, Princeton, NJ, 1998. Cited in A. Fisher, "Am I Too Old to Be a Tech Expert?... What Are Employers Really Looking For?" *Fortune,* May 25, 1998, p. 202.

2. O. Pollar, "Keeping Sane in Workplace Full of Change," *San Francisco Examiner,* July 27, 1997, p. J-3.

3. A. Zimmerman, "Costco's Dilemma: Be Kind to Its Workers, or Wall Street?" *The Wall Street Journal,* March 26, 2004, pp. B1, B3; J. Flanigan, "Costco Sees Value in Higher Pay," *Los Angeles Times,* February 15, 2004, www.latimes.com/business/la-fi-flan15feb15,1,61048 (accessed March 29, 2004); and C. Frey, "Costco's Love of Labor: Employees' Well-being Key to Its Success," *Seattle Post-Intelligencer,* March 29, 2004, http://seattlepi.nwsource.com/business/166680_costco29.html (accessed March 29, 2004); S. Greenhouse, "How Costco Became the Anti-Wal-Mart," *The New York Times,* July 17, 2005, sec. 7, p. 1; and C. Migden, "Wal-Mart Must Pay Its Share," *San Francisco Chronicle,* March 16, 2006, p. B9.

4. J. Useem, "Should We Admire Wal-Mart?" *Fortune,* March 8, 2004, pp. 118–120. See also A. Harrington, "America's Most Admired Companies," *Fortune,* March 8, 2004, pp. 80–82.

5. Zimmerman, 2004, p. B1.

6. D. Leonhardt, "The Economics of Henry Ford May Be Passé," *The New York Times,* April 5, 2006, pp. C1, C12.

7. R. B. Reich, "The Company of the Future," *Fast Company,* November 1998, pp. 124–150.

8. For more on Employee Stock Ownership Plans (ESOPs), see I. DeBare, "Stock Plan Transfers Ownership to Employees," *San Francisco Chronicle,* May 15, 2006, pp. C1, C4; J. Raymond, "Unlikely Pioneers," *BusinessWeek SmallBiz,* Spring 2006, pp. 56–59; and W. C. Taylor, "These Workers Act Like Owners (Because They Are)," *The New York Times,* May 21, 2006, sec. 3, p. 5.

9. M. J. Driver, "Careers: A Review of Personnel and Organizational Research," in C. L. Cooper and I. Robertson, eds., *International Review of Industrial and Organizational Psychology* (New York: Wiley, 1988).

10. Christopher Hart, author of *Extraordinary Guarantees,* quoted in A. Comarow, "Broken? No Problem," *U.S. News & World Report,* January 11, 1999, pp. 68–69.

11. Lieber, 1998.

12. "Banking Against Wal-Mart," editorial, *The Wall Street Journal,* January 4, 2006, p. A10; and M. Gordon, "Consumers and Banks Gang Up on Wal-Mart," *San Francisco Chronicle,* April 11, 2006, p. C3.

13. M. Barbaro, "Wal-Mart Offers Aid to Rivals," *The New York Times,* April 5, 2006, pp. C1, C12; and A. Zimmerman, "Wal-Mart Unveils Urban-Aid Plan in Bid to Quell Expansion Criticism," *The Wall Street Journal,* April 5, 2006, p. B3.

14. Bureau of Labor Statistics, U.S. Department of Labor, "Union Members in 2005," *Union Members Summary,* January 20, 2006; www.bls.gov/news.release/union2.nr0.htm (accessed June 14, 2006).

15. R. Pollin, "In Politics: Savvy Organizers Win 'Living Wage' Across U.S.," *San Jose Mercury News,* December 6, 1998, pp. 1P, 6P.

16. L. Atkinson and J. Galaskiewicz, "Stock Ownership and Company Contributions to Charity," *Administrative Science Quarterly,* vol. 33, 1988, pp. 82–100.

17. J. M. Peters and M. Maynard, "Company Town Relies on G. M. Long After Plants Have Closed," *The New York Times,* February 20, 2006, pp. A1, A12.

18. N. Shirouzu, "As Detroit Slashes Car Jobs, Southern Towns Pick Up Slack," *The Wall Street Journal,* February 1, 2006, pp. A1, A12.

19. E. Brazil, "300 Protest Gap in S.F.," *San Francisco Examiner,* March 7, 1999, p. A-2.

20. For a discussion of how politically passionate consumers take aim at certain businesses, see R. S. Dunham, "Companies in the Crossfire," *BusinessWeek,* April 17, 2006, pp. 30–33.

21. See, for example, F. Barringer, "$92 Million More Is Sought for Exxon Valdez Cleanup," *The New York Times,* June 2, 2006, p. A13.

22. Associated Press, "Productivity, Wages Both Up," CBS News, May 4, 2006, http://www.cbsnews.com/stories/2006/05/04/business/main1585477.shtml (accessed June 20, 2006); J. Aversa, "Fed Chief Explains Why Productivity Is Up," *San Francisco Chronicle,* June 10, 2006, pp. C1, C2.

23. Doug, quoted in C. Sutton, "Designing Women Show Off Their Marks," *San Francisco Examiner,* March 7, 1999, p. W-33.

24. M. Kabel, "Diet Trends Affect U.S. Meat Glut," *Reno Gazette-Journal,* May 16, 2006, p. 4D.

25. D. Foote and A. Murr, "Back on the Block," *Newsweek,* May 6, 2002, pp. 42–47. See also L. Buchanan, "The 2006 Inner City 100," *Inc. Magazine,* June 2006, pp. 109–118.

26. M. Galanter, reported in W. Glaberson, "When the Verdict Is Just a Fantasy," *The New York Times,* June 6, 1999, sec. 4 pp. 1, 6.

27. P. Geitner, "Microsoft Says EU Stepping on U.S. Turf," *The Globe & Mail,* March 24, 2004, p. B9.

28. American Council on Education, reported by P. Wingert, "'F' in Global Competence," *Newsweek,* May 20, 2002, p. 11. See also D. J. Lynch, "U.S. Firms Becoming Tongue-Tied," *USA Today,* February 9, 2006, p. 6B; and "Execs Learning to Speak Second Language," *Reno Gazette-Journal,* May 5, 2006, p. 6D.

29. G. Allred, quoted in S. Armour, "Facing a Tough Choice: Your Ethics or Your Job," *USA Today,* September 21, 1998, p. B1.

30. L. T. Hosmer, *The Ethics of Management* (Homewood, IL: Irwin, 1987).

31. S. Saul, "Unease on Industry's Role in Hypertension Debate," *The New York Times,* May 20, 2006, pp. A1, B9; and C. Arnst, "Hey, You Don't Look So Good," *BusinessWeek,* May 8, 2006, pp. 30–32.

32. B. Kabanoff, "Equity, Equality, Power, and Conflict," *Academy of Management Review,* April 1991, pp. 416–441.

33. D. Fritzsche and H. Baker, "Linking Management Behavior to Ethical Philosophy: An Empirical Investigation," *Academy of Management Journal*, March 1984, pp. 166-175.

34. S. H. Verhovek, "Northwest Confronts Its Growth: Wild Salmon Called Endangered," *The New York Times*, March 16, 1999, pp. A1, A13; Associated Press, "Pacific Salmon to Stay on Endangered List," May 28, 2004, http://msnbc.msn.com/id/5085081, accessed June 12, 2006.

35. J. Sandberg, "Monitoring of Workers Is Boss's Right but Why Not Include Top Brass," *The Wall Street Journal*, May 18, 2005, p. B1.

36. G. Morgenson, "The Big Winner, Again, Is 'Scandalot,'" *The New York Times*, January 1, 2006, sec. 3, pp. 1, 7; C. Said, "From White Collars to Prison Blues," *San Francisco Chronicle*, May 26, 2006, pp. D1, D6; G. Morgenson, "Are Enrons Bustin' Out All Over?" *The New York Times*, May 28, 2006, sec. 3, pp. 1, 8; K. Clark and M. Lavelle, "Guilty as Charged!" *U.S. News & World Report*, June 5, 2006, A. Sloan, "Laying Enron to Rest," *Newsweek*, June 5, 2006, pp. 25-30, pp. 44-45; M. Gimein, "The Skilling Trap," *BusinessWeek*, June 12, 2006, pp. 31-32. See also S. Labaton, "Four Years Later, Enron's Shadow Lingers as Change Comes Slowly," *The New York Times*, January 5, 2006, pp. C1, C4; J. H. Zamansky, "At the Least, Former Enron Chiefs Are Guilty of Moral Bankruptcy," *USA Today*, February 1, 2006, p. 11A; A. Shell, "Enron Verdicts Good for Investors," *USA Today*, May 30, 2006, p. 1B; K. Eichenwald and A. Barrionuevo, "Enron Shows Businesses Face Tough Tactics," *The New York Times*, May 27, 2006, pp. A1, B4.

37. See D. R. Dalton and C. M. Dalton, "Sarbanes-Oxley Legislation and the Private Company: If Not a Marriage, Then Certainly an Engagement," *Journal of Business Strategy*, February 2005, pp. 7-8; E. Iwata, "CEOs Report Stricter Rules," *USA Today*, March 20, 2006, p. 1B; D. A. Moore, "SarbOx Doesn't Go Far Enough," *BusinessWeek*, April 17, 2006, p. 112; V. Anand and L. Arnold, "Sarbanes-Oxley Hurts Some Firms, Says GAO," *San Francisco Chronicle*, May 9, 2006, p. C3; J. H. Quigley, "Please Be Patient," *The Wall Street Journal*, May 25, 2006, p. A14; "SOX: No One-Size-Fits-All Solution to Dishonest Accounting," Knowledge@W.P.Carey, June 7, 2006, http://knowledge.wpcarey.asu.edu/index.cfm?fa=viewArticle&id=1259 (accessed June 23, 2006); "Research Supports Value of IT Consults in Post-SOX Age," Knowledge@W.P. Carey, June 7, 2006, http://knowledge.wpcarey.asu.edu/index.cfm?fa=viewArticle&id=1261 (accessed June 23, 2006).

38. F. J. Evans, quoted in C. S. Stewart, "A Question of Ethics: How to Teach Them?" *The New York Times*, March 21, 2004, sec. 3, p. 11.

39. Research by the Center for Academic Integrity, Kenan Institute for Ethics, Duke University, cited in H. Oh, "Biz Majors Get an F for Honesty," *BusinessWeek*, February 6, 2006, p. 14.

40. L. Kohlberg, "Moral Stages and Moralization: The Cognitive-Developmental Approach," in T. Lickona, ed., *Moral Development and Behavior: Theory, Research, and Social Issues* (New York: Holt, Rinehart and Winston, 1976), pp. 31-53; and J. W. Graham, "Leadership, Moral Development and Citizenship Behavior," *Business Ethics Quarterly*, January 1995, pp. 43-54.

41. M. C. Gross, quoted in C. Hymowitz, "CEOs Set the Tone for How to Handle Questions of Ethics," *The Wall Street Journal*, December 22, 1998, p. B1.

42. A. Bennett, "Ethics Codes Spread Despite Criticism," *The Wall Street Journal*, July 15, 1988, p. 13.

43. C. Wiley, "The ABC's of Business Ethics: Definitions, Philosophies, and Implementation," *Industrial Management*, January/February 1995, pp. 22-27.

44. T. R. Mitchell, D. Daniels, H. Hopper, J. George-Falvy, and G. R. Ferris, "Perceived Correlates of Illegal Behavior in Organizations," *Journal of Business Ethics*, April 1996, pp. 439-455. See also M. W., "Ethics Training Works," *Training*, November 2005, p. 15; L. Paine, R. Deshpandé, J. D. Margolis, and K. E. Bettcher, "Up to Code: Does Your Company's Conduct Meet World-Class Standards?" *Harvard Business Review*, December 1, 2005, pp. 122-135; and J. Brockner, "Why It's So Hard to Be Fair," *Harvard Business Review*, March 1, 2006, p. 122-132.

45. R. Pear, "Whistleblowers Likely to Get Stronger Federal Protections," *The New York Times*, March 15, 1999, pp. A1, A17.

46. Study by C. C. Masten, inspector general, U.S. Department of Labor, reported in Pear, 1999.

47. L. Greenhouse, "Some Whistle-Blowers Lose Free-Speech Protections," *The New York Times*, May 31, 2006, p. A14; and D. G. Savage, "Ruling Limits Free Speech at Work," *San Francisco Chronicle*, May 31, 2006, p. A3, reprinted from *Los Angeles Times*. See also "Blow the Whistle, Loudly" [editorial], *The New York Times*, May 31, 2006, p. A22; and "Blow to Whistle-Blowers" [editorial], *San Francisco Chronicle*, June 2, 2006, p. B10.

48. "Tsunami: Anatomy of a Disaster," BBC News, March 27, 2005, http://news.bbc.co.uk/2/hi/science/nature/4381395.stm; and "Asian Tsunami: One Year On," BBC News, December 20, 2005, http://newsforums.bbc.co.uk/nol/thread.jspa?threadID=617&&edition=2&ttl=20060722180237 (both accessed July 22, 2006).

49. C. Chandler, "A Wave of Corporate Charity," *Fortune*, January 24, 2005, pp. 21-22.

50. Ibid.

51. Roper Starch Worldwide Inc. and Cone Communications 1996 survey, reported in Schatz and Poole, 1998.

52. A. B. Carroll, "The Pyramid of Corporate Responsibility: Toward the Moral Management of Organizational Stakeholders," *Business Horizons*, July/August 1991, p. 42.

53. M. Friedman, *Capitalism and Freedom* (Chicago: University of Chicago Press, 1962). See also S. Gallagher, "A Strategic Response to Freidman's Critique of Business Ethics," *Journal of Business Strategy*, January 2005, pp. 55-60.

54. P. Samuelson, "Love that Corporation," *Mountain Bell Magazine*, Spring 1971.

55. A. B. Carroll, *Business & Society: Ethics and Stakeholder Management* (Cincinnati: South-Western, 1989), p. 60.

56. E. Gatewood and A. B. Carroll, "The Anatomy of Corporate Social Response," *Business Horizons*, September–October, 1981, pp. 9-16.

57. D. Eisenberg, "Eyeing the Competition," *Time*, March 22, 1999, pp. 58-59.

58. "Tech Companies to Customers: Privacy Is History" [editorial], *USA Today*, March 12, 1999, p. 14A.

59. J. Collins and J. Porras, *Built to Last: Successful Habits of Visionary Companies* (London: Century Business, 1996).

60. Jed Emerson, quoted in C. Dahle, "60 Seconds with Jed Emerson," *Fast Company*, March 2004, p. 42.

61. J. Emerson, "The Nature of Returns: A Social Capital Markets Inquiry into Elements of Investment and the Blended Value Proposition," *Social Enterprise Series No. 17* (Boston: Harvard Business School Press, 2000), p. 36.

62. T. Howard, "Being Eco-Friendly Can Pay Economically," *USA Today*, August 15, 2005, p. 7B; D. Fonda, "G.E.'s Green Awakening," *Time Inside Business*, August 2005,

pp. AlO–Al6; "The Business of Green" [special section], *The New York Times,* May 17, 2006, pp. El–12.

63. A. Gore, *An Inconvenient Truth* (Emmaus, PA: Rodale, 2006). See also A. Gore and D. Blood, "For People and Planet," *The Wall Street Journal,* March 28, 2006, p. A20.

64. This definition of *sustainability* was developed in 1987 by the World Commission on Environment and Development.

65. M. L. Wald, "What's Kind to Nature Can Be Kind to Products," *The New York Times,* May 17, 2006, pp. El, E5.

66. Wald, 2006, p. E5. See also J. Carroll, "Exxon Faces Pressure over Environment and Gay Rights," *San Francisco Chronicle,* May 31, 2006, p. C3.

67. J. Markoff and S. Lohr, "Gates to Reduce Microsoft Role as Era Changes," *The New York Times,* June 16, 2008, pp. Al, C8; and J. Guynn, "He's Opening Windows to Philanthropy," *San Francisco Chronicle,* June 18, 2006, pp. Fl, F5.

68. T. L. O'Brien and S. Saul, "Buffet to Give Bulk of Fortune to Gates Charity," *The New York Times,* June 26, 2006, pp. Al, Al5; and D. G. McNeil Jr. and R. Lyman, "Buffet's Billions Will Aid Fight Against Disease," *The New York Times,* June 27, 2006, pp. Al, C4.

69. S. LaFraniere, "Business Joins African Effort to Cut Malaria," *The New York Times,* June 29, 2006, pp. Al, A9.

70. A.-A. Jarvis, "Pulling Off an Impressive Feet," *Newsweek,* July 3–10, 2006, p. 64.

71. R. Gildea, "Consumer Survey Confirms Corporate Social Action Affects Buying Decisions," *Public Relations Quarterly,* Winter 1994, pp. 20–21.

72. Caravan survey from Opinion Research developed by LRN of 2,037 adults, reported in "Ethics vs. Price," *USA Today,* June 14, 2006, p. 1B.

73. Results can be found in "Tarnished Employment Brands Affect Recruiting," *HR Magazine,* November 2004, pp. 16, 20.

74. 2003 National Business Ethics Survey, cited in *The Hidden Costs of Unethical Behavior* (Los Angeles: Josephson Institute of Ethics, 2004), p. 3, www.josephsoninstitute.org/ pdf/workplace-flier_0604.pdf (accessed June 23, 2006). See also D. Turban and G. Greening, "Corporate Social Performance and Organizational Attractiveness to Prospective Employees," *Academy of Management Journal,* 40 (1997), pp. 658–672.

75. M. Baucus and D. Baucus, "Paying the Piper: An Empirical Examination of Longer-Term Financial Consequences of Illegal Corporate Behavior," *Academy of Management Journal,* 40 (1997), pp. 129–151.

76. 2003 survey by Wirthlin Worldwide, cited in *The Hidden Costs of Unethical Behavior,* p. 2.

77. 2000 National Business Ethics Survey, cited in *The Hidden Costs of Unethical Behavior,* p. 3.

78. "ACFE's Highly-Anticipated Report to the Nation to Be Published in June," preview of *2006 ACFE Report to the Nation on Occupational Fraud & Abuse,* Association of Certified Fraud Examiners http://www.acfe.com/ announcement-rttn-preview.asp (accessed June 23, 2006).

79. Ernst & Young survey 2002 and KPMG Fraud Survey 2003, both cited in *The Hidden Costs of Unethical Behavior,* p. 2.

80. 2003 survey by Wirthlin Worldwide, cited in *The Hidden Costs of Unethical Behavior,* p. 2.

81. D. M. Long and S. Rao, "The Wealth Effects of Unethical Business Behavior," *Journal of Economics and Finance,* Summer 1995, pp. 65–73.

82. A discussion of ethics and financial performance is provided by R. M. Fulmer, "The Challenge of Ethical Leadership," *Organizational Dynamics,* August 2004, pp. 307–317.

83. J. Cloud, "Why Coors Went Soft," *Time,* November 2, 1998, p. 70. See also J. Ryan, J. Hawdon, and A. Branick, "The Political Economy of Diversity: Diversity Programs in Fortune 500 Companies," *Sociological Research Online,* May 31, 2002, http://www.socresonline.org.uk/7/l/ryan.html; Diversity/Careers, "At Coors, Diverse Markets Help Drive Hiring," http://www.diversitycareers.com/articles/pro/ 04-febmar/dia_coors.htm; and Coors Brewing Company, "Diversity Business Strategy & Implementation Plan," 2002, http://www.coorsjobs.com/diversity/ COORSDIVrevl203.pdf (all accessed July 20, 2006).

84. O. Pollar, "Why Diversity Improves the Bottom Line," *San Francisco Examiner,* November 1, 1998, p. J-1.

85. M. Loden, *Implementing Diversity* (Chicago: Irwin, 1996), pp. 14–15.

86. H. Collingwood, "Who Handles a Diverse Work Force Best?" *Working Woman,* February 1996, p. 25.

87. See A. Karr, "Work Week: A Special News Report about Life on the Job—and Trends Taking Shape There," *The Wall Street Journal,* June 1, 1999, p. Al.

88. B. Schlender, "Peter Drucker Takes the Long View," *Fortune,* September 28, 1998, pp. 162–173.

89. H. W. French, "As China Ages, a Shortage of Cheap Labor Looms," *The New York Times,* June 30, 2006, pp. Al, AlO.

90. T. Henricks, "Country Is Aging a Bit, Becoming More Diverse," *San Francisco Chronicle,* May 10, 2006, p. A4. See also U.S. Census Bureau, "Nation's Population One-Third Minority," U.S. Census Bureau News, May 10, 2006; www.census.gov/Press-Release/www/releases/archives/ population/006808.html (accessed July 1, 2006).

91. E. Porter, "Stretched to Limit, Women Stall March to Work," *The New York Times,* March 2, 2006, pp. Al, C2.

92. I. DeBare, "A Female Success Story," *San Francisco Chronicle,* January 26, 2006, pp. Cl, C2.

93. Study by Hilary Lips, Radford University, reported in B. Morris, "How Corporate America Is Betraying Women," *Fortune,* January 10, 2005, pp. 64–74.

94. Catalyst, cited in Morris, 2005, p. 66.

95. Catalyst, cited in "Breaking into the Boardroom," *The Wall Street Journal,* March 27, 2006, p. B3.

96. J. S. Lublin, "Women at the Top Are Still Distant from CEO Jobs," *The Wall Street Journal,* February 28, 1996, pp. Bl, B4. For further discussion of various aspects of the glass ceiling, see also R. Morris, "To Get Ahead, Own the Store," *The New York Times,* November 18, 2004, p. Cl0; R. E. Herzlinger, "A Corporate Push—Against Women," *USA Today,* December 7, 2004, p. 13A; C. H. Deutsch, "Are Women Responsible for Their Own Low Pay?" *The New York Times,* February 27, 2005, sec. 3, p. 7; T. L. O'Brien, "Up the Down Staircase," *The New York Times,* March 19, 2006, sec. 3, pp. 1, 4; and E. White, "Why Few Women Run Plants," *The Wall Street Journal,* May 1, 2006, pp. Bl, B5.

97. R. Sharpe, "As Leaders, Women Rule," *BusinessWeek,* November 20, 2000, pp. 75–84.

98. K. Wisul, "The Bottom Line on Women at the Top," *BusinessWeek,* January 26, 2004; www.businessweek.com/ bwdaily/dnflash/jan2004/nf20040126_3378_db035.htm (accessed April 7, 2006).

99. U.S. Census Bureau, 2000 Census, cited in National Center for Public Policy and Higher Education, Policy Alert, "Income of U.S. Workforce Project to Decline If Education Does Not Improve," November 2005, p. 2; http://www. highereducation.org/reports/pa_decline/pa_decline.pdf (accessed July 1, 2006).

100. "Worker Health Chartbook 2004," National Institute for Occupational Safety and Health, Table 1-3, NIOSH

Publication No. 2004-146; http://www2.cdc.gov/nioshChartbook/imagedetail.asp?imgid=401 (accessed July 22, 2006).

101. C. DeNavas-Walt, B.D. Proctor, and C. H. Lee, U.S. Census Bureau, Current Population Reports, P60-229, *Income, Poverty, and Health Insurance Coverage in the United States: 2004* (Washington, DC: U.S. Government Printing Office, 2005), Table I; www.census.gov/prod/2005pubs/p60-229.pdf (accessed July 22, 2006).

102. J. I. Sanchez and P. Brock, "Outcomes of Perceived Discrimination among Hispanic Employees: Is Diversity Management a Luxury or a Necessity?" *Academy of Management Journal,* June 1996, pp. 704-719.

103. F. J. Milliken and L. L. Martins, "Searching for Common Threads: Understanding the Multiple Effects of Diversity in Organizational Groups," *Academy of Management Review,* April 1996, pp. 402-433.

104. Results can be found in E. H. James, "Race-Related Differences in Promotions and Support: Underlying Effects of Human and Social Capital," *Organization Science,* September–October 2000, pp. 493-508.

105. Results are reported in C. Daniels, "Young, Gifted, Black—and Out of Here," *Fortune,* May 2004, p. 48.

106. J. S. Passel, "The Size and Characteristics of the Unauthorized Migrant Population in the U.S. : Estimates Based on the March 2005 Current Population Survey," Research Report, Pew Hispanic Center, March 7, 2006; http://pewhispanic.org/files/reports/61.pdf (accessed July 1, 2006).

107. B. Grow, "A Body Blow to Illegal Labor?" *BusinessWeek,* March 27, 2006, pp. 86-87. See also E. Porter, "Who Will Work the Farms?" *The New York Times,* March 23, 2006, pp. C1, C4; A. Goodnough, "Crackdown on Workers Brings Dismay and Anxiety," *The New York Times,* April 22, 2006, p. A8; "Yes, the Law Can Be Enforced, but Will You Like the Result?" [editorial], *USA Today,* April 26, 2006, p. 12A; and A. Bernstein, "Hiring Illegals: Inside the Deal Ahead," *BusinessWeek,* May 29, 2006, pp. 35-36.

108. B. E. Whitley, Jr., and M. E. Kite, "Sex Differences in Attitudes toward Homosexuality: A Comment on Oliver and Hyde (1993)," *Psychological Bulletin,* January 1995, pp. 146-154.

109. October 1, 2003, study by Harris Interactive Inc. and Witeck Combs Communications Inc., reported in C. Edwards, "Coming Out in Corporate America," *BusinessWeek,* December 15, 2003; www.businessweek.com:/print/magazine/content/03_50/b3862080.htm?bw (accessed April 7, 2006).

110. J. M. Croteau, "Research on the Work Experiences of Lesbian, Gay, and Bisexual People: An Integrative Review of Methodology and Findings," *Journal of Vocational Behavior,* April 1996, pp. 195-209; and L. Badgett, "The Wage Effects of Sexual Orientation Discrimination," *Industrial and Labor Relations Review,* July 1995, pp. 726-739.

111. Human Rights Campaign survey, reported in I. DeBare, "Gay, Lesbian Workers Gradually Gain Benefits," *San Francisco Chronicle,* June 30, 2006, pp. D1, D2.

112. D. Braddock and L. Bachelder, *The Glass Ceiling and Persons with Disabilities* (Washington, DC: Glass Ceiling Commission, U.S. Department of Labor, 1994).

113. K. Springen, "A Boost for Braille," *Newsweek,* May 20, 2002, p. 13.

114. D. L. Stone and A. Colella, "A Model of Factors Affecting the Treatment of Disabled Individuals in Organizations," *Academy of Management Review,* April 1996, pp. 352-401; and G. C. Pati and E. K. Baily, "Empowering People with Disabilities: Strategy and Human Resource Issues in Implementing the ADA," *Organizational Dynamics,* Winter 1995, pp. 52-69.

115. Survey by CollegeGrad.com, reported in "Underemployment Affects 18 Percent of Entry Level Job Seekers," September 9, 2004; www.collegegrad.com/press/underemployed.shtml (accessed July 2, 2006).

116. D. C. Feldman and W. H. Turnley, "Underemployment among Recent Business College Graduates," *Journal of Organizational Behavior,* November 1995, pp. 691-706.

117. "High School Dropout Rates," Child Trends DataBank; http://www.childtrendsdatabank.org/indicators/1HighSchoolDropout.cfm (accessed July 23, 2006).

118. "Facts on Literacy," *National Literacy Facts,* August 1998. See also S. Reese, "Illiteracy at Work," *American Demographics,* April 1996, pp. 14-15. Literacy statistics can be found in D. Baynton, "America's $60 Billion Problem," *Training,* May 2001, pp. 51-56.

119. T. L. Smith, "The Resource Center: Finding Solutions for Literacy," *HRFocus,* February 1995, p. 7. See also A. Bernstein, "The Time Bomb in the Workforce: Illiteracy," *BusinessWeek,* Febraury 25, 2002, p. 122.

120. M. Loden, 1996; E. E. Spragins, "Benchmark: The Diverse Work Force," *Inc.,* January 1993, p. 33; and A. M. Morrison, *The New Leaders: Guidelines on Leadership Diversity in America* (San Francisco: Jossey-Bass, 1992).

121. G. Dell'Orto, "Special Classes Help 3M Workers Learn How to Get Along," *San Francisco Chronicle,* June 2, 2000, p. B4.

122. S. Shellenbarger, "Please Send Chocolate: Moms Now Face Stress Moving In and Out of Work Force," *The Wall Street Journal,* May 9, 2002, p. D1. See also A. Bernstein, "Too Many Workers? Not for Long," *BusinessWeek,* May 20, 2002, pp. 126-130.

CHAPTER 4

1. Survey by the Zimmerman Agency for Residence Inn by Marriott, in "Things You Love to Miss," *USA Today,* March 1, 1999, p. 1B.

2. C. Bowman, "Commuter Flier Is No Longer a Rare Bird," *San Francisco Chronicle,* April 12, 1999, pp. A1, A15.

3. P. Saffo, quoted in G. P. Zachary, "It's a Bird. It's a Plane. It's a Commuter!" *San Francisco Examiner,* September 20, 1998, pp. J-1, J-2; reprinted from *The Wall Street Journal.*

4. P. Garfinkel, "Travel Is a Race Won by Seconds," *The New York Times,* July 4, 2006, p. C5.

5. V. Schubert-Martin, quoted in S. Armour and K. L. Alexander, 1997.

6. H. Lancaster, "Global Managers Need Boundless Sensitivity, Rugged Constitutions," *The Wall Street Journal,* October 13, 1998, p. B1.

7. These events are described in K. Maney, "Economy Embraces Truly Global Workplace," *USA Today,* December 31, 1998, pp. 1B, 2B.

8. Cellular Telecommunications Industry Association, cited in A. Dunkin, "Smart, Useful—and They Won't Put a Sag in Your Suit," *BusinessWeek,* May 30, 1994, p. 141.

9. TIA *2006 Telecommunications Marketing Review and Forecast,* cited in "U.S. Wireless Subscriber Level Reaches 194.5 Million in 2005; Expected to Grow to 270 Million by 2009," Telecommunications Industry Association, April 7, 2006; http://www.tiaonline.org/business/media/press_releases/2006/PR06-33.cfm (accessed July 4, 2006).

10. U.S. Central Intelligence Agency, "Field Listing—Internet Users," *The World Factbook,* last updated June 29, 2006; http://www.cia.gov/cia/publications/factbook/fields/2153.html (accessed July 4, 2006).

11. See J. Quittner, "Tim Berners-Lee," *Time,* March 29, 1999, pp. 193–194.

12. Study by Leadpile.com, reported in D. Comiskey, "Report: 2006 Online Retails Sales to Hit $100 Billion," Ecommerce-Guide.com, April 11, 2006; http://www.ecommerce-guide.com/news/trends/article.php/3598281 (accessed July 4, 2006).

13. R. Hof, "Amazon's Brighter Horizon?" BusinessWeek online, April 26, 2006; http://www.businessweek.com/technology/content/apr2006/tc20060426_550117.htm (accessed July 4, 2006).

14. R. M. Kantor, quoted in K. Maney, 1998.

15. Maney, 1998.

16. N. Birdsall, quoted in C. Kleiman, "Global Knowledge Helps in Making Career Decisions," *San Jose Mercury News,* September 24, 1995, p. 1PC.

17. K. Pennar, "Two Steps Forward, One Step Back," *Business-Week,* August 31, 1998, pp. 116–119.

18. Bill Gates, quoted in T. L. Friedman, "U.S. Is Losing the Race to Flatten Globe," *Arizona Republic,* May 4, 2006, p. B9; reprinted from *The New York Times.*

19. C. Smadja, "Living Dangerously," *Time,* February 22, 1999, pp. 94–95. Globalization is a subject of intense debate. Some recent books on the subject are S. B. Berger and the MIT Industrial Performance Center, *How We Compete: What Companies Around the World Are Doing to Make It in Today's Global Economy* (New York: Currency/Doubleday, 2006); D. Cohen, *Globalization and Its Enemies,* J. B. Baker trans. (Cambridge, MA: MIT Press, 2006); J. Faux, *The Global Class War: How America's Bipartisan Elite Lost Our Future—and What It Will Take to Win It Back* (New York: John Wiley, 2006); J. A. Frieden, *Global Capitalism: Its Fall and Rise in the Twentieth Century* (New York: W. W. Norton, 2006); and B. C. Lynn, *End of the Line: The Rise and Coming Fall of the Global Corporation* (New York: Doubleday, 2006). For two antithetical views, see also J. Owens, "Embrace Globalism," *The Wall Street Journal,* April 17, 2006, p. A17; and D. Gross, "Invest Globally, Stagnate Locally," *The New York Times,* April 2, 2006, sec. 3, p. 3.

20. N. Negroponte, quoted in Maney, 1998.

21. A. Sloan, "In the Land of Giants," *Newsweek,* August 10, 1998, pp. 42–43. See also A. Rozens, "Record Year of Mergers Expected," *San Francisco Chronicle,* March 1, 2006, p. C5; D. K. Berman, "Blizzard of Deals Heralds New Era of Megamergers," *The Wall Street Journal,* June 27, 2006, pp. A1, A16.

22. A. R. Sorkin, "Telecom Giants in Europe Plan $30 Billion Deal," *The New York Times,* June 19, 2006, pp. A1, A9.

23. S. Weimer, "Mannequin Madness," California Materials Exchange, Integrated Waste Management Board, April 23, 2004, http://www.ciwmb.ca.gov/CalMAX/Creative/2003/Winter.htm (accessed July 4, 2006); I. DeBare, "New Lease on Life for Mannequins," *San Francisco Chronicle,* July 29, 2006, p. J2; S. L. Thomas, "Warehouse Visit Spawns Mannequin Madness," *East Bay Business Times,* February 24, 2006, http://eastbay.bizjournals.com/eastbay/stories/2006/02/27/smallb1.html (accessed July 4, 2006).

24. L. M. Hughes, quoted in C. Kleiman, "Women Can Raise Their Visibility by Pursuing Overseas Assignments," *San Jose Mercury News,* November 29, 1998, p. PC1; reprinted from *Chicago Tribune.*

25. J. Androshick, quoted in H. Chura, "A Year Abroad (or 3) as a Career Move," *The New York Times,* February 25, 2006, p. B5.

26. T. Chea, "Americans Seek Opportunity in Bangalore," *Reno Gazette-Journal,* April 3, 2006, p. 3E.

27. S. Stapleton, quoted in R. Erlich, "Going Far in the East," *San Francisco Chronicle,* June 24, 2006, pp. C1, C2.

28. R. C. Carter, senior vice president for human resources at A&E Television Networks, quoted in Chura, 2006. For more about Americans working overseas, particularly in India, see J. S. Lublin, "Job Hopping Overseas Can Enhance a Career, but It Takes Fortitude," *The Wall Street Journal,* June 7, 2005, p. B1; N. Lakshman, "Subcontinental Drift," *Business-Week,* January 16, 2006, pp. 42–43; and R. J. Newman, "Coming and Going," *U.S. News & World Report,* January 23, 2006, pp. 50–52.

29. K. Reinhard, quoted in S. McCartney, "Teaching Americans How to Behave Abroad," *The Wall Street Journal,* April 11, 2006, pp. D1, D4.

30. DDB Worldwide survey, cited in J. Clark, "That 'Ugly American' Image Is Getting a Makeover Guide," *USA Today,* April 28, 2006, p. 9D.

31. A. B. Isaacs, "Tact Can Seal a Global Deal . . .," *The New York Times,* July 26, 1998, sec. 3, p. 13.

32. E. Schmitt, "A Man Does Not Ask a Man about His Wife," *The New York Times,* January 8, 2006, sec. 4, p. 7.

33. T. Rivas, "Name Game Hits a Global Roadblock," *The Wall Street Journal,* May 30, 2006, p. B5.

34. T. L. Speer, "Gender Barriers Crumbling, Traveling Business Women Report," *USA Today,* March 16, 1999, p. 5E.

35. The Wats House for Select Appointments, North America, in "Skills in Demand," *USA Today,* July 7, 1998, p. 1B.

36. Anne Fisher, "Readers Weigh In on Work and Women Abroad," *Fortune,* March 29, 1999, p. 200.

37. A. Fisher, "Think Globally, Save Your Job Locally," *Fortune,* February 23, 2004, p. 60.

38. D. A. Heenan and H. V. Perlmutter, *Multinational Organization Development* (Reading, MA: Addison-Wesley, 1979).

39. R. Kopp, "International Human Resource Policies and Practices in Japanese, European, and United States Multinationals," *Human Resource Management,* Winter 1994, pp. 581–599.

40. D. Barboza, "Pluralism under Golden Arches," *The New York Times,* February 12, 1999, pp. C1, C7.

41. S. McCartney, "Who's Inspecting Your Airplane?" *The Wall Street Journal,* March 3, 2004, pp. D1, D12.

42. Study of government data by Economic Policy Institute, Washington, DC, cited in R. Keil and L. Arnold, "New Jobs Created at Low End," *San Francisco Chronicle,* April 13, 2004, p. C5.

43. "Outsourcing Jobs: Is It Bad?" *BusinessWeek,* August 25, 2003, p. 36; "Where Are the Jobs?" *BusinessWeek,* March 22, 2004, p. 37.

44. S. Zuckerman, "Some Jobs May Not Return," *San Francisco Chronicle,* February 22, 2004, pp. I-1, I-14; J. Madrick, "As Job Exports Rise, Some Economists Rethink the Mathematics of Free Trade," *The New York Times,* March 18, 2004, p. C2; J. C. Cooper, "The Price of Efficiency," *BusinessWeek,* March 22, 2004, pp. 38–42; and J. E. Hilsenrath, "Behind Outsourcing Debate: Surprisingly Few Hard Numbers," *The Wall Street Journal,* April 12, 2004, pp. A1, A7.

45. H. R. Varian, "With Free Trade, What Goes Abroad Usually Finds Its Way Back, to Everyone's Benefit," *The New York Times,* March 11, 2004, p. C2.

46. B. Schlender, "Peter Drucker Sets Us Straight," *Fortune,* January 12, 2004, pp. 115–118. See also P. Engardio, "The Future of Outsourcing," *BusinessWeek,* January 30, 2006, pp. 50–58; E. White, "Smaller Companies Join the Outsourcing Trend," *The Wall Street Journal,* May 8, 2006, p. B3; and L. Buchanan, "The Thinking Man's Outsourcing," *Inc. Magazine,* May 2006, pp. 31–33.

47. Forrester Research, "Losing Our Edge? Estimated Number of High-Skilled U.S. Jobs Moving Offshore," reported in K. Madigan, "Yes: This Is No Longer About a Few Low-Wage or Manufacturing Jobs. Now One Out of Three Jobs Is At Risk," *BusinessWeek,* August 25, 2003, pp. 37–38.

48. J. Thottam, "Is Your Job Going Abroad?" *Time,* March 1, 2004, pp. 26–34.

49. F. Levy, quoted in D. Wessel, "The Future of Jobs: New Ones Arise, Wage Gap Widens," *The Wall Street Journal,* April 2, 2004, pp. A1, A5.

50. K. B. Mitchell, quoted in Fisher, 2004.

51. A. M. Chaker, "Where the Jobs Are," *The Wall Street Journal,* March 18, 2004, pp. D1, D3; J. Shinal, "Which Types of Jobs Will Be in Demand?" *San Francisco Chronicle,* March 25, 2004, pp. C1, C4; and D. Wessel, "The Future of Jobs: New Ones Arise, Wage Gap Widens," *The Wall Street Journal,* April 2, 2004, pp. A1, A5.

52. Association for Computing Machinery, reported in C. Kirby, "Tech Jobs Still Plentiful in U.S.," *San Francisco Chronicle,* February 24, 2006, pp. D1, D6.

53. J. Spohrer, quoted in Shinal, 2004.

54. Drucker, quoted in Schlender, 2004.

55. L. Uchitelle, "College Degree Still Pays, but It's Leveling Off," *The New York Times,* January 17, 2005, pp. C1, C2.

56. M. Mendenhall, B. J. Punnett, and D. Ricks, *Global Management* (Cambridge, MA: Blackwell, 1995).

57. U.S. Census Bureau, International Data Base, "IDB—Rank Countries by Population," updated April 26, 2005; http://www.census.gov/ipc/www/idbrank.html (accessed July 4, 2006).

58. R. J. Bowman, "Are You Covered?" *World Trade,* March 1995, pp. 100–104.

59. J. Ewinger, "Steel, Tariffs, and Politics Mix at U.S.-Canada Conference," *Cleveland Plain Dealer,* April 18, 2004; www.cleveland.com/news/plaindealer/index.ssf?/base/news/1082282265327050.xml (accessed April 18, 2006).

60. "China to Cancel Car Import Quota in 2005," *China Daily,* February 13, 2004; www.chinadaily.com.cn/english/doc/2004-02/13/ content_305954.htm (accessed April 18, 2006).

61. J. Bhagwati, *Protectionism* (Cambridge, MA: MIT Press, 1988).

62. "WTO Telecoms Deal Will Ring in the Changes on 5 February 1998," *World Trade Organization,* January 26, 1998.

63. C. Koch, "It's a Wired, Wired World," *Webmaster,* March 1997, pp. 50–55.

64. E. Iritani, "NAFTA 10 Years Later: U.S. Reaps Bittersweet Fruit of Merger," *Los Angeles Times,* January 19, 2004, p. A1.

65. J. Audley, *Learning Lessons Taught by NAFTA* (Washington, DC: Carnegie Endowment for International Peace, 2003); originally published in the *San Diego Union-Tribune,* November 25, 2003; www.ceip.org/files/publications/2003-11-25-sdut.asp (accessed April 20, 2006). See also Iritani, 2004; "Happy Birthday, NAFTA," *BusinessWeek,* December 22, 2003; www.businessweek.com/@@8Im9*4cQBOOUSwOA/magazine/content/03_51/b3863147_mz029.htm (accessed April 20, 2006); J. E. Garten, "At 10, NAFTA Is Ready for an Overhaul," *BusinessWeek,* December 22, 2003; www.businessweek.com/@@8Im9*4cQBOOUSwOA/magazine/content/03_51/b3863044_mz007.htm (accessed April 20, 2006); and G. Smith and C. Lindblad, "Mexico: Was NAFTA Worth It?" *BusinessWeek,* December 22, 2003; www.businessweek.com/@@8Im9*4cQBOOUSwOA/magazine/content/03_51/b3863008.htm (accessed April 20, 2006).

66. F. Vivano, "EU Nations Seek Harmony on Immigrants," *San Francisco Chronicle,* March 5, 1999, p. A10.

67. S. Porjes, "Strengthening Diversity," *International Business,* November 1996, pp. 18–24; and M. Elliott, "Hey, Can You Spare a 'Euro'?" *Newsweek,* February 17, 1997, pp. 48–49.

68. "Fair's Fair" [letters], *West, San Jose Mercury News,* April 4, 1999, pp. 3–4.

69. Peter Lowry, quoted in P. Sarkar, "Big Money Behind Big Malls," *San Francisco Chronicle,* April 9, 2006, pp. G1, G2.

70. "Going Global? Stifle Yourself!" *Training,* August 1995, p. 14.

71. "How Cultures Collide," *Psychology Today,* July 1976, p. 69.

72. See P. R. Harris and R. T. Moran, *Managing Cultural Differences,* 4th ed. (Houston: Gulf Publishing, 1996), pp. 223–228; and M. Hilling, "Avoid Expatriate Culture Shock," *HR Magazine,* July 1993, pp. 58–63.

73. For complete details, see G. Hofstede, *Culture's Consequences: International Differences in Work-Related Values,* abridged ed. (Newbury Park, CA: Sage, 1984); "The Interaction between National and Organizational Value Systems," *Journal of Management Studies,* July 1985, pp. 347–357; and "Management Scientists Are Human," *Management Science,* January 1994, pp. 4–13.

74. M. Javidan and R. J. House, "Cultural Acumen for the Global Manager: Lessons from Project GLOBE," *Organizational Dynamics,* Spring 2001, pp. 289–305; R. J. House, P. J. Hanges, M. Javidan, P. W. Dorfman, and V. Gupta, eds., *Culture, Leadership, and Organizations: The GLOBE Study of 62 Societies* (Thousand Oaks, CA: Sage, 2004); and M. Javidan, P. W. Dorfman, M. S. de Luque, and R. J. House, "In the Eye of the Beholder: Cross Cultural Lessons in Leadership from Project GLOBE," *Academy of Management Perspectives,* February 2006, pp. 67–90.

75. A discussion of Japanese stereotypes in America can be found in L. Smith, "Fear and Loathing of Japan," *Fortune,* February 26, 1990, pp. 50–57.

76. G. A. Michaelson, "Global Gold," *Success,* March 1996, p. 16.

77. Harris Poll, National Foreign Language Center, reported in "Lingua Franca?" *USA Today,* February 23, 1999, p. 1A.

78. D. J. Lynch, "U.S. Firms Becoming Tongue-Tied," *USA Today,* February 9, 2006, p. 6B.

79. "How Cultures Collide," 1976.

80. E. T. Hall, *The Hidden Dimension* (New York: Doubleday, 1966).

81. R. W. Moore, "Time, Culture, and Comparative Management: A Review and Future Direction," in S. B. Prasad, ed., *Advances in Comparative Management,* vol. 5. (Greenwich, CT: JAI Press, 1990), pp. 7–8.

82. R. Wartzman, "In the Wake of NAFTA, a Family Firm Sees the Business Go South," *The Wall Street Journal,* February 23, 1999, pp. A1, A10.

83. C. Woodward, "AP Poll Paints Portrait of Impatient American," *Reno Gazette-Journal,* May 29, 2006, pp. 1C, 7C.

84. Results adapted from and value definitions quoted from S. R. Safranski and I.-W. Kwon, "Religious Groups and Management Value Systems," in R. N. Farner and E. G. McGoun, eds., *Advances in International Comparative Management,* vol. 3 (Greenwich, CT: JAI Press, 1988), pp. 171–183.

85. J. Pohl, "Readers' Views Differ on Buying Japanese," letter to the editor, *Reno Gazette-Journal,* December 5, 2001, p. 9A.

CHAPTER 5

1. P. Sandman, reported in C. J. Farley, "Guarding Against Day-to-Day, Often Deadly Risks," *USA Today,* March 28, 1991, p. 6D.

2. W. F. Vitulli, quoted in R. Bahr, "Stack the Deck," *Men's Health,* August 1991, pp. 82–84.

3. Bahr, 1991.

4. Bahr, 1991.

5. D. G. Myers, *The Pursuit of Happiness: Who Is Happy—and Why* (New York: William Morrow, 1992).

6. R. Kreitner, *Management,* 7th ed. (Boston: Houghton Mifflin, 1998), p. 160.

7. M. Dell, quoted in C. Farkas and P. DeBacker, *Maximum Leadership: The World's Leading CEOs Share Their Five Strategies for Success* (New York: Henry Holt, 1996).

8. Kreitner, 1998, p. 162.

9. R. E. Miles and C. C. Snow, *Organizational Strategy, Structure, and Process* (New York: McGraw-Hill, 1978).

10. Jorma Ollila, quoted in K. Maney, "For CEO Who Remade Nokia, One Bold Departure Deserves Another," *USA Today,* April 5, 2006, p. 3B.

11. Maney, 2006.

12. M. Specter, "The Phone Guy," *The New Yorker,* November 26, 2001, pp. 62–72; and J. Guyon, "Nokia Rocks Its Rivals," *Fortune,* March 4, 2002, pp. 115–118.

13. R. O. Crockett, A. Reinhardt, and M. Ihlwan, "Cell Phones: Who's Calling the Shots?" *BusinessWeek,* April 26, 2004, pp. 48–49.

14. A. R. Sorkin, "Telecom Giants in Europe Plan $30 Billion Deal," *The New York Times,* June 19, 2006, pp. A1, A9; E. Sutherland, "Nokia/Siemens: The New Bully on the Block?" Internetnews.com, June 19, 2006, http://www.internetnews.com/bus-news/article.php/3614521 (accessed July 8, 2006); and "Nokia, Siemens Join Forces," Wired News, June 19, 2006, http://www.wired.com/news/technology/0,71189-0.html?tw=rss.technology (accessed July 8, 2006).

15. D. Pogue, "Going Online on the Go: Options," *The New York Times,* May 6, 2006, pp. E1, E5; T. J. Fitzgerald, "Going Wireless Most Places You Go," *The New York Times,* May 18, 2006, p. C7; and L. Yuan, A. Sharma, and M. Marr, "Cellphone Start-ups Struggle as Media Services Fail to Catch On," *The Wall Street Journal,* June 20, 2006, pp. A1, A16.

16. D. C. Hambrick, "On the Staying Power of Defenders, Analyzers, and Prospectors," *Academy of Management Executive,* November 2003, pp. 115–118. For more about the four basic strategy types, see also D. J. Ketchen Jr., "Introduction: Raymond E. Miles and Charles C. Snow's *Organizational Strategy, Structure, and Process,*" *Academy of Management Executive,* November 2003, pp. 95–96; D. J. Ketchen Jr., "An Interview with Raymond E. Miles and Charles C. Snow," *Academy of Management Executive,* November 2003, pp. 97–104; S. E. Brunk, "From Theory to Practice: Applying Miles and Snow's Ideas to Understand and Improve Firm Performance," *Academy of Management Executive,* November 2003, pp. 105–108; and S. Ghoshal, "Miles and Snow: Enduring Insights for Managers," *Academy of Management Executive,* November 2003, pp. 109–114.

17. D. Leider, "Purposeful Work," *Utne Reader,* July/August 1988, p. 52; excerpted from *On Purpose: A Journal about New Lifestyles & Workstyles,* Winter 1986.

18. P. F. Drucker, *The Practice of Management* (New York: Harper & Row, 1954), p. 122.

19. J. Bezos, "From Zero to 10 Million in Less Than Four Years: Amazon.com to Pass E-Commerce Milestone Today," June 7, 1999, PRNewswire, Amazon.com online press release.

20. P. de Jonge, "Riding the Wild, Perilous Waters of Amazon.com," *New York Times Magazine,* March 14, 1999, pp. 36–41, 54, 68, 79–80; and Amazon.com, AMZN Investor Relations, FAQs, http://phx.corporate-ir.net/phoenix.zhtml?c=97664&p=irol-faq#14296 (accessed July 7, 2006).

21. Amazon.com 2005 Annual Report, reprinting letter from 1997 Annual Report, http://library.coporate-ir.net/library/97/976/97664/items/193688/AMZN2005AnnualReport.pdf (accessed July 7, 2006).

22. Web site, Nest Fresh Eggs, "Cyd's NestFresh," mission statement, http://www.nestfresh.com/story.html (accessed July 27, 2006).

23. T. A. Stewart, "A Refreshing Change: Vision Statements That Make Sense," *Fortune,* September 30, 1996, pp. 195–196.

24. F. Gibney Jr., "Pepsi Gets Back in the Game," *Time,* April 26, 1999, pp. 38–40.

25. For application of vision to nonprofits, see A. Kilpatrick and L. Silverman, "The Power of Vision," *Strategy & Leadership,* February 2005, pp. 24–26.

26. de Jonge, 1999.

27. J. Bezos, quoted in D. Eisenberg, "Now It's One Big Market," *Time,* April 5, 1999, pp. 64–65.

28. Amazon.com 1998 Annual Report. See also Amazon.com, AMZN Investor Relations, FAQs.

29. Nest Fresh Eggs Web site, vision statement.

30. P. J. Below, G. L. Morrisey, and B. L. Acomb, *The Executive Guide to Strategic Planning* (San Francisco: Jossey-Bass, 1987), p. 2.

31. Survey conducted by the Society for Human Resource Management and the Balance Scorecard Collaborative, reported in J. Mullich, "Get in Line," *Workforce Management,* December 2003, pp. 43–44.

32. S. Khan and B. Hansen, "Routes, Type of Fliers Affect Range in Airfare Costs," *USA Today,* May 11, 1999, p. 9B; and B. De Lollis, "Southwest Plans Non-stop, Coast-to-Coast Flights," *USA Today,* May 8, 2002, p. 1B.

33. A. Serwer, "Southwest Airlines: The Hottest Thing in the Sky," *Fortune,* February 23, 2004, www.fortune.com/fortune/subs/article/0,15114,590780,00.html (accessed June 21, 2004).

34. "How Herb Keeps Southwest Hopping," *Money,* June 1999, pp. 61–62.

35. Willie Wilson, quoted in J. Bailey, "On Some Flights, Millionaires Serve the Drinks," *The New York Times,* May 15, 2006, pp. A1, A16.

36. H. Kelleher, quoted in "How Herb Keeps Southwest Hopping," 1999.

37. S. Warren, "Keeping Ahead of the Pack," *The Wall Street Journal,* December 19, 2005, pp. B1, B3; and A. Johnson, "Low-Cost Airlines Raise Fares," *The Wall Street Journal,* April 25, 2006, pp. D1, D3.

38. Adapted from N. Wingield, "At Apple, Secrecy Complicates Life but Maintains Buzz," *The Wall Street Journal,* June 28, 2006, pp. A1, A11.

39. See E. A. Locke and G. P. Latham, "Building a Practically Useful Theory of Goal Setting and Task Motivation," *American Psychologist,* September 2002, pp. 705–717.

40. Drucker, 1954.

41. Lock and Latham, 2002.

42. R. Rodgers and J. E. Hunter, "Impact of Management by Objectives on Organizational Productivity," *Journal of Applied Psychology,* April 1991, pp. 322–336.

43. J. Greene, "Microsoft's Midlife Crisis," *BusinessWeek,* April 19, 2004, pp. 88–98.

44. M. Frishberg, "Microsoft Strategy 'in the Cloud,'" Wired News, June 23, 2006, http://www.wired.com/news/business/1,37178-0.html (accessed July 9, 2006).

45. TheFreeDictionary.com, 2004, http://encyclopedia.thefreedictionary.com/project%20management (accessed June 23, 2004).

46. R. Gandossy, "The Need for Speed," *Journal of Business Strategy,* January/February 2003, pp. 29–33. See also

M. B. Lippitt, "Six Priorities That Make a Great Strategic Decision," *Journal of Business Strategy,* January/February 2003, pp. 21–24.

47. See P. B. Marren, "Business in the Age of Terrorism," *Journal of Business Strategy,* July/August 2002, pp. 19–23.

48. A. Toffler, *Powershift: Knowledge, Wealth, and Violence at the Edge of the 21st Century* (New York: Bantam Books, 1990), pp. 196–197.

49. M. Campbell-Kelly and W. Aspray, *Computer: A History of the Information Machine* (New York: Basic Books, 1996), pp. 253–256.

50. B. Elgin, "Google," *BusinessWeek,* May 3, 2004, pp. 82–90.

51. B. Elgin, "So Much Fanfare, So Few Hits," *BusinessWeek,* July 10, 2006, pp. 26–29; and V. Kopytoff, "In Other Ventures, Google Has to Search Harder for Success," *San Francisco Chronicle,* July 9, 2006, pp. F1, F6.

52. C. Wahlstrom and B. K. Williams, *Learning Success: Being Your Best at College & Life,* 3rd ed. (Belmont, CA: Wadsworth, 2002).

53. C. Shavers, "Detail vs. Strategic Thinking Can Put Workers at Odds," *San Jose Mercury News,* November 1, 1998, p. 3E.

CHAPTER 6

1. D. K. Rigby, "What's Today's Special at the Consultant's Café?" *Fortune,* September 7, 1998, pp. 162–163.

2. D. Rigby and B. Bilodeau, "The Bain 2005 Management Tool Survey," *Strategy & Leadership,* April 2005, pp. 4–12.

3. A. J. Slywotzky and D. J. Morrison, quoted in G. Colvin, "The Most Valuable Quality in a Manager," *Fortune,* December 29, 1997, pp. 279–280.

4. John A. Byrne, "Going Where the Money Is," *BusinessWeek,* January 26, 1998, p. 14; review of A. J. Slywotzky and D. J. Morrison, with B. Andelman, *The Profit Zone* (New York: Times Business, 1998).

5. "Intel vs. TI: Guess Who's the Underdog" *BusinessWeek On-line,* April 26, 2004, www.businessweek.com/technology/content/apr2004/tc20040426_6980_tc119.htm (accessed May 18, 2004); and H. Green, "Intel's Telecom Weapon: WiMax," *BusinessWeek Online,* April 26, 2004, www.businessweek.com/magazine/content/04_17/b3880606.htm (accessed May 18, 2006).

6. Colvin, 1997.

7. J. Pfeffer and R. I. Sutton, "Profiting from Evidence-Based Management," *Strategy & Leadership* 34, no. 2 (2006), pp. 35–42.

8. B. W. Barry, "A Beginner's Guide to Strategic Planning," *The Futurist,* April 1998, pp. 33–36; from B. W. Barry, *Planning Workbook for Nonprofit Organizations* (St. Paul, MN: Amherst H. Wilder Foundation, 1997).

9. A. A. Thompson Jr. and A. J. Strickland III, *Strategic Management: Concepts and Cases,* 6th ed. (Homewood, IL: BPI/Irwin, 1992); and Barry, 1998.

10. N. Byrnes and P. C. Judge, "Internet Anxiety," *BusinessWeek,* June 28, 1999, pp. 79–88.

11. A. Busch III, quoted in interview with G. Hamel, "Turning Your Business Upside Down," *Fortune,* June 23, 1997, pp. 87–88.

12. Barry, 1998. See also L. G. Hrebiniak, "Obstacles to Effective Strategy Implementation," *Organizational Dynamics,* February 2006, pp. 12–31.

13. H. Mintzberg, "The Strategy Concept II: Another Look at Why Organizations Need Strategies," *California Management Review,* vol. 30, no.1, 1987, pp. 25–32.

14. Adapted from M. Myser, "Marketing Made Easy," *Business 2.0,* June 2006, pp. 43–45.

15. G. Hamel, "Killer Strategies That Make Shareholders Rich," *Fortune,* June 23, 1997, pp. 70–84.

16. J. Surowiecki, "The Return of Michael Porter," *Fortune,* February 1, 1999, pp. 135–138.

17. M. E. Porter, "What Is Strategy?" *Harvard Business Review,* November–December 1996, pp. 61–78.

18. Porter, 1996.

19. Byrne, 1998.

20. "Reputation Renewal," *The Wall Street Journal,* March 30, 2004, pp. B1, B7; adopted from R. J. Alsop, *The 18 Immutable Laws of Corporate Reputation: Creating, Protecting, and Repairing Your Most Valuable Asset* (New York: Free Press, 2004).

21. S. V. Brull, "DVD and Conquer: Why One Technology Prevailed," *BusinessWeek,* July 5, 1999, p. 34; J. Brinkley, "Few Tears Are Shed as DivX Joins the 8-Track," *The New York Times,* June 24, 1999, p. D6; M. Fleeman, "Net Flics Soon Will Be Mouse Click Away," *San Francisco Chronicle,* May 31, 1999, pp. E1, E3.

22. D. Pogue, "Why the World Doesn't Need Hi-Def DVD's," *The New York Times,* May 11, 2006, pp. C1, C10; K. Belson, "A Star May Be Fading," *The New York Times,* June 13, 2006, pp. C1, C10; N. Wingfield, "Format Faceoff: Bringing the DVD War Home," *The Wall Street Journal,* June 30, 2006, pp. D1, D5; and S. Manes, "The Next Picture Show," *Forbes,* July 24, 2006, pp. 64–72.

23. W. Disney, quoted in B. Nanus, *Visionary Leadership: Creating a Compelling Sense of Direction for Your Organization* (San Francisco: Jossey-Bass, 1992), p. 28; reprinted from B. Thomas, *Walt Disney: An American Tradition* (New York: Simon & Schuster, 1976), p. 247.

24. C. A. O'Reilly III and M. L. Tushman, "A Clear Eye for Innovation," *Harvard Business School Working Knowledge,* April 26, 2004; excerpted from "The Ambidextrous Organization," *Harvard Business Review,* April 2004, http://hbswk.hbs.edu/item.jhtml?id=4097&t=leadership&nl=y (accessed May 18, 2006).

25. Nanus, 1992, pp. 28–29.

26. R. Kreitner, *Management,* 7th ed. (Boston: Houghton Mifflin, 1998), p. 206.

27. C. H. Roush Jr. and B. C. Ball Jr., "Controlling the Implementation of Strategy," *Managerial Planning,* November–December 1980, p. 4.

28. Barry, 1998.

29. Barry, 1998, p. 36.

30. Booz, Allen & Hamilton study, cited in S. Winston, *The Organized Executive: New Ways to Manage Time, Paper, People & the Electronic Office,* updated and revised for the nineties (New York: W. W. Norton, 1994), p. 152.

31. K. Maher, "Running Meetings," *The Wall Street Journal,* January 13, 2004, p. B6.

32. C. L. Romero, "Tedious Meetings Top Time-Waster," *Arizona Republic,* April 22, 2003, p. D2.

33. P. M. Lencioni, *Death by Meeting: A Leadership Fable . . . About Solving the Most Painful Problem in Business* (San Francisco: Jossey-Bass, 2004).

34. P. Lencioni, reported in D. Murphy, "Making Sense of Meetings," *San Francisco Chronicle,* April 3, 2004, p. 1C.

35. O. Pollar, "Questions on Peers, Time, and Meetings," *San Francisco Examiner,* June 27, 1999, p. J-3.

36. Winston, 1994, pp. 152–157, 163–164; G. English, "How About a Good Word for Meetings?" *Management Review,* June 1990, pp. 58–60; L. G. McDougle, "Conducting a Successful Meeting," *Personnel Journal,* January 1981; D. Batstone, "Right Reality: Most Meetings Stink . . . 5 Tips for Making Yours Useful," The Wag, December 21, 2005,

http://www.reightreality.com/wag_items/issues/05122lwag.html (accessed July 11, 2006); S. G. Rogelberg, D. J. Leach, P. B. Warr, and J. L. Burnfield, "'Not Another Meeting!' Are Meeting Time Demands Related to Employee Well-Being?" *Journal of Applied Psychology,* January 2006, pp. 86–96; and M. Linksky, "The Morning Meeting Ritual," *Harvard Management Communication Letter,* June 19, 2009, http://hbswk.hbs.edu/archieve/5388.html (accessed July 11, 2006).

37. Kreitner, 1998, p. 214.

38. R. Gibson, "Starbucks Holders Wake Up, Smell the Coffee and Sell," *The Wall Street Journal,* July 2, 1999, p. B3; C. Emert, "Why Starbucks Bid for Williams-Sonoma," *San Francisco Chronicle,* June 29, 1999, pp. C1, C7; N. Deogun, "Joe Wakes Up, Smells the Soda," *The Wall Street Journal,* June 8, 1999, pp. B1, B16; C. Burress, "Coffee Heavyweight Rattles Berkeley's 'Gourmet Ghetto,'" *San Francisco Chronicle,* June 1, 1999, p. A12; N. D. Schwartz, "Still Perking After All These Years," *Fortune,* May 24, 1999, pp. 203–210.

39. B. Horovitz, "Starbucks Aims Beyond Lattes to Extend Brand," *USA Today,* May 19, 2006, http://www.usatoday.com/money/industries/food/2006-05-18-starbucks-usat_x.htm (accessed July 11, 2006).

40. "'Commercial Jet Fuel Supply: Impact & Cost on the U.S. Airline Industry' Hearing Scheduled for Wednesday Morning," press release, U.S. House Committee on Transportation and Infrastructure, Washington, DC, February 14, 2006, http://www.house.gov/transportation/press/press2006/release5.html (accessed July 12, 2006).

41. D. Levin, "Hedging Helps Low-Cost Airlines Hold Down Price of Aviation Fuel," *Detroit News,* March 18, 2004, www.detnews.com/2004/business/0403/18/c01-95805.htm (accessed June 7, 2006).

42. T. Romo, quoted in E. Roston, "Hedging Their Costs," *Time,* June 20, 2005, http://www.time.com/time/globalbusiness/article/0.9171,1074147,00.html (accessed July 12, 2006).

43. See K. L. Alexander, "Southwest Pushes Fares Higher, Blaming Fuel Costs," *Washington Post,* July 6, 2006, p. D1.

44. M. E. Porter, *Competitive Strategy* (New York: The Free Press, 1980).

45. Example from Michael J. Silverstein, *Treasure Hunt,* cited in M. Archer, "Author Finds 'Value Calculus' at Work," *USA Today,* June 12, 2006, p. 7B.

46. P. L. Brown, "Surfers in Turmoil with the Loss of a Major Supplier," *The New York Times,* December 30, 2006, p. A12; and M. Overfelt, "Rough Surf," *USA Today,* February 17, 2006, http://money.cnn.com/magazines/fsb/fsb_archive/2006/02/01/8368201/index.htm (accessed July 12, 2006).

47. L. Rohter, "With Big Boost from Sugar Cane, Brazil Is Satisfying Its Fuel Needs," *The New York Times,* April 10, 2006, p. A1.

48. J. Greenberg, quoted in B. Horovitz, "Restoring the Golden-Arch Shine," *USA Today,* June 16, 1999, p. 3B.

49. Horovitz, 1999.

50. P. Connors, "J&J Decides to Discontinue Its Hismanal," *The Wall Street Journal,* June 22, 1999, p. B9.

51. M. Arndt, "A Tall Order for McDonald's New Chief," *Business-Week Online,* April 20, 2004, www.businessweek.com/bwdaily/dnflash/apr2004/nf20040420_7253_db035.htm (accessed May 18, 2006); Associated Press, "McDonald's Pulls Spicy Chicken Sandwich," BusinessWeek Online, July 12, 2006: http://www.businessweek.com/ap/financialnews/D8IQM4S85.htm?chan=search (accessed July 28, 2006); and Dave Carpenter, "McDonald's Stock Up on 2Q Profit Forecast," BusinessWeek Online, July 17, 2006; http://www.businessweek.com/ap/financialnews/D8ITVBH80.htm?chan=search (accessed July 28, 2006).

52. R. S. Kaplan and D. P. Norton, "The Balanced Scorecard—Measures that Drive Performance," *Harvard Business Review,* January–February 1992, pp. 71–79.

53. "The End Again for Indian Motorcycle Corporation," *American Motorcycle Network,* September 22, 2003, www.americanmotor.com/news.cfm?newsid=2236 (accessed May 20, 2006).

54. L. Bossidy and Ram Charan, with C. Burck, *Execution: The Discipline of Getting Things Done* (New York: Crown Business, 2002).

55. Bossidy and Charan, 2002, pp. 27–28.

56. Bossidy and Charan, 2002, p. 86.

CHAPTER 7

1. H. Lancaster, "How Life Lessons Have Helped a Successful Manager," *San Francisco Sunday Examiner & Chronicle,* August 15, 1999, p. CL-33; reprinted from *The Wall Street Journal.*

2. R. L. Keeney, reported in D. Murphy, "When to Make Decisions—or Delay Them," *San Francisco Examiner,* December 6, 1998, p. J-2.

3. O. Pollar, "Six Steps for Making Tough Choices," *San Francisco Examiner and Chronicle,* April 4, 1999, p. J-3.

4. P. Thomas, "Be Prepared for Surges of a Volatile Business," *The Wall Street Journal,* May 11, 2004, p. B4; and "Windowbox.com: Making the World a Better Place; Ben Swett—Founder & CEO Biography," www.windowbox.com/contact/pr_benbio.html (accessed May 29, 2006).

5. A. S. Grove, *High Output Management* (New York: Random House, 1983), p. 98.

6. Thomas, 2004.

7. Thomas, 2004.

8. Muriel Niederle, quoted in J. Tierney, "What Women Want," *The New York Times,* May 24, 2005, p. A25.

9. M. Niederle and L. Vesterlund, "Do Women Shy Away from Competition? Do Men Compete Too Much?" May 30, 2006, conditionally accepted subject to minor revisions at the *Quarterly Journal of Economics,* http://www.stanford.edu/~niederle/Women.Competition.pdf (accessed July 16, 2006).

10. The discussion of styles was based on material contained in A. J. Rowe and R. O. Mason, *Managing with Style: A Guide to Understanding, Assessing and Improving Decision Making* (San Francisco: Jossey-Bass, 1987), pp. 1–17.

11. See Rowe and Mason, 1987; and M. J. Dollinger and W. Danis, "Preferred Decision-Making Styles: A Cross-Cultural Comparison," *Psychological Reports,* 1998, pp. 755–761; and K. R. Brousseau, M. J. Driver, G. Hourihan, and R. Larsson, "The Seasoned Executive's Decision-Making Style," *Harvard Business Review,* February 2006, p. 111, http://custom.hbsp.com/custom/KORNFRO602F2006012769.pdf;jsessionid=BBCU302NQJFKOAKRGWCB5VQBKEOYIIPS (accessed July 16, 2006).

12. Q. Hardy, "Iridium Shares Fall After News of Missed Goals," *The Wall Street Journal,* May 17, 1999, p. B6; D. Barboza, "Motorola Rolls Itself Over," *The New York Times,* July 14, 1999, pp. C1, C2; S. Rosenbush, "Iridium Bets on New Structure," *USA Today,* August 4, 1999, p. 3B; L. Cauley, "Iridium's Downfall: The Marketing Took a Back Seat to Science," *The Wall Street Journal,* August 18, 1999, pp. A1, A6; and M. B. Lippitt, "Six Priorities That Make a Great Strategic Decision," *Journal of Business Strategy,* January–February 2003, pp. 21–24.

13. K. Liebeskind, "In the Fast Lane," *Selling Power,* September 1997, pp. 16–17.

14. A. Farnham, "Teaching Creativity Tricks to Buttoned-Down Executives," *Fortune,* January 10, 1994, pp. 94–100.

15. I. DeBare, "The Business May Change, but the Values Are the Same," *San Francisco Chronicle,* April 2, 2006, p. G5.

16. C. Hymowitz, "Everyone Likes to Laud Service to the Customer; Doing It Is the Problem," *The Wall Street Journal,* February 27, 2006, p. B1.

17. The Retail Customer Dissatisfaction Study 2006, conducted by the Jay H. Baker Retailing Initiative, Wharton, University of Pennsylvania, and the Verde Group, Toronto, reported in "Beware of Dissatisfied Customers: They Like to Blab," Knowledge@Wharton, http://knowledge.wharton.upenn.edu/index (accessed July 15, 2006).

18. Hymowitz, 2006.

19. S. Holmes, "The 787 Encounters Turbulence," *BusinessWeek,* June 19, 2006, pp. 38-40. See also S. Holmes, "Cleaning Up Boeing," *BusinessWeek,* March 13, 2006, pp. 63-68; and S. Holmes, "Boeing Straightens Up and Flies Right," *BusinessWeek,* May 8, 2006, pp. 69-70.

20. H. A. Simon, *Administrative Behavior,* 3rd ed. (New York: Free Press, 1996); and H. A. Simon, "Making Management Decisions: The Role of Intuition and Emotion," *The Academy of Management Executive,* February 1987, pp. 57-63.

21. W. Miller, "Building the Ultimate Resource," *Management Review,* January 1999, pp. 42-45; J. S. Brown and P. Duguid, "Balancing Act: How to Capture Knowledge without Killing It," *Harvard Business Review,* May-June 2000, pp. 73-80; and D. W. De Long and P. Seemann, "Confronting Conceptual Confusion and Conflict in Knowledge Management," *Organizational Dynamics,* Summer 2000, p. 33.

22. S. A. Akhter, "Strategic Planning, Hypercompetition, and Knowledge Management," *Business Horizons,* January-February 2003, pp. 19-24.

23. R. Lubit, "Tacit Knowledge and Knowledge Management: The Keys to Sustainable Competitive Advantage," *Organizational Dynamics* 29, no. 3(2001), pp. 164-178.

24. P. Babcock, "Shedding Light on Knowledge Management," *HR Magazine,* May 2004, pp. 47-50.

25. A. Mulcahy, quoted in E. E. Gordon, "Bridging the Gap," *Training,* September 2003, p. 32.

26. J. Pfeffer and R. I. Sutton, "Profiting from Evidence-Based Management," *Strategy & Leadership,* 34, no. 2(2006), pp. 35-42; and J. Pfeffer and R. I. Sutton, "Evidence-Based Management," *Harvard Business Review,* January 2006, pp. 63-74. Pfeffer and Sutton have also produced a book, *Hard Facts, Dangerous Half-Truths, and Total Nonsense* (Cambridge, MA: Harvard Business School Press, 2006). For a discussion of the book, see C. Hymowitz, "Executives Must Stop Jumping Fad to Fad and Learn to Manage," *The Wall Street Journal,* May 15, 2006, p. B1.

27. D. M. Rousseau, "Is There Such a Thing as 'Evidence-Based Management'?" *Academy of Management Review,* April 2006, pp. 256-269.

28. Pfeffer and Sutton, "Profiting from Evidence-Based Management," 2006.

29. R. I. Sutton, interviewed in "Asked & Answered: Prove It," *Stanford Magazine,* May/June 2006, http://www.stanfordalumni.org/news/magazine/2006/mayjun/dept/management.html (accessed July 15, 2006).

30. Pfeffer and Sutton, "Profiting from Evidence-Based Management," 2006.

31. Pfeffer and Sutton, "Evidence-Based Management," 2006, pp. 66-67.

32. G. Loveman, "Diamonds in the Data Mine," *Harvard Business Review,* May 2003, pp. 109-113. See also G. Loveman, *Diamonds in the Data Mine* (Cambridge, MA: Harvard Business School Press, 2003).

33. T. H. Davenport, "Competing on Analytics," *Harvard Business Review,* January 2006, pp. 99-107.

34. M. Lewis, *Moneyball: The Art of Winning an Unfair Game* (New York: W.W. Norton, 2004).

35. For comment on the Oakland A's and *Moneyball,* see J. Manuel, "Majoring in Moneyball," Baseball America Features, December 23, 2003, http://www.baseballamerica.com/today/features/031223collegemoneyball.html; J. Zasky, "Pay for Performance, Stupid," *Failure Magazine,* June 2003, http://failuremag.com/archives_business_sports_moneyball.html; R. Van Zandt, "Billy Beane's Perfect Draft: A Baseball Revolution?" BaseballEvolution.com, April 13, 2006, http://baseballevolution.com/guest/richard/rvzbeanel.html; and "Moneyball: The Art of Winning an Unfair Game," Wikipedia, July 12, 2006, http://en.wikipedia.org/wiki/Moneyball (all accessed July 14, 2006).

36. Davenport, 2006.

37. M. B. Zuckerman, "Policing the Corporate Suites," *U.S. News & World Report,* January 19, 2004, p. 72.

38. C. McNamara, "Complete Guide to Ethics Management: An Ethics Toolkit for Managers," www.mapnp.org/library/ethics/ethxgde.htm (accessed May 29, 2006).

39. C. E. Bagley, "The Ethical Leader's Decision Tree," *Harvard Business Review,* February 2003, pp. 18-19.

40. A.-M. Cusac, "U.S. Companies Trick Retirees out of Health Benefits," *UNI In Depth,* September 4, 2001, www.union-network.org/uniindep.nsf/0/54491a47e00ad956c1256a2900282ebe?OpenDocument (accessed May 29, 2006).

41. J. Appleby, "More Companies Trim Retiree Health Benefits," *USATODAY.com,* January 14, 2004, www.usatoday.com/money/industries/health/2004-01-15-retiree_x.htm (accessed May 29, 2006).

42. Bagley, 2003, p. 19.

43. K. Hodgson, *A Rock and a Hard Place: How to Make Ethical Business Decisions When the Choices Are Tough* (New York: AMACOM, 1992), pp. 66-77.

44. G. W. Hill, "Group versus Individual Performance: Are $n + 1$ Heads Better Than 1?" *Psychological Bulletin,* May 1982, pp. 517-539.

45. N. F. R. Maier, "Assets and Liabilities in Group Problem Solving: The Need for Integrative Function," *Psychological Review* 74(1967) pp. 239-249.

46. Maier, 1967.

47. Methods for increasing group consensus were investigated by R. L. Priem, D. A. Harrison, and N. K. Muir, "Structured Conflict and Consensus Outcomes in Group Decision Making," *Journal of Management,* December 22, 1995, pp. 691-710.

48. See D. L. Gladstein and N. P. Reilly, "Group Decision Making under Threat: The Tycoon Game," *Academy of Management Journal,* September 1985, pp. 613-627.

49. These conclusions were based on the following studies: J. H. Davis, "Some Compelling Intuitions about Group Consensus Decisions, Theoretical and Empirical Research, and Interpersonal Aggregation Phenomena: Selected Examples, 1950-1990," *Organizational Behavior and Human Decision Processes,* June 1992, pp. 3-38; and J. A. Sniezek, "Groups Under Uncertainty: An Examination of Confidence in Group Decision Making," *Organizational Behavior and Human Decision Processes,* June 1992, pp. 124-155.

50. Supporting results can be found in J. R. Hollenbeck, D. R. Ilgen, D. J. Sego, J. Hedlund, D. A. Major, and J. Phillips, "Multilevel Theory of Team Decision Making: Decision Performance in Teams Incorporating Distributed Expertise," *Journal of Applied Psychology,* April 1995, pp. 292-316.

51. See D. H. Gruenfeld, E. A. Mannix, K. Y. Williams, and M. A. Neale, "Group Composition and Decision Making: How

Member Familiarity and Information Distribution Affect Process and Performance," *Organizational Behavior and Human Decision Processes,* July 1996, pp. 1–15.

52. "Jack Welch's Lessons for Success," *Fortune,* January 25, 1993, p. 86.

53. See D. Pojidaeff, "Human Productivity and Pride in Work: The Core Principles of Participative Management," *Journal for Quality and Participation,* December 1995, pp. 44–47; and N. A. Holland, "A Pathway to Global Competitiveness and Total Quality: Participative Management," *Journal for Quality and Participation,* September 1995, pp. 58–62.

54. Results are presented in J. T. Delaney, "Workplace Cooperation: Current Problems, New Approaches," *Journal of Labor Research,* Winter 1996, pp. 45–61.

55. For an extended discussion, see M. Sashkin, "Participative Management Is an Ethical Imperative," *Organizational Dynamics,* Spring 1984, pp. 4–22.

56. Supporting results can be found in C. R. Leana, R. S. Ahlbrandt, and A. J. Murrell, "The Effects of Employee Involvement Programs on Unionized Workers' Attitudes, Perceptions, and Preferences in Decision Making," *Academy of Management Journal,* October 1992, pp. 861–873; and D. Plunkett, "The Creative Organization: An Empirical Investigation of the Importance of Participation in Decision Making," *Journal of Creative Behavior,* Second Quarter 1990, pp. 140–148. Results pertaining to role conflict and ambiguity can be found in C. S. Smith and M. T. Brannick, "A Role Replication and Theoretical Extension," *Journal of Organizational Behavior,* March 1990, pp. 91–104.

57. See J. A. Wagner III, "Participation's Effects on Performance and Satisfaction: A Reconsideration of Research Evidence," *Academy of Management Review,* April 1994, pp. 312–330.

58. A thorough discussion of this issue is provided by W. A. Randolph, "Navigating the Journey to Empowerment," *Organizational Dynamics,* Spring 1995, pp. 19–32.

59. G. M. Parker, *Team Players and Teamwork: The New Competitive Business Strategy* (San Francisco: Jossey-Bass, 1990).

60. These recommendations were obtained from G. M. Parker, *Team Players and Teamwork.*

61. A. F. Osborn, *Applied Imagination: Principles and Procedures of Creative Thinking,* 3rd ed. (New York: Scribners, 1979). See also W. H. Cooper, R. Brent Gallupe, S. Pollard, and J. Cadsby, "Some Liberating Effects of Anonymous Electronic Brainstorming," *Small Group Research,* April 1998, pp. 147–178.

62. A complete description of the nominal group technique can be found in A. L. Delbecq, A. H. Van de Ven, and D. H. Gustafson, *Group Techniques for Program Planning: A Guide to Nominal Group and Delphi Processes* (Glenview, IL: Scott Foresman, 1975).

63. See N. C. Dalkey, D. L. Rourke, R. Lewis, and D. Snyder, *Studies in the Quality of Life: Delphi and Decision Making* (Lexington, MA: Lexington Books, 1972).

64. Benefits of the Delphi technique are discussed by N. I. Whitman, "The Committee Meeting Alternative: Using the Delphi Technique," *Journal of Nursing Administration,* July–August 1990, pp. 30–36.

65. A thorough description of computer-aided decision-making systems is provided by M. C. Er and A. C. Ng, "The Anonymity and Proximity Factors in Group Decision Support Systems," *Decision Support Systems,* May 1995, pp. 75–83; and A. LaPlante, "Brainstorming," *Forbes,* October 25, 1993, pp. 45–61.

66. Results can be found in J. S. Valacich and C. Schwenk, "Devils' Advocacy and Dialectical Inquiry Effects on Face-to-Face and Computer-Mediated Group Decision Making," *Organizational Behavior and Human Decision Processes,*

August 1995, pp. 158–173; R. B. Gallupe, W. H. Cooper, M. Grise, and L. M. Bastianutti, "Blocking Electronic Brainstorms," *Journal of Applied Psychology,* February 1994, pp. 77–86; and A. R. Dennis and J. S. Valacich, "Computer Brainstorms: More Heads Are Better Than One," *Journal of Applied Psychology,* August 1993, pp. 531–537.

67. L. Thompson, "Improving the Creativity of Organizational Work Groups," *Academy of Management Executive,* February 2003, pp. 96–109.

68. Applications of the Delphi technique can be found in A. Alahlafi and S. Burge, "What Should Undergraduate Medical Students Know about Psoriasis? Involving Patients in Curriculum Development: Modified Delphi Technique," *British Medical Journal,* March 19, 2005, pp. 633–636; and A. M. Deshpande, R. N. Shiffman, and P. M. Nadkarni, "Metadata-Drive Delphi Rating on the Internet," *Computer Methods and Programs in Biomedicine,* January 2005, pp. 49–56.

69. Supportive results can be found in S. S. Lam and J. Schaubroeck, "Improving Group Decisions by Better Polling Information: A Comparative Advantage of Group Decision Support Systems," *Journal of Applied Psychology,* August 2000, pp. 565–573; and I. Benbasat and J. Lim, "Information Technology Support for Debiasing Group Judgments: An Empirical Evaluation," *Organizational Behavior and Human Decision Processes,* September 2000, pp. 167–183.

70. B. B. Baltes, M. W. Dickson, M. P. Sherman, C. C. Bauer, and J. S. LaGanke, "Computer-Mediated Communication and Group Decision Making: A Meta-Analysis," *Organizational Behavior and Human Decision Processes,* January 2002, pp. 156–179.

71. A description of the work of Daniel Gilbert appears in P. J. Hilts, "In Forecasting Their Emotions, Most People Flunk Out," *The New York Times,* February 16, 1999, p. D2.

72. D. D. Wheeler and I. L. Janis, *A Practical Guide for Making Decisions* (New York: Free Press, 1980), pp. 34–35; and I. L. Janis and L. Mann, *Decision Making: A Psychological Analysis of Conflict, Choice, and Commitment* (New York: The Free Press, 1977).

73. H. Lancaster, "Academics Have to Do Their Own Homework on Job Opportunities," *The Wall Street Journal,* July 13, 1999, p. B1.

74. E. Porter and G. Winter, "'04 Graduates Learned Lesson in Practicality," *The New York Times,* May 30, 2004, sec. 1, pp. 1, 18.

75. A. Levin and L. Parker, "Human, Mechanical Flaws Cut Off Path to Survival," *USA Today,* July 12, 1999, pp. 1A, 8A, 9A. Sometimes observers speak of a "fog of war," in which too much information or scattered information overwhelms decision-making abilities. See, for example, E. Lipson, "Hurricane Investigators See 'Fog of War' at White House," *The New York Times,* January 28, 2006, p. A8. Decision makers may also often be unable to discriminate between relevant and irrelevant alternatives, including extraneous considerations in their probability judgments. See M. R. Dougherty and A. Sprenger, "The Influence of Improper Sets of Information on Judgment: How Irrelevant Information Can Bias Judged Probability," *Journal of Experimental Psychology: General,* May 2006, pp. 262–281.

76. Wheeler and Janis, 1980.

77. M. Mangalindan, "PayPal Prepares for a Challenge from Google," *The Wall Street Journal,* February 6, 2006, pp. B1, B3.

78. D. Kahnemann and A. Tversky, "Judgment under Uncertainty: Heuristics and Biases," *Science* 185(1974), pp. 1124–1131; A. Tversky and D. Kahneman, "Availability: A Heuristic for Judging Frequency and Probability," *Cognitive Psychology*

5(1975), pp. 207–232; A. Tversky and D. Kahneman, "The Belief in the Law of Numbers," *Psychological Bulletin* 76(1971), pp. 105–110; C. R. Schwenk, "Cognitive Simplification Processes in Strategic Decision Making," *Strategic Management Journal* 5(1984), pp. 111–128; K. McKean, "Decisions," *Discover,* June 1985, pp. 22–31; J. Rockner, "The Escalation of Commitment to a Failing Course of Action: Toward Theoretical Progress," *Academy of Management Review* 17(1980), pp. 39–61; D. R. Bobocel and J. P. Meyer, "Escalating Commitment to a Failing Course of Action: Separating the Roles of Choice and Justification," *Journal of Applied Psychology,* June 1994, pp. 360–363; B. M. Shaw, "The Escalation of Commitment to a Course of Action," *Academy of Management Review,* October 1981, pp. 577–587; and M. Useem and J. Useem, "Great Escapes," *Fortune,* June 27, 2005, pp. 97–102; and J. T. Horn, D. P. Lovallo, and S. P. Viguerie, "Learning to Let Go: Making Better Exit Decisions," *The McKinley Quarterly,* no. 2, 2006, http://www.mckinseyquarterly.com/article_page.aspx?ar=1768&L2=21&L3=37 (accessed July 16, 2006).

79. W. Goodman, "How Gambling Makes Strange Bedfellows," *The New York Times,* June 10, 1997, p. B3.

80. P. Slovic, "The Construction of a Preference," *American Psychologist* 50(1995), pp. 364–371; K. J. Dunegan, "Framing, Cognitive Roles, and Image Theory: Toward an Understanding of a Glass Half Full," *Journal of Applied Psychology* 78(1993), pp. 491–503 and K. F. E. Wong, M. Yik, and J. Y. Y. Kwong, "Understanding the Emotional Aspects of Escalation of Commitment: The Role of Negative Affect," *Journal of Applied Psychology,* March 2006, pp. 282–297.

81. S. Thurm, "Seldom-Used Executive Power: Reconsidering," *The Wall Street Journal,* February 6, 2006, p. B3.

82. M. H. Bazerman, *Judgment in Managerial Decision Making* (New York: Wiley, 1990); D. E. Vell, H. Raiffa, and A. Tversky, *Decision Making* (Cambridge, UK: Cambridge University Press, 1988).

83. H. J. Einhorn and R. M. Hogarth, "Confidence in Judgment: Persistence in the Illusion of Validity," *Psychological Review* 85(1978), pp. 395–416.

84. B. Fischoff, "Hindsight≠Foresight: The Effect of Outcome Knowledge on Judgment under Uncertainty," *Journal of Experimental Psychology: Human Perception and Performance* 1(1975), pp. 288–299.

CHAPTER 8

1. Development Dimension International (DDI) Global Leadership Forecast of 4,561 respondents from 42 countries, reported in "Mentoring Impact," *USA Today,* March 22, 2006, p. 1B.

2. M. Cottle, "Minding Your Mentors," *The New York Times,* March 7, 1999, sec. 3, p. 8; C. Dahle, "HP's Mentor Connection," *Fast Company,* November 1998, pp. 78–80; I. Abbott, "If You Want to Be an Effective Mentor, Consider These Tips," *San Francisco Examiner,* October 18, 1998, p. J-3; D. A. Thomas, "The Truth about Mentoring Minorities—Race Matters," *Harvard Business Review,* April 2001, pp. 99–107; J. E. Wallace, "The Benefits of Mentoring for Female Lawyers," *Journal of Vocational Behavior,* June 2001, pp. 366–391; S. A. Mehta, "Best Companies for Minorities: Why Mentoring Works," *Fortune,* July 9, 2001, www.fortune.com/fortune/diversity/articles/0,15114,370475,00.html (accessed July 4, 2006); F. Warner, "Inside Intel's Mentoring Movement," *Fast Company,* April 2002, p. 116; B. Raabe and T. A. Beehr, "Formal Mentoring versus Supervisor and Coworker Relationships: Differences in Perceptions and Impact," *Journal of Organizational Behavior* 24 (2003), pp. 271–293; and A. Fisher, "A New Kind of Mentor," *Fortune,* July 28, 2004, www.fortune.com/fortune/annie/0,15704,368863,00.html (accessed July 4, 2006).

3. A. E. Hayden, quoted in Cottle, 1999.

4. C. Hymowitz, "Today's Bosses Find Mentoring Isn't Worth the Time and the Risks," *The Wall Street Journal,* March 13, 2006, p. B1.

5. K. K. Reardon, *The Secret Handshake: Mastering the Politics of the Business Inner Circle* (New York: Doubleday, 2002) and *It's All Politics: Winning in a World Where Hard Work and Talent Aren't Enough* (New York: Currency/Random House, 2005).

6. K. K. Reardon, interviewed by J. Vishnevsky, "Ask the Expert: Kathleen Kelley Reardon," *U.S. News & World Report,* July 25, 2005, p. EE10. See also C. Bush, "Learn How to Work with Others," *Arizona Republic,* August 21, 2005, p. EC1.

7. E. H. Schein, "Organizational Culture," *American Psychologist,* 45 (1990), pp. 109–119; E. H. Schein, *Organizational Culture and Leadership* (San Francisco: Jossey-Bass, 1985); and E. H. Schein, "The Role of the Founder in Creating Organizational Culture," *Organizational Dynamics,* Summer 1983, pp. 13–28.

8. B. Breen, "The Thrill of Defeat," *Fast Company,* June 2004, pp. 76–81. A comprehensive article about companies that cultivate cultures that embrace failure and learn from it is J. McGregor, "How Failure Breeds Success," *BusinessWeek,* July 10, 2006, pp. 42–52.

9. S. S. Watkins, in testimony before the Oversight and Investigations Subcommittee of the House Energy and Commerce Committee, U.S. Congress, February 14, 2002.

10. G. L. Neilson, B. A. Pasternack, and K. E. Van Nuys, "The Passive-Aggressive Organization," *Harvard Business Review,* October 2005, pp. 83–94.

11. Reward systems are discussed in J. Kerr and J. W. Slocum, "Managing Corporate Culture through Reward Systems," *Academy of Management Executive,* November 2005, pp. 130–138.

12. See C. Ostroff, A. Kinicki, and J. Tamkins, "Organizational Culture and Climate," in W. C. Borman, D. R. Ilgen, and R. J. Klimoski, eds., *Handbook of Psychology,* vol. 12 (New York: John Wiley & Sons, 2003), pp. 565–593.

13. P. Burrows, "Carly's Last Stand?" *BusinessWeek,* December 24, 2001, pp. 63–70; and R. Gaitonde, "An Analysis of HP's Future Strategy, Post Carly Fiorina," *OS News,* February 2, 2005; http://www.osnews.com/story.php?news_id=9810 (accessed August 3, 2006).

14. T. E. Deal and A. A. Kennedy, *Corporate Cultures: The Rites and Rituals of Corporate Life* (Reading, MA: Addison-Wesley, 1982), p. 22.

15. R. Jacob, "Corporate Reputations: The Winners Chart a Course of Constant Renewal and Work to Sustain Cultures that Produce the Very Best Products and People," *Fortune,* March 6, 1995, pp. 54–64.

16. D. Maraniss, "Lombardi's Way," *Vanity Fair,* September 1999, pp. 206–226, 231–246; excerpted from D. Maraniss, *When Pride Still Mattered: A Life of Vince Lombardi* (New York: Simon & Schuster, 1999).

17. A. Farnham, "Mary Kay's Lessons in Leadership," *Fortune,* September 20, 1993, pp. 68–77.

18. Deal and Kennedy, 1982.

19. Adapted from L. Smircich, "Concepts of Culture and Organizational Analysis," *Administrative Science Quarterly,* September 1983, pp. 339–358.

20. S. McCarney, "Airline Industry's Top-Rated Woman Keeps Southwest's Small-Fry Spirit Alive," *The Wall Street Journal,* November 30, 1996, pp. B1, B11.

21. D. Anfuso, "3M's Staffing Strategy Promotes Productivity and Pride," *Personnel Journal,* February 1995, pp. 28–34.

22. J. and S. Welch, "Dear Graduate . . . ," *BusinessWeek,* June 19, 2006, p. 100.

23. E. Holton, S. Naquin, and E. Holton, *So You're New Again: How to Succeed When You Change Jobs* (San Francisco: Berrett-Koehler Publishers, 2001); M. Watkins, *The First 90 Days: Critical Success Strategies for New Leaders at All Levels* (Watertown, MA: Harvard Business School Press, 2003); J. S. Lublin, "How to Win Support from Colleagues at Your New Job," *The Wall Street Journal,* November 25, 2003, p. B1; and "Dip, Before Diving, into That New Job," *Business-Week Online,* July 3, 2004, http://www.businessweek.com/bschools/content/jun2004/bs20040628_9967_bs001.htm (accessed August 4, 2006).

24. M. Sunnafrank and A. Ramirez Jr., "At First Sight: Persistent Relational Effects of Get-Acquainted Conversations," *Journal of Social and Personal Relationships,* June 1, 2004, pp. 361–379. See also J. Zaslow, "First Impressions Get Faster," *The Wall Street Journal,* February 16, 2006, p. D4.

25. G. Lingaard, G. Fernandes, C. Dudek, and J. Brown, "Attention Web Designers: You Have 50 Milliseconds to Make a Good First Impression," *Behaviour & Information Technology,* March–April 2006, pp. 115–126.

26. R. Ailes, in "Your First Seven Seconds," *Fast Company,* June–July 1998, p. 184.

27. J. Denrell, "Why Most People Disapprove of Me: Experience Sampling in Impression Formation," *Psychological Review,* October 2005, pp. 951–978. See also M. Krakovsky, "Researcher Disputes Notion You Have Only One Chance to Make a Good Impression," *Stanford Report,* August 18, 2004, http://newsservice.stanford.edu/news/2004/august18/impressions-818.html (accessed August 4, 2006).

28. L. P. Frankel, in "Your First Impression," *Fast Company,* June–July 1998, p. 188.

29. The strength perspective was promoted by T. E. Deal and A. A. Kennedy, *Corporate Cultures: The Rites and Rituals of Corporate Life* (Reading, MA: Addison-Wesley, 1982).

30. The HP Way is thoroughly discussed in J. Dong, "The Rise and Fall of the HP Way," *Palo Alto Weekly Online Edition,* April 10, 2002; http://www.paloaltoonline.com/weekly/morgue/2002/2002_04_10.hpway10.html (accessed August 4, 2006).

31. S. Berfield, "Less Insult from Injury," *BusinessWeek,* August 14, 2006, pp. 62–63.

32. J. P. Kotter and J. L. Heskett, *Corporate Culture and Performance* (New York: Free Press, 1992).

33. The mechanisms are based on material contained in E. H. Schein, "The Role of the Founder in Creating Organizational Culture," *Organizational Dynamics,* Summer 1983, pp. 13–28.

34. Wal-Mart's values are stated on its corporate Web site, "About Wal-Mart," http://www.walmart.com/catalog/catalog.gsp?cat=131473#null (accessed August 7, 2006).

35. A. B. Goldberg and B. Ritter, "Costco CEO Finds Pro-Worker Means Profitability," ABC News, August 2, 2006; http://abcnews.go.com/2020/Business/story?id=1362779 (accessed August 7, 2006).

36. J. Stossel and G. Silber, "Sexy Sweats without the Sweatshop," ABC News, July 31, 2006; http://abcnews.go.com/2020/Business/story?id=2257111 (accessed August 7, 2006).

37. W. Zellner, "Dress to Kill . . . Competitors," *BusinessWeek,* February 21, 2005, pp. 60–61.

38. D. F. Kuratko, R. D. Ireland, and J. D. Hornsby, "Improving Firm Performance through Entrepreneurial Actions: Acordia's Corporate Entrepreneurship Strategy," *Academy of Management Executive,* November 2001, p. 67.

39. F. Arner and L. Young, "Can This Man Save Putnam?" *BusinessWeek,* April 19, 2004, p. 103.

40. J. Ball, "Might Profit Maker," *The Wall Street Journal,* April 8, 2005, p. B1.

41. T. Galvin, "Birds of a Feather," *Training,* March 2001, p. 60.

42. C. I. Barnard, *The Functions of the Executive* (Cambridge, MA: Harvard University Press, 1938), p. 73.

43. P. M. Blau and W. R. Scott, *Formal Organizations* (San Francisco: Chandler, 1962).

44. S. Steklow, "Management 101," *The Wall Street Journal,* December 9, 1994, p. B1.

45. O. Pollar, "Don't Overlook the Importance of Delegating," *San Francisco Examiner,* August 8, 1999, p. J-3; D. Anderson, "Supervisors and the Hesitate to Delegate Syndrome," *Supervision,* November 1992, pp. 9–11; and E. Raudsepp, "Why Supervisors Don't Delegate," *Supervision,* May 1979, pp. 12–15.

46. S. Caudron, "Delegate for Results," *Industry Week,* February 6, 1995, pp. 27–30; R. Morgan, "Guidelines for Delegating Effectively," *Supervision,* April 1995, pp. 20–22; J. Ninemeier, "10 Tips for Delegating Tasks," *Hotels,* June 1995, pp. 20–22; Pollar, 1999; R. Wild, "Clone Yourself," *Working Women,* May 2000, pp. 79–80; C. M. Avery, M. A. Walker, and E. O'Toole, *Teamwork Is an Individual Skill: Getting Your Work Done When Sharing Responsibility* (San Francisco: Berrett-Koehler, 2001); S. Gazda, "The Art of Delegating: Effective Delegation Enhances Employee Morale, Manager Productivity, and Organizational Success," *HR Magazine,* January 2002, pp. 75–79; R. Burns, *Making Delegation Happen: A Simple and Effective Guide to Implementing Successful Delegation* (St. Leonards, Australia: Allen & Unwin, 2002); D. M. Genett, *If You Want It Done Right, You Don't Have to Do It Yourself! The Power of Effective Delegation* (Sanger, CA: Quill Driver Books, 2003).

47. E. H. Schein, *Organizational Psychology,* 3rd ed. (Englewood Cliffs, NJ: Prentice-Hall, 1980).

48. For an overview of the span of control concept, see D. D. Van Fleet and A. G. Bedeian, "A History of the Span of Management," *Academy of Management Review,* July 1977, pp. 356–372.

49. T. A. Stewart, "CEOs See Clout Shifting," *Fortune,* November 6, 1989, p. 66.

50. Pollar, 1999.

51. D. Machalaba, "After Crippling Chaos, Union Pacific Can See the Proverbial Light," *The Wall Street Journal,* August 25, 1999, pp. A1, A8.

52. L. Grant, "New Jewel in the Crown," *U.S. News & World Report,* February 28, 1994, pp. 55–57; H. Rothman, "The Power of Empowerment," *Nation's Business,* June 1993, pp. 49–52; and J. Galbraith, *Designing Complex Organizations* (Reading, MA: Addison-Wesley, 1973).

53. A. Lashinsky, "RAZR's Edge," *Fortune,* June 12, 2006, pp. 124–132.

54. "Virtual Organization," Whatis.com, http://whatis.techtarget.com/definition/0,,sid9_gci213301,00.html (accessed June 12, 2006). See also J. A. Byrne, "The Virtual Corporation," *BusinessWeek,* February 8, 1993, pp. 98–102; G. Lorenzoni and C. Baden-Fuller, "Creating a Strategic Center to Manage a Web of Partners," *California Management Review,* Spring 1995, pp. 146–163.

55. R. Walker, quoted in B. Richards, "The Business Plan," *The Wall Street Journal,* November 18, 1996, pp. R10, R16.

56. J. Hyatt, "The Soul of a New Team," *Fortune,* June 12, 2006, pp. 134–143.

57. P. F. Drucker, quoted in J. A. Byrne, "Advice from the Dr. Spock of Business," *BusinessWeek,* September 28, 1987, p. 61.

58. K. Deveny, "Bag Those Fries, Squirt That Ketchup, Fry That Fish," *BusinessWeek,* October 13, 1986, p. 86.

59. T. Burns and G. M. Stalker, *The Management of Innovation* (London: Tavistock, 1961). See also W. D. Sine, H. Mitsuhashi, and D. A. Kirsch, "Revisiting Burns and Stalker: Formal Structure and New Venture Performance in Emerging Economic Sectors," *Academy of Management Journal,* February 2006, pp. 121–132.

60. T. J. Peters and R. H. Waterman, *In Search of Excellence* (New York: Harper & Row, 1982).

61. Inc.com, "Virtual Company Advice," *101 Great Ideas for Managing People from America's Most Innovative Small Companies,* October 1999, http://www.inc.com/articles/1999/10/19238. html (accessed August 9, 2006); and M. Puente, "Direct Selling Brings It All Home," *USA Today,* October 27, 2003, http://www.usatoday.com/life/2003-10-27-home-shopping_x.htm (accessed August 9, 2006).

62. P. R. Lawrence and J. W. Lorsch, *Organization and Environment* (Homewood, IL: Irwin, 1967).

63. D. S. Pugh and D. J. Hickson, *Organization Structure in Its Context: The Aston Program* (Lexington, MA: D. C. Heath, 1976); and R. Z. Gooding and J. A. Wagner III, "A Meta-Analytic Review of the Relationship between Size and Performance: The Productivity and Efficiency of Organizations and Their Subunits," *Administrative Science Quarterly,* December 1985, pp. 462–481.

64. L. Smith, "Does the World's Biggest Company Have a Future?" *Fortune,* August 7, 1995, p. 124.

65. M. Fackler, "Cutting Sony, a Corporate Octopus, Back to a Rational Size," *The New York Times,* May 29, 2006, pp. C1, C4.

66. Peters and Waterman, 1982, pp. 272–273.

67. P. Parker, quoted in C. Palmeri, "A Process that Never Ends," *Forbes,* December 21, 1992, p. 55.

68. J. Woodward, *Industrial Organization: Theory and Practice* (London: Oxford University Press, 1965).

69. J. R. Kimberly, R. H. Miles, and associates, *The Organizational Life Cycle* (San Francisco: Jossey-Bass, 1980).

70. P. Gruber, quoted in A. Muoio, ed., "My Greatest Lesson," *Fast Company,* June–July 1998, pp. 83–92.

71. D. A. Garvin, "Building a Learning Organization," *Harvard Business Review,* July-August 1993, pp. 78–91; and R. Hodgetts, F. Luthans, and S. Lee, "New Paradigm Organizations: From Total Quality to Learning to World-Class," *Organizational Dynamics,* Winter 1994, pp. 5–19.

72. P. Senge, *The Fifth Discipline* (New York: Doubleday, 1990), p. 1.

73. J. B. Keys, R. M. Fulmer, and S. A. Stumpf, "Microworlds and Simuworlds: Practice Fields for the Learning Organization," *Organizational Dynamics,* Spring 1996, pp. 36–49; and F. Kogman and P. M. Senge, "Communities of Commitment: The Heart of Learning Organizations," *Organizational Dynamics,* Autumn 1993, pp. 5–23.

74. J. Case, "A Company of Businesspeople," *Inc.,* April 1993, p. 86.

CHAPTER 9

1. K. Lingle, national work-life director for KPMG, an accounting and consulting firm, quoted in C. Kleiman, "Work-Life Rewards Grow," *San Francisco Examiner,* January 16, 2000, p. J-2; reprinted from *Chicago Tribune.*

2. See H. R. Nalbantian, R. A. Guzzo, D. Kieffer, and J. Doherty, *Play to Your Strengths: Managing Your Internal Labor Markets for Lasting Competitive Advantage* (New York: McGraw-Hill, 2004).

3. M. Buckingham and C. Coffman, *First, Break All the Rules: What the World's Greatest Managers Do Differently* (New York: Simon & Schuster, 1999).

4. Kimberly Scott, project leader for Hewitt Associates, which helps compile the *Fortune* list, reported in D. Murphy, "Can Morale Contribute to Safer Skies?" *San Francisco Examiner,* February 11, 2000, p. J-1.

5. M. Boyle, "The Wegmans Way," *Fortune,* January 24, 2005; http://money.conn.com/magazines/fortune/fortune_archive/2005/01/24/8234048/index.htm (accessed August 11, 2006). *Fortune's* Best Places to Work annual list is compiled by the Great Place to Work Institute in San Francisco. See R. Levering, "Creating a Great Place to Work: Why It Is Important and How It Is Done," *Corrections Today* 66, no. 5 (2004), pp. 86–89.

6. J. Welch, quoted in N. M. Tichy and S. Herman, *Control Your Destiny or Someone Else Will: How Jack Welch Is Making General Electric the World's Most Competitive Corporation* (New York: Doubleday, 1993), p. 251.

7. P. Capelli and A. Crocker-Hefter, "Distinctive Human Resources Are Firms' Core Competencies," *Organizational Dynamics,* Winter 1996, pp. 7–22.

8. G. Bollander, S. Snell, and A. Sherman, *Managing Human Resources,* 12th ed. (Cincinnati, OH: SouthWestern Publishing, 2001), pp. 13–15; and B. E. Becker, M. A. Huselid, and D. Ulrich, *The HR Scorecard: Linking People, Strategy, and Performance* (Boston: Harvard Business School Press, 2001), p. 4. See also D. Stamps, "Measuring Minds," *Training,* May 2000, pp. 76–85; C. A. Bartlett and S. Ghoshal, "Building Competitive Advantage through People," *MIT Sloan Management Review,* Winter 2002, pp. 34–41; and R. Rodriguez, "Meet the New Learning Executive," *HR Magazine,* April 2005, pp. 64–69.

9. B. E. Becker, M. A. Huselid, and D. Ulrich, *The HR Scorecard: Linking People, Strategy, and Performance* (Boston: Harvard Business School Press, 2001), p. 4.

10. Inspired by P. S. Adler and S. Kwon, "Social Capital: Prospects for New Concept," *Academy of Management Review,* January 2002, pp. 17–40. See also D. Lidsky, "Winning the Relationship Game," *Fast Company,* October 2004, pp. 113–115; J. Steinberg, "One Heart at a Time," *Fast Company,* November 2004, p. 49; K. H. Hammonds, "A Lever Long Enough to Move the World," *Fast Company,* January 2005, pp. 60–63; and A. C. Inkpen and E.W.K. Tsang, "Social Capital, Networks, and Knowledge Transfer," *Academy of Management Review,* January 2005, pp. 146–165.

11. R. Levering and M. Moskowitz, "The 100 Best Companies to Work For," *Fortune,* January 12, 2004, p. 68.

12. R. J. Mirabile, "The Power of Job Analysis," *Training,* April 1990, pp. 70–74; and S. F. Mona, "The Job Description," *Association Management,* February 1991, pp. 33–37.

13. For a thorough discussion of affirmative action, see F. J. Crosby, A. Iyer, S. Clayton, and R. A. Downing, "Affirmative Action," *American Psychologist,* February 2003, pp. 93–115.

14. E. H. James, A. P. Brief, J. Dietz, and R. R. Cohen, "Prejudice Matters: Understanding the Reactions of Whites to Affirmative Action Programs Targeted to Benefit Blacks," *Journal of Applied Psychology,* December 2001, pp. 1120–1128.

15. For a thorough review of relevant research, see M. E. Heilman, "Affirmative Action: Some Unintended Consequences for Working Women," in B. M. Staw and L. L. Cummings, eds., *Research in Organizational Behavior,* vol. 16 (Greenwich, CT: JAI Press, 1994), pp. 125–169.

16. M. Rotundo, D.-H. Nguyen, and P. R. Sackett, "A Meta-Analytic Review of Gender Differences in Perceptions of Sexual Harassment," *Journal of Applied Psychology,* October 2001, pp. 914–922.

17. M. Maremont, "A Case Puts a Value on Touching and Fondling," *The Wall Street Journal,* May 25, 1999, pp. B1, B4; S. Armour, "More Men Say They Are Sexually Harassed at Work," *USA Today,* September 17, 2004, p. 1B; C. A. Pierce and H. Aguinis, "Legal Standards, Ethical Standards, and

Responses to Social–Sexual Conduct at Work," *Journal of Organizational Behavior* 26 (2005), pp. 727–732; L. A. Baar, "Harassment Case Proceeds Despite Failure to Report," *HR Magazine*, June 2005, p. 159; and S. Shellenbarger, "Supreme Court Takes on How Employers Handle Worker Harassment Complaints," *The Wall Street Journal*, April 13, 2006, p. D1.

18. J. Useem, "For Sale Online: You," *Fortune*, July 5, 1999, pp. 67–78.

19. Survey of 703 Americans by Taylor Nelson Sofres Intersearch, released January 2003, reported in "How Workers Found Their Latest Jobs," *USA Today*, February 3, 2003, p. 1B; and "Job Hunting the Old-Fashioned Way," *BusinessWeek*, February 17, 2003, p. 10.

20. G. McWilliams, "The Best Way to Find a Job," *The Wall Street Journal*, December 6, 1999, pp. R16, R22.

21. K. Maher, "Online Job Hunting Is Tough. Just Ask Vinnie," *The Wall Street Journal*, June 24, 2003, pp. B1, B10.

22. L. Stern, "New Rules of the Hunt," *Newsweek*, February 17, 2003, p. 67.

23. S. Armour, "Firms Key Up PCs for Job Screening," *USA Today*, October 20, 1997, p. 6B.

24. B. Weinstein, "Prescreened Interviews Are Catching On," *San Francisco Sunday Examiner & Chronicle*, February 21, 1999, p. CL-21.

25. Survey by Society for Human Resource Management, reported in J. Schramm, "Background Checking," *HR Magazine*, January 2005, p. 128.

26. M. Conlin, "You Are What You Post," *BusinessWeek*, March 27, 2006, pp. 52–53; and A. Finder, "When a Risqué Online Persona Undermines a Chance for a Job," *The New York Times*, June 11, 2006, pp. A1, A24.

27. J. McGregor, "Background Checks That Never End," *BusinessWeek*, March 20, 2006, p. 40.

28. B. M. Meglino, A. S. DeNisi, S. A. Youngblood, and K. J. Williams, "Effects of Realistic Job Previews: A Comparison Using an Enhancement and a Reduction Preview," *Journal of Applied Psychology* 73 (1981), pp. 259–266.

29. Survey by InfoLink Screen Services, reported in H. B. Herring, "On Our Résumés, Couldn't We All Have Gone to Yale?" *The New York Times*, March 12, 2006, sec. 3, p. 2.

30. Survey by ResumeDoctor.com, reported in C. Soltis, "Eagle-Eyed Employers Scour Résumés for Little White Lies," *The Wall Street Journal*, March 21, 2006, p. B7.

31. Survey by Society of Human Resource Management, reported in M. Villano, "Served as King of England, Said the Résumé," *The New York Times*, March 19, 2006, sec. 3, p. 9.

32. Survey by Background Information Services, reported in Villano, 2006.

33. C. W. Nevius, "If You Like Fiction, Read the Job Resumes," *San Francisco Chronicle*, February 28, 2006, pp. B1, B2. See also D. Koeppel, "That Padded Résumé Won't Help Break Your Fall," *San Francisco Chronicle*, April 23, 2006, p. F5; reprinted from *The New York Times*.

34. Report by Automatic Data Processing, Roseland, NJ, cited in J. L. Seglin, "Lies Can Have a (Long) Life of Their Own," *The New York Times*, June 16, 2002, sec. 3, p. 4. See also S. Armour, "Security Checks Worry Workers," *USA Today*, June 19, 2004, p. 1B.

35. J. S. Lublin, "Job Hunters with Gaps in Their Résumés Need to Write Around Them," *The Wall Street Journal*, May 6, 2003, p. B1.

36. M. Conlin, "Don't Hedge Your Age," *BusinessWeek*, October 6, 2003, p. 14. See also C. Dahle, "A Nip and Tuck for the Résumé," *The New York Times*, April 17, 2005, sec. 3, p. 10.

37. S. McManis, "Little White-Collar Lies," *San Francisco Chronicle*, October 1, 1999, pp. B1, B3.

38. D. Stamps, "Cyberinterviews Combat Turnover," *Training*, August 1995, p. 16.

39. D. S. Chapman, K. L. Uggerslev, and J. Webster, "Applicant Reactions Face-to-Face and Technology-Mediated Interviews: A Field Investigation," *Journal of Applied Psychology* 88 (2003), pp. 944–953.

40. E. D. Pursell, M. A. Campion, and S. R. Gaylord, "Structured Interviewing: Avoiding Selection Problems," *Personnel Journal*, November 1980.

41. M. C. Blackman, "Personality Judgment and the Utility of the Unstructured Employment Interview," *Basic and Applied Social Psychology* 24 (2002), pp. 241–250.

42. J. G. Rosse and R. A. Levin, *High-Impact Hiring* (San Francisco: Jossey-Bass, 1997); D. Murphy, "Choice Advice," *San Francisco Examiner*, November 15, 1998, pp. J-1, J-2; "Biggest Interviewing Mistakes," *USA Today*, November 19, 2001, p. 1B; D. Murphy, "Interviewers Just Don't Get the Importance of Failure," *San Francisco Chronicle*, May 19, 2002, pp. J1, J3B; Rosner, "Turning Your Job Interview into a Circus Isn't Always Bad," *San Francisco Chronicle*, June 2, 2002, p. J2; L. Adler, *Hire with Your Head: Using POWER Hiring to Build Great Teams*, 2nd ed. (New York: John Wiley, 2002); and R. W. Wendover, *Smart Hiring: The Complete Guide to Finding and Hiring the Best Employees*, 3rd ed. (Naperville, IL: Sourcebooks, 2002).

43. H. Lancaster, "Making a Good Hire Takes a Little Instinct and a Lot of Research," *The Wall Street Journal*, March 3, 1998, p. B1.

44. L. G. Otting, "Don't Rush to Judgment," *HR Magazine*, January 2004, pp. 95–98.

45. M. P. Cronin, "This Is a Test," *Inc.*, August 1993, pp. 64–68.

46. D. P. Shuit, "At 60, Myers-Briggs Is Still Sorting Out and Identifying People's Types," *Workforce Management*, December 2003, pp. 72–74.

47. S. Adler, "Personality Tests for Salesforce Selection: Worth a Fresh Look," *Review of Business*, Summer/Fall 1994, pp. 27–31.

48. Survey by Management Recruiters International, 2003, reported in L. Daniel, "Use Personality Tests Legally and Effectively," *Staffing*, April–June 2005, http://www.shrm.org/ema/sm/acrticles/2005/apriljune05cover.asp (accessed August 14, 2006).

49. B. Rose, "Critics Wary as More Jobs Hinge on Personality Tests," *Chicago Tribune*, October 31, 2004, p. 15.

50. S. Clifford, "The Science of Hiring," *Inc. Magazine*, August 2006, pp. 90–98.

51. V. Knight, "More Employers Are Using Personality Tests as Hiring Tools," *CareerJournal.com*, March 21, 2006; http://www.careerjournal.com/jobhunting/interviewing/20060321-knight.html (accessed August 14, 2006).

52. D. Cadrain, "Are Your Employee Drug Tests *Accurate?*" *HR Magazine*, January 2003, pp. 41–45.

53. S. Shellenbarger, "Companies Are Finding It Really Pays to Be Nice to Employees," *The Wall Street Journal*, July 22, 1998, p. B1. For more about *The Jungle*, see C. Phelps, "How Should We Teach 'The Jungle'?" *The Chronicle of Higher Education*, March 3, 2006, pp. B10–B11.

54. Brookings Institution, cited in Shellenbarger, 1998.

55. MCI Communications surveys, reported in Shellenbarger, 1998.

56. G. R. Jones, "Organizational Socialization as Information Processing Activity: A Life History Analysis," *Human Organization* 42, no. 4 (1983), pp. 314–320.

57. E. Lawler, reported in S. Ross, "Worker Involvement Pays Off," *San Francisco Examiner*, November 15, 1998, p. J-2.

58. C. McNamara, "Employee Training and Development: Reasons and Benefits," Free Management Library, 1999; http://www.managementhelp.org/trng_dev/basics/reasons.htm (accessed August 14, 2006).

59. Eduventures, cited in D. Goldenk, "Degrees @ StateU.edu," *The Wall Street Journal*, May 9, 2006, pp. B1, B4.

60. L. Koss-Feder, "Brushing Up from the Boardroom to the Back Office," *Time*, July 20, 1998, p. B5.

61. R. Van Liew, quoted in "E-Learning's Dirty Little Secret," *Training*, February 2006, p. 6. See also J. Gordon, "Seven Revelations about E-Learning," *Training*, April 2006, pp. 28–31.

62. B. Muirhead, "Looking at Net Colleges" [letter], *USA Today*, November 12, 1999, p. 14A.

63. M. W., "What If You Held a Training Session and No One Showed Up?" *Training*, January 2006, p. 10.

64. C. Hymowitz, "Why Managers Take Too Long to Fire Employees," *San Francisco Examiner*, February 21, 1999, p. J-2; reprinted from *The Wall Street Journal*.

65. L. B. Combings and D. P. Schwab, *Performance in Organizations: Determinants and Appraisal* (Glenview, IL: Scott Foresman, 1973).

66. D. J. Cohen, "HR Metrics: A Must," *HR Magazine*, February 2003, p. 136.

67. A meta-analysis of 24 360-degree feedback studies appears in J. W. Smither, M. London, and R. R. Reilly, "Does Performance Improve Following Multisource Feedback? A Theoretical Model, Meta-Analysis, and Review of Empirical Findings," *Personnel Psychology*, Spring 2005, p. 33.

68. D. E. Coates, "Don't Tie 360 Feedback to Pay," *Training*, September 1998, pp. 68–78. See also A. S. Wellner, "Everyone's a Critic," *Inc.*, July 2004, pp. 38, 41; and W. C. Byham, "Fixing the Instrument," *Training*, July 2004, p. 50.

69. "Dell: Home Schooled by the Brass," *BusinessWeek Online*, October 10, 2005; http://www.businessweek.com/magazine/content/05_41/b3954007.htm (accessed August 14, 2006).

70. C. S. Peck, "360-Degree Feedback: How to Avoid a Disaster," Workinfo.com, http://www.workinfo.com/free/downloads/71.htm (accessed August 14, 2006).

71. M. Boyle, "Performance Reviews: Perilous Curves Ahead," *Fortune*, May 15, 2001, www.fortune.com/fortune/subs/print/0,15935,374010,00.html (accessed June 6, 2006); C. M. Ellis, G. B. Moore, and A. M. Saunier, "Forced Ranking: Not So Fast," *Perspectives*, June 30, 2003, www.imakenews.com/eletra/mod_print_view.cfm?this_id=162170&u=sibson&issue_id=000034313 (accessed June 6, 2006); and A. Meisler, "Dead Man's Curve," *Workforce Management*, July 2003, pp. 45–49.

72. S. Scherreik, "Your Performance Review: Make It Perform," *BusinessWeek Online*, December 17, 2001, http://www.businessweek.com/magazine/content/01_51/b3762136.htm?chan=search (accessed August 14, 2006); and J. McGregor, "The Struggle to Measure Performance," *BusinessWeek Online*, January 9, 2006, http://www.businessweek.com/magazine/content/06_02/b3966060.htm?chan=search (accessed August 14, 2006). See also criticism of forced ranking in J. Pfeffer and R. I. Sutton, *Hard Facts, Dangerous Half-Truths & Total Nonsense: Profiting from Evidence-Based Management* (Boston: Harvard Business School Press, 2006).

73. *Employee Benefits Study, 2005* (Washington, DC: U.S. Chamber of Commerce, 2006).

74. Adapted from D. L. McClain, "Tricks for Motivating the Pay to Motivate the Ranks," *The New York Times*, November 15, 1998, sec. 3, p. 5.

75. A. Etzioni, "Americans Could Teach Austrians about Diversity," *USA Today*, February 14, 2000, p. 19A.

76. A. Fisher, "Dumping Troublemakers, and Exiting Gracefully," *Fortune*, February 15, 1999, p. 174.

77. Hymowitz, 1999.

78. R. Moss Kanter, "Show Humanity When You Show Employees the Door," *The Wall Street Journal*, September 21, 1997, p. A22.

79. Moss Kanter, 1997.

CHAPTER 10

1. T. J. Fadem, quoted in O. Port and J. Carey, "Getting to 'Eureka!'" *BusinessWeek*, November 10, 1997, pp. 72–75.

2. C. Hymowitz, "Task of Managing in Workplace Takes a Careful Hand," *The Wall Street Journal*, July 1, 1997, p. B1.

3. T. Peters, "A Brawl with No Rules," *Forbes ASAP*, February 21, 2000, p. 155.

4. M. McGuinn, quoted in Hymowitz, 1997.

5. P. Carbonara, "What Do You Do with a Great Idea?" *Your Company*, August–September 1998, pp. 26–31; G. Kawaski with M. Moreno, *Rules for Revolutionaries: The Capitalist Manifesto for Creating and Marketing New Products and Services* (New York: HarperBusiness, 1999); M. Weinstein, "Innovate or Die Trying," *Training Magazine*, May 2006, pp. 38–44; D. Hall, "The Customer Is Clueless," *BusinessWeek SmallBiz*, Spring 2006, p. 20; D. Brady, "Ideas That Bloom," *BusinessWeek SmallBiz*, Spring 2006, pp. 46–53; and P. Loewe and J. Dominiquini, "Overcoming the Barriers to Effective Innovation," *Strategy & Leadership* 34, no. 1 (2006), pp. 24–31.

6. Anthony Creed, quoted in D. Kirkpatrick, "Throw It at the Wall and See If It Sticks," *Fortune*, December 12, 2005, pp. 142–150.

7. Bruce Judson, quoted in J. M. Pethokoukis, "Bootstrapping Your Way into Business," *U.S. News & World Report*, March 27, 2006, p. 58.

8. E. Hoffer, *Ordeal of Change* (New York: Harper & Row, 1963).

9. P. Drucker, "The Future That Has Already Happened," *The Futurist*, November 1998, pp. 16–18.

10. Drucker, ibid.; and L. Jennings and J. Minerd, "Cybertrends Shaping Tomorrow's Marketplace," *The Futurist*, March 1999, pp. 12–14.

11. Some of these trends are based on K. Albrecht, "Eight Supertrends Shaping the Future of Business," *The Futurist*, September–October 2006, pp. 25–29.

12. C. Anderson, quoted in A. T. Saracevic, "Economic Theories in 'The Long Tail' Don't Deserve Short Shrift," *San Francisco Chronicle*, July 16, 2006, pp. F1, F5. See also C. Anderson, *The Long Tail: Why the Future of Business Is Selling Less of More* (New York: Hyperion, 2006).

13. S. Hamm, "Speed Demons," *BusinessWeek*, March 27, 2006, pp. 68–75.

14. C. M. Christensen, *The Innovator's Dilemma: When New Technologies Cause Great Firms to Fail* (Boston, MA: Harvard Business School Press, 1997). See also F. Arner and R. Tiplady, "'No Excuse Not to Succeed,'" *BusinessWeek*, May 10, 2004, pp. 96–98.

15. P. Engardio, "The Future of Outsourcing," *BusinessWeek*, January 30, 2006, pp. 50–58.

16. Ibid, p. 58.

17. Albrecht, 2006.

18. A. Toffler and H. Toffler, *Revolutionary Wealth* (New York: Alfred A. Knopf, 2006).

19. P. Mintz and F. Di Meglio, "Bausch & Lomb: Crisis Management 101," *BusinessWeek Online*, April 17, 2006, http://www.businessweek.com/investor/content/apr2006/pi20060417_741558.htm (accessed August 22, 2006).

20. B. J. Feder, "From Asia to America, How Bausch's Crisis Grew," *The New York Times*, May 18, 2006; http://www.corpwatch.org/article.php?id=13598 (accessed August 22, 2006).

21. A. Zimm and J. Tannembaum, "Bausch & Lomb Chops Its Forecast," *International Herald Tribune*, August 9, 2006;

http://www.iht.com/articles/2006/08/08/bloomberg/bxlens.php (accessed August 22, 2006).

22. "J&J Is on a Roll," *Fortune,* December 26, 1994, pp. 178-192; S. Siwolop and C. Eklund, "The Capsule Controversy: How Far Should the FDA Go?" *BusinessWeek,* March 3, 1986, p. 37; and "After Its Recovery, New Headaches for Tylenol," *BusinessWeek,* May 14, 1984, p. 137.

23. P. Robertson, D. Roberts, and J. Porras, "Dynamics of Planned Organizational Change: Assessing Empirical Support for a Theoretical Model," *Academy of Management Journal* 36, no. 3 (1993), pp. 619-634.

24. S. Moran, "The Range Gets Crowded for Natural Beef," *The New York Times,* June 10, 2006, pp. B1, B4.

25. M. Warner, "When It Comes to Meat, 'Natural' Is a Vague Term," *The New York Times,* June 10, 2006, p. B4.

26. "RFID: On Track for a Rapid Rise," *BusinessWeek Online,* February 4, 2004, www.businessweek.com/technology/content/feb2004/tc2004024_8389_tc165.htm (accessed June 7, 2006); "Like It or Not, RFID Is Coming," *BusinessWeek Online,* March 18, 2004, www.businessweek.com/technology/content/mar2004/tc20040318_7698_tc121.htm (accessed June 7, 2006); and S. Crane, "RFID: Symbol's Growth Engine?" *BusinessWeek Online,* March 19, 2004, www.businessweek.com/investor/content/mar2004/pi20040319_2070_pi044.htm (accessed June 7, 2006).

27. P. Dusenberry, "The Challenges of Managing Creative People," *USA Today,* November 20, 1997, p. 4B.

28. R. D. Hof, "Online Extra: Trading in a Cloud of Electrons," *BusinessWeek Online,* May 20, 2004, www.businessweek.com/@@TUSaZYUQTmOUSwOA/magazine/content/04_19/b3882621.htm (accessed June 8, 2006).

29. The term "Web 2" was popularized by Tim O'Reilly, CEO of O'Reilly Media Inc. See T. O'Reilly, "What Is Web 2.0," O'Reilly, September 30, 2005; http://www.oreillynet.com/pub/a/oreilly/tim/news/2005/09/30/what-is-web-20.html (accessed August 22, 2006).

30. R. D. Hof, "Web 2.0: The New Guy at Work," *BusinessWeek,* June 19, 2006, pp. 58-59.

31. M. Fugate, A. Kinicki, and C. L. Scheck, "Coping with an Organizational Merger over Four Stages," *Personnel Psychology,* Winter 2002, pp. 905-928.

32. G. A. Neuman, J. E. Edwards, and N. S. Raju, "Organizational Development Interventions: A Meta-Analysis of Their Effects on Satisfaction and Other Attitudes," *Personnel Psychology,* Autumn 1989, pp. 461-490.

33. W. G. Dyer, *Team Building: Current Issues and New Alternatives,* 3rd ed. (Reading, MA: Addison-Wesley, 1995).

34. See R. Rodgers, J. E. Hunter, and D. L. Rogers, "Influence of Top Management Commitment on Management Program Success," *Journal of Applied Psychology,* February 1993, pp. 151-155.

35. R. J. Schaffer and H. A. Thomson, "Successful Change Programs Begin with Results" *Harvard Business Review,* January-February 1992, pp. 80-89.

36. P. J. Robertson, D. R. Roberts, and J. I. Porras, "Dynamics of Planned Organizational Change: Assess Empirical Support for a Theoretical Model," *Academy of Management Journal,* June 1993, pp. 619-634.

37. C.-M. Lau and H.-Y. Ngo, "Organization Development and Firm Performance: A Comparison of Multinational and Local Firms," *Journal of International Business Studies,* First Quarter 2001, pp. 95-114.

38. Survey by Development Dimensions International Inc., 2005, reported in "The Big Picture: All Talk? Despite Management's Focus on Innovation, U.S. Executives Say Their Companies Give It Short Shrift," *BusinessWeek,* March 6, 2006, p. 13.

39. L. Selden and I. C. MacMillan, "Manage Customer-Centric Innovation—Systematically ," *Harvard Business Review,* April 2006, pp. 108-116.

40. C. B. Rabe, *The Innovation Killer: How What We Know Limits What We Can Imagine—and What Smart Companies Are Doing about It* (New York: Amacom, 2006).

41. C. R. Carlson and W. W. Wilmot, *Innovation: The Five Disciplines for Creating What Customers Want* (New York: Crown Business, 2006).

42. W. M. Bulkeley, "Can Linux Take Over the Desktop?" *The Wall Street Journal,* May 24, 2004, pp. R1, R4; and S. Hamm, "Software Shift," *BusinessWeek,* May 10, 2004, p. 90.

43. T. O'Reilly, quoted in W. C. Taylor, "Here's an Idea: Let Everyone Have Ideas," *The New York Times,* March 26, 2006, sec. 3, p. 3. See also R. E. Miles, G. Miles, and C. C. Snow, "Collaborative Entrepreneurship: A Business Model for Continuous Innovation," *Organizational Dynamics,* February 2006, pp. 1-11.

44. P. Warrior, cited in M. Lev-Ram, "Unwiring Motorola," *Business 2.0,* September 2006, pp. 103 -105.

45. R. Cohen, "Vive La Dolce Vita," *The New York Times,* April 16, 2006, sec. 4, pp. 1, 4.

46. K. Maney, "Tech Start-ups Don't Grow on Trees Outside USA," *USA Today,* June 28, 2006, pp. 1B, 2B.

47. J. Guynn, "Grunge Inc.," *San Francisco Chronicle,* July 30, 2006, pp. A1, A12.

48. S. Perman, "The Entrepreneurial Melting Pot," *BusinessWeek Online,* June 6, 2006; http://www.businessweek.com/smallbiz/content/jun2006/sb20060606_980521.htm (accessed August 22, 2006).

49. S. Baker, "How to Keep the Idea Pot Bubbling," *BusinessWeek,* October 20, 1997, pp. 15-18.

50. G. C. O'Connor, quoted in Port and Carey, 1997.

51. A. V. Bhidé, quoted in G. Gendron, "The Origin of the Entrepreneurial Species," *Inc.,* February 2000, pp. 105-114.

52. J. Yaukey, "Disposable Cell Phones Will Reach Retail Soon," *Reno Gazette-Journal,* October 22, 2001, p. 1E; and D. Pogue, "Cellphones for a Song, Just in Case," *The New York Times,* September 27, 2001, pp. D1, D7.

53. B. Evangelista, "Movies by Mail: Netflix.com Makes Renting DVDs Easy," *San Francisco Chronicle,* January 26, 2002, p. B1; and V. Kopytoff, "Successful Netflix Faces Competition," *San Francisco Chronicle,* March 8, 2004, pp. E1, E4.

54. J. McGregor, "The World's Most Innovative Companies," *BusinessWeek,* April 24, 2006, pp. 63-74.

55. R. Moss Kanter, *The Change Masters* (New York: Simon & Schuster, 1983).

56. T. Kuczmarski, "Inspiring and Implementing the Innovation Mind-Set," *Planning Review,* September–October 1994, pp. 37-48; L. K. Gundry, J. R. Kickul, and C. W. Prather, "Building the Creative Organization," *Organizational Dynamics,* Spring 1994, pp. 22-36; and T. M. Burton, "By Learning from Failures, Lilly Keeps Drug Pipeline Full," *The Wall Street Journal,* April 21, 2004, pp. A1, A9.

57. McGregor, 2006.

58. T. J. Martin, "Ten Commandments for Managing Creative People," *Fortune,* January 16, 1995, pp. 135-136; B. Schneider, S. K. Gunnarson, and K. Niles-Jolly, "Creating the Climate and Culture of Success," *Organizational Dynamics,* Spring 1994, pp. 22-36; T. Katauskas, "Follow-Through: 3M's Formula for Success," *R&D,* November 1990; and R. Mitchell, "Masters of Innovation: How 3M Keeps Its New Products Coming," *BusinessWeek,* April 10, 1989, pp. 58-63.

59. J. Denrell, "Vicarious Learning, Undersampling of Failure, and the Myths of Management," *Organizational Science,* May–June 2003, pp. 227-243.

60. Carbonara, 1998.

61. T. J. Allen and S. I. Cohen, "Information Flow in Research and Development Laboratories," *Administrative Science Quarterly,* March 1969, pp. 12–19.

62. Moss Kanter, 1983.

63. This three-way typology of change was adapted from discussion in P. C. Nutt, "Tactics of Implementation," *Academy of Management Journal,* June 1986, pp. 230–261.

64. Radical organizational change is discussed by T. E. Vollmann, *The Transformational Imperative* (Boston: Harvard Business School Press, 1996); and J. A. Neal and C. L. Tromley, "From Incremental Change to Retrofit: Creating High-Performance Work Systems," *Academy of Management Executive,* February 1995, pp. 42–53.

65. Adapted in part from B. W. Armentrout, "Have Your Plans for Change Had a Change of Plan?" *HR Focus,* January 1996, p. 19; and A. S. Judson, *Changing Behavior in Organizations: Minimizing Resistance to Change* (Cambridge, MA: Blackwell, Inc., 1991).

66. See "Vulnerability and Resilience," *American Psychologist,* January 1996, pp. 22–28. See also T. Kiefer, "Feeling Bad: Antecedents and Consequences of Negative Emotions in Ongoing Change," *Journal of Organizational Behavior,* December 2005, pp. 875–897.

67. See R. Moss Kanter, "Managing Traumatic Change: Avoiding the 'Unlucky 13,'" *Management Review,* May 1987, pp. 23–24.

68. Details of this example are provided by B. Schlender, "Inside the Shakeup at Sony," *Fortune,* April 4, 2005, pp. 94–104.

69. K. Lewin, *Field Theory in Social Science* (New York: Harper & Row, 1951).

70. The role of learning within organizational change is discussed by C. Hendry, "Understanding and Creating Whole Organizational Change through Learning Theory," *Human Relations,* May 1996, pp. 621–641; and D. Ready, "Mastering Leverage, Leading Change," *Executive Excellence,* March 1995, pp. 18–19.

71. C. Goldwasser, "Benchmarking: People Make the Process," *Management Review,* June 1995, p. 40; and *Cambridge Advanced Learner's Dictionary* (Cambridge: Cambridge University Press, 2004), http://dictionary.cambridge.org/define.asp?key=94109&dict=CALD (accessed July 5, 2004).

72. R. Kreitner and A. Kinicki, *Organizational Behavior,* 4th ed. (Burr Ridge, IL: Irwin/McGraw-Hill, 1998), p. 619.

73. These errors are discussed by J. P. Kotter, "Leading Change: The Eight Steps to Transformation," in J. A. Conger, G. M. Spreitzer, and E. E. Lawler III, eds., *The Leader's Change Handbook* (San Francisco: Jossey-Bass, 1999), pp. 87–99.

74. The type of leadership needed during organizational change is discussed by J. P. Kotter, *Leading Change* (Boston: Harvard Business School Press, 1996); and B. Ettorre, "Making Change," *Management Review,* January 1996, pp. 13–18.

CHAPTER II

1. Bureau of Labor Statistics, reported in P. O'Connell, "Ready for a Worker Shortage?" *BusinessWeek online,* March 22, 2006, www.businessweek.com/bwdaily/dnflash/mar2004/nf20040321_5457_db079.htm (accessed July 12, 2004). See also R. E. Herman, T. G. Olivo, and J. L. Gioia, *Impending Crisis: Too Many Jobs, Too Few People* (Winchester, VA: Oakhill Press, 2003); B. Tulgan and C. A. Martin, *Managing Generation Y: Global Citizens Born in the Late Seventies and Early Eighties* (Amherst, MA: Human Resource Development Press, 2001). See also S. Eisner, "Teaching Generation Y—Three Initiatives," *Proceedings in 2004 College Teaching and Learning Conference,* http://phobos.ramapo.edu/~seisner/Teaching.htm (accessed July 12, 2006).

2. Survey by Gallup Organization, reported in S. L. Lynch, "Gen Xers Sharpen Work Skills," *San Francisco Chronicle,* September 7, 1998, p. A2.

3. O. Pollar, "Managing the MTV Generation," *San Francisco Examiner & Chronicle,* June 15, 1997, p. J-3.

4. Tulgan and Martin, 2001. See also S. Baker, "Channeling the Future," *BusinessWeek,* July 12, 2004, pp. 70–71; R. Zemke, C. Raines, and B. Filipczak, *Generations at Work: Managing the Clash of Veterans, Boomers, Xers and Nexters in Your Workplace* (New York: AMACOM, 1999); "19 to 33 Years Old," *San Francisco Examiner,* March 7, 1999, special section, pp. W-1-W-34; Lynch, 1998.

5. See M. Rokeach, *Beliefs, Attitudes, and Values* (San Francisco: Jossey-Bass, 1968), p. 168.

6. M. Rokeach, *The Nature of Human Values* (New York: Free Press, 1973).

7. Families and Work Institute, cited in C. Shavers, "Qualities that Make Working with Gen Xers a Special Challenge," *San Jose Mercury News,* December 6, 1998, p. 3E; see also Tulgan and Martin, 2001.

8. For a discussion of the difference between attitudes and values, see B. W. Becker and P. E. Connor, "Changing American Values—Debunking the Myth," *Business,* January–March 1985, pp. 56–59.

9. M. Fishbein and I. Ajzen, *Belief, Attitude, Intention and Behavior: An Introduction to Theory and Research* (Reading, MA: Addison-Wesley Publishing, 1975), p. 6.

10. B. M. Shaw and J. Ross, "Stability in the Midst of Change: A Dispositional Approach to Job Attitudes," *Journal of Applied Psychology,* August 1985, pp. 469–480; see also J. Schaubroeck, D. C. Ganster, and B. Kemmerer, "Does Trait Affect Promote Job Attitude Stability?" *Journal of Organizational Behavior,* March 1996, pp. 191–196.

11. J. S. Becker, "Empirical Validation of Affect, Behavior, and Cognition as Distinct Components of Attitude," *Journal of Personality and Social Psychology,* May 1984, pp. 1191–1205; the components or structure of attitudes is thoroughly discussed by A. P. Brief, *Attitudes in and around Organizations* (Thousand Oaks, CA: Sage, 1998), pp. 49–84.

12. L. Festinger, *A Theory of Cognitive Dissonance* (Stanford, CA: Stanford University Press, 1957).

13. J. Hempel, "Big Blue Brainstorm," *BusinessWeek Online,* July 28, 2006, p. 70.

14. These five job dimensions are developed by researchers at Cornell University as part of the Job Descriptive Index. For a review of the development of the JDI, see P. C. Smith, L. M. Kendall, and C. L. Hulin, *The Measurement of Satisfaction in Work and Retirement* (Skokie, IL: Rand McNally, 1969).

15. See A. J. Kinicki, F. M. McKee-Ryan, C. A. Schriesheim, and K. P. Carson, "Assessing the Construct Validity of the Job Descriptive Index: A Review and Meta-Analysis," *Journal of Applied Psychology,* February 2002, pp. 14–32.

16. "Middle Managers Unhappy," *HR Magazine,* July 2006, p. 16.

17. The various models are discussed in T. A. Judge, C. J. Thoresen, J. E. Bono, and G. K. Patton, "The Job Satisfaction-Job Performance Relationship: A Qualitative and Quantitative Review," *Psychological Bulletin,* May 2001, pp. 376–407.

18. Ibid. One example is provided by D. J. Schleicher, J. D. Watt, and G. J. Greguras, "Reexamining the Job Satisfaction-Performance Relationship: The Complexity of Attitudes," *Journal of Applied Psychology,* February 2004, pp. 165–177. See also "Waking Up on the Wrong Side of the Desk: The Effect of Mood on Work Performance," *Knowledge@Wharton,*

July 26, 2006, http://knowledge.wharton.upenn.edu/article.dfm?articleid=1531 (accessed August 27, 2006).

19. See S. P. Brown, "A Meta-Analysis and Review of Organizational Research on Job Involvement," *Psychological Bulletin,* September 1996, pp. 235–255.

20. This recommendation is supported by K. W. Thomas, *Intrinsic Motivation at Work* (San Francisco: Berrett-Koehler, 2000).

21. Survey of adults conducted for Adecco Staffing North America, reported in K. Gurchiek, "Good News for Moms Reconsidering Work," *HR Magazine,* July 2006, p. 30.

22. See R. P. Tett and J. P. Meyer, "Job Satisfaction, Organizational Commitment, Turnover Intention, and Turnover: Path Analysis Based on Meta-Analytic Findings," *Personnel Psychology,* Summer 1993, pp. 259–293.

23. See J. E. Mathieu and D. Zajac, "A Review and Meta-Analysis of the Antecedents, Correlates, and Consequences of Organizational Commitment," *Psychological Bulletin,* September 1990, pp. 171–194; see also M. Riketta, "Attitudinal Organizational Commitment and Job Performance: A Meta-Analysis," *Journal of Organizational Behavior,* March 2002, pp. 257–266.

24. D. W. Organ, "The Motivational Basis of Organizational Citizenship Behavior," in B. M. Staw and L. L. Cummings, eds., *Research in Organizational Behavior* (Greenwich, CT: JAI Press, 1990), p. 46.

25. J. A. LePine, A. Erez, and D. E. Johnson, "The Nature and Dimensionality of Organizational Citizenship Behavior: A Critical Review and Meta-Analysis," *Journal of Applied Psychology,* February 2002, pp. 52–65.

26. See P. W. Hom and A. J. Kinicki, "Toward a Greater Understanding of How Dissatisfaction Drives Employee Turnover," *Academy of Management Journal,* October 2001, pp. 975–987. Also see R. W. Griffeth, P. W. Hom, and S. Gaertner, "A Meta-Analysis of Antecedents and Correlates of Employee Turnover: Update, Moderator Tests, and Research Implications for the Next Millennium," *Journal of Management* 26, no. 3 (2000), pp. 463–488; and J. D. Shaw, M. K. Duffy, J. L. Johnson, and D. E. Lockhart, "Turnover, Social Capital Losses, and Performance," *Academy of Management Journal,* August 2005, pp. 594–606; K. W. Mossholder, R. P. Settoon, and S. G. Henagan, "A Relational Perspective on Turnover: Examining Structural, Attitudinal, and Behavioral Predictors," *Academy of Management Journal,* August 2005, pp. 607–618; D. G. Allen, K. P. Weeks, and K. R. Moffitt, "Turnover Intentions and Voluntary Turnover: The Moderating Roles of Self-Monitoring, Locus of Control, Proactive Personality, and Risk Aversion," *Journal of Applied Psychology,* September 2005, pp. 980–990.

27. Costs of turnover are discussed by R. W. Griffeth and P. W. Hom, *Retaining Valued Employees* (Thousand Oaks, CA: Sage, 2001).

28. M. Littman, "Best Bosses Tell All," *Working Woman,* October 2000, pp. 48–56.

29. 2000 study by Development Dimensions International, Pittsburgh, reported in "Replacing Key People Has Many Hidden Costs," *San Francisco Chronicle,* December 24, 2000, p. J1; reprinted from *Boston Globe.*

30. For a thorough discussion of personality psychology, see D. P. McAdams and J. L. Pals, "A New Big Five: Fundamental Principles for an Integrative Science of Personality," *American Psychologist,* April 2006, pp. 204–217.

31. The landmark report is J. M. Digman, "Personality Structure: Emergence of the Five-Factor Model," *Annual Review of Psychology* 41 (1990), pp. 417–440. Also see M. R. Barrick and M. K. Mount, "Autonomy as a Moderator of the Relationships between the Big Five Personality Dimensions and Job Performance," *Journal of Applied Psychology,* February 1993, pp. 111–118; C. Viswesvaran and D. S. Ones, "Measurement Error in 'Big Five Factors' Personality Assessment: Reliability Generalization across Studies and Measures," *Education and Psychological Measurement,* April 2000, pp. 224–235; M. K. Mount, M. R. Barrick, S. M. Scullen, and J. Rounds, "Higher-Order Dimensions of the Big Five Personality Traits and the Big Six Vocational Interest Types," *Personnel Psychology,* Summer 2005, pp. 447–478; P. Warr, D. Bartram, and A. Brown, "Big Five Validity: Aggregation Method Matters," *Journal of Occupational and Organizational Psychology,* September 2005, pp. 377–386; and A.H.B. De Hoogh, D. N. Den Hartog, and P. L. Koopman, "Linking the Big Five-Factors of Personality to Charismatic and Transactional Leadership; Perceived Dynamic Work Environment as a Moderator," *Journal of Organizational Behavior,* November 2005, pp. 839–865; A. B. Bakker, K. I. Van Der Zee, K. A. Lewig, and M. F. Dollard, "The Relationship Between the Big Five Personality Factors and Burnout: A Study Among Volunteer Counselors," *Journal of Social Psychology,* February 2006, pp. 31–50; and H. Zhao and S. E. Seibert, "The Big Five Personality Dimensions and Entrepreneurial Status: A Meta-Analytical Review," *Journal of Applied Psychology,* March 2006, pp. 259–271.

32. M. R. Barrick and M. K. Mount, "The Big Five Personality Dimensions and Job Performance: A Meta-Analysis," *Personnel Psychology,* Spring 1991, pp. 1–26.

33. Barrick and Mount, 1991, p. 18; also see H. Moon, "The Two Faces of Conscientiousness: Duty and Achievement Striving in Escalation of Commitment Dilemmas," *Journal of Applied Psychology,* June 2001, pp. 533–540; M. R. Barrick, G. L. Stewart, and M. Piotrowski, "Personality and Job Performance: Test of the Mediating Effects of Motivation among Sales Representatives," *Journal of Applied Psychology,* February 2002, pp. 43–51; and L. A. Witt, L. A. Burke, M. R. Barrick, and M. K. Mount, "The Interactive Effects of Conscientiousness and Agreeableness on Job Performance," *Journal of Applied Psychology,* February 2002, pp. 164–169.

34. See M. P. Cronin, "This Is a Test," *Inc.,* August 1993, pp. 64–68.

35. J. M. Crant, "Proactive Behavior in Organizations," *Journal of Management,* no. 3, 2000, pp. 439–441; and J. M. Crant, "The Proactive Personality Scale as a Predictor of Entrepreneurial Intentions," *Journal of Small Business Management,* July 1996, pp. 42–49.

36. For an overall view of research on locus of control, see P. E. Spector, "Behavior in Organizations as a Function of Employee's Locus of Control," *Psychological Bulletin,* May 1982, pp. 482–497; the relationship between locus of control and performance and satisfaction is examined in D. R. Norris and R. E. Niebuhr, "Attributional Influences on the Job Performance–Job Satisfaction Relationship," *Academy of Management Journal,* June 1984, pp. 424–431; salary differences between internals and externals were examined by P. C. Nystrom, "Managers' Salaries and Their Beliefs about Reinforcement Control," *The Journal of Social Psychology,* August 1983, pp. 291–292.

37. D. Sacks, "60 Seconds with Erik Weihenmayer," *Fast Company,* May 2004, p. 40.

38. See, for example, V. Gecas, "The Social Psychology of Self-Efficacy," in W. R. Scott and J. Blake, eds., *Annual Review of Sociology,* vol. 15 (Palo Alto, CA: Annual Reviews, 1989), pp. 291–316; and C. K. Stevens, A. G. Bavetta, and M. E. Gist, "Gender Differences in the Acquisition of Salary Negotiation Skills: The Role of Goals, Self-Efficacy, and Perceived Control," *Journal of Applied Psychology,* October 1993, pp. 723–735; D. Eden and Y. Zuk, "Seasickness as a Self-Fulfilling Prophecy: Raising Self-Efficacy to Boost

Performance at Sea," *Journal of Applied Psychology,* October 1995, pp. 628–635; and S. M. Jex, P. D. Bliese, S. Buzzell, and J. Primeau, "The Impact of Self-Efficacy on Stressor-Strain Relations: Coping Style as an Explanatory Mechanism," *Journal of Applied Psychology,* June 2001, pp. 401–409.

39. J. Barling and R. Beattle, "Self-Efficacy Beliefs and Sales Performance," *Journal of Organizational Behavior Management,* Spring 1983, pp. 41–51.

40. For more on learned helplessness, see M. J. Martinko and W. L. Gardner, "Learned Helplessness: An Alternative Explanation for Performance Deficits," *Academy of Management Review,* April 1982, pp. 195–204; C. R. Campbell and M. J. Martinko, "An Integrative Attributional Perspective of Employment and Learned Helplessness: A Multimethod Field Study," *Journal of Management,* no. 2, 1998, pp. 173–200; and A. Dickerson and M. A. Taylor, "Self-Limiting Behavior in Women: Self-Esteem and Self-Efficacy as Predictors," *Group and Organization Management,* June 2000, pp. 191–210.

41. W. S. Silver, T. R. Mitchell, and M. E. Gist, "Response to Successful and Unsuccessful Performance: The Moderating Effect of Self-Efficacy on the Relationship between Training and Newcomer Adjustment," *Journal of Applied Psychology,* April 1995, pp. 211–225.

42. See P. C. Earley and T. R. Lituchy, "Delineating Goal and Efficacy Effects: A Test of Three Models," *Journal of Applied Psychology,* February 1991, pp. 81–98; and J. B. Vancouver, C. M. Thompson, and A. A. Williams, "The Changing Signs in the Relationships among Self-Efficacy, Personal Goals, and Performance," *Journal of Applied Psychology,* August 2001, pp. 605–620.

43. The positive relationship between self-efficacy and readiness for retraining is documented in L. A. Hill and J. Elias, "Retraining Midcareer Managers: Career History and Self-Efficacy Beliefs," *Human Resource Management,* Summer 1990, pp. 197–217; also see S. P. Brown, S. Ganesan, and G. Challagalla, "Self-Efficacy as a Moderator of Information-Seeking Effectiveness," *Journal of Applied Psychology,* October 2001, pp. 1043–1051.

44. V. Gecas, "The Self-Concept," in R. H. Turner and J. F. Short Jr. eds., *Annual Review of Sociology;* vol. 8 (Palo Alto, CA: Annual Reviews, 1982); also see N. Branden, *Self-Esteem at Work: How Confident People Make Powerful Companies* (San Francisco: Jossey-Bass, 1998).

45. P. G. Dodgson and J. V. Wood, "Self-Esteem and the Cognitive Accessibility of Strengths and Weaknesses after Failure," *Journal of Personality and Social Psychology,* July 1998, pp. 178–197; and D. B. Fedor, J. M. Maslyn, W. D. Davis, and K. Mathieseon, "Performance Improvement Efforts in Response to Negative Feedback: The Roles of Source Power and Recipient Self-Esteem," *Journal of Management,* January–February 2001, pp. 79–97; see also S. Begley, "Real Self-Esteem Builds on Achievement, Not Praise for Slackers," *The Wall Street Journal,* April 18, 2003, p. B1.

46. B. R. Schlenker, M. F. Weigold, and J. R. Hallam, "Self-Serving Attributions in Social Contest: Effects of Self-Esteem and Social Pressure," *Journal of Personality and Social Psychology,* May 1990, pp. 855–863; and P. Sellers, "Get Over Yourself," *Fortune,* April 2001, pp. 76–88.

47. J. W. McGuire and C. V. McGuire, "Enhancing Self-Esteem by Directed-Thinking Tasks: Cognitive and Affective Positivity Asymmetries," *Journal of Personality and Social Psychology,* June 1996, p. 1124.

48. M. Snyder and S. Gangestad, "On the Nature of Self-Monitoring: Matters of Assessment, Matters of Validity," *Journal of Personality and Social Psychology,* July 1986, p. 125.

49. Data from M. Kilduff and D. V. Day, "Do Chameleons Get Ahead? The Effects of Self-Monitoring on Managerial Careers," *Academy of Management Journal,* August 1994, pp. 1047–1060.

50. See F. Luthans, "Successful vs. Effective Managers," *Academy of Management Executive,* May 1988, pp. 127–132; also see W. H. Turnley and M. C. Bolino, "Achieving Desired Images While Avoiding Undesired Images: Exploring the Role of Self-Monitoring in Impression Management," *Journal of Applied Psychology,* April 2001, pp. 351–360.

51. D. Goleman, *Emotional Intelligence* (New York: Bantam, 1995).

52. D. Goleman, "What Makes a Leader," *Harvard Business Review,* November–December 1998, pp. 93–102.

53. S. Fox and P. E. Spector, "Relations of Emotional Intelligence, Practical Intelligence, General Intelligence, and Trait Affectivity with Interview Outcomes: It's Not All Just 'G,'" *Journal of Organizational Behavior,* March 2000, pp. 203–220.

54. M. D. Davies, L. Stankov, and R. D. Roberts, "Emotional Intelligence: In Search of an Elusive Construct," *Journal of Personality & Social Psychology,* October 1, 1998, pp. 989–1015; I. Goldenberg, K. Matheson, and J. Mantler, "The Assessment of Emotional Intelligence: A Comparison of Performance-Based and Self-Report Methodologies," *Journal of Personality Assessment,* February 2006, pp. 33–45; and J. E. Barbuto Jr. and M. E. Burbach, "The Emotional Intelligence of Transformational Leaders: A Field Study of Elected Officials," *Journal of Social Psychology,* February 2006, pp. 51–64.

55. Canadian Cancer Society 2002 study, cited in J. Gillum, "Strong Words, Images Target Smoking," *USA Today,* July 13, 2004, p. 10D.

56. D. Dearborn and H. Simon, "Selection Perception: A Note on the Departmental Identification of Executives," *Sociometry* 21 (1958), pp. 140–144.

57. Definition adapted from C. M. Judd and B. Park, "Definition and Assessment of Accuracy in Social Stereotypes," *Psychological Review,* January 1993, p. 110. See also D. T. Wegener, J. K. Clark, and R. E. Petty, "Not All Stereotyping Is Created Equal: Differential Consequences of Thoughtful Versus Nonthoughtful Stereotyping," *Journal of Personality and Social Psychology,* January 2006, pp. 42–59.

58. I. K. Broverman, S. Raymond Vogel, D. M. Broverman, F. E. Clarkson, and P. S. Rosenkrantz, "Sex-Role Stereotypes: A Current Appraisal," *Journal of Social Issues,* 1972, p. 75.

59. B. P. Allen, "Gender Stereotypes Are Not Accurate: A Replication of Martin (1987) Using Diagnostic vs. Self-Report and Behavioral Criteria," *Sex Roles,* May 1995, pp. 583–600.

60. J. Landau, "The Relationship of Race and Gender to Managers' Ratings of Promotion Potential," *Journal of Organizational Behavior,* July 1995, pp. 391–400.

61. S. R. Rhodes, "Age-Related Differences in Work Attitudes and Behavior: A Review and Conceptual Analysis," *Psychological Bulletin,* March 1983, p. 38.

62. See G. M. McEvoy, "Cumulative Evidence of the Relationship between Employee Age and Job Performance," *Journal of Applied Psychology,* February 1989, pp. 11–17; D. A. Waldman and B. J. Avolio, "Aging and Work Performance in Perspective: Contextual and Developmental Considerations," in G. R. Ferris, ed., *Research in Personnel and Human Resources Management*, vol. 11 (Greenwich, CT: JAI Press, 1993), pp. 133–162; and B. J. Avolio, D. A. Waldman, and M. A. McDaniel, "Age and Work Performance in Nonmanagerial Jobs: The Effects of Experience and Occupational Type," *Academy of Management Journal,* June 1990, pp. 407–422.

63. J. J. Martocchio, "Age-Related Differences in Employee Absenteeism: A Meta-Analysis," *Psychology and Aging,* December 1989, pp. 409–414; and M. C. Healy, M. Lehman, and M. A. McDaniel, "Age and Voluntary Turnover: A

Quantitative Review," *Personnel Psychology,* Summer 1995, pp. 335–345.

64. "U.S. Median Age Highest Ever," *U.S. Government Info/ Resources,* http://usgovinfo.about.com/library/weekly/aa05180la.htm (accessed August 26, 2006).

65. K. Helliker, "The Doctor Is Still In: Secrets of Health from a Famed 96-Year-Old Physician," *The Wall Street Journal,* March 8, 2005, p. D1.

66. M. Galen and A. T. Palmer, "Diversity: Beyond the Numbers Game," *Business Week,* August 14, 1995, pp. 60–61.

67. J. C. Brigham, "Limiting Conditions of the 'Physical Attractiveness Stereotype': Attributions about Divorce," *Journal of Research and Personality* 14 (1980), pp. 365–375; H. Hatfield and S. Sprecher, *Mirror, Mirror . . . The Importance of Looks in Everyday Life* (Albany, NY: State University of New York Press, 1986).

68. M. M. Clifford and E. H. Walster, "The Effect of Physical Attractiveness on Teacher Expectation," *Sociology of Education* 46 (1973), pp. 248–258.

69. T. Cash and L. H. Janda, "The Eye of the Beholder," *Psychology Today,* December 1984, pp. 46–52.

70. M. M. Mobius and T. S. Rosenblat, "Why Beauty Matters," *American Economic Review,* March 2006, pp. 222–235. A prepublication version of the paper is available at http://trosenblat.web.wesleyan.edu/home/beauty2005.pdf (accessed August 26, 2006).

71. Ibid.

72. H. R. Varian, "Beauty and the Fattened Wallet," *The New York Times,* April 6, 2006, http://www.nytimes.com/2006/04/06/business/06scene.html?ex=1301976000&en=a5f0aall31668f77&ei=5090&partner=rssuserland&emc=rss (accessed August 26, 2006).

73. S. J. Linton and L. E. Warg, "Attributions (Beliefs) and Job Satisfaction Associated with Back Pain in an Industrial Setting," *Perceptual and Motor Skills,* February 1993, pp. 51–62.

74. W. S. Silver, T. R. Mitchell, and M. E. Gist, "Responses to Successful and Unsuccessful Performance: The Moderating Effect of Self-Efficacy on the Relationship between Performance and Attributions," *Organizational Behavior and Human Decision Processes,* June 1995, pp. 286–299; and D. Dunning, A. Leuenberger, and D. A. Sherman, "A New Look at Motivated Inference: Are Self-Serving Theories of Success a Product of Motivational Forces?" *Journal of Personality and Social Psychology,* July 1995, pp. 58–68.

75. L. Woellert, "The-Reporter-Did-It Defense," *BusinessWeek,* May 8, 2006, p. 34.

76. See D. Eden and Y. Zuk, "Seasickness as a Self-Fulfilling Prophecy: Raising Self-Efficacy to Boost Performance at Sea," *Journal of Applied Psychology,* October 1995, pp. 628–635. For a thorough review of research on the Pygmalion effect, see D. Eden, *Pygmalion in Management: Productivity as a Self-Fulfilling Prophecy* (Lexington, MA: Lexington Books, 1990), ch. 2.

77. D. B. McNatt, "Ancient Pygmalion Joins Contemporary Management: A Meta-Analysis of the Result," *Journal of Applied Psychology,* April 2000, pp. 314–322.

78. See B. Schlender, "How Bill Gates Keeps the Magic Going," *Fortune,* June 18, 1990, pp. 82–89.

79. These recommendations were adapted from J. Keller, "Have Faith—in You," *Selling Power,* June 1996, pp. 84, 86; and R. W. Goddard, "The Pygmalion Effect," *Personnel Journal,* June 1985, p. 10.

80. *The Wirthlin Report,* reported in "Job Stress Can Be Satisfying," *USA Today,* April 19, 1999, p. 1B.

81. Study by The Medstat Group appearing in the *American Journal of Health Promotion,* October 3, 2000, reported in

82. Study in *Circulation,* March 1998, reported in "Managers at Risk from Work Stress," *San Jose Mercury News,* April 12, 1998, p. 5E; reprinted from *The New York Times.*

83. See A. J. Kinicki, F. M. McKee-Ryan, C. A. Schriesheim, and K. P. Carson, "Assessing the Construct Validity of the Job Descriptive Index: A Review and Meta-Analysis," *Journal of Applied Psychology,* February 2002, pp. 14–32; M. A. Cavanaugh, W. R. Boswell, M. V. Roehling, and J. W. Boudreau, "An Empirical Examination of Self-Reported Work Stress among U.S. Managers," *Journal of Applied Psychology,* February 2000, pp. 65–74; and J. R. Edwards and N. P. Rothbard, "Work and Family Stress and Well-Being: An Examination of Person-Environment Fit in the Work and Family Domains," *Organizational Behavior and Human Decision Processes,* February 1999, pp. 85–129.

84. R. S. Schuler, "Definition and Conceptualization of Stress in Organizations," *Organizational Behavior and Human Performance,* April 1980, p. 1980; and R. S. Lazarus, *Psychological Stress and Coping Processes* (New York: McGraw-Hill, 1966).

85. H. Selye, *Stress without Distress* (New York: Lippincott, 1974), p. 27.

86. R. S. Lazarus and S. Folkman, "Coping and Adaptation," in W. D. Gentry, ed., *Handbook of Behavioral Medicine* (New York: Guilford, 1982).

87. R. S. Lazarus, "Little Hassles Can Be Hazardous to Health," *Psychology Today,* July 1981, p. 61.

88. Selye, 1974, pp. 28–29.

89. M. Friedman and R. H. Rosenman, *Type A Behavior and Your Heart* (Greenwich, CT: Fawcett Publications, 1974), p. 84.

90. See M. S. Taylor, E. A. Locke, C. Lee, and. M. E. Gist, "Type A Behavior and Faculty Research Productivity: What Are the Mechanisms?" *Organizational Behavior and Human Performance,* December 1984, pp. 402–418; S. D. Bluen, J. Barling, and W. Burns, "Predicting Sales Performance, Job Satisfaction, and Depression by Using the Achievement Strivings and Impatience–Irritability Dimensions of Type A Behavior," *Journal of Applied Psychology,* April 1990, pp. 212–216; and C. Lee, L. F. Jamieson, and P. C. Earley, "Beliefs and Fears and Type A Behavior: Implications for Academic Performance and Psychiatric Health Disorder Symptoms," *Journal of Organizational Behavior,* March 1996, pp. 151–177.

91. S. A. Lyness, "Predictors of Differences between Type A and B Individuals in Heart Rate and Blood Pressure Reactivity," *Psychological Bulletin,* September 1993, pp. 266–295; S. Booth-Kewley and H. S. Friedman, "Psychological Predictors of Heart Disease: A Quantitative Review," *Psychological Bulletin,* May 1987, pp. 343–362; and T. Q. Miller, T. W. Smith, C. W. Turner, M. L. Guijarro, and A. J. Hallet, "A Meta-Analytic Review of Research on Hostility and Physical Health," *Psychological Bulletin,* March 1996, pp. 322–348.

92. T. D. Schellhardt, "Company Memo to Stressed-Out Employees: 'Deal with It,'" *The Wall Street Journal,* October 2, 1996, pp. B1, B4; see also L. A. Wah, "An Executive's No. 1 Fear," *American Management Association International,* January 1998, p. 87.

93. J. A. Davy, A. J. Kinicki, and C. L. Scheck, "A Test of Job Security's Direct and Mediated Effects on Withdrawal Cognitions," *Journal of Organizational Behavior,* July 1, 1997, p. 323.

94. G. Graen, "Role-Making Processes within Complex Organizations," in M. D. Dunnette, ed., *Handbook of Industrial and Organizational Psychology,* (Chicago: Rand McNally, 1976), p. 1201.

95. T. D. Wall, P. R. Jackson, S. Mullarkey, and S. K. Parker, "The Demands-Control Model of Job Strain: A More Specific Test,"

K. Fackelmann, "Stress, Unhealthy Habits Costing USA," *USA Today,* October 3, 2000, p. 5A.

Journal of Occupational and Organizational Psychology, June 1996, pp. 153–166; and R. C. Barnett and R. T. Brennan, "The Relationship between Job Experiences and Psychological Distress: A Structural Equation Approach," *Journal of Organizational Behavior,* May 1995, pp. 250–276.

96. "Lousiest Bosses," *The Wall Street Journal,* April 4, 1995, p. A1.

97. J. Schaubroeck and D. C. Ganster, "Chronic Demands and Responsivity to Challenge," *Journal of Applied Psychology,* February 1993, pp. 73–85; E. Demerouti, A. B. Bakker, F. Nachreiner, and W. B. Schaufeli, "The Job Demands-Resources Model of Burnout," *Journal of Applied Psychology,* June 2001, pp. 499–512.

98. J. M. Plas, *Person-Centered Leadership: An American Approach to Participatory Management* (Thousand Oaks, CA: Sage, 1996).

99. M. Patsalos-Fox, quoted in W. J. Holstein, "Tension Headaches in the Corner Office," *The New York Times,* March 12, 2006, sec. 3, p. 1.

100. N. E. Adler, T. Boyce, M. A. Chesney, S. Cohen, S. Folkman, R. L. Kahn, and S. L. Syme, "Socioeconomic Status and Health: The Challenge of the Gradient," *American Psychologist,* January 1994, pp. 15–24.

101. The link between stress and depression is discussed by P. Freiberg, "Work and Well-Being: Experts Urge Changes in Work, Not the Work," *The APA Monthly,* January 1991, p. 23.

102. M. Staver, quoted in C. H. Deutsch, "Winning the Battle Against Burnout," *The New York Times,* August 27, 2006, sec. 3, p. 5.

103. Absenteeism and stress are discussed by S. Shellenbarger, "Work & Family: Was That 24-Hour Flu That Kept You Home Really Just the Blahs?" *The Wall Street Journal,* July 24, 1996, p. B1.

104. "Workplace Drug Use Appears on Decline," *Arizona Republic,* July 7, 2003, p. D1; reprinted from *The New York Times.*

105. M. Ferri, L. Amato, and M. Davoli, "Alcoholics Anonymous and Other 12-Step Programmes for Alcohol Dependence (Review)," *Cochrane Database of Scientific Reviews,* 2006, Issue 3. See also report in N. Bakalar, "Review Sees No Advantage in 12-Step Programs," *The New York Times,* July 25, 2006, p. D6.

106. Recommendations for reducing burnout are discussed by M. Wylie, "Preventing Worker Burnout while Supporting the Users," *MacWeek,* October 4, 1993, pp. 12–14; and "How to Avoid Burnout," *Training,* February 1993, pp. 15, 16, 70.

107. These examples and techniques are discussed by R. L. Rose, "Time Out: At the Menninger Clinic, Executives Learn More About Themselves—and Why They're So Unhappy," *The Wall Street Journal,* February 26, 1996, p. R5; and L. Landon, "Pump Up Your Employees," *HR Magazine,* May 1990, pp. 34–37.

108. F. Luthans, *Organizational Behavior* (New York: McGraw-Hill, 1985), pp. 146–148.

CHAPTER 12

1. A. Zipkin, "The Wisdom of Thoughtfulness," *The New York Times,* May 31, 2000, pp. C1, C10; L. Brenner, "Perks that Work," *BusinessWeek Frontier,* October 11, 1999, pp. F.22–F.30; L. Alderman, "And We'll Even Throw In . . . ," *BusinessWeek Frontier,* October 11, 1999, pp. F.34–F.37; L. Stern, "Talent Trawl: What's the Best Bait?" *BusinessWeek Enterprise,* December 7, 1998, pp. ENT22–ENT24; and S. Schafer, "Battling a Labor Shortage? It's All in Your Imagination," *Inc.,* August 1997, p. 24.

2. Adapted from definition in T. R. Mitchell, "Motivation: New Directions for Theory, Research, and Practice," *Academy of Management Review,* January 1982, p. 81.

3. See R. M. Ryan and E. L. Deci, "Intrinsic and Extrinsic Motivations: Classic Definitions and New Directions," *Contemporary Educational Psychology,* January 2000, pp. 54–67.

4. D. Katz and R. L. Kahn, *The Social Psychology of Organizations* (New York: Wiley, 1966).

5. K. Down and L. Liedtka, "What Corporations Seek in MBA Hires: A Survey," *Selections,* Winter 1994, pp. 34–39; see also S. Armour, "Companies Get Tough on Absent Employees," *Arizona Republic,* February 7, 2003, p. A2; reprinted from *USA Today.*

6. T. Van Tassel, "Productivity Dilemmas," *Executive Excellence,* April 1994, pp. 16–17.

7. A. Maslow, "A Theory of Human Motivation," *Psychological Review,* July 1943, pp. 370–396.

8. C. C. Pinder, *Work Motivation: Theory, Issues, and Applications* (Glenview, IL: Scott, Foresman, 1984), p. 52.

9. H. Benson, "In an Era of High Technology, Low Commitment, One Man Says He's Found a Way to Measure Integrity," *San Francisco Chronicle,* June 21, 2006, pp. E1, E3.

10. P. H. Ray and S. R. Anderson, *The Cultural Creatives: How 50 Million People Are Changing the World* (New York: Harmony Books, 2000).

11. D. E. Meyerson, *Tempered Radicals: How Everyday Leaders Inspire Change at Work* (Boston: Harvard Business School Press, 2003). For examples of the need for achievement, see M. R. della Cava, "Answering Their Calling," *USA Today,* March 13, 2006, pp. 1D, 2D.

12. D. C. McClelland, *Human Motivation* (Glenview, IL: Scott, Foresman, 1985).

13. D. McClelland and H. Burnham, "Power Is the Great Motivator," *Harvard Business Review,* March/April 1976, pp. 100–110.

14. D. C. McClelland and R. E. Boyatsis, "The Leadership Motive Pattern and Long Term Success in Management," *Journal of Applied Psychology* 67 (1982), pp. 737–743.

15. Recent studies of achievement motivation can be found in H. Grant and C. S. Dweck, "A Goal Analysis of Personality and Personality Coherence," in D. Cervone and Y. Shoda, eds., *The Coherence of Personality* (New York: Guilford Press, 1999), pp. 345–371.

16. S. A. Flaum and J. A. Flaum, with M. Flaum, *The 100-Mile Walk: A Father and Son on a Quest to Find the Essence of Leadership* (New York: Amacom, 2006). See also J. C. Mead, "How to Succeed in Business: Walk," *The New York Times,* January 29, 2006, sec. 14LI, p. 6; S. Berfield, "Walk 100 Miles in My Shoes," *BusinessWeek,* June 26, 2006, pp. 80–81.

17. F. Herzberg, B. Mausner, and B. B. Snyderman, *The Motivation to Work* (New York: Wiley, 1959); and F. Herzberg, "One More Time: How Do You Motivate Employees?" *Harvard Business Review,* January–February 1968, pp. 53–62.

18. J. S. Adams, "Toward an Understanding of Inequity," *Journal of Abnormal and Social Psychology,* November 1963, pp. 422–436; and J. S. Adams, "Injustice in Social Exchange," in L. Berkowitz, ed., *Advances in Experimental Social Psychology,* 2nd ed. (New York: Academic Press, 1965), pp. 267–300.

19. U.S. Department of Commerce, cited in A. Salkever, "An Easy Antidote to Employee Theft," *BusinessWeek online,* May 20, 2003, www.businessweek.com/smallbiz/content/may2003/sb20030520_9328_sb018.htm (accessed July 10, 2004). See also J. Greenberg, "Employee Theft as a Reaction to Underpayment Inequity: The Hidden Cost of Pay Cuts," *Journal of Applied Psychology* 75 (1990), pp. 561–568.

20. See M. A. Korsgaard and L. Roberson, "Procedural Justice in Performance Evaluation: The Role of Instrumental and Non-Instrumental Voice in Performance Appraisal Decisions," *Journal of Management,* 1995, pp. 657–669; the role of

voice in justice perceptions was investigated by D. R. Avery and M. A. Quiñones, "Disentangling the Effects of Voice: The Incremental Roles of Opportunity, Behavior, and Instrumentality in Predicting Procedural Fairness," *Journal of Applied Psychology,* February 2002, pp. 81–86.

21. B. J. Tepper, "Health Consequences of Organizational Injustice: Tests of Main and Interactive Effects," *Organizational Behavior and Human Decision Processes,* November 2001, pp. 197–215; and S. Fox, P. E. Spector, and D. Miles, "Counterproductive Work Behavior (CWB) in Response to Job Stressors and Organizational Justice: Some Mediator and Moderator Tests for Autonomy and Emotions," *Journal of Vocational Behavior,* December 2001, pp. 291–309.

22. V. H. Vroom, *Work and Motivation* (New York: Wiley, 1964).

23. J. S. Lublin, "Boards Tie CEO Pay More Tightly to Performance," *The Wall Street Journal,* February 21, 2006, pp. A1, A14.

24. A Hudson survey of 10,000 employees March 20–26, 2006, found that 48% of managers but only 31% of nonmanagers agreed with the statement "Employees who do a better job get paid more"; 46% of managers but only 29% of nonmanagers agreed with the statement "My last raise was based on performance." Information cited in "Reasons for Raises," *BusinessWeek,* May 29, 2006, p. 11.

25. Research supporting the need to establish a direct relationship between pay and performance can be found in M. L. Williams, M. A. McDaniel, and N. T. Nguyen, "A Meta-Analysis of the Antecedents and Consequences of Pay Level Satisfaction," *Journal of Applied Psychology,* March 2006, pp. 392–413; and R. Kuvaas, "Work Performance, Affective Commitment, and Work Motivation: The Roles of Pay Administration and Pay Level," *Journal of Organizational Behavior,* May 2006, pp. 365–385.

26. Community Training and Assistance Center, *Catalyst for Change: Pay for Performance in Denver—Final Report,* January 2004; http://www.ctacusa.com/denvervol3-front-section.pdf (accessed September 1, 2006). See also Community Training and Assistance Center, "Teacher Pay for Performance: Catalyst for Change," press release, *CTAC News,* February 9, 2004; http://www.ctacusa.com/news3.html (accessed September 1, 2006).

27. P. Whoriskey, "Fla. to Link Teacher Pay to Students' Test Scores," *Washington Post,* March 22, 2006, p. A1; R. Tomsho, "More Districts Pay Teachers for Performance," *The Wall Street Journal,* March 23, 2006, pp. B1, B5; R. Grover and A. Bernstein, "Arnold Gets Strict with the Teachers," *BusinessWeek,* May 2, 2005, pp. 84–85; and E. W. Green, " More Apples for the Very Best Teachers," *U.S. News & World Report,* September 18, 2006, p. 40.

28. For a thorough discussion of goal-setting theory and application, see E. A. Locke and G. P. Latham, "Building a Practically Useful Theory of Goal Setting and Task Motivation," *American Psychologist,* September 2002, pp. 705–717.

29. B. Melin, U. Lundberg, J. Söderlund, and M. Granqvist, "Psychological and Physiological Stress Reactions of Male and Female Assembly Workers: A Comparison between Two Different Forms of Work Organization," *Journal of Organizational Behavior,* January 1999, pp. 47–61; and S. Melamed, I. Ben-Avi, J. Luz, and M. S. Green, "Objective and Subjective Work Monotony: Effects on Job Satisfaction, Psychological Distress, and Absenteeism in Blue-Collar Workers," *Journal of Applied Psychology,* February 1995, pp. 29–42.

30. M. A. Campion and C. L. McClelland, "Follow-Up and Extension of the Interdisciplinary Costs and Benefits of Enlarged Jobs," *Journal of Applied Psychology,* June 1993, pp. 339–351.

31. Herzberg et al., 1959.

32. S. Phillips and A. Dunkin, "King Customer," *BusinessWeek,* March 12, 1990, p. 91.

33. J. R. Hackman and G. R. Oldham, *Work Redesign* (Reading, MA: Addison-Wesley, 1980).

34. A. Taylor III, "Rally of the Dolls: It Worked for Toyota. Can It Work for Toys?" *Fortune,* January 11, 1999, p. 36.

35. See E. L. Thorndike, *Educational Psychology: The Psychology of Learning, Vol. II* (New York: Columbia University Teachers College, 1913); B. F. Skinner, *Walden Two* (New York: Macmillan, 1948); *Science and Human Behavior* (New York: Macmillan, 1953); and *Contingencies of Reinforcement* (New York: Appleton-Century-Crofts, 1969).

36. Taisdeal, quoted in Benson, 2006. For an article about the importance of congeniality, see D. Brady, "Charm Offensive," *BusinessWeek,* June 26, 2006, pp. 76–80.

37. Zipkin, 2000.

38. Gallup Organization study, reported in Zipkin, 2000.

39. E. White, "The Best vs. the Rest," *The Wall Street Journal,* January 30, 2006, pp. B1, B3; and J. Pfeffer, "Stopping the Talent Drain," *Business 2.0,* July 2006, p. 80.

40. See, for example, J. Anderson, "Tying One's Pay to Performance. What a Concept," *The New York Times,* July 15, 2005, p. C7. Also see M. J. Canyon, "Executive Compensation and Incentives," *Academy of Management Perspectives,* February 2006, pp. 25–44.

41. B. E. Graham-Moore and T. L. Ross, *Productivity Gainsharing* (Englewood Cliffs, NJ: Prentice-Hall, 1983).

42. "Take Stock of Stock Options," *Human Resource Executive Magazine,* June 3, 2004, workindex.com; www.workindex.com/editorial/ hre/hre0406-03.asp (accessed July 12, 2006).

43. K. Clark, "Too Safe a Bet?" *U.S. News & World Report,* June 19, 2006, pp. 37–38.

44. Lewis, 2000.

45. PricewaterhouseCoopers survey, reported in S. Shellenbarger, "What Job Candidates Really Want to Know: Will I Have a Life?" *The Wall Street Journal,* November 17, 1999, p. B1.

46. K. W. Smola and C. D. Sutton, "Generational Differences: Revisiting Generational Work Values for the New Millennium," *Journal of Organizational Behavior,* June 2002, p. 379.

47. Walker Information survey, reported in Lewis, 2000.

48. Spherion and Louis Harris Associates 1999 survey, reported in Zipkin, 2000.

49. See P. Falcone, "Doing More with Less: How to Motivate and Reward Your Overworked Staff During Lean Times," *HR Magazine,* February 2003, pp. 101–103; D. Kehrer, "Here Are Some Keys to Keeping Good Employees," *Reno Gazette-Journal,* March 30, 2004, p. 4D; and J. Noveck, "Do Bosses Need to Be Mean to Get Work Done?" *Nevada Appeal,* July 9, 2006, pp. D1, D2.

50. B. L. Ware, quoted in Zipkin, 2000.

51. B. Moses, quoted in Lewis, 2000.

52. K. Lingle, quoted in C. Kleiman, "Work-Life Rewards Grow," *San Francisco Examiner,* January 16, 2000, p. J-2; reprinted from *Chicago Tribune.*

53. S. Shellenberger, "Companies Retool Time-Off Policies to Prevent Burnout, Reward Performance," *The Wall Street Journal,* January 5, 2006, p. D1.

54. C. Kleiman, "CEO of Family-Friendly Firm Tells Others to 'Just Do It,'" *San Jose Mercury News,* September 19, 1999, p. PC-1; and D. Dallinger, "Battling for a Balanced Life," *San Francisco Chronicle,* November 14, 1999, "Sunday" section, p. 9; see also A. Fisher, "The Rebalancing Act," *Fortune,* October 6, 2003, pp. 110–113; D. Cadrain, "Cash vs. Non-cash Rewards," *HR Magazine,* April 2003, pp. 81–87; C. Hymowitz, "While Some Women Choose to Stay Home, Others Gain Flexibility," *The Wall Street Journal,* March 30, 2004, p. B1; J. Shramm,

"Fuel Economy," *HR Magazine,* December 2005, p. 120; S. Armour, "Cost-Effective 'Homesourcing' Grows," *USA Today,* March 13, 2006, p. 1B; S. E. Needleman, "Pick Worker Rewards Carefully," *The Wall Street Journal,* March 28, 2006, p. B8; and M. P. McQueen, "Employers Expand Elder-Care Benefits," *The Wall Street Journal,* July 27, 2006, pp. D1, D6.

55. A. Hedge, quoted in P. Wen, "Drab Cubicles Can Block Workers' Creativity, Productivity," *San Francisco Chronicle,* March 10, 2000, pp. B1, B3; reprinted from *Boston Globe.*

56. J. Sturges, N. Conway, D. Guest, and A. Liefooghe, "Managing the Career Deal: The Psychological Contract as a Framework for Understanding Career Management, Organizational Commitment, and Work Behavior," *Journal of Organizational Behavior,* November 2005, pp. 821–838; and J. Badal, "'Career Path' Programs Help Retain Workers," *The Wall Street Journal,* July 24, 2006, pp. B1, B4.

57. J. P. Smith, "Sabbaticals Pervade Business Sector," *Reno Gazette-Journal,* February 22, 2004, p. H1; M. Arndt, "Nice Work If You Can Get It," *BusinessWeek,* January 9, 2006, pp. 56–57; and L. Chao, "Sabbaticals Can Offer Dividends for Employers," *The Wall Street Journal,* July 17, 2006, p. B5.

CHAPTER 13

1. K. W. Thomas, "Conflict and Conflict Management," in M. Dunnette, ed., *Handbook of Industrial and Organizational Psychology* (Chicago: Rand McNally, 1976), pp. 889–935; K. W. Thomas "Toward Multiple Dimensional Values in Teaching: The Example of Conflict Behaviors," *Academy of Management Review,* July 1977, pp. 484–490; and M. A Rahim, "A Strategy for Managing Conflict in Complex Organizations," *Human Relations,* January 1985, p. 84.

2. Rahim, 1985.

3. "Once the Best, U.S. Settles for Bronze," *The New York Times,* September 3, 2006; http://www.nytimes.com/aponline/sports/AP-BKO-Worlds-U.S.html (accessed September 4, 2006).

4. A. Bagnato, "Greek Tragedy: Team USA's Dreams of Gold Gone," *Reno Gazette-Journal,* September 2, 2006, p. 2B.

5. M. Sokolove, "One Team, Indivisible?" *Play* (special edition of *The New York Times Magazine*), September 2006, p. 18.

6. "Top 10 Leadership Tips from Jeff Immelt," *Fast Company,* April 2004, p. 96.

7. P. F. Drucker, "The Coming of the New Organization," *Harvard Business Review,* January–February 1988, pp. 45–53.

8. T. Kelley, quoted in P. Sinton, "Teamwork the Name of the Game for Ideo," *San Francisco Chronicle,* February 23, 2000, pp. D1, D3.

9. This definition is based in part on one found in D. Horton Smith, "A Parsimonious Definition of 'Group': Toward Conceptual Clarity and Scientific Utility," *Sociological Inquiry,* Spring 1967, pp. 141–167.

10. E. H. Schein, *Organizational Psychology,* 3rd ed. (Englewood Cliffs, NJ: Prentice-Hall, 1980), p. 145.

11. J. R. Katzenbach and D. K. Smith, *The Wisdom of Teams: Creating the High-Performance Organization* (Boston: Harvard Business School Press, 1993), p. 45.

12. J. R. Katzenbach and D. K. Smith, "The Discipline of Teams," *Harvard Business Review,* March–April 1995, p. 112.

13. D. Krackhardt and J. R. Hanson, "Informal Networks: The Company Behind the Chart," *Harvard Business Review,* July–August 1993, p. 104.

14. Study by Center for Workforce Development, Newton, MA, reported in M. Jackson, "It's Not Chitchat, It's Training," *San Francisco Chronicle,* January 7, 1998, p. D2.

15. Center for Workforce Development, *The Teaching Firm: Where Productive Work and Learning Converge* (Newton, MA: Education Development Center, 1998). For more on informal learning, see D. W. Livingstone and R. Roth, "Workers' Knowledge: An Untapped Resource in the Labour Movement," paper presented at the International Conference on Union Growth, Toronto, April 30–May 1, 2001, http://www.oise.utoronto.ca/depts/sese/csew/nall/res/31workers.htm (accessed September 4, 2006); V. J. Marsick and K. E. Watkins, "Informal and Incidental Learning," *New Directions for Adult and Continuing Education,* February 26, 2002, pp. 25–34; and M. B. Twidale, "Over the Shoulder Learning: Supporting Brief Informal Learning," *Computer Supported Cooperative Work,* December 2005, pp. 505–547.

16. G. Marty, "Exploring the Frontiers of Learning and Work," *Brief,* May 11, 2005; http://www1.umn.edu/umnnews/Feature_Stories/Exploring_the_frontiers_of_learning_and_work.html (accessed September 4, 2006).

17. E. Sundstrom, K. P. DeMeuse, and D. Futrell, "Work Teams," *American Psychologist,* February 1990, pp. 120–133.

18. See K. Buch and R. Spangler, "The Effects of Quality Circles on Performance and Promotions," *Human Relations,* June 1990, pp. 573–582; and G. R. Ferris and J. A. Wagner III, "Quality Circles in the United States: a Conceptual Reevaluation," *The Journal of Applied Behavioral Science,* no. 2, 1985, pp. 155–167. See also E. E. Lawler III and S. A. Mohrman, "Quality Circles: After the Honeymoon," *Organizational Dynamics,* Spring 1987, pp. 42–54; and E. E. Lawler III, "Total Quality Management and Employee Involvement: Are They Compatible?" *Academy of Management Executive,* February 1994, pp. 68–76.

19. G. L. Stewart and M. R. Barrick, "Team Structure and Performance: Assessing the Mediating Role of Intrateam Process and the Moderating Role of Task," *Academy of Management Journal,* April 2000, p. 135.

20. Good background discussions can be found in P. S. Goodman, R. Devadas, and T. L. Griffith Hughson, "Groups and Productivity: Analyzing the Effectiveness of Self-Managing Teams," in J. P. Campbell, R. J. Campbell, and Associates, eds., *Productivity in Organizations* (San Francisco: Jossey-Bass, 1988), pp. 295–327; also see E. G. Rogers, W. Metlay, I. T. Kaplan, and T. Shapiro, "Self-Managing Work Teams: Do They Really Work?" *Human Resource Planning,* no. 2, 1995, pp. 53–57; and V. U. Druskat and S. B. Wolff, "Effects and Timing of Developmental Peer Appraisals in Self-Managing Work Teams," *Journal of Applied Psychology,* February 1999, pp. 58–74.

21. See C. Douglas and W. L. Gardner, "Transition to Self-Directed Work Teams: Implications of Transition Time and Self-Monitoring for Managers' Use of Influence Tactics," *Journal of Organizational Behavior* 25 (2004), pp. 47–65; and K. Kraiger, "Perspectives on Training and Development," in W. C. Borman, D. R. Ilgen, and R. J. Klimoski, eds., *Handbook of Psychology,* vol. 12 (New York: John Wiley, 2003), pp. 176–177.

22. C. Douglas and W. L. Gardner, "Transition to Self-Directed Work Teams: Implications of Transition Time and Self-Monitoring for Managers' Use of Influence Tactics," *Journal of Organizational Behavior* 25 (2004), pp. 47–65.

23. See B. S. Bell and S. W. J. Kozlowski, "A Typology of Virtual Teams: Implications for Effective Leadership," *Group & Organization Management,* March 2002, pp. 14–49.

24. Review of J. Lipnack and J. Stamps, *Virtual Teams: Reaching Across Space, Time, and Organization with Technology* (New York: John Wiley, 1997), in "Virtual Teams Transcend Space and Time," *The Futurist,* September–October 1997, p. 59.

25. W. Arnold, "Cathay Pacific Is Lesson in Culture, Computing," *The Wall Street Journal,* November 25, 1998, p. B6.

26. Adapted from "Managing the Challenge of a Virtual Work-place," box in C. Sandlund, "Remote Control," *BusinessWeek Frontier,* March 27, 2000, pp. F.14–F.20; see also C. Joinson, "Managing Virtual Teams," *HR Magazine,* June 2002, p. 71; A. Salkever, "Home Truths about Meetings," *BusinessWeek Online,* April 24, 2003, www.businessweek.com/smallbiz/content/apr2003/sb20030424_0977_sb010.htm (accessed July 12, 2006); J. Gordon, "Do Your Virtual Teams Deliver Only Virtual Performance?" *Training,* June 2005, pp. 20–26; Y. Shin, "Conflict Resolution in Virtual Teams," *Organizational Dynamics,* November 2005, pp. 331–345; H. Green, "It Takes a Web Village," *BusinessWeek,* September 4, 2006, p. 66; and D. L. Duarte and N. T. Snyder, *Mastering Virtual Teams: Strategies, Tools, and Techniques That Succeed,* 3rd ed. (San Francisco: Jossey-Bass, 2006).

27. See B. W. Tuckman, "Developmental Sequence in Small Groups," *Psychological Bulletin,* June 1965, pp. 384–399; and B. W. Tuckman and M. A. C. Jensen, "Stages of Small-Group Development Revisited," *Group & Organization Studies,* December 1977, pp. 419–427. An instructive adaptation of the Tuckman model can be found in L. Holpp, "If Empowerment Is So Good, Why Does It Hurt?" *Training,* March 1995, p. 56. See also C. Gersick, "Marking Time: Predictable Transitions in Task Groups," *Academy of Management Journal,* June 1989, pp. 274–309; and S. Wait, "Team Building Is Critical for Successful Growth," *Reno Gazette-Journal,* August 5, 2006, p. 5E.

28. See F. P. Morgeson, M. H. Reider, and M. A. Campion, "Selecting Individuals in Team Settings: The Importance of Social Skills, Personality Characteristics, and Teamwork Knowledge," *Personnel Psychology,* Autumn 2005, pp. 583–611.

29. Practical advice on handling a dominating group member can be found in M. Finley, "Belling the Bully," *HR Magazine,* March 1992, pp. 82–86; see also B. Carey, "Fear in the Workplace: The Bullying Boss," *The New York Times,* June 22, 2004, pp. D1, D6.

30. J. Case, "What the Experts Forgot to Mention," *Inc.,* September 1993, pp. 66–78.

31. M. Erez, "Is Group Productivity Loss the Rule or the Exception? Effects of Culture and Group-based Motivation," *Academy of Management Journal* 39 (1996), pp. 1513–1537.

32. "Is Your Team Too Big? Too Small? What's the Right Number?" *Knowledge@Wharton,* June 14, 2006, Wharton School, University of Pennsylvania, http://knowledge.wharton.upenn.edu/article.cfm?articleid=1501&CFID=1653072&CFTOKEN=14318984 (accessed September 1, 2006).

33. "A Team's-Eye View of Teams," *Training,* November 1995, p. 16.

34. M. E. Shaw, *Group Dynamics,* 3rd ed. (New York: McGraw-Hill, 1981); G. Manners, "Another Look at Group Size, Group Problem-Solving and Member Consensus," *Academy of Management Journal* 18 (1975), pp. 715–724.

35. H.-S. Hwang and J. Guynes, "The Effect of Group Size on Group Performance in Computer-Supported Decision Making," *Information & Management,* April 1994, pp. 189–198.

36. S. J. Karau and K. D. Williams, "Social Loafing: Research Findings, Implications, and Future Directions," *Current Directions in Psychological Science,* October 1995, pp. 134–140; S. J. Zacarro, "Social Loafing: The Role of Task Attractiveness," *Personality and Social Psychology Bulletin* 10 (1984), pp. 99–106; P. W. Mulvey, L. Bowes-Sperry, and H. J. Klein, "The Effects of Perceived Loafing and Defensive Impression Management on Group Effectiveness," *Small Group Research,* June 1998, pp. 394–415; and L. Karakowsky and K. McBey, "Do My Contributions Matter? The Influence of Imputed Expertise on Member Involvement and Self-Evaluations in the Work Group," *Group & Organization Management,* March 2001, pp. 70–92.

37. B.-C. Lim and K. J. Klein, "Team Mental Models and Team Performance: A Field Study of the Effects of Team Mental Model Similarity and Accuracy," *Journal of Organizational Behavior,* January 2006, pp. 403–418.

38. J. L. Yang, "The Power of Number 4.6," *Fortune,* June 12, 2006, p. 122.

39. Deutschman, 1994.

40. J. R. Hackman, *Leading Teams: Setting the Stage for Great Performances* (Boston: Harvard Business School Press, 2002).

41. J. R. Hackman and N. J. Vidmar, "Effects of Size and Task Type on Group Performance and Member Reactions," *Sociometry* 33 (1970), pp. 37–54.

42. K. J. Klein, cited in "Is Your Team Too Big? Too Small? What's the Right Number?" June 14, 2006.

43. K. D. Benne and P. Sheats, "Functional Roles of Group Members," *Journal of Social Issues,* Spring 1948, pp. 41–49.

44. D. C. Feldman, "The Development and Enforcement of Group Norms," *Academy of Management Review,* January 1984, pp. 47–53.

45. D. Kahneman, "Reference Points, Anchors, Norms, and Mixed Feelings," *Organizational Behavior and Human Decision Processes,* March 1992, pp. 296–312.

46. Adapted from N. Byrnes, "The Art of Motivation," *BusinessWeek,* May 1, 2006, pp. 57–62.

47. Feldman, 1984.

48. See, for example, P. Jin, "Work Motivation and Productivity in Voluntarily Formed Work Teams: A Field Study in China," *Organizational Behavior and Human Decision Processes* 54, no. 1 (1993), pp. 133–155.

49. L. Janis, *Groupthink,* 2nd ed. (Boston: Houghton Mifflin, 1982), p. 9.

50. V. Kemper, "Groupthink Viewed as Culprit in Move to War," *Los Angeles Times,* July 10, 2004; www.latimes.com/la-na-groupthink10jul10,1,4397696.story (accessed July 12, 2006).

51. J. Surowiecki, quoted in J. Freeman, "Books," *The Christian Science Monitor,* May 25, 2004; www.csmonitor.com/2004/0525/p15s01-bogn.html (accessed July 12, 2004). Also see J. Surowiecki, *The Wisdom of Crowds: Why the Many Are Smarter Than the Few and How Collective Wisdom Shapes Business, Economies, Societies, and Nations* (New York: Doubleday, 2004).

52. V. H. Palmieri, quoted in L. Baum, "The Job Nobody Wants," *BusinessWeek,* September 8, 1986, p. 60.

53. Surowiecki, quoted in Kemper, 2004. See also J. A. LePine, "Adaptation of Teams in Response to Unforeseen Change: Effects of Goal Difficulty and Team Composition in Terms of Cognitive Ability and Goal Orientation," *Journal of Applied Psychology* 90 (2005), pp. 1153–1167.

54. M. R. Callway and J. K. Desser, "Groupthink: Effects of Cohesiveness and Problem-Solving Procedures on Group Decision Making," *Social Behavior and Personality,* no. 2, 1984, pp.157–164.

55. Adapted from N. Byrnes, P. Burrows, and L. Lee, "Dark Days at Dell," *BusinessWeek,* September 4, 2006, pp. 26–29.

56. G. A. Moore, quoted in Byrnes, Burrows, and Lee, 2006, p. 27. Moore is author of *Dealing with Darwin: How Great Companies Innovate at Every Phase of Their Evolution* (New York: Portfolio/Penguin, 2006).

57. D. H. Freedman, "Collaboration Is the Hottest Buzzword in Business Today. Too Bad It Doesn't Work," *Inc. Magazine,* September 2006, pp. 61–62.

58. B. Rosner, "How to Avoid Violence from a Fired Worker," *San Francisco Sunday Examiner & Chronicle,* November 15, 1998, p. CL-13.

59. D. Loomis, S. H. Wolf, C. W. Runyan, S. W. Marshall, and J. D. Butts, "Homicide on the Job: Workplace and Community De-

terminants," *American Journal of Epidemiology,* September I, 2001, pp. 410–417. See also J. Carpenter, "Killer Jobs: New Study Finds Risk in Retail," abcnews.com, August 29, 2001, http://abcnews.go.com/sections/business/DailyNews/workplace_mortality_010829.html (accessed July 12, 2006).

60. J. A. Wall Jr. and R. Robert Callister, "Conflict and Its Management," *Journal of Management,* no. 3, 1995, p. 517.

61. C. Alter, "An Exploratory Study of Conflict and Coordination in Interorganizational Service Delivery Systems," *Academy of Management Journal,* September 1990, pp. 478–502; S. P. Robbins, "'Conflict Management' and 'Conflict Resolution' Are Not Synonymous Terms," *California Management Review,* Winter 1978, p. 70.

62. Cooperative conflict is discussed in D. Tjosvold, *Learning to Manage Conflict: Getting People to Work Together Productively* (New York: Lexington, 1993); and D. Tjosvold and D. W. Johnson, *Productive Conflict Management Perspectives for Organizations* (New York: Irvington, 1983). See also A. C. Amason, K. R. Thompson, W. A. Hochwarter, and A. W. Harrison, "Conflict: An Important Dimension in Successful Management Teams," *Organizational Dynamics,* Autumn 1995, pp. 20–35; and A. C. Amason, "Distinguishing the Effects of Functional and Dysfunctional Conflict on Strategic Decision Making: Resolving a Paradox for Top Management Teams," *Academy of Management Journal,* February 1996, pp. 123–148.

63. L. Lange, quoted in J. Noveck, "Do Bosses Need to Be Mean to Get Work Done?" *Nevada Appeal,* July 9, 2006, pp. D1, D2. See also D. Brady, "Charm Offensive," *BusinessWeek,* June 26, 2006, pp. 76–80.

64. Study by B. Tepper, April 2004, reported in B. Carey, "Fear in the Workplace: The Bullying Boss," *The New York Times,* June 22, 2004, pp. D1, D6.

65. See B. J. Tepper, M. K. Duffy, C. A. Henle, and L. S. Lambert, "Procedural Injustice, Victim Precipitation, and Abusive Supervision," *Personnel Psychology,* March 2006, pp. 101–123. See also K. L. Zellars, B. J. Tepper, and M. K. Duffy, "Abusive Supervision and Subordinates' Organizational Citizenship Behavior," *Journal of Applied Psychology* 87 (2002), pp. 1068–1076; B. J. Tepper and E. C. Taylor, "Relationships Among Supervisors' and Subordinates' Procedural Justice Perceptions and Organizational Citizenship Behaviors," *Academy of Management Journal,* February 2003, pp. 97–105; B. J. Tepper, M. K. Duffy, J. Hoobler, and M. D. Ensley, "Moderators of the Relationship between Coworkers' Organizational Citizenship Behavior and Fellow Employees' Attitudes," *Journal of Applied Psychology,* June 2005, pp. 455–465; B. J. Tepper, M. Uhl-Bien, G. F. Kohut, S. G. Rogelberg, D. E. Lockhart, and M. D. Ensley, "Subordinates' Resistance and Managers' Evaluations of Subordinates' Performance," *Journal of Management,* April 1, 2006, pp. 185–209.

66. R. I. Sutton in "Breakthrough Ideas for 2004: The HBR List," *Harvard Business Review,* February 2004, pp. 13–24, 32–37. Sutton's topic was headed "More Trouble Than They Are Worth." His book based on these ideas is *The No Asshole Rule: Building a Civilized Workplace and Surviving One That Isn't* (New York: Warner, in press).

67. R. I. Sutton, "R. I. Sutton: Nasty People," *CIO Insight,* May 1, 2004; http://www.cioinsight.com/article2/0,1217,a=126979,00.asp (accessed September 3, 2006).

68. A. M. O'Leary-Kelly, R. W. Griffin, and D. J. Glew, "Organization-Motivated Aggression: A Research Framework," *Academy of Management Review,* January 1996, pp. 225–253.

69. L. R. Pondy, "Organizational Conflict: Concepts and Models," *Administrative Science Quarterly* 2 (1967), pp. 296–320.

70. P. Burrows, "Carly's Last Stand?" *BusinessWeek,* December 24, 2001, pp. 63–70. See B. Pimentel, "Heftier HP Is Ready to Forge Ahead," *San Francisco Chronicle,* May 5, 2002, pp. G1, G4.

71. R. A. Cosier and C. R. Schwenk, "Agreement and Thinking Alike: Ingredients for Poor Decisions," *Academy of Management Executive,* February 1990, p. 71. Also see J. P. Kotter, "Kill Complacency," *Fortune,* August 5, 1996, pp. 168–170.

72. See "Facilitators as Devil's Advocates," *Training,* September 1993, p. 10; and C. R. Schwenk, "Devil's Advocacy in Managerial Decision Making," *Journal of Management Studies,* April 1984, pp. 153–168.

73. S. G. Katzenstein, "The Debate on Structured Debate: Toward a Unified Theory," *Organizational Behavior and Human Decision Processes,* June 1996, pp. 316–332.

74. W. Kiechel III, "How to Escape the Echo Chamber," *Fortune,* June 18, 1990, p. 130.

CHAPTER 14

1. R. E. Kelley, *How to Be a Star at Work: Nine Breakthrough Strategies You Need to Succeed* (New York: Times Books, 1999); A. M. Webber, "Are You a Star at Work?" *Fast Company,* June 1998, p. 114; C. Shavers, "Being a Star at Work Requires Self-Management," *San Jose Mercury News,* December 13, 1998, p. 4E; I. DeBare, "How to Become a Star in the Workplace," *San Francisco Chronicle,* July 20, 1998, p. D2; L. M. Sixel, "So You Want to Be a Star at Your Job," *San Francisco Examiner & Chronicle,* September 13, 1998, p. CL-17; reprinted from *Houston Chronicle;* and C. Smith, "'Star' Traits Aren't Always Obvious Ones," *San Francisco Examiner & Chronicle,* August 15, 1999, p. CL-17.

2. C. A. Schriesheim, J. M. Tolliver, and O. C. Behling, "Leadership Theory: Some Implications for Managers," *MSU Business Topics,* Summer 1978, p. 35. See also G. Yukl, "Managerial Leadership: A Review of Theory and Research," *Journal of Management* 15 (1989), pp. 251–289.

3. T. Peters and N. Austin, *A Passion for Excellence* (New York: Random House, 1985), pp. 5–6; but see also B. Kellerman, "Leadership—Warts and All," *Harvard Business Review,* January 1, 2004, pp. 40–45.

4. B. M. Bass, *Bass & Stogdill's Handbook of Leadership: Theory, Research, and Managerial Applications,* 3rd ed. (New York: Free Press, 1990), p. 383.

5. J. P. Kotter, "What Leaders Really Do," *Harvard Business Review,* December 2001, pp. 85–96; the role of leadership within organizational change is discussed in J. P. Kotter, *Leading Change* (Boston: Harvard Business School Press, 1996).

6. F. Smith, quoted in "All in a Day's Work," *Harvard Business Review,* December 2001, pp. 54–66.

7. N. Tichy and C. DeRose, "Roger Enrico's Master Class," *Fortune,* November 27, 1995, pp. 105–106.

8. L. H. Chusmir, "Personalized versus Socialized Power Needs among Working Women and Men," *Human Relations,* February 1986, p. 149.

9. D. Leonhardt, "Don't Mess with This Maytag Repairman," *Business Week,* August 9, 1999, p. 70.

10. R. M. Kramer, "The Great Intimidators," *Harvard Business Review,* February 2006, pp. 88–96.

11. "Push-Button Age," *Newsweek,* July 9, 1990, p. 57.

12. R. E. Tedlow, "The Education of Andy Grove," *Fortune,* December 12, 2005, pp. 117–138.

13. A. S. Grove, *Only the Paranoid Survive: How to Exploit the Crisis Points That Challenge Every Company and Career* (New York: Currency/Doubleday, 1996). Grove is also the author of *High Output Management* (New York: Random House, 1983).

14. "Remaking Intel from Top to Bottom," *BusinessWeek,* January 9, 2006, p. 49.

15. Tedlow, 2005, p. 138.

16. Based on Table I in G. Yukl, C. M. Falbe, and J. Y. Youn, "Patterns of Influence Behavior for Managers," *Group & Organization Management,* March 1993, pp. 5–28.

17. G. Yukl, H. Kim, and C. M. Falbe, "Antecedents of Influence Outcomes," *Journal of Applied Psychology,* June 1996, pp. 309–317.

18. B. Schlender, "A Conversation with the Lords of Wintel," *Fortune,* July 8, 1996, p. 44.

19. R. M. Stogdill, "Personal Factors Associated with Leadership: A Survey of the Literature," *Journal of Psychology* 25 (1948), pp. 35–71; and R. M. Stogdill, *Handbook of Leadership* (New York: Free Press, 1974).

20. B. Bass, *Stogdill's Handbook of Leadership,* rev. ed. (New York: Free Press, 1981).

21. J. M. Kouzes and B. Z. Posner, "The Credibility Factor: What Followers Expect from Their Leaders," *Business Credit,* July–August 1990, pp. 24–28; J. M. Kouzes and B. Z. Posner, *The Leadership Challenge: How to Get Extraordinary Things Done in Organizations* (San Francisco: Jossey-Bass, 1995); and J. M. Kouzes and B. Z. Posner, *Credibility* (San Francisco: Jossey-Bass, 1993).

22. L. Bossidy, "The Job No CEO Should Delegate," *Harvard Business Review,* March 2001, pp. 47–49.

23. Results can be found in T. A. Judge, J. E. Bono, R. Ilies, and M. W. Gerhardt, "Personality and Leadership: A Qualitative and Quantitative Review," *Journal of Applied Psychology,* August 2002, pp. 765–780.

24. See T. A. Judge, A. E. Colbert, and R. Ilies, "Intelligence and Leadership: A Quantitative Review and Test of Theoretical Propositions," *Journal of Applied Psychology,* June 2004, pp. 542–552.

25. A summary of this research is provided by B. J. Avolio, J. J. Soskik, D. I. Jung, and Y. Berson, "Leadership Models, Methods, and Applications," in W. C. Borman, D. R. Ilgen, and R. J. Klimoski, eds., *Handbook of Psychology,* vol. 12 (Hoboken, NJ: John Wiley & Sons, 2003) pp. 277–307.

26. Study by Catalyst, New York, reported in J. S. Lublin, "Women Aspire to Be Chief as Much as Men Do," *The Wall Street Journal,* June 28, 2004, p. D2.

27. R. Sharpe, "As Leaders, Women Rule," *BusinessWeek,* November 20, 2000, pp. 75–84.

28. Study by Hagberg Consulting Group, Foster City, California, reported in Sharpe, 2000, p. 75.

29. B. R. Ragins, B. Townsend, and M. Mattis, "Gender Gap in the Executive Suite: CEOs and Female Executives Report on Breaking the Glass Ceiling," *Academy of Management Executive,* February 1, 1998, pp. 28–42.

30. L. Tischler, "Where Are the Women?" *Fast Company,* February 2004, pp. 52–60.

31. P. Sellers, "Power: Do Women Really Want It?" *Fortune,* October 13, 2003, p. 88.

32. See M. Conlin, "Self-Deprecating Women," *BusinessWeek,* June 14, 2004, p. 26. For more on this subject, see also "The 'Masculine' and 'Feminine' Sides of Leadership and Culture: Perception vs. Reality," *Knowledge@Wharton,* http://knowledge.wharton.upenn.edu/index.cfm?fa=printArticle & ID (accessed September 22, 2005); "Guiding Aspiring Female Execs Up the Ladder," *HR Magazine,* January 2006, p. 14; T. G. Habbershon, "It's a Man's World," *BusinessWeek SmallBiz,* Spring 2006, p.16; Q.M. Roberson and C.K. Stevens, "Making Sense of Diversity in the Workplace: Organizational Justice and Language Abstraction in Employees' Accounts of Diversity-Related Incidents," *Journal of Applied Psychology,* March 2006, pp. 379–391; E. Porter, "Women in Workplace—Trend Is Reversing," *San Francisco Chronicle,* March 2, 2006,

p. A2, reprinted from *The New York Times;* T. L. O'Brien, "Up the Down Staircase: Why Do So Few Women Reach the Top of Big Law Firms?" *The New York Times,* March 19, 2006, sec. 3, pp. 1, 4; "Breaking into the Boardroom," *The Wall Street Journal,* March 27, 2006, p. B3; E. White, "Why Few Women Run Plants," *The Wall Street Journal,* May 1, 2006, pp. B1, B5; J. Zaslow, "A New Generation Gap: Differences Emerge Among Women in the Workplace," *The Wall Street Journal,* May 4, 2006, p. D1; W.A. Holstein, "Glass Ceiling? Get a Hammer," *The New York Times,* June 18, 2006, sec. 3, p. 12; C. Hymowitz, "Women Swell Ranks as Middle Managers, but Are Scarce at Top," *The Wall Street Journal,* July 24, 2006, p. B1; S. Vedantam, "Glass Ceiling Breaks When Women Are in Charge, Study Says," *San Francisco Chronicle,* August 13, 2006, p. A17, reprinted from *Washington Post.*

33. R. House, M. Javidan, P. Hanges, and P. Dorfman, "Understanding Cultures and Implicit Leadership Theories Across the Globe: An Introduction to Project GLOBE," *Journal of World Business,* Spring 2004, p. 4.

34. R. Likert, *New Patterns of Management* (New York: McGraw-Hill, 1961); and R. Likert, *The Human Organization* (New York: McGraw-Hill, 1967).

35. C. A. Schriesman and B. J. Bird, "Contributions of the Ohio State Studies to the Field of Leadership," *Journal of Management Studies* 5 (1979), pp. 135–145; and C. L. Shartle, "Early Years of the Ohio State University Leadership Studies," *Journal of Management* 5 (1979), pp. 126–134.

36. V. H. Vroom, "Leadership," in M. D. Dunnette, ed., *Handbook of Industrial and Organizational Psychology* (Chicago: Rand McNally, 1976).

37. H. Lancaster, "New Managers Get Little Help Tackling Big, Complex Jobs," *The Wall Street Journal,* February 10, 1998; and C. Hymowitz, "New Top Managers Often Find They Miss Close Peers, Counsel," *The Wall Street Journal,* November 25, 1997, p.B1; see also M. Stettner, *Skills for New Managers* (New York: McGraw-Hill, 2000); J. H. Grossman and J. R. Parkinson, *Becoming a Successful Manager: How to Make a Smooth Transition from Managing Yourself to Managing Others* (New York: McGraw-Hill, 2001); and L. A. Hill, *Becoming a Manager: How New Managers Master the Challenges of Leadership,* 2nd ed. (Boston: Harvard Business School Press, 2003).

38. F. E. Fiedler, "Assumed Similarity Measures as Predictors of Team Effectiveness," *Journal of Abnormal and Social Psychology* 49 (1954), pp. 381–388; F. E. Fiedler, *Leader Attitudes and Group Effectiveness* (Urbana, IL: University of Illinois Press, 1958); and F. E. Fiedler, *A Theory of Leadership Effectiveness* (New York: McGraw-Hill, 1967).

39. A recent review of the contingency theory and suggestions for future theoretical development is provided by R. Ayman, M. M. Chemers, and F. Fiedler, "The Contingency Model of Leadership Effectiveness: Its Levels of Analysis," in F. Dansereau and F. J. Yamminrino, eds., *Leadership: The Multiple-Level Approaches* (Stamford, CT: JAI Press, 1998), pp. 73–94.

40. R. J. House, "A Path-Goal Theory of Leader Effectiveness," *Administrative Science Quarterly,* September 1971, pp. 321–338; and R. J. House and T. R. Mitchell, "Path-Goal Theory of Leadership," *Journal of Contemporary Business,* Autumn 1974, pp. 81–97. The most recent version of the theory is found in R. J. House, "Path-Goal Theory of Leadership: Lessons, Legacy, and a Reformulated Theory," *Leadership Quarterly,* Autumn 1996, pp. 323–352.

41. These studies are summarized in House, 1996.

42. Supportive results can be found in D. Charbonneau, J. Barling, and E. K. Kelloway, "Transformational Leadership

and Sports Performance: The Mediating Role of Intrinsic Motivation," *Journal of Applied Social Psychology,* July 2001, pp. 1521–1534.

43. Results can be found in P. M. Podsakoff, S. B. MacKenzie, M. Ahearne, and W. H. Bommer, "Searching for a Needle in a Haystack: Trying to Identify the Illusive Moderators of Leadership Behaviors," *Journal of Management,* 1995, pp. 422–470.

44. A thorough discussion is provided by P. Hersey and K. H. Blanchard, *Management of Organizational Behavior: Utilizing Human Resources,* 5th ed. (Englewood Cliffs, NJ: Prentice-Hall, 1988).

45. Results can be found in J. R. Goodson, G. W. McGee, and J. F. Cashman, "Situational Leadership Theory," *Group & Organization Studies,* December 1989, pp. 446–461.

46. C. Adams, "Leadership Behavior of Chief Nurse Executives," *Nursing Management,* August 1990, pp. 36–39.

47. See D. C. Lueder, "Don't Be Misled by LEAD," *Journal of Applied Behavioral Science,* May 1985, pp. 143–154; and C. L. Graeff, "The Situational Leadership Theory: A Critical View," *Academy of Management Review,* April 1983, pp. 285–291.

48. For a complete description of the full range leadership theory, see B. J. Bass and B. J. Avolio, *Revised Manual for the Multi-Factor Leadership Questionnaire* (Palo Alto, CA: Mindgarden, 1997).

49. A definition and description of transactional leadership is provided by J. Antonakis and R. J. House, "The Full-Range Leadership Theory: The Way Forward," in B. J. Avolio and F. J. Yammarino, eds., *Transformational and Charismatic Leadership: The Road Ahead* (New York: JAI Press, 2002), pp. 3–34.

50. M. Arndt, "3M's Rising Star," *BusinessWeek,* April 12, 2004, p. 65.

51. U. R. Dundum, K. B. Lowe, and B. J. Avolio, "A Meta-Analysis of Transformational and Transactional Leadership Correlates of Effectiveness and Satisfaction: An Update and Extension," in B. J. Avolio and F. J. Yammarino, eds., *Transformational and Charismatic Leadership: The Road Ahead* (New York: JAI Press, 2002), p. 38.

52. Supportive results can be found in T. A. Judge and J. E. Bono, "Five-Factor Model of Personality and Transformational Leadership," *Journal of Applied Psychology,* October 2000, pp. 751–765.

53. Supportive research is summarized by Antonakis and House, 2002.

54. Arndt, 2004, p. 65.

55. These definitions are derived from R. Kark, B. Shamir, and C. Chen, "The Two Faces of Transformational Leadership: Empowerment and Dependency," *Journal of Applied Psychology,* April 2003, pp. 246–255. See also R. T. Keller, "Transformational Leadership, Initiating Structure, and Substitutes for Leadership: A Longitudinal Study of Research and Development Project Team Performance," *Journal of Applied Psychology,* January 2006, pp. 202–210.

56. B. Nanus, *Visionary Leadership* (San Francisco: Jossey-Bass, 1992), p. 8. See also B. R. Agle, N. J. Nagarajan, J. A. Sonnenfeld, and D. Srinivasan, "Does CEO Charisma Matter? An Empirical Analysis of the Relationships among Organizational Performance, Environmental Uncertainty, and Top Management Team Perceptions of CEO Charisma," *Academy of Management Journal,* February 2006, pp. 161–174.

57. See R. E. Quinn, "Moments of Greatness: Entering the Fundamental State of Leadership," *Harvard Business Review,* July–August 2005, pp. 75–83.

58. See K. B. Lowe, K. G. Kroeck, and N. Sivasubramaniam, "Effectiveness Correlates of Transformational and Transac-

tional Leadership: A Meta-Analytic Review of the MLQ Literature," *Leadership Quarterly,* 1996, pp. 385–425.

59. Results can be found in Dundum, Lowe, and Avolio, 2002.

60. See Kark, Shamir, and Chen, 2003.

61. Supportive results and can be found in B. M. Bass, B. J. Avolio, D. I. Jung, and Y. Berson, "Predicting Unit Performance by Assessing Transformational and Transactional Leadership," *Journal of Applied Psychology,* April 2003, pp. 207–218; J. E. Bono and T. A. Judge, "Self-Concordance at Work: Toward Understanding the Motivational Effects of Transformational Leaders," *Academy of Management Journal,* October 2003, pp. 554–571; and D. Charbonneau, J. Barling, and E. K. Kelloway, "Transformational Leadership and Sports Performance: The Mediating Role of Intrinsic Motivation," *Journal of Applied Social Psychology,* July 2001, pp. 1521–1534.

62. See A. J. Towler, "Effects of Charismatic Influence Training on Attitudes, Behavior, and Performance," *Personnel Psychology,* Summer 2003, pp. 363–381; and M. Frese and S. Beimel, "Action Training for Charismatic Leadership: Two Evaluations of Studies of a Commercial Training Module on Inspirational Communication of a Vision," *Personnel Psychology,* Autumn 2003, pp. 671–697.

63. These recommendations were derived from J. M. Howell and B. J. Avolio, "The Ethics of Charismatic Leadership: Submission or Liberation," *The Executive,* May 1992, pp. 43–54.

64. G. Graen and J. F. Cashman, "A Role-Making Model of Leadership in Formal Organizations: A Developmental Approach," in J. G. Hunt and L. L. Larson, eds., *Leadership Frontiers* (Kent, OH: Kent State University Press, 1975), pp. 143–165; F. Dansereau Jr., G. Graen, and W. J. Haga, "A Vertical Dyad Linkage Approach to Leadership Within Formal Organizations: A Longitudinal Investigation of the Role-Making Process," *Organizational Behavior and Human Performance,* February 1975, pp. 46–78; and R. M. Dienesch and R. C. Liden, "Leader–Member Exchange Model of Leadership: A Critique and Further Development," *Academy of Management Review,* July 1986, pp. 618–634.

65. See D. Duchon, S. G. Green, and T. D. Taber, "Vertical Dyad Linkage: A Longitudinal Assessment of Antecedents, Measures, and Consequences," *Journal of Applied Psychology,* February 1986, pp. 56– 60.

66. See C. A. Schriesheim, S. L. Castro, and F. J. Yammarino, "Investigating Contingencies: An Examination of the Impact of Span of Supervision and Upward Controllingness on Leader–Member Exchange Using Traditional and Multivariate within—and between—Entities Analysis," *Journal of Applied Psychology,* October 2000, pp. 659–677; K. Sherony and S. Green, "Coworker Exchange: Relationships between Coworkers, Leader–Member Exchange, and Work Attitudes," *Journal of Applied Psychology* 87 (2002), pp. 542–548; O. Janssen and N. W. V. Yperen, "Employees' Goal Orientations, the Quality of Leader–Member Exchange, and the Outcomes of Job Performance and Job Satisfaction," *Academy of Management Journal,* June 2004, pp. 368–384; B. Erdogan, M. I. Kraimer, and R. C. Liden, "Work Value Congruence and Intrinsic Career Success: The Compensatory Roles of Leader–Member Exchange and Perceived Organizational Support," *Personnel Psychology,* Summer 2004, pp. 305–332; and T. N. Bauer, B. Erdogan, R. C. Liden, and S. J. Wayne, "A Longitudinal Study of the Moderating Role of Extraversion: Leader–Member Exchange, Performance, and Turnover During New Executive Development," *Journal of Applied Psychology,* March 2006, pp. 298–310.

67. A turnover study was conducted by G. B. Graen, R. C. Liden, and W. Hoel, "Role of Leadership in the Employee With-

drawal Process," *Journal of Applied Psychology,* December 1982, pp. 868–872. The career progress study was conducted by M. Wakabayashi and G. B. Braen, "The Japanese Career Progress Study: A 7-Year Follow-Up," *Journal of Applied Psychology,* November 1984, pp. 603–614.

68. R. J. House and R. N. Aditya, "The Social Scientific Study of Leadership: Quo Vadis?" *Journal of Management* 23 (1997), pp. 409–473.

69. A thorough discussion of shared leadership is provided by C. L. Pearce, "The Future of Leadership: Combining Vertical and Shared Leadership to Transform Knowledge Work." *Academy of Management Executive,* February 2004, pp. 47–57.

70. This research is summarized in B. J. Avolio, J. J. Soskik, D. I. Jung, and Y. Benson, "Leadership Models, Methods, and Applications," in W. C. Borman, D. R. Ilgen, and R. J. Klimoski, eds. *Handbook of Psychology,* vol. 12 (Hoboken, NJ: John Wiley & Sons, 2003) pp. 277–307.

71. L. L. Berry, "The Collaborative Organization: Leadership Lessons from Mayo Clinic," *Organizational Dynamics,* August 2004, pp. 230–231.

72. A. Taylor III, "Bill's Brand-New Ford," *Fortune,* June 28, 2004, p. 74.

73. P. Gollner, "Dell: CEO Rollins Has 'Full Support' of Chairman," CRN, August 23, 2006; http://www.crn.com/sections/breakingnews/dailyarchives.jhtml?articleId=192203421 (accessed September 12, 2006).

74. A. Ignatius, "Meet the Google Guys," February 12, 2006, http://www.time.com/time/magazine/article/0,9171,1158956,00.html (accessed September 12, 2006); and Google Corporate Information, "Google Management," http://www.google.com/corporate/execs.html (accessed September 12, 2006).

75. P. Sellers, "MySpace Cowboys," *Fortune,* September 4, 2006, pp. 66–74. See also J. Kornblum, "Teens Hang Out at MySpace," *USA Today,* January 9, 2006; http://www.usatoday.com/tech/news/2006-01-08-myspace-teens_x.htm (accessed September 12, 2006).

76. An overall summary of servant leadership is provided by L. C. Spears, *Reflections on Leadership: How Robert K. Greenleaf's Theory of Servant-Leadership Influenced Today's Top Management Thinkers* (New York: Wiley, 1995).

77. D. L. Moore, "Wooden's Wizardry Wears Well," *USA Today,* March 29, 1995, pp. 1C, 2C.

78. B. Saporito, "And the Winner Is Still . . . Wal-Mart," *Fortune,* May 2, 1994, pp. 62–70.

79. M. De Pree, quoted D. Gergen, "Bad News for Bullies," *U.S. News & World Report,* June 19, 2006, p. 54. The quote is from M. De Pree, *Leadership Is an Art* (New York: Dell, 1989).

80. Gergen, 2006.

81. F. F. Reichheld and T. Teal, *The Loyalty Effect: The Hidden Force Behind Growth, Profits, and Lasting Value* (Boston: Harvard Business School Press, 2001); see also F. F. Reichheld, *Loyalty Rules! How Today's Leaders Build Lasting Relationships* (Boston: Harvard Business School Press, 2001); and *The Loyalty Effect: The Hidden Force Behind Growth* (Boston: Harvard Business School Press, 1996).

82. F. F. Reichheld, "Lead for Loyalty," *Harvard Business Review,* July–August 2001, pp. 76–84.

83. J. Kerstetter and P. Burrows, "Sun: A CEO's Last Stand," *BusinessWeek Online,* July 26, 2004; http://www.business-week.com/magazine/content/04_30/b3893001_mz001.htm (accessed September 12, 2006).

84. D. Fost, "'Mr. Sun' Ends a Chapter in Saga of Silicon Valley," *San Francisco Chronicle,* April 25, 2006, p. A1.

85. B. Pimentel, "McNealy Resigns as CEO of Sun Microsystems," *San Francisco Chronicle,* April 25, 2006, p. C1.

86. P. Burrows, "Sun's New Boss: The Same as the Old Boss?" *BusinessWeek Online,* April 25, 2006; http://www.businessweek.com/technology/content/apr2006/tc20060425_843283.htm (accessed September 12, 2006).

87. P. Sealey, quoted in Fost, 2006, p. A1.

88. A. T. Saracevic, "Sun's McNealy Has Been a Bright, Shining Example of Leadership," *San Francisco Chronicle,* April 23, 2006, pp. F1, F2.

89. J. Collins, *Good to Great* (New York: Harper Business, 2001).

90. J. Collins, "Level 5 Leadership," *Harvard Business Review,* January 2001, p. 68.

91. Collins, *Good to Great,* 2001, p. 21.

92. See Collins, *Good to Great,* 2001.

93. See B. J. Avolio, J. J. Sosik, D. I. Jung, and Yair Berson, 2003, pp. 295–298.

94. D. MacRae, "Six Secrets of Successful E-Leaders," *Business Week online,* September 6, 2001; www.businessweek.com/technology/content/sep2001/tc2001096_619.htm (accessed July 23, 2004).

95. D. Q. Mills, *E-Leadership: Guiding Your Business to Success in the New Economy* (Paramus, NJ: Prentice Hall Press, 2001). See also R. Hargrove, *E-Leader: Reinventing Leadership in a Connected Economy* (Boulder, CO: Perseus Books Group, 2001); S. Annunzio, *eLeadership: Bold Solutions for the New Economy* (New York: Simon & Schuster, 2001); and T. M. Siebel, *Taking Care of eBusiness: How Today's Market Leaders Are Increasing Revenue, Productivity, and Customer Satisfaction* (New York: Doubleday, 2001).

96. L. Capotosto, "Millenial Management," *Darwin,* www2.darwinmag.com/connect/books/book.cfm?ID-188 (accessed July 24, 2004).

CHAPTER 15

1. See C. Kanchier, "Telephone Skills Crucial for Success," *San Francisco Examiner,* May 2, 1999, p. J-2; C. Kanchier, "How to Make Effective Phone Calls," *San Francisco Examiner,* September 26, 1999, p. J-3; B. Roserner, "The Right Tone for When You Use the Phone," *San Francisco Examiner & Chronicle,* August 29, 1999, p. CL-13; and O. Pollar, "How to Be a Winner at Phone Tag," *San Francisco Examiner & Chronicle,* May 2, 1999, p. J-3.

2. R. Todd, quoted in A. Fisher, "Readers Speak Out on Illiterate MBAs and More," *Fortune,* March 1, 1999, p. 242.

3. See D. Fenn, "Benchmark: What Drives the Skills Gap?" *Inc.,* May 1996, p. 111.

4. September 1998 survey by Office Team, reported in S. Armour, "Failure to Communicate Costly for Companies," *USA Today,* September 30, 1998, p. B1.

5. J. R. Hinrichs, "Communications Activity of Industrial Research Personnel," *Personnel Psychology,* Summer 1964, pp. 193–204.

6. J. Kotter, "Power, Dependence, and Effective Management," *Harvard Business Review* 55 (1977), pp. 125–136.

7. Communication noise is discussed by J. Sandberg, "Office Minstrels Drive the Rest of Us Nuts but Are Hard to Silence," *The Wall Street Journal,* February 14, 2006, p. B1.

8. R. L. Daft, and R. H. Lengel, "Information Richness: A New Approach to Managerial Behavior and Organizational Design," in B. M. Staw and L. L. Cummings, eds., *Research in Organizational Behavior,* (Greenwich, CT: JAI Press, 1984), p. 196; and R. H. Lengel and R. L. Daft, "The Selection of Communication Media as an Executive Skill," *Academy of Management Executive,* August 1988, pp. 225–232.

9. E. Goode, "Old as Society, Social Anxiety Is Yielding Its Secrets," *The New York Times,* October 20, 1998, pp. D7, D11.

10. Goode, 1998; for more on social anxiety disorder, see T. J. Bruce and S. A. Saeed, "Social Anxiety Disorder: A Common, Underrecognized Mental Disorder," *American Family Physician,* November 15, 1999, pp. 2311–2320, 2322.

11. H. Lancaster, "Workday Etiquette: Know the Right Fork and Watch That E-Mail," *The Wall Street Journal,* April 21, 1998, p. B1; J. Flaherty, "Finding Your Manners," *The New York Times,* February 13, 1999, pp. B1, B14; C. Smith, "How Clean Underwear Aids Your Career," *San Francisco Examiner,* February 28, 1999, p. CL-13; B. Rosner, "Giving Thanks without Looking Like a Phony," *San Francisco Examiner & Chronicle,* March 7, 1999, p. CL-13; E. White, "Lessons in Shaking Hands, Twirling Spaghetti Await Some Workers," *The Wall Street Journal,* December 7, 1999, pp. B1, B16; J. Blais, "Mind Your Manners, Even If You're at Work," *USA Today,* January 17, 2000, p. 5B; M. Brody, "Test Your Etiquette," *Training & Development,* February 2002, pp. 64–66; P. Post and P. Post, *Emily Post's The Etiquette Advantage in Business* (New York: HarperCollins, 2000); and S. Jayson, "Are Social Norms Steadily Unraveling?" *USA Today,* April 13, 2006, p. 4D. See also B. Dela Vega, "Tattoos in Business: OK? Or Taboo?" *Reno Gazette-Journal,* March 5, 2006, pp. 1E, 7E.

12. S. Merchant, quoted in S. Srivastava, "Why India Worries about Outsourcing," *San Francisco Chronicle,* March 21, 2004, p. E3.

13. The role of jargon in communication is discussed by R. Spragins, "Don't Talk to Me That Way," *Fortune Small Business,* February 2002, p. 26; and C. Hymowitz, "Mind Your Language: To Do Business Today, Consider Delayering," *The Wall Street Journal,* March 27, 2006, p. B1.

14. Some of these barriers are discussed in J. P. Scully, "People: The Imperfect Communicators," *Quality Progress,* April 1995, pp. 37–39.

15. A. Farnham, "Trust Gap," *Fortune,* December 4, 1989, p. 70.

16. C. R. Rogers and F. J. Roethlisberger, "Barriers and Gateways to Communication," *Harvard Business Review,* July–August 1952, pp. 46–52.

17. Rogers and Roethlisberger, 1952, p. 47.

18. W. D. St. John, "You Are What You Communicate," *Personnel Journal,* October 1985, p. 40.

19. The importance of nonverbal communication is discussed by D. Arthur, "The Importance of Body Language," *HRFocus,* June 1995, pp. 22–23; and N. M. Grant, "The Silent Shroud: Build Bridges, Not Barriers," *HRFocus,* April 1995, p. 16. Problems with interpreting nonverbal communication are discussed by A. Pihulyk, "Communicate with Clarity: The Key to Understanding and Influencing Others," *The Canadian Manager,* Summer 2003, pp. 12–13.

20. This statistic was provided by A. Fisher, "How Can I Survive a Phone Interview?" *Fortune,* April 10, 2004, p. 54.

21. See N. Morgan, "The Kinesthetic Speaker: Putting Action into Words," *Harvard Business Review,* April 2001, pp. 113–120.

22. R. E. Axtell, *Gestures: The Do's and Taboos of Body Language Around the World* (New York: John Wiley & Sons, 1998).

23. "How Cultures Collide," *Psychology Today,* July 1976, p. 14.

24. Norms for cross-cultural eye contact are discussed by C. Engholm, *When Business East Meets Business West: The Guide to Practice and Protocol in the Pacific Rim* (New York: John Wiley & Sons, 1991).

25. See J. A. Russell, "Facial Expressions of Emotion: What Lies Beyond Minimal Universality?" *Psychological Bulletin,* November 1995, pp. 379–391.

26. Related research is summarized by J. A. Hall, "Male and Female Nonverbal Behavior," in A. W. Siegman and S. Feldstein, eds. *Multichannel Integrations of Nonverbal Behavior* (Hillsdale, NJ: Lawrence Erlbaum, 1985), pp. 195–226.

27. A thorough discussion of cross-cultural differences is provided by Axtell, 1998. Problems with body language analysis also are discussed by C. L. Karrass, "Body Language: Beware the Hype," *Traffic Management,* January 1992, p. 27; and M. Everett and B. Wiesendanger, "What Does Body Language Really Say?" *Sales & Marketing Management,* April 1992, p. 40.

28. Results can be found in Hall, 1985.

29. J. W. Lee and L. K. Guerrero, "Types of Touch in Cross-Sex Relationships between Coworkers: Perceptions of Relational and Emotional Messages, Inappropriateness, and Sexual Harassment," *Journal of Applied Communication Research* 29 (2001), pp. 197–220. See also D. Jones, "Female Bosses Can Touch More Freely," *USA Today,* February 19, 2002, p. 9B.

30. See J. S. Lublin, "Women Fall Behind When They Don't Hone Negotiation Skills," *The Wall Street Journal,* November 4, 2003, p. B1.

31. J. C. Tingley, *Genderflex: Men & Women Speaking Each Other's Language at Work* (New York: American Management Association, 1994), p. 16.

32. D. Tannen, "The Power of Talk: Who Gets Heard and Why," in *Negotiation: Readings, Exercises, and Cases,* 3rd ed., eds. R. J. Lewicki and D. M. Saunders (Burr Ridge, IL: Irwin/McGraw-Hill, 1999), pp. 147–148; research on gender differences in communication can be found in E. L. MacGeorge, A. R. Graves, B. Feng, S. J. Gillihan, and B. R. Burleson, "The Myth of Gender Cultures: Similarities Outweigh Differences in Men's and Women's Provision of Responses to Supportive Communication," *Sex Roles* 50 (2004), pp. 143–175; and V. N. Giri and H. O. Sharma, "Brain Wiring and Communication Style," *Psychological Studies* 48 (2003), pp. 59–64.

33. C. Clarke, quoted in A. Pomeroy, "Female Executives May Have a Business Edge," *HR Magazine,* August 2005, p. 16. See also C. Clarke, "A (Necessary) End to Male Dominance," *post-gazette.com,* March 21, 2006, http://www.post-gazette.com/pg/06080/673640-334.stm (accessed September 21, 2006).

34. R. Sharpe, "As Leaders, Women Rule," *BusinessWeek,* November 20, 2000, pp. 75–84.

35. A. Cummings, reported in "The 'Masculine' and 'Feminine' Sides of Leadership and Culture: Perception vs. Reality," *Knowledge@Wharton,* October 5, 2005, knowledge.wharton.upenn.edu/article.cfm?articleide=1287 (accessed September 21, 2006).

36. D. Jones, "Male Execs Like Female Coaches," *USA Today,* October 24, 2001, p. 3B.

37. G. M. Goldhaber, *Organizational Communication,* 4th ed. (Dubuque, IA: W. C. Brown, 1986).

38. Early research is discussed by K. Davis, "Management Communication and the Grapevine," *Harvard Business Review,* September–October 1953, pp. 43–49; and R. Rowan, "Where Did *That* Rumor Come From?" *Fortune,* August 13, 1979, pp. 130–137. The most recent research is discussed in "Pruning the Company Grapevine," *Supervision,* September 1986, p. 11; and R. Half, "Managing Your Career: 'How Can I Stop the Gossip?'" *Management Accounting,* September 1987, p. 27.

39. T. J. Peters and R. H. Waterman Jr., *In Search of Excellence* (New York: Harper & Row, 1982); and T. Peters and N. Austin, *A Passion for Excellence: The Leadership Difference* (New York: Random House, 1985).

40. W. H. Bulkeley, "The View from the Top," *The Wall Street Journal,* June 21, 1999, p. R6.

41. D. Kirkpatrick, "Life in a Connected World," *Fortune,* July 10, 2006, pp. 98–100.

42. International Data Corp., *U.S. Intranet Usage and User Intentions, 1998-1999,* reported in Michael Pastore, "Companies Expanding Intranet Uses," ClickZ Network, September 3, 1999, www.clickz.com/stats/big_picture/hardware/article.php/192561 (accessed July 30, 2006).

43. See J. Useem, "For Sale Online: You," *Fortune,* July 5, 1999, pp. 67–78.

44. "Websmart," *BusinessWeek e.biz,* May 14, 2001, p. EB56.

45. J. S. Lublin, "Some Dos and Don'ts to Help You Hone Video-conference Skills," *The Wall Street Journal,* February 7, 2006, p. B1.

46. Results can be found in S. A. Rains, "Leveling the Organizational Playing Field—Virtually: A Meta-Analysis of Experimental Research Assessing the Impact of Group Support System Use on Member Influence Behaviors," *Communication Research,* April 2005, pp. 193–234.

47. Challenges associated with virtual operations are discussed by S. O'Mahony and S. R. Barley, "Do Digital Telecommunications Affect Work and Organization? The State of Our Knowledge," in R. I. Sutton and B. M. Straw, eds. *Research in Organizational Behavior,* vol. 21, (Stamford, CT: JAI Press, 1999), pp. 125–161.

48. R. Balu, "Work Week: A Special News Report about Life on the Job," *The Wall Street Journal,* July 20, 1999, p. A1; D. E. Baily and N. B. Kurland, "A Review of Telework Research: Findings, New Directions, and Lessons for the Study of Modern Work," *Journal of Organizational Behavior,* June 2002, pp. 383–400; and S. Shellenbarger, "Work and Family: This Time, Firms See Work-Life Plans as Aid During the Downturn," *The Wall Street Journal,* March 28, 2001, p. B1.

49. Deloitte, *Eye to the Future—How Technology, Media, and Telecommunications Advances Could Change the Way We Live in 2010,* reported in A. Donoghue, "2010: The Year of the Techie," *ZDNet UK,* May 17, 2006, http://news.zdnet.co.uk/business/0,39020645,39269493,00.htm (accessed September 21, 2006). More statistics on telecommuting are available at Canadian Telework Association, *InnoVisions Canada,* http://www.ivc.ca/studies/us.html (accessed September 21, 2006).

50. Report by the Reason Foundation, reported in "Will More of Us Be Telecommuting?" *The Week,* January 13, 2006, p. 11.

51. R. O. Crockett, "Multimedia Phones," *BusinessWeek,* May 16, 2005, pp. 100–104; C. Conkey, "Parking Meters Get Smarter," *The Wall Street Journal,* June 30, 2005, pp. B1, B54; K. Maney, "Melding of Cellphones and Wi-Fis Will Be Cosmic, Man," *USA Today,* August 24, 2005, p. 3B; K. Maney, "One Fine Day a Cellphone Could Find You a Parking Spot," *USA Today,* May 3, 2006, p. 3B; and J. Markoff and M. Fackler, "With a Cellphone as My Guide," *The New York Times,* June 28, 2006, pp. C1, C7.

52. M. Marriott and K. Hafner, "It's Not Just a Phone, It's an Adventure," *The New York Times,* March 17, 2005, p. C9.

53. J. Garofoli, "The Truth About Blogging," *San Francisco Chronicle,* July 20, 2006, pp. A1, A11.

54. V. Hoang, "Youngsters Fuel Boom in Cyberspace 'Blogs,'" *Arizona Republic,* February 4, 2006, p. D3.

55. See M. Gunn, "The Original Executive Blogger," *The Always On Generation,* March 13, 2006, http://www.alwayson-network.com/comments.php?id=13807_0_1_0_C (accessed September 21, 2006). See also R. Buckman, "How Tech Start-Ups Tap Blogs as Cheerleaders," *The Wall Street Journal,* February 9, 2006, p. B6.

56. See, for example, "Firms Taking Action against Worker Blogs," *MSNBC News,* March 7, 2005, www.msnbc.msn.com/id/7116338 (accessed September 21, 2006).

57. J. Fine, "Polluting the Blogosphere," *BusinessWeek,* July 10, 2006, p. 20.

58. Surfwatch Checknet, cited in K. Daughton, J. Raymond, K. Shulman, and D. Struzzi, "Cyberslacking," *Newsweek,* November 29, 1999, pp. 62–65.

59. Survey by Salary.com and America Online, reported in S. Toomey, *Suntimes.com,* August 9, 2006; http://www.suntimes.com/output/news/cst-nws-slack09.html (accessed September 21, 2006).

60. N. H. Nie, A. Simpser, I. Stepanikova, and L. Zheng, *Ten Years After the Birth of the Internet, How Do Americans Use the Internet in Their Daily Lives?* (Stanford, CA: Stanford Institute for Quantitative Study of Society, 2004).

61. The Radicati Group, *Hosted Email Market 2004–2008* (Palo Alto, CA: The Radicati Group, 2004).

62. Daniel Yankelovich Group report, cited in B. P. Noble, "Electronic Liberation or Entrapment?" *The New York Times,* June 15, 1994, p. C4.

63. K. Maney, "No Time Off? It's Tech Giants' Fault," *USA Today,* July 21, 2004, p. 4B.

64. D. Greenfield, quoted in M. Conlin, "Take a Vacation from Your BlackBerry," *BusinessWeek,* December 20, 2004, p. 56.

65. See M. Burley-Allen, "Listen Up," *HR Magazine,* November 2001, pp. 115–120.

66. Burley-Allen, 2001; see also C. G. Pearce, "How Effective Are We as Listeners?" *Training & Development,* April 1993, pp. 79–80; and R. A. Luke Jr., "Improving Your Listening Ability," *Supervisory Management,* June 1992, p. 7.

67. Research by The Discovery Group, reported in "Hey, I'm Talking Here," *Training,* December 2005, p. 9.

68. See the discussion on listening in G. Manning, K. Curtis, and S. McMillen, *Building Community: The Human Side of Work* (Cincinnati, OH: Thomson Executive Press, 1996), pp. 127–154.

69. Derived from J. R. Goldon, *A Diagnostic Approach to Organizational Behavior,* 2nd ed. (Boston: Allyn and Bacon, 1987), p. 230; P. Slizewski, "Tips for Active Listening," *HRFocus,* May 1995, p. 7; G. Manning, K. Curtis, and S. McMillen, *Building the Human Side of Work Community* (Cincinnati, OH: Thomson Executive Press, 1996), pp. 127–154; and J. Sandberg, "What Exactly Was It That the Boss Said? You Can Only Imagine," *The Wall Street Journal,* September 19, 2006, p. B1.

70. C. Vinzant, "Messing with the Boss' Head," *Fortune,* May 1, 2000, pp. 329–331.

71. M. Price, "Effective Communication Begins with Listening," *Reno Gazette-Journal,* November 27, 2000, p. 1F.

72. D. Stiebel, *When Talking Makes Things Worse! Resolving Problems When Communication Fails,* reported in O. Pollar, "Talk Is Cheap If You Have Big Disagreements," *San Francisco Examiner & Chronicle,* February 21, 1999. p. J-3.

73. M. Just, P. A. Carpenter, and M. Masson, reported in J. Meer, "Reading More, Understanding Less," *Psychology Today,* March 1987, p. 12.

74. K. Alesandrini, *Survive Information Overload* (Homewood, IL: Irwin, 1992), pp. 191–202.

75. Alesandrini, 1992, p. 197.

76. K. Tyler, "Toning Up Communications," *HR Magazine,* March 2003, pp. 87–89.

77. T. Alessandra and P. Hunsaker, *Communicating at Work* (New York: Fireside, 1993), p. 231.

78. Alessandra and Hunsaker, 1993, p. 241.

79. Cited in Alessandra and Hunsaker, 1993, p. 169.

80. G. Lindenfield, "Don't Be Nervous," *Management Today,* June 2003, p. 81.

81. P. Theibert, "Speechwriters of the World, Get Lost!" *The Wall Street Journal,* August 2, 1993, p. A16. This section adapted from C. Wahlstrom and B. Williams, *Learning Success: Being Your Best at College & Life,* 3rd ed. (Belmont, CA: Wadsworth, 2002), pp. 243–245.

82. L. Waters, *Secrets of Successful Speakers: How You Can Motivate, Captivate, and Persuade* (New York: McGraw-Hill, 1993), p. 203.

CHAPTER 16

1. Some new ideas are found in J. McGregor, "How Failure Breeds Success," *BusinessWeek*, July 10, 2006, pp. 42–52; B. Morris, "The New Rules," *Fortune*, July 24, 2006, pp. 70–87; S. Clifford, "The New Science of Hiring," *Inc. Magazine*, August 2006, pp. 90–99; and R. D. Hof, "How to Hit a Moving Target," *BusinessWeek*, August 21/28 2006, pp. 80–83.

2. See, for example, G. Colvin, "Who Wants to Be the Boss?" *Fortune*, February 20, 2006, pp. 76–78.

3. W. A. Ruch, "Productivity Measurement," *Arizona Business*, February 1981, p. 20.

4. When labor costs rise, productivity slows down, unless other variables are changed. See M. Crutsinger, "Growth of Productivity Slows Down," *San Francisco Chronicle*, August 9, 2006, p. C3.

5. J. Welch, quoted in T. A. Stewart, "U.S. Productivity: First but Fading," *Fortune*, October 1992, p. 54.

6. M. Mandel, "Bad News and Good News on Productivity," *BusinessWeek Online*, August 8, 2006, http://www.businessweek.com/the_thread/economicsunbound/archives/2006/08/bad_news_and_go.html (accessed September 19, 2006).

7. L. Uchitelle, "Productivity Finally Shows the Impact of Computers," *The New York Times*, March 12, 2000, sec. 3, p. 4; J. Reingold, M. Stepanek, and D. Brady, "Why the Productivity Revolution Will Spread," *BusinessWeek*, February 14, 2000, p. 112–118; G. S. Becker, "How the Skeptics Missed the Power of Productivity," *BusinessWeek*, January 1, 2004, p. 26; and J. Aversa, "Bernanke Bullish on Productivity Gains," *BusinessWeek Online*, August 31, 2006, http://www.businessweek.com/ap/financialnews/D8JRJTJOO.htm?chan=search (accessed September 19, 2006).

8. See study by B. P. Bosworth and J. E. Triplett, "Productivity Measurement Issues in Services Industries: 'Baumol's Disease' Has Been Cured," *The Brookings Institution*, September 1, 2003, www.brookings.org/views/articles/bosworth/200309.htm (accessed August 1, 2006). Also see H. R. Varian, "Information Technology May Have Been What Cured Low Service-Sector Productivity," *The New York Times*, February 12, 2004, p. C2.

9. See W. W. Lewis, *The Power of Productivity: Wealth, Poverty, and the Threat to Global Stability* (Chicago: University of Chicago Press, 2004). Also see V. Postrel, "Why Do Certain Countries Prosper? A New Study Looks at Productivity and Comes Up with Some Contrarian Conclusions," *The New York Times*, July 15, 2004, p. C2.

10. W. Taylor, "Control in an Age of Chaos," *Harvard Business Review*, November–December 1994, pp. 64–70.

11. E. Byron, "Snack 'n' Shop," *The Wall Street Journal*, July 13, 2004, pp. B1, B9.

12. S. Rosenbush, "Time Warner: Still Searching for Answers," *BusinessWeek Online*, December 19, 2005, http://www.businessweek.com/technology/content/dec2005/tc20051217_665912.htm?chan=search (accessed September 20, 2006).

13. A. P. Sloan Jr., *My Years with General Motors* (New York: Doubleday, 1964).

14. "Behind the UPS Mystique: Puritanism and Productivity," *BusinessWeek*, June 6, 1990, pp. 66–73; see also D. Foust, "Big Brown's New Bag," *BusinessWeek*, July 19, 2004, pp. 54–56.

15. I. G. Seidenberg, quoted in S. E. Ante, "Giving the Boss the Big Picture," *BusinessWeek*, February 13, 2006, pp. 48–51.

16. R. S. Kaplan and D. P. Norton, "The Balanced Scorecard—Measures That Drive Performance," *Harvard Business Review*, January–February 1992, pp. 71–79.

17. Kaplan and Norton, 1992.

18. R. S. Kaplan and D. P. Norton, "Having Trouble with Your Strategy? Then Map It," *Harvard Business Review*, September–October 2000, pp. 167–176. See also R. Kaplan and D. Norton, "Plotting Success with 'Strategy Maps,'" *Optimize*, February 2004, http://www.optimizemag.com/article/showArticle.jhtml?articleId=18200733 (accessed September 18, 2006).

19. R. Quinn, quoted in J. H. Lingle and W. A. Schiemann, "From Balanced Scorecard to Strategic Gauges: Is Measurement Worth It?" *American Management Association*, March 1996, pp. 56–61.

20. Lingle and Schiemann, 1996.

21. For discussions of how to measure services and intangible assets, see R. S. Kaplan and D. P. Norton, "Measuring the Strategic Readiness of Intangible Assets," *Harvard Business Review*, February 2004, pp. 52–63; K. M. Kroll, "Repurposing Metrics for HR," *HR Magazine*, July 2006, pp. 65–69; and B. Hindo, "Satisfaction Not Guaranteed," *BusinessWeek*, June 19, 2006, pp. 32–36.

22. W. G. Ouchi, "The Transmission of Control Through Organizational Hierarchy," *Academy of Management Journal*, June 1978, pp. 173–192; and R. E. Walton, "From Control to Commitment in the Workplace," *Harvard Business Review*, March–April 1985, pp. 76–84.

23. A description of Genentech's culture is provided by B. Morris, "The Best Place to Work Now," *Fortune*, January 23, 2006, pp. 79–86.

24. L. J. Shinn and M. S. Sturgeon, "Budgeting from Ground Zero," *Association Management*, September 1990, pp. 45–58; J. V. Pearson and R. J. Michael, "Zero-Based Budgeting: A Technique for Planning Organizational Decline," *Long Range Planning*, June 1981, pp. 68–76; P. A. Pyhrr, "Zero-Based Budgeting," *Harvard Business Review*, November–December 1970, pp. 111–118; and "Zero-Based Budgeting," *Small Business Report*, April 1988, pp. 52–57.

25. D. Jones, "Baldrige Winners Named," *USA Today*, November 24, 1999, p. 3B. See also D. Jones, "Baldrige Award Honors Record 7 Quality Winners," *USA Today*, November 26, 2003, p. B6; and R. O. Crockett, "Keeping Ritz Carlton at the Top of Its Game," *BusinessWeek Online*, May 29, 2006, http://www.businessweek.com/magazine/content/06_22/b3986130.htm?chan=search (accessed September 20, 2006).

26. R. N. Lussier, *Management: Concepts, Applications, Skill Development* (Cincinnati, OH: South-Western College Publishing, 1997), p. 260.

27. The Japanese have taken efficiency to a high level. See the example of Matsushita Electric Industrial Co., described in K. Hall, "No One Does Lean Like the Japanese," *BusinessWeek*, July 10, 2006, pp. 40–41.

28. O. Port, "The Push for Quality," *BusinessWeek*, June 8, 1987, pp. 130–136.

29. H. Rothman, "You Need Not Be Big to Benchmark," *Nation's Business*, December 1992, pp. 64–65.

30. K. Chang, "Enlisting Science's Lessons to Entice More Shoppers to Spend More," *The New York Times*, September 19, 2006, p. D3.

31. J. Pfeffer and R. I. Sutton, *Hard Facts, Dangerous Half Truths & Total Nonsense: Profiting from Evidence-Based Management* (Boston: Harvard Business School Press, 2006).

32. J. B. Quinn and F. Hilmer, "Strategic Outsourcing," *Sloan Management Review*, Summer 1994, pp. 43–52; and S. Tully, "You'll Never Guess Who Really Makes . . .," *Fortune*, October 3, 1994, pp. 124–128.

33. C. L. Mann, "Globalization of I.T. Services and White-Collar Jobs: The Next Wave of Productivity Growth," December 2003, International Economics Policy Briefs, No. PB03-11, www.iie.com/publications/pb/pb03-11.pdf (accessed August 1, 2006). See also V. Postrel, "A Researcher Sees an Upside in the Outsourcing of Programming Jobs," *The New York Times,* January 29, 2004, p. C2.

34. H. Menzies, "Quality Counts When Wooing Overseas Clients," *Fortune,* June 1, 1997, www.fortune.com/fortune/subs/article/0,15114,378797,00.html (accessed August 1, 2006).

35. D. B. Henriques, "'Privatized' Doesn't Always Mean Perfect," *San Francisco Examiner,* May 14, 2000, p. B-10; reprinted from *The New York Times.*

36. E. Sclar, *You Don't Always Get What You Pay For: The Economics of Privatization* (Ithaca, NY: Cornell University Press, 2000).

37. B. Ekeler, quoted in Menzies, 1997. See also M. V. Uzumeri, "ISO 9000 and Other Metastandards: Principles for Management Practice?" *Academy of Management Executive* 11, no 1. (1997), pp. 21–28; and T. B. Schoenrock, "ISO 9000: 2000 Gives Competitive Edge," *Quality Progress,* May 2002, p. 107.

38. A. Fisher, "Rules for Joining the Cult of Perfectability," *Fortune,* February 7, 2000, p. 206.

39. J. E. Morehouse, quoted in C. H. Deutsch, "Six Sigma Enlightenment," *The New York Times,* December 7, 1998, pp. C1, C7. For more on Six Sigma, see M. S. Sodhi and N. S. Sodhi, "Six Sigma Pricing," *Harvard Business Review,* May 2005, pp. 135–142; and J. Gordon, "Take *That* to the Bank," *Training,* June 2006, p. 41.

40. D. Jones, "Firms Aim for Six Sigma Efficiency," *USA Today,* July 21, 1998, pp. 1B, 2B.

41. See M. Poppendieck, "Why the Lean in Lean Six Sigma?" *The Project Management Best Practices Report,* June 2004, www.poppendieck.com/pdfs/Lean_Six_Sigma.pdf (accessed August 1, 2006).

42. Arner and Aston, 2004; and A. Aston, J. Carey, and O. Kharif, "Online Extra: The New Factory Floor, and Tomorrow's," *BusinessWeek Online,* May 3, 2004; www.businessweek.com/@@vr3DfocQkImUSwOA/magazine/content/04_18/b3881601.htm (accessed August 1, 2006).

43. K. Day and J. Howard, "Albertsons Officials to Implement New Efficiency Program," *Reno Gazette-Journal,* February 25, 2004, pp. 1D, 3D.

44. L. Clifford, "Why You Can Safely Ignore Six Sigma," *Fortune,* January 22, 2001; www.fortune.com/fortune/investing/articles/0,15114,367825,00.html (August 1, 2006).

45. See R. J. Aldag and T. M. Stearns, Management (Cincinnati, OH: South-Western Publishing, 1987), pp. 653–654; D. Robertson and E. Anderson, "Control System and Task Environment Effects on Ethical Judgment: An Exploratory Study of Industrial Salespeople," *Organizational Science,* November 1993, pp. 617–629.

46. K. A. Merchant, *Control in Business Organizations* (Boston: Pitman, 1985), pp. 10–11; K. M. Bartol and D. C. Martin, *Management,* 3rd ed. (Burr Ridge, IL: Irwin/McGraw-Hill, 1998), pp. 533–534; and J. R. Schermerhorn Jr., *Management for Productivity,* 3rd ed. (New York: John Wiley & Sons, 1993), p. 592.

47. J. Epstein, "Corporations Enlisted in Battle to Save Rain Forests," *San Francisco Chronicle,* July 7, 1999, pp. A8, A10.

48. Bartol and Martin, 1998, pp. 532–533; S. C. Certo, *Modern Management,* 8th ed. (Upper Saddle River, NJ: Prentice Hall, 2000), pp. 435–436; and Griffin, 1997, pp. 384–386.

49. J. P. Kotter, L. A. Schlesinger, and V. Sathe, *Organization: Text, Cases, and Readings on the Management of Organizational Design and Change* (Homewood, IL: Irwin, 1979).

50. K. Merchant, *Control in Business Organizations* (Boston: Pitman, 1985).

51. D. Murphy, "A Show of Initiative," *San Francisco Examiner,* February 13, 2000, pp. J-1, J-2; H. Lancaster, "Take on Tough Jobs, Assess Your Own Work, and Other Life Lessons," *The Wall Street Journal,* December 7, 1999, p. B1; O. Pollar, "These Crucial Skills Make You a 'Keeper,'" *San Francisco Examiner & Chronicle,* November 28, 1999, p. J-3; B. Weinstein, "Define What Product You Can Deliver," *San Francisco Examiner & Chronicle,* January 17, 1999, p. CL-21; and D. Murphy, "To Manage Well, Break a Few Rules," *San Francisco Examiner,* May 24, 1999, p. J-1.

glossary

A

absenteeism When an employee doesn't show up for work.

accommodative approach One of four managerial approaches to social responsibility; management does more than the law requires, if asked, and demonstrates moderate social responsibility.

acquired-needs theory Theory that states that there are three needs—achievement, affiliation, and power—that are the major motives determining people's behavior in the workplace.

action plan Course of action needed to achieve a stated goal.

adaptive perspective Perspective of organizational culture that assumes that the most effective cultures help organizations anticipate and adapt to environmental change.

adjourning One of five stages of forming a team; the stage in which members of an organization prepare for disbandment.

administrative management Management concerned with managing the total organization.

affective component of an attitude The feelings or emotions one has about a situation.

affirmative action The focus on achieving equality of opportunity within an organization.

Americans with Disabilities Act Passed by the U.S. in 1992, act that prohibits discrimination against the disabled.

analyzers Organizations that allow other organizations to take the risks of product development and marketing and then imitate (or perhaps slightly improve on) what seems to work best.

analytics (business analytics) Term used for sophisticated forms of business data analysis, such as portfolio analysis or time-series forecast.

anchoring and adjustment bias The tendency to make decisions based on an initial figure.

Asian-Pacific Economic Cooperation (APEC) Group of 21 Pacific Rim countries whose purpose is to improve economic and political ties.

assessment center Company department where management candidates participate in activities for a few days while being assessed by evaluators.

attitude A learned predisposition toward a given object; a mental position with regard to a fact, state, or person.

authority The right to perform or command; also, the rights inherent in a managerial position to make decisions, give orders, and utilize resources.

availability bias Tendency of managers to use information readily available from memory to make judgments; they tend to give more weight to recent events.

B

balance sheet A summary of an organization's overall financial worth—assets and liabilities—at a specific point in time.

balanced scorecard Gives top managers a fast but comprehensive view of the organization via four indicators: (1) customer satisfaction, (2) internal processes, (3) the organization's innovation and improvement activities, and (4) financial measures.

base pay Consists of the basic wage or salary paid employees in exchange for doing their jobs.

behavior Actions and judgments.

behavioral component of an attitude Also known as *intentional component,* this refers to how one intends or expects to behave toward a situation.

behavioral leadership approach Attempts to determine the distinctive styles used by effective leaders.

behavioral science Relies on scientific research for developing theories about human behavior that can be used to provide practical tools for managers.

behavioral viewpoint Emphasizes the importance of understanding human behavior and of motivating employees toward achievement.

behavioral-description interview Type of structured interview in which the interviewer explores what applicants have done in the past.

behaviorally anchored rating scale (BARS) Employee gradations in performance rated according to scales of specific behaviors.

benchmarking A process by which a company compares its performance with that of high-performing organizations.

benefits (fringe benefits) Additional nonmonetary forms of compensation.

Big Five personality dimensions They are (1) extroversion, (2) agreeableness, (3) conscientiousness, (4) emotional stability, and (5) openness to experience.

birth stage The nonbureaucratic stage, the stage in which the organization is created.

blended value The idea that all investments are understood to operate simultaneously in both economic and social realms.

blog Online journal in which people write about whatever they want about any topic.

bonuses Cash awards given to employees who achieve specific performance objectives.

boundaryless organization A fluid, highly adaptive organization whose members, linked by information technology, come together to collaborate on common tasks; the collaborators may include competitors, suppliers, and customers.

bounded rationality One type of non-rational decision making; the ability of decision makers to be rational is limited by numerous constraints.

brainstorming Technique used to help groups generate multiple ideas and alternatives for solving problems; individuals in a group meet and review a problem to be solved, then silently generate ideas, which are collected and later analyzed.

break-even analysis A way of identifying how much revenue is needed to cover the total cost of developing and selling a product.

break-even point The amount of sales revenue at which there is no profit but also no loss to your company.

budget A formal financial projection.

buffers Administrative changes that managers can make to reduce the stressors that lead to employee burnout.

bureaucratic control The use of rules, regulations, and formal authority to guide performance.

burnout State of emotional, mental, and even physical exhaustion.

C

cascading Objectives are structured in a unified hierarchy, becoming more specific at lower levels of the organization.

causal attribution The activity of inferring causes for observed behavior.

centralized authority Organizational structure in which important decisions are made by upper managers—power is concentrated at the top.

change agent A person inside or outside the organization who can be a catalyst in helping deal with old problems in new ways.

charisma Form of personal attraction that inspires acceptance and support.

classical viewpoint In the historical perspective, the viewpoint that emphasizes finding ways to manage work more efficiently; it has two branches—scientific and administrative.

closed system A system that has little interaction with its environment.

code of ethics A formal, written set of ethical standards that guide an organization's actions.

coercive power One of five sources of power; the power held by all managers, which results from their authority to punish their subordinates.

cognitive component of an attitude The beliefs and knowledge one has about a situation.

cognitive dissonance Term coined by social psychologist Leon Festinger to describe the psychological discomfort a person experiences between what he or she already knows and new information or contradictory behavior, or by inconsistency among a person's beliefs, attitudes, and/or actions.

cohesiveness The tendency of a group or team to stick together.

collective bargaining Negotiations between management and employees regarding disputes over compensation, benefits, working conditions, and job security.

command economy   In a planned economy or a central-planning economy, the government owns most businesses and regulates the amounts, types, and prices of goods and services.

common purpose   A goal that unifies employees or members and gives everyone an understanding of the organization's reason for being.

communication   The transfer of information and understanding from one person to another.

compensation   Payment comprising three parts: wages or salaries, incentives, and benefits.

competitive intelligence   Gaining information about competitors' activities so that one can anticipate their moves and react appropriately.

competitive advantage   The ability of an organization to produce goods or services more effectively than its competitors do, thereby outperforming them.

competitors   People or organizations that compete for customers or resources.

computer-assisted instruction (CAI)   Training in which computers are used to provide additional help or to reduce instructional time.

conceptual skills   Skills that consist of the ability to think analytically, to visualize an organization as a whole and understand how the parts work together.

confirmation bias   Biased way of thinking in which people seek information to support their point of view and discount data that does not.

conflict   Process in which one party perceives that its interests are being opposed or negatively affected by another party.

conglomerate structure   The fourth type of organizational structure, whereby divisions are grouped around similar businesses or activities.

consensus   General agreement; group solidarity.

constructive conflict   Functional conflict that benefits the main purposes of the organization and serves its interest.

contemporary perspective   In contrast to the historical perspective, the business approach that includes three viewpoints—systems, contingency, and quality-management.

content perspectives   Also known as *need-based perspectives;* theories that emphasize the needs that motivate people.

contingency approach to leadership   The belief that the effectiveness of leadership behavior depends on the situation at hand.

contingency design   The process of fitting the organization to its environment.

contingency leadership model   Fiedler's theory (1951) that leader effectiveness is determined by both the personal characteristics of leaders and by the situations in which leaders find themselves; the leader's style is either task-oriented or relationship-oriented, and it must be determined which style fits the situation at hand.

contingency planning   Also known as *scenario planning* and *scenario analysis;* the creation of alternative hypothetical but equally likely future conditions.

contingency viewpoint   In opposition to the classical viewpoint; a manager's approach should vary according to—that is, be contingent on—the individual and the environmental situation.

continuous improvement   Ongoing, small, incremental improvements in all parts of an organization.

continuous-process technology   A highly routinized technology in which machines do all of the work, to produce highly routinized products.

control process   The four steps in the process of controlling: (1) establish standards; (2) measure performance; (3) compare performance to standards; and (4) take corrective action, if necessary.

control standard   The first step in the control process; the performance standard (or just standard) is the desired performance level for a given goal.

controlling   Monitoring performance, comparing goals, and taking corrective action as needed.

coordinated effort   The coordination of individual efforts into a group or organization-wide effort.

core principles of TQM   In total quality management, (1) everyone involved with the organization should focus on delivering value to customers (people orientation), and (2) everyone should work on continuously improving the work processes (improvement orientation).

cost-leadership strategy   One of Porter's four competitive strategies; keeping the costs, and hence prices, of a product or service below those of competitors and targeting the wider market.

cost-focus strategy   One of Porter's four competitive strategies; to keep the costs, and hence prices, of a product or service below those of competitors and to target a narrow market.

countertrading   Bartering goods for goods.

cross-functional team A team that is staffed with specialists pursuing a common objective.

culture A shared set of beliefs, values, knowledge, and patterns of behavior common to a group of people.

culture shock Feelings of discomfort and disorientation associated with being in an unfamiliar culture.

customer division A divisional structure in which activities are grouped around common customers or clients.

customers Those who pay to use an organization's goods or services.

D

database Computerized collection of interrelated files.

decentralized authority Organizational structure in which important decisions are made by middle-level and supervisory-level managers—power is delegated throughout the organization.

decentralized control An approach to organizational control that is characterized by informal and organic structural arrangements, the opposite of bureaucratic control.

deciding to decide A manager agrees that he or she must decide what to do about a problem or opportunity and take effective decision-making steps.

decision A choice made from among available alternatives.

decision making The process of identifying and choosing alternative courses of action.

decision-making style A style that reflects the combination of how an individual perceives and responds to information.

decision tree Graph of decisions and their possible consequences, used to create a plan to reach a goal.

decisional role One of three types of managerial roles: managers use information to make decisions to solve problems or take advantage of opportunities. The four decision-making roles are entrepreneur, disturbance handler, resource allocator, and negotiator.

decline stage The fourth stage in the product life cycle; period in which a product falls out of favor, and the organization withdraws from the marketplace.

decoding Interpreting and trying to make sense of a message.

defenders Experts at producing and selling narrowly defined products or services.

defensive approach One of four managerial approaches to social responsibility; managers make the minimum commitment to social responsibility—obeying the law but doing nothing more.

defensive avoidance When a manager cannot find a good solution and follows by (a) procrastinating, (b) passing the buck, or (c) denying the risk of any negative consequences.

defensive strategy Also called *retrenchment strategy;* one of three grand strategies, this strategy involves reduction in the organization's efforts.

delegation The process of assigning managerial authority and responsibility to managers and employees lower in the hierarchy.

Delphi group A problem-solving technique in which a group of physically dispersed experts fills out questionnaires to anonymously generate ideas; the judgments are combined and averaged to achieve a consensus of expert opinion.

democratic governments Governments that rely on free elections and representative assemblies.

demographic forces Influences on an organization arising from changes in the characteristics of a population, such as age, gender, ethnic origin, and so on.

developed countries Countries with a high level of economic development and generally high average level of income among their citizens.

development The education of professionals and managers in the skills they will need to do their jobs.

devil's advocacy Taking the side of an unpopular point of view for the sake of argument.

diagnosis Analysis of underlying causes.

dialectic method The process of having two people or groups play opposing roles in a debate in order to better understand a proposal.

differentiation The tendency of the parts of an organization to disperse and fragment.

differentiation strategy One of Porter's four competitive strategies; offer products or services that are of a unique and superior value compared to those of competitors and to target a wide market.

discrimination Prejudicial outlook; when people are hired or promoted—or denied hiring or promotion—for reasons not relevant to the job.

distributor A person or an organization that helps another organization sell its goods and services to customers.

diversification Strategy by which a company operates several businesses in order to spread the risk.

diversity All the ways people are unlike and alike—the differences and similarities in age, gender, race, religion, ethnicity, sexual orientation, capabilities, and socioeconomic background.

division of labor Also known as *work specialization;* arrangement of having discrete parts of a task done by different people. The work is divided into particular tasks assigned to particular workers.

divisional structure The third type of organizational structure, whereby people with diverse occupational specialties are put together in formal groups according to products and/or services, customers and/or clients, or geographic regions.

downward communication Communication that flows from a higher level to a lower level.

dumping A foreign company's practice of exporting products abroad at a price lower than the home-market price, or even below the costs of production, in order to drive down the price of the domestic product.

E

e-business Using the Internet to facilitate every aspect of running a business.

e-commerce Electronic commerce; the buying and selling of goods and services over computer networks.

e-mail Electronic mail; text messages and documents transmitted over a computer network.

e-leadership Leadership that involves one-to-one, one-to-many, and within- and between-group and collective interactions via information technology.

economic forces General economic conditions and trends—unemployment, inflation, interest rates, economic growth—that may affect an organization's performance.

effect uncertainty One of three types of uncertainty; when the effects of environmental changes are unpredictable.

effective To achieve results, to make the right decisions and to successfully carry them out so that they achieve the organization's goals.

efficient Using resources—people, money, raw materials, and the like—wisely and cost-effectively.

electronic brainstorming (brainwriting) Technique in which members of a group come together over a computer network to generate ideas and alternatives.

embargo A complete ban on the import and/or export of certain products.

emotional intelligence The ability to cope, to empathize with others, and to be self-motivated.

employee assistance program Program designed to help employees overcome personal problems affecting their job performance.

employment tests Tests legally considered to consist of any procedure used in the employment selection process.

encoding Translating a message into understandable symbols or language.

entrepreneur Someone who sees a new opportunity for a product or service and launches a business to try to realize it.

entrepreneurship The process of taking risks to try to create a new enterprise.

Equal Employment Opportunity (EEO) Commission U.S. panel whose job it is to enforce antidiscrimination and other employment-related laws.

equity theory In the area of employee motivation, the focus on how employees perceive how fairly they think they are being treated compared to others.

escalation of commitment bias When decision makers increase their commitment to a project despite negative information about it.

ethical behavior Behavior accepted as "right" as opposed to "wrong" according to recognized ethical standards.

ethical dilemma A situation in which you have to decide whether to pursue a course of action that may benefit you or your organization but that is unethical or even illegal.

ethics Generally accepted standards of right and wrong that influence behavior; these standards may vary among countries and cultures.

ethics officer A person trained about matters of ethics in the workplace, particularly about resolving ethical dilemmas.

ethnocentric managers Managers who believe that their native country, culture, language, and/or behavior are superior to others.

ethnocentrism The belief that one's native country, culture, language, abilities, and/or behavior are superior to those of another culture.

European Union (EU)   Union of 25 trading partners in Europe.

evidence-based management   Kind of management that believes organizations will perform better if managers face the hard facts about what works and doesn't, understand the dangerous half-truths that constitute so much conventional wisdom about management, and reject the total nonsense that too often passes for sound advice.

exchange rate   The rate at which one country's currency is exchanged for another country's currency.

execution   As proposed by Larry Bossidy and Ram Charan, execution is not simply tactics, it is a central part of any company's strategy; it consists of using questioning, analysis, and follow-through in order to mesh strategy with reality, align people with goals, and achieve results promised.

expatriate manager   A manager living or working in a foreign country.

expectancy   The belief that a particular level of effort will lead to a particular level of performance.

expectancy theory   Theory that suggests that people are motivated by two things: (1) how much they want something and (2) how likely they think they are to get it.

expert power   One of five sources of power; the power resulting from one's specialized information or expertise.

explicit knowledge   Information that can be easily put into words, graphics, and numbers and shared with others.

exporting   Producing goods domestically and selling them outside the country.

expropriation   A government's seizure of a foreign company's assets.

external audit   Formal verification by outside experts of an organization's financial accounts and statements.

external dimensions of diversity   Human differences that have an element of choice; they consist of the personal characteristics that people acquire, discard, or modify throughout their lives.

external recruiting   Attracting job applicants from outside the organization.

external stakeholders   People or groups in the organization's external environment that are affected by it. This environment includes the task environment and the general environment.

extinction   The withholding or withdrawal of positive rewards for desirable behavior, so that the behavior is less likely to occur in the future.

extranet   An extended intranet that connects internal employees with selected customers, suppliers, and other strategic partners.

extrinsic reward   The payoff, such as money, that a person receives from others for performing a particular task.

F

Fair Labor Standards Act   Legislation passed in 1938 that established minimum living standards for workers engaged in interstate commerce, including provision of a federal minimum wage.

feedback   The receiver's expression of his or her reaction to the sender's message. Also, the information about the reaction of the environment to the outputs that affect the inputs; one of four parts of a system, along with inputs, outputs, and transformational processes.

financial statement   Summary of some aspect of an organization's financial status.

first-line managers   One of three managerial levels; also called *supervisory managers;* they make the short-term operating decisions, directing the daily tasks of nonmanagerial personnel.

fit perspective   Perspective of organizational culture that assumes that an organization's culture must align, or fit, with its business or strategic context.

fixed budget   Allocation of resources on the basis of a single estimate of costs.

focused-differentiation strategy   One of Porter's four competitive strategies; to offer products or services that are of unique and superior value compared to those of competitors and to target a narrow market.

forced ranking performance review systems   Performance review systems whereby all employees within a business unit are ranked against one another, and grades are distributed along some sort of bell curve, like students being graded in a college course.

forecast   A projection of the future.

Foreign Corrupt Practices Act of 1977   An act that makes it illegal for employees of U.S. companies to bribe political decision makers in foreign nations.

formal appraisals   Appraisals conducted at specific times throughout the year and based on performance measures that have been established in advance.

formal communication channels Communications that follow the chain of command and are recognized as official.

formal group A group, headed by a leader, that is established to do something productive for the organization.

forming One of five stages of forming a team; the first stage, in which people get oriented and get acquainted.

four management functions The management process that "gets things done": planning, organizing, leading, and controlling.

franchising A form of licensing in which a company allows a foreign company to pay it a fee and a share of the profit in return for using the first company's brand name and a package of materials and services.

free market economy Economic model in which production of goods and services is controlled by private enterprise and the interaction of the forces of supply and demand rather than by the government.

free trade The movement of goods and services among nations without political or economic obstruction.

full-range leadership Approach that suggests that leadership behavior varies along a full range of leadership styles, from take-no-responsibilty (*laissez-faire*) "leadership" at one extreme through transactional leadership, to transformational leadership at the other extreme.

functional managers Managers who are responsible for just one organizational activity.

functional structure The second type of organizational structure, whereby people with similar occupational specialties are put together in formal groups.

fundamental attribution bias Tendency whereby people attribute another person's behavior to his or her personal characteristics rather than to situational factors.

G

gainsharing The distribution of savings or "gains" to groups of employees who reduce costs and increase measurable productivity.

general environment Also called *macroenvironment*; in contrast to the task environment, it includes six forces: economic, technological, sociocultural, demographic, political-legal, and international.

general managers Managers who are responsible for several organizational activities.

geocentric managers Managers who accept that there are differences and similarities between home and foreign personnel and practices and that they should use whatever techniques are most effective.

geographic division A divisional structure in which activities are grouped around defined regional locations.

glass ceiling The metaphor for an invisible barrier preventing women and minorities from being promoted to top executive jobs.

global economy The increasing tendency of the economies of the world to interact with one another as one market instead of as many national markets.

global outsourcing Using suppliers outside the United States to provide labor, goods, and/or services.

global village The "shrinking" of time and space as air travel and electronic media make it easier for the people of the globe to communicate with one another.

globalization The trend of the world economy toward becoming a more interdependent system.

GLOBE project Massive, ongoing cross-cultural investigation of nine cultural dimensions involved in leadership and organizational processes. Started by Robert J. House, GLOBE stands for Global Leadership and Organizational Behavior Effectiveness.

goal Also known as *objective;* a specific commitment to achieve a measurable result within a stated period of time.

goal displacement The primary goal is subsumed to a secondary goal.

goal-setting theory Employee-motivation approach that employees can be motivated by goals that are specific and challenging but achievable.

government regulators Regulatory agencies that establish ground rules under which organizations may operate.

grand strategy Second step of the strategic-management process; it explains how the organization's mission is to be accomplished. Three grand strategies are growth, stability, and defensive.

grapevine The unofficial communication system of the informal organization.

greenfield venture A wholly-owned foreign subsidiary that the owning organization has built from scratch.

group Two or more freely interacting individuals who share collective norms, share collective goals, and have a common identity.

group cohesiveness A "we feeling" that binds group members together.

group support systems (GSSs) Use of state-of-the-art computer software and hardware to help people work better together.

groupthink A cohesive group's blind unwillingness to consider alternatives. This occurs when group members strive for agreement among themselves for the sake of unanimity and avoid accurately assessing the decision situation.

growth stage The second stage of the product life cycle. This, the most profitable stage, is the period in which customer demand increases, the product's sales grow, and (later) competitors may enter the market.

growth strategy One of three grand strategies, this strategy involves expansion—as in sales revenues, market share, number of employees, or number of customers or (for nonprofits) clients served.

H

halo effect An effect in which we form a positive impression of an individual based on a single trait.

hero A person whose accomplishments embody the values of the organization.

heuristics Strategies that simplify the process of making decisions.

hierarchy of authority Also known as *chain of command*; a control mechanism for making sure the right people do the right things at the right time.

hierarchy of needs theory Psychological structure proposed by Maslow whereby people are motivated by five levels of needs: (1) physiological, (2) safety, (3) belongingness, (4) esteem, and (5) self-actualization.

high-context culture Culture in which people rely heavily on situational cues for meaning when communicating with others.

historical perspective In contrast to the contemporary perspective, the view of management that includes the classical, behavioral, and quantitative viewpoints.

Hofstede model of four cultural dimensions Model proposed by Geert Hofstede that identified four dimensions along which national cultures can be placed: individualism/collectivism, power distance, uncertainty avoidance, and masculinity/femininity.

horizontal communication Communication that flows within and between work units; its main purpose is coordination.

human capital Economic or productive potential of employee knowledge, experience, and actions.

human relations movement The movement that proposed that better human relations could increase worker productivity.

human resource inventory A report listing an organization's employees by name, education, training, languages, and other important information.

human resource (HR) management The activities managers perform to plan for, attract, develop, and retain a workforce.

human skills The ability to work well in cooperation with other people in order to get things done.

hybrid structure Fifth type of organizational structure, whereby an organizational form uses functional and divisional structures in different parts of the same organization.

hygiene factors Factors associated with job dissatisfaction—such as salary, working conditions, interpersonal relationships, and company policy—all of which affect the job context or environment in which people work.

I

import quota A trade barrier in the form of a limit on the numbers of a product that can be imported.

importing Buying goods outside the country and reselling them domestically.

incentives Benefits used to move people to action, such as commissions, bonuses, profit-sharing plans, and stock options.

income statement Summary of an organization's financial results—revenues and expenses—over a specified period of time.

incremental budgeting Allocating increased or decreased funds to a department by using the last budget period as a reference point; only incremental changes in the budget request are reviewed.

incremental innovations The creation of products, services, or technologies that modify existing ones.

incremental model One type of nonrational model of decision making; managers take small, short-term steps to alleviate a problem.

indigenization laws   Laws that require that citizens within the host country own a majority of whatever company is operating within that country.

individual approach   One of four approaches to solving ethical dilemmas; ethical behavior is guided by what will result in the individual's best long-term interests, which ultimately is in everyone's self-interest.

informal appraisals   Appraisals conducted on an unscheduled basis and consisting of less rigorous indications of employee performance than those used in formal appraisals.

informal communication channels   Communication that develops outside the formal structure and does not follow the chain of command.

informal group   A group formed by people seeking friendship that has no officially appointed leader, although a leader may emerge from the membership.

information overload   An overload that occurs when the amount of information received exceeds a person's ability to handle or process it.

informational role   One of three types of managerial roles: managers receive and communicate information with other people inside and outside the organization as monitors, disseminators, and spokespersons.

infrastructure   The physical facilities that form the basis of a country's level of economic development.

innovation   Introduction of something new or better, as in goods or services.

inputs   The people, money, information, equipment, and materials required to produce an organization's goods or services; one of four parts of a system, along with outputs, transformation processes, and feedback.

instrumentality   The expectation that successful performance of the task will lead to the outcome desired.

integration   The tendency of the parts of an organization to draw together to achieve a common purpose.

interacting group   A problem-solving technique in which group members interact and deliberate with one another to reach a consensus.

internal audit   A verification of an organization's financial accounts and statements by the organization's own professional staff.

internal dimensions of diversity   The human differences that exert a powerful, sustained effect throughout every stage of people's lives (gender, age, ethnicity, race, sexual orientation, physical abilities).

internal locus of control   The belief that one controls one's own destiny.

internal recruiting   Hiring from the inside, or making people already employed by the organization aware of job openings.

internal stakeholders   Employees, owners, and the board of directors, if any.

international forces   Changes in the economic, political, legal, and technological global system that may affect an organization.

international management   Management that oversees the conduct of operations in or with organizations in foreign countries.

International Monetary Fund (IMF)   One of three principal organizations designed to facilitate international trade; its purpose is to assist in smoothing the flow of money between nations.

Internet   Global network of independently operating but interconnected computers, linking hundreds of thousands of smaller networks around the world.

interpersonal role   One of three types of managerial roles; managers interact with people inside and outside of their work units. The three interpersonal roles include figurehead, leader, and liaison activities.

intervention   Interference in an attempt to correct a problem.

intranet   An organization's private, internal Internet.

intrapreneur   Someone who works inside an existing organization who sees an opportunity for a product or a service and mobilizes the organization's resources to try to realize it.

intrinsic reward   The satisfaction, such as a feeling of accomplishment, a person receives from performing a task.

introduction stage   The first stage in the product life cycle; a new product is introduced into the marketplace.

intuition model   Form of nonrational decision making whereby a manager quickly sizes up a situation and makes a decision based on his or her experience or practice.

ISO 9000 series Set of company quality-control procedures, developed by the International Organization for Standardization in Geneva, Switzerland, that deals with all activities—from purchasing to manufacturing to inventory to shipping—that can be audited by independent quality-control experts, or "registrars."

J

jargon Terminology specific to a particular profession or group.

job analysis The determination of the basic elements of a job.

job characteristics model The job design model that consists of five core job characteristics that affect three critical psychological states of an employee that in turn affect work outcomes—the employee's motivation, performance, and satisfaction.

job description A summary of what the holder of the job does and how and why he or she does it.

job design The division of an organization's work among its employees and the application of motivational theories to jobs to increase satisfaction and performance.

job enlargement Increasing the number of tasks in a job to increase variety and motivation.

job enrichment Building into a job such motivating factors as responsibility, achievement, recognition, stimulating work, and advancement.

job involvement The extent to which one is personally involved with one's job.

job posting Placing information about job vacancies and qualifications on bulletin boards, in newsletters, and on the organization's intranet.

job satisfaction The extent to which one feels positively or negatively about various aspects of one's work.

job simplification The process of reducing the number of tasks a worker performs.

job specification Description of the minimum qualifications a person must have to perform a job successfully.

joint ventures Organizations that join forces to realize strategic advantages that neither could have achieved alone; a U.S. firm may form a joint venture, also known as a *strategic alliance,* with a foreign company to share the risks and rewards of starting a new enterprise together in a foreign country.

justice approach One of four approaches to solving ethical dilemmas; ethical behavior is guided by respect for impartial standards of fairness and equity.

K

knowledge management Implementation of systems and practices to increase the sharing of knowledge and information throughout an organization; also, the development of an organizational structure—and the tools, processes, systems, and structures—that encourages continuous learning and sharing of knowledge and information among employees, for the purpose of making better decisions.

knowledge worker Someone whose occupation is principally concerned with generating or interpreting information, as opposed to manual labor.

L

large-batch technology Routinized products made by highly mechanized organizations; mass-production assembly-line technology.

leader–member exchange (LMX) model of leadership Model proposed by George Graen and Fred Dansereau that emphasizes that leaders have different sorts of relationships with different subordinates.

leadership The ability to influence employees to voluntarily pursue organizational goals.

leading Motivating, directing, and otherwise influencing people to work hard to achieve the organization's goals.

lean Six Sigma Quality-control approach that focuses on problem solving and performance improvement—speed with excellence—of a well-defined project; *see also* Six Sigma.

learned helplessness The debilitating lack of faith in one's ability to control one's environment.

learning organization An organization that actively creates, acquires, and transfers knowledge within itself and is able to modify its behavior to reflect new knowledge.

legitimate power One of five sources of power; all managers have this power, which results from their formal positions with the organization.

less-developed countries Also known as *developing countries;* nations with low economic development and low average incomes.

Level 5 leadership Leadership situation in which an organization is led by a Level 5 executive who possesses the paradoxical characteristics of humility and a fearless will to succeed, as well as the capabilities associated with levels 1–4: highly capable, contributing, competent, effective.

licensing Company X allows a foreign company to pay it a fee to make or distribute X's product or service.

line managers Managers who have the authority to make decisions and usually have people reporting to them.

locus of control Measure of how much people believe they control their fate through their own efforts.

loss Total costs exceed total sales revenue.

low-context culture Culture in which shared meanings are primarily derived from written and spoken words.

M

maintenance role Relationship-related role consisting of behavior that fosters constructive relationships among team members.

management The pursuit of organizational goals efficiently and effectively by integrating the work of people through planning, organizing, leading, and controlling the organization's resources.

management by exception Control principle that states that managers should be informed of a situation only if data shows a significant deviation from standards.

management by objectives (MBO) Four-step process in which (1) managers and employees jointly set objectives for the employee, (2) managers develop action plans, (3) managers and employees periodically review the employee's performance, and (4) the manager makes a performance appraisal and rewards the employee according to results.

management by wandering around (MBWA) Style of management whereby a manager literally wanders around the organization and talks with people across all lines of authority.

management process Performing the planning, organizing, leading, and controlling necessary to get things done.

management science Sometimes called *operations research;* branch of quantitative management; method of solving management problems by using mathematics to aid in problem solving and decision making.

maquiladoras U.S. manufacturing plants allowed to operate in Mexico with special privileges in return for employing Mexican citizens.

matrix structure Sixth type of organizational structure, which combines functional and divisional chains of command in a grid so that there are two command structures—vertical and horizontal.

maturity stage A stage when the organization becomes very bureaucratic, large, and mechanistic. Also the third stage in the product life cycle; period in which the product starts to fall out of favor, and sales and profits fall off.

means-end chain A hierarchy of goals; in the chain of management (operational, tactical, strategic), the accomplishment of low-level goals are the means leading to the accomplishment of high-level goals or ends.

mechanistic organization Organization in which authority is centralized, tasks and rules are clearly specified, and employees are closely supervised.

media richness Indication of how well a particular medium conveys information and promotes learning.

medium The pathway by which a mes-sage travels.

Mercosur The largest trade bloc in Latin America, with four core members: Argentina, Brazil, Paraguay, Uruguay.

message The information to be shared.

meta-analysis Statistical pooling technique that permits behavioral scientists to draw general conclusions about certain variables from many different studies.

middle managers One of three managerial levels; they implement the policies and plans of the top managers above them and supervise and coordinate the activities of the first-line managers below them.

midlife stage A period of growth evolving into stability when the organization becomes bureaucratic.

mission An organization's purpose or reason for being.

mission statement Statement that expresses the purpose of the organization.

mixed economy An economy in which most of the important industries are owned by the government, but others are controlled by private enterprise.

monochronic time The standard kind of time orientation in U.S business; preference for doing one thing at a time.

moral-rights approach One of four approaches to solving ethical dilemmas; ethical behavior is guided by respect for the fundamental rights of human beings.

most favored nation This trading status describes a condition in which a country grants other countries favorable trading treatment such as the reduction of import duties.

motivating factors Factors associated with job satisfaction—such as achievement, recognition, responsibility, and advancement—all of which affect the job content or the rewards of work performance.

motivation Psychological processes that arouse and direct goal-directed behavior.

multinational corporation Business firm with operations in several countries.

multinational organization Nonprofit organization with operations in several countries.

N

National Labor Relations Board Legislated in 1935, U.S. commission that enforces the procedures whereby employees may vote to have a union and collective bargaining.

need-based perspectives Also known as *content perspectives;* theories that emphasize the needs that motivate people.

needs Physiological or psychological deficiencies that arouse behavior.

network structure Eighth type of organizational structure, whereby a central core is linked to outside independent firms by computer connections, which are used to operate as if all were a single organization.

noise Any disturbance that interferes with the transmission of a message.

nominal group A group whose purpose it is to generate ideas and evaluate solutions by writing down as many ideas as possible. The ideas are listed on a blackboard, then discussed, then voted on in a secret ballot.

nonprogrammed decisions Decisions that occur under nonroutine, unfamiliar circumstances.

nonrational model of decision making A model of decision-making style that explains how managers make decisions; they assume that decision making is nearly always uncertain and risky, making it difficult for managers to make optimum decisions.

nonverbal communication Messages in a form other than the written or the spoken word.

norming One of five stages of forming a team; stage three, in which conflicts are resolved, close relationships develop, and unity and harmony emerge.

norms General guidelines or rules of behavior that most group or team members follow.

North American Free Trade Agreement (NAFTA) Formed in 1994, the trading bloc consisting of the United States, Canada, and Mexico.

not bat an eye *To not seem to see; to not react.*

O

objective See *goal.*

objective appraisal Also called *results appraisal;* form of performance evaluation that is based on facts and that is often numerical.

obstructionist approach One of four managerial approaches to social responsiblity; managers put economic gain first and resist social responsibility as being outside the organization's self-interest.

open system System that continually interacts with its environment.

operating plan Typically designed for a one-year period, this plan defines how a manager will conduct his or her business based on the action plan; the operating plan identifies clear targets such as revenues, cash flow, and market share.

operational control Monitoring performance to ensure that operational plans—day-to-day goals—are being implemented and taking corrective action as needed.

operational goals Goals that are set by and for first-line managers and are concerned with short-term matters associated with realizing tactical goals.

operational planning Determining how to accomplish specific tasks with available resources within the next 1-week to 1-year period; done by first-line managers.

operations management A branch of quantitative management; effective management of the production and delivery of an organization's products or services.

opportunities Situations that present possibilities for exceeding existing goals.

organic organization Organization in which authority is decentralized, there are fewer rules and procedures, and networks of employees are encouraged to cooperate and respond quickly to unexpected tasks.

organization A group of people who work together to achieve some specific purpose. A system of consciously coordinated activities or forces of two or more people.

organization chart Box-and-lines illustration of the formal relationships of positions of authority and the organization's official positions or work specializations.

organization development (OD) Set of techniques for implementing planned change to make people and organizations more effective.

organizational behavior (OB) Behavior that is dedicated to better understanding and managing people at work.

organizational citizenship behaviors Employee behaviors that are not directly part of employees' job descriptions—that exceed their work-role requirements, such as constructive statements about the department.

organizational culture Sometimes called *corporate culture;* system of shared beliefs and values that develops within an organization and guides the behavior of its members.

organizational life cycle Four-stage cycle with a natural sequence of stages: birth, youth, midlife, and maturity.

organizational opportunities The environmental factors that the organization may exploit for competitive advantage.

organizational size Measurement of a group's size according to the number of full-time employees.

organizational strengths The skills and capabilities that give the organization special competencies and competitive advantages in executing strategies in pursuit of its mission.

organizational threats The environmental factors that hinder an organization's achieving a competitive advantage.

organizational weaknesses The drawbacks that hinder an organization in executing strategies in pursuit of its mission.

organizing Arranging tasks, people, and other resources to accomplish the work.

orientation Process of helping a newcomer fit smoothly into the job and the organization.

outputs The products, services, profits, losses, employee satisfaction or discontent, and the like that are produced by the organization; one of four parts of a system, along with inputs, transformation processes, and feedback.

outsourcing Subcontracting of services and operations to an outside vendor. Using suppliers outside the company to provide goods and services.

owners Those who can claim the organization as their legal property.

P

panic Situation in which a manager reacts frantically to get rid of a problem that he or she cannot deal with realistically.

paradigm Generally accepted way of viewing the world.

parochialism Also known as *ethnocentrism;* narrow view in which people see things solely from their own perspective.

participative management (PM) The process of involving employees in (1) setting goals, (2) making decisions, (3) solving problems, and (4) making changes in the organization.

path–goal leadership model Contingency approach that holds that the effective leader makes available to followers desirable rewards in the workplace and increases their motivation by clarifying the paths, or behavior, that will help them achieve those goals and providing them with support.

pay for knowledge Situation in which employees' pay is tied to the number of job-relevant skills they have or academic degrees they earn.

pay for performance Situation in which an employee's pay is based on the results he or she achieves.

perception Awareness; interpreting and understanding one's environment.

performance appraisal Assessment of an employee's performance and the provision of feedback.

performing One of five stages of forming a team; stage 4, in which members concentrate on solving problems and completing the assigned task.

personality The stable psychological traits and behavioral attributes that give a person his or her identity.

personalized power Power directed at helping oneself.

philanthropy Act of making charitable donations to benefit humankind.

piece rate Pay based on how much output an employee produces.

planning Setting goals and deciding how to achieve them. Also, coping with uncertainty by formulating future courses of action to achieve specified results.

planning/control cycle A cycle that has two planning steps (1 and 2) and two control steps (3 and 4), as follows: (1) Make the plan. (2) Carry out the plan. (3) Control the direction by comparing results with the plan. (4) Control the direction by taking corrective action in two ways—namely, (a) by correcting deviations in the plan being carried out, or (b) by improving future plans.

policy Standing plan that outlines the general response to a designated problem or situation.

political risk The risk that political changes will cause loss of a company's assets or impair its foreign operations.

political-legal forces Changes in the way politics shape laws and laws shape the opportunities for and threats to an organization.

polycentric managers Managers who take the view that native managers in foreign offices best understand native personnel and practices, and so the home office should leave them alone.

polychronic time Kind of time orientation common in Mediterranean, Latin American, and Arab cultures; preference for doing more than one thing at a time.

Porter's four competitive strategies (four generic strategies) (1) Cost-leadership, (2) differentiation, (3) cost-focus, (4) focused-differentiation. The first two strategies focus on wide markets, the last two on narrow markets.

Porter's model for industry analysis Model proposed by Michael Porter for determining competitiveness within a particular industry; suggests that business-level strategies originate in five primary competitive forces in a firm's environment: (1) threats of new entrants, (2) bargaining power of suppliers, (3) bargaining power of buyers, (4) threats of substitute products or services, and (5) rivalry among competitors.

positive reinforcement The use of positive consequences to encourage desirable behavior.

power The measure of the extent to which a person is able to influence others so that they respond to orders.

predictive modeling Data mining technique used to predict future behavior and anticipate the consequences of change.

privatization The making private of business activities, as when state-owned activities are performed by private enterprise.

proactive approach One of four managerial approaches to social responsibility; managers actively lead the way in being socially responsible for all stakeholders, using the organization's resources to identify and respond to social problems.

proactive change Planned change; making carefully thought-out changes in anticipation of possible or expected problems or opportunities; opposite of *reactive change.*

proactive personality Someone who is apt to take initiative and persevere to influence the environment.

problems Difficulties that inhibit the achievement of goals.

procedure Also known as *standard operating procedure;* a standing plan that outlines the response to particular problems or circumstances.

process innovation A change in the way a product or service is conceived, manufactured, or disseminated.

process perspectives Theories of employee motivation concerned with the thought processes by which people decide how to act: expectancy theory, equity theory, and goal-setting theory.

product division A divisional structure in which activities are grouped around similar products or services.

product innovation A change in the appearance or the performance of a product or a service or the creation of a new one.

product life cycle A model that graphs the four stages of a product or service during the "life" of its marketability: (1) introduction, (2) growth, (3) maturity, and (4) decline.

profit The amount by which total revenue exceeds total costs; a valuable return.

profit sharing The distribution to employees of a percentage of the company's profits.

program A single-use plan encompassing a range of projects or activities.

programmed conflict Conflict designed to elicit different opinions without inciting people's personal feelings.

programmed decisions   Decisions that are repetitive and routine. Contrast *nonprogrammed decisions.*

project   A single-use plan of less scope and complexity than a program.

project life cycle   Cycle of a project with four stages from start to finish: definition, planning, execution, and closing.

project management   Achieving a set of goals by planning, scheduling, and maintaining progress of the activities that constitute a project.

project management software   Programs for planning and scheduling the people, costs, and resources to complete a project on time.

project planning   Preparation of single-use plans, or projects.

prospectors   Managers who develop new products or services and seek out new markets, rather than waiting for things to happen.

punishment   The application of negative consequences to stop or change undesirable behavior.

Q

quality   The total ability of a product or service to meet customer needs.

quality assurance   A means of ensuring quality that focuses on the performance of workers, urging employees to strive for "zero defects."

quality circles   Small groups of volunteer workers and supervisors who meet intermittently to discuss workplace and quality-related problems.

quality control   A means of ensuring quality whereby errors are minimized by managing each state of production.

quality-management viewpoint   Perspective that focuses on quality control, quality assurance, and total quality management.

quantitative management   An evolutionary form of operations research, whereby quantitative techniques, such as statistics and computer simulations, are applied to management. Two branches of quantitative management are management science and operations management.

R

radical innovations   New products, services, or technologies that replace existing ones.

ratio analysis   The evaluation of financial ratios (the relationship of two or more things); includes liquidity ratios, debt management ratios, asset management ratios, and return ratios.

rational model of decision making   Also called the *classical model;* the style of decision making that explains how managers should make decisions; it assumes that managers will make logical decisions that will be the optimum in furthering the organization's best interests.

reactive change   Change made in response to problems or opportunities as they arise. Compare *proactive change.*

reactors   Managers who make adjustments only when finally forced to by environmental pressures.

readiness   The extent to which a follower possesses the ability and willingness to complete a task.

realistic job preview   A picture of both positive and negative features of the job and organization given to a job candidate before he or she is hired.

receiver   The person for whom a message is intended.

recruiting   The process of locating and attracting qualified applicants for jobs open in the organization.

reduced cycle time   The reduction of steps in the work process.

referent power   One of five sources of power; power deriving from one's personal attraction.

reinforcement   Anything that causes a given behavior to be repeated or inhibited; the four types are positive, negative, extinction, and punishment.

reinforcement theory   The belief that behavior reinforced by positive consequences tends to be repeated, whereas behavior reinforced by negative consequences tends not to be repeated.

related diversification   Strategy by which an organization under one ownership operates separate businesses that are related to one another.

relaxed avoidance   The situation in which a manager decides to take no action in the belief that there will be no great negative consequences.

relaxed change   The situation in which a manager realizes that complete inaction will have negative consequences but opts for the first available alternative that involves low risk.

reliability   Degree to which a test measures the same thing consistently, so that an individual's score remains about the same over time, assuming the characteristics being measured also remain the same.

representativeness bias The tendency to generalize from a small sample or a single event.

response uncertainty One of three types of uncertainty; when the consequences of a decision are uncertain.

responsibility The obligation one has to perform the assigned tasks.

reward power One of five sources of power; all managers have this power, which results from their authority to reward their subordinates.

risk propensity Willingness to gamble or to undertake risk for the possibility of gaining an increased payoff.

rites and rituals The activities and ceremonies, planned and unplanned, that celebrate important occasions and accomplishments in an organization's life.

role A socially determined expectation of how an individual should behave in a specific position; set of behaviors that people expect of occupants of a position.

rule Standing plan that designates specific required action.

S

sales commissions The percentage of a company's earnings as the result of a salesperson's sales that is paid to that salesperson.

Sarbanes-Oxley Act of 2002 Often shortened to *SarbOx* or *SOX;* act establishing requirements for proper financial record keeping for public companies and penalties for noncompliance.

satisficing model One type of nonrational decision-making model; managers seek alternatives until they find one that is satisfactory, not optimal.

scientific management Management approach that emphasizes the scientific study of work methods to improve the productivity of individual workers.

selection process The screening of job applicants to hire the best candidate.

selective perception The tendency to filter out information that is discomforting, that seems irrelevant, or that contradicts one's beliefs.

self-efficacy Personal ability to do a task.

self-esteem Self-respect; the extent to which people like or dislike themselves.

self-fulfilling prophecy Also known as the *Pygmalion effect;* the phenomenon in which people's expectations of themselves or others leads them to behave in ways that make those expectations come true.

self-managed teams Groups of workers who are given administrative oversight for their task domains.

self-monitoring Observing one's own behavior and adapting it to external situations.

self-serving bias The attributional tendency to take more personal responsibility for success than for failure.

semantics The study of the meaning of words.

sender The person wanting to share information.

servant leaders Leaders who focus on providing increased service to others—meeting the goals of both followers and the organization—rather than on themselves.

sexual harassment Unwanted sexual attention that creates an adverse work environment.

shared leadership Simultaneous, ongoing, mutual influence process in which people share responsibility for leading.

simple structure The first type of organizational structure, whereby an organization has authority centralized in a single person, as well as a flat hierarchy, few rules, and low work specialization.

single-product strategy Strategy by which a company makes and sells only one product within its market.

single-use plan Plan developed for activities that are not likely to be repeated in the future; such a plan can be either a program or a project.

situational interview A structured interview in which the interviewer focuses on hypothetical situations.

situational leadership theory Leadership model that holds that leaders should adjust their leadership style according to the readiness of the followers.

skunkworks A project team whose members are separated from the normal operation of an organization and asked to produce a new, innovative product.

small-batch technology System in which goods are custom-made to customer specifications in small quantities.

SMART goal A goal that is Specific, Measurable, Attainable, Results oriented, and has Target dates.

social capital Economic or productive potential of strong, trusting, and cooperative relationships.

social loafing The tendency of people to exert less effort when working in groups than when working alone.

social responsibility Manager's duty to take action that will benefit society's interests as well as the organization's.

socialized power Power directed at helping others.

sociocultural forces Influences and trends originating in a country, society, or culture; human relationships and values that may affect an organization.

spam Unsolicited e-mail jokes and junk mail.

span of control The number of people reporting directly to a given manager.

special-interest groups Groups whose members try to influence specific issues.

special-purpose team A team that meets to solve a special or one-time problem.

stability strategy One of three grand strategies, this strategy involves little or no significant change.

staff personnel Staff with advisory functions; they provide advice, recommendations, and research to line managers.

stakeholders People whose interests are affected by an organization's activities.

standing plan Plan developed for activities that occur repeatedly over a period of time; such a plan consists of policies, procedures, or rules.

state uncertainty One of three types of uncertainty; when the environment is considered unpredictable.

statistical process control A statistical technique that uses periodic random samples from production runs to see if quality is being maintained within a standard range of acceptability.

stereotype A standardized mental picture resulting from oversimplified beliefs about a certain group of people.

stereotyping The tendency to attribute to an individual the characteristics one believes are typical of the group to which that individual belongs.

stock options The right to buy a company's stock at a future date for a discounted price; often a benefit given to key employees.

storming One of five stages of forming a team; stage two, the emergence of individual personalities, roles, and conflicts within the group.

story A narrative based on true events, which is repeated—and sometimes embellished upon—to emphasize a particular value.

strategic allies Describes the relationship of two organizations that join forces to achieve advantages that neither can perform as well alone.

strategic control Monitoring performance to ensure that strategic plans are being implemented and taking corrective action as needed.

strategic goals Goals that are set by and for top management and focus on objectives for the organization as a whole.

strategic human resource planning The development of a systematic, comprehensive strategy for (1) understanding current employee needs and (2) predicting future employee needs.

strategic management A five-step process that involves managers from all parts of the organization in the formulation and implementation of strategies and strategic goals: establish the mission and the vision; establish the grand strategy; formulate the strategic plans; carry out the strategic plans; maintain strategic control.

strategic map A visual representation of the four perspectives of the balanced scorecard that enables managers to communicate their goals so that everyone in the company can understand how their jobs are linked to the overall objectives of the organization.

strategic planning Determining what an organization's long-term goals should be for the next 1–10 years with the resources it expects to have available; done by top management.

strategic positioning Strategy that, according to Michael Porter, attempts to achieve sustainable competitive advantage by preserving what is distinctive about a company.

strategy A large-scale action plan that sets the direction for an organization.

strategy formulation The process of choosing among different strategies and altering them to best fit the organization's needs.

strategy implementation The execution of strategic plans.

strength perspective Perspective of organizational culture that assumes that the strength of a corporate culture is related to a firm's long-term financial performance.

stress The tension people feel when they are facing or enduring extraordinary demands, constraints, or opportunities and are uncertain about their ability to handle them effectively.

stressor The source of stress.

structured interview Interview in which the interviewer asks each applicant the same questions and then compares the responses to a standardized set of answers.

subjective appraisal Form of performance evaluation based on a manager's perceptions of an employee's traits or behaviors.

subsystems The collection of parts that make up the whole system.

sunk-cost bias (sunk-cost fallacy) Biased way of thinking in which managers add up all the money already spent on a project and conclude it is too costly to simply abandon it.

supplier A person or organization that provide supplies—raw materials, services, equipment, labor, or energy—to other organizations.

sustainability Economic development that meets the needs of the present without compromising the ability of future generations to meet their own needs.

SWOT analysis The search for the Strengths, Weaknesses, Opportunities, and Threats that affect an organization.

symbol An object, act, quality, or event that conveys meaning.

synergy Situation in which the economic value of separate, related businesses under one ownership and management is greater than the businesses are worth separately.

system A set of interrelated parts that operate together to achieve a common purpose.

systems viewpoint Perspective that regards the organization as a system of interrelated parts.

T

360-degree assessment A performance appraisal in which employees are appraised not only by their managerial superiors but also by peers, subordinates, and sometimes clients.

tactical control Monitoring performance to ensure that tactical plans—those at the divisional or departmental level—are being implemented and taking corrective action as needed.

tactical goals Goals that are set by and for middle managers and focus on the actions needed to achieve strategic goals.

tactical planning Determining what contributions departments or similar work units can make with their given resources during the next six months to two years; done by middle management.

tacit knowledge Knowledge that is individual-based, intuitive, acquired through considerable experience, and hard to express and to share.

tariff A trade barrier in the form of a customs duty, or tax, levied mainly on imports.

task environment Eleven groups that present you with daily tasks to handle: customers, competitors, suppliers, distributors, strategic allies, employee groups, local communities, financial institutions, government regulators, special-interest groups, and mass media.

task role Behavior that concentrates on getting the team's task done.

team A small group of people with complementary skills who are committed to a common purpose, performance goals, and approach to which they hold themselves mutually accountable.

team-based structure Seventh type of organizational structure, whereby teams or workgroups, either temporary or permanent, are used to improve horizontal relations and solve problems throughout the organization.

technical skills Skills that consist of the job-specific knowledge needed to perform well in a specialized field.

technological forces New developments in methods for transforming resources into goods or services.

technology All the tools and ideas for transforming material, data, or labor (inputs) into goods or services (outputs). It applies not just to computers but any machine or process that enables an organization to gain a competitive advantage in changing materials used to produce a finished product.

telecommute To work from home or remote locations using a variety of information technologies.

top managers One of three managerial levels; they make the long-term decisions about the overall direction of the organization and establish the objectives, policies, and strategies for it.

total quality management (TQM) A comprehensive approach—led by top management and supported throughout the organization—dedicated to continuous quality improvement, training, and customer satisfaction. It has four components: (1) Make continuous improvement a priority. (2) Get every employee involved. (3) Listen to and learn from customers and employees. (4) Use accurate standards to identify and eliminate problems.

totalitarian governments Governments ruled by a dictator, a single political party, or a special-membership group.

trade protectionism The use of government regulations to limit the import of goods and services.

trading bloc Also known as an *economic community;* a group of nations within a geographical region that have agreed to remove trade barriers with one another.

training Educating technical and operational employees in how to better do their current jobs.

trait approaches to leadership Attempts to identify distinctive characteristics that account for the effectiveness of leaders.

transactional leader One who focuses on the interpersonal transactions between managers and employees.

transactional leadership Leadership style that focuses on clarifying employees' roles and task requirements and providing rewards and punishments contingent on performance.

transformation processes The organization's capabilities in management and technology that are applied to converting inputs into outputs; one of four parts of a system, along with inputs, outputs, and feedback.

transformational leadership Leadership style that transforms employees to pursue organizational goals over self-interests.

trend analysis A hypothetical extension of a past series of events into the future.

turnover The movement of employees in and out of an organization when they obtain and then leave their jobs.

two-factor theory Herzberg's theory that proposes that work satisfaction and dissatisfaction arise from two different work factors—work satisfaction from so-called motivating factors and work dissatisfaction from so-called hygiene factors.

Type A behavior pattern Behavior describing people involved in a chronic, determined struggle to accomplish more in less time.

U

underemployed Working at a job that requires less education than one has.

unity of command Principle that stresses an employee should report to no more than one manager in order to avoid conflicting priorities and demands.

unrelated diversification Operating several businesses that are not related to one another under one ownership.

unstructured interview Interview in which the interviewer asks probing questions to find out what the applicant is like.

upward-communication Communication that flows from lower levels to higher levels.

utilitarian approach One of four approaches to solving ethical dilemmas; ethical behavior is guided by what will result in the greatest good for the greatest number of people.

V

valence The value or the importance a worker assigns to a possible outcome or reward.

validity Extent to which a test measures what it purports to measure and extent to which it is free of bias.

value system The pattern of values within an organization.

values Abstract ideals that guide one's thinking and behavior across all situations; the relatively permanent and deeply held underlying beliefs and attitudes that help determine a person's behavior.

variable budget Allowing the allocation of resources to vary in proportion with various levels of activity.

variable costs Expenses that vary directly depending on the numbers of the product that one produces and sells.

videoconferencing Using video and audio links along with computers to enable people located at different locations to see, hear, and talk with one another.

virtual bank A bank with no building to go to; an Internet bank.

virtual organization Organization whose members are geographically apart, usually working with e-mail, collaborative computing, and other computer connections, while often appearing to customers and others to be a single, unified organization with a real physical location.

vision statement Statement that expresses what the organization should become and where it wants to go strategically.

W

whistleblower An employee who reports organizational misconduct to the public.

wholly owned subsidiary A foreign subsidiary, or subordinate section of an organization, that is totally owned and controlled by the organization.

work teams Teams that engage in collective work requiring coordinated effort; they are of four types, which may be identified according to their basic purpose: advice teams, production teams, project teams, and action teams.

World Bank One of three principal organizations designed to facilitate international trade; its purpose is to provide low-interest loans to developing nations for improving transportation, education, health, and telecommunications.

World Trade Organization (WTO) One of three principal organizations designed to facilitate international trade; it is designed to monitor and enforce trade agreements.

Y

youth stage The stage in which the organization is in a prebureaucratic phase, one of growth and expansion.

Z

zero-based budgeting (ZBB) Forcing each department to start from zero in projecting its funding needs for the coming budget period.

credits

CHAPTER 1

Photos: Page 4, AP/Wide World Photos; 5, © Royalty-Free/CORBIS; 6, © Chip Somodevilla/Getty Images; 7, © Walter Hodges/Getty Images; 9, © Jacques Munch/AFP/Getty Images; 10, © Brian Williams & Stacey Sawyer; 11, 13, AP/Wide World Photos; 15, © Everett Kennedy Brown/epa/CORBIS; 16, AP/Wide World Photos; 17, © Mark Leet Photography; 18, © Mark Peterson/Redux; 19, 20, AP/Wide World Photos; 22, © Jim Wilson/The New York Times/Redux; 24t, AP/Wide World Photos; 24b, © 2002 Morton Buildings, Inc./Courtesy of Woodward Camp, 25, 27, AP/Wide World Photos.

CHAPTER 2

Photos: Page 43, © Bettmann/CORBIS, 44, © Underwood & Underwood/CORBIS; 45, © Digital Vision/PunchStock; 46, © Bettmann/CORBIS; 47, Courtesy of AT&T Corporate Archives; 48, Courtesy of Debra's Natural Gourmet; 50, © Najlah Feanny/CORBIS SABA; 54t, © Mark Richards/PhotoEdit; 54b, © The McGraw-Hill Companies, Inc./John Flournoy, photographer; 57, © Cyndy Freeman/© Starbuck Coffee Co. All Rights reserved.; 59, Courtesy MIT Press.

Logo: Page 41, Oticon logo, used by permission.

CHAPTER 3

Photos: Page 74, © Mark Peterson/CORBIS; 76, © The McGraw-Hill Companies, Inc./John Flournoy, photographer; 79, © Tim Boyle/Getty Images; 80, © Andre Jenny/The Image Works; 81, AP/Wide World Photos; 82, © Rob Melnychuk/Getty Images; 84, © Brand X Pictures/Getty Images; 87, © Reuters/CORBIS; 89, © The McGraw-Hill Companies, Inc./John Flournoy, photographer; 90, © Eric Millette Photography; 95, © Digital Vision/Getty Images; 96, AP/Wide World Photos; 97, © Scott T. Baxter/Getty Images; 98, Courtesy of Johnson & Johnson.

CHAPTER 4

Photos: Page 110, © Brian Williams & Stacey Sawyer; 111, © Justin Sullivan/Getty Images; 112, © Jacobs Stock Photography/Getty Images; 114, © PhotoDisc/Getty Images; 116, © Hoang Dinh Nam/AFP/Getty Images; 120, AP/Wide World Photos; 122, © Deborah Harse/The Image Works; 123, © Joseph Van Os/Getty Images; 125, AP/Wide World Photos; 129, © Aaron C. Anderer; 134, Robert Sullivan/AFP/Getty Images.

Logo: Page 109, The Amazon.com logo and Amazon.com are registered trademarks of Amazon.com, Inc. or its affiliates.

CHAPTER 5

Photos: Page 147, © Evan Agostini/Getty Images; 149, 150, © The McGraw-Hill Companies, Inc./Jill Braaten, photo-

grapher; 163, © Catherine Karnow/CORBIS; 164, © image100/PunchStock.

Logo: Pages 152, 153, The Amazon.com logo and Amazon.com are registered trademarks of Amazon.com, Inc. or its affiliates.; 156, Southwest Airlines logo courtesy of Southwest Airlines, Co.

CHAPTER 6

Photos: Page 176, © Ryan McVay/Getty Images; 178, © The McGraw-Hill Companies, Inc./Jill Braaten, photographer; 182, © Spike Mafford/Getty Images; 183, © Reuters/CORBIS; 185, © The McGraw-Hill Companies, Inc./John Flournoy, photographer; 189, © The McGraw-Hill Companies, Inc./Jill Braaten, photographer; 190, Courtesy of Southwest Airlines; 193, © Steve Mason/Getty Images; 195, © Brian Williams & Stacey Sawyer; 198, © Justin Sullivan/Getty Images.

CHAPTER 7

Photos: Page 210, © Rhona Wise/epa/CORBIS; 211, © Tina-Marie Lacava/Courtesy of Camden County College; 213, Courtesy of Southwest Airlines; 216, © Royalty-Free/CORBIS; 217, © Digital Vision; 219, © image100/PunchStock; 226, © Digital Vision; 231, © PhotoDisc/PunchStock.

CHAPTER 8

Photos: Page 248, © Ryan McVay/Getty Images; 249, Courtesy of Hewlett-Packard Company; 252, © Digital Vision; 256, © Erik Freeland/CORBIS; 258, © Eric Audras/Photoalto/PictureQuest; 262, © Skip Nall/Getty Images; 265, © The McGraw-Hill Companies, Inc./John Flournoy, photographer; 270, AP/Wide World Photos; 271, © Najlah Feanny/CORBIS; 272, AP/Wide World Photos.

CHAPTER 9

Photos: Page 290, © The McGraw-Hill Companies, Inc./John Flournoy, photographer; 291, © Chevron Corporation and used with permission; 300, Lafayette Instrument Company, Inc.; 301, 303, 304, © Digital Vision; 308, © PhotoDisc/Getty Images; 309, © Royalty-Free/CORBIS.

CHAPTER 10

Photos: Page 325, © The McGraw-Hill Companies, Inc./John Flournoy, photographer; 330, © Edward Bock/CORBIS; 333, © Digital Vision; 335, AP/Wide World Photos; 343, Courtesy of Southwest Airlines.

Logo: Page 338, 3M logo reprinted with permission of 3M Corporation.

CHAPTER 11

Photos: Page 356, Courtesy of New School University, NY, NY; 357, © Najlah Feanny/CORBIS; 359, © Ben Van Hook; 360, © Liquidlibrary/Dynamic Graphics/Jupiterimages; 368, © Digital Vision; 370, © Royalty-Free/CORBIS; 373, © Ryan McVay/Getty Images.

CHAPTER 12

Photos: Page 386, © Tony Freeman/PhotoEdit; 394, © Chuck Savage/CORBIS; 396, © Kay Nietfeld/epa/CORBIS; 397, © Ryan McVay/Getty Images; 400, © Stockbyte Platinum/Getty Images; 403, © Keith Brofsky/Getty Images; 404, Photo by Howard Sokol/Courtesy of The Boppy Pillow; 407, © PhotoDisc/Getty Images.

CHAPTER 13

Photos: Page 420, © Digital Vision; 422, Courtesy of Volvo Car Corporation; 426, Courtesy of NASCAR Public Relations; 430, © Tom Prettyman/PhotoEdit; 432, © The McGraw-Hill Companies, Inc./John Flournoy, photographer; 434, © Ramin Talaie/CORBIS; 437, © Brand X Pictures/PunchStock.

CHAPTER 14

Photos: Page 449, © Thomas Engstrom/Getty Images; 451, © Anne Knudsen/Getty Images; 458, © John A. Rizzo/Getty Images; 460, © PhotoDisc/Getty Images; 464, AP/Wide World Photos; 466, © Doug Menuez/Getty Images; 468, AP/Wide World Photos; 474, © David Paul Morris/Getty Images.

CHAPTER 15

Photos: Page 488, © Ryan McVay/Getty Images; 492, 496, © PhotoDisc/Getty Images; 500, © Ryan McVay/Getty Images; 502, © Digital Vision; 505, © Zigy Kaluzny/Getty Images; 508, 510, © PhotoDisc/Getty Images; 512, © image100/PunchStock.

CHAPTER 16

Photos: Page 525, © Royalty-Free/CORBIS; 529, © Pixtal/Superstock; 536, © Royalty-Free/ CORBIS; 537, © Oscar Sabetta/Getty Images; 539, © Vince Bucci/Getty Images; 541, Photo courtesy of Viking Range Corporation; 546, Courtesy of Instituto Pro-Natura; 548, Kim Steele/Getty Images.

name index

Page numbers followed by n indicate notes.

company &
organization index

subject index

Health care software, 254
Health clinics, onsite, 410
Health insurance, 224, 293; *see also*
　　Fringe benefits
Health Insurance Portability & Accountability
　　Act (HIPAA), 293
Heart attacks, 370
Hedging fuel prices, 190
Heroes, **250**
Hersey-Blanchard situational leadership
　　theory, 464–465
Herzberg's two-factor theory, 390–391, 398
Heuristics, **234**–236
Hierarchies
　　career paths in, 77
　　communicating through, 500–501
　　of needs, 48, 386–388
　　in organizational structures, 257, **259**
　　traditional support for, 41
Hierarchy of human needs, 48
High-context cultures, **130**
High-control situations, 461
High-performance cultures, 253–255
High-road companies, 474
High school dropouts, 97
High-speed wireless technology, 175
High touch service, 284
Higher-level needs, 388
Highlighting in written pieces, 511
Hinduism, 134
Hiring
　　discrimination prohibited, 292–294
　　as management function, 448
　　selection process overview, 296–300
Hismanal, 194–195
Hispanic workers, obstacles for, 96
Historical perspectives of management
　　behavioral, 46–49
　　classical, 42–45
　　defined, **40**
　　quantitative, 50–51
Hofstede model of four cultural dimensions,
　　130–131
Home health care workers, 434
Homicides, 433
Homosexual workers, 97
Honesty, 225, 454
Horizontal communication, **501**–502
Horizontal loading, 399
Horizontal specialization, 257
Horse trading, 229
Hospital management, 51
Hostile environment harassment, 294
Hotels, 23, 51
Hours of work, 19
House's path–goal leadership model,
　　461–464
HP Way, 249, 253
Human capital, **61**, 289
The Human Equation, 57
Human life, respecting dignity of, 225
Human relations movement, **48**–49
Human resource inventories, **291**
Human resource management; *see also*
　　Employees; Performance appraisal;
　　Training
　　advancement and discipline issues,
　　310–312, 315–316
　　compensation and benefits issues,
　　308–309
　　control tools for, 536
　　legal issues in, 292–294
　　major elements, **288**–291

Human resource management—*Cont.*
　　orientation, training and development,
　　301–303
　　performance appraisal, 304–307
　　recruitment and selection, 295–300
Human skills, **26**–27
Humane orientation, 132
Humaneness, 225
Humility, 475–476
Hybrid cars, 168–170
Hybrid structures, **265**–266
Hygiene factors, **390**, 391
Hypocrisy, 356

I

Idea generation, 62, 230–231, 431; *see also*
　　Innovation
Identity, from organizational culture, 251
Ignoring-randomness bias, 237
Illegal immigration, 96
Illiteracy, 97
Illusion-of-control bias, 237
Illusion of unanimity, 431
Imagery, 28
Imagination breakthroughs, 281
Immigration Reform & Control Act, 293
Impartial controls, 547
Implementation
　　in rational decision-making model,
　　216–217
　　of strategies, 185, 197–200
Import quotas, 117, 125, 126
Important tasks, urgent versus, 73
Importing, **118**
Improvement objectives, 160
Improvement orientation of TQM, 541–542
In-group collectivism, 131
In-group exchange, 470
Incentives; *see also* Motivation; Rewards
　　aligning with company goals, 309
　　defined, 308
　　with employee monitoring, 359
　　need for change, 330
　　personality and, 362
　　popular approaches, 404–407
　　to spur constructive conflict, 437
　　tying to team building, 429
Income statements, **539**
An Inconvenient Truth, 91
Incremental budgeting, **537**
Incremental innovations, **336**
Incremental model of decision making, **219**
Independent learning opportunities, 353
India
　　general impact on markets, 325
　　population growth, 122
　　software services, 114, 117
Indigenization laws, 122
Indirectness, 498
Individual approach to ethics, **85**
Individualism, 130, 131
Indonesia, 122, 127
Industrial psychology, 46
Ineffective responses to problems, 232–233
Influence, leadership and, 450–452
Informal appraisals, **307**
Informal communication channels, **502**
Informal groups, **420**
Information, incomplete, 218–219
Information management, 20
Information overload, 20, 491, 507
Information resource controls, 536

Information sharing, 499
Information technology; *see also* Technology
　　historic development, 108–109
　　infrastructures, 122–123
　　key management challenges of, 10–11,
　　60–61
　　knowledge sharing via, 219
　　leadership based on, 476–477
　　overview of communication tools,
　　503–507
　　productivity gains from, 525
　　teamwork via, 11, 421, 423
　　use in recruiting and selection, 295, 296
Informational roles of management, **20**–21
Infrastructures, **122**–123
Ingratiating tactics, 452
Inhibition, **401**
Initiating structure, 459
Initiative, 447, 549
Initiators, 428
Innovate system, 335
Innovation
　　defined, **8**
　　growing emphasis on, 61
　　means of promoting, 334–339, 523, 532
　　organizational cultures promoting, 161,
　　251, 335, 337–338
　　overcoming resistance to, 340–343
　　risking failure for, 281
　　as strategic planning benefit, 178–179
　　from teams, 427, 440–441
Innovation Jam, 357
Innovative change, **340**
The Innovator's Dilemma, 325
Inputs
　　defined, **53**
　　in equity theory, 392
　　in productivity formula, 525
Inspections, 545
Inspiration; *see* Motivation
Inspirational appeals, 452
Instability, political, 124
Institutional collectivism, 131
Institutional power, 389
Instrumentality, **395**
Insurance, political risk, 123
Integrated product development, 268
Integration, 47, **272**
Integrity, 361, 468
Intellectual stimulation, 226
Intelligence, 364, 455
Interaction facilitation, 463
Interaction in teams, 427
Internal audits, **539**
Internal business processes, monitoring, 532
Internal dimensions of diversity, **94**–95
Internal forces of change, 328–329
Internal locus of control, **25**, 362, 462
Internal recruiting, **295**, 296
Internal stakeholders, **76**
Internal strengths and weaknesses, 188, 189
International Data Corp., 10
International forces, **83**
International management, 112–115
International Monetary Fund, **127**
International Organization for
　　Standardization, 543–544
Internet
　　car buying via, 191
　　competitive intelligence on, 196
　　defined, **10**
　　impact on communications, 10–11,
　　503–504

Management theory
    applications for learning organizations, 60–63
    contemporary perspectives, 41, 52–59
    historical perspectives, 40, 42–51
    reasons to study, 41
Management tools, 175
Managers
    abusive, 434
    benefits of becoming, 4–7
    entrepreneurs versus, 23–25
    line versus staff, 261
    major challenges of, 8–11
    principal functions of, 12–13
    required skills, 26–27
    roles of, 18–21
    as stressors, 372
    tips for the newly promoted, 459
Manager's Toolboxes, purpose of, 3
Manners, 494
Maquiladoras, **117**
Masculine terms, 499
Masculinity/femininity dimension, 130, 499
Maslow's hierarchy of needs, 48, 386–388
Mass markets, 324
Mass media, as stakeholders, 81
Material culture, 143
Matrix structures, **266**–267
Maturity stage (organizational life cycle), **274**
Maturity stage (product life cycle), **194**
MBO technique, 160–161
McClelland's acquired needs theory, 388–390
Means-end chains, **154**
Means versus ends, in control process, 548
Measurability of goals, 157
Measurement
    in basic control process, 529, 532–534
    of goals, 157
    for improving productivity, 359, 523
    in performance appraisal, 304
    of success, 17
    transmitting culture through, 255
Measurement-managed firms, 532–534
Meat industry, 82
Mechanistic organizations, **271**
Mectizan, 90
Media
    in communication process, **489,** 493
    selecting for effective communication, 490–491
    as stakeholders, 81
Media richness, **491**
Medical Expense Manager, 254
Medical imaging, 68–69
Medical model of organization development, 331–332
Medium-size companies, 270
Meetings
    streamlining, 186
    videoconferencing, 504–505
    of virtual teams, 423
Megamergers, 111
Memory chips, 451
Memory skills, 28
Men's Health, 23
Mental imagery, 28
Mentoring, 247
Mercosur, **128**
Mergers, 110–111, 149, 331
Messages, 487, **489**
Meta-analyses, **455**
Metro 7 jeans, 55

Mexico
    governmental system, 124
    as major U.S. trading partner, 125
    manufacturing in, 117, 133
    as NAFTA member, 127
Microbreweries, 178
Microprocessors, 451
Middle managers, **15**–16, 154
Midlife stage, **274**
Millennium Generation, 55
Mindfulness, 39
Mindguards, 431
Mindlessness, 39
Minifirms, 111
Minimum wage, 292
Minorities, 96, 294; *see also* Discrimination; Diversity
Mintzberg's study, 18–19
Mission
    defined, **152**
    establishing, 181–183
    introducing new employees to, 302
    statements of, 151, **152,** 181–182, 183
Mistake proofing, 51
Mistakes; *see also* Failure
    controlling for, 51, 527
    as necessary risk, 279–281
Mistrust, climates of, 341
Misunderstandings, 436
Misuse of technology, 506
Mixed economies, **121**–122
Modeling, predictive, 222
Moderate-control situations, 461
MoistureLoc cleaner, 326
Momentum, 178
Moneyball, 222
Monitor role, 20–21
Monochronic time, **132**–133
Moral development, 86; *see also* Ethics
Moral principles, 225
Moral-rights approach, **85**
Morale, 427, 553; *see also* Attitudes; Motivation
Most favored nation trading status, **128**
Motion studies, 43
Motivating factors, in Herzberg's theory, 390–391
Motivating potential score, 400
Motivation; *see also* Incentives; Productivity; Rewards
    compensation for, 404–406
    importance to behavioral viewpoint, 46–49
    job design and, 398–400
    as leadership function, 449, 467–468
    MBO technique, 160–161, 304–305
    needs-based theories, 386–391, 398–399
    from organizational culture, 250
    overview, **384**–385
    in privatization, 544
    process views of, 392–397
    reinforcement perspectives, 401–403
    for team performance, 426
Movements, in communication, 497
MRI technology, 68–69
Multinational corporations, **112**
Multinational organizations, **112**
Multiplier effect, 5–6
Multitasking, 18, 20, 133, 507
Multivariable testing, 543
Mutual accountability, 426
Mutual-benefit organizations, 17, 256
Myers-Briggs Type Indicator, 299–300
Myths, 254

N

Namibia, 120
Narrow span of control, 260
NASCAR racing, 65–66, 426
National Labor Relations Board, **292**
Natural beef, 327
Necessity entrepreneurs, 25
Need for achievement, 25, 389–390
Needs, role in motivation, **386**–391
Needs hierarchy, 48, 386–388
Negative conflict, **433,** 434
Negative reinforcement, **401**–402
Negotiations, 498
Negotiator role, 21
Nervousness while speaking, 511
Network structures, **268**–269
Network television, 9
Networking, 447
Neuromarketing, 69
New Coke, 181, 205
New competitors, 191
The New Yorker, 23
News leaks, 159
Newspaper advertising effectiveness, 543
Newspapers, 509–510
Newton Messagepad, 54
Niche products, 324
Nigeria, population growth in, 122
Nintendo, 55
No-jerk rule, 434
Noise, in communication process, **490**
Nominal group technique, **230,** 231
Nonmonetary budgets, 538
Nonmonetary incentives, 406–407
Nonprofit organizations
    basic attributes, 17, 256
    boards of directors, 76
    CEO compensation, 6
    economic value of, 90
    general management, 17
Nonprogrammed decisions, **211**
Nonrational decision making, **218**–219
Nonverbal communications, 130, 490, **496**–497
Nonwork demands, 372
Norming stage (team), **425**
Norms, **429**–430
North American Free Trade Agreement, **127**–128
Note taking, 29
Numbered lists, 30

O

Oakland Athletics, 222
Obedience, 260
Objective appraisals, **304**–305
Objective controls, 547
Objective test-taking skills, 30
Objectives; *see also* Goals
    conflicts over, 435
    defined, **154**
    in expectancy theory, 396
    imprecise, 534
    management by, 160–161, 304–305
Observable culture, 250
Obstructionist managers, **89**–90
Occupational Safety and Health Act, 292, 293
Occupational Safety and Health Administration, 87
Off-the-job training, 303
Office politics, 248

Examples